February 7–10, 2010
Hong Kong, China

**Association for
Computing Machinery**

Advancing Computing as a Science & Profession

IUI 2010

Proceedings of the 14th ACM International Conference on
Intelligent User Interfaces

Sponsored by:
ACM SIGCHI & ACM SIGART

Supported by:
**IBM Research, RedWhale Software, Microsoft Research,
The Hong Kong Polytechnic University, The University of Hong Kong,
Hong Kong Baptist University,
and The Hong Kong University of Science and Technology**

In cooperation with:
Association for the Advancement of Artificial Intelligence

**Association for
Computing Machinery**

Advancing Computing as a Science & Profession

The Association for Computing Machinery
2 Penn Plaza, Suite 701
New York, New York 10121-0701

Notice to Past Authors of ACM-Published Articles

ISBN: 978-1-60558-515-4

Additional copies may be ordered prepaid from:

ACM Order Department
PO Box 30777
New York, NY 10087-0777, USA

Phone: 1-800-342-6626 (US and Canada)
+1-212-626-0500 (Global)
Fax: +1-212-944-1318
E-mail: acmhelp@acm.org
Hours of Operation: 8:30 am – 4:30 pm ET

ACM Order Number 608010

Printed in the USA

Foreword

IUI has successfully established itself as a unique, interdisciplinary conference, at the intersection of Artificial Intelligence and Human-Computer Interaction. The Conference receives contributions from many traditional as well as hot topics in the field, ranging from Multimodal Interfaces and Recommender Systems, to Affective Computing and Brain-Computing Interfaces.

Because of this ever-increasing diversity of topics, this edition has seen further changes to our reviewing process. We have introduced a rebuttal phase for Long Papers, following a trend adopted by several high-quality conferences. The objective of the rebuttal is to ensure greater transparency and fairness, as the authors' responses should influence the discussion phase moderated by a Senior Program Committee (SPC) member.

In order to ensure that all topics were adequately covered over 200 reviewers have contributed to the selection of this year's program and we trust that this had a very positive impact on the relevance and quality of individual reviews.

We have retained the successful format of the conference with Long Papers, Short Papers and Demonstrations. In addition, we have addressed the issue of conversion of Long Papers into Short Papers by explicitly requesting authors' approval at submission time.

The accepted submissions cover a wide range of topics, including personalized information systems, intelligent user interaction for information search and browsing, affective computing, gesture-based systems, and multimodal user interfaces. Geographically, the accepted work also represents researchers and institutions in many countries across four continents, including China, Japan, Korea, Singapore, Canada, Netherlands, Ireland, France, Germany, Australia, New Zealand, United Kingdom, and the United States of America.

As always, the selection process has been the object of careful consideration and multiple discussions. We have asked the SPC moderators to formulate recommendations for acceptance and in the vast majority of cases it has been straightforward for us to endorse their choice. It is always down to the Program Chairs to make final decisions, sometimes difficult ones, on the total number of papers to be accepted. We have adopted a continuity policy from previous editions (around 22% for Long Papers), this year's overall acceptance rate achieves the right balance between selectivity and openness to innovative papers.

The conference program highlights two invited talks: Paul Sajda, from Columbia University and Kazuo Yano, from Hitachi's Advanced Research Laboratory.

This year's Conference will also feature five full-day and one half-day workshops, covering several hot topics in the area of IUI, with strong emphasis on semantics, social aspects and multimodality of interfaces, including:
-    Social Recommender Systems
-    Intelligent Visual Interfaces for Text Analysis
-    Multimodal Interfaces for Automotive Applications
-    Interoperability and Interaction on the Social and Semantic Web
-    Eye Gaze in Intelligent Human Machine Interaction
-    Semantic Models for Adaptive Interactive Systems

The demonstration program accepted fifteen regular submissions. We would like to thank Tyler Baldwin and Brian Romanowski for their help in organizing the demo session.

Once again, we acknowledge the support of the ACM through its special interest groups SIGART and SIGCHI, and of AAAI who have assisted with publicizing the Conference. We also wish to thank our corporate sponsors Red Whale, Microsoft and IBM. We gratefully acknowledge the support of our four academic sponsors: The Hong Kong Polytechnic University, The University of Hong Kong, Hong Kong Baptist University and The Hong Kong University of Science and Technology.

Finally, we thank Brandon Hung of Red Whale for assisting with the Conference web site and Lisa Tolles of Sheridan printing for the preparation of the proceedings.

We hope that you find this year's program exciting and we are looking forward to meeting you in Hong Kong!

Charles Rich and Qiang Yang
General Co-Chairs

Marc Cavazza and Michelle Zhou
Program Co-Chairs

Tsvi Kuflik and Patrick Gebhard
Workshops Co-Chairs

Joyce Chai
Demonstration Chair

Li Chen
Publicity Chair

Wenyin Liu and Philips F.L. Wang
Local Arrangements Co-Chairs

Table of Contents

Invited Talk

Session 1: Access/Brain Interfaces

Session 2: Smart Reading

Session 3: Intelligent Agent

Invited Talk

Session 4: Mobile Interaction

Session 5: Multimodal Interaction

Session 6: Smart Web Apps

Session 7: Enhanced Search

Session 8: UI for the Masses

Session 9: User-Centered Design

Short Paper Presentations (Posters)

Demonstrations

Workshops

IUI 2010 Conference Organization

General Co-Chairs: Charles Rich *(Worcester Polytechnic Institute, USA)*
Qiang Yang *(Hong Kong University of Science & Technology, China)*

Program Co-Chairs: Marc Cavazza *(Teesside University, UK)*
Michelle Zhou *(IBM Research, China)*

Workshops Co-Chairs: Tsvi Kuflik *(University of Haifa, Israel)*
Patrick Gebhard *(DFKI, Germany)*

Demonstration Chair: Joyce Chai *(Michigan State University)*

Local Arrangements Co-Chairs: Wenyin Liu *(City University of Hong Kong, China)*
Philips F.L. Wang *(City University of Hong Kong, China)*

Publicity Chair: Li Chen *(Hong Kong Baptist University, China)*

Treasurer: Huamin Qu *(Hong Kong University of Science & Technology, China)*

Registration Chair: Howard Leung *(City University of Hong Kong, China)*

Sponsorship Chair: Doug Riecken *(IBM Research)*

Senior Program Committee: Elisabeth Andre *(Augsburg University, Germany)*
Brian Bailey *(University of Illinois, USA)*
Sumit Basu *(Microsoft Research , USA)*
Mark Billinghurst *(HIT Lab NZ, University of Canterbury, New Zealand)*
Andreas Butz *(Ludwig-Maximilians-Universität Munich, Germany)*
Ed Chi *(PARC, USA)*
Cristina Conati *(University of British Columbia, Canada)*
Mary Czerwinski *(Microsoft Research, USA)*
Krzysztof Gajos *(Harvard University, USA)*
Andreas Girgensohn *(FX Palo Alto Laboratory, USA)*
Anthony Jameson *(DFKI, Germany)*
Gareth Jones *(Dublin City University, Ireland)*
Antonio Krüger *(Saarland University, Germany)*
Alejandro Jaimes *(University Carols III, Spain)*
Jennifer Lai *(IBM Research, USA)*
Tessa Lau *(IBM Almaden Research Center, USA)*
Gary Geunbae Lee *(POSTECH, Korea)*
Helen Meng *(The Chinese University of Hong Kong, Hong Kong SAR)*
Anton Nijholt *(University of Twente, The Netherlands)*
Nuria Oliver *(Telefonica R&D, Spain)*
Helmut Prendinger *(National Institute of Informatics, Japan)*
Pearl Pu *(EPFL, Switzerland)*
John Riedl *(University of Minnesota, USA)*
Candace Sidner *(Worcester Polytechnic Institute, USA)*
Robert St. Amant *(North Carolina State University, USA)*
Hongan Wang *(Chinese Academy of Sciences, China)*

Program Committee: Cecilia Aragon *(Lawrence Berkeley National Laboratory, USA)*
Lora Aroyo *(VU University Amsterdam, The Netherlands)*
Joerg Baus *(DFKI, Germany)*
Nadia Berthouze *(University College London, UK)*
Timothy Bickmore *(Northeastern University, USA)*
Jacob Biehl *(FX Palo Alto Laboratory, Inc., USA)*
Jeffrey Bigham *(University of Washington, USA)*
Andrea Bunt *(University of Manitoba, Canada)*
Robin Burke *(DePaul University, USA)*
Giuseppe Carenini *(University of British Columbia, Canada)*
Sylvain Castagnos *(EPFL, Switzerland)*
Joyce Chai *(Michigan State University, USA)*
Fang Chen *(NICTA, Australia)*
Li Chen *(Hong Kong Baptist University, Hong Kong SAR)*
Keith Cheverst *(Lancaster University, UK)*
Karen Church *(Telefonica R&D, Spain)*
Dan Cosley *(Cornell University, USA)*
Steven Drucker *(Microsoft Research, USA)*
Henry Duh *(National University of Singapore, Singapore)*
Patrick Ehlen *(CSLI, Stanford University, USA)*
Jacob Eisenstein *(MIT CSAIL, USA)*
Berna Erol *(Ricoh Innovations, California Research Center, USA)*
George Ferguson *(University of Rochester, USA)*
James Fogarty *(University of Washington, USA)*
Luciano Gamberini *(University of Padova, Italy)*
Daniel Gatica-Perez *(IDIAP Research Institute, Switzerland)*
Melinda Gervasio *(SRI International, USA)*
Werner Geyer *(IBM Research, USA)*
Yolanda Gil *(University of Southern California, USA)*
Andrew Gordon *(University of Southern California, USA)*
Dirk Heylen *(University of Twente, The Netherlands)*
Chao Huang *(Microsoft Research Asia, China)*
Shamsi Iqbal *(Microsoft Research, USA)*
Yuri Ivanov *(Honda Research Institute US, USA)*
Giulio Jacucci *(Helsinki Institute for Information Technology, Finland)*
Kristiina Jokinen *(University of Helsinki, Finland)*
Nicolas Jones *(Swiss Federal Institute of Technology, Switzerland)*
Ece Kamar *(Harvard University, USA)*
Shaun Kane *(University of Washington, USA)*
Jussi Karlgren *(Swedish Institute of Computer Science, Sweden)*
Henry Kautz *(University of Rochester, USA)*
Aisling Kelliher *(Arizona State University, USA)*
Andruid Kerne *(Texas A&M Computer Science Department, USA)*
Michael Kipp *(DFKI, Germany)*
Per Ola Kristensson *(University of Cambridge, UK)*

Program Committee (continued): Bernd Kroger *(Aachen University, Germany)*

Marc Latoschik *(University of Bayreuth, Germany)*

Alison Lee *(Nokia Research Center - Palo Alto, USA)*

James Lester *(North Carolina State University, USA)*

Tsai-Yen Li *(National Chengchi University, Taiwan)*

Henry Lieberman *(Massachusetts Institute of Technology, USA)*

Chin-Yew Lin *(Microsoft Research Asia, China)*

Christine Lisetti *(Florida International University, USA)*

Jiming Liu *(Hong Kong Baptist University, Hong Kong SAR)*

Julian Looser *(Human Interface Technology Lab NZ, New Zealand)*

Jean-Claude Martin *(LIMSI-CNRS & University of Paris South, France)*

Judith Masthoff *(University of Aberdeen, UK)*

Wolfgang Minker *(Ulm University, Germany)*

Louis-Philippe Morency *(University of Southern California, USA)*

Christian Mueller *(DFKI, Germany)*

Mark Neerincx *(TNO Human Factors, The Netherlands)*

Mark Newman *(University of Michigan, USA)*

Jeffrey Nichols *(IBM Research, USA)*

Toyoaki Nishida *(Kyoto University, Japan)*

Pierre-Yves Oudeyer *(INRIA, France)*

Antti Oulasvirta *(Helsinki Institute for Information Technology, Finland)*

Sharon Oviatt *(Incaa Designs, USA)*

Cecile Paris *(CSIRO/ICT Centre, Australia)*

Shwetak Patel *(University of Washington, USA)*

Catherine Pelachaud *(CNRS – ParisTech, France)*

Paolo Petta *(OFAI, Austria)*

Rui Prada *(INESC-ID and IST-UTL, Portugal)*

Christopher Raphael *(Indiana University, USA)*

Patrick Rau *(Tsinghua University, China)*

Xiangshi Ren *(Kochi University of Technology, Japan)*

Mark Riedl *(Georgia Institute of Technology, USA)*

Michael Rohs *(Deutsche Telekom Laboratories; TU Berlin, Germany)*

Doree Seligmann *(Avaya Labs, USA)*

Shilad Sen *(Macalester College, USA)*

Jianqiang Shen *(Pearson, USA)*

Frank Shipman *(Texas A&M University, USA)*

Rainer Stiefelhagen *(Universität Karlsruhe, Germany)*

Oliviero Stock *(FBK-IRST, Italy)*

Didier Stricker *(DFKI, Germany)*

Bongwon Suh *(Palo Alto Research Center, USA)*

Hari Sundaram *(Arizona State University, USA)*

Arun Surendran *(Microsoft, USA)*

Jacques Terken *(Eindhoven University of Technology, The Netherlands)*

Mariet Theune *(University of Twente, The Netherlands)*

Program Committee (continued): Bruce Thomas *(University of South Australia, Australia)*
Feng Tian *(Chinese Academy of Sciences, China)*
Mercan Topkara *(IBM T. J. Watson Research, USA)*
Julita Vassileva *(University of Saskatchewan, Canada)*
Hannes Vilhjálmsson *(Reykjavik University, Iceland)*
Guoping Wang *(Peking University, China)*
Woontack Woo *(Gwangju Institute of Science and Technology, Korea)*
R. Michael Young *(North Carolina State University, USA)*
Kai Yu *(Cambridge University, UK)*
John Zaientz *(Soar Technology, USA)*
Massimo Zancanaro *(FBK-IRST, Italy)*
Shengdong Zhao *(National University of Singapore, Singapore)*

IUI 2010 Additional Reviewers

Piotr Adamczyk
Jason Alexander
Ching Man Au Yeung
Dominikus Baur
Russell Beale
Nikolaus Bee
Tony Bergstrom
Shlomo Berkovsky
Michael Bernstein
James Blustein
Dan Bohus
Sebastian Boring
Stephen Brewster
Gregor Broll
Anne-Marie Brouwer
Margaret Burnett
Fabio Buttussi
Stefania Castellani
Fred Charles
Jilin Chen
Mauro Cherubini
Georgios Christou
Mark Claypool
Lorcan Coyle
Aba-Sah Dadzie
Nicholas Diakopoulos
Dean Eckles
Dominik Ertl
Danyel Fisher
Wai-Tat Fu
Xin Fu
Gersende Georg
Werner Geyer
Giuseppe Ghiani
Stephen Gilroy
Gloria Gomez
Liang Gou
Joshua Hailpern
Björn Hartmann

Kirstie Hawkey
Christopher Healey
Erik Hofer
Peter Holt
Lichan Hong
Hung-Pin Hsu
Pui-Yu Hui
Jee Yeon Hwang
Amy Hurst
Vikramaditya Jakkula
Arnav Jhala
Sasa Junuzovic
Gerrit Kahl
Santosh Kalwar
Takayuki Kanda
Bridget Kane
Amy Karlson
Kostas Karpouzis
Harish Katti
Melanie Kellar
Hadi Kharrazi
Si-Jung Kim
Sung-Hee Kim
Seung Wook Kim
Jonghwa Kim
Peter Klein
Christian Kray
Benjamin Lafreniere
Shyong Lam
Silke Lang
Georgios Lappas
Marc Le Pape
Hyowon Lee
Sandro Leuchter
Leilah Lyons
José Macías Iglesias
Walter Mankowski
Stefan Marti
Reed Martin

Michael Massimi
Michael Mateas
Tara Matthews
Marilyn McGee-Lennon
Andrew Miller
Jim Miller
Elena Minina
Michael Muller
Jörg Müller
Hideyuki Nakanishi
Carman Neustaedter
Alena Neviarouskaya
Patrick Olivier
Bernt Ivar Olsen
Jeff Orkin
Patrizia Paggio
Wai-Man Pang
Kayur Patel
Fabio Paternò
Adam Perer
Mark Pfaff
Jeffrey Pierce
Emmanuel Pietriga
Luke Plurkowski
Mannes Poel
Christopher Power
Andreas Rath
Janet Read
Tim Regan
Boris Reuderink
Ian Ruthven
Kathy Ryall
Nithya Sambasivan
Thomas Schlegel
Johannes Schöning
Michael Sedlmair
Yuechuan She
Sylvia Sheppard
Mei Si

Ian Smith
Tal Sobol Shikler
Junehwa Song
Lübomira Spassova
Molly Stevens
James Stewart
Simone Stumpf
Sriram Subramanian
Xiao Hua Sun
Elisabeth Sylvan
Jaime Teevan
Joe Tullio
E.M.A.G. van Dijk
Jan Van Erp
Radu Vatavu
Ravi Vatrapu
Thurid Vogt
Yi Wang
Xiaoyu Wang
Jingtao Wang
Ning Wang
Zhen Wen
Jackie Wheeler
Andrew Wilson
Fei Wu
Jun Xiao
Rachel Yang
Koji Yatani
Tom Yeh
Ji Soo Yi
Nelson Zagalo
Thorsten Zander
Xiaolong Zhang
Li Zhang
Juergen Ziegler
Job Zwiers

IUI 2010 Sponsors & Supporters

Event Sponsors:

SIGCHI
ACM Special Interest Group on
Human-Computer Interaction

SIGART
ACM Special Interest Group on
Artificial Intelligence

Corporate Supporters:

IBM Research

RedWhale Software

Microsoft Research

Academic Supporters:

**The Hong Kong Polytechnic
University**

The University of Hong Kong

Hong Kong Baptist University

**The Hong Kong University
of Science and Technology**

In Cooperation With:

AAAI
Association for the Advancement of
Artificial Intelligence

A POMDP Approach to
P300-Based Brain-Computer Interfaces

Jaeyoung Park
Dept. of Computer Science
KAIST
Daejeon, Korea
jypark@ai.kaist.ac.kr

Kee-Eung Kim
Dept. of Computer Science
KAIST
Daejeon, Korea
kekim@cs.kaist.ac.kr

Sungho Jo
Dept. of Computer Science
KAIST
Daejeon, Korea
shjo@cs.kaist.ac.kr

ABSTRACT

Most of the previous work on non-invasive brain-computer interfaces (BCIs) has been focused on feature extraction and classification algorithms to achieve high performance for the communication between the brain and the computer. While significant progress has been made in the lower layer of the BCI system, the issues in the higher layer have not been sufficiently addressed. Existing P300-based BCI systems, for example the P300 speller, use a random order of stimulus sequence for eliciting P300 signal for identifying users' intentions. This paper is about computing an optimal sequence of stimulus in order to minimize the number of stimuli, hence improving the performance. To accomplish this, we model the problem as a partially observable Markov decision process (POMDP), which is a model for planning in partially observable stochastic environments. Through simulation and human subject experiments, we show that our approach achieves a significant performance improvement in terms of the success rate and the bit rate.

Author Keywords

P300, brain-computer interface (BCI), partially observable Markov decision process (POMDP)

ACM Classification Keywords

H.5.2 [Information Interfaces and Presentation (e.g., HCI)]: User Interfaces --- Brain-Computer Interfaces; I.2.8 [Artificial Intelligence]: Problem Solving, Control Methods, and Search --- Partially Observable Markov Decision Processes

General Terms

Algorithms, Design, Experimentation, Performance

INTRODUCTION

A brain-computer interface (BCI) aims to provide a communication channel for conveying messages and commands from the brain to the external system by interpreting brain

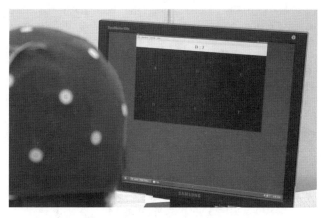

Figure 1. Human sitting in front of EEG-based BCI with a [2x3] stimulus matrix.

activities [22]. There are a variety of devices and methods for BCI, including non-invasive methods such as using encephalography (EEG). The EEG-based BCI is perhaps the most popular method to date, because it is relatively easy and cheap to set up the system [15]. One of the most reliable signal features of EEG is the P300 evoked potential [14], which is a positive peak in the signal amplitude at about 300ms after a stimulus is given to the user's attention [6, 22].

A number of BCI systems using P300 have been proposed in the literature, including the P300 speller [6]. In the P300 speller system, the user faces a 6x6 matrix of letters, and the user gazes at one of the 36 letters that one desires to select. The letters in a row or a column are flashed (stimulated) in a random order. If the letter that the user is gazing at flashes, P300 is generated at about 300ms later. We can thus train a classifier to detect this P300 to identify the desired letter. Some BCI systems with a smaller matrix may flash one letter at a time, e.g., [3].

Figure 1 shows a typical setup of EEG-based BCIs. These traditional systems generate flashes in a random order. For example, the P300 speller generates the same number of flashes for every row and column in a random order. We can note that however, by determining the optimal sequence of flashes, we can identify the desired selection from a smaller number of flashes. For example, based on the history of flashes and the P300 detection results, if the probability that the first row contains the desired selection is very low compared to other rows, there is no reason to flash the first row. In contrast, if the probability is high for both the second and the third row, it is desirable to flash the second or the third row in order to resolve the uncertainty. Bell et al. [3] suggests that, since we can identify the most likely selection during flashes by maintaining a running sum of P300 classifier output, we may be able to reduce the number of flashes in identifying the desired selection.

This paper presents a systematic approach to finding an optimal sequence of flashes in order to identify the desired selection using the fewest possible number of flashes in EEG-based BCIs. Determining the best flash sequence based on the accumulated results of P300 detection is viewed as a sequential decision making problem, and we adopt the partially observable Markov decision process (POMDP) model [11] for the representation of the problem. The POMDP model provides a rigorous framework for representing sequential decision making problems under limited sensory capabilities of agents. It perfectly fits our purpose since we have to deal with P300 classifier errors. Although it is computationally infeasible to find an optimal solution from POMDPs, the recent development of fast approximate algorithms such as point-based value iteration (PBVI) [16], and heuristic search value iteration (HSVI) [19], has made the POMDP approach practical for a wide variety of real-world applications such as spoken dialogue management [22] and assisted daily living [9].

Most of the previous works on EEG-based BCIs have been focused on the lower level of the interface. Whereas they are concerned with better feature extraction or classification methods for detecting single P300 from EEG while relying on a simple, random order of flashes, our focus is on finding an optimal sequence of flashes given a P300 classifier which is already implemented. Hence our work addresses the higher level of the interface, which is an important but currently missing part for an effective BCI.

BACKGROUND
In this section, we briefly review the facts about P300 in EEG and the common settings used in EEG-based BCIs which we will also be adopting in our work. We also review the standard definition of POMDPs for the sake of presenting our work.

Electroencephalography (EEG) and P300 Interfaces
EEG signals are the electrical signals recoded from the scalp and produced by the electrical activity of neurons in the brain. The electric potentials reflect the summation of the synchronous electrical activity of thousands or millions of neurons that are near the electrode for recording the EEG signals [20].

Event related potential (ERP) is elicited by an infrequent or particularly significant somatosensory stimulus. P300 is the positive peak component of ERP at about 300ms after the

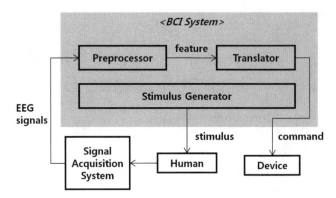

Figure 2. A typical architecture of the P300-based BCIs.

stimulus [6, 22]. P300 is known as one of the most reliable signals for composing BCI systems. However, the P300 elicited by the stimulus cannot be obtained easily, because EEG captures the brain activities from numerous sources and the P300 may be buried deeply [8]. Fortunately, there exist several P300 feature extraction methods and classification methods for detecting the P300 component of ERP. The feature extraction methods include the averaging of EEG signals [8], the Mexican hat wavelet [8, 17], and the spatial filter algorithm [10]. Once the relevant features are extracted, classification methods such as Fisher's linear discriminant, stepwise linear discriminant analysis (SWLDA), and support vector machine (SVM) [13] are used to detect the existence or absence of P300 in the EEG.

BCI systems based on P300 have a typical architecture as shown in Figure 2. There are components for stimulus generation, signal acquisition, preprocessing, and translation. The stimulus generator component gives stimuli to a user to elicit P300 on the desired situation. The signal acquisition component records the EEG signal for the given stimulus. The preprocessing component carries out feature extraction for detecting P300 from the given EEG signal. The translation component classifies the existence of P300, and sends appropriate commands to the external devices.

Partially Observable Markov Decision Processes (POMDPs)
A POMDP is a mathematical model for sequential decision making problems under uncertainty in the observation. It is defined by 8-tuple $\langle S, A, Z, b_0, T, O, R, \gamma \rangle$: S is the set of environment states; A is the set of actions available to the agent; Z is the set of all possible observations; b_0 is the initial belief where $b_0(s)$ denotes the probability that the environment starts in state s; T is the transition probability where $T(s, a, s')$ denotes the probability that the environment changes from state s to state s' when executing action a; O is the observation probability where $O(s, a, z)$ denotes the probability that the agent makes observation z when executing action a and arriving at state s; R is the reward function where $R(s, a)$ denotes the reward received by the agent when executing action a in state s; γ is the discount factor such that $0 \leq \gamma \leq 1$.

Since we assume that the agent cannot directly know the environment state, it maintains the probability distribution of the states based on the history of observations and actions. The probability distribution is defined as a belief state b where $b_t(s)$ denotes the probability that the state is s at time-step t. The belief state b_t can be regarded as the posterior distribution of states given the initial belief b_0 and the history $\{a_0, z_1, a_1, z_2, \ldots, a_{t-1}, z_t\}$:

$$b_t(s) = P(S_t = s | a_0, z_1, a_1, z_2, \ldots, a_{t-1}, z_t)$$

Upon execution action a_t and making observation z_{t+1} in belief state b_t, the belief state $b_{t+1} = \tau(b_t, a_t, z_{t+1})$ at the next time-step is computed by the Bayes rule,

$$b_{t+1}(s') = \frac{O(s', a_t, z_{t+1}) \sum_{s \in S} T(s, a_t, s') b_t(s)}{P(z_{t+1} | b_t, a_t)},$$

where $P(z_{t+1} | b_t, a_t)$ is the normalizing constant such that $\sum_s b_{t+1}(s) = 1$.

A policy determines the actions to be executed by the agent. Specifically, a policy π of a POMDP can be defined as a mapping from belief states to actions, i.e., $\pi : \Delta S \to A$. Every policy has an associated value function, which is (in the case of infinite horizon problems) the expected cumulative discounted reward by following the policy starting from a given belief state. When solving a POMDP, we search for an optimal policy that maximizes the value for each belief state. The maximum value for the belief state can be computed recursively

$$V^*(b) = \max_a \left[R(b, a) + \gamma \sum_z P(z|b, a) V^*(\tau(b, a, z)) \right],$$

where $P(z|b, a) = \sum_{s'} O(s', a, z) \sum_s T(s, a, s') b(s)$ and $R(b, a) = \sum_s R(s, a) b(s)$. The optimal value function V^* can be obtained by a series of dynamic programming back-up

$$V_t(b) = H V_{t-1}(b)$$
$$= \max_a \left[R(b, a) + \gamma \sum_{z \in Z} P(z|b, a) V_{t-1}(\tau(b, a, z)) \right],$$

for every belief state $b \in \Delta S$. We can also derive that value function V_t is piecewise linear and convex, hence it is represented as a set of α-vectors $\Gamma_t = \{\alpha_1, \ldots, \alpha_m\}$ and the value at a particular belief state b is calculated as

$$V_t(b) = \max_{\alpha \in \Gamma_t} \sum_{s \in S} \alpha(s) b(s) .$$

Once we compute the optimal value function V^*, the optimal policy is obtained by

$$\pi^*(b) = \arg\max_a \left[R(b, a) + \gamma \sum_z P(z|b, a) V^*(\tau(b, a, z)) \right].$$

Since there are infinitely many belief states, it is intractable to compute the optimal value function and the optimal policy. Some of the POMDP algorithms such as the witness algorithm [11] exploit the piecewise linear and convex property of value functions, but they are still limited to problems of small sizes. Instead, we settle for approximate algorithms such as point-based value iteration (PBVI) [16] or heuristic search value iteration (HSVI) [19], which focus the computational effort around the reachable belief states. These approximate algorithms are scalable, yet the solutions found are almost optimal in various benchmark POMDP problems. A complete review of exact and approximate algorithms for POMDPs is outside the scope of this paper, so we refer the readers to the references mentioned above.

SYSTEM ARCHITECTURE

Figure 3 shows the architecture of our BCI system. It is similar to the system described in Bell et al. [3], except that our system uses the POMDP policy for determining which letter to flash (stimulate).

The flash scheme of our system follows the paradigm similar to that of the P300 speller system: The user gazes at the target letter and the letters in the matrix are flashed in 250ms intervals, one letter at a time. Each flash turns on the letter for 125ms and turns off for another 125ms. A test consists of a series of flashes for identifying the target letter, and a pause interval of 2.5s is given between consecutive tests.

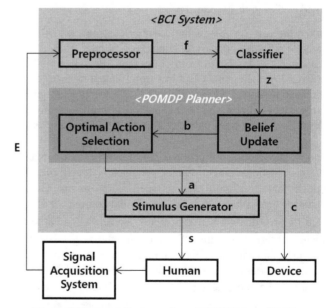

Figure 3. The architecture of our POMDP-based BCI system. 'f' is a feature vector, 'z' is the output from the P300 classifier and also the observation of POMDP, 'b' is the current belief, 'a' is the action to flash a letter or make a decision (i.e. conveying a command to device), 'c' is the command issued to a back-end device, and 'E' is the EEG signal.

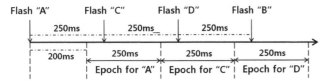

Figure 4. Time course of stimulus events and the corresponding epochs in EEG signals.

The EEG signals are acquired by the Biopac MP 150 data acquisition system [2] from 16 channels with 1kHz sampling rate. An epoch of EEG signals corresponding to a flash is the window of the 16-channel signal data between 200ms and 450ms after the flash is given (Figure 4), since P300 is expected to appear approximately at 300ms after the stimulus.

This epoch data is fed into the *preprocessor* to extract relevant features from the raw signal data, and then passed to the *classifier* to detect the existence of P300. The output of the classifier is used as the observation of the *POMDP planner*, which will perform the belief update and decide which letter to flash. In this section, we provide the details on how the preprocessor and classifier are constructed. The description of the POMDP planner deserves a separate section since it is the central component of our system.

Preprocessor

In order to construct the preprocessor and the classifier, we first prepare the training data consisting of P300 epoch instances each labeled either a target or a non-target. This training data is gathered using the same flash scheme outlined earlier in this section.

Since the raw signals contain a significant amount of high frequency noise, they are band-pass filtered (0.5-30Hz) with a 6th order Butterworth filter and down-sampled to 100Hz. We then extract features from the epoch data using the spatial projection algorithm [10]. This algorithm generates a set of filters which maximally discriminates between target and non-target epoch instances in the training data. More formally, given m channels and n time points of an epoch, the spatial projection algorithm generates a maximum of m linear filters. Each filter linearly transforms the epoch data from multi-channel (i.e. epoch) to one virtual channel. Each filter f_j (an m-dimensional column vector) is said to have discriminative power d_j, which is the value of Fisher criterion for linearly separating the target and the non-target instances in the training data. Given an epoch instance E_i (an $m \times n$ matrix) for the i-th flash, the feature vector of the epoch using filter f_j is computed by $f_j^T E_i$ (an n-dimensional row vector). The exact number of filters is usually determined by cross-validation. In our case, we limit the maximum number of filters to 5, since this number was sufficiently large for most of the subjects participating in this study and guaranteed timely processing of data for the computational resource available.

Classifier

To identify whether an epoch instance contains P300, we trained a classifier on the preprocessed feature vectors using the LIBLINEAR package [5]. Specifically, we used the L2-regularized logistic regression to map the binary output to a real value between 0 and 1, which represents the posterior probability that the feature vector is a target (i.e., the epoch contains P300). The parameters of the classifier are decided by 5-fold cross-validation on training data.

POMDP PLANNER

The POMDP planner plays the central part of our BCI system. In order to compute the optimal sequence of flashes using POMDP, we first need to model the problem. Once the modeling is done, we use a POMDP algorithm to obtain an optimal policy, which will determine the flash sequence. However, our approach is more sophisticated than plain models and algorithms since we have to take into account some important constraints of the system, such as *the delay in the P300* (the relevant observation is not available throughout the next two flashes) and *the repetition blindness* (P300 may not be elicited if two flashes is given on a target letter within 500ms).

POMDP Modeling of BCI

Our problem in hand is to find the target letter as accurately as possible while using as a small number of flashes as possible. Conceptually, this problem can be considered as an extension of the tiger problem in the POMDP literature [11], where the number of doors matches the number of letters in the stimulus matrix. The exact description is given below.

Let N be the number of letters in the matrix. In this paper, we consider [2x2] and [2x3] matrices, hence $N = 4$ and $N = 6$, respectively. The states in the POMDP correspond to the target letters, hence a total of N states. For each letter in the matrix, we can either flash it in the hope of detecting P300 (N flash actions) or claim that it's the target letter (N select actions), hence a total of $2N$ actions. The output value from the P300 classifier serves as the observation, where the real value between 0 and 1 is discretized into intervals of size 0.1 (e.g., z_1 for the output value in [0.0, 0.1), z_2 for the output value in [0.1,0.2), etc.), hence a total of 10 observations.

To make the system identify the target letter as soon as possible, we give -0.1 reward for the flash actions, +1 reward for the select actions that make a correct claim of the target letter, and -10 rewards for the select actions that incorrectly make a claim on a non-target letter.

We define the transition probability for each flash action as an identity matrix: we assume that the target does not change to some other letter within a test. Hence, we assign the transition probability of 1 if the state at the current time step is the same as the state at the next time-step, and 0 if the state at the current time-step is different from the state at the next time-step. For select actions, the transition probabilities are uniform: we assume that the target letter will reset to any letter in the matrix with the same probabilities between consecutive tests.

The errors in the P300 classification results are modeled as observation probabilities. Specifically, we assume that the classifier output follows the beta distribution when flashing the target letter. The parameters α and β of the beta distribution are obtained from the training data. We also assume that the distribution of output values when flashing a non-target letter is symmetric to the case when flashing the target letter. Hence, if α_{target} and β_{target} are the parameter values of the beta distribution for flashing the target letter, we set $\alpha_{\text{non-target}} = \beta_{\text{target}}$ and $\beta_{\text{non-target}} = \alpha_{\text{target}}$ for the beta distribution for flashing a non-target letter. Since these parameter values are different among the subjects, and POMDP algorithms take hours to find the optimal policy, we set the observation probability to 9 (and 11) different beta distributions that can appear in the human experiments on the system with [2x2] (and [2x3]) matrix. Hence, we have 9 (and 11) POMDP models with different observation probabilities for [2x2] (and [2x3]). The discount rate is set to 0.99, and the initial belief is set to the uniform distribution. This completes the specification of the POMDP model.

We briefly summarize how the model works. The state corresponds to the target letter in the current test, of which the BCI system does not have the direct knowledge. Hence, the system has to infer which letter is the target by some sequence of flash actions and the corresponding classification output values. When the system flashes a letter, and if the letter happens to be the target, then the probability is high for the classification output value close to 1. If the letter happens to be a non-target, then the probability is high for the classification output value close to 0. Thus, from a flash action and the corresponding classification output value (i.e., observation), the system can infer the probability distribution on target letters using the belief state of the POMDP. If a letter has a significant probability to be the target, the system repeatedly flashes the letter to increase the certainty that the letter is indeed the target. If the probability gets higher than some threshold, the system selects the letter as the target to maximize the expected return.

Solving the POMDP model

When we obtain the POMDP policy that determines the flash sequence, we have to address two constraints that come from the nature of the P300, namely the delay in P300 and the repetition blindness. We describe how these constraints are handled while implementing the POMDP algorithm.

Delay in P300

Standard definition of POMDPs assumes that the relevant observation is obtained before the execution of the next action. This assumption does not hold in our BCI system. As shown in Figure 4, the relevant P300 epoch ends at 450ms after the flash. Since a small amount of additional

delay is incurred by the data acquisition system, the preprocessor and the classifier, the observation is available at almost 510ms after the flash. Hence, the relevant observation is not available throughout the next two actions.

We can handle this constraint by using POMDPs with delayed observations [1]. Solving the model essentially requires finding the best action sequence of size equal to the delay in time-steps (in our case, sequence of length 2) during each dynamic programming backup, in contrast to finding the best single action in standard POMDPs without delayed observations.

Repetition blindness

The repetition blindness refers to the situation where P300 may not be elicited when two flashes on the target letter are given within 500ms [7, 12]. For example, when the target letter "A" is flashed and the "A" is flashed again within 500ms, the EEG signal corresponding to the second flash may not contain P300. A simple way to avoid this phenomenon is to make sure that the flash is not given on the same letter within 500ms. Since our flash scheme makes two flashes in 500ms, the flash at the current time-step should be different from the previous two flashes. In terms of our POMDP model, the action at the current time-step should be different from the previous two actions.

This constraint can also be handled by modifying the standard dynamic programming backup operation in POMDP algorithms: when we compute the best action that yields the best value, we only consider the actions that were not executed in the previous two time-steps.

POMDP algorithm for BCI

We now present our implementation of POMDP algorithm that addresses the P300 delay and the repetition blindness.

Basically our implementation is a modified version of the PBVI algorithm [16], which we refer to as BCI-PBVI. Figure 5 shows the main loop of the algorithm. As in PBVI, this algorithm requires the set B of randomly sampled belief states (i.e., belief set) for restricting the dynamic programming backup to those belief states (i.e., point-based

---

Algorithm BCI-PBVI(B, K, D, ϵ)
  INPUTS: belief set B; attentional blink length K; observation delay D; required precision ϵ
  for all action sequence $\langle a_1, \ldots, a_D \rangle$ of length D **do**
    Initialize $\Gamma_{a_1,\ldots,a_D} = \{\vec{0}\}$
  end for
  repeat
    for all action sequence $\langle a_1, \ldots, a_D \rangle$ of length D **do**
      $\Gamma'_{a_1,\ldots,a_D} = \text{backup}(B, K, D, \Gamma, a_1, \ldots, a_D)$
    end for
    $\delta = \text{difference}(B, \Gamma, \Gamma')$
    $\Gamma = \Gamma'$
  until $\delta < \epsilon$
  return Γ

Figure 5. Top-level pseudocode of BCI-PBVI.

```
Algorithm backup(B, K, D, Γ^{t-1}, a_1, ..., a_D)
  INPUTS: belief set B; attentional blink length K; observation delay D; set of α-vectors for (t-1)-step value
  function Γ^{t-1}; the action sequence of interest ⟨a_1, ..., a_D⟩
  A_allow = A - {a_{D-K+1}, ..., a_D}
  for all action a ∈ A_allow do
    for all observation z_D ∈ Z do
      for all α-vector α_i ∈ Γ^{t-1}_{a_2,...,a_D,a} do
        a_i^{a,z_D}(s) = γ Σ_{s'} T(s, a_1, s')O(s', a_1, z_D)α_i(s'),   ∀s ∈ S
      end for
      Γ^{t,a,z_D}_{a_1,...,a_D} = ∪_i {α_i^{a,z_D}}
    end for
  end for
  for all belief state b ∈ B do
    for all action a ∈ A_allow do
      α_b^a = Σ_{s_1∈S,...,s_D∈S} T(s,a_1,s_1)T(s_1,a_2,s_2) ··· T(s_{D-1},a_D,s_D)R(s_D,a) + Σ_{z∈Z} argmax_{α∈Γ^{t,a,z}_{a_1,...,a_D}} Σ_{s∈S} b(s)α(s)
    end for
    α_b = argmax_{α_b^a, a∈A_allow} Σ_{s∈S} b(s)α_b^a(s)
    Γ^t_{a_1,...,a_D} = Γ^t_{a_1,...,a_D} ∪ {α_b}
  end for
  return Γ^t_{a_1,...,a_D}
```

Figure 6. The backup operator for BCI-PBVI.

backup). Whereas the standard PBVI maintains the best α-vector and the corresponding best action for each sampled belief, the BCI-PBVI maintains α-vector for all length-D action sequences for each sampled belief state. It is like computing the action-value function rather than the state-value function. This is necessary in order to prevent the same action being executed within K time-steps, i.e., handle repetition blindness.

For every possible length-D action sequence, we update the corresponding set of α-vectors using the backup procedure. Figure 6 shows the pseudocode of the procedure, and it is the central part of our algorithm. Assuming that the current time-step is T, we first compute the set A_{allow} of actions that are allowed to execute at time-step $T + D$, i.e., the set of actions except those appearing in the last K steps in the sequence. Among the set of α-vectors that are computed in the previous iteration, only those with action sequences ending with allowed actions are valid α-vectors for the backup. The first loop in the pseudocode carries out this task. The second loop performs the actual point-based backup on the belief set B. For action sequence $a_1,...,a_D$, and a belief state b, we compute α_b such that $\sum_s b(s)\alpha_b(s)$ is the maximum expected value gathered *after D-steps in the future*, if, starting from the current belief state b, we execute the action sequence $a_1,...,a_D$. Cautious readers may question that α_b should also consider the rewards gathered *within D-steps in the future*, but as we will see shortly, it is not necessary to do so.

Belief update

Assume that, at time-step t, we have executed an action sequence $a_{t-D},...,a_{t-1}$, and deciding which action a_t to execute. According to the definition of α-vectors in BCI-PBVI, we cannot use the current belief state b_t. Instead, we need the belief state b_{t-D} of D-steps in the past, and this is the belief state we maintain while executing the policy.

Once we execute a_t and observe z_t, the belief state b_{t-D} is updated by

$$b_{t-D+1}(s') = \frac{O(s', a_{t-D}, z_t)\sum_s T(s, a_{t-D}, s')b_{t-D}(s)}{P(z_t|b_{t-D}, a_{t-D})}$$

where $P(z_t|b_{t-D}, a_{t-D})$ is the normalizing constant. Hence, in order to perform appropriate belief update, we need to remember the past belief state b_{t-D} as well as the action sequence $a_{t-D},...,a_{t-1}$.

Optimal action selection

At this point, selecting the optimal action for execution is quite straightforward. Assume once again that, at time-step t, we have executed an action sequence $a_{t-D},...,a_{t-1}$, and deciding on which action a_t to execute. Since we have the belief state b_{t-D} at hand, we compute $\sum_s b_{t-D}(s)\alpha(s)$ for $\forall\alpha \in \Gamma_{a_{t-D},...,a_{t-1}}$, and execute the best action associated with the α-vector that yields the best value.

SIMULATION EXPERIMENTS

Methods

Baseline

The baseline method follows a flash sequence decided by random order and hence it is equivalent to the method used in traditional BCI systems including Bell et al. [3]: the flash sequence is randomized among the letters that are not flashed within the current trial, where the trial refers to a subsequence of length equal to the letters in the matrix, hence each letter is flashed once per trial. However, our baseline method additionally takes repetition blindness into account: if a letter was flashed within 500ms, it will not be considered as a candidate for the current flash. The decision is made by the total score from the classifier: the output value of the classifier is regarded as the posterior probability, and the letter with the largest sum throughout trials is selected as the target letter. Hence, the method can be stopped at the end of any trial during a test, and determine the most likely target letter. The total score of a letter can be regarded as the posterior probability of being the target letter given the history of flashes and classifier output values. Note that the baseline method has no explicit "stop and select" decision making mechanism.

POMDP with select actions (PWSA)

The PWSA method uses the optimal flash policy computed from POMDP. The select actions represent the explicit decision making mechanism.

POMDP without select actions (PWOSA)

The PWOSA method uses the same set of actions as PWSA except the select actions. When stopped, we determine the target letter with the highest belief state probability. We prepared this method for the sake of performance comparison with the baseline method when the same number of flashes is used. Ideally, this method will be more efficient than the baseline method in terms of the number of flashes because the flash sequence is determined by the POMDP policy, rather than by some random distribution. Conceptually, this method can be considered as an optimal policy from a POMDP model with negative infinite rewards for selecting an incorrect target letter.

Setup

We performed 20 simulations on [2x2] and [2x3] matrices, each simulation consisting of 10000 tests. Output values from the classifier (i.e. observations) are sampled from the beta distribution with parameters $\alpha_{\text{target}} = \beta_{\text{non-target}} = 1.228$ and $\beta_{\text{target}} = \alpha_{\text{non-target}} = 0.625$, which were obtained from the pilot experiment involving one of the human subjects.

Each test consists of 40 flashes for the [2x2] matrix and 60 for the [2x3] matrix. For the baseline method, these numbers correspond to 10 observations for each letter in the matrix, whereas the PWSA and PWOSA methods may have different number of observations for each letter. Note also that the baseline and PWOSA methods run until the test ends, whereas the PWSA method can terminate early when the final select action is executed.

Measurements

We measured the performance of each method using the success rate and the bit rate.

Success rate

The success rate is defined by the percentage of tests in the simulation with correct identification of the target letters. We stopped the methods at the end of each trial (4 flashes for [2x2] and 6 flashes for [2x3]), and measured the success rate. Note that the PWSA method can terminate before the specified number of flashes. In this case, we extended the results until the end of tests. For example, if the PWSA method terminated during the 5th trial with an incorrect target letter, the method is regarded as selecting an incorrect target letter for all subsequent trials, and vice versa.

For all three methods, if the method has the same total score or the same maximum belief value for K letters, we gave a partial success of $1/K$.

Bit rate

The bit rate represents the quantity of transferred information per unit time during communication [18, 21]. The bit rate is defined as $B \cdot D$, where B is the number of bits per decision and D is the number of decisions per unit time. Let N be the total number of letters in the matrix and P be the success rate. Then we have

$$B = \log_2 N + P \log_2 P + (1 - P) \log_2 \frac{1 - P}{N - 1} .$$

In order to measure D, we used the following scheme: For the baseline method, since the decision has to be delayed (260ms) until the result of the last flash is available, we add the delay to the time spent on flashes. For example, if we have flashed 40 times, then the total time spent for the decision is calculated as 250ms * 40 flashes + 260ms. For the PWSA and PWOSA methods, since it takes an additional 115ms delay for updating the belief state, we add a delay of 375ms to the time spent on flashes. For example, if we have flashed 40 times, the total time for the decision is 250ms * 40 flashes + 375ms. D is calculated as the reciprocal of the total time.

Since the bit rate changes depending on the success rate, we calculated the bit rates for different success rates. The tradeoff here is that we can improve the success rate by increasing the number of flashes, but more time is accordingly spent per decision. For the PWSA method, since it has its own explicit termination mechanism, we will report only one value for the bit rate measurement.

Results

Figure 8 shows the success rate results for the three methods. The performance gap between the baseline method

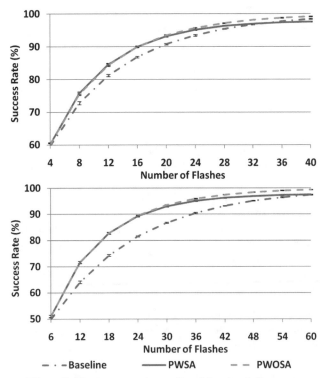

Figure 8. The success rate results of the simulation experiments. The top graph shows the result on [2x2] matrix and the bottom graph shows the result on [2x3] matrix.

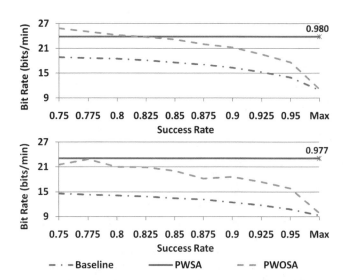

Figure 7. The bit rate results of the simulation experiments. The top graph shows the results on [2x2] matrix and the bottom graph shows the results on [2x3] matrix.

	[2x2] Matrix	[2x3] Matrix
Baseline†	18.879 (75.0%)	14.612 (75.0%)
Baseline‡	10.867 (98.4%)	9.257 (98.4%)
PWSA	23.840 (98.0%)	23.080 (97.7%)
PWOSA†	25.830 (75.0%)	22.859 (77.5%)
PWOSA‡	11.102 (99.2%)	9.820 (99.2%)

Table 1. Bit rate results of simulation experiment for each system. '†' denotes for maximum bit rate and '‡' denotes the bit rate on maximum success rate. The percentage in parenthesis is the corresponding success rate.

and the PWSA/PWOSA method is larger in the [2x3] matrix than in the [2x2] matrix. We conjecture that the performance gap will become even larger when we experiment on larger stimulus matrices. The baseline and the PWOSA methods will converge to a 100% success rate as the number of flashes goes to infinity. In contrast, the success rate of the PWSA method doesn't due to the bias inherent in the reward function. However, having an infinite number of flashes is not a practical assumption, and this kind of bias is necessary if we ever want the method to have some explicit termination mechanism. In our experiments, the PWSA method converges to a success rate close to 100% very quickly when forced not to terminate before the specified number of flashes, which is sufficient to demonstrate the validity of our approach. Figure 7 shows the bit rate results. The PWOSA method is always significantly better than the base line method. The PWSA method yields the success rates of 0.980 for [2x2] and 0.977 for [2x3], which correspond to 23.840 bits/min and 23.080 bits/min respectively. Table 1 summarizes the bit rate results of the three methods. Comparing the bit rates at the best achievable success rates, the PWSA method improves the bit rates by 220% to 249%. Comparing to the best bit rates achievable by the baseline method [1], the PWSA method achieves improvements of 126% to 158%.

---

[1] The baseline and PWOSA methods can achieve higher bit rates by lowering the success rate, but we set the minimum to 75% since we also want a sufficiently high success rate.

HUMAN SUBJECT EXPERIMENTS

Subjects and Experimental Setup

Nine (9) able-bodied male students at the Korea Advanced Institute of Science and Technology (KAIST) participated in the human subject experiments.

We compared the performances of the baseline and PWSA methods on the [2x2] and [2x3] matrices for these human subjects. Each test randomly assigned a target letter, while making sure that each letter was selected as the target letter exactly 10 times for the [2x2] matrix and 5 times for the [2x3] matrix. Hence, we performed a total of 40 tests for the [2x2] matrix and 30 tests for the [2x3] matrix. As in the simulation experiments, each test consisted of 40 flashes for the [2x2] matrix and 60 for the [2x3] matrix.

Procedure

We first prepared a number of different POMDP models with varying observation probabilities, since the classifier showed different error rates depending on the human subject. By varying the parameters of the beta distribution, we obtained 9 different models of the [2x2] matrix, and 11 for

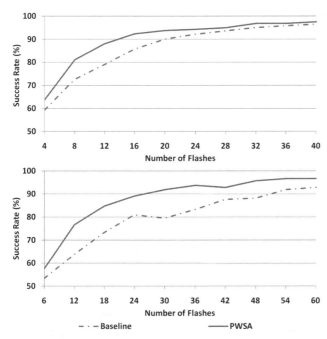

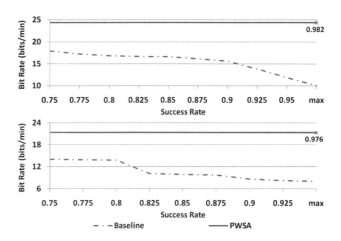

Figure 9. The bit rate results from the human subject experiments. The top graph shows the result on [2x2], and the bottom graph shows the result on [2x3].

	[2x2] Matrix	[2x3] Matrix
Baseline†	17.951 (75.0%)	14.070 (75.0%)
Baseline‡	10.065 (96.4%)	8.052 (92.9%)
PWSA	24.368 (98.2%)	21.367 (97.6%)

Table 2. Bit rate results on human experiment for each system. '†' denotes for maximum bit rate and '‡' denotes the bit rate on maximum success rate. The percentage in parenthesis is the corresponding success rate.

Figure 10. The success rates from the human subject experiments. The top graph shows the result on [2x2] matrix, and the bottom graph shows the result on [2x3] matrix.

the [2x3] matrix. We pre-computed the optimal policy for each model, since our implementation of the POMDP algorithm currently takes hours to finish. This is due to the fact that the point-based backup requires enumerating all possible action sequences of length D. Further optimization via pruning useless action sequences is left as a future work. We used 1028 randomly selected belief states for the [2x2] matrix, and 1030 for the [2x3] matrix.

At the onset of the experiment for each subject, we carried out a short pilot experiment where we gathered the training data for the preprocessor/classifier. Once they were trained, we performed cross-validation evaluation, chose the POMDP model with the minimum KL-divergence, and used the corresponding optimal POMDP policy.

We measured the success rates and the bit rates for comparing the performances of the baseline and PWSA methods.

Results

We originally involved nine (9) human subjects, but two (2) of them had beta distributions very far from any of the pre-computed models. Hence we use the data from seven (7) human subjects.

Figure 10 shows the success rate results of the human experiments. The success rate for the PWSA method is higher than the baseline method on any number of available flashes and the performance gap becomes larger as the matrix gets larger, which is consistent with the results from the simulation experiments.

Figure 9 shows the bit rate results. The PWSA method yielded an average success rate of 98.2% for the [2x2] ma-

trix and 97.6% for the [2x3] matrix. The corresponding bit rate is 24.368 bits/min for the [2x2] matrix, and 21.367 bits/min for the [2x3] matrix. In the case of the baseline method, we can control the success rate by changing the number of flashes, and the maximum average success rates are 96.4% for the [2x2] matrix and 92.9% for the [2x3] matrix. Regardless of how we set the success rate for the baseline method, the PWSA yielded higher bit rates. The summary of the bit rate results is shown in Table 1. Compared to the bit rates at the best achievable success rates, the PWSA method improves the bit rates by 242% to 265%. Compared to the best bit rates achievable by the baseline method, the PWSA method achieves improvements of 135% to 151%. These results are similar to those from the simulation experiments.

DISCUSSION

In this paper, we have presented a P300-based BCI system that uses POMDP for calculating the optimal flash sequence. In contrast to the previous body of research that concentrate on obtaining better feature extraction and classification algorithm from the raw EEG signals, our work provides a unified framework for building the BCI system. Bell et al. [3] have roughly suggested the idea of using the confidence values from the P300 classifier for optimizing the flash sequence, but to the best of our knowledge, our work is the first to address the problem in a principled way.

The contributions of this paper are as follows: First, we provided a formal decision-making model for P300-based BCI. Specifically, we showed how the POMDP model with observation delays can be adapted to BCI. Although we explained in the context of P300-based BCI systems, we believe that our approach is general enough to be easily applied to other BCI paradigms. Second, we presented a novel point-based algorithm for solving POMDPs with observation delays. The algorithm extends the standard point-based backup operator to handle observation delays. Third, we report experimental results using simulation as well as human subjects. Our POMDP-based method achieves significant performance improvement over the baseline method currently used in other BCI systems.

Currently, we are working on improving the speed of the algorithm for POMDPs with observation delays. One of the most time-consuming aspects of our algorithm is in the enumeration of all possible action sequence of length equal to the delay. Since some action sequences may be inferior to others, a combination of forward search and dynamic programming may yield substantial improvement in the speed. We are also working on applying the technique to P300 speller, where the user intentions exhibit more regularity. We strongly believe that we can achieve a magnitude of order improvement in performance (bit rate) if we embed the bigram/trigram model of alphabets into the intention-level transition probability of the POMDP. Finally, we are investigating into the methods [4] that enable the adaption of model to individual subjects without explicit pilot trial experiments or pre-computing optimal policies by enumerating candidate models.

ACKNOWLEDGMENTS
This work was supported by the National Research Foundation of Korea Grant 2009-0069702 and by the Defense Acquisition Program Administration and the Agency for Defense Development of Korea under contract UD080042AD.

REFERENCES

1. Bander, J.L. and White III, C.C. Markov decision processes with noise-corrupted and delayed state observations. *J. Operational Research Society 50* (1999).

2. Biopac System Inc. http://www.biopac.com

3. Bell, C.J., Shenoy, P., Chalodhorn, R. and Rao, R.P.N. Control of a humanoid robot by a noninvasive brain-computer interface in humans. *J. Neural Eng. 5* (2008).

4. Doshi, F., Pineau, J. and Roy, N. Reinforcement learning with limited reinforcement: Using Bayes risk for active learning in POMDPs. *Int. Conf. on Machine Learning* (2008).

5. Fan, R.E., Chang, K.W., Hsieh, C.J., Wang, X.R. and Lin, C.J. LIBLINEAR – A library for large linear classification. (2008), http://www.csie.ntu.edu.tw/~cjlin/liblinear/

6. Farwell, L.A. and Donchin, E. Talking off the top of your head: toward a mental prosthesis utilizing event-related brain potentials. *Electroencephalogr. Clin. Neurophysiol 70* (1988).

7. Fazel-Rezai, R. Human error in P300 speller paradigm for brain-computer interface. *Proc. 29th Annual Int. Conf. of the IEEE EMBS.* (2007).

8. Fazel-Rezai, R. and Peters, J.F. P300 wave feature extraction: preliminary results. *Proc. 18th Annual Canadian Conf. on Electrical and Computer Eng.* (2005).

9. Hoey J., Poupart, P., von Bertoldi, A., Craig, T., Boutilier, C. and Mihailidis, A. Automated handwashing assistance for persons with dementia using video and a partially observable Markov decision process. *Computer Vision and Image Understanding* (2009).

10. Hoffmann, U., Vesin, J.M. and Ebrahimi, T. Spatial filters for the classification of event-related potentials. *Proc. 14th ESANN* (2006).

11. Kaelbling, L.P., Littman, M.L. and Cassandra, A.R. Planning and acting in partially observable stochastic domains. *Artificial Intelligence 101* (1998).

12. Kanwisher N.G. Repetition blindness: Type recognition without token individuation. *Cognition 27* (1987).

13. Krusienski, D.J., Sellers, E.W., Cabestaing, F., Bayoudh, S., McFaland, D.J., Vaughan, T.M. and Wolpaw, J.R. A comparison of classification techniques for the P300 Speller. *J. Neural Eng. 3* (2006).

14. Krusienski, D.J., Sellers, E.W., McFaland, D.J., Vaughan, T.M. and Wolpaw, J.R. Toward enhanced P300 speller performance. *J. of Neuroscience Methods 167* (2008).

15. Mason, S.G., Bashashati, A., Fatourechi, M., Navarro, K.F. and Birch, G.E. A comprehensive survey of brain interface technology designs. *Annals of Biomedical Engineering 35*, 2 (2007).

16. Pineau, J., Gordon, G. and Thrun, S. Anytime point-based approximations for large POMDPs. *J. Artificial Intelligence Research 27* (2006).

17. Ramanna, S. and Fazel-Rezai, R. P300 wave detection based on rough sets. *Lecture Notes in Computer Science 4100*, Springer (2006).

18. Serby, H., Yom-Tov, E. and Inbar, G.F. An improved P300-based brain-computer interface. *IEEE Trans. Neural. Syst. Rehabil. Eng. 13* (2005).

19. Smith, T. and Simmons, R. Point-based POMDP algorithms: Improved analysis and implementations. *Proc. 21st Conf. on Uncertainty in Artificial Intelligence* (2005).

20. Wikipedia. http://en.wikipedia.org/wiki/Electroencephalography

21. Wolpaw, J.R., Birbaumer, N., Heetderks, W.J., McFarland, D.J., Peckham, P.H., Schalk, G., Donchin E., Quatrano, L.A., Robinson C.J. and Vaughan, T.M. Brain-computer interface technology: A review of the first international meeting, *IEEE Trans. Rehabil. Eng. 8* (2000).

22. Wolpaw, J.R., Birbaumer, N., McFarland, D.J., Pfurtscheller, G. and Vaughan, T.M. Brain-computer interfaces for communication and control. *Clin. Neurophysiol. 113* (2002).

23. Williams, J.D. and Young, S. Partially observable Markov decision processes for spoken dialog systems. *J. Computer Speech and Language 21* (2007).

Automatically Identifying Targets Users Interact with During Real World Tasks

Amy Hurst   Scott E. Hudson   Jennifer Mankoff
Human Computer Interaction Institute, Carnegie Mellon
5000 Forbes Ave, Pittsburgh, PA 15213
{akhurst, scott.hudson, jmankoff}@cs.cmu.edu

 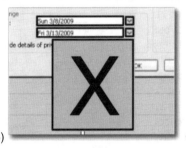 

A)   B)   C)

Figure 1: Our hybrid technique is able to identify significantly more targets than the Accessibility API alone. **A)** A screenshot of an open dropdown calendar object in Microsoft Outlook 2003. Interactive targets visible in this image include: two textboxes (with dates); two dropdown handles next to the textboxes; arrows on either side of the month; the month and year; any of the dates in the calendar; and the Today button. **B)** The Microsoft Accessibility API can identify 4 targets correctly (shown with a framed rectangle) and cannot identify 46 targets (shown with a filled gray rectangle). **C)** Our hybrid technique can identify all but one of targets in this example. All of the days of the month and the "Today" button change appearance when clicked on – something we can capture by calculating the difference image; and the arrows on either side of the month can be found with template matching.

ABSTRACT

Information about the location and size of the targets that users interact with in *real world settings* can enable new innovations in human performance assessment and software usability analysis. Accessibility APIs provide some information about the size and location of targets. However this information is incomplete because it does not support all targets found in modern interfaces and the reported sizes can be inaccurate. These accessibility APIs access the size and location of targets through low-level hooks to the operating system or an application. We have developed an alternative solution for target identification that leverages visual affordances in the interface, and the visual cues produced as users interact with targets. We have used our novel target identification technique in a hybrid solution that combines machine learning, computer vision, and accessibility API data to find the size and location of targets users select with 89% accuracy. Our hybrid approach is superior to the performance of the accessibility API alone: in our dataset of 1355 targets covering 8 popular applications, only 74% of the targets were correctly identified by the API alone.

ACM Classification Keywords: H5.2 [Information interfaces and presentation]: User Interfaces - Graphical user interfaces.

General Terms: Design, Human Factors

Author Keywords: Computer Accessibility, Usability Analysis, Target identification, Pointing Input.

INTRODUCTION

The ability to analyze user actions in any software environment is necessary to answer research questions regarding software usability, human performance, and how computers are used in daily life. Furthermore, the size and location of targets used in any real world application is crucial to this analysis. Target size and location is necessary to assess the pointing performance of an individual with motor impairments [14], perform usability evaluations of real world software [13], and to compare preference and performance of multiple interactor designs [7]. Many researchers either collect this data in controlled laboratory settings with custom or adapted software [7,14,15] which is easy to analyze, or deploy studies in the real world and capture and hand code the interaction [13]. While frequently more difficult to analyze, data about real world computer use can provide a welcome balance to the more artificial data gathered in laboratory studies. We have developed a technique that enables evaluators to automatically collect the size and location of the full range of targets a user interacted with during real world use.

Accessibility APIs such as the widely deployed *Microsoft Active Accessibility API (MSAA API)* [20] are designed to provide information about interactors in Graphical Users Interfaces and are available on many operating systems and programming platforms. While these APIs can be extremely accurate at identifying some targets, in practice many real world targets are not supported by these accessibility APIs [2]. Unfortunately, this includes targets in commonly used, popular applications such as Microsoft Outlook (Figure 1). Frequently, tools that need this information avoid API limitations by operating in constrained settings where targets are known or have been manually defined. For example, the Eggplant Functional Tester [23] has experimenters manually define a target they are interested in and uses computer vision (template matching) to find all occurrences of that target in a given interface. Another approach is to ignore the API entirely and use only visual information about the interface to identify targets. Seminal work in the area of visual analysis for identifying user interface targets has been done by Amant *et al.* [2, 3, 28] to support cognitive modeling and programming by example tools. Unfortunately, we cannot compare the accuracy of our hybrid technique to their vision-only approach because the accuracy numbers for their evaluations are not available. Recently, Yeh *et al.* [27] have explored using icon matching to identify user-selected targets in a GUI.

The primary contribution of this paper is a technical approach to the problem of finding the size and location of interactive targets from real world interactions that can step in where accessibility APIs leave off. This solution is flexible in that it can work across any application because it leverages visual cues that are ubiquitous across interfaces. We developed this technique using Microsoft Windows XP, but since it requires information that is relatively easy to acquire, it can be extended to other platforms. In this paper we describe how our technique, illustrated in Figure 1, successfully detects targets with 89% accuracy. We use a realistic dataset of 1355 targets gathered from a small representative set of real-world applications. Only 74% of the target selections in this dataset are accessible from the standard accessibility API. In comparing the difference between the size of targets found by the Accessibility API alone to those found by our hybrid technique, we show that the height of the targets found by the hybrid technique are significantly closer to the real size of the targets than the those found by the Accessibility API alone with an average difference of 7.2 pixels (or 19.6% of the average height of all targets in our dataset).

Approach: Leveraging "free" visual cues

When a mouse or other *locator* device is used to select a target, most graphical user interfaces (GUIs) provide standard visual cues (*e.g.,* change the appearance of the item once selected, such as the rectangle around the number 9 in Figure 1A). It is also common to visually change the ap-

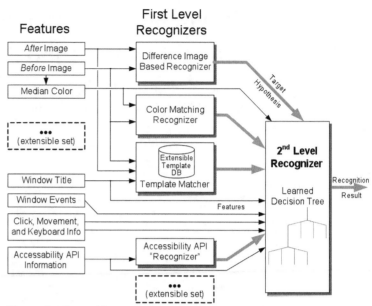

Figure 2: The architecture of our two-level recognizer. Thick gray lines represent target hypotheses, while thin black lines are features. Boxes at left represent feature generators. Middle column boxes are first level recognizers. Right hand box is the second level recognizer (classifier).

pearance of the target during the interaction (*e.g.,* change the color of a button when a mouse button is pressed, such as in Figure 3). These visual cues can help the user to interpret the function of the targets or catch errors and misunderstandings.

These cues can also be used to automatically find targets that are not available through the Accessibility API by analyzing screenshots of the interface with computer vision techniques. For example, the change in a button's shadow when a user clicks on it is easily detectable using *Difference Images*. *Template Matching* [6] can use samples of common targets to detect others with similar shapes. *Color Matching* uses a target's color to estimate its boundaries.

Our approach leverages an extensible combination of techniques including computer vision, input event data and accessibility data. Machine learning is used to combine the information provided by these techniques. This allows us to take advantage of their respective strengths, while avoiding their weaknesses, and performs better than any of the individual techniques alone.

Overview

In this paper we first present our hybrid technique to target identification that leverages an accessibility API and three computer vision algorithms. Next we present our evaluation of this hybrid technique on real world interfaces. Finally, we discuss some potential uses for our technique and conclude with future work discussing how this technique could be used in other platforms including mobile devices.

RECOGNITION ARCHITECTURE

Our approach defines *targets* as interactive elements that the user clicks on. This fits the structure of the vast majority of GUIs, but does not support advanced interaction activities such as gesture based interaction or crossing activities [1]. Further, our current implementation does not support dragging (where button press and release events are widely separated). However, the techniques developed here should be able to support more advanced interactions in the future.

As stated earlier, our work leverages computer vision to find targets. Screen images are relatively noise free and well suited to even simple image processing techniques. However, no single technique is capable of identifying all targets with high accuracy. Instead, as shown in Figure 2, we have implemented an extensible set of techniques each of which produces a guess about a probable target (a *target hypothesis*). We then use machine learning techniques to make a choice between these candidate targets.

There is a range of well understood machine learning techniques [21] that can be used to intelligently choose the most likely target from multiple target hypotheses. Generally, these techniques make use of *labeled training data* to create (or *learn*) a statistical model. This learned model *predicts* which hypothesis is correct based on information that describes a particular interaction. This information is expressed in terms of a set of *features* derived from the interaction (such as the window title, input event data about user motions towards the target, or an image of the screen just before the click on the target).

The feature information and a ground truth label indicating the correct size and location of the target are needed for each interaction instance used in training. A learning algorithm processes this training data and produces a *classifier* – an executable entity that can take the features from a new interaction and use those to produce a predicted target size and position.

In our case we have created a two-level classification scheme. At the first level we use a set of classifiers each of which identifies some types of targets well, but others less well. We refer to these as *recognizers* to distinguish them from the *learned classifier* that intelligently picks from among these results based on features from the interaction. We use ADABoosting [8] on a decision tree (created with a variant of the well known C4.5 algorithm [21]) to implement this second level classifier. Our architecture is sufficiently general that first level recognizers can be added over time. Some examples of first level recognizers we have currently implemented include:

Accessibility API: This returns the size and location of the lowest level object under the cursor that is returned from the accessibility API.

Difference Image: Comparison of two images is a standard computer vision technique [6]. Visual feedback can be captured by comparing the screen image taken just before the locator button press event to a screen image taken just before the locator button release event. The

bounding box around those screen pixels that are different is a potential target.

Color Matching: After blurring an image, the target often stands out as a region of color different from the surrounding image. This is especially so when the target is highlighted in response to the user's click. Standard computer vision techniques can be used to find the boundaries of regions of color that match the color under the cursor at the time of the click.

Template Matching: A known target can be used as a pattern or template by breaking it into its constituent corners and edges so that it can be compared to the image of an unknown target. This enables a single template to help find the borders of many similar targets of varying sizes.

IMPLEMENTATION

Data collection

The first piece of our target finding system is the capture component. CRUMBS (Capture Real-world User Mouse BehaviorS) captures information about interaction activities including (1) all locator, keyboard, and window events (2) any accessibility API information that is available and (3) two 300x300 screen captures that are centered on the cursor during a button event.

CRUMBS, written in C++, is based on DART (Disruption Awareness and Recovery Tracker) [11]. CRUMBS probes the MSAA API for the type and size of interactive targets. An API hook is used to take a 300x300 pixel screen capture (centered on the cursor) immediately before each button press event is dispatched, and immediately after each release event is dispatched. This limit is set for efficiency reasons, and because it is large enough to capture most targets (92% in our data set). If the cursor moves between press and release the second image is centered on the new cursor location. CRUMBS has been deployed in the field continuously since January 2008 and can also be used for laboratory data collection.

Two level classifier

Our implementation leverages the Weka toolkit [26], and we use the C4.5 Decision Tree learning algorithm [21] with binary splits (which suit our data well as it is a mix of numeric, nominal, and string features). The data used for training is hand labeled (details on the training data and results are given in the validation section). Our implementation currently runs offline, but could easily be augmented to run as data is collected. Below we describe various components of the implementation.

Feature Generation

We use features as a way to describe an interaction. Features are used by the first level recognizers to create their hypotheses, and potentially again by the second level classifier to help choose the correct target size or location from among these hypotheses. Features reduce the complexity of the decision problem while also highlighting the most important information. We extract the following features for each interaction:

Accessibility API features: The Accessibility API reports the size, location and type of the lowest level accessible object under the cursor.

Locator features: For each interactive sequence (starting from the previous sequence's release event and ending after the user presses and releases the locator button in the current sequence), the following features are reported:

Click features: Which locator button was pressed during the current press/release; click duration (time the locator button was held down between the current press and release); and distance slipped (amount of movement between locator button press and release).

Movement features: Euclidean distance moved (between the previous release and the current press); total distance moved (along the actual path of the locator during the same period); duration of movement (from the previous release until the current press); average velocity of movement (same period); and total sequence duration (time between the previous release and the first movement after the current release).

Keyboard features: Because it sheds light on what the target was used for, in the case of keyboard activity we are interested in what happens after the release rather than leading up to it. Consequently, keyboard features are measured from current release through the press of the next sequence. These include: a count of the number of keys pressed, a count of various special keys (including arrow, letter, number, enter, tab), a string of all keys pressed, and the time before first key press (after the click). Note that because this feature makes use of information occurring after the target is selected it will not be suitable for use in some real-time applications. As shown in our results (Figure 10), these features turned out not to be of high value for target finding, meaning that applications that operate in real time could operate without them.

Window event features: Like keyboard features, information about the window in use sheds light on what a target might have been selected for. The window title of the window currently in focus is reported as a feature. Window events that take place immediately after the locator button is released are also important indications of the user's goals. Any window events, including window title and whether it was minimized, maximized, gain focus, *etc.* are reported. These may occur anytime between the current release and the first move of the next sequence.

Additional possible targets: Each first level recognizer returns its best estimate for target size and position. However, additional features are generated indicating the presence of "second best" targets, the total number of targets found, and how many of the viable targets contain the point where there locator button press occurred.

Visual features: Features are generated indicating whether only one or many areas of visual change were present, the median RGB color value near the button press, the presence of a specific known interactor (as detected by a template), and whether that template was fixed or variable in size.

First Level Recognizers

The features described above feed into an extensible set of *first level recognizers*. Each first level recognizer is responsible for providing a hypothesized target size and position (or an indication that it finds no viable target) from those features. Details for each of our current recognizers follow.

Accessibility API recognizer

This first level recognizer simply returns a hypothesis matching the best information available from the Accessibility API. Specifically, the size and location of the lowest level accessible object under the cursor, during a pointing device's button press, is used as the target hypothesis.

For the work described here we make use of the *Microsoft Active Accessibility API (MSAA API)* and associated OS hooks. This is a cross-application Windows operating system level solution for getting low-level information about targets including push buttons, menus, textboxes and html links.

Limitations of the MSAA API: As previously stated, not all interactors are supported by the MSAA API. Examples of some of these unsupported targets include the entire editing area of Microsoft PowerPoint, the full playing area of Windows games such as Solitaire and Minesweeper, and specialty dialogs including the Character Map, custom color selector panels, and the Microsoft Paint controls. In addition, not all applications support the API in the same way. For example, two popular web browsers, Microsoft's Internet Explorer and Open-source Firefox, treat content in a very different way, limiting the API's access to them. Internet Explorer treats embedded Flash applets in such a way that the API is able to access most of the targets, however Firefox embeds Flash in such a way that the targets are not accessible through the API by clicking on them.

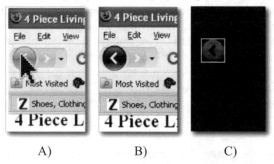

Figure 3: Selected Target found by calculating the difference between images taken during a locator button's press and release events. **A)** The user is pressing on the "Back" button in Firefox (the cursor here is for illustration only and not captured in our data). **B)** The image captured after the user releases the button. **C)** After subtracting A from B, the resulting difference is the correct target (shown with a bounding box).

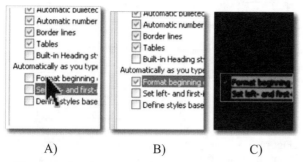

A)   B)   C)

Figure 4: Overlap error with difference imaging: The difference image accidentally joins the targets because the top edge in **A)** overlaps with the bottom edge in **B)**. **C)** shows the resulting target which is too big.

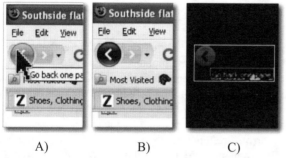

A)   B)   C)

Figure 5: Visual change error in difference imaging: New visual content appears that overlaps or is near the target. **A)** Tooltip in the press image very near target **B)** Tooltip is not present in release image **C)** Resulting difference region includes both the target and the tooltip, which is incorrect.

Difference image recognizer

A difference image is a subtraction of all the pixel values in two images [6]. Targets that produce a salient visual change upon interaction may be detected by calculating the difference between the image before the press event of a click is dispatched and the one found after the release event is dispatched.

Recall that CRUMBS captures an image immediately before the mouse press and immediately after the mouse release in an interaction sequence (Figure 3 A and B). Difference imaging compares these two images. Since it is common for users to *slip*, or accidentally move the pointing device a few pixels during the click, we automatically align the images according to the amount and direction of motion between press and release. Any overlap is cropped so that both images are the same size. At this point, a Gaussian blur is applied to both images. Applying this blur helps minimize the impact of very small visual elements (such as letters) that are really part of a larger targets (such as a button).

After the images have been prepared, we iterate through each image and subtract the pixel values from one image to another at the corresponding locations. This subtraction yields an output image of only the differences between the two images. Next we apply a connected component filter [6] to group changes into contiguous regions (or *blobs*). The results of the connected component filter are analyzed

to find the bounding box of the smallest sufficiently large blob (at least 5x5 pixels) that overlaps the cursor position. If no blobs are sufficiently large then the bounding box of all pixels that differed between the two images is returned.

This technique, along with template matching and color matching techniques, is written using a combination of the JAVA Advanced Image library [12] and ImageMagick [10].

Limitations of the difference image recognizer: If there was only one region of visual change (such as in Figure 3) and it is sufficiently large (either its height or its width is greater than 5 pixels), then the bounding box of this region is given as the hypothesis target size. However, sometimes multiple visual changes occur, and the boundaries of these targets overlap in the difference image. For example, Figure 4 shows how difference imaging fails when the boundaries of the two targets touch after blurring.

Difference imaging also has difficulty when the button press triggers additional animations or otherwise changes the targets. Examples include displaying tooltips, non-target interactors losing their focus, or visual changes unrelated to the pointing device occurring. Figure 5 illustrates when a tooltip window appears too close to a target.

Color matching recognizer

The color matching technique searches for a color region in the image associated with the current sequence press event that could indicate the bounds of a target (Figure 6). The image is prepared using a median blur filter of 10 pixels (Figure 5B). This has a similar effect to the Gaussian blur used in difference imaging – removing small differences – but tends to choose a single color rather than continuously varying one. Once the image is blurred, the color of the pixel directly under the cursor (at the center of the image) is used as the color to match. The match algorithm may return multiple regions. These regions are handled similarly to difference imaging (the bounding box of the smallest region greater than 5 pixels in either height or width is selected). If no blobs are sufficiently large, a bounding box around all matched pixels is used.

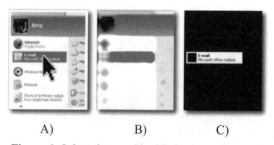

A)   B)   C)

Figure 6: Selected target identified using color matching. Difference imaging failed to find this target because images captured from the button down and button up events were identical. **A)** Original image. **B)** Image after median blur. The color over the cursor (dark blue) is selected for color matching **C)** The matching algorithm selects the smallest blob of that color over the cursor (the correct target).

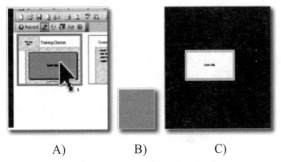

A)   B)   C)

Figure 7: Example of false positive from color matching from Microsoft PowerPoint. Target in image **A)** was the thumbnail of slide 1 which is highlighted by the interface with a blue square. **B)** Color chosen to use for color matching after applying median blur to A. **C)** Results of color matching. In this example, choosing the color of the center pixel after applying the median blur yielded an incorrect result because the bounds of the selected color were much smaller than the target size.

Limitations of the color matching recognizer: This technique complements difference imaging because it works even when there is no visual change. However it currently does not support targets with a mutli-color background (such as a gradient or shading as found on the Microsoft Windows Start Button). Additionally, it does not support targets that are not surrounded by a differently colored background (such list items or checkboxes that share the same background). Figure 7 illustrates an example where color matching failed to identify the correct target because it matched a color that was connected to a smaller shape within the target.

Template matching recognizer

Template matching is a relatively simple computer vision technique that matches a prepared set of pattern or *template* images against a source image (captured by CRUMBS) and finds occurrences of the template image within the source image (Figure 8). Given the image of a target, it can be used as a fixed sized image (or icon) template. It can also be processed into a variable sized template by automatically extracting the corners and edges of the icon. By convolving the source image with a template, it is possible to

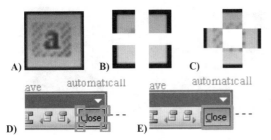

A)   B)   C)
D)   E)

Figure 8: Example of corner template matching. Where template **A)** is used to identify target in **E)**. **B)** Corner templates: 5x5 pixels. **C)** Edge templates 6x6 Pixels. **D)** Source image with found corners marked with squares. **E)** Source image with line around found target. Note that this technique is size independent, as the aspect ratio in **E)** is different from **A)**.

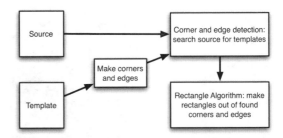

Figure 9: Corner and edge template matching algorithm takes in source and template images, extracts the edges and corners from template, and searches source for template corners and edges. Finally rectangles are formed from matched corners and edges.

quickly identify all regions where template pixels match the target image.

Systems using the techniques described here should be delivered with a set of templates designed to match many common toolkit components appearing on various platforms. Templates can then be added to the template set on an as needed basis. We envision this happening when users detect and correct errors made by the system. In particular, when errors are reported, the user might be asked to correct or disambiguate [16] the system by drawing a bounding box around the correct target. The system may also ask the user to indicate which if any part of the current window title string is indicative of the application being used (see discussion of application groupings below). The training and validation section below will discuss our investigation of the effects of adding more templates on accuracy.

Template matching is a multi-step process. First we check for an exact (icon) template match on both screen captures associated with the interaction activity. Next, the template matching algorithm searches for variable size matches by comparing each corner and edge of the template to the corresponding region around the spot where the locator button click occurred (Figure 9). Additional corners are created by connecting any two strongly matching adjacent edges even where a corner was not found. The algorithm takes all corner template matches and corners created from adjacent edges, and searches this set for possible resulting rectangles. Finally, the smallest rectangle is returned as the resulting target hypothesis.

The sets of possible templates to match against are grouped by application or application class. Applications are determined by examining window titles (which frequently include the application name and the active file name) using application indicator strings delivered with the system or subsequently identified by end users. For efficiency reasons, we restricted the list of potential templates matched based on the indicated application. Window titles that do identify a recognized application are put into an "unknown title" category.

Limitations of the template matching recognizer: Fixed size (*icon matching*) works best on icons or unique targets that don't have a border. Variable size (*corner and edge matching*)

Application	% of data
MS Outlook	39.9%
Web Browsing (IE and Firefox)	23.5%
MS Word	12.2%
Windows Explorer (files & customization)	9.3%
Media Player	7.6%
MS PowerPoint	7.6%

Table 1: Distribution of test data by application

works best on targets with clear borders and is able to handle items that differ in size from the original template, something icon matching cannot do. Thus the two techniques complement each other. However, both have difficulty finding the correct target in cases where an animation has not completed when the screenshot is taken, because in that case the screenshot may not contain the final image that the template matches.

TRAINING AND ACCURACY VALIDATION

Recall that the creation of a classifier depends on a training stage in which labeled data is needed. In our case, the data is example interaction activity, and the labels are the correct target size and location for each activity. Here we will describe how we acquired this training data, how the classifier was trained, and present results of accuracy tests.

Data acquisition

Although the CRUMBS data acquisition component of our system has been field deployed for a year as a part of a related project, the deployment setting is not Internet enabled and targets a population of users with motor impairments who spend much of their time playing games on the computer. While this data set is interesting for many reasons, we did not feel that it was sufficiently diverse to demonstrate our technique.

To account for this, we generated what we believe to be a

1. Window title
2. API result type
3. Width of target found by Template Matching
4. Height of target found by Template Matching
5. Area of target found by Template Matching
6. Color used for color Matching
7. Technique (connected component, or bounding box) used to analyze blobs in difference image
8. Velocity before button press
9. Distance moved before button press
10. Time elapsed between last button release and next movement
11. Count of valid targets found by difference image
12. Area of target found by difference image
13. Width of target found by difference image
14. Height of target found by difference image
15. Count of occurrence of a window focus event immediately after the button release.

Figure 10. Top 15 features used as by the second level classifier, sorted by information gain.

realistic and representative training and test corpus. We carried out the exact steps specified in a set of tutorials for Windows and Microsoft Office products (called the Step By Step Tutorials). These tutorials give clear, step-by-step instructions for how to accomplish common tasks. Because they provide instructions for what to do, they remove any potential bias on the part of the experimenters in selecting targets. Because they focus on common tasks for common products, they provide reasonably representative data. We used portions of the following tutorials to create our initial dataset: Microsoft Office Outlook [17], Microsoft Office: PowerPoint 2003 [18], Microsoft Office: Word 2003 [19], and Learning Windows XP [24].

Data from Internet interactions was added to this set by having our colleagues interact with several of the websites on the Alexa.com Top sites in the United States. Our participants selected websites they used normally from our list of top websites, and performed tasks they would normally do on them. They chose to use 7 of the 10 most popular sites (as of March 2009): google.com, yahoo.com, facebook.com, youtube.com, Wikipedia.com, eBay.com, craigslist.com. The relative proportion of interactions from each application is shown in Table 1.

Next we segmented the data into interaction sequences ending with a click. Since our initial implementation explicitly does not support drag interactions, and training on them would produce anomalous results, we also removed any interaction activity with a movement between press and release longer than 10 pixels. (We should be able to remove this limitation and consider drags in a later release.) Clicks that could not be assigned to a specific target after careful human examination of the data were also removed; these were frequently focus clicks or accidental clicks. The result was a data set of 1355 interaction sequences. These were processed offline to generate the features needed for the training phase.

Labeling of ground truth

To establish labels for training, our dataset was hand coded by one of the authors by selecting the "click sensitive" screen region for each target within the images captured with our data. The distribution of interactor types which make up targets in our data is shown in Table 2.

Training

The Weka machine learning system [26] was used to create the classifier using the ADABoost.M1 algorithm [7] with 10 iterations using the C.45 decision tree algorithm [21] as its base classifier. Overall, on average, the decision tree for each iteration from training on our interactive target labels contained 136.2 decision nodes. Figure 10 indicates the top 15 features used in the resulting classifier, ordered by information gain.

Interactor Type	% data	Interactor Type	% data
pushbutton	50.1%	tree view item	1.0%
menu item	9.8%	outlook date item	0.9%
list item	8.4%	table cell	0.5%
text link (webpage)	7.2%	window (focus click)	0.5%
image link (webpage)	6.3%	combo box	0.4%
text box (1 line)	4.4%	icon	0.4%
check box	3.2%	radio button	0.4%
scroll bar arrow	2.5%	desktop	0.2%
tab	1.3%	equation	0.1%
text (single word)	1.1%	spin box	0.1%
text area (multi-line)	1.0%		

Table 2: Distribution of interactor types acting as targets in the training dataset.

Accuracy results

In assessing accuracy we considered the size and position of each classification made by the system. We considered a classification to be correct if it contained the click point of the interaction and was within 15% or 5 pixels (whichever was larger) of both the width and height of our human labeled ground truth.

To estimate the overall accuracy of the resulting classifier we used the common 10-fold stratified cross validation method – we estimate the accuracy of the final classifier as the average accuracy found in 10 classifiers, each built from 90% of the test data and tested against the remaining 10%. Our tests indicate an overall accuracy of 89% (kappa = .8), and Figure 11 illustrates the overall accuracy of our hybrid approach compared to the accuracy of each individual recognizer.

As mentioned earlier, the current implementation of CRUMBS logging software only captures images that are 300x300 pixels. Not only does this cover 92% of our targets, but for a number of applications, the details of large

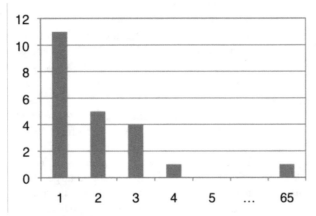

Figure 12: Distribution of number of targets covered by a single template. Most templates (11) found only one target (the one they were created from). The most successful template of the 22 we created found 65 targets, and the rest found four or fewer targets. While it is true that a relatively small number of targets is found by each template, the cost of creating each one is small.

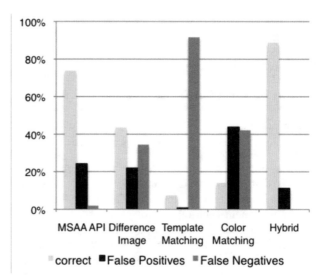

correct ■ False Positives ■ False Negatives

Figure 11: Raw accuracies of four first level recognizers (API, Difference Image, Template Matching, Color Matching) and the overall accuracy of our hybrid technique.

targets are of less interest (*e.g.,* they are easy to select). However, this limitation does cause some misclassification, since in the end 7.9% of the targets in our dataset ended up being larger than 300 pixels in some dimension (and so are clipped in the images our classifier uses). Of these, 2.6% are actually misclassified (with the remaining 5.3% being correctly identified by the API without the need for images). As a result, it may be possible to improve overall accuracy by capturing larger images if the performance issues regarding taking full-sized screenshots can be resolved.

Because templates may be added over time, it is useful to consider the impact of templates on overall accuracy. Our intuition was that a fairly small number of templates will provide sufficient accuracy benefits, and that this will allow us to distribute a manageable library of initial templates with a system and still get high accuracy from the beginning.

To create an initial set of templates, we considered each target which failed the preliminary version of the system without template matching. For each of these failures we semi-automatically created a template. In particular, we manually outlined the bounding rectangle of the target -- much as a user might in providing correction feedback -- then the system automatically extracted corner and edge images to create a template. As we progressed through 154 initial error cases (in random order) we eventually created 22 distinct templates. These templates successfully covered 102 of the initial 154 error cases, illustrated in Figure 12.

DISCUSSION

Based on systematic tests with realistic data, our results demonstrate the viability of a hybrid approach to finding the location and size of targets. Even though our algorithm is relatively computationally simple, it managed to correctly identify most of the targets in our dataset. As illustrated in Figure 11, our hybrid approach was more accurate than any of our first level recognizers -- only missing 11% of targets, compared to lower accuracy for all of the component first level recognizers it is built from, including the accessibility API. This suggests that our overall approach might be further improved by adding additional first level recognizers, even if those recognizers don't themselves perform better than our current system. For example, we might include rule-based techniques such as those of Amant et al. [2,3,28].

Another addition to our technique would be to design first level recognizers to handle targets that demonstrate systematic types of errors. For example, one common error in our data set involved targets with multiple unconnected visual components, such as checkboxes with adjacent clickable labels. When the user clicked on either the checkbox or the label, the label received a blue highlight, and a check was added to the box. Our difference image algorithm had difficulty with these targets because it tended to see them as separate visual elements. Template matching is best suited to find icons, so it could find the checkbox but not its accompanying label. Finally, color matching identified the label, but missed the checkbox. Based on these findings, a combined target hypothesis created from the results of two first level recognizers may be a better hypothesis than either recognizer can provide alone.

Another error that happens systematically in our data is caused by the choice to capture only 300x300 pixel images. Although we did this for efficiency reasons, as mentioned earlier this choice is responsible for 2.6% of our errors. By adjusting the capture size based on runtime information from the API to extend to the full width of the proposed API target, we could make it possible to eliminate many of these errors.

APPLICATIONS AND FUTURE WORK

Identifying the size and location of targets interacted with during real world use can enable novel additions to existing technology. Below we present three areas that can benefit from accurate target identification of user interfaces.

Improving Computer Accessibility

Having more reliable information about the size and location of targets a user interacts with provides opportunities to assess and adapt to performance metrics during real world use. One approach to assess pointing accuracy is to use metrics drawn from characterizations of data with respect to Fitts' Law [5]. Historically this metric has been explored in the laboratory, but our hybrid technique could expand on research that looks at this metric during real world use [4]. Additionally, there are many target-specific pointing performance metrics that have yet to be studied out of the laboratory [13,15]. Finally, knowing the size and location of targets interacted with could greatly expanded the ability to understand real world pointing performance of motor impaired individuals [9].

We are interested in using automatic assessments of pointing performance to suggest adaptations to a computer environment to increase computer accessibility. For example,

accurate information about target selection performance could help identify when a user slips off a target during a click. With accurate assessment of this pointing problem, a software adaptation that froze the locator position during a click, such as Steady Clicks [24], could be deployed.

Supporting Automatic Extraction of a Task Sequence

In usability evaluations, having a list, or *task sequence*, of the targets a user interacted with to achieve a goal is desirable. Task sequence can be analyzed to reveal differences in the steps a user performed and a pre-defined sequence, or to compare the actions of multiple users. Experimenters typically generate a task sequence through logging software built into a custom application [7] or by hand coding video logs [13]. Our technique could help usability specialists by automatically extracting these sequences from real world use, and be used in existing video annotation tools such as Transana (http://www.transana.org).

Automatically Scripting Common Actions

During real world use, it is common to encounter repeated sequences of UI interactions. Tools such as Automise (http://www.automise.com) enable users to easily generate scripts to perform multiple UI tasks. We envision automatic target identification being incorporated into these tools to automatically identify targets in frequently performed task sequences and suggest scripts to automate these tasks. Yeh et al. have begun to explore this domain with Sikuli, which allows users to graphically write GUI automation scripts [27].

Future Work

In future work, we plan to leverage our results to improve computer access in real world interactions. Specifically, we plan on using our hybrid technique to identify the size and locations of real world targets encountered in daily life to automatically assess the pointing performance of individuals with pointing problems.

Our solution is currently limited to Windows platforms because CRUMBS only works with the MSAA API. However, the visual characteristics of interaction that we leverage are not limited to the Windows operating system. Other platforms (including mobile phones) utilize the same visual affordances our technique is designed to detect: strong visual changes on interaction, color highlights, common borders, and repeated graphics. As future work we would like to develop our technique to other platforms, using their respective accessibility APIs.

CONCLUSIONS

We have presented a new application independent technique to identify targets a user interacts with. This technique uses a hybrid of accessibility API information and of several computer vision techniques to identify these targets. In a dataset that was collected from realistic interactions with real applications, our technique was able to identify 89% of the targets, and the underlying accessibility API could only identify 74% of these targets.

ACKNOWLEDGMENTS
This work was supported in part by the National Science Foundation under grants EEC-0540865, IIS-0713509, IIS-0325351, IIS-0205644, the first author's NSF Graduate Student Research Fellowship; IBM Research; and the Pennsylvania Infrastructure Technology Alliance.

REFERENCES

1. Accot, J. and Zhai, S., (2002), More than dotting the i's – foundations for crossing-based interfaces. In *Proceedings of the SIGCHI conference on Human factors in computing systems,* ACM Press, pp. 73-80.

2. St. Amant, R., Lieberman, H., Potter, R., and Zettlemoyer, L., (2000), Programming by example: visual generalization in programming by example. In *Communications of the ACM*, ACM Press, 43, 3, pp. 107-114.

3. St. Amant, R. and Riedl, M. O., A perception/action substrate for cognitive modeling in HCI. In *International Journal of Human-Computer Studies*, Elsevier, 55(1), pp. 15-39.

4. Chapuis, O., Blanch, R., and Beaudouin-Lafon, M., (2007), Fitts' Law in the Wild: A Field Study of Aimed Movements. Technical Report n.1480, LRI, Univ. Paris-Sud, France, December 2007, 11 pages.

5. Fitts, P.M., (1954), The Information Capacity of the Human Motor System in Controlling the Amplitude of Movement. In *Journal of Experimental Psychology,* 47, pp. 381-391.

6. Forsyth, D. and Ponce, J., (2002), *Computer Vision – A Modern Approach,* 1st edition, Prentice Hall.

7. Findlater, L. and McGrenere, J., (2004), A comparison of static, adaptive, and adaptable menus. In *Proceedings of the SIGCHI Conference on Human Factors in Computing Systems*, ACM Press, pp. 89-96.

8. Freund, Y. and Schapire. R.E., (1996), Experiments with a new boosting algorithm. In *Proceedings of Machine Learning*, Morgan Kaufmann, pp. 148-156.

9. Hurst, A., Mankoff, J., and Hudson, S. E., (2008), Understanding pointing problems in real world computing environments. In *Proceedings of the ACM SIGACCESS conference on Computers and Accessibility*, ACM Press, pp. 43-50.

10. ImageMagick software suite: http://www.imagemagick.org (Accessed 09/17/09)

11. Iqbal, S. T. and Horvitz, E., (2007), Disruption and recovery of computing tasks: field study, analysis, and directions. In *Proceedings of the SIGCHI conference on Human Factors in Computing Systems*, ACM Press, pp. 677-686.

12. JAVA Advance Imaging, Template Matching https://jaistuff.dev.java.net/ (Accessed 09/17/09)

13. Kaufman, D. R., Patel, V. L., Hilliman, C., Morin, P. C., Pevzner, J., Weinstock, R. S., Goland, R., Shea, S., and Starren, J., (2003), Usability in the real world: assessing medical information technologies in patient's homes. In *Journal of Biomedical Informatics,* 36, 1/2, pp. 45-60.

14. Keates, S., Hwang, F., Langdon, P., Clarkson, P. J., and Robinson, P., (2002), Cursor measures for motion-impaired computer users. In *Proceedings of the ACM SIGACCESS conference on Computers and Accessibility*, ACM Press, pp. 135-142.

15. MacKenzie, I. S., Kauppinen, T., and Silfverberg, M., (2001), Accuracy measures for evaluating computer pointing devices. In *Proceedings of the SIGCHI conference on Human factors in Computing Systems,* ACM Press, pp. 9-16.

16. Mankoff, J., Hudson, S. E., and Abowd, G.D., (2000), Interaction techniques for ambiguity resolution in recognition-based interfaces. In *Proceedings of the ACM Symposium on User Interface Software and Technology (UIST)*, ACM Press, pp. 11-20.

17. *Microsoft Office Outlook 2003 Step By Step*, Microsoft Press, 2004.

18. *Microsoft Office Powerpoint 2003 Step By Step*, Microsoft Press, 2004.

19. *Microsoft Office Word 2003 Step By Step*, Microsoft Press, 2004.

20. Microsoft Active Accessibility API, http://msdn2.microsoft.com/en-us/library/ms697707(VS.85).aspx, accessed 9/17/09.

21. Mitchell, T., (1997), *Machine Learning*, McGraw-Hill.

22. Quinlan, J.R., (1993), *C4.5: Programs for Machine Learning*, Morgan Kaufmann.

23. *Testplant Software,* Eggplant Functional Tester, http://www.redstonesoftware.com/, accessed 9/17/09.

24. Trewin, S., Keates, S., and Moffatt, K., (2006), Developing steady clicks: a method of cursor assistance for people with motor impairments. In *Proceedings of the ACM SIGACCESS conference on Computers and Accessibility*, ACM Press, pp. 26-33.

25. *Windows XP Step By Step,* 2nd edition, Microsoft Press, 2005.

26. Witten, I.H. and Frank, E., (2005), *Data Mining: Practical machine learning tools and techniques,* 2nd Edition, Morgan Kaufmann.

27. Yeh, T., Chang, T., and Miller, R. C., (2009), Sikuli: using GUI screenshots for search and automation. In *Proceedings of the ACM Symposium on User Interface Software and Technology*, ACM Press, pp. 183-192.

28. Zettlemoyer, L. S. and St. Amant, R., (1999), A visual medium for programmatic control of interactive applications. In *Proceedings of the SIGCHI Conference on Human Factors in Computing Systems*, ACM Press, pp. 199-206.

Addressing the Problems of Data-Centric Physiology-Affect Relations Modeling

Roberto Legaspi, Ken-ichi Fukui, Koichi Moriyama, Satoshi Kurihara, Masayuki Numao
The Institute of Scientific and Industrial Research, Osaka, University
8-1 Mihogaoka, Ibaraki, Osaka, 567-0047, Japan
{roberto, fukui, koichi, kurihara, numao}@ ai.sanken.osaka-u.ac.jp

Merlin Suarez
Center for Empathic Human-Computer Interactions, College of Computer Studies, De La Salle University-Manila
2401 Taft Avenue, 1004 Manila, Philippines
merlin.suarez@delasalle.ph

ABSTRACT

Data-centric affect modeling may render itself restrictive in practical applications for three reasons, namely, it falls short of feature optimization, infers discrete affect classes, and deals with relatively small to average sized datasets. Though it seems practical to use the feature combinations already associated to commonly investigated sensors, there may be other potentially optimal features that can lead to new relations. Secondly, although it seems more realistic to view affect as continuous, it requires using continuous labels that will increase the difficulty of modeling. Lastly, although a large scale dataset reflects a more precise range of values for any given feature, it severely hinders computational efficiency. We address these problems when inferring physiology-affect relations from datasets that contain 2-3 million feature vectors, each with 49 features and labelled with continuous affect values. We employ automatic feature selection to acquire near optimal feature subsets and a fast approximate kNN algorithm to solve the regression problem and cope with the challenge of a large scale dataset. Our results show that high estimation accuracy may be achieved even when the selected feature subset is only about 7% of the original features. May the results here motivate the HCI community to pursue affect modeling without being deterred by large datasets and further the discussions on acquiring optimal features for accurate continuous affect approximation.

ACM Classification Keywords

H.1.2. User/Machine Systems: Human Factors. Human information processing.
Models and Principles.

General Terms

Human Factors, Experimentation, Algorithms

IUI'10, February 7–10, 2010, Hong Kong, China.
Copyright 2010 ACM 978-1-60558-515-4/10/02...$10.00.

INTRODUCTION

The motivation behind affective computing in human computer interaction (HCI) is that the knowledge of user affective states can help make the computer interact more effectively with the user. Various research works in affective computing have underlined evidence of strong relationships between physiological reactions and human affective states (e.g., [5,12,15,25-29,41,43,47]). The data-centric problem of mapping physiological patterns to specific affect types, however, remains unresolved due to solutions being partial or restrictive. The data-centric approach collects readings of emotion changes together with the change in activity in the autonomic nervous system that accompanies the emotion and then finds physiology-emotion relations by mining the recorded data. Data-centric affect modeling can render itself restrictive in practical applications for three reasons, namely, it falls short to investigate feature optimality, focuses on inferring discrete, rather than continuous, affect classes and deals with small to average sized datasets.

The fundamental issue of finding the physiological feature that is actually indicative of an affective state remains to be compelling. Given the high cost of sensors, it seems reasonable that the majority of works in physiological signal-based affect modeling have employed commonly investigated features from physiological sensors that have already been proved useful, e.g., the mean and standard deviation computed from raw and/or normalized signals of the electromyogram (EMG), electrocardiogram (ECG), blood volume pulse (BVP), skin conductance (SC) and/or respiration sensors (as evidenced by the literature cited here, among others). The primary issue with this, which renders it problematic, is that there may be other potentially useful features that can pave the way for discovering new relation possibilities. Moreover, it is uncertain if these commonly employed features are indeed optimal. A feature can be considered optimal if it is relevant, i.e., its correlation with the class label is high and non-redundant, i.e., its correlation with other features is low [10,11], and effective, which means that it improves the estimation or prediction accuracy, i.e., the recognition rate on test data when describing concepts of physiology and affect relations. An irrelevant feature does not influence the formulation of the target concept and a redundant feature provides no added value to the target concept [6]. High estimation accuracy will validate the effectiveness of relevant and non-redundant features. With only relevant and non-redundant features, a more general concept and a significant reduction in the algorithm's execution time can be obtained [6].

Emotion theorists have long been divided on whether to view human affect as categorical or dimensional [36]. The latter suggests that it is insufficient to describe affective states in discrete categories and can be better represented as continuous trajectories in a multi-dimensional space [44]. This view that emotion is a continuous phenomenon seems more realistic and practical. Core affect, which is the heart of any emotional phenomenon [37] and has been identified as a primitive concept that is the foundation of all other affective concepts, is continuous [35]. Although people can report emotions in distinct and discrete categories, this is not consistent with what is really neural and physiological, i.e., what actually exists is core affect. Furthermore, certain novel applications thrive with a core affect point of view such as in modeling relationships between emotion and the dynamic nature of its elicitor (e.g., in automated affect-based music composition [34] and interactive art [33]) and in assistive robotics (e.g., [31]), among others. In machine learning perspective, however, to represent the affective states with continuous values will make the modeling task more difficult since it will lead to regression analysis.

Lastly, it may be that the dataset from which the relation models are inferred is significantly restricted in size. The issue here is that the machine learning task cannot take into account what could be the more precise range of values for any given feature since the full spectrum of physiological readings were not accounted for. Furthermore, because of a relatively small amount of data, the empirical validation method can become restrictive, e.g., settling for a leave-one-out rather than a full 10-fold cross validation. However, to address these will consequently lead to a large scale learning problem where the inference of useful information may be severely hindered by the computational complexity of the learning algorithm, i.e., the algorithm must scale at worst linearly with the n training patterns. Most state-of-the-art nonparametric machine learning algorithms have a computational complexity of either $O(n^2)$ or $O(n^3)$. In other words, the huge amount of data can significantly slow down the learning task.

This paper reports our attempt to address these problems when inferring physiology-affect relations from datasets that contain two to more than three million sample patterns, with each pattern represented as a feature vector with 49 features and labeled with a continuous affect value. We applied automatic feature selection to acquire the near optimal features and a fast approximate matching algorithm to solve the regression problem and cope with the challenge of a large scale dataset. This approach leads to a solution that is cost effective, i.e., it minimizes the number of features and

sensors, and efficient, i.e., the relation models are obtained in less time with high prediction accuracy. We intentionally resorted to existing algorithms since our main objective is to show how this kind of approach can actually work in the physiology-affect relations modeling domain. As far as our knowledge of the literature is concerned, we have yet to encounter a similar application within this target domain. Table 1 shows a snapshot of the literature; obviously not exhaustive, but may be representative of the usually employed methodologies. The affect types D and C refer to discrete and continuous, respectively. The number of sample patterns refers to the total number of feature vectors used to train and test the classification (affect recognition) algorithms. The classifiers usually used by research works in this domain demand high computational cost even for average sized data.

Work	#Subj.	Aff.	#Feat.	#Patterns	Auto. Feat. Sel./Red.	Classi.
[9]	1	C	13	1000	n/a	MLP
[26]	29	D	3	140	n/a	kNN, DFA, MBP
[12]	9	C	22	112	Fisher	LDP
[41]	1	D	32	100	SFS Fisher	kNN, LDF, MLP
[14]	3	D	110	360	SBS	LDA

Table 1: Related works on physiology-affect modeling

Clearly, with few features and limited number of patterns, our methodology is insignificant, not until the learning algorithm encounters the curse of dimensionality, i.e., several features and millions of sample patterns.

EXPERIMENTATION METHODOLOGY

Physiological readings were collected from two subjects using the wearable sensors in Figure 1 as the subjects listened continuously to affect-eliciting sounds for about 25 minutes. The electroencephalography (EEG) helmet can infer affective states automatically from analyses of brainwave productions, and the other sensors can measure the BVP, respiratory movement (RS), skin responses - i.e., SC, temperature (ST), heat flux (HF) and near-body temp (NT), and movements of the corrugator (EMG$_1$) and left/right masseter (EMG$_2$) muscles that accompany the emotion. Since the heart rate variability (HR), which is a strong indicator of affect arousal and valence, can be directly computed from the BVP, we conveniently omitted the use of ECG in our experiments.

Research have shown that music is an effective means of emotion induction, manipulation and regulation (refer to [48] for a good review). Also, [14] related together music, emotion and physiological signals. However, [48] also stated that not all individuals react to music. Hence, we specifically advised the subjects to choose the particular musical pieces that will elicit in them the targeted affective states. This is similar to the approach taken by [41] and [14].

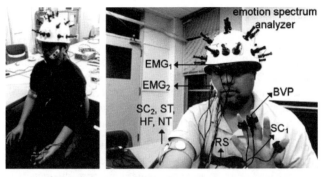

Figure 1. Subject (left) wearing physiological sensors (right) while listening to affect-eliciting sounds.

Feature Set

From the collected readings, feature vectors were constructed. Each vector consists of 49 attribute values. Table 2 summarizes the set of features and their source sensors. (Note: The reader is referred to the manufacturers' websites[1] and to an additional document[2] for the meaning of the features). The software used with these sensors can automatically compute from the acquired raw signals cepstral attribute values within a specified epoch as indicated by a sliding time-slice window (e.g., 20s). This greatly spared us from manually extracting these features from the raw signals and permitted us to avoid dealing with the intricacies of low-level signal processing.

Sensor	Features
BVP (35 features)	• BVP: amplitude mean(μ), peak freq μ (Hz), LF/HF (μs), LF/HF (epoch μs), • inter-beat interval(IBI): peak freq, std(σ)/SDDR, epoch σ, peak amplitude, peak amplitude max, NN interval • HR from IBI: HR μ, HR σ, HR_{MAX}-HR_{MIN}, HR epoch μ, HR_{MAX}-HR_{MIN} μ (b/min) • HR standard freq bands (VLF,LF,HF): %power, total power, %power μ, total power μ, %power epoch μ, total power epoch μ
RS (4)	• rate, rate μ (br/min), rate epoch μ, amplitude μ
SC_1 (2)	• μ (microS), epoch μ
$EMG_{1,2}$ (4)	• μ (microV), epoch μ
SC_2, ST, HF, NT (4)	• individual averages (μs)

Rows 1-4: Stand-alone sensors by Thought Technology Ltd.
Last row: Wireless packaged sensors by BodyMedia Inc.

Table 2: Complete set of features

Continuous Affect Labels

To label the feature vectors with affect values, we employed another device, which is an EEG that uses emotion spectrum analysis[3] to induce from brainwave signals the user affective states. EEG features are extracted into a set of 45 cross-

[1] Thought Technology Ltd HP: http://www.thoughttechnology.com/; BodyMedia Inc HP: http://www.sensewear.com/BMS/solutions_bms.php

[2] Available in http://www.thoughttechnology.com/pdf/Mar648-00%20 Virtual%20Channel%20Computation%20Explanation.pdf

[3] Brains Functions Laboratory Inc., http://www.bfl.co.jp/english/top.html

correlation coefficients calculated for each of the frequency components, namely, θ(5-8 Hz), α(8-13 Hz) and β(13-20 Hz), forming a 135-dim EEG state vector. Operating a transformation matrix on this multidimensional state vector linearly transforms it to a 4-dim vector $E=<a_1,a_2,a_3,a_4>$, with the four components representing continuous levels of stress, joy, sadness and relaxation, respectively. The time resolution of emotion analysis done in real-time was 5.12s. The chart in Figure 2 graphically shows series of emotion readings that were taken over time. More discussions regarding this device can be found in [25, 34].

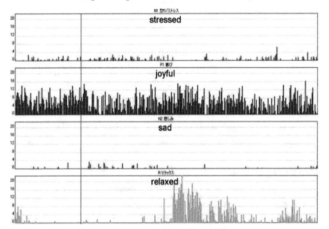

Figure 2. Affect readings from emotion spectrum analyses of brainwave signals

We regard the readings provided by this device as credible since it has been found suitable for medical/clinical purposes (e.g., being used for dementia research) [42,24,20] and its brainwave analyses is user independent making it commercially viable. We treated the outputs of this device as ground truth in our experimentation.

Data Set

In effect, the affective states and accompanying physiology changes were recorded simultaneously. Hence, any feature vector representing the physiological signals at time t can be labeled with the affect values at t. Consequently, four datasets were constructed, one for each affect type, that have the same physiological attribute values but different continuous affect labels.

Prior to the regression task, all labeled feature vectors were normalized into the range [0,1] since their components differ in the scales in which their values lie:

$$A_{normalized} = \frac{A - \min(A)}{\max(A) - \min(A)} \quad (1)$$

To account for the baseline measurement, i.e., the condition against which physiological changes can be compared, periods of silence were inserted at the start (30s) and in between sounds (15s). Even before the actual measurements were made the subject was instructed to rest. It is plausible that in these rest periods the subject experienced minimum level of autonomic nervous system activity which then accounted for the $min(A)$ in (1).

From each dataset, one containing more than two million (subject A), and the other, more than three million (subject B), training and test datasets were constructed for a 10-fold cross validation, i.e., for each fold (a) 10% of the data was reserved for testing and the rest for training the regression classifier, and (b) the test patterns changed as the 10%-window slid across the original dataset. Furthermore, two versions of each dataset were constructed, one using all 49 features and the other using the subset of supposedly optimal features. The feature subset was obtained by the feature selection algorithm from the training dataset.

Having few subjects at this time can be justified by our taking the common practice of a user-centered classification that is supposed to provide better results when the classifiers are trained exclusively on data captured from a particular user as this reduces variability. Our approach can be optimal in a user-centered paradigm since it considers a large scale dataset for a single user.

MACHINE LEARNING TASK

We leveraged the effectiveness of sequential forward floating selection [30] with a correlation-based filter [10,11] to select the subset of near optimal features and a fast approximate nearest neighbor algorithm [1,22] to find the k nearest neighbors. The regression problem is solved by computing the predictive value as the average of the continuous affect labels of the k nearest neighbors.

Feature Selection

Feature selection reveals which subset of the existing features in the test bed is most useful for analysis and prediction [6,10,11,13,17,21], and consequently, these few features can be retained for the final implementation. Fewer features help improve concept generalization and reduce computational costs. We chose feature selection over feature extraction/ reduction (e.g., principal component analysis (PCA), linear discriminant analysis (LDA), Fisher projection, and projection pursuit, among others), since the latter can allow history of interpretations, origins of analyses in the application domain or information about the underlying structures of the data to be lost or allow parts of noisy features to be inherited during transformation. Feature extraction transforms all the existing features to new features, as opposed to selection where no new feature is created, consequently creating a new search space with lower dimensions but can result to the new features not having clear physical meaning or interpretation.

Feature selection requires a search strategy to explore the space of all possible features and select candidate feature subsets, and an objective function to evaluate these candidates. [13] examined different feature selection methods and found that the sequential floating selection algorithm proposed by [30] is superior to other algorithms. These floating methods are sequential search algorithms characterized by dynamically changing and improving the feature subset membership at each step by means of backtracking. These methods were shown to be effective and computationally more efficient than other search (e.g., branch and bound) methods [13,30]. Although we are aware that these floating search methods have been formulated some ten years ago, still, these methods remain robust and widely used, hence, a good place to start our theories with.

As for the objective function, several categories have been defined by various works with the most common categories being filters and wrappers. While wrappers evaluate the candidate subsets based on the approximation accuracy of the learning algorithm through statistical resampling or cross validation, filters evaluate feature subsets by their information content and the intrinsic characteristics of the data (e.g., interclass distance, statistical dependence, information theoretic measures, consistency, etc.) with regard to the target concept independent of any learning algorithm. Table 3 compares these two based on their performance. Because filter-based methods aim to screen candidate subsets while preserving the original information as possible, which also makes it suitable for body sensor network applications [46], and due to the nature of our task that has more than 2-3M instances, hence, computationally intensive but requires fast execution, the use of a filter is suitable in our experiments, except for one aspect, i.e., most existing filters only work with discrete class problems.

Filter	Advantage
	▪ Computationally simple and fast: non-iterative computations
	▪ Can easily scale to high-dimensional datasets
	▪ Independent of any induction algorithm
	Disadvantage
	▪ Tendency to select large candidate subsets
	▪ Ignores feature dependencies
Wrapper	Advantage
	▪ Accurate
	▪ Ability to generalize concepts
	Disadvantage
	▪ Computationally intensive
	▪ Vulnerable to classifier biases

Table 3. Comparison of filter and wrapper

Although in itself is a filter, the correlation-based filter algorithm of [10,11] can easily extend to continuous class problems as it applies the suitable correlation measures. Its heuristic is that good feature subsets contain features that are highly correlated (predictive) with the continuous labels yet have minimal or no correlation (not predictive) with each other (considers feature dependencies). The goodness of a feature subset S with m features is computed as:

$$Merit_S = \frac{m\overline{r_{fl}}}{\sqrt{m + m(m-1)\overline{r_{ff}}}} \qquad (2)$$

$$r_{xy} = \frac{\sum xy}{n\sigma_x\sigma_y} \qquad (3)$$

where n is the number of training samples and r_{fl} and r_{ff} are the average feature-to-label correlation and feature-to-feature intercorrelation, respectively. This heuristic will reveal the irrelevant features as poor indicators of the target concept and will discriminate against redundant attributes. Even though the wrapper is considered to produce better feature subsets, this correlation-based filter compares favorably with it but demands less computational cost [11].

Fast Approximate Nearest Neighbor Algorithm

Learning from data, as one of the basic ways to perceive the world and acquire knowledge, is true both for humans and machine learners that try to model computationally how the human mind works. Unfortunately, unlike the human mind, the machine learner will struggle on two critical problems when it attempts to operate in large scale problems, namely, the dramatic increase in learning time and strict demand for more memory due to the dimensionality and size of the data.

Various algorithms have been formulated to reduce time complexity and space requirement without the need to sacrifice estimation accuracy, such as kernel-based (e.g., in [2,3,7,8,38-40,45]) and improved nearest neighbor (e.g., [2,4,18,19,23,32]) algorithms. After performing initial runs with kernel-based, Bayesian regression, and clustering algorithms, we found that the approximate k-nearest neighbor algorithm provided us excellent initial partial results while offering excellent computational efficiency.

The k-nearest neighbor (kNN) problem has been applied in a wide range of real-world settings such as knowledge discovery and datamining, pattern recognition, machine learning, database querying, document retrieval, data compression, bioinformatics, multimedia databases, statistics and data analysis [1,19,23]. The kNN classification is easy to understand and implement due to its simplicity. Evidence suggests that it performs well in many situations, even better at times than Bayesian and support vector machine approaches [45]. Also because of its simplicity, it is effortless to modify it for a regression task by assigning the predictive value for the query point to be the average of the values of its k nearest neighbors. However, to perform a linear search over a large scale dataset to find the nearest neighbors is impractical. Furthermore, the curse of high-dimensionality is the long standing problem of NN algorithms [19]. A linear search over a dataset of n instances with d dimensions has a running time of $O(nd)$.

One approach to deal with the intractability due to large and high-dimensional datasets is to define a variation of the problem. Instead of finding the exact nearest neighbors, the problem is modified to that of finding an approximate nearest neighbor, i.e., a neighbor within $1+\varepsilon$ (where ε is any positive real value) of the distance to the true nearest neighbor: a point $p \in P$ is an approximate nearest neighbor of a query point $q \in P$ if the distance $dist(p, q) \leq (1+\varepsilon) \cdot dist(p^*, q)$ where p^* is the true nearest neighbor. For any given q, p can be obtained quickly. Approximate NN algorithms can be orders of magnitude faster than the exact exhaustive linear search with only minor loss (near optimal) in accuracy [23]. In our experiments, we used the latest version of a library [22] for approximate NN search.

RESULTS AND ANALYSES

We performed a 10-fold cross validation over the datasets using our methodology. We measured the performance of the regression analysis in terms of root mean squared error (RMSE) and coefficient of determination (R^2). RMSE and R^2 both show the strength of prediction or forecast of future outcomes through a model or an estimator on the basis of observed related information. The latter also shows how good the approximation function might be constructed from the target model. We used a correlation measure since we are also concerned on whether the predictions will behave, i.e., increase or decrease, correspondingly with the target values. A 0.6 to 0.8 correlation can be considered strong especially for a noisy variable (e.g., physiological signal). We consider here strong the RMSE ≤ 0.05 and $R^2 \geq 0.8$.

Table 4 shows the feature subsets selected by the sequential forward floating selection with correlation-based filter (SFFS+CF) algorithm we used. A ■ indicates that the feature appeared in the corresponding i^{th} fold. The table also indicates the reduction in the number of features and sensors, with the percentage values in the "% of sel. feat." row indicating the portion of selected features, i.e., feature subset size over the number of original features, that was retained after SFFS+CF was applied. The size and membership of the subsets differ due to the varying behavior of the data among folds and subjects. In other words, the subsets vary according to the characteristics of the dataset and the user-specific affective state.

Since our approach is data-centric, we shall not attempt to interpret the meaning of the identified [inter]correlations. Instead, we wish to leave the interpretation to the experts in the emotion field. While we agree that a data mining task reflecting on the identified features on the basis of a large number of studies already available is important, we believe that interesting generalizations can be inferred through an automatic analysis of the data alone in the absence of theoretical or expert knowledge, consequently evading the cost of expert knowledge construction. We do not intend to present the results here in the more conventional way, i.e., affect A is characterized by high P and low S physiological signals, since our objective is how to automatically infer the affective state from the discovered optimal features without attempting to observe the physical behavior of the signals.

Subject A

Stressed	1	2	3	4	5	6	7	8	9	10
LF/HF (ep μs)										
IBI pk freq										
IBI σ / SDDR										
IBI ep σ										
IBI pk ampl max										
IBI NN intervals										
HR μ										
HR σ										
LF % pow										
HF % pow										
VLF % pow μ										
LF % pow ep μ										
VLF % pow ep μ										
LF tot pow ep μ										
EMG$_1$ μ										
RS rate μ										
RS ep μ										
ST μ										
% of sel. feat.	14	16	20	12	14	18	18	22	18	14
No. of sensors	1	3	3	2	2	2	2	3	2	2

Joyful	1	2	3	4	5	6	7	8	9	10
HR$_{MAX}$-HR$_{MIN}$ μ										
VLF % pow										
RS ampl μ										
EMG$_2$ ep μ										
Heat flux μ										
% of sel. feat.	6	6	8	6	6	8	6	8	6	6
No. of sensors	3	3	4	3	3	3	3	3	3	3

Sad	1	2	3	4	5	6	7	8	9	10
BVP ampl μ										
IBI pk ampl max										
IBI NN intervals										
HR										
HR μ										
HF % pow										
RS rate μ										
SC$_1$ μ										
ST μ										
NT μ										
Heat flux μ										
% of sel. feat.	12	10	8	10	8	6	10	10	12	8
No. of sensors	3	3	3	2	2	3	3	3	3	3

Relaxed	1	2	3	4	5	6	7	8	9	10
BVP ampl μ										
LF/HF (ep μs)										
IBI pk ampl max										
LF % pow										
VLF % pow										
VLF total pow										
LF % pow μ										
VLF % pow μ										
HF % pow ep μ										
VLF % pow ep μ										
LF tot pow μ										
HF tot pow μ										
VLF tot pow μ										
HF tot pow ep μ										

Subject B

HR$_{MAX}$-HR$_{MIN}$ μ										
RS Ampl μ										
SC$_1$ μ										
EMG$_1$ μ										
EMG$_2$ μ										
SC$_2$ μ										
% of sel. feat.	16	12	22	18	12	12	12	16	16	18
No. of sensors	2	1	5	3	1	1	1	1	3	2

Stressed	1	2	3	4	5	6	7	8	9	10
LF/HF (ep μs)										
IBI NN intervals										
HF % pow										
VLF total pow										
VLF % pow ep μ										
SC$_1$ ep μ										
EMG$_1$ μ										
EMG$_2$ μ										
SC$_2$ μ										
% of sel. feat.	12	8	10	8	8	8	8	12	12	8
No. of sensors	5	3	3	3	3	3	3	5	5	2

Joyful	1	2	3	4	5	6	7	8	9	10
BVP ampl μ										
HF % pow ep μ										
EMG$_1$ ep μ										
EMG$_2$ μ										
Heat flux μ										
% of sel. feat.	2	2	2	2	2	2	8	2	4	4
No. of sensors	1	1	1	1	1	1	3	1	2	2

Sad	1	2	3	4	5	6	7	8	9	10
IBI										
IBI σ / SDDR										
HR σ										
LF % pow										
HF % pow ep μ										
SC$_1$ ep μ										
SC$_1$ μ										
Heat flux μ										
% of sel. feat.	10	8	8	8	6	10	12	8	6	6
No. of sensors	2	3	3	3	3	3	3	3	1	2

Relaxed	1	2	3	4	5	6	7	8	9	10
BVP Ampl μ										
LF/HF (ep μs)										
IBI NN intervals										
LF total pow										
HF total pow										
VLF total pow										
VLF % pow										
LF tot pow ep μ										
VLF tot pow ep μ										
EMG$_1$ μ										
RS rate μ										
NT μ										
SC$_2$ μ										
% of sel. feat.	12	12	12	12	12	10	10	10	12	10
No. of sensors	3	3	3	3	3	3	3	3	3	3

Table 4. Feature subsets selected by the SFFS+CF algorithm

Table 5 shows the strength of prediction when all 49 features were used and compares this when SFFS+CF was applied. It can be seen here that even at times when the average size of the feature subsets, as averaged across 10 folds per affective state, is only about 7% of the original features, as shown in Table 6, the predictions are equally strong as when all 49 features were employed.

	Subject A				Subject B			
	49 Features		SFFS+CF		49 Features		SFFS+CF	
Aff	RMSE	R^2	RMSE	R^2	RMSE	R^2	RMSE	R^2
St	0.034	0.888	0.038	0.890	0.042	0.887	0.055	0.876
J	0.033	0.890	0.034	0.892	0.039	0.897	0.126	0.429
Sa	0.023	0.890	0.026	0.893	0.041	0.890	0.043	0.864
R	0.037	0.892	0.028	0.919	0.040	0.889	0.042	0.892

*Stressed, Joyful, Sad, Relaxed

Table 5. Accuracy of prediction

Aff	Subject A (%)	Subject B (%)
St	17	10
J	7	3
Sa	10	8
R	16	11

Table 6. Average (rounded off) sizes of the feature subsets

The poor approximation of the joy levels of subject B is an indication that the selected feature subset was not at all optimal perhaps due primarily to the insufficiently small feature membership suggesting that there should be a threshold on the minimum number of features. We tried a stopgap measure for this problem, i.e., we applied the feature subset that appeared in fold 7 of subject B's joyful states (in Table 4) since the estimation accuracy here is high: RMSE=0.025 and R^2=0.955. Although the results we obtained indicate a significant improvement, i.e., the RMSE improved from 0.126 to 0.045 and the R^2 from 0.429 to 0.873, this stopgap measure is rather intuitive and we have yet to automate this second level selection task.

The next important aspect that we need point out is the significant reduction in training time when our method was applied. Table 7 shows the averaged time in minutes it took our learning algorithm to infer the nearest neighbors using the approximate kNN with and without the SFFS+CF outputs and the percentage of time saved when SFFS+CF was applied. Note that this percentage is the average of the time saved in every fold per affect: %time_saved$_{fold\_i,affect\_a}$ = $(1 - t_{49}/t_{SFFS+CF}) \times 100\%$. For example, due to the feature subsets provided by SFFS+CF, inference time was reduced to an average of about 89% and 92% per fold per affective state for subjects A and B, respectively. The reduction is even more significant if we compare this to when we were initially trying the exhaustive kNN algorithm, i.e., it took about five days to obtain the nearest neighbors from a single fold of one affective state using all 49 features.

This efficiency aspect is relevant for at least two reasons. First, it allows an experimenter to spend more time analyzing the results that were obtained quickly rather than being idle waiting for the learning algorithm to finish. Secondly, a quick-to-learn algorithm becomes viable for a system that needs to update its model online in real-time. Here, an initial model that is partial can be constructed before deployment but with the system improving the model incrementally online after each interaction with the user. Since any user interface that is perceived to be ineffective or slow to adapt is undesirable, it is necessary for the system to learn online, as rapidly as feasible without compromising effectiveness. We discussed in a prior paper, in [16], how extremely non-trivial this problem is and the kind of research that can be pursued along this line.

	Time to infer the k NNs		Ave. % of time saved
	49 Features	SFFS+CF	
Subject A	11.28	1.15	88.71
Subject B	15.75	1.13	92.25

Table 7. Efficiency of the learning algorithm

Our next experiment involved treating the source sensors separately. Many research works immediately suggest working with multisensory inputs for multimodal modeling. The motivation for multimodal input is to offset the weakness and uncertainty associated with only a single measure by the contributions of other inputs [28]. However, we also wanted to find out the individual contributions of each sensor to the model induction task. Table 8 summarizes the accuracy of prediction through each sensor as averaged over using the two datasets. The results show that accurate predictions were obtained through the BVP, followed by the RS and then the EMG on the masseter. The results also confirm that the features from the sensors that performed poorly did not introduce any new or helpful information, nor did these influence the classification task.

Aff	BVP	RS	SC_1	EMG_1	EMG_2	BM
			RMSE			
St	0.041	0.055	0.111	0.099	0.080	0.219
J	0.035	0.055	0.108	0.095	0.081	0.100
Sa	0.034	0.047	0.091	0.072	0.060	0.081
R	0.042	0.058	0.103	0.087	0.072	0.089
			R^2			
St	0.890	0.849	0.537	0.633	0.750	0.580
J	0.895	0.847	0.545	0.687	0.762	0.633
Sa	0.892	0.859	0.618	0.672	0.773	0.671
R	0.891	0.852	0.580	0.683	0.750	0.651

Table 8. Average RMSE and R^2 for 2 subjects

The results further suggest that the use of BVP or RS sensor alone is sufficient. This is relevant since we used only four features for the RS sensor. If the BVP sensor is to be used over the RS for some reason (e.g., availability), then our methodology can once again be applied. While Table 9 shows a significant reduction from the original number of BVP features, Table 10 presents the estimation accuracy of the regression model using the extracted near optimal BVP feature subsets.

Subject A										
Stressed	1	2	3	4	5	6	7	8	9	10
BVP ampl μ		■	■	■	■	■	■	■	■	■
BVP pk freq μ	■	■				■	■	■	■	■
IBI σ / SDDR	■	■	■	■	■	■	■	■	■	■
IBI ep σ	■									
IBI pk ampl max	■	■	■	■	■	■	■	■	■	■
HR						■		■	■	
HR μ		■	■	■	■	■		■	■	
LF % pow	■	■	■	■	■	■	■	■	■	■
VLF % pow	■	■	■	■	■	■	■	■	■	■
VLF % pow ep μ	■	■	■			■	■	■	■	■
HF tot pow ep μ					■					
% of sel. feat.	20	23	20	17	20	26	20	26	26	20
Joyful	1	2	3	4	5	6	7	8	9	10
IBI pk freq	■	■	■	■	■	■	■	■	■	■
VLF % pow μ	■									
LF tot pow μ	■	■	■	■	■	■	■	■	■	■
VLF tot pow μ		■	■	■	■	■	■	■	■	■
% of sel. feat.	9	9	9	9	9	9	9	9	9	9
Sad	1	2	3	4	5	6	7	8	9	10
BVP ampl μ	■	■	■	■	■	■	■	■	■	■
LF/HF (ep μs)	■	■	■	■	■	■	■	■	■	■
IBI									■	■
IBI pk ampl	■	■	■	■	■	■	■	■	■	
LF % pow	■	■	■	■	■	■	■	■	■	■
% of sel. feat.	11	11	11	11	11	11	11	11	14	11
Relaxed	1	2	3	4	5	6	7	8	9	10
LF/HF (ep μs)	■									
IBI pk freq	■	■	■	■	■	■	■	■		■
IBI ep σ		■	■				■	■	■	■
HF % pow									■	
VLF % pow		■	■			■	■	■	■	■
VLF tot pow	■			■	■					
LF % pow ep μ	■	■	■		■		■	■	■	■
LF tot pow μ	■	■	■	■	■		■	■	■	■
VLF tot pow μ	■	■	■	■	■	■	■		■	■
% of sel. feat.	17	17	17	11	14	9	17	14	17	17
Subject B										
Stressed	1	2	3	4	5	6	7	8	9	10
IBI pk ampl max	■	■	■	■	■	■	■	■	■	■
HF % pow										■
% of sel. feat.	3	3	3	3	3	3	3	3	3	6
Joyful	1	2	3	4	5	6	7	8	9	10
LF/HF (ep μs)	■									
HR										■
HF % pow μ	■	■	■	■	■	■				
LF % pow ep μ	■	■	■	■	■	■	■	■	■	■
% of sel. feat.	9	6	6	6	6	6	3	3	3	6
Sad	1	2	3	4	5	6	7	8	9	10
BVP pk freq μ			■		■	■			■	■
HR μ	■	■	■	■	■	■	■	■		
LF % pow ep μ	■	■	■	■	■	■	■	■	■	■
% of sel. feat.	6	6	9	6	9	9	6	6	6	6
Relaxed	1	2	3	4	5	6	7	8	9	10
IBI pk ampl max	■	■	■	■	■	■	■		■	■
HR ep μ								■		
HF % pow	■	■	■	■		■	■			
HF tot pow ep μ	■	■	■					■	■	
VLF tot pow ep μ	■	■	■	■	■	■	■	■	■	
LF/HF (ep μs)	■	■	■	■	■	■	■	■	■	
% of sel. feat.	14	14	14	11	9	11	11	11	11	3

Table 9: Selected BVP feature subsets

	Subject A				Subject B			
	49 Features		SFFS+CF		49 Features		SFFS+CF	
Aff	RMSE	R^2	RMSE	R^2	RMSE	R^2	RMSE	R^2
St	0.035	0.891	0.037	0.891	0.046	0.888	0.138	0.460
J	0.030	0.896	0.032	0.891	0.041	0.894	0.086	0.623
Sa	0.024	0.895	0.026	0.892	0.044	0.890	0.070	0.770
R	0.044	0.893	0.040	0.890	0.041	0.890	0.058	0.856

Table 10. Accuracy of prediction using the BVP features

Aff	Subject A (%)	Subject B (%)
St	22	3
J	9	5
Sa	12	7
R	15	11

Table 11. Average size of the BVP feature subsets

Even with the reduced number of features, the accuracy obtained for subject A dataset is equally excellent. The performance with subject B dataset, however, deteriorated when the stressed and joyful levels were approximated. Again, we suspect the insufficient feature subset membership, as shown in Table 11, as contributing to this problem.

The traces above further suggest that instead of proceeding immediately with the modeling task using all sensors at hand, it is reasonable to test first the performance of each individual sensor since a multimodal input may not work advantageously just like here. In other words, here is a case where a multimodal model may not be necessary.

CONCLUSION AND FUTURE WORK

A great majority of related recognition systems are not yet advanced enough to be taken out of the labs and be deployed in realistic applications due to the limitations we have specified in this paper. Not only do we agree with [41] that automatic feature selection is desirable for a realistic online application, we also point out that it is still prohibitive if the system does not consider the full spectrum of values because of a limited database. Our paper's main contribution is the benefit of using sequential forward floating selection with a correlation-based filter and fast approximate matching algorithms in the target domain.

The results reported here show that high estimation accuracy may be achieved even when the average size of the feature subsets is only 7% of the original features. We hope that the results here can motivate the HCI community to pursue affect modeling without being deterred by large datasets and further the discussions on acquiring optimal features for accurate continuous affect approximation so that works along these lines can be further pursued for more conclusive solutions.

Apart from constructing intelligent data-centric means to determine the minimum feature subset size for it to be near optimal and implement the stopgap measure we used, we also need to obtain empirical validations over several subjects in order to obtain a more conclusive generalization.

ACKNOWLEDGMENTS
This research is supported in part by the Japan Society for the Promotion of Science (JSPS) and the Global COE (Centers of Excellence) Program of the Ministry of Education, Culture, Sports, Science and Technology, Japan.

REFERENCES
1. Arya, S., Mount D.M., Netanhayu, N.S., Silverman, R. and Wu, A.Y. (1998). An optimal algorithm for approximate nearest neighbor searching in fixed dimensions. *Journal of the ACM*, 45(6):891-923.

2. Auton Lab, School of Computer Science, Carnegie Mellon University, Fast EM Clustering Software. http://www.autonlab.org/autonweb/10466.html?branch=1&language=2.

3. Bradley, P.S., Fayyad, U.M. and Reina, C.A. (1998) Scaling clustering algorithms to large databases. *4th KDD 1998*, 9-15.

4. Chen, Y.-S., Hung, Y.-P., Yen, T.-F. and Fuh, C.-S. (2007). Fast and versatile algorithm for nearest neighbor search based on a lower bound tree. *Pattern Recognition*, 40(2):360-375.

5. Conati, C. and Maclaren, H. (2009). Empirically building and evaluating a probabilistic model of user affect. *User Modeling and User-Adapted Interaction*, 19(3):267-303.

6. Dash, M. and Liu, H. (1997). Feature selection for classification. *Intelligent Data Analysis*, 1:131-156.

7. Dong, J.-X., Krzyżak, A. and Suen, C.Y. (2005). Fast SVM training algorithm with decomposition on very large data sets. *IEEE Transactions on Pattern Analysis and Machine Intelligence*, 27(4):603-618.

8. Ester, M., Kriegel, H.-P., Sander, J. and Xu, X. (1996). A density-based algorithm for discovering clusters in large spatial databases with noise. *2nd KDD 1996*, 226-231.

9. Haag, A., Goronzy, S., Schaich, P. and Williams, J. (2004). Emotion recognition using bio-sensors: First step towards an automatic system. *Affective Dialogue Systems, Tutorial and Research Workshop, ADS 2004*, 36-48.

10. Hall, M.A. (2000). Correlation-based feature selection for discrete and numeric class machine learning. *ICML 2000*, 359-366.

11. Hall, M.A. and Smith, L.A. (1999) Feature selection for machine learning: Comparing a correlation-based filter approach to the wrapper. *FLAIRS-99*, 235-239.

12. Healey, J.A. and Picard, R.W. (2005). Detecting stress during real-world driving tasks using physiological sensors. *IEEE Transactions on Intelligent Transportation Systems*, 6(2):156-166.

13. Jain, A. and Zongker, D. (1997). Feature selection: Evaluation, application, and small sample performance. *Journal of Machine Learning Research*, 3:1157-1182.

14. Kim, J. and André, E. (2008). Emotion recognition based on physiological changes in music listening. *IEEE Transactions on Pattern Analysis and Machine Intelligence*, 30(12):2067-2083.

15. Kim, K.H., Bang, S.W. and Kim, S.R. (2004). Emotion recognition system using short-term monitoring of physiological signals. *Medical and Biological Engineering and Computing*, 42(3):419-427.

16. Legaspi, R., Kurihara, S., Fukui, K.-I., Moriyama, K. and Numao, M. (2008) An empathy learning problem for HSI: To be empathic, self-improving and ambient. *HSI*, 209-214.

17. Liu H. and Yu, L. (2002). *Feature Selection for Data Mining*. Research Technical Report, Arizona State University.

18. Liu, T., Moore, A.W. and Gray, A. (2006). New algorithms for efficient high-dimensional nonparametric classification. *The Journal of Machine Learning Research*, 1135-1158.

19. Liu, T., Moore, A.W., Gray, A. and Yang, K. (2004). An investigation of practical approximate nearest neighbor algorithms. *NIPS 2004*.

20. Luo, Z. and Inoue, S. (2000). A short daytime nap modulates levels of emotions objectively evaluated by the emotion spectrum analysis method. *Psychiatry and Clinical Neurosciences*, 54:207-212.

21. Molina, L.C., Belanche, L. and Nebot, À. (2002). Feature selection algorithms: A survey and experimental evaluation. *ICDM 2002*, 306-313.

22. Mount, D.M. and Arya, S. ANN: A library for approximate nearest neighbor search, v.1.1.1 Aug. 4, 2006 release. http://www.cs.umd.edu/~mount/ANN/

23. Muja, M. and Lowe, D.G. (2009). Fast approximate nearest neighbors with automatic algorithm configuration. *VISAPP 2009*.

24. Musha, T., Kimura, S., Kaneko, K.-I., Nishida, K. and Sekine, K. (2000). Emotion spectrum analysis method (ESAM) for monitoring the effects of art therapy applied on demented patients. *CyberPsychology and Behavior*, 3(3):441-446.

25. Musha, T., Terasaki, Y., Haque, H.A. and Ivanitsky, G.A. (1997). Feature extraction from EEGs associated with emotions. *Artif Life Robotics*, 1:15-19.

26. Nasoz, F., Alvarez, K., Lisetti, C.L. and Finkelstein, N. (2004). Emotion recognition from physiological signals

using wireless sensors for presence technologies. *Cognition, Technology, and Work*, 6:4-14.

27. Picard, R.W. (1997). *Affective Computing*. MIT Press.

28. Picard, R.W. and Daily, S.B. (2005). Evaluating affective interactions: Alternatives to asking what users feel. *CHI Workshop on Evaluating Affective Interfaces: Innovative Approaches*. http://affect.media.mit.edu/pdfs/05.picard-daily.pdf

29. Prendinger, H. and Ishizuka, M. (2007). Symmetric multimodality revisited: Unveiling user's physiological activity. *IEEE Transactions on Industrial Electronics*, 54(2):692-698.

30. Pudil, P., Novovičová, J. and Kittler, J. (1994). Floating search methods in feature selection. *Pattern Recognition Letters*, 15(11):1119-1125.

31. Sancho-Pradel D.L. and Nikolova, E.G. (2008). Probabilistic multisensory emotion estimation framework for assistive robotic applications. *2008 AAAI Fall Symposium – AI in Eldercare: New Solutions to Old Problems*, 92-99.

32. Sankaranarayanan, J., Samet, H. and Varshney, A. (2007). A fast all nearest neighbor algorithm for applications involving large point-clouds. *Computer & Graphics*, 31:157-174.

33. Shugrina, M., Betke, M. and Collomosse, J.P. (2006). Empathic painting: Interactive stylization through observed emotional state. *NPAR 2006*, 87-96.

34. Sugimoto, T., Legaspi, R., Ota, A., Moriyama, K. and Numao, M. (2008). Modelling affective-based music compositional intelligence with the aid of ANS analyses. *Knowledge Based Systems*, 21(3):200-2008.

35. Sun, H. and Zhang, P. (2006). The role of affect in information systems research: A critical survey and a research model. *Human-Computer Interaction and Management Information Systems: Foundations*, Series of *Adavances in Management information Systems*, 295-329.

36. Takehara, T. (2007). Dimensional structure of emotional facial expression recognition and complex system. *Focus on Nonverbal Communication Research*, 65-88.

37. Timmermans, T., Mechelen, I.V. and Nezlek, J.B. (2009). Individual differences in core affect reactivity. *Personality and Individual Differences*, 47:510-515.

38. Tresp, V. (2001). Scaling kernel-based systems to large datasets. *Data Mining and Knowledge Discovery*, 5:197-211.

39. Tsang, I.W., Kocsor, A. and Kwok, J.T. (2007). Simpler core vector machines with enclosing balls. *ICML 2007*, 911-918.

40. Tsang, I.W., Kwok, J.T. and Cheung, P.-M. (2005). Core vector machines: Fast SVM training on very large data sets. *Journal of Machine Learning Research*, 6:363-392.

41. Wagner, J., Kim, J. and André, E. (2005). From physiological signals to emotions: Implementing and comparing selected methods for feature extraction and classification. *ICME 2005*, 940-943.

42. Wei, D., Musha, T., Ono, S., Shimizu, N., Hara, J. and Shankle, W. (1999). Alpha rhythm dipolarity: An index in quantitative prediction of degree of Alzheimer's disease. *38th JSMEBE*.

43. Wilhelm, F.H., Pfaltz, M.C. and Grossman, P. (2006). Continuous electronic data capture of physiology, behavior and experience in real life: Towards ecological momentary assessment of emotion. *Interacting with Computers*, 18(2):171-186.

44. Wöllmer, M., Eyben, F., Reiter, S., Schuller, B., Cox, C., Douglas-Cowie, E. and Cowie, R. (2008). Abandoning emotion classes – Towards continuous emotion recognition with modelling of long-range dependencies. *9th Interspeech 2008, Incorporating SST 2008*, 597-600.

45. Wu, X. and Kumar, V. (2009). *The Top Ten Algorithms in Data Mining*. Chapman & Hall/CRC Press.

46. Yang, G.-Z. and Hu, X. (2006). Multi-sensor fusion. *Body Sensor Networks*, 239-286.

47. Zakharov, K. (2007). *Affect recognition and support in intelligent tutoring systems*. Masters Thesis, Dept. of Computer Science and Software Engineering, University of Canterbury. http://www.cosc.canterbury.ac.nz/research/reports/MastTheses/2007/mast_0708.pdf

48. Zentner, M., Grandjean, D. and Scherer, K.R. (2008). Emotions evoked by the sound of music: Characterization, classification and measurement. *Emotion*, 8(4):494-521.

Personalized News Recommendation Based on Click Behavior

Jiahui Liu, Peter Dolan, Elin Rønby Pedersen
Google Inc.
1600 Amphitheatre Parkway, Mountain View, CA 94043, USA
{jiahui, peterdolan, elinp}@google.com

ABSTRACT

Online news reading has become very popular as the web provides access to news articles from millions of sources around the world. A key challenge of news websites is to help users find the articles that are interesting to read. In this paper, we present our research on developing personalized news recommendation system in Google News. For users who are logged in and have explicitly enabled web history, the recommendation system builds profiles of users' news interests based on their past click behavior. To understand how users' news interests change over time, we first conducted a large-scale analysis of anonymized Google News users click logs. Based on the log analysis, we developed a Bayesian framework for predicting users' current news interests from the activities of that particular user and the news trends demonstrated in the activity of all users. We combine the content-based recommendation mechanism which uses learned user profiles with an existing collaborative filtering mechanism to generate personalized news recommendations. The hybrid recommender system was deployed in Google News. Experiments on the live traffic of Google News website demonstrated that the hybrid method improves the quality of news recommendation and increases traffic to the site.

Author Keywords
Personalization, user modeling, news trend.

ACM Classification Keywords
H.3.3. Information Search and Retrieval: Information filtering.

General Terms
Algorithms, Design, Experimentation

INTRODUCTION

News reading has changed with the advance of the World Wide Web, from the traditional model of news consumption via physical newspaper subscription to access to thousands of sources via the internet. News aggregation

websites, like Google News and Yahoo! News, collect news from various sources and provide an aggregate view of news from around the world. A critical problem with news service websites is that the volumes of articles can be overwhelming to the users. The challenge is to help users find news articles that are interesting to read.

Content-based recommendation is a technology in response to this challenge of information overload in general. Based on a profile of user interests and preferences, systems recommend items that may be of interest or value to the user. Content-based methods plays a central role in recommender systems, as it is able to recommend information that has not been rated before and accommodates the individual differences between users [3, 8]. This technique has been applied in various domains, such as email [16], news [4, 5, 20], and web search [15, 18]. In the domain of news, this technology particularly aims at aggregating news articles according to user interests and creating a "personal newspaper" for each user.

An accurate profile of users' current interests is critical for the success of content-based recommendation systems. Some systems [1, 19] require users to manually create and update profiles. This approach places an extra burden on users, something very few are willing to take on. Instead, systems can construct profiles automatically from users' interaction with the system.

In this paper, we describe our research on developing a personalized news recommendation system based on profiles learned from user activity in Google News. The Google News website, available at http://news.google.com, is one of the most popular news websites in the world, receiving millions of page views and clicks from users around the world

The nature of news reading makes news recommendation distinctive from content-based recommendation in other domains. When visiting a news website, the user is looking for *new information*, information that was not known before, or even surprising. Since user profiles are inferred from past user activity, it is important to know how users' news interests change over time and how effective it would be to use the past user activities to predict their future behavior.

To understand this issue, we conducted a large scale log analysis of Google News users to measure the stability of users' news interests. We found that their interests do vary over time but follow the aggregate trend of news events. Based on these findings, we develop a Bayesian model to predict the news interests of an individual user from the activities of that particular user and the news trend demonstrated in activities of a group of users. To recommend news stories to users, the system takes into account of the genuine interests of individual users and the current news trend. Therefore, the user will receive news tailored to her interests without missing the important news events, even when those events do not strictly match the user's particular interests.

We combined the content-based method with the collaborative filtering method previously developed for Google News [7] to generate personalized recommendations for news access. The hybrid method was evaluated in a live experiment: a subset of the live traffic at Google News used the hybrid method; the result showed significant improvement over the existing collaborative filtering method. The experiment on live traffic also revealed a number of interesting issues related to recommendations, serendipitous exploration and user satisfaction. We will discuss these issues later in this paper.

The contribution of this paper is three-fold. First, we report a large-scale log analysis of the consistency of users' news interest. Second, we propose a novel method for predicting a user's news interests based on click behavior which combines the genuine interests of the user and the current news trend. Third, we presented a hybrid system that combines content-based and collaborative filtering method for personalized news recommendation and ran an experiment on the live traffic, showing improved results.

PERSONALIZATION IN GOOGLE NEWS

Google News is a computer-generated news website that aggregates headlines from news sources worldwide. It classifies news articles into different topic categories (e.g. "world", "sport", "entertainment", etc.) and displays them in corresponding sections, as do standard news websites, but with fully automated text-based classification. Google News serves millions of users around the world, and provides numerous editions for different countries and languages.

Users usually visit Google News starting from the homepage. The homepage of the standard edition has the *Top Stories* section on the top of the homepage, followed by topic based sections of news articles, like "world" and "sport".

If a user signs in to her Google Account and explicitly enables Web History, the system will record her click history and generate a personalized section for her, named "Recommended for [*account*]", containing stories recommended based on her click history in Google News.

The recorded click histories were fully anonymized and kept secure according to the Google Privacy Policy.

A previous Google News recommendation system was developed using a collaborative filtering method [7]. It recommends news stories that were read by users with similar click history. This method has two major drawbacks in recommending news stories. First, the system cannot recommend stories that have not yet been read by other users, a problem that is often referred to as the *first-rater problem* [7, 8]. For news recommendations, this is a serious problem, as news service websites strive to present the most updated information to users in a timely manner. News articles presented in Google News are usually published within one hour. However, the collaborative filtering method has to wait several hours to collect enough clicks to recommend the news story to users, resulting in undesirable time lags between break-out news and recommendations. Second, not all users are equal to each other, and the collaborative filtering method may not account for the individual variability between users [3]. For example, we observed that entertainment news stories are constantly recommended to most of the users, even for those users who never clicked on entertainment stories. The reason is that entertainment news stories are generally very popular, thus there are always enough clicks on entertainment stories from a user's "neighbors" to make the recommendation.

A solution to these two problems would be to build profiles of user's genuine interests and use them to make news recommendations. The profiles would help the system filter out the stories that are not of interest to the user, such as the entertainment news mentioned above. A news story may also be recommended to the user if it matches her interest, even if the story has not been clicked on by other users.

In this paper, we describe an content-based method to recommend news articles according to their topic categories, which is assigned by text classifiers. Based on a user's news reading history the recommender predicts the topic categories of interest to her each time she visit Google News. News articles in those categories are ranked higher in the candidate list and will be recommended to the user. We chose to recommend news stories at the general level of topic categories instead of fine grained topics because of the nature of news reading: most users visit news websites with the attitude of "show me something interesting," rather than having any specific information goals [7]. Over-specializing the user profile may limit the recommendations to news that the user already knew, which is obviously undesirable for news reading.

The user activities that Google News records are the user's clicks on the Google News website. The system records the event and the time when a user clicks on the page. Each click on a news article is treated as a positive vote for the topic category of that article.

There are two practical constraints on our content-based news recommendation algorithm. First, a user's news interests may change over time. The system should be able to incrementally update the user's profile to reflect change in interest. Second, there is a large variance in the click history size of the users. A successful algorithm needs to degrade gracefully, i.e. be able to provide reasonable recommendations even when there is little information about the user.

RELATED WORK

Two different technologies are commonly used in recommender systems: content-based recommendation and collaborative filtering. The content-based approach recommends information based on profiles; these profiles are built by analyzing the content of items that the user accessed and favored in the past. In contrast, the collaborative filtering approach does not consider the content of items, but uses the opinions of peer users to generate recommendations. In this paper, we focus on developing effective content-based mechanism for news recommendation in a large-scale website.

The content-based approach has been applied to provide personalized selection of news information in various forms such as personal news agents [1], news readers for wireless devices [2, 3] and web-based news aggregators [19]. These systems build user profiles from information explicitly provided by the user or implicitly observed in user activities. The profiles are then compared with the content of news articles to generate personalized recommendations.

Tan and Teo [19] presented a personalized news system, named PIN. PIN retrieves and ranks news articles according to the user's profile, which is initially defined by the user as a list of keywords and then learned from user feedback using neural network technology. When interacting with PIN, users provide explicit feedback by rating the articles. A similar system, News Dude [1], reads news to users, supporting a series of feedback options such as "interesting", "not interesting", "I already know this", etc. A special purpose news browser for PDAs, named WebClipping2, is implemented by Carreira et al. [3]. WebClipping2 uses a Bayesian Classifier in order to calculate the probability that a specific article would be interesting to the user. Rather than requiring users to provide explicit feedbacks, WebClipping2 observes the total reading time, number of lines read and some other characteristics of user behavior to infer the user's interests. Another personal news agent, PVA [8], uses a proxy to collect user's page clicks and the browsing time, in order to construct a "personal view" that reflects user interests. PVA is applied and evaluated to provide personalized news access.

Unlike these news personalization systems, our news recommendation system infers user interest based on their click behavior on the news website. There are no ratings or negative votes to gauge what the user dislikes. For privacy protection reasons, Google News does not record detailed information about the clicks, such as the amount of time

spent on the page. Thus, the system needs to make reasonable prediction with the limited and noisy information of user activity on the website.

Recently, there has been some research on user modeling based on click histories, mostly with the aim of enhancing personalized web search. For instance, Qiu and Cho [13] presented a formal framework and a method to automatically learn user interest based on past click history. The learned user interest is integrated in Topic-Sensitive PageRank to generate personalized ranking. Speretta and Gauch [17] classified queries and snippets of clicked search results to create user profiles, which were then used to re-rank search results. Kim and Chan [9] proposed to model user interest in a hierarchy of concepts, going from general to specific. The hierarchy is learned from the web pages bookmarked by the user using clustering methods.

An important issue in user modeling, particularly for news access, is the changes in user interest over time. Billsus and Pazzani [1] found that there are two types of user interest in news reading: short-term and long-term. The short-term interest usually is related to hot news events and changes quickly. In contrast, long term interest often reflects actual user interest. Accordingly, News Dude [1] uses a multi-strategy machine learning approach to create separate models of short-term and long-term interest. Chen et al. [8] analyzed the change of user interest in news over time and used special mechanisms to update user profiles to reflect user's current interests. Liang and Lai [14] proposed a time-based approach to build user profiles from browsing behavior, which took into account of the time spent by the user on reading the articles and the recency of user activity.

Compared to the above methods, our method is unique in that it captures the dynamic changes of user interest in the context of news trend. The system discovers the genuine interest of users and combines the genuine interest with the current news trend to predict the user's current news interest.

The second technology for recommender systems is collaborative filtering. Collaborative filtering has been applied to personalized news reading applications, such as GroupLens [12] and the first version of Google News recommender.

The content-based and collaborative filtering each has their advantages and limitations [3]. Some research tried to combine both methods and achieved encouraging results [3, 6]. The hybrid method benefits from both methods, providing early predictions that cover all items and users, and improving the recommendations as the number of users and ratings increases. In Google News, we combined our new content-based method with the collaborative filtering method previously developed for Google News [7] to generate personalized recommendations for news access. The live traffic experiment showed that the hybrid method improved the quality of news recommendation.

LOG ANALYSIS OF USER INTEREST

The basic assumption of personalization is that users have reasonably consistent interests. A user's history will only be useful if the history help us predict her future actions.

Wedig and Madani [21] performed a large-scale analysis of Yahoo! search engine query logs to determine the consistency of user interests and answer other questions related to personalization. They found that the distribution of users' interest over 22 general topic categories (e.g. "travel", "computing", etc.) converge to a stationary distribution after hundreds of queries are observed. However, news reading is very different from web search. Users usually have specific information goals when issuing queries to search engines, but users visit news website with the attitude of "show me something interesting" [7]. News readers' interest is influenced by the big news events [1]. Many news personalization systems assume that users' news interest change over time [1, 8, 14]. However, to our knowledge, there are no formal studies about how the interest changes. To gain a deep understanding of this issue, we conducted a large-scale log analysis of click behavior on Google News.

Data

We examine the anonymized click logs of those Google News users who were signed into their Google account and explicitly enabled history tracking over 12-month period, from 2007/7/1 to 2008/6/30. From users who made at least 10 clicks per month in that period, we randomly sampled 16,848 users. These users are from more than 10 different countries and regions.

Click Distribution

As we described in the previous section, Google News classifies news articles into a predefined set of topic categories, $C = \{c_1, c_2, ..., c_n\}$, including "world", "sports", and "entertainment". In our log analysis, we computed the click distribution over the set of topic categories for individual users as well as the group of users in a country. We divided the time period into 12 months. Then, for each user u, we computed the distribution of her clicks in every month t, $D(u,t)$, represented as a vector over the set of topic categories:

$$D(u,t) = (\frac{N_1}{N_{total}}, \frac{N_2}{N_{total}}, ..., \frac{N_n}{N_{total}}), \quad \text{where } N_{total} = \sum_i N_i \text{ (1)}$$

N_i is the number of clicks on articles classified into category c_i made by user u in month t. N_{total} is the total number of clicks made by the user in the time period. Thus, $D(u,t)$ represents the proportion of time the user spent

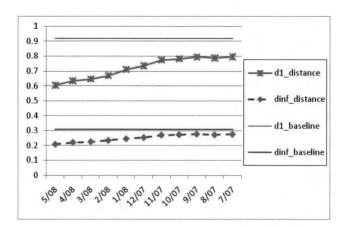

Figure 1. Comparison between the click distribution of the month to be predicted and those of previous months

reading about each topic category and reflects the interest distribution of the user in that month.

Change of User's News Interests over Time

If a user's news interests are stable, her click distributions in each month should be consistent over time. Particularly, we are interested in using her history to predict her future behavior. Thus, for each user, we compared her click distribution of the most recent month (2008/6/1-2008/6/30) to her click distributions of all the previous months. The comparison demonstrates how well the historical click distribution predicts the future click distribution. Similar to the search log analysis by Wedig and Madani [21], we used d_1 and d_∞, based on l_1 and l_∞, to measure the distance between the click distributions. The d_1 and d_∞ distance of two vectors X and Y is defined as follows:

$$d_1(X,Y) = \sum_i |x_i - y_i| \quad \text{and} \quad d_\infty(X,Y) = \max_i(|x_i - y_i|) \text{ (2)}$$

Figure 1 shows the average d_1 and d_∞ distance between the click distribution of the most recent month and those of previous months. Larger value of d_1 and d_∞ distance in a month implies bigger differences between the click distribution of that month and the most recent month. As baselines, we use the d_1 and d_∞ distance of an individual user and the general public in the same location, computed in the next section. As is evident in figure 1, the difference between the click distribution of the most recent month and a past month increased as we go back into the history. Compared to the month of 5/08, the d_1 distance in 7/07 increased 31.9%, and the d_∞ distance increased 32.1%. The figure shows that users' news interests do change over time and their clicks in older history become much less useful in predicting their future interests.

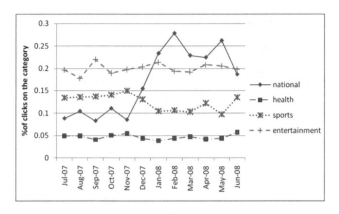

Figure 2. Interest distribution of US users over time

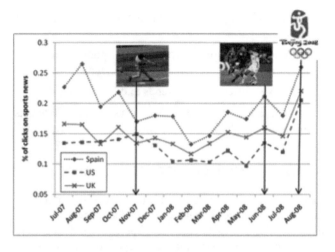

Figure 3. Change of interests in sports news over time

News Trend

In addition to the click distribution of individual users, we calculated the click distributions of the general public in various countries where Google News is served. For each country, the general interests can be represented by the distribution of all the clicks made by the users from that country in a past time period t, represented as $D(t)$.

Figure 2 plots the click distribution for the United States population over time. For the clarity of the figure, only 4 most representative categories are shown in the figure. Figure 2 shows many fluctuations in the news interests of the general public in the US, which was also observed in plots of other countries (not shown in this paper). Furthermore, some topic categories (e.g. "national") showed greater variation than others (e.g. "health"). This phenomenon may be explained by the fact that there are more and bigger break-out news in national politics than health.

We hypothesize that the interest change of a country's general public corresponds to the big news events in that country. The log analysis provided empirical evidence for this hypothesis. For example, the US election campaign starting in late 2007 attracted a large amount of attention to national political news. Figure 2 shows that the percentage of national news clicks doubled during the election campaign compared to before the campaign. Those users who usually paid little attention to national politics probably read more news about the election campaign because of the importance of the event. Similarly, the 2008 Olympic Games in August 2008 produced a spike in the general interest in sports news in several different countries, as shown in Figure 3.

Moreover, the log analysis shows that there are regional differences in the news trend represented in the click distributions of general public. Figure 3 shows the change of interests in sports news in three different countries: United Kingdom, Spain and United States. Overall, Spanish users read more sports news than British and American users. Figure 3 shows spikes in June 2008 and August 2008, which correspond to the Euro Cup in June and Olympic

Games in August respectively. But the American users showed much lower interests in the Euro Cup than the two European countries. On the other hand, the American users' interests in Sports news dropped dramatically in November 2007, when the baseball season ended. However, there were no such trend in Spain and UK.

Influence of the General News Trends on Individual Interest Change

The previous subsections analyze the interest change of individual users and the general public. A natural question that follows is whether the general news trends influence the interest change of individual users. To understand this question, we compare the click distribution of individual users with the click distribution of the general public in the same time period. We also computed the d_1 and d_∞ distance of an individual user and the general public in a randomly picked different location. If the user's interest is influenced by the local news trend, her click distribution should be more similar to general click distribution of the location that she belongs to than to those of other locations. The average d_1 and d_∞ distance is presented in table 1.

Table 1. Comparison in click distributions between individual users and the general public

	d_1 distance	d_∞ distance
Same location	0.92	0.31
Different location	1.13	0.39

As shown in the table, an individual user's click distribution is more similar to the click distribution of the general public in the same location than to a randomly selected location. Using t-test, both the d_1 and d_∞ distance in the same location are significantly lower than those in the different location, at the confidence level of 99%.

We can draw the following conclusions from this log analysis:

- The news interests of individual users do change over time.

- The click distributions of the general public reflect the news trend, which correspond to the big news events.

- There exist different news trends in different locations.

- To a certain extent, the individual user's news interests correspond with the news trend in the location that the user belongs to.

BAYESIAN FRAMEWORK FOR USER INTEREST PREDICTION

The log analysis reveals that the click distributions of individual users are influenced by the local news trend. For example, Spanish users read more sports news during Euro Cup. Similar phenomena were also reported in a user study of the lifecycle of news interests [8]. Based on these findings, we decompose user's news interests into two parts: users' genuine interests and the influence of local news trend. The user's genuine interests originate from the personal characteristics of the user, such as gender, age, profession, etc. and are thus relatively stable over time. On the other hand, when deciding what to read, users are also influenced by the news trend in the location that they belong to. This kind of influence produces short-term effects and changes over time. The genuine interests and news trend influence correspond to the "long-term" and "short-term" interests discussed in [1]. However, we used distinct methods to predict user's news interests. More importantly, we model the "short-term" interests from the perspective of news trend using the click patterns of the general public, instead of only using the user's own feedbacks.

We developed an approach using Bayesian frameworks [10] to predict users' current news interest based on the click patterns of the individual users and the group of users in the country. The predicted interests are used in news recommendation. The approach works as follows: first, the system predicts user's genuine news interests regardless of the news trend, using the user's clicks in each past time period; second, the predictions made with data in a series of past time periods are combined to gain an accurate prediction of the user's genuine news interests; finally, the system predicts the user's current interests by combining her genuine news interests and the current news trend in her location.

Predicting User's Genuine News Interest

For a specific time period t in the past, we observed the click distribution of individual users, $D(u,t)$, and the click distribution of all the users in a country, $D(t)$, which represents the news trend in that country in the time period. We would like to learn the user's genuine interests revealed in $D(u,t)$ regardless of the influence of $D(t)$. The genuine interest of a user in topic category c_i is modeled as $p^t(click \mid category = c_i)$, the probability of the user

clicking on an article about c_i. Using a Bayesian rule, $p\ (click \mid category = c_i)$ is computed as follows:

$$interest^t(category = c_i) = p^t(click \mid category = c_i)$$

$$= \frac{p^t(category = c_i \mid click)\,p^t(click)}{p^t(category = c_i)} \quad (3)$$

$p^t(category = c_i \mid click)$ is the probability that the user's clicks being in category c_i. It can be estimated by the click distribution $D(u,t)$ observed in time period t, as computed in Equation 1.

$p^t(category = c_i)$ is the prior probability of an article being about category c_i. This is the proportion of news articles published about that category in the time period, which correlates with the news trend in the location. As more news events happen in a given topic category, more news articles will be written in that category. Thus, we can approximate this probability with the click distribution of the general public $D(t)$.

$p^t(click)$ is the prior probability of the user clicking on any news article, regardless of the article category.

According to Equation 3, $p(click \mid category = c_i)$ represents the extent to which the user's interest in the topic category differs from the general public of the same location. If the user reads a lot of sports news while a lot of users are reading it, the user may not be particularly interested in sports but read the sports news because of some hot sports event. In contrast, an extraordinary large proportion of clicks on sports news is a strong signal for the user's genuine interests in sports.

Combining Predictions of Past Time Periods

Equation 3 computes the user's genuine news interest based on the click distributions in a particular time period. To accurately gauge the user's genuine interests, we combine the predictions made over multiple time periods as follows:

$$interest(category = c_i) = \frac{\sum_t \left(N^t \times interest^t(category = c_i) \right)}{\sum_t N^t}$$

$$= \frac{\sum_t \left(N^t \times \dfrac{p^t(category = c_i \mid click)\,p^t(click)}{p^t(category = c_i)} \right)}{\sum_t N^t}$$

$$(4)$$

The more clicks we have recorded about the user, the better the prediction is going to be. Therefore, we normalize the predictions made in time periods t by N^t, the total number of clicks by the user in time period t.

We can assume that the prior probability of a user clicking on any article is constant over time. Thus, Equation 4 becomes Equation 5:

$$interest(category = c_i)$$

$$= \frac{p(click) \times \sum_t \left(N^t \times \frac{p^t(category = c_i \mid click)}{p^t(category = c_i)} \right)}{\sum_t N^t} \qquad (5)$$

Predicting User's Current News Interest

As we discussed before, the user's news interest is decomposed into two parts: the genuine news interest and the influence of news trends. The previous section calculated the user's genuine news interests based on her past click behaviors. To gauge the current news trend, we use the click distribution of the general public in a short current time period (e.g. in the past hour), represented as $p^0(category = c_i)$. Because of the large number of users, there are enough clicks in the short current time period to accurately estimate the popular topic categories in the location.

The ultimate goal is to predict the click distribution of the user for the near future. Again, we use the Bayesian law:

$$p^0(category = c_i \mid click)$$

$$= \frac{p^0(click \mid category = c_i) p^0(category = c_i)}{p^0(click)} \qquad (6)$$

We estimate $p^0(click \mid category = c_i)$ with the genuine news interests, $interest(category = c_i)$, computed in Equation 5, and assume the probability a user clicking on any news article is constant, thus,

$$p^0(category = c_i \mid click)$$

$$\propto \frac{interest(category = c_i) p^0(category = c_i)}{p(click)} \qquad (7)$$

$$\propto \frac{p^0(category = c_i) \times \sum_t \left(N^t \times \frac{p^t(category = c_i \mid click)}{p^t(category = c_i)} \right)}{\sum_t N^t}$$

In addition to the user's past clicks, we add a set of virtual clicks, with the same click distribution as that of current news trend, i.e. $p^0(category = c_i)$. Thus, the final estimation of the user's news interests in the near future is

$$p^0(category = c_i \mid click)$$

$$\propto \frac{p^0(category = c_i) \times \left(\sum_t \left(N^t \times \frac{p^t(category = c_i \mid click)}{p^t(category = c_i)} \right) + G \right)}{\sum_t N^t + G}$$

$$(8)$$

G is the number of virtual clicks (set to be 10 in the system), which can be regarded as a smoothing factor. When the system observes very few (even zero) clicks from the user, the system will predict the user's interest mostly based on the current news trend, which is still a reasonable estimation. On the other hand, if $\sum_t N^t$ is the much larger than G, the estimation is mainly based on the user's own click distribution in the past.

Another advantage of the proposed approach is that the user's interests can be updated incrementally. The system can save the values of N^t and $\frac{p^t(category = c_i \mid click)}{p^t(category = c_i)}$ for each past time period. When updating the user's profile, the system only needs to compute the value for the most recent time period and recompute the weighted sum with the saved values.

NEWS RECOMMENDATION

In order to rank the list of candidate articles to be recommended, the system generates an content-based recommendation score, $CR(article)$, and a collaborative filtering score, $CF(article)$, for each article. $CR(article)$ is based on the topic category of that article and the predicted user's interest using Equation 8. The collaborative method implemented in [7] computes $CF(article)$. The two scores are combined in ranking the candidates for news recommendation:

$$Rec(article) = CR(article) \times CF(article) \qquad (9)$$

Combining the content-based method and the collaborative method offers the advantages of both methods and shows improved performance over using the collaborative method alone. In the next section, we describe our evaluation of the hybrid method on the live traffic of Google News.

LIVE TRAFFIC EXPERIMENT

To evaluate the performance of the hybrid methods and understand the user experience with personalized news recommendation, we conducted experiments on a fraction (about 10,000 users) of the live traffic at Google News. The users were randomly assigned to a control group and a test group. The two groups had about the same number of users. When a logged-in Google News user (who also explicitly has enabled web history) visits the website, a section of recommended news is generated particularly for that user. In our experiment, the users in the control group get recommended news from the existing collaborative filtering method; while the new hybrid method is used for the test group. Aggregate click-through rate analysis was then performed over fully anonymized click logs.

The experiment was run for 34 days, from 1/10/2009 to 2/17/2009. The user's clicks in the past 12 months are used as history to compute the user's interests. To gain greater accuracy in estimating the news trend in the past, we

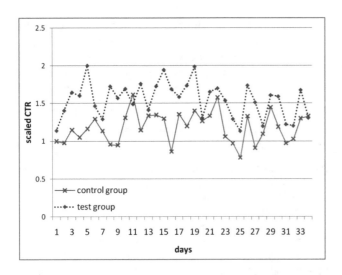

Figure 4. CTR of the recommended news section

calculated the click distributions of the general public for each week. The current news trend, $p^0(category = c_i)$, is estimated with the click distribution of the general public in the past day.

Three different metrics are used to measure the performance of the recommender and the user's experience: click-through rates (CTR) of the recommended news section, CTR of the Google News homepage, and frequency of visiting Google News website. We calculated the three metrics for each user on daily basis. The performance of the control and test group was derived by averaging the measurements of all the users in the corresponding group. We report the experiment results for the three aspects below.

CTR of the recommended news section is calculated as the number of clicks on the recommended news articles every time the user visits the Google News website. It directly measures the quality of the recommendations as how many of the recommendations are clicked on, thus liked, by the user. Figure 4 shows the CTR of the recommended news section for the control and test group in the 34 days. The values are scaled so that the CTR of the control group in the first day is 1. As shown in the figure, the CTR in the test group is consistently higher than the CTR in the control group, in 33 of 34 days in the experiment. This shows that the proposed news interest prediction method improved the quality of news recommendations. On average, the hybrid method that incorporates the information filtering method improves the CTR upon the existing collaborative method by 30.9%. The improvement is significant at the 99% confidence level according to t-test.

The recommended news section is only one part of the Google News website, which presents to the user many other standard non-personalized news sections along with the recommended news section, such as top stories, world news, business news, etc. We would like to analyze the

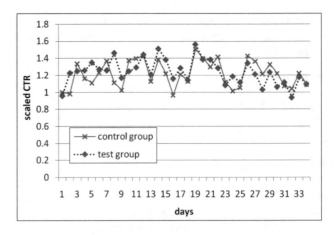

Figure 5. CTR of the Google News homepage

effect of the improved recommender on the user experience of the whole website. Two metrics are computed to evaluate the news recommender in the larger context of news reading: CTR of the Google News homepage and the frequency of visiting the Google News site.

The CTR of the Google News homepage is calculated as the total number of clicks for each page visit made by the user. Figure 5 plots the measurements for the control and test groups in the experiment. Interestingly, there is not much difference in the CTR of the homepage for the two groups. Although the test group clicked on more news articles in the recommended news section (shown in figure 4), the total number of articles that a user is willing to click on in each website visit seems to be constant. In other words, the improved recommender "stole" clicks from other non-personalized sections, rather than increasing the overall number of clicks. The experiment demonstrated that the improved news recommender created a more focused news reading in the test group. As the recommender was improved to present news articles that better matched the user's interests, the users seemed to pay more attention to the recommended news section and spend less time and effort in finding interesting news articles in the non-personalized sections.

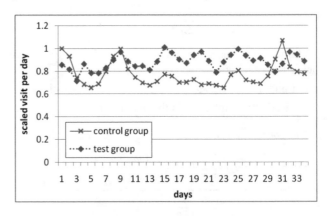

Figure 6. Frequency of website visit per day

We measure the overall satisfaction of the Google News website with the frequency of website visits, calculated as the number of times the user visits the website in a day. Figure 6 shows the frequency of website visit for the control and test group. It is evident in the figure that the test group visited Google News more often than the control group in most of the days in the experiment period. On average, the frequency of website visits in the test group is 14.1% higher than the control group. The improvement is significant at the 99% confidence level according to t-test.

In summation, the proposed news interest prediction method improved the quality of news recommendations. More recommended news articles were clicked on by the users in the test group using the new hybrid method than the control group using the existing collaborative filtering method. As a result, users seemed to like Google News more and visited the website more often. However, the total amount of attention that users are willing to pay per visit seems to be constant. As users clicked on more recommended news articles, they clicked on fewer articles in the standard non-personalized sections. More research of in-depth user studies would be needed to understand the effects of personalization on information exploration and serendipitous discovery.

CONCLUSION AND FUTURE WORK

In this paper, we present our research on developing an effective information filtering mechanism for news recommendations in a large-scale website such as Google News. We first conducted a log analysis on the change of user's interests in news topics over time. The log analysis demonstrated variations in users' news interests and shows that the news interests of individual users are influenced by the local news trend. Based on these findings, we decompose users' news interests into two parts: the genuine interests and the influence of local news trends. A Bayesian framework is proposed to model a user's genuine interests using her past click history and predict her current interests by combining her genuine interest and the local news trend. The method for predicting user's interests was used in content-based news recommendation, and it was combined with the existing collaborative filtering method to generate personalized news recommendations. We conducted an experiment with the news recommender using the hybrid method on a fraction of live traffic on the Google News website. Compared with the existing collaborative filtering method, the experiment showed that the hybrid method improved the quality of news recommendations and attracted more frequent visits to the Google News website.

The research can be extended in the following directions in the future. Position bias can be investigated and incorporated in modeling users' interests using the click behavior. More advanced methods for combining the information filtering and collaborative filtering mechanisms can also be studied to better leverage the advantages of both mechanism. In addition, our live traffic experiment revealed

that the improved recommender increased the CTR of the recommended news sections while reducing the CTR of other standard sections. Further user studies can be conducted to investigate this phenomenon to better understand the effect of personalization on news exploration.

REFERENCE

1. Billsus, D. and Pazzani, M. J. A hybrid user model for news story classification. In Proceedings of the Seventh International Conference on User Modeling. 1999.

2. Billsus, D. and Pazzani, M. J., User Modeling for Adaptive News Access, User Modeling and User-Adapted Interaction, v.10 n.2-3, p.147-180, 2000

3. Carreira, R., Crato, J. M., Gonçalves, D., Jorge, J. A. Evaluating adaptive user profiles for news classification, Proceedings of the 9th international conference on Intelligent user interfaces, 2004.

4. Chen, C. C., Chen, M. C., Sun, Y. PVA: a self-adaptive personal view agent system, Proceedings of the seventh ACM SIGKDD international conference on Knowledge discovery and data mining, 2001.

5. Chen, Y-S., Shahabi, C.: Automatically improving the accuracy of user profiles with genetic algorithm. In: Proceedings of IASTED International Conference on Artificial Intelligence and Soft Computing, 2001.

6. Claypool, M., Gokhale, A., Miranda, T., Murnikov, P., Netes, D. and Sartin, M. Combining Content-Based and Collaborative Filters in an Online Newspaper. In Proceedings of ACM SIGIR Workshop on Recommender Systems, 1999.

7. Das, A. S., Datar, M., Garg, A., Rajaram, S. Google news personalization: scalable online collaborative filtering, Proceedings of the 16th international conference on World Wide Web, 2007

8. Good, N., Schafer, J. B., Konstan, J. A., Borchers, A., Sarwar, B., Herlocker, J., Riedl, J. Combining collaborative filtering with personal agents for better recommendations, Proceedings of the 16th national conference on Artificial intelligence and the 11th Innovative applications of artificial intelligence conference innovative applications of artificial intelligence, 1999.

9. Kim, H. R., Chan, P. K. Learning implicit user interest hierarchy for context in personalization, Proceedings of the 8th international conference on Intelligent user interfaces, January 12-15, 2003.

10. Jensen, V. Bayesian Networks and Decision Graphs. Springer, 2001

11. Katakis, I., Tsoumakas, G., Banos, E., Bassiliades, N., Vlahavas, I. An adaptive personalized news

dissemination system. In Journal of Intelligent Information Systems, Volume 32, Issue 2. 2009.

12. Konstan, J. A., Miller, B.N., Maltz,D., Herlocker, J. L.,Gordon, L. R., and Riedl, J. Group-Lens: Applying collaborative filtering to usenet news. Commun. ACM 40, 77-87. 1997.

13. Lee, U., Liu, Z., Cho, J. Automatic identification of user goals in Web search, Proceedings of the 14th international conference on World Wide Web, 2005

14. Liang, T.-P. and Lai, H.-J. Discovering User Interests from Web Browsing Behavior: An Application to Internet News Services, IEEE Computer Society, Los Alamitos, CA, USA, 2002.

15. Liu, F., Yu, C., Meng, W. Personalized Web Search For Improving Retrieval Effectiveness. In: IEEE Transactions on Knowledge and Data Engineering, 2004.

16. Maes, P. Agents that reduce work and information overload, Communications of the ACM, v.37 n.7, p.30-40, July 1994.

17. Speretta, M., Gauch, S.: Personalized Search based on User Search Histories. In: IEEE/WIC/ACM International Conference on Web Intelligence, 2005.

18. Sugiyama, K., Hatano, K., Yoshikawa, M. Adaptive web search based on user profile constructed without any effort from users. In: Proceedings 13th International Conference on World Wide Web, 2004.

19. Tan, A. and Tee, C. "Learning User Profiles for Personalized Information Dissemination," Proceedings of 1998 IEEE International Joint conference on Neural Networks, pp. 183- 188, May 1998

20. Tan, A., Teo, C.: Learning user profiles for personalized information dissemination. In: Proceedings of 1998 IEEE International Joint Conference on Neural Networks, 1998.

21. Wedig, S., Madani, O. A large-scale analysis of query logs for assessing personalization opportunities, Proceedings of the 12th ACM SIGKDD international conference on Knowledge discovery and data mining, 2006.

Aspect-level News Browsing: Understanding News Events from Multiple Viewpoints

Souneil Park
KAIST
spark@nclab.kaist.ac.kr

SangJeong Lee
KAIST
peterlee@nclab.kaist.ac.kr

Junehwa Song
KAIST
junesong@nclab.kaist.ac.kr

ABSTRACT

Aspect-level news browsing provides readers with a classified view of news articles with different viewpoints. It facilitates active interactions with which readers easily discover and compare diverse existing biased views over a news event. As such, it effectively helps readers understand the event from a plural of viewpoints and formulate their own, more balanced viewpoints free from specific biased views. Realizing aspect-level browsing raises important challenges, mainly due to the lack of semantic knowledge with which to abstract and classify the intended salient aspects of articles. We first demonstrate the feasibility of aspect-level news browsing through user studies. We then deeply look into the news article production process and develop framing cycle-aware clustering. The evaluation results show that the developed method performs classification more accurately than other methods.

Author Keywords Media Bias, Aspect-level News Browsing, Aspect-level Classification.

ACM Classification Keywords

K.4 Computers and Society: Social Issues, H.4 Information Systems Applications: Communication Applications

General Terms Algorithms, Design

INTRODUCTION

Bias in news articles is a major obstacle in keeping the public well informed. The reality of news events is inevitably filtered and reframed by the subjective valuation of journalists. They select different aspects of reality, cover them in different tones, and present them in different styles. Their valuation is continuously influenced by their political and ideological views, as well as external factors of news production such as owners and advertisers. It is very difficult for ordinary readers to build a comprehensive, balanced understanding of a news event. The resulting widespread biases intensify political extremism [2], and distort public debate on contentious issues such as the health care reform [14].

Our work aims to provide a computational solution to the media bias problem. We are developing a novel news service

framework that mitigates the effects of media bias. The framework automatically creates and promptly provides readers with multiple classified viewpoints on news events. In our previous paper [11], we discussed an early prototype of the framework and its service process. The prototype collects news articles from diverse news sources, classifies and presents articles with different viewpoints. The effectiveness of the prototype was evaluated and reported through various user studies. The results showed that the prototype helps readers compare and contrast different viewpoints and develop their own views.

In this paper, we elaborate on the core function of the framework, *aspect-level news browsing*. Aspect-level news browsing provides readers with a classified view of news articles with different viewpoints. It facilitates active interactions with which readers easily discover and compare diverse existing biased views over a news event. As such, it effectively helps readers understand the event from a plural of viewpoints and formulate their own, more balanced viewpoints free from specific biased views.

Aspect-level news browsing differs from conventional event-level browsing as it engages readers in critical news reading for a selected event. Existing news services, such as GoogleNews, organize news articles based on the reported events. They do not expose the different viewpoints among articles covering a common event. The users of an event-level browsing service are likely to finish browsing without comparing and contrasting different viewpoints. In contrast, aspect-level news browsing enables readers to be aware of different articles on the selected event, and critically read and compare them with the other articles.

Aspect-level news browsing effectively reveals different viewpoints through *aspect-level classification* of news articles. News producers with different viewpoints frame news events by covering different aspects at different depths [18]. Thus, to reveal diverse viewpoints, aspect-level classification identifies the salient aspects, and classifies articles by the similarity of their aspects.

Realizing aspect-level classification raises several important challenges. First, the feasibility of aspect-level classification has to be studied. If people interpret and classify aspects of news articles differently, aspect-level classification would be infeasible; hence, a computational method will also be impossible to develop. We conduct experiments and demonstrate that people agree on i) the articulated aspects of individual articles, and ii) the classification of articles.

Second, computational methods need be developed for two tasks: *aspect extraction*, extracting the articulated aspects of individual articles; and *article classification*, classifying the articles based on the extraction results. The tasks are technically involved, mainly due to the lack of semantic knowledge with which to abstract and classify the intended salient aspects of articles. We look deeply into the news article production process and identify important characteristics. Based on these characteristics, we develop two novel methods, namely, news structure-based extraction (NSE) and framing cycle-aware clustering (FCAC). NSE [11] exploits well known news writing rules to automatically abstract the aspects of an article. We observe that a news article is usually written to fit an inverted pyramid structure (Figure 3). As this structure is general in news articles, NSE can broadly be applied to many articles regardless of their topics and languages.

FCAC effectively reveals the diversity of different aspects of a news event. By examining the framing cycle of news events, we observe an important characteristic, namely the head-tail characteristic; similar aspects are commonly covered by many articles at the head of the framing cycle, and diverse uncommon aspects abound over time in later articles. The method increases the sensitivity of classification by identifying and selectively applying the common keywords reflecting the common, head-side aspects and the uncommon keywords reflecting the uncommon, tail-side aspects. It especially acknowledges the importance of the uncommon keywords and delicately captures the diversity of the uncommon aspects, which is the source of the richness in the viewpoints. We evaluate the developed method and show that the method outperforms other widely used text clustering methods.

As an early solution to aspect-level classification, the method leaves room for further improvement. The method is developed mainly based on the domain knowledge of news production, i.e., the news writing rules and the framing cycle. Thus, the performance of the method provides a baseline that can be achieved without advanced IR and NLP techniques. We believe the method can be further improved by adopting these techniques on top of it.

BACKGROUND AND RELATED WORK

A comprehensive overview of the media bias problem and its solution space is provided in [11]. We briefly review them and discuss related work.

The media bias problem has been investigated in mass communication and journalism studies. The studies argue that media bias is an inevitable structural problem of the news industry rather than a temporary phenomenon. A survey by the American Society of Newspaper Editors [19] revealed that 78 percent of the public believed that there was bias in news reporting. The impact of media bias on distorting social awareness on critical public issues and collective decision making processes, such as elections [5], has also been reported. The problem grows more serious as

people do not make efforts to overcome bias. Arguments have been made that people do not actively seek diverse newspapers or TV news [17], or different political books [6]. While media bias has been studied extensively, no clear solution has been developed.

Following [11], the potential solutions to the problem can be viewed at two different points, i.e., during production or in post-production. While the production stage approaches try to avoid the creation of bias, the post-production stage approaches deal with the created biases of published contents. News producers have established journalism ethics and standards, and developed alternative reporting formats such as point-counterpoint, and roundtable discussions. However, the approaches entirely depend on the efforts of individual journalists or require significant changes in the news production process. These approaches have not succeeded in resolving the problem. Media bias is still widespread [19].

The post production approaches are classified into bias correction, bias diagnosis, and bias mitigation, which is the approach we take. Though not focused on news issues, Wikipedia makes attempts for bias correction through collaborative review. However, bias correction is intrinsically difficult as it is hard or impossible even to clearly define what an unbiased news report is. Bias diagnosis attempts to examine and explain the bias of produced news articles. However, the scale of analyses is limited as they are conducted by only a few experienced researchers. The studies are mostly confined to single issues, and the scope of analyzed articles is limited to those of a few big news outlets. Bias mitigation takes a practical approach while admitting the prevalence of biases. It attempts to reduce the effect of the biases on the reader's experience rather than to prove or correct them. Our framework realizes the approach by effectively revealing a diversity of existing biased views to readers. Importantly, it automates the delivery process and quickly handles recent news events, keeping up with the news production cycle.

Aspect-level news browsing has high potential to reveal different viewpoints and mitigate bias. Researches in mass communication indicate that selection of aspects is central in the development of viewpoints [4][14]. This applies especially to straight news, the most common article type which is our current focus. As straight news concentrates on delivering facts, selection of aspects is a major determinant in shaping a story.

News Article Processing

Much research effort has been made on news articles in various topics; news clustering [16], topic detection and tracking of news stories [1], news summarization [12], news categorization [15], etc. They have mainly targeted helping users efficiently browse a vast quantity of news articles and easily acquiring the intended information. Hence, these researches mostly were concerned with the relation between news documents and readers, and did not look deeply into how the problems occurring in the news production process are propagated to the readers.

The goal of news categorization [15] is to help readers search for articles by creating a topic directory, and then classifying a volume of news articles into the proper categories. These works sort news articles into a set of pre-defined categories at different levels of granularity. For example, coarse-grained categorizes such as politics, business, sports, and technology may be used while the business category may be further divided into fine-grained categories such as world business, markets, and company research. However, articles on a common news event are included in the same category regardless of their viewpoints and readers can not easily find different views on the event.

Researches on news summarization [12] focus on automatic generation of a summary of an article or multiple articles related to a news event. Summaries help readers identify whether articles are relevant to their interests or understand the overall story. The summaries are created by selecting and organizing important sentences, phrases, or words from the articles. The sentences, phrases, or words that commonly appear in many articles are usually considered important and selected for the summaries. The resulting summaries may show the commonly covered aspects of the articles but will not reveal the different aspects. In spite of this difference, they can be complementary to our work if a summarization technique is applied to sum up articles within an aspect group after aspect-level classification.

News clustering has been studied as a specific domain of document clustering [16]. Various news clustering techniques have been investigated especially in the context of new event detection (NED), which is a part of the topic detection and tracking (TDT) program [1]. News clustering has also been explored in multi-document summarization (MDS) research [12][21]. In NED, clustering techniques are used to identify new events from a stream of news. In MDS, the clustering techniques are used to collect news articles relevant to a given event before creating a summary. Such clustering techniques group articles mainly based on news events. Thus, they cannot effectively capture and reveal multiple aspects of an event. For example, GoogleNews, a popular news clustering service, provides users with a flat list of articles associated with an event. Users need to look through the list and read a number of articles to understand multiple aspects of the event.

A recent work by Wagner et al. attempts to develop a news browsing interface providing the context of the reported events [20]. While our work aims to give readers different viewpoints on news events, Wagner's work aims to give background of the news events. When browsing a news article, the interface provides the history (i.e., related events in the past) and biography of the participants to contextualize the reported event.

Though not focused on news articles, there is a growing body of work on opinion mining and sentiment analysis [9]. They attempt to automatically identify and classify sentiments in text documents. Many of them narrow the sentiments of interest down to positive and negative, and deal with documents which explicitly reveal such sentiments, e.g., product reviews in blogs. The bias problem in news articles is different from detecting sentiments. In news reports, journalists rarely reveal their subjective opinions or sentiments, especially in straight news articles. Bias can be expressed through objective sentences by selecting facts they prefer to deliver. For example, a news article can give a negative impression about a government program just by covering the increase of deficit caused by it. Even if journalists express their subjective opinion, it is difficult to computationally analyze it as positive or negative. They make various arguments or interpretations rather than explicitly expressing their positive or negative sentiments. For example, a journalist who criticized the sin tax wrote "the introduction of the sin tax is likely to be intended to make up the deficit with working class' money", instead of simply writing "I'm opposed to the sin tax".

ASPECT-LEVEL NEWS BROWSING INTERFACE

In this section, we describe the interface of aspect-level browsing in more detail. For a selected news event, aspect-level news browsing provides a structured overview of the articles covering different aspects of the event (Figure 1(b)). It supports users in easily discovering and understanding more diverse facts about the event. Note that the service is different from conventional news aggregation services. Existing services, e.g., Google News, are limited to supporting event-level browsing. The articles referring to a common event are grouped altogether and presented in a simple list interface (Figure 1(a)). It is hard to expect ordinary users to intentionally search for different articles and understand different viewpoints in such an environment.

We use the example news event "Announcement of new property tax plan" to describe the aspect-level news browsing interface in more detail. The event was a contentious issue which received intense media coverage. It involved a nationwide debate on whether the plan will lead to a massive tax increase or normalization of the property tax. When the event occurred, many articles emphasized the tax increase for high-priced houses.

Figure 1 contrasts the aspect-level browsing interface from GoogleNews for the selected event. The article list of GoogleNews is filled with the articles emphasizing the aspect "The government's plan will increase property tax for houses …" However, in the aspect-level browsing interface (Figure 1(b)), those articles are clustered in the top left corner and articles with different aspects are presented in the other areas. The article presented in the top right corner articulates the aspect "Chief policy secretary says the tax will increase further to stabilize home prices". The article in the bottom right corner covers the aspect

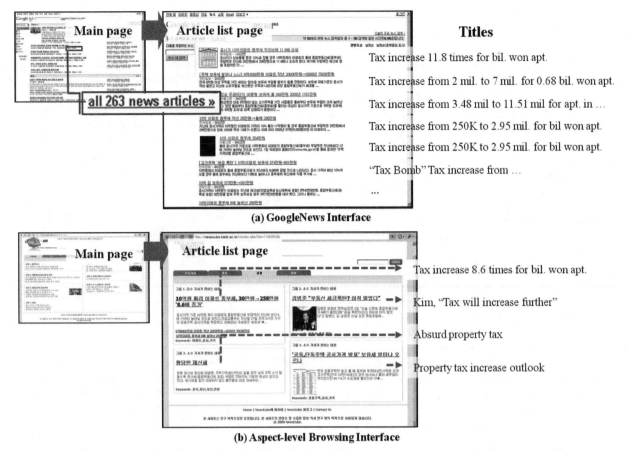

(a) GoogleNews Interface

(b) Aspect-level Browsing Interface

Figure 1. Interface Comparison for Example Event "Government announcement of property tax"

"The government's plan doesn't affect houses in most districts". Browsing these different articles, users can understand the announced tax plan from multiple viewpoints.

Our user study showed the effectiveness of aspect-level browsing for bias mitigation [11]. It helps users read more diverse articles in terms of aspects. The delivered aspects had an impact on the development of users' viewpoints.

FEASIBILITY OF ASPECT-LEVEL CLASSIFICATION

Aspect-level classification of news articles is central in supporting aspect-level news browsing. In this section, we first model an 'aspect' of a news event, then study the feasibility of aspect-level browsing.

Aspects of News Events

Different biased views of reporters result in different news storylines for an identical event. The reporters select different aspects of the event for their news storylines [4]. We conceptualize an 'aspect' of an event to be Rhee's [14] "thematic proposition", composed of the elements of a news storyline shown in Figure 2.

The proposition has the element 'agent' as its subject, and other elements as its predicate. For example, an article reporting on a presidential debate may mainly articulate the aspect "Obama has proposed a tax cut plan", where Obama becomes the agent and the tax cut proposal becomes the action. An article may articulate multiple aspects. The article

on the debate may further include another aspect "McCain criticized its efficacy" in the later part.

> **Agent**: Who does the act? (need not to be a human)
> **Action**: What is the agent's action about?
> **Agency**: How is the agent's action done?
> **Scene**: What is the agent's background of the action?
> **Implications**: What are the consequences?

Figure 2. Elements of news story-line

According to Entman [4], 'news framing' is an activity of selecting and emphasizing certain aspects of an event while organizing a news storyline. A specific framing of an event selects some aspects and discards others, and gives a limited perception of the event. Thus, different news frames can be distinguished by comparing the covered aspects in news articles.

Feasibility of Aspect-level Classification

Before we develop techniques for aspect-level classification, we test whether commonly agreed-upon results can be made for it. Aspect-level classification would be infeasible if people interpret aspects of articles differently and classify them in different ways. We demonstrate the feasibility in two stages. First, we show agreement in interpreting the articulated aspects of individual articles. Second, we show agreement in the classification of a set of articles.

1) **Agreement in interpretation of aspects**: Agreement in aspect interpretation is demonstrated through a sentence selection study. We had multiple participants select the

sentences which represent the articulated aspects. Then the commonness of the selections between the participants was analyzed. If the selected sentences overlapped much, it is possible to conclude that they interpreted the articulated aspects similarly. Four students were recruited for the test. For impartiality, three of them were recruited from outside the research team, those who are unaware of this research.

The concept of an "aspect" was first explained to the participants. They were then given 120 straight news articles, which were sampled from diverse topics in politics, business, and local sections. After reading each article, they selected sentences that represented aspects. They were allowed to choose multiple sentences for an article.

The participants were allowed to perform the task whenever and wherever they preferred over the course of nearly a week. A simple web interface was provided to support the task, and the participants read the articles and selected the sentences through the interface.

To measure the commonness in sentence selection, we used the widely used F-measure. The F-measure is the harmonic mean of the precision and the recall. It measures the similarity between two sentence selection results. For a given article, consider the selection results of two participants, $S_i=\{s_i^1, s_i^2, ..., s_i^n\}$ and $S_j=\{s_j^1, s_j^2, ..., s_k^m\}$, where s_i^k and s_j^l each represent a selected sentence. The F-measure between S_i and S_j is

$$f(S_i, S_j) = \frac{2 \times precision(S_i, S_j) \times recall(S_i, S_j)}{precision(S_i, S_j) + recall(S_i, S_j)} \quad where,$$

$$precision(S_i, S_j) = \frac{|S_i \cap S_j|}{|S_j|} \quad recall(S_i, S_j) = \frac{|S_i \cap S_j|}{|S_i|},$$

For each article, we calculated the *Avr f*, the average $f(S_i, S_j)$ over all pairs of sentence selection sets, i.e.,

$$Avr\ f = \frac{1}{_4C_2} \sum_{\substack{i,j, \\ i \neq j}} f(S_i, S_j)$$

For most of the articles (86%), we observed a high level of similarity between the sentence selection results. For those articles, the *Avr f* value was greater than 0.5, and their average was 0.8. A value of 0.8 can be achieved when most sentence selections overlap, e.g., for two selection results, $S_1=\{a, b, c\}$ and $S_2=\{a, b\}$. The results indicate that the participants interpret the articulated aspect similarly for most of the articles. The results further indicate that aspect extraction is feasible for those articles. By selecting the words of those sentences agreed on by the participants, a quality aspect extraction could be achieved.

We also observed that news structure-based extraction (NSE) is effective for aspect extraction. Recall that NSE selects the keywords from between the head and the lead. The participants made the sentence selections mostly from sentences between the head and the lead of an article. In nearly 90% of the articles (107/120), sentences in that area were selected. Among 1229 selections in total, 1000 of them were made in that area.

2) **Agreement in article classification:** A document level study was conducted to demonstrate agreement in article classification. We had multiple participants manually classify a set of news articles. Five participants performed aspect-level classification. Again, four of them were recruited from outside the research team for impartiality. As a preliminary result, the similarity between the created results was analyzed and reported in [11]. We here present the inter-rater agreement between the participants.

The concept of an "aspect" was first explained to the participants and they were then asked to group articles which articulate similar aspects. Then they performed the task through a simple web interface. They could read and classify articles through the interface. They were allowed to perform the task whenever and wherever they preferred over a near two week period.

The task was performed on 30 article sets, sampled via GoogleNews (460 articles in total). Each set consists of topically related articles published on the same date. They were collected from the politics, business, and local sections: ten sets from politics, nine from business, and eleven from local. The article sets cover many important events such as the 2007 Korean presidential campaign, the special prosecutor's investigation of Samsung corp., and the railroad strike, just to name a few.

We show the commonness between classification results using the kappa measure, a widely used inter-rater agreement measure for classification tasks. We used the free-marginal multi-rater kappa [13], which is a variation of the Fleiss kappa[1]. As a rule of thumb, kappa values greater than 0.6 are considered to show substantial agreement [7]. In our experiments, the measured kappa value was greater than 0.6 for all 30 test sets. Table 1 shows the distribution of the kappa value of the 30 test sets.

Table 1. Distribution of kappa value of the 30 test sets

Kappa value	No. of article sets
>= 0.9	3
>= 0.8	14
>= 0.7	23
>= 0.6	30

ASPECT-LEVEL CLASSIFICATION METHOD

Aspect-level classification requires two steps: *aspect extraction*, extracting the articulated aspects of individual articles; and *article classification*, classifying the articles based on the extraction results. In this section, we describe the developed method for each step, *news structure-based extraction* and *framing cycle-aware clustering*.

Aspect Extraction

Interpreting aspects from news texts becomes very difficult when it is performed computationally. It requires complex

---

[1] The selected kappa measure is used when the number of raters is greater than two. Free-marginal kappa is recommended when the raters do not know a priori the number of items that should be assigned to each category. Fixed-marginal kappa is recommended otherwise.

semantic knowledge as well as domain knowledge related to the reported news events, e.g., characteristics of agents, relations between agents, connected events in the past, etc. News topics generally span over various broad domains and they are newly generated every day. It is impractical to encode and update such broad semantic knowledge.

To be practical, we approach the approximation of aspects using the keyword-weight vector model. Although this may not fully capture the semantic meaning of aspects, it is possible to distinguish the difference between covered aspects by sorting out important keywords and comparing them. For example, consider the articles presented in the top left corner and the top right corner in Figure 1(b). Keywords such as "government announcement, tax increase" and "chief policy advisor, stabilize house price" directly reveal the difference between covered aspects.

News Structure-based Extraction

The main idea of News Structure-based Extraction (NSE) was introduced in [11]. In this section, we review the key feature of the method and articulate its procedure in detail.

The key feature of NSE is the utilization of the 'inverted pyramid style' news writing rule. This rule guides journalists in arranging information and facts in descending order of importance within an article. From this rule, we can obtain conclusive hints for aspect extraction; the location of semantically meaningful keywords and how much importance they are given.

The inverted pyramid structure is composed of head, subhead, lead and main text (Figure 3). The head and the sub-head are decisive factors in deciding whether or not to read an article. They usually contain core terms which reflect the aspects being focused on in the article. The lead is usually the first sentence of the article, or the first two sentences in some cases. To quickly inform readers, the information ordering principle is especially applied to the lead and guides reporters to reveal the most interesting facts. The main text is organized with collected information which supports the lead in order of decreasing importance. NSE is performed through three stages: meta-data annotation, keyword extraction, and weight calculation. NSE first annotates structural information of a news article: such as "<Title>…</Title>" and "<Lead>…</Lead>". The structural information is used in both keyword selection and weight calculation. In addition, word class information, i.e., the POS tag, is annotated to assist keyword extraction.

Figure 3. Components of Inverted pyramid structure.

Second, keywords are carefully extracted in order to select only the words constituting aspects. As aspects are detailed and subtle, inclusion of irrelevant terms seriously degrades the accuracy of extraction. NSE uses the structural characteristics and the class of words to select relevant terms accurately. Considering the structural characteristics, NSE confines the area of extraction to the core parts of an article, i.e., head, sub-head and lead.

The word class information is used to select the words which have the potential to act as elements of aspects, such as agents or actions. For example, proper nouns and non-descriptive nouns are selected since they could be possible agents. Similarly, verbs and descriptive nouns are also selected to reflect descriptions of agents. NSE further identifies noun phrases to better capture the element 'agent'. Agents are often represented as noun phrases, e.g. "President Bush", "Military Base", "Justice Department", etc. These phrases are identified through syntactic parsing. Individual words of a phrase are considered as instances of the same keyword and share the same weight value.

Third, the weight of each keyword is calculated based on the structural characteristics of the main text. The contents of the main text support the lead more the earlier it appears and the more information is written. Thus, NSE not only considers the number of occurrences of keywords, but also considers the locations of occurrences, and the amount of text used relating to the keywords.

A keyword is considered to be important if the following conditions hold. First, if the keyword is covered in the front part of the main text. Second, if the keyword appears repeatedly. Third, if the keyword appears in a long sentence or a long paragraph. The notations and equations for the weight calculation are summarized in Table 2 and Equations (1)-(3). For each appearance, the weight of a keyword w_n is given based on the length of a paragraph $Lp(i, j)$, and a sentence $Ls(i, k)$ relative to the length of the article $La(i)$. In

Table 2. Notations

Symbol	Description
$A(i)$	i-th article in a set of news articles
$Aspect(i)$	Approximation of $A(i)$'s aspects
$W(i)$	Set of keywords which reflect elements of aspects of $A(i)$
$La(i)$	Length of $A(i)$
$Lp(i, j)$	Length of j-th paragraph in $A(i)$
$Ls(i, l)$	Length of l-th sentence in $A(i)$
k_n	n-th keyword in $W(i)$
w_n	Weight value of k_n
d_{Pj}	Diminishing factor of j-th paragraph in $A(i)$
d_{Sk}	Diminishing factor of l-th sentence in $A(i)$

$Aspect(i) = \{(k_n, w_n) \mid k_n \in W(i) \text{ and } w_n \in \mathbf{R}\}, \text{ where}$

$$1) \quad w_n = \sum_{j,k} \left(\frac{Lp(i,j)}{La(i)} d_{Pj} + \frac{Ls(i,k)}{La(i)} d_{Sk} \right),$$

$$2) \quad d_{Pj} = 1 - \sum_{m=1}^{j-1} \frac{Lp(i,m)}{La(i)} \quad , where \ d_{P1} = 1$$

$$3) \quad d_{Sk} = 1 - \sum_{m=1}^{k-1} \frac{Ls(i,m)}{La(i)} \quad where \ d_{S1} = 1$$

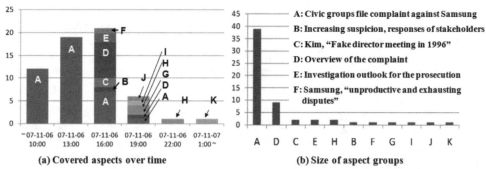

Figure 4. Aspect coverage analysis for the event "complaint against Samsung Corp."

order to differentiate weights according to the locations in the structure, the diminishing factor d_{Pj} and d_{Sk} is multiplied to $Lp(i, j)$ and $Ls(i, k)$, respectively. The values of the two factors decrease as the keywords appear in the latter parts of an article.

To support similarity measures to be robust to the variance of article lengths, the number of keywords and weight scales among articles are normalized. These variations can distort similarity calculations and cause erroneous classification results. The number of keywords is controlled either by lengthening the lead or filtering out a few keywords whose weight is low. Weight values in each article are also normalized to follow a normal distribution.

Article Classification

We approach the classification of articles with an unsupervised classification method, i.e., clustering. Supervised classification methods require a predefined category. However, it is impossible to predict and construct predefined aspect categories for a news event.

In our previous work [11], we applied and evaluated widely used clustering methods such as k-means, hierarchical clustering, etc. From our experience, we note that aspect-based clustering requires more delicate similarity analysis than plain comparison of overlapping keywords and their weights. We developed a new method called *framing cycle-aware clustering (FCAC)*, customized to aspect-based clustering of news articles.

The Framing Cycle of News Events

Through an extensive data analysis, we examined the framing cycle of news events. Our analysis shows that the same aspects are commonly covered at an early stage of news reporting and the covered aspects diverge over time. Figure 4(a) shows an example with the event "complaint against Samsung Corp.". Until 1 pm, all news articles reported the filing of the complaint done by the civic and lawyers' groups (denoted as A). After that, some articles started to deliver different aspects (denoted from B to K) such as Samsung's response.

The framing cycle is closely related with the news gathering behaviors of reporters. News reporters often rely on identical news sources such as press releases, news agency reports, or public relations departments [3]. According to our observation, identical sources are used to collect basic facts of an event especially at the early stage of the event. Later,

some reporters reach out for different news sources, e.g., stakeholders or related experts. In addition, different participants of the event also try to access reporters and gain visibility with facts and interpretations in favor of their positions [8].

As a result of the framing cycle, the set of articles on an event shows a *head-tail characteristic*: a good many articles at the head side of the framing cycle cover common aspects, and the rest of the articles at the tail side cover diverse uncommon aspects. Figure 4(b) shows the size of the article groups classified by the covered aspects for the example event. Such a characteristic is also found in other article sets. We have collected all article sets which were available from GoogleNews on the same date. 58 article sets of 1122 articles in total were collected from politics, business, and local sections. Each set showed a similar pattern, i.e., the head-tail characteristic. In 53 sets (91%), the largest group included more than 50% of the articles.

From the head-tail characteristic, we developed a Head-Tail model for the news articles of an event. Let A be a set of news articles for an event. Then, A can be partitioned into a Head group, Hg, and multiple Tail groups, Tg_i.

Head-Tail model of news articles

1) $A = Hg \cup (\bigcup_{i=1}^{n} Tg_i)$ 2) $|Hg| = HgP \times |A|$ 3) $\left| \bigcup_{i=1}^{n} Tg_i \right| = (1 - HgP) \times |A|$,   *where*

- n is the number of Tail groups, $n \geq 0$
- $Hg, Tg_1, \ldots, Tg_n$ are all disjoint
- HgP (Head group proportion) is the proportion of the Head group

Framing Cycle-Aware Clustering

Knowing the head-tail characteristic, we identify and separate the common keywords, the keywords reflecting the common, head-side aspects, and the uncommon keywords, the keywords reflecting the uncommon, tail-side aspects. Based on this distinction, the FCAC is performed in two stages; head-tail partitioning and tail-side clustering. Head-Tail partitioning separates the Head group, the articles with the common aspects, and the non-Head group, the articles covering uncommon aspects. Tail-side clustering classifies the articles in the non-Head group to different Tail groups according to the covered aspects, delicately capturing the differences in the uncommon keywords.

As it is sensitive to the head-tail characteristic, this approach is advantageous in supporting aspect-level browsing of news articles, i.e., it reveals more effectively the diversity of different aspects of a news event. For example, it prevents the articles in the Head group from being scattered into different aspect groups. Even if articles share only a small number of keywords, they can be grouped together if the keywords are common keywords. Conventional clustering methods easily classify such articles into different groups as their keyword-weight vectors will show low similarity. It also increases the sensitivity of classification of the uncommon aspects. It acknowledges the importance of the uncommon keywords and better recognizes the uncommon tail-side aspects. The diversity of the uncommon aspects is the source of the richness in the viewpoints and is crucial for bias mitigation.

The applicability of FCAC is not limited to news events that are identified as complete, i.e., the events at the end of the framing cycle. Applied to an event at an early stage, FCAC will present fewer tail-side aspects. However, FCAC can be applied multiple times as the event evolves. As such, recently revealed aspects can be updated in the results.

Head-Tail Partitioning: Careful partitioning of the Head group and the non-Head group is important to achieve high quality clustering. The Head group includes the most articles. Thus, a poor partitioning of the Head group is likely to result in many redundant groups with the common aspects. It may also induce noise into tail-side aspect groups.

For the partitioning, we develop two metrics, *Commonness* (*Cn*) and *Uncommonness* (*Un*), to denote the degree of inclination of each article to the Head group and the non-Head group, respectively (Def. 3). An article which includes many common keywords with high weight values will have a high *Cn* value. An article including many uncommon keywords with high weight values will have a high *Un* value. To carefully separate out only the articles which belong to the non-Head group, the method selects out the articles which show a high *Un* value and a low *Cn* value.

Definition 1. Common keyword set, *cK,* and uncommon keyword set, *uK*.
- $cK = \{cK_i \mid cK_i \in K \text{ and } app\_r(cK_i) \geq HgP\}$
- $uK = \{uK_i \mid uK_i \in K \text{ and } app\_r(uK_i) < HgP\}$, where

$$app\_r(k_i) = \frac{app\_c(k_i)}{n},$$

$app\_c(k_i)$ is the number articles which include k_i,
n is the number of articles in the article set, and
K is the set of keywords for an article set.

Definition 2. (*Un*)*Commonness* of a (un)common keyword cK_i/uK_i
- $Cn(cK_i) = app\_r(cK_i) \cdot avg\_w(cK_i)$
- $Un(uK_i) = (1 - app\_r(uK_i)) \cdot avg\_w(uK_i)$, where

$$avg\_w(k_i) = \frac{\sum_{m=1}^{app\_c(k_i)} w(m)}{app\_c(k_i)}, \text{ and } w(m) \text{ is the } k_i\text{'s weight in an article } a_m.$$

Definition 3. *Commonness* and *Uncommonness* of an article a_m
- $Cn(a_m) = \sum Cn(k_j) \cdot w_j$, where

k_j is a keyword of a_m, $k_j \in cK$, and w_j is the weight of k_j in a_m.

- $Un(a_m) = \sum Un(k_l) \cdot w_l$, where

k_l is a keyword of a_m, $k_l \in uK$, and w_l is the weight of k_l in a_m.

The *Cn* and *Un* values of an article are computed in two steps. First, the *Cn* or *Un* values are computed for each keyword (Def. 2). Then, the *Cn* and *Un* values of the article are computed to be the weighted sum of the *Cn* and *Un* values of its keywords (Def. 3).

To calculate the *Cn* and *Un* values of keywords, the keywords of an article set are first divided into two sets, i.e., the common keyword set *cK* and the uncommon keyword set *uK*. They are divided based on their appearance ratio over the article set and the Head group proportion, *HgP*. If a keyword appears in the article set with a ratio greater than or equal to *HgP*, it is classified as a common keyword. Otherwise, it is an uncommon keyword (Def. 1).

For each common keyword, a *Cn* value is computed and for each uncommon keyword, a *Un* value is computed. The values are computed using the appearance ratio of the keywords and their average weight over the appearing articles (Def. 2). The *Cn* value of a common keyword cK_i increases with its appearance ratio, i.e., as the keyword appears frequently in the article set. On the contrary, the *Un* value of an uncommon keyword, uK_i, increases as its appearance ratio decreases.

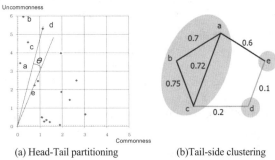

(a) Head-Tail partitioning   (b)Tail-side clustering
Figure 5. Framing cycle-aware clustering example

The Head group is identified by selecting out articles which show a high *Un* value relative to their *Cn* value. The articles are selected in decreasing order of *Un/Cn* rate until the number of remaining articles corresponds to *HgP*. Figure 5(a) shows the *Un* and *Cn* values of an example article set with 16 articles. In the example, the *HgP* is set to 0.25, and the articles *a*, *b*, *c*, *d* are selected out.

HgP is important to Head-Tail partitioning. We select the *HgP* value which can most clearly separate the two groups, the Head group and the non-Head group. The degree of separation is measured by the difference of *Un/Cn* rates between the Head group and non-Head group. In the example in Figure 5(a), the degree of separation is θ between the articles *d* and *e*. The degree of separation is computed iteratively, and the *HgP* value which maximizes the degree of separation is selected.

Tail-side Clustering: Tail-side clustering should delicately capture the differences in covered aspects and partition different Tail groups. However, the Tail groups are usually composed of a small number of articles and a few errors in the partitioning process can easily hide different aspects.

Tail-side clustering focuses on capturing the differences among the uncommon aspects. It uses only uncommon keywords in similarity analysis. The uncommon keywords appear only in a few articles. Articles which cover different aspects have little chance of sharing such keywords. Thus, this method can avoid combining articles which belong to different Tail groups. On the other hand, articles covering the same uncommon aspects are likely to share several uncommon keywords and thus can be grouped together.

For clustering, we employ a similarity graph-based clustering technique. The widely used Cosine measure is adopted for the similarity metric. Each article becomes a vertex, and the cosine similarity value between a pair of articles is considered as the weight of an edge. To partition the articles into Tail groups, the method cuts the edges with similarity values lower than a threshold. We use the average of non-zero similarity values as the threshold. Figure 5(b) shows a graph made with five articles, a, b, c, d, and e. The edges which have a non-zero weight are shown in the graph. The thick edges, (a,b), (b,c), (a,c), and (a,e) are those with higher weights than the threshold. The vertices that form a complete graph are identified as a Tail group; five articles are partitioned into three groups, {a,b,c}, {d}, and {e}.

PERFORMANCE EVALUATION

In this section, we measure the performance achieved by the developed method, i.e., NSE combined with FCAC. We compare the method with three representative clustering methods; Hierarchical Agglomerative Clustering (HAC), K-means clustering, and Spectral clustering. To see the benefit of NSE, each comparison clustering method is combined with NSE and a simple term frequency-based extraction (TF). TF simply selects keywords from the whole article and assigns weights by counting the number of occurrences.

For evaluation, we made ground truth classification results based on manually created classification results. Recall that five participants made manual classification results on 30 article sets for the feasibility test. Based on those results, the ground truths were made by grouping the articles into groups that four or more participants had agreed on. We denote the ground truth classification result of the 30 article sets as $G^1, ..., G^{30}$.

The performance of the methods is assessed from three perspectives. First, we measure the accuracy of classification results, i.e., similarity of the classification results to the ground truth results. Second, we measure the diversity of the aspects revealed in the classification results. Revealing diverse aspects is important to provide users with different viewpoints. Third, we measure the redundant article groups in the classification results. A redundant article group is a critical error which can annoy users and make them mistrust the overall results.

Accuracy of classification: The accuracy is evaluated by comparing the classification results to the ground truth results. We used the weighted average F-measure, a variation of the F-measure [21]. It is calculated for each cluster of the ground

truth as follows. Consider an article set A, a clustering result, $C = \{c_1, c_2, ..., c_l\}$, and a ground truth $G = \{g_1, g_2, ..., g_k\}$, where c_i and g_i each represent a cluster of articles. For each g_i, the maximum F-measure over all the clusters c_is in C is taken. Then, the *weighted average F-measure*, denoted as $F[G,C]$, is calculated as the weighted average of such maximum F-measures, i.e., $F[G,C] = \sum_i \frac{|g_i|}{|A|} \max_j \{f(g_i, c_j)\}$. The results of other methods except FCAC are taken from our previous work [11].

Table 2. Mean $F[G,C]$ values and number of winning sets

	mean $F[G,C]$	No. of winning sets		mean $F[G,C]$	No. of winning sets
Spectral(NSE)	0.542	0	Spectral(TF)	0.527	0
K-means(NSE)	0.587	0	K-means(TF)	0.567	0
HAC (NSE)	0.683	6	HAC(TF)	0.654	3
FCAC(NSE)	**0.777**	**21**			

Table 3 compares our method with six different extraction-clustering methods. We calculate the mean value of $F[G,C]$ over the 30 article sets, *i.e.,* $mean F = \frac{1}{30} \sum_{k=1}^{30} F[G^k, C^k]$. In addition, we identify the winning method for each article set, i.e., the method which generates the clustering result with the highest $F[G,C]$. The table shows that our method (NSE-FCAC) achieves the highest *mean $F[G,C]$* value. The method also generates the best clustering results for most of the sets, 21 sets among 30. While not shown in the table, in the other 9 article sets, the differences in $F[G,C]$ between our method and the winning method were relatively small. Figure 6 shows the distribution of $F[G,C]$ values for each extraction-clustering method. The portions with higher $F[G,C]$ values are larger in NSE-FCAC.

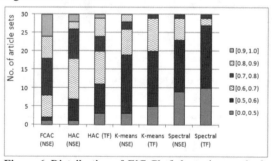

Figure 6. Distribution of $F[G,C]$ of clustering methods

Diversity of the revealed aspects: To present diverse aspects to users, the classification results should present the tail-side aspects. Thus, we assess how many tail-side clusters of the ground truth are presented in the classification results. We consider a tail side cluster as presented if the classification result has an article group whose member articles all overlap with those of the tail-side cluster, i.e., the article group has no false positive error. Such groups help users understand the aspect covered in the group without confusion as all member articles cover the same aspect.

For the 30 article sets, we measure the ratio of the tail-side clusters presented in the classification results. Figure 7 shows the distribution of the ratio over the 30 article sets. It shows that NSE-FCAC presents more tail-side aspects compared to other methods. The portions with higher ratio values are larger in NSE-FCAC.

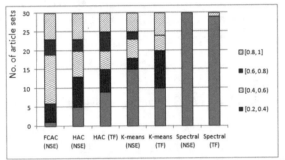

Figure 7. Distribution of the presented tail-side cluster ratio

Redundant article groups: Redundant groups hinder users in making sense of the overall classification results. Thus, it is also important not to produce redundant article groups. We measure the redundant article groups in the classification results and compare it to the other methods.

To count the number of redundant article groups, we first map the article groups of the classification results to those of the ground truths. The article groups are mapped to the most similar group according to the f-measure value. The groups mapped to the same group are considered redundant.

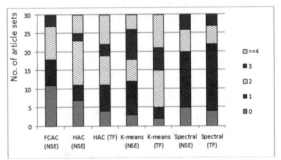

Figure 8. Distribution of the redundant article group count

For the 30 article sets, we counted the redundant article groups of the classification results. Figure 8 shows the distribution of the counted number of redundant article groups over the 30 article sets. NSE-FCAC produces fewer redundant article groups than the HAC and K-means methods. NSE-FCAC also does not present any redundant article group for more article sets (11 sets) than other methods. In the case of the Spectral methods, the number of redundant groups was relatively small as its classification results had fewer article groups compared to other methods.

CONCLUSION

In this paper, we present aspect-level browsing, a novel news browsing method designed for mitigation of media bias. It achieves its goal by classifying aspects and presenting articles with contrasting aspects. Readers can understand news events from a plural of viewpoints and formulate their own, more balanced viewpoints free from specific biased views.

There are a number of issues worthy of future investigation. We mainly deal with one typical form of bias in straight news articles, i.e., aspect selection. There are other types of bias embodiments which require further exploration, such as labeling, tone, space allocation, etc. Different types of news articles, e.g., editorials, are open for investigation.

ACKNOWLEDGEMENT

This research was supported by the Ministry of Knowledge Economy, Korea, under the Information Technology Research Center support program supervised by the National IT Industry Promotion Agency (grant number: NIPA-2009-C1090-0902-0006)

REFERENCES

1. Allan, J., et al. Topic Detection and Tracking Pilot Study: Final Report. In *Proc. of DARPA Broadcast News Transcription and Understanding Workshop*, 1998.
2. Bernhardt, D., et al. Political Polarization and the Electoral Effects of Media Bias. *CESifo Working Paper Series* No. 1798.
3. Curtin, P. A. Reevaluating public relations information subsidies: Market driven journalism and agenda-building theory and practice. *Journal of Public Relations Research*, 11, 53-90. 1999.
4. Entman R.M. Framing: Toward Clarification of a Fractured Paradigm. *Journal of Communication* 43 (4): 51-8, 1993.
5. Gerber, A., et al. Does the Media Matter? A Field Experiment Measuring the Effect of Newspapers on Voting Behavior and Political Opinions. *Yale Economic Applications and Policy Discussion Paper* No. 12.
6. Krebs, V. Political Polarization in Amazon.com Book Purchases. orgnet.com. 2008.
7. Landis JR, Koch G. The measurement of observer agreement for categorical data. *Biometrics* 1977;33:159-174.
8. Miller, M. M. et al. Spiral Opportunity and Frame Resonance: Mapping Issue Cycle in News and Public Discourse. In *Framing Public Life*, NJ: Lawrence Erlbaum Asso.
9. Pang, B. et al. Thumbs up? sentiment classification using machine learning techniques. In *Proc. of EMNLP*. 2002.
10. Park. S, et al. Mitigating media bias: a computational approach. In *Proc. of the hypertext 2008 workshop on Collaboration and collective intelligence*. 2008.
11. Park. S, et al. NewsCube: Delivering Multiple Aspects of News to Mitigate Media Bias. In *Proc. of ACM CHI*, 2009.
12. Radev, D.R. et al. NewsInEssence: Summarizing Online News Topics.*Communication of the ACM* 48(10)
13. Randolph, J. J. Free-marginal multirater kappa: An alternative to Fleiss' fixed-marginal multirater kappa. *Joensuu University Learning and Instruction Symposium*. 2005.
14. Rhee, J. W. Framing the Health Care Reform Campaign of 1993-94: News Frame, Interpretation and Public Opinion Change. *Political Comm.*, vol 15: 274-76. 1998.
15. Sebastiani, F. Machine learning in automated text categorization. *ACM Computing Survey*:1-47, 2002.
16. Steinbach, M., et al. A Comparison of Document Clustering Techniques. In *Proceedings of TextMining Workshop, KDD*. 2000.
17. Sunstein, C. *Republic.com*. Princeton, New Jersey: Princeton University Press. 2001.
18. Son, S.C. The Revolution of News Reading. Kaemagowon, 2006 (in Korean).
19. Urban. C. Examining Our Credibility: Perspectives of the Public and the Press. *American Society of Newspaper Editors*, 1999.
20. Wagner. E. Rich Interfaces for Reading News on the Web. In *Proc. of ACM IUI*. 2009.20
21. Wan, X., et al. CollabSum: Exploiting Multiple Document Clustering for Collaborative Single Document Summarization. In *Proc. of ACM SIGIR*. 2007.

Personalized Reading Support for Second-Language Web Documents by Collective Intelligence

Yo Ehara
Graduate School of Information Science and
Technology
The University of Tokyo
ehara@r.dl.itc.u-tokyo.ac.jp

Nobuyuki Shimizu
Takashi Ninomiya
Hiroshi Nakagawa
Information Technology Center
The University of Tokyo
{shimizu,ninomi}@r.dl.itc.u-tokyo.ac.jp
nakagawa@dl.itc.u-tokyo.ac.jp

ABSTRACT

Novel intelligent interface eases the browsing of Web documents written in the second languages of users. It automatically predicts words unfamiliar to the user by collective intelligence and glosses them with their meaning in advance. If the prediction succeeds, the user does not need to consult a dictionary; even if it fails, the user can correct the prediction. The correction data are collected and used to improve the accuracy of further predictions. The prediction is personalized in that every user's language ability is estimated by a state-of-the-art language testing model, which is trained in a practical response time with only a small sacrifice of prediction accuracy. Evaluation results for the system in terms of prediction accuracy are encouraging.

Author Keywords

Reading Support, Web Page, Item Response Theory, Glossing System, Collective Intelligence

ACM Classification Keywords

H.5.4 Information Interfaces and Presentation: Hypertext/Hypermedia—*User issues*

General Terms

Design, Experimentation, Human Factors, Languages

INTRODUCTION

More and more users are now browsing Web pages, using English word glossing systems, which eliminate the need to consult a dictionary every time an unknown word is encountered. A glossing system presents the user with the meaning of an unknown word in a pop-up window when the user clicks on or mouses over it. Take "pop jisyo", shown in Figure 1, as an example. The background sentences that begin with "A group of Han Chinese" are sentences on a Web page

that we assume the user is reading. Suppose that the user encounters the word "paramilitary" and does not know its meaning. If the user mouses over the word, a pop-up window opens and the meaning of the word "paramilitary" is displayed in it.

While useful, existing English glossing systems do not utilize the user's vocabulary. They waste valuable data about the user's vocabulary, which could be accumulated. Instead, we may harness collective intelligence by utilizing the accumulated word click logs from many users. We are developing a system that can accumulate this kind of knowledge and make full use of it to help users to read English Web pages by predicting the words that the user does not know and displaying their meanings [1]. Our aim is to combine an English word glossing system and word difficulty prediction in an integrated and intelligent user interface. Existing research on word difficulty relies heavily on corpus frequency. However, corpus frequency may not reflect the difficulty that users actually feel: some words occur frequently in corpora, but actually may not be known to the users, while some words are rarely seen in corpora, but actually may be known to the users. By accumulating the word click logs from many users and uncovering the "collective intelligence" beneath the logs, we can get the collective intelligence to adjust the weight for each word to reflect the difficulty that users actually feel; even if some words occur frequently in corpora, those words are regarded as difficult if many users frequently click them to see their glosses. Even if some words are rarely seen in corpora, those words are regarded as easy if many users click those words to hide their glosses. Thus, we can regard our system as using the collective intelligence embedded in the click log to correct the corpus-frequency-based word difficulty.

The main contribution of this study is a mechanism for predicting words unknown to a user. We use logistic regression to estimate which words on the Web page are unknown to the user because it is widely used to test language ability in "item response theory" (IRT). This theory lets one estimate both a user's language ability θ and a word's difficulty d at the same time. To train the logistic regression faster, we

---

[1] http://www.socialdict.com/

Figure 1. Example of word glossing in pop-jisyo.

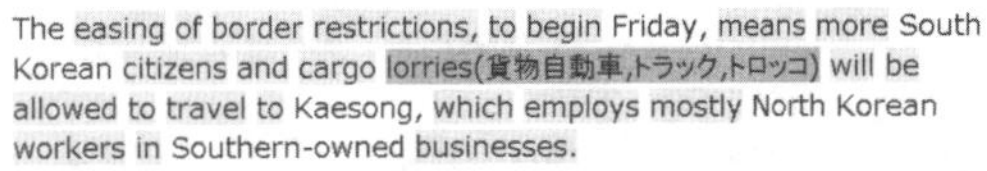

The easing of border restrictions, to begin Friday, means more South Korean citizens and cargo lorries(貨物自動車,トラック,トロッコ) will be allowed to travel to Kaesong, which employs mostly North Korean workers in Southern-owned businesses.

Figure 2. Example of word glossing in our system.

chose stochastic gradient descent (SGD) from among many parameter optimization methods because it is an online algorithm. An online algorithm can perform training faster than a batch method because it accesses a datum in the data set only once whereas a batch method accesses the data many times.

In summary, our system is characterized as follows.

1. Accumulates knowledge about the vocabulary of each user and fully utilizes it

2. Has a machine-learning-based mechanism for predicting words unknown to a user

This paper is organized as follows. First, we introduce related work. Second, we introduce the design and implementation issues of our system. We then explain the relationships among IRT, logistic regression, and the Rasch model, which is a special case of IRT and also a special case of logistic regression, which our system uses. We then explain the methods for estimating the parameters of logistic regression and the derivation of SGD. We then describe an experimental evaluation of our system. Finally, we conclude this paper by briefly summarizing the main points and mentioning future work.

RELATED WORK

This section describes previous work related to this paper.

Glossing systems for Web pages have been implemented in two forms: as desktop applications that retrieve Web pages and perform the glossing on the user's local machine and as Web applications in which Web page retrieval and glossing is performed on a Web proxy server instead of on the user's local machine. While desktop glossing systems are fast because they do not require communication between the Web proxy server and the user's local machine, they are not suitable for accumulating the user click logs because the logs are distributed across many local machines in desktop applications. Since we accumulate and utilize the click logs, we implemented our system as a Web application.

Desktop glossing systems are usually implemented as add-ons for Web browsers, such as: **FireDictionary** [12], and **popIn** [16]. They work as add-ons for the **Firefox** Web browser.

Notable Web-based glossing systems include **popjisyo** [5], which we used as an example, **rikai.com** [20]. In particular, **popjisyo** supports glossing between multiple languages [2].

However, as far as we know, no application estimates the users' language ability or predicts the words unknown to the users from the accumulated click logs, though some applications may simply accumulate them for quick access to the words previously clicked. Our application is novel in that it assesses the user's language ability and predicts words unknown.

Our approach also differs from machine translation in that our system glosses only those words predicted to be unknown to the user whereas machine translation does not utilize the user's language ability and translates the entire text including words known to the user.

SYSTEM OVERVIEW

This section explains the operation of our system and implementation issues.

The way our system operates is schematically illustrated in Figure 3. It is a glossing system that uses "CGI-proxy" and predicts words unknown to the user by machine learning. In use, it operates as follows.

(0) The user passes user identifier u to the system. Note that a user identifier is not necessary in previous systems because they do not perform user adaptation.

(1) The user passes document identifier $l \in URL$ to the system.

(2) The system finds the Web server hosting the target document by following l.

(3) The system tries to retrieve document D specified by l from the Web server. If the system fails to retrieve the document, it simply returns an error message to the browser in step (4).

(4) The system extracts words from document D and returns the document with the words predicted to be unfamiliar to user u glossed with their meanings.

Web documents are usually have tags like "<html>" and "<body>". Thus, they can be represented by a tree, as shown in Figure 4 (a). Let Dom_D be the set of all Web pages and Dom_T be the set of trees. We define $Parse(D)$ as a function that takes a Web page $D \in Dom_D$ and returns tree $R' \in Dom_T$, that corresponds to D. Conversely, we define $Unparse(R'')$ as a function that takes tree $R'' \in Dom_T$ and returns the Web page that corresponds to R''.

Step (4) in Figure 3 involves a tokenization function "Tokenize" and a prediction and glossing function "PredictGloss". "Tokenize" takes tree $R \in Dom_T$ and returns a tree whose sentences are tokenized into words. An example is shown in

[2]Japanese to English, Japanese to German, English to Japanese, English to Korean, English to Spanish, Chinese to Korean, Chinese to English, and Korean to English.

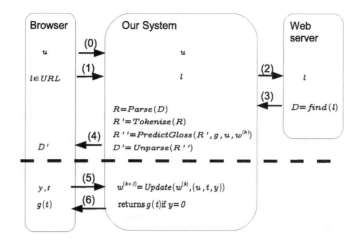

Figure 3. System operation.

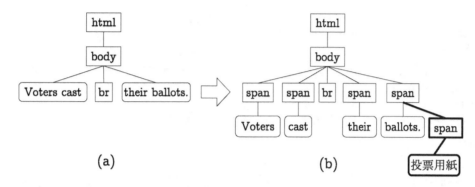

Figure 4. (a) Example of a tree, (b) Tree passed back to the browser. The bold part is an example of a gloss, showing the meaning of ballots in Japanese.

Figure 4: "Tokenize" takes Figure 4(a) and returns the tree in Figure 4(b) except for the bold parts. "Tokenize" also tags every token by "<span>" and embeds a JavaScript script that enables the user to consult a dictionary simply by clicking the word.

"PredictGloss" takes tokenized tree $R' \in Dom_T$, glosser function g, user identifier u, and the weight of classifier $w^{(k)}$ and g takes token t and returns its gloss (meaning) $g(t)$. For all the leaves, i.e., tokens, in tree R', "PredictGloss" first predicts the words unfamiliar to user u and then glosses only unfamiliar ones with g. The prediction is determined by the sign of the function $h(u, t, w^{(k)})$.

While previous systems do not require any communication with the browser after (4), our system communicates with the browser in (5) and (6) to collect the "click log" (y, t) (defined below) to train $w^{(k)}$. This communication is made possible by the use of "AJAX", asynchronous JavaScript, and XML (extensible markup language). We used "jQuery"[3] for the library for AJAX.

(5) When token t in a different Web document D' is clicked, the embedded JavaScript script in D' sends the pair of y and t to the system.

---

[3] http://jquery.com/

(6) If $y = 0$, i.e., the user does not know word t, so its gloss is sent back to user u.

Here, y codes whether or not user u knows word t. It is defined as follows: $y = 0$ is sent to the system if word t was predicted to be unfamiliar to user u prior to the click and is clicked for the first time after this prediction. $y = 0$ means that the system regards user u as not knowing word t because user u is now requesting the gloss for word t even though the system first regarded user u as knowing word t in (4). If word t is predicted to be known to user u and is clicked for the first time, the exact opposite happens: $y = 1$ is sent to the system, which means that the system regards user u as knowing word t because user u is now hiding word t even though the system first regarded user u as not knowing word t in (4). The data (u, t, y) is used to update the value of $w^{(k)}$ for training, as shown in Figure 3. The function $Update(w^{(k)}, u, t, y)$ is explained later.

MODEL

Logistic regression is used to model our system because it includes the Rasch model, which is a basic IRT. IRT is widely used to test language ability. To predict the words unknown to a user, it is necessary to model the user's language ability. Thus, logistic regression is suitable for use in this application.

Item Response Theory

This section explains IRT and how it is involved in our system. IRT is a statistical method for analyzing the results of tests of human abilities including language tests. Indeed, IRT is thought to be used in TOEFL (Test of English as a Foreign Language) and TOEIC (Test of English for International Communication). Details of the mathematical aspects of IRT are given in [1].

IRT has been used to generate fill-in-the-blank questions automatically from text retrieved from the Web [19].

First, IRT calculates "parameters" from human ability test results. Once the parameters have been calculated, IRT can then estimate the following probabilities.

- probability that a user will answer a "different" question correctly

- probability that a "different" user will answer the original question correctly

Here, "different" means that no record with the same pair of user and question is found in the previous test results. This covers the user or question being a new one and the user or question existing but the user not answering that question in the previous test.

Definition of IRT

IRT involves three concepts: "users", "items", and "responses". Users are simply the set of users. Items correspond to the questions in a test. The response indicates how correctly the user responded to an item.

Given user $u \in U$ and item $t \in T$, Eq. 1 models user u's response y to item t, where U and T are finite sets of users and items, respectively, and y is the response given u and t.

Eq. 1 codes y as a binary random variable (though in some variations of IRT, y can take more than two states); that is, $y = 1$ when user u answers item t correctly and $y = 0$ otherwise. Eq. 1 shows a typical IRT formulation. Eq. 1 shows a typical item response theory.

$$P(y = 1|u, t) = c_t + (1 - c_t)\sigma (a_t (\theta_u - d_t)) \quad (1)$$

Here, σ is a logistic sigmoid function, which is widely used in probabilistic models because, for a value $x \in \mathcal{R}$, $0 < \sigma(x) < 1$ holds.

$$\sigma(x) = \frac{1}{(1 + \exp(-x))} \quad (2)$$

Eq. 1 has four parameters to estimate, as listed and explained below.

θ_u Ability parameter of the user u.

d_t Difficulty parameter of the item t.

a_t Discrimination parameter of the item t.

c_t Guessing parameter of the item t

The ability of every user $u \in U$ is modeled by user parameter θ_u. The higher θ_u is, the greater is the ability that our system regards user u as having.

The difficulty of each item $t \in T$ is modeled by d_t. The higher d_t is, the more difficult item t is and the fewer users can answer correctly.

The latter parameters are optional. Discrimination parameter a_t determines how steep the item characteristic curve of item t is. The higher a_t is, the steeper the item characteristic curve is.

Guessing parameter c_t determines the probability of test takers guessing the correct answer. This parameter is typically used to model multiple choice items. For example, if a test taker is supposed to choose one item from five choices, then $c_t = \frac{1.0}{5.0} = 0.20$.

Rasch Model

Our system simply assumes items to be words.

$$P(y = 1|u, t) = \sigma (\theta_u - d_t) \quad (3)$$

By comparing Eq. 1 with Eq. 3, you can find that Eq. 3 is a special case of Eq. 1. Indeed, Eq. 3 is derived from Eq. 1 by substituting $a_t = 1$ and $c_t = 0$ for $\forall t \in T$, where $a_t = 1$ means that all the questions are regarded as equally discriminative and $c_t = 0$ means that the model assumes that it is impossible to guess the correct answer.

Logistic Regression

This section introduces logistic regression, which is a kind of "supervised classification" in machine learning literature [2].

In supervised classification, a "classifier" is first trained with "training data". A training datum can be represented as $(y, \boldsymbol{x})$, which is a pair of "input vector" $\boldsymbol{x}$ and "class" $y \in \mathcal{Y}$, where $\mathcal{Y}$ is the "domain" of the classes and $\mathcal{X}$ is the domain of input vectors. A classifier has a "parameter" vector, $\boldsymbol{w}$, that stores all the information for the current status of the training, where $\boldsymbol{w}$ determines the classifier. Given another input vector $\boldsymbol{x}$ and parameter vector $\boldsymbol{w}$, the classifier further predicts the class of the input vector.

Supervised classification methods can be categorized into two types: probabilistic or non-probabilistic. Probabilistic methods calculate the probability that y belongs to a certain class given input vector $\boldsymbol{x}$. They then classify $\boldsymbol{x}$ as the most probable class in domain $\mathcal{Y}$. Logistic regression is one of the most typical of these methods. Non-probabilistic methods such as Support Vector Machines (SVM) do not use probability explicitly but simply maps $\boldsymbol{x}$ to some $y \in Y$. For our system, probabilistic classification is preferable because, even if the prediction fails, it tells us how significant the failure is in the form of a probability. This is beneficial in this application because it enables users to prioritize the predictions to correct.

Given a training datum $(y, \boldsymbol{x})$, logistic regression directly models the conditional probability of y given $\boldsymbol{x} \in \mathcal{X}$ by a sigmoid function. In this application, input vector $\boldsymbol{x}$ consists of two components: the index of user $u \in \{1, \ldots, |U|\}$ and the index of word $t \in \{1, \ldots, |T|\}$. Thus, $\boldsymbol{x} = (u, t)$.

Random variable y represents how well user u knows word t. In this study, we simply assumed that this is represented by two states: "know" and "don't know". That is, $y = 1$ when user u knows word t and $y = 0$ otherwise. Thus, the domain of y is $\mathcal{Y} = \{1, 0\}$ in this application. Limiting y to be a binary random variable has a benefit: it reduces the number of variables to optimize. In our system, we need to optimize vector $\boldsymbol{w}$ so that it fits the data. If y can take more than two classes, say K classes, then $(K-1)|\boldsymbol{w}|$ variables need to be optimized. However, if y is binary, then optimizing $|\boldsymbol{w}|$ variable is sufficient; the probability of one class, $y = 1$ in Eq. 4, also determines the probability of the other class $y = 0$, as shown by Eq. 4.

$$
\begin{aligned}
P(y=1|\boldsymbol{\phi}; \boldsymbol{w}) &= \sigma\left(\boldsymbol{w}^{\mathrm{T}}\boldsymbol{\phi}(\boldsymbol{\phi})\right) \\
P(y=0|\boldsymbol{\phi}; \boldsymbol{w}) &= 1 - \sigma\left(\boldsymbol{w}^{\mathrm{T}}\boldsymbol{\phi}\right) \\
&= \left(1 - \sigma\left(\boldsymbol{w}^{\mathrm{T}}\boldsymbol{\phi}\right)\right)^{1-y}
\end{aligned}
\tag{4}
$$

Eq. 4 conveniently allows the following notations. First, Eq. 4 enables binary classifier h to be represented as

$$
h(u, t; \boldsymbol{w}^{(k)}) = \log \frac{P(y=1|\boldsymbol{\phi}(u,t); \boldsymbol{w}^{(k)})}{P(y=0|\boldsymbol{\phi}(u,t); \boldsymbol{w}^{(k)})}
\tag{5}
$$

Second, the notation introduced in Eq. 4 also combines $P(y=1|\boldsymbol{\phi}; \boldsymbol{w})$ and $P(y=0|\boldsymbol{\phi}; \boldsymbol{w})$ into one representation $P(y|\boldsymbol{\phi}; \boldsymbol{w})$, as shown in Eq. 6.

$$
P(y|\boldsymbol{\phi}; \boldsymbol{w}) = \sigma\left(\boldsymbol{w}^{\mathrm{T}}\boldsymbol{\phi}\right)^{y}\left(1 - \sigma\left(\boldsymbol{w}^{\mathrm{T}}\boldsymbol{\phi}\right)\right)^{1-y}
\tag{6}
$$

Thus, the negative log likelihood $E(\boldsymbol{w})$ of Eq. 6 is derived as shown in Eq. 7. The maximum likelihood estimator of Eq. 6 is given by minimizing Eq. 7.

$$
\begin{aligned}
E(\boldsymbol{w}) &= -\log\left(\prod_{n=1}^{N} P(y_n|\boldsymbol{\phi}_n; \boldsymbol{w})\right) \\
&= -\sum_{n=1}^{N} \log\left(P(y_n|\boldsymbol{\phi}_n; \boldsymbol{w})\right)
\end{aligned}
\tag{7}
$$

Relation to Rasch Model

This section shows that IRT is a special case of logistic regression when parameter vector $\boldsymbol{w}$ and feature vector $\boldsymbol{\phi}$ are modeled as follows. Let $|A|$ denote the size of set A. Let $\oplus$ denote the direct sum of two vectors; i.e., given two vectors

$$
\begin{aligned}
\boldsymbol{v}_x &= (v_{x_1}, \ldots, v_{x_{N_{v_x}}}) \in \mathbb{R}^{N_{v_x}} \\
\boldsymbol{v}_y &= (v_{y_1}, \ldots, v_{y_{N_{v_y}}}) \in \mathbb{R}^{N_{v_y}}
\end{aligned}
\tag{8}
$$

Eq. 9 shows $\boldsymbol{v}_x \oplus \boldsymbol{v}_y$.

$$
\boldsymbol{v}_x \oplus \boldsymbol{v}_y = (v_{x_1}, \ldots, v_{x_{N_{v_x}}}, v_{y_1}, \ldots, v_{y_{N_{v_y}}}) \in \mathbb{R}^{N_{v_x}+N_{v_y}}
\tag{9}
$$

In addition, this paper uses the following notation: a vector representing user language ability,

$$
\boldsymbol{\theta} = (\theta_1, \ldots, \theta_u, \ldots, \theta_{|U|})
\tag{10}
$$

and a vector of the difficulty of the words,

$$
\boldsymbol{d} = (-d_1, \ldots, -d_t, \ldots, -d_{|T|})
\tag{11}
$$

and $\boldsymbol{e}_u \in \mathbb{R}^{|U|}$, which denotes a unit vector whose u'th element is 1 while all the other elements are 0.

The Rasch model is a special case of logistic regression where $\boldsymbol{w}$ and $\boldsymbol{\phi}(u, t)$ in Eq. 4 are defined as in Eq. 12.

$$
\begin{aligned}
\boldsymbol{w} &= \boldsymbol{\theta} \oplus \boldsymbol{d} \\
\boldsymbol{\phi}(u, t) &= \boldsymbol{e}_u \oplus \boldsymbol{e}_t
\end{aligned}
\tag{12}
$$

Eq. 12 can be improved by adding additional features, as shown in Eq. 13.

$$
\begin{aligned}
\boldsymbol{w} &= \boldsymbol{\theta} \oplus \boldsymbol{d} \oplus \boldsymbol{w}_a \\
\boldsymbol{\phi}(u, t) &= \boldsymbol{e}_u \oplus \boldsymbol{e}_t \oplus \boldsymbol{\phi}_a(u, t)
\end{aligned}
\tag{13}
$$

Here, $\boldsymbol{\phi}_a$ is an additional feature vector that depends on u and t, and $\boldsymbol{w}_a$ is the weight vector for $\boldsymbol{\phi}_a$. When selected appropriately, the additional feature vector improves the systems prediction performance.

Our system uses $\boldsymbol{\phi}_a$ to introduce word difficulty. An appropriate choice of $\boldsymbol{\phi}_a$ improves accuracy. Remember that our system needs to estimate user language ability $\boldsymbol{\theta}$ and word difficulty $\boldsymbol{d}$. Among these two, not much information about language ability is expected to be available ahead of time because many users are anonymous by the nature of the Web community. In contrast, much is known about word difficulty $\boldsymbol{d}$. While many measures of word difficulty have been proposed, most of them are based on word frequency in a large corpus because word frequency has been demonstrated to be good measure of word difficulty for ESL (English as a second language) learners [21]. Thus, we used two kinds of features for word difficulty: "Google 1-gram" and "SVL". Google 1-gram is created from the raw word frequency taken from [3]. Taken from approximately a trillion Web pages, [3] is one of the largest word frequency lists known. Specifically, we used the value of normalized $-\log(\frac{f_t}{\sum_t f_t})$, where f_t is the word frequency of word t in [3]. Although also based on word frequency, SVL [18] is a word difficulty measure manually checked by English native speakers for Japanese ESL learners. SVL12000 covers 12,000 words and has 12 levels.

A Rasch model is not simply applicable to this system because the input data are too sparse. However, by using the notation used for logistic regression, we can tackle this problem by just adding more features to $\boldsymbol{\phi}$. In particular, we can approximate average word difficulty by using word frequencies; there are many report that word frequency can be used as a measure of word difficulty [21]. We used word frequencies from the Google corpus [3], whose n-gram counts are claimed to have been "generated from approximately 1 trillion word tokens of text from publicly accessible Web pages".

PARAMETER ESTIMATION

This section introduces parameter estimation methods for logistic regression. The main parameter estimation algorithms are shown in Table 1. To train the classifier for our system, online learning methods are preferable to batch learning methods because the click logs of our system are accumulated in an online manner. Batch learning may, however, be applicable to our system, for example, for training the classifier periodically.

Table 1. Parameter estimation methods for logistic regression.

	Optimal	Batch/Online
L-BFGS [11]	√	Batch
Trust Region [10]	√	Batch
SGD [2]		Online

The "Optimal" column shows whether the algorithm can find the global optimal solution of the objective function of a logistic regression. The "Batch/online" column shows whether the algorithm is a batch algorithm or an online algorithm.

L-BFGS [11] is a widely used method of estimating logistic regression parameters. It is a variant of quasi-Newton method. It consumes a memory space only linear to the number of features while a naïve method consumes a memory space squared to the number of features.

Trust region [10] is another recently proposed batch method for optimizing binary logistic regression parameters. It can optimize the parameters faster than L-BFGS, but it is limited to logistic regression whereas L-BFGS is more general and more widely applicable. An implementation of Trust region is given in [9] and this implementation was used for the evaluation later described.

Stochastic Gradient Descent (SGD)

The proposed system uses SGD (Stochastic Gradient Descent) to estimate the parameters because it is an online algorithm. While a batch algorithm requires the whole training data to be given from the beginning to the end, an online algorithm can process every record of the data one by one. An online algorithm suits for a Web application, because users of a Web application do not feed the whole data at a time.

SGD is derived from steepest gradient descent, a batch algorithm, by removing summation over the data points. The steepest gradient descent for logistic regression is shown in Eq. 14 where $\nabla E_n(\boldsymbol{w}) = \left(y_n - \sigma\left(\boldsymbol{w}^{\mathrm{T}}\boldsymbol{\phi}_n\right)\right)\boldsymbol{\phi}_n$.

$$\boldsymbol{w}^{(k+1)} = \boldsymbol{w}^{(k)} - \eta \sum_{n=1}^{N} \nabla E_n(\boldsymbol{w}^{(k)}) \qquad (14)$$

Eq. 14 contains the summation of E_n over all the data, so it is a batch algorithm. In this case, an online algorithm is easily

derived by removing the summation over n from Eq. 14. The resulting online algorithm is SGD, the algorithm used in our system. SGD is given by

$$\mathbf{w}^{(k+1)} = \mathbf{w}^{(k)} - \eta_k \nabla E_n(\mathbf{w}^{(k)}) \qquad (15)$$

In Eq. 15, η_k is defined as $\eta_k = \frac{1}{\lambda(k+k_0)}$, where λ, k_0 are the parameters of SGD and η_k is defined in this way so that Eq. 15 converges [13]. Note that η is usually a constant in Eq. 14. $Update(\boldsymbol{w}^{(k)}, u, t, y)$ in Figure 3 is defined by Eq. 15.

EXPERIMENTS

This section presents the results of our experiments and discusses them.

Evaluation Data

We developed a database of the vocabulary knowledge of 16 human subjects for 12,000 words for training and evaluating our system. This database is a matrix of the numbers representing the degree of vocabulary knowledge, where the rows correspond to the human subjects and the columns correspond to the words. The vocabulary knowledge was obtained by assessing the *language ability of humans* introduced in [17].

The database was developed by firstly determining the set of words for assessing the language ability of humans. The word set was selected from the Standard Vocabulary List 12000 (SVL12000) [18]. SVL12000 lists the most fundamental 12,000 words that an English learner should learn and they have been checked by native English speakers. Then, the questions for assessing the subject's language ability were developed. Each human subject answered the question for every word in SVL12000.

In [17], two methods are introduced to make questions for measuring the degree of human language ability.

Multiple-choice items A question consists of a word and multiple choices. The subjects are told to choose the choice that has the same meaning as the word.

Self-report scale A question consists of a word and multiple choices. The subjects are told to choose the choice that has the same meaning as the word.

The Self-report scale was used for developing the evaluation data because creating and answering multiple-choice items for 12,000 words has a much higher cost burden than the Self-report scale.

There have been several studies on designing scales for the Self-report scale. The scale shown in Table 2 was proposed in early research by Dale [7]. Paribakht & Wesche [15] proposed the scale shown in Table 3. Although the first four ranks on the scales show some correspondence between Dale's scale and Paribakht & Wesche's scale, the latter has one more additional rank, rank V, which tests the subject's writing ability by testing whether the subject can use the word correctly in a sentence. Rank V is additional to the

Table 2. Dale's scale	
Stage 1	"I never saw it before."
Stage 2	"I've heard of it, but I don't know what it means."
Stage 3	"I recognize it in context - it has something to do with ..."
Stage 4	"I know it."

Table 3. Paribakht & Wesche's elicitation scale	
I	"I don't remember having seen this word before."
II	"I have seen this word before, but I don't know what it means."
III	"I have seen this word before, and I think it means (synonym or translation)."
IV	"I know this word. It means (synonym or translation)."
V	"I can use this word in a sentence: (Write a sentence.) (If you do this section, please also do Section IV)"

other ranks; those who do rank V must also do rank IV, as described in the note in Table 3. We created the scale shown in Table 4. It is based on both Dale's scale and Paribakht & Wesche's scale with two major modifications. The first modification is that we omitted rank V because that exists for testing writing ability rather than testing reading ability, which our system tries to support. The second modification is that knowledge of synonyms and translations is omitted in our ranks. The reason for this is to prevent bias in the results. As it takes time for the subjects to give a synonym or translation, they may hesitate to choose an item that requires one, especially if the test covers many words. Another modification to Dale's scale is that we divided this Rank 2 into two ranks: 2.1 and 2.2. This modification was introduced because we wanted to discriminate the case where the subject has tried to learn the word before from the case where the subject simply has seen the word before. Dale's scale does not discriminate these two because it was originally for testing L1 language ability, and words are usually learned incidentally in L1 acquisition.

16 students mostly from graduate schools of the University of Tokyo participated in the test as human subjects. Each student answered 12,000 questions corresponding to the 12,000 words using our scale (Table 4). Note that the ranks in Table 4 are numbered to correspond to those of Dale's scale (Table 2) and Paribakht & Wesche's scale (Table 3). The subjects saw a simple ordinal numbering $1, 2, 3, 4, 5$, so that numbering did not affect their results.

The scale in Table 4 needs to be binarized to evaluate our system because our system eventually classifies words into "known" and "unknown" to a user. This scale binarization was performed as follows: Only rank 4 in Table 4 was regarded as $y = 1$, i.e., the case where user u knows word t. All the other ranks were regarded as $y = 0$, i.e., the case where user u does not know word t.

EVALUATION SETTING

The database was divided into a training set, development set, and test set. 600 words were randomly chosen for the training set, 1400 words were randomly chosen for the development set, and 9999 words were randomly chosen for the test set. Accuracy was defined as the percentage of the

words that our system correctly answered among the 9999 words in the test set. The remaining 600 words were used as training data.

The evaluation setting simulated the case where a new user starts using our system with a specified log. Every user among the 16 subjects was assumed to start using the system as a new user and to click at most 600 words. This number 600 was chosen so that everyone could click them within about 5 minutes.

The system was trained with data from **smart.fm** [4] instead of our system's log because no log had been accumulated at the start. **smart.fm** is an implementation of a computer-assisted vocabulary acquisition (CAVOCA) system in the field of computer-assisted language learning (CALL). The purpose of a CAVOCA system is to support its users, typically ESL learners, so that they can learn as many English words as possible in a fixed period. A CAVOCA system works as follows: First, the CAVOCA system gives the user a word list and the user selects words in the list to learn. If the user finds words that he/she already knows, he/she can check them and skip them. For our system, we used the checked words as training data because they are regarded as known words and the unchecked words in the word list are regarded as unknown words. Note that words absent from the word list were not used. Once the set of words to learn has been determined, the CAVOCA system automatically generates a set of questions about the words and presents these questions to the user. The CAVOCA system continues generating questions and the user continues answering them until he/she is able to answer the whole set of questions correctly. The question types include multiple-choice questions and spelling questions. While we obtained the records for 10,526 **smart.fm** users, we eventually chose 675 users from amongst these and used their records because many users simply tried **smart.fm** and did not use it seriously and repeatedly. These 675 users were chosen according to the following criteria: selection of at least 100 words for learning and 15% or more skipped words out of the total number of words in the word lists.

Our system was trained with data created from **smart.fm** and at most 600 new user words as training data. The hy-

Table 4. Our scale for evaluation.

1	never seen the word before
2.1	probably seen the word before
2.2	absolutely seen the word before but don't know its meaning / tried to learn the word before but forgot its meaning
3	probably know the word's meaning / able to guess the word's meaning
4	absolutely know the word's meaning

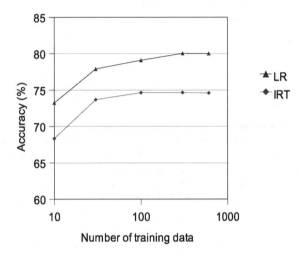

Figure 5. Comparison of logistic regression and IRT.

perparameters were tuned for the development set, and the accuracy of our system was measured on the test set. The accuracy was defined as the average percentage for the case where the classifier predicted correctly over the test sets of the 16 subjects.

EVALUATION OF THE PROPOSED SYSTEM

The Rasch model is a kind of IRT that can be defined as a logistic regression by providing user-IDs and word-IDs as features in logistic regression. Our model is an extension of the Rasch model with the addition of word difficulty features in logistic regression. This section describes how we evaluated the effectiveness of the word difficulty features. [9] was used for both IRT and LR with L2-regularization. The regularization parameter was selected from $1.0, 0.5, 2.0$ and the value that gave the highest accuracy in the development set was used in the test. Note that since IRT is a logistic regression that does not use word difficulty features, evaluating the case where no word difficulty features are used corresponds to evaluating the effectiveness of IRT.

Table 5. Values of accuracy (%) for IRT and LR.

	$N = 10$	30	100	300	600
IRT	68.33	73.69	74.65	74.65	74.60
LR	**73.25**	**77.89**	**79.09**	**80.03**	**80.01**

The results are shown in Table 5 and Figure 5. Both show that "LR", the case that includes word difficulty features, exhibited considerably higher accuracy than "IRT". This means that word difficulty features are effective because the difference between "LR" and "IRT" lies only in the word difficulty features. Thus, the use of word difficulty features is confirmed to be reasonable.

Another observation from Figure 5 is that the accuracy of both settings seemed to saturate in the range where the number of training data was over 300. "LR" achieved about 5% higher accuracy than "IRT" as a result of using word difficulty features.

Comparing Logistic Regression with Other Classifiers

There are many algorithms for binary classification besides logistic regression. Our system can be trained with them by using the same features. This section compares logistic regression with other binary classification algorithms in terms of accuracy. The following algorithms were compared with logistic regression.

1. SVM (Linear)

2. SVM (RBF)

3. Confidence Weighted

"SVM (Linear)" is a support vector machine with a linear kernel. This algorithm was chosen for the comparison because a support vector machine is a state-of-the-art algorithm for binary classification. Unlike a support vector machine with a Gaussian kernel, a support vector machine with a linear kernel cannot fully classify nonlinear data. However, this does not cause much problem with high-dimensional data because there are enough dimensions to classify the given data linearly. Explanations of support vector machines are found in [6]. Again, [9] was used for the implementation. The performance of a support vector machine is known to be affected by the value of regularization parameter C. In this evaluation, C was chosen from $1.0, 2.0, 0.5$. The value was tuned for the development set.

"SVM (RBF)" is a support vector machine with a Gaussian kernel, so it is another state-of-the-art algorithm for binary classification. [9] was used for the implementation. Unlike all the other algorithms, "SVM (RBF)" takes hours to optimize. The value of regularization parameter C was set to 1.0.

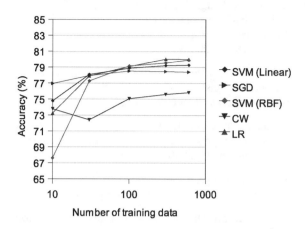

Figure 6. Comparison of logistic regression and other algorithms.

"Confidence Weighted" (CW) is a recently proposed online algorithm [8]. Its classification performance was reported to be high [8]. Here, [14] was used for the implementation. The performance of Confidence Weighted, and more generally that of any online algorithm, varies with the number of iterations, i.e., the number of times the classifier sees the whole data. The number of iterations was chosen from $1, 10, 20$. Confidence Weighted also has a regularization parameter, usually denoted by C. This parameter was chosen from $1.0, 0.1, 10.0$. For both these parameters, the values giving the best accuracy in the development testing were used for the test.

"Stochastic Gradient Descent" (SGD) is the SGD described so far. Note that no regularization is performed in SGD.

Finally, "LR" denotes the results for logistic regression. Again, LR was optimized with L2-regularization using [9]. The regularization parameter was selected from $1.0, 0.5, 2.0$, and the value that gave the highest accuracy in the development set was used for the test.

Table 6. Prediction accuracy (%) for various algorithms.

	$N_1 = 10$	30	100	300	600
SVM (Linear)	74.78	**78.08**	78.88	79.20	79.27
SVM (RBF)	67.61	77.27	**79.16**	79.55	79.91
CW	73.77	72.40	75.06	75.60	75.82
SGD	**76.95**	77.94	78.52	78.46	78.39
LR	73.25	77.89	79.09	**80.03**	**80.01**

Accuracy values for logistic regression and other algorithms are listed in Table 6. Logistic regression achieved the highest accuracy when the number of the training data was 300 and 600. It also achieved nearly the highest accuracy for $30, 100$. This means that logistic regression is sufficiently accurate compared with the other algorithms. Thus, the use of logistic regression is reasonable for this application.

When the numbers of the training data were 10 and 30, SGD outperformed LR and achieved the highest and the second

highest accuracy respectively. This result is encouraging because it suggests that SGD is quick to adapt to a user. SVM (RBF) had the lowest accuracy when the number of training data was set to 10. We attributed this to the amount of training data being too small and to parameter C of the SVM (RBF) being fixed to 1. CW achieved the lowest accuracy among all the algorithms.

As shown in Figure 6, all the algorithms saturated in the range where the number of training data exceeded 300 and even the highest of accuracy was only about 80%. This shows that about 80% is the accuracy limit owing to the nature of the given data.

DISCUSSION

Although state-of-the-art online learning achieves accuracy close to that of batch learning, batch learning is still usually considered to achieve higher accuracy than online learning. However, when the number of training data was lower than 100, SGD outperformed LR in terms of accuracy. This seems to be the result of the online learning and the existence of the regularization term: while LR is L2-regularized, SGD is not regularized.

Thus, the choice of online or batch learning depends on the environment and implementation. Note that we could also use a hybrid method of both online and batch learning by using the same model for both online and setting up the initial weight vector of the online learning by using the weight vector resulting from the batch training. We currently use only SGD, an online learning, since no significant problem with accuracy has been reported. As SGD is quick to adapt to a user, we think that SGD offers an advantage in terms of user satisfaction compared to other algorithms.

While we have so far explained how our system adapts to the users, one might come up with a simpler system that performs no adaptation to users: first, the system would be given a static list of "difficult" words, i.e., the system would be informed which words are "difficult" and it would then simply gloss those "difficult" words. This simpler system corresponds to the case where a specific and static weight vector is used in our model. In fact, this simpler system can be obtained by adding a feature that is triggered when the word is in the given list and by setting the element of the weight vector for that feature to 1 and setting all the other elements of the weight vector, including the elements for the users' features, to 0. Since our system optimizes the weight vector on the fly, we assume it would outperform this simpler system in terms of accuracy.

CONCLUSIONS

We described a new glossing system that can predict words unknown to the user by utilizing logs that contain valuable information about a user's vocabulary. Although existing glossing systems are helpful for English learners because they provide the meaning of a word by displaying it in a pop-up window when the user encounters an unknown word and clicks on or mouses over it, they waste this log information.

We investigated models for our system's prediction. The use of logistic regression was found to be appropriate because the Rasch model, a simple form of item response theory (IRT) widely used to assess human language ability, is also a logistic regression that employs a specific feature vector. We extended IRT by introducing word difficulty features and achieved accuracy higher than that of straight-forward IRT.

For estimating the parameters of the model, we found that stochastic gradient descent (SGD) was appropriate because it is an online algorithm and the click logs of our system are accumulated in an online manner. When a user newly starts using the system, if the system does not learn the user's behavior well, it is likely that the user ends up with not using the system. Thus, the system needs to adapt to the user quickly. Our evaluation simulated the case where new users start using the system after a click log has already been accumulated. The average accuracy over 16 users was observed. We compared SGD with other binary classification algorithms in terms of accuracy. SGD achieved the highest and the second highest accuracy compared with the other algorithms when the number of training data was 10 and 30, respectively. Suggesting SGD adapts quickly to the user, this result is encouraging.

REFERENCES

1. F. Baker and S. Kim. *Item response theory: Parameter estimation techniques*. CRC, 2004.

2. C. M. Bishop. *Pattern recognition and machine learning*. Springer, 2006.

3. T. Brants and A. Franz. *Web 1T 5-gram Version 1*. Linguistic Data Consortium, Philadelphia, 2006.

4. Cerego Japan Inc. smart.fm, 2009. http://smart.fm/.

5. Coolest.com Inc. popjisyo.com, 2002. http://www.popjisyo.com/.

6. N. Cristianini and J. Shawe-Taylor. *An introduction to support Vector Machines: and other kernel-based learning methods*. Cambridge Univ Pr, 2000.

7. E. Dale. Vocabulary measurement: techniques and major findings. *Elementary English*, 42:895–901, 948, 1965.

8. M. Dredze, K. Crammer, and F. Pereira. Confidence-weighted linear classification. In *ICML '08: Proceedings of the 25th international conference on Machine learning*, pages 264–271, New York, NY, USA, 2008. ACM.

9. R. Fan, K. Chang, C. Hsieh, X. Wang, and C. Lin. LIBLINEAR: A library for large linear classification. *The Journal of Machine Learning Research*, 9:1871–1874, 2008.

10. C. Lin, R. Weng, and S. Keerthi. Trust region Newton method for logistic regression. *The Journal of Machine Learning Research*, 9:627–650, 2008.

11. D. Liu and J. Nocedal. On the limited memory BFGS method for large scale optimization. *Mathematical Programming*, 45(1):503–528, 1989.

12. Nori. Firedictionary.com, 2005. http://www.firedictionary.com/.

13. A. B. Novikoff. On convergence proofs for perceptrons. In *Proceedings of the Symposium on the Mathematical Theory of Automata*, volume 12, pages 615–622, 1963.

14. D. Okanohara. *oll: Online-Learning Library*, 2008. http://code.google.com/p/oll/.

15. T. Paribakht and M. Wesche. Vocabulary enhancement activities and reading for meaning in second language vocabulary acquisition. *Second language vocabulary acquisition: A rationale for pedagogy*, pages 174–200, 1997.

16. popIn Inc. popin, 2008. http://www.popin.cc/en/home.html.

17. J. Read. *Assessing Vocabulary*. Cambridge University Press, 2000.

18. SPACE ALC Inc. Standard vocabulary list 12,000, 1998. http://www.alc.co.jp/goi/PW_top_all.htm.

19. E. Sumita, F. Sugaya, and S. Yamamoto. Measuring non-native speakers' proficiency of English by using a test with automatically-generated fill-in-the-blank questions. In *Proceedings of the Second Workshop on Building Educational Applications Using NLP*, pages 61–68, Ann Arbor, Michigan, June 2005. Association for Computational Linguistics.

20. T. D. Rudick. Rikai, 2001. http://www.rikai.com/.

21. J. M. Tamayo. Frequency of use as a measure of word difficulty in bilingual vocabulary test construction and translation. *Educational and Psychological Measurement*, 47(4):893–902, 1987.

Agent-Assisted Task Management
that Reduces Email Overload

Andrew Faulring, Brad Myers, Ken Mohnkern, Bradley Schmerl, Aaron Steinfeld,
John Zimmerman, Asim Smailagic, Jeffery Hansen, and Daniel Siewiorek
School of Computer Science, Carnegie Mellon University
{faulring, bam, kem, schmerl, astein, johnz, asim, hansen, dps}@cs.cmu.edu

ABSTRACT

RADAR is a multiagent system with a mixed-initiative user interface designed to help office workers cope with email overload. RADAR agents observe experts to learn models of their strategies and then use the models to assist other people who are working on similar tasks. The agents' assistance helps a person to transition from the normal email-centric workflow to a more efficient task-centric workflow. The Email Classifier learns to identify tasks contained within emails and then inspects new emails for similar tasks. A novel task-management user interface displays the found tasks in a to-do list, which has integrated support for performing the tasks. The Multitask Coordination Assistant learns a model of the order in which experts perform tasks and then suggests a schedule to other people who are working on similar tasks. A novel Progress Bar displays the suggested schedule of incomplete tasks as well as the completed tasks. A large evaluation demonstrated that novice users confronted with an email overload test performed significantly better (a 37% better overall score with a factor of four fewer errors) when assisted by the RADAR agents.

Author Keywords

Agents, email classification, email overload, intelligent planning, learning, RADAR, task management.

ACM Classification Keywords

H.5.2 [Information Interfaces and Presentation]: User Interfaces---Interaction styles, Graphical user interfaces (GUI); I.2.11 [Artificial Intelligence]: Distributed Artificial Intelligence---Intelligent agents, Multiagent systems.

General Terms

Design, Experimentation, Human Factors.

INTRODUCTION

Email plays a central role in the work of many people. Unfortunately email client software is poorly suited to support the "collaborative quality of e-mail task and project man-

agement," which results in people suffering from "email overload" [2]. When faced with a large number of emails, people can find it difficult to choose an order in which to handle them. Possible strategies include handling each email in the order received, scanning the list of email subjects and senders for ones that appear to match various criteria (important, quick to handle, and so forth), or using filters to file emails into folders. The order in which emails are handled can significantly affect the efficiency of the strategy, since performing similar tasks together reduces the overhead of switching between different types of tasks. People find it difficult to create an efficient order when sorting their inbox using email-centric properties, such as sender, subject, or date, because sorting by those properties will usually not group similar tasks together nor will it account for inter-task dependencies. Email threads can help in some situations, and other times people can rely on "crutches" such as asking senders to use a specific subject line in the email. However in general, a person would need to inspect each email, manually create task metadata, and then generate an order for handling the emails. Several research projects have explored adding task-management features to email clients [2, 12, 23], and some email clients do provide features that facilitate task management such as tagging and separate to-do lists. The primary drawback of this approach is that users resist doing that additional work [24], and it forces them to read each email at least twice: once when creating the tasks, then again to actually do the task. Temporal factors further complicate email processing. High priority emails might need to be handled independent of efficiency concerns. Additionally, when time is tight people must decide which emails to ignore.

We have developed a mixed-initiative email system, which uses Artificial Intelligence (AI) learning techniques, to help mitigate these problems and thereby reduce email overload. We evaluated our system in an experiment in which RADAR was trained by observing people who were not the test participants. While this tests a situation where a novice is filling in for an expert, we are also interested in how well our techniques will help when a person is processing their own email. The Email Classifier observes the types of tasks an expert creates from emails and then learns a model that it uses to automatically find tasks within new emails. Next, the Multitask Coordination Assistant (MCA) observes expert users perform the tasks found by the Email Classifier. The MCA uses these training observations to learn models describing how to efficiently perform a set of tasks. The MCA uses these learned models to assist users working on a similar set of tasks. Its advice includes a suggested order for performing tasks and warnings when the user's behavior differs significantly from the expert's behavior. This approach reduces the number of times a person has to read an email and allows the tasks to be performed efficiently.

This mixed-initiative email system was a central feature of the **R**eflective **A**gents with **D**istributed **A**daptive **R**easoning (RADAR) project. RADAR was a large interdisciplinary project to build a suite of intelligent agents that help office workers complete tasks more efficiently. Over 100 faculty, staff, and students worked on RADAR components including the Email Classifier [25] and Multitask Coordination Assistant, along with other components including a Natural Language Processor [17], a Knowledge Base [7], a Schedule Optimizer [9], a Webmaster [27], a Briefing Assistant [15], and a Task Management Architecture [11]. Freed provides a more detailed description of the overall RADAR approach, architecture, and agents [10]. We have previously described some of the user interfaces in a case study on usability issues for AI systems [8]. The current paper provides more details on the interface design and a significantly more detailed analysis of the user study results.

A large-scale user test evaluated several versions of RADAR over three years [19]. The test measured RADAR's performance using quantitative metrics acquired through data logging, including an evaluation score that summarizes overall performance along with qualitative metrics collected with a post-test user survey [20].

The post-test user survey for the RADAR 1.1 system found that RADAR's AI had little impact on user perceptions of the system. Although RADAR 1.1 included the Email Classifier, tasks were embedded as objects in each email. The system also exhibited usability and performance problems. It was hypothesized that the poor user interface was masking the potential benefit of the AI [20]. For RADAR 2.0, we designed a mixed-initiative task-centric email client in which the user's inbox is augmented with a separate task list. The post-test survey for the RADAR 2.0 study found that the AI technologies now positively impacted user perceptions of RADAR. In particular, participants were more confident that they had done tasks well, had found tasks easier to complete, and had been more immersed in the test. These qualitative metrics were supported by a significant improvement in the test's evaluation score.

While participants were more successful at performing individual tasks, many still struggled to find an efficient order for performing a group of tasks. We observed a wide variance in performance including a long-tail of poor scores from participants who struggled. To address this problem, the RADAR 3.0 system introduced a task strategy component called the Multitask Coordination Assistant. The MCA proposes a schedule for performing tasks, emphasizes highly-important "critical" tasks, recommends tasks to skip if

time is tight, and issues warnings if the user's behavior deviates significantly from expert behavior. The results of testing RADAR 3.0 showed another significant increase in performance accompanied by a noticeable drop in variance.

These results suggest that adding AI technologies to interactive systems can benefit users, a conclusion that has been met with skepticism within the HCI community [18]. While some of the concern focuses specifically on anthropomorphic agent interfaces, a major complaint against interactive AI is that it interferes with a user's ability to easily *predict*, *control*, and *monitor* the system's behavior. When the AI technologies make mistakes, will the user notice and correct the errors? When the system does act correctly, will the user notice what has been done? A related concern is that people will have difficulty *understanding* why an intelligent system made a particular decision or suggestion, which might lower a user's trust or confidence in the system. However, the benefits of predictability and understandability need to be weighed against the benefits of automation [13]. A direct manipulation system can be slower and have *more* errors than an intelligent system [21]. Predictability and understandability are subgoals of the ultimate goal, usable systems, and must be weighed against other subgoals such as performance, which also impact usability.

RADAR makes specific contributions to address these issues. The automatically detected tasks are presented in a list view and in a detail view along with the original email message, so that users can easily understand, check and perform the tasks. The recommended ordering of the tasks is clear from the sort order in the task view and in a novel Progress Bar that shows future as well as completed tasks. Additionally, RADAR is generally not allowed to take autonomous actions when such actions would be visible to other people or systems. RADAR has considerable flexibility to work on the user's behavior without risking costly mistakes that might embarrass the user or leak private information.

A user study showed that the user interfaces presented the AI assistance in a helpful manner: users who received AI assistance performed 37% better compared with users who did not. Additionally, users were able to recognize when RADAR made errors, correctly handling 89% of the tasks that the Email Classifier erroneously suggested. Overall, these users incorrectly completed 2.6 tasks per user. In contrast, the users without AI assistance *incorrectly* completed 10.3 tasks on average, which accounted for 19% of the tasks they did. This is a factor of four *more* errors.

RELATED WORK

Much task-management research has studied adding task-management features to email client software [2, 12, 23] and making it easy to move tasks from email client software to dedicated task managers [21, 23, 27]. This work focuses on email because users often use email client software as a task manager since many tasks arrive as emails and the information necessary to complete a task is commonly contained in the email as well. Hence, the inbox becomes an informal to-do list [6]. Unfortunately, email applications are not designed to perform the task-management duties that users demand from them [24]. For example, when an inbox collects a large number of emails, it can become difficult to find information. Email software allows users to create folders and email filters, label emails, perform searches, and so forth. Unfortunately these features are not always implemented in a way that makes task management easy [23]. For example, Gwizdka found that most of the Microsoft Outlook users he studied did not use many of Outlook's features, such as the to-do list, email flags, reminder flags, and journal [12]. Dedicated task-management applications do not provide the answer to this problem since users dislike the tedious process of entering task metadata such as dependencies, due dates, and priorities [1]. TaskMaster [2], which did not use AI, took a hybrid approach like RADAR, providing features of both email clients and task managers.

Task managers generally display to-do tasks in a list [1, 3, 16], as does RADAR. One notable exception is TaskView [12], which displays future tasks within an email client by arranging emails in a grid where time runs along the horizontal axis and an email property, such as sender or subject, runs along the vertical axis. However, TaskView requires that task information be manually entered, whereas RADAR calculates task priorities and orders tasks automatically in both the Action List and the Progress Bar. Towel [4], the user interface for the PExA time- and task-management tool [16], allows the user to delegate tasks to humans or software agents. RADAR automatically creates tasks from emails and fills in the forms used to do the tasks.

The SmartMail system automatically identifies sentences in emails that contain tasks and flags the emails in the inbox [5]. However, it does not classify the tasks by type nor does it add the tasks to a to-do list. RADAR implements both of those features as part of its task-centric user interface.

The Priorities system used email headers, content, and recipient availability to calculate the urgency of an email [14]. RADAR orders emails based upon the associated tasks, which include information from the email.

TASK-CENTRIC EMAIL PROCESSING

Initial Contextual Inquiries

We began exploring how to address the email overload problem by performing a set of contextual inquiries with approximately two dozen office workers to understand the problems that they encountered when handling their email. We quickly saw a pair of roles emerge, which we labeled *Initiator*, the person who needs assistance, and *Human Service Assistant* (HSA), the person who can provide the help. HSAs regularly received email requests that are performed by filling out forms, so their work serves as a good example for informing the design of the Action List interface. Observations of HSAs processing requests revealed that they would regularly save a small set of related tasks and then perform them together as a group. They claimed that this saved them time by sharing the overhead costs of connecting to different IT systems among multiple tasks.

Inspired by these observations, we designed the Action List as a mechanism for transforming the processing of email requests from the traditional email-centric workflow to a task-centric workflow. This new perspective offered two distinct advantages over current email systems for an HSA. First, by providing a view of all tasks to be processed, HSAs could focus on completing one type of task at a time. We hypothesized that this would reduce the amount of context switching taking place, allowing HSAs to work more efficiently. Second, by interacting with a task-level view of incoming requests, HSAs could better prioritize their work.

We employed an iterative design process, building multiple working versions of the system. This approach helped us to assess both what kinds of errors the agents would make and to learn how well our users could recognize and repair these errors. One important discovery from the usability testing was that the term "action" works better than "task," so we used the former term in the user interface. However, we will continue to use the term "task" throughout this paper, except when referring to specific user interface elements.

The Action List

The Action List design supports a mixed-initiative interaction style for creating and completing tasks contained within emails. The Email Classifier examines the content of each email for evidence that it contains any requests of the eight known task types [25]. The Email Classifier dumps all available tokens and knowledge features of the email into one bag-of-words model and uses a regularized logistic regression algorithm, which scales to thousands of labels [26]. When it finds sufficient evidence for a given task type, it applies the label for that task type to the email. The classifier considers the evidence that supports each task type independently, and so it applies zero, one, or more different labels to each email. However, it cannot determine if an email contains multiple tasks of the same type. To improve classification performance, Scone [7], which is RADAR's knowledge base, provides additional ontological information that is not contained in the email's content. Examples include basic facts, such as "the Connan room is in the University Center," and higher-level concepts, such as "a peanut is kind of food that people might be allergic to."

The RADAR evaluation uses novice users, who may have difficulty effectively judging whether the email classifier's labels are correct. We were concerned that too many false positives might confuse them, so we tuned the classifier to favor precision over recall. An examination of the classifier's behavior showed that it did perform as desired. The latest evaluation had 123 emails, which contained 102 task labels. The classifier correctly found 47 task labels and incorrectly suggested 6 other task labels (false positives): *precision* = 0.887 (47/53) and *recall* = 0.461 (47/102).

Figure labels (left margin): (a), (a.i), (a.ii), (a.iii), (a.iv), (b), (c), (d), (e), (f), (g)

Incomplete Actions (11)

Order ▼	Description	Subject	Sender	Created	Modified	Creator
1	Modify Event: *Demo M1: Driver Monitoring Systems*	Attendance figures and new #	Amy Lim <lim12@ardra.org>	Today, 3:32 PM		RADAR
2	Modify Event	note schedule chagnes	Spence Pierro <spierro@ardra.org>	Today, 3:54 PM		RADAR
3	Modify Room: *Flagstaff: Sternwheeler*	Sternwheeler Capacity	Meredith Lorenz <lorenze@pittsburgh.flagstaff.com>	Today, 4:07 PM		RADAR
4	Modify Room: *Flagstaff: Vandergrift*	Sternwheeler Capacity	Meredith Lorenz <lorenze@pittsburgh.flagstaff.com>	Today, 4:10 PM		USER
5	Optimize the Schedule	no email		Today, 3:45 PM		RADAR
6	Website Update (VIO): Modify Person: *Austin Parton*	Webpage	Austin Parton <aparton@ardra.org>	Today, 3:37 PM		RADAR
7	Website Update (VIO): Modify Person	Attendance figures and new #	Amy Lim <lim12@ardra.org>	Today, 3:32 PM		RADAR
8	Website Update (VIO)	Organization Wrong	Sonal Malhotra <smalh@ardra.org>	Today, 4:32 PM		RADAR
9	Website Update (WbE)	change phone numbers	Emily Halwizer <halwizer@ardra.org>	Today, 4:47 PM		RADAR
10	Place a Vendor Order	Tech. Request - flip charts	Maggie Foxenreiter <mfox@ardra.org>	Today, 3:33 PM		RADAR
11	Send a Briefing	Brief me, please	Jonathon Robertson <jrobertson@ardra.org>	Today, 4:42 PM		RADAR

Overflow Actions (1)

Order	Description ▼	Subject	Sender	Created	Modified	Creator
	Reply to Question	Vegetarian options?	Sandra Nubanks <snubanks@ardra.org>	Today, 4:02 PM		RADAR

Completed Actions (1)

Order	Description	Subject	Sender	Created	Modified ▼	Creator
	Modify Event: *Workshop 1a: Intermodal Passenger Screening*	Attendance figures	Amy Lim <lim12@ardra.org>	Today, 3:21 PM	Today, 3:45 PM	RADAR

Deleted Actions (1)

Order	Description	Subject	Sender	Created	Modified ▼	Creator
	Modify Speaker's Availability	Planning for History Week	Michelle Randal <mich-randal@gmail.com>	Today, 4:28 PM	Today, 4:34 PM	RADAR

Possibly Conference-Related Emails (1)

Read	Subject	Sender	Date ▼	
•	for my presentation	Laura Timdale <laurat2@ardra.org>	Today, 3:24 PM	Add an Action

Blake, I didnt know who to contact about making sure to have a laptop available, and connected to teh AV equipment - ie projector. I want all that ready on the ...

Other Emails (1)

Read	Subject	Sender	Date ▼	
•	car arrangements	Angie Randal <angiednacer6@gmail.com>	Today, 3:23 PM	Add an Action

Ms K is counting on me to help out with the kids' dance class. The car is still in the shp. Can you drop me off over there? thanks :-)

Deleted Emails (1)

Read	Subject	Sender	Date ▼	
	Precipitation Update	Weather Alerts <weather@weather.gov>	Today, 3:56 PM	Add an Action

There is a 70% probability for thunderstorms with heavy rain in ALLEGHENY COUNTY this evening through tomorrow. Plan accordingly and be safe! Go to www.weather.gov ...

Figure 1: The RADAR Action List provides a task-centric view of an email inbox. The "Incomplete Actions" (a), "Overflow Actions" (b), and "Completed Actions" (c) tables list the tasks contained within email messages, allowing the user to sort by task-centric properties. The three email tables contain emails for which no tasks have been created (e, f, and g).

For each task label applied to an email, RADAR creates a task object, which is managed by the Task Manager [11]. Information stored includes the web form for that kind of task, if applicable. As we observed for real-life HSAs, in RADAR, many tasks require filling out web-based forms. RADAR's Natural Language Processor [17] attempts to specify task-specific parameters in the form, including the database record that the form should modify, if applicable. If RADAR can identify the record, then it will also try to fill in the other fields in the form. This novel integration of a to-do list with the forms for completing the tasks removes unnecessary steps from the process of performing a task.

The resulting tasks are displayed by the Action List, which provides a task-centric view of the user's email inbox (see Figure 1). The Action List allows a user to inspect the tasks that RADAR created, add ones that were missed, delete ones that should not have been created, and launch web pages to perform some of the tasks. The Action List contains seven tables divided into two groups: the first for tasks, and the second for emails (see Figure 1). The task group contains four tables that list "Incomplete" (a), "Overflow" (b), "Completed" (c), and "Deleted" (d) tasks. Tasks that the user has yet to perform are split between the Incomplete and Overflow table, with the latter table containing tasks that the MCA (to be described later) recommends that the user should skip due to time constraints. An email message will appear multiple times in the Action List if it is associated with multiple tasks of the same type (a.ii and a.iii), multiple tasks of different types (a.i and a.iv), or both. Tasks completed by the user appear in the Completed table, which provides the user with a record of their progress and allows them to go back and revisit previous tasks.

The tabular task display allows the user to sort their tasks with respect to task-centric properties such as "Description" or "Order" (by clicking on the column title), in addition to standard email-centric properties such as sender, subject, and date. The "Description" column sorts tasks alphabetically by type and within each type by the date of the associated email. When an email contains multiple tasks of different types, each of those tasks will be grouped with the other tasks of the same type when the table is sorted by the Description column. The other columns use a standard sort order based upon their data type.

The second set of tables (e, f, and g) display emails that are not associated with any non-deleted tasks. These tables are designed like a traditional inbox, with columns for the subject, sender, and date. The row for each email includes an excerpt from the beginning of the email body to help the user determine whether an email contains a task without opening the email. The user opens an email by clicking on either the subject or the "Add an Action" link. The email display includes the header and body sections along with the list of tasks that the user can add to the email.

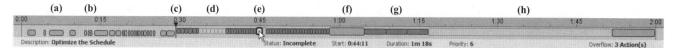

Figure 2: The Progress Bar shows completed (a) and deleted (b) tasks to the left of the current time (c), and the suggested schedule to the right. Noncritical tasks are blue (a, b, and g), critical tasks are orange (f), and expected tasks are gray (d and h). Details about the highlighted task (e) are shown in the status bar at the bottom.

The emails are divided among the three tables. The "Possibly Conference-Related Emails" table contains emails that RADAR thinks may contain tasks but for which it could not confidently identify the exact task type (e). This partial classification focuses the user's attention on emails likely to contain tasks without risking errors that might result if RADAR incorrectly classified the task as being of a particular type. The second table contains other emails that RADAR did not identify as task-related (f). The third table contains emails that the user deleted (g).

PROVIDING TASK ORDERING ADVICE

The evaluation of the RADAR 2.0 system showed that the task-centric workflow enabled by the AI technologies helps users. However, user performance varied significantly. Based upon analyses of the data logs, we hypothesized that some users had had difficulty finding a high-level strategy for completing the work. The novice users likely lacked meta-knowledge about tasks such as task importance, expected task duration, and task ordering dependencies. An expert user with that knowledge should be able to make good decisions about which tasks to work on at any given time and which tasks to skip when time is limited.

The MCA, a new component for RADAR 3.0, was built to address this problem by providing guidance about the order in which to work on a set of tasks. The MCA was designed to supports both near-term deadlines on the order of 1–8 hours, which would be encountered during a typical HSA's workday, and situations in which the amount of work exceeds the time allotted. The MCA learns task models upon which the advice is based by passively observing experts performing similar tasks. The MCA includes a novel visualization called the Progress Bar (see Figure 2), which shows a suggested schedule for performing incomplete tasks. The MCA's goal is to provide advice that improves performance and reduces overall performance variance, hopefully cutting off the long-tail of poor performance.

User Interfaces for Suggesting a Schedule

The primary advice provided by the MCA is a suggested schedule, which specifies an order in which to perform outstanding tasks. The MCA suggests which tasks to skip when it calculates that not enough time remains to perform all incomplete tasks. The MCA learns which tasks are generated after other tasks are completed, and so it also adds such "expected" tasks to the schedule. Including the expected tasks in the schedule provides the user with a more realistic understanding of upcoming work and eliminates major changes to the schedule that would otherwise occur

when an expected task actually becomes necessary. Additionally, the MCA identifies "critical" tasks, which are particularly important for the user to complete. The suggested schedule is displayed by the Progress Bar (see Figure 2) and in the "Order" column of the Action List (see Figure 1).

The Progress Bar (see Figure 2) appears at the bottom of the screen just above the Windows Taskbar and always remains on top without obscuring other windows. Time is represented on the horizontal axis, which in this case spans two hours. An inverted black triangle and a vertical red line represent the current time (c), which increases from left to right. Each rectangular box represents a task. Task boxes to the left of the current time represent completed (a) or deleted (b) tasks, providing a record of the user's progress so far. The width of a task box represents the time that the user spent working on that task. The suggested schedule is visualized by the task boxes to the right of the current time. The width of each of these task boxes represents the amount of time that the MCA expects the task to require. Blue task boxes represent noncritical tasks (g). Orange task boxes, which are also slightly taller, represent critical tasks (f). Gray boxes represent expected tasks (d); expected critical tasks appear as taller gray boxes (h). The user can quickly inspect any task by moving the mouse over its task box (e), which updates the status bar at the bottom to show the task's description, status, actual/planned start time, actual/planned duration, and priority. That task, along with all other tasks of the same type, is drawn with a thicker border to allow the user to see where that type of task is distributed throughout the schedule. Double-clicking on a task box opens the corresponding task. The number of overflow tasks, which are the ones the MCA proposes to skip due to time constraints, appears at the bottom right.

MCA advice also appears in other parts of the RADAR user interface. First, the Action List's "Order" column shows the position of each future task within the suggested schedule (see Figure 1(a)). Only tasks in the "Incomplete Actions" table are included in the suggested schedule; the "Order" column is blank in the other tables. Sorting the "Incomplete Actions" table by the "Order" column shows the schedule as an ordered to-do list. Second, tasks that the MCA suggests that the user skip are shown in the "Overflow Actions" table. Third, after the user completes or deletes a task, RADAR redisplays the task's form in a finished state to provide feedback that the command succeeded. This confirmation screen also includes a link to the next suggested task in the schedule, which allows the user to navigate to the next task that the MCA recommends without having to return to the Action List. Finally, the MCA displays popup warning dialogs when the user significantly deviates from the suggested schedule. The warnings are issued if the user works on a critical task much earlier than experts did (Early Critical), if the user has not yet started working on a critical task by the time most experts had (Late Critical), or if the user starts working on a critical task that is not the next critical task on the suggested schedule (Wrong Critical).

Training the MCA

The MCA learned a model of expert behavior by passively observing experts performing tasks using the same user interfaces that test participants will later use. To train the system, experts did the two-hour study using a version of the system for which the MCA learning components were watching rather than recommending. Other AI components operated normally. For example, the Email Classifier had analyzed the emails to identify tasks. The training used three different email sets (none of which was the test email set), which provided variability to prevent overtraining.

Since there were no actual experts for the test tasks, we trained RADAR team members who had not worked on the MCA to be experts. People with detailed knowledge of how the MCA worked might behave in a way that aids the learning algorithm and hence would not be representative of real experts. We taught the experts how to use the RADAR components with the same instruction that novice test participants received. Additionally, the experts had significant exposure to the problem domain, detailed knowledge of some of the fixed stimuli (for example, available buildings), and were given more time to practice, all of which are consistent with the idea that they have more experience performing the test tasks. We also gave them some high-level strategy advice that a real expert would know based on knowledge of the scenario and evaluation methodology.

The primary goal of the MCA training process was to provide the MCA with an opportunity to infer the high-level strategy from passive observations of experts using that strategy to perform the two-hour study. The MCA learns the following information. First, the average *duration* to complete a task, along with the variance, is recorded per task type. Second, the MCA identifies *critical* tasks, which are tasks with a small number of instances and for which the mix of tasks changes after the critical task is completed, and computes an expected completion time for each critical task. Third, it learns task *phases*, which are the mix of tasks between critical tasks. Fourth, the MCA infers *prerequisites* among task types by looking for transitions between task types that are observed to occur with high probability. Each high probability transition is encoded as a directed edge within a partial ordering of the task types. Fifth, the MCA learns a *contextual task ordering*, which predicts the ordering among individual tasks. Sixth, the MCA computes *generate dependencies* among task types, which are the expected number of tasks of each type created after the completion of a task, with self-looping edges being allowed.

Collectively, this information, which is computed using a variety of statistical machine learning algorithms, forms the MCA's learned model of expert behavior.

Generating the Suggested Schedule

Given the learned model and the current collection of tasks (both completed and incomplete) the MCA computes a suggested schedule for performing the tasks within the remaining time. Its goal is to produce a schedule representative of how an expert would perform the same collection of tasks. The process works as follows. First, the *generate dependencies* are used to create expected tasks. Second, the *prerequisites* (task-type ordering constraints) and output of the *contextual task ordering* predictor (individual-task ordering constraints) are passed into an Advice Integrator. Each constraint includes a weight that the Advice Integrator uses to compare against other constraints to produce a consensus schedule. The consensus schedule is a total ordering of the incomplete tasks, including expected tasks. Third, the Task Shedder [22] uses the learned task *durations* and task importance, along with the observed user's speed relative to the experts' speed, to decide which tasks to shed from the consensus schedule. The Task Shedder's algorithm generally sheds noncritical and expected tasks while shortening the planned duration of compressible tasks, but it never reorders individual tasks. The Task Shedder outputs the suggested schedule, which is presented to the user in the Progress Bar and Action List user interfaces.

EVALUATION

We evaluated RADAR using a conference planning test to determine how effective it is at assisting novice users based upon learned models of expert performance. This section describes the study design and then reports results from the evaluation of the RADAR 3.0 system.

The Conference Planning Test

A key challenge was designing an evaluation that measured how well RADAR reduced email overload. Since the project was planned to run for several years, we wanted to conduct carefully controlled, repeatable user studies that would allow us to measure progress over time. We initially considered designing an evaluation that used people's actual email, but decided against it. Such an evaluation would make comparisons difficult because of the vast differences among people's workloads. Additionally, any study would have to carefully protect the privacy of both the participants and those with whom they communicated via email.

Project members, in cooperation with external evaluators, developed a system-wide user test to evaluate how well RADAR's user interface and AI technologies assist a novice user. This section provides an overview of the test; a complete description can be found elsewhere [19]. The evaluation was designed to present participants with a challenging email overload workload that satisfied the following criteria. First, the tasks should be heterogeneous, just like in real-life. Second, some tasks could be handled quickly, while others would require significant effort. Third, dependencies should exist between some tasks, and doing those tasks out of order should result in wasted work or incorrect results. Fourth, email-centric properties such as subject lines should not be very helpful for grouping similar tasks or discerning efficient task orders. Fifth, users should not be expected to finish the test within the allotted time, so as to prevent ceiling effects in performance results.

The test presents participants with a simulated conference-planning scenario. Participants assume the role of the conference planner, filling in for the regular planner, Blake, who is indisposed. The simulated four-day, multitrack conference has keynotes, plenary talks, banquets, paper sessions, poster sessions, workshops, and so forth. Participants in our study must handle the outstanding conference planning tasks which have arrived in email, including many requests from the conference attendees. Blake's inbox contains these emails, which can be categorized as follows:

- **Scheduling:** Participants must update the database of event *constraints* (A/V requirements, meal preferences, attendee availabilities, and so forth) and conference room *properties* using an appropriate web form.
- **Website:** Attendees request changes to their contact information on the conference website. The participants must also update the website with the latest schedule.
- **Informational:** Attendees request information about the conference, generally concerning how the schedule has changed. The participants must author a reply email.
- **Vendors:** Attendees specify meal preferences and A/V requirements for events which then have to be forwarded to vendors using the vendor's web forms.
- **Briefing:** The conference chair requests a briefing summarizing the participant's progress at the end of the test. The inbox contains just one such request.

Participants also must deal with a conference crisis, which involves the loss of use of a significant number of rooms in which conference events had already been scheduled. Participants now need to find new rooms for the conference and adjust the schedule such that each event is placed in a room that satisfies the event's constraints, such as capacity, available equipment, seating arrangement, and so forth.

The tasks satisfy the criteria described earlier. Some tasks, such as informational requests, can be handled in around a minute, whereas other tasks, such as updating the conference schedule on the website, can take 15 minutes. Some emails contained over 20 tasks. An example of an intra-task dependency is that participants should handle the scheduling emails before updating the schedule on the website. Additionally, updating vendor orders requires submitting requests and waiting for email responses.

The test emails included anonymized real emails and fabricated ones, the latter necessary in part to make the emails consistent with the simulated world [19]. A team of under-graduate English majors was employed to create a detailed backstory email corpus, independent messages detailing one or more tasks, and noise messages, which were unrelated to the conference. The students were given a series of story arcs, guidelines, and a handful of characters with some specific assigned personalities (for example, formal, annoying, and so forth). Each study used the same backstory email corpus. However, to increase the validity of the tests, each study used a different *email set* of task and noise emails. An outside consultant customized those emails for each study. The consultant designed the emails to have comparable difficulty and task distribution. Between studies the stacks differed in the exact nature of the crisis—the specific rooms and times lost—and the details of the other email requests. These emails were kept secret until the test, so AI components could not train on them.

The test is designed to be hard—and it is. Over the past three years, approximately 400 people participated in the four major evaluations of different versions of RADAR; an additional 300 more people participated in interim evaluations. None of these people, including RADAR researchers, have been able to complete all of the tasks within the allotted time. We therefore think this evaluation approximates what a real person experiences, where it is often impossible to handle in one sitting all the emails that are pending.

The email set for the RADAR 3.0 study had 123 emails, of which 83 contained 153 tasks. The number of tasks is greater than the 102 task labels mentioned earlier, since some emails contained multiple tasks of the same type. The other 40 "noise" emails were unrelated to the conference.

Method

Conditions
The test used a between-subjects design with a single independent variable, *Assistance*, which had three levels: *Without Learning*, *Without MCA*, and *With MCA*.

In the *Without Learning* condition, most of RADAR's intelligent components were disabled. Specifically, the Action List initially had no email-based tasks since the Email Classifier was disabled, all the MCA advice was disabled, and the Progress Bar only showed the completed or deleted tasks. The main differences from the Action List in Figure 1 were that the "Order" column, the "Overflow Actions" table, and "Possibly Conference-Related Emails" table were not displayed, and the action tables were initially empty.

In the *Without MCA* condition, all of RADAR's AI components were enabled except for the MCA. The Action List contained the tasks that the Email Classifier found, and the "Possibly Conference-Related Actions" table contained emails. Again, the Progress Bar only showed the completed or deleted tasks. This condition was similar to RADAR 2.0. The main differences from the Action List in Figure 1 were that the "Order" column and the "Overflow Actions" table were not displayed.

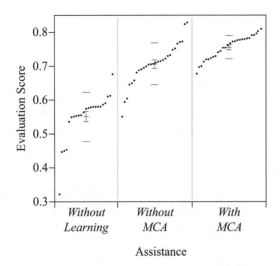

Figure 3: The evaluation scores show that the MCA advice in the *With MCA* condition significantly improved performance, reduced performance variation, and eliminated the long-tail of poor performance.

In the *With MCA* condition, all MCA functionality was enabled, as described in the previous sections.

Sessions
Each test session included up to 15 participants, who worked independently, and lasted up to 4.25 hours. In the first phase, which lasted 1.5 hours, participants learned about the test and received hands-on training with the software. After a break, participants started the two-hour testing session, which included another break after one hour. Then participants completed a survey and received payment, including extra payments for achieving specified milestones.

Participants
Participants were recruited from local universities and the general population using a human participant recruitment website. Participants were required to be between the ages of 18 and 65, be fluent in English, and not be affiliated with or working on RADAR. The study included 23 participants in the *Without Learning* condition, 28 participants in the *Without MCA* condition, and 28 participants in the *With MCA* condition. The number of participants varied among conditions since not all sessions yielded 15 usable data sets due to no-shows, participants who dropped out, participants who failed to make a good-faith effort, and software crashes or configuration issues that invalidated the data.

Results

Evaluation Score
An evaluation score, designed by external program evaluators, summarized overall performance into a single objective score ranging from 0.000 to 1.000, with higher scores reflecting better performance (for full details, see [10, 19]). It was important that this score be tied to objective conference planning performance rather than a technology-

specific algorithm (for example, F1 for classification). This technology-agnostic approach allowed us to compare performance across conditions given any technology. The score was calculated from points earned as a result of satisfying certain conditions, coupled with costs and penalties. These included the quality of the conference schedule (for example, constraints met, special requests handled), adequate briefing to the conference chair, accurate adjustment of the web site (for example, contact information changes, updating the schedule on the website), costs for the rooms, food, and equipment for the conference, and penalties for requesting that others give up existing room reservations. The score coefficients were two-thirds for the schedule, one-sixth for website updating, and one-sixth for briefing quality. On this measure, *With MCA* participants clearly outperformed *Without MCA* participants, who in turn outperformed *Without Learning* participants (ANOVA, $F(2,76) = 83.7$, $p < 0.0001$) (also see Figure 3).

Assistance	N	Mean	Std Dev
Without Learning	23	0.550	0.072
Without MCA	28	0.706	0.063
With MCA	28	0.754	0.035

A subsequent Tukey post-hoc test found that the three conditions were significantly different from each other. All but 3 of the 28 *With MCA* participants earned higher scores than the average score of the *Without MCA* participants. Additionally, the standard deviation of the evaluation score dropped 44% from the *Without MCA* to *With MCA* condition and the long-tail of poor performance in the *Without MCA* condition disappeared, as we had hoped.

Email Classification and the Task-Centric Action List
We examined how well the task-centric user interfaces helped participants evaluate the suggestions of the Email Classifier. The following table lists the average number of tasks for each outcome.

	Without MCA		With MCA	
True Positives (TP)	47.0		47.0	
Viewed	43.6	100.0%	38.4	100.0%
Completed	38.4	88.0%	34.1	89.0%
Deleted	2.0	4.5%	1.9	4.8%
Ignored	3.3	7.5%	2.4	6.1%
Not Viewed	3.4		8.6	
False Positives (FP)	6.0		6.0	
Viewed	5.8	100.0%	5.3	100.0%
Completed	0.7	12.3%	0.8	14.3%
Deleted	2.7	46.9%	2.5	48.3%
Ignored	2.5	42.6%	2.0	37.4%
Not Viewed	0.6		0.7	
False Negatives (FN)				
Completed	4.5		2.0	
True Negatives (TN)				
Completed	4.3		1.8	
FP & TN Completed	**5.0**		**2.6**	

Of the 47 correctly classified tasks (TP) that participants inspected (Viewed), participants completed the majority of them, and rarely erroneously deleted any. Additionally, of the six incorrectly classified tasks (FP) that the participants inspected (Viewed), participants deleted or ignored the vast majority of them, only occasionally erroneously completing one. However, participants did not complete many tasks that the classifier missed (FN). They also created and completed some tasks when they should not have (TN: emails that actually did not contain any tasks). The *Without MCA* participants completed over twice as many TN compared with the *With MCA* participants (4.3 vs. 1.8; $t(54) = 2.5152$, $p < 0.02$). Overall, combining both commission errors (FP Completed + TN Completed), the *Without MCA* participants incorrectly completed on average 5.0 tasks, and the *With MCA* participants incorrectly completed 2.6 tasks.

In the *Without Learning* condition the Email Classifier was disabled, so participants had to inspect emails to find tasks. These participants correctly completed on average 43.7 tasks but incorrectly completed 10.3 tasks (equivalent to TN); the errors accounted for 19% of the completed tasks. While the *With MCA* participants made errors based upon incorrect AI suggestions, the participants without the assistance made up to four times *more* mistakes (10.3 vs. 2.6).

Effects of the MCA's Task Strategy Recommendations
Since participants earned significantly better evaluation scores in the *With MCA* condition than in the *Without MCA* condition, we examined the completed tasks to see how MCA advice may have impacted their scores.

The MCA identified five critical task types: "Optimize the Schedule" (run the Schedule Optimizer), "Publish the Schedule" (run script that updates the schedule on the conference website), "Bulk Website Update" (change the same type of information for many people on the website), "Reschedule Vendor Orders" (fix the vendors associated with events that moved in the schedule), and "Send a Briefing" (write a briefing for the conference chairperson). The following table shows the number of participants in each condition who completed each of the critical tasks at least once.

Task Type	Without MCA	With MCA
Optimize the Schedule	27	28
Publish the Schedule	27	28
Bulk Website Update	13	25
Reschedule Vendor Orders	3	6
Send a Briefing	25	28

The "Reschedule Vendor Orders" task takes about 30 minutes to complete so few participants in either condition finished it. However, the percentage of correctly scheduled vendor orders (a measure of partial progress on this task) was significantly higher in the *With MCA* condition than in the *Without MCA* condition (51% vs. 29%; $t(54) = 2.3400$, $p < 0.05$). Additionally, the percentage of money wasted on incorrectly scheduled vendor orders (another measure of partial progress) significantly dropped in the *With MCA* condition (30% vs. 66%; $t(54) = 3.3061$, $p < 0.01$).

Participants in the *Without MCA* condition completed more total tasks (65.5 vs. 55.3; $t(54) = 2.4770$, $p < 0.02$) and more noncritical tasks (54.0 vs. 44.9; $t(54) = 2.671$, $p < 0.02$) than the *With MCA* participants did. Yet, the *With MCA* participants earned higher scores, because they did the more important tasks rather than just doing more tasks.

The following table shows that participants generally complied with the critical task warnings that the MCA issued.

Task Type	Issued	Complied	%
Late Critical	93	83	89%
Wrong Critical	25	14	56%
Early Critical	1	0	0%
Total	112	97	83%

Compliance with the "Late Critical" warnings was high. However, participants did not allows follow the "Wrong Critical" alerts. Five of these participants seemed to be averse to quitting what they were currently working on. This could be exacerbated by the fact that participants are instructed that critical tasks are special, and therefore they might believe that finishing the current one is more important than following the warning's advice.

In the *With MCA* condition, the average position of a task in the suggested schedule at the time that it was finished (either completed or deleted) was 5.0. Finished tasks were in the top position 21% of the time and within the top five 62% of the time. Since the *Without MCA* condition does not provide a suggested schedule, we computed the position of the task in the Action List when it was finished. In the *Without MCA* condition, the average position of tasks when it was finished was 11.6. Finished tasks were in the top position 18% of the time and within the top five 37% of the time. Finally, we found no significant difference for the number of times that participants followed the "next suggested task" link (19.2 in *With MCA* vs. 17.8 in *Without MCA*; $t(54) = 0.3246$, n.s.).

Discussion
The participants clearly found the AI systems helpful in performing their tasks. They were able to understand the AI component's suggestions and override them when in error. We looked for reasons why participants did not seem to be following the MCA's recommendation for the specific next task to do. It appears that users often were skipping the top one or two tasks over and over, suggesting that they did not want to do those specific tasks for some reason. Thus, participants were relying on the MCA to give them strategic advice of an overall order, but felt comfortable looking within the top few recommendations. This lends support to our mixed-initiative user interface rather than one that just presented the next task. Our pop-up alerts for critical tasks also were successful in focusing the user's attention on critical tasks they were ignoring in the other views.

CONCLUSION AND FUTURE WORK

Now that the RADAR techniques have proven so successful in our lab study that simulated a HSA's workload, we are eager to transition these techniques to a real email system with online learning. The main hurdle will be making the AI components robust enough for use with real-world tasks and emails, and integrating the AI technologies and the user interface with the real forms that are used to perform the tasks. Additionally, the HSA workload represents a subset of the work performed by office workers, and we are interested to see how our techniques apply to other workloads.

ACKNOWLEDGMENTS

The authors thank Michael Freed, Geoff Gordan, Jordan Hayes, Javier Hernandez, Matt Lahut, Pablo-Alejandro Quinones, Nicholas Sherman, Stephen Smith, Fernando de la Torre, Pradeep Varakantham, Jigar Vora, Yiming Yang, Shinjae Yoo, and Gabriel Zenarosa. This material is based upon work supported by the Defense Advanced Research Projects Agency (DARPA) under Contract No. NBCHD030010.

REFERENCES

1. Bellotti, V., Dalal, B., Good, N., Flynn, P., Bobrow, D.G. and Ducheneaut, N. What a To-Do: Studies of Task Management Towards the Design of a Personal Task List Manager. *Proc. CHI*, ACM Press (2004), 735–742.

2. Bellotti, V., Ducheneaut, N., Howard, M., Smith, I. and Grinter, R.E. Quality Versus Quantity: E-Mail-Centric Task Management and Its Relation With Overload. *Human-Computer Interaction 20*, 1/2 (2005), 89–138.

3. Bellotti, V. and Thornton, J.D. Managing Activities with TV-ACTA: TaskVista and Activity-Centered Task Assistant. *Proc. SIGIR Workshop on PIM*, (2006), 8–11.

4. Conley, K. and Carpenter, J. Towel: Towards an Intelligent To-Do List. *Proc. AAAI Spring Symposium on Interaction Challenges for Artificial Assistants*, AAAI Press (2007), 26–32.

5. Corston-Oliver, S., Ringger, E., Gamon, M. and Campbell, R. Task-focused Summarization of Email. *Proc. ACL Workshop on "Text Summarization Branches Out"*, Association for Computational Linguistics (2004), 43–50.

6. Ducheneaut, N. and Bellotti, V. E-mail as Habitat: An Exploration of Embedded Personal Information Management. *interactions 8*, 5 (2001), 30–38.

7. Fahlman, S.E. Marker-Passing Inference in the Scone Knowledge-Base System. *Proc. KSEM*, Springer (2006), 114–126.

8. Faulring, A., Mohnkern, K., Steinfeld, A. and Myers, B.A. The Design and Evaluation of User Interfaces for the RADAR Learning Personal Assistant. *AI Magazine 30*, 4 (2009), 74–84.

9. Fink, E., Bardak, U., Rothrock, B. and Carbonell, J.G. Scheduling with Uncertain Resources: Collaboration with the User. *Proc. IEEE SMC*, IEEE Press (2006), 11–17.

10. Freed, M., Carbonell, J., Gordon, G., Hayes, J., Myers, B., Siewiorek, D., Smith, S., Steinfeld, A. and Tomasic, A. RADAR: A Personal Assistant that Learns to Reduce Email Overload. *Proc. AAAI-08*, AAAI Press (2008), 1287–1293.

11. Garlan, D. and Schmerl, B. The RADAR Architecture for Personal Cognitive Assistance. *IJSEKE 17*, 2 (2007), 171–190.

12. Gwizdka, J. TaskView: Design and Evaluation of a Task-based Email Interface. *Proc. CASCON*, IBM Press (2002), 4.

13. Horvitz, E. Principles of Mixed-Initiative User Interfaces. *Proc. CHI*, ACM Press (1999), 159–166.

14. Horvitz, E., Jacobs, A. and Hovel, D. Attention-Sensitive Alerting. *Proc. UAI 1999*, Morgan Kaufman (1999), 305–313.

15. Kumar, M., Das, D. and Rudnicky, A.I. Summarizing Non-textual Events with a 'Briefing' Focus. *Proc. RIAO*, Centre De Hautes Etudes Internationales D'Informatique Documentaire (2007).

16. Myers, K., Berry, P., Blythe, J., Conley, K., Gervasio, M., McGuinness, D., Morley, D., Pfeffer, A., Pollack, M. and Tambe, M. An Intelligent Personal Assistant for Task and Time Management. *AI Magazine 28*, 2 (2007), 47–61.

17. Nyberg, E., Riebling, E., Wang, R.C. and Frederking, R. Integrating a Natural Language Message Pre-Processor with UIMA. *Proc. LREC Workshop on "Towards Enhanced Interoperability for Large HLT Systems: UIMA for NLP"*, (2008), 28–31.

18. Shneiderman, B. and Maes, P. Direct Manipulation vs. Interface Agents. *interactions 4*, 6 (1997), 42–61.

19. Steinfeld, A., Bennett, S.R., Cunningham, K., Lahut, M., Quinones, P.-A., Wexler, D., Siewiorek, D., Hayes, J., Cohen, P., Fitzgerald, J., Hansson, O., Pool, M. and Drummond, M. Evaluation of an Integrated Multi-Task Machine Learning System with Humans in the Loop. *Proc. PerMIS*, NIST (2007).

20. Steinfeld, A., Quinones, P.-A., Zimmerman, J., Bennett, S.R. and Siewiorek, D. Survey Measures for Evaluation of Cognitive Assistants. *Proc. PerMIS*, NIST (2007).

21. Stylos, J., Myers, B.A. and Faulring, A. Citrine: Providing Intelligent Copy and Paste. *Proc. UIST*, ACM Press (2004), 185–188.

22. Varakantham, P. and Smith, S. Linear Relaxation Techniques for Task Management in Uncertain Settings. *Proc. ICAPS*, AAAI Press (2008), 363–371.

23. Whittaker, S., Bellotti, V. and Gwizdka, J. Email in Personal Information Management. *CACM 49*, 1 (2006), 68–73.

24. Whittaker, S. and Sidner, C. Email Overload: Exploring Personal Information Management of Email *Proc. CHI*, ACM Press (1996), 276–283.

25. Yang, Y., Yoo, S., Zhang, J. and Kisiel, B. Robustness of Adaptive Filtering Methods in a Cross-Benchmark Evaluation. *Proc. SIGIR*, ACM Press (2005), 98–105.

26. Yang, Y., Zhang, J. and Kisiel, B. A Scalability Analysis of Classifiers in Text Categorization. *Proc. SIGIR*, ACM Press (2003), 96–103.

27. Zimmerman, J., Tomasic, A., Simmons, I., Hargraves, I., Mohnkern, K., Cornwell, J. and McGuire, R.M. VIO: A Mixed-initiative Approach to Learning and Automating Procedural Update Tasks. *Proc. CHI*, ACM Press (2007), 1445–1454.

An Adaptive Calendar Assistant Using Pattern Mining for User Preference Modelling

Alfred Krzywicki, Wayne Wobcke and Anna Wong
School of Computer Science and Engineering
University of New South Wales
Sydney NSW 2052, Australia
{alfredk,wobcke,annawong}@cse.unsw.edu.au

ABSTRACT

In this paper, we present SmartCal, a calendar assistant that suggests appointment attributes, such as time, day, duration, etc., given any combination of initial user input attributes. SmartCal uses closed pattern mining to discover patterns in past appointment data in order to represent user preferences and adapt to changing user preferences over time. The SmartCal interface is designed to be minimally intrusive: users are free to choose or ignore suggestions, which are dynamically updated as users enter new information. The user model as a collection of patterns is intuitive and transparent: users can view and edit existing patterns or create new patterns based on existing appointments. SmartCal was evaluated in a user study with four users over a four week period. The user study shows that pattern mining makes appointment creation more efficient and users regarded the appointment suggestion feature favourably.

Author Keywords

Data Mining, Personal Assistants, Calendar Management

ACM Classification Keywords

H.5.2 Information Interfaces and Presentation: User Interfaces—*Graphical user interfaces (GUI)*; H.2.8 Information Systems: Database Applications—*Data mining*; I.2.11 Distributed Artificial Intelligence: Intelligent agents

General Terms

Algorithms, Design, Experimentation, Human Factors

INTRODUCTION

The problem of scheduling meetings is difficult because of the number and complexity of interrelated constraints needed to be resolved. Maes [10] proposed the idea of personal assistants to perform such complex tasks on behalf of users. Personal assistants not only aim to hide task complexity from the user, but also to learn user preferences and adapt to changing preferences over time. In the domain of time manage-

ment, early work by Dent *et al.* [4] advocated the use of decision tree learning or a combination of learning and predefined rules for the suggestion of appointment features. Typically these methods can achieve reasonable accuracy, but require many training cases before an acceptable level of accuracy is reached, a serious impediment to deployment.

Generating useful suggestions for appointment features is difficult because there are usually many conflicting preferences that must be consistently combined to produce coherent suggestions compatible with the user's existing schedule. The desired scenario is where a user initially specifies values for any number of attribute(s) of an appointment, e.g. the category, day or attendees, and the task of the system is to predict any or all of the remaining attribute values. Moreover, the number and types of the intended specified attributes in an appointment solution is not fixed; some appointments may require values only for mandatory attributes such as the title, time, date and duration, while others may also have optional attributes specified, such as location, attendees, priority, etc. The requirement that the input/output set of attributes be flexible makes the problem harder to solve.

In this paper, we present SmartCal, a calendar assistant that generates appointment feature suggestions from initial user input attribute values. SmartCal uses *closed frequent patterns* as a representation of user preferences to provide the flexibility of allowing arbitrary user input attributes. A pattern is simply a relation between any number of attribute values that typically occur together, e.g. research meetings are on Wednesdays at 10:30am. Critical to usability is the development of suitable methods for ranking solutions (i.e. potential appointments) and computing suggestions from solutions for presentation to the user (i.e. solutions consistent with the user's schedule), because users will typically only examine a very small number of suggestions.

The rest of the paper is structured as follows. We first summarize the definitions relating to closed pattern mining, describe how pattern mining is used to generate solutions in SmartCal, and briefly summarize an initial validation of the approach. Next we discuss the design of the SmartCal interface. Then we present a user study of SmartCal with four users over a four week period focusing on suggestion accuracy, usability and the effectiveness of the ranking algorithm. Finally, we discuss related research and summarize our results and potential future work.

APPOINTMENT FEATURE GENERATION

In this section, we summarize the data mining and appointment feature generation methods used in SmartCal. The algorithms are described in more detail in Krzywicki and Wobcke [8].

Definitions

The underlying theory of closed patterns is based on Formal Concept Analysis, Wille [15]. Pasquier *et al.* [13] extended the theory and introduced the idea of *closed patterns*, applying Formal Concept Analysis to data mining. The key terminology of this theory as well as the basic definitions related to the calendar domain are summarized below.

The basic element of a calendar appointment is an attribute-value pair, called a ***feature***, for example: Category="Team Meeting". The attributes used in the calendar domain are Title, Category, Period, Day, AmPm (either "am" or "pm"), Time, Duration, Location and Attendees (a list of names). The AmPm attribute is useful for representing general user preferences for meeting times. An attribute may appear in an appointment at most once and may not occur at all.

For the purpose of illustrating the data mining concepts used in this paper, we use the following example features:
Category="Meeting" or "Lecture",
Period="Semester" or "Break",
Day="Monday" or "Wednesday",
Time=10:00 or 14:00,
Location="Room 401k" or "Room 501"

A ***pattern*** is any part of an appointment, more precisely, a set of features containing at least one feature, but in practice at least two features.

A ***closed frequent pattern*** is a maximal set of features common to a maximal set of objects. Since objects in the calendar domain are appointments, a closed frequent pattern encapsulates a largest possible chunk of information, which can be treated as a user preference. We therefore use closed frequent patterns as building blocks to construct future calendar appointments. The concept of closed patterns in the calendar domain is illustrated in Figure 1.

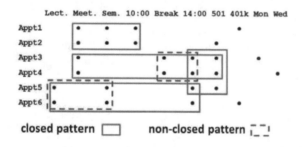

Figure 1. Closed vs Non-Closed Patterns

In this figure, each pattern is a set of at least two calendar features occurring in at least two appointments. For example a pattern:
Category="Meeting", Period="Semester", Time=10:00

occurs in appointments 1 and 2. Since no other appointment has this exact set of features and since no other features are common to this exact set of appointments, this pattern is a closed pattern. In contrast, the pattern:
Category="Lecture", Period="Semester"
which is common to appointments 5 and 6 is not closed, as the feature:
Time=14:00
is also common to these appointments.

A candidate for an appointment created by SmartCal from initial user input features is called a ***solution***. A number of solutions can be selected by the system and presented to the user as ***suggestions***. Solutions may be built from more than one pattern. A critical issue is how to combine patterns to create solutions. In our prior work, we investigated a number of possibilities based on whether patterns are overlapping or conflicting with one another and/or the initial user input feature set.

Two features are ***overlapping*** if they have the same attribute.

Two features are ***conflicting*** if they have the same attribute with different values.

Two patterns are ***conflicting*** if they contain at least one pair of conflicting features. We also call two conflicting patterns ***inconsistent***.

Two patterns are ***overlapping*** if they contain overlapping features.

Our solution generation algorithm uses either non-conflicting or non-overlapping patterns. Note that conflicting patterns are always overlapping, therefore non-overlapping implies non-conflicting. Examples of pairs of patterns illustrating the remaining possibilities are shown in Figure 2, where features in green (bold) are overlapping and features in red (italics) are conflicting.

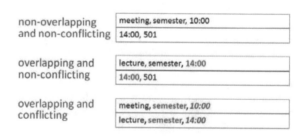

Figure 2. Conflicting and Overlapping Patterns

Mining Closed Frequent Patterns

The data mining algorithm used in SmartCal is based on the FP-Growth algorithm introduced by Han, Pei and Yin [6]. For compatibility with our earlier software, we used the Java implementation of FP-Growth by Coenen, Goulbourne and Leng [3]. The algorithm uses an FP-Tree (Frequent Pattern Tree) to store all itemsets and find frequent patterns. In order to find closed frequent patterns, we filter out all non-closed patterns as they arrive from the FP-Growth method.

More precisely, closed frequent patterns are mined in two steps: (1) build an FP-Tree from the database of past cases, and (2) retrieve frequent patterns from the FP-Tree, filtering out all non-closed patterns. Coenen, Goulbourne and Leng [3] use a T-Tree structure (Total Support Tree) to store frequent patterns and their support. In our implementation, we store only closed frequent patterns in the T-Tree, which provides fast access to the set of closed frequent patterns. We modified the algorithm to generate the frequent patterns in order of size from largest to smallest. This allows us to filter out non-closed patterns using the following property, due to Pasquier *et al.* [13]: the support of any pattern is the same as the support of the smallest closed pattern containing it. Therefore any frequent pattern properly contained in the smallest closed pattern is not a closed pattern. By testing this condition as frequent patterns are generated, our algorithm discovers all closed frequent patterns.

Generating Solutions

Patterns found in the data mining process are used as building blocks to construct calendar appointment solutions. Individual patterns may complement one another, conflict or overlap (as defined above). In order to generate useful suggestions, we aim to efficiently find solutions that make use of as many patterns as possible. We examined two methods for generating solutions: the "non-conflicting" and the "non-overlapping" methods. The "non-conflicting" method combines only patterns that do not have conflicting features. The "non-overlapping" method is more strict and does not allow overlapping features. The algorithm presented below uses the "non-conflicting" method for pattern selection, which was shown to give higher accuracy in initial validation.

Algorithm 1 (Generating solutions)
1   SolutionList = {}
2   InitialSolution = initial user features
3   PatternList = all patterns not conflicting and having
4   common feature(s) with InitialSolution
5   UnusedPatternList = PatternList
6   **Do Until** UnusedPatternList is empty
7   Solution = InitialSolution
8   Patterns = non-conflicting patterns from
9   UnusedPatternList that do not conflict with
10   Solution patterns
11   Add Patterns to Solution
12   Patterns = non-conflicting patterns from PatternList
13   that do not conflict with Solution patterns
14   Add Patterns to Solution
15   Add Solution to SolutionList
16   Remove all Solution patterns from
17   UnusedPatternList
18 **End Do**

The algorithm is not guaranteed to find all possible solutions, though it has been experimentally verified to provide sufficient time performance and solution quality, and importantly, generates a variety of solutions (i) that the user can easily distinguish from one another, and (ii) that are more likely to include a useful suggestion amongst the top five generated. The algorithm first computes a set of all patterns that do not conflict with, but have at least one common fea-

ture with, the initial user features. The algorithm heuristically finds subsets of these patterns jointly consistent with the initial user features; each such set is extended to one maximal set of non-conflicting features.

As an example, suppose the initial features are as follows:
Category="Meeting", Period="Semester"
Further suppose that the existing patterns are as follows (the closed patterns from Figure 1 with some additional patterns):
P1. Category="Meeting", Period="Semester", Time=10:00
P2. Category="Meeting", Period="Break", Time=14:00,
Location="Room 501"
P3. Category="Lecture", Period="Semester", Time=14:00,
P4. Time=14:00, Location="Room 501"
P5. Period="Semester", Day="Monday", Time=10:00,
Location="Room 401k"
P6. Category="Meeting", Day="Wednesday", Location="Room 501"

The initial solution (line 2) is just the initial set of features entered by the user. Since patterns P2 and P3 are conflicting with the initial solution and P4 has no common features with the initial solution, the PatternList and UnusedPatternList sets (lines 3–5) contain only patterns P1, P5 and P6. Solutions always start with an initial user solution (line 7). A new solution is generated in lines 8–14. In lines 8–10, P1 and P5 are retrieved as not conflicting with InitialSolution and having common features with InitialSolution. They also do not conflict with each other. Since the initial solution has no associated patterns, P1 and P5 are added and the solution becomes:

Category="Meeting", Period="Semester", Day="Monday",
Time=10:00, Location="Room 401k"

The procedure then continues to add patterns from the PatternsList set (lines 12–14), but there is nothing new to add at this stage. Therefore the first solution is complete and UnusedPatternList is updated (lines 16–17). UnusedPatternList is still not empty, so the solution generation iterates again, this time adding P6 to the initial solution, generating the second solution, as follows:

Category="Meeting", Period="Semester", Day="Wednesday",
Location="Room 501"

As with the first solution, the procedure checks if there is anything to add from PatternsList set (lines 12–14) and finds P1 as non-conflicting with the current solution, therefore the second solution becomes:

Category="Meeting", Period="Semester", Day="Wednesday",
Time=10:00, Location="Room 501"

At this stage UnusedPatternList becomes empty, therefore the algorithm concludes with two solutions stored in SolutionList.

Initial Validation

We briefly summarize the results of an experimental validation of the closed pattern mining approach for solution generation (see Krzywicki and Wobcke [8] for more details). To determine the best approach, plus to compare pattern mining with decision tree and other learning methods, we ran a simulation of a calendar system on 16 months of real data taken from a single user's calendar.

We examined two methods for combining patterns to generate solutions: one that uses non-conflicting patterns and another that uses non-overlapping patterns. The simulation results showed that the accuracy of prediction was much higher for solutions generated from non-conflicting patterns than from non-overlapping patterns. This can be explained by the way solutions are created. It is generally easier to find overlapping patterns in a solution than non-overlapping, hence the former method creates a higher number and variety of solutions.

By comparing the prediction results for closed pattern mining and decision tree learning, we observed that closed pattern mining gave significantly better prediction in the first 200 cases, which is an important difference for interactive calendar users (corresponding to roughly 3 months of appointments). Moreover, decision tree learning prediction is less stable, showing greater sensitivity to user preference changes in transition periods. One important reason for this instability is that each attribute is predicted separately, which, in some cases, makes the solution incompatible with user preferences. The closed pattern mining method, in contrast, due to the closedness property, uses maximal and consistent patterns.

THE CALENDAR ASSISTANT

In this section, we state the SmartCal design objectives, describe the method for ranking solutions and provide an example of user interaction with SmartCal in the process of creating an appointment.

SmartCal Design

The primary purpose of SmartCal is to assist the user with creating appointments based on user preferences represented as patterns mined from previous appointment data. In contrast to other calendar assistants, where the user is, to some degree, required to provide feedback from which the system learns (Dent *et al.* [4], Berry *et al.* [1]), our objective was that the calendar assistant is completely non-intrusive, allowing the user to define appointments with or without the assistance of the system. An additional requirement is that the suggestions should be updated dynamically as the user input changes, without the need for user intervention. Another important design factor is that, in order to maintain the user's trust in the system, the presentation of the preferences to the user must be understandable and transparent: the user should be able to see preference patterns for any appointment and a list of all patterns. In addition, some users may wish to manage their patterns, including addition, deletion, editing and creating new patterns. We aimed at providing all this functionality to the user. We chose closed frequent patterns for the representation of user preferences to meet the requirement of flexible input/output attributes: the user may start defining an appointment from any attribute as an input and the system must be able to supply any or all of the remaining attributes. Note that this flexibility could not be provided using association rules because of their fixed antecedent-consequent structure. The "non-conflicting" method was used for generating appointment solutions.

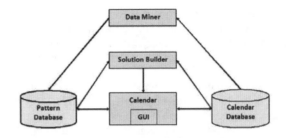

Figure 3. SmartCal System Components

The overall system design of the calendar assistant is shown in Figure 3. After each completed field in the new appointment form, SmartCal runs the Solution Builder to check if any new suggestions can be made to the user. If so, and if the Suggestion window is not displayed, a new pop-up window is displayed with the suggestions. If the Suggestion window is already displayed, the window is updated with the new suggested features. An important issue is exactly *when* to first display the Suggestion window. We need to have confidence that the suggestions are valid and that the window does not distract the user from entering data. Reliable suggestions can be generated from just one feature, but we need to ensure that the user has completed the input to that field before showing any suggestions. In SmartCal, the Suggestion window is displayed after the user moves to edit another field or after a few seconds with no typing or other mouse activity. This delay is intended to ensure that the user has completed the input in the current field.

The Suggestion pop-up window is non-intrusive, so the user can continue editing without interruption. The Suggestion window is displayed at an early stage of appointment creation to give the user a chance to select a suggestion as soon as possible. At any time, the user can also trigger suggestion generation manually. If the user accepts a suggestion, the suggestion data is copied to the appointment form and the user can continue editing until the new appointment is fully defined. After the appointment is stored in the Calendar Database, SmartCal re-rates the patterns associated with the new appointment. This occurs only if the system suggestion has been accepted or the Suggestion window was closed by the user. Next, the Data Miner runs its mining program and adds new closed frequent patterns, if any, to the Pattern Database.

Apart from creating appointments, SmartCal enables the user to create new patterns based on existing appointment data, to edit existing patterns and to view a number of highest weighted patterns. In addition, the user can also define appointments directly from selected patterns. However, we expected that these functions would not be often used.

A suggestion always includes a time and date for the appointment, since every appointment must have these features specified eventually. If, for a given suggestion, these features are not determined by the solution, SmartCal adopts the strategy of presenting the next available free slot that is consistent with the generated solution. This heuristic is valid

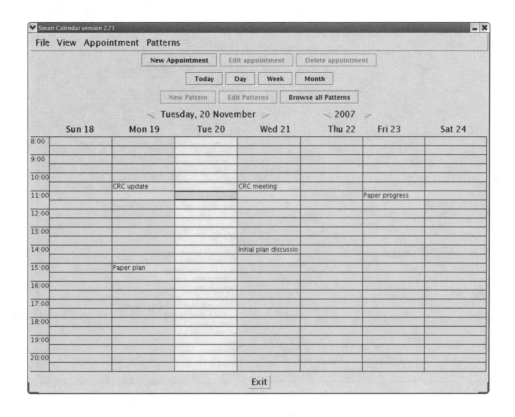

Figure 4. SmartCal Week View

in some contexts (such as doctor's appointments), but was not expected to be universally applicable. The idea was that presenting some time and date was better than presenting no time and date, and that eventually the right patterns would be discovered to enable personalized time and date suggestion.

Another design issue is whether to allow overlapping appointments. SmartCal does allow overlapping appointments as it was felt that this feature would be useful, as indeed was the case (see below). However, the system never gives the user any suggestions for meeting times that overlap with appointments in the calendar. When the user enters an appointment that overlaps with another, a warning is issued.

Ranking Solutions

SmartCal must include a mechanism for ranking solutions, since only a few suggestions are ever likely to be examined by the user when creating an appointment. Pattern weighting is used for ranking solutions in order to select the best appointment suggestions. The weight of a pattern is a number between 0 and 1 expressed as a percentage. Patterns receive an initial weight based on their support in previous appointment data. For example, a pattern present in 60 appointments out of 100 would have an initial weight of 60%.

During user sessions, a pattern's weight is adjusted up or down (or remains unchanged) according to the following rules:

Rule 1: Increment the weight of all patterns used to build a solution selected by the user (to a maximum of 1).

Rule 2: Decrement the weight of all patterns used to build solutions presented to the user but not selected (to a minimum of 0).

Rule 2 is also applicable if the user rejects all suggestions by closing the Suggestion window. The weight remains unchanged if the user ignores the suggestions, that is, if the user neither selects anything nor closes the Suggestion window. If a pattern occurs on both selected and non-selected solutions, the pattern weight is both increased and decreased.

The selection of the increments and decrements affects the system's time to adjust weights to accommodate change in user preferences. If the values are high, the re-ranking of solutions occurs sooner, but may cause the system to "forget" previously learnt information and result in less stable behaviour. If, on the other hand, the values are too low, the changes would be fine-grained but too slow to be useful for the user. A value of 0.1 was chosen for both increment and decrement based on the results of simulation over one user's calendar data.

Note that if the user selects a suggestion and then modifies the features, the pattern weight is still increased (even though the pattern is somehow "wrong"). However, the new appointment is entered into the Calendar Database, so the Data Miner will discover a new pattern covering these new features, which, as it is used, will eventually become more highly ranked than the original "incorrect" pattern. In this way, even incorrect patterns can be of benefit to the user, and SmartCal can adapt to the user's real preferences.

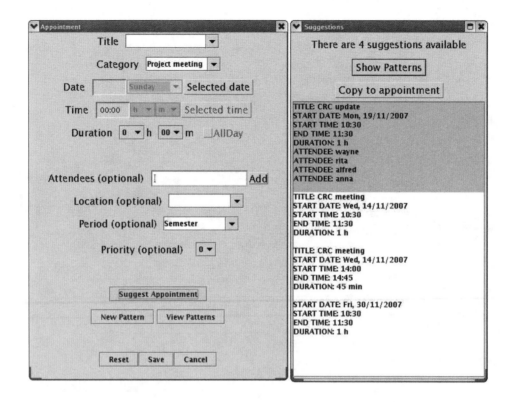

Figure 5. New Appointment and Suggestion Windows

User Interaction

The solutions generated using pattern mining and ranked according to pattern weightings must be turned into specific suggestions given to the user in the context of creating an appointment. This requires finding a free timeslot in the user's calendar compatible with each selected solution. SmartCal takes all features of the solution related to the date and time, i.e. Day, AmPm, Time and Duration, and evaluates these features against available timeslots in the calendar. If a matching timeslot is found, the candidate appointment is assigned its time and date (if there are several matches, the earliest is chosen) and presented to the user as a suggestion. Suggestions from the top five ranked solutions (only the new predicted attributes) are presented to the user: when there are equally ranked solutions, the suggestions are presented in time order. The choice of five presented suggestions is based on what users can see in the Suggestion window.

The way SmartCal works is illustrated in the following example. Suppose that the calendar already contains a number of appointments, as shown in the week view in Figure 4. Now suppose the user opens the New Appointment window and enters the following attribute values (see Figure 5):

Category="Project meeting",
Period="semester"

The Suggestion window pops up displaying four suggestions, as shown in Figure 5. No user action is required at this point; if the user chooses to continue entering data, the Suggestion window remains open, updating suggestions dynamically. Alternatively, the user may select the most suitable suggestion and then click the "Copy to Appointment" button to supplement already entered features with the suggested ones. If the user chooses the first suggestion from the list, the New Appointment window is updated, showing the following details:

Title="CRC update",
Category="Project meeting",
Date = "19 Nov, Monday",
Time = 10:30,
Duration = 1 h,
Attendees = "wayne, rita, alfred, anna",
Category="Project meeting",
Period="semester"

The user may also display the Suggestion window on request by clicking on the "Suggest Appointment" button if the window was previously closed. Patterns used to generate the selected suggestion, shown below, can be displayed by clicking on the "Show Patterns" button.

90%	Category="Project meeting", Time=10:30, AmPm="am"
80%	Day="Monday", Duration=60, Period="semester"
50%	Day="Monday", Period="semester"
50%	AmPm="am", Period="semester"
40%	Time=1030, AmPm="am", Period="semester"
30%	Category="Project meeting", AmPm="am"
20%	Title="CRC update", Category="Project meeting", Time=1030, AmPm="am", Day="Monday"
10%	Time=1030, AmPm="am", Day="Monday", Period="semester"
0%	Time=1030, AmPm="am", Day="Monday", Attendees="wayne, rita, alfred, anna", Period="semester"

The left column shows the weight of the pattern. Note that the last pattern has zero weight as an effect of rejecting associated suggestions in previous user sessions. As can be seen, all patterns in this list contain at least one attribute in common with the initial solution, do not conflict with the initial solution, and contribute new features to the solution.

USER STUDY

To evaluate the SmartCal calendar assistant, a small-scale user study was conducted. Our main goal was to assess the quality of the appointment suggestions provided by the assistant. The secondary goals were to assess the usability of the calendar assistant and observe how users interacted with the system and made use of the suggestions.

Method

There were four participants in the study, one male and three female, ranging from 18 to 55 years old, with a variety of occupations. Users 1 and 2 were students with a computing background. User 3 was a postdoctoral fellow and user 4 a department secretary, both with limited computing experience. Users 1–3 were heavily involved in organizing extra-curricular activities in addition to their work, so defined a mixture of regular and one-off meetings during the study. User 4 was defining appointments on behalf of the department head. Most users had some experience using other software calendaring systems. All users had Smart-Cal installed on their computers and were asked to perform a series of tasks typically done in a calendaring application, e.g. adding, changing and cancelling appointments. Users were then asked to use the suggestions, with guidance given by the experimenter where necessary. Information on how to add, delete and change new patterns was also explained to them, although this functionality was not essential for normal calendar usage. SmartCal was used continuously for four weeks by participants, with weekly interviews assessing their impressions of the accuracy of the suggestions offered, the system's performance, and any usability or technical issues they came across during the week. At the end of the four weeks, users were administered a final questionnaire, with questions focusing on the quality of the suggestions produced and their satisfaction with the general performance of the system over the whole period.

Results and Discussion

Table 1 provides a summary of user and system activity over the period of the study. On average, users manually entered about 41 appointments, out of which 59% were defined using system suggestions. Users 1 and 2 imported a large number of appointments from their existing calendar system before using SmartCal. The number of patterns per appointment for these users is lower than for users 3 and 4. This may suggest two things. Firstly, appointments for users 1 and 2 may have a higher degree of regularity and consistency than users 3 and 4, therefore a smaller number of patterns are needed to cover the appointments. This is particularly evident for user 3, who started a new project during the user study, enabling the system to generate more patterns. Secondly, as we expected, the number of patterns shows a tendency to saturate as the number of appointments increased.

This may suggest that most of the useful patterns have been discovered.

The last two columns in the table show the average rank of selected suggestions and the average number of suggestions per appointment for each user. In order to evaluate the ranking mechanism, we counted only cases where more than two suggestions were presented to the user. Generally, selected suggestions were ranked highly, with variations that can be explained by the way suggestions were used. We expected that users would use the title and category features to trigger the generation of other features, such as duration, location and time of day. We also expected that users would ignore all useless suggestions. By analysing activity logs, we found however that users selected suggestions that were partially correct and then changed some values for the final appointment. This resulted in the ranking for incorrect patterns being increased and less accurate subsequent suggestions. This is evident for users 1 and 4, who tended to enter a large number of initial attributes and accepted suggestions with little additional information. User 3, on the other hand, often entered the title and/or category and had the largest number of useful suggestions.

Considering the general usability of the calendar assistant, most users were easily able to perform tasks considered standard (e.g. add, delete and change an appointment): all users rated the basic functionality positively (average responses: add 4.5, delete 4.25, change 3.5 on a 5-point Likert scale where the question is whether it was easy to perform the function, and 1=strongly disagree, 3=neither agree nor disagree, 5=strongly agree). Users 1 and 3 experimented with creating and editing their own patterns. A detailed examination of user logs revealed that user 1 added 4 patterns, of which two were actually used in later appointments. User 3 added one pattern, which was not used in any later appointments.

To evaluate the user perception of the suggestions generated, users were asked about the suggestions presented to them by SmartCal both weekly and at the end of the four week period. Users liked that the assistant provided suggestions for their appointments (average rating 4.25 on a 5-point Likert scale where 1=strongly disagree, 3=neither agree nor disagree, 5=strongly agree), typically receiving suggestions for appointments some to most of the time (average rating 2.75 on a 5-point Likert scale where 1=none of the time, 3=some of the time, 5=all the time). Inspection of data files after testing showed that, as expected, SmartCal tended to generate more suggestions as the number of defined appointments increased, as shown in Figure 6.

Initially, users 1 and 2, who imported their appointments from other calendars, had more suggestions. However, after about 15 appointments were entered manually, a similar number of suggestions were generated for users 3 and 4. This shows that SmartCal was able to adapt quickly to user preferences by generating useful patterns.

User	Appointments	Appointments defined by user	Appointments defined using suggestions	Patterns	Patterns per appointment	Rank of used suggestions	Suggestions per appointment
User 1	460	25	12	433	0.94	1.0	3.0
User 2	407	39	25	296	0.73	1.4	3.5
User 3	48	48	26	112	2.33	1.9	4.1
User 4	54	54	38	57	1.05	1.0	3.4

Table 1. Accuracy and Use of Suggestions

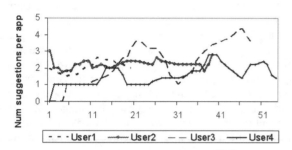

Figure 6. Number of Suggestions

User	Accurate	Inaccurate	% correct
User 1	11	0	100
User 2	8	9	47
User 3	10	8	55
User 4	13	11	54

Table 2. Duration Prediction Accuracy

Over the course of several weeks, the attributes which individual users found to be most useful often changed. In particular, the schedule of user 3 changed considerably over the four weeks, where a project finished and another started. The user found that the usefulness of attributes changed from title and duration to category and title. During the week where the projects changed, the quality and quantity of the calendar's suggestions was affected. However, during the remaining weeks of the study, it is interesting to note (Figure 6) that SmartCal was able to adapt to the change and produce more reliable suggestions for title and category by the end of the user study. A similar issue was reported by Mitchell *et al.* [11], where the calendar prediction accuracy decreased around the boundaries of semester and break periods.

The question of how often suggestions were used varied from user to user (responses ranged from a little to a lot of the time, average rating 2.75 on a 5-point Likert scale where 1=none of the time, 3=some of the time, 5=all the time). The use of patterns is highly dependent on the nature of the appointments created by the users and does not necessarily reflect the quality of the patterns discovered. In particular, since users 1–3 defined a number of one-off meetings in addition to their regular appointments, it was less likely that these one-off meetings could be covered by previously discovered patterns. Further information derived from the interviews found that frequency of use was dependent on the

quality of the suggestions produced. Inspection of the data logs showed that on average, users defined their appointments using suggestions 59% of the time (Table 1), indicating that SmartCal was producing relatively accurate suggestions.

All users found that some attributes had more accurate suggestions than others. For the majority of users, on a week-by-week basis as well as averaged over the four weeks, the duration attribute produced the most accurate suggestions. This result is consistent with that of Mitchell *et al.* [11], who found that duration was relatively easy to predict accurately. Table 2 shows the results for duration accuracy. The average accuracy is 52% for users 2, 3 and 4. User 1 decided to select only suggestions with accurate duration; therefore the number of incorrect duration values was not available for this user.

Finally, in the post-study questionnaire, users provided some general feedback on the features they would have liked in SmartCal. As SmartCal was not intended to be a fully functional calendar system, we do not regard the lack of these features as limitations of SmartCal or of the pattern mining technique, but are reported here as interesting possibilities for future work. Some of the users' comments reflect the particular way they used the system, so cannot be taken as general requirements.

User 1 would have liked a means to specify deadlines: this user worked around the lack of support for deadlines by turning an end-of-day deadline into a single day-long appointment, effectively preventing the system from suggesting other meetings on the same day. What was desired was a way to specify that the day should include an amount of appointment-free time to work on the task due by the deadline. Similarly, user 4 would have liked a way to specify all-day events that were not appointments, so would not prevent the system from suggesting appointments on that day. Our earlier work on this type of problem, Wobcke [16], considered scheduling longer "activities" with fuzzy deadlines over several blocks of time, however this is not quite what was required.

User 4 made special use of overlapping meetings. In particular, the department head is often obliged to attend meetings that overlap. However, rather than viewing this as a conflict in the calendar, the department head would typically attend the first meeting, then decide during that meeting whether to leave early to attend the second meeting, or whether to continue at the first meeting and arrive late to the second meeting. This scenario shows that calendaring cannot be regarded as simply a traditional scheduling problem where tasks cannot overlap. In SmartCal, overlapping appointments are allowed (however were never suggested to users), but it was not clearly visible in the interface when appointments were overlapping (prompting the user's comment in the questionnaire). User 2 also made use of overlapping meetings.

User 4 also arranged a number of short "drop in" meetings, where people wanted to see the department head for a short time. The user wanted a way to indicate in the calendar that several such meetings would occur at unspecified times in a single timeslot, allowing the department head the means of confining such "scheduled interruptions" to certain periods of the day. As far as we know, no current calendar system adequately supports such a feature.

In addition, user 4 wanted a convenient way of defining a series of repeated meetings (such as weekly management meetings). However, suggesting times for such meetings would have required more complex patterns, and so was not included in the current version of the system.

RELATED WORK

As far as we know, there are no other calendar applications supported by pattern mining, however there are examples of research where some kind of machine learning has been applied for the representation of user preferences. One of the first papers on this topic was Kozierok and Maes [7], where memory-based reasoning was used to predict user actions in particular situations involving the use of a calendar system. Typically, however, the tasks considered were simpler than appointment feature generation, such as determining whether the user would accept, reject or request renegotiation of a proposed meeting request.

Dent *et al.* [4] used a number of methods in the CAP system to provide suggestions for various appointment parameters. For learning they used two competing methods: neural networks and ID3. The results from both methods were converted into rules and stored in the system. The learnt rules were supplemented with hand-coded rules, which gave better accuracy in the first 150 cases. After that, the learnt rules generally achieved higher accuracy. Our pattern based calendar system achieved a reasonable prediction accuracy for duration (52% on average, Table 2) after about 30 cases. Another difference is that CAP predicts each attribute of the appointment separately, which may have potential consistency problems.

Another preference learning calendar assistant is PTIME, Berry *et al.* [1]; a more recent overview of PTIME as incorporated into the CALO project is given in Myers *et al.* [12]. PTIME is designed to schedule meetings in the open calendar environment. Unlike our calendar system, designed to build and present suggestions non-intrusively, PTIME requires the user to choose amongst suggestions in order to generate training data for learning user preferences. To generate useful suggestions before sufficiently many training examples are provided, PTIME also enables the user to explic-

itly specify general preferences and constraints (e.g. Tuesday is preferred to Wednesday, all else being equal). A more sophisticated approach is given in Berry *et al.* [2], where multi-attribute utility theory is used to define a user preference function, but again in terms of a mixture of explicitly expressed preferences and information implicit in user selections from amongst several alternatives presented during system operation. However, we believe preferences elicited in this way may be unreliable and/or incomplete, because they are typically specified in advance and out of the context of a particular appointment, so users will have difficulty articulating them. Moreover, the Choquet integral approach used in Berry *et al.* [2] simplifies for computational reasons the complexity of the preference model, but potentially at the cost of being unable to express some of the user's real preferences. SmartCal also provides a function allowing the user to define patterns representing preferences, but these patterns are extracted from existing appointments, when users are aware of at least one context in which the pattern will apply; moreover, such patterns can be arbitrarily complex (involve any number of attributes) over the possible features.

None of the above approaches to preference modelling take into account the context of the user's calendar as input to the learning. The work of Gervasio *et al.* [5] and Weber and Pollack [14] on PLIANT (as part of a different version of PTIME) aims to learn a more complex model that incorporates such features, again using implicit user feedback from selection from amongst alternative presented schedules. However, the feature space for learning is very large, so in practice any system would require a long learning time before an accurate model could be learnt. Indeed, this mode of learning has only ever been tested in simulation. In contrast, with the patterns used in SmartCal, useful suggestions can be given as soon as one pattern is recognized. Weber and Pollack [14] focus on the question of which candidate schedules to present to the user to gain maximum feedback for the learner, basing the choice of method on the degree of diversity of the solution set. It is interesting to note that SmartCal's Solution Builder automatically generates a diverse range of solutions, which is especially important as users will only ever see around 5 suggestions; however, the motivation of obtaining useful feedback for adjusting the weights is the same.

The only work we know of that attempts to learn general patterns over multiple appointments in a calendar scenario is Maclaren [9], where Inductive Logic Programming (ILP) is used to learn common sequences of appointments and, moreover, learn constraints over their features represented as logic programming clauses. When the user defines an appointment that matches an element of a known sequence, further appointments in the sequence conforming to the constraints could be suggested (unfortunately the method has not been tested in an interactive calendar system so it is unknown how well this would work in practice). The work considered various approaches to representing background knowledge and generating "near misses" for use in guiding the learner, which is essential to the success of any ILP approach.

CONCLUSION AND FUTURE WORK

We have built and evaluated a calendar assistant, SmartCal, which uses closed pattern mining for the suggestion of appointment features given arbitrary initial user-supplied attribute values. The suggestions are completely non-intrusive and are updated dynamically without the need for user interaction. We used a modified FP-Growth method for user preference mining and closed pattern mining for representing user preferences. Simulation results showed that this method of pattern mining is superior to decision tree learning in three important respects: (i) pattern mining better supports creating multiple solutions with consistent structures, (ii) pattern mining converges more rapidly to a similar level of accuracy, and (iii) pattern mining is more stable to user preference changes over time.

We conducted a small-scale user study showing that Smart-Cal is able to suggest useful appointments and that the ranking algorithm is able to learn to rank highly the suggestions most useful to the user. The system was able to adapt relatively quickly to user preference changes and demonstrated great flexibility in users' selection of input/output attributes. The suggestions were also regarded highly in user feedback.

Future research relating to data mining includes improving suggestion accuracy using the temporal aspects of appointments and mining frequent sequences of appointments. The issues raised by the user study participants discussed above also provide opportunities for further work.

Acknowledgements

This work was funded by the CRC for Smart Internet Technology. We would like to thank Frans Coenen for his open source implementation of the data mining algorithm. and Ben Fortuna for the iCal import/export open source utility used in the calendar. Thanks also to the anonymous reviewers of this paper for helpful suggestions that improved the quality of the presentation.

REFERENCES

1. Berry, P., Conley, K., Gervasio, M., Peintner, B., Uribe, T. and Yorke-Smith, N. Deploying a Personalized Time Management Agent. In *Proceedings of the Fifth International Joint Conference on Autonomous Agents and Multiagent Systems*, pp. 1564–1571, 2006.

2. Berry, P. M., Gervasio, M., Peintner, B. and Yorke-Smith, N. A Preference Model for Over-Constrained Meeting Requests. In *Proceedings of the AAAI 2007 Workshop on Preference Handling for Artificial Intelligence*, pp. 7–14, 2007.

3. Coenen, F., Goulbourne, G. and Leng, P. Tree Structures for Mining Association Rules. *Data Mining and Knowledge Discovery*, vol. 8, pp. 25–51, 2004.

4. Dent, L., Boticario, J., Mitchell, T. M. and Zabowski, D. A. A Personal Learning Apprentice. In *Proceedings of the Tenth National Conference on Artificial Intelligence (AAAI-92)*, pp. 96–103, 1992.

5. Gervasio, M. T., Moffitt, M. D., Pollack, M. E., Taylor, J. M. and Uribe, T. E. Active Preference Learning for Personalized Calendar Scheduling Assistance. In *Proceedings of the 2005 International Conference on Intelligent User Interfaces*, pp. 90–97, 2005.

6. Han, J., Pei, J. and Yin, Y. Mining Frequent Patterns without Candidate Generation. In *Proceedings of the 2000 ACM SIGMOD International Conference on Management of Data*, pp. 1–12, 2000.

7. Kozierok, R. and Maes, P. A Learning Interface Agent for Scheduling Meetings. In *Proceedings of the International Workshop on Intelligent User Interfaces*, pp. 81–88, 1993.

8. Krzywicki, A. and Wobcke, W. R. Closed Pattern Mining for the Discovery of User Preferences in a Calendar Assistant. In Nguyen, N. T. and Katarzyniak, R., editors, *New Challenges in Applied Intelligence Technologies*, pp. 67–76, Springer-Verlag, Berlin, 2008.

9. Maclaren, H. *A Divide and Conquer Approach to Using Inductive Logic Programming for Learning User Models*. PhD thesis, Department of Computer Science, University of York, 2003.

10. Maes, P. Agents That Reduce Work and Information Overload. *Communications of the ACM*, vol. 37(7), pp. 31–40, 1994.

11. Mitchell, T., Caruana, R., Freitag, D., McDermott, J. and Zabowski, D. Experience with a Learning Personal Assistant. *Communications of the ACM*, vol. 31(7), pp. 80–91, 1994.

12. Myers, K., Berry, P., Blythe, J., Conley, K., Gervasio, M., McGuinness, D., Morley, D., Pfeffer, A., Pollack, M. and Tambe, M. An Intelligent Personal Assistant for Task and Time Management. *AI Magazine*, vol. 28(2), pp. 41–67, 2007.

13. Pasquier, N., Bastide, Y., Taouil, R. and Lakhal, L. Efficient Mining of Association Rules Using Closed Itemset Lattices. *Information Systems*, vol. 24, pp. 25–46, 1999.

14. Weber, J. S. and Pollack, M. E. Entropy-Driven Online Active Learning for Interactive Calendar Management. In *Proceedings of the 2007 International Conference on Intelligent User Interfaces*, pp. 141–150, 2007.

15. Wille, R. Formal Concept Analysis as Mathematical Theory of Concepts and Concept Hierarchies. In Ganter, B., Stumme, G. and Wille, R., editors, *Formal Concept Analysis*, Springer-Verlag, Berlin, 2005.

16. Wobcke, W. R. A Calendar Management Agent with Fuzzy Logic. In Zhong, N., Liu, J., Ohsuga, S. and Bradshaw, J., editors, *Intelligent Agent Technology: Research and Development*, World Scientific, Singapore, 2001.

Tell Me More, not just "More of the Same"

Francisco Iacobelli
f-iacobelli@u.northwestern.edu

Larry Birnbaum
birnbaum@cs.northwestern.edu

Kristian J. Hammond
hammond@cs.northwestern.edu

Intelligent Information Lab.
Northwestern University
2133 Sheridan Rd.
Evanston, IL 60208, U.S.

ABSTRACT

The Web makes it possible for news readers to learn more about virtually any story that interests them. Media outlets and search engines typically augment their information with links to similar stories. It is up to the user to determine what new information is added by them, if any. In this paper we present Tell Me More, a system that performs this task automatically: given a seed news story, it mines the web for similar stories reported by different sources and selects snippets of text from those stories which offer new information beyond the seed story. New content may be classified as supplying: *additional quotes, additional actors, additional figures* and *additional information* depending on the criteria used to select it. In this paper we describe how the system identifies new and informative content with respect to a news story. We also show that providing an explicit categorization of new information is more useful than a binary classification (new/not-new). Lastly, we show encouraging results from a preliminary evaluation of the system that validates our approach and encourages further study.

Author Keywords

New information detection, Information Retrieval, Dimensions of Similarity

ACM Classification Keywords

H.4 Information Systems Applications: Miscellaneous; H.3 Information Storage and Retrieval: Information Search and Retrieval—*Information Filtering*

General Terms

Design, Human Factors, Reliability

INTRODUCTION

The Web offers tremendous opportunities to contextualize information through aggregation and hyperlinks, making it possible for news readers to learn more about virtually any story that interests them. And indeed most online news sources take advantage of these opportunities by presenting, alongside their stories, lists of "Related Stories" or other media related in some way to those stories. The potential advantages are clear: For users, to create a richer news experience, providing more background, or more detail, than any single story can present. For publishers, to increase the utilization of their content.

However, in many online news outlets the additional information that is presented to audiences is explicitly determined by human editors using their expert judgment. The problem with this approach is that it isn't scalable. Additionally, when content is automatically generated, the quality of the results often suffers. Yes, readers are presented with "related" information, but too often this information is just a rehash of the story they started with [23] and no guide is provided as to what they add to the main story, if anything.

In this paper we present Tell Me More. A system that doesn't just present readers with "more of the same." Instead, it selects stories that go beyond the initial story and presents them in a way that creates a genuinely richer news experience. Tell Me More uses the content of those stories to select and display only stories containing information that is new with respect to the original news story.

In particular, we claim that Tell Me More selects and displays paragraphs from other news stories containing details and background information that are new with respect to the original story. More specifically, the system retrieves new actors, new quotes and new figures which, by themselves, are important kinds of new information.

In terms of the presentation of new information, prior systems aim at detecting new information based on a single score that determines whether a piece of information is new or not. In this paper, however, we provide evidence that presenting this new information in categories that make the selection criteria visible, is more useful than aggregating snippets in one big list with no clues to assess the new information contained in them.

The following sections present the architecture of Tell Me More, a small user study on the value of categorizing information and an initial evaluation of the user experience with Tell Me More. We, then, discuss related work and finish with conclusions and future work.

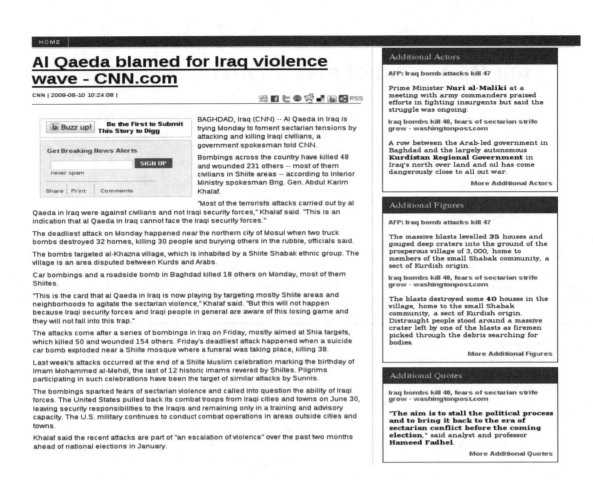

BAGHDAD, Iraq (CNN) -- Al Qaeda in Iraq is trying Monday to foment sectarian tensions by attacking and killing Iraqi civilians, a government spokesman told CNN.

Bombings across the country have killed 48 and wounded 231 others -- most of them civilians in Shiite areas -- according to Interior Ministry spokesman Brig. Gen. Abdul Karim Khalaf.

"Most of the terrorists attacks carried out by al Qaeda in Iraq were against civilians and not Iraqi security forces," Khalaf said. "This is an indication that al Qaeda in Iraq cannot face the Iraqi security forces."

The deadliest attack on Monday happened near the northern city of Mosul when two truck bombs destroyed 32 homes, killing 30 people and burying others in the rubble, officials said.

The bombs targeted al-Khazna village, which is inhabited by a Shiite Shabak ethnic group. The village is an area disputed between Kurds and Arabs.

Car bombings and a roadside bomb in Baghdad killed 18 others on Monday, most of them Shiites.

"This is the card that al Qaeda in Iraq is now playing by targeting mostly Shiite areas and neighborhoods to agitate the sectarian violence," Khalaf said. "But this will not happen because Iraqi security forces and Iraqi people in general are aware of this losing game and they will not fall into this trap."

The attacks come after a series of bombings in Iraq on Friday, mostly aimed at Shia targets, which killed 50 and wounded 154 others. Friday's deadliest attack happened when a suicide car bomb exploded near a Shiite mosque where a funeral was taking place, killing 38.

Last week's attacks occurred at the end of a Shiite Muslim celebration marking the birthday of Imam Mohammed al-Mehdi, the last of 12 historic imams revered by Shiites. Pilgrims participating in such celebrations have been the target of similar attacks by Sunnis.

The bombings sparked fears of sectarian violence and called into question the ability of Iraqi forces. The United States pulled back its combat troops from Iraqi cities and towns on June 30, leaving security responsibilities to the Iraqis and remaining only in a training and advisory capacity. The U.S. military continues to conduct combat operations in areas outside cities and towns.

Khalaf said the recent attacks are part of "an escalation of violence" over the past two months ahead of national elections in January.

Figure 1. Screenshot of Tell Me More showing three kinds of new information

ARCHITECTURE

The goal of our system, given a seed news article, is to find other sources reporting on the same situation and then to present only the paragraphs that contain supplementary information reported by these sources that is not present in the seed article. Figure 1 shows Tell Me More's interface with three of four possible kinds of new information: additional actors, additional figures and additional quotes.

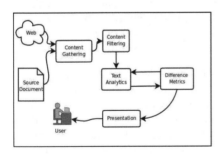

Figure 2. System architecture

Core Modules

Tell Me More employs five core modules to extract and present new information to the user. Given a source document, the system uses it as a seed for retrieval of similar stories and comparison. At the end of the cycle the user is presented with a categorization of the new information discovered, if any. The five modules (see Figure 2) are described next.

1. **Content Gathering:** This module can gather documents from search engines as well as from user defined sources. The implementation presented in this paper develops a basic model of the source article through text analytics (see module 3 below) and uses this to form a query that is sent to the Google News API. When Google News finds a news story, it usually returns a cluster of very similar stories embedded in the result set. The module then scrapes the text from the highest ranked story and the cluster of stories associated with it. The system has a number of strategies for forming queries so that if the first query does not return results, it is always possible to form a second and a third query to this effect. These techniques are based on our previous work [2, 7] and are described in some detail in the next section.

2. **Content Filtering:** This module filters results and eliminates documents that are exactly the same as the seed document or documents that are too different, and hence probably concern different situations. Content filtering also takes care of discarding articles that look like compendia of articles or spam using simple heuristics.

3. **Text Analytics:** This module is used to develop a statistical and heuristic model both at the paragraph and at the

document level on the source article, as well as analytics on every incoming new article. For every new source that it examines, it detects entities, quotes, figures and also computes a vector representation of each paragraph.

4. **Difference Metrics** After the text analytics are gathered for a new document, this module compares them with the previously seen text and determines which paragraphs contain new information. In addition, the Difference Metrics module keeps track of the kind of new information contained on each selected paragraph.

5. **Presentation** This module categorizes and ranks the new information based on the output of the Difference Measures module.

The following sections treat each of these modules in detail.

Content Gathering

Once a seed document is provided, this module uses text analytics [2] to extract key features from it, specifically, the title, named entities and a histogram of content bearing words. This module, as implemented for this paper, tries to search Google News (at this point the system is able to also use Google, Yahoo News and user specified websites) using the title of the news story as a query. If Google News has indexed the given story, it is likely that its URL will be at the top of the result set and, associated with it, Google returns a cluster of URLs of the most similar stories.

It may be the case that Google News has not indexed many similar stories and therefore it will not return the cluster of stories associated with the search query. The content gathering module detects this situation and then performs, in order, the following additional queries:

1. A query with the most frequently occurring words from the histogram plus the named entity most frequently mentioned. Once Google returns a result set, the module looks for the highest ranked result and its cluster, if present.

2. If a cluster is still not present, the module retains the top five URLs returned by Google.

After the URLs of these additional news resources have been gathered, they are processed by a webpage scraper which obtains the text of the news by looking into the DOM tree of the webpage and selects the ¡div¿ tag with most readable text in it (i.e. not scripts nor tags). These methods are largely based on our previous work [2, 7]. The scraped content is then stored and handed on to the next module: Content Filtering.

Content Filtering

Because a web search can produce sets with documents that are not too similar, Tell Me More takes a further step by filtering documents based on their similarity to the seed story. We compute this similarity using Latent Semantic Analysis[12] (LSA). LSA[1] extracts semantic information of words

based on contextual information provided by the training data. Therefore, we trained LSA on actual news stories – 1000 news stories about popular topics from the web [7]– to provide a good context for semantic comparison of news stories. Content Filtering, then, creates a multi dimensional vector representation of the seed document, and of each additional document gathered in the previous module, using this LSA space. Each vector is computed by averaging the LSA vectors of the individual words of the story excluding stop-words. With this corpus and our implementation of LSA, a document similar enough that it is likely to be referring to the same situation as the original seed article, but that contains meaningful differences, can have a similarity score of about 0.8 when compared to the seed article. Therefore, Content Filtering will only allow documents with similarity score x where $0.8 \leq x < 1.0$. In addition, this module has simple heuristics, based on [7], to exclude articles that look like news summaries and articles that may be spam.

Text Analytics

Tell Me More is based on the premise that the presence of new named entities, new quantifiers, and additional quotes are important kinds of new information. It is necessary, then, to have a module that analyzes the textual information accordingly. In addition, this module computes a semantic representation of each paragraph using LSA.

Thus, each paragraph in each document retrieved is represented as a vector with four features (a) a latent semantic representation of the paragraph; (b) a list of entities; (c) a list of quantifiers and (d) a list of quotes present in the paragraph. Each of these features is discussed in further detail below:

A Latent Semantic Representation of The Paragraph

Sometimes, new information may be present in a paragraph at a semantic level. Therefore, to account for the semantic representation of a paragraph, this module computes an LSA representation of each new paragraph. This module associates each representation with its corresponding paragraph.

List of Entities

When named entities are introduced in a paragraph of a news stories they usually signal important information such as evidence supporting claims in the news story[1]. Based on this idea, our system tracks entities mentioned in each paragraph within a few categories: persons, places, cities and organizations. These are computed for each paragraph. Entities that refer to the same base entity (e.g. "O.A.S." and "Organization of American States") are normalized. That is, mapped to a single entity. We detect and categorize entities using a boosting approach to entity detection based on two named entity recognizers (NERs) described below. Finally, this approach allows the system to tag some entities as "well-known."

---

[1]LSA is based on singular value decomposition (SVD) of the term x document matrix. SVD is an algebraic transformation on a matrix such that a term-document matrix T can be decomposed as follows:

$T = USV^T$. Then the dimensions of S, U and V are reduced to produce an approximation of T. Finally, the matrix TT^T is used as a term co-occurrence matrix[5].

Boosting an entity detection system

Due to its robust support for entity recognition, we used OpenCalais[2], an off the shelf commercial entity detection system that works very well for detecting instances of common categories such as people, places and organizations. However, because OpenCalais lacks good normalization capabilities, we augmented it with a modified version of WPED, an in-house entity detection system based on Wikipedia entries that does a good job at detecting different instances of the same entity. WPED has been used previously in other intelligent systems [15].

OpenCalais is a Thomson-Reuters free web service that performs named entity recognition and extracts relationships and events from text. OpenCalais uses natural language processing techniques and machine learning to recognize instances of named entities. Because OpenCalais is not based solely on hand-crafted databases of entities it can recognize new entities that may not yet be incorporated in any database, but that can be detected based on surface features of the text such as capitalization. The main weakness of OpenCalais is that it doesn't always normalize instances of entities. For example, *"Ted Kennedy"* and *"Senator Kennedy"* are detected as two different entities by OpenCalais when in reality, they are two instances of the same entity.

WPED, on the other hand, matches text to Wikipedia entries and therefore can normalize entity names with multiple instances —as long as they are pointing to the same wikipedia article. In a departure from other wikipedia named entity recognizers[10] or "wikifiers" [14, 3], WPED maps entities to overarching categories such as "person," "location," "organization," etc. thus, making uniform the, far-from-standard, default classifications provided by Wikipedia users. This allows compatibility with the classifications used by OpenCalais.

In sum, OpenCalais can detect people's names and organizations that may not appear in Wikipedia. Therefore it is the main entity detection method used. We, then, boosted the entity recognition process using WPED as follows: if any of the entities from OpenCalais can be mapped to an instance of an entity detected by WPED, we use the WPED base entity for annotation in the Text Analytics module.

Lastly, we considered the entities detected by both Open-Calais and WPED to be "well known" compared with those detected only by OpenCalais. This becomes relevant for a later discussion ranking paragraphs.

List of Quantifiers

Bell [1] argues that numbers in a new story are a marker of evidence and relevance. In particular, numbers that serve as quantifiers are a strong indication of relevant information.

For example: the number 100 could be a quantifier of time, money, or people involved in an accident or it could carry a different semantic content altogether as in the phrase "100

percent successful" where it serves as a synonym for "totally" and carries little information.

By discriminating and choosing only quantifiers, the system ensures it has detected a true piece of evidence or a fact related to the story.

For the present version of the system, we decided that any number that was in the proximity of a proper noun was a quantifier. It is usually the case that in news stories quantifiers and the object they quantify are in the same sentence. Using Montylingua, a part of speech tagger (POS) developed at MIT [13] we detect whether plural proper nouns occur in the same sentence together with a number. When this happens we add the number to the list of quantifiers. This gives us the desired effect: In the case of "100 percent successful", the system will ignore the number "100" as a quantifier.

List Of Quotes

Additional quotes usually indicate the opinion of experts, witnesses or relevant officials with respect to an event. Therefore, one of the analytics we collect are quotes. The system collects a list of text between quotation marks or ***&quote;***HTML markers per each paragraph.

To summarize, Text Analytics computes LSA vectors of the paragraphs, and collects quantifiers, entities and quotes. This conforms the four features of a vector of meta information about the paragraph that is then handed to the difference metrics module.

Difference Metrics

The difference metrics module compares the vector for each paragraph to the vectors of all previously selected paragraphs, including all the paragraphs of the seed story, and determines which ones contain new information based on meaningful differences.

The comparison of paragraphs with the previously seen documents occurs at two levels: At the paragraph level and at the document level. At the paragraph level, the system compares each new paragraph with each of the previously collected paragraphs using LSA and determines whether the new paragraph is sufficiently semantically different, below a threshold, to be considered new information. At the document level, each new paragraph's entities, quantifiers and quotes are compared to those detected in the previously seen text as a whole.

Each of the features of a paragraph (LSA representation, entities, quantifiers and quotes) has its own difference metric that will be computed and stored. Later on, the presentation module will use these scores to categorize the difference and present the paragraphs in the correct category. Each difference metric is now discussed in detail.

Semantic difference with LSA

To determine semantic difference we compare each new paragraph with all the previously seen ones. The most different paragraphs will naturally be least similar. Therefore, if

[2]http://www.opencalais.com

paragraphs score below a threshold in similarity, they are considered semantically different. For each paragraph we keep track of the highest similarity score obtained as a proxy for how similar or different the paragraph is with respect to other paragraphs. The highest similarity score is obtained by a cross-paragraph comparison between any new paragraph and those previously retrieved. The maximum similarity score is computed as follows:

$$Score_i = \max_{k \subseteq P}(sim(v_i, v_k)); \ P = \{0...i-1\}$$

Where v_i is the LSA vector representation of paragraph i, v_k is a vector of any of the previously seen paragraphs. The similarity function sim is the cosine similarity between the two LSA representations.

This score allows us to determine a baseline similarity between a new paragraph and the previously seen text. If the similarity is below the threshold of 0.3, the paragraph is considered to be semantically different from any other paragraph and therefore a candidate for containing new information. Conversely, high similarity scores indicate little semantic difference between the new paragraph and the previously seen text and, therefore, it is not a candidate for new information by this metric. This threshold has been pre-tested and works well in practice with our LSA space.

Different Entities

When a new paragraph is processed, its entities are compared to all entities associated with previously seen paragraphs. This is a straight string comparison except for one caveat. If an entity detected in the new paragraph is a substring of an entity already seen, both entities are considered to be the same. The rationale for this is that because the articles being compared are very similar, it is very probable that a substring of an entity is a reference to that entity. For example, if an article mentions *"Barack Obama"* and later on mentions *"Obama"* it is likely that it is referring to the same entity.

If a paragraph mentions at least one new entity, the paragraph is considered sufficiently different and therefore, containing new information. The score for this metric is equal to the number of new entities detected.

Different Quantifiers

This algorithm is similar to that for entities. The system compares the quantifiers of the new paragraphs with those previously collected from the processed documents. Again, if a paragraph includes a new quantifier, it is considered to be different than the rest due to this new information. The score of this metric is equal to the number of new quantifiers detected. Although previous systems have used dollar amounts as a measure of novelty [18], Ours is, to the best of our knowledge, the first to use quantifiers in a more general sense.

Different Quotes

Again, a similar algorithm compares the quotes present in the new paragraph with quotes previously seen in the collected text. However, for this feature one cannot rely on straight string comparison of the quotes under consideration and the previously collected ones.

When journalists transcribe quotes obtained orally, they make editorial choices and it may be the case that transcriptions come out slightly differently or that the quotes are edited at slightly different points. For example, one quote may start with "You know, when I was (...)" and another source may quote the same person omitting the initial "You know."

Because we compare quotes in the current paragraph against all previously contributed quotes we have to take into account these minor editorial choices. Therefore, straight string comparison is not enough. Comparisons need to be somewhat flexible. To address this, we scored string similarity using the Smith Waterman algorithm [11] commonly used in bio-informatics to align DNA sequences. Smith Waterman is a variant of the longest common sub-sequence algorithm that detects the longest common alignment of letters between two strings. The similarity score consisted in the percentage of aligned letters with respect to the longest string. We set a threshold of 70% which, empirically, was the lowest score at which we considered both quotes to be the same. Therefore, a quote is considered different if it matches less than 70% of any pre existing quote in previously seen documents.

When quotes are found to be different, they are scored by dividing the length of the quote with respect to the length of the paragraph in terms of letters. Because paragraphs are usually complete units of thought, this score is a good proxy of the prominence of the quote in that context. Therefore, more prominent and less edited quotes should obtain higher scores.

To the best of our knowledge, novelty detection systems have not considered quotes as a unit of differentiation for new paragraphs and we believe they are a valuable source of new information in the detection of novel information with respect to a news stories.

In sum, the Difference Metrics module compares the meta information about paragraphs obtained in the Text Analytics module. Namely, the LSA representations from previously seen paragraphs and the previously seen entities, figures and quotes. It assigns a score to each of these comparisons that establishes how different the new paragraphs are compared with to previously seen text, and, more importantly, along which dimensions.

Presentation: More than single scores

In our view, presenting new information based on a binary classification (new/not-new) provided by a single, all encompassing score lacks the usefulness that comes from making the criteria for novelty selection visible. A binary classification assumes that the new information should be obviously new to all users. However, this is not necessarily the case. People may not be in agreement of what constitutes novel information when they compare news stories.

Individual differences in the perception of novelty vary greatly. This is evident when researchers have looked at human assessments of what counts as new information. For the TREC conferences that hosted a novelty track, inter rater reliability scores, that incorporate agreement as well as correction for disagreements, measured by Cohen's Kappa, were 0.54[3] for relevance and even lower for novelty[20]. Schiffmann [17] tried to build a corpus of pairs of documents for the detection of new information and obtained a Kappa of 0.24 on judgments of novelty. Other methods to improve reliability have been explored, such as evaluating agreement on the answers to questions about the different texts (fact-focused novelty detection) but the Kappa scores are still low[16].

Because people do not always agree on judgments of information novelty, we think it is particularly important to make the selection criteria for new information visible to users. Research on presenting search results suggests that categorizing the results in meaningful ways helps user navigate them more easily [4, 8]. Thus, Tell Me More recommends paragraphs in one of four sections based on the difference metrics obtained earlier: (a) "additional actors" are new proper names, countries, cities and organizations; (b) "new numbers" which in this first iteration are any numbers not appearing in the story that the user is reading; (c) "additional quotes" are quotes not appearing in the source document and (d) "supplementary information" is text that is semantically different from previously seen text. Later in this paper we present a user study in which we compare our approach to a binary classification version of our system.

Currently, the system presents at most two paragraphs with new information per category on the front page (see Figure 1); however, it gives the users the opportunity to explore other new paragraphs within each category by clicking on "more additional $< category\_name >$."

To be able to know the category for a paragraph, the system looks at the difference metrics and determines its score in each category. Currently, the system has one rule for classifying paragraphs: if the new paragraph contains a new quote of length greater than 80% of the paragraph, then the paragraph should be classified as "additional quotes." Otherwise, the paragraph should be classified under the difference metric that is most distinctive of the paragraph –that is, the one with the highest score.

Because only two paragraphs show on the main webpage it is necessary to have a ranking mechanism that attempts to put the most relevant new paragraphs there.

Ranking new information

When presenting paragraphs with new information in categories, we rank these paragraphs according to the counts of new information detected by the Difference Metrics module in descending order. There are two exceptions:

1. **additional actors**: Because research suggests that there are entities that may matter more to the average reader,

---
[3]Usually, a Kappa above 0.65 is considered decent reliability.

and that these entities tend to be the most well known or influential [1] we think that having a wikipedia page (i.e. WPED finds them) is a good proxy to measure reader interest in the entity. Therefore, we rank first the paragraphs by number of popular actors present and then by the number of non-popular actors.

2. **Supplementary Information**: Because low scores indicate greater semantic difference, supplementary information is ranked by its scores in ascending order.

In the next sections we present a user studies to evaluate the validity of our approach in terms of categorizing results and a survey on the user experience with Tell Me More.

USER STUDY. BINARY CLASSIFICATION VERSUS MULTIPLE DIMENSIONS

When evaluating new information, most systems judge novelty with a single score and determine whether the information is new or not with respect to some seed document. As explained in Section , We believe that a single score is not informative enough for the task of reading news stories and that systems should make the dimensions of novelty visible to users.

Methodology

To test this hypothesis we conducted a small user study where participants saw a Tell Me More webpage with new information on the side. Users were told to read the new information and find two names that did not appear in the main article and at least one new fact that did not appear in the main article. Then they were told to look at the same news story with a different version of the interface. Users were then asked: "Do you think this format would have made finding the previous information easier or harder?" The two interfaces were: (a) MH: information of the sidebar is categorized under multiple headings: additional actors, additional figures and additional quotes and bolded entities, quotes and figures when applicable; and (b) OH: the new information was presented without any formatting or categorization and the only heading of the sidebar read "New Information." We counter balanced the order in which users saw each interface. 11 adults participated in this study.

Results and discussion

All but one participant preferred the interface with multiple headings (MH). This difference is significant ($\chi^2(1) = 11.63; P < 0.001$). Despite the small sample size, due to the huge difference in percentages (9% preferred OH versus 91% who preferred MH), the statistical power, considering a significance level of 0.05, is 92%, which is a very strong suggestion that no matter how big the sample size, the results are bound to suggest that users prefer the information when it is presented in a categorized manner and when it highlights the new information contained.

In other words, we find strong support for the hypothesis that users prefer an interface that makes visible the criteria for selecting new information, when the task consists of finding names or other supplementary facts. This is a departure from previous approaches to the detection and presentation of new information which do not make the selection criteria visible to users in the presentation [6, 17].

EVALUATION OF THE INTERFACE

At this point we believe that comparing Tell Me More with standard news readers would not be the as informative as we would like. The reason for this is the lack of a truly comparable news reading interface free of, or with few, confounds and that can provide ecological validity to our results.

Therefore, for this evaluation we are concerned with the subjective user experience and trust on Tell Me More. In particular, we are interested in users' initial reaction to the following questions: does Tell Me More help users understand news better? Does it provide a trusted source of news? Does it provide relevant detail or background information with respect to the main story? And, do people like the ability to see new information side by side with the news?

Methodology

To evaluate the user interface of Tell Me More more generally, we asked participants to read a news story and respond a questionnaire with respect to their experience. The stories were chosen at random from among 25 stories that were, themselves, chosen randomly from stories utilized by the system. Their only requirement is that they had at least one piece of new information in them. There were at least two stories in each of the following topics: politics, entertainment, world news, business, technology, health, sports and crime. The questionnaire asked people to evaluate their experience in terms of organization of new information, ease or difficulty of finding new information and trust in the information presented (as a whole and separately for the seed article and new information snippets). The questionnaire also asked people to rate the truth of statements about relevant background information in the snippets and relevant details. It then asked the users to rate their understanding of the topic after reading new information snippets and whether they would like to have an interface with new information in their news readers. Finally we collected some demographic information such as how often did users read news online, from how many sources, participant's age, occupation and gender. 24 adults responded the survey and all, except one, read news online at least once a day. 79% of the respondents actually consult more than 1 source. There were 13 females and 11 males and approximately 54% were between 25 and 35 years of age, 29% were younger than 25 and 17% older than 35.

Results

To answer the question of whether Tell Me More helps users understand news better, we analyzed the response to the item "I have a better understanding of the topic of the news story thanks to snippets of new information presented." which was responded to using a 5 point Likert scale that went from "Strongly disagree" to "Strongly Agree." We grouped the entries in three groups that can be seen in Figure 3: (a) people who disagree with the statement, that is, scores of 1 or 2; (b) people that neither agree nor disagree, that is responses

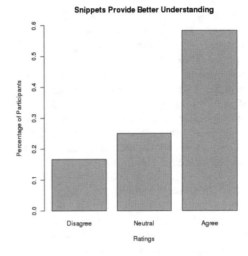

Figure 3. Level of agreement over having a better understanding of the news thanks to the snippets of new information. Difference between agreeing and other responses is significant to the $p < 0.05$ level.

of score 3; and (c) people that agreed with the statement, that is, scores of 4 or 5. A test for equality of proportions $\chi^2(2) = 10.5; p < 0.01$ reveals that the difference between the percentages of the three groups are significant. Post hoc analysis, using a test for equality of proportions, shows that the difference between (a) and (b) was not significant, but the differences between those groups and those who agree (c) was significant at least at the $p < 0.05$ level.

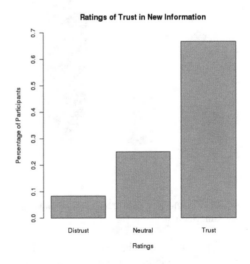

Figure 4. Ratings of trust of the new information presented. All differences are significant to the $p < 0.005$ level, except for Neutral>Distrust

Approximately 66.7% of the respondents rated the item "Rate your trust with respect to the webpage as a whole" with a 4 or a 5. A linear regression shows, not surprisingly, that trusting the new information sections is the main driver for people to trust the webpage as a whole ($F(2, 21) = 10.37; p < 0.01$) Therefore, we analyzed the responses to the item "Rate your level of trust with regards to the new information presented."

The item had ratings on a 5 point Likert scale that went from "totally distrust" to "totally trust." Again, for the purpose of analysis we grouped the responses in three groups. (a) Those who distrusted the information (scores 1 and 2); (b) those that remained neutral, that is neither trusted nor distrusted (score 3); and (c) those who trusted the information (scores 4 and 5). Figure 4 shows these ratings. A test for equality of proportions ($\chi^2(2) = 19.5; p < 0.001$) shows that the differences in ratings are significant. A more detailed analysis shows that all differences are significant at the $p < 0.005$ level, except for the difference between group (a) and (b) which were not significant.

Our next question had to do with the relevance of the information presented in terms of background information and additional details. Participants were asked whether they agreed or disagreed, on a five point Likert scale, with the following statements: "Relevant background information was contained in the new information snippets" and "Relevant additional details were contained in the new information snippets." By analyzing the data using the same methodology of grouping the ratings in three, we found that most respondents agreed with those two statements: 62.5% agreed with the statement about relevant background information ($\chi^2(2) = 13.85; p < 0.005$) and 75% agreed with the statement about relevant details ($\chi^2(2) = 28.5; p < 0.001$). See Figure 5

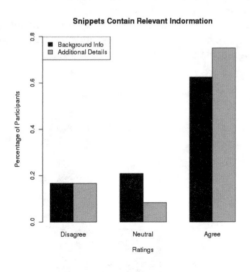

Figure 5. Agreement over the relevancy of background and details contained in the new information.

Our last question was to see whether people would like to have an interface like this one in their regular news reading experiences. Participants had to rate their agreement with the item "I would like to see an interface like this in my online news sources" on a five point Likert scale from "Strongly disagree" to "Strongly agree." Again, for the analysis we grouped them in three: (a) disagree (scores 1 and 2); (b) neutral or neither agree nor disagree (score 3); and (c) agree (scores 4 and 5). Approximately 58% of the respondents agreed with the statement. A test for equality of proportions show that there is a significant difference in the scores ($\chi^2(2) = 10.5; p < 0.05$) and detailed analysis shows

that the difference between group (c) and (a) is significant to the $p < 0.005$; the difference between groups (c) and (b) is slightly significant ($p < 0.07$) and the difference between groups (a) and (b) was not significant. See Figure 6

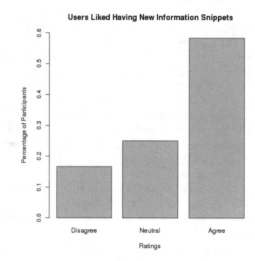

Figure 6. Users liked the ability to have new information snippets along with the news

Users were allowed to freely write feedback on the project. Most feedback had to do with the names of the headings, how little attention they pay to headings on a side bar, how the highlighting of a quote and a name were misplaced under "Additional Actors." Other feedback included suggestions on clustering and ranking. Positive feedback had to do with users liking the "Additional Quotes" section and the overall utility of the system.

Discussion

The evaluation of the interface suggests that users trust the new information presented. Because 96% of the participants read news online, and 76% of them consult more than one source, it is plausible to assume that when they responded the trust questions, they may have had their usual news sources in mind for comparison. Respondents reported that Tell Me More contains relevant details and background information and that the interface is one that they would like to see in their news reading experience. This suggests that Tell Me More is a feasible and potentially interesting news-reading interface and that it is worth optimizing its individual components and studying their effects on the overall news reading experience.

Relevance is a hard concept to define in terms of user experience, so it would be hard to quantify the "amount" of relevant information. However, the fact that the new information helped people get a better understanding of the news story, suggests that whatever relevant information is contained in the paragraphs is easy to access and augments the main news story in useful ways.

Additionally, the good feedback on the "Additional Quotes" section suggests that this is a meaningful criteria for selecting new information. To the best of our knowledge, Tell Me More is the first system to use quotes, and quantifiers, as indicators of new information.

Further analysis is needed to explore which topics are better served with the current implementation of Tell Me More. Lastly, given the user feedback, better wording and, at times, different organization can make the experience even more useful and pleasant.

RELATED WORK

Systems that detect new information based on one score have produced low to moderate precision rates. Significant research on detecting new information has been carried out as part of the TREC novelty track competitions which ran from 2002 to 2004. The novelty track is comprised of several tasks related to new and relevant sentence retrieval. At TREC 2002 and 2003, the first task was: "given an ordered set of 25 relevant documents, systems should return the relevant and new sentences from this set"[19]. In this task, the highest precision and recall measures were around 0.55 and 0.78.[19] Among the techniques used, the team from the University of Maryland Baltimore[9] used a similar technique to our LSA representation. They used a vector-space model based on SVD to create a matrix of word co-occurrence. Then they used it to compare sentences from each new document to the sentences previously contributed by other documents. On the same task at TREC 2004 the team from The University of Massachusetts scored sentences based on a combination of vector-space model using TFIDF and the mentions of new named entities with respect to previously mentioned ones. Their F measure scores was 0.61. By considering named entities, they consider some of the context of the previously retrieved documents. All this signals the difficulty of systems that use traditional, vector based, similarity measures to judge what is considered new information.

Schiffman [17] argues that, to detect novel information it is necessary to consider both sentence-level information and contextual information. At TREC 2004 Schiffman did not use a vector-space model. Instead he incorporated the detection of named entities, cash amounts, nouns and verbs and the notion that new information usually comes in consecutive phrases or is contained within a phrase in a few words. He employed hill climbing algorithms to detect thresholds that indicated new content. The best precision scores obtained by his team were around 0.6 [18]. Our system, however, makes use of quotations and quantifiers as additional units of information.

New information detection research has largely been used for news summarization software[22, 17]. However, because summarization systems aggregate information from various sources, it is hard to tell why the system includes the texts it does. In the realm of news, researchers have detected new information comparing the word distribution of different documents. Swan [21] used this technique to build time lines of events. Kuo [24] detected new information not only by comparing the distribution, but by assigning different weights to different kinds of terms, such as named entities, dates,

etc. skewing the document vector representations. However, many of these approaches have been used in hand processed corpora and have selected new information based on a single score model.

The system that is most similar to Tell Me More is NewsJunkie [6]. NewsJunkie utilizes vector representations and entity detection to judge novel content in news, however the novelty detection is used to provide readers with updates, developments and recaps of news stories. In contrast to our system, Newsjunkie does not specify what exactly is new information in the articles presented. Another difference is that Newsjunkie operates on the document as a whole, ranking it according to "how different" it is to the seed story. Tell Me More ranks paragraphs, thus pointing out specific new information contained within additional news stories. Lastly, in a user study of NewsJunkie users expressed the opinion that it was hard to judge the novelty of articles because of their relevance with respect to the seed story. We believe that making the selection criteria visible to users can help bridge that obstacle.

In sum, finding relevant new information is not a trivial task. Previous systems have used different criteria than we do, and none have made their selection criteria visible to users. We believe this is an essential component of a usable system that presents new information about news articles to users.

CONCLUSIONS

In this paper we presented Tell Me More, a rich news reading system that displays new information alongside a news story. We showed that Tell Me More, as designed, selects and displays paragraphs from other news stories containing information that is new with respect to the original story. New actors, new quotes and new figures are important kinds of new information retrieved and presented by the system. An initial evaluation of the system validates our approach and encourages us to continue development and research.

Our second claim, and the point of user study 1, is narrower yet: to provide evidence that presenting this new information in categories is more useful than aggregating snippets as one big list with no indication as to the nature of the new information contained in them.

In this paper we also propose that quotations and quantifiers are valuable kinds of new information in news reading.

Tell Me More aims to realize the promise of the Web by delivering a truly richer news-reading experience in a scalable and economical way.

REFERENCES

1. A. Bell. *The Language of News Media*. Language in Society. Wiley-Blackwell, September 1991.

2. J. Budzik, K. J. Hammond, and L. Birnbaum. Information access in context. *Knowledge-Based Systems*, 14(1-2):37–53, March 2001.

3. S. Cucerzan. Large-scale named entity disambiguation

based on Wikipedia data. In *Proceedings of the 2007 Joint Conference on Empirical Methods in Natural Language Processing and Computational Natural Language Learning (EMNLP-CoNLL)*, pages 708–716, Prague, Czech Republic, June 2007. Association for Computational Linguistics.

4. S. Dumais, E. Cutrell, and H. Chen. Optimizing search by showing results in context. In *CHI '01: Proceedings of the SIGCHI conference on Human factors in computing systems*, pages 277–284, New York, NY, USA, 2001. ACM.

5. G. W. Furnas, S. Deerwester, S. T. Dumais, T. K. Landauer, R. A. Harshman, L. A. Streeter, and K. E. Lochbaum. Information retrieval using a singular value decomposition model of latent semantic structure. In *SIGIR '88: Proceedings of the 11th annual international ACM SIGIR conference on Research and development in information retrieval*, pages 465–480, New York, NY, USA, 1988. ACM Press.

6. E. Gabrilovich, S. Dumais, and E. Horvitz. Newsjunkie: providing personalized newsfeeds via analysis of information novelty. In *WWW '04: Proceedings of the 13th international conference on World Wide Web*, pages 482–490, New York, NY, USA, 2004. ACM Press.

7. F. Iacobelli, K. Hammond, and L. Birnbaum. Makemypage: Social media meets automatic content generation. In *ICWSM 2009*, 2009.

8. M. Käki. Findex: search result categories help users when document ranking fails. In *CHI '05: Proceedings of the SIGCHI conference on Human factors in computing systems*, pages 131–140, New York, NY, USA, 2005. ACM.

9. S. Kallurkar, Y. Shi, R. S. Cost, C. Nicholas, A. Java, C. James, S. Rajavaram, V. Shanbhag, S. Bhatkar, and D. Ogle. Umbc at trec 12. In *TREC Notebook Proceedings*, 2003.

10. J. Kazama and K. Torisawa. Exploiting wikipedia as external knowledge for named entity recognition. In *EMNLP-CoNLL*, 2007.

11. D. E. Krane and M. L. Raymer. *Fundamental Concepts of Bioinformatics (The Genetics Place Series)*. Benjamin Cummings, 1 edition, September 2002.

12. T. K. Landauer and S. T. Dumais. A solution to plato's problem: The latent semantic analysis theory of acquisition, induction, and representation of knowledge. *Psychological Review*, 104(2):211–240, April 1997.

13. H. Liu. Montylingua: An end-to-end natural language processor with common sense. Available at: http://web.media.mit.edu/hugo/montylingua, 2004.

14. R. Mihalcea and A. Csomai. Wikify!: linking documents to encyclopedic knowledge. In *CIKM '07: Proceedings of the sixteenth ACM conference on Conference on information and knowledge management*, pages 233–242, New York, NY, USA, 2007. ACM.

15. N. Nichols and K. Hammond. Machine-generated multimedia content. In *ACHI '09: Proceedings of the 2009 Second International Conferences on Advances in Computer-Human Interactions*, pages 336–341, Washington, DC, USA, 2009. IEEE Computer Society.

16. J. Otterbacher and D. Radev. Exploring fact-focused relevance and novelty detection. *Journal of Documentation*, 64(4):496–510, 2008.

17. B. Schiffman. *Learning to identify new information*. PhD thesis, Columbia University, 2005.

18. B. Schiffman and K. R. Mckeown. Columbia university in the novelty track at trec 2004. In *Proceedings of the TREC 2004*, 2004.

19. I. Soboroff and D. Harman. Overview of the TREC 2003 novelty track. In *Proceedings of TREC-2003*. Citeseer, 2003.

20. I. Soboroff and D. Harman. Novelty detection: the trec experience. In *HLT '05: Proceedings of the conference on Human Language Technology and Empirical Methods in Natural Language Processing*, pages 105–112, Morristown, NJ, USA, 2005. Association for Computational Linguistics.

21. R. Swan and D. Jensen. Timemines: Constructing timelines with statistical models of word usage. In *ACM SIGKDD 2000 Workshop on Text Mining*, pages 73–80, 2000.

22. S. Sweeney, F. Crestani, and D. Losada. 'show me more': Incremental length summarisation using novelty detection. *Information Processing & Management*, 44(2):663–686, March 2008.

23. The Associated Press and The Context-Based Research Group. A new model for news: Studying the deep structure of young-adult news consumption. Technical report, 2008.

24. K. Zhang, J. Zi, and L. G. Wu. New event detection based on indexing-tree and named entity. In *SIGIR '07: Proceedings of the 30th annual international ACM SIGIR conference on Research and development in information retrieval*, pages 215–222, New York, NY, USA, 2007. ACM.

Rush: Repeated Recommendations on Mobile Devices

Dominikus Baur
University of Munich
dominikus.baur@ifi.lmu.de

Sebastian Boring
University of Munich
sebastian.boring@ifi.lmu.de

Andreas Butz
University of Munich
andreas.butz@ifi.lmu.de

ABSTRACT

We present *rush* as a recommendation-based interaction and visualization technique for repeated item selection from large data sets on mobile touch screen devices. Proposals and choices are intertwined in a continuous finger gesture navigating a two-dimensional canvas of recommended items. This provides users with more flexibility for the resulting selections. Our design is based on a formative user study regarding orientation and occlusion aspects. Subsequently, we implemented a version of rush for music playlist creation. In an experimental evaluation we compared different types of recommendations based on similarity, namely the top 5 most similar items, five random selections from the list of similar items and a hybrid version of the two. Participants had to create playlists using each condition. Our results show that top 5 was too restricting, while random and hybrid suggestions had comparable results.

Author Keywords

Interaction technique, mobile; recommender systems

ACM Classification Keywords

H5.m. Information interfaces and presentation (e.g., HCI): Miscellaneous.

General Terms

Design, Experimentation, Human Factors

INTRODUCTION

Recommender Systems have come a long way [2]: while initially conceived as a way to handle email information overload by collaborative filtering [9], they soon were adapted by online retailers (most prominently Amazon.com) to increase sales. With this history, recommender systems continued to be used mainly in web interfaces and for reducing large data sets to well-chosen subsets in order to conserve bandwidth and prevent information overload.

Despite broadband internet connection and increased processing power in mobile devices, explicit research on user

interfaces for mobile recommender systems is scarce: existing systems ([14],[18]) mostly rely on established desktop interaction metaphors (e.g., critique-based recommendation [21]) and examine issues of mobility such as loss of connection ([19],[8]) and decentralization [13]. Peculiarities of mobile device interaction, such as occlusion problems [35], the influence of the reduced screen space [30] and possibly abrupt endings (e.g., when the bus arrives at the station) have mostly been ignored.

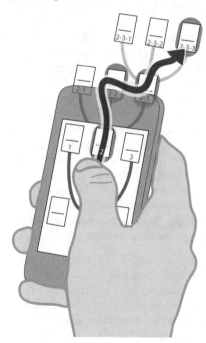

Figure 1. Repeated selection from recommendation sets

Ward et al. presented Dasher [36], a visual tool for text entry based on language models that has also been successfully ported to Pocket PCs. A continuous gesture allows selecting letters to form words and sentences. The underlying language model is used to enlarge more probable items and make selecting the correct one easier. With up to 60 words per minute in its original version, it is an efficient way to enter text. Despite being used in a variety of other ways (e.g., with an eye-tracker [37]), the original task of text entry has never been changed, though.

In this paper, we present rush (see Figure 1), a variation on Dasher, as an interaction technique for mobile touch-screen devices for repeatedly selecting items from a set of recommendations.

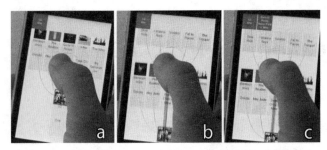

Figure 2. Rush overview: a) Starting from a seed item five recommendations are displayed. b) Touching the middle item causes a new set of recommendations tailored to this item to appear above. c) By completing the crossing gesture, the middle item is added to the selected set.

Similar to Dasher, rush's interaction takes place on a virtual two-dimensional canvas. Starting from a seed item, related items are selected by the underlying recommender engine and displayed close to it. The user can then select one of these suggestions, which in turn generates recommendations related to this item (see Figure 2). This iterative expansion of a recommendation tree continues until the user is satisfied with the set of selections. Navigation and selection happens with a single finger gesture: the canvas moves below the finger depending on the distance and angle to the screen's center. For example, the user's finger in the upper right part of the screen causes the canvas to slide towards the lower left. To allow fluid gestures and prevent the need to lift a finger, we used crossing gestures [1] for the selection of items instead of pointing. Selecting an item in rush is performed by drawing a line through it. In theory, the user's interaction thus limits itself to moving the finger on the screen: putting the finger down starts the process and lifting it again means the collection is finished.

In the following, we discuss the issues of device and interface orientation and a formative evaluation that led to rush's final design. We also present a user study where we examined a rush implementation for music playlists and the influence of the underlying recommendation on user satisfaction. Finally, we discuss possible extensions.

RELATED WORK

Interaction for recommender systems is often combined with approaches from information retrieval and visualization. O'Donovan et al. [22] built an interactive visualization as a way to provide users with explanations of the collaborative filtering process and as a way to influence the results.

Swearingen et al. [32] analyzed eleven online recommender systems and identified the importance of transparency, familiarity with items and providing details. The advantages of transparency and explanations in recommender systems and a design adapted towards them have been addressed by Pu et al. [27] and Tintarev et al. [33]. The longstanding GroupLens and MovieLens projects also analyzed how to gather information on users through different interface additions (e.g., [34]).

Conversational recommenders and mixed initiative systems [31] ask questions or make repeated suggestions to help the user understand an item set and ultimately make a choice. They are used to specify the requirements of the user and make more refined recommendations. Still, their goal is to recommend a single item and not multiple ones. The recommendation process is over if this item has been found.

Recommending collections

Hansen et al. discuss the challenges and present the design space of automatically recommending collections [11]: In addition to finding suitable items, such systems also have to consider how well these items fit together and in which order they should be presented. The music domain already provides multiple systems for recommending song collections, mostly commercially driven: Websites like Last.FM, imeem or Pandora let users listen to a dynamically generated web-radio based on a chosen seed song. Similarly, playlist generators like iTunes Genius or Microsoft's Smart DJ produce playlists for desktop or mobile music players.

The underlying method for generating such playlists is mostly based on collaborative filtering ([24], [17]), but there are also systems that analyze user interaction, such as skipping behavior [23], audio similarity [26] or patterns in authored streams (e.g., radio playlists) [28]. While automatic playlist generation is fast and convenient, its results often lack variety or ignore the importance of song order.

Apart from fully automatic processes, the user can be involved to varying degrees: Aucouturier et al. [6] let the user define constraints and generate a playlist based on them. SatisFly [25] is an interface that is also based on constraints. Downsides of the constraint-based approach are: (1) it becomes complex if more elaborate constraints are used and (2) all constraints have to be known beforehand.

Music on Mobile Devices

Music has become mobile with the proliferation of handheld MP3-devices such as Apple's iPod. But with the growing storage space on such devices the problem of accessing items became worse. Mobile visualization of music promises to make collections manageable: Mapping approaches such as Artist Map [40], PocketSOMPlayer [20] or Mobile Music Explorer [10] visualize music items using dimensionality reduction techniques and provide an overview of the whole collection. Generating playlists in such visualizations is mostly done by drawing lines through the map [39], [10], thus causing the system to choose a list of songs following this trajectory. Due to the abstraction of the visualization, the user can influence the resulting playlist only on a very high level (mostly genre).

FORMING RUSH

In contrast to desktop user interfaces, mobile applications face additional problems such as readability issues due to the device's orientation. As mobile devices mostly have rectangular shapes, there are two ways of holding them: (1) vertically and (2) horizontally. In the latter case, users can either grip both sides with both hands and interact with their thumbs or hold one side with the non-dominant hand while interacting with the dominant one. One-handed interaction on the whole screen is only possible in the former case.

		Interface Orientation	
		Vertical	Horizontal
Interface Direction	Up-Right	Up	Right
	Down-Left	Down	Left

Table 1. Which interface directions are available depends on the interface orientation. The "forward" direction where new items appear is based on these two factors.

Occlusion introduces a further problem when interacting with small screens: if important parts of the interface are regularly occluded by fingers, the performance drops [35]. Several solutions to this problem have been proposed: most of them require additional screen space (thus occluding other parts of the interface) [35] or special hardware [38]. One obvious solution is to re-arrange the interface content so that occlusion is minimized.

In rush, the interaction happens mostly in one direction: forward movements show new suggestions for a specific item and select it. When moving backwards, users can undo a selection or receive recommendations for a different item. However, as the latter case is rare, the forward direction should be optimized. The four directions, namely up, down, left and right, are feasible candidates for forward movement, leading to different kinds of occlusion: if new items appear to the right of an item, then right-handers will occlude them, while left-handers have no problems. The bottom-direction is mostly occluded with either hand, as the device is held there. The up-direction should not suffer from any occlusion-problems.

Two solutions to the problem of occlusion thus are feasible, namely shaping interaction towards the upper side of the device or flipping the interface for left- and right-handers. This last solution should lead to no problems with nominal data such as products, which are typically found in recommendation situations. For ordinal data such as letters (as in Dasher [36]), the reading direction might have an influence on the performance. This makes flipping for right-handers less attractive if they have a Western background (and thus a reading direction from left to right).

In order to find an optimal design for rush, we wanted to clarify these uncertainties. Therefore, we performed a pre-study to examine the influence of (1) device and interface orientation, (2) interface direction, (3) used hand and (4) handedness on the user's performance.

Method

We implemented a version of rush that was focused on these interface attributes. We chose all selectable items to represent single digits (see Figure 3). We then generated sets that contained random numbers and orders and presented them to each participant.

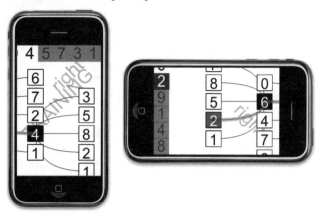

Figure 3. Two different conditions for the rush pre-study. Left: vertical device, horizontal interface, direction right. Right: horizontal device, horizontal interface, direction left (the "right" label in the background tells participants to use their right hand for interaction)

This version of rush supported two different orientations for the device (horizontal and vertical). We divided the four possible movement directions into interface orientation (horizontal, i.e. sets of recommended items appear to the left or right of the current item (see Figure 3) and vertical, i.e. sets of recommended items appear above or below (see Figure 1)) and the two resulting interface directions (horizontal interface orientation: either left or right direction, vertical interface orientation: either up or down direction, see Figure 3 for two examples). The available directions are dependent on the interface orientation, so we combined the up and right (up-right) and down and left (down-left) directions to turn interface direction into a variable with two states. In addition to that, participants were told to use either their left or right hand for a task. The movement speed on the canvas depended on the finger's distance to the center of the screen, so that twice the distance resulted in twice the speed. Our test device was an Apple iPhone 3G, with a screen resolution of 320 × 480 pixels. To keep all orientations comparable, the movement speed was capped at a distance of 160 pixels to the center of the screen. Otherwise, interaction in the longer direction would have allowed higher movement speeds and thus better results.

Task and Study Design

Participants had to select ten numbers using the rush interface. For each item, five suggestions were given out of which only one item was the correct one. The location where new items appeared ("forward") depended on the interface orientation as well as the interaction direction (see Table 1). By forcing participants to use both of their hands, we partially provoked occlusion and were able to measure its effects on performance.

We measured task time and error rates for each trial. The task time began as soon as the participant put a finger on the screen and ended when the last item was selected. Errors were counted for both selecting a wrong item as well as deselecting a correct one. All participants performed this task for every combination of display orientation, interface orientation, interface direction and used hand. The order of the tasks was randomized to counter learning effects. Before each task, participants performed a practice run with a different sequence of numbers using the identical interface condition.

We used a within-subjects study design. We had a *2 Device Orientations* (*Horizontal*, and *Vertical*) × *2 Interface Orientations* (*Horizontal*, and *Vertical*) × *2 Interface Directions* (*up-right*, and *down-left*) × *2 Used Hand* (*Left*, and *Right*) design. For each combination, participants had one practice block and one timed block. In each task, we measured task time and error rate. The resulting design was:

> *2 Device Orientations* (*Horizontal*, and *Vertical*) ×
> *2 Interface Orientations* (*Horizontal*, and *Vertical*) ×
> *2 Interface Directions* (*up-right*, and *down-left*) ×
> *2 Used Hand* (*Left*, and *Right*) ×
> *2 Blocks* (*Training*, and *Timed*)
>
> = 32 (16 timed) data points per participant.

Participants

We recruited 12 participants (3 female, 10 right-handed) from our institution with their age ranging from 21 to 32 (average age was 27.4 years). All participants had at least some previous experience with touch screens.

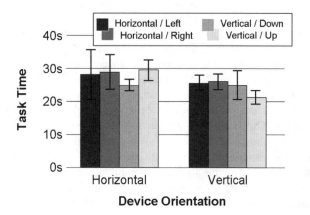

Figure 4. Task times from the pre-study

Hypotheses

Based on our understanding of performance of mobile interfaces we had three hypotheses: occlusion in general leads to higher task times as users have to adjust their hand's position to identify items (H1). The dominant hand outperforms the non-dominant one in both task times and error rates (H2). The interface and device orientation correlate with faster task times (H3).

Results

We conducted a repeated measures ANOVA test on mean completion times (see Figure 4 for results) and error rates. To identify the nature of interaction effects, we performed additional tests on subsets of our data. All post hoc pairwise comparisons used Bonferroni corrected confidence intervals for comparisons against α = 0.05.

We first analyzed whether the handedness of users had any influence on the results. The mean completion time of left-handers was 24.12 seconds when they used their left hand and 26.46 when they used their right hand respectively. There was almost no difference for right-handers (26.34 seconds for the right hand compared to 26.39 seconds for the left hand respectively). However, we did not find any significant main effects or interactions for this between-subject factor on both task time and error rate. Thus, we excluded the handedness for sub-sequent analysis. This is contradictory to our hypothesis H2 as the handedness does not have any significant effects on task times or error rates.

We found significant main effects on completion time for both *Device Orientation* ($F_{1,10} = 13.056$, $p < 0.005$) and *Interface Orientation* ($F_{1,10} = 7.094$, $p < 0.024$). There were no significant interaction effects in our data. Overall, the *Vertical Device Orientation* (M=24.49, SD=1.29) was faster than the *Horizontal* one (M=27.85, SD=1.28). The *Vertical Interface Orientation* (M=25.16, SD=1.23) was also faster than the *Horizontal Orientation* (M=27.17, SD=1.28). The combination of both vertical directions was the fastest one (M=23.13, SD=1.76) with an average improvement of 4.05 seconds (≈ 15%) compared to all other combinations of device and interface orientations.

As there was no significant effect or interaction for *Interface Direction* we decided to use bottom to top as it is the fastest one when both the device and the interface are oriented vertically (M=21.23, SD=1.16). On average, participants were 4.7 seconds (≈ 18%) faster when using this direction compared to horizontal movements. In general, H1 is confirmed as the *Vertical Device Orientation* in combination with the *Vertical Interface Orientation* does not lead to occlusion effects.

When analyzing the error rate we found a significant main effect for *Device Orientation* ($F_{1,10} = 6.139$, $p < 0.033$) but no significant interaction effects. Post-hoc multiple means comparisons revealed that the *Vertical Device Orientation* (M=0.53, SD=0.15) performs better than the *Horizontal* one (M=0.86, SD=0.14). Considering low error rates and short task times, H3 is supported by our results.

Discussion

The higher error rates and task times for conditions where occlusion was a problem for participants can be explained as follows: (1) participants touched an item which caused recommended items to appear beyond the display's boundaries and were thus invisible. (2) They put their finger to the far end of the screen to reach those as fast as possible. (3) Participants then had to precisely pick the moment when the items appeared, but sometimes still selected the wrong item, which increased the error rate. Furthermore, the task time got higher as they had to deselect the item and select the correct one. For the final design of rush, this implies separating interaction into getting recommendations for an item and selecting an item.

Another effect we observed in the study was that participants were either not aware of all suggested items or had to pan orthogonally to the *Interface Direction* to see all of them. This caused frustration among our participants. Hence, in the final design of rush, we decided to restrict panning to one dimension and only show one set of recommendations at one time.

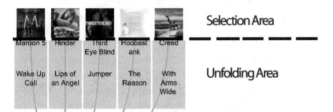

Figure 5. Representation of items

RUSH: DESIGN

The results of the pre-study led to the final design of the rush interaction technique (see Figures 1 and 2) with vertical device and interface orientation and interaction direction from bottom to top.

Touch interaction and Crossing-based interfaces

In the final version, one finger is still sufficient for navigating the complete item set and select items. The distance from the screen's center determines the speed, the angle the direction of movement (but as mentioned above, only along the vertical dimension). This movement is indirect and caused by a sliding of the underlying canvas into the opposite direction. After launching the application and choosing a seed item from a list or entering it manually, it is displayed in the center of the screen.

Figure 6 Selecting multiple items with one stroke

The visual representation of items is separated into two areas (see Figure 5): One area triggers the display of recommended items ("unfolds" the item) while the other one can be used to select the item for the result set. Also, the items are no longer squares but rectangles and aligned with the movement direction, making it harder to erroneously select them by drawing a complete line.

As soon as the user touches an item, recommendations are presented, but the item is not selected until a full line is drawn through it. Accot and Zhai have shown in [1] that continuous crossing-based interaction is comparable in performance to pointing-based alternatives. As the user's finger is on the screen anyway, crossing-based selection is an obvious choice for rush: the finger on the touch-screen not only causes navigation on the item plane, but also produces an (invisible) line that can be used for selecting items. In addition to that, continuously drawing a line contains additional information: the user is, for example, able to select multiple items in a row by simply drawing a longer line through them instead of repeatedly lifting, aiming and lowering the finger (see Figure 6). Also, instead of just hitting a single (more or less random) point within an item, a crossing line has an entering and exiting side which also can be used as a way for "richer semantics" [1]: We decided to minimize the number of erroneous de-selections by coupling the interface direction with the crossing direction: Drawing a line from bottom to left, top or right (along the interface direction) selects an item, while drawing a line from top to bottom (against the interface direction) deselects it.

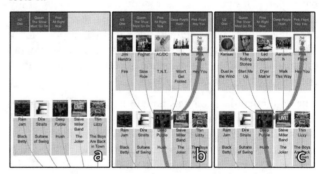

Figure 7. On-screen item layout while unfolding and selecting: a) initially, only row 1 is visible. b) After unfolding and selecting two songs from rows 1 and 2. c) After unfolding a different song from row 1 the recommendations in row 2 change.

We found that while in theory a complete interaction process can be started and ended by putting the finger down and up again, it is strenuous for users to keep their fingers pressed to the screen. To end the process, the user can alternatively wait for a short time to allow a dialog to pop up asking him if he wants to quit or shake the device, which can be detected by the integrated accelerometers and is sufficiently diametric to the regular interaction to not be triggered unintentionally.

As rush is intended for building collections of items, providing an overview of recently selected items is necessary to reduce the cognitive load and prevent the necessity to memorize recent decisions. The alternative of going back and following the trail of previous choices is time-consuming, so we preferred the alternative of using a portion of the screen space to display these recent choices. Similar to the version used for the pre-study, we used the top of the screen to display a textual representation of the last five selected items (see top of Figure 7).

Recommendation sets

By crossing either of the two areas with his finger, the item is unfolded and a set of recommended items is displayed. When thinking about the purpose of rush, the number of recommended items is crucial: As an information reduction technique, the number of items reflects the trade-off between freedom of choice and time spent deciding and browsing (cf. [29]). A small number of suggestions heavily restrict the possible choices, while a large one increases the time necessary for each decision. As every item has to be visually scanned, this time increases linearly with the number of items. The unsorted items allow no subdivision, so logarithmic decisions as in the Hick-Lyman Law cannot be applied [15]. Additionally, the available screen space is a restricting factor: To display many items they either have to become very small (and possibly unreadable) or disappear beyond the screen borders (making panning necessary to reach them). We decided for five items in our implementation as a compromise between choice and convenience. The participants of our second user study (see below) generally appreciated this choice (58% of them said that the number of suggestions was neither too high nor too low). The new set of suggestions appears in a row above the original item, using the available screen space as well as possible (see Figure 7).

One additional decision was how to handle a change in selection of the original item. With every row containing five items, five corresponding sets of recommendations are available. While in the regular case only one of these sets will be required (the one building on the selected item), the user is free to access the other sets as well. Displaying all 25 available items would lead to a large panning overhead and make it almost impossible to gather which item originated from where, so only one set of recommendations is available at one time. If a different item is unfolded, all unselected items from the last visible set are hidden and available spots are filled with new recommendations (see Figure 7b) and c)). Already selected items from the old set stay put. Every time an item is touched its recommendations are displayed, which means that when selecting multiple items using a single stroke only the last item's recommendations are visible afterwards.

An additional issue is the arrangement of recommended items, as the horizontal dimension (i.e., the order of the five items) can be used to encode additional information. We used the similarity of the recommended items for that and placed in one setup (*Hybrid*, see user study) the most similar item in the middle of the screen, next to two items that were reasonably similar but not too much and finally two items with a very low similarity as a way to "break out" of a certain direction. With this layout, the user is able to replicate the work of an automatic playlist creator based on similarity such as [26] by drawing a straight line up, thus always selecting the most similar item.

Sorting the items based on the probability returned by the recommendation engine allows users to have a clear conception about the relevance and changing their visual scanning depending on the current task. We compared the hybrid layout to one displaying the top five items in our study and found that chances were high that users had no way to maneuver out of a certain direction with the latter. In the hybrid layout, we circumvent the common "more of the same" problem of recommender systems and allow serendipity ([12], [5]) - but, of course, only if the user chooses to.

IMPLEMENTATION

For our second user study, we chose the domain of playlist creation. We implemented rush for the Apple iPhone 3G which has a 3.5" touch screen with a resolution of 320 x 480 pixels. We used the iPhone SDK and Objective-C for the implementation and OpenGL ES 1.1 for drawing. All songs and their relations were saved in a 10 Megabyte SQLite database directly on the device. Also, album covers or, if not available, artist photos were deployed as JPEG images together with the application to increase the loading speed. We wanted to allow participants to listen in on songs to make it easier for them to decide whether they fit in the current context or to help them recall a song if cover, artist and title name are not enough. For this purpose, we streamed 30 second samples from a web server through the phone's wireless LAN connection, which decreased the application's performance slightly but was received favorably by our study's participants.

USER STUDY

Rush is in the middle of the spectrum between fully automated and manual. Naturally, this hybrid approach causes longer task times than a fully automatic one (which effectively takes no time at all). We further assumed that the results were better in terms of quality. Our expectation for the manual approach, however, was that it produces the highest quality but is by far the slowest technique.

In a user study we investigated whether our assumptions were correct. We wanted to examine how well rush performed compared against automatic and manual playlist construction and what influence the choice of suggestion sets had on the user's satisfaction and performance.

Song Set Used in the Study

To give a realistic scenario and show that recommendation was indeed useful (i.e., browsing is not sufficient), we created a data set of 3900 songs, including samples and representative images. Our goal for the data set was to create a collection that only includes songs which are commonly known. With this, participants were not confronted with completely unknown recommendations. The alternative of asking participants for sufficiently large song sets would have made the results less comparable. Therefore, we started with a manual selection of all time favorites from the genres rock, pop and R'n'B. Based on that, a script extracted similar songs from Last.FM[1]. We only considered songs that had been listened to at least 500,000 times, which made them sufficiently popular. For each song in the set, we created a list of similar songs (again based on Last.FM data). Songs with less than ten connections to songs by different artists were erased and we arrived at a final set of 3900 songs (from originally 4500).

While the similarity was based on Last.FM data, we added two constraints to improve the quality of resulting playlists. First, songs that were already in the playlist were not suggested again. Second, suggestions for a song did not have the same artist. Additional constraints on, for example, tempo or genre were not used.

Conditions, Task and Study Design

During the study, participants had to create four playlists: three using rush in different conditions and one manually. The three different versions of rush were identical regarding the interface, but the approach to recommendation changed: The *Top 5* condition presented users with the five most similar songs for an item. The *Random* condition took five songs at random from the list of similar songs. The already mentioned *Hybrid* condition presented the top similar song, two songs from the middle of the similarity list and two songs from the bottom. In the manual condition, participants had access to a web browser on a desktop PC with a list of all 3900 available songs. In order to keep the results comparable, participants were able to see the (full) list of similar items for each song. They also had the option to listen to samples of those. The last set of conditions was automatic playlists, created out of the 3900 songs. The playlist generator replicated the user's choices in rush but picked a random song from the five suggestions. In the automatic condition, there were also three suggestion strategies (*Top 5*, *Random*, and *Hybrid*).

In all conditions the task was the same: (1) participants initially chose a seed song which was the same in all conditions. (2) Starting from this song, they had to construct a playlist with ten songs. We asked the participants to create a playlist for other people (e.g., a social event) to make them think about what constitutes a good playlist.

We used a within-subject study design. Our independent variable was the used *Tool* with 7 factors: *Manual, Rush*

---

[1] Last.FM is a platform for tracking listening behavior and based on this data, similarity values are created by collaborative filtering.

Top 5, Rush Random, Rush Hybrid, Automatic Top 5, Automatic Random, and *Automatic Hybrid*. Prior to the study, participants were allowed to get comfortable using the system. The order of the three rush conditions was counterbalanced across our participants and the automatic ones were created in the background during the study. When they completed the playlists using the rush conditions, participants had to manually create another playlist. We measured the completion time for each of the rush tools and the time spent using the manual condition.

In the beginning of the study, participants chose their seed song. They then created the playlists using each rush condition. However, after each constructed playlist, they had to fill out a questionnaire on how useful they rated the suggestions and how random they appeared. They then built their final one manually. In the end, participants had to fill out a post-questionnaire with a modified set of the IBM Computer Usability Satisfaction questions and statistical data. Also, they were asked to rank the rush and manual tools (as the automatic versions allowed no interaction) and the resulting seven playlists.

Participants

We recruited 12 participants for our second user study (4 female, 2 left-handed, 4 had participated in the pre-study). All participants declared they had experience with touch screens. Their age ranged from 24 to 35 (average: 28 years).

Hypotheses

We had three hypotheses: playlists can be constructed fastest using the automatic tools, the slowest using the manual version. Rush takes a time between the two (H1). The quality of the resulting playlists is higher with rush than the *Automatic* conditions (H2). And, *Rush Hybrid* gives better results and is preferred to *Rush Random* (H3).

Results

The creation time of automatic is, of course, always 0 seconds. The average times for rush were 123.8 (*Rush Top 5*), 142.1 (*Rush Hybrid*), and 162.3 seconds (*Rush Random*). The manual condition – as expected the slowest one – had an average time of 388.6 seconds. This supports our hypothesis H1.

The participants were overall satisfied with rush's usability as the operation speed was the only point of criticism (average ranking of 2 on a 5-point Likert-scale where 1 translates into "too slow"). Analyzing the tool's quality ranking using the Condorcet Ranked-Pairs system reveals the *Manual* as the winning candidate (3 wins), followed by *Rush Hybrid* (2 wins, 1 loss), *Rush Random* (1 win, 2 losses) and *Rush Top 5* (3 losses).

Measuring the quality of playlists is hard ([4],[3]), as the results are always personal and thus should be evaluated by their creators only. On the other hand, we would add a bias because participants are expected to rank the playlists they were involved with better and the automatic playlists worse.

This "emotional bond" can be explained by the fact that participants would generally rank playlists better if they had spent time on their creation. The "novelty effect" could further explain this bias. Thus – to learn about the impartial playlist quality – we started an online questionnaire where everyone was asked to rank a random set of playlists from the study. We received 10 ranked sets of playlists.

An analysis of the study participants' rankings using the Condorcet Ranked-Pairs system showed that playlists built manually were clearly favored (6 wins), followed by *Rush Hybrid* (5 wins, 1 loss), *Rush Random* (4 wins, 2 losses), *Automatic Random* (3 wins, 3 losses), *Rush Top 5* (2 wins, 4 losses), *Automatic Top 5* (1 win, 5 losses), and *Automatic Hybrid* (6 losses). As expected, the online participants had different opinions: *Rush Hybrid*, *Rush Random* and *Automatic Hybrid* are tied for first place (4 wins, 2 unresolved), followed by *Automatic Random* (3 wins, 3 losses), *Manual* (2 wins, 4 losses), *Rush Top 5* (1 win, 5 losses), and at the last position *Automatic Top 5* (6 losses).

Our conclusion is that the participants were clearly biased towards their own playlists and thus ranked the automatic results negatively. The more independent online vote shows that the *Hybrid* and *Random Automatic* and *Rush* versions yielded better results than the *Manual* and *Top 5* versions. We suppose these results stem from the participants' lack of experience in playlist building: Thus, adding recommendations helped to improve the quality of produced playlists, but only if the suggestions were not too restricting (as in the *Top 5* versions). The freedom that participants gained from the manual version had the downside of reducing the quality. Restricting the participants' choices might decrease the tool's satisfaction but actually helps them in producing (objectively) better results. Thus, *Rush Hybrid* and *Rush Random* brought the overall best results in subjective and objective quality. Unfortunately, we were not able to confirm H3, which means that a random set of suggestions and the more elaborate hybrid set ranked equally well.

DISCUSSION
Rush's flexibility is inherently restricted: The convenience of only having to choose between five and not all items of a collection can also be seen as the limitation of only *being able* to choose between five items. As the second study showed, depending on the underlying recommendation engine rush can yield very different results. In general, the suggestions by rush can be local, i.e., personalized for the user with one of the various recommendation techniques like collaborative filtering (for an overview see [7]). Yet, with rush being an (interactive) recommendation technique itself, suggestions can also be global (identical for each user) and thus based on, for example, a similarity metric. While we used the second approach in the user study to keep the results comparable, we suppose that introducing personalized suggestions might improve the user experience.

Shaping Recommendations
Depending on the use case several adaptations of the recommendation engine might be useful. First of all, chosen items can be interpreted as votes, thus adapting the user profile while he interacts with the system. Every item that is chosen receives a positive rating, while other items from the same set are downgraded, thus refining the adaptation to the user. The downside of this approach is the growing restriction in suggestions, with diminishing serendipity being a common problem of recommender systems [12].

Second, constraints might be applied to the set of suggestions depending on the use case. In addition to the design space for recommending collections proposed by Hansen et al. [11] we suggest two main categories based on the time frame of consumption: Items in a *concurrent* collection are consumed at the same time (e.g., apparel, extras for a car or a hotel room). Items in a *sequential* collection are consumed sequentially (e.g., a song playlist, travel plans, dinner courses). The type of collection leads to different constraints: For concurrent collections, order is not applicable but all items have to work together all the time. For sequential collections, internal consistency is important as well, but can be alleviated by a clever use of sequence. This sequence, on the other hand, adds additional constraints in that sequential items have to work after one another.

Finally, for certain user tasks and requirements, additional rule-based constraints might be added to the generation of suggestions. One such rule might be that a playlist should not contain songs twice or two songs by the same artist in a row. Also, constraints like "two sequential songs have to be similar in tempo or rhythm" might be applied. Such constraints can be used to minimize the number of inappropriate suggestions that otherwise take up one of the five precious slots. But they can also help an inexperienced user (who does not know these rules that guarantee quality) produce suitable results.

Steerable Recommendations
Rush provides users with "steerable" recommendations: The choice of an item not only makes it part of the current selection but also shapes the form of the newly suggested set as these are related to it, thus guaranteeing a certain coherence of the resulting set.

The major advantage of making recommendations interactive is the flexibility that it brings. First of all, the user is able to shape the results of the recommendation process to his liking at every step of the process. Items that the recommendation engine might find suitable but the user clearly knows he does not like can immediately be skipped and the recommendations can also be adapted to the current mood of the user - something that recommendations based on a user profile are not able to do without additional questioning. But flexibility is not only restricted to this local level: The sum of all these small decisions, the resulting collection, can also be actively adapted to the likings of the user: While other tools allow setting a general mood or tone of the items [25], rush adds a temporal flexibility to that: Depending on the underlying recommendation strategy, musical playlists that start with a certain mood and change over time in a gradual buildup are possible. Also, there is no predefined length of the collection, which lets users add items as long as they like. Lastly, the user is also flexible in its interaction with the tool: Depending on temporal constraints, the user can quickly finish building a collection, spend some more time exploring the recommendations and choosing more deliberately, or switch between the two whenever appropriate.

In addition to flexibility, rush provides users with an easy way to generate collections: Constraint-based recommender systems might also be able to yield similarly complex results but demand more mental effort from users: All constraints have to be known beforehand and expressing, for example, a gradual buildup in mood in a music playlist might be hard to express in the underlying constraint language. Also, a spontaneous change of plan is only possible by repeating the complete process, while rush users have no problem with adapting their preferences in the middle of the process. Finally, rush has the "I know it when I see it" advantage: Users can decide what they want on the go and listen to their gut feeling instead of having to decide and rationalize beforehand (cf. [16]).

Conclusion

We have presented rush, an interaction technique for creating item collections on mobile devices. An underlying recommendation algorithm decreases the user's options and thus makes it easier to build suitable collections. Still, compared to fully automatic recommendation, the user is able to influence the resulting set in a less complicated way than with constraint-based recommenders. One-touch and crossing-based interaction makes rush suitable for mobile use. Our studies showed that the vertical orientation performed best for interface and device. We also found that the choice of suggestions had a strong influence on the user's liking of the system and the quality of the results. Too restricting suggestions should be avoided in order not to frustrate the users (as one participant put it: "There are always the same songs!"). We evaluated rush in a playlist scenario but the technique itself is applicable to various recommendation tasks.

An alternate use of rush might lead to a single item selection instead of that of a whole collection: Using a "navigation by proposing" [31] approach, each row of suggestions and succeeding choices can be interpreted as a vote, thus more and more restricting the search space. We plan to evaluate this version as well.

It might also be interesting to see if a different type of interaction (e.g., panning by finger flicking, selection by tapping) has an influence on user performance.

Lastly, we plan to evaluate rush in a real-world mobile context and not just the laboratory.

ACKNOWLEDGMENTS

We thank the state of Bavaria for funding. We would also like to thank the participants of our studies, Alexander De Luca for helping with the evaluation and Petteri Nurmi for valuable feedback on the paper.

REFERENCES

1. Accot, J. and Zhai, S. More than dotting the i's - foundations for crossing-based interfaces. *Proc. SIGCHI conference on Human factors in computing systems*, (2002), 73-80.

2. Adomavicius, G. and Tuzhilin, a. Toward the next generation of recommender systems: a survey of the state-of-the-art and possible extensions. *IEEE Transactions on Knowledge and Data Engineering* 17, 6 (2005), 734-749.

3. Andric, A. and Haus, G. Estimating Quality of Playlists by Sight. *First International Conference on Automated Production of Cross Media Content for Multi-Channel Distribution (AXMEDIS'05)*, (2005), 68-74.

4. Andric, A. and Haus, G. Automatic playlist generation based on tracking user's listening habits. *Multimedia Tools and Applications* 29, 2 (2006), 127-151.

5. André, P., Teevan, J., and Dumais, S. From x-rays to silly putty via Uranus: serendipity and its role in web search. *Proc. 27th international conference on Human fac-tors in computing systems*, ACM (2009), 2033–2036.

6. Aucouturier, J. and Pachet, F. Scaling up music playlist generation. *Proc. IEEE International Conference on Multi-media and Expo*, IEEE (2002), 105–108.

7. Burke, R. Hybrid recommender systems: Survey and experiments. *User Modeling and User-Adapted Interaction* 12, 4 (2002), 331–370.

8. Cöster, R. and Svensson, M. Incremental collaborative filtering for mobile devices. *Proc. 2005 ACM symposium on Applied computing - SAC '05*, ACM Press (2005), 1102.

9. Goldberg, D., Nichols, D., Oki, B., and Terry, D. Using collaborative filtering to weave an information tapestry. *Communications of the ACM* 61, 10 (1992), 1-10.

10. Goussevskaia, O., Kuhn, M., and Wattenhofer, R. Exploring Music Collections on Mobile Devices. *Proc. 10th international conference on Human computer interaction with mobile devices and services*, ACM (2008), 359-362.

11. Hansen, D.L. and Golbeck, J. Mixing It Up: Recommending Collections of Items. *Proc. 27th international con-ference on Human factors in computing systems*, ACM (2009), 1217-1226.

12. Herlocker, J.L., Konstan, J.A., Terveen, L.G., and Riedl, J.T. Evaluating Collaborative Filtering Recom-mender Systems. *Transactions on Information Systems (TOIS)* 22, 1 (2004), 5-53.

13. Jacobsson, M., Rost, M., and Holmquist, L.E. When Media Gets Wise: Collaborative Filtering with Mobile Media Agents. *World Wide Web Internet And Web Information Systems*, (2006).

14. Kim, C.Y., Lee, J.K., Cho, Y.H., and Kim, D.H. VISCORS: A Visual-Content Recommender for the Mobile Web. *IEEE Intelligent Systems* 19, 06 (2004), 32-39.

15. Landauer, T. and Nachbar, D. Selection from alphabetic and numeric menu trees using a touch screen: breadth, depth, and width. *Proceedings of the SIGCHI conference on Human factors in computing systems*, ACM New York, NY, USA (1985), 73–78.

16. Lehrer, J. How We Decide. Houghton Mifflin, New York, 2009.

17. Lehtiniemi, A. and Seppänen, J. Evaluation of Automatic Mobile Playlist Generator. *Proc. Mobility*, (2007), 452-459.

18. Miller, B., Konstan, J., and Riedl, J. Pocketlens: Toward a personal recommender system. *ACM Transactions on Information Systems* 22, 3 (2004), 437–476.

19. Miller, B.N., Albert, I., Lam, S.K., Konstan, J.A., and Riedl, J. MovieLens Unplugged: Experiences with an Oc-casionally Connected Recommender System. *Proc. IUI*, (2000), 263-266.

20. Neumayer, R., Dittenbach, M., and Rauber, A. Playsom and pocketsomplayer, alternative interfaces to large music collections. *Proc. ISMIR*, (2005), 618–623.

21. Nguyen, Q. and Ricci, F. Long-term and session-specific user preferences in a mobile recommender system. *Proc. 13th international conference on Intelligent user interfaces*, ACM New York, NY, USA (2008), 381–384.

22. O'Donovan, J., Smyth, B., Gretarsson, B., Bostandjiev, S., and Höllerer, T. PeerChooser: Visual Interactive Recommendation. *Proc. twenty-sixth annual SIGCHI conference on Human factors in computing systems*, (2008), 1085-1088.

23. Pampalk, E., Pohle, T., and Widmer, G. Dynamic Playlist Generation Based on Skipping Behaviour. *Proc. ISMIR*, (2005), 634-637.

24. Pauws, S. and Eggen, B. PATS: Realization and user evaluation of an automatic playlist generator. *Proc. 3rd International Conference on Music Information Retrieval*, (2002), 222–230.

25. Pauws, S. and Wijdeven, S.V. User evaluation of a new interactive playlist generation concept. *Proc. ISMIR*, (2005).

26. Pohle, T., Pampalk, E., and Widmer, G. Generating similarity-based playlists using traveling salesman algorithms. *Proc. 8th International Conference on Digital Au-dio Effects (DAFx-05)*, (2005), 1-6.

27. Pu, P. and Chen, L. Trust building with explanation interfaces. *Proc. 11th international conference on Intelli-gent user interfaces*, ACM Press (2006), 93.

28. Ragno, R., Burges, C.J., and Herley, C. Inferring similarity between music objects with application to playlist generation. *Proc. 7th ACM SIGMM international workshop on Multimedia information retrieval*, ACM Press New York, NY, USA (2005), 73-80.

29. Schwartz, B. The paradox of choice: Why more is less. Harper Perennial, New York, 2005.

30. Smyth, B. and Cotter, P. Personalized adaptive navigation for mobile portals. *Proc. ECAI*, (2002), 608–612.

31. Smyth, B. Case-based recommendation. *In Lecture Notes in Computer Science*. Springer, Berlin / Heidelberg, 2007, 342-376.

32. Swearingen, K. and Sinha, R. Interaction design for recommender systems. *Proc. of Designing Interactive Systems*, ACM (2002).

33. Tintarev, N. and Masthoff, J. Effective explanations of recommendations: user-centered design. *Proc. 2007 ACM conference on Recommender systems*, ACM New York, NY, USA (2007), 153–156.

34. Vig, J., Sen, S., and Riedl, J. Tagsplanations: explaining recommendations using tags. *Proc. 13th international conference on Intelligent User Interfaces*, ACM (2009), 47-56.

35. Vogel, D. and Baudisch, P. Shift: a technique for operating pen-based interfaces using touch. *Proc. SIGCHI conference on Human factors in computing systems*, ACM (2007), 657-666.

36. Ward, D.J. and Blackwell, A.F. Dasher---a data entry interface using continuous gestures and language models. *Proc. 13th annual ACM symposium on User interface software and technology - UIST '00*, ACM Press (2000), 129-137.

37. Ward, D.J. and MacKay, D. Fast Hands-free Writing by Gaze Direction. *Nature* 838, August (2002), 4-6.

38. Wigdor, D., Forlines, C., Baudisch, P., Barnwell, J., and Shen, C. Lucid touch: a see-through mobile device. *Proc. 20th annual ACM symposium on User interface software and technology*, ACM (2007), 269-278.

39. van Gulik, R. and Vignoli, F. Visual playlist generation on the artist map. *Proc. ISMIR*, (2005), 520-523.

40. van Gulik, R., Vignoli, F., and van De Wetering, H. Mapping music in the palm of your hand, explore and dis-cover your collection. *Proc. ISMIR*, (2004).

SocialSearchBrowser: A novel mobile search and information discovery tool

Karen Church, Joachim Neumann, Mauro Cherubini and Nuria Oliver
Telefonica Research
Via Augusta 177, 08021 Barcelona, Spain
{karen, joachim, mauro, nuriao}@tid.es

ABSTRACT

The mobile Internet offers anytime, anywhere access to a wealth of information to billions of users across the globe. However, the mobile Internet represents a challenging information access platform due to the inherent limitations of mobile environments, limitations that go beyond simple screen size and network issues. Mobile users often have information needs which are impacted by contexts such as location and time. Furthermore, human beings are social creatures that often seek out new strategies for sharing knowledge and information in mobile settings. To investigate the social aspect of mobile search, we have developed SocialSearch-Browser (SSB), a novel proof-of-concept interface that incorporates social networking capabilities with key mobile contexts to improve the search and information discovery experience of mobile users. In this paper, we present the results of an exploratory field study of SSB and outline key implications for the design of next generation mobile information access services.

Author Keywords

Mobile search, social search, social networks, location-based services, context, field study, user evaluation

ACM Classification Keywords

H.5.2 Information interfaces and presentation (e.g., HCI): User Interface, H.3.3 Information Storage and Retrieval: Information Search and Retrieval.

General Terms

Design, Evaluation, Human Factors

INTRODUCTION

There are more mobile phones in the world than personal computers. They allow communication across remote locations and ubiquitous access to a wealth of information sources. Yet, most of the information retrieval systems that are available within the mobile space today are simple adaptations of their desktop counterparts and as such are not well-suited to handle the complexities of mobile contexts. In particular, geographical information is intimately related to mo-

bile devices, as they are typically carried by their owners in their daily lives. Contextual information of this nature is too fined grained and too dynamic to be captured by web technologies. Often, we seek and share local information through other communication channels and word-of-mouth appears to be the most reliable and efficient communication medium in certain information seeking tasks [28]. For instance, standard search tools have difficulties providing answers to questions such as finding information about an upcoming friends birthday or what is the most populated club in a city after a major sporting event.

Furthermore, humans are social beings who often seek new and improved ways of sharing information with their peers. In the last few years, several research projects have attempted to exploit the social dimension of search by designing interfaces that allow users to collaboratively help each other in finding the information they need [13, 22, 25]. However, these prototypes were designed with the desktop experience in mind. Conversely, prototypes that were built to improve mobile search did not exploit the social dimension of information seeking [16, 18].

In this regard, we are interested in understanding whether people's information needs while on-the-go could be addressed by providing a readily available connection to a user's social network. We believe that friends and family, who are trusted information sources, are likely to be able to draw on their experiences to provide interesting, valuable and relevant answers to the user's queries while on-the-go [15].

To explore this research space, we have developed **Social-SearchBrowser** (SSB in short), a proof-of-concept, map-based mobile search prototype designed to enhance the search and information discovery experience of mobile users by allowing them to (1) see the queries and interactions of peers and to (2) pose queries of their own (see detailed description in Section "SSB prototype"). SSB gives users the ability to connect with friends or family members while on-the-go and ask them questions. Interactions are handled on a rich map-based interface, which enables the use of deictic gestures between the remote peers [6]. Furthermore, SSB provides novel methods for filtering the queries displayed based on the level of the friendship among users.

SSB was deployed in a live field study in Ireland during the first week of April 2009. We decided to run the study in Ireland because Facebook and iPhone usage is higher in Ireland than in Spain and the authors had previous experience in recruiting participants within Ireland.

Sixteen participants tested the application and generated approximately 300 messages. Their interactions with the application were logged and time stamped in the SSB server which allowed objective analysis of their usage of the system. These measures were complemented by a post-study survey allowing us to elicit subjective information regarding the experiences of participants and based on these results we were able to draw a number of important implications for the design of social mobile applications of this nature.

The rest of this paper is organized as follows: Firstly, we summarize related studies that inspired and guided our approach and methodology. Secondly, we describe the SSB prototype. Next, we outline the methodology that we employed to conduct the field study. Then, we report the main results of the study, starting with the objective measures of the users' interaction with the system, followed by key findings of the surveys. Finally, we describe the implications for design that emerged from this research.

RELATED WORK

In this section we highlight key papers in four related areas: exploratory search, mobile search, social search and location-based annotation services.

Exploratory Search

In standard Web search, users submit a query via a search box and view a textual list of results. More recently, a new class of search has emerged, called *exploratory search* [29], which supports the exploration and discovery of information through both querying and browsing strategies. In that regard, Marchionini [21] identified three types of search activities: (1) lookup, (2) learn and (3) investigate. Lookup searches can be thought of as traditional search, while learn and investigate searches relate to discovery-oriented tasks.

In recent years, a few desktop exploratory search systems have been proposed in the literature. Yee *et al.* [30] presented an alternative interface for exploring large collections of images using hierarchical faceted metadata and dynamically generated query previews. Similarly, Alonso *et al.* [1] described an interface that utilizes timeline data to enable effective presentation and navigation of search results. Finally, Tvaroek & Bielikov [23] proposed a personalized faceted browser that facilitates exploratory search by providing users with an integrated search and navigation interface that combines full text, faceted, content-based and collaborative search. However, these prototypes were not built specifically for mobile devices, nor the user experience of interacting with them adapted to location-specific information. This particular aspect was explored by the projects described in the next section.

Mobile Search

Another area of research related to this paper concerns innovative approaches to mobile search. **FaThumb** [18] is a mobile search application designed for navigating through large data sets on mobile devices. A user evaluation demonstrated how the facet-based navigation is faster for less specific queries. Heimonen and Käki [16] examined the use of search result categorization to improve presentation on mobile devices through an interface called **Mobile Findex**.

The **Questions not Answers (QnA)** prototype [17] represents an interesting alternative to traditional mobile search. QnA allows users to access previous queries posted from the user's current location by means of a map-based interface, providing users with an *enriched sense of place*. By clicking on the queries, users can execute the displayed search. However, users cannot interact with the author of a particular query. In a live user study [2], users found the interface to be useful and they enjoyed the proactive display the interface enabled. However, there is a social component to search that these prototypes were missing and that was addressed by other projects described in the next section.

Social Dimensions of Search

More recently, researchers are investigating the social side to search. Collaborative Web Search (CWS) involves using the search histories (*i.e.*, queries and result-selections) of communities of like-minded individuals. In [12], Freyne *et al.* integrated CWS with social browsing in order to produce an effective social information access service. Preliminary results indicated that the use of social cues helps users to access relevant information in an easy and efficient manner.

Alternative approaches involve exploiting Web 2.0 technologies, specifically Web annotations, to improve Web search. The basic premise is that by allowing users to annotate search results and share these annotations with others, the search experience may be improved. Boa *et al.* [3] proposed two novel algorithms to explore the role of social annotations on similarity ranking and static ranking respectively.

Another related area of interest is *social search*. Social search in this context involves exploiting different forms of human judgements, ratings and interactions to improve the overall search experience. There have been a number of social search services developed recently, including **Stumbleupon**[1], **Wikia Search**[2] and Microsoft's **U Rank**[3].

The prototypes listed above employ an extended definition of the "social context" of users as in these cases the social context also includes *strangers* and relates more to the definition of *social navigation* [11]. In the work presented in this paper, *social* refers to the group of friends or contacts with which we maintain communication through social networks.

Most relevant to our current work is the use of social networks to enhance search results and online interactions. Mislove *et al.* presented **PeerSpective** [22], an experimental prototype which exploits both the hyperlinks of the Web and the social links within communities of users to inform a new search result ranking approach. An evaluation of the PeerSpective search engine showed that it performs well in terms of disambiguation, ranking and serendipity of search results.

Pujol & Rodriguez [25] presented **Porqpine**, a distributed social search engine which crawls, indexes and ranks content implicitly and collaboratively as users browse and search. Porqpine utilizes multiple social network sources such as Facebook, twitter and email contacts.

---

[1]See http://www.stumbleupon.com, last retrieved Sept 2009.

[2]See http://search.wikia.com, last retrieved Sept 2009.

[3]See http://research.microsoft.com/projects/urank/, last retrieved Sept 2009.

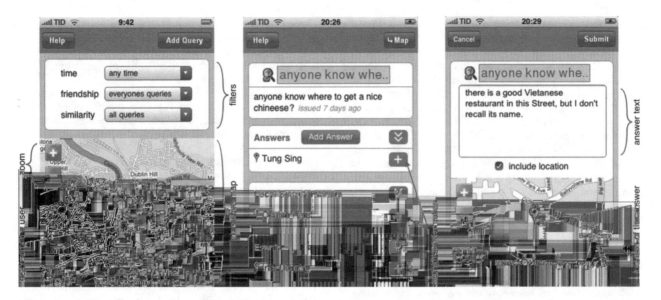

Figure 1. Screenshots of the SocialSearchBrowser (SSB) Application: (*left*) The map screen is the main screen of the SSB application. Queries are overlaid on a Google maps visualization (own queries are show with a green semi-transparent background) and three drop down menus that allow the user to filter the displayed queries; (*center*) The query detail screen shows three categories of answers: (1) answers by other users, (2) results from Google local search and (3) results from Eventful API; (*right*) When a query is answered, the user can optionally add a location.

Location-based social search

Lastly, it is worth mentioning several projects that aim to connect electronic information, (*e.g.*, a Wikipedia article describing a monument), to the physical location to which the information refers. The most relevant projects in this domain have enabled users to generate textual content in digitial form linked to a physical location, such as **GeoNotes** [24], **ActiveCampus** [14], **E-graffiti** [5], and **UrbanTapestries** [19]. All these interfaces allow users to express opinions, preferences, recommendations, *and questions* — all connected to a physical place.

More recently, commercial applications appeared on the market. **Loopt**[4] or **BrightKite**[5] enable social serendipitous encounters and keeping track of what your friends are up to. Other applications allow people to share recommendations on restaurants or other commercial activities (**Yelp**[6], **Food-Buzz**[7], or **Tabelog**[8]). Google and Yahoo also provide generic location sharing services (**Latitude**[9] or **Fireeagle**[10]).

Most relevant to our work is the prototype developed by Bilandzic *et al.* [4] called **CityFlocks** which allows users visiting a new city to pose questions —via phone calls and SMS, to local citizens. The trial of the application was successful although users reported misgivings in posing questions to complete strangers. We believe that an important dimension of information seeking is the *level of trust* that is associated to the information provider. Hence, the importance of leveraging social networks in the context of social search.

Our Proposal

The work presented in this paper builds upon earlier work presented in [7, 9]. The SSB prototype is similar in nature to the QnA prototype. The QnA system tags queries with a location. These queries are displayed on a map-based interface enabling users to visualize the search space. The QnA prototype does not, however, provide any means for a user to filter queries, other than by location. Given that the volume of queries at specific locations is likely to be high and there is no means to filter queries, the QnA prototype raises a new interface / presentation challenge. In our prototype, we address this issue by offering the user three types of filters. Additionally, although QnA pioneered the proactive display of queries on a map, the application did not allow users to issue their own queries nor to communicate with the author(s) who generated the queries being displayed. Thus, the realism of their user study is limited in some regards. The proposed SSB prototype allows its users to add and respond to queries, and to interact with other users.

Additionally, our work is related to the CityFlocks approach, although the SSB prototype focuses the interaction to the group of peers that can provide *trusted* information to the user [15]. A key contribution of our work is to explore the *social side* to mobile search, not only through a social query filter, but also by studying mobile search mediated interactions with peers (*e.g.*, members of the user's social network).

In summary our research questions can be stated as follows: *RQ1: How do mobile users interact with proactive mobile information access applications?*, and *RQ2: What are the implications of these types of applications on the design of mobile search services?*

SSB PROTOTYPE

SSB is designed to enhance information search and discovery by displaying what other users have been searching for on an interactive map-based interface. The software archi-

[4]See http://loopt.com, last retrieved Sept 2009.

[5]See http://brightkite.com/, last retrieved Sept 2009.

[6]See http://www.yelp.com/, last retrieved Sept 2009.

[7]See http://www.foodbuzz.com/, last retrieved Sept 2009.

[8]See http://tabelog.com/, last retrieved Sept 2009.

[9]See www.google.com/latitude, last retrieved Sept 2009.

[10]See http://fireeagle.yahoo.net/, last retrieved Sept 2009.

tecture of SSB consists of three components: (1) an iPhone application that allows users to browse, answer and add queries; (2) a Facebook application that allows a given user's social network to browse queries and add new answers to those queries; and (3) a server that synchronizes and stores all queries in the SSB database [11]. The server feeds applications (1) and (2) with an up-to-date list of all queries and answers. When a new query is issued by a user, the server submits the query to the Google Local Search API and the Eventful API for a set of possible search results[12]. The server also comprises an SMS notification facility that informs members of the appropriate social network about new queries and new human generated answers. In addition, the server logs all the interactions between the user and the GUI of the iPhone application for off-line analysis of user behaviour.

Figure 2. Query icons: (a) queries without any answers or result selections, (b) queries with at least one search result selection, (c) queries with answers and (d) queries with both answers and result selections.

Mobile application

The main interface of the SSB mobile application consists of a Google Maps visualization of the user's current location (Figure 1, left) with overlaid queries. This map-based interface provides users with a *sense of place* at a glance by allowing them to visualize the kind of queries that other users have issued while they were at the same location. The map indicates the user's current location by a blue circle. A tiny red circle positioned at the center of the map marks the location that new queries will be associated with. As users pan or zoom within the map, the set of visible queries is updated.

An *icon* is assigned to each query to indicate what kind of information is available about the query. This icon is displayed to the left of the query text (long query texts are truncated on the map interface). A small magnifying glass icon is assigned to a query that does not result in the selection of any search result[13] (Figure 2a). A query that resulted in the selection of at least one search result is identified by the globe icon (Figure 2b). If a query has been answered by a user of the SSB application, the associated icon is augmented with a small image that depicts a user (Figure 2c and d).

A semi-transparent background colour conveys the *origin* of the query: queries are either issued by the user (*green background*), friends (*red background*) or other people (*blue background*). Furthermore, the size of the query icon reflects the *popularity* of a query based on the number of answers that the query has received and the number of times the details of a query have been accessed by the users (Figure 1).

Interactive filters

Three filters positioned above the map allow the user to control the queries that are displayed (Figure 1, left). The filters may be used to reduce the number of queries on a crowded map or to focus on queries that fulfill specific criteria.

The *time* filter enables a form of temporal visualisation of queries. For example, users can view queries that have been submitted in the last two of hours (setting *now*), in the last 24 hours (*today*), the last week, etc.

A similar principle applies to the *friendship* filter. This filter allows users to show queries submitted by *everyone* or only by *friends*. This social filter has several degrees of 'levels of friendship'. The premise behind this filter is that in some situations, users might prefer to see queries that have been generated by friends. The level of friendship is determined by SSB as number of wall posts, tags and comments that have been exchanged between the two peers within Facebook[14].

The *similarity* filter allows users to limit the queries to those that are similar to queries that have been previously entered by the user him/herself. For a given user and a given query, SSB calculates the *similarity* as the number of words that match between the query in question and all other queries issued by the user in question[15]. Queries are displayed only if the number of matching words is equal or greater than the threshold value that is set through the similarity filter.

Query details and answers

Double-tapping on a query brings the user to the query details screen (Figure 1) which consists of 4 components:

1. *Full query details*: Showing the complete query string, the timestamp when the query was issued and the name of the user who issued the query only if this user is a *friend* of the current user.

2. *Answers*: A list of all answers that have been submitted by other users. Answers can be submitted by users via the mobile application or via the Facebook application (see below).

3. *Local search results*: A list of localized search results extracted from Google's local search service[16].

4. *Event search results*: A list of related events extracted from the Eventful API[17].

Tapping on the "plus" icon beside any of the individual query details expands additional information about the associated answer, local search result or event search result. These details include a map with a location, phone numbers and a "more info" link to an external webpage (Figure 1, right).

Facebook application

Queries submitted via the mobile application can also be answered by the user's friends through a Facebook application. The Facebook application lists all queries that have

[11]We use Tomcat for the server requirements of the application and all data is stored in a MySQL database.

[12]We define search results returned by the Google Local Search API and the Eventful API as *machine generated answers*, while answers submitted by other users or friends within a given social network are defined as *human generated answers*

[13]A *search result* in this case is defined as one of the results returned by either the Google Local Search API or the Eventful API. Eventful is an API which provides access to localized event listings.

[14]We currently use Facebook as a source of social network information, however, other online social network information could also be exploited. Upon registration, users grant SSB access to their social network. This information is stored in SSB's server and the user's original social network is never accessed again.

[15]The similarity is calculated after stemming and stopword removal

[16]http://code.google.com/apis/ajaxsearch/local.html

[17]http://eventful.com/

been submitted by any friend together with the name of the user who issued the query, the timestamp and location of the query (Figure 3). Mobile Facebook clients do not support Facebook applications and were not used in this study.

Clicking on a query opens a detailed information page (See Figure 3) that shows additional query details and a Google map of the location of the query. Additionally, it displays a list of all the answers submitted for the query and an input form for entering new answers. Facebook users can also add a location to their answer, generating what we call a *geo-answer* [6], simply by clicking on the point of the map where the resource was located. Therefore, Facebook users are able to see what queries their friends have executed while on-the-go, where and when their friends executed these queries and any answers provided to these queries.

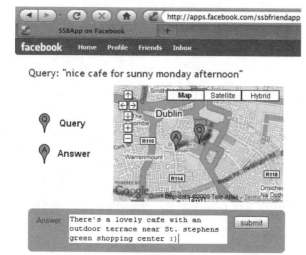

Figure 3. A friend received an SMS notification and uses the Facebook desktop application to submit the answer and a location to a query.

EVALUATION OF THE SSB PROTOTYPE

Understanding the impact of applications such as SSB on users' behavior is challenging because these applications support novel types of mobile experiences that lie beyond the scope of established practices and social conventions. Therefore, we deployed a *breaching experiment* [10]. In a breaching experiment, new technologies are deployed in the wild, allowing them to provoke new practices and reveal contingencies between activities and technological interactions.

Hence, we carried out an exploratory field study involving 16 participants in Dublin, Ireland. Our goal was to investigate how mobile users react to this type of application and to highlight implications for the design of future mobile information access services. Although 16 subjects might be considered too few to generalize results, we have observed similar results in more recent evaluations of SSB which involved a larger group of users. Given that our evaluations were conducted *in-the-wild*, we believe that these early results are valid and help us shed light on how such novel mobile services might be used among groups of friends.

Participants

Due to our design choices, participants were required to own an iPhone and be active Facebook users. We recruited par-

ticipants using an online questionnaire which we advertised in various Internet boards and mailing lists within Ireland. From a pool of more than 100 respondents, we selected a subset that matched our requirements. Participants were informed that a small incentive — in the form of a gift voucher — would be provided for taking part in the study and that they would be rewarded for involving their friends in the study. This additional incentive provided a motivation to have friends installing the Facebook application.

In total, 16 participants took part in the study (14 male and 2 female) who ranged in age between 18 and 54, with an average age of 29 (stdev 8.8). The participants lived in various counties in Ireland and had a diverse set of occupations, including undergraduate students, a PhD student, a musician, a nurse, a factory coordinator, a car salesperson, a porter and a few IT/Technical support specialists.

Most of the participants owned the 3G version of the iPhone ($> 87\%$). Most users ($> 60\%$) had their Facebook account for more than a year. The vast majority of participants accessed their Facebook accounts at least once per day ($> 87\%$) and the majority of them ($> 87\%$) stated that Facebook is part of their daily routine. All but one participants have more than 10 Facebook friends (median number of friends $51 - 100$). When we examined the social connections between the participants, we found that 9 of the 16 participants were connected through Facebook with at least one other participant of the study. We identified 3 social groups; 1 highly connected group of 5 participants and 2 smaller groups consisting 2 participants each.

The majority of the participants declared to access the Internet multiple times per day through their mobile phone ($\sim 87\%$). Also, the majority declared to have used a search engine via their mobile phone in the past ($\sim 97\%$).

Procedure

Before the field test began, users were asked to: (1) Access an online application which extracted social network details from their Facebook account; (2) install the Facebook application and ask their Facebook friends to also install the application; and (3) install the SSB iPhone application.

Once the mobile application was installed, users were given some time to explore the interface, execute queries, etc. and to ask us any questions or express any concerns that they had in using the application. Users were informed that this was a "test/training" period[18] and that all queries/interactions generated during the training period would be deleted when the live field study began. The live field study ran for a one-week period, from the 31st of March 2009 until the 6th of April 2009. Participants had access to a website which included full details on each phase of the user study and a frequently asked questions page for the duration of the study.

One of the authors was based in Dublin, Ireland, for the entire duration of the study to address any issues the participants had. Users were sent regular reminders and updates regarding the user study via email[19]. Finally, participants

---

[18]The "test/training" period took place over a weekend.

[19]We emailed participants on 5 occasions over the 7-day test period.

were asked to complete a post-study survey to gather subjective information on their experiences with the application[20].

SMS notifications

The SSB application employed an SMS notification facility to keep users informed of the interactions of other users. Any time a user issued a new query in the mobile application, an SMS notification was sent to all his/her friends that had installed the Facebook application. Likewise, users of the mobile application were informed via SMS as soon as someone answered their query.

RESULTS

Basic usage patterns

Table 1 shows the basic usage statistics generated by our study. In total, participants generated 56 queries, 171 query lookups[21] and 66 answers, which corresponds to almost 300 messages over the 1-week period. We found that users were more active in the early days of the study when compared to the latter days. If we examine the distribution of queries and answers generated per participant, as shown in Figure 4, we see asymmetry in user behaviour, with some users generating lots of queries and other users generating more answers.

Measure	Queries	Lookups	Answers
Total #	56	171	66
Mean (per-user)	3.5	10.7	3.3
Mean (per-day)	8	24.4	9.4

Table 1. The total and average number of queries, query lookups and answers. Note the average number of answers per user reported above is across the 20 unique participants who provided at least one answer.

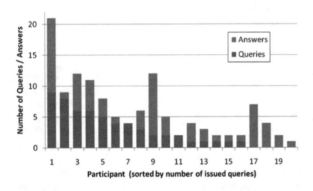

Figure 4. Number of queries & answers per participant over the 7 days.

Interestingly, we find that the two *standard* search results, *i.e.* Google local search and Eventful search results, provided results to the users' queries *less frequently* than anticipated by the authors: only 79% of queries returned one or more local search result (in average 4) and only 7% of the queries returned one or more event search result. Additionally, users *seldom interacted* with the search results, in particular the event search results: only six (38%) participants interacted with at least one local search result, while only

---

[20]Some of the participants took it upon themselves to setup a Facebook group to discuss the prototype and user study.

[21]A query lookup corresponds to the user requesting the query details page by double-tapping on the query.

one participant interacted with an event search result. Furthermore, only a single user made use of the external *"more info"* link of the search results[22].

Conversely, participants were significantly more active when providing answers to posted queries. At least one answer was submitted for 73% of the queries, generating a total of 66 answers with an average of 9.4 per day and 3.3 per user, see Table 1. Interestingly, half of the answers were generated from the SSB mobile application and the other half were generated from the Facebook application. These answers were generated by 18 unique users: 14 were participants of the SSB mobile application, while the other 4 users corresponded to Facebook friends who had installed the Facebook application. Participants engaged frequently with the *answers* facility in the mobile application: 10 (62%) of the participants interacted with at least one answer.

Types of Interactions & motivations to use the SSB

In order to gain an insight into the types of interactions our participants were involved in, we manually classified all queries and answers according to their type. We identified five types of queries within the dataset and five types of answers. Their frequency of occurrence is illustrated in Table 2.

1. Location Specific Queries: We found that 57% of the queries are location specific; they refer to a specific geographical location and geographical information is needed in order to satisfy the user's information need. The vast majority of these queries include the interrogative keyword 'where', such as *"Where is nice to go for breakfast?"* and *"Where can I buy an incase slider cover for the iPhone 3G?"*.

2. General Queries: General queries are queries which are not explicitly dependent on location. Examples include *"anything good in the cinema?"* and *"what time is it?"*. We found that 36% of queries correspond to this type.

3. Status Update Queries: Interestingly, 16% of queries correspond to this type. These queries fulfill a similar purpose to twitter tweets or Facebook/Instant messenger status updates. Instead of satisfying an information need, users are informing others about what they are currently doing or how they are currently feeling. Examples include *"waiting in the car"* and *"nice chicken roll :)"*. One user reflected on his experience with SSB and wrote *"you can see conversations starting based on queries which reminds me a little of my twitter experience"*. Note that we cannot conclude whether this behavior was primed by previous exposures to other social applications. It would have been interesting to understand whether our participants creatively adapted their use of SSB in order to achieve their goals or whether they were unclear about how to use the application which lead to a more exploratory use case. We would like to explore this further as part of future work.

4. Application Related and *5. Miscellaneous Queries*: Application related queries (4%) relate to comments about the mobile application itself, *"does this work?"*, whereas miscellaneous queries (2%) could not be classified into one of the other types (*e.g.* jokes).

---

[22]This "more info" link corresponds to a search result-selection. Clicking on this link brings the user to an external website

Queries		Answers	
Location Specific Query	57%	General Answer	53%
"Where is nice to go for breakfast?"		*"Cafe lucia is good I hear"*	
General Query	36%	Conversational Answer	26%
"Is there anything good on tv this evening?"		*"having fun?"*	
Status Update Query	16%	Status Update Answer	23%
"waiting in the car"		*"I'm hear"*	
Application Related Query	4%	Miscellaneous Answer	14%
"does this wrok"		*"hello"*	
Miscellaneous Query	2%	Application Related Answer	9%
"jacob"		*"The accuracy can vary a bit too"*	

Table 2. Queries and answers classified by their type along with examples

These observations indicate that SSB served both as a tool for inter-group communication as well as a search and information discovery tool while on-the-move. Despite the application's original design, *i.e.,* helping users satisfy their mobile information needs, it appears that the social aspects provided by the application (*i.e.* the involvement of friends, the social filter, the answers facility), inspired unexpected forms of social interactions among participants. Table 3 shows two examples that emphasize this observation. For example, it appears that a few general queries evolved into short conversations between participants. These findings suggest that our participants would have enjoyed support for conversations and not only for bulletin-board type messages.

Following the same methodology used for the queries we categorized the provided answers into 5 categories. Table 2 shows these five types with examples.

1. General Answers: The most popular type of answers (53%) are general answers in which the user is attempting to provide a valid and relevant answer that may or may not be location-specific.

2. Conversational Answers: 26% of answers belong to this category. Conversational answers are probes for additional details or statements/comments that appear to be motivated by the desire to chat. For example, the query *"cinema"*, generated the conversational answer *"are you looking to go see something?"*. Another example is the (status update type) query *"waiting in the car"*, to which a friend answered *"having fun?"*. While these queries and answers are not satisfying an information need in a traditional sense, they seem to be relevant as starting points of conversations.

3.Status Update Answers: We also identified a status update type in 23% of the answers. Examples include *"It's wonderful here :-)"* and *"I'm here"*.

4. Application Related and *5. Miscellaneous Answers*: Application related answers (9%) again correspond to comments about the application itself, for example *"Yeah I noticed this since getting the iPhone. The accuracy can vary a bit too"*, whereas miscellaneous answers (14%) could not be classified into any of the other categories (e.g. *"hello"*).

It is worth pointing out that some of the queries and answers fall into more than one category, particularly when it comes to *status updates*. For example, in the query *"just got caught by april fools. anyone have a good idea for one?"*, we find

that the first statement is a status update, while the second statement is a general query. The answer to this query was also a combination of types: *"my boyfriend proposed this morning....and then said April Fools! he's lucky I saw the funny side"*. In this answer, the user is informing the other participant of what happened (status update), but the statement is also an attempt to provide an answer to the query.

Example 1
Q: *"where will i find a 3G signal?"*
A1: *"I found one here! 3 bars too!"*
A2: *"good man I was going to say move into the city"*
Example 2
Q: *"where is the luas?"*
A1: *"at the entrance to james' hospital"*
A2: *"cheers buddy"*

Table 3. Examples of queries and answers that correspond to little conversations among participants

Qualitative Feedback and Experiences

Our participants filled out a post-task questionnaire designed to elicit their experiences with SSB. The questionnaire included several open questions where participants could freely express their experience with the SSB prototype.

Some participants reported speed and responsiveness of the application to be a concern, in particular relating to the maps component. However, despite these issues, there were many aspects of the application that users enjoyed.

One user described his experience with SSB as a means of bridging connections with others: *"I liked the ability to see where friends were, what they were doing. It gave me the opportunity to feel as if I was involved even though I wasn't there, or indeed to join them if they were doing something I enjoyed."*. Another user likened SSB to an extension of his social network: *"I found the SSB App to be an extension of my normal social network. It was great to approach trading information between people and the time scale between the query and answer seemed to be much shorter than in any other social network because I had sms and email updates. The physical location was a great addition because you could appreciate the context of location in a users query. In turn giving a more helpful answer."*

Some users explicitly expressed that they saw the potential in an SSB-like approach to search: *"I can really see the usefulness of this app once more people are using it"*, *"I think*

Question	Mean	Median	Mode	Frequency				
				1	2	3	4	5
Q1	3.8	4	4	1	0	1	13	1
Q2	3.8	4	4	1	0	4	7	4
Q3	3.8	4	4	1	0	4	8	3
Q4	3.4	4	4	1	1	5	9	0
Q5	2.9	3	3	1	4	6	5	0

Table 4. Questionnaire results: users' reactions to the proactive display.

Question	Mean	Median	Mode	Frequency				
				1	2	3	4	5
Q1	3.8	4	4	1	1	2	9	3
Q2	3.9	4	4	1	0	3	8	4
Q3	3.9	4	4	1	0	2	9	4
Q4	3.9	4	4	1	0	4	6	5
Q5	4.1	4	4	1	0	1	8	6
Q6	3.3	3	3	1	1	9	3	2

Table 5. Questionnaire results: users' reactions to the answers facility.

it is an excellent idea and use of the technology at hand" and *"The more people that use it, the more interaction and information you would get."*.

One of the goals of our open field study was to explore what types of experiences a proactive mobile interface like SSB is generating. Results to these questions are shown in table 4. When asked about viewing other people's queries and interactions, participants rated this experience as interesting ($Q1 = 4$) on a 5-point Likert scale (1=strongly disagree, 5=strongly agree and 3=neutral)[23]. Subjects also indicated that it enabled them to discover new interesting content ($Q2 = 4$), it encouraged them to think of their own new queries ($Q3 = 4$) and it allowed them to learn about the area in question ($Q4 = 4$). However, participants were somewhat neutral when asked if it allowed them to learn about people in a given location ($Q5 = 3$).

We explicitly asked participants if they liked viewing other people's queries and interactions and found that 13 users ($> 80\%$) indicated *yes*. In accordance, we found *curiosity* to be the main reason why SSB was seen as appealing. Participants liked to know what other people were doing and where they were. One participant commented *"I could tell what people were getting up to and where exactly they had been or were going. A bit like a story of their day..."*.

The reactions to the filters were mixed. It appears that some users were confused and others could see their potential but felt the filters would only be truly useful if there were more queries. However, some participants indicated that the filters provided them with complete control over the set of queries displayed on the map. Although the usefulness of the filters was difficult to test, given the low number of queries displayed on the map, we found that the *time* filter was interacted with most frequently (60% of cases), highlighting the importance of temporal information on the mobile platform.

The most highly rated feature of SSB was the answers facility. Table 5 shows details on user responses to a series of

---

[23] All ratings reported are the median rating across all participants.

post-task survey questions. Users found the ability to add answers to queries useful ($Q1 = 4$), they liked being able to answer queries ($Q2 = 4$) and enjoyed the ability to add a location to their answers ($Q3 = 4$). Users appeared to find answers with a location more useful than answers without a location ($Q4 = 4$) and participants really liked the fact that their friends could answer their queries ($Q5 = 4$). Interestingly, users were neutral in their response when asked whether the answers provided by other people helped them satisfy their information need ($Q6 = 3$). It appears that although participants liked the answers feature, not all the answers they received were useful or relevant.

Additionally, sharing knowledge and helping other people was frequently mentioned as a positive aspect of the answers component. A few exemplary comments by participants: *"I found I could share my knowledge with others"*, *"if I could answer their queries I was glad to help"* and *"it was good being able to help other people with their queries"*.

When asked what they liked most about SSB, 40% of participants pointed to either the answers facility or the SMS notifications. As described above, every time a query was answered, the person that issued the query received an SMS. Likewise, when a participant submitted a new query, their friends were notified via SMS. Comments on this topic: *"The fact that it notified answers to queries by SMS"* and *"Receiving texts when queries had been answered"*.

IMPLICATIONS

SSB has proven to be a useful showcase of proactive map-based mobile social search and has allowed us to evaluate new search paradigms with real mobile users. Our results have showed that mobile users enjoyed the proactive, social nature of the SSB prototype. In the following section we outline key findings and implications for the design of future mobile information access services.

Location, privacy & curiosity

Participants found the map-based interface to be an intuitive way to browse queries. Some users explicitly mentioned that they liked the ability to share their location with friends. For example, one participant commented: *"Knowing locations of friends when they execute queries can be helpful but also gives you the feeling that the distance between people is reduced."*. Participants also liked the location-based aspect of SSB because it allowed them to learn about the location of others. Our participants liked that they could see exactly where other people were when they executed queries, allowing them to *track* or *watch* others. One user commented: *"you can keep tabs on people :)"*.

Conversely, the availability of location information raised a few negative reactions: 4 participants (25%) reported that revealing one's location raised privacy concerns. Participants also asked for more control over the location component of the application. In particular, they were interested in being able to conceal or obscure their own location. When asked what they liked *least* about the application, one participant commented *"using my location and everyone seeing it."*. Another participant made a more general comment: *"it can also be a little unnerving if you post a query at home knowing that others can find where you live."*. Previous work in this area has found similar privacy concerns [20].

However, it came as a surprise to the authors that revealing one's location was significantly more problematic in terms of privacy than the actual content of the queries and answers. Participants seemed very relaxed with respect to the types of queries and answers they submitted, with very little regard for the tone and language used. In fact, some users posted queries and answers that might be considered quite personal in nature. This behavior might be explained by the fact that all our participants were active Facebook users and hence were used to sharing status updates, comments, photos and other personal content with their online friends.

One outcome from our study is that future location-based systems of this nature need to consider the importance of location-privacy trade-offs. Curiosity about our peers' whereabouts and activities seems to be part of human nature. However we tend to be reluctant to reveal these details about ourselves. One approach to address these concerns could be to allow the user to selectively decide whom a query or a location will be visible to. Alternatively, a facility for users to *offset* or *obfuscate* their current physical location could be provided. Note that 57% of the queries in our study were location specific, whereas the rest of queries did not require others to know the user's location in order to be answered. Finally, as mobile location-based services become more pervasive, we expect the users' sensitivities about sharing location information to change.

Unique characteristics of mobile information needs
Previous research has shown that mobile information needs differ significantly from standard web needs [8, 27]. The results of our user study confirm this and in fact, help us increase our understanding of what it is that makes mobile information needs so unique.

The SSB prototype leverages a user's social network to enable friends to answer queries and provide recommendations to other users. Ten users preferred this human-generated content over both the local and event search listings. Although local search engines such as Google local are very good at answering specific queries like *"starbucks"*, they are less equipped to satisfy information needs that are personal in nature or that require access to very *fresh* content. For example, queries like *"Is there anything good on tv this evening?"* and *"is anyone else on this ssb on boards?"*[24] could not be answered by a standard search engine. Hence, it's important for mobile information access services to consider alternative approaches to helping mobile users. Such approaches should look beyond traditional search engine indices and incorporate a human component for access to the most relevant, personal and up-to-date content.

Existing technologies & real-time notifications
The SMS notifications were used within SSB to inform friends of new query submissions and new answers. The authors thought of the SMS notification as a rather unimportant add-on and were surprised by the overwhelmingly positive reaction from the SSB users. Possible explanations for this reaction are: (1) Mobile phone users know from their own experience that text messages (almost) always reach the recipient.

---

[24]*boards* is a well known online forum within Ireland and as such the participant wanted to know if anyone else using the SSB application was also a users of boards.ie.

This reliability gives users reassurance that their SSB queries and answers reach their friends; (2) SMS messages are semi-instantaneous. This speeds up response time and transforms SSB from a information-pull search application to an information-push application with high interaction speeds. When waiting for an answer from a friend (or non-friend) after issuing a query, the SMS notification allows the user to shut down the SSB application and focus on something else while waiting for an answer as opposed to requiring the user to wait with no responses or updates from SSB. Finally, (3) text messages are perceived as direct human-to-human communication as opposed to other types of computer mediated human-to-human interaction such as playing in gaming networks or interacting in second life. Thus, the SMS notification shifts the perception of SSB from a search engine service towards a tool to communicate with real people.

These findings imply that utilizing trusted and reliable technologies is welcomed by users. Therefore, when designing future mobile services researchers should consider the integration of existing approaches that work well and are understood by their users. It appears that push-based information services are key within the mobile space, providing users with easier access to relevant and interesting content.

CONCLUSION
Mobile information access is challenging, particularly from a search perspective. Key contexts such as location, time and social interactions have significant impact on mobile information needs. In this paper, we have described a proof-of-concept research prototype called SocialSearchBrowser (SSB) which explores the social context of mobile search. SSB incorporates social networking capabilities with key mobile contexts to improve the search and information discovery experience of mobile subscribers, providing users with proactive access to interesting content. In this paper, we have presented key results from an exploratory field study of SSB and outlined a number of implications for the design of next generation mobile information access services.

We are currently investigating a few areas of future work related to the SSB prototype. We are in the process of implementing an improved version of SSB which incorporates some of the lessons we have learned. Specifically, we plan to strengthen the social interaction between participants and to address privacy issues by allowing users to *obfuscate* their current physical location. We plan to carry out a longitudinal live mobile field study involving more participants and more groups of friends. We have also identified interesting research directions that explore the social context of mobile search in more detail. For example, we found that a significant percentage of the queries and answers lead to conversations among participants. We would like to explore these social interactions in more detail and devise new approaches to utilizing these human-interactions to improve the information access experiences of mobile users.

ACKNOWLEDGEMENTS
We would like to thank the participants of this study for sharing their needs and opinions with us, Alejandro Gutierrez for helping debugging the application and Pamela Fox for insights related to Google maps.

REFERENCES

1. ALONSO, O., BAEZA-YATES, R., AND GERTZ, M. Exploratory search using timelines. In *Proc. CHI'07, Workshop on Exploratory Search and HCI* (2007).

2. ARTER, D., BUCHANAN, G., HARPER, R., AND JONES, M. Incidental information and mobile search. In *Proc. of MobileHCI'07* (2007), ACM, pp. 413–420.

3. BAO, S., XUE, G., WU, X., YU, Y., FEI, B., AND SU, Z. Optimizing web search using social annotations. In *Proc. of WWW'07* (2007), ACM, pp. 501–510.

4. BILANDZIC, M., FOTH, M., AND DE LUCA, A. Cityflocks: designing social navigation for urban mobile information systems. In *Proc. of DIS '08* (New York, USA, 2008), ACM, pp. 174–183.

5. BURRELL, J., AND GAY, G. K. E-graffiti: evaluating real-word use of a context-aware system. *Interacting with Computers*, 14 (2002), 301–312.

6. CHERUBINI, M. *Annotations of Maps in Collaborative Work at a Distance.* PhD thesis, n. 4116, Swiss Federal Institute of Technology (EPFL), Lausanne, Switzerland, June 2008.

7. CHURCH, K. AND SMYTH, B. Who, what, where & when: a new approach to mobile search. In *Proc. of IUI'08* (2008), ACM, pp. 309-312.

8. CHURCH, K. AND SMYTH, B. Understanding the intent behind mobile information needs. In *Proc. of IUI'09* (2009), ACM, pp. 247-256.

9. CHURCH, K. AND SMYTH, B. AND OLIVER, N. Visual Interfaces for Improved Mobile Search. In *Workshop on Visual Interfaces to the Social and the Semantic Web (VISSW), part of IUI'09* (2009).

10. CRABTREE, A. Design in the absence of practice: breaching experiments. In *Proc. DIS '04* (New York, NY, USA, 2004), ACM Press, pp. 59–68.

11. DOURISH, P., AND CHALMERS, M. Running out of space: Models of information navigation. In *Proc. of HCI'04* (Glasgow, UK, 1994).

12. FREYNE, J., FARZAN, R., BRUSILOVSKY, P., SMYTH, B., AND COYLE, M. Collecting community wisdom: integrating social search & social navigation. In *Proc. of IUI '07* (2007), ACM, pp. 52–61.

13. GOLBECK, J., AND WASSER, M. M. Socialbrowsing: integrating social networks and web browsing. In *Proc. CHI '07* (2007), ACM, pp. 2381–2386.

14. GRISWOLD, W. G., SHANAHAN, P., BROWN, S. W., AND BOYER, R. T. Activecampus: Experiments in community-oriented ubiquitous computing. *IEEE Computer 37*, 10 (2003).

15. HEATH, T. *Information-seeking on the Web with Trusted Social Networks: from Theory to Systems.* PhD thesis, The Open University, Milton Keynes, UK, January 2008.

16. HEIMONEN, T., AND KÄKI, M. Mobile findex: supporting mobile web search with automatic result categories. In *Proc. MobileHCI '07* (2007), ACM, pp. 397–404.

17. JONES, M., BUCHANAN, G., HARPER, R., AND XECH, P.-L. Questions not answers: a novel mobile search technique. In *Proc. of CHI '07* (2007), ACM, pp. 155–158.

18. KARLSON, A. K., ROBERTSON, G. G., ROBBINS, D. C., CZERWINSKI, M. P., AND SMITH, G. R. FaThumb: a facet-based interface for mobile search. In *Proc. of CHI '06* (2006), ACM, pp. 711–720.

19. LANE, G., THELWALL, S., ANGUS, A., PECKETT, V., AND WEST, N. Urban tapestries: Public authoring, place and mobility. Project final report, Proboscis, UK, London, UK, 2005.

20. LUDFORD, P. J., PRIEDHORSKY, R., REILY, K., AND TERVEEN, L. Capturing, sharing, and using local place information. In *Proc. of CHI'07* (2007), ACM, pp. 1235–1244.

21. MARCHIONINI, G. Exploratory search: from finding to understanding. *Communications of the ACM 49*, 4 (2006), pp. 41–46.

22. MISLOVE, A., GUMMADI, K. P., AND DRUSCHEL, P. Exploiting social networks for internet search. In *Proc. HotNets '06* (2006).

23. TVAROŽEK, M. AND BIELIKOVÁ, M. Collaborative multi-paradigm exploratory search. In *Proc. of WebScience '08* (2008), ACM, pp. 29–33.

24. PERSSON, P., AND FAGERBERG, P. Geonotes: a real-use study of a public location-aware community system. Technical Report SICS-T–2002/27-SE, SICS, University of Göteborg, Sweden, 2002.

25. PUJOL, J.P., AND RODRIGUEZ, P. Porqpine: a distributed social search engine. In *Proc. of WWW'09* (2009).

26. YEE, K.-P., SWEARINGEN, K., LI, K., AND HEARST, M. Faceted metadata for image search and browsing. In *Proc. of CHI'03* (2003), ACM, pp. 401–408.

27. SOHN, T. AND LI, K. A. AND GRISWOLD, W. G. AND HOLLAN, J. D. A diary study of mobile information needs. In *Proc. of CHI'08* (2008), ACM, pp. 433–442.

28. SHARDANAND, U. AND MAES, P. Social information filtering: algorithms for automating "word of mouth" In *Proc. of CHI'95* (1995), ACM, pp. 210–217.

29. WHITE, R. W., KULES, B., DRUCKER, S., AND SCHRAEFEL, M. Supporting exploratory search: Special issue. *Communications of the ACM 49*, 4 (2006).

30. YEE, K.-P., SWEARINGEN, K., LI, K., AND HEARST, M. Faceted metadata for image search and browsing. In *Proc. of CHI'03* (2003), ACM, pp. 401–408.

Usability Guided Key-Target Resizing for Soft Keyboards

Asela Gunawardana
Microsoft Research
Redmond, WA 98052
aselag@microsoft.com

Tim Paek
Microsoft Research
Redmond, WA 98052
timpaek@microsoft.com

Christopher Meek
Microsoft Research
Redmond, WA 98052
meek@microsoft.com

ABSTRACT

Soft keyboards offer touch-capable mobile and tabletop devices many advantages such as multiple language support and space for larger graphical displays. On the other hand, because soft keyboards lack haptic feedback, users often produce more typing errors. In order to make soft keyboards more robust to noisy input, researchers have developed key-target resizing algorithms, where underlying target areas for keys are dynamically resized based on their probabilities. In this paper, we describe how overly aggressive key-target resizing can sometimes prevent users from typing their desired text, violating basic user expectations about keyboard functionality. We propose an anchored key-target method which aims to provide an input method that is robust to errors while respecting usability principles. In an empirical evaluation, we found that using anchored dynamic key-targets significantly reduce keystroke errors as compared to the state-of-the-art.

Author Keywords

source-channel key-target resizing, language model, touch model

ACM Classification Keywords

H.5.2 Information Interfaces and Presentation: User Interfaces—*Input devices and strategies*

General Terms

Experimentation, Human Factors, Performance

INTRODUCTION

Mobile and tabletop devices with touchscreens have become increasingly widespread in the commercial market, such as the Apple iPhone [1] and the Microsoft Surface [2]. These devices often utilize a graphically rendered image of a keyboard, or a *soft keyboard* (see [10] for a survey), for text input. Because soft keyboards have no physical manifestation, more space can be devoted to larger displays, and because they are driven by software, soft keyboards can easily support multiple languages, key layouts, and screen orientations

[8]. On the other hand, soft keyboards lack tactile feedback, which enable users to know when they have touched, clicked and slipped away from a key. These physical affordances have been shown to be critical for touch-typing [17]. For mobile devices, smaller key sizes exacerbate the situation. Mobile users not only type slower on a soft keyboard than on a miniature physical keyboard [8], but they also generate more errors and fail to notice them [4].

A number of interesting approaches to mitigating errors on soft keyboards involve making the rendered keys larger or smaller depending on their likelihood [3]. Some approaches even visually highlight keys [3, 15, 14], though some studies [7] report that users could find this distracting. A different kind of approach, which we focus on here, is *key-target resizing*, where underlying target areas for keys, rather than the keys themselves, are dynamically resized based on their probabilities. Notably, the soft keyboard of the popular iPhone, which actually markets key-target resizing as one of its key features [16], uses this approach. For example, in the case of a standard QWERTY layout, touches on parts of the rendered "y" key may return "t" if the previous input was "habi" because "habit" is more probable than "habiy." This makes it seem as if the target area for the "t" key has grown while the hit target for the "y" key has shrunk. In order to estimate the probability of keys for key-target resizing, Goodman et al. [6] introduced a *source-channel approach* which combines a *language model* for predicting the likelihood of different intended key sequences with a *touch model* for predicting the likelihood of different finger touch or pen locations on the screen given the user's intended key. When a touch event occurs, the source-channel approach uses both the touch location and the likelihood of various continuations of the key stream in order to determine the most likely key the user intended to type.

While this approach has been shown to improve typing accuracy [6], we argue that it also makes the behavior of the keyboard less predictable to users. Since the key-targets are dynamic and do not correspond to the rendered keys, it is unclear to users where they should touch the keyboard in order to register their desired keys. In extreme cases, overly aggressive key-target resizing may even cause certain key sequences to be impossible to type. For example, it may be impossible to type the "y" key after "habi," even if the user actually intends to type "habiy" (e.g., as a proper name). This violates basic user expectations about keyboard functionality. It is therefore desirable that key-target resizing be guided by the usability principle that every key can reliably be typed in every context, and that the location that returns each key is intuitive. In this paper, we propose an anchored key-target resizing method that accomplishes this within the source-channel approach, so that soft keyboards can remain robust to errors while respecting usability principles.

This paper consists of three sections. In the first section, we provide a summary of the source-channel approach [6] to key-target resizing. In the second, we detail how we modified this approach to yield anchored dynamic key-targets. In the third section, we empirically evaluate our anchored dynamic key-targets in simulation experiments on mobile soft keyboard data, showing improvements in keystroke error rate over the state-of-the-art. After discussing our results, we conclude with opportunities for future research.

BACKGROUND

Related Research

As mentioned in the introduction, a number of researchers have explored making the language model component of key prediction explicit in the interface by visually highlighting the next likely keys. Al Faraj et al. [3] increased the visual size of the keys of a QWERTY soft keyboard on a ultra-mobile PC and found that users were faster and more accurate. Similarly, Magnien et al. [15] found that by bolding the next likely keys for keyboard layouts unfamiliar to users, showing correctly predicted keys increased speed. However, they did not examine performance on a QWERTY layout. MacKenzie and Zhang [14] also highlighted the next likely keys on a QWERTY soft keyboard with different colors for an eye-typing interface. They found that coloring combined with their gaze fixation algorithm significantly reduced error rates. One nice side effect of visually highlighting the next likely keys is that it can sometimes assist users who are unsure of how to spell a word to type correctly.

Unfortunately, in the above studies, none of the researchers investigated the effect of using the key predictions as just a language model weight for noisy input without visual highlighting. As such, it is difficult to tease apart how much the visual aspect contributed to performance above and beyond what would have been gained by leveraging the language model. For key prediction, the above studies employed either character-level bigrams [3] or prefix-based word completions [15][14]. They did not consider ways of incorporating models of touch or eye-gaze input into estimating the overall likelihood of different keys, as is possible with the source-channel approach.

Because different users can and do generate different touch observations for intended keys, Himberg et al. [7] explored personalizing soft keyboards based on individual touch patterns. For a nine-key numeric layout, they visually adjusted the centroids and borders of each key according to different adaptation schedules. Although they did not measure performance, they assessed qualitative feedback from users and concluded that any adaptation of soft keyboard layouts should be sensitive to user expectations so that it is not distracting. We concur with this sentiment and consider personalization an important future direction.

Finally, various researchers have sought to overcome noisy input on soft keyboards by augmenting them with hardware for vibro-tactile feedback [8][4]. Others have developed alternative keyboard layouts based on Fitt's law and character-level bigrams such as the Metropolis [19] and OPTI [13] layouts.

Source-Channel Key-Target Resizing

We now review the source-channel approach to key-target resizing described in [6]. This approach utilizes a language model that predicts the likelihood of intended key sequences, and a touch model that predicts the likelihood of different touch locations for each intended key. The model is fairly general, and subsumes some other probabilistic models such as that of [7].

Suppose that $l_1, \cdots, l_n$ is a sequence of n touch locations, where each $l \in \mathbb{R}^2$ is an x and y coordinate pair. The task is to output a good estimate $k_1^*, \cdots, k_n^*$ of the user's intended sequence of keys, from a key alphabet $\mathcal{K}$. In this paper, we address the case where there are no insertion or deletion errors, where an unintended touch is spuriously registered or an intended touch is not registered. The most likely intended key sequence given the sequence of touch locations is given by

$$k_1^*, \cdots, k_n^* = \underset{k_1, \cdots, k_n}{\arg\max}\, p(k_1, \cdots, k_n | l_1, \cdots, l_n) \quad (1)$$

Using Bayes' rule,

$$p(k_1, \cdots, k_n | l_1, \cdots, l_n) = \\ \frac{p(k_1, \cdots, k_n) p(l_1, \cdots, l_n | k_1, \cdots, k_n)}{p(l_1, \cdots, l_n)} \quad (2)$$

Since the denominator is a positive constant with respect to $k_1, \cdots, k_n$, it can be ignored in the maximization of equation (1) to yield

$$k_1^*, \cdots, k_n^* = \\ \underset{k_1, \cdots, k_n}{\arg\max}\, p(k_1, \cdots, k_n) p(l_1, \cdots, l_n | k_1, \cdots, k_n) \quad (3)$$

The first term is referred to as the *language probability* while the second term is the *touch probability*.

Using the chain rule we can decompose the language probability as

$$p(k_1, \cdots, k_n) = \\ p(k_1) p(k_2 | k_1) \cdots p(k_n | k_1, \cdots, k_{n-1}) \quad (4)$$

Following [6], the language probability is modeled using an N-gram language model which makes the approximation

$$p(k_i | k_1, \cdots, k_{i-1}) \approx p_L(k_i | k_{i-N+1}, \cdots, k_{i-1}) \quad (5)$$

That is, we assume that the probability of a key given all the keys so far is approximated by the probability of that key given only the last $N - 1$ keys. Since we do not wish key-target resizing to rule out any key at any time, it is important that the language model be "smooth." That is, it is important

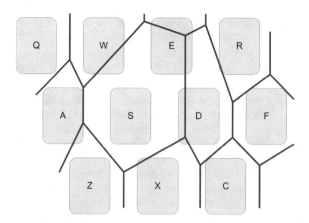

Figure 1. A schematic example where key-target resizing has made it difficult for the user to type the key 'e' because the language model predicts that it is very unlikely compared to the key 's'. The key-target outlines are shown in heavy lines.

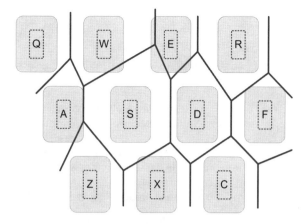

Figure 2. An schematic example where target areas respect each key's anchor. The target area outlines are shown in heavy sold lines, while the anchor outline are shown in broken lines.

that $p_L(k_i = k | k_{i-N+1}, \cdots, k_{i-1}) > 0$ for all k and all histories. As described in [5], we estimate $p_L(k_i | k_{i-N+1}, \cdots, k_{i-1})$ using the interpolated Knesser-Ney technique.

With respect to the touch probability, we again follow [6] and assume that

$$p(l_1, \cdots, l_n | k_1, \cdots, k_n) = p_T(l_1 | k_1) \cdots p_T(l_n | k_n) \quad (6)$$

That is, we assume that given the intended key, the touch location for a key press is independent of the intended keys and touch locations for other key presses. The touch probability $p_T(l|k)$ for a single key press will be modeled as a bivariate normal distribution.

For key-target resizing, the keyboard needs to return a key for every keystroke it receives in an online manner, instead of returning a key sequence after receiving an entire sequence of keystrokes, as implied by equation (3). In this case, the most likely intended key is given by

$$k_i^* = \arg\max_{k_i} p_L(k_i | h) p_T(l_i | k_i) \quad (7)$$

where we have denoted the language model history by h.

For each key k, the *key-target* $\mathcal{T}_k(h)$ is the region of the keyboard that returns k, and is given by

$$\mathcal{T}_k(h) = \Big\{ l | p_L(k|h) p_T(l|k) >$$
$$p_L(k'|h) p_T(l|k'), \forall k' \neq k \Big\} \quad (8)$$

Notice that the key-targets $\mathcal{T}_k(h)$ change with the key history $h = k_{i-N+1}, \cdots, k_{i-1}$.

ANCHORED DYNAMIC KEY-TARGETS

A standard soft keyboard has a predictable user interface–the keys are rendered on the interface and correspond closely to their visual target areas. This guarantees to users that a touch within the rendered boundaries of a key will return that key. Since the target areas on a soft keyboard utilizing key-target resizing change with the key history, the rendered keyboard

must either change with the target areas as discussed above, or no longer match the target areas. As was found in [7], users can find dynamic rendering of the keyboard distracting. If the target areas no longer match the rendered keys, users may not always be able to unambiguously predict the response of the interface to different touch locations. In extreme cases, keys which the language model predicts will be very improbable may have target areas that become very small, or even vanish altogether, so that it becomes difficult or impossible for the user to type these keys. For example, Figure 1 shows an instance where the target area of the 's' key has grown at the expense of the 'e' key, leaving the 'e' key's target area small and in an unexpected position.

Such problems will be rare if the language model only made such predictions when the user is truly unlikely to attempt to type these keys. However, even rare occurrences can be quite frustrating to a user. Furthermore, making accurate predictions of the continuations of text is a difficult problem; one that has been the subject of active research for over half a century [18][5]. We therefore present an approach for ensuring that each key has a central *anchor* that is always included in its target area irrespective of the language model history. This provides at least some level of predictability for the user, since touch locations within each key's anchor (typically at the center of the rendered key) are guaranteed to return that key. Figure 2 shows an instance where each key has a central anchor that is always included in its target.

More formally, we wish to associate an anchor $\mathcal{A}_k \subset \mathbb{R}^2$ with each key $k \in \mathcal{K}$ such that $\mathcal{A}_k \subset \mathcal{T}_k(h)$ for all h for any choice of smooth language model or history.

PROPOSITION 1. $\mathcal{A}_k \subseteq \mathcal{T}_k(h)$ *for any choice of smooth language model and history if and only if* $p_T(l|k) > 0$ *for all* $l \in \mathcal{A}_k$ *and* $p_T(\mathcal{A}_k | k') = 0$ *for all* $k' \neq k$.

PROOF. To prove the "if" portion of the result, recall that smoothness means $p_L(k|h) > 0$ for all k and h. Therefore, all $l \in \mathcal{A}_k$ have

$$p_T(l|k) p_L(k|h) > 0$$

and

$$p_T(l|k')p_L(k'|h) = 0$$

for any $k' \neq k$, so that $l \in \mathcal{T}_k(h)$ by the definition of equation (8).

To prove the "only if" portion of the result by contradiction, we consider two cases. In the first case, we suppose there exists an $l \in \mathcal{A}_k$ such that $p_T(l|k) = 0$. In this case, If the user touches location l it cannot be the case that $\mathcal{A}_k \subseteq \mathcal{T}_k(h)$ and we have a contradiction. In the second case, we suppose there exists $k' \in \mathcal{K}$ such that $p_T(\mathcal{A}_k|k') = A > 0$. If $\mathcal{A}_k \subseteq \mathcal{T}_k(h)$ for all histories and smooth language models, we have that

$$p_T(l|k)p_L(k|h) > p_T(l|k')p_L(k'|h)$$

for all $k \in \mathcal{A}_k$ and all choices of language model and history. Integrating both sides over $\mathcal{A}_k$ we get

$$p_T(\mathcal{A}_k|k)p_L(k|h) > p_T(\mathcal{A}_k|k')p_L(k'|h)$$

$$p_T(\mathcal{A}_k|k) > A\frac{p_L(k'|h)}{p_L(k|h)}$$

Since this holds for any choice of language model and history, it must hold when $\frac{p_L(k'|h)}{p_L(k|h)} > \frac{1}{A}$. This implies $p_T(\mathcal{A}_k|k) > 1$, which is the contradiction.

This completes the proof. $\square$

Proposition 1 is an important result because it maintains that the only way to guarantee that an anchor returns its corresponding key irrespective of the language model is to restrict the support of the touch model to disallow the anchor for all other keys. In particular, this means that Gaussian touch models, as described in [6], would need to be restricted in order to guarantee some degree of predictability.

DATA COLLECTION AND EVALUATION

In this section, we describe how we collected mobile soft keyboard data for training and testing our language and touch models. We also discuss the results of simulation experiments we conducted comparing our anchored key-target resizing method against the state-of-the-art approach and a baseline of having no key-target resizing at all.

Data Collection

For both data collection and evaluation, we sought to create a soft keyboard prototype which would allow participants to enter text in a "natural" fashion. If the prototype had no key-target resizing, it might generate too many errors, causing users to change their typing behavior so as to be more deliberate for each keystroke. This would not only upset the naturalness of the data, but we might not generate enough noisy touch input to train a touch model. Therefore, we created a prototype with simulated "ideal" key-target resizing: as long as participants touched keys that were adjacent to their intended key on the QWERTY layout, we registered the correct key. This enabled us to collect data for building a key-target resizing system without having such a system to collect data from. Following traditional text entry tasks

[12], we gave users text to copy so that we always knews what keys they were intending to hit.

Procedure
On a touchscreen mobile device, participants were instructed to type in a short phrase that appeared above the soft keyboard as "quickly and as accurately as possible". As participants typed each letter of the phrase, the phrase would subtract that letter. For example, when the user typed "p" for "prevailing winds from the east", the screen would then show "revailing winds from the east". As long as the user touched a key that was adjacent to the one they were supposed to touch, the letter would be subtracted. For example, instead of "p", the user might accidentally hit "o" or "l", both of which constitute adjacent keys on a QWERTY layout. This procedure gave participants a sense that they could type on the soft keyboard in a "natural" fashion, despite its lack of tactile feedback. From follow-up discussions, we found that most participants did not even notice that this occurred and among those who did, they just assumed that the soft keyboard had "awesome intelligence", which is indeed what we were striving to create from their data. Participants finished with the phrase when there were no letters left to subtract.

Note that this procedure allows us to obtain useful distribution data for training touch models because we are effectively learning that when users try to type "p", they sometimes hit "o" with some frequency and "l" with some frequency. Given that we subtract letters only when users touch that letter or an adjacent key, one problem that might occur is that users might type in long sequences of keystrokes that are off by one letter. For example, if the user types "irevailing" instead of "prevailing", we might falsely assume that in addition to hitting "i" for "p", which is not an adjacent key, the user also intended to hit "r" for "p", "e" for "p", and so forth. In order to circumvent this problem, we played a beep sound every time the user touched a key that was neither the expected key nor its adjacent keys.

The touchscreen mobile device we used was a prototype pre-market phone with a 4.2 inch resistive screen with 800 x 480 pixels. For comparison, we note that the iPhone sports a 3.5 inch capacitive screen with 480 x 320 pixels.

Stimuli
We presented four types of stimuli phrases. We obtained *standard* phrases from MacKenzie and Soukoreff's phrase set [11], which contains short phrases of English text from 16 to 43 characters whose unigram and bigram frequency correlation with an English corpus is high at $r = 0.954$. Additionally, in order to make sure that participants had a chance to hit every letter on the keyboard, we wrote a script to select the shortest sequences of phrases that covered the entire alphabet from "a" through "z". We used these *standard-training* phrases as training data for our touch models. We treated the rest of the standard phrases as *standard-testing* data for evaluation. Furthermore, we sought to obtain phrases for common mobile tasks. As such, we obtained frequent *urls* sampled from a corpus of web browser logs and search

queries sampled from a corpus of Bing search query logs. We also obtained snippets of *emails* culled from an email corpus, which contained at least one word which was either a proper noun or technical jargon (e.g., "anoo regarding dev budget").

Note that none of the stimuli phrases contained any capitalization, punctuation or other symbols. We did this to avoid having to require users to switch to an alternative keyboard layout (e.g., for selecting symbols), which would also complicate our touch modeling.

Participants received three sets of stimuli with relaxation breaks in between. We used three sets in order to capture three common ways in which users held mobile devices. For each set, participants were asked to type using either two thumbs, one thumb on one hand, or one hand holding the device and another hand for typing. We counter-balanced the order of these three conditions. Each set of stimuli contained 50 phrases consisting of 15 standard-training phrases, 10 standard-testing phrases, 11 email phrases, 7 query phrases, and 7 url phrases. The order of the phrases was randomized.

Participants

We recruited 9 participants (5 males and 4 females) between the ages of 21 and 40 using a professional contracting service. Participants hailed from a wide variety of occupational backgrounds. All participants were compensated for their time. 3 owned touchscreen phones sometime in their life, 3 owned QWERTY phones sometime in their life, and 3 owned 12-key numeric phones only. During recruiting, all participants answered that they were familiar with the QWERTY layout and could type on a normal-size keyboard without frequently looking at the keys.

Training Data and Model Building

We use the *standard-training* phrases, which were specifically chosen to cover all the letter keys of a QWERTY keyboard, to train our touch models. The touch models were full-covariance bivariate Gaussians as described in [6]. They were trained using maximum a posteriori estimation with conjugate priors. The priors for the means were centered at the center of each key. A single shared diagonal covariance matrix was computed for all keys and used to center the prior for the covariance matrix. Models with different equivalent sample sizes were evaluated on the *standard-testing* data and the best model chosen.

The language models used were Kneser-Ney smoothed interpolated key 8-grams (see [6] and [5]). This model was trained using 8.5 million characters of text culled from the USENET. There was no overlap between this text and any of the test phrases. The language model probabilities were exponentially weighted, to balance the dynamic range of the language model and touch model probabilities. In other words, we used $p_L^w(k|h)$ instead of the language model $p_L(k|h)$, as is commonly done in areas such as speech recognition [9]. The weighted language models can be renormalized, but this will have no effect on the maximization of equation (7). The weight w was optimized on the *standard-testing* data.

Key-Target Resizing Evaluation

From our data collection, we obtained logs containing the key participants were supposed to hit as well as their actual touch inputs for that key. Touch inputs were averaged (x, y) pixel coordinates from the touch drivers. With these logs, we are able to conduct simulation experiments examining how we would have performed using different key-target resizing approaches.

Simulation Procedure

The logs contain three types of key outcomes. Using a standard layout in which key boundaries lie halfway between the visible boundaries of each key, the participant could have either 1) typed the expected key, which we denote as a *match*, 2) typed an adjacent key, which we denote as a *fuzzy-match*, or 3) typed a non-adjacent key that was not the expected key, which we denote as a *no-match*. For these outcomes, we used the following procedure for simulating how we would have performed using different key-target resizing approaches.

As we process each keystroke from the first expected key to the last, if the user typed a match, we get one chance to also correctly predict the expected key given the (x, y) touch input. This is because the match typed in by the user gets accepted and the letter is subtracted from the phrase, as described in the data collection procedure. Similarly, for fuzzy-matches, we get only one chance to predict the correct key because adjacent keys get accepted.

On the other hand, if the user has typed a no-match, then the next keystroke will have the same expected key as before since the key would not have been accepted and a beep would have been played. Consecutive sequences of no-matches end only when the user types either a match or a fuzzy-match. For each no-match, we attempt to predict the expected key until we either guess correctly using a key-target resizing approach or we run into a match or fuzzy-match.

For example, suppose the user has typed "iiiprevailing", which includes three nomatches in the beginning. Using the (x, y) coordinates of the first "i", our key-target resizing approach might also incorrectly predict an "i". For the second (x, y) coordinates, however, we might correctly predict a "p", in which case, we do not need to guess on the third character "i" nor the fourth character "p" since we already correctly predicted the expected key.

Evaluation Metrics

At the end of our simulation procedure, we obtain a final input stream, which we can then compare against the expected phrase. For accuracy, we evaluated two metrics. First, we assessed *KeystrokeErrorRate* which measures the degree to which we incorrectly predicted the expected key:

$$\text{KeystrokeErrorRate} = 1 - \frac{|\text{match}|}{|IS|} \qquad (9)$$

where |match| denotes the number of correctly predicted keys, and $|IS|$ denotes the length of the final input stream.

We also assessed *MSDErrorRate*, which measures error rate as a function of the minimum string distance (MSD) between two strings. MSD computes the distance between two strings in terms of the lowest number of edit operations required to convert one string into the other (see [12] for more details). Turned into an error rate measure, MSDErrorRate is calculated as:

$$\text{MSDErrorRate} = \frac{\text{MSD}(T, IS)}{\max(|T|, |IS|)} \quad (10)$$

where T denotes the target expected phrase, and MSD is the minimal edit distance between T and IS.

RESULTS

We first performed a series of experiments to determine the effect of anchor size on KeystrokeErrorRate on the *standard-testing* data set. We then evaluated the best anchor size chosen on the *standard-testing* data set on the *emails*, *queries*, and *urls* data sets to ensure that the improvements we observed generalized to other data sets.

Varying Anchor Size

We experimented with restricting the support of the Gaussian touch models to bigger and bigger rectangles centered at the center of each key. The smallest such rectangles corresponded to the static key-targets, and the rectangles grew in height and width by 2 pixel increments until they reached the center of a neighboring key. Because most keys were 46 pixels wide and 100 pixels high, this occurred when the rectangles were 46 pixels wider than the static targets. Each of these increments corresponded to key targets having anchors that began at 46 pixels by 100 pixels (i.e. that enveloped the entire static target of each key), and then shrank in height and width at 2 pixels per step. Thus, the anchor sizes examined ranged from 0 pixels to 4600 pixels (46×100).

Figure 3 shows the average key error rate on the *standard-testing* data set as a function of anchor size. The best anchor size was 6 pixels by 60 pixels, which corresponded to restricting touch models to rectangles 40 pixels wider and 40 pixels higher than the static key targets.

An error analysis of the static, dynamic, and anchored dynamic systems revealed that anchored key-target resizing corrected 22% of the cases where the static system was correct but the state-of-the-art unanchored dynamic system was incorrect, while maintaining 96% of the corrections the unanchored dynamic system made and making no new errors.

Generalization

Finally, we compared the performance of static key-targets, the state-of-the-art unanchored dynamic key-targets, and the anchored dynamic key-targets on the *standard-testing* set, where we optimized the anchored system as well as the independent *emails*, *queries*, and *urls* sets to ensure that the choices made on the *standard-testing* data set gave good results on these other data sets.

As shown in Figure 4, using the anchored dynamic key-

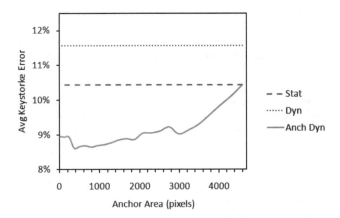

Figure 3. The average key error rate of anchored dynamic key-targets on the *standard-testing* data set as a function of the area of the key anchors (solid line). The performance of the state-of-the-art dynamic key-targets is shown in the dotted line, while the performance of static key-targets is shown in the broken line. At an area of 0, the key-targets are constrained to not extend beyond the center of the neighboring keys. At an anchor area of 4700, the anchors coincide with the static key targets, so that no resizing takes place. The optimal anchor area was 360 pixels.

targets obtains relative improvements of 17%, 6%, 8%, and 13% respectively over the static system on the *standard-testing*, *emails*, *queries*, and *urls* sets with respect to average keystroke error. In contrast, the state-of-the-art unanchored key-target resizing method had an average keystroke error which was 10% *worse* than the static system on the *standard-testing* and *emails* tasks. Note that these difference are all statistically significant at the $p < .01$ level according to McNemar's test.

DISCUSSION

Although the anchored key-target resizing method significantly reduced keystroke errors compared to the static system across the different test sets, the state-of-the-art unanchored system performed worse than the baseline with respect to the *standard-testing* and *emails* tasks. This may be due to a mismatch between the text from these two tasks and the USENET training corpus. Interestingly, the anchored system outperformed the state-of-the-art in al ofl the data sets, but the advantage was not so great with *urls*. Again, this may be explained by the fact that the USENET corpus already contains a fair number of urls. Note that both the anchored and unanchored dynamic systems, which leverage the source-channel approach to key-target resizing, had generally low average keystroke errors.

The anchored and unanchored dynamic systems did not differ much in terms of average MSD error rate. Note that keystroke error rate measures how frequently the keystrokes typed by users do not match what they are intending to type, whereas MSD error rate measures how distant their typed output is from their desired text in terms of required edit operations. Although one could argue that MSD error rate matters most because it represents the amount of work users have to do in order to convert their typed output into the de-

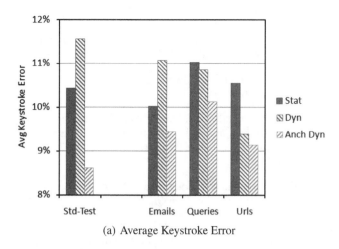

(a) Average Keystroke Error

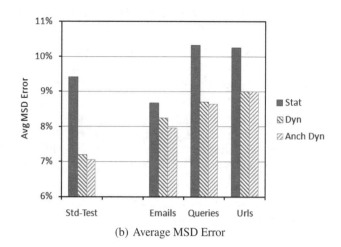

(b) Average MSD Error

Figure 4. The performance of static key-targets, state-of-the-art dynamic key-targets, and anchored dynamic key-targets on the *standard-testing* set as well as the independent *emails*, *queries*, and *urls* sets.

sired text, this assumes that users type without monitoring their output and only later go back to edit their text. However, previous research [8] suggests that because touchscreen keyboards lack haptic feedback, users are likely to spend more time monitoring their text. Nevertheless, this certainly should be validated in a user study. In fact, we acknowledge that while we have laid the theoretical and empirical grounds for a usability guided key-target resizing method, we still need to verify that real users indeed find the anchors more "usable" in practice. Indeed, we plan to conduct such user studies in the future.

With respect to the data collection we used for our simulation experiments, one problem we encountered was that we obtained far fewer noisy input than we expected. This was due to the fact that we used a mobile device with a large screen and high resolution. We plan to collect more data on a mobile device with a smaller, lower resolution screen (similar to the iPhone) where the need for key-target resizing may be even greater.

CONCLUSION AND FUTURE DIRECTIONS

We have described how state-of-the-art key-target resizing can cause soft keyboards to violate user expectations about keyboard functionality, and how restricting the touch model to yield anchored dynamic key-targets can alleviate this problem. In fact, our theoretical results showed that any source-channel approach that is guaranteed to alleviate this problem must restrict the touch model. We then gave empirical results that showed that anchored dynamic key-targets achieve significant keystroke error reductions as compared to the state-of-the-art.

Our paper described one class of restricted touch model; namely, Gaussians with support restricted to a rectangle around each key. One direction for future research is to explore other restricted touch models, such as models with non-rectangular anchors or non-Gaussian distributions. Distributions could also depend on additional information such as previous keystrokes.

Another area for future work is the adaptation of the touch model, including the anchor sizes, as well as the language model to the user. Furthermore, because users vary in terms of their hand size and consequently their finger touch points, it will be interesting to see if adaptation can improve key-target resizing. In any case, whatever adaptation we pursue will certainly be guided by usability principles, as is the case with our current approach.

REFERENCES

1. Apple iPhone, 2009. http://www.apple.com/iphone/.

2. Microsoft Surface, 2009. http://www.microsoft.com/surface/.

3. K. Al Faraj, M. Mojahid, and N. Vigouroux. Bigkey: A virtual keyboard for mobile devices. In *Proceedings of the 13th International Conference on Human-Computer Interaction. Part III*, pages 3–10, Berlin, Heidelberg, 2009. Springer-Verlag.

4. S. Brewster, F. Chohan, and L. Brown. Tactile feedback for mobile interactions. In *CHI '07: Proceedings of the SIGCHI conference on Human factors in computing systems*, pages 159–162, New York, NY, USA, 2007. ACM.

5. J. Goodman. A bit of progress in language modeling. *Computer Speech & Language*, 15(4):403–434, 2001.

6. J. Goodman, G. Venolia, J. Steury, and C. Parker. Language modeling for soft keyboards. In *AAAI*, 2002.

7. J. Himberg, J. Häkkilä, P. Kangas, and J. Mäntyjärvi. On-line personalization of a touch screen based keyboard. In *IUI*, 2003.

8. E. Hoggan, S. A. Brewster, and J. Johnston. Investigating the effectiveness of tactile feedback for mobile touchscreens. In *CHI '08: Proceeding of the twenty-sixth annual SIGCHI conference on Human factors in computing systems*, pages 1573–1582, New York, NY, USA, 2008. ACM.

9. F. Jelinek. *Statistical Methods for Speech Recognition*. MIT Press, 1998.

10. M. Klsch and M. Turk. Keyboards without keyboards: A survey of virtual keyboards. Technical report, In: Proceedings of Sensing and Input for Media-centric Systems, 2002.

11. I. S. MacKenzie and R. W. Soukoreff. Phrase sets for evaluating text entry techniques. In *CHI '03: CHI '03 extended abstracts on Human factors in computing systems*, pages 754–755, New York, NY, USA, 2003. ACM.

12. I. S. MacKenzie and K. Tanaka-Ishii. *Text entry systems: Mobility, accessibility, universality*. Morgan Kaufmann, San Francisco, 2007.

13. I. S. MacKenzie and S. X. Zhang. The design and evaluation of a high-performance soft keyboard. In *CHI '99: Proceedings of the SIGCHI conference on Human factors in computing systems*, pages 25–31. ACM, 1999.

14. I. S. MacKenzie and X. Zhang. Eye typing using word and letter prediction and a fixation algorithm. In *ETRA '08: Proceedings of the 2008 symposium on Eye tracking research and applications*, pages 55–58, New York, NY, USA, 2008. ACM.

15. L. Magnien, J. Bouraoui, and N. Vigouroux. Mobile text input with soft keyboards: optimization by means of visual clues. In *Proceedings of Mobile HCI*, pages 337–341, Berlin, Heidelberg, 2004. Springer-Verlag.

16. D. Pogue. iPhone keyboard secrets. *The New York Times*, June 2007.

17. E. Rabin and A. M. Gordon. Tactile feedback contributes to consistency of finger movements during typing. *Experimental Brain Research*, 155:362–369, 2004.

18. C. E. Shannon. Prediction and entropy of printed English. *Bell Sys. Tech. J.*, 30, 1951.

19. S. Zhai, M. Hunter, and B. A. Smith. The metropolis keyboard - an exploration of quantitative techniques for virtual keyboard design. In *UIST '00: Proceedings of the 13th annual ACM symposium on User interface software and technology*, pages 119–128, New York, NY, USA, 2000. ACM.

Intelligent Understanding of Handwritten Geometry Theorem Proving

Yingying Jiang[1] Feng Tian[1] Hongan Wang[1,2]
[1] Intelligence Engineering Lab,
Institute of Software,
Chinese Academy of Sciences
Beijing, China
{jyy,tf,wha}@iel.iscas.ac.cn

Xiaolong Zhang[3] Xugang Wang[1] Guozhong Dai[1,2]
[2] State Key Laboratory of Computer Science,
Institute of Software, Chinese Academy of
Sciences
{wxg,dgz}@iel.iscas.ac.cn
[3] The Pennsylvania State University
lzhang@ist.psu.edu

ABSTRACT

Computer-based geometry systems have been widely used for teaching and learning, but largely based on mouse-and-keyboard interaction, these systems usually require users to draw figures by following strict task structures defined by menus, buttons, and mouse and keyboard actions. Pen-based designs offer a more natural way to develop geometry theorem proofs with hand-drawn figures and scripts. This paper describes a pen-based geometry theorem proving system that can effectively recognize hand-drawn figures and hand-written proof scripts, and accurately establish the correspondence between geometric components and proof steps. Our system provides dynamic and intelligent visual assistance to help users understand the process of proving and allows users to manipulate geometric components and proof scripts based on structures rather than strokes. The results from evaluation study show that our system is well perceived and users have high satisfaction with the accuracy of sketch recognition, the effectiveness of visual hints, and the efficiency of structure-based manipulation.

Author Keywords

Geometry theorem proving, hand-drawn figures, hand-written proof scripts, recognition, structure based manipulation.

ACM Classification

H5.2. Information Interfaces and Presentation: User Interfaces. - Interaction styles; I.5.4. Pattern Recognition: Applications. - Signal processing.

General Terms Design, Algorithms, Human Factors

INTRODUCTION

Geometry theorem proving is one of the most challenging skills for students to learn in secondary school mathematics

[5, 18]. Senk found that the results of geometry education in secondary school were disappointing, even in the second semester of learning geometry [26]. About a quarter of students gave up on problems of geometry proving, and only about 30% of students can complete 75% or more of geometry proofs correctly. Many students find it difficult to write down a formal proof because they do not understand the geometric properties involved in the proof [29].

Computer-assisted geometry proving has been studied by many researchers [2, 7, 9, 12, 19, 23]. Dynamic geometry systems are developed to assist users to create geometric constructions, explore geometry graphs, formulate conjectures, check facts [9, 12, 19, 23], and even build proofs [2, 7]. These tools are useful in helping users understand geometric properties, generate theorem proving ideas, and discover interesting geometry propositions. However, built upon the traditional WIMP interaction style, they impose pre-defined interaction styles and task structures that are defined by menus, buttons, mouse and keyboard actions, and so on. These interaction styles and task structures often do not match what students usually do in geometry proving in their real-life. Being forced to follow unfamiliar interaction styles and task structures, students may be distracted from the major task of exploring and understanding the relationships between proof steps and geometry figures, which is an important factor to improve the understanding of geometry proving [30].

Pen-based interaction offers an opportunity to enhance the learning of geometry proofs by leveraging advanced computational techniques and at the same time, by allowing students to follow the natural and traditional hand-written approach. With pen-based tools, students can write proof scripts and geometric figures on computer screens, just as what they do with pen and paper in real life. Computational tools can understand their hand-writing and offer intelligent help based on their actions and action contexts.

In this paper, we explore an approach to support pen-based geometry proving. A sketch recognition method is proposed to understand the hand-drawn geometry graphs and handwritten geometry proof scripts and build the correspondence between geometric components and proof scripts. Based on the algorithm, we develop a system to provide dynamic and intelligent visual assistance to help users understand the process of proving and support structure-based manipulation of proof scripts. Figure 1 demonstrates some key features of our approach. Lines in Figure 1 are the recognition results of hand-written lines; when a geometry proof step, $AB \perp AC$, is selected, the corresponding geometry representation, the perpendicular lines AB and AC, are highlighted.

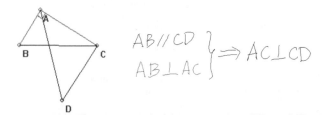

Figure 1. An example of intelligent visual hints that highlights the geometry representation of a selected proof step.

The paper is structured as the following. First, we review related research, and then outline the key factors in geometry proofs by analyzing a proving example. Next, we describe the detail of the recognition algorithm and intelligent tools to assist geometry proving. Furthermore, we present the evaluation of a prototype system of geometry proving. Finally, we discuss the results of our research and conclude the paper with future research directions.

RELATED WORK

Geometry Systems
Computer assisted teaching and learning systems are important to education. In geometry education, interactive geometry software environments [4, 9, 11, 12, 23] have offered new methods for teaching and learning geometry theorem proving [13]. For example, MMP/Geometer [9] and GeoProof [23] support automatic geometry theorem proving; GeoProof [23] used an automatic theorem prover to check facts. Although these systems are useful, they are based on the mouse-and-keyboard interaction, which is unnatural and imposes task structures that do not match what students do in real-life.

Researchers have studied pen-based geometry systems to support more natural interactive activities. Liu et al [22] developed a pen-based geometry teaching system, which supported only geometry drawing but neglected geometry proving. GeoAssistor [10] is a pen-based geometry proving system, but the system cannot understand hand-written proof scripts.

Sketch Recognition
Sketch understanding systems have been used in education area. These systems made learning activities more interesting. MathPad2 [20] is a system to support the creation and exploration of mathematical sketches. Ouyang [24] studied the recognition of hand-drawn chemical diagrams and the generation of the 3D structure of the organic substance based on recognition results to support the interaction with and understanding of the substance. Alvarado [1] built a system to simulate physical phenomenon based on pen-based sketches. Sim-U-Sketch and VibroSketch [16] can assist the learning of the circuit and vibration knowledge by recognizing hand-drawn circuit and vibration diagrams. Research has also been done to recognize handwritten formulae, such as mathematical expression [20] and chemical expression [24,28]. However, these systems are domain-specific, and cannot be easily extended to other domains, such as plane geometry.

A geometry proof consists of hand-drawn geometry figures and handwritten proof scripts. Recognizing hand-drawn graphs has been researched. Paulson [25] studied the recognition of primitive sketches. Li [21] investigated synchronized recognition of graphs with real-time user feedback. However, little research has been done to recognize handwritten geometry proof scripts and build the correspondence between geometry figures and proof scripts.

GEOMETRY THEOREM PROOF IN PLANE GEOMETRY
To prove geometry theorem in plane geometry, a student usually draws the corresponding geometry graph, and writes the proof scripts step by step to prove the theorem. Sometimes, assistant lines are constructed to help the proof.

We collected ten geometry exercise books from junior-high students who were studying plane geometry, and analyzed these manuscripts to get students' typical handwritten proving styles on the paper. Figure 2 demonstrates a snippet from a geometry student's exercise book, which is the typical proving style in these exercise books.

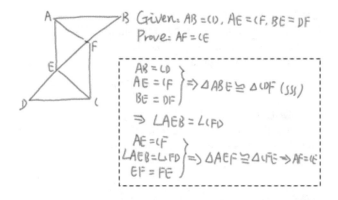

Figure 2. A snippet from a student's geometry exercise book.

As shown in the figure, the proving scripts are on the right of the hand-drawn graph and are within the blue dashed box. The proof scripts consist of a serial of preconditions and conclusions that are combined by the deduction symbols. We define each precondition or conclusion as a proof step. Deduction symbols, such as "}=>" and "=>", are between proof steps. The reason for a deduction is often behind the conclusion item and enclosed by a pair of brackets.

For the structure of a proof step, each proof step usually specifies two geometry objects and their relationship. The type of a geometry object can be "line", "circle", "triangle", "point", and so on. The relationships include "parallel", "perpendicular", "similar", "same", "equal", etc.

In this paper, we propose a computer-based approach to support such geometry proving. Our work focuses on an algorithm to understand geometry proving styles, shown in Figure 2, and to provide assistance to geometry proving by establishing the correspondence between geometry figures and geometry proof scripts. The recognition of handwritten deduction reason is not addressed in this research.

UNDERSTANDING HANDWRITTEN PROOFS

As shown in the preceding section, handwritten geometry proofs include hand-drawn geometry figures and handwritten geometry proof scripts. Both of them are composed of a serial of strokes. Our algorithm recognizes them respectively and then builds the correspondence between them.

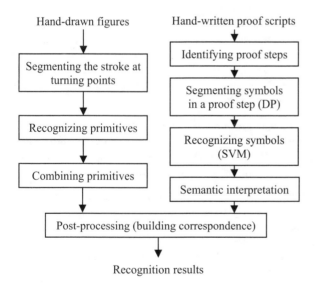

Figure 3. Architecture of hand-drawn geometry proof understanding.

Figure 3 shows the architecture of our algorithm. The hand-drawn figure recognition method deals with each stroke separately. It consists of three steps: stroke segmentation, primitive recognition, and primitive combination. The

recognition of hand-written proof scripts is based on proof step identification. For each proof step, DP-based (Dynamic Programming) symbol segmentation [8] and SVM-based symbol recognition [6] are performed to understand the handwritten proof step. After that, the meaning of the proof is created through semantic interpretation. A post-processing step builds the correspondence between the figures and the proofs.

Recognition of Hand-Drawn Geometry Figures

In plane geometry, a geometry figure is usually composed of points, lines, and circles. Our figure recognition method treats each stroke separately. For each stroke, our algorithm first segments it into sub-strokes at turning points. Then each sub-stroke is recognized separately to be a shape primitive (point, line, or circle). Furthermore, a hierarchy of the primitives is constructed. Combining all the recognition results of strokes leads to a geometry figure.

Stroke segmentation

A stroke contains a serial of points. For each stroke, it is re-sampled according to the equal between-point distance criterion. The re-sampled stroke can be represented as $\{P_0, P_1, ..., P_N\}$. $P_i(x, y)$ indicates the position of the *ith* point in the stroke. Figure 4 gives an example of a re-sampled stroke.

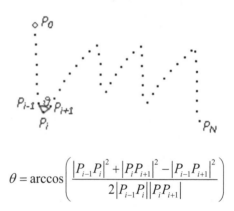

$$\theta = \arccos\left(\frac{|P_{i-1}P_i|^2 + |P_iP_{i+1}|^2 - |P_{i-1}P_{i+1}|^2}{2|P_{i-1}P_i||P_iP_{i+1}|}\right)$$

Figure 4. Re-sampled points of a stroke and an angle between two adjacent lines of this stroke.

To judge whether P_i is a turning point in a stroke, the algorithm calculates the angle θ between Line $P_i P_{i-1}$ and Line $P_i P_{i+1}$ using the law of cosines as shown in Figure 4. If the angle θ is smaller than a given threshold angle – *angleThres*, P_i is a turning point in the stroke; otherwise, P_i is not a turning point. In our research, *angleThres* is set to be $4\pi/5$.

After finding all turning points in a stroke, the stroke is divided into several sub-strokes separated by turning points. If the number of re-sampled points of a sub-stroke is less than a given threshold, *ptThres*, the sub-stroke is added to its preceding sub-stroke. After segmentation, each sub-stroke constitutes a shape primitive. In our research, *ptThres* is set to be 5.

Primitive recognition

A shape primitive could be a point, a line, or a circle. The following formula defines how the type of a stroke is found.

$$type = \begin{cases} Point, & if\,(pointNum < ptThres) \\ Line, & if\,(density > lDenThres\,\&\,density < hDenThres) \\ Circle, & else \end{cases}$$

When the stroke in a shape primitive has less than *ptThres* points, the primitive is a point. Line recognition is based on stroke density. Here, we define the density of a stroke as the ratio of the stroke's length to its bounding box's diagonal length. When the density of a stroke in a primitive is between two given thresholds, *lDenThres* and *hDenThres*, the primitive is a line. If a stroke is not recognized as either a point or a line, it is taken as a circle. In our algorithm, *lDenThres* and *hDenThres* are set to be 0.7 and 1.3 respectively.

Letter labels are assigned to shape primitives. A point only needs one letter to be separated from other points. A line has two labels, each of which corresponds to an end of the line. A circle also has two labels: one for the center and the other for a point on the circle. Our algorithm keeps track of what letters have been assigned and guarantees the uniqueness of letter labels.

Primitive combination

After knowing shape primitives, the algorithm combines these primitives to form a high level geometry figure. For example, when the endpoint of a line is very close to the endpoint of another line, the two lines are linked by a common endpoint.

Figure 5 illustrates the recognition results of some hand-drawn geometry figures. Figure 5(a) is a hand-drawn curve, and Figure 5(b) shows its recognition result, a poly-line and letter lables on individual lines. The quadrangle in Figure 5(d) is the recognition result of the drawing in Figure 5(c). The hand-drawn graph in Figure 5(e) is recognized as a circle in Figure 5(f).

Recognition of Handwritten Geometry Proof Scripts

The basic unit of a geometry proof script is proof step. Our geometry proof script recognition method is based on proof step identification. The following sections describe proof step identification, symbol partition in a geometry item, symbol recognition, and semantic interpretation.

Proof step identification

A proof step is usually followed by a deduction symbol or by another step in a new line. We use this feature to identify individual proof steps.

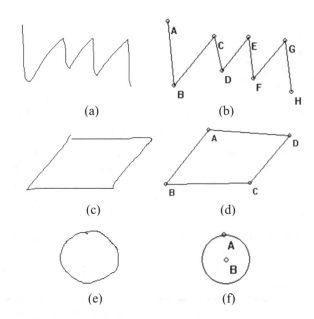

Figure 5. Hand-drawn geometry graphs and their recognition results.

When the pen is up, the algorithm judges whether the current stroke is the deduction symbol '}' by the SVM-based recognition method, which will be introduced below, or whether it is a stroke in a new line by the spatial relations to the current proof step. If the stroke is '}', the current proof step is finished. If the stroke is in a new line, the current proof step is finished and a new proof step is created. Otherwise, the DP and SVM based symbol segmentation and recognition process are performed to get the recognition result of the current handwritten proof step. If the last symbol is '=>', a proof step has been finished and the user is going to start a new proof step. Otherwise, the user is still working on the current proof step.

Symbol partition in a proof step

Dynamic programming is typically applied to optimization problems [8]. It is used to segment a handwritten proof step to several symbols in our algorithm.

Before symbol partitioning, the strokes in the proof step are sorted according to the left borders of their bounding boxes. Thus, the writing order of the symbols in a proof step is not restricted. After stroke sorting, overlapped strokes are merged to stroke blocks. The merged stroke blocks can be represented as $\{b_1, b_2... b_N\}$.

The following formula describes the approach to find optimal symbol segmentations by dynamic programming.

$$D(i,j) = \min\{D(i,k) + D(k+1,j), d(i,j)\}$$

$$i,j,k \in [1,N], i \le j, i \le k < j$$

where $D(i, j)$ is the reliability corresponding to the optimal symbol segmentation of stroke blocks $\{b_i, ..., b_j\}$ and $d(i, j)$ is the reliability of the candidate symbol that is composed of stroke blocks $\{b_i, ..., b_j\}$.

The symbols in a proof step have the following characteristics: first, they have similar widths and heights; second, the distances between stroke blocks in a symbol are often smaller than the distances between stroke blocks in different symbols; third, the width of a symbol is often not too large. Thus, $d(i,j)$ can be calculated by the following formula:

$$d(i, j) = a * intraDF(i, j) + b * \frac{1}{interDF(i, j)} + c * wF(i, j)$$

$$i, j \in [1, N], i \leq j$$

where intraDF is the intra-distance factor between stroke blocks in a symbol. *interDF* describes the inter-distance between adjacent symbols; wF is the width of a candidate symbol; and a, b, c are weights of these factors in the overall distance(In our algorithm, these three factors are treated equally: a=0.33, b=0.33 and c=0.33).

Suppose $d'(i,j)$ is the normalized distance between the bounding boxes of the stroke block b_i and the stroke block b_j, $intraDF(i,j)$ and $interDF(i,j)$ can be calculated by the following formulae.

$$intraDF(i, j) = \sum_{k=i+1}^{j} d'(k-1, k)$$

$$interDF(i, j) = \begin{cases} d'(i-1,i) + d'(j, j+1) & if\ (i > 0\ \&\ j < N) \\ d'(i-1,i) + \overline{d'} & if\ (i > 0\ \&\ j = N) \\ d'(j, j+1) + \overline{d'} & if\ (i = 0\ \&\ j < N) \end{cases}$$

The following formula describes the calculation of $wF(i,j)$. It is normalized by the average height and the maximum width of the stroke blocks.

$$wF(i, j) = \frac{width(i, j) - \frac{1}{N}\sum_{k=0}^{N} height(k)}{\max_{k \in [1, N]} \{width(k)\}}$$

Symbol recognition
SVM classifier is proved to be effective to recognize hand-drawn mathematical symbols [17]. As most symbols in geometry proof are mathematical symbols, this research also adopts a SVM classifier to recognize handwritten

geometry symbols. In particular, the multi-class classification is accomplished with Libsvm [6] and the classifier uses the RBF kernel. A handwritten symbol can contain online features that include sequential information about points and strokes, and offline features that are based on the symbol's corresponding image. As online features and offline features could complement each other [17, 27], both online features and offline features are used by our classifier.

Before extracting features for the SVM input, normalization is performed for the handwritten symbols. The normalized symbols have fixed size and contain the same number of points. Moreover, the image of the symbol is also generated.

Our algorithm uses the angles between adjacent points in the strokes as the online features and uses the ratios of black pixels as the offline features. Suppose the strokes in a symbol have pN points and the image is partitioned into $m*m$ sub-images. The features used by the classifier can be represented as follows:

$$F = \begin{cases} \sin_1, \cos_1, \sin_2, \cos_2 ... \sin_{pN-1}, \cos_{pN-1}, \\ density_1, density_2, ..., density_{m*m} \end{cases}$$

$$\sin_i = \frac{y_{i+1} - y_i}{\sqrt{(x_{i+1} - x_i)^2 + (y_{i+1} - y_i)^2}}$$

$$\cos_i = \frac{x_{i+1} - x_i}{\sqrt{(x_{i+1} - x_i)^2 + (y_{i+1} - y_i)^2}}$$

where $density_i$ is the ratio of black pixels in the *ith* sub-image.

Currently, the geometry symbols that can be recognized by our algorithm include 10 digits, 26 English letters – both lower and upper cases, and some special symbols in geometry ($\because \therefore \angle \triangle \square \cong \perp \backsim + - \llcorner = // \} \Rightarrow$).

Semantic interpretation
After getting the proof recognition result, semantic meanings of a proof step can be extracted. For example, "$\triangle ABC$" are not just four symbols, but have the meaning of a triangle consisting of three linked lines.

Our algorithm uses a semantic interpretation table to look up semantic meanings. The semantic interpretation table mainly includes two parts. One part defines the semantic meaning of symbols that indicate geometry shapes, such as '$\angle$', '$\llcorner$', '$\triangle$', and '$\square$'. The other part explains the relationship symbols that describe relationships between geometry components, such as '$\because$', '$\therefore$', '$\cong$', '$\perp$', '$\backsim$', '$+$', '$-$', '$=$', '$//$', and '$\Rightarrow$'.

Figure 6 shows the recognition result of a handwritten geometry proof.

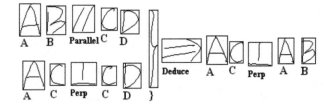

Item1: Parallel<Line(A,B), Line(C,D)>

Item2: Perpendicular<Line(A,C), Line(C,D)>

Item3: Perpendicular<Line(A,C), Line(A,B)>

Deduce<<Item1,Item2>,Item3>

Figure 6. Recognition result of handwritten geometry proof.

Post-processing

With the recognition results, our algorithm builds the correspondence between the geometry graphs and the geometry proof scripts. The recognized figures are represented as a serial of graph primitives and their relationships.

After recognizing handwritten proof scripts, our algorithm connects a proof step with geometry objects. The correspondence between them is established by matching the recognized letters in proof step with the labels of graph primitives.

Such correspondence can also help to correct some errors in the recognition of handwritten proof scripts. As the proof scripts should be consistent with the graph, our algorithm uses the knowledge extracted from the graph to identify potential text recognition errors. For example, when "CD" is incorrectly recognized as "CP", the result can be corrected by knowing that there's a line "CD" in the graph and there's no line "CP" in the graph.

ASSISTANCE TO GEOMETRY PROOF

If a student does not understand the conditions of a proposition, she cannot really judge the correctness of the proposition [13, 14]. Moreover, the student may fail to relate each proof step in a text book proof to the accompanying figure [30]. To help students understand geometry proof, we provide intelligent visual hints and structure-based manipulation technique.

Intelligent hints for geometry proof

By using the correspondence between geometry figures and geometry proof scripts, we provide intelligent hints to help users understand geometry proving processes. The hints update when the pen is up (Figure 7) or object manipulation happens (Figure 1).

Figure 7 shows how intelligent hints work. When a user writes the geometry proof scripts, the current proof step as well as its corresponding figure is highlighted. The figures

at the top of Figure 7 are the formal geometry figures recognized from hand-drawn figures. The bottom shows the geometry proof scripts. The recognition result of the handwritten geometry proof scripts is used implicitly and not shown in the figure. In Figure 7(a), when the step of *AB//CD* is written and recognized, Lines *AB* and CD in the geometry figure are highlighted. In Figure 7(b), handwritten *AB* in a new proof step is recognized, and Line *AB* in the geometry figure is highlighted. In Figure 7(c), the proof step of *AB⊥AC* is recognized, and the perpendicular lines of *AB* and *AC* in the geometry figure are highlighted.

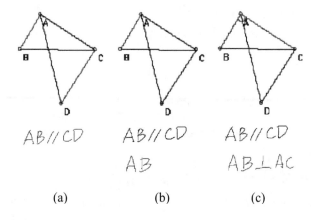

(a)   (b)   (c)

Figure 7. Highlighting the proof step the user is writing and its corresponding figure.

Intelligent hints also appear when the user manipulates the geometry proofs. For example, as shown in Figure 1, when the user selects a proof step, the step and its corresponding figure are highlighted.

With the intelligent hint technique, a proving process can be replayed by highlighting each geometry proof step with its corresponding figure. This approach can help to overcome the difficulty in relating the proof step in a text book proof to the accompanying figure, a big barrier in learning geometry proof [30].

Efficient manipulation of geometry proofs

In geometry proving, some geometry proof steps may be used several times and the user need to write the same steps several times. Sometimes, the user may find errors in proofs and want to delete some proof steps. Thus, it is important to provide efficient methods to manipulate geometry proofs.

Structure-based manipulation methods of sketches are proved to be more efficient than stroke-based approaches [3, 15]. In plane geometry, a proof consists of geometry figures and geometry proof scripts. By recognizing hand-drawn geometry figures and extracting the structure of handwritten proof scripts, structured manipulation can be supported. We designed pen gestures for structure-based selecting, deleting, moving, cutting, and pasting operations in handwritten geometry proofs. These structure-based methods allow the operations of handwritten geometry proof scripts at the granularity of proof step.

For example, with structure-based manipulation, deleting a geometric component in geometry figures can also lead to the deletion of related proof scripts. Figure 8 demonstrates an example of deleting a line in geometry figures. Figure 8(a) shows the selected line (in red color), its corresponding geometry proof scripts, *DE* (in red color), and the deleting gesture (in green color). Figure 8(b) is the effect after the operation. Both the selected line and the related geometry proof steps are deleted.

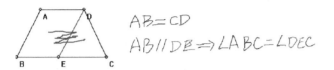

(a) Deleting a line in the geometry figure

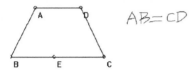

(b) Geometry figure and proof scripts after deleting

Figure 8. An example of deleting a line in geometry figure.

EVALUATION

With the proposed sketch understanding algorithm and the assistance technique in plane geometry proof, we built a pen-based geometry proving tool – PenProof (Figure 9).

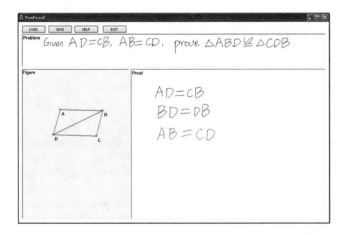

Figure 9. The user interface of PenProof.

In PenProof, there are three separate areas for defining geometry problems, drawing geometry figures, and writing geometry proofs. In the figure area, the hand-drawn figures are recognized into formal figures and dynamic geometry is supported based on MMP/Geometer [9]. In the proof area, handwritten proof scripts are recognized in the background to provide assistance to geometry proving.

We conducted a study to evaluate the PenProof system. The study had two goals: to test the recognition accuracy of our sketch understanding algorithm, and to obtain user feedback on the system.

Task, Subjects, Apparatus, and Procedure
The test task was to write down geometry proofs provided by us and did not require any knowledge beyond secondary schools, so we recruited twelve graduate students who possessed the required geometry knowledge. The test was on a machine equipped with a 2.4GH CPU, 4G memory and a Wacom screen.

To test the recognition accuracy of our sketch understanding algorithm, we provided each subject 10 figures and 10 proofs, and each subject was asked to select and finish 4 figures and 4 proofs in PenProof. The provided figures consisted of points, lines, and circles. The provided proofs consisted of proof steps and deduction symbols. However, the provided proofs did not include all the geometry symbols supported in this paper. An additional evaluation of the symbol recognition accuracy was conducted by asking each subject to draw all the geometry symbols twice.

After trying the PenProof tool, each subject was asked to answer a post-test questionnaire to grade the graph recognition accuracy, the structured interaction, the visual hints, the comfort, and the enjoyment of the tool, all in a 7-level Likert scale (1-vary bad, 7-very good).

Recognition accuracy
The evaluation results show that accuracy of hand-drawn figure recognition is 92.1%. Most errors were at the juncture of the graphs due to the warp of the points. Users could correct the errors either by manipulating the formal figures or by deleting and redrawing the figures. As for the proof recognition, the total recognition accuracy is 87.3%. The errors include the proof step identification errors, symbol segmentation errors, and symbol recognition errors. The errors of proof step identification were mainly caused by the misrecognition of the deduction symbols. Segmentation errors occurred because some users wrote adjacent symbols too close. Symbol recognition errors were due to irregularly written symbols.

As for the geometry symbol recognition, our SVM-based geometry symbol recognizer used 20 samples for each symbol to train the classifier. These samples were collected from one user and were written regularly. The evaluation results show that the recognition accuracy for the same person achieves 96.4%. When using the classifier to recognize symbols collected from subjects, the average accuracy is 90.1%. The errors are caused by symbols written with irregular stroke orders or irregular symbol shapes.

User Feedback

Figure 10 exhibits the results of subjective evaluation. As shown, the recognition accuracy, the structured interaction, and the dynamic visual hints all received good feedback from subjects. In addition, the subjects thought it was comfortable and enjoyable to use the tool.

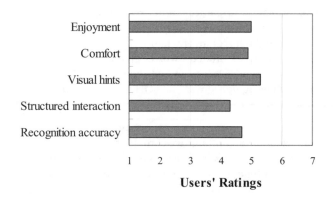

Figure 10. Users' ratings

While all subjects thought the tool was useful, they also offered some constructive suggestions. Currently, the letter labels for shape primitives are generated automatically by the PenProof system. Some users suggested that the tool allow a user-controlled labeling design. Some users pointed out that the tool should support more proving styles, such as proofs written in a two-column form.

DISCUSSION

As seen, the error rates of our current approach are relative low. The recognition accuracies of hand-drawn figures and hand-written proofs are 92.1% and 87.3%, respectively.

The most serious errors were related to incorrect deduction symbols. This may frustrate subjects when they used structured manipulation techniques and lead to relatively low ratings on structured manipulation compared with other ratings.

Figure 11 shows one error caused by incorrect recognition of deduction symbols. Here, a subject tried to select the item "AC//BD" and reuse it in a proof that followed. However, the structured selection that operates at the granularity of proof step selected "AC//BD}", instead of "AC//BD". This error was because the deduction symbol "}" was incorrectly recognized as "1" and consequently, led to incorrect identification of proof items.

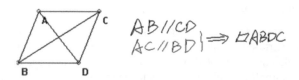

Figure 11. An error caused by incorrect recognition of deduction symbol.

In addition to these errors related to recognition algorithms, we also observed some errors produced by subjects when they wrote proofs inconsistent with the figures. The mismatch between drawn figures and written proofs can cause conflict interpretations. In this situation, subjects received no hint or even wrong hints. Figure 12 is an example of errors caused by conflicting figure and proof. Here, the proof step of "∠ABD=∠CDB" were written down, but "∠ABD" did not exist in the geometry figure. Thus, no visual hint in the geometry figure can be provided.

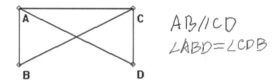

Figure 12. An error due to conflicting figure and proof.

To address these errors, we need to enhance our algorithms in several ways. First, the accuracy of deduction symbols should be further improved. Second, new algorithms are required to detect conflicting figures and proofs.

It should be noted that in our evaluation, we did not measure the influence of errors on performance quantitatively. This is because of the lack of comparable systems. We have not found any system that offers the same level of support for hand-written geometry proof. Thus, we focused on the evaluation of the design concept first, rather than quantified user performance.

CONCLUSION

This paper presented a pen-based geometry proving system. We proposed a sketch recognition algorithm to recognize and correlate hand-drawn geometry figures and hand-written geometry proof scripts. While the hand-drawn figure recognition is based on the detection of shape primitives using turning points, the hand-written geometry proof scripts recognition is based on the identification of proof steps. Based on the recognition results, we designed intelligent visual hints and structured manipulation technique to assist the understanding of geometry proving. Results from our evaluation study show that the algorithm is effective and the assistance is useful. This pen-based geometry theorem proving approach has the potential to enhance the learning of geometry proofs by following the natural and traditional proving approach and meanwhile provide intelligent help to users.

The contribution of this research lies in two aspects. Technically, we have developed algorithms to establish the connections between hand-drawing and hand-written structures. While we applied our techniques in a geometry proving system, our algorithms can be expanded into other areas that have similar tasks.

Cognitively, the proposed "intelligent hint" design suggests a way to reduce cognitive loads in pen-based user interfaces by leveraging intelligent methods. In conventional user interfaces, such as WIMP-based designs, techniques to help reducing cognitive loads (e.g., highlighting relevant objects) are mature. However, objects in pen-based UI are usually not well-structured and well-recognized, so it is a challenge to use these techniques to assist users. Our approach shows that based on user action contexts and object correspondence, we can provide useful cues to reduce cognitive loads.

In the future, we are interested in extending our research in the following directions. First, we will enhance our recognition algorithms to address the limitation of our current algorithms. The current method could only recognize a limited set of symbols, and only support limited graph types and proving styles. In the future, we will try to recognize more characters besides current geometry symbols.

Second, we will explore other error correction strategies for PenProof. Currently, users are allowed to correct errors by erasing and rewriting the geometry proof. In the future, other error correction strategies, such as the multimodal methods, would be explored.

Third, we will extend our research into other areas. Although this research focuses on pen-based geometry theorem proving in plane geometry, pen-based proving techniques could be used in solid geometry theorem proving as well. In the future, we will support proving in solid geometry by recognizing and understanding hand-drawn solid geometry figures.

ACKNOWLEDGMENTS
This research is supported by National Key Basic Research and Development Program of China under Grant No. 2009CB320804, the National Natural Science Foundation of China under Grant No. U0735004, No.60603073, and the National High Technology Development Program of China under Grant No. 2007AA01Z158, No.2009AA01Z337.

REFERENCES
1. Alvarado, C. and Davis, R. (2001). Resolving ambiguities to create a natural sketch based interface. In *Proc. IJCAI 2001*, AAAI Press, 1365-1371.

2. Anderson, J.R., Boyle, C.F., Yost, G. (1985). The geometry tutor. In *Proc. IJCAI 1985*, 1–7.

3. Ao, X., Li, J.F., Wang, X.G. and Dai, G.Z. (2006). Structuralizing digital ink for efficient selection. In *Proc. IUI 2006*, ACM Press, 148-154.

4. Cabri Geometry. http://www.cabri.com/

5. Chazan, D. (1993). High school geometry students' justification for their views of empirical evidence and mathematical proof. *Educational Studies in Mathematics*, 24(4), 359-387.

6. Chang, C.C. and Lin, C.J. (2001). LIBSVM: a library for support vector machines, 2001. http://www.csie.ntu.edu.tw/_cjlin/libsvm.

7. Chou, S.C., Gao, X.S. and Zhang, J.Z. (1996). Automated Generation of Readable Proofs with Geometric Invariants. *J. Autom. Reasoning.* 17(3), 349-370.

8. Cormen, T.H., Leiserson, C.E., Rivest, R.L. and Stein, C. (2001). *Introduction to Algorithms, 2nd ed.* MIT Press, Cambridge, USA, 2001.

9. Gao, X.S. and Lin, Q. (2002). MMP/Geometer - a software package for automated geometry reasoning. In *Proceedings of ADG 2002*, Springer-Verlag, 44-46.

10. GeoAssistor: A Pen-based Geometry Learning Tool for Students. http://research.microsoft.com/en-us/um/beijing/projects/research/education/penbased.aspx

11. Geometer's Sketchpad. http://www.dynamicgeometry.com/

12. Geometry Explorer. http://homepages.gac.edu/~hvidsten/explorer/

13. Hanna, G. (1998). Proof as understanding in geometry. *Focus on Learning Problems in Mathematics.* 20(2&3), 4-13.

14. Hoyles, C. and Healy, L. (1999). Linking informal argumentation with formal proof through computer-integrated teaching experiences. In *Proceedings of the 23rd conference of the international group for the psychology of mathematics education*, 1999, 105-112.

15. Jiang, Y.Y., Tian, F., Wang, X.G., Zhang, X.L., Dai, G.Z. and Wang, H.A. (2009). Structuring and manipulating hand-drawn concept maps. In *Proc. IUI 2009*, ACM Press, 457-462.

16. Kara L.B. (2004). *Automatic parsing and recognition of hand-drawn sketches for pen-based computer interfaces*. Doctor's dissertation, Department of Mechanical Engineering, Carnegie Mellon University, Pittsburgh, PA, USA, 2004.

17. Keshari, B. and Watt, S.M. (2007). Hybrid mathematical symbol recognition using support vector machines. In

Proc. ICDAR 2007, IEEE Computer Society Press, 859-863.

18. Knuth, E.J. (2002). Teachers' conception of proof in the context of secondary school mathematics. *Journal of Mathematics Teacher Education*, 5(1), 61-88.

19. Kortenkamp, U. and Richter-Gebert, J. (2004). Using automatic theorem proving to improve the usability of geometry software. In *Proceedings of the Mathematical User Interfaces Workshop 2004*, 2004.

20. LaViola, J. and Zeleznik, R. (2004). MathPad2: A System for the Creation and Exploration of Mathematical Sketches. *ACM Transactions on Graphics*. 23(3), 432-440.

21. Li, J.F., Zhang, X.W., Ao, X. and Dai, G.Z. (2005). Sketch recognition with continuous feedback based on incremental intention extraction. In *Proc. IUI 2005*, ACM Press, 145-150.

22. Liu, Y.Y., Lin, Q. and Dai, G.Z. (2007). PIGP: A Pen-Based Intelligent Dynamic Lecture System for Geometry Teaching. In *Proc. Edutainment 2007*. Springer Berlin / Heidelberg, 381-390.

23. Narboux, J. (2007). A graphical user interface for formal proofs in geometry. *Journal of Automated Reasoning*. 39(2), 161-180.

24. Ouyang, T.Y. and Davis, R. (2007). Recognition of Hand Drawn Chemical Diagrams. In *Proc. AAAI 2007*, AAAI Press, 846-851.

25. Paulson, B. and Hammond, T. (2008). PaleoSketch: accurate primitive sketch recognition and beautification. In *Proc. IUI 2008*, ACM Press, 1-10.

26. Senk, S.L. (1985). How well do students write geometry proofs? *The mathematics teacher*. 78(6), 448-456.

27. Tanaka, H., Nakajima, K., Ishigaki, K., Akiyama, K. and Nakagawa, M. (1999). Hybrid pen-input character recognition system based on integration of online-offline recognition. In *Proc. ICDAR 1999*, ACM Press, 209–212.

28. Wang, X., Shi, G.S. and Yang, J.F. (2009). The understanding and structure analyzing for online handwritten chemical formulas, In *Proc. ICDAR 2009*, IEEE Computer Society Press, 1056-1060.

29. Wong, W.K., Chan, B.Y. and Yin, S.K. (2005). A Dynamic Geometry Environment for Learning Theorem Proving. In *Proceedings of the 5th IEEE International Conference on Advanced Learning Technologies (ICALT) 2005,* IEEE Computer Society Press, 15-17.

30. Yang, H.H., Wong, W.K. and Chan, B.Y. (2006) Using computer-assisted instruction for the visualization of proof tree to improve the reading comprehension of geometry proofs. In *International Workshop on Human-Computer Interaction and Learning Technologies 2006*, 1431-1436.

Usage Patterns and Latent Semantic Analyses for Task Goal Inference of Multimodal User Interactions

Pui-Yu Hui, Wai-Kit Lo and Helen M. Meng
Human-Computer Communications Laboratory
The Chinese University of Hong Kong
Shatin, Hong Kong SAR of China
{pyhui, wklo, hmmeng}@se.cuhk.edu.hk

ABSTRACT

This paper describes our work in usage pattern analysis and development of a latent semantic analysis framework for interpreting multimodal user input consisting speech and pen gestures. We have designed and collected a multimodal corpus of navigational inquiries. Each modality carries semantics related to domain-specific task goal. Each inquiry is annotated manually with a task goal based on the semantics. Multimodal input usually has a simpler syntactic structure than unimodal input and the order of semantic constituents is different in multimodal and unimodal inputs. Therefore, we proposed to use semantic analysis to derive the latent semantics from the multimodal inputs using latent semantic modeling (LSM). In order to achieve this, we parse the recognized Chinese spoken input for the spoken locative references (SLR). These SLRs are then aligned with their corresponding pen gesture(s). Then, we characterized the cross-modal integration pattern as 3-tuple multimodal terms with SLR, pen gesture type and their temporal relation. The inquiry-multimodal term matrix is then decomposed using singular value decomposition (SVD) to derive the latent semantics automatically. Task goal inference based on the latent semantics shows that the task goal inference accuracy on a disjoint test set is of 99%.

Author Keywords

Multimodal input, spoken input, pen gesture, task goal inference, latent semantic modeling (LSM), singular value decomposition (SVD).

ACM Classification Keywords

H.5.2 [User Interfaces]: Input devices and strategies, Natural language, User-centered design.

General Terms

Algorithms, Human Factors, Languages

1. INTRODUCTION

This paper describes our initial attempt in developing a semantic analysis framework for multimodal user input with speech and pen gestures. Each modality in the multimodal user input presents a different abstraction of user's informational or communicative goal as one or more input events. Semantic interpretation of multimodal inputs captured with the mobile devices requires syntactic, semantics, temporal and contextual information derived from multiple modalities. Previous work in semantic interpretation of multimodal input include frame-based heuristic integration [1, 2], unification parsing [3, 4], hybrid symbolic-statistical approach [5, 6], weighted finite-state transducers [7], probabilistic graph matching [8, 9] and the salience-driven approach [10]. We leveraged such experiences to devise a computationally efficient approach based on score-based, cross-modal integration that incorporates semantic and temporal information [11]. The approach does not present high demands for training data. The current work extends cross-modal integration with semantic interpretation. More specifically, our aim is to infer the domain-specific task goal(s) of the multimodal input. The task goal is characterized by terms used in the spoken modality, as well as particular term co-occurrence patterns across modalities. Previously, we have applied Belief Networks [12, 13] for task goal inference based on unimodal (speech-only) inputs. However, previous studies [11, 19] that compare the spoken part of multimodal inputs with unimodal (speech-only) inputs shows that the former generally has simpler syntactic structures, more diverse vocabularies and different term ordering. Therefore, we explore the use of latent semantic modeling (LSM) for task goal inference, with the objective of uncovering the associations between (unimodal or multimodal) terms and task goals through a data-derived latent space.

LSM [14] is a data-driven approach that models the underlying semantics of word usages from available corpora. It has been applied unimodally to text or transcribed speech for language modeling [15], document clustering [16], spoken document retrieval [17], document summarization [18], etc. The objective of our current work is to apply LSM in capturing the latent semantics of the multimodal user inputs. In LSM, the associations of between terms and inquiries are represented as a term-inquiry matrix. This can be factorized into a term-semantics and an inquiry-semantics matrix using singular value decomposition (SVD) [14]. These two matrices associate terms and inquiries through an automatically derived space of semantics, instead of directly relating the terms with inquiries.

We represent a multimodal input by means of lexical or multimodal terms. Multimodal terms are decided base on cross-modality integration patterns elicited from the user inputs. We then perform LSM to analyze the content of a multimodal input. Each input is associated with every latent semantic category by a weight. The weights are used for task goal inference. There are a total of nine task goals in our experimental domain.

In the following, we introduce latent semantic analysis, present the collected multimodal corpus and discuss the process of task goal inference and related experimentation.

2. THE LATENT SEMANTIC ANALYSIS FRAMEWORK

We apply latent semantic analysis for task goal inference based on multimodal input. The latent semantic model (LSM) uses Singular Value Decomposition (SVD) to derive a latent semantic space that relates multimodal terms (combined lexical and gestural terms) with the users' inputs. Correlations between cross-modal terms are captured from the training data. During testing, multimodal terms are extracted from the input and the vector is projected into the latent space. Thereafter, the task goal is inferred based on a combination of latent semantics.

2.1 Association Matrices

Associations between terms and inquiries can be summarized in a term–inquiry matrix G. Given M terms (details of the multimodal terms will be presented in section 4.5) and N inquiries, we form an $M \times N$ matrix G. Each column represents an inquiry. The element $g_{m,n}$, is the weight (i.e. normalized term frequency using TF-IDF) for the term m in the nth inquiry.

$$G = \begin{bmatrix} g_{1,1} & \cdots & g_{1,n} & \cdots & g_{1,N} \\ \vdots & \ddots & \vdots & \cdot^{\cdot^{\cdot}} & \vdots \\ g_{m,1} & \cdots & g_{m,n} & \cdots & g_{m,N} \\ \vdots & \cdot^{\cdot^{\cdot}} & \vdots & \ddots & \vdots \\ g_{M,1} & \cdots & g_{M,n} & \cdots & g_{M,N} \end{bmatrix} \quad (1)$$

where $g_{m,n} = (1 - \varepsilon_m)\dfrac{\kappa_{m,n}}{\lambda_n}$,

$$\varepsilon_m = -\frac{1}{\log N}\sum_{n=1}^{N}\frac{\kappa_{m,n}}{\tau_m}\log\frac{\kappa_{m,n}}{\tau_m}$$

$\kappa_{m,n}$ denotes the number of times the term m occurs in the nth inquiry,

λ_n is the total number of terms in the nth inquiry,

ε_m denotes the normalized entropy of term m in the data set; and

τ_m is the total number of times that term m occurs in the training set.

G may be decomposed into a product of three matrices, with methods such as singular value decomposition (SVD), probabilistic latent semantic analysis (PLSA) [20] and latent Dirichlet allocation (LDA) [21]. We propose to focus on the use of SVD of order R, as shown in Equation 2.

$$G = USV^T$$

$$= \begin{bmatrix} u_{1,1} & \cdots & u_{1,R} \\ \vdots & \ddots & \vdots \\ u_{M,1} & \cdots & u_{M,R} \end{bmatrix}\begin{bmatrix} s_{1,1} & 0 & 0 \\ 0 & \ddots & 0 \\ 0 & 0 & s_{R,R} \end{bmatrix}\begin{bmatrix} v_{1,1} & \cdots & v_{1,R} \\ \vdots & \ddots & \vdots \\ v_{N,1} & \cdots & v_{N,R} \end{bmatrix}^T \quad (2)$$

where U is the left unitary matrix of dimensions $M \times R$,

S is the diagonal matrix of singular values sorted in descending order with dimensions $R \times R$,

V^T is the right unitary matrix of dimensions $R \times N$,

$R = \min\{M, N\}$ is the order of decomposition and

T is the transpose of the matrix.

Each column of U contains the estimated weight of each term m that corresponds to the latent semantic category r while each column of V^T contains the estimated weight of each inquiry n that corresponds to the latent semantic category r. Equation 2 projects the space of terms and inquiries onto a reduced R-dimensional space which is defined by the orthonormal basis given by the column vectors u_m and v_n from matrices U and V respectively. In order to collapse the terms that are "semantically similar", we always choose $R' < R$. The smaller the value R', the more pronounced is the reduction of semantic redundancy in the latent semantic space. Based on the latent semantic space, we may re-construct the space of terms and inquiries, denoted as $\hat{G}$ in Equation 3.

$$G \approx \hat{G} = U\hat{S}V^T \quad (3)$$

where $\hat{S}$ is the reduced diagonal matrix of singular values with optimized value of R'.

We need to find an "optimal" choice of R' that minimizes the distortion between the re-constructed space $\hat{G}$ and the original space G, in the implementation of Equation 3 in the training procedure. We plan to optimize R' through empirical analysis of the latent space.

2.2 Relating Task Goals with Latent Semantics

In the training procedure, we represent the nth inquiry by the column vector g_n. The weights for latent semantic category r can then be obtained by a dot product between g_n and the corresponding column vector of the left unitary matrix U, u_r. Therefore, from the vector g_n, we can obtain a vector of weights w_n for each latent semantic category by Equation 4:

$$w_n = g_n^T U \quad (4)$$

where $w_n = \begin{bmatrix} w_{n,1} & \cdots & w_{n,R'} \end{bmatrix}$, $g_n = \begin{bmatrix} g_{1,n} & \cdots & g_{M,n} \end{bmatrix}^T$ and

$w_{n,r}$ is the weight of latent semantic category r for the nth inquiry.

We use A to denote the total number of task goals within the application domain, a_n to denote the task goal of the nth inquiry, and R' to denote the number of dimensions in the latent semantic space. We attempt to compute a projection matrix F that can transform the vector of weights for the latent semantic categories w_n into a vector of weights for the A task goals (see Equation 5).

$$h_n = w_n F \qquad (5)$$

where $F = \begin{bmatrix} f_{1,1} & \cdots & f_{1,A} \\ \vdots & \ddots & \vdots \\ f_{R',1} & \cdots & f_{R',A} \end{bmatrix}$,

$f_{r,a}$ is the weight of a latent semantic category r that would correspond to a task goal a and

$$h_n = \begin{bmatrix} h_{n,1} & \cdots & h_{n,A} \end{bmatrix}$$

where $h_{n,a}$ is the weight of the nth inquiry would correspond to a task goal a.

According to Equation 5, associations between inquiry and latent semantic categories can be summarized in an inquiry-latent semantic categories matrix W (an NxR' matrix) and the associations between inquiry and task goal can be summarized in an inquiry-task goal matrix H (an NxA matrix). Therefore, we can obtain Equation 6 as follows.

$$H = WF \qquad (6)$$

where $W = \begin{bmatrix} w_1 \\ \vdots \\ w_N \end{bmatrix} = \begin{bmatrix} w_{1,1} & \cdots & w_{1,R'} \\ \vdots & \ddots & \vdots \\ w_{N,1} & \cdots & w_{N,R'} \end{bmatrix}$ and

$$H = \begin{bmatrix} h_1 \\ \vdots \\ h_N \end{bmatrix} = \begin{bmatrix} h_{1,1} & \cdots & h_{1,A} \\ \vdots & \ddots & \vdots \\ h_{N,1} & \cdots & h_{N,A} \end{bmatrix}.$$

Mathematically, the projection matrix F can be found using Equation 7.

$$F = W^{-1}H' \qquad (7)$$

where $H' = \begin{bmatrix} h'_1 \\ \vdots \\ h'_N \end{bmatrix} = \begin{bmatrix} h'_{1,1} & \cdots & h'_{1,A} \\ \vdots & \ddots & \vdots \\ h'_{N,1} & \cdots & h'_{N,A} \end{bmatrix}$,

h'_n is a vector of manually labeled task goal for n^{th} inquiry,

$h'_{n,a}$ is the manually labeled task goal of inquiry n, in which $h'_{n,a} = \{0,1\}$ and $\sum_{a=1}^{a=A} h'_{n,a} = 1$ and

W^{-1} is the pseudo inverse of the matrix W.

Through the projection matrix F and Equation 5, we can obtain the weight of each inquiry that would correspond to each task goal. A task goal a_n^* will be assigned as the automatic derived task goal for inquiry n where $a_n^* = \arg\max_a \{h_{n,a}\}$.

The performance of task goal inference of the training data can then be evaluated by comparing a_n^* to the manually annotated task goal a_n. Moreover, we may examine the structural relations between latent semantic category and task goals in the transformation matrix F.

In the testing procedure, we also represent the nth inquiry by a vector g_n. We obtain the weights for the r latent semantic categories by Equation 4 where the left unitary matrix U is obtained from the training procedure. The vector of weights for each latent semantic category lies in the R'-dimensional space. We transform it to A-dimensional space and automatically derived task goal a_n^* for the nth inquiry using Equation 5. The task goal inference performance can be evaluated by comparing the a_n^* assigned and task goal a_n manually annotated of the nth inquiry.

3. MULTIMODAL CORPUS

We collected a multimodal corpus with speech and pen gestures in the city navigation domain. We invited 23 Mandarin-speaking subjects, each of whom was asked formulate 66 task-oriented multimodal inputs according to a set of instructions. The tasks are designed based on nine task goals including:

- BUS_INFORMATION
- CHOICE_OF_VEHICLE
- MAP_COMMANDS
- OPENING_HOURS
- RAILWAY_INFORMATION
- ROUTE_FINDING
- TIME_CONSTRAINT
- TRANSPORTATION_COSTS and
- TRAVEL_TIME

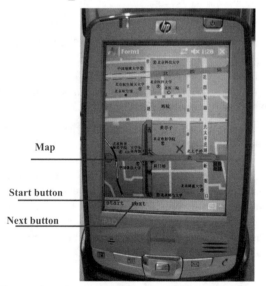

Figure 1. Data collection interface of the Pocket PC, augmented with soft buttons for logging functions (start/stop) and loading the next map.

Each inquiry may involve up to n ($n=6$ in this work) locations. They may refer to target locations shown on a Pocket PC interface (see Figure 1) by speech and/or pen gestures. Both speech and pen input are recorded directly by the Pocket PC. Captured multimodal inputs involve disfluencies in the speech modality (e.g. filled pauses and repairs), spurious pen gestures (e.g. repetitive pen gesture inputs) and recognition errors in both modalities. These imperfections have adverse effects on cross-modality semantic integration. Table 1 shows an example task and a multimodal input obtained during data collection. We collected a total of 1518 user inquiries, which include 1442 multimodal and 76 speech-only (unimodal) inputs. All speech and pen data are *manually* transcribed. Furthermore, subjects were presented with their own multimodal data and asked to indicate (based on their original intentions) the correspondences between the spoken locative references (e.g. *here*, *the nearest station*, etc.) and pen gestures. These cross-modality correspondences are referenced as we annotate the cross-modal integration patterns. We divided the 1,442 multimodal inputs randomly into disjoint training and test sets in a 7:3 ratio. Hence we have 999 inputs as the training set and 443 inputs as the test set. As a first step, we apply the task goal inference framework to the *manual* transcriptions of speech (which is equivalent to having perfect speech recognition) and will defer handling speech recognition errors to a later step.

Information category: TRAVEL_TIME
Task: 告知系統你所在的位置，查詢從那裡到另外四所大學需要多長時間。 "*Specify your current location. Find the time it takes to travel to four universities of your choice.*"
Multimodal input: **S**: 我在 <u>北郵</u> 從 <u>這裡</u> 出發到 <u>這四個大學</u> 要多久？ **P**:　　• (*a point*)　　•••• (*four points*) "*I'm at <u>BUPT</u>. From <u>here</u>, I want to visit <u>these four universities</u>. How long will it take?*"

Table 1. Example of a multimodal input with speech (S) and pen gestures (P). Translations are provided in italics and corresponding SLRs are underlined.

4. CHARACTERIZING AND ANNOTATING CROSS-MODAL INTEGRATION PATTERNS

A navigational inquiry in the multimodal corpus may include one or more SLRs and/or pen gestures that indicate specific locations on the map. As will be explained later, there is no straightforward correspondence between SLRs and pen gestures. Therefore, we need to understand the characteristics of each modality and their temporal relationships, in order to appropriately obtain cross-modal integration patterns.

4.1 Spoken Locative References

An SLR can be a direct (full name, abbreviated name or a contextual phrase such as "*my current location*") or an indirect one [11]. It may also be a singular, aggregated, plural reference or unspecified on number:

- A **singular reference** can be a direct reference with a full name or an abbreviated name. It may also be a singular indirect reference (e.g. 這個公園 "*this park*"), which may optionally include information about the location type (i.e. a park in the given example).
- An **aggregated reference** is an indirect reference with a specific numeric value (which is greater than 1) and

an optional location type feature (e.g. 這四個地方 "*these four locations*").

- A **plural reference** is an indirect reference with the numeric feature set to plural (i.e. NUM=*plural*), as well as an optional location type feature (e.g. 這些大學 "*these university*").
- An **unspecified reference** is an indirect reference with unspecified numeric and location type features (e.g. 這裡 "*here*").

Analysis of the training set shows that it contains 2442 SLRs among the 999 multimodal inputs. Their distribution is shown in Figure 2.

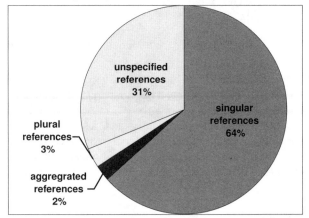

Figure 2. Distribution of the types of SLRs in the training set.

Spoken Terms Regularization
Analysis of the spoken inputs also shows that there are many synonymous terms and aliases. For example, the word "route" in Chinese consists of two characters (i.e. 路線), which may also be reversed (as 線路) and the meaning of the word remains the same. Similarly, SLRs may have synonymous terms. For example, the full name 北京郵電大學 (i.e. *Beijing University of Post and Telecommunications*) may be abbreviated as 北郵 (i.e. *BUPT*). There is also a variety of verbalization to express the contextual phrase of "current location", including: 目前的所在地, 當前的位置, 所在的地方, 所在地, etc. Other contextual phrases may differ by a "measure word" which is characteristic of Chinese, e.g. 這間大學 and 這所大學 both mean "*this university*". In order to simplify processing, synonymous terms and aliases are collapsed into a single category. In other words, we have created a category for each group of semantically equivalent terms. It is conceivable that this categorization may be implemented through the use of SVD if sufficient data is available. Since we only have limited training data for the time being, we choose to design regularization rules (56 rules in all) for categorization.[1] As such, we have reduced

---

[1] This step forms equivalence classes that group together terms with the same meaning. We expect that this step should help task goal inference because it reduces term diversity given the limited amount of training data. We plan to perform an analogous experiment without term regularization for comparison.

the number of lexical terms[2] significantly. Since we also have pen gestures with their corresponding SLRs, we are able to form "multimodal terms". Each is a 3-tuple consisting of an SLR, the corresponding pen gesture and their temporal relationship. We will elaborate on this later.

The statistics of the lexical and multimodal terms in the training set are shown in Table 2. After regularization, the number of multimodal terms can be reduced by around 66%. The number of (SLR and pen) multimodal terms is fewer than expected. There are 22 multimodal terms that contain only an SLR with no pen gesture. This is because of an anaphoric reference (which can be resolved with contextual information). There are also 6 multimodal terms that contain pen gestures only and no SLR, due the use of ellipsis.

	Before term regularization	After term regularization
# of Multimodal terms	456	261
(SLR and pen)	407	233
(SLR only)	43	22
(Pen only)	6	6
# of Lexical terms	260	216
Total number of terms	716	477

Table 2. Statistics of the lexical and multimodal terms (count by type).

4.2 Pen Gestures

A pen gesture can be recognized as a point, circle or stroke. Using these three types of pen gestures, subjects can indicate different semantics such as a single location, an area with multiple locations or a route (see Table 3). There can be up to n (=6) locations in an inquiry and the mapping between SLRs and pen gestures may be one-to-many or many-to-one. Analysis of the training set shows that it contains 2480 pen gestures. 95% of the multimodal inputs contain a single pen gesture, i.e. POINT, CIRCLE or STROKE. The remaining multimodal inputs (i.e. 5%) contain multiple pen gestures, to which we refer as MULTI-POINT, MULTI-CIRCLE and MULTI-STROKE. Table 3 shows examples of pen gestures and their semantics.

4.3 Correspondence between Spoken Locative References and Pen Gestures

We derive the correspondence between SLRs and pen gestures based on temporal ordering and semantic compatibility. Analysis of the training data shows that in a multimodal input, SLR and pen gesture that (jointly) refer to the same intended location may not always overlap in time. Hence our approach only enforces the temporal ordering of SLRs and pen gestures when deriving their associations.

Additionally, the association between SLRs and pen gestures also enforce semantic compatibility. Our approach checks the numeric value (NUM) of an SLR and ensures that

it is associated with a compatible number of pen gestures. For the case of one-to-many mapping between the SLR and its associated pen gestures, the pen gestures are considered together as a group (i.e. MULTI-POINT, MULTI-CIRCLE or MULTI-STROKE) in cross-modality integration. The reverse is also true when mapping a pen gesture to multiple SLRs. Furthermore, our approach also checks for agreement in the location type features (LOC_TYPE) in the cross-modality association.

Semantics	Gesture type	Illustration(s)
A single location	POINT	
	CIRCLE	
	STROKE	
An area / multiple locations	CIRCLE (a big circle)	
Multiple locations	MULTI-POINT (four points correspond to one SLR)	
	MULTI-CIRCLE (four circles correspond to one SLR)	
	MULTI-STROKE (three strokes correspond to one SLR)	
A route	STROKE (a stroke indicates the start and end points)	
	MULTI-STROKE (a long stroke with one or more turning points indicate a route)	

Table 3. Examples of different pen gesture types and their semantics.

4.4 Temporal Relationships

Temporal integration patterns [19] between corresponding SLRs and pen gestures, as observed in our training set, include two main types: simultaneous (SIM) and sequential patterns (SEQ). Simultaneous SLRs and pen gestures have temporal overlap. Sequential associations do not. A 3-tuple that consists of corresponding SLR(s) and pen gesture(s), together with their temporal relationship, i.e., <SLR | pen_gesture_type | temporal_relationship> is referred as a multimodal term. Among the 2261 multimodal terms found in the training set, 74% are simultaneous and 26% are sequential. For example, consider the multimodal expression:

---

[2] A lexical term refers to a tokenized Chinese word from the speech modality but which is not an SLR. Examples include: 開放時間 *"opening hours"*, 路線 *"route"*, 從 *"from"*, etc.

從 我所在的地方 到 這裡 可以怎麼走？

● ● ● ● ●

"How can I go from my current location to here?"
Its multimodal terms include <我所在的地方|POINT |SIM>
and <這裡|MULTI-POINT|SIM>.

Speech (as parsed SLR)	Pen (as transcribed gesture)	Temporal Relationship (SIM / SEQ)	Count
Singular (1550/2480, 62.5%)	Single (1417/1550, 91.4%)	SIM (1024/1417, 72.3%)	1024
		SEQ (393/1417, 27.7%)	393
	Multiple (0/1550, 0%)	SIM	0
		SEQ	0
	∅ (133/1550, 8.6%)	∅	133
Aggregated (56/2480, 2.3%)	Single (9/56, 16%)	SIM (7/9, 77.8%)	7
		SEQ (2/9, 22.2%)	2
	Multiple (44/56, 78.6%)	SIM (25/44, 56.8%)	25
		SEQ (19/44, 43.2%)	19
	∅ (3/56, 5.4%)	∅	3
Plural (75/2480, 3%)	Single (21/75, 28%)	SIM (12/21, 57.1%)	12
		SEQ (9/21, 42.9%)	9
	Multiple (54/75, 72%)	SIM (35/54, 64.8%)	35
		SEQ (19/54, 35.2%)	19
	∅ (0/75, 0%)	∅	0
Unspecified (761/2480, 30.7%)	Single (715/761, 94%)	SIM (569/715, 79.6%)	569
		SEQ (146/715, 20.4%)	146
	Multiple (1/761, 0.1%)	SIM (1/1, 100%)	1
		SEQ (0/1, 0%)	0
	∅ (45/761, 5.9%)	∅	45
∅ (38/2480, 1.5%)	Single (34/38, 89.5%)	∅	34
	Multiple (4/38, 10.5%)	∅	4

Table 4. Statistics of cross-modal integration patterns in the training set. There are altogether 2480 multimodal terms (count by token) in total. Among them, 2261 contain both SLR and pen gesture, 181 contain only SLRs and 38 of them contain only pen gestures.

4.5 Cross-Modal Integration Patterns

Recall that SLRs may be singular, aggregated, plural and unspecified references. Recall also that an SLR may correspond to one or more pen gestures. We analyze the statistics in the training set as shown in Table 4. From the statistics, we observe that users predominantly prefer to use a single reference in the SLR (62.5%). Furthermore, a single SLR generally corresponds to a single pen gesture, as none were found mapping to multiple pen gestures. As regards aggregated references (e.g., <這四個大學> or <*these four universities*>), 79% were found to correspond with multiple pen gestures to indicate multiple locations. The other 16% are used with a circle (i.e. a single pen gesture) that encompasses multiple locations. An example is the multimodal term <這四個大學|CIRCLE|SIM> or <*these four universities |CIRCLE/SIM*>. For plural references, 72% are used with multiple pen gestures to indicate multiple locations. The remaining 28% are used with a single pen gesture, with the majority (19/21) being circles and the remaining two are points. SLRs with an unspecified numeric features should correspond to both single and multiple pen gestures. Within the training set, however, an unspecified reference predominantly (94%) occurs in association with a single pen gesture.

User input with deictic and anaphoric references (the second "*here*" is an anaphora to the first "*here*"):
S: 我 在 這裡 從 這裡 到 這裡 要 多久 ***P***:　　　● 　　　　　　　　　○ *"I'm now here. How much time will it take to go from here to here?"*
Annotated user input with multimodal terms:
我 　 在 　 <這裡|POINT|SIM> 　 從 　 <這裡|∅|∅> 　 到 <這裡|CIRCLE|SEQ> 要 多久 *"I'm now at <here/POINT/SIM>. How much time will it take from <here/∅/∅> to <here/CIRCLE/SEQ>?"*
User input with elliptic locative references (the SLR is omitted in speech):
S: 　　　　開放時間 *"Opening hours?"* ***P***: ● ● ●
Annotated user input with a multimodal term:
<∅|MULTI-POINT|∅> 開放時間 *"<∅/MULTI-POINT/∅> Opening hours?"*

Table 5. Examples on 3-tuple multimodal term annotation with speech (*S*) and pen gesture (*P*). Translations are italicized and quoted.

The above refers to SLRs that are deictic or anaphoric expressions. Deictic expressions need to be interpreted jointly with the associated pen gestures. Anaphoric references are interpreted based on contextual information and do not correspond to any pen gestures. The first row in Table 5 presents examples of these two types of expressions. Additionally, there are also elliptic expressions, where the SLR is completely omitted but the pen gesture is present. For such cases, the cross-modal temporal relationship is irrelevant (and indicated by "∅"). Table 5 shows some examples.

The number of multimodal terms is much fewer than the exhaustive combinations between SLRs and pen gestures. Some of the terms are not available in the corpus, while others may be implausible combinations, such as:

A singular reference with multiple pen gestures (e.g. <這個大學|MULTI-POINT|SIM> "<*this university |MULTI-POINT|SIM>*") – a singular SLR refers to one location and corresponds to one pen gesture. Multiple pen gestures should correspond to an aggregated or plural reference. Therefore, this combination involves incompatibility in the numeric feature.

An aggregated reference with a single point or a single stroke (e.g. <這三個地方|POINT|SIM> "<*these three places |POINT|SIM>*") – an aggregated SLR refers to multiple locations and should correspond to multiple pen gestures or a circle. Again, this combination involves incompatibility in the numeric feature.

An unspecified reference with multiple circles or strokes (e.g. <這裡|MULTI-STROKE|SIM> "<*here|MULTI-STROKE /SIM>*") – empirically, we have found that about 94% of the unspecified references are used to indicate a single location (as shown in Table 4). A possible reason may be that unspecified SLRs have short durations, during which the subjects may find it difficult to gesture multiple circles or strokes simultaneously.

5. TASK GOAL INFERENCE

In the previous section, we examined the associations between SLRs and pen gestures, leading to the definition of a multimodal term that captures cross-modal integration patterns and their temporal relationships. In this section, we present a framework for inferring the task goal based on an input inquiry.

As a reference baseline, we apply the vector-space model [22] for task goal inference. For each task goal a, we consider all of its training expressions and their multimodal terms. We create a vector j_a of weights, using the normalized term frequency TF-IDF of the multimodal terms. For an input multimodal expression, we create a vector g_n, similar to the column vector of G in Equation 1. The similarity between an inquiry g_n and task goal vector j_a is calculated as the inner product of the two vectors. Long inquiries contain more terms. Since the dot product favors long inquiries by generating higher similarity scores, we apply cosine normalization (see Equation 7) to reduce the adverse effect of term repetition.

$$Similarity_{cosine}(j_a, g_n) = \frac{j_a \cdot g_n}{\|j_a\| \|g_n\|} \quad (7)$$

where j_a is the weight for all terms in the ath task goal and
g_n is the weight for all terms in the nth inquiry.

The input expression is assigned to the task goal a_n^* which has the maximum similarity score, as shown in Equation 8.

$$a_n^* = \arg\max_a \left\{ Similarity_{cosine}(j_a, g_n) \right\} \quad (8)$$

Experiments show that vector-space model can correctly infer task goals for 85% and 90% of the inquiries in training and test sets respectively.

Recall that the proposed approach using LSM involves setting up a term-inquiry matrix G. We include both lexical (unimodal, speech only) terms and multimodal terms with speech and pen gestures. There are a total of 216 unimodal terms and 261 multimodal terms in our training corpus. Hence the non-negative matrix G (in Equation 1) is of dimensions 477x999. As described in Section 2, we apply SVD to G and factorize it into U, S and V.

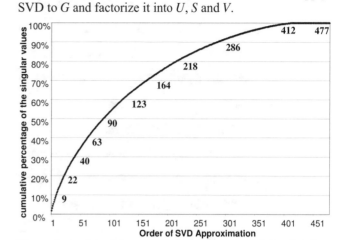

Figure 3. A plot of the cumulative percentage of the singular values against the values of R'.

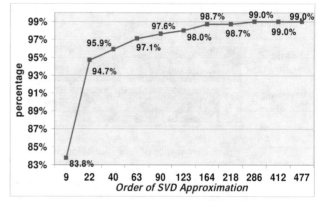

Figure 4. A plot of task goal inference accuracy of multimodal inputs in training set against the order of SVD approximation

5.1 Optimization of R'

Recall that the total number of lexical and multimodal terms sum to $R=477$. We may consider that the original semantic space to be determined by these terms and attempt to determine the optimal number of dimensions for the latent space. We may choose the order of SVD approximation (R') with reference to the percentage of the cumulative sum of retained singular values over the maximum at $R'=477$. We plot the percentage of the cumulative sum of preserved singular values over the total sum of all singular values (i.e. at $R'=477$). In Figure 3, we show the R' values corresponding to the cumulative sum of singular values, at multiples of 10%.

We also perform task goal inference on the multimodal inputs in the training set at the different values of R' (see Figure 4). The performance of task goal inference increases with R'. The rate of increase slowed down as R' becomes higher, reaching saturation approximately at R'=286 with a performance of task goal inference at 99% correct. The choice of R'=286 as the dimensionality of the latent space implies a reduction of 40% with respect to the original space.

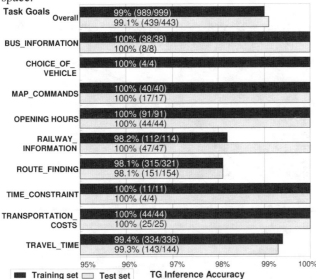

Figure 5. Performance of task goal inference for each of the nine task goals in the application domain. Results are based on the latent space with 286 dimensions.

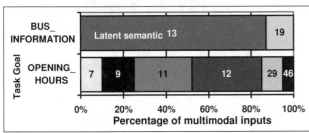

Figure 6. Percentage of multimodal inputs that belong to different latent semantic categories, within two task goals BUS_INFORMATION and OPENING HOURS. The numbers inside the bars are the labels (indexed by r) of the latent semantic categories.

5.2 Performance Evaluation

Overall performance in task goal inference for the training and test sets are 99%[3] and 99.1%[4] respectively. Detailed analyses of the results are shown in Figure 5. The test set lacks inqueries that fall under the task goal of CHOICE_OF_VEHICLE (i.e., asking the user what type of vehicle he/she wishes to take). Performance of task goal inference remains high for all the other task goals (at 98% or above).

---

[3] Improvements in task goal inference accuracies brought about by LSM is statistically significant from 85% to 99% ($\alpha=0.01$, one-tailed z-test).

[4] Improvements in task goal inference accuracies brought about by LSM is statistically significant from 90% to 99.1% ($\alpha=0.01$, one-tailed z-test).

5.3 Analysis of the Latent Semantic Space
5.3.1 Sub-categorization of task goals

Analysis of the latent semantic space shows that it has subdivided some of the task goals into logical sub-types. For example, the task goal BUS_INFORMATION contains two latent semantic categories (see Figure 6):

- The latent semantic category (r=13) refers to BUS_INFORMATION along a street; e.g. 經過 <這條大街|STROKE|SEQ> 的 所有 公交 線路 是 哪些 *"what are the bus routes that pass through <this street/STROKE/SEQ>?"*
- The category (r=19) refers to BUS_INFORMATION within an area; e.g. 告訴我 所有 在 <這個範圍|CIRCLE|SIM> 行走 的 公交路線 *"please tell me all the bus routes in <this area/CIRCLE/SIM>."*

Another example is the task goal OPENING_HOURS, which contains six latent semantic categories:

- The latent semantic category (r=11) refers to OPENING_HOURS of one location; e.g. 我想知道 <這個 公園|POINT|SIM> 的 開放時間 *"I would like to know the opening hours of <this park/POINT/SIM>."*
- The category (r=46) refers to OPENING_HOURS of multiple locations using ellipsis; e.g. <∅|POINT|∅> 開 放時間 *"<∅|POINT|∅> opening hours."*
- The categories (r=7 and 29) refer to OPENING_HOURS of multiple locations using multiple singular SLRs; e.g. 我 想 知 道 <這個市場|POINT|SIM> <這個廣場|POINT|SIM> <這個購物中心|POINT|SIM> 的 開放時間 *"I would like to know the opening hours of <this plaza/POINT/SIM>, <this plaza/POINT/SIM> and <this shopping center/POINT/SIM>."*
- The category (r=9) refers to OPENING_HOURS of multiple locations using one aggregated SLR; e.g. 勞駕 你告訴我 <這三個地方|MULTI-POINT|SEQ> 的 營業時 間 *"Please tell me the opening hours of <these three locations/MULTI-POINT/SEQ>."*
- The category (r=12) refers to OPENING_HOURS of multiple locations using one plural SLR; e.g. 我 想 知 道 <這幾個地方|MULTI-POINT|SEQ> 的 營運時間 *"I would like to know the opening hours of <these locations/ MULTI-POINT/SEQ>."*

We observe that latent semantic modeling has produced subcategories of specific task goals based on the ways in which users compose their inquiries. This is potentially advantageous because finer semantics categorization can enhance understanding and will facilitate automatic generation of system responses.

5.3.2 Capturing key terms for task goals

We examine the term weights in the latent semantic space to identify key terms that are indicative of each task goal. Illustrative examples include:

- For the task goal MAP_COMMAND, key terms with the highest LSM weights are 放大 (i.e. *"zoom in"*), 縮小 (i.e. *"zoom out"*), 拉遠 (i.e. *"zoom out"*), as well as related standalone pen gestures expressed as the multimodal terms <∅|POINT|∅> and <∅|CIRCLE|∅>.

- For the task goal ROUTE_FINDING, key terms with the highest LSM weights are 到 (i.e. "*to*"), 從 (i.e. "*from*"), 怎樣走 "*how to get to*", 最快 "*the fastest*", 依次 "*in sequence*", as well as the multimodal terms <這裡|POINT|SEQ> (i.e. <*here*|POINT|SEQ>) and <這個大學|POINT|SIM> (i.e. <*this university*|POINT|SIM>).

5.3.3 Generalizing across related multimodal terms

Upon further examination of the LSM weights, we observe their ability to generalize across related multimodal terms, even if the correlations are not directly found in the training data. To describe the underlying mechanism – the LSM framework draws upon the co-occurrences between terms A and B, as well as the co-occurrences between B and C, in order to obtain the correlation between terms A and C.

As an illustration, we can refer to two multimodal inputs by which the user wishes to zoom in on a map:

- 放大 CIRCLE (i.e. the verb phrase "*zoom in*" followed by a circle), corresponding respectively to the lexical and multimodal terms 放大 and <∅|CIRCLE|∅>"
- 放大 POINT (i.e. the verb phrase "*zoom in*" followed by a point), corresponding respectively to the lexical and multimodal terms 放大 and <∅|POINT|∅>".

The column vectors of these two input expressions, as extracted from the original term-inquiry matrix, are shown in Table 7. We compare these vectors with their counterparts in the reconstructed term-inquiry matrix $\hat{G}$ (with R'=286), as shown in Table 8. We observe that the reconstructed column vector of the multimodal input "放大 CIRCLE" in Table 8 carry additional weighting (≥0.06) for several additional multimodal terms, namely:

- <這個地方|CIRCLE|SIM>
- <這個範圍|CIRCLE|SEQ>
- <這個範圍|CIRCLE|SIM> and
- <這幅圖|POINT|SIM >

These additional multimodal terms with non-zero weights (see Table 8) did not appear in the original user inputs (see Table 7). But these terms are commly used to convey the task goal MAP_COMMAND, according to the training data (13 out of 40 multimodal inputs). LSM captures the new correlations among <∅/CIRCLE/∅>, 放大 "*zoom in*", <這個地方|CIRCLE|SIM> "*this location*", <這個範圍|CIRCLE|SEQ> "*this area*", <這個範圍|CIRCLE|SIM> "*this area*" and <這幅圖|POINT|SIM > "*this map*" and put them into correlated latent semantics. The weights in Table 8 reflect that the circling action can be used to indicate a single location (這個地方) or an area (這個範圍).

Similarly, we also observe that the feature vector of the multimodal input "放大 POINT in Table 8 introduces additional multimodal terms with non-zero weights (e.g. ≥0.05) for several additional multimodal terms:

- <這個地方|CIRCLE|SIM >
- <這個地方|POINT|SIM > and
- <這幅圖|POINT|SIM >

	放大 "*zoom in*" <∅|CIRCLE|∅>	放大 "*zoom in*" <∅|POINT|∅>
<∅/CIRCLE/∅>	0.44	0
<∅/POINT/∅>	0	0.34
放大 "*zoom in*"	0.37	0.37
<這個地方|CIRCLE|SEQ> "*this location|CIRCLE/SEQ*"	0	0
<這個地方|CIRCLE|SIM> "*this location|CIRCLE/SIM*"	0	0
<這個地方|POINT|SEQ> "*this location|POINT/SEQ*"	0	0
<這個地方|POINT|SIM> "*this location|POINT/SIM*"	0	0
<這個範圍|CIRCLE|SEQ> "*this area|CIRCLE/SEQ*"	0	0
<這個範圍|CIRCLE|SIM> "*this area|CIRCLE/SIM*"	0	0
<這個範圍|POINT|SIM> "*this area|POINT/SIM*"	0	0
<這個範圍|STROKE|SEQ> "*this area|STROKE/SEQ*"	0	0
<這幅圖|POINT|SIM > "*this map/POINT/SIM*"	0	0

Table 7. An excerpt of the term-inquiry matrix G corresponding to two multimodal inputs. The weights (shown up to 2 decimal places) are obtained using Equation 1. Translations are in quotes and italics.

	放大 "*zoom in*" <∅|CIRCLE|∅>	放大 "*zoom in*" <∅|POINT|∅>
<∅|CIRCLE|∅>	0.18	**0.11**
<∅|POINT|∅>	0.06	0.28
放大 "*zoom in*"	0.51	0.44
<這個地方|CIRCLE|SEQ> "*this location|CIRCLE/SEQ*"	0.00	0.00
<這個地方|CIRCLE|SIM> "*this location|CIRCLE/SIM*"	**0.07**	**0.05**
<這個地方|POINT|SEQ> "*this location|POINT/SEQ*"	0.00	0.00
<這個地方|POINT|SIM> "*this location|POINT/SIM*"	0.03	**0.05**
<這個範圍|CIRCLE|SEQ> "*this area|CIRCLE/SEQ*"	**0.07**	0.04
<這個範圍|CIRCLE|SIM> "*this area|CIRCLE/SIM*"	**0.07**	0.04
<這個範圍|POINT|SIM> "*this area|POINT/SIM*"	0.00	0.00
<這個範圍|STROKE|SEQ> "*this area|STROKE/SEQ*"	0.00	0.00
<這幅圖|POINT|SIM > "*this map/POINT/SIM*"	**0.06**	**0.06**

Table 8. An excerpt of the reconstructed term-inquiry matrix $\hat{G}$ corresponding to two multimodal inputs as in Table 7. The estimated weights (shown up to 2 decimal places) of $\hat{G}$ are obtained using Equation 3 with R'=286. Translations are in quotes and italics

These additional multimodal terms with non-zero weights (see Table 8) did not appear in the original user inputs (see Table 7). But these terms are commonly used to convey the task goal MAP_COMMAND (11 out of 40 multimodal inputs). LSM captures the new correlations among <∅|POINT|∅>, 放大 *zoom in*, <這個地方|CIRCLE|SIM> "*this location*", <這個地方|POINT|SIM> "*this location*" and <這幅圖|POINT|SIM > "*this map*" and put them into correlated latent semantics.

map" and put them into correlated latent semantics. The weights in Table 8 reflect that the pointing action can be used to indicate a single location (這個地方).

6. CONCLUSIONS

This paper describes our work in the usage pattern and latent semantic analyses of multimodal user inputs with speech and pen gestures. Our investigation is based on a multimodal corpus that we have designed and collected, which consists of over a thousand navigational inquiries. The inquiries cover nine task goals. The task goal of each multimodal input is hand-labeled as a gold standard. We begin with an analysis of the usage patterns and designed the format of a multimodal term to be a 3-tuple, consisting of a spoken locative reference, pen gesture(s) and their temporal relationship). Such multimodal terms can represent the cross-modality integration patterns adopted by the user. Then, we apply latent semantic analysis for task goal inference. Characteristic cross-modal integration patterns are derived from the training set to form multimodal terms. We also derive lexical terms from the speech portion of the multimodal expression. We use a non-negative term-inquiry matrix to capture the associations between terms (lexical and multimodal) and inquiries. Decomposition of the term-inquiry matrix using singular value decomposition captures the associations between terms and inquiries through a latent semantic space. We project the latent semantic space into the space of task goals through a matrix derived from training data. An input multimodal inquiry can be projected into the latent semantic space and then into the task goal space. This gives a vector with which we can use the highest weighting element to select the inferred task goal. We experimented with this approach based on the multimodal corpus. Analysis shows structural relations between latent semantic categories for certain task goals. Furthermore, the weights of the lexical and multimodal terms in the latent semantic space an also help us identify key terms for specific task goals. The latent semantic approach achieves around 99% accuracy in task goal inference, for both the training and test sets. This is significantly higher that the reference baseline obtained with a vector-space model, which achieves 85% and 90% for the training and test sets respectively.

ACKNOWLEDGMENTS

This work is partially supported by a grant from the HKSAR Government Research Grants Council (Project Number 415609). This work is affiliated with the CUHK MoE-Microsoft Key Laboratory of Human-centric Computing and Interface Technologies.

REFERENCES

1. Nigay, L. and J. Coutaz, "A Generic Platform for Addressing the Multimodal Challenge," in the *Proc. of CHI*, 1995.
2. Wang, S. "A Multimodal Galaxy-based Geographic System," S.M. Thesis, MIT, 2003.
3. Johnston, M. et al., "Unification-based Multimodal Integration," in the *Proc. of COLING-ACL*, 1997.
4. Johnston, M., "Unification-based Multimodal Parsing," in the *Proc. of COLING-ACL*, 1998.
5. Wu, L. et al., "Multimodal Integration – A Statistical View," *IEEE Transactions on Multimedia*, 1(4), pp.334-341, 1999.
6. Wahlster, W. et al., SmartKom (www.smartkom.org)
7. Johnston, M. & S. Bangalore, "Finite-state Multimodal Parsing and Understanding," in the *Proc. of COLING*, 2000.
8. Chai, J. et. al., "A Probabilistic Approach to Reference Resolution in Multimodal User Interfaces," in *the Proc. of IUI*, 2004.
9. Chai, J. et. al., "Optimization in Multimodal Interpretation," in *the Proc. of ACL*, 2004.
10. Qu, S. and J. Chai, "Salience Modeling based on Non-verbal Modalities for Spoken Language Understanding," in *the Proc. of ICMI*, 2006.
11. Hui, P. Y. and H. Meng, "Cross-Modality Semantic Integration with Hypothesis Rescoring for Robust Interpretation of Multimodal User Interactions," *IEEE Trans. on Audio, Speech and Language Processing*, Vol. 17, No. 3, 2009.
12. Meng, H., et al., "To Believe is to Understand," in the *Proc. of the Eurospeech*, 1999.
13. Chan, S. F. and H. Meng, "Interdependencies among Dialog Acts, Task Goals and Discourse Inheritance in Mixed-Initiative Dialog," in the *Proc. of the HLT*, 2002.
14. Bellegarda, J. R., "Latent Semantic Mapping: Principles and Applications," *Synthesis Lectures on Speech and Audio Processing*, Vol. 3, No. 1, 2007.
15. Naptali, W., et al., "Word Co-occurrence Matrix and Context Dependent Class in LSA based Language Model for Speech Recognition," *International Journal of Computers*, Issue 1, Volume 3, 2009.
16. Song, W. and S. C. Park, "A Novel Document Clustering Model Based on Latent Semantic Analysis," in the *Proc. of the ICSKG*, 2007.
17. Chen, B., "Word Topic Models for Spoken Document Retrieval and Transcription," *ACM Trans. on Asian Language Information Processing*, Vol. 18, No. 1, 2009.
18. Lee, J. H., et al., "Automatic Generic Document Summarization based on Non-negative Matrix Factorization," *International Journal on Information Processing and Management*, Vol. 45, Issue 1, 2009.
19. Oviatt, S., et al., "Integration and Synchronization of Input Modes during Multimodal Human-Computer Interaction," in the *Proc. of the CHI*, 1997.
20. Hofmann, T., "Probabilistic Latent Semantic Analysis," in the *Proc. of UAI*, 1999.
21. Blei, D. M., et. al., "Latent Dirichlet allocation," *Journal of Machine Learning Research 3*, 2003.
22. Salton, G. and M. McGill, *Introduction to Modern Information Retrieval*, McGraw-Hall, New York, New Jersey, USA, 1983.

Estimating User's Engagement from Eye-gaze Behaviors in Human-Agent Conversations

Yukiko, I. Nakano
Dept. of Computer and Information Science
Seikei University
y.nakano@st.seikei.ac.jp

Ryo Ishii
NTT Cyber Space Laboratories

ishii.ryo@lab.ntt.co.jp

ABSTRACT

In face-to-face conversations, speakers are continuously checking whether the listener is engaged in the conversation and change the conversational strategy if the listener is not fully engaged in the conversation. With the goal of building a conversational agent that can adaptively control conversations with the user, this study analyzes the user's gaze behaviors and proposes a method for estimating whether the user is engaged in the conversation based on gaze transition 3-gram patterns. First, we conduct a Wizard-of-Oz experiment to collect the user's gaze behaviors. Based on the analysis of the gaze data, we propose an engagement estimation method that detects the user's disengagement gaze patterns. The algorithm is implemented as a real-time engagement-judgment mechanism and is incorporated into a multimodal dialogue manager in a conversational agent. The agent estimates the user's conversational engagement and generates probing questions when the user is distracted from the conversation. Finally, we conduct an evaluation experiment using the proposed engagement-sensitive agent and demonstrate that the engagement estimation function improves the user's impression of the agent and the interaction with the agent. In addition, probing performed with proper timing was also found to have a positive effect on user's verbal/nonverbal behaviors in communication with the conversational agent.

Author Keywords

conversational engagement, eye-gaze, conversational agent, dialogue management.

ACM Classification Keywords

H.5.2 Information Systems: User Interfaces

General Terms

Algorithms, Design, Human Factors

INTRODUCTION

Recent studies on virtual agents and communication robots have revealed that conversational engagement is fundamental and indispensable in communication between human users and humanoid interfaces [1, 2]. By engagement, we refer to "the process by which two (or more) participants establish, maintain and end their perceived connection", as defined in [3]. If the user is not fully engaged in the conversation, information presented by the system (agent) will not be properly conveyed to the user. Thus, in order to establish natural interactions between users and agents, displaying bodily expressions, such as facial expressions and gestures, to signal that the agent is listening to the user and perceiving nonverbal engagement signals, such as eye gaze and head nods, from the user as a listener are indispensable. If the system can monitor the user's attitude toward the conversation and detect whether the user is engaged in the conversation, then the system can adapt its behavior and communication strategy according to the user's attitude. This is critical in information providing systems, such as explanatory agents, kiosk agents, and instructor agents. If the user does not listen to the agent, the system cannot construct a reliable user model. While tailoring explanations based on the user's understanding is one of the main goals of information providing systems, few studies have considered user engagement as a basis for modeling communication with the user.

To build conversational agents that are sensitive to user engagement, there are two primary aspects to be considered. First, the system must perceive the user's nonverbal behaviors and estimate user engagement based on the sensed information. Thanks to progress in computer vision and human sensing technologies, accurate measurement of human behavior is possible in real time. For example, in an ideal circumstance, eye trackers can recognize the user's gaze points to an accuracy of 0.5 degrees at more than 100 Hz. However, few studies have investigated the interpretation of communication signals or the extraction of communication signals from an enormous number of data.

The second aspect is that the system should exploit the recognized communicative signals in dialogue management and determine the agent's behaviors properly according to the user's engagement status. For instance, if the user is not engaged in the conversation, the system needs to attract the user's attention by changing the topic of conversation. For this purpose, we propose a dialogue management mechanism that works with an eye-tracking system and presents a prototype system of an automatic conversational agent that can estimate user engagement and determine the agent's response according to the results of the estimation.

In summary, with the goal of improving naturalness in human-agent communications, this paper proposes a method of estimating the degree of engagement by measuring the user's attentional behavior in real time and implementing a conversational agent that decides the agent's response according to the user's level of engagement. Related research is reviewed in the following section. Then, a Wizard-of-Oz experiment on data collection using an eye-tracker is described. After describing the empirical results of analyzing the gaze data, an engagement estimation method is proposed. The second half of this paper describes the implementation of a multimodal dialogue model, as well as a multimodal dialogue manager that can work with an eye-tracking system. The results of evaluating the prototype system are also reported. Finally, we discuss future research.

RELATED WORK

Eye gaze as a communicative signal in face-to-face conversation

During dialogues, two participants repeatedly alternate roles between speaker and listener. Psychological studies reported that eye gazing, specifically accompanied by head nods, serves as positive feedback to the speaker [4] and demonstrates that the listener is paying attention to the conversation. Eye gazing also contributes to smooth turn-taking [5]. Furthermore, Novick, et al. [6] reported that during conversational difficulties, mutual gaze was held longer at turn boundaries. In studies of face-to-face communication, Kendon [7] described various eye gaze functions from an ethnomethodological point of view. These results suggest that speakers distinguish different types of listener's gaze. In fact, Argyle, et al. [8] claimed that gaze is used to send positive feedback accompanied by nods, smiles, and other facial expressions, as well as to collect information from the partner.

Looking at the partner is not the only signal of engagement. When conversational participants share the same physical environment and their task requires complex reference to, and joint manipulation of physical objects, participants do not frequently pay attention to the partner, but rather look at the shared object most of the time [9, 10]. In such situations, paying attention to the shared object signals the listener's engagement in the conversation.

These findings in psychology and communication science provide the basis of the present study. However, to build conversational humanoids, it is also necessary to establish computational models and methods to implement a mechanism that can automatically interpret the user's nonverbal signals from the enormous amount of data obtained by sensing devices.

Sensing user behaviors in conversational systems

The use of head/eye trackers as a component of multimodal conversational interfaces has been successfully demonstrated in previous studies of conversational systems. Prasov and Chai [11] proposed a probabilistic model for reference resolution by combining speech and eye-gaze information. In some studies, eye-gaze information was used to estimate user interest. In Qvarfordt and Zhai [12], maps and pictures are shown on the user's desktop computer display, and based on eye-tracking data, the system estimates the focus of the user's interest and provides information about that place. Eichner, et al. [13] incorporated this user interest estimation mechanism into a presentation system with virtual agents. This system changes the conversational content presented by a pair of virtual agents according to the object of interest. As a conversational agent that communicates directly with a user, Nakano and Nishida [14] used a head-tracker to estimate user interest on a 70-inch big screen, and a tour guide conversational agent changed the topic according to the user's interest. In these systems, using the eye gaze, the user can specify interesting objects even if the name of the object is unknown.

These studies suggest that off-the-shelf head/eye tracking systems are sufficiently accurate and sufficiently stable to use as a component in complex agent systems. Thus, we believe that by combining these sensing technologies with a dialogue management mechanism, conversational agents can become sensitive to the user's level of engagement.

Interpreting nonverbal communicative signals in conversational agents

In previous studies on conversational agents, determining and generating proper communicative signals by the agents has been one of the main issues, and having the agents display nonverbal communicative signals as a listener was demonstrated to be effective in human-agent communications. Pelachaud and Bilivi [15] proposed a gaze model for generating appropriate agent gaze behaviors. Gratch, et al. [16] reported that backchannel feedback from a listener agent is effective in establishing a sense of rapport between a user and a virtual character.

However, in order to determine appropriate nonverbal signals, agents need to be able to sense and interpret signals from the user, because communication is a bilateral process between two parties. As a study focusing on the sensing aspect, Nakano, et al. [17] proposed a gaze model for nonverbal grounding in conversational agents, and, using a head tracker, implemented an agent that can judge whether the information provided from the agent is grounded. The agent also selects a direction giving strategy according to the results of grounding judgment. Morency, et al. [18] used a head tracker to recognize a user's head-nodding behavior. They reported that by combining linguistic contextual information with the results of computer vision processing, the performance of head nod detection was improved. They also applied this technology to a communication robot [19]. More recently,

Bohus and Horvitz [20] proposed a method of predicting the user's engagement intention in multiparty situations using a head tracker. Their system predicts that the user(s) will be engaged in the conversation with a reception agent if the user approaches the system from an F-formation position [21].

In these studies, the user's gaze direction was roughly estimated from the head direction measured by a head tracker. This study attempts to build an information-providing agent that demonstrates and explains products on a display as a virtual salesperson, which must accurately sense the user's attentional behavior. Thus, we use an eye (pupil) tracker to measure gaze information more accurately and estimate the user's level of engagement during the conversation with the agent.

WIZARD-OF-OZ EXPERIMENT TO COLLECT VERBAL AND NONVERBAL DATA

As the first step towards engagement estimation in human-agent communication, it is necessary to collect eye-gaze data and investigate whether eye-gaze behaviors would be useful in estimating user engagement. For this purpose, we use a Wizard-of-Oz experiment. In a Wizard-of-Oz experiment, the agent's actions are limited to the actions that the autonomous agent (to be implemented) can perform, and most of the subjects believe that they are interacting with a real autonomous agent. Therefore, the collected corpus can be used as a basis for designing human-agent interactions.

Since we are interested in information providing systems, the Wizard-of-Oz agent was designed as a salesperson in a mobile phone store in which new models are displayed and the users (subjects) want to collect useful information from the virtual sales agent.

Experiment

Experimental set-up: The experimental set-up is shown in Figure 1. Two people participated in the experiment. One of the subjects was standing in front of a sales agent displayed on a 120-inch screen and communicated with the sales agent. This subject is referred to as the "user". The distance between the sales agent and the user was 1.5 m. The other subject observed the interaction between the user and the agent through a one-way mirror. This subject is referred to as the "observer". The observer was standing 1.5 m from the user. The total number of subjects was 10, and seven of the subjects participated in the next session as an observer after being a user.

User task: Users were instructed to guess the most popular design for specific users (e.g., high school girls, businessmen). The users were promised 1,000 yen for each correct guess. Therefore, users were motivated to carefully listen to the agent's descriptions of all of the cell phones.

Experimental materials: The agent's behaviors shown on the screen were very monotonic. The agent described each of the cell phones while looking at and pointing to the cell phone

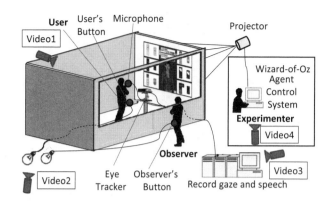

Figure 1. Experimental set-up for data collection

being described. The agent faced the user for 3 seconds after every 10 utterances.

Verbal/nonverbal data

We collected 10 conversations, the average length of which was 16 minutes. The number of utterances by the agent was 951, and the number of utterances by the user was 61. The user's speech was recorded using a pin microphone. We videotaped the user's upper body and the video of the agent's displayed on the screen. The user's gaze data was collected using a Tobii-X50 eye tracker. The frame rate was 50 fps, and the freedom of head movement was 30 x 15 x 20 cm. The eye tracker has an accuracy of 0.5 degrees.

In addition, a push-button device was given to both the user and the observer. The user was instructed to press the button when the agent's explanation was boring and the user would like to change the topic. On the other hand, the observer was instructed to press the button when the user looked bored and distracted from the conversation. Since the button was small and completely hidden in the user's hand, the observer was not able to see whether the user was pressing the button. When these buttons were pressed, lights went on in another room, and these lights were recorded as video data[1].

ANALYSIS

Construction of gaze 3-grams:

We defined four labels to categorize the user gaze direction:

T: looking at the object that the agent is explaining. This object is referred to as the target object. Since the agent is looking at the current target object most of the time, it is presumed that joint attention is established between the user and the agent when the user's gaze label is T.

AH: looking at the agent's head

AB: looking at the agent's body

F: looking at non-target objects, such as other cell phones or advertisement posters ($F1{\neq}F2{\neq}F3$).

---

[1] We recorded the engagement judgments by video, which is the simplest method, although other methods are possible.

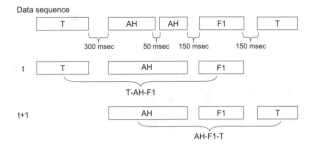

Figure 2. 3-gram construction

During blinking or completely looking down, the eye-tracker cannot measure the pupils' movements. If missing data (blank) occurs for a very short time period (less than 200 msec) and the gaze labels before and after the blank are the same, then these two consecutive gaze data were combined into one block. In contrast, if the gaze label changes after a short blank or if the blank is longer than 200 msec, then these two gaze data are not combined. For example, as shown in Figure 2, suppose that the user's gaze direction shifts as follows: *T*-(300-msec blank)-*AH*-(50-msec blank)-*AH*-(150-msec blank)-*F1*. In this case, the two *AH*s before and after the 50-msec blank are combined into one block. As a result, at time *t*, a 3-gram *T-AH-F1* is constructed from this sequence. If the blank is longer than 1 sec and a 3-gram is not complete, then we ignore the sequence as an incomplete 3-gram and start a new 3-gram at the next gaze data. In our corpus, most of the gaze data construct a 3-gram, and incomplete 3-grams are not very frequent.

Analysis of 3-grams with respect to the degree of disengagement

As part of the nonverbal data, we recorded the button pressing behaviors of the user and the observer as human judgments of disengagement. The reason for collecting reports from both parties is that using self reporting alone is not reliable and using only the observer's report is not reliable because the observer is an overhearer [22], who may not consider the user's nonverbal behaviors as signals directed toward herself/himself. Investigation of the overlap between the user's judgment and the observer's judgment revealed that the observer pressed the button 39.0% of the time when the user also pressed the button, and the user pressed the button 54.4% of the time when the observer also pressed the button. Since the agreement was not high, we decided to use the sum of the judgments, and judged that the user was disengaged if either the user or the observer pressed her/his button.

The average probability of button pressing was then calculated for each type of 3-gram and was used as the degree of disengagement (Figure 3). For example, *F1-AH-AH* co-occurs with button pressing 82% of the time. Thus, the degree of disengagement of this pattern is 82%. For the *AH-T-T* 3-gram, the degree of disengagement was only 45%. This scale indicates that 3-grams with higher degrees violate

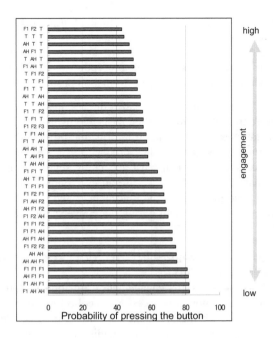

Figure 3. Probability of pressing the engagement judgment button

proper engagement gaze rules and those with lower degrees contribute to the conversation in a proper manner. Note that, as shown in Figure 3, 3-grams containing *T* have lower degrees of disengagement. This suggests that looking at the target object or establishing joint attention with the agent is a positive sign of user engagement. A further analysis of 3-gram patterns is presented in [23].

Analysis of individual difference

As the next step, we investigated the individual difference of the 3-gram distribution. Figure 4 plots the observed 3-grams with respect to degree of disengagement. The X-axis is the timeline (sec), and the Y-axis indicates the degree of disengagement. The rectangles at the top of each graph indicate the time period during which user disengagement was reported (i.e., when either the user or the observer pressed her/his button).

As shown in the graphs, for both User A and User B, 3-grams with higher disengagement values co-occur with human judgments of disengagement. Based on this observation, we set a threshold in order to estimate whether the user is engaged in the conversation.

However, comparison of User A and User B revealed that the distribution of the 3-grams differed depending on the user. In the graph for User A, 3-grams that co-occurred with human judgments of disengagement are shaded (areas (a), (b), and (c)), and the other areas indicate 3-grams that occurred during user engagement (areas (1), (2), (3), and (4)). To distinguish the disengaged areas from the engaged areas, the threshold should be set higher than the upper bound of the engaged areas and lower than the lowest upper bound among the disengaged areas. For example, for User A, the upper

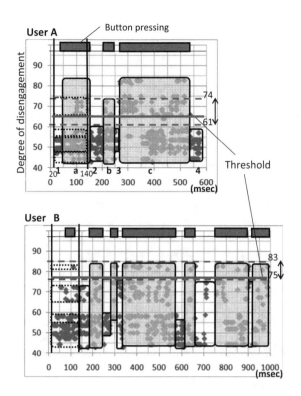

Figure 4. Individual difference of 3-gram distribution

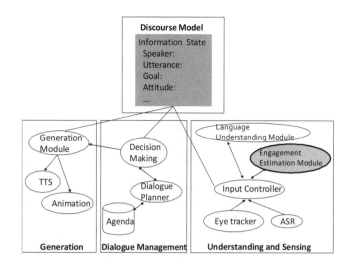

Figure 5. System architecture

bound of area (b) is the lowest among the shadowed areas (areas (a) through (c)), and the upper bound of area (2) is the highest among areas (1) through (4). In this case, the threshold should be set between the upper bound of area (2) (61%) and the upper bound of area (b) (74%). Likewise, for User B, the threshold should be set between 75% and 83%. The proper threshold ranges are marked with dashed lines and double-headed arrows.

Based on the above analysis, the threshold can be specified as the degree of disengagement that is assigned based on the button pressing probability and should be adapted according to the individual characteristics of the users.

ESTIMATING USER ENGAGEMENT

In order to adapt the threshold for disengagement judgment to individual users, we use a clustering technique. To determine an appropriate threshold according to the user in real time, the clustering algorithm uses the first 120 seconds of gaze data from the beginning of the explanatory conversation. Since the actual explanatory conversation starts 20 second after the greeting, the data sampling ends 140 second from the start of the interaction. In Figure 4, the 3-gram data used in determining a threshold are surrounded by dotted lines.

The data points are clustered according to the degree of disengagement. We use a simple centroid method for this purpose. The clustering procedure is as follows. First, starting with individual data points as a cluster, the Euclidean

distance between the centroids of two clusters is calculated, and the closest clusters are merged. The centroid of the new cluster is then calculated by weighting the centroids of the original clusters according to the number of data points. When the number of clusters becomes four, the process is terminated.

After the clustering procedure, four clusters are obtained. The midpoint between the centroid of the highest disengagement cluster and the centroid of the second highest disengagement cluster is used as the threshold. For example, using this algorithm, the threshold of User A in Figure 4 is determined to be 65, and that of User B is determined to be 76. Note that both of these thresholds fall within the proper ranges, as indicated by the dashed lines in Figure 4.

We evaluated the proposed user adapted engagement estimation method and found that the predictive accuracy is much higher when using the user-adaptive threshold than when applying the same threshold to all users. The details of this evaluation are described in [23].

ARCHITECTURE OF AN ENGAGEMENT-SENSITIVE CONVERSATIONAL AGENT

In this section, we describe the system architecture of the proposed conversational agent. The agent serves as a sales person at a cell phone store and explains about the cell phones in the store one by one. In addition to speech-based communication, this system can estimate the user's conversational engagement through attentional information. Moreover, this system uses the results of estimation in determining the agent's next action. The system architecture is shown in Figure 5. The primary components are described below.

Understanding and Sensing:

Input Controller: The Input Controller receives various types of data from multiple components and updates the state of the dialogue (using the Information State, which will be

```
< InfoState Version="0.0.0">
        <Cell ID="1" name="cVerbal">
...


        <Cell ID="2" name="cNonVerbal">
                <variable varName="cUser1" type="cell"/>
        </Cell>
        <Cell ID="3" name="cUser1">
                <variable varName="Gaze" type="cell"/>
        </Cell>
        <Cell ID="4" name="Gaze">
                <variable varName="Time" type="obj"/>
                <variable varName="CorX" type="obj"/>
                <variable varName="CorY" type="obj"/>
        </Cell>
</InfoState >
```

Figure 6. XML for customizing IS and information flow in the dialogue manager

explained later). The Input Controller receives the recognition results from input devices, such as a speech recognition system and an eye tracker, and obtains the interpretation results from language understanding and engagement estimation. The Input Controller processes these inputs using a queue for their synchronization.

Input Devices: At present, the proposed system has two input devices, namely, a speech recognition system (ASR) and an eye tracker. We use julius-4.0.2 for Windows [9] for Japanese speech recognition. We defined simple recognition rules to recognize user questions, such as questions related to the price and functions of the cell phones. The second input device is the Tobii X-120 eye tracker, which measures the user's gaze behavior. The eye tracker measures the user's gaze points at 50 Hz.

Engagement Estimation Module: We implemented the engagement estimation method proposed in the previous sections as an Engagement Estimation Module. The Engagement Estimation Module receives eye-gaze information from the eye tracker, and, based on the gaze information, this component judges whether the user is engaged in the conversation with the agent. The results of judgment are sent to the Input Controller to update the state of the dialogue.

Discourse Model

The Discourse Model maintains the state of the dialogue. We use the concept of the Information State (IS) [24] to keep track of the state of the dialogue. We modified the original IS to manipulate heterogeneous verbal and nonverbal information, such as symbolic verbal information updated at each utterance and numeric data for gaze points received 50 times per second. The details of the Multimodal Dialogue Management Mechanism are described later.

Dialogue Management

The Dialogue Planner uses a request to explain a cell phone as input and generates a plan for explaining the cell phone. All the communicative goals to be accomplished are added to the Agenda, which is implemented as a stack. The Agenda is

also accessed by the Decision Making to determine the agent's next action.

Generation

Recipes of the agent's speech are synthesized by Hitachi Hit-Voice TTS and are saved as .wav files. A sequence of animation commands for each speech is saved as a script file, which is automatically generated by the CAST system [25]. Each animation script is interpreted by the Haptek animation system to generate agent animations that are synchronized with speech.

MULTIMODAL DIALOGUE MANAGEMENT MECHANISM

This section describes the details of the Multimodal Dialogue Management Mechanism (MDMM), which has two primary functions: (1) maintaining the state of the dialogue and (2) determining the agent's next action.

In the engagement-sensitive agent of the present study, the MDMM must update the state of the dialogue according to verbal and nonverbal information, which have different grain sizes. In the current system, gaze information is sent to the Input Controller 50 times per second. On the other hand, verbal information is updated upon each utterance, which is normally several seconds long.

In order to integrate and maintain such heterogeneous information in the MDMM, we use an Information State-based discourse model. The Information State-based dialogue management tool has already been developed as TrindiKit [26] and Midiki [27] in Java implementation. Since these tools were designed to process verbal information in text-based or speech-based dialogue systems, some modifications are necessary in order to process a large amount of nonverbal information, i.e., numerical data sent from motion/eye/head tracking systems.

Multimodal information management: In order to synchronize different types of information that have different grain sizes, a unique time stamp is assigned to all of the information. This allows us to refer to any type of information by specifying the time. For example, by specifying the start and end times of an utterance, the system can access the gaze point information and engagement status during the utterance.

Customizing IS specification: In multimodal dialogue systems, input devices differ depending on the system. Therefore, the IS specification needs to be customizable. The MDMM provides an XML-based IS configuration file that can be edited by system developers. Figure 6 shows an example. The top level contains the "cVerbal" cell and "cNonverbal" cell. In "cNonverbal" cell, one user, "cUser1", is defined, and this cell has a sub cell, "Gaze". Then, the "Gaze" cell has three variables, namely, Time (time stamp), CorX (X coordinate of the gaze point), and CorY (Y coordinate of the gaze point). Subscription and trigger relationships are also defined in XML to specify which component subscribes which cell and which information

(15) A: I have this model, and I found that the peep preventing function is particularly useful.
<User asked a question by interrupting the agent's explanation>
(16) U: What is the price of the D904i?
(17) A: The D904i is 35,300 Yen if you start a new contract.
(18) A: Can I continue explaining?
(19) U: Yes.
(20) A: Let us resume the previous explanation.
...
(25) A: This design is both beautiful and useful. It is 17 mm-thick and fits comfortably in your hands.
<A person interrupted the conversation and the system detected the distraction>
(26) A: Would you like to move on to the next cell phone?
(27) U: Yes.
<Changing the topic after obtaining the user's agreement>
(28) A: Let us resume the explanation. At your left is the kid's model which has many safety features.
< The system detected distraction >
(29) A: Do you understand so far?
< User asked a question after prompting by the agent >
(30) U: What are the game functions like on the kid's model?
(31) A: Both the D904i and the SH904i have intuitive game functions. Can I continue the explanation?
(32) U: Yes.
(33) A: Let us resume the explanation. This phone is easy to handle...

A: Agent's utterance, U: User's utterance
Target objects are marked with squares.
User's gaze points are marked with circles.

Figure 7. Example of user-agent interaction

triggers which component. For example, when the Gaze call is updated, a message is sent to the Engagement Estimation Module, which processes the message to judge whether the user is engaged in the conversation.

<u>Decision Making Module:</u> The Decision Making in the MDMM decides the agent's next action by referring to the IS and the Agenda to find possible subsequent communication goals. As a special case, when the user's distraction is reported to the IS, the Decision Making Module does not choose the next goal in the Agenda, but rather adds a new communicative goal whereby the user is posed a probing question, such as "Do you have any questions?" or "Would you like to move on to the next cell phone?"

EXAMPLE

Figure 7 shows a conversation between a user and the proposed agent. During the agent's explanation of a cell phone, at (16), the user asked a question by interrupting the agent's explanation, at which point the agent responded to the user. This is a typical speech-based interaction between

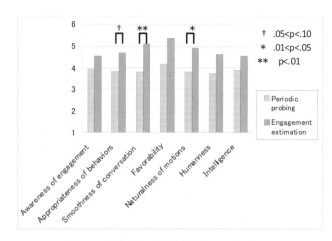

Figure 8. Rating of subjective evaluation

a user and a dialogue system. Just before an utterance at (26), another person approached the user, grabbing his attention. At this time, by processing the eye-tacking data, the engagement estimation module detected that the user was not engaged in the conversation. Then, by referring to the Information State, the MDMM discerned that the user was distracted from the conversation. Based on this information, the Decision Making Module decided to ask the probing question, "Would you like to move on to the next cell phone?" at the next turn. Since the user accepted this proposal, the system changed the topic of conversation to the next cell phone. Later, at (29), the disengagement gaze pattern was detected again. This time, the system asked another probing question, "Do you understand so far?" The system then released its turn to the user, and the user had the chance to ask a question without interrupting the agent's explanation.

EVALUATION

Experimental procedure
To examine whether the agent's capability of estimating user engagement improves the effectiveness of the system and the naturalness of the interaction with a user, we conducted an evaluation experiment. We used three female and six male subjects. None of the subjects had participated in the previous data collection experiment. The subject's task was the same as in the previous experiment, namely, listening to the agent's explanation and guessing the most popular model for female high school students or businessmen. This time, the subject did not report her/his disengagement by pressing a button (because disengagement was judged automatically by the system). A list of questions that the user can ask (regarding, for example, price, game functions, and display size) was displayed in front of the user, and the user wore a headset microphone that was used for the speech input. In the experiment, however, the user's speech was interpreted by an experimenter in order to avoid speech recognition errors that would influence the quality of the interaction. Each subject interacted with the agent under the following two conditions:

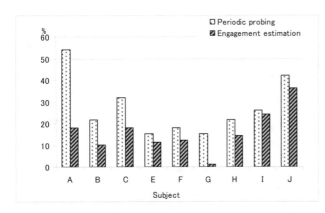

Figure 9. Frequency of disengagement gaze patterns

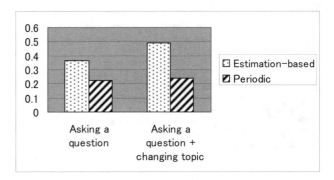

Figure 10. Frequency of user's verbal behaviors triggered by agent's probe

- Probing based on engagement estimation (engagement estimation condition): The agent generates probing questions when the Engagement Estimation Module detects the user's disengagement

- Periodic probing: The agent periodically asks probing questions (after every 10 utterances).

In the engagement estimation condition, a threshold is calculated using the data collected during the first 120 seconds of the explanatory conversation, and the threshold is determined at 140 seconds, as explained in previous sections. For each condition, three cell phones were displayed on the screen as the targets of the agent's explanations.

We used both subjective and objective (behavioral) evaluation measures. As the nonverbal objective measure, the frequency of disengagement gaze patterns was counted. The frequency of asking questions by the subjects was used as the verbal objective measure. As a subjective measure, we used a six-point Likert scale to ask the subjects about their impression towards the agent and the interaction with the agent. The questionnaire contained 33 questions, which were classified into the seven categories shown in Appendix A. Thus, four or five questions were asked for each category, and average values were used in the analysis. Since this experiment uses a within-subject design, each subject completes this questionnaire twice, once after each condition. In order to cancel the order effect, half of the subjects started with the engagement estimation condition and the other half started with the periodic probing condition.

Results

Subjective evaluation

The averages for each question category are shown in Figure 8. All of the scores were higher in the engagement estimation condition than in the periodic probing condition. Specifically, for Appropriateness of behavior and Smoothness of conversation, we found a statistical significance or trend in the two-tailed t-test (t (8) = 1.96; p < 0.10 for Appropriateness of behavior, and t (8) = 3.90; p < 0.01 for Smoothness of conversation). These results suggest that

selecting the agent's behaviors according to the results of engagement estimation is effective in human-agent interaction.

Another interesting finding is that the subjects felt the agent's animated motions to be more natural in the engagement estimation condition than in the periodic probing condition (t (8) = 2.32; p < 0.05), although the animations were exactly the same. This suggests that the agent's verbal behavior presented with proper timing improve the user's impression of the agent's nonverbal expressions.

Objective evaluation of nonverbal behaviors

Figure 9 shows the percentage of disengagement gaze patterns in each session for each subject. Note that for all of the subjects (Subjects A through J), the percentage of disengagement gaze patterns decreased in the engagement estimation condition. This difference was found to be statistically significant in a two-tailed t-test (t (8) = 3.26; p < 0.05). This result suggests that agent's probing questions presented with proper timing prevent subjects from becoming distracted from the conversation.

Objective evaluation of verbal behaviors

As the second behavioral measure, we investigated the subjects' verbal behaviors. We hypothesized that if the agent were to pose probing questions with proper timing, then the subject would be more likely to ask a question or request a change of topic during her/his turn provided by the agent's question. Therefore, such behaviors are expected to be more frequently observed in the engagement estimation condition than in the periodic probing condition. Figure 10 shows the average ratios of (a) subject's asking a question and (b) asking a question and then requesting a change of topic with respect to the total number of the agent's probing questions. In the engagement estimation condition, the subjects asked questions for 37% of the time when an opportunity was presented, although in periodic probing condition, the subjects asked questions 22% of the time when an opportunity was presented. A statistical trend was observed in a two-tailed T-test (T (8) =2.066, p < 0.1). Similarly, in engagement estimation condition, the user changed the topic of conversation 49% of the time when an opportunity was presented, whereas, in the periodic probing condition, the user changed the topic of conversation 24% of the time when an opportunity was presented (T (8) = 2.387, p < 0.05). This difference is statistically significant. These results suggest that the agent's probes effectively provide opportunities for the subjects to talk to the agent.

Discussion

In the evaluation experiment, we found that, in the engagement estimation condition, not only that the user's impression of the agent was improved, but also that the subjects were less distracted from the conversation than in the periodic probing condition, and that the users asked more questions. These findings suggest that the proposed engagement estimation mechanism can work well in a complex conversational agent system and is useful for improving the quality of the interaction between the user and the agent.

CONCLUSION AND FUTURE WORK

By analyzing gaze patterns observed in a Wizard-of-Oz experiment, we observed that patterns of gaze transition 3-grams are strongly correlated with human subjective or observational judgment of a user's engagement in the conversation. Based on these findings, we applied a clustering technique to gaze 3-gram data and proposed a method of automatically detecting whether the user is engaged in the conversation. Then, we incorporated this mechanism into a conversational agent serving as a salesperson and conducted an evaluation experiment. By using subjective and objective measures for the evaluation, we obtained positive results suggesting that the proposed engagement-sensitive agent improved the human-agent interaction.

Although the proposed method focuses on the transitions of gaze direction, another important aspect is the duration of gaze fixation. Therefore, the proposed method might be improved by weighting each 3-gram according to its temporal duration. As such, whether the model extension contributes to improving the engagement estimation should be investigated.

Finally, we intend to address issues related to how to select the most appropriate probing question according to the user's level of disengagement. In addition to the agent asking probing questions, there may be other possibilities for reacquiring user engagement, such as asking the user's preference or telling the user to disregard other objects. More basic research is necessary in order to select an effective probe. This research may include collecting various types of probes and investigating the correlation between the conversational context and the probe.

ACKNOWLEDGMENTS

This study was supported by the Japan Society for the Promotion of Science (JSPS) through a Grant-in-Aid for Scientific Research in Priority Areas "i-explosion" (21013042).

REFERENCES

1. Sidner, C.L., et al., *Explorations in engagement for humans and robots.* Artificial Intelligence, (2005). 166(1-2): pp. 140-164.

2. Peters, C. *Direction of Attention Perception for Conversation Initiation in Virtual Environments.* in *Intelligent Virtual Agents.* (2005). p. 215-228.

3. Sidner, C.L., et al. *Where to Look: A Study of Human-Robot Engagement.* in *ACM International Conference on Intelligent User Interfaces (IUI).* (2004). p. 78-84.

4. Argyle, M. and Cook, M., *Gaze and Mutual Gaze.* (1976), Cambridge: Cambridge University Press.

5. Duncan, S., *On the structure of speaker-auditor interaction during speaking turns.* Language in Society, (1974). 3: pp. 161-180.

6. Novick, D.G., Hansen, B., and Ward, K. *Coordinating turn-taking with gaze.* in *ICSLP-96.* (1996). Philadelphia, PA. p. 1888-1891.

7. Kendon, A., *Some Functions of Gaze Direction in Social Interaction.* Acta Psychologica, (1967). 26: pp. 22-63.

8. Argyle, M., et al., *The different functions of gaze.* Semiotica, (1973). 7: pp. 19-32.

9. Argyle, M. and Graham, J., *The Central Europe Experiment - looking at persons and looking at things.* Journal of Environmental Psychology and Nonverbal Behaviour, (1977). 1: pp. 6-16.

10. Anderson, A.H., et al., *The effects of face-to-face communication on the intelligibility of speech.* Perception and Psychophysics, (1997). 59: pp. 580-592.

11. Prasov, Z. and Chai, J.Y. *What's in a Gaze? The Role of Eye-Gaze in Reference Resolution in Multimodal Conversational Interfaces.* in *the 13th international conference on Intelligent user interfaces* (2008). p. 20-29.

12. Qvarfordt, P. and Zhai, S. *Conversing with the User Based on Eye-Gaze Patterns.* in *the Conference on Human-Factors in Computing Systems, CHI 2005.* (2005).

13. Eichner, T., et al. *Attentive Presentation Agents.* in *The 7th International Conference on Intelligent Virtual Agents (IVA).* (2007). p. 283-295.

14. Nakano, I.Y. and Nishida, T., *Attentional Behaviors as Nonverbal Communicative Signals in Situated Interactions with Conversational Agents*, in *Engineering Approaches to Conversational Informatics*, Nishida, T., Editor. (2007), John Wiley & Sons Inc.

15. Pelachaud, C. and Bilvi, M. *Modelling Gaze Behavior for Conversational Agents.* in *IVA03 International Working Conference on Intelligent Virtual Agents.* (2003). Germany.

16. Gratch, J., et al., *Virtual Rapport*, in *6th International Conference on Intelligent Virtual Agents*. (2006), Springer: Marina del Rey, CA.

17. Nakano, Y.I., et al. *Towards a Model of Face-to-Face Grounding*. in *the 41st Annual Meeting of the Association for Computational Linguistics (ACL03)*. (2003). Sapporo, Japan. p. 553-561.

18. Morency, L.-P., Kok, I.d., and Gratch, J. *Predicting Listener Backchannels: A Probabilistic Multimodal Approach*. in *The 8th International Conference Intelligent Virtual Agents (IVA'08)*. (2008): Springer. p. 176-190.

19. Morency, L.-P., et al., *Head gestures for perceptual interfaces: The role of context in improving recognition*. Artificial Intelligence (2007). 171(8-9): pp. 568-585.

20. Bohus, D. and Horvitz, E. *Learning to Predict Engagement with a Spoken Dialog System in Open-World Settings*. in *SIGdial'09*. (2009). London, UK.

21. Kendon, A., *Spatial organization in social encounters: the F-formation system, Conducting Interaction: Patterns of behavior in focused encounters*. Studies in International Sociolinguistics, ed. Gumperz, J.J. (1990): Cambridge University Press.

22. Schober, M.F. and Clark, H.H., *Understanding by addressees and overhearers*. Cognitive Psychology, (1989). 21: pp. 211-232.

23. Ishii, R. and Nakano, Y. *Estimating User's Conversational Engagement based on Gaze Behaviors*. in *The 8th International Conference Intelligent Virtual Agents (IVA'08)*. (2008): Springer. p. 200-207.

24. Matheson, C., Poesio, M., and Traum, D. *Modelling Grounding and Discourse Obligations Using Update Rules*. in *1st Annual Meeting of the North American Chapter of the Association for Computational Linguistics (NAACL2000)*. (2000). p. 1-8.

25. Nakano, Y.I., et al. *Converting Text into Agent Animations: Assigning Gestures to Text*. in *Human Language Technology Conference of the North American Chapter of the Association for Computational Linguistics (HLT-NAACL 2004), Companion Volume*. (2004). Boston. p. 153-156.

26. Larsson, S., et al., *TrindiKit 1.0 (Manual)*. (1999). p. http://www.ling.gu.se/projekt/trindi//.

27. *MIDIKI*. [cited; Available from: http://midiki.sourceforge.net/.

Appendix A. List of questions used in subjective evaluation

Labels	Definitions
(a) Awareness of engagement	1. Did you feel that the sales agent was aware of your attitude during her explanation? 8. Did you feel that the sales agent was aware of your bored with the conversation? 17. Did you feel that the sales agent catch the atmosphere? 23. Did you feel that the sales agent was aware of your gaze? 31. Did you feel that the sales agent was aware of your facial expressions?
(b) Appropriateness of behavior	2. Did the sales agent adapt her explanation according to your attitude? 9. Did you feel that the sales agent continued her description when you were not bored with the conversation and behaved appropriately when you were bored? 11. Was the timing of the agent's questions (e.g., "Do you understand so far?") proper? 18. Were the contents of the agent's questions (e.g., "Do you understand so far?") proper? 24. Was the number/frequency of the agent's questions (e.g., "Do you understand so far?") proper?
(c) Smoothness of conversation	3. Did you feel that the sales agent was easy to talk to? 12. Did you feel that the conversation with the sales agent was smooth? 25. Did you feel that the conversation was natural? 33. Was it easy to have a conversation with the sales agent? 29. Did you feel that the agent posed too many questions (e.g., "Do you understand so far?") or posed questions too frequently? 32. Did you feel that the agent posed too few questions (e.g., "Do you understand so far?") or did not pose questions frequently enough?
(d) Favorability	4. Did you have a good impression of the sales agent? 13. Did you want to talk to the agent again? 19. Did you feel that the sales agent was friendly? 30. Did you have good impressions of the sales agent's service?
(e) Naturalness of motion	5. Did you feel that the sales agent's actions were natural? 14. Did you feel that the sales agent's motions were smooth? 20. Did you feel that the gestures of the sales agent were natural? 26. Did you feel that the facial expressions of the sales agent were natural?
(f) Humanness	6. Did you feel human likeliness to the sales agent? 10. Did you feel that the sales agent is getting closer to human beings? 15. Did you feel humanity to the sales agent? 21. Did you feel that the sales agent was alive? 27. Did you feel that the sales agent had social skills?
(g) Intelligence	7. Did you feel that the sales agent was intelligent? 16. Did you feel that the sales agent was smart? 22. Did you feel that the sales agent had the ability to learn? 28. Did you feel that the sales agent had the ability to think?

Embedded Media Markers: Marks on Paper that Signify Associated Media

Qiong Liu, Chunyuan Liao, Lynn Wilcox, Anthony Dunnigan, Bee Liew
FX Palo Alto Laboratory
3400 Hillview Avenue, Bldg.4
{liu, liao, wilcox, tonyd, bee}@fxpal.com

ABSTRACT

Embedded Media Markers, or simply EMMs, are nearly transparent iconic marks printed on paper documents that signify the existence of media associated with that part of the document. EMMs also guide users' camera operations for media retrieval. Users take a picture of an EMM-signified document patch using a cell phone, and the media associated with the EMM-signified document location is displayed on the phone. Unlike bar codes, EMMs are nearly transparent and thus do not interfere with the document appearance. Retrieval of media associated with an EMM is based on image local features of the captured EMM-signified document patch. This paper describes a technique for semi-automatically placing an EMM at a location in a document, in such a way that it encompasses sufficient identification features with minimal disturbance to the original document.

Author Keywords

Augmented paper, barcode, camera phone, document recognition, marker on paper, vision-based paper interface.

ACM Classification Keywords

H.5.1 Multimedia Information Systems: Artificial, augmented, and virtual realities. H.5.2 User Interfaces: Interaction styles.

General Terms

Algorithms, Design, Documentation, Human Factors.

INTRODUCTION

Although paper is one of the most widely used devices for viewing information, it cannot play dynamic media such as video and audio. On the other hand, cell phones are increasingly used to play audio and video but cannot match paper's high resolution, large display size, flexibility in spatial organization, outdoor-readability and robustness for

static content. It is now possible to combine the two, using image recognition technology to link paper documents to corresponding dynamic media. A cell phone camera is used to capture an image of a document patch. The document patch is identified using features in the image, and digital media linked to that location in the document is retrieved and then played on the cell phone.

A common method for creating this type of media link on a paper document is to print markers on the document. Examples are 2D bar codes [13] or printed grids of dots [5]. However, these markers are visually obtrusive and interfere with the document content layout. Microsoft Tag [22] alleviates this issue by merging data cells with the user-specified image background, but still requires an opaque black-white border for the decoder to locate the data cells. DataGlyphs [16] overcome these problems by printing a nearly invisible machine-recognizable pattern on the paper. However, this type of marker requires high resolution printers and cameras to identify document locations. Electronic markers like RFID can be used too [18], but this approach increases the production costs.

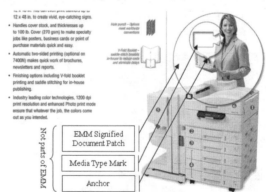

Figure 1. Partial image of an EMM enhanced paper page. In this EMM usage example, the circle shape EMM printed on paper (top-right of the figure) signifies that there is a video corresponding to the magazine in the person's hand. (the bottom-left callouts are not parts of an EMM)

Other systems compute features of the document content itself for identifying the document patch and thus creating a media link. HotPaper [2] and Mobile Retriever [9] use features based on document text such as the spatial layout of words. Other systems such Bookmarkr [6] and MapSnapper [4] use pixel level image features, such as the

SIFT [10] algorithm, to recognize generic document content such as pictures and graphic elements. With these systems, visually obtrusive marks are not required for identification.

Both marker-based methods and document-appearance-based methods fall short in providing visual guidance for users. Although bar codes and Data Glyphs are visible, they do not directly indicate the existence or type of media associated with them. When appearance-based feature are used, there is no on-paper indication at all to the user that there is media linked to the document. As a result, a HotPaper [2] user has to pan a camera phone over the paper document to look for hotspots until feedback such as a red dot or vibration is presented on the cell phone.

To solve this problem, we augment paper with meaningful awareness-marks, called Embedded Media Markers (EMMs) that indicate the existence, type, and capture guidance of media links. On seeing an EMM, the user knows to capture an image of the EMM-signified document patch with a cell phone in order to view associated digital media. This is analogous to Web pages that use underlines, font differences, or image tags to indicate the existence of links that users then click for additional information. Unlike barcodes, EMMs are nearly transparent and thus do not interfere with the document appearance. Unlike Embedded Data Glyphs [16] or Anoto patterns [17], EMMs can be printed with a regular low-resolution printer and identified from an image captured by a normal cell phone camera. Unlike other appearance-based approaches, EMMs clearly indicate signified document patches and locations. The design of EMMs also indicates what type of media (e.g. audio, video, or image) is associated with the EMM-signified document location. Furthermore, by requiring the captured image to cover the whole mark, we can improve feature construction accuracy, matching accuracy, and efficient resource usage.

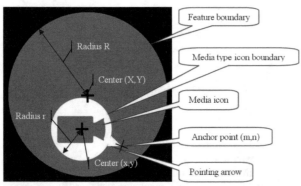

Figure 2. Basic components of an EMM

Figure 1 shows an EMM added in a printer description brochure. The EMM signifies that there is a video corresponding to the magazine in the person's hand. The portion of the document inside the big EMM feature boundary circle is named EMM-signified document patch (Figure 2). This patch should be completely included in a snapshot for successful retrieval. Within the EMM-signified document patch is the media type mark, a smaller

boundary (a circle in this implementation) containing a graphic that indicates the type of media associated with this EMM, in this case video. The arrow connected to the smaller circle points to the exact location in the document that is associated with the media, and is called the anchor, or the EMM-signified document location (Figure 2).

In the next section, we explain the requirements for EMMs construction. We then describe the algorithm for semi-automatic arrangement of the EMM on the document. The EMM system and several applications are described, followed by an evaluation. We end with conclusions and discussions for future work.

EMM CONSTRUCTION

EMMs are marks on paper that signify the existence of media associated with specific locations. For usability purposes, EMMs should have the following properties:

1. EMMs should be visible to the human. An EMM should be a visible mark that signifies the existence of multimedia information associated with the document

2. EMMs should be meaningful to human. An EMM should indicate the type of media, e.g. audio, video, text, image, and annotation, that is associated with it.

3. EMMs should not take up extra space on the paper, nor should the document layout be changed to accommodate the EMMs.

4. EMMs should minimize the semantic change to original paper content.

5. EMMs should not significantly change the document patch appearance, as identification is mainly based on the visual features of document appearance, which must be well preserved.

Feature Boundary Mark

When barcodes are not available, features in the image can be used to identify the document patch. These features may be generic image features such as SIFT [10], PCA-SIFT [15], SURF [1], FIT [8] etc. They may also be features based on word center relations [2] or stroke-center arrangements in a text patch [11]. These features are derived from the local appearance of the document image and are distributed non-uniformly. Thus a feature boundary is needed to tell users what part of the document to capture. Without a clear feature boundary, users of an augmented paper system may capture a document patch without sufficient features for the system to identify the patch. To tackle this problem, we guide the user's capture with an artificial boundary. More specifically, we use this boundary to set the minimum capture region for patch identification. With the help of this capture region guidance, we can dramatically reduce indexed features in our database. This feature reduction is very helpful for improving the accuracy and speed of an EMM identification.

To guarantee sufficient features in different capturing directions (we assume the camera optical axis is perpendicular to the paper), we tentatively use a feature boundary circle, illustrated in Figure 2, as an artificial feature boundary. From paper patch identification aspect, the larger the circle is, the more features we can use to facilitate the paper patch identification. On the other hand, the larger the circle is, the less EMMs we can put in every page and the less benefit we can get from feature reduction. Moreover large circle beyond certain size cannot be fully used by camera phones because of field-of-view and resolution limitations.

Besides circle size (radius R in Figure 2), the circle position (center (X,Y) in Figure 2) is also important for patch identification. If a circle is positioned at a place with dense feature distribution, the circle radius R can be greatly reduced while the identification accuracy is not compromised. On the other hand, a large circle placed at a blank location may lead to degraded recognition accuracy. The procedure and algorithm proposed here provides a method for finding an optimal circle center (X,Y) and radius R.

Media Type Mark

Besides cameraphone capture guidance, the media type (e.g. audio, video, weblink, 3D model, or company mark etc.) information is also useful for readers of enhanced paper document. For different media (e.g. audio) associated with an EMM, different media type icons are adopted to reflect the distinction. The EMM in Figure 2 has a video icon to graphically depict a video link associated with this EMM. The iconic information of media type is within a small interior circle, which aims to emphasize the iconic information. On the other hand, it is also visually consistent with the feature boundary mark.

A media type information mark must have a certain size to attract user's attention. We currently use a fixed size. On the other hand, this mark shouldn't obscure features for document patch identification. In this paper, we provide a method for finding an optimal iconic mark center (x,y).

Anchor Point and Pointing Arrow

The relatively small circle in Figure 2 does not include any specific position on a paper. This makes it difficult to convey information to a user at an exact position in the document. For example, if there are several machine parts close to each other in a figure and we have associated digital 3D models for the parts, it is difficult for people to associate the circle surrounded iconic marks with their corresponding parts. To solve this problem, we allow the document creator to select a specific location as an anchor point (m,n) and add an arrow that points to the anchor point from the circle surrounded icon. The arrow's appearance exactly matches that of the circle it is associated with so that the arrow and the circle surrounded icon form a callout for the specific location (m,n).

Graphical Effects

To reduce the interference with the original document, we use skeletons instead of colored regions to represent media type icons. Since human are good at separating alpha-blended images, alpha-blending media-type-icons with the original document can further reduce semantic impacts on the original document. By changing the alpha-blending coefficients for different color channels and regions, we can also change the text color or picture color in an EMM-signified region. Moreover, because graphical objects in a paper document are mainly in 2D space, adding 3D graphical effects to EMMs may further facilitate the separation of EMMs and other graphical objects in the original document.

In our current implementation, shown in Figure 2, all EMMs have a similar appearance: a large circle surrounding a smaller circle. The smaller circle features a simple icon and an attached arrow (Figure 2). This homogeneity in appearance is designed to allow users to find the EMMs on a page very quickly. The function of an EMM is similar to the simple colored and underlined hyperlink on a traditional web page. Unlike a hyperlink, an EMM is printed on physical paper and uses a meaningful icon to indicate available media associated with the EMM-signified document location.

In our current implementation, occlusion of images and text has been mitigated by adjusting only the luminance channel of the file used to print a page containing EMMs. The EMM varies the luminance of the underlying image in a limited range. Luminance information was chosen because it is reproduced with good fidelity by both color and monochrome copy machines and printers. In the implementation both the large bounding circle and the smaller circle add to the underlying image's luminance while a drop shadow effect diminishes it.

Image Feature Descriptor

Many image local features such as SIFT [10], PCA-SIFT [15], SURF [1], and FIT [8] can be used for EMM indexing. We use FIT[8] in our current system. FIT is an image local feature descriptor related to the well known SIFT[10] descriptor. Similar to SIFT, FIT finds keypoints (locations for feature computation) based on extremes in the Difference of Gaussian (DOG) image pyramid. Unlike SIFT which accumulates histograms of Gaussian weighted gradients at a key point level, the FIT descriptor directly computes its features at multiple scales higher than the key point scale. This approach can greatly reduce the number of image-pixel-operations involved in feature extraction. Moreover, FIT uses the pre-computed pyramid to save computational cost on the expensive Gaussian weighting process [8]. Through early comparison between SIFT and FIT, FIT was reported to have comparable recognition accuracy to SIFT on document recognition task, with less than 1/3 of SIFT's storage space and much shorter construction and search time.

EMM PLACEMENT PROCEDURE AND ALGORITHM

The EMM construction mainly focuses on readers' requirements for multimedia enhanced paper. We also need to consider the requirements from the identification algorithm. More specifically, we want to arrange an EMM to improve instead of degrading a paper patch identification process. To achieve this goal, an algorithm is needed to adjust parameters for an EMM arrangement.

EMM Placement Rules and Procedures

There are three basic sets of parameters for an EMM adjustment: feature-boundary-circle center (X,Y), feature-boundary-circle radius R, and media-type-circle center (x,y). Since the patch identification accuracy does not change much if the number of patch-covered feature points is over a certain threshold, the boundary-circle optimization goal is to achieve good patch-identification accuracy with minimum cost of paper surface area. Small EMM boundary circles have the following benefits to our system:

1) The EMM will create less distortion in the original document appearance.

2) Small surface area occupation makes it easier to put more separated EMMs in every page.

3) Since we only need to index the keypoints, such as SIFT[10]/SURF[1]/FIT[8] keypoints, in the circle for patch identification, small surface area occupation reduces the number of keypoints saved on the index server. The reduced number of keypoints is helpful for increasing query image identification accuracy and speed.

4) The small marked area may guide a reader to submit a patch without too much computation (the number of keypoints is controlled by the circle), and require less time for retrieving multimedia data.

5) Keeping the capture-area-low-limit small also makes it more convenient for cell phone capture. More specifically, capturing a large circle needs a large distance between the cell phone and paper while capturing a small circle is more flexible in a large dynamic range.

To get a small radius for the feature-boundary-circle, our algorithm will locate the boundary-circle at a place with high keypoint density and shrink the radius to meet the minimum keypoint number requirement.

With paper patch identification algorithms described in the previous sections, the feature-boundary-circle is normally much larger than the minimum visibility requirement. In our algorithm, we set the media-type-icon-circle inside the feature-boundary-circle to make sure readers consider them as one EMM. To reduce the disturbances caused by the icon-circle, our algorithm tries to move this circle to a place with minimum keypoint density. More specifically, with the icon-circle size fixed, we expect the circle to include a minimum number of keypoints in the original document.

This procedure has the following benefits for the patch identification process.

1) The media-type-icon and its surrounding circle create less distortion to important features. We think this is helpful for a reader to separate the original content and the icon so that the reader can have a better understanding to the original document.

2) Since the media-type-callout is mainly formed with semi-transparent skeletons and shadows, the callout and original document content may form more distinctive keypoints in sparse-keypoint regions. This keypoint density balancing process is useful for removing matching outliers and further improving patch identification accuracy.

Besides these basic optimization approaches, we also set some rules to make an EMM look more attractive and more consistent in various situations. These rules include:

1) The anchor point should be inside the feature-boundary-circle. It makes the EMM more intuitive. It reduces our circle searching space. Moreover, it avoids merging multiple EMMs on the same page to the same location (a global optimal position).

2) The media-type-icon and its surrounding circle shouldn't cover the anchor point. In this way, we can always have the arrow pointing outside from the circle and that gives EMMs more consistent look at various locations.

3) To make the arrow shorter, the algorithm forces the iconic callout to move closer to the anchor point.

4) All EMMs uses the same lighting source at infinite distance for their shadows.

5) In our current implementation, we assume an EMM model has a three-level construction in a 3D space for shadows. This construction model is illustrated in Figure 5.

In our current design, the light for shadows comes from up-left at an infinite distance.

A Fast Algorithm for Estimating the Number of Points in a Circle

To get an optimal location and size for a feature-boundary-circle or an optimal location for an iconic callout circle, the system has to count the number of keypoints inside a circle. If an EMM changes the image local features dramatically, the system has to re-compute all features in an EMM-signified patch when a set of new parameters (i.e. location and size) is tested. This kind of procedure will make it difficult to get an optimal parameter set in reasonable time. Since our EMM mainly includes edges and shadows, we believe that adding an EMM in a document patch will not decrease the number of keypoints much. Since an EMM edge can form new features with original contents close to the edge and an EMM transparent region will not have much impact to the original features, it is more probable that an EMM will increase the number of keypoints in its local region. With this consideration in mind, we can safely use keypoint distribution in a page without an EMM to estimate the number of real features in an EMM feature boundary circle or an EMM media-type-icon boundary.

Even though our system can skip feature re-computation for testing each set of EMM parameters, the system still has to count the number of keypoints inside a circle with many different circle parameters. More specifically, the system may need to try the position of every pixel as a circle center. Moreover, it may also try multiple radiuses before an optimal solution is reached. Therefore, the algorithm for estimating the number of points in a circle has to be fast for a practical application.

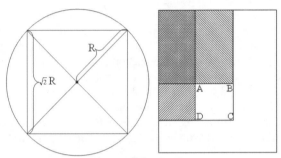

Figure 3. (left) Use the number of keypoints in the square to approximate the number of keypoints in the circle.
(right) Use a cumulative keypoint distribution to compute the number of keypoints in a square.

The number of keypoints, n, of a normally scanned 100DPI (dots per inch) page may reach several thousands. Assume we use a brute-force searching approach, the computational complexity for estimating the number of keypoints in a circle will be O(n). For example, if we want to search an optimal circle center in a 500 by 500 patch and the number of keypoints in the whole page is 5000, the number of math operations used by the system will be over 10^9. If we try multiple circle radiuses and consider the computation for the icon circle, the number of math operations may reach 10^{10} or more.

To overcome this computational complexity, we designed a fast algorithm for estimating the number of points in a circle. The algorithm is based on the integral image of a keypoint distribution histogram. To use this algorithm, we approximate the number of keypoints in a circle with the number of keypoints in a square inside the circle. The relationship between the circle and the square is illustrated in Figure 3 (left). Denote N_c as the number of keypoints in the circle and N_s as the number of keypoints in the square, we can get $N_s \leq N_c$. This approximation can guarantee enough keypoints in the circle for patch identification when the number of keypoints in the square reaches the patch identification low limit.

Figure 4 (left) shows keypoints overlaid on top of a brochure image. Corresponding to the image in Figure 4

(left), Figure 4 (right) shows the cumulative keypoint distribution map, in which the value at each point equal to the number of keypoints in its top-left region. Assume the number of pixels in an image is N, the computational complexity for getting this cumulative keypoint distribution map is O(N). Since the algorithm only needs to compute this map once and the system can pre-compute this map for each image, the computational complexity of this map will not affect the optimization much when a document creator uses this approach to get an optimal EMM arrangement.

Figure 4. (left) keypoints overlaid on top of a brochure image, and (right) cumulative keypoint distribution of the same page.

With the cumulative keypoint distribution map, the system can compute the number of keypoints in a square in constant time. Assume a square, ABCD in Figure 3 (right), has its sides parallel to one image boundary or the other and the values for the points A, B, C, and D on the cumulative distribution map are N_A, N_B, N_C, N_D respectively. The system can get the number of keypoints in the square ABCD, N_{SQ}, with the following equation:

$$N_{SQ} = N_A + N_C - N_B - N_D$$

The computation consists of only one addition and two subtractions. This is much more efficient than the brute force approach.

Optimal Feature-boundary-circle

With the fast algorithm for estimating the number of keypoints in a circle, the system can try a circle center at the position of every pixel. Moreover, the system also needs to know the optimal radius for the best feature-boundary-circle. To get the optimal radius, we used the following binary search approach for optimization:

```
while ((radiushigh-radiuslow)>SMALLMARGIN)
    Get a circle center location that allows the circle to
    include the anchor point and the maximum number of
    keypoints with this radius;
    if maximum number of keypoints with this radius >
    KEYNUMLOWLIMIT
        radiushigh = currentradius;
    else
        radiuslow = currentradius;
    end
    currentradius = (radiushigh + radiuslow)/2;
end
```

Optimal Surrounding Circle for an Media-type-icon

Since a media-type-icon has a fixed size, getting the optimal location of this circle is a circle location that allows the circle to include minimum number of keypoints. Besides this optimization, we also need to consider rules in the previous paragraphs to make an EMM look nicer. In other words, the distance between the surrounding circle center and the anchor point should be larger than the radius of the surrounding circle. Moreover, the surrounding circle should be 'close' to the anchor point for a short pointing arrow. There are several ways to make the arrow short. One way is to set the maximum distance between the anchor point and the surrounding circle center. Another approach is to compute a vector from (X,Y) to (x,y) and a vector from (X,Y) to (m,n), and force the angle between these two vectors smaller than 90°. We take the second approach in our current implementation.

Generate Graphical Effects for an EMM

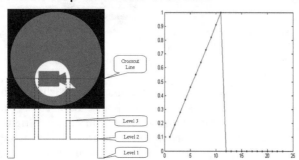

Figure 5. (left) A three-level EMM construction in a 3D space. (right) The filter diagonal coefficient shape for shadow generation.

Because graphical objects in a paper document are mainly in 2D space, adding 3D graphical effects to EMMs may further facilitate the visual separation of overlaid marks from other graphical objects in original document. In our current implementation, we use a three-level EMM model in 3D space for shadows. The three-level EMM model is illustrated in Figure 5 (left). For shadows, we assume the light comes from the top-left of a document. To mimic this effect, we used a sobel filter followed by a 2D filter. The sobel filter has coefficients [1 0; 0 -1]. The 2D filter has the shape shown in Figure 5 (right) in its diagonal direction, and has zero coefficients for all other filter positions.

Figure 6. Generate graphical effect for an EMM. (a) A black and white multimedia icon. (b) An EMM decorated with graphical effects.

By combining the filtering result with an EMM edge, the system can generate proper EMM graphical effects based on each black and white multimedia icon. Figure 6 showed a typical black and white multimedia icon and an EMM decorated with graphical effects. Because the arrow is dynamically added to the 3-level EMM model after the optimal EMM parameter set is found, the arrow's graphical effects are properly blended with graphical effects for other EMM parts. From Figure 1, readers may see the effect of alpha blending an EMM with a document page.

THE EMM SYSTEM AND APPLICATIONS

To demonstrate the feasibility and applications of EMMs, we have built a system to support the complete workflow for creating and using EMMs. As illustrated in Figure 7, the system consists of three major interaction entities, namely Authoring Client, EMM Server and Retrieving Client.

The EMM Authoring Client

The authoring client is a PC application for authors to add EMMs to a document with the previously presented algorithm. With this tool, an EMM author can open a document file, specify an anchor point in a page via a mouse-click, type the URL of associated media, and get an EMM overlaid image. This tool also allows users to change the media type mark, adjust the EMM alpha-blending coefficient, adjust the document DPI, or view keypoint distribution on the image. Currently, our system supports

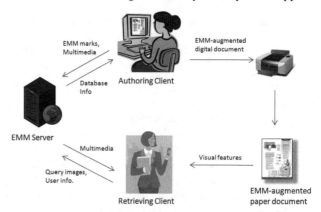

Figure 7. The architecture of the EMM system

five types of media links: audio, video, text, webpage, and image.

The generated EMMs and their associated multimedia URLs are uploaded to the EMM server, which indexes the marks in a database and stores the link information. The authoring client might retrieve information from the server, e.g. the existing features in the database, for verification.

The resulting EMM-augmented digital document can then be printed and delivered to end users, who run a retrieving client application on a camera phone. With the application, an end user takes a snapshot of an EMM on paper to capture its visual features. The snapshot and the user information are then submitted to the EMM server to fetch the associated multimedia. Upon successful retrieval, the user can review and interact with the multimedia data. Based on the system, we have developed several applications in the areas of maps, manuals and advertisements.

Augmented Maps

A paper map offers a large high-quality display of geographic information. It is outdoor readable, foldable, and easy to share with other people [4, 21]. However, it lacks dynamic location-specific information, such as video clip about a restaurant, weather forecast for a park, and currently available discounts for a hotel.

Figure 8. (left) A map augmented with a video EMM (right) The associated YouTube video

With EMMs, such dynamic multimedia can be easily brought to paper maps. As illustrated in Figure 8, on a map of Tokyo in Japan, a famous restaurant Ginza Sky Lounge is augmented by an EMM, which points to a YouTube video clip about the history and highlights of the place. Similarly, the EMM may point to a customer review site or the detailed menus, and allow the user to make a reservation right away. Note that the EMM does not change the original map layout and has minimal appearance interference, which differentiates EMMs from the existing barcode-based techniques [13, 14]. Besides, overlaying an in-place EMM right on top of a POI (point of interest) is especially useful to retain the context of the POI in the map.

In-situ Multimedia Manuals

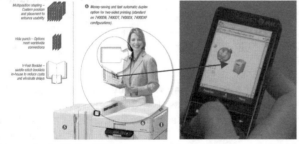

Figure 9. (left) An EMM in a cartridge installation manual (right) The associated step-by-step video tutorial

Due to paper's high display quality, robustness, instant accessibility, and spatial flexibility, printed manuals are extensively used by in-the-field workers such as automobile mechanics and airplane electricians, who often bring to the working space the manual as quick references for specific parts. This in-situ use of manuals is also quite common with average customers who are learning to operate appliances or perform maintenance, say replacing cartridge of a

printer. The paper manuals, however, often falls short of presenting intuitive instructions (e.g. a video clip demonstrating the cartridge installation steps) or up-to-date information about the parts and devices (e.g. the availability of a type of tires at local stores). And a computer is not always accessible in the working spaces.

An EMM-enhanced manual and a mobile phone can help address the dilemma. Figure 9 exemplifies such a printer manual, with which a user can easily retrieve and play the video tutorial of cartridge inspection. If a new cartridge is necessary, the user can also immediately place an order through the web site associated with an EMM.

Multimedia Advertisement on Paper

EMMs open the door to a wide range of interactive paper applications. Besides their use in maps and manuals, EMMs can also be applied to multimedia advertisements (Ads) on paper bills, flyers or catalogs. EMMs not only bring to paper more expressive media for Ads (e.g. video, audio and animations), but also allow users to proactively interact with the Ads and start the shopping workflow immediately. For example, after watching the associated video of a cash bonus promotion for opening a checking account, the user can activate the enrollment by simply clicking the video (Figure 10). Moreover, the Ads can be customized based on the user's personal information, including preferences, shopping history and events (e.g. birthdays and anniversaries). EMMs can be also used to augment textbooks, kids' story books, calendars, magazines etc.

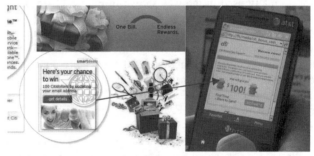

Figure 10 (left) An EMM Ad on a bill. (right) The personalized web page for the user to interact with the Ad.

EMM EVALUATION

For early stage deployment and evaluation, we currently focus on using EMMs for pages within a publication such as a book or magazine and use our image local features FIT [8] for EMM identification. Users scan the book ISBN, or capture the cover page, or input other similar publication index. Then, EMMs within the publication can be used. For this purpose, we choose the ICME06 proceedings as our target document for an early stage performance evaluation of the EMM design and the semi-automatic EMM construction algorithm. The proceeding has 2188 letter-size (8.5"x11") document pages with text, images, and figures. With the large page collection and content variation in the

Setup \ Batch #	1	2	3	4	5	6	7	8	9	10
Printer	BW	BW	BW	BW	Color	Color	Color	Color	Color	Color
Capture Environment	Office	Patio	Office	Patio	Office	Patio	Office	Patio	Office	Patio
Printing Software	Irfan-View	Irfan-View	Printing Wizard	Printing Wizard	Irfan-View	Irfan-View	Printing Wizard	Printing Wizard	Printing Wizard	Printing Wizard
Pages / Paper	1	1	1	1	1	1	1	1	4	4
Query #	20	10	10	10	10	10	10	10	10	10
Correct Identification #	20	10	10	10	10	10	10	10	10	9

Table 1. EMM testing results for different setups.

experiment, we believe that our test results will be reliable EMM-performance evaluations at the book level.

Before giving the demo system to many users for a more complete testing, we need to make sure the system is robust to commonly used printing devices, printing software, image coding mechanisms, and lighting conditions. Therefore, our preliminary EMM evaluation will focus on impacts of these factors.

The EMM Capture Assumptions and Implications

The feature-boundary-circle of an EMM is used to guide a user's capture of the EMM image. We assume that EMMs are normally used in the way shown in Figure 11. In other words, when a user captures an EMM, the user roughly has the EMM feature-boundary-circle filled the captured image. With this assumption, we may limit the feature extraction to the relatively small neighborhood of the feature-boundary-circle. This simplification can save us memory, disk space and computation time. For each EMM, we crop a square region that includes the EMM feature-boundary-circle for visual feature indexing. Because most cameras have 4:3 aspect ratio and an EMM needs 6% more space for shadows, we set the square side 1.06*4/3≈1.414 times the EMM feature-boundary-circle diameter. We also align the center of the square with the center of the feature-boundary-circle for consistent margin around the circle.

Figure 11. A typical EMM usage scenario.

A main purpose of an EMM is to signify the existence of media associated with that part of the document. For that

purpose, an EMM must occupy a sufficiently large region on a page to attract user's attention. We set the diameter size of the EMM inner circle to 1" for clear indication of the media type. Moreover, the minimum diameter size of an EMM feature-boundary-circle is set to 2.5". Based on our experience, this minimum size or a larger size is easy for a user to focus a camera phone on a marker and fill the captured image with a small neighborhood of the marker. For example, when we use an AT&T FUZE to capture a 2.5" EMM, the distance between the camera phone and the paper is about 4". We also tested the Google G1 phone. Its shortest distance for auto focus is also around 3". Therefore, we think that the 2.5" diameter setup is reasonable for existing technology.

Since most camera phones have the 640-by-480 resolution, we assume the captured EMM image has this resolution. To efficiently use captured EMM images (around 2.5" diameter in physical space) at this resolution, we use 480dots/2.5inch=192DPI≈ 200DPI resolution images in our database. Corresponding to each EMM, the minimum neighborhood size for visual feature computation will be 1.414*2.5*200=707-pixel by 707-pixel in our database. For space saving, all images in our database are saved in JPEG format.

The Factor for Balancing Accuracy and Resources

For practical applications, EMM designers are responsible for reasonable retrieval accuracy and speed. On one hand, using more keypoints makes the EMM identification system more robust to capture noise caused by illumination changes and occlusions etc. On the other hand, designers should also restrict the memory consumption by each page on the server for query speed and overall page indexing volume. In our EMM construction algorithm, we use the minimum number of keypoints within the feature-boundary-circle to address this issue. In our experiment, we set this minimum number to 100.

EMM Testing against Printing Software, Paper Size, Printer, and Lighting Condition

In practice, EMM enhanced documents may be rendered with different printing software, and print on different size papers with different printers. People may also use EMMs in indoor environments or outdoor environments.

For testing these factors, we *randomly* generate 2188 2D locations for 2188 document pages. By using these 2188 locations as EMM anchor points, our EMM construction algorithm creates 2188 non-overlapping EMMs and computes FIT features in all EMM-neighborhood squares for indexing. From these 2188 pages, we also *randomly* selected 110 EMM overlaid pages for real query image capture. These 110 testing pages were saved in JPEG format with 1700 by 2200 resolution.

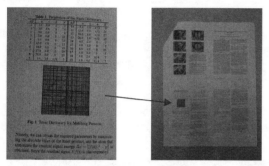

Figure 12. (left) The EMM capture that is failed to find its corresponding link. (right) The hardcopy used for this capture.

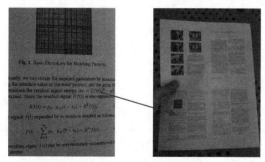

Figure 13. (left) The capture of an adjusted EMM. (right) The hardcopy used for this capture.

For testing the EMM sensitivity to printing software, we tried the IrfanView and the Windows XP Photo Printing Wizard. To check the EMM sensitivity to paper size, we print 90 pages on letter-size paper, and fit 4 pages on each letter-size paper for all other 20 pages. Because the EMM sizes on these 4-page/paper hardcopies are relatively small, filling the captured image with an EMM is a little difficult. Our AT&T FUZE camera showed the red 'x' for all these captures at the camera focus stage. For data collection, we forced these captures on our camera phone.

The 110 hardcopies were generated with either Xerox Workcentre 255 black-and-white printer or Xerox Docucolor 240 color printer. On the black-and-white printer generated hardcopies, we can clearly see halftone effects.

The 110 testing query images were captured either in an office or on an open patio. By capturing EMMs in these different environments, we can learn the EMM sensitivity to normal indoor and outdoor lightings. Because we assumed that EMMs are used in normal reading conditions, we did not capture EMMs in extreme lighting conditions for this test.

Table 1 reports our EMM performance evaluations when we change various factors described in this section. In the table, we use 'BW' to indicate the Xerox Workcentre 255 black-and-white printer and use 'Color' to indicate the Xerox Docucolor 240 color printer. In all these 110 EMM query images, the system failed on only one image. This image is shown in Figure 12. According to the log of our code, the failure is caused by insufficient matching points. In several million keypoints saved in our database, this image input only finds two matching points. To handle similar problems in practice, we may consider increasing the EMM diameter size or forcing the EMM feature-boundary-circle center to a different location for EMM rearrangement. We tried the second approach in our experiment. In this experiment, we kept the anchor point unchanged and adjusted the EMM center location for the failed document. Our EMM arrangement algorithm re-computed all other EMM parameters, such as the feature-boundary-circle diameter, and the media type mark location, and regenerated the EMM overlaid page (Figure 13). After that, we captured the regenerated EMM under similar conditions of the previous capture, and the captured EMM was correctly recognized. For future research, we will explore the causes of insufficient matches in this case.

Comparisons with Early Tests without EMMs

The FIT paper [8] tested the algorithm by randomly rotating and scaling training-images in a certain range. The test dataset was the ICME2006 proceeding, and recognition test was on the page-level. In the test presented in this paper, we adopted the same proceeding, but used real camera captures instead of synthetic images. Moreover, the EMM recognition is performed on patch-level instead of page-level. People may expect much lower recognition rate for this test. However, after the EMM adjustment illustrated in Figure 13, the document recognition result is even better than the result presented in the FIT paper [8]. We think that is caused by following reasons:

1. The indexing image dimension that we used in this experiment is 707x707, instead of 306x396 used in the previous experiment in [8]. This larger image size gives the system more details for matching.

2. We prepared indexing images at similar resolutions of the captured images. This strategy can help us to reduce the feature-construction interpolation error, and the matching noise caused by irrelevant scales.

In another early experiment which allows novice users to interact with paper via an unguided (without EMM)

320x240 image capture, the first snapshot success rate is about 81.6% (finding an image with at least six matching points). The result we get from the EMM experiment is much improved over that early experiment. We think this improvement is also caused by increasing the indexing image size, the query image size, and providing EMM capture guidance.

CONCLUSION AND FUTURE WORK

This paper describes the use of Embedded Media Markers printed on paper to signify the existence of media associated with documents and guide user to interact with the printout. To facilitate the use of EMMs, we introduce a procedure and algorithm to semi-automatically arrange visible EMMs on paper. The algorithm can help editors to build quality EMMs that are user friendly, machine friendly, and document friendly. The EMMs can then be overlaid on other document contents for printout of enhanced paper. A user can then get extra multimedia information on an active screen by capturing an EMM-signified document patch on paper. Besides the EMM idea and the semi-automatic EMM construction tool, we also discussed potential EMM applications and evaluated the EMM performance.

There are still a number of research issues surrounding the accuracy, scalability, and usability of EMMs. These depend on database size, image local features (FIT, SIFT, SURF, etc.) used for recognition, resolution of the original indexed images and the printed EMM-enhanced documents, resolution and quality of captured images, size of EMMs, and number of image features used for indexing. In order to optimize these parameters for usability, we need to collect a large number of captured EMMs from a variety of documents, users, cell-phone cameras, and environments. In addition, we need to identify other methods for scalability in addition to the publication identification method proposed in the paper. Finally, we need to do user studies on real tasks to better understand and focus the value of this technology.

REFERENCES

1. Bay, H., Ess, A., Tuytelaars, T., Van Gool, L. "SURF: Speeded Up Robust Features", Computer Vision and Image Understanding (CVIU), Vol. 110, No. 3, pp. 346-359, 2008.

2. Erol, B., Emilio Antunez, and J.J. Hull. HOTPAPER: multimedia interaction with paper using mobile phones. In Proceedings of ACM Multimedia'08, pp. 399-408.

3. Pixazza, Now a picture is worth more than a thousand words. http://pixazza.com/.

4. Hare, J., P. Lewis, L. Gordon, and G. Hart. MapSnapper: Engineering an Efficient Algorithm for Matching Images of Maps from Mobile Phones. Proceedings of Multimedia Content Access: Algorithms and Systems II, 2008.

5. Hecht, B., M. Rohs, J. Schöning, and A. Krüger. Wikeye – Using Magic Lenses to Explore Georeferenced Wikipedia Content. PERMID 2007.

6. Henze, N. and S. Boll. Snap and share your photobooks. In Proceedings of ACM Multimedia'08, pp. 409-418.

7. Hull, J.J., B. Erol, J. Graham, Q. Ke, H. Kishi, J. Moraleda, and D.G.V. Olst. Paper-based Augmented Reality. Proceedings of IEEE ICAT 2007, pp. 205-209.

8. Liu, Q., H. Yano, D. Kimber, C. Liao, and L. Wilcox. High Accuracy and Language Independent Document Retrieval With A Fast Invariant Transform. In Proceedings of IEEE ICME'09, pp. 386-389.

9. Liu, X. and D. Doermann, Mobile Retriever: access to digital documents from their physical source. Int. J. Doc. Anal. Recognit., 2008. 11(1): pp. 19-27.

10. Lowe, D.G., Distinctive Image Features from Scale-Invariant Keypoints. Int. J. Comput. Vision, 2004. 60(2): pp. 91-110.

11. Nakia, T., K. Kise, and M. Iwamura. Use of affine invariants in locally likely arrangement hashing for camera-based document image retrieval. LNCS, Vol. 3872, pp. 541-552.

12. Parikh, T.S., P. Javid, S. K., K. Ghosh, and K. Toyama. Mobile phones and paper documents: evaluating a new approach for capturing microfinance data in rural India. Proceedings of ACM CHI'06, pp. 551-560.

13. Rekimoto, J. and Ayatsuka, Y. 2000. CyberCode: designing augmented reality environments with visual tags. In Proceedings of ACM DARE 2000, pp. 1-10.

14. Rohs, M. Real-world interaction with camera-phones. LNCS, Vol. 3598, pp. 74-89.

15. Ke, Y. and Sukthankar, R., PCA-SIFT: A More Distinctive Representation for Local Image Descriptors. Proceedings of IEEE CVPR 2004.

16. Hecht D. L., Embedded Data Glyph Technology for Hardcopy Digital Documents. SPIE -Color Hard Copy and Graphics Arts III, Vol. 2171, pp. 341-352.

17. Wikipedia, Digital paper. http://en.wikipedia.org/wiki/Digital_paper

18. Reilly, D., M. Rodgers, R. Argue, et al., Marked-up maps: combining paper maps and electronic information resources. Personal and Ubiquitous Computing, 2006. 10(4): pp. 215-226.

19. Costanza, E., J. Huang., Designable Visual Markers, Proceedings of ACM CHI'09, pp. 1879-1888.

20. NODA TSUGIO, MOROO JUN, CHIBA HIROTAKA, Print-type Steganography Technology, Fujitsu 2006, Vol. 57. No. 3, pp. 320-324.

21. Morrison, A., Oulasvirta, A., Peltonen, P., Lemmela, S., Jacucci, G., Reitmayr, G., Näsänen, J., and Juustila, A., Like bees around the hive: a comparative study of a mobile augmented reality map. In Proceedings of ACM CHI '09, pp. 1889-1898.

22. Microsoft Tag. http://www.microsoft.com/tag/

WildThumb: A Web Browser Supporting Efficient Task Management on Wide Displays

*Shenwei Liu**
Information Science
Cornell University
301 College Avenue, Ithaca, NY 14850-4623
sl2277@cornell.edu

Keishi Tajima
Graduate School of Informatics
Kyoto University
Sakyo, Kyoto, Japan 606-8501
tajima@i.kyoto-u.ac.jp

ABSTRACT

Nowadays the Web and Web browsers have become the most important and universal platform for people to search, view, process, and exchange various kinds of information. Consequently, today's users usually open many Web pages simultaneously in order to perform multiple tasks in parallel, which makes Web browsers crucial in our daily task management. However, no existing Web browser provides users with sufficient support for the management of many tabs or windows of opened pages. On the other hand, wide displays have become more affordable and prevalent, while extra space on those displays is not utilized effectively in Web browsing. In this paper, we propose a new Web browser interface aiming to support efficient task management in Web browsing on wide displays. In order to help users switch between opened Web pages, we show thumbnails of the pages in the extra space around the currently focused page. In the page thumbnails, we emphasize distinctive elements in each page in order to make the selection of the thumbnails easier. In addition, we calculate the relevance between pages based on users' switching history, and emphasize pages relevant to the current page by adjusting the size or opacity of the thumbnails. This further helps users find the thumbnails of needed pages, and also helps users get the overview of the page set related to the current task.

Author Keywords

multitask, task switching, task grouping, working set, augmented thumbnail, site logo, tab-browser, window system

ACM Classification Keywords

H.5.2 Information Interfaces and Presentation: User Interfaces—*Graphical user interfaces, Screen design, Windowing systems*

General Terms

Design, Human Factors

*This work was done while the author was at Kyoto University.

INTRODUCTION

Since the Web is now the biggest information resource, and most intellectual labor today relies heavily on information search on the Web, Web browsers have become the most important application for many users. In addition, recent evolution of the Web are making Web browsers even more important. First, Web browsers have become the standard platform for information access. They are used not only for Web pages but also for various data repositories on the Internet/intranets, or for various hardware, such as printers, sensors, and network devices. Secondly, Web browsers have also become a platform for running applications. Because of the recent browser technologies that enable more functional applications, and the recent paradigm shift to the cloud computing, many Web-based equivalents of traditional applications have acquired popularity over their predecessors. Thirdly, the success of many Web 2.0 applications, such as, blogs, micro-blogs, and social network services, has made the Web also a platform for information publishing.

As a result of these changes, today's users use Web browsers even longer and even more frequently than before. Another important consequence of these changes is that today's users usually work on many tasks simultaneously on Web browsers [18]. In order to work on many tasks, users open one or more (sometimes many) pages for each task, and switch back and forth among those many pages. Because of this trend, *tab-browsers* have recently become very popular. A tab-browser holds many Web pages within one browser window, and users can switch among them by clicking their *tabs* or by some keyboard shortcuts. There are also users who open many browser windows, and switch between them by using keyboard shortcuts or by using functions of the window systems, such as TaskBar of Microsoft Windows. It has also been observed that users who use larger displays tend to open more windows at a time [13].

In existing browsers, however, it becomes difficult to switch among tabs or windows as the number of them increases. The difficulty of page switching is attributable to three problems. First, as tabs or window icons (such as, TaskBar buttons) become smaller, the page titles shown in them are truncated, which makes different Web pages indistinguishable. Secondly, as the number of tabs or icons increases, it takes longer time for users to scan through all of them to find the needed one. Although human beings have very effective spatial memory, it is hard to remember the positions of all the tabs or window icons, when we have many of them. It is especially hard when a user has not been switching to some pages for long time, or when the positions have changed after opening or closing some pages. Thirdly, smaller tabs or icons are harder to select using pointing devices.

Another defect of existing browsers is lack of functions for organizing many opened pages into tasks. As mentioned above, each task corresponds to one or more pages. We call a set of pages involved in a task *the working set* of the task. When a user is browsing a page, the user sometimes needs to know what other pages are involved in the same task. In order to provide users with such an overview of each task, we need functions for grouping pages into working sets. Such a task overview is also useful when a user switches back to a task from another task after long interruptions, and has to restore the information related to the task into their working memory. Nowadays business users are frequently interrupted during the work, such as in every several minutes [3, 1]. Therefore, it is important to reduce overhead in task resumption, but existing browsers do not have much support for that. Notice that page grouping also relieves the scan problem explained before because intra-task page switching happens more often than inter-task page switching.

In this way, existing Web browsers have four problems in multitask management: difficulty in page recognition, inefficient scan of page lists, difficulty in page pointing, and lack of page organization. On the other hand, wide displays have recently become very popular. However, most Web pages are still designed for traditional displays in order to maximize accessibility. This results in the ineffective use of screen space: most Web pages cause unused empty margins when displayed on wide displays. Accordingly, in this research, we leverage extra space on wide displays to solve these four problems in multitask management.

First, in order to make recognition and pointing of pages easier, we display thumbnails, instead of small tabs or window icons, of all the opened pages all the time in marginal spaces at the both sides on wide displays, as shown in Figure 1.

In order to further improve the recognizability of thumbnails, we also augment ordinary thumbnails: we extract distinctive elements from each Web page, and overlay them onto the ordinary thumbnails. Figure 3 shows an example of the augmentation of the thumbnail shown in Figure 2.

Even if we display such augmented thumbnails, we still have the problem of the linear scan of many thumbnails. To solve this problem, we calculate the relevance between pages based on the past switching history, and we emphasize thumbnails of pages with higher relevance to the currently focused page. We expect that we can reduce the average number of thumbnails that a user actually scan through by emphasizing pages that the user is more likely to switch to.

Emphasizing relevant thumbnails also relieves the problem of the lack of page organization. Because we can expect that pages involved in the current task have higher relevance to

Figure 1. Screen Shot of Our System

Figure 2. Thumbnail   **Figure 3. Augmented Thumbnail**

the currently focused page, users can get the overview of the current task by watching only emphasized thumbnails.

To validate our method, we conducted two user experiments. In the first experiment, we measured average switching time when participants use tabs, ordinary thumbnails, and augmented thumbnails. In the second experiment, participants were asked to perform simple work consisting of multiple tasks, and to respond a semi-structured interview afterward. By the first experiment, we quantatively confirmed the effectiveness of our augmented thumbnails, and in the second experiment, we obtained subjective opinions on the satisfying and undesirable aspects of our approach.

RELATED WORK

In Web browsing, a task usually corresponds to a set of pages. In more general context, a user task on computers usually corresponds to a set of windows. We call those sets of pages or windows *working sets*. According to the observation by González and Mark, users in multitask activities very frequently switch from a working set to another, and save and restore functions of them are important [3]. Czerwinski et al. also observed that users in multitask activities have difficulty when they return to tasks after some interruption [1].

The most popular approach to multitask management in the past research is to provide users with facilities for grouping windows. Rooms [4] is pioneering research on multiple virtual workspaces. Rooms provides multiple virtual workspaces in order to reduce space contention, and users manage working sets by manually assigning windows to virtual workspaces. On the contrary, we show thumbnails of all pages in order to make full use of extra space on wide displays, and automatically predicts pages in the current working set without users' burden of manually defining working sets. Additional advantage of such an approximation approach is that it naturally supports overlapping groups.

In Scalable Fabric [14], while the user is focusing on one window, other windows are shown in small size in the periphery areas on the display. GroupBar [16], which extends TaskBar of Microsoft Windows, also allows users to manually group windows by drag-and-dropping a task button onto another task button. In tab-browsers, we can manually group pages by creating one browser window for each task, and opening pages related to the task as tabs within that window. These approaches also require users to manage working sets.

TaskTracer [2] provides automatic grouping similar to ours. It automatically groups resources (files, Web pages, etc.) related to each task, and create a kind of virtual folders. We introduce the similar approach to Web browsers, but one important difference is that we model a working set of each task as a fuzzy set, and emphasize each page in accordance with their membership degree. One advantage of this fuzzy approach is errors in automatic group detection do not cause a fatal problem. SWISH [12] and RelAltTab [11] also provide a similar automatic window grouping, and Iqbal and Bailey proposed a method of automatically detecting breakpoints between tasks [5], but they also create crisp, non-fuzzy sets.

In CAL [6], when a user selects a keyword in a text editor, and triggers the "content-aware layout," the system shows only windows containing the selected keyword. This can be regarded as another approach to the automatic window grouping, but it can define groups only by keywords.

Recently, popular operating systems have introduced thumbnails of windows for task management, such as Aero of Microsoft Windows Vista and Exposé of Mac OS X. There are also many systems that use thumbnails for documents or Web pages. In Data Mountain [15], users can store thumbnails of a large number of Web pages in a 3D space for efficient later retrieval. Woodruff et al. proposed a method of enhancing thumbnails of Web pages [19]. They show thumbnails of pages when showing search results of search engines, and enhance the thumbnails by emphasizing the occurrences of query keywords within them. In their context, emphasized query keywords are very useful for users to judge the relevance of each page to their information need. However, our purpose is to help users match thumbnails with the pages in their memory. Therefore, thumbnails enhanced by distinctive visual elements are more effective.

Web page "caricatures" [20] represent Web pages by their titles, representative images, and so on. Their caricatures, however, do not show the original appearance of the pages, although the original appearance is very helpful when users match caricatures with the pages in their memory. Similarly, Clipping Lists [10] extracts the most important portions of application windows, and show them in the periphery on the display, but they also pointed out that their approach removes spatial layout information of windows, which must be useful for users. Our approach uses both thumbnails showing the original appearance and extracted important portions.

We first reported our idea of augmenting thumbnails with site logs and salient images in a bachelor thesis [8] and an unrefereed workshop paper [7]. Recently, Teevan et al. have also proposed very similar idea in [17]. They use titles, site logos, and salient images to create compact *visual snippet* of Web pages. Their experiments have confirmed that their visual snippets are more useful than ordinary thumbnails, especially when users revisit some known pages.

AUGMENTED THUMBNAILS
In this section, we first analyze advantages and disadvantages of existing methods of representing windows or pages, and explain in more detail why our augmented thumbnails explained in the introduction solve these disadvantages. Next, we discuss what kind of page elements are the most useful to augment thumbnails, and then we explain our heuristic method of extracting such salient elements from Web pages.

Why Augmented Thumbnails?
Existing systems use some GUI objects as buttons for switching windows or pages. Some systems show titles in those GUI objects, and other systems show icons or thumbnails. While titles are text, icons and thumbnails are visual representation. Because humans have very high ability for remembering and recognizing visual representation, icons and thumbnails have long been used in various kinds of user interface. It has been shown that thumbnails are also very effective for documents or Web pages [15, 19].

Text and icons/thumbnails also differ in the shape of regions needed to display them on screens. To display text titles, long narrow boxes are usually used. On the other hand, icons or thumbnails usually have shapes which are closer to squares. According to [9], square regions are easier to point to than long narrow rectangles of the same area size.

Although we use thumbnails because of these two advantages, one disadvantage of thumbnails is that they are often redundant and include much unnecessary information, while text is usually more compact representation including only necessary information. Their size on screens is not a problem for us because our purpose is to leverage extra space on wide displays, but the redundancy may cause inefficiency in users' recognition of the information. We expect that our augmented thumbnails, which emphasize important parts in the Web pages, alleviate this problem.

One problem common to all these three types of representation is that windows or pages represented by them are sometimes indistinguishable. In systems that show titles in buttons or tabs, we usually show only their beginning parts. When we have many buttons or tabs, shown parts often become too short to understand its meaning. Furthermore, if some titles share a common prefix, they may become completely indistinguishable. As many sites prefix the site names

Figure 4. Top Parts of Two Pages

Figure 5. Lower Parts of The Pages

Figure 6. Their Augmented Thumbnails

to the titles of their pages, this situation happens very often. Similarly, in systems that use icons, windows of the same application, or pages from the same site are usually represented by the same icon, and thus indistinguishable.

Thumbnails of windows or pages are also sometimes indistinguishable, e.g., when they are full of text without salient layout structure. In addition, even when there are some distinctive parts, if thumbnails do not include those parts, we have the same problem. Therefore, how to choose parts to include in thumbnails is an important issue.

There are two approaches used in the existing systems. First, Microsoft Windows Vista or Exposé of Mac OS produces thumbnails of windows by using their current views. However, "the currently focused part" is not necessarily the most distinctive nor the most impressive parts of the page. For example, many pages from news Web sites or Wikipedia include some distinctive images only at the top parts, and the lower parts are full of text in a similar layout. Therefore, if we create thumbnails when a user is reading their lower parts, we cannot distinguish their thumbnails. For example, two Wikipedia pages shown in Figure 4 have distinctive photos at their tops, but thumbnails created from their lower parts are indistinguishable, as shown in Figure 5.

On the other hand, many file browsers create thumbnails of PDF or Word files by using their first pages. This does not always work, either. Many technical documents have similar appearance in their first pages (e.g., titles and authors), and include salient figures mainly in the later pages.

In this way, the most distinctive parts of documents differ from documents to documents. Therefore, in order to create distinguishable thumbnails, we need to automatically detect the most distinctive elements in th given documents.

In addition, distinctive elements in Web pages are sometimes so small that we cannot recognize them when their size is reduced in thumbnails. In such cases, thumbnails may become indistinguishable even if they include those distinctive elements. One approach to this problem is to change the resizing factor depending on the importance of each component, just as in the well-known fisheye visualization. Fisheye visualization, however, destructs the original appearance of

pages, which is also useful for users to recognize the thumbnails. To avoid that, we use a special reducing factor only for two distinctive elements for each page, as explained later.

What Elements to Extract for Augmentation?

An important issue in our approach is what page elements are most useful for augmenting thumbnails. We augment thumbnails in order to make them distinguishable from the other currently shown thumbnails. In that sense, we should select distinctive elements by comparing the Web page with the other opened Web pages. Such an approach, however, has the following drawback. If we emphasize different elements in a thumbnail of the same page depending on the other currently opened pages, it confuses the user. For example, suppose we open a page p_1, show its thumbnail, then close p_1, also open or close some other pages, and then re-open p_1. In that case, it is not a good idea to choose different elements from p_1 when it is first opened and when it is re-opened later, even if the set of opened pages has changed.

Therefore, we select elements from Web pages independently of the other opened pages. In order to choose elements that are useful in most cases irrespective of other opened pages, we consider the following two typical situations, which cover most cases where a user opens many Web pages:

- The user is collecting or comparing information on something, and opens many pages on it from various Web sites.

- The user is searching something in some Web site, and opens many pages of that site.

For example, a user who wants to buy an iPod usually compares prices by viewing pages of iPod from many online shopping sites. Main images of those pages may be identical, i.e., the image of iPod provided by Apple Inc. In such a case, logo images of the online shopping sites are very useful to distinguish those pages. On the other hand, when a user wants to buy some books about iPod programming, he may open many pages of Amazon. Similarly, when a user collects information about something from Wikipedia, he may open many pages of Wikipedia. In these cases, the site logos are useless, and main images of these pages are more useful.

Considering these two cases, we extract two elements from each page: an element representing its site logo, and a main image related to the topic of the page. We call the latter *the featured image* of the page. Figure 6 shows augmented thumbnails of the two Wikipedia pages in Figure 4, and Figure 7 shows augmented thumbnails of two pages about the same product but from two different online shopping sites.

Logo and Featured Image Extraction

In this research, we extract site logos and featured images by using heuristics based on the properties of HTML elements listed in Table 1. When computing offsets, we exclude the margin width because page margin varies depending on the browser window size. We create *featureStr* by extracting strings surrounded by predefined delimiter characters.

Our method uses constraints and scoring functions. Given

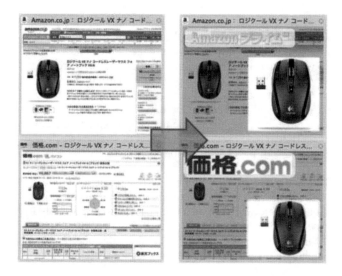

Figure 7. Two Pages on the Same Product from Two Sites

Table 1. Properties Used by Heuristics

area	(width * height) of the element
aspect	(width / height) of the element
hOffset	horizontal offset in pixels from the left edge of the page to the left edge of the element
hOffsetC	horizontal offset in pixels from the center of the page to the center of the element
vOffset	vertical offset in pixels from the top edge of the page to the top edge of the element
tag	tag name of the element, such as `img` or `div`
featureStr	a set of strings extracted from CSS class name, `href` value, and `src` value

Table 2. Precision of Logo and Featured Image Extraction

	Logo	Featured Image
# of pages	62	62
# of pages with no answer	0	22
Precision	83%	76%

a Web page, we first collect elements in it that satisfy the constraints. Then we compute a score of each of them, and select the one with the highest score. If no element has a score higher than a predefined threshold, no element is chosen. A score is given by the weighted sum of scores defined for each property above. We manually tuned weights and thresholds, but we plan to determine more appropriate values by machine learning with larger data set in future work.

For extracting logo elements, we use the following constraint:

$$
\begin{aligned}
500 &\leq area \leq 40000 \\
1 &\leq aspect \leq 8 \\
-100 &\leq hOffset \leq 0.5 * \text{page width} \\
-100 &\leq vOffset \leq 200
\end{aligned}
$$

Negative offsets are used in many pages for various tricks. For elements satisfying these constraints, we compute scores by using the following formula:

$$ score = areaScr * 2 + offsetScr + tagScr + strScr $$

where

$$
\begin{aligned}
areaScr &= area/10000 && \text{if } area \leq 10000 \\
&= 9/8 - (area/80000) && \text{if } 10000 < area < 90000 \\
&= 0 && \text{if } 90000 \leq area \\
vFactor &= (250 - vOffset)/100 && \text{if } vOffset > 150 \\
&= 1 && \text{otherwise} \\
offsetScr &= vFactor && \text{if } hOffset \leq 1/4 * \text{page width} \\
&= vFactor && \text{if } |hOffsetC| \leq 50 \\
&= vFactor*0.5 && \text{if between two regions above} \\
&= vFactor*0.2 && \text{otherwise} \\
tagScr &= 1 && \text{if } tag=\texttt{img} \\
&= 0 && \text{otherwise} \\
strScr &= 3 && \text{if "logo"} \in featureStr \\
&= -3 && \text{else if "ad"} \in featureStr \\
&= -1.5 && \text{else if "ad*"} \in featureStr \\
&= -1.5 && \text{else if "banner*"} \in featureStr \\
&= 0 && \text{otherwise}
\end{aligned}
$$

We give bigger scores to `img` elements, but do not exclude other tags because many pages represent site logos by `a` tags or `div` tags, with style sheets assigning images to them. There are also site logos represented by text.

For featured images, we use the following constraints:

$$
\begin{aligned}
-100 &\leq hOffset \\
80 &\leq vOffset \leq 1000 \\
tag &= \texttt{img}
\end{aligned}
$$

and use the following score function:

$$ score = aspectScr + areaScr + offsetScr + strScr $$

where

$$
\begin{aligned}
aspectScr &= aspect && \text{if } aspect \leq 1 \\
&= 1/aspect && \text{otherwise} \\
areaScr &= area/50000 && \text{if } area < 50000 \\
&= \max(0, (250000 - area)/200000) && \text{otherwise} \\
hFactor &= 0.7 && \text{if } hOffset < \text{body width}/8 \\
&= 1.0 && \text{else if } hOffsetC < 0 \\
&= 0.5 && \text{otherwise} \\
vFactor &= vOffset/150 && \text{if } vOffset < 150 \\
&= (1000 - vOffset)/850 && \text{otherwise} \\
offsetScr &= (hFactor + 2 * vFactor)/3 \\
strScr &= 2 && \text{if "product"} \in featureStr \\
&= -5 && \text{else if "ad"} \in featureStr \\
&= -1.5 && \text{else if "ad*"} \in featureStr \\
&= -3 && \text{else if "banner*"} \in featureStr
\end{aligned}
$$

We evaluated the accuracy of our method by using a data set collected in the following way. First, we select the top 100 sites of the traffic-based access ranking published by Alexa.com. From this list, we removed a couple of inappropriate sites (porn sites) and duplicate sites (e.g., google.com and google.co.jp), and instead, we added 4 sites that are popular in Japan (social network service, video sharing, online shopping, message board). Then we create a page set by choosing two representative pages from each site (or only one page if all pages of the sites have same layouts). The correctness of extracted elements was judged manually. The results are shown in Table 2. When a page does not have an appropriate element to extract, we excluded it from the calculation of the precision. The number of such pages are shown in the third row of the table. Notice that the precision shown in this table means how often we can extract the most appropriate elements. Our method sometimes extract the second or third best ones, which are often useful enough for users to distinguish pages, but they are not regarded as correct answers in the calculation of the precision.

EMPHASIZING RELEVANT THUMBNAILS

As we explained, one of the best-known and very successful approaches to task management in window systems is to provide multiple virtual workspaces. Users can create one workspace for each task, and assign windows related to a task to the corresponding workspace. Then, while a user is working on a task, he only sees its working set, i.e., the windows (and icons or buttons for them) related to that task. This reduces the number of window icons or buttons to scan when the user wants to switch to another window in the same task. In addition, when the user wants to switch to another task, he switches the workspace to the corresponding one. By that, the user can switch not only from a window to a window, but also from a working set to a working set.

That approach, however, requires additional cost of managing workspaces and assigning windows to them. In order to provide users with similar benefit without that cost, we introduce automatic task management where we dynamically emphasize thumbnails that are likely to be of interest to the user at the time. Another advantage of this approach over the virtual workspace approach is that we can handle pages belonging to multiple working sets more naturally.

Here, we assume a user wants to see the thumbnails of the following two sets of pages:

- pages to which the user wants to switch next, or

- pages involved in the working set of the current task.

We emphasize the former in order to help users switch pages. We emphasize the latter in order to provide the overview of the current task. Notice that the former may include some pages in other working sets. In the multiple workspace approach, we usually provide a separate function for switching workspaces, and for switching windows within a workspace. On the other hand, in our approach, we emphasize these two kinds of pages in order to help users perform these two kinds of operations. When a user switches to a page in another task, soon all the pages in that task are emphasized, so the user can switch from a working set to a working set, as in the multiple workspace approach.

In this section, we first describe how we predict such pages, and then we explain how we emphasize their thumbnails.

Estimation of Relevance between Pages

Both of the two page sets above are difficult to predict accurately, so we model those two sets as fuzzy sets, and for each page, we compute its membership degree to the two

fuzzy sets. For the former set, we approximate the membership degree of each page by the probability of page switching from the current page to that page, which takes a value between 0 and 1 inclusive. For the latter set, we approximate the membership degree of a page to the current working set by the relevance between the page and the currently focused page, which also takes a value between 0 and 1. Then, for each page, we compute its membership degree to the union of these two fuzzy sets, and based on this value, we display thumbnails of pages with various emphasis degree.

This is the basic idea, but in the current implementation, we further approximate the membership degree to the former set by the relevance between each page and the currently focused page, i.e., the same value as the membership degree to the latter set. Therefore, we just compute this one value, and emphasize page thumbnails in accordance with this value.

Now we explain how we compute the relevance between two pages. Suppose we have n pages denoted by $p_1, \ldots, p_n$. Then we store users' page switching history in an array H of the following form:

$$H = [p_{h_1}, p_{h_2}, \ldots, p_{h_l}].$$

That is, if the user switched from p_8 to p_5 at the second page switching, $h_2 = 8$ and $h_3 = 5$. The length of the currently available switching history is denoted by l.

Then, for each pair of p_i and p_j, we first compute $r_{i,j}$ defined by the following formula:

$$r_{i,j} = \frac{|switch(i,j) \cup switch(j,i)|}{|pre(p_i) \cup post(p_i) \cup pre(p_j) \cup post(p_j)|}$$

where

$$
\begin{aligned}
switch(i,j) &= \{t \mid 1 \le t \le l-1, h_t = i, h_{t+1} = j\} \\
pre(i) &= \{t \mid 1 \le t \le l-1, h_t = i\} \\
post(i) &= \{t \mid 1 \le t \le l-1, h_{t+1} = i\}
\end{aligned}
$$

That is, $r_{i,j}$ is the ratio of page switching between p_i and p_j to all page switching from/to p_i or p_j. Notice that $r_{i,j} = r_{j,i}$.

$r_{i,j}$ is a primary approximation of the relevance between p_i and p_j, and we refine $r_{i,j}$ into $s_{i,j}$ as follows. Let P be a $n \times n$ matrix whose i,j entry is $r_{i,j}$. We compute the refined approximation $s_{i,j}$ by computing another $n \times n$ matrix Q, whose i,j entry gives $s_{i,j}$, defined by the following formula:

$$Q = (1 - \epsilon)P + \epsilon * P \times P$$

$P \times P$ is the relevance between pages intermediated by some other pages, and we take a weighted average of P and $P \times P$. In another interpretation, if we regard $r_{i,j}$ as the probability of page switch from p_i to p_j, P is the transition matrix of page switching sequence modeled as a Markov chain, and the refined approximation $s_{i,j}$ takes into consideration the page switch in two steps. Inclusion of two-hop switches is effective to compensate the approximation especially when we do not have a long enough history data. It also captures the cases where the user opens several pages, which are related to each other, from a hub page such as a search result

Table 3. Accuracy of Our Page Switch Prediction

rank	1	2	3	4	5	all zero	total
# of switches	23	21	16	5	2	35	102

page. In such a case, the user may switch among those related pages only in two steps through that "hub" page.

There are various other factors we should take into consideration when computing page relevance. Because of the space limitation, here, we only briefly explain how we can include the following two factors: task evolution and link navigation.

When we perform tasks, they often evolve. For example, one complicated task might break up into several subtasks for ease to handle, and the subtasks might be merged into a single task back again when their complexities are reduced to an acceptable level. There are also cases where the original goal of a task evolves during the process. If we want to take this aspect into consideration, we can apply sliding windows to the switching history data. In order to keep enough information on each page pair, we use a separate window for each page pair. That is, for each page pair (p_i, p_j), we record a predefined number of the most recent switches including p_i or p_j. In addition to the sliding windows, we can also give bonus scores to the last two pages in the history. This bonus score is especially effective when working sets are very small, such as consisting of two or three pages.

As we focus on Web browsing in this research, we also should pay more attention to features of Web pages. The most important feature of Web pages is that they are connected by links, and users open new pages mainly by following links [18]. The most typical scenario is opening new tabs or windows to load pages linked from some kind of a hub page, e.g., a search result page. In such a case, the new page and the hub page are usually in the same working set. In addition, after opening the new page, with a very high probability, the user immediately returns to the hub page either to try another link or to close the hub page. Following this observation, when a user open a new page p_j by following a link in a page p_i, we give a bonus score to that page pair. In the current implementation, we always set their relevance to 1.0.

As a preliminary experiment to measure the accuracy of our relevant page prediction method, we recorded the page switching history of a user (the first author of the paper) in the daily use, and calculated how often the user switched to the page that had the highest predicted relevance. We started to record the history when there were 12 opened pages, and recorded 102 page switches to some already opened pages. We did not include page switches opening new pages because our method cannot predict relevance of such new pages, and in addition, when users switch to new pages, even if we emphasize wrong thumbnails of already opened pages, it does not hinder users in opening new pages.

Among the recorded 102 page switches, in 35 switches, all the thumbnails had relevance 0. This happens when there is no opened page from/to which the user had ever switched to/from the current page. For example, the user may open a

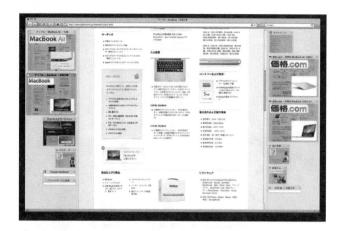

Figure 8. Dynamic-Size Mode

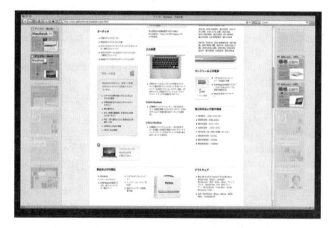

Figure 9. Dynamic-Opacity Mode

new page p_1 from some page p_0, and then close p_0. In 23 switches, our method was correctly giving the highest relevance to the page to which the user actually switched. Similarly, in 21, 16, 5, and 2 switches, the user actually switched to pages with the second, third, fourth, and fifth highest relevance. The average number of opened pages in these 102 switches was 11.9. The result is summarized in Table 3.

In this experiment, the correct answer was never ranked at 6 or lower, while there were 11.9 pages in average. On the other hand, we could not predict any page relevance in 35 cases. This is because we use only information on the switching history. In future work, we will improve our method by also including information on the page contents.

How to Emphasize Thumbnails
Given the relevance, we emphasize thumbnails of pages with higher relevance. We propose two ways to emphasize them.

Dynamic-size mode: In dynamic-size mode, thumbnails are shown in size that is proportional to the relevance to the currently focused page, as shown in Figure 8. This has two advantages. First, larger thumbnails draw more attention, and it shortens the time to find it. Secondly, larger thumbnails are easier to select by pointing devices.

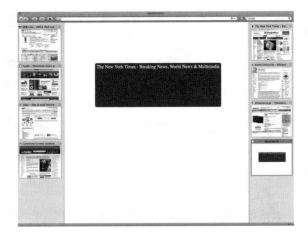

Figure 10. Screenshot in Experiment 1

Dynamic-opacity mode: In dynamic-opacity mode, opacity of thumbnails are changed in accordance with the relevance, as shown in Figure 9. As in the dynamic-size mode, thumbnails with higher opacity draw more attention, and thus shorten the time to find needed pages.

USER EXPERIMENTS

We implemented a research prototype as a Firefox add-on. To validate our approach, we conducted two experiments:

Experiment 1 : We measured page switching time in order to quantatively evaluate the effectiveness of our method.

Experiment 2 : We obtained subjective feedbacks from users of the prototype by semi-structured interviews.

We had 9 participants, 8 males and 1 female, from 22 to 26 years old, all undergraduate or graduate students in engineering, and experienced Web browser users. The experiment environment consists of a Macbook Pro and a 24-inch LCD with 1920×1200 pixels. We asked all participants to use a prepared Logicool mouse. Because all experiments were run on a Firefox window, Microsoft Windows users experienced no unfamiliarity. In these experiments, we did not use sliding windows for switching history because the task scenarios used in the experiments includes no task evolution.

Experiment 1

In Experiment 1, we measured page switching time for three methods of showing opened Web pages: tabs, ordinary thumbnails, and our augmented thumbnails. In each case, we used two page sets consisting of 7 pages and 15 pages. Therefore, each user had $3 * 2 = 6$ experiment runs. After each run, we had a one-minute break. In each run, the participant is asked to perform page switch 50 times. At each switch, title of some opened page is displayed at the center of the screen as shown in Figure 10. If the participant switches to a correct page, he is asked to move the cursor back to the center of the screen, and then, the title of the next target page is shown. If the participant switches to a wrong page, an error message is shown, and the participant has to select a page again.

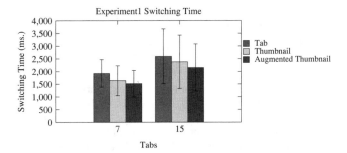

Figure 11. Result of Experiment 1: Switching Time

Table 4. Result of Experiment 1 (μ = average, σ = standard deviation)

	switching time			
	7 pages		15 pages	
	μ	σ	μ	σ
tabs	1928	542	2592	1079
thumbnails	1637	591	2376	1051
augmented thumbnails	1520	525	2152	929

We used page sets consisting of 7 pages because 7 is the average working memory volume. Therefore, in runs with 7 pages, we expect that users remember locations of most tabs or thumbnails. On the other hand, users usually cannot remember locations of all 15 tabs or thumbnails. We used the same page set in three runs for 7 pages, and another page set in three runs for 15 pages, in order to make a fair comparison of tabs, thumbnails, and augmented thumbnails, but we use different pages in these two page sets in order to avoid memorization of pages. We also interlaced 3 runs for 7 pages and 3 runs for 15 pages so that participants cannot use the memory from the previous runs with the same page set. To further avoid order influence, we shuffled the order of runs for tabs, thumbnails, and augmented thumbnails. Before starting the experiment, participants had several minutes to browse the page contents and remember the page titles.

We used pages whose logos and featured images were correctly extracted in order to isolate and measure the effectiveness of augmented thumbnails. In addition, we chose pages whose titles never share the same prefix because such pages can make tabs especially useless. Because search engines are so frequently used, we included search result pages of Google initiated by various keywords in each set.

Table 4 and Figure 11 shows the results. We excluded outliers, which are less than 0.8 sec or greater than 8 sec, from the statistics in order to exclude cases where the user happened to click on the correct thumbnails by mistake, and cases where the user could not concentrate on the experiment. The excluded outliers were less than 5% of the data. Below is the summary of the results:

- Thumbnails achieved shorter switching time than tabs with a significant difference (in t-test, t=7.225 and p=1.183e-12 for 7 pages; t=2.8493 and p=4.496e-3 for 15 pages).

- Augmented thumbnails achieved even shorter switching

time than thumbnails with a significant difference (t=2.9629, p=3.14e-3 for 7 pages; t=3.1849, p=1.505e-3 for 15 pages).

- Even in the experiments with 7 pages, where the participants can remember locations of most thumbnails, augmented thumbnails outperformed thumbnails.

Experiment 2

In Experiment 2, we asked participants to use our prototype to perform a simple multitask scenario, and after that, we conducted a semi-structured interview. In the scenario, the participants switch among the following four working sets.

- Compare the specification of Macbook and Macbook Air, and read some review threads about them.

- Collect information from pages about the biography and the past career of Barack Obama.

- Find similarities among four famous people in the history of Kyoto University.

- Collect information from Google's top results for "Olympic 2008".

In order to simulate frequent interruptions in the real world, we made a sign for participants to switch to the next working set every three minutes. To compare dynamic-size mode and dynamic-opacity mode, half of users start with the former, while the other half start with the latter, and we asked users to switch the mode in the middle of the experiment.

After the completion of the task, we interviewed participants, and asked them to respond to a questionnaire consisting of 17 queries. In the questionnaire, the participants choose their answers from five-level Likert measure: agree, partly agree, hard to say, partly disagree, disagree. We assign values 5 to 1 to these options. Table 5 shows the results. For Q4 and Q5, we had answers from only 6 participants.

The result of Q1 shows that our system was preferred over ordinary tab-browsers for page switching. Q2 and Q3 also show that thumbnail enlarging was effective. However, Q4 and Q5 show that dynamic-opacity mode was not very effective. According to the interview, this is because User 1 and 2 did not notice the change of opacity, or could not immediately understand what it means. User 5 and 7 also pointed out that thumbnails in dynamic-opacity mode were sometimes too transparent to recognize. On the other hand, User 1 and 2 also showed disfavor towards location changes caused by size change in dynamic-size mode, while User 4 and 7 were not concerned with it. The result of Q6 reflects these results. The result of Q9 shows that augmented thumbnails do not compromise the visibility of ordinary thumbnails. Q10 to Q12 also confirmed that our system is easy to use, Q13 to Q15 confirmed the overall usefulness of our system, and Q16 shows high satisfaction of the participants.

DISCUSSION AND CONCLUSION

In this research, we proposed a new method of supporting efficient task management in Web browsing on wide displays. First, we proposed augmented thumbnails, and sec-

Table 5. Questionnaire Results (μ = average, σ = standard deviation)

Page Switching	μ	σ
Q1. Our system makes page switching faster than ordinary tab-browsers.	4.50	0.71
Q2. In dynamic-size mode, the thumbnail of the page to switch to was enlarged.	4.00	0.50
Q3. Larger thumbnails are easier to find.	4.63	0.89
Q4. In dynamic-opacity mode, the thumbnail of the page to switch to was more opaque.	3.67	0.78
Q5. More opaque thumbnails are easier to find.	3.33	0.91
Q6. Change of size and location of thumbnails upon page switching does not cause a problem.	2.13	0.94
Thumbnails	μ	σ
Q7. Thumbnails are easier to find than tabs.	4.63	0.48
Q8. Augmented thumbnails are easier to distinguish and easier to find than ordinary thumbnails.	4.63	0.48
Q9. Overlaying logos and featured images does not make it harder to see the page contents.	4.00	0.79
Usage Easiness	μ	σ
Q10. This system is easy to use.	4.75	0.71
Q11. The usage of this system is easy to learn	4.38	0.48
Q12. The usage of this system is easy to remember	4.38	0.48
Usefulness	μ	σ
Q13. This system is useful.	4.50	0.71
Q14. This system makes page switch easier.	4.38	0.67
Q15. This system improves the productivity.	4.00	0.61
Overall Satisfaction	μ	σ
Q16. I am satisfied with this system.	4.25	0.61
Q17. I will use this system if I have a wide display.	4.38	0.82

ondly, we proposed automatic task management by emphasizing pages that have higher predicted relevance to the current task, instead of manual task management like multiple virtual workspaces. Experiment 1 quantatively attests that our system are more useful than tabs or ordinary thumbnails in page switching. Despite the importance of spatial memory, augmented thumbnails are more efficient than ordinary thumbnails, even when there are only 7 pages, which means users can remember positions of most thumbnails. We suppose that users take time to confirm the identity of thumbnails after they quickly locate them by using spatial memory, and in this final confirmation stage, augmented thumbnails require shorter time than ordinary thumbnails. The result of Experiment 2 also shows the participants have strong preference for augmented thumbnails over ordinary thumbnails.

We tested two methods of emphasizing thumbnails: changing their size, and changing their opacity. According to Experiment 2, the main problem of dynamic-size mode is the location changes caused by size changes. Oliver et al. has reported that the change of the order of window thumbnails can deteriorate the efficiency of users window switching because spatial memory of users plays an important role in window switching [11]. In our dynamic-size mode, the order of thumbnails does not change, but even moderate location change invalidated users' spatial memory.

On the other hand, dynamic-opacity mode is disfavored by some users because thumbnails are sometimes too transparent to recognize. To solve this problem, we should use a higher minimum value for the opacity. However, there were also users who did not notice the opacity change. Therefore, we need to fine-tune the function to compute the opacity, and in that computation, we may need to consider visual properties of pages, such as, their background colors.

There were also users who did not understand that our system was emphasizing relevant pages. We should improve the way to emphasize thumbnails so that new users can soon understand the meaning of the emphasis even without explicit explanation. Some participants also suggested that showing thumbnails at the both ends of wide displays may harm efficiency of page switching. In order to solve this problem, we need to improve the screen layout of our system.

Another problem we found so far is that many pages are switched to for only a few times before closed. In that case, its relevance to other pages cannot be predicted correctly. In future work, we plan to leverage content similarity between pages to improve the prediction accuracy. In addition, we need more experiments to measure the accuracy of our page relevance prediction, and we also need experiments to confirm whether the thumbnail emphasis is really contributing to make users page switch faster in Experiment 1.

Application of our methods to other contexts, such as file browsers, window systems, or result pages of search engines, is also an interesting issue for future work.

ACKNOWLEDGEMENT

We would like to thank the anonymous reviewers for their valuable comments, which greatly improved the paper.

REFERENCES

1. M. Czerwinski, E. Horvitz, and S. Wilhite. A diary study of task switching and interruptions. In *Proc. of CHI*, pages 175–182, Apr. 2004.

2. A. N. Dragunov, T. G. Dietterich, K. Johnsrude, M. R. McLaughlin, L. Li, and J. L. Herlocker. TaskTracer: a desktop environment to support multi-tasking knowledge workers. In *Proc. of IUI*, pages 75–82, Jan. 2005.

3. V. M. González and G. Mark. "constant, constant, multi-tasking craziness": managing multiple working spheres. In *Proc. of CHI*, pages 113–120, Apr. 2004.

4. D. A. Henderson, Jr. and S. Card. Rooms: the use of multiple virtual workspaces to reduce space contention in a window-based graphical user interface. *ACM Trans. Graph.*, 5(3):211–243, July 1986.

5. S. T. Iqbal and B. P. Bailey. Understanding and developing models for detecting and differentiating breakpoints during interactive tasks. In *Proc. of CHI*, pages 697–706, Apr.–May 2007.

6. E. W. Ishak and S. Feiner. Content-aware layout. In *CHI '07 Extended Abstracts on Human Factors in Computing Systems*, pages 2459–2464, Apr.–May 2007.

7. S. Liu and K. Tajima. Support of efficient task switching in Web browsing on large displays. In *DEIM*, Mar. 2009. (Unreferred workshop paper in Japanese. http://db-event.jpn.org/deim2009/proceedings/files/E4-6.pdf.)

8. S. Liu. WildTab: A Web browser supporting efficient task management on large displays. Bachelor thesis, Kyoto University, Feb. 2009. In Japanese.

9. I. S. MacKenzie and W. Buxton. Extending Fitts' law to two-dimensional tasks. In *Proc. of CHI*, pages 219–226, May 1992.

10. T. Matthews, M. Czerwinski, G. G. Robertson, and D. S. Tan. Clipping lists and change borders: improving multitasking efficiency with peripheral information design. In *Proc. of CHI*, pages 989–998, Apr. 2006.

11. N. Oliver, M. Czerwinski, G. Smith, and K. Roomp. RelAltTab: assisting users in switching windows. In *Proc. of IUI*, pages 385–388, Jan. 2008.

12. N. Oliver, G. Smith, C. Thakkar, and A. C. Surendran. SWISH: semantic analysis of window titles and switching history. In *Proc. of IUI*, pages 194–201, Jan.–Feb. 2006.

13. G. Robertson, M. Czerwinski, P. Baudisch, B. Meyers, D. Robbins, G. Smith, and D. Tan. The large-display user experience. *IEEE Comput. Graph. Appl.*, 25(4):44–51, Jul.–Aug 2005.

14. G. Robertson, E. Horvitz, M. Czerwinski, P. Baudisch, D. R. Hutchings, B. Meyers, D. C. Robbins, and G. Smith. Scalable Fabric: flexible task management. In *Proc. of AVI*, pages 85–89, May 2004.

15. G. G. Robertson, M. Czerwinski, K. Larson, D. C. Robbins, D. Thiel, and M. van Dantzich. Data Mountain: Using spatial memory for document management. In *Proc. of UIST*, pages 153–162, Nov. 1998.

16. G. Smith, P. Bausdich, G. Robertson, M. Czerwinski, B. Meyers, D. Robbins, and D. Andrews. GroupBar: The TaskBar evolved. In *Proc. of OZCHI*, pages 34–43, Jan. 2003.

17. J. Teevan, E. Cutrell, D. Fisher, S. M. Drucker, G. Ramos, P. André, and C. Hu. Visual snippets: summarizing Web pages for search and revisitation. In *Proc. of CHI*, pages 2023–2032, Apr. 2009.

18. H. Weinreich, H. Obendorf, E. Herder, and M. Mayer. Not quite the average: An empirical study of Web use. *ACM Trans. Web*, 2(1):1–31, Feb. 2008.

19. A. Woodruff, A. Faulring, R. Rosenholtz, J. Morrsion, and P. Pirolli. Using thumbnails to search the Web. In *Proc. of CHI*, pages 198–205, Apr. 2001.

20. M. J. Wynblatt and D. Benson. Web page caricatures: Multimedia summaries for WWW documents. In *Proc. of IEEE Intl. Conf. on Multimedia Computing and Systems*, pages 194–199, June–July 1998.

Lowering the Barriers to Website Testing with CoTester

Jalal Mahmud and Tessa Lau

IBM Almaden Research Center
650 Harry Rd,
San Jose, CA 95120, USA
{jumahmud, tessalau}@us.ibm.com

ABSTRACT

In this paper, we present CoTester, a system designed to decrease the difficulty of testing web applications. CoTester allows testers to create test scripts that are represented in an easy-to-understand scripting language rather than a complex programming language, which allows tests to be created rapidly and by non-developers. CoTester improves the management of test scripts by grouping sequences of low-level actions into subroutines, such as "log in" or "check out shopping cart", which help testers visualize test structure and make bulk modifications. A key innovation in CoTester is its ability to automatically identify these subroutines using a machine learning algorithm. Our algorithm is able to achieve 91% accuracy at recognizing a set of 7 representative subroutines commonly found in test scripts.

ACM Classification Keywords

H.3.3 Information Systems: Search and Retrieval; H.5.2 Information Interfaces and Presentation: User Interfaces

General Terms

Algorithms, Design, Human Factors, Experimentation

Author Keywords

Website Testing, Test Script, Instruction, Subroutine

INTRODUCTION

The web has become an indispensible part of our daily activities. As more and more applications move to the web, there is a growing need for tools to assist with web application development and testing. However, today's web testing tools, such as Rational's Functional Tester [3] and HP's Mercury [2], present several barriers to use. First, they require programming ability: tests are recorded in programming languages such as Java or Visual Basic. Second, maintaining a corpus of tests can be time-consuming, particularly during iterative development as applications change and tests need to be kept in sync. As a result of these barriers, testing tools are not as widely used as they could be.

CoTester, which is built on the CoScripter [17, 16] platform, provides testers with features specifically targeted at functional web testing, including test management and support for assertions. By applying CoScripter's easy-to-understand scripting language (ClearScript) to the domain of web testing, CoTester enables testers with a wide variety of skill levels to create and maintain test scripts. CoTester extends the ClearScript language with support for assertions [18], which are an important aspect of functional testing.

Once a set of tests has been created, they may need to be updated frequently as the application under test (*e.g.*, a website) changes. Updating tests may require much manual effort by testers, who have to manually inspect each test and make the required changes to update it for the new application. Global search and update is typically not sufficient in these cases. For example, a web application may change its checkout process such that a new checkbox "notify by email" is added to the checkout page. If the checkout process could be automatically identified, a tester would be able to easily add an assertion to test the presence of this checkbox across all instances of this process. As another example, a tester may want to add an assertion after the login process to check that a user has successfully logged in to the website. This can not be done automatically unless the login process is identified from the test scripts.

Subroutines group together a sequence of low-level actions within a test (*e.g.*, entering a username, entering a password, and clicking on a "Sign in" button) into a conceptual unit representing a higher-level action, such as "Log in to the website". They enable better test management and help testers visualize test structure. For example, Figure 2 shows the subroutines identified from the scripts in Figure 1. Subroutines have the promise to make test maintenance easier by enabling testers to automatically apply a similar change to all instances of a subroutine across all test scripts. For example, the instruction *check the "notify by email" checkbox* in a checkout subroutine could be added automatically across all the test scripts which have a checkout process. In addition, assertions [18] could be automatically added to the start/end of each subroutine to ensure that certain conditions hold before/after every instance of the subroutine (*e.g.*, asserting that the user's name is displayed on the page after a login has been completed, asserting that a radiobutton "delivery method" is present before the checkout).

- go to "http://www.southwest.com"
- click the "MySouthwest Login" link
- enter "678899532" into the "Account Number" textbox
- enter your password into the second textbox
- turn on the "Remember my account number for future login." checkbox
- click the "Login" button
- assert there is an element containing "Account"
- click the "Online Checkin" link

(a)

- go to "http://www.southwest.com"
- click the "Book Travel" link
- assert there is an element containing "My Southwest Login"
- enter "456712345" into the "Account Number" textbox
- assert there is a "Password" textbox
- enter your password into the "Password" textbox
- click the "Login" button
- assert there is an element containing "Account Snapshot"

(b)

Figure 1. Example test scripts for two tasks on southwest.com

---

* go to "http://www.southwest.com"

Login

   * click the "MySouthwest Login" link

   * enter "678899532" into the "Account Number" textbox

   * enter your password into the second textbox

   * "turn on the "Remember my account number for future login." checkbox

   * click the "Login" button

   * assert there is an element containing "Account"

* click the "Online Checkin" link

(a)

* go to "http://www.southwest.com"

* click the "Book Travel" link

Login

   * assert there is an element containing "My Southwest Login"

   * enter "456712345" into the "Account Number" textbox

   * assert there is a "Password" textbox

   * enter your password into the "Password" textbox

   * click the "Login" button

   * assert there is an element containing "Account Snapshot"

(b)

Figure 2. Subroutine identified from scripts in Figure 1. Instructions grouped together as a subroutine are shown as right indented under the subroutine.

To help testers maintain large corpora of test scripts, we have designed and implemented a machine learning algorithm to *automatically identify subroutines* in test scripts. Using apriori labelled samples of subroutines collected from a number of scripts, we learn models of subroutines. Such models are used to automatically recognize subroutines within a test script.

In this paper, we make the following contributions:

- An implemented system, CoTester, which builds on Co-Scripter [17, 16] to provide a lightweight, easy-to-use system for web test automation.

- Extensions to the ClearScript language for representing assertions, which are fundamental for functional testing.

- A machine learning algorithm for automatic subroutine identification from test scripts.

- An empirical evaluation of our algorithm, showing that it is capable of recognizing a set of 7 subroutines with 91% accuracy when the algorithm is trained and tested on scripts recorded from the same website.

RELATED WORK
Here we present prior work related to our contributions.

Website Testing Tools
There are a number of commercial and open source tools available which assist in the automation of web testing [3, 21, 1]. Most of the commercial testing tools (*e.g.*, SilkTest [1], Rational Functional Tester (RFT) [3]) are made for website developers and testers with programming knowledge. For example, SilkTest [1], developed by Borland Software, uses the proprietary 4Test language for automation scripting. Rational Functional Tester (RFT) [3] records test scripts in the Java language. HP's QuickTest [2] records test scripts

written in the Visual Basic language. Other functional testing tools include Selenium [21], Sahi [19], Concordian [7].

However, test scripts recorded by these tools require some amount of programming knowledge to be able to understand and edit them. In contrast, by leveraging CoScripter's [17, 16] easily understandable scripting language, CoTester enables testers without programming ability to create and edit test scripts. In addition, CoTester can improve test script maintenance by identifying the subroutines from test scripts. Most often developers do not use functional testing until the application is mostly complete, since the application changes too often during the development phase. Subroutine detection could improve test script maintenance during such a phase and thus enable testing during the iterative development of an application.

End User Programming and Task Learning
Subroutine identification from test scripts is related to research on programming by demonstration [8, 15], and task learning [4, 5, 6, 13, 10, 22, 12].

Programming by demonstration [8, 15] allows users to construct a program by simply performing actions in the user interface, with which they are already familiar. For example, Eager is a PBD system that observes a user executing a task one or more times and then infers a general procedure to do the task [8]. However, it assumes a fixed structure of the task (fixed number of steps, e.g., steps to fill out a form) and can generalize only if the user repeats the steps (e.g., a user may demonstrate the same sequence of steps multiple times and the system infers a general procedure). PBD trace generalization using a machine learning technique is described by Lau and Weld [15]. However, such generalization also learns a single pattern within a task and can not learn variability of the structure of the task, *e.g.*, different ways of doing a checkout in an e-commerce website, different ways of adding an item to a shopping cart. In contrast, subroutine learning learns conceptual units from already existing executable scripts. It does n't assume any fixed structure of the subroutine and can learn variance of the structure (i.e.

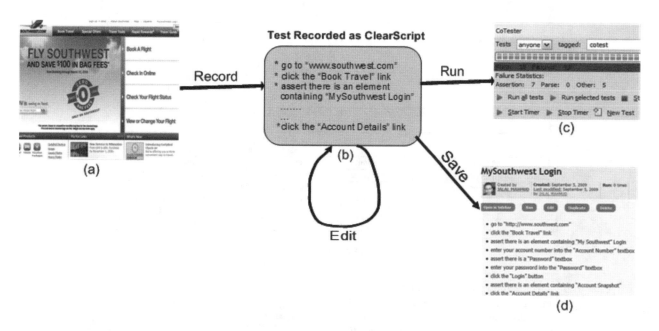

Figure 3. Testing using CoTester - (a) A webpage (b) Test script (c) CoTester sidebar (d) CoTester shared repository

sequence of instructions) of a subroutine from its instances collected from a number of test scripts. In addition, subroutine identification can identify one or more instances of subroutines from a test script, which is in contrast to PBD systems that can detect only one task at a time.

Task learning systems learn task models from users' examples. Huffman et al. illustrate how an intelligent agent can be taught to perform tasks [12]. Tailor [5] enables users to modify task information through instruction. A framework for learning hierarchical models of web service procedures is described in [6]. Sheepdog [13] learns procedures by demonstration by watching multiple experts performing the same procedure across different conditions. PLOW [4] is a collaborative task learning system that learns task models by demonstration, explanation, and dialog. Lapdog [10] learns procedures in emails from one or more examples. Spaulding et al. describe a task learning system that learns executable procedures from user demonstration and instruction [22].

Subroutine identification from test scripts is different from all of the above mentioned research in the following ways. First, task learning systems learn executable tasks from users actions. Their goal is to automate such tasks. Most of them use special semantics of a task (*e.g.*, precondition, postcondition) to learn the task models. In contrast, we learn conceptual units from already existing executable scripts to help testers visualize test structure and maintain test scripts. In addition, learning subroutines does not use the above mentioned special semantics. Second, most of the task learning systems require a lot of human interaction and language-rich demonstration from users as part of the learning process. In contrast, we try to minimize the amount of information user has to provide during the learning process.

However, the fundamental difference between our work and all of the above mentioned research is that subroutine identi-

fication from test scripts is focused on improving test script maintenance which is not the goal of the existing task learning systems. To the best of our knowledge, there is no prior research that automatically identifies such subroutines from scripts.

THE COTESTER SYSTEM

CoTester is built on top of CoScripter [17, 16] and allows testers to create test scripts that are represented in the ClearScript language, an easy-to-understand scripting language. To better support testing, we have extended the original ClearScript language used in CoScripter with assertions, which are used to test the presence or absence of elements on the page and are fundamental for functional testing. Table 1 shows examples of CoTester assertions.

Figure 3 illustrates a high level picture of the CoTester system. Figure 3 (a) shows the homepage of "www.southwest.com". The example test script of the picture is recorded from this website. The recording of such a script is done by doing actions on web pages, and generating an instruction for each of them (Figure 3 (b)). As users interact with the browser performing a process, CoTester records all the forms filled, links and buttons clicked, and generates instructions for each action. In addition, users can also insert assertions in a test script, and edit instructions. Assertions can be inserted in the following ways: i) manually editing the script, or ii) using our interface as illustrated in Figure 4. In Figure 4, a user first clicks the assert toolbar button of the sidebar. When the user is in assertion mode and moves the mouse pointer over a web page element, our system highlights that element by showing a red rectangle surrounding it. The user can click the highlighted element to insert an assertion. Therefore, highlighting and clicking "Manage Your Travel" inserts an assertion for this text in the script.

Type	Example
Presence of an Object	assert there is a link
	assert there is a button
	assert there is a checkbox
Absense of an Object	assert there is no link
	assert there is no radiobutton
	assert there is no listbox
Presence of an Object with a Caption	assert there is a "southwest" link
	assert there is a "go" button
Absense of an Object with a Caption	assert there is no "address" textbox
	assert there is no "Image Search" link
Presence of an Object with a Caption and a Value	assert there is a text "san jose" into the "city" textbox
Absense of an Object with a Caption and a Value	assert there is no "CA" into the "state" listbox
Presense of a Text	assert there is a td that contains "Please enter"
	assert there is a div that starts with "Almaden"
	assert there is an element that ends with "Click here"
Absense of a Text	assert there is no element that contains "Pay bill"

Table 1. CoTester Assertions

The CoTester user interface allows saving the recorded script in a centralized shared repository where a community of users can share, run and collaboratively develop test scripts (Figure 3 (d)). It also allows easy management of test scripts (Figure 3 (c)). Users can tag test scripts in the shared repository and select the scripts tagged by them, or anyone. They can run a single test script, or a batch of scripts. When a script is executed, each instruction (either assertion or regular instruction) is parsed and the Document Object Model [9] of the web page is analyzed to find the desired element. In case of a successful match of the element, the system highlights the matched element on the web page, and executes the instruction. However, in case of a non-match, the instruction is not executed and the test fails. If all such instructions are successful, we say that the result of the test is a "Success". Otherwise, it is a "Failure". When a test fails, the system outputs the reason for the failure (*e.g.*, could not find the element with label "Place Order"). Figure 5 shows the output of CoTester after a set of test scripts has been executed. After a batch of scripts have been run, users can save the test report as a spreadsheet (see Figure 6). In the next section, we will describe how subroutines from test scripts are identified.

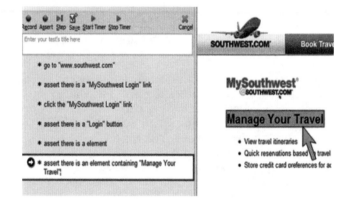

Figure 4. Inserting assertions to scripts using CoTester interface

SUBROUTINE IDENTIFICATION FROM TEST SCRIPTS

Once a set of tests has been created, they may need to be updated frequently as the website changes. To reduce the manual effort to update test scripts, we have designed and implemented a machine learning algortihm to identify subroutines from test scripts. Our algorithm could make test maintenance easier by enabling testers to automatically apply a similar change to all instances of a subroutine across all test scripts. In this section, we describe our subroutine identification algorithm. First, we discuss a few preliminary concepts.

Technical Preliminaries

The *Vector Space Model* (VSM) is widely used in Information Retrieval systems for document retrieval [20]. In this model, a document is represented as a vector, where each dimension corresponds to a separate term. Typically terms are single words, bigrams, trigrams, or even longer text strings.

Figure 5. Test Management using CoTester

	A	B		C
1	total tests completed	4		
2	total tests succeeded	2		
3	total tests failed	2		
4	total tests failed for assertion	1		
5	total tests failed for parse	1		
6				
7	Individual Test Statistics			
8				
9	Test Title	TimeStamp (hh:mm:ss m		Test Result
10				
11	Apply for San Jose Library Card	4::07::8pm	7/ 23/ 2009	Assertion Failure
12				
13	Change BluePages name capitalization	4::07::9pm	7/ 23/ 2009	Success
14				
15	Apply for San Jose Library card	4::07::22pm	7/ 23/ 2009	Success
16				
17	Find a San Jose library branch	4::07::27pm	7/ 23/ 2009	Parse Failure

Figure 6. An example test report saved by CoTester

Each term appearing in the document is assigned a non-negative weight. One popular weighting scheme is TF*IDF [20]. It uses the following expression to assign weights:

$$w_{t,d} = \text{tf}_t \cdot \log \frac{|D|}{|\{t \in d\}|} \qquad (1)$$

In the expression, $w_{t,d}$ is the weight of term t in document d; tf_t is the term frequency of term t in document d; $|D|$ is the total number of documents; $\log \frac{|D|}{|\{t \in d\}|}$ is the inverse document frequency; $|\{t \in d\}|$ is the total number of documents containing the term t.

Suppose $1, 2, .., N$ denote the terms of a document d. Then the weighted document vector $\mathbf{v}_d$ for d is:

$$\mathbf{v}_d = [w_{1,d}, w_{2,d}, \ldots, w_{N,d}] \qquad (2)$$

We use cosine similarity to measure the degree of "semantic closeness" between the two vectors. Given a query vector v_q, the cosine of the angle between this vector and a document vector d is the expression:

$$\cos \theta = \frac{\mathbf{v_q} \cdot \mathbf{v_d}}{\|\mathbf{v_q}\| \, \|\mathbf{v_d}\|} \qquad (3)$$

A value of 1 means the vectors are identical, and it is 0 if they are orthogonal. Two vectors are considered to be *similar* if their cosine similarity is above some set threshold.

We introduce the notion of an *Instruction-Class*, which is a class of similar instructions in test scripts and members of which perform similar functions across tests (*e.g.*, entering a password into a textbox in a login form). We map each instruction i_j in a script to an Instruction-Class $IC(i_j)$. For example, the instruction *enter "12345" into the second textbox* is different from the instruction *enter "xyzabc" into the "Password" textbox*. However, both of them indicate entering password into a textbox. Since they are similar, we would like them to be mapped to the same Instruction-Class. For simplicity, we will denote $IC(i_j)$ as l_j throughout the paper.

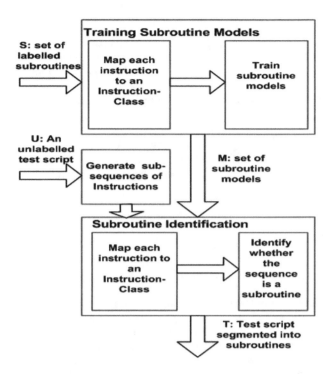

Figure 7. High level overview of the algorithm

Overview of the Proposed Approach

The goal of subroutine identification is to automatically identify subroutines contained within a repository of scripts. We assume that a user has previously labeled several instances of each desired subroutine within a separate training repository. Let S denote the set of such labelled subroutines. The goal of the algorithm is to recognize instances of these subroutines within the unlabeled scripts in the main repository. Figure 7 illustrates the high level overview of our algorithm.

Each labeled subroutine consists of a sequence of instructions. Our algorithm works as follows. First, each instruction is mapped to an Instruction-Class. Second, sequences of Instruction-Classes which are labeled as being instances of the same subroutine are used to train the subroutine model. The output of this step is the set of subroutine models, M. Finally, given an unlabeled script U, which may contain subroutines, all possible subsequences of instructions in that script are examined and compared against each of the subroutine models. If a match is found, the algorithm concludes that the matching instruction sequence is an instance of the matching subroutine. The output of this process is the script T, which is segmented into subroutines. The next subsections describe each of the components of this algorithm in detail.

Mapping Instructions to Instruction-Classes

Given a set of instructions I = $\{i_1, i_2, ...\}$ and a set of Instruction-Classes IC = $\{l_1, l_2, ...\}$, each instruction i_j is mapped to the Instruction-Class in IC to which it is most similar.

This is a clustering problem where each Instruction-Class is a cluster. Such clusters are constructed from instructions in scripts. Features of the instruction are action type, object type, words and word combinations (unigrams, bigrams, trigrams) from object label. We represent these instructions as vectors. Features of the instruction become the terms of the vector representing that instruction.

We use the parser described by Lau et al. [14] to parse the instructions and identify the type of action, type of the object, object label and value. For example, the instruction *click the "add to cart" button* is parsed into the following information:

- Action Type: click

- Object Type: button

- Object Label: "add to cart"

The features of this instruction are the following: (click, button, "add", "cart", "add to", "to cart", "add to cart"). Here, words and word combinations (bigrams, trigrams) are computed from the object label. These features become the terms of the vector representing the instruction. The vector which represents this instruction is: <click, button, "add", "cart", "add to", "to cart", "add to cart">. These terms are weighted using a TF*IDF weighting scheme. If the action type of an instruction is "assert", we do not add the "assert" keyword to the vector representing that instruction. This is to ensure that an assertion can be considered to be similar to any other instruction that acts on similar objects. Thus, the vector which represents *assert there is a "add to cart" button* is: <button, "add", "cart", "add to", "to cart", "add to cart">.

To compute similarity of an instruction to an Instruction-Class, we do the following:

- If the action type of the instruction is not "assert" and is different from the action type of the Instruction-Class, then the instruction is not similar to the Instruction-Class. Thus, the instruction *click the "username" textbox* is not similar to the instruction *enter name into the "username" textbox*.

- Otherwise, we compute a cosine similarity score between the vectors computed from the instruction and the Instruction-Class. If this is above the cosine similarity threshold of clustering (determined experimentally), then the instruction is considered to be similar to the Instruction-Class.

Each instruction is assigned to the Instruction-Class to which it is most similar. When an instruction is assigned to an Instruction-Class, we update the terms of the corresponding vector with the terms of the instruction and adjust the TF*IDF score of the Instruction-Class vectors. However, it is possible that an instruction may not be assigned to any Instruction-Class (i.e. the cosine similarity is below the threshold for every Instruction-Class or the set of Instruction-Classes is empty). In that case, we create a new Instruction-Class from that instruction.

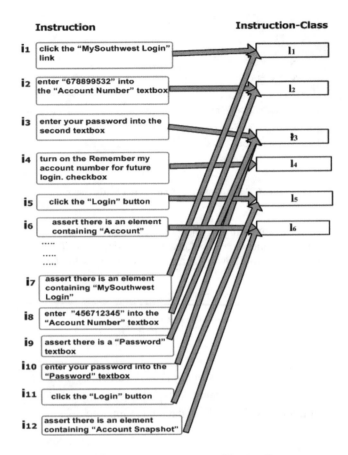

Figure 8. Mapping instructions to Instruction-Classes

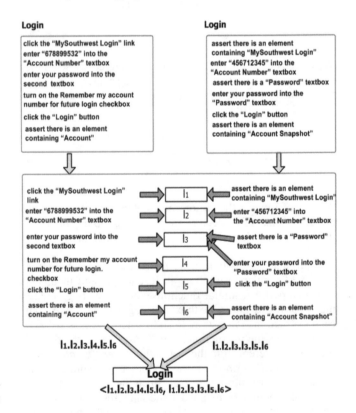

Figure 9. Training "Login" subroutine vector

Let us illustrate the algorithm with the instructions for the "Login" subroutine as illustrated in Figure 2 (a) and (b). Initially the set of Instruction-Classes is empty. Therefore, we create an Instruction-Class vector from the terms of the first instruction i_1 and assign a machine-generated identifier (l_1) to that Instruction-Class. The term vector of the next instruction i_2 is compared with the term vector of this Instruction-Class. But the similarity value is below the threshold. As a result we create another Instruction-Class vector from the terms of that instruction and assign it an identifier (l_2). Similarly, Instruction-Class vectors are created from the next four instructions and assigned machine generated identifiers (l_3, l_4, l_5, l_6).

The first instruction of the "Login" subroutine in Figure 2 (b) is found to be similar to the first Instruction-Class. As a result, we add the terms of that instruction to the Instruction-Class vector. The next instruction i_8 is found to be similar to the second instruction class l_2, and the terms of this instruction is added to the Instruction-Class vector. The next two instructions are found to be similar to the third Instruction-Class and the final two instructions are found to be similar to the fifth and sixth Instruction-Classes. Figure 8 shows the Instruction-Class labels constructed from these instructions.

Training Subroutine Models

Training a subroutine model[1] consists of constructing a vector for that subroutine from the labelled instances collected from test scripts. For each subroutine instance, we identify the Instruction-Class from each of the instructions. We construct the terms of the subroutine vector from the resulting Instruction-Class sequences. Given a sequence of Instruction-Classes $l_1.l_2.l_3$ labelled as an instance of subroutine S, the term of the subroutine vector V_S is the sequence $l_1.l_2.l_3$. Note that terms are typically words and word combinations in a vector space model. However, in our representation, each term of the subroutine vector is a sequence of Instruction-Class labels.

Figure 9 shows how a subroutine vector is constructed from labelled instances of the "Login" subroutine collected from the scripts shown in Figure 1. Two labelled instances of the "Login" subroutine are given as examples. The instructions from each subroutine are mapped to Instruction-Classes. As a result, an Instruction-Class sequence is retrieved from each subroutine instance. For example, the sequence $l_1.l_2.l_3.l_4.l_5.$-l_6 is retrieved for the first subroutine. This sequence becomes a term of the "Login" subroutine vector. Similarly, the sequence $l_1.l_2.l_3.l_3.l_5.l_6$ becomes another term of the "Login" subroutine vector. We weight each such term using a standard TF*IDF weighting scheme (which computes a weight using the frequency of this sequence in this particular subroutine vector and all the other subroutine vectors). For lack of space, Figure 9 does not show the other subroutine vectors (*e.g.*, a "Checkout" subroutine vector) constructed from the scripts recorded from that website.

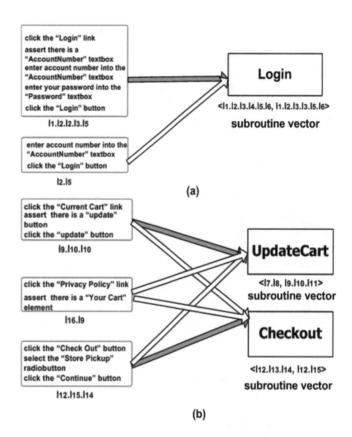

Figure 10. Subroutine Identification

Subroutine Identification

Trained subroutine models are then used to identify unlaballed instances of subroutines. To determine whether a sequence of instructions in a test script is an instance of a learned subroutine, we do the following:

First, we identify the Instruction-Class for each of the instructions. Next, we construct a term from the resulting Instruction-Class sequence and build a vector with that term. Then, we compute the cosine similarity of this vector with each of the trained subroutine vectors. If the similarity score between them is above the cosine similarity threshold for subroutine identification (determined experimentally), the sequence of instructions is identified as an instance of that subroutine. If the sequence is identified as an instance of multiple subroutines (i.e. cosine similarity is above the thresholds for multiple subroutine vectors), then the highest scoring vector is picked as the final classification.

However, we modify the definition of cosine similarity in order to capture the variability of instruction sequences of a subroutine. The usual cosine similarity measure considers two terms in a vector to be equal iff they are exactly identical. We extend this and consider two terms to be equal iff any of the following conditions are satisfied:

- The terms are identical.

- One of the terms is a generalization of the other term.

---

[1] In this paper, we use the terms subroutine vector and subroutine model interchangeably.

175

- One of the terms is a partial match of the other term.

To compute whether a term (i.e. the Instruction-Class sequence) is a generalization of another term, we remove any repeated subsequence from it, and see whether this is identical to the other one. For example, removing the repeated occurances of l_4 from the term $l_1.l_2.l_3.l_4.l_4.l_5$ makes it identical to the term $l_1.l_2.l_3.l_4.l_5$.

To compute whether a term (i.e. the Instruction-Class sequence) partially matches another term, we compute the edit distance [11] between them, normalize the edit distance by the length of the larger term and conclude a partial match if the normalized distance is below the threshold set for edit distance (determined experimentally). For example, the edit distance between the terms $l_1.l_2.l_2.l_3.l_5$ and $l_1.l_2.l_3.l_4.l_5$ is 2. The normalized value is 0.4 which is below the edit distance threshold 0.5. Hence this is a partial match.

Figure 10 (a) and (b) illustrate subroutine identification. For Figure 10 (a), the first sequence of instructions is identified as an instance of the "Login" subroutine. In Figure 10 (b), the first sequence is identified as "UpdateCart", the third sequence is identified as "Checkout" and the second sequence is not identified as any of the subroutines.

Segmenting a Script into Subroutines

Given a test script as input, our algorithm can determine the subroutines from it and segment the entire script into subroutines. It generates consecutive subsequences of instructions from the script in descending order of the size and identifies whether the subsequences are subroutines. Algorithm *SegmentScript* illustrates the high-level abstract pseudo-code.

Algorithm *SegmentScript*
Input: *Script*: A Test Script
Input: *Models*: Trained Models of Subroutines
Output: *ScriptWithSubroutines*: Script which has Subroutines identified
1. $Instructions \leftarrow$ Instructions of $Script$
2. $ScriptWithSubroutines \leftarrow Script$
3. **for** $i \leftarrow 1$ **to** $Instructions.Length$
4.   **do for** $j \leftarrow Instructions.Length$ **downto** i
5.   **do** $CurSeq \leftarrow$ Sequence of Instructions from i to j
6.   IdentifySubroutine ($CurSeq, Models$)
7.   **if** $CurSeq$ is a $Subroutine$
8.   **then** Label $CurSeq$ as $Subroutine$
9.   Add this Label to $Script$
10. $i \leftarrow j + 1$
11. **return** $ScriptWithSubroutines$

Algorithm *SegmentScript* starts with the largest subsequence, i.e. the entire script and checks whether this is a subroutine. In case of a match, it labels the subsequence as a subroutine and does not check for more subroutines inside it. Otherwise, it generates subsequences of length $n - 1$, and checks for subroutines. If a subroutine is found, it labels the subsequence with the subroutine name and checks for more subroutines outside the subsequence. Otherwise, the algorithm

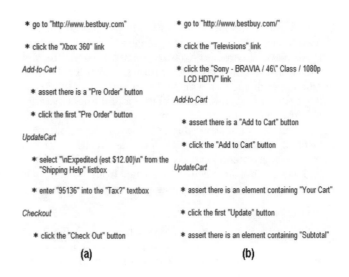

Figure 11. Test scripts segmented into subroutines

generates smaller subsequences ($n - 2$, $n - 3$, ..., 2, 1) and checks for subroutines.

For example, Figure 11 shows a test script segmented into subroutines.

EVALUATION

We present the experiments we have done to evaluate the subroutine identification feature of CoTester and a preliminary lab study that illustrates the value of the system.

Dataset

We used 70 scripts recorded from 12 websites for our experiments. They were recorded by active users of the CoScripter system [16]. We manually identified 144 subroutines from the scripts. Table 2 shows the experimental dataset. The first column of this table shows the websites, the second column shows the total number of scripts (in our dataset) which were recorded from that website, the third column shows the number of subroutines manually identified from those scripts, the fourth column shows the training set, and the final column shows the testing set. Each comma-seperated item in these sets specifies a subroutine and its number of instances in the set.

Baseline Algorithm

We wanted to justify our use of Instruction-Class sequences as terms of the subroutine vector. To do that, we also implemented a simpler baseline algorithm, Subroutine-Identification-Simple, which ignored the sequences, constructed subroutine models using the bag of words from the instructions, and used only the bag of words from instruction sequences to identify subroutines.

Performance

Website testers usually create a test suite from scripts recorded from a single website. Therefore, we assessed the performance of our algorithm by constructing website-specific subroutine models. Subroutine identification from scripts

Website	Scripts	Subroutines	Training Set	Testing Set
Amazon	7	16	Login:2, Add-to-Cart:2, Checkout:2, Search:1	Login:3, Add-to-Cart:2, Checkout:2, Search:2
BN	5	13	Login:2, Search:2, Add-to-Cart:1,Continue:2	Login:2, Search:2, Add-to-Cart:1, Continue:1
OfficeMax	6	15	Search:2, Add-to-Cart:2, Checkout:2, Register:1	Search:2, Add-to-Cart:2, Checkout:2, Regiser:2
Typetees	8	19	Login:3, Search:2, Register:2, Continue:2, Logout:1	Login:2, Search:2, Register: 1, Continue:2, Logout:2
Walmart	7	11	Search:2, Continue:3, Checkout:2	Search:2, Continue:1, Checkout:1
OfficeDepot	5	11	Login:2, Logout:2, Register:1	Login:2, Logout:2, Register:2
CircuitCity	5	10	Add-to-Cart:2, Continue:2, Checkout:1	Add-to-Cart:2, Continue:2, Checkout:1
Bestbuy	4	8	Checkout:2, Register:2	Checkout:2, Register:2
Shop	6	12	Checkout:2, Logout:2, Login:2	Checkout:2, Logout:2, Login:2
Buy	7	10	Login:2, Add-to-Cart:2, Search:2	Login:2, Add-to-Cart:1, Search:1
Threadless	4	9	Add-to-Cart:2, Register:1, Checkout:1	Add-to-Cart:2, Register:2, Checkout:1
Theselectseries	6	10	Search:2, Register:3	Search:2, Register:3

Table 2. Experimental Dataset

across multiple websites is more challenging since instructions in the scripts may show a lot of variability across websites.

We constructed such subroutine models for each website in our dataset and tested their performance. We computed how many subroutines were identified correctly, how many were identified incorrectly, how many were not identified. From this computation, we measured recall/precision and F-measure of the learned subroutine models. We averaged these values across websites. On average, our algorithm achieved 94% precision, 89% recall and 91.8% F-measure for subroutine identification.

We compared this performance with that of our baseline algorithm. We found that F-measure performance was 14% lower for this simpler approach. (see Figure 12, overall F-measure for the simpler approach is 77.8%). The performance differences are statistically significant (two-tailed p value is less than 0.0001, 95% confidence, t = 6.4920, degrees of freedom = 10, standard error of difference = 0.021). This justifies our use of sequences to identify subroutines.

We were interested to find whether the use of cosine similarity instead of simple equality checking between an instruction and instruction-class was really needed. Since cosine similarity with a threshold of 1.0 is equivalent to equality checking, we varied the cosine similarity threshold of clustering from 0 to 1.0 by an increment of 0.1 and computed the performance. A cosine similarity threshold of 0.4 for clustering resulted in the highest performance when the other two thresholds (edit distance threshold and cosine similarity threshold of subroutine identification) were set to 0.5 (the performance reported in this paper is for these threshold values). Performance drops by 12% when the cosine similarity threshold of clustering was set to 1.0 (which is equality checking), when the other thresholds were 0.5. This performance drop is statistically significant (two-tailed p value is less than 0.0001, 95% confidence, t = 6.3095, degrees of freedom = 12, standard error of difference = 0.018). This justifies the use of cosine similarity instead of simple equality checking between an instruction and the Instruction-Class.

User Study

We also did a preliminary user study of the system. The goal of this study was to find whether the easy-to-understand

scripting language and subroutine identification features of CoTester would be useful to users. 4 users participated in the study. They were experienced computer users and regularly browse the web. 3 of them had previous web development experience. 2 users were familiar with web testing tools and 1 user previously used a web testing tool. We showed them the user interface of CoTester and some example test scripts. We also introduced them to the subroutine learning feature. Each participant recorded 2 scripts from an e-commerce website (a total of 4 websites were used in the study, 1 website per participant) such that each script contained at least the following subroutines: "Login", "Add-to-Cart", "Checkout". They also added assertions to each of the scripts in two ways: i) using the graphical user interface ii) manually editing the scripts. Participants mentioned that they would prefer the first approach to insert assertions. Then, we used our algorithm to identify the subroutines from the scripts and showed the modified scripts to the participants. They noted that subroutines segmented the scripts in conceptual units, and helped them to better understand the higher level tasks performed by instructions. They also ran the scripts in batch mode and saved the test reports. One of the participants mentioned that our test report should contain information about the subroutine when a failure occured within that subroutine (e.g., the "Login" button is not found). This can be a novel benefit of subroutines we did not anticipate. Finally, we asked them to edit the recorded scripts. They noted that although they had to look at the repository of other scripts to get the correct syntax of instructions, editing was quite easy since the scripts were understandable. Overall, all of them liked the simple language of the CoTester system. One of the participants mentioned that she would like to write test scripts using our system to test her personal website.

CONCLUSIONS AND FUTURE WORK

We have presented CoTester, a lightweight web testing tool which can help testers easily create and maintain test scripts. CoTester's easy-to-understand scripting language and subroutine identification feature can reduce, if not eliminate, the barrier to web application testing.

There are many possible avenues of future research: First, CoTester's assertions check for presence or absence of web page elements based on textual properties (e.g., caption of a button). In the future, we would like to add other forms of

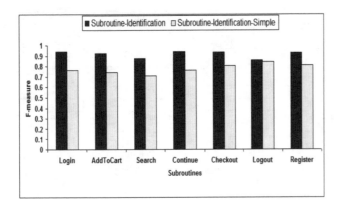

Figure 12. Subroutine Identification Performance

assertions, *e.g.*, an assertion that can check whether a submit button is disabled, or an assertion that can perform a bitmap comparison. Second, the subroutine identification feature is not yet deployed to functional testers. We like to deploy this feature to functional testers and see whether this can improve test script maintenance by enabling them to automatically apply similar changes to a large corpus of scripts (bulk modification), when websites change. Towards that, we will extend the user interface of CoTester with a bulk modification component, so that testers can select the scripts or the test suite and specify the desired change (e.g., adding an assertion in a login process) and the system can do the modification in all the matching scripts. Third, we have trained and tested subroutine models for a few subroutines. In the future, we will train more subroutine models, conduct thorough experiments with a larger dataset, and explore the usage of subroutine models trained from multiple websites. Finally, we will perform a thorough user study of the deployed system.

ACKNOWLEDGEMENT

We thank Jeffrey Nichols for his insightful comments about this paper.

REFERENCES

1. Borland SilkTest. http://www.borland.com/us/products/silk/silktest/.

2. Hp QuickTest Professional. http://www.hp.com.

3. IBM Rational Functional Tester. http://www-01.ibm.com/software/awdtools/tester/functional/.

4. J. F. Allen, N. Chambers, G. Ferguson, L. Galescu, H. Jung, M. D. Swift, and W. Taysom. Plow: A Collaborative Task Learning Agent. In *Proc. of AAAI*, 2007.

5. J. Blythe. Task Learning by Instruction in Tailor. In *Proc. of the 10th Intl. Conf. on Intelligent user interfaces*, pages 191–198, New York, NY, USA, 2005. ACM.

6. M. H. Burstein, R. Laddaga, D. McDonald, M. T. Cox, B. Benyo, P. Robertson, T. Hussain, M. Brinn, and

D. V. McDermott. Poirot - Integrated Learning of Web Service Procedures. In D. Fox and C. P. Gomes, editors, *AAAI*, pages 1274–1279. AAAI Press, 2008.

7. http://www.concordion.org/.

8. A. Cypher. Watch What I Do: Programming by Demonstration. *MIT Press*, 1993.

9. http://www.w3.org/DOM/DOMTR.

10. M. Gervasio, T. J. Lee, and S. Eker. Learning Email Procedures for the Desktop. In *AAAI 2008 Workshop on Enhanced Messaging*, Chicago, IL, July 2008.

11. D. Gusfield. *Algorithms on Strings, Trees, and Sequences: Computer Science and Computational Biology*. Cambridge University Press, January 1997.

12. S. B. Huffman and J. E. Laird. Flexibly Instructable Agents. Technical report, Price Waterhouse, 1995.

13. T. Lau, L. Bergman, V. Castelli, and D. Oblinger. Sheepdog: Learning Procedures for Technical Support. In *Proc. of Intl. Conf. on Intelligent user interfaces*, pages 109–116, 2004.

14. T. Lau, C. Drews, and J. Nichols. Interpreting Written How-to Instructions. In *Proceedings of the International joint conference on Artificial Intelligence*, 2009.

15. T. A. Lau and D. S. Weld. Programming by Demonstration: An Inductive Learning Formulation. In *Proc. of Intl. Conf. on Intelligent User Interfaces*, pages 145–152, 1999.

16. G. Leshed, E. M. Haber, T. Matthews, and T. Lau. Coscripter: automating and sharing how-to knowledge in the enterprise. In *CHI '08: Proceeding of the twenty-sixth annual SIGCHI conference on Human factors in computing systems*, pages 1719–1728, 2008.

17. G. Little, T. A. Lau, A. Cypher, J. Lin, E. M. Haber, and E. Kandogan. Koala: Capture, Share, Automate, Personalize Business Processes on the Web. In *CHI '07: Proceedings of the SIGCHI conference on Human factors in computing systems*, pages 943–946, 2007.

18. D. S. Rosenblum. A Practical Approach to Programming With Assertions. *IEEE Trans. Softw. Eng.*, 21(1):19–31, 1995.

19. http://sahi.co.in/w/.

20. G. Salton, A. Wong, and C. S. Yang. A Vector Space Model for Automatic Indexing. *Commun. ACM*, 18(11):613–620, 1975.

21. http://seleniumhq.org/.

22. A. Spaulding, J. Blythe, W. Haines, and M. Gervasio. From Geek to Sleek: Integrating Task Learning Tools to Support End Users in Real-world Applications. In *IUI '09: Proceedings of the 13th international conference on Intelligent user interfaces*, pages 389–394, 2009.

Towards a Reputation-based Model of Social Web Search

Kevin McNally, Michael P. O'Mahony, Barry Smyth, Maurice Coyle, Peter Briggs
CLARITY: Centre for Sensor Web Technologies
School of Computer Science and Informatics
University College Dublin, Ireland
{firstname.lastname}@ucd.ie

ABSTRACT

While web search tasks are often inherently collaborative in nature, many search engines do not explicitly support collaboration during search. In this paper, we describe *HeyStaks* (www.heystaks.com), a system that provides a novel approach to collaborative web search. Designed to work with mainstream search engines such as Google, HeyStaks supports searchers by harnessing the experiences of others as the basis for result recommendations. Moreover, a key contribution of our work is to propose a reputation system for HeyStaks to model the value of individual searchers from a result recommendation perspective. In particular, we propose an algorithm to calculate reputation directly from user search activity and we provide encouraging results for our approach based on a preliminary analysis of user activity and reputation scores across a sample of HeyStaks users.

Author Keywords

Collaborative Web Search, Reputation Model, HeyStaks

ACM Classification Keywords

H.4.0 Information Systems Applications: General

General Terms

Algorithms, Experimentation, Security

INTRODUCTION

The world of web search is usually viewed as a solitary place. Although millions of searchers use services like Google and Yahoo everyday, their individual searches take place in isolation. Recently, researchers have begun to question the solitary nature of web search, proposing a more collaborative search model in which groups of users can cooperate to search more effectively [10, 11, 12, 13, 17]. Indeed, recent work by [4] highlights the inherently collaborative nature of more general purpose web search. Despite the absence of explicit collaboration features from mainstream search engines, there is clear evidence that users implicitly engage in many different forms of collaboration as they

search – although these collaboration "work-arounds" are often frustrating and inefficient [4]. Naturally, this has motivated researchers to consider how different types of collaboration might be supported by future editions of search engines. *HeyStaks* is one such model of collaborative web search (www.heystaks.com) which has been designed to work with mainstream search engines, such as Google, and which has recently been deployed online. HeyStaks takes the form of a browser toolbar to allow users to capture and share their search experiences with other users and, in so doing, facilitates the creation of search communities. In turn, members of these search communities benefit from recommendations that are derived from the activities of other community members.

During the initial trials of HeyStaks it has become clear that different users engage in, and benefit from, different degrees of search collaboration [19, 20]. For example, clear *search leaders* and *search followers* often emerge, the former being consistently first to contribute search knowledge for the latter to consume in the form of recommendations. In this paper, we consider the notion of *reputation* as a measure of how reliable a searcher is when it comes to the production of useful search knowledge. For example, if a particular searcher contributes search knowledge that is frequently selected by others during future searches, then the reputation of that searcher should be credited. In this paper, we describe one such reputation model and discuss the results of a preliminary evaluation across a subset of collaborating users. First, however, we review recent work in the area of collaborative information retrieval and summarise the HeyStaks system that forms the basis for this work.

COLLABORATIVE INFORMATION RETRIEVAL

Collaborative information retrieval research takes a fresh look at information retrieval and web search, which highlights the potential for collaboration between searchers during extended search tasks. Recent work by [4] highlights the inherently collaborative nature of more general purpose web search. For example, during a survey of just over 200 respondents, clear evidence for collaborative search behaviour emerged. More than 90% of respondents indicated that they frequently engaged in collaboration at the level of the *search process*. For example, 87% of respondents exhibited "backseat searching" behaviours, where they watched over the shoulder of the searcher to suggest alternative queries. Some 30% of respondents engaged in search coordination activities, by using instant messaging to coordinate searches. Furthermore, 96% of users exhibited collaboration at the level of *search products*, that is, the results of searches. For example, 86% of respondents shared the results they had found during searches with others by email. Indeed, almost 50% of respondents telephoned colleagues directly to share web search results, while others prepared summary documents and/or web pages in order to share results with others.

Thus, despite the absence of explicit collaboration features from mainstream search engines, there is clear evidence that users implicitly engage in many different forms of collaboration as they search, although, as reported by [4], these collaboration "work-arounds" are often frustrating and inefficient. This has motivated researchers to consider how different types of collaboration might be supported by future editions of search engines. The resulting approaches to *collaborative information retrieval* can be distinguished in terms of two dimensions – *time* and *place*. In terms of the former, collaborative search systems can be designed to support *sychronous* or *asynchronous* collaborative search. And in terms of the latter, systems can be designed to support either *co-located* or *remote* forms of collaborative search.

Co-located systems offer a collaborative search experience for multiple searchers at a single location, often via a single PC [1] or, more recently, by taking advantage of computing devices that are more naturally collaborative, such as table-top computing environments [16]. In contrast, remote approaches allow searchers to perform their searches at different locations across multiple devices [5, 6, 20]. While co-located systems enjoy the obvious benefit of an increased facility for direct collaboration that is enabled by the face-to-face nature of co-located search, remote services offer a greater opportunity for collaborative search.

Synchronous approaches are often characterised by systems that broadcast a "call to search" in which specific participants are requested to engage in a well-defined search task for a well defined period of time [15]. In contrast, asynchronous approaches are characterised by less well-defined, ad-hoc search tasks and provide for a more open-ended approach to collaboration in which different searchers contribute to an evolving search session over an extended period of time [5, 18]. In this paper we will focus on a community-based approach to collaborative web search in which the *asynchronous* search experiences of communities of like-minded *remote* searchers are harnessed to provide an improved search experience that is more responsive to the learned preferences of a community of searchers.

HEYSTAKS: A SEARCH UTILITY

In designing HeyStaks our primary goal is to provide social web search enhancements, while at the same time allowing searchers to continue to use their favourite search engine. As such, a key component of the HeyStaks architecture is a browser toolbar that permits tight integration with search engines such as Google, allowing searchers to search as normal while providing a more collaborative search experience via targeted recommendations. In this section we will outline the basic HeyStaks system architecture and summarize

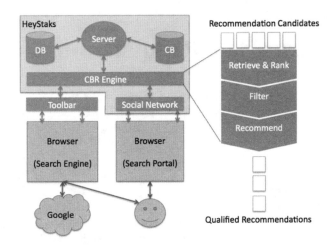

Figure 1. The HeyStaks system architecture and outline recommendation model.

how result recommendations are made during search. In addition, we will make this discussion more concrete by briefly summarizing a worked example of HeyStaks in action.

System Architecture

HeyStaks adds two important collaboration features to any mainstream search engine. First, it allows users to create *search staks* as a type of folder for their search experiences. These staks can then be shared with others so that their own searches will also be added to the stak. Second, HeyStaks uses staks to generate recommendations that are added to the underlying search results that come from the mainstream search engine. These recommendations are results that stak members have previously found to be relevant for similar queries and help the searcher to discover results that friends or colleagues have found interesting – results that may otherwise be buried deep within Google's default result-list.

As per Figure 1, HeyStaks takes the form of two basic components: a client-side *browser toolbar* and a back-end *server*. The toolbar allows users to create and share staks and provides a range of ancillary services, such as the ability to tag or vote for pages. The toolbar also captures search result click-thrus and manages the integration of HeyStaks recommendations with the default result-list. The back-end server manages the individual stak indexes (indexing individual pages against query/tag terms and positive/negative votes), the stak database (stak titles, members, descriptions, status etc.), the HeyStaks social networking service and, of course, the recommendation engine. In the following sections we will briefly outline the basic operation of HeyStaks and then focus on some of the detail behind the recommendation engine.

A Worked Example

To make HeyStaks more concrete, it is useful to consider a worked example. With this in mind, consider the scenario where the leader of a recommender systems research group wishes to harness the search knowledge of his/her group to help other group members, particularly new researchers, to search more productively.

This is the scenario illustrated in Figure 2. To begin with, the group leader creates a new search stak by selecting the "Create a New Stak" option from the "Staks" menu in the HeyStaks toolbar. As per Figure 2(a), creating a stak is a straightforward process: the stak creator needs to provide a stak name and some helpful description information; the stak can be configured to be public (anyone can join) or private (invitation only); and the creator can invite initial members by providing their email addresses. In this case the user creates the public *RecSys* stak and invites a group of researchers via the *postgrads@clarity-centre.org* group-email address. If the researchers accept this invitation, then the RecSys stak will be added to their HeyStaks toolbar.

At search time, HeyStaks users can select an active stak from their toolbar to provide a context for their search. For example, in Figure 2(b) the searcher has selected the *RecSys* stak in a search for "collaborative filtering" and the result list returned by Google has been augmented by HeyStaks promotions. In this case the top 3 results have been promoted by HeyStaks because they have each been found to be relevant to stak members, either during previous searches for similar queries or through their tagging activities. In addition to these primary recommendations, RecSys can also make a larger set of *additional* recommendations available. These may be drawn from the *RecSys* stak or indeed from other staks that the user has joined; in this case, HeyStaks has found additional recommendations from the *RecSys* stak and also from the user's personal *My Searches* stak.

In this way, as stak members submit queries and select results, these search experiences are captured in the *RecSys* stak. As mentioned above, HeyStaks also allows users to more explicitly interact with search results and web pages. For example: users can vote for (or against) particular results; users can email a page directly to another user without leaving the page or their search; and users can explicitly tag any page that they find interesting (see Figure 2(c)). This combination of *implicit* click-thru data and *explicit* voting, sharing, or tagging data permits staks to capture a variety of important interaction types, which HeyStaks uses to infer the *relevance* of a page to a given stak; see [19] for details.

Separately from the toolbar, HeyStaks users also benefit from the HeyStaks *search portal*, which provides a social networking service built around people's search histories. For example, Figure 2(d) shows the portal page for the *RecSys* stak, which is available to all stak members. It presents an activity feed of recent search history and a query cloud that makes it easy for the user to find out about what others have been searching for. The search portal also provides users with a wide range of features such as stak maintenance (e.g., editing, moving, copying results in staks and between staks), various search and filtering tools (see Figure 2(e)), and a variety of features to manage their own search profiles and find new search partners.

The HeyStaks Recomendation Engine

In HeyStaks, each search stak (S) serves as a profile of the search activities of the stak members. Each stak is made up of a set of result pages ($S = \{p_1, ..., p_k\}$) and each page is anonymously associated with a number of implicit and explicit interest indicators, including the total number of times a result has been selected (sel), the query terms ($q_1, ..., q_n$) that led to its selection, the number of times a result has been tagged (tag), the terms used to tag it ($t_1, ..., t_m$), the votes it has received (v^+, v^-), and the number of people it has been shared with ($share$) as indicated by Eq. 1.

$$p_i^S = \{q_1, ..., q_n, t_1, ..., t_m, v^+, v^-, sel, tag, share\} \quad (1)$$

In this way, each page is associated with a set of *term data* (query terms and/or tag terms) and a set of *usage data* (the selection, tag, share, and voting count). The term data is represented as a Lucene (*lucene.apache.org*) index, with each page indexed under its associated query and tag terms, and provides the basis for retrieving and ranking *promotion candidates*. The usage data provides an additional source of evidence that can be used to filter results and to generate a final set of recommendations. At search time, recommendations are produced in a number of stages: first, relevant results are retrieved and ranked from the stak index; next, these promotion candidates are filtered based on the usage evidence to eliminate noisy recommendations; and, finally, the remaining results are added to the Google result-list according to a set of *recommendation rules*.

Retrieval & Ranking. Briefly, there are two types of promotion candidates: *primary promotions* are results that come from the active stak S_t; whereas *secondary promotions* come from other staks in the searcher's stak-list. To generate these promotion candidates, the HeyStaks server uses the current query, q_t, as a probe into each stak index, S_i, to identify a set of relevant stak pages, $P(S_i, q_t)$.

Each candidate page, p, is scored against the query, q_t, using a *term frequency–inverse document frequency* (TF-IDF) based retrieval function. TF-IDF is a well-known weighting scheme from the field of information retrieval and is a measure used to weight the importance of a term within a collection of documents [14]. The value of this weight is proportionate to the frequency of the term in a particular document, but is offset by its frequency across the entire corpus. Such an approach serves as the basis for an initial recommendation ranking in HeyStaks, as per Equation 2.

$$score(q_t, p) = \sum_{t \epsilon q_t} tf(t \epsilon p) \bullet idf(t)^2 \quad (2)$$

Evidence-Based Filtering. Staks are inevitably noisy, in the sense that they will frequently contain pages that are not on topic. As a result, the retrieval and ranking stage may select pages that are not strictly relevant to the current query context. To avoid making spurious recommendations, HeyStaks employs an *evidence filter*. This filter uses a variety of threshold models to evaluate the relevance of a particular result in terms of its usage evidence. For example,

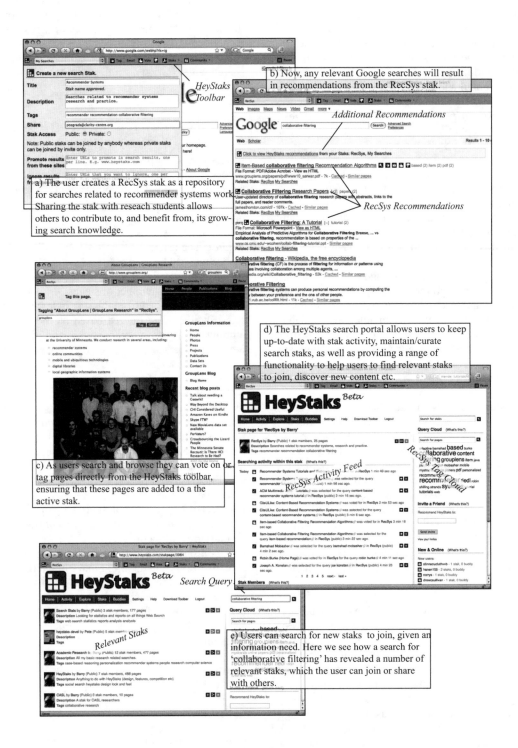

Figure 2. HeyStaks in action: a) stak creation; b) result recommendations; c) tagging a web page; d) stak activity on the HeyStaks portal; e) finding new staks.

tagging evidence is considered more important than voting, which in turn is more important than implicit selection evidence. Pages that have only been selected once, by a single stak member, are not automatically considered for recommendation by HeyStaks and, all other things being equal, will be filtered out at this stage. In turn, pages that have received a high proportion of negative votes will also be eliminated. The precise details of this model are beyond the scope of this paper but suffice it to say that any results which do not meet the necessary evidence thresholds are eliminated from further consideration.

Recommendation Rules. After evidence pruning we are left with revised primary and secondary promotions and the final task is to add these *qualified recommendations* to the Google result-list. HeyStaks uses a number of different recommendation rules to determine how and where a promotion should be added. Once again, space restrictions prevent a detailed account of this component but, for example, the top 3 primary promotions are always added to the top of the Google result-list and labelled using the HeyStaks promotion icons. If a remaining primary promotion is also in the default Google result-list then this is labeled in place. If there are still remaining primary promotions then these are added to the secondary promotion list, which is sorted according to HeyStaks relevance values. These recommendations are then added to the Google result-list as an optional, expandable list of recommendations.

Summary Discussion

HeyStaks is designed to help users to collaborate during web search tasks and, importantly, it succeeds in integrating collaborative recommendation techniques with mainstream search engines. In preceding sections, we have provided an overview of the various functionality that HeyStaks provides and have discussed the ranking, filtering and recommendation techniques that are used to make result promotions. Further details on the precise techniques employed can be found in previous research [2, 18]. The HeyStaks system has recently moved into public-beta and during this time approximately 500 users have registered, leading to the creation and sharing of thousands of search staks. In the next section, we introduce a reputation model for HeyStaks users and we show how this model can be used to identify the search leaders in a community and also how user reputation can be used to enhance the ranking of result promotions.

A REPUTATION MODEL FOR SOCIAL SEARCH

As described in the previous section, the many and varied different types of activities that a user can perform (click-thrus, tagging, voting, sharing) on a web page are ultimately combined and leveraged by HeyStaks to make recommendations at search time. And, while the recommendation algorithm used differentially weights different activity types (so that tagging, for example, is considered a more reliably indicator of interest that a simple result click-thru), the source of the activity (that is, the user performing the activity) is not considered explicitly. Intuitively, we might expect that some users are more experienced searchers and, as such, perhaps their activities should be considered as more reliable at rec-

ommendation time, so that promotion candidates that hail from the activities of very experienced users might be considered ahead of candidates that come from the activity of less experienced users. This is particularly important given the potential for malicious users to disrupt stak quality by introducing dubious results to a stak.

In this section then, we describe how user activities in HeyStaks can be harnessed to generate a computational model of user reputation, based on the collaboration events that naturally occur between HeyStaks users who share their search experiences. We describe an algorithm for maintaining an up-to-date reputation model at search time and go on to propose a simple mechanism for incorporating reputation into the HeyStaks result recommendation subsystem.

From Activities to Reputation

It seems natural that the reputation of a searchers should be linked to the search knowledge that they contribute to HeyStaks. In simple terms this search knowledge is based on the creation and sharing of search staks and, ultimately, the web pages that are added to these staks according to a variety of different types of user activities, which include:

- *Click-thrus (Result Selections)* – that is, a user selects a search result (whether *organic* or *promoted*);

- *Voting* – that is, a user positively votes on a given search result or the current web page;

- *Sharing* – that is, a user chooses to share a specific search result or web page with another user (via email or by posting to their Facebook Wall etc.);

- *Tagging/Commenting* – that is, the user chooses to tag and/or comment on a particular result or web page.

Each of these activities results in the creation of new search knowledge. If the target page is new to a stak, then its selection, sharing, voting, or tagging will cause it to be added to the stak for the first time. If the page is already represented, as a result of an earlier activity, then the page's stak record will be updated to reflect the additional activity. As mentioned previously, not all of these activities are equal with respect to their reliability as indicators of relevance/quality. For example, the act of selecting a search result (a click-thru) is considered to be an *implicit* activity, which may or may not indicate that the user views the page to be relevant; for example, if the user quickly dismissed the selected page and returns to searching then it is unlikely that the page was considered to be particularly useful or relevant. In contrast, the other activities (sharing, voting, tagging) are *explicit* and thus tend to be more reliable indicators of page relevance.

What then is the relationship between search activity and searcher reputation? Under the heading of *"more search knowledge is better than less search knowledge"* it might make sense to model reputation as a direct function of the sheer volume of activity that a given searcher engages in. This would be a mistake. For a start, just because a user is creating a lot of search knowledge, by adding many pages to search staks, it does not mean that this new knowledge is useful, especially to others. On the contrary, one of the major concerns in any social recommender is the potential for misuse through the actions of malicious users, a problem that would no doubt be exacerbated by valuing the contribution of very 'productive' malicious users.

Ultimately, in a social media context, reputation is a form of *incentive*. It allows HeyStaks to communicate the value of a user's contributions to that user, and potentially to others, and this can help significantly to drive further contributions [8, 9]. (Related to this is the concept of trust in recommender systems and social networks [3, 7] where, for example, the accumulation of trust scores can motivate users to enhance the quantity and quality of their contributions.) But like any incentive, reputation can be *gamed* and thus it is vitally important that the incentive is tightly coupled to the sort of behaviour that benefits the system and its users as a whole. A reputation model that is the sum of all user activities does not meet this requirement since it is not necessarily to anyone's benefit to create a system that is measured simply by the volume of its search knowledge. Instead, it is the quality of this search knowledge that is important, and so our model of reputation must model search knowledge quality. The long-term value of HeyStaks as a social search service depends critically on the ability of users to benefit from its quality search knowledge and if, for example, all of the best search experiences are tied up in private staks and never shared, then this long-term value will be greatly diminished.

Reputation as Collaboration

Thus, our model of reputation must recognise the *quality* of *shared* search knowledge. Fortunately there is a way to capture this notion in a manner that serves to incentivise users to behave in just the right way to grow long-term value for all. The key idea is that, ultimately, the quality of shared search knowledge can be estimated by looking at the frequency of *search collaborations* within HeyStaks.

If HeyStaks recommends a result to a searcher, and the searcher chooses to act on (select, tag, vote on or share) this result, then we can view this as a single instance of search collaboration. The current searcher who chooses to act on the recommendation is known as the *consumer* and, in the simplest case, the original searcher whose earlier action on this result caused it to be added to the search stak is known as the *producer*. In other words, the producer created search knowledge that was deemed to be useful enough for the consumer to act upon it. And the basic idea behind our reputation model is that this act of implicit collaboration between producer and consumer confers a *unit of reputation* on the producer (Figure 3). If a given user is a regular producer of search knowledge that is frequently recommended to, and acted on by, many other users, then this producer will enjoy a high reputation score. Moreover, if users create lots of staks and share these staks with many other users, or simply join staks that have been created by others, then they create an opportunity for more collaboration; and if users contribute good search knowledge to shared staks then their reputation score will benefit from the realisation of these frequent

collaboration opportunities. In this way, this collaboration-based model of reputation is incentivizing users not just to create search knowledge but also to share it with others.

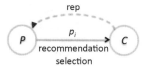

Figure 3. Producer (P) and consumer (C) collaboration: C selects page p_i, which has been recommended to C based on P's previous activity. In turn, C confers reputation on P.

The conferral of reputation by a consumer is a little more complicated than just described because, in the general case, at the time when the consumer acted on the promoted result, there may have been a number of different producers who each contributed part of the search knowledge that caused this result to be promoted. An original producer may have been the first to select the result in question, but subsequent users may have selected it for different queries, or they may have voted on it or tagged it or shared it with others independently of its other producers. In the case of our reputation model we share the unit of reputation between the other producers. So, if at time t, when the consumer acts on a promoted result, we can identify k producers then the reputation score of each of these producers is incremented by $1/k$.

An Example

To illustrate our user reputation model, consider the simple scenario as depicted in Figure 4. Here, the activity of four users, $\{u_1, \ldots, u_4\}$, with respect to a single search result page p is shown at four points in time t_i, where $t_4 > t_3 > t_2 > t_1$. Further, assume that all four users are members of a particular stak S, which is currently the active stak for each of these users. The sequence of events at each time step t_i is as follows:

t_1: User u_1 organically selects page p for some search query q, causing page p to be added to stak S.

t_2: User u_2 selects page p, which has been promoted by HeyStaks, for a search query that is related to q. Since user u_1 is the only user to have previously selected page p in stak S, we say that user u_1 (the *producer*) has *promoted* page p to user u_2 (the *consumer*). Consequently, user u_2 assigns a *reputation* score of 1 to user u_1.

t_3: User u_3 organically selects page p for an unrelated search query q'. This time, page p is not promoted by HeyStaks and hence no reputation is assigned by user u_3 to any of the other users.

t_4: Finally, user u_4 selects page p, which has been promoted by HeyStaks, for a search query that is again related to q. Since users u_1, u_2 and u_3 have all previously selected (either organically or by promotion) page p, on this occasion reputation is assigned by user u_4 to each of these users. Thus, in Figure 4, the reputation score is distributed equally among the three users, such that each user receives a score of $1/3$.

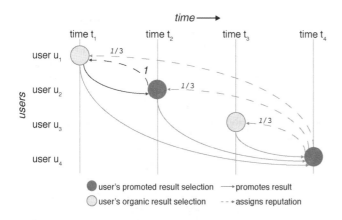

time $\longrightarrow$

Figure 4. Simple example of user reputation calculations in HeyStaks

At the end of the time period, overall user reputation is calculated by simply summing the individual reputation components that each user has received. For example, in the above scenario, the overall reputation scores for users u_1, u_2, u_3 and u_4 are $4/3$, $1/3$, $1/3$ and 0, respectively.

The complete user reputation algorithm is given in Figure 5. For the purposes of simplicity, this algorithm shown is one suitable for offline execution. The algorithm can be readily modified such that user reputation scores are updated in real time when new activities are performed by users. In future work, we plan on integrating such a version into the HeyStaks application.

The algorithm takes as input a temporally ordered set of user activities $\mathcal{A}$ which are retrieved from the HeyStaks activity feed (e.g. Figure 2(d)). Each entry $a \in \mathcal{A}$ is a tuple $\langle u, p, t, S, type \rangle$, where $a.u$ is the user who performed the activity, $u.p$ is the associated result page, $u.t$ is the time when the activity occurred, $u.S$ is the active stak at the time of the activity and $a.type$ indicates whether or not the activity relates to a HeyStaks promotion. In addition, the set of all staks $\mathcal{S}$ and the current (previously calculated) set of user reputation scores $\mathcal{R}$ are provided as a starting point.

For each promotion activity $a \in \mathcal{A}$ (line 3), the set of staks S_c that the current user u_c is a member of is retrieved (line 8). Then, the set of prior activities relating to the current page p_c, in any of the staks in S_c, is determined (line 9) and the users who performed these activities are identified (line 10). Finally, a unit of reputation is distributed equally among these users and added to their existing reputation score (lines 12–14). This process continues until all activities are processed and the array $\mathcal{R}$, which contains each user's updated reputation score, is returned.

Result Promotion

We now consider how user reputation can be employed to influence the ranking of promoted results in HeyStaks. Currently, pages are selected for promotion as follows. For a given search query q_t submitted by a user u, a set of candidate pages, $\{p_1, p_2, \ldots, p_k\}$, are identified for promotion

---

Input: Set $\mathcal{A}$ of user activity tuples $\langle u, p, t, S, type \rangle$, set S of all staks, array $\mathcal{R}$ of user reputation scores
Output: Updated array $\mathcal{R}$ of user reputation scores

1.   UserReputation($\mathcal{A}$, S, $\mathcal{R}$)
2.   **begin**
3.   **foreach** activity $a \in \mathcal{A}$
4.   **if** $a.type$ = promotion
5. $u_c \leftarrow a.u$
6. $p_c \leftarrow a.p$
7. $t_c \leftarrow a.t$
8. $S_c \leftarrow$ staks(S, u_c)
9. $A \leftarrow \{a' \in \mathcal{A} : a'.p = p_c \,\& \, a'.S \in S_c \,\& \, a'.t < t_c\}$
10. $U \leftarrow \{a'.u : a' \in A\} - \{u_c\}$
11.
12.   **foreach** $u \in U$
13. $\mathcal{R}[u] \leftarrow \mathcal{R}[u] + 1/|U|$
14.   **end**
15.   **end**
16.   **end**
17.   **end**

Figure 5. User reputation algorithm

and a relevance score, $score(q_t, p_i)$, is computed for each page (Eqn. 2). These scores are then used to rank order candidate pages, and the pages with the highest scores are promoted to the user.

We propose to incorporate user reputation into the above ranking process as follows. Let $rep(p_i)$ denote the reputation accruing to candidate page p_i. Candidate pages can now be ranked according to:

$$rank(p_i) = w \times rep(p_i) + (1 - w) \times score(q_t, p_i) , \quad (3)$$

where w lies in the interval $[0, 1]$. Higher values of w increase the influence of page reputation on overall rankings.

The reputation of a candidate page p_i at time t is calculated as follows. Let U be the set of users who had selected, voted up, shared or tagged page p_i prior to time t. Further, let $\mathcal{R}$ be an array containing the reputation scores for each user $u \in U$, where $\mathcal{R}$ is the (normalised) output of the user reputation algorithm described above. The reputation of page p_i is calculated as:

$$rep(p_i) = \frac{\sum_{u \in U} \mathcal{R}[u]}{|U|} . \quad (4)$$

Eqn. 4 assigns larger scores to candidate pages that have been previously selected by users with high user reputations. Thus, by incorporating page reputation into the HeyStaks' page ranking process as per Eqn. 3, the relevance of promoted pages can be further enhanced.

PRELIMINARY EVALUATION

Ultimately it is our intent to evaluate this reputation model as an integrated component within HeyStaks as part of a long-term user trial. Accordingly it will be possible to determine just how important a role reputation can play when it comes to influencing recommendations and user engagement. For example, will a reputation-based recommendation model lead to improved recommendations that attract more frequent click-thrus? And would exposing reputation statistics to users help to deepen their engagement with the system, leading to more collaboration in the long-run?

Unfortunately, this level of integration is beyond the scope of this work. However, we do have an opportunity to evaluate the reputation model with respect to a limited user community in order to explore and better understand the relationship between users, their activities, and their reputation scores.

Dataset & Methodology

For this initial evaluation, we considered 26 HeyStaks users who have been using the system over the course of the last 9 months. These users were invited to try out the system and can be said to be typical of early adopters of new systems. As such, they may be more technically knowledgeable than the average user and thus our findings may not fully generalise to regular users. Nonetheless, our test group is typical of that used in many system trials (e.g. [20]) and useful findings and insights can be obtained from our study.

The activity data associated with our user group captures a wide range of information about user activity within HeyStaks, including stak creation, joining and sharing as well as page selection, tagging, voting and sharing. In total, some 20,472 individual activity records are included and these provide the basic input to the reputation model described above to form the basis of our evaluation. Note that we focus on these 26 users as the *holders* of reputation, but it is important to realise that they may have received this reputation from a wider set of users who do not form part of this test-group.

User Activity

Overall, user activity in HeyStaks is dominated by selection actions, where the user selects a particular search result, be it an organic result or a recommended/promoted result. Figure 6 presents the total number of selections, tags, votes and shares that have been performed by the 26 users. Selections are of course a natural type of search activity (approximately 90%) and so it is unsurprising that they dominate compared to the other activities such as tagging (3.5%), voting (1.6%), and sharing (4%).

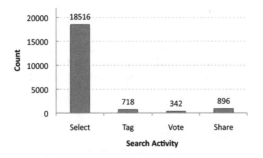

Figure 6. User search activity versus count

Figure 7(a) shows summary statistics in relation to the total activity (i.e. selection, tagging, voting, sharing) carried out

by the 26 users. The median total activity across the users is 638 with the most active user performing as many as 3528 activities, while the least active user performed only 11 actions. This suggests a reasonable spread of activity across the 26 test users.

Another important issue to consider is the extent to which users engage in the sort of activities that ultimately facilitate search collaboration. Do they create and join staks, for example? How many other users are they connected with (their *network size*)? All other things being equal, if a user creates and joins many staks, then they are more likely to be connected to a greater number of other users and thus will benefit from a larger collaboration network to act as a source of recommendations. Figures 7(b) to 7(d) presents the summary statistics for the number of staks created and joined and the network size for the 26 test users.

We can see that the median number of staks created is 3 versus 8 staks joined. So the typical user tends to join more staks (which others have created) than they create. This is an important indication that users are recognising the potential value of other staks which other users have created and is a first step towards meaningful search collaboration. Once again there are some significant outliers with, at one extreme, a user creating 36 staks while another joined 49, whilst, at the other extreme, one user only created a single stak while another joined only 2. It is worth highlighting that there is a strong correlation (0.97) between the number of staks created and the number of staks joined.

The median network size – that is, the number of other users a given user is *connected* with by virtue of sharing staks – is 30 (this value includes other users who were not part of this particular analysis). Indeed one user is connected to 89 others while another is only connected to 11. These summary statistics suggest that not only are users engaged in a significant level of search activity within HeyStaks, they have also created the conditions (shared staks) for meaningful collaboration.

User Reputation

The results of applying the reputation model to the 26 users are shown in Figure 8, with users ordered by decreasing reputation score. Remember that the reputation score is basically a weighted sum of the number of times a particular user has contributed to the promotion of a result that has been subsequently been acted on (i.e. selected, shared etc.). If the user in question was the sole producer of the promotion then they gain a full unit of reputation, but more often than not they are partly responsible for the promotion and so only share in a fraction of the reputation along with the promotion's other producers.

The results in Figure 8 tell a tale of two user types. On the one hand, about 20% of the users (5 out of 26) have achieved reputation scores of 60 or higher, with one user achieving a reputation score in excess of 105. These are clearly users who are engaged in a significant amount of search collaboration as distinct from the other users (21 out of 26) who have

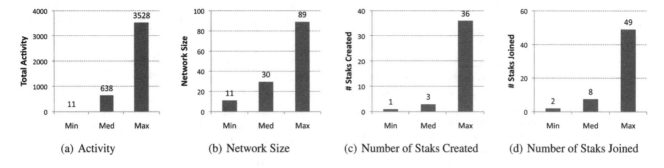

Figure 7. Maximum, median and minium scores for activity metrics across 26 users

helped to drive some, although a relatively small amount of, collaboration. These users have reputation scores between 1 and 25 and as such have proven to be less important when it comes to producing search knowledge that is of use to others (although no doubt these users are consuming promotions that others have produced). We view the smaller subset of high-reputation users as the *search leaders* within HeyStaks, while there is a larger subset of *search followers* who are more likely to consume than produce search knowledge.

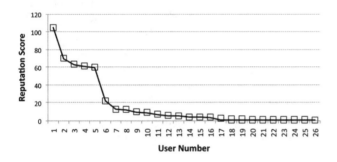

Figure 8. Reputation scores for 26 users

Activity versus Reputation

Earlier in the paper, we cautioned against reputation models that reward users purely on the basis of the accumulation of some activity. Such models can be readily exploited to reward unproductive activity that does not contribute to the core value of a service in and of itself. In this paper we have strived to develop a reputation model that is closely linked with the type of activities that are likely to reward the good behaviour of users whose actions contribute to the long-term value of the system. In HeyStaks this long-term value is ultimately invested in the ability of the system to support meaningful collaboration between searchers.

Nonetheless, it is interesting to understand the strength of the relationship between factors such as activity, staks created/joined, network size and user reputation scores. This correlation information is presented in Figure 9 and it is interesting to note that there is a clear relationship between the factors and the user reputation score. Overall, the degree of user activity comes out on top compared to the number of staks created or joined and network size. This shows that

creating and joining staks may be necessary but it is not sufficient to drive reputation, at least in the absence of the contribution of the user, through their activity, to their search network's knowledge. Correlation with network size across users is comparatively low, suggesting that while having a large network does indeed provide a user with a good opportunity to collaborate, some users may prefer to work together in more tightly-knit search communities.

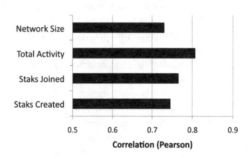

Figure 9. The correlation between activity, staks created/joined, network size and user reputation scores.

CONCLUSIONS

Even though mainstream search engines do not explicitly support collaboration during search, there is much evidence that many search tasks are inherently collaborative. One contribution of this paper is a description of a novel approach to collaborative web search that is fully compatible with mainstream web search engines. The HeyStaks system (www.heystaks.com) helps users to create search networks as a platform for search collaboration.

The main contribution of this paper, however, is the proposal of a reputation system for HeyStaks as a way to model the value of individual searchers, in terms of a reputation score, in order to weight their contributions during result recommendation. The key insight behind the proposed model is that the reputation of a user can be best measured by looking at how often the user is responsible for result recommendations that are ultimately selected. We have described how reputation can be calculated directly from user activity and we have provided some preliminary results based on an analysis of user activity and reputation scores across a sample of HeyStaks users. In summary the reputation model, while correlated with factors such as the number of staks created/joined, the size of a users network, and the activity level of the user, is not dominated by any single factor and so should help to preserve the integrity of the model.

This reputation model will be especially important as a way to protect HeyStaks from malicious users who are motivated to game the system. While we accept that no system is totally foolproof, the HeyStaks system does provide a significant degree of protection against gaming. For example, search knowledge is partitioned into staks that have separate memberships, and this makes it difficult for a user to universally influence search results. HeyStaks also permits stak owners to curate their staks; owners can edit and delete stak contents and ban certain users if they are attempting to game a stak. Furthermore, the reputation algorithm confers reputation on a user u if and only if some other user v ($<> u$) selects a promotion that was derived from the search actions of u. Thus, if u is a spammer and contributes irrelevant or self-interested results to a stak, then these results are unlikely to be promoted and so u never benefits from a reputation increase.

Our paper is just a starting point for this work. The evaluation provided is of a preliminary nature, although it points in the right direction. Our next steps include a tight integration of the reputation system with the deployed HeyStaks system as the basis for a longer-term study that will focus on, for example, the following important issues: (1) does the reputation model lead to improved recommendations with higher click-thru rates; (2) does the availability of reputation statistics, on a user-by-user basis, help to provide users with useful feedback abour their *search value* and does this deepen their engagement with HeyStaks and its search communities; (3) identifying the types of gaming activities and strategies that are likely to be carried out against HeyStaks and developing the reputation model to provide robustness against such activities.

ACKNOWLEDGEMENTS
Based on works supported by Science Foundation Ireland, Grant No. 07/CE/I1147 and HeyStaks Technologies Ltd.

REFERENCES
1. S. Amershi and M. R. Morris. Cosearch: a system for co-located collaborative web search. In *CHI*, pages 1647–1656, 2008.

2. O. Boydell and B. Smyth. Capturing community search expertise for personalized web search using snippet-indexes. In *CIKM*, pages 277–286, 2006.

3. U. Kuter and J. Golbeck. SUNNY: A new algorithm for trust inference in social networks, using probabilistic confidence models. In *AAAI*, pages 1377–1382, 2007.

4. M. R. Morris. A survey of collaborative web search practices. In *CHI*, pages 1657–1660, 2008.

5. M. R. Morris and E. Horvitz. S^3: Storable, shareable search. In *INTERACT (1)*, pages 120–123, 2007.

6. M. R. Morris and E. Horvitz. Searchtogether: an interface for collaborative web search. In *UIST*, pages 3–12, 2007.

7. J. O'Donovan and B. Smyth. Trust in recommender systems. In *IUI*, pages 167–174, 2005.

8. J. Preece and B. Shneiderman. The reader to leader framework: Motivating technology-mediated social participation. *AIS Trans. on Human-Computer Interaction*, 1(1):13–32, 2009.

9. A. M. Rashid, K. Ling, R. D. Tassone, P. Resnick, R. Kraut, and J. Riedl. Motivating participation by displaying the value of contribution. In *CHI*, pages 955–958, 2006.

10. M. C. Reddy and P. Dourish. A finger on the pulse: temporal rhythms and information seeking in medical work. In *CSCW*, pages 344–353, 2002.

11. M. C. Reddy, P. Dourish, and W. Pratt. Coordinating heterogeneous work: Information and representation in medical care. In *ECSCW*, pages 239–258, 2001.

12. M. C. Reddy and B. J. Jansen. A model for understanding collaborative information behavior in context: A study of two healthcare teams. *Inf. Process. Manage.*, 44(1):256–273, 2008.

13. M. C. Reddy and P. R. Spence. Collaborative information seeking: A field study of a multidisciplinary patient care team. *Inf. Process. Manage.*, 44(1):242–255, 2008.

14. G. Salton and M. J. McGill. *Introduction to modern information retrieval*. McGraw-Hill, 1983.

15. A. F. Smeaton, C. Foley, D. Byrne, and G. J. F. Jones. ibingo mobile collaborative search. In *CIVR*, pages 547–548, 2008.

16. A. F. Smeaton, H. Lee, C. Foley, and S. McGivney. Collaborative video searching on a tabletop. *Multimedia Syst.*, 12(4-5):375–391, 2007.

17. B. Smyth. A community-based approach to personalizing web search. *IEEE Computer*, 40(8):42–50, 2007.

18. B. Smyth, E. Balfe, J. Freyne, P. Briggs, M. Coyle, and O. Boydell. Exploiting query repetition and regularity in an adaptive community-based web search engine. *User Modeling and User-Adapted Interaction: The Journal of Personalization Research*, 14(5):383–423, 2004.

19. B. Smyth, P. Briggs, M. Coyle, and M. P. O'Mahony. A case-based perspective on social web search. In *ICCBR*, 2009.

20. B. Smyth, P. Briggs, M. Coyle, and M. P. O'Mahony. Google? shared! a case-study in social search. In *User Modeling, Adaptation and Personalization*. Springer-Verlag, June 2009.

DocuBrowse: Faceted Searching, Browsing, and Recommendations in an Enterprise Context

Andreas Girgensohn[1], Frank Shipman[2], Francine Chen[1], Lynn Wilcox[1]

[1]FX Palo Alto Laboratory, Inc.
3400 Hillview Avenue
Palo Alto, CA 94304, USA

[2]Department of Computer Science &
Center for the Study of Digital Libraries
Texas A&M University
College Station, TX 77843-3112

{andreasg, chen, wilcox}@fxpal.com, shipman@cs.tamu.edu

ABSTRACT

Browsing and searching for documents in large, online enterprise document repositories are common activities. While internet search produces satisfying results for most user queries, enterprise search has not been as successful because of differences in document types and user requirements. To support users in finding the information they need in their online enterprise repository, we created Docu-Browse, a faceted document browsing and search system. Search results are presented within the user-created document hierarchy, showing only directories and documents matching selected facets and containing text query terms. In addition to file properties such as date and file size, automatically detected document types, or genres, serve as one of the search facets. Highlighting draws the user's attention to the most promising directories and documents while thumbnail images and automatically identified keyphrases help select appropriate documents. DocuBrowse utilizes document similarities, browsing histories, and recommender system techniques to suggest additional promising documents for the current facet and content filters.

Author Keywords

Document retrieval, document management, faceted search, document visualization, document recommendation.

ACM Classification Keywords

H5.2. Information interfaces and presentation: User Interfaces; H3.3. Information storage and retrieval: Information search and retrieval.

General Terms

Algorithms, Design, Human Factors.

INTRODUCTION

Enterprise search has been defined in different ways, including search of an organization's intranet, search of an organization's external web site, and search of any text content in electronic form, such as email and databases [6]. In this

paper we focus on search of unstructured information in a corporate document repository. In this type of enterprise search, an employee typically knows or remembers some attributes of the target results [12]. Locating documents in an enterprise often involves finding specific documents that either the user created or the user knows or expects that they were created. In these activities, the user's knowledge of the organization, its history, and its policies and practices can be valuable in locating the desired documents. This is in contrast to Internet users who are searching among a set of unfamiliar documents. Additionally, Internet users are often searching for a fact, such as the phone number for the local restaurant, or a general discussion of a topic, such as what is happening with a particular politician.

In this paper, we present a method for providing search and navigation options to the user through the use of metadata and the document collection file structure. Enterprise document collections are often organized in hierarchies similar to directory trees in file systems. These hierarchies are representations of the policies and practices of the organization, often partly mapping to the structure, roles, and activities in the organization. While newer interfaces allow for access to documents within multiple categories via tags or other mechanisms, the user experience is still relatively similar: users view the set of categories or directories and navigate through the options displayed to locate documents of interest.

To improve system support for navigation and selection in enterprise document collections, we combine data-oriented document analysis with novel interface design. A facet-based interface designed to run in a web browser provides a rich user experience enabling a combination of search and navigation-based location strategies. Because the document type, e.g., spreadsheet, is a useful facet for search, we automatically identify the genre based on features of the page images. Document analysis is also used to determine representative keyphrases of documents to provide a quick overview of each document. These capabilities are part of the new DocuBrowse environment.

In the next section, we elaborate on our vision for enterprise search. The following sections present an overview of the mixed-initiative interface for browsing and searching document collections and discuss recommendation approaches appropriate to the enterprise context. This is followed by a description of the document analysis component with an emphasis on genre identification. We conclude with a vision of how such technologies will change the way people and businesses will store and retrieve documents.

ENTERPRISE SEARCH

Enterprise search is often aided by the user's memory of some properties of the document or the circumstances under which it was presented. We describe two typical examples of this. An employee needs to find information from a past project review presentation. He does not know where the presentation material is located, who gave the presentation, or even which organization in the company created the material. He does recall information in table format in a slide presentation last spring. Another employee is working on solving a problem in product design and remembers a similar problem that was solved in another product several years ago. She would like to find information on the solution, including how it was solved and who solved it. Since the product manager has since left the company, she needs to search the document repository for the information. She knows the product name, the rough time frame, and the nature of the problem.

Unlike in enterprise searches, in typical internet searches the user does not have any prior knowledge of the documents but looks for facts such as a restaurant's phone number or background about a politician. For these types of requests, many different documents meet their needs. In addition to the restaurant's web site, the restaurant phone number could be found on a restaurant review site or a Yellow Pages site. Similarly, articles about the politician can be found on many different news papers and blogs. Another difference is that a Web search result that gets the user close to the result often includes links for browsing to the desired content. In contrast, documents in an enterprise context do not include links with which to browse between documents and that can be used to compute relevance. As the above differences imply, the content-based search techniques used on the Web, while helpful, do not fully address the problem of enterprise search and document access. Thus, other techniques to enhance web-type text queries are needed.

Enterprise search also has to deal with scanned paper documents. While most enterprise documents start in digital form, they often have a period of their life-cycle as paper documents. They need to be signed, annotated, or handed from one person to another. As a result, a document that starts in an easily processable electronic document format (e.g., Microsoft Word) often becomes a scanned document later. The content of the scanned document may be mostly reconstructed through OCR but the result is that all types of documents, whether they start out in a word processor, a spreadsheet, a database, or presentation software, end up as the same document format.

Recommender systems are useful in many contexts and have become common tools for people finding movies, books, etc. Thus, it is natural to apply recommender techniques to the enterprise context. Unfortunately, most recommender techniques are not directly applicable due to assumptions about information availability and access homogeneity. Typically, recommender techniques rely on individuals having access to the same set of resources. In a

corporate context, each employee is likely to have access to a different subset of resources. This may undermine some of the statistical analysis techniques commonly used. These systems also rely on users being willing to share evaluations of resources and interests. Such information is unlikely to be available in the enterprise context. The enterprise social setting makes it inappropriate for employees to rate each other's (or their boss's) documents. Likewise, issues of privacy and compartmentalization makes it unlikely for information that can be used to determine who is working on what to be centralized. However, we can use certain types of recommendations such as documents matching the query that other users with similar queries viewed or documents that were recently viewed by other users in the same organization.

DOCUBROWSE

Our DocuBrowse system supports faceted searching, browsing, and recommendations in an enterprise context. It combines well-known techniques for supporting document access, including browsing the structure of the document collection, searching content, filtering based on metadata, and presenting recommendations based on past user or group activity (see Figure 1). We have deployed the system internally to provide access to 9,000 office documents and 50,000 images created over the past ten years.

Browsing the Document Collection

Enterprise workers typically organize their document collections into sub-collections that group documents based on characteristics of their content, generation, or use. In file system-based document stores, the collection structure is the directory hierarchy. For documents with metadata, documents may be placed based on an ontology of the metadata concepts (e.g., MeSH Terms for the National Library of Medicine).

Acknowledging the centrality of browsing through collections, we created DocuBrowse as a web-based interface that makes browsing such structures easy and intuitive. As such, the majority of DocuBrowse's display is used to present the contents of the user's current location in the document collection. Subcollections (e.g. directories) are presented above the individual documents. DocuBrowse employs modern web technologies to quickly respond to user requests in an asynchronous fashion, for example, by retrieving additional information about a document to be displayed in a tool tip.

Unlike traditional file systems, DocuBrowse allows users to put a document into more than one "directory" and, unlike Windows short cuts, each document entry provides direct access to the original document. In the DocuBrowse prototype, documents are identified by a content hash. This enables automatic duplicate detection so that only one copy of the document has to be stored. As a change to a document changes its identifier, all entries for that document have to be updated. A history mechanism can point to previous versions of a document. To explicitly point to an older version of a document, an entry has to be marked to prevent updates for new document versions.

The document hierarchy is stored in a database. To speed up queries that need to check all documents in a directory sub-

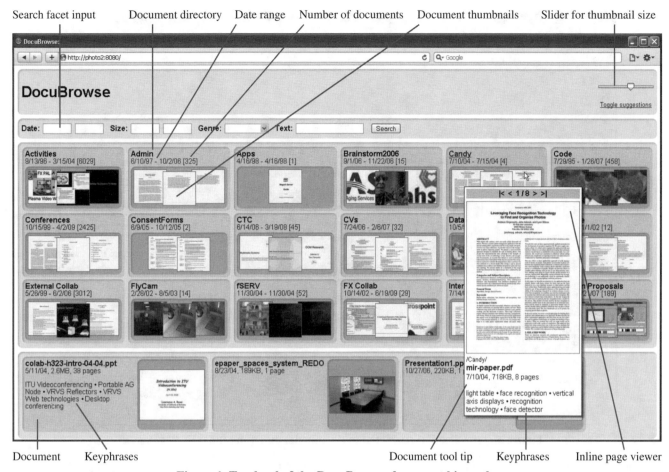

Search facet input Document directory Date range Number of documents Document thumbnails Slider for thumbnail size

Document Keyphrases Document tool tip Keyphrases Inline page viewer

Figure 1. Top-level of the DocuBrowse document hierarchy.

tree, e.g., for selecting thumbnails for directories, we also store the containment closure by directly storing all parent directories for each document and directory. That enables us to retrieve all documents or directories in a directory tree with a single query. While the initial document hierarchy is modeled after the file system hierarchy provided by the user, multiple hierarchies can be supported. Each hierarchy is stored in database tables so that no changes to the flat document storage area are required when a hierarchy is added or changed. Other hierarchies may be based on document properties or on external semantic hierarchies such as the Library of Congress classification for books.

Visualizing Documents

Documents are visualized by a box including the document name, metadata, and automatically selected keyphrases on the left and a thumbnail of the first page of the document on the right (see Figure 2). Clicking anywhere in the document opens the document in the document viewer. The document thumbnails and the information text are offered in different sizes that can be changed quickly by using a slider (see Figure 1). This slider employs dynamic web technologies to zoom in or out without having to reload the whole page. Thumbnails are created in many different sizes when documents are added to the collection so that thumbnails of a requested size can be shown quickly. Figure 4 shows a page with larger thumbnails.

Subcollections, or more simply collections, are visualized by three thumbnails of selected documents in that collection (see Figure 2). Those thumbnails are cropped to squares to better fill the directory box. If fewer than three documents

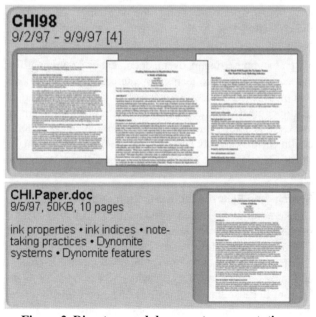

Figure 2. Directory and document representations.

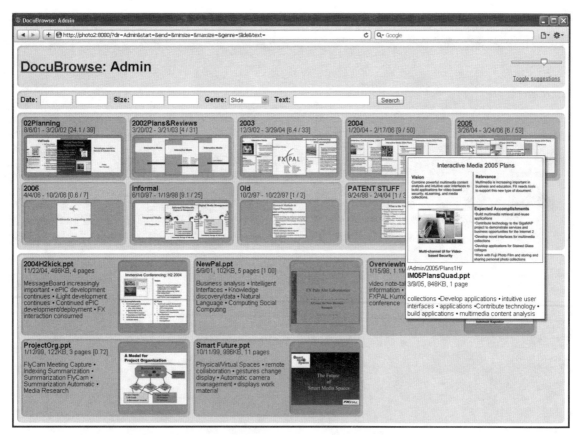

Figure 3. Subcollection restricted to documents matching the "slide" genre.

exist in that collection, then only that number of thumbnails is presented. Thumbnails are selected such that a good sample of the documents in the collection is provided. If a keyword or facet search is active, directory thumbnails are chosen among the documents that best match the search query. In addition to the thumbnails, the collection's name and statistics about its contents are shown. The statistics include the number of documents and the date range. Clicking on the collection visualization navigates to that subcollection, replacing the current list of collections and documents.

When the mouse lingers over a document or a thumbnail for a document in a subcollection, an interactive tool tip appears that provides easy access to more detailed information about that document. The tool tip also includes a small document viewer that allows the user to flip through images of the document pages. This lets the user quickly verify if this is the desired document before opening the full-size document viewer.

Search- and Filter-Based Navigation Support

Unlike traditional search systems that display a list of matching documents, DocuBrowse uses a combination of filtering, color-coding, and browsing to present search results. This approach keeps matching documents in context and makes it easy to narrow or widen a search for a subcollection. Because the document organization tends to reflect the structure and practices of organizations, we maintain that structure in the visualization of results.

To find documents with certain characteristics or contents, DocuBrowse provides filters for different facets of the documents. An important facet is the type, or genre, of a document. Our automatic genre detector is trained to identify technical papers, slides, tables, and photos that correspond roughly to the file formats MS Word, PowerPoint, Excel, and JPEG. By selecting a genre, only documents matching the genre and directories containing those documents are shown. For fuzzy genre matches, color coding is used to indicate the strength of the match.

In addition to genres, DocuBrowse can filter the results based on document size and date. More options can be provided for document collections where additional metadata facets are available. When the user specifies values for a facet, only those documents that fit those values are shown in the browser. DocuBrowse also supports full-text search, so documents that partially or completely match the terms in the query are displayed in the browser while non-matching documents are filtered out. As with fuzzy genre matches, color coding indicates the quality of the match.

When a search or filter is active, the visualization of subcollection is colored to show where large numbers of matching documents are located (see Figure 3). The score for a directory tree combines the score of the best-matching document with the total number of matching documents and the density of the match scores. The match score for a directory is given by:

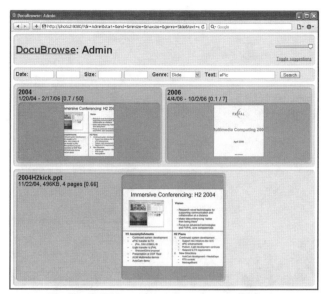

Figure 4. Slides containing the text "ePIC."

$$s = b \cdot \sqrt{\frac{d^2 + c^2}{2}}$$

where b is the best match score among documents in the directory tree, d is the normalized density, and c is the normalized count. The density is the average match score, including documents with a match score of zero. The count is the number of documents with a non-zero match score. Both d and c are normalized relative to the greatest value from the subdirectories being compared. For combining d and c, we chose the quadratic mean because it comes close to picking the maximum of the two values without completely ignoring the other value. Document thumbnails for each directory are chosen from those documents that best match the query while balancing the selection from different branches of the directory tree. Documents with multiple paths to them are only included once.

Multiple document facets can be combined to further restrict the matching documents. For example, after having located slides in a document collection, the user can further restrict the matching documents to those that also contain the specified text string (see Figure 4). Note that each directory in Figure 4 is only visualized by a single document thumbnail even though multiple documents are contained in those directories. This is due to the fact that only a single document matches the query in each of those directories. For combining the results of fuzzy facet searches, we multiply the individual document scores. That produces results consistent with conjunctions in boolean contexts.

Document Viewer

The DocuBrowse viewer provides access to the document pages without requiring other software such as Flash or Adobe Acrobat. It offers two fairly traditional views. One view provides thumbnails of all pages in the documents. Just like in the collection view, a slider allows the user to quickly change the size of the thumbnails. While such a view is available in applications such as Microsoft Power-

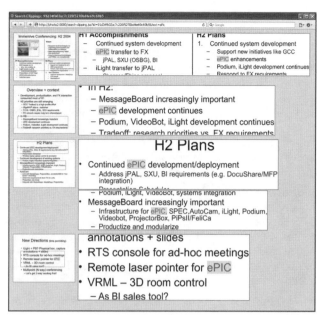

Figure 5. Clippings of pages containing search text.

Point, it is less common in document viewers. The reading view includes thumbnails on the left with a large view of a single page on the right. It is quite similar to a view provided by Adobe Acrobat.

The snippet view displays more details for full text search results. It shows the thumbnails of pages with matching terms and a larger view of the snippets of text in which those terms appeared (see Figure 5). This view provides a quick view of text matches that are too small to see in a thumbnail view. By showing the outlines of snippets in the page thumbnails, context for the snippets is provided.

Search Scenario

To illustrate our approach to search, we describe a use scenario. The Director of Research at a research laboratory wants to access details about a presentation system that was created a few years ago. When looking at the top-level view presented by DocuBrowse (Figure 1), she notices the "Admin" directory and realizes that project reviews stored in that directory would be a good source for the desired information. After navigating to that directory, she restricts the view to documents in the "slide" genre (Figure 3). Among the keyphrases displayed for one of the documents is the word "ePIC" that sounds familiar. To make sure that this is indeed the desired system, she performs a text search with that term. This reduces the view to two subcollections and one document (Figure 4). Clicking on the document displays search clippings that provide sufficient information to identify the system (Figure 5).

ENTERPRISE-ORIENTED RECOMMENDATIONS

Designing mechanisms to generate suggestions requires an understanding of the structure of activity within an enterprise. We look at different properties of corporate organizations. Once appropriate recommender groups have been identified, we base our recommendations on recency, type of access, and document similarity. We present recommendations within DocuBrowse and indicate the basis for each recommendation.

Defining Recommender Groups in a Corporate Setting

As described by Simon, the hierarchic structures of organizations are meant to limit the need for information flow between parts of the organization [15]. As a result, only very general documents such as phone lists, policy descriptions, and guidelines are likely to be widely available across an organization. This raises the problem of identifying activity in the organization's information access that is predictive of future needs of an individual.

Instead of using interaction history of the whole user community to recognize people with similar information needs, as is generally true in recommender algorithms, we propose to use subgroups of the organization chosen based on an understanding of information access in organizations. Two attributes of individuals are being used to identify subgroups:

- *Organizational structure.* As the basis of Simon's argument about the effects of bounded rationality on organizational structure, the information needs of people in the same part of the organization are likely to be indicative of the needs of others in that part of the organization. The first subgroup considered are those individuals that are part of the same organizational component. Determination of the organizational levels used for this grouping requires knowledge of the organization.

- *Job classification.* Simon notes that the organizational structure is not the only hierarchic decomposition of an enterprise. A classification indicative of the type of activity one is involved in is one's job title and different types of activities (e.g. accounting, purchasing, administration, etc.). Thus, our second subgroup used to generate suggestions is the set of people with the same or similar job title. Again, some knowledge of the organization is required to determine which job titles (e.g. assistant professor, associate professor, professor) should be combined into a single group.

To generate suggestions based on each of these groups, we aggregate individual access histories into relevance scores as described below. Thus, all of the individuals in a specified organizational layer are included in organizational structure recommendations. If a complete organizational structure is available, the individual assessments can be weighted by distance from the individual accessing the document store. Otherwise, all individuals within that structure are equally weighted. Similarly, all individuals within the set of job titles defined as equivalent for this purpose are included for generating job classification recommendations.

A final change with regard to traditional recommender algorithms is that suggestions can be for directories as well as individual documents. Directories are important in organizations as the location where documents in a particular sequence are kept. Thus, while past interactions with the January, February, and March accounting files for a office would not point to the April accounting file in a traditional recommender approach, they will point to the directory that includes the April file.

Figure 6. Suggestions for relevant documents.

Computing Document Value

Our recommendations are provided based on recency, type of access, and document similarity. There are three methods to generate suggestions. The first is based on the individual's past interactions with documents. The second and third are based on access and viewing by the subgroups of the organization just described. To compute the likely interest value of a document for a particular individual, we currently use a simple model to incorporate the type and history of access by that individual. DocuBrowse distinguishes between documents that have been viewed in the interactive tool tip and those that were opened in the document viewer. We consider the former to be a quick glance and the latter a more detailed exploration. To differentiate between those types of access, we record the most recent view event for each and then apply an exponential decay to an initial score. In our current implementation, both types start with the same score. Tool tip views have a half life of 30 minutes and detailed views have a half life of 60 minutes. This framework can be expanded to include additional forms of access as they become available in DocuBrowse. Also, instead of only considering the most recent view, more of the interaction history could be considered. For example, the decaying scores for all views could be added.

Computing the interest value of a directory is based on the interest of the files within that directory. When a significant fractions of documents in a directory would be suggested, we instead suggest the whole directory. This approach is applied recursively such that the parent directory is recommended if most subdirectories and documents in it are deemed to be relevant.

Presenting Suggestions in DocuBrowse

DocuBrowse presents suggestions in a floating pane below the main browsing interface (see Figure 6). If a directory is suggested instead of an individual document, the directory is visualized in a fashion similar to the directory listing. The thumbnails of the three most relevant documents are shown with the most relevant one in the front (see second suggestion in Figure 6).

Because there are multiple methods used to generate suggestions, DocuBrowse exposes the form of reasoning used to generate each suggestion through color coding. We currently indicate the following types of suggestions:

- Suggestions based on personal interaction history.
- Suggestions based on the interaction history of members of one's organizational branch.
- Suggestions based on the interaction history of employees with similar job titles.
- Suggestions based on multiple lines of reasoning.

Users of the system do not need to know the specifics of the reasoning approaches. It is natural that some forms of reasoning are more valuable for some jobs than others. Experiences examining suggestions with different color codings will lead users to learn which classes of suggestions work best for them.

KEYPHRASE SELECTION

Keyphrases that give a sense of the content of a document are used in the document summaries presented in DocuBrowse. A small number of keyphrases that can be compactly presented are needed. We decided that a larger number of shorter keyphrases would be more informative, and so five keyphrases that are up to three words long are selected for each document.

Our method identifies sequences of words between stop words and other textual cues, such as punctuation, including PowerPoint bullets, and changes in font style and size, as candidate keyphrases. For each document, the candidate keyphrases are scored and the best N keyphrases selected, where N is prespecified and may be dependent on the amount of screen space available to the application.

To select the best keyphrases, a weighted combination of features is used. The features are text based and include: (1) number of times a term occurs in the document, (2) number of documents in which a term occurs at least once in an English corpus, (3) number of tokens in the keyphrase, (4) location of first mention of the term in the document, measured as paragraph number.

The weighted combination of features is given by:

$$Score(k_j) = \sum_i \lambda_i f_i(k_j, d)$$

where λ_i is the weight given a feature and $f_i(k_j, d)$ is the value of feature i for keyphrase candidate k_j in document d. Once each of the keyphrases is scored, they are then ranked against each other and the best keyphrases are selected for each document.

Evaluation of the keyphrase selection has been limited to visual inspection of the keyphrases displayed by Docu-Browse (Figures 1, 2, and 3). As with sentence-based summarization tasks, there are generally many more keyphrases that are suitable keyphrases for conveying the gist of a document than can be displayed, and evaluation is a tricky

endeavor. For technical papers and slides, the keyphrases displayed by DocuBrowse have been found to be good.

Although we have described keyphrase selection by document, the approach can be applied to other units of text. Our keyphrase selection system has been used to select keyphrases for each page of a document. In these cases, the keyphrases are selected within a document, and additional features and methods are used to reduce redundancy in the selected keyphrases. On the other hand, our keyphrase selection system could also be used to select keyphrases for larger units, such as a subdirectory, although the usefulness would depend on the coherence of the documents in each directory.

GENRE IDENTIFICATION

Documents are often classified and searched for based on words and topics. However, documents can also be classified by another independent attribute: genre. Example genres in literature include poetry, fiction, and drama. In enterprise search and browsing, a different set of document genres than those used to describe literature are needed.

Documents in the DocuBrowse repository are created using a variety of tools that produce documents in different formats, including PDF, DOC, XLS, JPG, and PPT. In a simplistic approach to genre identification, the different document formats roughly correspond to different genres, and a document filename extension could be a surrogate for document genre. However, a document creation tool is often used to create documents in more than one genre. In addition, some extensions, such as PDF, are associated with many genres, since files created in different formats are often converted to PDF for its portable representation. Thus, using only file extensions would result in a user looking for slides to see PowerPoint files that are not slides. Furthermore, the user will not see slides that are in other formats, such as PDF. Similarly, scanned document pages may be JPEG files, so that their genre is unknown.

In genre identification for DocuBrowse, the documents are automatically categorized into a small number of genres, roughly corresponding to the genres usually associated with document format types: technical paper, slides, table, and photo. Figure 7 shows examples of pages from each of the four genres that our Genre Identification and Estimation system (GenIE) has been trained to identify. Note the variation within a genre and that, while the text might not be large enough to read, the genre of each page is readily apparent.

The GenIE System

In the GenIE system, documents are classified based on features extracted from page images. Those images are either generated by scanning paper documents or by rendering electronic documents. Our approach tries to capture layout features without explicitly performing layout analysis. In particular, each page image is tiled and document-based image features are extracted to characterize each tile. Genre identification is performed per page, and then document genre is estimated based on the genre estimates for the pages in the document.

Figure 7. Sample document pages from the genres of technical papers, photos, tables, and slides.

We developed GenIE using a corpus of documents crawled from the web, some of them printed and scanned by us, and some directly converted to JPEG. GenIE was trained to identify the four genres of interest: technical papers, slides, photos, and tables.

We developed a set of features that capture local document characteristics, such as lines of text or text size, within a tile. The tiles must be large enough to extract document characteristics within each tile and at the same time small enough so that the different region types (e.g., heading, figure, body text) remain distinct. Empirically, we have found that dividing each page image into a grid of 5 tiles horizontally by 5 tiles vertically, for a total of 25 tiles, meets our requirements.

The following features are computed for each tile: (1) image density [10], (2) horizontal pixel projection, (3) vertical pixel projection, and (4) color correlogram. Three page-based features are computed: (1) horizontal line lengths, (2) vertical line lengths, and (3) image size.

Each document may be tagged with zero or more genres. To handle tagging with multiple genres, a separate classifier was trained for independently identifying each genre. In developing the genre identification classifiers, a corpus of documents composed of 5098 pages from 1081 documents was labeled with the targeted genres with a total of 3670 labels. Because of the competitive performance of support vector machines (SVM) for many classification tasks, we used an SVM classifier, SVMlight [8]. A separate classifier using a one-against-many model was trained for each genre. We reimplemented Kim and Ross' algorithm [10] as a baseline for comparing performance of our GenIE system and observed that GenIE performed noticeably better (mean precision of 0.59 vs. 0.94 and F1 of 0.51 vs 0.84 for Kim and Ross vs. GenIE, respectively).

To tag the documents in the DocuBrowse corpus, the four GenIE document genre identifiers were used to score each page of all the documents in the corpus. For the Docu-Browse task, the emphasis is on high recall, and our method of combining the page scores for tagging documents by genre bears this in mind. A document genre score, $S_d(g)$, for document d being genre g is computed for each genre as the average of the individual page scores for a document. A page score is the averaged SVM score, clipped to a minimum value of 0.0 and a maximum value of 1.0.

$$S_d(g) = \frac{1}{2P}\sum_{p,c} max(min(s(p, g, c), 0.0), 1.0)$$

where $s(p,g,c)$ is the SVM score for page p being classified as genre g by classifier c and P is the total number of pages in a document. We used two classifiers per genre where each classifier was trained on a separate data partition.

In addition to GenIE's good performance in comparison to a baseline implementation, we also found that it provided a major contribution in the context of DocuBrowse. The offered genres are intuitive and filter the document collection in a useful fashion. For example, restricting the document hierarchy to just slides is very helpful for finding project presentations.

RELATED WORK

There has been much work in several areas related to our work presented here. In this section, we highlight how our work draws from and extends this earlier work, and how we tailor it to address the characteristics of enterprise search.

Document Browsers and Faceted Search

Facets have been presented and used in search and browsing systems in a variety of ways, and the set of facets supported varies, depending on the contents of the document repository. A study by Wilson and schraefel [18] found that "a balance of exploratory and keyword searches" was performed using the mSpace faceted browser both during early use of the system and in later use, indicating that both browsing and search should be supported. This is a feature in both our system and the faceted search systems that we will contrast with ours.

The mSpace faceted browser lays out categorical facet values in columns which can be moved to indicate the priority of filtering relationships. Our system also provides for user-ordered filtering by facet, but the ordering is determined by the order that a user specifies facet values of interest.

Hearst [5] provides recommendations for the design and layout of hierarchical, categorical facets in the Flamenco system and also comments on the use of facets in the eBay Express interface. In Flamenco, which was developed on a collection of fine art images, the result set is shown on the right half of the interface, with result items grouped by the most recently selected facet.

Microsoft's FacetLens system [11] lays out facets and their attribute values in rectangular regions, with the result set also presented on the right side of the interface. FacetMap [16], a predecessor to FacetLens, was also developed at Microsoft for personal information stores with rich metadata. It uses facets for organizing dataset items and dynamically allocates screen space based on the distributions of attributes among the search result set. FaThumb [9] was also developed at Microsoft and provides faceted mobile search.

In contrast with these systems, our system relies on the directory hierarchy to provide the grounding context for users, and results are presented by filtering out parts of the directory hierarchy and by highlighting directories to indicate those that are good matches. In addition, the facets in our system are a mix of pre-specified categories and facets with many values, such as a date range or range of file sizes.

These earlier systems were developed for a browsing task with a relatively homogenous collection of item types, while our "enterprise" document collection contains a variety of document types, such as technical papers and slides. The UpLib system [7] is a "personal digital library system" that also contains a variety of document types, such as technical papers and slides, similar to our document corpus. In UpLib, metadata can be stored with each document. Documents are accessed either by viewing all the documents in the repository or by search over the text and metadata, such as "authors" or "keywords" using the Lucene system. The search-based approach is in contrast to the faceted systems that prompt the user to select a facet value and so reduce the cognitive load on the user.

DocuBrowse draws from the work of these earlier faceted search and browsing systems. Each of these earlier systems was developed for collections with rich metadata that is a significantly stronger organizational factor than the file directory hierarchy. For our task context of enterprise collections, the file hierarchy plays a significant role, and we developed DocuBrowse to integrate faceted search and browsing with a file hierarchy. As with the other faceted systems, facet selection narrows the repository items presented. But unlike earlier systems, the presentation of documents is integrated with the file hierarchy.

Enterprise-Oriented Recommendations

DocuBrowse also provides recommendations, unlike the earlier faceted search systems. Although recommendation systems for different types of data have been developed, we have not seen a recommendation system for enterprise collections. DocuBrowse uses enterprise-based subgroups to generate different types of suggestions. Abecker et al. [1] present an information architecture designed to support the active delivery of resources in an enterprise but do not explore the availability of information necessary to support the active delivery process. Plu et al. [13] describe using recommender techniques to suggest contacts in a corporate

environment. More related to DocuBrowse, Zhen et al. [20] focus on fact-oriented recommendations, such as experiences with a particular vendor or with a specific product.

Keyphrase Selection

Although some documents contain keyphrases, many do not. The automatic selection of document keyphrases provides for greater coverage in the use of keyphrases when visualizing documents. There are a number of ways to identify keyphrases (e.g., [17]). A straight-forward method is by tagging the part-of-speech (POS) of the text and then identifying POS tag sequences that correspond to a noun phrase [17]. Another method is to identify sequences of words between "stop words," or non-content words [3]. More recently, supervised methods which learn how to combine different features have been successfully used. One such system is the KEA system [19]. These systems require a training set of documents labeled with keyphrases. Since we do not have a labeled corpus and it would have been time-consuming to manually label a reasonable size corpus for training a system, we took an unsupervised approach that produces reasonable keyphrases.

Genre Identification

The data collections used by the earlier systems were rich in metadata, where much of the metadata was manually entered. For enterprise collections, the work practice of employees generating documents usually does not include entering metadata for each document. Additionally, when metadata is entered in an ad hoc manner by many people, it is often inconsistent. By automatically extracting metadata, such as genre, from a document collection, more consistent metadata is available for use in faceted search. Although genre identification systems have been developed, the genres covered were not a good match to our enterprise collection and the performance was not good enough for use as facets. Automatic genre identification based on text and markup features has been proposed for web search improvements [2]. Other systems have been developed for classifying page images into different genres.

Shin and Doermann [14] perform document layout analysis to label and identify the boundaries of different types of document regions (e.g., text, image, graphics) and extract features for use in a decision tree classifier. Their identified "genres" correspond to page types: cover page, reference, table of contents, and form pages.

Although layout analysis can be successfully performed for limited domains, general layout analysis is still not robust. Two other image-based approaches to genre identification that do not require layout analysis have been developed by Gupta and Sarkar [4] and by Kim and Ross [10]. Gupta and Sarkar identified salient feature points and performed classification based on the points' locations and local image characteristics. However, their genre classifier was tested on discriminating between only two types of genres: journal articles and memos.

Kim and Ross [10] developed an image-based genre classifier for the first page of a document. They divide the page into a uniform grid of 62 by 62 tiles, count the number of non-white pixels in each tile to compute black pixel density, and use the tile densities as classifier features. They compared the performance of the count feature using Naïve Bayes, Random Forest, and support vector machine (SVM) classification methods. Their best-performing image-based genre classifier performance was Naïve Bayes, but the performance was relatively poor and is meant to be used in conjunction with a text-based genre classifier.

FUTURE WORK

Our system has been in internal use for several months to provide access to historical research documents of our laboratory. We have anecdotal evidence that our approach for combining searching and browsing helps in locating documents that would be missed in a pure search. For example, we located slides depicting Japanese visitors from a previous visit ten years ago. We do not have a sufficient history of interactions with this set of research documents to fully evaluate our algorithms and interfaces for recommending documents. Furthermore, our laboratory is small and has a flat organization, so we could not test recommendations based on organization. We are currently exploring ways to deploy DocuBrowse in a larger organization and are determining requirements for additional security measures and tools.

CONCLUSIONS

We presented a new approach for searching and browsing enterprise document collections that combines faceted filtering and search with navigation of the document collection structure. These techniques are part of a web-based system for accessing document collections. Unlike traditional document search systems, our system presents search results within the user-created document hierarchy by only showing matching documents and directories and highlighting promising areas. To support scanned-in documents and to better classify electronic documents, we utilize an automatic genre identifier that can determine genres such as papers, slides, tables, and photos. We also automatically determine keyphrases that provide users with a quick overview of the document content. We look at access histories, job roles, and document similarities to recommend additional documents that may be useful to the user. We expect this novel approach to simplify access to enterprise document collections.

REFERENCES

1. A. Abecker, A. Bernardi, K. Hinkelmann, M. Sintek. Enterprise Information Infrastructures for Active, Context-Sensitive Knowledge Delivery, in *Knowledge Management Systems: Theory and Practice*, S. Barnes (ed.), Thomson Learning, pp. 146-160, 2002.

2. E.S. Boese and A.E. Howe. Effects of web document evolution on genre classification. In *Proc. of ACM CIKM 2005*, pp. 632-639, 2005.

3. F. Chen, S. Putz, D. Brotsky. Automatic method of selecting multi-word key phrases from a document. US Patent 5745602.

4. M.D. Gupta and P. Sarkar. A shared parts model for document image recognition. In *Proc. of the Ninth International Conference on Document Analysis and Recognition*, pp. 1163-1172, 2007.

5. M. Hearst. Design Recommendations for Hierarchical Faceted Search Interfaces. In *Proc. of the ACM SIGIR Workshop on Faceted Search*, pp. 26-30, 2006.

6. D. Hawking. Challenges in Enterprise Search. In *Proc. of Australasian Database Conference,* pp. 15-24, 2004.

7. W. Janssen and K. Popat. UpLib: a universal personal digital library system. *Proc. of ACM Symposium on Document Engineering*, pp. 234-242, 2003.

8. T. Joachims, Making large-Scale SVM Learning Practical. *Advances in Kernel Methods - Support Vector Learning*, B. Schölkopf and C. Burges and A. Smola (ed.), MIT-Press, pp. 169-184, 1999.

9. A. Karlson, G. Robertson, D. Robbins, M. Czerwinski, and G. Smith. FaThumb: a facet-based interface for mobile search. In *Proc. of CHI'06*, pp. 711-720, 2006.

10. Y. Kim and S. Ross. Examining variations of prominent features in genre classification. In *Proc. of Hawaii International Conference on System Sciences*, p. 132. 2008.

11. B. Lee, G. Smith, G. Robertson, M. Czerwinski, D. Tan. FacetLens: exposing trends and relationships to support sensemaking within faceted datasets. In *Proc. of CHI '09*, pp. 1293-1302, 2009.

12. R. Mukherjee and J. Mao. Enterprise search: Tough stuff. *Queue*, pp. 36-46, 2004.

13. M. Plu, L. Agosto, L. Vignollet, J.-C. Marty, A Contact Recommender System for a Mediated Social Media, *Enterprise information systems VI*, Vol. 58, I. Seruca, J. Cordeiro, S. Hammoudi (ed.), Springer, 293-300, 2006.

14. C. Shin and D. S. Doermann. Classification of document page images based on visual similarity of layout structures. In *Proc. SPIE 2000*, pp. 182-190, 2000.

15. H. Simon. *Sciences of the Artificial, 3rd Edition*. MIT Press, Cambridge, Massachusetts, 1996.

16. G. Smith, M. Czerwinski, B. Meyers, D. Robbins, G. Robertson, D. Tan. FacetMap: A scalable search and browse visualization. *IEEE Trans. Visualization and Computer Graphics*, 12, 5, pp. 797-804, 2006.

17. P. Turney. Extraction of Keyphrases from Text: Evaluation of Four Algorithms. *National Research Council of Canada Technical Report ERB-1051*, 1997.

18. M.L. Wilson and m.c. schraefel. A longitudinal study of exploratory and keyword search. In *Proc. of JCDL*, pp. 52-56, 2008.

19. I. Witten, G. Paynter, E. Frank, C. Gutwin, C. Nevill-Manning. KEA: practical automatic keyphrase extraction, In *Proc. of ACM DL*, pp.254-255, 1999.

20. L. Zhen, G. Huang, Z. Jiang, An Inner-Enterprise Knowledge Recommender System, *Expert Systems with Applications*, Elsevier, pp. 1703-1712, 2009.

Facilitating Exploratory Search by Model-Based Navigational Cues

Wai-Tat Fu, Thomas G. Kannampallil, and Ruogu Kang
Applied Cognitive Science Lab
University of Illinois at Urbana-Champaign
405 N. Mathews Ave., Urbana, IL 61801
wfu@illinois.edu

ABSTRACT

We present an extension of a computational cognitive model of social tagging and exploratory search called the *semantic imitation model*. The model assumes a probabilistic representation of semantics for both internal and external knowledge, and utilizes social tags as navigational cues during exploratory search. We used the model to generate a measure of information scent that controls exploratory search behavior, and simulated the effects of multiple presentations of navigational cues on both simple information retrieval and exploratory search performance based on a previous model called *SNIF-ACT*. We found that search performance can be significantly improved by these model-based presentations of navigational cues for both experts and novices. The result suggested that exploratory search performance depends critically on the match between internal knowledge (domain expertise) and external knowledge structures (folksonomies). Results have significant implications on how social information systems should be designed to facilitate knowledge exchange among users with different background knowledge.

Author Keywords

Semantic Imitation, SNIF-ACT, exploratory learning, knowledge exchange, social tagging

ACM Classification Keywords

H.5.3 Group and Organization Interfaces: Collaborative computing. H5.4. Information interfaces and presentation (e.g., HCI): Hypertext/Hypermedia.

General Terms

Design, Theory, Performance

INTRODUCTION

In the domain of computer science, representations of data are known to determine implementation of control structures and computations. Similarly, in the domain of

cognitive science, representations and processes of mental contents and skills are shown to have significant impact on human cognitive activities, development, and acquisition of knowledge structures. These observations lead naturally to the thesis that different interface representations and interaction methods will have significant impact on shaping the structure, performance, and emergent behavior of human-computational systems.

The goal of this paper is to show how a computational cognitive model of social tagging and exploratory search can generate useful predictions on the effects of different presentations of navigational cues on facilitating exploratory search and knowledge exchange. Results are useful for informing engineering decisions on how navigational cues should be presented to make knowledge search more effective or efficient, or, in other words, to create more intelligent interfaces.

Social Tags as Navigational Cues

Recent advances have made the Web a more participatory social-computational systems that allow people to explore, learn, and share information with others. A good example is the increasing popularity of social bookmarking systems such as del.icio.us CiteULike.org, and Bibsonomy.org, which allow users to annotate, organize and share their web-based resources using short textual labels called tags. Many have argued that social tagging systems can provide navigational cues or "way-finders" [6, 10, 14, 15, 20, 24] for other users to explore information. The notion is that, given that social tags are labels that users create to represent topics extracted from Web documents, interpretation of these tags should allow other users to predict contents of different documents efficiently. Social tags are arguably more important in exploratory search, in which the users may engage in iterative cycles of goal refinement and exploration of new information (as opposed to simple fact-retrievals), and interpretation of information contents by others will provide useful cues for people to discover topics that are relevant.

One significant challenge that arises in social tagging systems is the rapid increase in the number and diversity of the tags. As opposed to structured annotation systems, tags provide users an unstructured, open-ended mechanism to annotate and organize web-content. As users are free to create any tag to describe any resource, it leads to what is referred to as the *vocabulary problem* [9]. Because users may use different words to describe the same document or extract different topics from the same document based on their own background knowledge, the lack of a top-down mediation may lead to an increase in the use of incoherent tags to represent the information resources in the system. In other words, the inherent "unstructuredness" of social tags may hinder their potential as navigational cues for searchers because the diversities of users and motivation may lead to diminishing tag-topic relations as the system grows.

Descriptive Models of Social Tagging

Despite this potential vocabulary problem, recent research has found that at the aggregate level, tagging behavior seemed relatively stable and that the tag choice proportions seemed to be converging rather than diverging [2, 11]. While these observations provided evidence against the proposed vocabulary problem, they also triggered a series of research investigating how and why tag proportions tended to converge over time.

One explanation for the stability was that there was an inherent propensity for users to "imitate" word use of others as they create tags. This propensity may act as a form of *social cohesion* that fosters the coherence of tag-topic relations in the system, and leads to stability in the system. Golder and Huberman showed that the stochastic urn model by Eggenberger and Polya [3] was useful in explaining how simple imitation behavior at the individual level could explain the converging usage patterns of tags. Specifically, convergence of tag choices was simulated by a process in which a colored ball was randomly selected from an urn and was replaced in the urn along with an additional ball of the same color, simulating the probabilistic nature of tag reuse. The simple model, however, does not explain why certain tags would to be "imitated" more often than others, and therefore cannot provide a realistic mechanism for tag choices and how social tags could be utilized as navigational cues during exploratory search, not to mention the obviously over-simplified representation of individual users by balls in an urn.

The memory-based Yule-Simon (MBYS) model of Cattuto [2] attempted to explain tag choices by a stochastic process. They found that the temporal order of tag assignment has an impact on users' tag choices. Similar to the stochastic urn model, the MBYS model assumed that at each time step a tag would be randomly sampled: with probability p the sampled tag was new, and with probability $1-p$ the sampled tag was copied from existing tags. When copying, the probability of selecting a tag was assumed to decay with time, and this decay function was found to follow a power law distribution. Thus, tags that were recently used had a higher probability of being reused than those used in the past. One major finding by Cattuto et al. was that semantically general tags (e.g., "blog") tended to co-occur more frequently with other tags than semantically narrower tags (e.g., "ajax"), and this difference could be captured by

the decay function of tag reuse in their model. Specifically, they found that a slower decay parameter (when the tag is reused more often) could explain the phenomenon that semantically general tags tended to co-occur with a larger set of tags. In other words, they argued that the "semantic breadth" of a tag could be modeled by a memory decay function, which could lead to different emergent behavioral patterns in a tagging system.

A Predictive Process Model of Social Tagging

Results from previous models were based on analyses of word-word relations as revealed by the various statistical structures in the organization of tags (e.g., how likely one tag would co-occur with other tags or how likely each tag was reused over time). These models are therefore *descriptive* models at the aggregate level, and have little to offer about *predictions* at the level of interface interactions and cognitive processes of individual. To this end, we attempted to adopt a slightly different approach. Rather than describing aggregate behavioral patterns, we drew on research results from the domain of cognitive science to develop a computational cognitive model that characterized knowledge representation and tag choices at the individual level, then studied how their effects could generate useful predictions on search performance.

In our previous work [6-8], we argued that, rather than imitating other users at the word level, one possible explanation for this kind of social cohesion could be grounded on the natural tendency for people to process tags at the semantic level, and it was at this level of processing that most *imitation* occurred. This explanation was supported by research in the area of reading comprehension [17], which showed that people tended to be influenced by meanings of words, rather than the words themselves during comprehension. Assuming that background knowledge of people in the same culture tend to have shared structures (e.g., using similar vocabularies and their corresponding meanings in order to conform and communicate with each), users of the same social tagging system may also share similar semantic representations of words and concepts, even when the use of tags may vary across individuals at the word level. In other words, we argued that part of the reason for the stability of social tagging systems can be attributed to the shared semantic representations among the users, such that users may have relatively stable and coherent interpretation of information contents and tags as they interact with the system. Based on this assumption, we developed the *semantic imitation model* [7, 8] that predicts how different semantic representations may lead to differences in individual tag choices and eventually different emergent properties at the aggregate behavioral level. The model also predicts that the *folksonomies* (i.e., knowledge structures) in the system reflect the shared semantic representations of the users.

In the current paper, we propose an extension of the semantic imitation model to predict how different presentations of navigational cues may influence search performance. We will first describe performance in an exploratory search task and contrast it with a standard information retrieval task using traditional search engines. We will then introduce the details of the semantic imitation model and how it can be applied to characterize social tagging and search behavior. We will then describe how the model can be combined with our previous SNIF-ACT model of Web search [5] to generate predictions on the effects of different presentations of navigational cues on search performance. We will also show how this potential improvement in performance may differ in systems that are mostly used by domain experts and novices.

SIMULATING SEARCH PERFORMANCE

Figure 1 shows a scenario in which a user is performing a search task in a simplified social tagging system. For simple information retrieval, the searcher may utilize some keywords to locate a single piece of information (e.g., address of a movie theatre). For exploratory search, the searcher may be looking for information related to a particular topic (e.g., financial crisis), but he or she may not know exactly where and what to look for information relevant to this topic. The searcher can begin by inputting the topic and selecting one of the tags that are associated with the topic as suggested by the social tagging system. The searcher may then click on one of the tags to access the list of documents associated with the tag. Each of the documents will also contain a list of tags created by other users, so the searcher can use these tags to evaluate whether the document may contain information relevant to their information goal, as well as to gain some ideas about what other tags/keywords may be related to the topic that he or she is searching for. In contrast to information retrieval, in exploratory search the information that the searcher is looking for is seldom contained in a single document. Rather, the searcher will likely need to collect and integrate a set of documents related to the topics (and subtopics) during their search, and may need to iteratively refine their search goals to learn more about the topic as they navigate in the system [6-8, 15, 16, 20].

In many ways, the tag-based exploratory search as depicted in Figure 1 is similar to information retrieval in a traditional search engine, in which a user types in a keyword and a list of documents will be returned from the search engine. There are, however, three main differences between searching in a traditional search engine and in a social tagging system. First, in a social tagging system, users can browse through tags created by others to pick one that is closest to the topic that they are interested in, but in a traditional search engine users have to come up with their own keywords as they browse through the documents. Second, the list of documents returned from a social tagging system are determined by tags created by other users, but in a traditional search engine the links between keywords and document are usually calculated by machine-learning algorithms, which may or may not be capturing the effect of social cohesion in a tagging system as discussed earlier.

Third, tags associated with the list of returned documents can help users to refine their information goal by interpreting the association of these tags (and the related topics) within and across documents, such that they can gain a better understanding of *not only* the topics that they are looking for, but *also the relations among these related topics* as they are distributed across documents tagged by users of the system [16]. In contrast, in traditional search engines, the list of documents returned are usually not semantically related and thus they do not inherently support this kind of *sensemaking* activity [6, 8, 10, 14, 16, 18, 20].

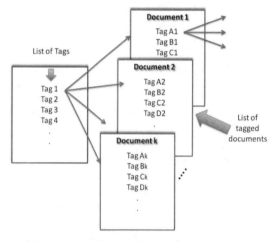

Figure 1. An example of exploratory search in a social tagging system. The list of tags are provided by the system, when a user clicks on a tag, a list of documents associated with that tag will be presented. Each of these documents also has a list of tags associated with it.

When the searcher is retrieving a single piece of information, search performance can be measured by the number of documents browsed before the target document can be found (the fewer the number of documents browsed, the better the performance). However, because in exploratory search the goal is not to find a single document, this measure of performance cannot be directly used. Instead, one can assume that the number of documents that the searcher collects (or saves as bookmarks) in a certain amount of time can be used as a measure of exploratory search performance. In other words, if system A allows a searcher to find more relevant documents in the same amount of time (or clicks) than system B, we assume that system A provides better support for exploratory search than system B. We will use this measure for exploratory search performance in our simulation.

Relation to Previous Information Search Models

Before discussing our model of tag-based exploratory search, it will be useful to review briefly previous models of information search [5, 22-24]. One important control variable in these models is the measure of information scent [5, 22]. Information scent is a general term describing the perception of the relevance of a link to the information goal of the searcher based on information cues presented by the system (e.g., link texts on the search-result page returned from either a search engine or social tagging system). There are different calculations of the measure of information scent, but most of them are derived from some forms of statistical text processing techniques that calculates the semantic distance between two words. Results from previous models suggest that the use of information scent as a control variable for searching behavior provides good match to navigational behavior.

THE SEMANTIC IMITATION MODEL

In this section, we will briefly review the major components of the semantic imitation model [7, 8] that explains the process of social tagging based on semantic interpretation of content. The model has properties that allow us to separately model the external and internal knowledge structures and effectively integrate it with a psychologically plausible choice mechanism. The model assumes that when users navigate in a social tagging system, they *look at existing tags* (created by previous users), *infer topics* related to the existing tags based on the semantic interpretation of the tags, *select the tags* that are most relevant to the topics that the user is interested in, *comprehend the content* of the document (resource) that is being tagged, and then *choose a tag* (or reuse an existing) that is appropriate for the resource (see Figure 2). We will first focus how the model represent semantic knowledge. We will then describe how the model interpret and create tags based on the semantic knowledge representations, before we describe how the model can simulate exploratory search in a social tagging system.

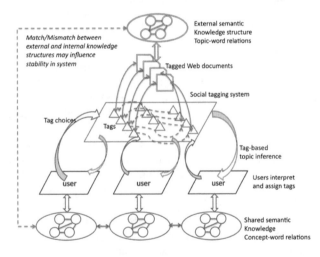

Figure 2. *Semantic Imitation Model*: Users interpret tags based on their knowledge and infer topics in a document and choose tags to represent the latent semantics in the documents.

Representation of semantic knowledge

There are three main components in the model: words, semantic concepts (or topics) underlying the words, and documents that contain both the words and the topics. It is assumed that concepts can be represented as a probability distribution of words. For example, the concept "health" can instantiate many associated words such as hospital, doctor, surgery, etc. If c represents the set of available concepts and w represents the set of words, then $p(w|c)$ is the probability distribution of words, given a set of concepts. Using Bayes theorem, we can then calculate the set of concepts given a set of words.

$$p(c_k \mid w) = \frac{p(\overline{w} \mid c_k)\, p(c_k)}{\sum_i p(w \mid c_i)\, p(c_i)} \qquad (1)$$

We assume that for each concept, c, the associated word in the multinomial distribution $p(w|c)$ is normally distributed. Thus, there will be words in a concept that are more "central" than others. For example, for the concept "money", the word "dollar" is more central than the word "exchange". By assuming that concepts have overlapping normal distributions over words, we can simulate different degrees of ambiguities of the semantic meanings of words.

One major advantage of the current semantic representation is that it is a generative model, in the sense that we can generate documents based on the assumed set of word-topic distributions. This means that we can use a unified framework to simulate both the internal and external knowledge structures in the system. For example, given a particular distribution of topics and words in a set of documents, we can simulate the differences in internal knowledge structures between experts and novices by varying the match between internal and external knowledge structures (i.e., experts will have a better match to the word-topic distributions in the documents than novices). Previous research has shown that the model can produce documents that match well with real documents in large corpora [13].

In the current simulations, we manipulated the standard deviations of the normal distributions of the word-concept distributions of the users. When the standard deviation was set to a higher value, there would be a decrease in the specificity of word use to represent a concept (e.g., when creating tags) as well as in word interpretation (e.g., when comprehending the meaning of words/tags). In other words, we assumed that experts will have higher specificity in both their word use and interpretation than novices. Note that this definition is consistent with research that adopts a network approach to define expertise [21].

Interpreting tags

As the user navigates through the system, existing tags of a resource act as retrieval cues for inferring the related concepts. As users browse through a set of tags that were previously created for a resource, semantic representations for those tags (words) are activated. This tag-based topic inference can be represented as a measure that estimates the probability that a set of tags will instantiate a specific set of topics (or concepts), $p(c|w)$, where c is the set of concepts and t are the tags that are associated with a resource. Substituting tags, t into equation (1) we get,

$$p(c_k \mid t) = \frac{p(t \mid c_k)\, p(c_k)}{\sum_i p(t \mid c_i)\, p(c_i)} \qquad (1a)$$

Equation 1a represents the probability that a given tag can predict a particular concept. This tag-based topic inference process will facilitate the evaluation of the relevance of the document, as well as the comprehension of the document if a document is selected, as we will discuss next.

Comprehension of document contents

The comprehension process consists of combining the concepts that the user abstracts from the tags and then combines it with the concepts extracted from the document. This final set of topics that are obtained uses the prior distributions of all concepts represented by $p(c_k|t)$ (calculated from 1a). This is represented by the posterior probability $p(c_k|d)$ extracted from document, d.

$$p(c_k \mid d) = \frac{p(\overline{w} \mid c_k)\, p(c_k \mid t)}{\sum_i p(\overline{w} \mid c_i)\, p(c_i \mid t)} \quad (2)$$

Assigning Tags

Tag creation is based on concept-word and word-concept relations. In order to do this, the probability of selecting a new tag given the set of existing tags and the words in the document is computed. In (3), w_{new} is the new tag created by the user and d represents the aggregate of all words in the document and the existing tags.

$$p(w_{new} \mid d) = \sum_i p(w_{new} \mid c_k)\, p(c_k \mid d) \quad (3)$$

Thus, $p(w_{new}|d)$ is the likelihood that the words and tags associated with a document will predict the creation of a new tag, w_{new}. An important element of the tag choice process is that it should mirror a behavioral decision making process. For this we used a random utility model (RUM) that has been used extensively to model human choice behavior [19]. We use the degree of representativeness of a tag as the measure of utility of the tag. The degree of representativeness of a tag provides a measure of how much a tag represents the semantic contents of a document. We also use a random variable, σ to incorporate a degree of uncertainty into the model.

$$U_w = p(w \mid d) + \sigma \quad (4)$$

where σ follows a double exponential distribution, and it can be shown that the probability that U_w is the maximum can be expressed as (b controls how likely a word with low utility will be chosen over one that has high utility)

$$p(U_w > U_j \text{ for all j}) = \frac{\exp(U_w/2b)}{\sum_j \exp(U_j/2b)} \quad (5)$$

A new tag assignment occurs only when the tag that has a higher utility was more representative than the existing tags.

$$\frac{\max[U_w]}{\max[U_t]} > h \quad (6)$$

In (6), $\max[U_w]$ is the maximum utility among all words and $\max[U_t]$ is the maximum utility among all existing tags. The assumption here is that users create new tags reflect the content of a document. Though in this paper we focus only on the informational value of the tags, previous research has shown that representativeness reflects the association between cues (a tag in this case) and an item retrieved from personal memory. Thus, it is possible to take into account cases where people use personal tags (e.g., to read) to qualify a resource.

As opposed to other models of social tagging, the semantic imitation model was based on a cognitively plausible tag choice mechanism that was coupled to the formal representations of semantic knowledge that exist in both external documents and internal knowledge structures of the users. The model provides an explanation on generally accepted concepts of tag convergence and stabilization based on a cognitive model of individual taggers (users). Additionally, it has a mechanism for generating testable predictions about behavioral patterns in systems generated by different user populations (e.g., experts vs. novices).

Exploratory search

To model exploratory search, we simulated a searcher who is searching for information related to a randomly selected topic. Because one can only measure the actual word use by the searcher, we cannot use (1a) to directly calculate information scent. Instead, when the searcher enters the first tag to search for or select a tag during navigation, we can use that to infer what this person may be looking for by summing over all possible topics that are related to the selected tag (see 3). Therefore, the measure of information scent of each of the tag $IS(tag)$ can be calculated by

$$IS(tag) = p(tag|tag_{selected})$$
$$= \sum_k p(tag|c_k)p(c_k|tag_{selected}) \quad (7)$$

in which $tag_{selected}$ represents the last tag selected, and tag represents each of the tag to be presented. We used $IS(tag)$ as a measure of how the searcher will perceive that a tag is relevant during exploratory search. However, in our previous work as well as others, it was found that the sequential order of links (or in this case, tags) had significant effect on search performance [5]. Specifically, it was found that people tended to engage in local cost-benefit tradeoffs [4] as they evaluated links sequentially, such that they would click on a link positioned at the top even when there was a higher-scent link positioned at a lower position.

Model-based Presentations of Navigational Cues

Figure 3 shows the three model-based presentations of navigational cues in a social tagging system. First, we simulated exploratory search performance in a system that presents tags based on its information scent. Under the assumption that tags are created to represent topics in documents, ranking tags based on their information scent should also increase the efficiency of search (in terms of amount of relevant information found per unit time).

In the simulation, we assumed that the model-searcher would start with a keyword (for information retrieval) or a word sampled from a topic (for exploratory search). This word would be used to generate a list of related tags by the system. In the *random arrangement* condition, the order of these tags will be randomized. Otherwise, the tags would be presented in the order of their information scent.

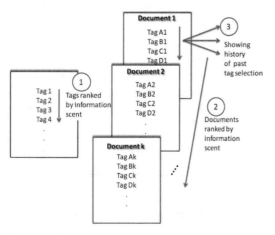

Figure 3. The three model-based presentations to be tested by the mode simulation during the exploratory search process: (1) ranking tags based on their information scent, (2) ranking documents based on the average information scent of tags, and (3) leaving a document when the information scent drops below threshold (i.e., satisficing).

Following the SNIF-ACT model [5], selection of tags would depend on *both* the sequential order of the tags *and* its information scent. Specifically, there were two competing actions as the model evaluated each tag and decide which tag to click. The *evaluate-next* action would move on to the next sequential link, and the *select-tag* action would click on a tag. The utilities for each action were calculated based on the Bayesian satisficing model (BSM, see [4, 5]) as:

$$U_{ev}(n+1) = \frac{U_{ev}(n) + IS(tag)}{1 + N(n)}, U_s(n+1) = \frac{U_s(n) + IS(best\ tag)}{1 + k + N(n)}$$
(8)

where U_{ev} and U_s were the utilities for the action evaluate-next and select-tag respectively. n represents the model cycle. After each cycle, the utilities would be updated according to (8). *IS(best tag)* represented the information scent of the tag that had the highest IS value among tags that were evaluated so far. $N(n)$ was the number of tags evaluated up to cycle n. k is a constant that controls the initial bias for the model to evaluate more links (i.e., initially U_s will be lower than U_{ev}, but as $N(n)$ increased, this difference diminished, such that the model would be biased to evaluate at least a few tags before selecting a tag). These two actions competed with each other, and at any model cycle one action would be selected based on the utilities of the actions (see the softmax equation in eqn 5).

When a tag was selected, the model would read through documents that were associated with the selected tags. When the model-searcher read a document, it would judge whether the document contained a relevant topic based on the calculation of $p(c_k|d)$. Specifically, the document would be saved if

$$p(c_k|d) > H_{relevant}$$
(9)

We set $H_{relevant} = 0.5$ throughout the simulation. Once a document was read (regardless it was saved or not), the model would go back to the previous page and continued with the next tag, and so on.

In the second model-based presentation, in addition to ranking tags according to their information scent, we also simulated the situation in which the interface also ranked the presentation of documents returned from a tag selection. The ranking was, however, based on the weighted sum of information scent between the selected tag and the set of tags associated with each of the documents. Following the SNIF-ACT model, the information scent of a document was calculated by

$$IS(document) = \sum_j IS(tag_j) * \exp(-dj)$$
(10)

in which d represents a decay parameter and was set to 0.5 as in [17], and the summation was for all tags j associated with the document. The exponential weighting was to control for the additive effect of the number of tags in a document to the measure of *IS(document)*.

Similar to the evaluation of tags, we also assumed that both the sequential order of documents and their information scent would influence how likely the documents would be read. The document selection process was similar to that in tag selection, and the same utility equations in (8) were used, except that *IS(tag)* was replaced by *IS(document)*.

The final model-based cue was to show the history of tag selection as the model navigated in the system. We assumed that when the history of tag selection was included, the searcher could have more integration of topics browsed during the navigation, and would be able to better distinguish what information was relevant. In addition, we assumed that the calculation of information scent would more accurately reflect the relevance of tags and documents when the history of tag selection was taken into account. Specifically, when subsequent tags were selected, we calculated information scent of each tag by including all tags selected in (7). Tags and documents would then be ranked according to the extent to which they matched the whole history of tags selected by the model-searcher.

SIMULATING THE MODEL

In this section, we describe the simulation set up for the semantic imitation model for testing the overall properties of folksonomies created by the semantic imitation model by experts and novices, as well as the exploratory search performance of an expert and novice model-searcher. We will first describe the basic simulation set up below.

Basic Simulation Set Up

Following the method by others [1, 13], a set of 100 documents was generated. Each document had a random set of topics assigned to it. The topics were randomly sampled from a set of 100 sample topics. As explained earlier, for each topic a set of words were sampled from a multinomial distribution of 2500 words. Each word had a prior probability that was normally distributed with a standard deviation of 1. Each document had 500 words.

At the start of simulation, a document was randomly selected. Using an unbiased topic inference process the probabilities for each of the 100 topics were computed. The probabilities for each of the topics were calculated based on the available words (w) in the document. This was the $p(c_k|w)$ for the document (for topics k=1 to 100)(see equation (1)). It was also assumed that at the start of the simulation there was no tag assigned to any document. The set of $p(c_k|w)$ for all documents was used to compute the $p(w_i|w)$ for all words in the vocabulary. The utilities of all possible words in the vocabulary were then calculated (using equation (4)).

In the second stage of the simulation, the tag-based topic inference process was invoked by the existing tag, which semantically primed the topic extraction and comprehension process. In order to achieve this, each $p(c_k)$ would be substituted by $p(c_k|w)$ from the previous iteration of equation (1). Additionally, instead of w, the previously assigned tag t would be used. The probability values of $p(c_k|t)$ would then be updated for all topics and used as the prior distribution of concepts during comprehension (using equation (2)). Utilities of all words would be calculated and the word that has the maximum utility was compared to the maximum utility of the existing tags. If the ratio exceeded the threshold parameter, h, the new word was added as a tag to the document. This process continued across 100 iterations for all documents. The threshold parameter h was set at 1 and b was set to 0.01 in all simulation runs.

The Expert and Novice Network

The major benefit of the semantic imitation model was its flexibility in creating different knowledge representations for users. As described earlier, by changing the spread of prior distributions of words over all the available words, different knowledge representations of the user could be created. The smaller spread (i.e., lower s.d.) in the probability distribution of words within each topic implied that the words were more accurate in predicting the concepts in the document, such that the simulated user would be better able to interpret a tag and infer the topic as well as to assign a tag to represent the topic. We assumed that this reflected the performance of domain experts.

The purpose of this simulation was to determine the differences in the overall properties of tags (i.e., the resulting folksonomy) created by experts and novices. The basic simulation parameters were the same as the basic set up (100 documents, 100 topics, 2500 words). There were two conditions that were tested in this simulation. In the

expert-network, 35 experts were simulated to create tags in the system, while in the *novice-network*, 35 novices were simulated to create tags in the system. The following properties were computed at the end of each simulation run: total number of tag applications (a tag application was the addition of a tag to a document), number of tags that were reused, number of unique tags that were created, and the variance in the number of tag applications.

The Expert and Novice Searcher

We also simulated search efficiency in both networks with different model-based presentations of navigational cues shown in Figure 3. We created the expert and novice searcher, each of which performed a simple document retrieval task and an exploratory search task in each network. We therefore had four different sets of simulation results from the combinations of expert and novice models searching in the expert and novice networks. In each set, separate simulations were conducted for each addition of the model-based presentations (i.e., they were cumulative). In addition, a condition in which tags and documents were randomly organized was simulated as a control condition. Therefore, we simulated performance in each of the four conditions in each of the four sets of simulations.

RESULTS

General Properties: Convergence, Stabilization of Tags

The most generally accepted property of social tagging systems is that the proportion of tags assigned to a document converges over time [12]. So, as the total number of tags increase in a system, the ratio of the frequency of a tag to the total number of tags remains fairly constant. This emergent property of tags, called *convergence*, was attributed to the social nature of the tagging process. In our previous simulations [7], we showed that the semantic imitation model produced not only the convergence, but also predicted how experts and novices could lead to different rates of convergence. To provide the background for the effects of the model-based presentation, we showed the results here to highlight the differences.

The two graphs on the top half of Figure 4 shows simulation results generated from the model. The graphs are based on simulation of 100 documents with each point representing the proportion of a tag (y-axis) at a certain time point during the simulation (x-axis). Similar to results obtained by Golder and Huberman [9], the tag proportions created from the semantic imitation model converged over time. The convergence of tags in the semantic imitation model can be explained as follows: users tag choices are driven by the degree of representativeness of a tag to the concepts extracted from the document. The extraction of concepts is influenced by the semantic interpretation of existing tags (rather than a direct imitation). The commonality in the semantic representation of words and concepts among all users will lead to a coherent interpretation and choice of tags that are perceived to be most representative of the documents.

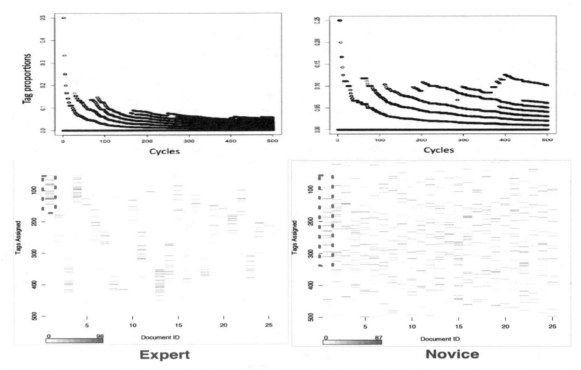

Figure 4. Convergence and stabilization in tags created by experts (top-left) and novices (top-right). The corresponding spread of tags created by experts and novices are shown at the bottom panels.

The faster convergence in the expert network can be explained as follows: the tags assigned by experts were more predictive of the topics in the document and experts could extract these topics better than novices. Additionally, other experts tagging the same resource tended to choose the same higher quality tags. In contrast, novices were less knowledgeable about the contents of the document and consequently less effective in extracting the appropriate topics (and therefore tags) from the documents. Novices therefore selected tags that were more diverse than experts and hence the slower convergence.

This phenomenon was further clarified in the graphs shown on bottom half of figure 2. The x-axis represents a subset of documents (25) from the 100 documents used for the simulation and the y-axis shows a subset of tags (500) from the total of 2500. The "spread" of the tags created by experts was much narrower than those created by novices (shown within the dashed box for one document). This means that experts' tag creation process was similar in nature and they reached a consensus much quicker than novices. In contrast, tags created by novices were more diverse, leading to slower convergence.

Performance on Simple Information Retrieval

We simulated the model's performance on information search for a single document to understand how different presentations of results could benefit experts and novices in the expert and novice network. Each model searcher would be given a keyword to search for a specific document in the network. The system would then return a set of tags most related to the keyword. The model would then select the tag

sequentially based on the order presented by the system (which varied depending on the condition). We then tabulated the number of documents browsed before the document was found for each condition, and average the results over 100 iterations.

Figure 5 shows the results for the expert and novice searcher in the networks. In the expert network, the expert searcher was much better at finding the document than novices. The three model-based navigational cues seemed to have helped the novices significantly in finding the document, as the number of documents browsed was much reduced when ranked tags were presented, and this number decreased even more as presentations of documents were ranked, and when tag history was presented to rank the documents. Given that the performance of the experts were already good even when tags were randomly presented, the improvement was smaller than that for the novice. However, we did see improvement as more model-based navigational cues were used.

The results showed that in the expert network, when the "quality" of tags was good, experts were very good at utilizing the tags as navigational cues to find the target document. Indeed, experts could find the target document much more efficiently than novices even in the random arrangement of tags. This suggested that experts were much better at evaluating which tags were good than novices (such that there was a much higher difference in the IS(tag) values for experts than novices, making them better at selecting the right tag to search as specified in eqn 8). On

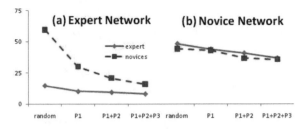

Figure 5. In simple information retrieval, mean number of documents *browsed* before the desired document was found in each of the presentation conditions for expert and novice searchers in the (a) expert and (b)novice network.

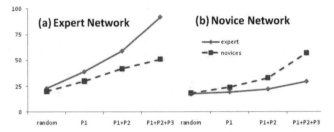

Figure 6. In exploratory search, the mean number of documents *saved* in each of the presentation conditions for expert and novice searchers in the (a) expert and (b)novice network.

the other hand, the model-based navigational cues did help the novices to find the target document more efficiently, suggesting that when novices could not evaluate which tags were good, ranking the high-quality tags for them would significantly help them to navigate to the target document. Indeed, when all three model-based navigational cues were used, novices could perform almost just as well as experts, suggesting that the model-based presentation of expert tags were effective in guiding novices to navigate in the system.

As Figure 5b shows, results were quite different in the novice network. Although the model-based navigational cues did help both expert and novice searchers, the improvement in efficiency was much smaller than that in the expert network. In addition, there was virtually no difference between performance by experts and novices. This suggested that when the quality of tags were low, users could not benefit much from the tags to help them navigate to the target document. In other words, the effectiveness of the model-based presentation techniques were impeded by the inherently low-quality tags generated by novices. Apparently, the ranking of tags and documents based on the noisy estimates of information scent was not very useful in guiding searchers to navigate in the system.

Performance on Exploratory Search

In exploratory search, the main performance measure was the number of relevant document saved within 100 tag selections. We assumed that the more number of document saved, the better was the performance. Figure 6 shows the number of documents saved during exploratory search for expert and novice searchers in the networks. In the expert network, model-based navigational cues apparently helped both experts and novices search for relevant information. Interestingly, for experts, as more model-based navigational

cues were introduced, the improvement was significantly more than for novices (as shown by the exponential increase in effectiveness in Figure 6a). This suggested that when experts were exploring for information with good quality tags, the model-based navigational cues significantly augmented the exploration of information much more than novices. This could be attributed to the fact that experts were much better at interpreting the tags. Thus, the estimation of information scent for experts was better than novices. Experts could therefore select more relevant tags within the same number of tag search compared to novices. Similarly, the ranking of documents and the inclusion of search history had significantly improved exploratory search performance for the expert searcher, as experts were better at interpreting the tags to navigate to the right documents. This was most salient when the history of tags was used, in which the number of documents found increased almost 4 times as much compared to the random arrangement condition.

Similar to performance in simple information retrieval, exploratory search performance in the novice network was much poorer than in the expert network. Interestingly, in contrast to performance in information retrieval, novices benefited more from the model-based navigational cues than experts. Apparently, novices found more relevant documents than experts when searching in a novice network. This could be attributed to the fact that novices were able to find more documents that had information scent values higher than the threshold than experts, but this was mostly caused by the fact that their estimation of information value was less accurate. Another way to interpret the results was that novices had a better match between their internal knowledge and the external knowledge in the novice network, and thus they were able to "better utilize" the navigational cues. However, given that the quality of tags in the novice network was poorer, the higher number of saved documents could be an artifact of poorer evaluation of relevance by the novices. In other words, novices might be "misguided" by the poorer tags. Nevertheless, both experts and novices did find more relevant information with the model-based navigational cues, suggesting that the presentations were useful in enhancing the navigational values of tags in the system.

CONCLUSION AND DISCUSSION

We presented an extension of the semantic imitation model to simulate an expert and a novice network, and simulated search performance of an expert and a novice searcher navigating in each of the networks. In general, we found that the model-based navigational cues were useful in facilitating both simple information retrieval and exploratory search, but this effect was more prominent in the expert network than in the novice network. The result suggested that both the quality of tags and the presentation formats of tags and documents could facilitate effective and efficient navigation in a social tagging system. We, however, did not imply that social tags are created only for navigational purposes, indeed others have showed that there are a number of other possibilities (e.g., [25]). Future research will include these other possibilities.

Our results showed that even when quality of tag was low, simple manipulation in the presentation of information could serve as good navigational cues to guide users to find the right information. Our results also highlighted the value of a predictive process model in generating testable interface features and representations that could significantly augment performance in a system.

The semantic imitation model presented in this paper shows a good example of how theories of cognitive science and artificial intelligence may provide researchers a strong theoretical basis for empirical investigations of behavior in social information systems, and how they can lead to potential design insights for future social tagging systems. The results from the simulations can also lead to testable predictions and guide the design of empirical studies to test the effects of different interface representations and interaction methods on performance.

REFERENCES

1. Blei, D., A. Ng, and M. Jordan, *Latent Dirichlet Allocation.* Journal of Machine Learning Research, 2003. 3: p. 993-1022.
2. Cattuto, C., V. Loreto, and L. Pietronero, *Semiotic dynamics and collaborative tagging.* Proceedings of National Academy of Sciences, 2007. 104: p. 1461-1464.
3. Eggenberger, F. and G. Polya, *Uber Die Statistik Verketter Vorgage.* Zeit. Angew. Math. Mech,, 1923. 1: p. 279-289.
4. Fu, W.-T. and W. Gray, *Suboptimal tradeoffs in information seeking.* Cognitive Psychology, 2006. 52(3): p. 195-242.
5. Fu, W.-T. and P. Pirolli, *SNIF-ACT: A cognitive model of user navigation on the World Wide Web.* Human-Computer Interaction, 2007. 22: p. 355-412.
6. Fu, W.-T., *The microstructures of social tagging: A rational model, in Proceedings of the ACM 2008 conference on Computer supported cooperative work.* 2008: San Diego, CA. p. 229-238.
7. Fu, W.-T., T.G. Kannampallil, and R. Kang, *A Semantic Imitation Model of Social Tag Choices. , in Proceedings of the IEEE conference on Social Computing.* 2009: Vancouver, BC. p. 66-72.
8. Fu, W.-T., et al., *Semantic Imitation in Social Tagging.* ACM Transactions on Computer-Human Interaction, in press.
9. Furnas, G.W., et al., *The vocabulary problem in human-system communication.* Communications of the ACM, 1987. 30(11): p. 964-971.
10. Furnas, G.W., et al. *Why do tagging systems work?* in *CHI '06 Extended Abstracts on Human Factors in Computing Systems.* 2006. Montréal, Québec, Canada.
11. Golder, S. and B. Huberman, *Usage patterns of collaborative tagging systems.* J. Inf. Sci., 2006. 32(2): p. 198-208.
12. Golder, S.A. and B.A. Huberman, *Usage patterns of collaborative tagging systems.* J. Inf. Sci., 2006. 32(2): p. 198-208.
13. Griffiths, T.L., et al., *Topics in Semantic Representation.* Psychological Review, 2007. 114(2): p. 211-244.
14. Kammerer, Y., et al. *Signpost from the masses: learning effects in an exploratory social tag search browser.* in *Proceedings of the 27th international Conference on Human Factors in Computing Systems CHI '09.* 2009. Boston, MA, USA.
15. Kang, R., et al., *Conformity out of Diversity: Dynamics of Information Needs and Social Influence of Tags in Exploratory Information Search, in Proceedings of the 13th International conference of Human-Computer Interaction.* 2009: San Diego, CA.
16. Kang, R. and W.-T. Fu, *Exploratory Information Search by Domain Experts and Novices, in Proceedings of the 2010 Conference on Intelligent User Interfaces.* 2010: Hong Kong, China.
17. Kintsch, W., *The role of knowledge in discourse comprehension: A construction-integration model.* Psychological Review, 1988. 95: p. 163-182.
18. Marchionini, G., *Exploratory search: from finding to understanding.* Commun. ACM, 2006. 49(4): p. 41-46.
19. McFadden, D., *Conditional Logit Analysis of Qualitative Choice Behavior, in Frontiers of Econometrics, P. Zarembka, Editor.* 1974, Academic Press: New York. p. 105-142.
20. Millen, D., et al., *Social bookmarking and exploratory search, in ECSCW 2007.* 2007. p. 21-40.
21. Noll, M.G., et al., *Telling experts from spammers: Expertise ranking in folksonomies, in Proceedings of the ACM conference on Information Retrieval (SIGIR).* 2009: MA: Boston. p. 612-619.
22. Pirolli, P. and S. Card, *Information Foraging.* Psychological Review, 1999. 106(4): p. 643-675.
23. Pirolli, P. *An elementary social information foraging model.* in *Proceedings of the 27th international Conference on Human Factors in Computing Systems CHI '09.* 2009. Boston, MA, USA.
24. Qu, Y. and G. Furnas, *Model-driven formative evaluation of exploratory search: A study under a sensemaking framework.* Inf. Process. Manage., 2008. 44(2): p. 534-555.
25. Sen, S., et al., *tagging, communities, vocabulary, evolution, in Proceedings of the 2006 20th anniversary conference on Computer Supported Cooperative Work.* 2006, ACM: Banff, Alberta, Canada.

Outline Wizard: Presentation Composition and Search

Lawrence Bergman, Jie Lu, Ravi Konuru, Julie MacNaught, Danny Yeh
IBM T.J. Watson Research Center
Hawthorne, NY USA
{bergmanl, jielu, rkonuru, jmacna, dlyeh}@us.ibm.com

ABSTRACT

Assembling electronic presentations from existing presentation material is a commonly-performed task. Yet current tools provide inadequate support – search tools are unable to return individual slides, and the linear model employed by presentation creation tools lacks structure and context. We propose a novel method for presentation creation, implemented in a tool called Outline Wizard, which enables outline-based composition and search. An Outline Wizard user enters a hierarchically-structured outline of a presentation; using that structure, the tool extracts user requests to formulate contextual queries, matches them against presentations within a repository, taking into account both content and structures of the presentations, and presents the user with sets of slides that are appropriate for each outline topic. At the heart of Outline Wizard is an outline-based search technique, which conducts content search within the context derived from the hierarchical structures of both user requests and presentations. We present a heuristic outline-extraction technique, which is used to reverse engineer the structures of presentations, thereby making the structures available for our search engine. Evaluations show that the outline-extraction technique and outline-based search both perform well, and that users report a satisfying experience when using Outline Wizard to compose presentations from libraries of existing material.

Author Keywords

Presentation composition, presentation search, outline-based search, context-sensitive information retrieval

ACM Classification Keywords

H.5.2 [Information Interfaces and Presentation]: User Interfaces — User interaction styles, User-centered design; H.3.3 [Information Storage and Retrieval]: Information Search and Retrieval — Query formulation, Search process

General Terms

Design, Human Factors

1. INTRODUCTION

Presentations, created and presented using software tools such as Microsoft PowerPoint[1] and OpenOffice Impress[2] are widely used, with millions produced each day [9]. In a series of informal interviews with corporate executives and managers, we have discovered that creating new presentations by assembling slides from previously existing presentations is a common practice. For example, slides from presentations of individual products may be needed for inclusion in a marketing presentation; slides from presentations of various projects may be required for a management report.

Using today's tools, collating slides into new presentations is a painful process. The user must first *search* for the slides. Current search tools are unable to operate at the level of individual slides, which causes two problems. First, because the search is at the presentation level, any presentation containing all search terms anywhere within it will be returned, even though the objective may be to obtain a single slide containing all search terms. Second, the user must sift through entire presentations returned by the search to find and extract relevant slides, which is often a time-consuming and difficult task.

In an attempt to address these issues, our group has developed a slide-level presentation repository, known as *SlideRiver*. Presentations (in PowerPoint or OpenOffice formats) are uploaded into SlideRiver, which automatically indexes individual slides within presentations. These slides can then be browsed, shared, and searched.

Simply providing a slide-level search facility, however, is not a panacea. First, presentations often include slides whose content does not contain sufficient context for slide-level search. Consider searching for a slide that contains *"goals"* for the *"SlideRiver"* project. Presentations on SlideRiver may contain slides that describe goals (and contain the word *"goals"*), but do not have the word *"SlideRiver"* in their content. As a result, these slides may not be considered relevant when judged on their content alone without considering context, i.e., the presentations they come from. An additional complication is introduced when the desired material for a given topic spans multiple slides. For instance, a scenario or use case may consist of a

---

[1] http://office.microsoft.com/en-us/powerpoint/default.aspx
[2] http://www.openoffice.org/product/impress.html

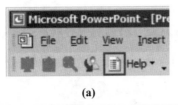

(a)

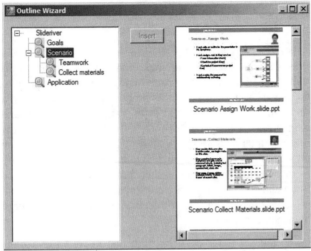

(b)

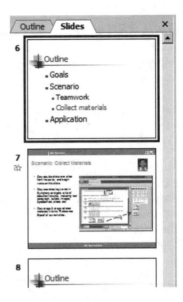

Figure 2. Presentation composition using Outline Wizard

process of opening each source presentation, then cutting-and-pasting between source and target using separate windows for each.

Our work attempts to provide support for search and composition through a new model of creating presentations from existing slides. Based on the common practice of structuring presentations via outlines, we present a methodology that unifies search and composition. In our system, entitled *Outline Wizard*, a user creates an outline, using text editing operations, which defines the structure of a presentation. As she does, a query is constructed at each level of the hierarchical outline, with nested context from the outline used to scope the query. To address the shortcomings of single-slide search discussed earlier, we employ a novel outline-based search technique. The technique matches scoped queries against sets of existing presentations to find candidate slides or groups of slides by considering both presentation content and structure. Since the structure of currently existing presentations is not typically available, we introduce an outline-extraction technique to reverse engineer presentation structures that can be used for search.

As an example of using Outline Wizard for presentation composition and search, we consider a user who wants to construct a presentation detailing the SlideRiver software system. She creates an outline (shown in Figure 1 (b) and (c)) that includes the title of the presentation – "*SlideRiver*," topics – "*Goals*," "*Scenario*," "*Application*," and subtopics (of "*Scenario*") – "*Teamwork*," "*Collect materials*." The hierarchically structured outline provides context used for search. In Figure 1(c), for example, the highlighted topic specifies that a "*Collect materials*" *scenario* is being sought for *SlideRiver*. Outline Wizard derives contextual queries based on the outline, conducts search over a repository of

(c)

Figure 1. Outline Wizard user interface

sequence of slides, but the search terms "*scenario*" or "*use case*" may not be present on all slides of the sequence. A slide-level search method that lacks knowledge of presentation structure will be incapable of identifying and returning relevant groups of slides under such circumstances.

Once slides are located, the new presentation must be *composed*. Composition consists of two portions – the structure of the presentation must be designed, and materials must be created/inserted into the structure. Current tools provide almost no support for designing presentation structure. Users often structure presentations hierarchically – this can be seen in the large number of presentations that begin with an agenda or outline slide. Yet, most of today's tools represent a presentation solely as a linear sequence of slides. Insertion of materials from multiple sources is typically accomplished by the laborious presentations, associates sets of search results with these contextual queries, and supplies them in-context. By clicking on a topic within the outline, the user is able to preview the content of retrieved slides associated with that topic (Figure 1(b)). Outline Wizard automatically constructs a series of outline slides for the presentation based on the user-specified outline. The user can select particular slides from the search results for inclusion at the appropriate place in the presentation, as shown in Figure 2.

Compared to existing tools, Outline Wizard offers users three distinct benefits. First, it provides a mechanism for the user to design a presentation using a much more structured representation than that provided by traditional linear presentation tools. Second, Outline Wizard automatically formulates queries and conducts search based on the outline specified by the user, which frees her from manually crafting and issuing multiple queries to search for content. Third, Outline Wizard allows the user to easily inspect search results, and incorporate selected results into the presentation without cutting-and-pasting between multiple windows.

Below, we briefly discuss related work, followed by an overview of Outline Wizard. We then describe Outline Wizard's key components and our evaluation.

2. RELATED WORK

Our work is related to several systems that extend the typical linear presentation model to support hierarchical or graph-based representations of presentation structures [1, 6, 8]. We go beyond these systems by addressing not only how to organize presentation materials, but also how to locate them through search. [5] addresses the issue of composing presentations from multiple versions of a particular presentation; our focus is on assembling presentations from heterogeneous sources.

Chen [3, 4] presents a system that uses extracted presentation structures to search a PowerPoint database. It focuses on finding particular items (slides, diagrams, images, etc.) with queries specified via a generated ontology. In contrast, our system allows the user to specify the complete presentation structure via free-text, and automatically formulates queries from the structure.

XML information retrieval matches "content and structure" (CAS) queries, which specify requested or required content structure, against Extensible Markup Language (XML) documents. In outline-based search, contextual similarity plays a bigger role than structural similarity in determining the relevance of a slide to a user request. In spite of this difference between outline-based search and XML retrieval, our work is inspired by the body of research in XML retrieval, particularly the work on extending the vector space model for structured-based search [2, 7].

Our outline-based search technique creates and uses context vectors to conduct context-sensitive information retrieval, which is related to work on context-aware, adaptive information retrieval [10]. Context-aware retrieval uses context vectors, created from a graph of user actions which represents the user's investigative context, to augment explicit user queries. In comparison, outline-based search creates context vectors based on user-specified outlines and presentation structures, and these context vectors are used to inform context-sensitive search.

3. SYSTEM DESCRIPTION

Here we provide an overview of Outline Wizard, starting with its user interface, followed by its system architecture.

User Interface

Outline Wizard was developed as a PowerPoint plug-in. When the user clicks the Outline Wizard toolbar button (highlighted in Figure 1(a)), a new PowerPoint presentation is initiated, and the Outline Wizard user interface is displayed (Figure 1(b)). The user enters a presentation outline in the panel on the left. The top-most item is the presentation title ("*SlideRiver*" in Figure 1), with presentation topics and subtopics contained in a nested tree structure. The outline tree is editable; with tree items indented or dedented via keystrokes.

As the user completes entry of each topic, a search is initiated; when results are obtained, a spyglass icon is presented to the left of the topic. In Figure 1(b), search results returned for the highlighted topic "*Scenario*" are presented in the right-hand panel as thumbnails, each representing a single PowerPoint slide. The user can select any of the slides, as shown in Figure 1(c), and then insert that slide into the PowerPoint presentation, by clicking on the "Insert" button. The user can see a larger preview of a slide thumbnail by double-clicking on it; the preview panel also contains an "Insert" button. Figure 2 shows a portion of the PowerPoint user interface, containing the presentation being constructed. Outline slides are automatically inserted for each topic, showing the current topic ("*Collect materials*" in Figure 2) highlighted within the full outline context. Slides that have been inserted are displayed immediately following the topic they represent.

System Architecture

Figure 3 shows the architecture of the Outline Wizard system. It has two subsystems comprised of five main components: a front end containing an input processor and output processor, and a back end containing an outline processor, outline searcher, and outline extractor.

As the user types a presentation outline into the Outline Wizard user interface, the *input processor* processes user input and creates an XML-based representation of the outline to send to the outline processor. Given the outline, the *outline processor* first constructs and updates a

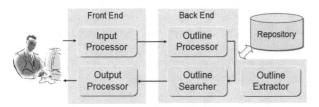

Figure 3. Outline Wizard architecture

hierarchical tree structure to represent the outline. Next it extracts content and context information from the hierarchy to formulate contextual queries. The *outline searcher* matches each query against context-sensitive representations of presentation content. Query results are passed to the *output processor*, which displays sets of results and supports user interaction with them.

The *outline extractor* is responsible for reverse engineering presentation outlines which are used for creating context-sensitive representations of presentation content. It reads and parses PowerPoint presentations stored in the repository, and infers an outline structure for each based on a variety of heuristic rules. Outline extraction is executed during an offline process.

4. OUTLINE EXTRACTION

Outline extraction is the process of reverse engineering an outline using content contained within an existing presentation. We began development of this component with an informal study of presentation structure. We examined about 100 presentations collected from colleagues. The presentations included project reviews and summaries, proposals, and technical materials. We noted a number of regularities in many of the presentations, including repeated structures (e.g., multiple slides in sequence with identical or similar titles indicating a slide group), and explicit organizational aids (e.g., introductory outline or agenda slides). Based on this examination, we initially focused on presentations containing agenda slides (slides typically titled "outline," "agenda," "table of contents," "roadmap," or "overview;" we will use the term *agenda* to refer to all of these).

We randomly selected 755 PowerPoint presentations from a large corporate information repository containing sales and

	Development	Test
Non-structural	**11**	**14**
Single agenda slide	**55**	**46**
Multiple agenda slides	**34**	**40**
Color/bold for current topic	(20)	(22)
Box/highlight for current topic	(9)	(11)
Other schemes for current topic	(5)	(7)
Total	**100**	**100**

Table 1. Types of agenda slides contained in presentation samples

marketing presentations. We developed an *automated agenda extractor* which identified 229 (30%) of these as having agenda slides. We randomly selected 100 of these agenda-containing presentations for use as a development set. A more detailed examination of these 100 yielded the results displayed in Table 1. This table displays both the results discussed here (in the column labeled "Development"), and the breakdown of a test set used for evaluation.

11% of the presentations had agenda slides that on inspection clearly did not indicate the structure of the presentation, but instead presented workshop timetables, gave product highlights, etc. Although we were able to distinguish these non-structural agenda slides from those that reflect presentation structure, we felt it would be difficult for an algorithm to do so.

55% of the presentations contained a single agenda slide near the start of the presentation. Often the agenda topics matched the titles of particular slides within the presentation, either exactly or near-exactly. In other cases, the agenda might contain the topic (e.g., "*Why it sells*") with the associated slides containing titles that give specific reasons, but with no keyword matches.

34% of the presentations contained multiple agenda slides. Typically, these multiples were replicas of the agenda slide marking the start of each topic. Often, the current topic would be highlighted, usually by changing the color or by bolding the font (59% of multiple-agenda presentations), or by visually changing the background via a box or background highlight (26% of multiple-agenda presentations).

Based on these results, we developed an *outline inference module*. Figure 4 shows a display of output from the module. The leftmost panel displays slide titles, one line per slide. The middle panel shows the topics on the agenda slide. The rightmost panel shows the inferred outline. Topics from the agenda slide have become group titles (shown in blue), with each group containing zero or more slides (shown in red).

The inference module extracts topics from an agenda slide, then assigns individual slides to agenda topics using a segmentation-based algorithm, which assumes that slides appear in the same order as agenda topics (usually, but not universally true). The segmentation algorithm seeks to find a starting slide for each topic, and assumes that all slides that follow belong to the topic, until the slide that starts the next topic. Note that this approach allows hierarchically nested topics.

For a presentation with a single agenda, the correspondences between slides and agenda topics are determined by matching agenda topics with slide titles

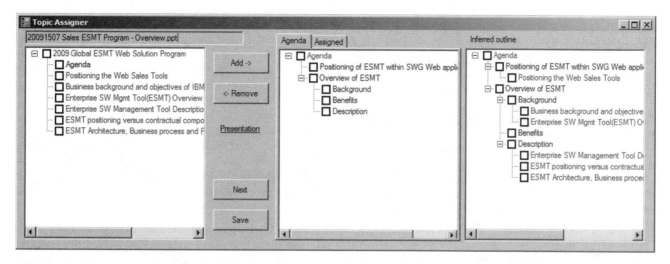

Figure 4. Outline extraction interface, showing slide titles, agenda topics, and extracted structure

based on the keywords extracted from each. Keywords are stopped with a stopword list derived from Lucene[3] and stemmed using the Snowball package[4]. Quoted strings are retained intact. A match score M between a slide title S and an agenda topic A is computed as the percentage of keywords from the slide title found in the topic:

$$M(S, A) = |K_s \cap K_a| / |K_s|$$

where K_s is the set of keywords in the slide title, and K_a is the set of keywords in the agenda topic. Any value of $M(S, A)$ that exceeds an empirically determined cutoff level is considered a match.

When there are multiple identical or near-identical agenda slides in a presentation, the inference module uses these slides to segment the presentation; each marks the start of a topic. The topic associated with each agenda slide is identified by recognizing color or bold highlighting. Details of this method are omitted due to space limitation.

If no color/bold highlighting is found, and the number of agenda slides is equal to the number of agenda topics, we assume a one-to-one correspondence between agenda slides and topics. Otherwise, the inference module ignores the multiple agenda slides, and segments the presentation via title matching as if it contains a single agenda slide, as described earlier.

5. OUTLINE-BASED SEARCH

In this section, we present our approach to outline-based search. First, we introduce the hierarchical tree-based representations used for modeling user-specified outlines and existing presentations. Second, we describe how we derive context-sensitive vectors from these representations to represent queries and presentation elements (e.g., slides or groups of slides). Third, we present the process that, given a user-specified outline, retrieves and ranks

presentation elements based on their estimated relevance to the queries, and determines which slides to return.

Hierarchical Representations of Outlines and Presentations

Any outline, whether user-specified, or derived from an existing presentation, is represented by a hierarchical tree of *nodes*. For a user-specified outline, a node corresponds to one topic in the hierarchical outline, e.g., "*Scenario*," "*Teamwork*," etc. in Figure 1(b). We refer to these as *query nodes*, since they are used to automatically formulate searches. For an outline derived from an existing presentation in the repository, a node corresponds to a presentation element, which can be the entire presentation, a group of slides associated with a topic in the presentation outline, or a single slide. We refer to these as *repository nodes*.

The *content* of a node is determined by the *type* of the node. For a repository node representing a presentation, its content corresponds to the title of the presentation. For a repository node that represents a slide or a query node that represents an outline topic, its content is the text contained in the slide[5] or the topic. For a repository node that represents a group of slides, its content corresponds to the group title, which comes from the presentation outline topic with which these slides are associated.

The links between nodes in the hierarchical tree are determined by the parent-child relations as indicated by the outline structure. A top-level outline topic such as "*Overview of ESMT*" shown in Figure 4 is a child of the node that corresponds to the entire presentation. An outline data structure organizes all the nodes of a hierarchical outline, and provides methods for its navigation.

---

[3] http://lucene.apache.org/
[4] http://snowball.tartarus.org/

---

[5] We extracted text from all text areas within a slide, but not text embedded within graphics or images, nor did we use text within the notes areas.

The representation of a user-specified outline is created and updated dynamically as the user creates and edits the outline structure. The representations of presentation elements in the repository are created and indexed by an offline process and are loaded on demand at run time.

Context-Sensitive Vector Representations of Queries and Presentation Elements

We employ a vector space model to capture both content and context of query nodes and repository nodes. The *context* of a node is defined as the aggregate content of all of its ancestors and descendants in the hierarchical tree of nodes. A node's *context-sensitive vector* integrates the node's content with its context. It is created in two steps. First, the *content term vector* of the node is created, based on the content it encodes, without considering its context. Second, this content term vector is integrated with all content term vectors from the node's context to create its context-sensitive vector. Next we describe these two steps in detail.

We construct a node's content term vector by removing punctuation marks and stopwords, then stemming the set of words and quoted strings. For a query node, the weight of a term is determined by the term's frequency in the node's content. For a repository node, the weight of a term is computed based on its frequency in the node's content as well as its location and overall popularity in the presentation. Location refers to the hierarchical nesting level of a term, from inner to outer – slide content, slide title, outline topic, presentation title. Following the common practice of assigning location-based term weights in information retrieval, we give a higher weight to a term when it occurs at an outer level than when it occurs at an inner level in the hierarchy. Specifically, the location-based weight $w_{location}$ of a term t in a node n's content is set to 1.0 for the node's content that corresponds to presentation title, 0.8 for outline topic, 0.6 for slide title, and 0.4 for slide content. The simple linear weighting scheme is used due to the lack of training data for determining the relative importance of terms at different locations in a presentation.

A term's overall popularity is inversely related to its discriminative power, which is typically measured by inverse document frequency (*idf*) in traditional information retrieval. Because the basic result unit for outline-based search is a slide, we use inverse slide frequency *isf* to measure a term t's discriminative power within a presentation p:

$$isf(p, t) = log(N_p / N_{p,t})$$

where N_p is the total number of slides in the presentation p, and $N_{p,t}$ is the number of p's slides containing the term t.

The weight w of a term t in the content term vector v_c of the node n for a presentation element is therefore calculated as the product of the term's frequency f in the node's content, its location-based weight $w_{location}$, and its inverse slide frequency *isf* in the presentation to which the node belongs:

$$w(t) = f(t) \times w_{location}(t) \times isf(p, t)$$

To create a context-sensitive vector v_s for the node n, its content term vector v_c is integrated with all of the content term vectors from n's context as follows:

$$v_s(n) = v_c(n) + \Sigma_{n' \in context(n)} \ min(0, 1 - 0.2d(n, n')) \times v_c(n')$$

where each content term vector $v_c(n')$ from the context is discounted based on the distance (i.e., path length) $d(n, n')$ between its node n' and the targeted node n in the hierarchical tree, so that terms located closer to the targeted node are given higher weights. The discount factor of 0.2 is determined empirically.

As with the node representations, context-sensitive vectors that represent queries are created dynamically as the user edits the outline; vectors that represent presentation elements are created and indexed offline then dynamically loaded at run time.

Process of Outline-Based Search

As the user creates and edits an outline in the interface, the outline topics are dynamically sent to the outline processor, which updates the hierarchical representation created for the outline, extracts from it a set of nodes for topics that have new/changed content or context, and creates context-sensitive query vectors for these nodes. Each query vector is passed to the outline searcher, which conducts search in three steps. First, the query is sent to a Lucene text search engine, which uses the traditional *tf.idf*-based ranking

---

Input: the list of ranked presentation elements L_e
Output: the list of slides to return as the search result L_s

Procedure:
  foreach presentation element e in L_e
    if $e.type == Slide$
      $L_s.add(e)$
    else if $e.type == SlideGroup \ || \ Presentation$
      L = all the slides that belong to e
      foreach slide s in L
        if $s.score < e.score$
          // boost the slide score
          $s.score = (s.score + e.score) / 2$
        endif
        $L_s.add(s)$
      endfor
    endif
  endfor
  L_s = sort(L_s)
  foreach slide s in L_s
    // normalize the score to be between 0 and 1
    $s.score = (s.score - min(L_s)) / (max(L_s) - min(L_s))$
  endfor
  L_s = sub-list of L_s including all the unique slides with ranks
      higher than a cutoff c or scores greater than a threshold t
  return L_s

Figure 5. The method for determining which slides to return as the search result for a query

algorithm to rank its indexed presentations and returns a list of top-ranked presentations as candidates. Second, the outline searcher retrieves the context-sensitive vectors of the presentation elements contained in these candidate presentations, and estimates the relevance r of each presentation element e to the query q based on a combination of the standard cosine similarity Sim_{cos} between the query vector and the vector of the presentation element, the Boolean similarity Sim_{bool} between them, and the relevance score of the presentation p to which the presentation element belongs:

$$r(e, q) = Sim_{cos}(v_s(e), v_s(q)) \times Sim_{bool}(v_s(e), v_s(q)) \times r(p, q)$$

The Boolean similarity Sim_{bool} is calculated as the percentage of query terms that are matched. It is introduced to favor presentation elements that match all query terms. Third, the outline searcher ranks the presentation elements by their relevance scores, and generates a result list.

Currently the basic result unit for outline-based search is a slide. Figure 5 describes the method used by the outline searcher to determine which slides to return as the search result for the query. It uses the scores of the presentation elements at the level of presentation or slide group to boost the scores of the slides that belong to them, so that a slide is more likely to be returned when it belongs to a presentation or a slide group that is deemed relevant, even if this slide seems less relevant judged on its own. Slides which exceed a rank-based cutoff, c, or a score-based threshold, t, (both constants determined empirically) are included in a ranked list of return results.

6. EVALUATION

The evaluation consisted of three portions: 1) evaluation of the outline-extraction technique, 2) evaluation of the outline-based search, and 3) evaluation of the Outline Wizard user experience.

Outline Extraction Evaluation: Methodology

Outline extraction was initially evaluated on the development set of 100 agenda-containing presentations described in Section 4. Two of the authors (Bergman and Lu) independently assigned slides to agenda topics using a manual assignment process. The tool shown in Figure 4 allowed us to select a set of slides, select a topic (from the automatically identified agenda slide), and assign the slides to the topic. We ran the automated outline extractor on the same 100 presentations.

We devised an outline similarity metric S for comparing two outlines o_1 and o_2 representing a presentation p. It calculates the average degree of agreement between two outlines as follows:

$$S(o_1, o_2) = \sum_{s \in p} A(t_1(s), t_2(s)) / |p|$$

where for each slide s in p, $t_1(s)$ and $t_2(s)$ denote the agenda topics to which s is assigned in the two representations, A

denotes the agreement between them, and $|p|$ denotes the number of slides in the presentation p.

A has a non-zero value if $t_1(s)$ and $t_2(s)$ are located on the same sub-tree in the topic hierarchy of p's agenda, with the degree of agreement discounted by a measure of their "distance" from each other. Specifically, it is computed as:

$$A(t_1, t_2) = 1 - min(1, 0.2 \times D(t_1, t_2))$$

where D is a measure of the "distance" between two agenda topics in the presentation agenda's topic hierarchy:

$$D(t_1, t_2) = max(d(t^*, t_1), d(t^*, t_2))$$

where t^* is the closest common topic to t_1 and t_2 among the set of agenda topics that includes t_1, t_2 and their ancestors in the topic hierarchy, and $d(\bullet, \bullet)$ is the distance (i.e., path length) between two topics. If t_1 and t_2 refer to the same topic, D is set to 0. The discount factor of 0.2 is determined empirically.

If a slide is assigned to a topic by the outline extractor but is left unassigned by manual assignment, A is set to 0.5. If a slide is assigned manually but is left unassigned automatically, A is set to 0.

For each presentation in the development set, we calculated similarity scores on three pairs – comparing the two manual assignments, and then comparing the automatic extract with each of the manual assignments.

Once we had completed development of the algorithm, we randomly selected an additional 100 agenda-containing presentations, and repeated this set of evaluation procedures.

Outline Extraction Evaluation: Results

Results comparing the assigned outlines are shown in Table 2. Note that the two human annotators (designated as Annotator 1 and Annotator 2) corresponded well (but not perfectly) in their assignments, both with the development set as well as the test set. The degree of agreement between the outline assignments of the automated outline extraction and both humans was satisfactory – about 70% for the development set, and about 60% for the test set, indicating the effectiveness of our outline-extraction technique.

The lower scores for the automated outline extraction can be attributed to several factors. First, there were errors in outline extraction for a small handful of presentations. This was primarily due to the algorithm looking for indented bullets, but being unable to recognize other form of indenting, such as tabs. Second, the algorithm did not handle all forms of structure marking within the presentation sets. In particular, some presentations with multiple agenda slides contained a different two-level structure on each agenda slide; our algorithm did not handle this case, and performed poorly. Finally, the keyword matching approach failed in some cases, particularly where the text in the agenda did not correspond well with the terms on the slide titles.

	Development set		Test set	
	Average	StDev	Average	StDev
Annotator 1 vs. Annotator 2	0.90	0.15	0.85	0.20
Annotator 1 vs. Automatic	0.71	0.25	0.60	0.28
Annotator 2 vs. Automatic	0.69	0.28	0.57	0.28

Table 2. Evaluation results of outline extraction

The lower scores on the test set (relative to the development set) can be attributed to a lack of homogeneity between the two sets. First, the test set had a higher number of non-structural agendas (14 vs. 11). Second, the test set had a larger number of multiple-agenda presentations highlighted with outline boxes (11 vs. 9) which we are currently not handling. Finally, the test set had a number of multiple-agenda presentations containing agenda slides with more than two highlights per slide; these were quite a bit less common in the development set, and we did not handle these in our algorithm.

Outline-Based Search Evaluation: Methodology

We evaluated search on two separate sets of presentations, which came from two different organizations within our corporation – sales and development. The presentations within each set shared a common theme, e.g., providing a profile of a potential corporate customer, or documenting a development process. Each set of presentations was specified by a template, but individuals who created the presentations were free to either delete elements of the template, or add additional elements. The presentations for customer profiles contained explicit agenda slides. Although the development process presentations did not contain explicit agenda slides, we asked two colleagues who are somewhat familiar with this development process to manually construct agendas for eight of them.

We simulated two use cases of presentation composition and search, one for each data set. The first use case was composing a presentation to compile particulars (e.g., executive summary, industry analysis, company overview) of several potential corporate customers. The second use case was constructing a presentation to summarize common development aspects (e.g., functional description, design requirements) of several projects. We simulated a two-level user-specified outline for each use case, with the outer level specifying various particulars/aspects required for composing the presentation, and the inner level specifying names of different customers/projects. The outlines resulted in a total of 30 queries, 18 for the first use case and 12 for the second.

We added both sets of presentations to the presentation repository, and created context-sensitive vectors of presentation elements based on the presentation outlines generated by the outline extractor. Then we ran our outline searcher to obtain a set of top-ranked slides for each outline topic query. We manually compiled a list of relevant slides by inspecting the presentations about targeted customers and projects. For each query, we calculated accumulative precision and recall as well as F-measure (the harmonic mean of precision and recall) for the top 20 ranked slides. The average number of relevant slides per topic was 8 for the first use case and 2.75 for the second use case.

As a baseline, we used the slide-level search facility provided by the SlideRiver system, which employed a Lucene text search engine to index both presentations and individual slides from these presentations as documents. Given a query, the search engine retrieved documents ranked using Lucene's default *tf.idf*-based ranking algorithm. The Boolean *AND* query operator was applied to multiple query terms. We measured precision and recall for the baseline results using two different methods. The first method measured the performance of slide-level search and ignored presentation results. The second method expanded each presentation result to include all the slides from this presentation in the search result. Here we refer to the evaluation result using the first method as "*baseline-slide*" and that using the second method as "*baseline-all*".

We also compared *context-sensitive search* – outline-based search using context-sensitive vectors (created from presentation structures) with *content-only search* – standard slide-level search using only content term vectors of slides without context.

Outline-Based Search Evaluation: Results

Figure 6 shows evaluation results of outline-based search in both use case 1 (composing a presentation to profile potential corporate customers) and use case 2 (constructing a presentation to summarize projects under development). Figure 6(a) and Figure 6(c) plot precision against recall, averaged over all the queries in each use case. Figure 6(b) and Figure 6(d) depict the change in F-measure as the document (slide) rank increased from top 1 to top 20. Because on average the number of slide results returned by the baseline approach was very small (1.72 per query for use case 1 and 1.58 for use case 2) due to the Boolean query constraint, "baseline-slide" had fewer data points than the other methods.

The results indicate that outline-based *context-sensitive search* performed well in both use cases, no matter whether it was recall-oriented (use case 1, with an average of 8 relevant slides per query) or precision-oriented (use case 2, with an average of 2.75 relevant slides per query). By contrast, *baseline-slide* (which only considered slide results) yielded very low recall in recall-oriented use case 1, while *baseline-all* (which included individual slide results and all the slides from presentation results) had very low precision in precision-oriented use case 2, indicating that no

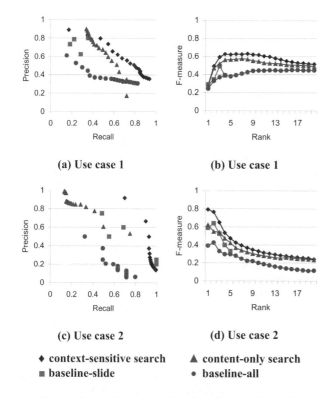

(a) Use case 1   (b) Use case 1

(c) Use case 2   (d) Use case 2

♦ **context-sensitive search**   ▲ **content-only search**
■ **baseline-slide**   ● **baseline-all**

Figure 6. Evaluation results of outline-based search

single strategy worked well in both cases for the SlideRiver baseline system.

For both use cases, *context-sensitive search* outperformed both the baseline and *content-only search*, demonstrating the promise of incorporating context information derived from outline structures for more effective slide-level search.

User Experience Evaluation: Methodology

We conducted an informal evaluation of the Outline Wizard user experience. We asked six people – five of them researchers or software engineers within our organization, one of them the retired head of corporate communications for a Fortune 50 company – to compose a presentation from existing materials using the Outline Wizard from within PowerPoint. Three of the participants were men, three women, all of whom use PowerPoint as part of their job. The repository used for this study was populated with the eight project development presentations used for evaluating outline-based search. The task involved constructing a presentation on a set of specified themes (e.g., "design requirements", "usage scenarios"), each theme to contain information on several projects. Thus, the task naturally contained a two-level information structure. After being given a short demo of Outline Wizard, the users were asked to use the tool to create a presentation outline and select slides. The users were observed using the tool, and then asked to complete a brief questionnaire. They were also

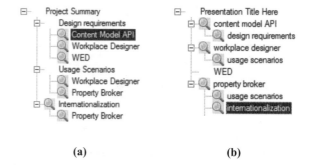

(a)   (b)

Figure 7. Different outline structures reflecting the same task

asked to comment on the tool, and to offer suggestions for improvement.

User Experience Evaluation: Results

The user study participants all successfully performed the task, with few difficulties. Four of the six produced hierarchical outlines. The remaining two produced flat structures, with all topics at the same level. When asked why, one had misinterpreted the instructions; the other stated that he had not read them carefully.

Three of the four participants that produced a two-level hierarchy, created one that very closely modeled the written structure of the task, which nested development projects within themes (such as "design requirements"). An example is shown in Figure 7(a). One participant re-factored the hierarchical structure – nesting themes within projects – to produce the outline shown in Figure 7(b). We noted that in both cases, similar sets of search results were returned, and the users were able to successfully complete the task. This indicates that our approach is not dependent on a particular hierarchical structure, but supports a variety of specifications.

We also noted two distinct working styles. Most participants typed in the outline, then when the outline was complete, went back and selected slides. A minority of the participants interleaved typing topics and selecting slides.

The users were all enthusiastic about Outline Wizard. Comments included, "*I like this very much,*" and "*It would be very useful for big worldwide companies; it could save hours of time.*" Several participants stated a belief that the tool would be particularly useful in sales, where assembling presentations to customers from libraries of presentation materials is a common practice.

Figure 8 shows results from the questionnaire. All questions received positive responses (numbers in parentheses are averages on a 1-5 Likert scale with 5 the most positive) – Q1: "*I could easily construct a presentation with Outline Wizard*" (4.3), Q2: "*The concept of outline-based search and composition is easy to understand and use*" (4.5), and Q3: "*I would use Outline Wizard for my own work, if available*" (4.3). The single response of "Undecided" for Q3 was from a participant who said that he always produces his

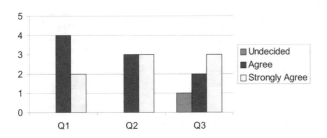

Figure 8. User responses to questionnaire items. Questions are documented in the text

presentations "from scratch", so would not find a tool that supports reuse of value to him.

The users had a number of suggestions for improvements to Outline Wizard. These included: 1) visual indicators showing that slides had been inserted into topics, 2) user selectable options to control formatting for the generated outline slides, including level-of-detail control, 3) the ability to add additional search specifications (keywords, Boolean operators, scope, etc.) in addition to the topic titles, 4) support for easy reorganization of an outline, perhaps via drag-and-drop operations, and 5) adding social networking functions, such as display of ratings, tags, comments, for individual slides returned from the search.

7. CONCLUSIONS AND FUTURE WORK

We have presented an outline-based model for composition of presentations based on searching existing material. The user composes a presentation by specifying a hierarchically-structured free-text outline. The outline provides both search terms and contextual structure for a contextual outline-based search. The content to be searched is also represented hierarchically, by means of extracted outlines which are reverse engineered from the existing presentations. We have shown the outline extraction process to perform reasonably well on a random selection of presentations. Furthermore, we have shown the outline-based search technique to be effective at returning appropriate individual slides. Users of the Outline Wizard system, which embodies the outline-based search, successfully used it to create "new presentations from old", and were enthusiastic about the tool. Although the system as presented operates only on English-language text, there is nothing in either the extraction or search algorithms that is inherently language-dependent.

We have plans to extend this research in several directions. First, we wish to extend the outline extraction algorithm to handle presentations that do not contain agendas. We note that many presentations contain local regularity – for example, repeated keywords in sequences of slides – that could be used to extract local structure. Because our search algorithm is layered on a standard keyword search, partial structures, even very minimal ones, should yield an improvement. Second, we wish to support more than single slide results. In many cases, the results of a query should be

a group of related slides, for example, several slides that compose a scenario. This would require identifying a tight relationship between these slides, delivering them together from the search engine, and providing the appropriate user interface elements for displaying and manipulating them. Related to this is our desire to support previously-created topics as searchable elements; the ability to search and compose using topics from a "topic library" would extend the power of the outline-based model. Finally, we would like to extend the outline-based model to include aspects of workflow typically encountered within an organization – enabling sharing, distribution, and collaborative editing via topics.

ACKNOWLEDGMENTS
We thank Rich Thompson and Robert Flavin of the SlideRiver team for suggestions and feedback, as well as development support. We also thank Jennifer Lai and Ramesh Gopinath for their support of this work.

REFERENCES

1. Apple Keynote '09, http://www.apple.com/iwork/keynote/

2. D. Carmel, Y. Maarek, M. Mandelbrod, Y. Mass, and A. Soffer. "Searching XML documents via XML fragments." In SIGIR 2003.

3. C. Y. Chen, R. Ribier, and S. P. Liou. "An automatic poster summarization for microsoft powerpoint presentation." In IASTED EuroIMSA, 2005.

4. C. Y Chen. "An integrated system supporting effective indexing, browsing and retrieval of Microsoft PowerPoint presentation database." In 22nd Intl. Conf. on Data Engineering Workshops (ICDEW'06).

5. S. M. Drucker, G. Petschnigg, and M. Agrawala. "Comparing and managing multiple versions of slide presentations." In UIST 2006.

6. D. Holman, P. Stojadinović, T. Karrer, and J. Borchers. "Fly: An organic presentation tool." In CHI 2006.

7. S. Liu, Q. Zou, and W. Chu. "Configurable indexing and ranking for XML information retrieval." In SIGIR 2004.

8. T. Moscovich, K. Scholz, J. F. Hughes, D. H. Salesin. "Customizable presentations." Technical Report CS-04-03, Computer Science Department, Brown University.

9. I. Parker. "Absolute PowerPoint: Can a software package edit our thoughts?" The New Yorker, 2001.

10. Z. Wen, M. Zhou, and V. Aggarwal. "Context-aware adaptive information retrieval for investigative tasks." In IUI 2007.

A Code Reuse Interface for Non-Programmer Middle School Students

Paul A. Gross[1], Micah S. Herstand[1], Jordana W. Hodges[2], Caitlin L. Kelleher[1]

Washington University in St. Louis[1]
One Brookings Dr., St. Louis, MO 63130
{grosspa, herstandm, ckelleher}@cse.wustl.edu

The University of North Carolina at Charlotte[2]
9201 University City Blvd, Charlotte, NC 28223
jwhodge1@uncc.edu

ABSTRACT

We describe a code reuse tool for use in the Looking Glass IDE, the successor to Storytelling Alice [17], which enables middle school students with little to no programming experience to reuse functionality they find in programs written by others. Users (1) record a feature to reuse, (2) find code responsible for the feature, (3) abstract the code into a reusable Actionscript by describing object "roles," and (4) integrate the Actionscript into another program. An exploratory study with middle school students indicates they can successfully reuse code. Further, 36 of the 47 users appropriated new programming constructs through the process of reuse.

Author Keywords

Code reuse, non-programmer, end user, middle school, Looking Glass, Storytelling Alice.

ACM Classification Keywords

H.5.2 [Information interfaces and presentation]: User Interfaces.

General Terms

Human Factors

INTRODUCTION

Middle school is a critical time when many students, particularly female students, decide whether they are interested in pursuing math- and science-based careers [7, 36]. At a time when the gap between male and female participation in undergraduate computer science is widening [37], the rarity of computer science teachers and opportunities to explore computing at the middle school level is unfortunate. Programming environments that provide a motivating and supportive context for learning to program may help increase the number of students interested in exploring computing.

Prior research on programming environments demonstrated that storytelling can provide a compelling context to learn computer programming, particularly for middle school girls [17]. A formal study of girls' programming behavior found

that users of Storytelling Alice were more than three times as likely to sneak extra time to program than users of a non-story based version of the same environment [18]. While encouraging, this study focused solely on users' first two to three hours of programming.

Enabling middle school students to learn new skills by reusing and adapting each others' code may encourage more of them to explore computer programming over the longer term. This paper introduces an interface that enables students to reuse others' code without requiring that they understand how the program code works.

Imagine that a user named Eva is creating an animation that tells a story about a girl named Melly who develops super strength. Eva remembers seeing a story in which a secret agent character jumped into an evil doctor and the doctor toppled over. Eva wants Melly to jump into a house and knock it over.

To enable this, our code reuse tool guides users through the processes of *selecting* and *integrating* code [13]. Specifically users:

1. Record the execution of the program containing the functionality of interest.
2. Identify the beginning and ending of the functionality of interest.
3. Abstract the code responsible for the functionality by describing the roles that each character in the functionality plays.

We save the abstracted version of the code as an intermediate code representation called an *Actionscript*. To use the Actionscript, the user selects characters from a new program to act out the roles in the Actionscript.

To explore the potential for code reuse tools in a social learning environment, we conducted an exploratory study in the context of a summer science camp for at-risk middle school students. We found that users were able to successfully reuse code with our tool. Further, the process of selecting code for reuse helped some users to develop an understanding of new programming constructs, which they successfully used outside of the context of Actionscripts. As a next step, we plan to generate tutorials that will guide users through reconstructing the Actionscript code in their new program.

RELATED WORK

Our related work spans two areas: software reuse and end-user program sharing.

Software Reuse

Researchers have identified a number of activities that are a part of code reuse [20, 26, 29]. Holmes [13] suggests that code reuse consists of three fundamental phases: *location*, *selection*, and *integration*. While much of the research in code reuse focuses on professional developers [35], some researchers have explored small-scale reuse [4]. Other work explores reuse through demonstration [10, 22].

Location

During the location stage, users search for software artifacts that may contain source code relevant to their task (not to be confused with searching in source code to determine if part of it is suitable for reuse). Many tools exist for assisting programmers in locating relevant source code (reviews in [14, 23, 27]). Some recent work focuses on finding code examples either on the web [11] or through tools integrated with an IDE [1, 8, 14, 31, 34].

Selection

In the selection phase, users try to identify the code responsible for functionality of interest, understand it, determine its reusability, and extract it for reuse.

The process of identifying and understanding the code responsible for particular functionality is difficult for non-programmers [9]. Systems for end user programmers, who typically have limited programming experience, employ a variety of techniques to help users identify and understand relevant code. FireCrystal [28] enables users to record web browser events and view the Javascript and CSS code that executed as a result of the events. The WYSIWYT spreadsheet environment [30] helps provides a visualization of cell dependencies. The Whyline [19] allows end users to pose "why" and "why not" questions about program behavior and receive answers directly related to runtime information.

Program understanding tools typically employ program visualizations to help professional programmers grapple with feature and fault localization (e.g., [21, 24, 32, 33]). Effective use of these visualizations requires knowledge that non-programmers are unlikely to have.

Integration

For the integration phase, users must insert the selected code into their own code and adapt it for their own context. For Java developers, Jigsaw [4] evaluates structural and semantic information from a code source to manage dependencies and recreate missing functionality during integration to a new program. CReN [15] and CloneTracker [5] attempt to manage variable references in multiple cloned code locations.

Currently there are no tools for general end-to-end software reuse [13]. However, d.mix, a recent web programming system, helps users with the selection and integration steps.

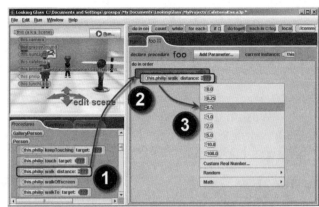

Figure 1. Looking Glass where a user programs by (1) dragging a method, (2) dropping it into the code pane, and (3) selecting parameters.

Using d.mix, a user can identify reusable components on an arbitrary web page, select components to reuse, and integrate them into a working wiki page [10]. Like d.mix, our system supports non-programmers through the selection and integration steps, however d.mix generates static web API calls where our system can capture and reuse dynamic behaviors.

End User Program Sharing

There is a long history of designing programming environments for novice programmers [16]. To the best of our knowledge, none of these systems focus on enabling code reuse. Users of MOOSE Crossing could copy and customize or extend scripts written by other users [2]. Scratch [25] directly supports sharing through a web repository, but users share entire programs and there is no integration support for reusing sprite behaviors dependent on other sprites.

LOOKING GLASS

We built our code reuse tools into Looking Glass, the successor to Storytelling Alice that is under development. Like Storytelling Alice, Looking Glass is designed to enable users to create interactive 3D animated stories. To prevent users from making syntax errors, Looking Glass users drag graphical tiles representing methods or programming constructs, drop them into a program editor area, and select parameter values through pop-up menus (see Figure 1). The environment supports common programming constructs such as loops and if-statements. Additionally, the do together construct enables users to have statements in Looking Glass execute concurrently.

CODE REUSE TOOLS

Enabling users to reuse functionality from programs created by others requires supporting them in three basic activities:

1. Finding the code responsible for the target functionality.
2. Extracting the responsible code from its original program.
3. Integrating the responsible code into a new context.

For experienced programmers, an intelligent copy and paste system might be sufficient to enable code reuse. However, our goal is to enable new programmers to reuse code without requiring that they understand how that code works. In an educational system, this may seem strange. Our eventual goal is to have users select functionality they want to reuse and then complete a tutorial guiding them through building that functionality in their own program. We believe the high level strategy of selecting code without fully understanding it and reconstructing the code to build understanding has two strong advantages:

1. If users build the selected functionality step by step, they will see the impact of each new line and each change. We believe it will be easier for users to understand new functionality by constructing it themselves rather than by exploring potentially complex, fully functional code.

2. Users are motivated to build their own stories [17]. We believe that enabling users to construct the new functionality in the context of their own story will align with their natural motivation.

To help users find the code responsible for functionality they want to reuse, we enable users to navigate the code based on observable output. After users identify the beginning and ending points of the functionality they want to reuse, they can extract the code responsible and integrate it into another program using wizard-style interfaces.

Identifying Functionality for Reuse

Previous research on how new programmers approach the problem of identifying the code responsible for observable output found that new programmers employ a cyclic search process. New programmers (1) identify a search target in the output (or code), (2) search for potentially matching lines of code (or output actions) and (3) repeat (changing from output to code or vice versa) until there are enough matches to form a solution. This process was not very successful for non-programmers; users successfully found the code responsible for a specific output feature only 41% of the time [9].

The study identified several barriers contributing to non-programmers lack of success, including:

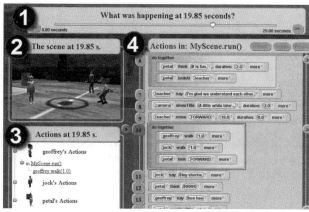

Figure 2. The History tool interface: (1) Time Slider for scrubbing through time, (2) Scene Viewer shows the scene at the selected time, (3) Current Actions Pane shows what actions characters did at the selected time, and (4) Annotated Code View selects the executing line(s) of code, affords block and statement playback, and navigational controls.

1. Users struggle to match their motion descriptions to method names and parameters in the code.
2. Users often fail to fully navigate relevant code.
3. Users do not recognize temporal relationships in programs containing constructs such as loops, do togethers (i.e., a concurrency block), or method calls.

We designed a history tool to address these barriers by helping users identify what code is executing and connect the code with visual output. This history tool is integrated into the code reuse process. The history tool interface includes four components: (1) the Time Slider, (2) the Scene Viewer, (3) the Current Actions Pane, and (4) the Code View Pane (see Figure 2).

The *Time Slider* (1) enables users to scrub forward and backward through the program's recorded history.

The *Scene Viewer* (2) displays the scene's appearance at the selected time. To find an action of interest, a user can scrub through recorded history using the Time Slider until he or she sees the action of interest shown in the scene viewer.

The *Current Actions Pane* (3) shows all methods executing

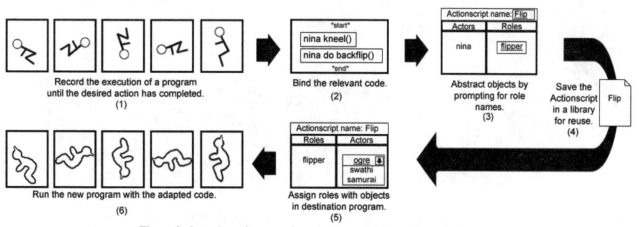

Figure 3. Overview of process for selecting and integrating code for reuse.

at the selected time, organized by character. To determine what a particular character (e.g., geoffrey) was doing at the selected time, the user can expand "geoffery's Actions." The expanded view shows which individual statements were executing and the methods from which they were called. The user can navigate to a statement or method call by clicking on it. The Code View Pane will update to display the statement that the user clicked.

Finally, the *Code View Pane* (4) presents a view of the executed code in the latest run of the program. The statement that executed at the selected time is highlighted in green. A play button next to the executing statement enables users to play back all of the images captured while that statement executed. Buttons on the right side of the interface enable users to zoom in on block statements

Wizards for Extraction and Integration

A wizard-style interface guides users through extracting the selected code. We abstract the extracted code and save it into an intermediary form we call an Actionscript.

A second wizard-style interface allows users to select which characters will perform the actions recorded in the Actionscript. After users assign characters to each role in the Actionscript, we generate the code necessary for the actions encoded in the Actionscript.

Figure 3 shows the process overview for identifying and reusing a section of code. In the remainder of this section, we describe the process of reusing a section of code.

Usage Scenario – Recording an Actionscript

In the introduction, we described a scenario in which a user named Eva wants to reuse an agent's action of jumping and knocking over an evil doctor in her story about super-strong Melly. Creating an Actionscript for the jump and knock over action requires five steps that are presented through a wizard-style interface.

Step 1: Eva records the actions occurring in the agent's story (i.e., the tool constructs a dynamic execution trace for the history tool) until after the agent's fall is complete. At the bottom of the record panel, Eva clicks a next button (see

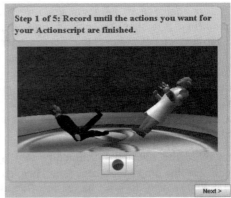

Figure 4. Recording the program to capture a feature for reuse.

Figure 4) which loads the history tool to help her find where the agent's jump and knock over begins and ends (see Figure 5).

Step 2: To find where the agent began to jump, Eva drags the Time Slider (Fig. 5a, circle 1) back until she sees the agent start to move up (Fig. 5a, circle 2). At the selected time, the Current Actions Pane (Fig. 5b) indicates the agent and the doctor are active. Users' programs often contain simultaneously executing statements using the do together construct [9].

Because Eva is interested in the agent's actions, she expands "agent's Actions" in the Current Actions Pane. In this example, Eva clicks on move up. This action occurs within the method **jumpkick**, which is not currently shown in the code view (Fig 5a, circle 4). When Eva clicks the link, the history tool opens the **jumpkick** method in the code view and selects the move up method in green (Fig. 5c). Eva clicks the play button to the statement's left, which animates through the series of images recorded while the line of code executed.

At this point, Eva has found the beginning of the actions that comprise the jump and knock over. She selects the "start" arrow next to the move up action to indicate that the code to reuse begins with this action.

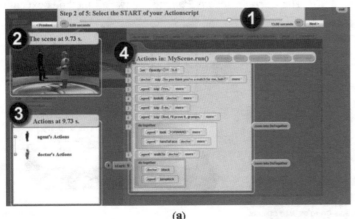

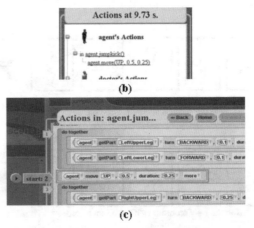

Figure 5. (a) The history tool for selecting the beginning of a feature. (b) After expanding an object's current actions to see action links. (c) After clicking an action link to show a new method in the code view and selecting a statement as the beginning.

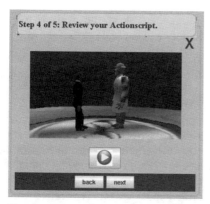

Figure 8. Choosing an Actionscript to reuse.

Melly program and her Actionscript library (see Figure 8). She selects the "Jump and Knock Down" Actionscript she recorded earlier.

To incorporate the jump and knock down action into her current program, Eva selects the character who she wants to jump and knock over another object (see Figure 9).

Once Eva assigns all roles and presses "Add Actionscript," Looking Glass generates all the code necessary for the chosen actors to perform the actions recorded in the script. The code is stored in a global method called "Jump_and_Knock_Down," which Eva can invoke or edit (see Figure 10). Looking Glass also adds an invocation of Jump_And_Knock_Down to the beginning of the program so Eva may immediately view it by running the program.

Figure 6. Reviewing an Actionscript to ensure the functionality is captured.

Step 3: To find the end action, Eva can scrub forward in time to find where the doctor falls. She can use a similar process as described in Step 2 to identify the final statement that is the end of the functionality to reuse.

Step 4: With the beginning and ending of the functionality she wants to reuse identified, Eva can play through the selected actions to confirm she selected the correct functionality (see Figure 6). If Eva decides that she prefers a different beginning or ending, she can return to the previous steps to make changes.

Step 5: In the final step, Eva names and describes her Actionscript (see Figure 7). The names and descriptions help her to remember the functionality in the Actionscript and what each character did. Eva names her Actionscript "Jump and Knock Down" and describes the roles each character played in the extracted code. In this example, she describes the agent's role as "Jumper" and the doctor's role as "Thing knocked over". Looking Glass saves the completed Actionscript in Eva's library for later use.

IMPLEMENTATION

Our system for selection and integration has five steps:

1. Based on the user's start and end statement selections, we extract the responsible code from an execution trace.
2. We ensure all local references in the extracted code are declared to prevent integration syntax errors.

Usage Scenario – Using an Actionscript
To use her Actionscript, Eva opens the super-strength

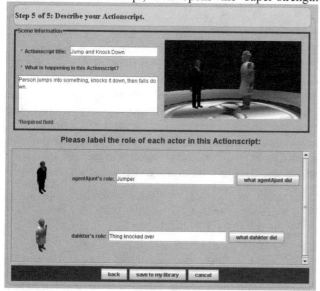

Figure 7. Abstracting the selected code into an Actionscript by naming object's roles.

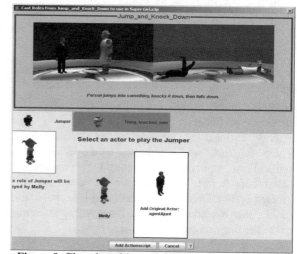

Figure 9. Choosing objects to play the roles that were recorded in the ActionScript.

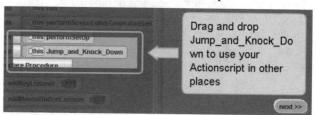

Drag and drop Jump_and_Knock_Down to use your Actionscript in other places

next >>

Figure 10. The Actionscript is added as a global method.

3. To enable type-safe integration, we determine the object types that can fill roles.
4. We parameterize the extracted code by roles to make it reusable and store it in an Actionscript.
5. When the user integrates an Actionscript, we generate new code with the characters and scenery objects the user selects to play each role.

Extracting the Responsible Code

To extract the code responsible for the functionality the user wants to reuse requires that we 1) enable the user to select functionality based on the observable output and 2) link the selected functionality to the program statements responsible for producing that output.

We continuously capture time-tagged screenshots of the output to enable users to select functionality to reuse. These images are used later in the interface to help the user choose the appropriate start and end statements executing at the appropriate times by showing what the scene looked like at a selected time.

To link the selected functionality to the program code responsible for it, we capture and structure the executed program into a tree that affords easily extracting the responsible code. The tree represents execution periods and program structure as subtrees. Each tree node contains a reference to a statement that executed and the statement's execution time range. Each child node's time range is contained in its parent's time range and its statement executed in its parent's context (e.g., a method call that executed within a loop). When a user selects start and end statements, we find the lowest common ancestor of the statements. We then quickly prune the subtree by traversing the common ancestor's time-sorted children and discarding nodes not in the start and end statement's time range.

We use the timing information to link the images and program execution events within the user interface.

Avoiding Compilation Errors in Extracted Code

The extracted code will not compile later if it contains references to locals not declared in the extracted code. To account for this, we record any local declarations and modifications occurring in children of the common ancestor that execute before the first relevant statement. If any extracted code references an undeclared local parameter or variable, then we add all recorded statements affecting the local to the beginning of the extracted code.

Avoiding Runtime Errors in Extracted Code

Allowing any object to fill any Actionscript's role can violate type safety during integration and cause run-time errors later. For instance, assume a user creates the role 'walker' from a person, like the agent, and the role invokes the walk method on the object filling the role. Then a user can only safely fill the 'walker' role with objects inheriting from the class implementing the walk method (i.e., the Person class). For example, an object like a table cannot fill the 'walker' role because a table does not extend the Person

class. If we assigned table to the 'walker' role, this would violate type safety and cause a run-time error.

To determine which characters and scenery objects can safely fill roles in an Actionscript, we must determine the class that implements a role's most specific type reference. To accomplish this, we crawl the extracted code to find expressions that directly and indirectly reference character and scenery objects. Because the extracted code is static, we use expressions' runtime evaluations from the captured program execution (e.g., function result, variable access) to resolve indirect references. The expressions' types determine a role's most specific type reference.

Creating an Actionscript

At this point in the process, we have extracted all the code responsible for the user's desired functionality and determined which object types are safe to fill the roles present in the code. Next, we need to store this information in a form that will allow us to easily reuse it at a later time: our Actionscript. Actionscripts contain a copy of the extracted code, parameterized by the roles, and role information. Because potential conflicts with local and dynamic dependencies have been resolved in the previous steps, we can use this information to perform a simple object substitution and code copy operation.

Integrating an Actionscript

To integrate an Actionscript into a new program requires two steps: 1) the user selects objects to fill the Actionscript's roles, and 2) we copy the Actionscript's code into the new program.

Because an Actionscript's code is parameterized by its roles, a user must choose objects to fill the Actionscript's roles to use the Actionscript. To ensure type safety while integrating an Actionscript, we use the roles' most specific type reference information to present users with a list of characters and scenery objects in their program that can safely fill the roles.

With the objects filling the roles selected, we can then copy the Actionscript's code and substitute in the chosen objects; but we must ensure all chosen objects are in scope for the contexts they will be used. We avoid the scope issue by copying the code into a new method of the program's Scene class. The Scene class has all program objects as fields; thus any object reference in a Scene class method is in scope. Additionally, every Looking Glass program contains a globally available Scene instance, allowing an invocation of a Scene class method in any context.

Differences in the body structure of different graphical objects create another potential source of integration problems. Because 3D objects can have different subparts, type safety does not prevent all possible errors. Suppose a user creates a role from a Samurai which turns the Samurai's helmet subpart. The user may later assign a Coach to safely fill this role, but the Coach does not have a helmet subpart to turn. If unchanged, a run-time error will occur when the program tries to turn the Coach's helmet. Because the error results from a role assignment, it cannot be resolved earlier. During copying, we match referenced subparts by name (e.g., the role references a helmet and the object filling the role has a helmet) but defer to the user when a suitable match is not found (e.g., user chooses a hat to substitute for the helmet).

Implementation Limitations

Our approach has two major limiting factors.

First, because Looking Glass is designed for middle school students, we elected not to support full inheritance through the programming environment. Hence our implementation cannot resolve class hierarchy conflicts like other systems for integration [4]. For instance, iterating over an array of Samurais to invoke the Samurai class method backflip cannot be abstracted to a super class with a backflip method for two roles to inherit from. Thus we cannot assign two different types of objects to fill the Samurais' roles later.

Second, Looking Glass programs provide rich visual output that users can utilize to find particular functionality. Applying these techniques to non-visual domains requires additional work to make program behavior observable.

CODE REUSE EVALUATION

To evaluate the potential use for our code reuse tools, we conducted an exploratory study to answer several questions:

1. Can middle school users with little or no previous programming experience successfully reuse code?
2. Does the process of selecting and reusing code help middle school users extend their programming skills?
3. Will animations propagate through social networks?

Participants

We conducted this study within the context of a class for the Exxon Mobil Bernard Harris Summer Science Camp held at Washington University. The camp provides opportunities to explore science and engineering for students with potential to succeed but who may be at risk due to limited academic opportunities in their school, family problems, or other issues. The camp works with St. Louis teachers to identify students who may benefit from attending. The camp accepts students based on teacher recommendations and an essay. The 47 camp attendees were rising sixth through eighth graders. The group was gender balanced and predominantly African-American.

Camp Course

During the two-week camp we oversaw two one-week classes: the first for 24 students and the second for 23 students. Each class was to include four two-hour sessions. The first week was limited to three sessions due to a network outage that made the lab unusable.

Evaluating Learning

To explore the potential for students to learn new programming skills through reusing code, we intentionally limited the formal instruction we provided the students. During the first session we demonstrated adding a 3D

Day 1	User methods, count loop, do together
Day 2	If/else, while loop, functions
Day 3	Sequential blocks in do togethers, sequential iteration over a list, parallel execution over a list

Table 1. Concepts and constructs in daily example programs

character, making characters perform actions by dragging and dropping method invocations, and running the program. We also introduced students to our code reuse interface.

To enable students to teach themselves new programming concepts through reuse, we provided each student with three example programs on each of the first three days. We designed the three example programs to contain motivating animations to be reused in other stories, and to illustrate a set of focus concepts for that day. The focal language concepts and constructs for each day are listed in Table 1. Each day, the students had access to the programs for the current day and all the previous days for that session.

To ensure example code was students' primary learning resource, researchers did not provide assistance to students. Instead, researchers responded to help requests by suggesting a relevant program in the example library.

Social Propagation

We are also interested in whether program functionality may spread through different social groups. We created two different types of groups: working groups and presentation groups. While students actively built programs, they sat with members of their working group. Toward the end of each session, we asked students to show the project they created that day to the members of their presentation group. Each working group contained eight students. Each presentation group contained six students.

On the first three days of each class, we asked each student to create a new program that incorporated two animations reused from other programs. Each day we created two example programs from which all working groups could reuse animations. We also provided a third example program, unique to each working group, intended to seed novel animations into the presentation groups.

Presentation groups contained two students from each working group. Students gathered in their presentation groups to view other student's programs constructed that day. We encouraged students to reuse animations they found captivating in their presentation group and offered prizes to anyone whose unique animation was reused more than once by other students.

Data

We collected three types of data: Actionscripts that participants captured, programs using those Actionscripts, and participants' performance on a programming quiz given during the final session of each camp class.

Scripts and Programs

Collecting participants' Actionscripts and programs enabled us to gather qualitative information about how users reuse code with our system, what kinds of actions they capture,

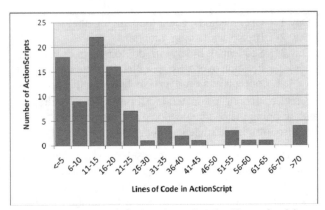

Figure 11. Frequency of Actionscript size (lines of code).

and how they use those actions within their own creations. We are interested in the potential for users to learn new programming constructs or concepts through the process of reuse. To ascertain the extent to which this happens, we collected quantitative information about the constructs participants use through their Actionscripts and independently in their programs.

Post-camp quiz

At the end of the final session, participants took an eleven-item forced-choice programming quiz in which we asked them to predict the behavior of short segments of Looking Glass code. Each question presented a small snippet of code and a series of four or five textual descriptions of how that code might behave. We asked participants to select the best description for each snippet of code. The questions on the quiz covered simple uses of sequential and parallel programming, count and while loops, iterating over a list, parameter passing, and method calls.

Based on an exploratory factor analysis of the quiz questions, we created a programming quiz scale that included six questions loading on the same factor (Cronbach's $\alpha = 0.60$). This factor reflects participants' ability to predict basic constructs behavior including sequential and parallel execution, parameter passing, loops, method calls, and iterating over lists. An additional two questions covered more advanced programming constructs: if statements and parallel execution over a list.

Results

Forty-six of our 47 participants successfully captured and reused code. The majority of their Actionscripts, 77%, contain more than five lines of code (Figure 11), which we consider non-trivial functionality. Typical script content focused on a single character or an exchange involving a small group of characters. This content indicates a focus on capturing functionality that can be used in a story that may be unrelated to the source.

Learning Through Reuse

We measured learning in two ways: (1) participants' modification or use of new programming constructs in their programs and (2) participants' performance on the post-workshop programming quiz.

Programming Construct	User Captured in Used Script	User Modified	User Added
Property Assign.	31	4	2
Function Call	38	1	10
Do Together	40	10	28
Count Loop	25	1	1
While Loop	2	0	0
For Each In Order	3	0	0
Each In Together	1	0	2
User Method Call	39	0	2

Table 2. Number of participants who captured a construct in an Actionscript they used, modified the construct in a program using the Actionscript, or added it independently.

Modification and Use of Programming Constructs

Thirty-six of our 47 participants either modified or independently used programming constructs which were only introduced through the process of reusing code.

Although our example programs used a variety of constructs, we saw a strong concentration of do together and loop constructs in the users' Actionscripts. This construct homogeneity limited the scope of learning. However, we observed evidence that participants used creating and modifying Actionscripts to learn new skills (see Table 2). Table 2 shows participants usage of programming constructs in their scripts and programs.

We observed three levels of programming construct usage. At the most basic level, users created Actionscripts including a particular construct. In the next level, users explored the code created by Actionscripts in their programs and modified one or more programming constructs. At the most advanced level, users created new sections of code that included programming constructs or techniques they discovered through reuse. Due to the emphasis on do together in the captured Actionscripts, we see the greatest number of modifications and independent uses of do together constructs. However, users also frequently learned how to call functions to request and animate the individual body parts of characters.

Programming Quiz Performance

We expect that learning will come primarily through modifying code from an Actionscript or using constructs discovered in an Actionscript to accomplish other goals. To investigate this, we divided our participants into two groups based on their programming behavior (see Table 3). The Low programming group (11 participants) includes participants who made no modifications to Actionscripts they used and did not use new programming constructs elsewhere in their programs. The High programming group (36 participants) includes participants who either modified

Programming Group	Basic Constructs	Advanced Constructs
Low (n = 11)	3.9	0.7
High (n = 36)	4.7	1.0

Table 3: Average number of correct answers on Post-camp Quiz by Programming Group

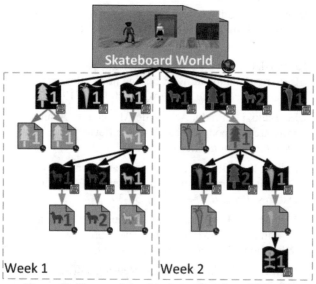

**Figure 12. Reuse originating from Skateboard World.
Black wave shapes are scripts and grey shapes are worlds.
Labels show creator ID, with color showing a creator's
working group and an object for their presentation group.**

the code in Actionscripts or used programming constructs introduced through the Actionscripts in other places of their program. We found that modification of code and use of new constructs correlates with better performance on the quiz for basic (r=2.67, p<.1) and advanced (r=2.95, p<.05) constructs. While this is not necessarily a causal relationship, we believe it suggests code reuse using our tools may be a learning pathway for new programmers.

Social Propagation of Functionality

We did see animations propagate through the camp's working and presentation groups. Figure 12 shows how participants captured and reused functionality from one source program, *Skateboard World*. During the first week of camp, three yellow working group users made Actionscripts containing animations from *Skateboard World*. Two of the three users created programs using these Actionscripts. The users shared their programs with their presentation groups at the end of the first day. On the second day, two red working group users and one blue working group user captured new Actionscripts from the yellow user's program and used the Actionscripts in their own prorgams. These users were in the same animal presentation group. We see a similar reuse pattern in week two for a purple working group user and *Skateboard World*.

This social propagation of functionality may provide a social channel through which users of Looking Glass can teach each other new programming constructs.

Study Limitations

The participants for the camp in which we conducted our study were selected because they had potential to be successful but were at risk for academic problems. The goal of the camp is to motivate these students to engage with academics. While we do not believe that our results are limited to this population and environment, more research

is necessary to explore the success of our tools with other populations.

FUTURE WORK

Our interface enables middle school students to successfully select and integrate code. Further, the results of our exploratory study suggest the reuse process helps users to build their repertoire of programming constructs.

Currently, our system does not support any customization or modification of an existing Actionscript. However, several users asked about modifications, such as including or excluding roles from an Actionscript or changing a property that is set within the Actionscript. To enable this type of interaction, we need to first understand what non-programmers want to modify in their Actionscripts and how they expect to accomplish this. Enabling users to remove a role or modify a specific action may increase the reusability and utility of Actionscripts. Communication with non-programmers about these modifications will be challenging.

Participants in our study selected Actionscripts that included only a subset of the programming constructs represented in the example set. We are considering an interaction for watching and automatically recording from a stream of Looking Glass programs called Looking Glass TV. A user simply stops watching when they see something they want and they can immediately begin the reuse process. By maintaining a history of programming constructs the user has experience with, we may be able to select examples for Looking Glass TV that help to introduce new programming concepts. Furthermore, this support for locating useful artifacts allows us to create a complete end-to-end software reuse tool.

While users seem to gradually increase their repertoire of programming constructs through reuse, we believe the process of constructing the code for an Actionscript may make the learning process faster and more effective. We plan to develop an automatic tutorial system that can guide users through building the code for a given Actionscript.

REFERENCES

1. Brandt, J., Dontcheva, M., Weskamp, M., and Klemmer, S.R. Example-Centric Programming: Integrating Web Search into the Development Environment. Stanford University Technical Report, CSTR-2009-01.

2. Bruckman, A. MOOSE Crossing: Construction, Community, and Learning in a Networked Virtual World for Kids. MIT Media Lab. Boston, MA., 1997.

3. Cottrell, R., Chang, J., Walker, R.J., and Denzinger, J. Determining detailed structural correspondence for generalization tasks. Proc. *SIGSOFT*, (2007), 165-174.

4. Cottrell, R., Walker, R.J., and Denzinger, J. Semi-automating small-scale source code reuse via structural correspondence. *Proc. SIGSOFT* (2008), 214-225.

5. Duala-Ekoko, E. and Robillard, M.P. Tracking Code Clones in Evolving Software. *Proc. ICSE* (2007), 158-167.

6. Fischer, G., Henninger, S., and Redmiles, D. Cognitive tools for locating and comprehending software objects for reuse. *Proc. ICSE* (1991), 318-328.

7. Gill, J. Shedding Some New Light on Old Truths: Student Attitudes to School in Terms of Year Level and Gender. *Proc. of the American Educational Research Association.* (1994).

8. Goldman, M. and Miller, R. Codetrail: Connecting source code and web resources. *Proc. VL/HCC* (2008), 65-72.

9. Gross, P. and Kelleher, C. Non-programmers Identifying Functionality in Unfamiliar Code: Strategies and Barriers. *Proc. VL/HCC* (2009), 75-82.

10. Hartmann, B., Wu, L., Collins, K., and Klemmer, S.R. Programming by a sample: rapidly creating web applications with d.mix. *Proc. UIST*, ACM (2007), 241-250.

11. Hoffmann, R., Fogarty, J., and Weld, D.S. Assieme: finding and leveraging implicit references in a web search interface for programmers. *Proc. UIST*, ACM (2007), 13-22.

12. Holmes, R., Walker, R., and Murphy, G. Approximate Structural Context Matching: An Approach to Recommend Relevant Examples. *IEEE Trans. On Soft. Eng.* (2006), 952-970.

13. Holmes, R., Cottrell, R., Walker, R.J., and Denzinger, J. The End-to-End Use of Source Code Examples: An Exploratory Study. *Proc. ICSM*, (2009), to appear.

14. Holmes, R., Walker, R.J., and Murphy, G.C. Strathcona example recommendation tool. *Proc. ESEC/FSE,* ACM (2005), 237-240.

15. Jablonski, P. and Hou, D. CReN: a tool for tracking copy-and-paste code clones and renaming identifiers consistently in the IDE. *Proc. OOPSLA*, ACM (2007), 16-20.

16. Kelleher, C. and Pausch, R. Lowering the barriers to programming: A taxonomy of programming environments and languages for novice programmers. *ACM Comput. Surv.* 37, 2 (2005), 83-137.

17. Kelleher, C. and Pausch, R. Using storytelling to motivate programming. *Comm. of ACM* 50, 7 (2007), 58-64.

18. Kelleher, C., Pausch, R., and Kiesler, S. Storytelling alice motivates middle school girls to learn computer programming. *Proc. CHI*, ACM (2007), 1455-1464.

19. Ko, A.J. and Myers, B.A. Designing the whyline: a debugging interface for asking questions about program behavior *Proc. CHI*, ACM (2004), 151-158.

20. Krueger, C.W. Software reuse. *ACM Comput. Surv.* 24, 2 (1992), 131-183.

21. Lanza, M. CodeCrawler-lessons learned in building a software visualization tool. *Proc. CSMR*, (2003), 409-418.

22. Leshed, G., Haber, E.M., Matthews, T., and Lau, T. CoScripter: automating & sharing how-to knowledge in the enterprise. *Proc. CHI,* ACM (2008), 1719-1728.

23. Lucredio, D., Prado, A., and de Almeida, E. A survey on software components search and retrieval. *Proc. Euromicro Conference* (2004), 152-159.

24. Lukoit, K., Wilde, N., Stowell, S., and Hennessey, T. TraceGraph: immediate visual location of software features. *Proc. ICSM*, (2000), 33-39.

25. Maloney, J., Burd, L., Kafai, Y., Rusk, N., Silverman, B., and Resnick, M. Scratch: a sneak preview [education]. *Proc. C^5* (2004), 104-109.

26. Mili, H., Mili, F., and Mili, A. Reusing software: issues and research directions. Software Engineering, *IEEE Trans. on Soft. Eng.* 21, 6 (1995), 528-562.

27. Mili, A., Mili, R., and Mittermeir, R. A survey of software reuse libraries. *Annals of Soft. Eng.* 5, 1 (1998), 349-414.

28. Olney, S. and Myers, B. FireCrystal: Understanding Interactive Behaviors in Dynamic Web Pages. *Proc. VL/HCC*, (2009), 105-108.

29. Prieto-Diaz, R. Status report: software reusability. IEEE *Software* 10, 3 (1993), 61-66.

30. Ruthruff, J., Creswick, E., Burnett, M., et al. End-user software visualizations for fault localization. *Proc. SoftVis*, ACM (2003), 123-132.

31. Sahavechaphan, N. and Claypool, K. XSnippet: mining for sample code. SIGPLAN Not. 41, 10 (2006), 413-430.

32. Schafer, T., Eichberg, M., Haupt, M., and Mezini, M. The SEXTANT Software Exploration Tool. *IEEE Trans. on Soft. Eng.* 32, 9 (2006), 753-768.

33. Storey, M. and Muller, H. Manipulating and documenting software structures using SHriMP views. *Proc. ICSM*, (1995), 275-284.

34. Thummalapenta, S. and Xie, T. Parseweb: a programmer assistant for reusing open source code on the web. *Proc. ASE*, ACM (2007), 204-213.

35. Yongbeom, Kim and Stohr, E.A. Software Reuse: Survey and Research Directions. *Journal of Management Info. Sys.* 14, 4 (1998), 113-147.

36. Zimmer, L. and Bennett, S. Gender differences on the California statewide assessment of attitudes and achievement in science. *Proc. of the American Educational Research Association*, (1987).

37. Zweben, S. 2007-2008 Taulbee Survey. *Computing Research News* 21, 3 (2009), 8-23.

Speeding Pointing in Tiled Widgets: Understanding the Effects of Target Expansion and Misprediction

Jaime Ruiz and Edward Lank
David R. Cheriton School of Computer Science
University of Waterloo
Waterloo, ON, Canada
{jgruiz,lank}@cs.uwaterloo.ca

ABSTRACT

Target expansion is a pointing facilitation technique where the users target, typically an interface widget, is dynamically enlarged to speed pointing in interfaces. However, with densely packed (tiled) arrangements of widgets, interfaces cannot expand all potential targets; they must, instead, predict the user's desired target. As a result, mispredictions will occur which may disrupt the pointing task. In this paper, we present a model describing the cost/benefit of expanding multiple targets using the probability distribution of a given predictor. Using our model, we demonstrate how the model can be used to infer the accuracy required by target prediction techniques. The results of this work are another step toward pointing facilitation techniques that allow users to outperform Fitts' Law in realistic pointing tasks.

Author Keywords

Pointing, target expansion, Fitts' Law, tiled widgets, human performance

General Terms

Human Factors, Performance

ACM Classification Keywords

H5.m. Information interfaces and presentation (e.g., HCI): Miscellaneous.

INTRODUCTION

Pointing, with a mouse, electronic stylus, touchpad, trackpoint, or trackball, is a frequent task in modern graphical user interfaces. Due to the frequency of pointing, even a marginal improvement in pointing performance can have a large effect on a user's overall productivity. As a result, researchers have explored various techniques to speed pointing, including bubble cursors [5], pointer warping [6], manipulation of motor space [7, 13, 2], and target expansion [10, 14]. While these techniques can speed pointing for sparsely spaced targets on a computer display, McGuffin and

Balakrishnan [10] note that these techniques provide less benefit for denser target arrangements, and, in the case of tiled targets, many provide no benefit. Several researchers have explored designing pointing facilitation techniques for tiled target arrangements [10, 14] with, as of yet, no success.

Tiled targets are, however, common in graphical interfaces. For example, widgets are frequently contained by toolbars, ribbons and menus, all multi-widget containers where no space exists between widgets. As well, widgets are not the only candidate targets in interfaces. The cells in a spreadsheet program or the words and letters in a word processing program also constitute legitimate locations for a user to target in a graphical interface. If these programs are displayed in full screen mode, the computer monitor is almost entirely covered with a tiled arrangement of potential targets.

In this paper, we explore the performance of one pointing facilitation technique, target expansion, for tiled targets. Target expansion works by expanding the target a user is pointing at on the display so the target is easier to acquire. However, as noted by McGuffin and Balakrishnan [10] and Zhai et al. [14], when targets are densely arranged on the screen, expanding all targets in a user's path results in no pointing advantage. With dense or tiled target arrangements, performance gains are only possible if one could reasonably predict the trajectory of the cursor such that the system can identify, in real time, the target a user is going to select [10]. To support target expansion for tiled targets, we need some technique for predicting the endpoint of a user's pointing motion in real time.

One sophisticated technique for endpoint prediction is *kinematic endpoint prediction* (KEP) [11, 8]. KEP uses the motion profile of a user to define a region of interest on the display. However, this region of interest is larger than an individual target: Ruiz and Lank [11] show that the region predicted by KEP is defined by a normal probability distribution. The normal distribution is centered on the maximally likely target, and targets surrounding that region have decreasing likelihoods. As a result, while the predicted target may be the actual intended target, surrounding targets are also likely.

Given that KEP cannot predict a single onscreen target, in this work we explore two issues associated with pointing in tiled target arrangements. First, is it possible to expand a small group of targets rather than an individual target to boost predictor accuracy? Second, given expansion of a set of targets, does the use of the KEP improve pointing performance?

It may be the case that the present KEP accuracy is sufficient to observe an improvement in performance in pointing tasks when expanding multiple targets. For example, if the KEP correctly predicts the user's target, the user's intended target will be at the center of the expansion region, and targeting will likely be faster. However, because the KEP predicts a region, offset errors are common, and, with an offset error, the expansion region will be centered on a target other than the user's desired target. If the offset is sufficiently small, the user's desired target will be expanded, but the target expansion will be confounded with target displacement – targets closer to the center of the expansion region will push the user's desired target either toward or away from the user. If the algorithm's prediction is off by a distance greater than the expansion region, a large offset error, the user's desired target will not be expanded *and the target will be shifted*. There is a probable benefit if the KEP algorithm is correct and expands a set of targets centered on the user's desired target. It is highly likely that large offset errors (where the user's desired target is shifted and not expanded) will increase the cost of a pointing task. The effect of small offset errors, where a target is enlarged and shifted on the display, is unknown. In this paper, we seek to determine whether Ruiz and Lank's KEP accuracies result in an *overall* improvement in pointing performance. We also wish to examine the costs of small and large-offset errors.

Through results from two experiments presented in this paper, we show that it is possible to expand a small set of targets on the computer screen to improve pointing performance. We also show that, when expanding a region, the benefits of expansion are affected by the target shift, i.e. the size of the offset error. We find a limit on shift of about 80 pixels on our 24 inch 1920x1200 displays. Finally, we demonstrate that, within the expansion region limit, any endpoint predictor must have an accuracy greater than 56.5% to realize a net benefit from expanding targets.

This paper is organized as follows. First we describe related work on expanding targets and endpoint prediction. Next we describe our design decisions for expanding a group of targets using screen expansion. We then describe and present results from a pilot study conducted to determine if performance benefits can be accrued when enlarging a candidate set of targets. This is followed by an experiment that uses a real time implementation of the KEP as described in Ruiz and Lank [11] for tiled targets. We conclude with a discussion on the implications and future directions of our work.

BACKGROUND

Fitts' Law [4] relates pointing time to target size and distance through a logarithmic term referred to as the *Index of Difficulty* or *ID*:

$$T = a + b \, log_2 \left(\frac{A}{W} + 1 \right) \quad (1)$$

In the above equation, A represents the distance to the target, and W represents the size of the target.

Given the reliability of Fitts' Law to predict movement times in interfaces [9], work in pointer facilitation can be categorized by techniques that reduce the distance to the target, increase the width of the target, or both decrease the distance and increase target width (see [1] for a review of these techniques). In this paper, we focus on techniques that increase the size of the target on the display.[1]

McGuffin and Balakrishnan [10] investigated the potential performance benefits of expanding target size. In their study they demonstrated that users are able to take advantage of enlarged targets even if target expansion occurs with only 10% of the distance left to travel. They also conclude that the required movement time to acquire a target can be accurately modeled by Fitts' law using the expanded target width to calculate the target's index of difficulty. In a replication study, Zhai et al. [14] pointed out that in McGuffin and Balakrishnan's experiment, users could anticipate the enlarging of a target. Therefore, observed benefits may be a result of anticipation of a larger target or may result from the enlarged target. Zhai et al. added additional conditions in which targets would expand, shrink, or remain static to prevent users from anticipating the final target size. Their results support McGuffin and Balakrishnan's results that users are able to take advantage of an expanding target as late as 90% of a movement even if the user is unable to anticipate the final target size. Despite the advantages of expanding targets on the display screen, facilitating the selection of tiled targets remains an open challenge. Unlike in isolated targets, where targets expand to fill empty screen space, in a tiled target arrangement targets cannot expand without either obstructing other neighboring targets or causing neighboring targets to be displaced on the screen.

When one considers target expansion of tiled targets, there exists a question of which targets to expand. Expanding every target is clearly no longer an option, as both McGuffin and Balakrishnan[10] and Zhai et al.[14] note. If every target is doubled in size, the screen space consumed by the tiled target arrangement doubles in size consuming too much screen real estate and will spill off the sides of the computer display. Furthermore, while the desired target becomes larger, all intervening targets also become larger, thus increasing the distance to the user's desired target. The benefits of a larger target are exactly offset by the increase in distance. For example, if all targets doubled in size on a display, to reach his or her desired target the user would need to traverse the intervening targets on the display. These intervening targets also double in size, effectively doubling the distance the user needs to travel to reach his or her goal (this assumes a fully tiled display). As shown in Equation 1, if both A and W are doubled, the overall pointing time remains unchanged from the initial distance and size. It is for precisely these reasons

---

[1]Targets can also be expanded in motor space (but not visually) [6] or visually (but not in motor space) [3]. While both of these techniques have shown benefits in isolated pointing tasks, we focus on display expansion in this paper.

that, to enable target expansion in tiled target arrangements, a predictor is needed to select a candidate target for expansion.

Recent work on endpoint prediction [8, 11] may enable pointing tasks even for dense or tiled target arrangements by predicting the target of a user's pointing motion. Using established kinematic models of motion, the researchers derived a kinematic endpoint prediction (KEP) algorithm. Lank et al. showed that their KEP was able to predict a user's target 42% of time and an adjacent target an additional 39% of the time (assuming tiled arrangements of targets) given a relatively small set of target sizes and distances. In follow up work, Ruiz and Lank [11] demonstrated that distance of motion has a significant effect on predictor accuracy. Therefore, while the KEP algorithm predicts a user's target 42% of the time for the distances tested by Lank et al., the accuracy decreases as the distance of motion increases. Ruiz and Lank also demonstrated that the region identified by KEP is defined by a normal probability distribution around the predicted endpoint. The standard deviation of the probability distribution is linearly correlated with distance of motion and is approximately 10% of motion distance.

Regardless, one drawback to any prediction technique is misprediction. For example, Lank et al.'s prediction technique results in correct prediction of their target sizes only 42% of the time and is accurate ± one target an additional 39% of the time. Ruiz and Lank extend this work, and show that the KEP yields a probability distribution over a region. While the KEP could be augmented with domain knowledge or user task models to improve its predictive power, there exists an open question on predictor accuracy. Clearly, more accurate target predictors are always to be preferred over less accurate predictors. However, how accurate must a predictor be to be useful for target expansion with tiled candidate target arrangements? Is the current state of the art in endpoint prediction, the KEP, accurate enough for generalized targeting tasks in interfaces? We seek to address these questions in the remainder of this paper.

TARGET EXPANSION FOR TILED TARGETS

A goal of this paper is to design expanding targets for tiled arrangements, for example, arrangements of targets in toolbars, menus, and ribbons in programs such as spreadsheets and word processors. As mentioned above, enlarging all targets in the user's path will result in no performance gain. Therefore, to enable target expansion in tiled target arrangements, a predictor is needed to select a candidate target for expansion. Given that KEP identifies a region of interest on the display and the region is typically larger then that of the user's intended target, the predicted target may not be the user's intended target.

To overcome the frequency of offset errors in endpoint prediction and increase the likelihood that the user's intended target is enlarged, we propose expanding a candidate set of targets. Expanding a group of targets will obviously improve the probability that any individual candidate target will be included in the expanded set. However, expansion of a group

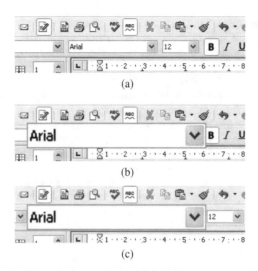

Figure 1. Font and point size selection widgets common in word processing programs. (a) The original unexpanded widget. (b) Expansion of the font widget using occlusion resulting in 100% occlusion of the point size widget. (c) Expansion of the font widget using displacement.

also results in having a greater effect on neighboring targets. In this section we describe our design decisions for expanding a group of targets.

Due to the limited amount of screen space around tiled targets, expansion of a target will have an effect on neighboring targets. There are two possible effects caused by the expansion of a target in tiled targets: occlusion and displacement.

Occlusion has been suggested as a technique to avoid excessive sideways shift of targets at the cost of interfering with the visibility of neighboring targets [10]. Previous designs using occlusion for tiled targets have been limited to targets of equal size. Therefore, doubling the height and width of one target results in a 50% occlusion of the adjacent targets. However, if target sizes differ, up to 100% occlusion of neighboring targets can occur. For example, a majority of word processing applications' toolbars include widgets for font and point size selection similar to the one shown in Figure 1(a). As shown in Figure 1(b), expansion of the font selector widget would result in the complete occlusion of the point size selection widget. Expanding multiple targets exacerbates the occlusion problem. If three targets are expanded to double their original width and height, then 1.5 targets of equal size are occluded on either side.

Due to both the heterogeneous size of widgets found in graphical user interfaces and our desire to expand multiple candidate targets, both of which would result in the total occlusion of possible targets, we choose to examine the use of displacement when expanding multiple targets in tiled arrangements. Displacement occurs when an expanding target causes neighboring targets to shift in order to make room for the target's new size. However, displacement is also not without limitations. Expanding a target that is not the user's intended target, what we call an offset error, results in the user needing to acquire a target that has shifted position. In the example of the font and point size widgets, expansion of the font selection widget results in the point size widget being displaced 100% of it's width (see Figure 1(c)).

Expanding multiple targets will cause an even larger co-linear displacement compared to expanding a single target, because the group of targets consume more space than a single target. Finally, visual disruption of the display is caused by expanding multiple targets, and this visual disruption may negate the performance benefits of expanding the target size.

Because of these potential risks, we describe two studies of target expansion with endpoint prediction. The first uses a simulated predictor with high accuracy, while the second uses the real-time KEP algorithm as described by Ruiz and Lank [11].

EXPANSION WITH SIMULATED ENDPOINT PREDICTION
The goal of our first experiment is to determine whether or not it is possible to expand a candidate set of targets, and whether any amount of target displacement is possible. To do this, we use a simulated predictor based on the accuracies reported in the original KEP paper of Lank et al. [8]. The original KEP was reported to have accuracies of 42% for the user's desired target and it predicted an adjacent target an addition 39% of the time. Our goal was to determine whether simulating these accuracies would result in a measurable performance improvement in pointing tasks. We also wished to determine how great the cost of displacement is with small offset errors (off-by-one) where the user's target is enlarged and shifted slightly, and large offset errors (off-by-two) where the user's target is not enlarged and is shifted.

In this section, we describe an experiment that shows that, if we expand a candidate set of three targets - the predicted target $\pm$ one target - in a tiled arrangement, it aids target acquisition based on Lank et al.'s initial probabilities. As aspects of this experimental design are replicated in our second study, we spend some time on the specific details of this study.

Method

Apparatus
The experiment was conducted on a generic desktop computer (P4, 2.0GHz) with a 24-inch 1920x1200 LCD display running custom software written in C# using Microsoft .NET. Input was collected using a Wacom Intuos3 five button mouse on a 12x19 inch tablet with cursor acceleration turned off.

Task
To test the performance of expanding a set of targets, we devised an experimental task that mimics that of previous work on target expansion [10, 14, 2]. Our task differs only in its use of seven tiled targets instead of an isolated target and in that target expansion occurs over more than one target.

The task for our experiments was a simple one-dimensional pointing task. Initially a green starting rectangle was randomly displayed close to one of the horizontal boundaries of the screen. The task began when the participant used the cursor to click within the starting location. At that time, seven tiled targets, would appear on the display orthogonal to the starting position. Participants were required to move the cursor to the red target and use the mouse button to click on the target. A successful target acquisition (i.e., clicking within the target region) was indicated by the target changing color. Users were told to acquire the target as quickly and accurately as possible, similar to other Fitts' Law tasks. To prevent users from always targeting the center of the multi-target widget, the location of the desired target was varied between the third, fourth, and fifth target.

Similar to previous work in expanding targets [14, 10], task ID ranged from 3.17 to 7.01 bits. However, our experiment contains fifteen Distance/Width (*D/W*) combinations resulting from presenting each task ID at three different distances. The three distances were chosen to correspond to close movements (512px), average movements (1024px), and distant targeting tasks (1526px). Our fifteen combinations of D/W (in screen pixels) were 512/4, 512/8, 512/16, 512/32, 512/64, 1024/8, 1024/16, 1024/32, 1024/64, 1024/128, 1536/12, 1536/24, 1536/48, 1536/96, and 1536/192.

Experimental Conditions
In our pilot study, there are two conditions. The first condition is a *Static/No Expansion* condition where the target size never changes during the movement. The other condition is an expansion condition where the candidate targets' widths expand by a factor of two when the cursor has covered 80% of the target distance (D). The targets expanded around a predicted target's center. To simulate predictor behaviour, 40% of the time the predicted target and the user's intended target were the same; 20% of the time one target before and 20% of the time one target after the intended target was the predicted target; and 10% of the time two targets before and 10% of the time two targets after were the predicted targets. As shown in Figure 2, mispredictions resulted in the intended target being shifted. If an off-by-two error occurred, the user's target was shifted and was not expanded.

Participants
Twelve adult volunteers, seven male and five female, between the ages of 18-32 (mean=24.7, SD=4.1) participated in the study. All participants were affiliated with a local university and received a $10 gift certificate for a local coffee shop for their participation.

Procedure and Misprediction Conditions
The experiment consisted of three blocks: one practice block (no expansion) and two experimental blocks: no expansion and expansion using the simulated predictor. The practice and no expansion block consisted of 15 D/W combinations presented six times (twice for each possible target location), resulting in 90 tasks per block. The expansion block consisted of each D/W combination being presented to the user ten times resulting in 150 tasks per block. The order of presentation of the combinations was randomized and the order of the experimental blocks was counterbalanced.

For the ten pointing tasks at each D/W combination, we introduce misprediction conditions to simulate the behaviour of Lank et. al's predictor. These conditions correspond to the conditions shown in Figure 2.

- *Correct Prediction:* In 4 of the 10 movements at each D/W combination, the predicted target was the user's intended target.

- *-1 Prediction:* In 2 of the 10 movements at each D/W combination, the predicted target was the target immediately before the user's intended target, along the user's path of motion.

- *+1 Prediction:* In 2 of the 10 movements at each D/W combination, the predicted target was the target immediately beyond the user's intended target.

- *-2 Prediction:* In 1 of the 10 movements at each D/W combination, the predicted target was two targets before the user's intended target, along the user's path of motion.

- *+2 Prediction:* In 1 of the 10 movements at each D/W combination, the predicted target was two targets beyond the user's intended target, along the user's path of motion.

The visual effect of each misprediction condition on the intended targets in screen space is illustrated in Figure 2.

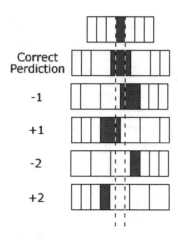

Figure 2. Illustrations of each of the five experimental conditions for expansion condition.

Results
Of the 2880 tasks recorded, 4.1% resulted in the user not correctly hitting the target. These tasks were removed from our analysis.

Figure 3 illustrates the overall movement time for experimental versus control conditions by ID. Figure 4 further segments movement time using each of the expanding conditions (Correct, +1, −1, +2, −2). Analysis of variance shows a significant effect for condition (expansion or no expansion) ($F_{1,11} = 8.51, p < 0.01$), misprediction condition (Correct, ± 1, ± 2) ($F_{4,8} = 27.73, p < 0.01$), and ID ($F_{4,8} = 396.20, p < 0.001$) on movement time. We also

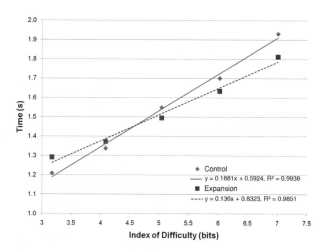

Figure 3. Movement times by Index of Difficulty by expanding condition for the user trial.

observed condition * misprediction interactions ($F_{4,20} = 24.15, p < 0.001$), and condition * ID interactions ($F_{8,16} = 5.97, p < 0.01$) on total movement time.

Analyzing Mispredictions
Results from our user trial indicate that even in the presence of mispredictions, users benefit from target expansion. Analysis of variance for tasks in the expansion condition show a significant effect for ID ($F_{4,8} = 154.18, p < 0.001$), misprediction error condition ($F_{4,8} = 59.21, p < 0.001$), order ($F_{2,10} = 18.17, p < 0.01$), and ID * misprediction interactions ($F_{4,24} = 2.507, p < 0.05$) on movement time. Post Hoc analysis using Bonferroni correction shows the −2 misprediction condition to result in the slowest mean movement time followed by the +2 condition. Post Hoc analysis also shows the −1 misprediction condition to be significantly slower than the the correct prediction and +1 condition. However, Bonferroni correction does not show a significant effect on movement time for the correct prediction and +1 misprediction condition. Finally, in all cases, when the target expands, the user outperforms the control condition. As well, overall the expansion condition outperform the control condition based on the simulated error rates we used. Qualitatively, we note that for all but the lowest IDs (largest, closest targets) the experimental condition was faster than the control condition.

As described by McGuffin and Balakrishnan[10], the maximum expected benefit of expanding a target can be calculated using Fitts' Law with the target's expanded size. Using the target's final width to calculate the task's Index of difficulty, represented as ID_{final}, we plot the effect on movement time by misprediction alongside the maximum expected benefit represented as a solid line (Figure 4). This line was calculated using Fitts' law coefficients from the static condition in Figure 3 assuming that we always predict and expand the correct target. In Figure 4, we see that correct prediction slightly outperforms the maximum expected benefit, and that the +1 condition, also outperforms the expected benefit for all but the lowest ID. The -1 condition performs, on aver-

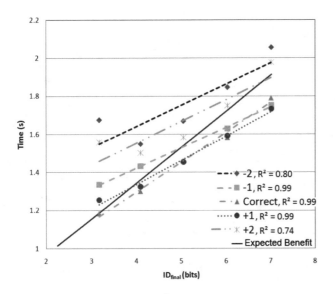

Figure 4. Movement time by final Index of difficulty for the screen expansion condition.

age, at the lower bound (slightly better for high ID tasks and slightly worse for low ID tasks). Finally, the +2 and -2 conditions do perform worse than the optimal expected benefit, but these conditions are relatively rare with current predictor accuracy (10% probability each).

REAL-TIME PREDICTION AND TARGET EXPANSION

Our results in our pilot study demonstrate that expanding a candidate set of targets on the computer screen coupled with optimistic endpoint prediction accuracies improves pointing performance in a tiled target pointing task. We have shown that the screen expansion of multiple targets improves pointing performance and that users are able to capitalize on an enlarged target despite the presence of mipredictions and target shifts. However, as mentioned above, follow up work by Ruiz and Lank [11] demonstrated that while high accuracies could be replicated at the distances used by Lank et al., as distance increased the distributions of predicted endpoints also increased, resulting in lower probabilities of the correct target being predicted. Therefore, at distances further than 512-pixels, even if three targets are expanded, it is much less likely that a user's target will be expanded. To increase the likelihood of target expansion in real world prediction, it is necessary to increase the size of the candidate set as distance increases.

In this section we describe an experiment conducted to examine expanding a region of targets using a real-time implementation of the kinematic endpoint prediction algorithm. In particular, the goal of the experiment is to answer the following questions:

- Will using a real-time predictor and a candidate set of targets, enable us to expand the user's intended target at accuracies defined by a normal probability distribution?

- Is there a limit to the amount of displacement that can occur before performance degrades?

- Finally, is the current state of the art in endpoint prediction accurate enough for enabling expanding targets in interfaces?

Kinematic Endpoint Prediction

To conduct this experiment, we implement the KEP algorithm and incorporate it into our pointing task. The KEP algorithm is described in [11], and is used to predict the endpoint of a user's motion. We summarize the implementation of this predictor here.

The KEP algorithm is a 3-step algorithm to determine user endpoint. The three steps are:

1. Given a partial gesture of length d toward a target, a quadratic equation is used to fit the data points $(d, s(d))$ along the partial gesture. Here d is the distance, and $s(d)$ is the speed at that distance. The quadratic equation is solved for it's 0-roots (x-intercepts). One x-intercept should occur at point $(0, 0)$, the start point. The other occurs at some distance from the start point, d_{calc}.

2. Calculate the *stability* of the predictor by comparing the previous endpoint predicted to the current predicted endpoint. If the prediction is not stable, return a value indicating an accurate prediction is not possible at this point in time.

3. If the predictor is stable, calculate the predicted percentage of gesture length completed by dividing the current distance traveled by d_{calc}. If the percentage is greater than a set threshold, return d_{calc}; otherwise return a value indicating a prediction is not possible at this time.

To return an endpoint, after curve fitting, we first estimate *stability* of our prediction. Our predictor is stable when the following equation holds:

$$\frac{l_n - l_{n-1}}{l_n} \approx 0 \qquad (2)$$

Here l_n is the current value of d_{calc}, and l_{n-1} is its previous value. Typically, this equation only approaches 0. Ruiz and Lank find that, as long as the value of the stability estimate is < 0.02, the prediction is sufficiently stable to give a reliable estimate.

If the prediction is stable, we then calculate where we are in motion. Based on previous work [10, 14], indicates that users are able to take advantage of an expanding target as late as 90% of a movement. We therefore typically predict before 90% of user movement. In our implementation of KEP, if the current distance traveled is 0.89 of d_{calc}, we return a predicted endpoint. For more details on the implementation of the KEP algorithm and the rationale for these design decisions, the interested reader is referred to [11], available on-line at the HCI lab website at the University of Waterloo, and to [8].

In Ruiz and Lank's KEP implementation, they show that the standard deviation of the predicted endpoint of a user's motion can be approximated by taking 10% of the distance a user travels. As a result, they recommend considering candidate targets within two standard deviations ($\pm10\%$) highly likely, i.e. 68.2% likelihood of target expansion. We base the expansion region of this experiment on this recommendation, as described below.

Method

Task

The task was the same task as described in pilot study with one exception. Instead of displaying seven targets, the whole screen was tiled with targets. As a result, the KEP predictor could choose any region on the screen as the predicted endpoint instead of limiting predictions to, for example, seven targets, as in the pilot study.

Expanding Conditions

Similar to our pilot study, our experiment has two conditions.

No Expansion/Control: Target size never changed during the movement.

Expansion: Using a real-time implementation of the kinematic endpoint prediction (KEP) algorithm, predictions were made continuously throughout the motion. At 89% of predicted distance (i.e. current distance is 89% of the predicted endpoint) a prediction was acted upon. At that time, the prediction was used to create a candidate set of targets around the predicted target by either determining the number of targets that can occupy a region defined by $\pm10\%$ of motion distance (D) or ±1 target, which ever was greater. For example, for an 8-pixel target at a distance of 512 pixels, a candidate set of 13 targets will be expanded because 6 targets fall within 51 pixels on each side of the predicted target. However, for a 64-pixel target at the same distance, only 3 targets will belong to the candidate set since each 64-pixel target is larger than the 51-pixel region defined by 10% of distance traveled. As mentioned above, 10% of motion distance is approximately one standard deviation of the probablity distribution for the region defined by Ruiz and Lank's KEP algorithm. Therefore, we would expect the user's intended target to be contained within a region of $\pm10\%$ of motion distance (or two standard deviations) approximately 68.2% of the time.

Procedure

The experiment consisted of three blocks: one practice block consisting of no expansion and two experimental blocks: control and expansion. Each block consisted of 15 D/W combinations presented ten times resulting in 150 tasks per block. The order of presentation of the combinations was randomized and the order of the experimental blocks was counterbalanced.

Participants

12 adult volunteers, 8 male and 4 female, between the ages of 21-33 (mean=25.8, SD=3.6) participated in the study. All participants were affiliated with a local university and received a $10 gift certificate for a local coffee shop for their participation.

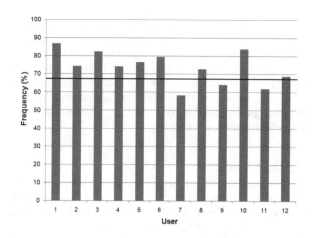

Figure 5. Frequency of the user's target expanding as part of the candidate set by user. The bold horizontal line represents the expected frequency of 68.2%

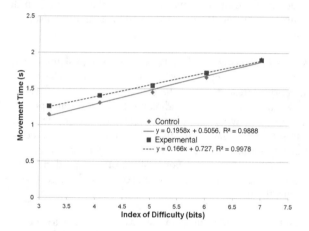

Figure 6. Movement times by Index of Difficulty by condition.

Results

Of the 3600 tasks recorded, 4.1% resulted in the user not correctly hitting the target. There was no significant difference between error rates in the control (5.1%) and expanding (3.1%) conditions. Errors were removed from our analysis.

In our experiment, candidate targets consisted of targets occupying $\pm10\%$ of motion distance around the predicted target. As mentioned above, the region predicted by the KEP algorithm is defined by a normal probablity distribution around the predicted target and approximately 10% of distance represents one standard deviation of the distribution. By expanding a region consisting of $\pm10\%$ of motion (i.e. two standard deviations), we would expect the user's target to be expanded 68.2% of the time. Results from our experiment indicated that the user's intended target was expanded 73.7% of the time. Figure 5 displays the accuracies by user. As shown in the figure, observed accuracies were typically better than expected, with only three users with frequencies below 68.2% (Users 7, 9 and 11). Accuracies reached as high as 86.9% for one user in our study.

Overall movement times by condition and ID are shown in Figure 6. Results from the experiment indicate that using the kinematic endpoint predictor to identify a candidate set of targets and expanding that set resulted in slower movement times than the control condition. To examine why, we now focus our attention on the analysis of how mispredictions, both small offset mispredictions and large offset mispredictions, affected movement time.

Analyzing Mispredictions

We examine the performance of target expansion for tiled targets by investigating the effect of offset errors on pointing speed. To perform this analysis, we normalize the time taken by motion by subtracting the average time taken in the control condition from the time taken for each individual motion. A value of 0 indicates that the movement speed was identical to the average control condition speed. Negative values indicate the user was faster than their average in the control condition. Positive values indicate that the user was slower.

We also categorize each data point into one of three categories: correct, negative off, and positive off. The correct category represents when the user's intended target was included in the expanded candidate set. Negative and positive off represent when the user's target was not in the candidate set. For Negative off, the algorithm underestimated the user's motion, so the user's intended target was moved farther away from the user. For Positive off, the predicted endpoint was beyond the user's target, so the user's target moved toward the user.

Offset error is measured in two ways, relative to the target's original width and in absolute pixels. Relative offset error defines offset error as a measure of the target's original width. For example, if the KEP predicts the correct target, then the target is not shifted and the relative offset error is 0. If the KEP is off by one target, the relative offset error would be equal to 1. For an error of k targets, the relative offset error is k.

The performance benefit/cost by relative offset error for the correct category is shown Figure 7. As illustrated by the figure, relative displacement has no correlation to the observed benefit/cost. For example, for a 4-pixel target a benefit is observed for relative offset errors as high as 11. Therefore, even though the user's intended target was displaced 11 times the original target's width (44 pixels), the user still capitalizes on the enlarged area of the target. In contrast, for 32-pixel targets, a relative target offset error as low as 1 (32 pixels) negates any benefit of an enlarged target.

Due to the lack of correlation for relative offset error on performance, we focus on absolute offset error, which, as shown in Figure 8, is more strongly correlated with benefit/cost. Absolute offset error is defined as the number of pixels the center of the target was shifted. For example, if the KEP predicts the correct target, then the absolute offset error is 0, the target is not shifted. If the KEP is off by one target, the

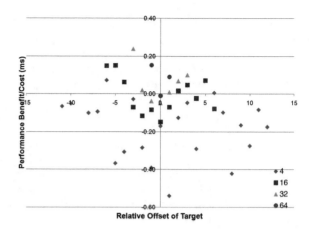

Figure 7. Performance Benefit/Cost by relative displacement of a user's target for targets of size 4, 16, 32, and 64-pixels for the correct experimental condition.

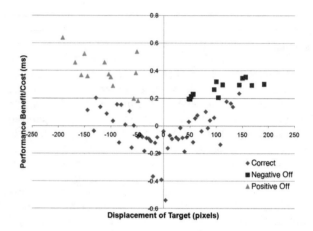

Figure 8. Performance Benefit/Cost by absolute displacement of user's target for each category in the experimental condition.

absolute offset error would be equal to W, the target width, and for an error of k targets, the absolute offset error is kW.

Examination of Figure 8 suggests that 0-pixel target displacement (displayed on the horizontal axis) is a point of reflection. Post-hoc analysis using Bonforroni correction confirms this, showing no significant difference between the negative and positive off categories. Therefore, we simplify our categories by taking the absolute value of target offset and combining the positive and negative off category into a single *Error* category. Figure 9 illustrates the normalized time taken versus offset error for each of our resulting categories, Correct, and Error. The solid line represents the best linear fit for each category.

As in the pilot study, we can calculate the expected best performance from expanding the user's intended target by using the Fitts' Law coefficients obtained from the control condition. Using these coefficients, we calculate the maximum performance benefit for our participants to be -0.20. As in the pilot study, when expansion occurs around the user's intended target, resulting in no horizontal displacement, we observed a performance benefit near the maximum benefit

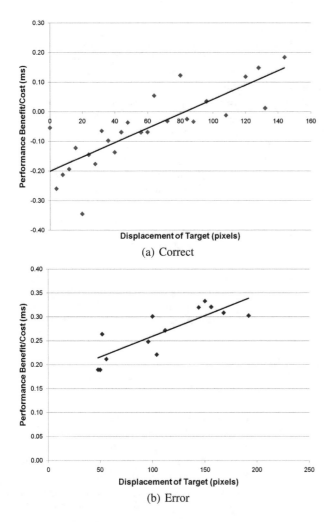

(a) Correct

(b) Error

Figure 9. Performance Benefit/Cost by absolute value of the displacement of user's target for the correct and error categories.

expected by Fitts' Law. However, the performance benefits of the enlarged target quickly degrades as the user's intended target shifts. When the offset error reaches 80 pixels (shown in Figure 9(a)), the time taken to acquire a target matches the control condition. For shifts greater than 80 pixels in our experimental configuration, the user performed worse than control, even if the correct target was expanded.

The performance cost for the error condition is shown in Figure 9(b). As shown in the figure, even at the lowest level of displacement (50 pixels), the performance is worse than the control condition, suggesting a significant cost for target displacement.

DISCUSSION

While our pilot study using a candidate set of three targets and the simulated prediction accuracies reported by Lank et al. [8] resulted in promising results, they did not extend to larger sets of targets using a real-time implementation of the KEP predictor. Results from our experiment demonstrate that there is a limit to the amount a user's target can shift when expanded. On our experimental setup, the limit on tar-

get displacement was approximately 80 pixels. If displacement was greater than 80 pixels, then target expansion did not result in a net benefit. Figure 9(a) plots this expected benefit as a linear function. While the 80-pixel limit on displacement is undoubtedly a function of the resolution of our computer monitor and input device, for any display/input device a relatively simple pointing task can be used to calculate the limits on target displacement for a specific user. See, for example, Wobbrock et al.'s work [12] calculating an error function for Fitts' Law pointing tasks, where they use a simple test to calibrate users.

As we note earlier, Ruiz and Lank [11] show that the KEP algorithm can be used to calculate a normal distribution around a predicted endpoint with standard deviation, σ_i, approximately equal to 10% of the user's movement. A normal distribution can be used to calculate specific probability of a value lying between the mean and any arbitrary number of standard deviations, s, using the erf function as follows:

$$p(x) = \frac{2}{\sqrt{\pi}} \int_0^s e^{-x^2} dx \qquad (3)$$

Using our 80 pixel limit for our monitor/input device configuration, we can use this to calculate the necessary accuracy of our predictor. At 0 pixels of displacement, we see a maximum benefit, calculated as about $1/5$ of a second, i.e. 0.20 seconds. This benefit shrinks to 0 seconds at 80 pixels, yielding a straight line equation of the form:

$$t_{saved} = -0.20 + \frac{0.20}{80}x \qquad (4)$$

Beyond 80 pixels, our targets are not expanded, yielding a constant cost based on 80 pixels of displacement of 0.25 seconds of additional time. We can claim the following:

$$p(x)t_{saved} > 0.25(1 - p(x)) \qquad (5)$$

Essentially, the probability of any time saving associated with expansion must *outweigh* the likely cost associated with 80-pixel target displacements when no expansion occurs. The probability of no expansion is exactly equal to $1 - p(x)$, where $p(x)$ is the probability that the target expands. Therefore, 80 pixels is equivalent to the number of standard deviations, s in Equation 3 such that the inequality, Equation 5 holds. Solving this analytically in Maple yields a result that $s = 0.729$. Our displacement limit, 80 pixels, is an arbitrary function of our hardware. However, the predictor accuracy must be greater than 56.5% for our maximum displacement limit. We obtain this calculation by evaluating the integral in Equation 3 with $s = 0.73$.

Considering the current standard deviations associated with the KEP, we see that only for distances less than 800 pixels will the predictor perform with sufficiently high accuracy to result in performance gain on our current experimental configuration. Therefore, for distances presented in Lank et al.'s original study [8], i.e. all distances less than 600 pixels, we would expect to see a net benefit. However, when implementing the real-time predictor on a larger display, only at 512 pixels is the KEP sufficiently accurate to allow a net improvement in performance, and then only if a region of 80 pixels is expanded. Expanding smaller regions will drop the predictor accuracy and limit some of the benefit, resulting in suboptimal benefit for expanding targets.

FUTURE WORK

We are in the process of exploring variants of expansion strategies to determine promising approaches to endpoint facilitation with expanding targets. While the KEP is currently not sufficiently accurate, it may be possible to increase the reliability of the KEP by combining its probabilities with additional information. For example, histories of command usage or user task modeling could allow the calculation of set of priors on the underlying interface widgets. This would allow the KEP to identify the maximally likely target within a candidate set using two independent probability distributions – one from command use and one from motion kinematics. Combining these probability distributions could significantly improve endpoint selection. In addition, in our experiment, we enlarged all candidate set targets around the predicted target. However, if underlying priors indicate that certain targets are highly unlikely, we could either not expand those targets, or we could even shrink less likely targets to make additional space available for expansion of more likely targets. This selective expansion would result in less displacement of expanded, likely target, and less overall displacement of unlikely but possible targets. Another strategy is to increase the size of the targets in proportion to the likelihood of the target as determined by the combined probability distributions, so that targets are of varying sizes. This will result in displacement of the user's intended target within the expansion region, but the displacement should be considerably less than expanding every target in the region the same amount.

Beyond target expansion, we also aim to explore additional pointing facilitation strategies. For example, one problem with display expansion is the visual disruption caused by targets moving on the screen. Motor expansion has been shown to improve performance in pointing tasks, and it may be the case that making targets "sticky" in motor space based on either KEP probabilities, or KEP probabilities in conjunction with underlying priors, could have a higher net benefit. One significant benefit of motor space expansion is that visual disruption of the display is entirely eliminated. We continue to explore techniques that effectively incorporate KEP into realistic pointer facilitation techniques for dense and tiled target configurations.

CONCLUSION

In this paper, we examine the effectiveness of expanding multiple candidate targets with a region on a computer display when the entire screen is covered with potential targets. We show that, if a predictor accuracy is sufficiently high (i.e. if a target is expanded with probability greater than 56.5%) and if the expansion region is sufficiently small (less than 80 pixels in our display configuration, or about 4% of the display resolution), then there is a net benefit to expanding

targets when using a real-time kinematic endpoint prediction algorithm in conjunction with expanding targets. As distances increase beyond about 800 pixels on our computer display, however, the error associated with our predictor increases, and endpoint prediction is no longer sufficiently accurate to support improved pointing speeds. Although kinematic endpoint prediction may not be, in itself, sufficient to support endpoint expansion for targets on typical desktop computer displays with resolutions of 1920x1200 pixels or greater, we argue that additional information in the form of underlying priors can be used to refine the underlying target probabilities. Generating an accurate set of target probabilities based on priors and motion kinematics should enable novel target expansion strategies, with the potential for significant improvements in user pointing performance in desktop computer displays.

ACKNOWLEDGMENTS

We thank the participants in our study and our colleagues in the HCI lab at the University of Waterloo for valuable suggestions. Funding for this research was provided by the Natural Science and Engineering Council of Canada (NSERC).

REFERENCES

1. R. Balakrishnan. "beating" fitts' law: virtual enhancements for pointing facilitation. *Int. J. Hum.-Comput. Stud.*, 61(6):857–874, 2004.

2. R. Blanch, Y. Guiard, and M. Beaudouin-Lafon. Semantic pointing: improving target acquisition with control-display ratio adaptation. In *CHI '04*, pages 519–526, 2004.

3. A. Cockburn and P. Brock. Human on-line response to visual and motor target expansion. In *Graphics Interface 2006*.

4. P. M. Fitts. The information capacity of the human motor system in controlling the amplitude of movement. *Journal of Experimental Psychology*, 47:381–391, 1954.

5. T. Grossman and R. Balakrishnan. The bubble cursor: enhancing target acquisition by dynamic resizing of the cursor's activation area. In *Proc. CHI '05*, pages 281–290.

6. Y. Guiard, R. Blanch, and M. Beaudouin-Lafon. Object pointing: a complement to bitmap pointing in guis. In *Graphics Interface 2004*.

7. D. V. Keyson. Dynamic cursor gain and tactual feedback in the capture of cursor movements. *Ergonomics*, 40(12):1287–1298, 1997.

8. E. Lank, Y. Cheng, and J. Ruiz. Endpoint prediction using motion kinematics. In *Proc. CHI '07*.

9. I. S. MacKenzie. Fitts' law as a research and design tool in human-computer interaction. *Human-Computer Interaction*, 7:91 – 139, March 1992.

10. M. McGuffin and R. Balakrishnan. Fitts' law and expanding targets: Experimental studies and designs for user interfaces. *ACM Transactions on Computer-Human Interaction*, 12(4):388–422, 2005.

11. J. Ruiz and E. Lank. Effects of target size and distance on kinematic endpoint prediction. Technical Report CS-2009-25, University of Waterloo, 2009.

12. J. O. Wobbrock, E. Cutrell, S. Harada, and I. S. MacKenzie. An error model for pointing based on fitts' law. In *CHI '08*, pages 1613–1622, New York, NY, USA, 2008. ACM.

13. A. Worden, N. Walker, K. Bharat, and S. Hudson. Making computers easier for older adults to use: area cursors and sticky icons. In *Proc. CHI '97*.

14. S. Zhai, S. Conversy, M. Beaudouin-Lafon, and Y. Guiard. Human on-line response to target expansion. In *Proc. CHI '03*.

Local Danger Warnings for Drivers: The Effect of Modality and Level of Assistance on Driver Reaction

Yujia Cao
Human Media Interaction
University of Twente
P.O. Box 217, 7500 AE,
Enschede, The Netherlands
y.cao@utwente.nl

Angela Mahr
German Research Center
for Artificial Intelligence
Building D3₂, Campus
Saarbrücken, Germany
angela.mahr@dfki.de

Sandro Castronovo
German Research Center
for Artificial Intelligence
Building D3₂, Campus
Saarbrücken, Germany
sandro.castronovo@dfki.de

Mariët Theune
Human Media Interaction
University of Twente
P.O. Box 217, 7500AE,
Enschede, The Netherlands
m.theune@utwente.nl

Christoph Stahl
Cluster of Excellence -
Multimodal Computing &
Interaction
Saarland University, Germ.
stahl@cs.uni-sb.de

Christian Müller
German Research Center
for Artificial Intelligence
Building D3₂, Campus
Saarbrücken, Germany
christian.mueller@dfki.de

ABSTRACT

Local danger warning is an important function of Advanced Driver Assistance Systems (ADAS) to improve the safety of driving. The user interface (the warning presentation) is particularly crucial to a successful danger avoidance. We present a user study investigating various warning presentations using a scenario of emergent road obstacles. Two presentation factors were selected: *modality* and *level of assistance*. The modality factor had 4 variants: speech warning, visual and speech warning, visual warning with blinking cue, and visual warning with sound cue. The level of assistance varied between with or without action suggestions (AS). In accordance with the ISO usability model, a total of 6 measurements were derived to assess the effectiveness and efficiency of the warnings and the drivers' satisfaction. Results indicate that the combination of speech and visual modality leads to the best performance as well as the highest satisfaction. In contrast, purely auditory and purely visual modalities were both insufficient for presenting high-priority warnings. AS generally improved the usability of the warnings especially when they were accompanied by supporting information so that drivers could validate the suggestions.

Author Keywords

automotive, multimodal interfaces, car2car communication

ACM Classification Keywords

H.5.2 Information interfaces and presentation: User Interfaces, User-centered design

General Terms

Design, Human Factors

INTRODUCTION

Local danger warning is an important function of Advanced Driver Assistance Systems (ADAS) to improve the safety of driving. Besides directly sensing the environment to detect danger [8], recent advances in inter-vehicle communication technology (e.g.wireless ad-hoc networks car-2-car communication) further allow the exchange of information between cars [2] [13]. This enables a much wider application of local danger warnings, as drivers can be alerted to approaching danger that is not yet visible. A crucial part of successful danger avoidance is the user interface – the presentation of the warning to the driver, which is investigated in this study. We focus on a scenario where drivers are warned about road obstacles that are a short distance ahead but not yet visible (e.g. due to a bend in the road or a leading vehicle), therefore requiring an immediate reaction.

According to the situation awareness (SA) theory from Endsley [6], driving can be considered as a dynamic decision making task based on real-time maintenance of SA. SA has three hierarchical phases which all contribute to 'knowing what is going on' ([6], p.36) in a dynamic environment. The first step, perception, is to perceive the dynamics of relevant elements in the environment. The second step, comprehension, is to obtain an understanding of the perceived elements, including their significance to the task. The third step, projection, is to predict the future states of the environment. Finally, based on this updated SA, a decision can be made on how to react. For example, a driver D perceives a newly-presented warning message in the car. D understands from the warning that there is a stationary vehicle on the road-side shortly ahead. Then D predicts that there might be people moving around that vehicle. Finally D decides on a significant decrease in driving speed in order to be able to pass safely. From this perspective, the presentation of local danger warnings should aim at assisting a timely update of the D's SA, as well as helping him or her to make proper decisions. Accordingly, we chose to investigate two presentation factors, namely *modality* and *level of assistance*. A user experiment was conducted to evaluate various presentation modes for obstacle warnings, manipulated by these two factors.

PRESENTATION FACTORS: MODALITY AND LEVEL OF ASSISTANCE

Modality is a factor that is known to influence the quality and efficiency of information perception, the very first phase of SA. In the context of in-vehicle warnings, the study in [21] showed that drivers appeared more vigilant for hazards when the warnings were delivered aurally (speech) rather than visually (text). It was also suggested in [12] that auditory modalities, sound in particular, are the most suitable for presenting warnings with a high priority, whereas visual modalities are not adequate. This can be explained from several aspects. Regarding the sensory resources, driving mainly consumes visual perception resources. Thus, auditory messages interfere less with the driving task and are less likely to cause mental overload [22]. Auditory modalities are also omnidirectional, so that the information can be picked up while the eyes are kept on the road [20]. In addition, auditory modalities have a very high salience and this means they can trigger an immediate attention shift to the warning messages [3]. However, sound warnings, if over-used or not well-designed, can cause annoyance [17]. They can produce faster reactions than visual modalities, but suffer from more inappropriate responses [9]. Speech might be too time-consuming in a situation where a real quick reaction is needed. For example, it was demonstrated in [4] that the duration of speech warning messages (less than 10 words, about 5 seconds) is longer than the time needed to obtain the same information through visual modalities (1.8 seconds for icons and 3.6 seconds for text). Regarding the visual presentation of warnings, the major weak point of visual modalities is a lack of salience so that a timely perception cannot be guaranteed. However, once attended to, well-designed visual messages can be more efficient time-wise in conveying information. Therefore, in this study, additional cues (a blinking bar in the peripheral visual field or a beep sound) were provided to enhance the salience of visual warning messages, which were then compared to pure speech warnings. Furthermore, we also investigated the combination of speech and visual warnings to see whether their somewhat complementary characteristics could bring together "the best of both worlds".

While the modality factor influences SA, the factor *level of assistance* plays a role in decision making. It manipulates whether a warning contains only the information of the approaching danger or also an action suggestion (e.g. brake, change lanes). Action suggestions are expected to shorten the time needed to infer a proper action from the latest status of SA. However, a few previous studies showed that a high level of assistance was not always favored. Using a headway maintaining scenario, [11] presented that the lowest level of assistance (providing information about leading cars) allowed the smoothest driving in terms of speed variance and was the best accepted by drivers. In contrast, the brake command to the drivers and the automated brake by the vehicle hampered the driving safety and were less acceptable. In their study, the usage of modality differed in all conditions.

Therefore, the findings might be confounded with a modality influence, as the authors also discussed. Another study [14] compared a command message style (e.g. "Reduce speed") with a notification style (e.g. "Curve ahead"). Results revealed that the command style increased the drivers' compliance to the ADAS. However, the trust in the ADAS and the self-confidence both declined when drivers were not provided with sufficient information and were forced to rely on the command messages. Based on the SA theory, the decision making process relies on an up-to-date SA. Therefore, when drivers are aware of an information lack, they cannot be confident in their decisions. In our study, the action suggestions were always presented in combination with warning messages. When receiving the action suggestion, drivers also had the opportunity to know why they were suggested so and to decide whether they should comply. The higher level of assistance was expected to enhance the effectiveness of local danger warnings.

EXPERIMENT

We conducted a user study in which obstacle warnings were presented in various modes. For evaluation, we followed the usability guidance from ISO (ISO 9241-11, [1]). In this ISO standard, the usability of a user interface is assessed in terms of effectiveness, efficiency and satisfaction. **Effectiveness** is the accuracy and completeness with which users achieve specified goals. In our driving context, it can be reflected by the performance of danger avoidance and the level of situation awareness. SA was assessed on-line by placing recall tasks along the driving course [5]. **Efficiency** is the (temporal and cognitive) resources expended to achieve the goals, which can be measured by the reaction time and the subjective evaluation of driving load. Finally, **Satisfaction** is the users' positive attitude towards the use of the interface, and can be obtained in terms of subjective rating.

Subjects. 32 drivers participated in this experiment, 16 men and 16 women. Their age varied between 20 years and 62 years (mean = 32.6, SD = 10.8). All participants had been in possession of a valid driver's licence for at least two years. They were all native German speakers. Each driver was paid 15 Euros for approximately 2 hours of experiment time.

Apparatus. To promote a realistic sensation of driving, the experiment was carried out inside a real car (Mercedes-Benz R Klasse). The simulator software was hosted by a normal PC. The driving scene was a one-way highway with two lanes. No extra traffic was involved. The scene was projected onto the windshield and was updated at approximately 25Hz. The vehicle stood indoors enclosed by extra shields to reduce ambient light. This ensured a good visibility of the projection at all times of the day. Visual warning messages were presented on a 10.6-inch head-down display mounted next to the steering wheel on the right hand side. The display was also a touch screen through which the recall task was performed. Auditory signals (speech and sound) were delivered through a PC speaker located in the center of the vehicle. A web camera was mounted on the dashboard to record the frontal facial view of the driver throughout the experiment. Figure 1 shows a subject driving.

Figure 1. A subject driving in the experiment.

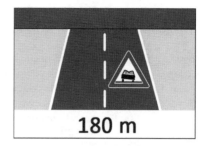

Figure 3. A visual warning displayed with a (blinking) top bar.

Messages and Presentations. A warning message described an obstacle in terms of its type (what), location (where) and distance (how far). Four types of obstacles were included: broken vehicle, fallen tree, rock and lost cargo. The location could be on the left lane, on the right lane or on the right roadside. The distance varied between 150m and 180m. In this experiment, these three information units were not equally relevant to the drivers' reaction (explained in the next section). In order to let drivers carefully perceive all three information units before reacting to the obstacles, we also presented irrelevant messages with one of the three units being 'out of range'. The irrelevant type, location and distance were air traffic, on the left roadside and more than 10km, respectively. Note that the irrelevant messages were included for experimental purposes only; it should never be a function of real ADAS systems to give false alarms.

The modality factor had 4 variants: visual + blinking cue, visual + sound cue, visual + speech, and speech only. For visual warnings, icons were designed for the four types of obstacles (Figure 2); the location of an icon on a road image indicated the obstacle location; and the distance was presented in text (Figure 3). This design was found to require shorter perception time in comparison with three other visual presentations [4]. The blinking cue was provided by a flashing red bar on top of the warning display area (Figure 3). The sound cue was a beep tone that lasted for about 350ms. All cues were delivered at the onset of a visual warning. Speech warnings narrated the obstacle type, distance and location sequentially, such as "Broken vehicle in 180 meters on the right roadside" (translated from German). This sequence was determined in an informal survey with 8 German native speakers.

Figure 2. Icon design of the four types of obstacles used in the study: broken vehicle, fallen tree, rock and lost cargo.

The level of assistance varied between with or without action suggestions (AS). AS were always given in speech, such

as "Change lanes" or "Brake" for warnings and "Attention" for irrelevant messages. A full factorial design of the two presentation factors resulted in 8 (4 × 2) presentation conditions. They are summarized in Table 1. In the visual channel, visual message and blinking bar started simultaneously, when both present. In the auditory channel, if more than one component was included, they were presented sequentially. The order from first to last was beep sound, AS and speech message.

Table 1. Presentation conditions used in the experiment.

Condition Index	1	2	3	4	5	6	7	8
Action Suggestion					×	×	×	×
Visual Message	×	×	×		×	×	×	
Speech Message	×			×	×			×
Beep Sound		×				×		
Blinking Bar			×				×	

Driving Task. The driving speed could be controlled at two levels (120km/h and 60km/h), using the gas pedal and the brake pedal. For example, when the speed was 120km/h, pressing the brake pedal would change it to 60km/h immediately. The basic driving requirement was to drive 120km/h in the nearside lane.

Obstacle warnings were presented at random intervals between 800m and 1300m. Drivers were required to change to the offside lane if the obstacle was on the nearside lane and brake if the obstacle was on the offside lane or on the right roadside. After passing the obstacle, they should change back to the nearside lane or accelerate to the higher speed again. When a warning started, the obstacle was not yet visible. It only appeared in the scene when it was 40 meters ahead of the vehicle, in the form of a colored box (Figure 4). Drivers were instructed not to wait for the obstacles to appear. Instead, they should react to the warnings immediately after they had decided on the right action to perform, because given the distance settings in the experiment there was no risk of acting unnecessarily early. Regarding the AS, they were given total freedoms from complying to it immediately to ignoring it and relying only on the warnings. Irrelevant messages did not require any reaction and were to be ignored in all conditions. In addition, brake or lane change actions should be completed at a safe distance from the obstacles. We defined a distance of more than 20m to be safe, which means the speed should have been decreased to 60km/m or the vehicle should be on the offside lane when the car reached 20m in front of the obstacle. A low pitch error sound was delivered in case of a late or missed reaction.

Speech messages all finished before the obstacles appeared and visual messages were taken off the display when the obstacles were passed. During the interval between two obstacles, drivers were asked to recall the situation of the most recent obstacle. A question was asked via speech, regarding either the type, the distance mentioned in the warning message, or the color of the obstacle. Drivers answered by pressing one of the four options displayed on the touch screen. No questions were asked after irrelevant messages.

Figure 4. An obstacle on the nearside lane. The color can be yellow, green, blue or red.

Procedure. The procedure of the experiment was as follows. When entering the car, the drivers first adjusted the seat to their comfort. Then the experiment was introduced, including the driving scenario, messages, presentations and task. Then the drivers drove two practice tracks of about 15 minutes in total. In the first track, obstacles appeared in the scene without warnings and the drivers had to react as soon as they saw them. The second track included all 8 types of warning presentations, as well as the irrelevant messages. The recall task was also practiced. The main part of the experiment started after the practicing section. First, a baseline drive was performed for 5 minutes. The drivers encountered 16 obstacles without warnings. Afterwards, based on a within subject design, the drivers drove 8 tracks with different presentation conditions. Each track lasted for about 5 minutes, containing 8 warning messages and 3 irrelevant messages. The message order was randomized. During a short break after each track, the drivers filled in a questionnaire, rating driving activity load and the satisfaction with the warning presentation. A size-8 Latin square was used to counterbalance the order of the 8 tracks. At the end of the experiment, an open questionnaire was provided to obtain more comments and feedback.

Measurements. Based on the ISO usability model [1], a total of 6 measurements were derived to assess effectiveness, efficiency and satisfaction, as summarized in Table 2.

An effective warning is supposed to enhance the driving safety and the driver's SA. Therefore, to assess effectiveness, we used one measurement for the driving safety and two measurements for drivers' SA. Regarding unsafe behaviors, 3 error types were distinguished: 1) incorrect reaction, such as lane change instead of braking; 2) late reaction, which was performed less than 20m in front of the obstacle; and 3) no reaction to the obstacle warning. The *unsafe behaviors* measured the total amount of these three types of behaviors in

Table 2. Summary of dependent measurements.

Parameter	Dependent Measurement
Effectiveness	Unsafe behaviors Correct recalls Reaction to irrelevant messages
Efficiency	Reaction Time Driving activity load (Effort of attention, Visual demand, Auditory demand, Temporal demand, Interference and Situational stress)
Satisfaction	Expected satisfaction with the warnings in real-life driving

each condition. The *correct recalls* assessed the amount of recall questions that were correctly answered in each condition as a measure of SA. The *reaction to irrelevant messages* refers to the unnecessary brake and lane change actions after irrelevant messages. It also reflects how well drivers were aware of the situation conveyed by the warnings.

The efficiency of warnings was evaluated by the reaction time and the subjective ratings of driving load. The reaction time was defined as the time interval between the moment when a warning presentation started and the moment when an action was performed. A brake action was identified when the speed changed from 120km/h to 60km/h. A lane change action was identified when the lateral displacement of the car reached 10% of the maximum lateral displacement during the course of a lane change (Figure 5). To obtain subjective evaluation of the driving load, we used the Driving Activity Load Index (DALI), which is a revised version of the NASA Task Load Index adapted to the driving task [18, 19]. It contains 6 workload factors as described in Table 3. Each factor can be rated on a 6-level scale from 0 (low) to 5 (high).

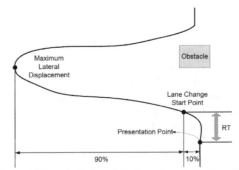

Figure 5. The calculation of the lane change starting point.

Finally, the subjective satisfaction with the usability of the warnings was obtained by a 9-level rating scale, from -4 (very unsatisfied) to 4 (very satisfied). Drivers were asked to base their judgements on the expected usability in a real-life driving situation. They always had access to the ratings they had already given, so that they could make adjustments to maintain the relative rankings between conditions.

Table 3. Description of DALI factors.

Factor	Description
Effort of attention	To evaluate the attention required by the driving activity – to think about, to decide, to choose, to look for etc.
Visual demand	To evaluate the visual demand necessary for the driving activity.
Auditory demand	To evaluate the auditory demand necessary for the driving activity.
Temporal demand	To evaluate the specific constraints due to timing demands when driving.
Interference	To evaluate the possible disturbance when driving simultaneously with any other supplementary task, such as perceiving the warning messages.
Situational stress	To evaluate the level of constraints / stress while driving – fatigue, insecure feeling, irritation, discouragement etc.

RESULTS

Unsafe Behaviors. During the baseline drive without obstacle warnings, all drivers except one showed unsafe behaviors. On average, 19.1% of the obstacles were not passed safely, because drivers reacted either incorrectly or too late. There were more unsafe lane change reactions than unsafe braking reactions. This baseline performance indicates that it is indeed a challenge for drivers to react to obstacles at short notice.

With the assistance of warnings, 18 drivers (56.3%) safely avoided all obstacles in all presentation conditions. The percentage of unsafe behaviors was reduced to 1.4% on average. The percentage within each condition is shown in Figure 6. When AS were provided, unsafe reactions only occurred in the speech condition (1.2%), because subjects did not immediately comply to the AS and did not act fast enough after the speech messages were over. When AS were not available, the number of unsafe behaviors increased in all modality conditions, especially when speech was used alone (9.0%). Figure 7 further shows the distribution of all unsafe behaviors over the two action types and three error types. Most unsafe situations were caused by incorrect actions, counting up to 58.6% from both action types. In another 31.1% of the cases, brake or lane change actions were performed correctly but too late. In the remaining 10.3% of the cases, subjects did not brake and passed the obstacles with the higher speed. Late actions and no actions all occurred in the pure speech conditions.

A two-way repeated-measure ANOVA further revealed a significant assistance effect ($F(1, 31) = 15.8, p < .001$) and a significant modality effect ($F(3, 29) = 5.1, p < .01$). The higher level of assistance (with AS) led to safer driving than the lower level (without AS). Among the four modality variants, the performance was equally good for the three variants that included visual modalities. However, driving safety de-

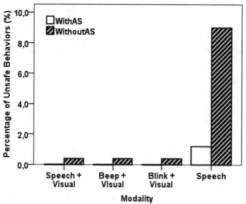

Figure 6. Percentage of unsafe behaviors in each condition.

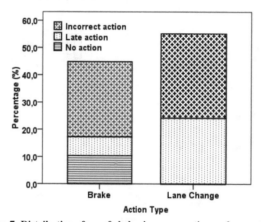

Figure 7. Distribution of unsafe behaviors over action and error types.

creased significantly when speech was used alone, compared to the other three variants ($F(1, 31) = 16.2, p < .001$ by Helmert contrast). There was also a significant interaction between modality and the assistance level ($F(3, 29) = 5.5, p < .01$), meaning that when drivers received assistance in the form of AS, presenting the warnings using speech alone was much less harmful to the driving safety.

Correct Recalls. The recall task was generally performed well. On average, 91.7% of the questions were answered correctly. The performance was the best when AS, speech and visual information were all provided (96.1% correct), and was the worst in the two pure speech conditions (87.9% correct). Repeated ANOVA was conducted and confirmed a significant modality effect on the quality of recall ($F(3, 29) = 3.5, p < .05$). Combining speech and visual messages led to significantly more correct recalls than the other three modality variants ($F(1, 31) = 10.2, p < .01$, by Helmert contrasts). This result suggests that the maintenance of SA could be assisted by presenting information through more than one sensory channel. Pure speech resulted in the worst recall performance ($F(1, 31) = 6.6, p < .05$). This might be due to the transience of speech, which does not allow repeated perception. No difference in recall was found between the two visual conditions with additional cues. The level of assistance did not influence the recall performance either ($F(1, 31) = 0.03$, n.s.). This is not surprising, because the action suggestions did not contain relevant information to the questions.

Besides modality, the topic of the questions also had an effect on the quality of recall ($F(2, 30) = 8.0$, $p < .01$). As shown in Figure 8, the color of obstacles was recalled the worst, compared to the type and the distance ($F(1, 31) = 8.9$, $p < .01$). A possible explanation is that of the three types of information, color was not mentioned by the warnings and was the least relevant to the driving task, so the users may have paid less attention to it. In addition, the obstacle type was recalled better than the distance ($F(1, 31) = 9.8$, $p < .01$). The reason might be that the icon presentations of obstacles were more vivid than the text presentations of distances, because shapes and colors have great salience to human information processors due to the sharp contrasts they are able to create [16].

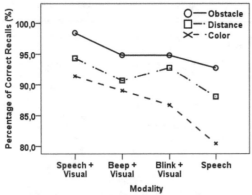

Figure 8. Percentage of correct recalls (averaged over the assistance levels for each modality variant).

Reactions to Irrelevant Messages. To obtain more insight into the level of SA created by the warning messages, we looked into drivers' reactions to irrelevant messages. On average, drivers reacted to 12.1% of irrelevant messages with unnecessary braking or lane changes. In most cases, drivers self-corrected their actions very soon. The number of unnecessary reactions was influenced by the modality factor ($F(3, 29) = 5.2$, $p < .01$) but not by the level of assistance ($F(1, 31) = 0.1$, n.s.). The latter finding is not surprising, since the irrelevant action suggestion ("Attention") did not refer to a physical driving action.

It can been seen in Figure 9 that unnecessary reactions occurred the most when messages were presented visually with the blinking cue ($F(1, 31) = 9.8$, $p < .01$, by Helmert contrast: blink + visual vs. other three). Since this is the only modality variant that is purely visual, this result might suggest that the lack of auditory modalities could make the drivers less vigilant (cf. [21]) and less careful. Interestingly, unnecessary reactions occurred the least when speech was used alone, which seems to contradict its negative impact shown by the measure of unsafe behaviors. However, a possible explanation is obtained when analyzing the three types of irrelevant information separately. As Figure 9 shows, when visual messages were provided (except speech only), drivers reacted more to irrelevant distances than to irrelevant obstacles and locations ($F(1, 31) = 29.5$, $p < .001$ by Helmert

contrast: distance vs. other two). Irrelevant obstacles again resulted in more reactions than irrelevant locations. This pattern suggests that drivers may have used a common sequence to scan the visual messages. Since the location of an obstacle was the most relevant to the driver's reaction, it was probably inspected first. Then the type of an obstacle would have been observed before the distance, because it was more spatially integrated with the location. Since early reactions could be performed at any time before all three information units were analyzed, the later the irrelevant unit was perceived, the more unnecessary reactions were performed. In the pure speech conditions, however, the sequence of perception was fixed, with the location information being presented last. This guaranteed the detection of irrelevant obstacles and distances before any action could be performed. However, this advantage does not mean that the speech modality is the most able to enhance drivers' SA. In contrast, when looking at those cases where the location was irrelevant, the speech condition still produced the most unnecessary reactions, which is consistent with the fact that 82.4% of the incorrect reactions to regular warnings occurred in the pure speech conditions. Finally, these results suggest that it takes more effort to interpret spatial information (e.g. locations) when it is presented only orally than when it is also presented visually. This is consistent with literature (e.g. [7]) stating that spatial information can be effectively presented by visual non-verbal modalities, such as image.

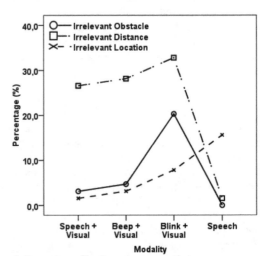

Figure 9. Percentage of irrelevant messages that were unnecessarily reacted to (averaged over the assistance levels for each modality variant).

Reaction Time. First, we looked at whether reaction time differed between the brake and the lane change actions. A three-way repeated measure ANOVA was conducted and revealed that the action type (brake/lane change) did significantly influence the reaction time. On average, the lane change actions were performed 0.24 seconds faster than the brake actions ($F(1, 31) = 15.4$, $p < .001$). This result falls in line with previous findings stating that steering is 0.15 to 0.3 seconds faster than braking, because of a lower response complexity [10]. Due to the difference, further analyses were conducted separately on the two types of actions.

When speech was used alone without AS, the reaction time

was particularly long, because no action could be performed before the end of the speech. (Remember that the location information, which was essential for deciding which action should be performed, was given at the end of the message.) As Figure 10 shows, the average reaction time was 5.1s (170m) for braking and 4.8s (160m) for lane change. When drivers were assisted with AS, the reaction time in the pure speech condition was reduced to 2.3s for braking and 2.1s for lane change. However, these reaction times are still the longest among the four conditions where AS were provided. It seems that the drivers hesitated to comply to the action suggestions when no visual information was available. Playing back the video recordings, we saw that when visual messages were provided, most drivers checked the display during the course of the action suggestion or shortly afterwards. This might explain their hesitation in the pure speech condition. Generally, drivers still chose to comply to the AS without the complete information of an obstacle. However the reaction was more or less delayed.

Besides the two pure speech conditions, the difference in reaction time among the other six conditions was relatively minor. However, ANOVA still revealed significant modality effects (braking: $F(2, 62) = 25.0, p < .001$; lane change: $F(2, 30) = 22.0, p < .001$) as well as significant assistance effects (braking: $F(1, 31) = 27.9, p < .001$; lane change: $F(1, 31) = 24.7, p < .001$). Regarding the level of assistance, both braking and lane change were performed faster with AS than without AS, as shown in Figure 10. On average, AS accelerated braking by 470ms (15.7m) and lane change by 130ms (4.3m). This finding suggests that although most drivers spent time on validating the action suggestions with the visual messages, it was still less time/effort consuming compared to making decisions without any suggestion. In this driving simulation, the structure of visual displays and the content of warning messages were rather simple, thus the benefit of AS in terms of reaction time was only below a half second. However, this benefit could be larger in a more dynamic situation where the warning messages are more diverse and less expected.

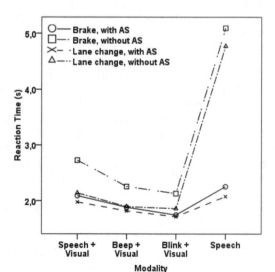

Figure 10. Average reaction time in each condition for brake and lane change respectively.

Among the three modality variants with the visual modality, the combined use of speech and visual messages led to the longest reaction time for both braking reactions ($F(1, 31) = 44.8, p < .001$) and lane change reactions ($F(1, 31) = 44.6, p < .001$). Comparing the two visual conditions with attentional cues, both types of reactions were faster with the blinking cue than with the beep cue. However, the difference was only significant for the lane change action ($F(1, 31) = 6.9, p < .05$).

A somewhat reversed pattern could be found when comparing the reaction time with the drivers' reactions to irrelevant messages (Figure 9). It seems that the longer the reaction time was, the fewer unnecessary reactions there were. This observation suggests a variation in the level of vigilance. When speech was presented with the visual information, drivers seemed the most willing to carefully inspect the visual messages before reacting to them. On the other hand, in the purely visual conditions, drivers reacted the fastest but most often overlooked the irrelevant items. As a couple of drivers commented, they found the purely visual condition boring. This again suggests that the lack of auditory signals could decrease the drivers' vigilance, causing them to be less attentive and behave less carefully.

Driving Activity Load. Using the DALI questionnaire, the load of driving activities (to avoid obstacles during driving) was rated on 6 dimensions: effort of attention, situational stress, visual demand, auditory demand, temporal demand, and interference. Each dimension could be rated from 0 (low) to 5 (high). First, we averaged the rating scores over all 6 dimensions as a global assessment of driving load. Repeated ANOVA revealed that the global driving load was influenced by both the modality ($F(3, 93) = 5.0, p < .01$) and the assistance level ($F(1, 31) = 23.4, p < .001$). As Figure 11 shows, the driving task was generally less demanding with AS than without AS. Regarding modality, the driving task was rated the least demanding when speech and visual modalities were combined ($F(1, 31) = 5.8, p < .05$, by Helmert contrast), and the most demanding when speech was used alone ($F(1, 31) = 5.3, p < .05$). No significant difference in the driving load was found between the visual conditions with attentional cues.

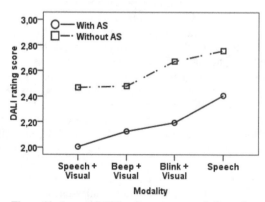

Figure 11. Average DALI rating scores over 6 dimensions.

When zooming into the DALI dimensions, we found that besides the two perceptional (visual and auditory) demands, the remaining 4 showed a common pattern over the 8 conditions. To validate this observation, we conducted the reliability analysis on these four variables in each of the 8 conditions. Results showed that the Cronbach's Alpha (coefficient of internal consistency) values were all greater than 0.8, indicating that ratings on these 4 DALI dimensions are indeed highly consistent. The common pattern among them obviously corresponds with the global driving load (Figure 11). In contrast, the variance in the perceptional demands was closely related to the manipulation of modalities (Figure 12). As expected, the visual demand was rated the lowest in the speech conditions. Additional demand was induced by visual warning messages, but the increment was at a minimum when the visual warnings were combined with speech. AS also generally reduced the visual demand, probably because less effort was needed to analyze the information on the display. Regarding auditory demand, the scores were the lowest in the purely visual condition and the highest in the pure speech conditions. Interestingly, the auditory demand induced by speech warnings was less when visual messages were provided at the same time. The reason might be that drivers spent less effort on listening to the speech because they could also get some information visually.

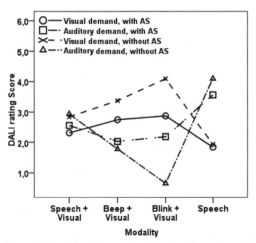

Figure 12. DALI ratings on visual and auditory demand.

Subjective Satisfaction. Drivers rated how satisfied they would be to use each warning presentation in real-life driving. On a 9-level rating scale from -4 (very unsatisfied) to 4 (very satisfied), the judgments were generally positive on average, except for the purely visual warnings without AS (Figure 13). The condition with speech, visual messages and AS was rated the highest. ANOVA confirmed that the subjective satisfaction was affected by both the modality ($F(3, 29) = 22.1$, $p < .001$) and the level of assistance ($F(1, 31) = 43.2$, $p < .001$). Subjects were more satisfied with the higher level of assistance than the lower one. Among the four modality variants, combing speech and visual messages was the most satisfying ($F(1, 31) = 33.0$, $p < .001$). The visual condition with beep cues was the second best ($F(1, 31) = 8.7$, $p < .01$). No significant difference was found between the purely auditory (speech) and the purely visual (with blinking cues) variants. This is due to an interaction between the modality and the level of assistance. When drivers were given suggestions on what to do, they preferred

the purely visual messages to the pure speech messages, because they could quickly validate the action suggestions and react with confidence. Without AS, on the other hand, the purely visual messages were rated lower than speech. Several drivers explained that the messages were less salient without any auditory signals. Although the blinking cue worked well in this experiment, it might be less effective when there are more distractions in the car, such as radio and conversations. It was also mentioned that when there was no action suggestion, it was more important to keep one's eyes on the road.

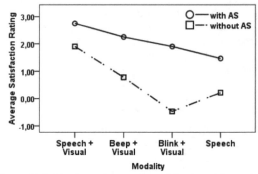

Figure 13. Subjective ratings on the satisfaction with warnings.

DISCUSSION

In this experiment, obstacle warnings were presented to drivers, in order to assist them to safely avoid emergent local dangers. It is shown that warnings presented in various modes all resulted in less unsafe behaviors, compared with the baseline condition where drivers were not warned in advance. This indicates that the safety of driving could indeed benefit from providing local danger warnings to drivers. In addition, this experiment also revealed that the way the warnings were presented, with regard to modality and level of assistance, could influence their effectiveness and efficiency, and drivers' satisfaction with them.

Level of Assistance. The level of assistance varied between with and without AS. The AS were supposed to directly assist drivers to decide on how to react to the obstacles. In this experiment, the advantage of using AS was consistently shown by various measurements. Less unsafe behaviors occurred with than without AS. AS accelerated both braking and lane change actions. Although the benefit was below a half second, it could be more pronounced when the warning messages are more dynamic and less expected and the situational decisions are more complex. Regarding the driving load ratings, the attentional effort, stress, visual demand, temporal demand and interference were all rated lower when AS were provided. Moreover, drivers expected the warnings to be more satisfying in real-life driving if AS would be available. In summary, based on the ISO usability model, adding AS made the warnings more effective, efficient and satisfying in this experiment.

This finding seems inconsistent with some previous studies which favored a lower level of assistance for drivers. In the headway assistant presented in [11], users either received braking commands that were presented in speech, or information about a leading car that was presented visually. Information was always presented much earlier than the commands so that there would be sufficient time to analyze it. Subjects in this study accepted the information style more than the command style. It is not surprising that drivers preferred to be notified as early as possible and decide on what to do themselves. However, in the situation of an emergent danger, action commands could be more effective because time might not always be sufficient for analyzing the information and deciding the next steps to take. In our study, the drivers were notified of the obstacles less than 10 seconds ahead, which might explain their strong preference for action suggestions. In addition, AS in our experiment always pointed to correct actions. Although aware of this fact, most drivers still validated the AS with the visual messages when they were available. This finding suggests that when integrating AS into real ADAS systems, it is important to provide relevant information at the same time, because the AS might not always be perfect and drivers should still have the chance to decide for themselves. In summary, we could say that AS are probably more beneficial when the situation is more urgent and they should be provided together with relevant information about the situation.

Modality. Regarding the four modality variants used in this experiment, our usability assessment generally suggests that the speech and visual modality combined variant is the most usable, speech alone is the least usable and the two visual variants with attentional cues lie in between. Speech has three major drawbacks when used in our scenario. First, the duration of the speech messages was too long, leaving the drivers only about 2 seconds to react. Second, speech does not allow multiple perception without a repeat function. Third, it is not suitable to convey spatial information such as object locations, which were the most relevant to this task. As a result, using only speech led to the most unsafe behaviors, the worst recall, the longest reaction times and the highest ratings on driving load. In line with previous findings [12], our result suggests that speech alone is not adequate for presenting high priority warnings.

Comparing the two kinds of attentional cues, although no significant difference was found in terms of effectiveness and efficiency, the beep cue was clearly preferred by the drivers. The satisfaction ratings showed that drivers expected the warnings with beep cues to be more satisfying in real-life driving than the warnings with blinking cues. In the general questionnaire at the very end of the experiment, drivers were asked to rate the usefulness of the two kinds of cues, on a 6-level scale from 0 (not useful) to 5 (very useful). The beep cue received significantly higher scores (mean=3.8, sd=1.3) than the blinking cue (mean=2.1, sd=1.8), shown by a t-test ($p < .001$). In addition, 15.6% of the drivers commented that they had not noticed the blinking top bar at all. This result confirms that visual modalities have a lack of salience, thus are less suitable for warning presentations than auditory modalities. In this experiment, this lack of salience did not harm the driving safety, because the warnings were always well expected, so no warning was missed even if the blinking cues were not detected. However, the visual cues might

be less useful in a real-life driving situation, because warnings are normally unexpected and thus are more likely to be missed.

Besides the lack of salience, our results also suggest that purely visual presentations could reduce the drivers' vigilance for hazards. In the condition with visual message, blinking cue and no AS, drivers reacted the fastest but overlooked the most irrelevant messages. It seems that they were less willing to check the warnings properly and were less careful with their reaction. Regarding the satisfaction rating, the purely visual condition was the only one that received a minus score on average. Several drivers described this condition as boring. These findings stand in line with the study in [21] where drivers appeared more vigilant when warnings were delivered aurally than visually. Therefore, it could be suggested that the presentation of high-priority warnings needs to include auditory signals.

Although pure speech and purely visual messages both have major drawbacks, the combination of the two significantly improved the usability of the warnings. Their complementary characteristics provided both salience and a freedom of perception. Consequentially, this modality variant had the best recall performance, the lowest driving load score and the highest satisfaction score. Although the reaction was not the fastest, drivers reacted the least to irrelevant messages (when presented visually), indicating a better awareness of the situation conveyed by the warnings. As several drivers explained, receiving information through multiple channels would let it be picked up more quickly, because there are more choices for perception and drivers could choose one that is compatible with the driving activities in that specific situation. It seems that a redundant use of multiple modalities did bring "the best of both world" in this study. This redundancy benefit was also previously obtained using an in-car navigation task [15], where drivers made the fewest errors and showed the most proper vehicle control when the navigation messages were delivered both visually and aurally (relative to the single modalities).

CONCLUSIONS AND FUTURE WORK
In this study, we investigated the presentation of local danger warnings to drivers. A user experiment was conducted in which obstacle warnings were presented in 8 modes, manipulated by four modality variants and two levels of assistance. In accordance with the ISO usability model, 6 measurements were derived to assess effectiveness and efficiency of the warnings and drivers' satisfaction. Based on the results, several suggestions are made for the design of local danger warnings in ADAS systems. First, regarding modality, purely auditory or purely visual modalities are both insufficient for presenting high-priority warnings. The combination of both can be beneficial, especially the combination of speech and well-designed visual messages. In speech messages, the critical information needs to be presented first. The speech should be kept short and a 'repeat' function might be worth consideration. If spatial information such as locations needs to be presented, it is better to present it visually and graphically. Second, if it is neces-

sary to use additional cues to attract drivers' attention to the warnings, auditory signals (e.g. sounds) are more suitable than visual signals (e.g. blinking objects), due to a higher level of salience. Finally, it could be beneficial to provide action suggestions in urgent situations. However, AS should always be accompanied by supporting information, because they might not always be perfect and thus drivers always need the opportunity to validate the suggested action.

Future work can be considered in the following directions: using a head-down display, we found that providing attentional cues in the peripheral visual field was not very effective. However, this finding needs to be reexamined using head-up displays, such as direct projection on the windshield. This is expected to enhance the effectiveness of visual cues. Moreover, the warning messages were relatively simplex in this experiment and there was no extra traffic involved. It would be useful to extend the current study with more diverse warnings and more dynamic driving scenarios.

ACKNOWLEDGEMENT
This work was funded by the Dutch Ministry of Economic Affairs (project Interactive Collaborative Information Systems, grant nr: BSIK03024) and the German Ministry of Education and Research (project Car-Oriented Multimodal Interface Architecture, grant number 01IW08004).

REFERENCES
1. ISO 9241: Ergonomic requirements for office work with visual display terminals (vdts) - part 11: Guidance on usability, 1998.

2. Identify intelligent vehicle safety applications enabled by DSRC. Technical Report DOT-HS-809-859, U.S. Department of Transportation, National Highway Traffic Safety Administration, Springfield, Virginia, USA, March 2005.

3. N. Bernsen and L. Dybkjaer. Exploring natural interaction in the car. In *CLASS Workshop on Natural Interactivity and Intelligent Interactive Information Representation*, pages 75–79, 2001.

4. Y. Cao, S. Castronovo, A. Mahr, and C. Müller. On timing and modality choice with local danger warnings for drivers. In *1st International Conference on Automotive User Interfaces and Interactive Vehicular Applications (AutomotiveUI 2009)*, pages 75–78, 2009.

5. M. R. Endsley. Measurement of situation awareness in dynamic systems: Situation awareness. *Human Factors*, 37(1):65–84, 1995.

6. M. R. Endsley. Towards a theory of situation awareness in dynamic systems. *Human Factors*, 37(1):32–64, 1995.

7. S. K. Feiner and K. R. McKeown. Automating the generation of coordinated multimedia explanations. *IEEE Computer*, 24:33–41, 1991.

8. D. M. Gavrila. Sensor-based pedestrian protection. *IEEE Intelligent Systems*, 16(6):77–81, 2001.

9. R. Graham. Use of auditory icons as emergency warnings: evaluation within a vehicle collision avoidance application. *Ergonomics*, 42(9):1233–1248, 1999.

10. M. Green. "How long does it take to stop?" Methodological analysis of driver perception-brake times. *Transportation Human Factors*, 2(3):195–216, 2000.

11. A. Kassner. Meet the driver needs by matching assistance functions and task demands. In *European Conf. on Human Centred Design for Intelligent Transport Systems*, pages 327–334, 2008.

12. C. Kaufmann, R. Risser, A. Geven, and R. Sefelin. Effects of simultaneous multi-modal warnings and traffic information on driver behaviour. In *European Conf. on Human Centered Design for Intelligent Transport Systems*, pages 33–42, 2008.

13. T. Kosch. Local danger warning based on vehicle ad-hoc networks: Prototype and simulation. In *1st International Workshop on Intelligent Transportation (WIT 2004)*, 2004.

14. J. D. Lee, B. F. Gore, and J. L. Campbell. Display alternatives for in-vehicle warning and sign information: message style, location and modality. *Transportation Human Factors*, 1(4):347–375, 1999.

15. Y. C. Liu. Comparative study of the effects of auditory, visual and multimodality displays on drivers performance in advanced traveller information systems. *Ergonomics*, 44(4):425–442, 2001.

16. N. H. Lurie and C. H. Mason. Visual representation: Implications for decision making. *Journal of Marketing*, 71:160–177, 2007.

17. D. C. Marshall, J. D. Lee, and P. A. Austria. Alerts for in-vehicle information systems: Annoyance, urgency, and appropriateness. *Human Factors*, 49(1):145–157, 2007.

18. A. Pauzié. Evaluating driver mental workload using the driving activity load index (DALI). In *Proc. of European Conference on Human Interface Design for Intelligent Transport Systems*, pages 67–77, 2008.

19. A. Pauzié and G. Pachiaudi. Subjective evaluation of the mental workload in the driving context. *Traffic and Transport Psychology*, pages 173–182, 1997.

20. N. Sarter. Multimodal information presentation: Design guidance and research challenges. *International journal of industrial ergonomics*, 36(5):439–445, 2006.

21. B. Seppelt and C. Wickens. In-vehicle tasks: Effects of modality, driving relevance, and redundancy. Technical Report AHFD-03-16/GM-03-2, GM Corp, 2003.

22. C. D. Wickens. Multiple resources and mental workload. *Human Factors*, 50(3):449, 2008.

Designing a Thesaurus-Based Comparison Search Interface for Linked Cultural Heritage Sources

Alia Amin[1], Michiel Hildebrand[1], Jacco van Ossenbruggen[1,3], Lynda Hardman[1,2]
[1]Centrum Wiskunde & Informatica (CWI), Amsterdam,
[2]University of Amsterdam (UvA),
[3]VU University Amsterdam,
firstname.lastname@cwi.nl

ABSTRACT

Comparison search is an information seeking task where a user examines individual items or sets of items for similarities and differences. While this is a known information need among experts and knowledge workers, appropriate tools are not available. In this paper, we discuss comparison search in the cultural heritage domain, a domain characterized by large, rich and heterogeneous data sets, where different organizations deploy different schemata and terminologies to describe their artifacts. This diversity makes meaningful comparison difficult. We developed a thesaurus-based comparison search application called LISA, a tool that allows a user to search, select and compare sets of artifacts. Different visualizations allow users to use different comparison strategies to cope with the underlying heterogeneous data and the complexity of the search tasks. We conducted two user studies. A preliminary study identified the problems experts face while performing comparison search tasks. A second user study examined the effectiveness of LISA in helping to solve comparison search tasks. The main contribution of this paper is to establish design guidelines for the data and interface of a comparison search application. Moreover, we offer insights into when thesauri and metadata are appropriate for use in such applications.

Author Keywords

comparison search, thesauri, cultural heritage

ACM Classification Keywords

H.5.2 Information Interfaces and Presentation

General Terms

Human Factors, Design

INTRODUCTION

In an in-depth study on information seeking needs in the cultural heritage domain, comparison search was identified as an example of an information seeking task that experts perform frequently for their work [3]. Comparison search involves examining objects or sets of objects for similarities and differences. The more objects there are to compare, and more properties to compare on, the more complex the task becomes. For such tasks, support tools are indispensable. Comparison search tasks are commonly found in the e-commerce domain. For example, a customer who wants to buy a product online might be interested in comparing products from different manufacturers using various properties, such as quality, price, features, and delivery time.

Comparison search also occurs in the cultural heritage domain. For example, consider an art historian doing comparative studies on Dutch paintings owned by different museum collections throughout the Netherlands. First, the historian needs to thoroughly *search* for all paintings made by Dutch artists in different archives and digital museum collections. Second, after all artworks are *selected*, the historian might need to *compare* the artworks by their distinguishing properties, such as by artist, materials used, art style or year of creation, to be able to identify trends. In practice, the scenario above is not trivial. First, there are difficulties in thoroughly searching for artworks in collections. Many museums have their own thesauri from which they use terms to annotate their artworks. As a result, a user needs to be familiar with the different terms in these thesauri and how they are used to annotate the artworks. This is unlikely, as typically, only the museum employees have such detailed knowledge. Second, most museum collections and archives offer poor support for complex search tasks such as comparison search. Most tools used only offer simple interaction, such as keyword search. This is found to be too restrictive for complex tasks such as comparison search [3].

In this paper, we discuss a user-centric approach to support cultural heritage experts in searching and comparing artworks. This research consists of several phases. We carried out a preliminary study to better understand how experts conduct comparison search in practice for their daily work. Based on this study, we derived design requirements and identified key features for a thesaurus-based comparison search tool that supports users to search, select and compare artworks. We then implemented LISA to help experts compare sets of artworks. Finally, we evaluate how well LISA supports the comparison search task. The contribution of this paper is to establish design requirements for the data and interface of a comparison search application. Moreover, we offer insights into when thesauri and metadata are appropriate to use for such applications.

RELATED WORK

To the best of our knowledge, no other tools currently support comparison search in the cultural heritage domain. We first discuss the state of the art information access tools in cross-collection cultural heritage search sites followed by support for comparison search in other domains.

As a result of many digitization projects, the collections of many museums, archives and libraries are now accessible online. Recently, new aggregated search applications allow users to search directly in multiple collections. Examples include portal sites such as europeana.eu and www.collectiewijzer.nl; and research prototypes such as MultimediaN E-Culture [14] and CultureSampo [8]. Such systems are useful, not only because they enable users to find pieces of information faster, but because of their potential for comparing objects from different collections. Most of these systems include interfaces for common information seeking tasks, namely searching, browsing and exploration [15]. Unfortunately, however, the interfaces of none of the systems mentioned above support comparison tasks directly. Rather, experts are forced to use the standard search and browse interfaces provided.

Related work on comparison search can be found, however, in other domains. For e-commerce applications, analysis of requirements for supporting comparison search has been well covered in the literature [5, 10, 11, 17]. One important requirement of a product comparison search interface is to allow users to extensively search and browse objects before comparing [5, 17]. Selection is also another crucial requirement and can be done in different ways. For example, a study on electronic catalogs [17] emphasizes the importance of allowing users to conduct incremental object selection in comparison search. Another example is to use interactive object filtering based on the available properties, such as in VOPC [11]. In this interface, the properties are visualized next to each other, providing the user with an overview of all possible properties to select from.

A visualization requirement for comparison search is the capability to present multiple properties [11, 17]. Different visualisations have different characteristics. Some presentations are able to show values of a single property (e.g. Bar charts, Dotplots, Histograms and Spinograms), two properties (e.g. Scatterplot, Mosaicplot), or multiple properties (e.g. Table) [19, 25]. Bar charts are simple and straight for-

ward. All values of a single property can be displayed in ascending or descending order. Scatterplots are mostly used when two important characteristics need to be displayed at once, such as in Gapminder [1] and in [12, 13]. Tables are still the most popular visualisations for comparison search in practice. Tables present information in a simple way: the products are presented all in one column, while the product properties are presented in a row (or vice versa) [16, 18]. This type of presentation allows a user to clearly see the values for multiple properties for multiple products at the same time.

The effects of different visualisations on user performance have also been studied, e.g. in [5, 10]. The experiment in [10] shows that table-like interfaces help users solve problems faster, while a scatterplot is better at guiding users to find correct answers. Callahan et al. [5] show that an interactive table (InfoZoom) helps users compare object properties faster than a hierarchical table. The hierarchical table interface, however, was found to be more pleasant to use. The study also suggests that the user's performance, while using a comparison search interface, depends on the type of task, the context and the ability of the user to translate the given problem while working with the system [5]. Thus, different domains and tasks might have different comparison search requirements.

PRELIMINARY STUDY: UNDERSTANDING COMPARISON SEARCH IN THE CULTURAL HERITAGE DOMAIN

We conducted the preliminary study with two goals in mind. First, to identify problems that experts face when they conduct comparison searches. Second, to derive realistic use cases about comparison search tasks that cultural heritage experts carry out during their work.

Setup

We carried out one to two hours semi-structured interviews that took place at the participant's working environment. Each interview consisted of several parts, starting with an introduction explaining the study and general demographic questions. We then asked questions related to accessing multiple cultural heritage sources and how to compare results coming from these sources. Next, we showed sketches of a hypothetical comparison search prototype. These were displayed on the computer to animate interactions with the interface. Finally, the participants were given the opportunity to ask any questions or address concerns about the sketches. In total, seven cultural heritage experts from three different institutions took part in the interviews (see Table 1). The participants' average age was 39 years. They had diverse roles: 2 researchers, 3 curators, 1 art historian and 1 consultant. Most participants had senior positions and had a good overview of the different expert roles within their organization. We hoped that our participants would thus be able to provide insights into the work of their colleagues as well as into their own. All interviews were voice recorded for documentation.

Results

We divide the participants' comments into two themes: the comparison search task use cases that experts conduct for

Table 1. Preliminary Study: Participants demography (total: 7 people)

Age:	35-42 years old (M=39.3, SD=2.8)
Gender:	1 male, 6 female
Affiliation	CH institution(6), museum(1),
Expert role:	researcher(2), curator(3)
	art historian(1), consultant(1)

their work, and challenges that experts face in conducting these tasks.

Comparison search use cases

In the interview, we asked participants for instances of comparison search tasks that they, or people in their community, would conduct as part of their daily work. To stimulate ideas, we showed them mock-ups of a comparison search tool. Based on the comparison search demonstrated in the mock-up, participants described several use cases along with the roles of those involved. These use cases can be either qualitative or quantitative comparisons.

Learning about collections — As a part of their education program in art history and museology, students are required to familiarize themselves with the variety of museum collections. Currently, this can only be done by browsing through different museum websites individually. *"Students study sculptures from different museums to get a first impression about what different museums have related to sculptures."* [P6]

Planning exhibitions — Whenever a curator needs to prepare for an exhibition, s/he needs to find and collect different artwork candidates. This is followed by a selection process where the curator compares and judges each artwork to find the most suitable ones to be displayed in the exhibition. *"I'm preparing an exhibition on [a painter], and need to make a selection and then from the selected items decide which ones should be finally picked for the exhibition."* [P4]

Museometry[1] — Museum collections change throughout time. Artworks may be loaned, borrowed, sent for restoration or donated. The museum management needs to have periodic quantitative reports of the distribution of artworks to allocate appropriate resources, e.g. for risk management or for expert training courses. *"A museum with diverse collections will benefit more from this interface [mock-up], in particular from the managerial perspective. If I can see, for example, that 80% of my collections are [made of] wood, then I know how many resources to allocate for wood preservation."* [P2].

Qualitative comparison — Experts often need to conduct qualitative comparisons on other experts' assumptions, opinions or recommendations. This task may require in-depth cognitive analysis and interpretation. For example, one participant often needs to analyze different point of views *"I would like to compare arguments between experts about a particular topic. First look at a lot of projects and look for best practices. Always choose from internationally recognized studies."* [P3]

Challenges in conducting comparison search tasks

The challenges mentioned by participants were primarily about: first, *searching* the terms (e.g. name aliases, multiple languages and multiple terms); second, *comparing* objects in multiple sets and multiple properties. Descriptions of these issues are presented below.

Name aliases — The participant may not always specify the correct name when searching because s/he does not know

---

[1]Museometry: research that emphasizes a quantitative approach to answer questions related to different aspects of museum information and its quality.

which variant is used in the collection. For example, location names change with time, e.g. Burma (old name), Myanmar (official name). Artists may also have different name aliases. *"The problem is you don't always know how to write the artist name that belongs in a specific collection."* [P2]

Multiple languages — A related problem is when artworks have multilingual annotations. Artworks coming from all parts of the world may be annotated in their vernacular terms or other languages (e.g. Spain, Spanje, España). In order to find these artworks, traditionally, the user needs to perform multiple searches using all possible terms and languages. Not only is this task tedious but also not always obvious for users. *"How could I search for artworks if the language is different?"* [P5]

Multiple terms — There are many potential terms that museums can use to annotate their work. To an outsider, even with some level of domain expertise, guessing which search terms to use is not obvious. One museum curator mentioned that she often needs to help website visitors with their searching. *"Sometimes visitors (of the museum collection website) do not know what to type. For example, to search for an Islamic collection, there are many different words: Islam, Islamic, Moslem, Muslim. Thus sometimes I do the searching for them and send the (search result) link."* [P6]

Comparing many sets — The tools used do not support the comparison of multiple sets of artworks e.g. comparing the differences between artworks from different museums. For example, one participant researching on museum management usually compares 77 contemporary art museums in the Netherlands at the same time. *"Most of the time I compare more than one museum."* [P6]. Comparison may be based on various characteristics, such as artworks from different museums or artworks from different artists.

Single and multiple property comparison — Tools do not support comparison search tasks using multiple properties: *"Compare collections of artworks by female artists from before and after the 1960's."* [P1]. In another example, the curator wants to highlight different aspects of African art collections in museums in the Netherlands, and wants to compare how different cultures (e.g. Akan, Gurma) predominately create different artwork types (e.g. mask, painting) and how this changes according to the history of the nation (e.g. pre-colonialism v.s. post-colonialism).

Key findings

The preliminary study provided us insights into comparison search tasks conducted by cultural heritage experts. Our intention was to see where a thesaurus-based comparison search tool can help the experts. Comparison search use cases, such as learning about collections, planning exhibitions and museometry, may require quantitative processing of artwork's metadata. Since there can be many homonyms and synonyms within the metadata, simple text matching is insufficient. Quantitative computation on the artwork's metadata taking the thesaurus that provides the metadata terms could yield more accurate results. Therefore, for these use cases, a thesaurus-based comparison search tool maybe useful. For other use cases, such as qualitative comparisons, a thesauri-based comparison tool might not be sufficient. Qualitative comparison requires in-depth analysis and interpretation of information primarily coming from non structured data, such as literature and articles. Thus, for these use cases, metadata and thesauri are insufficient information sources. This is confirmed by participants. For example, when asked about using metadata for comparing different experts' points of view, participants commented: *"Sometimes the information is just too basic."* [P5], *"This is not specific enough for the job."* [P2]

Tasks identified were searching and comparing. In order to compare sets results found have to be selected to become part of the comparison tasks. The three main challenges in comparison search: (1) to *search* using the terms that match with the variety in object's metadata, such as name aliases, multiple languages, multiple terms; (2) to *select* sets of objects to compare and (3) to *compare* objects belonging to multiple sets and having multiple properties.

DESIGN REQUIREMENTS
The preliminary study and related work gave us directions on the design requirements for a thesaurus-based comparison search tool for the cultural heritage domain: it should provide features that help users overcome the search, selection and comparison challenges:

Searching artworks — Most of the problems when searching for artworks, such as name aliases, multiple languages and multiple terms, are related to finding terms that match with the artwork's metadata. To help users find the matching terms, a *guided search*, such as an interactive query expansion interface [4], feature should be provided.

Selecting artworks — Selecting artworks is an important part of a comparison search task [11, 17]. Selection is an intermediate step where participants define sets of artworks to be compared against each other. While this activity is enabled in some museum collection websites that cultural heritage experts frequently use [2], the interface and interaction is often unintuitive and sluggish. There are two important requirements for the artwork selection process: first, the selection process has to be easy and convenient; second, to ensure a smooth selection process, the user has to be able to add and to remove any artwork from a selected set.

Comparing artworks — There are two requirements for this activity: first, a comparison search tool for the cultural heritage domain should support comparing multiple sets, where a set can contain many artworks. In the presentation, the differences and similarities between these sets should be clearly distinguishable. Second, it is important to support comparison of single and multiple properties. To focus our research, we concentrate on supporting one property (single property) and two properties (dual property) comparison. For different types of comparison search tasks (single and dual property) a suitable presentation type should be made available [19, 25].

LISA: DESIGN AND IMPLEMENTATION
The LISA application[2] is part of a suite of tools developed within the MultimediaN E-Culture project[3]. The project con-

centrates on providing intelligent access to distributed and heterogeneous cultural heritage collections. In the following sections we discuss LISA's technology infrastructure, the datasets and the user interface. We focus our discussion primarily on the interface and interaction. For an extensive discussion on the technological infrastructure, see [14, 24].

Design
Overview — To support the identified activities of comparison search, the LISA interface consists of four areas (see Fig.1 top left): (a) the search area, (g) the search result area, (k)(l) the selection areas, and (j) the comparison area. In the search area, the user incrementally formulates queries, and the results are shown in the search result area below. In the selection area, users can see two sets of artworks. In the comparison area, there are alternative visualizations that can be used to see the characteristics of the selected artworks. We discuss the three supported activities separately. As an example, we compare the self-portraits of Vincent van Gogh with the self-portraits of Rembrandt van Rijn (see Fig.1).

Search — To support search, we use a thesaurus-based guided search that consists of a property filter and autocompletion in the interface. The property filter is a pull down menu that shows all possible artwork properties, such as artwork creator, creation date or material, that can be selected (see Fig.1b). When a user types a keyword, the autocompletion interface will show suggestions of terms used by the museum collections. An alphabetical ordering is used for our autocompletion suggestions as we found it to be the most effective ordering for loosely structured thesauri [4]. The guided search takes the form of `property:value` pairs. Users can complete a search by selecting an autocompletion suggestion (Fig.1d). To assure full flexibility, the user can add and remove as many `property:value` pairs as s/he wishes. In the example of Fig. 1, to search for self-portraits of Rembrandt van Rijn, the user specified two guided searches: to search for all artworks having a `Creator:Rembrandt van Rijn` *and* `subject:zelfportret` (English: self-portrait) (see Fig 1c), and to search for all artworks having a `Creator: Vincent van Gogh` *and* `subject:zelfportret`.

Because related terms from different thesauri are linked, the system can provide a match even though the artworks' metadata are different as long as they are semantically equivalent. For example, there are 31 name aliases for 'Rembrandt van Rijn' in ULAN[4], e.g. 'Rembrandt van Ryn' or 'Rembrandt van Rhijn'. If a user specifies any of these alternative names, LISA will be able to retrieve the same artworks. Similarly, it is possible to thoroughly search with different geographical, art and architecture, and iconographic name aliases. For a list of all linked thesauri supported by LISA, refer to Table 2. For more information about designing and configuring a thesaurus-based autocompletion see [4] [5].

Selection — After the user is satisfied with the search results, s/he needs to select the artworks to compare. The

[2]The LISA prototype is accessible at: `http://e-culture.multimedian.nl/lisa/compsearch`.
[3]`http://e-culture.multimedian.nl/`

[4]Union List of Artist Names thesaurus, `http://www.getty.edu/research/conducting_research/vocabularies/ulan/`
[5]In this implementation, only syntactic matches are shown in the suggestions. This is, however, configurable to also suggest semantic matches, such as broader, narrower and related terms.

system allows the user to add multiple artworks in either set. In the current implementation, we only support comparison between two sets [6]. An artwork can be placed in any of the available sets (Set A or Set B). There are two easy ways to add an artwork to a selection: first, by dragging and dropping an artwork thumbnail from the search result panel to the selection panel (Fig. 1k,l); second, a bulk selection of all search results can be made by clicking the *Set A* or *Set B* button (Fig. 1f). To allow fine tuning of selections, adding or removing an artwork from the set is made possible. The search and selection process are typically done sequentially. For example, first the user searches for all self-portraits of Van Gogh (`creator: Vincent van Gogh, subject: zelfportrait`), places them on the Set A selection area (Fig. 1k). Afterwards s/he makes a second search of all self-portraits of Rembrandt (`creator: Rembrandt van Rijn, subject: zelfportrait`) and places the results in the Set B selection area (see Fig. 1l).

Comparison with visualizations — LISA currently supports single property comparison and dual property comparison. We choose the Bar chart (Fig. 1j3) for single property comparison and the Scatterplot (Fig. 1j1) for dual property comparison because these presentations are the most common from a variety of visualizations specified in [19, 25]. Additionally, we also implemented a Table visualization because this type of presentation is the default presentation for most comparison search applications (see Fig. 1j2). Whenever an object is placed in the selection area (Set A or Set B), the visualization area is updated. In all visualizations, we use color codes to indicate which sets the elements belong to (either Set A or Set B). Fig. 1j3 shows a Bar chart representation of artworks from both sets. The bar chart highlights the comparison between the two sets with respect to the chosen property:`material`. The x-axis represents the artworks organized by the selected property:`material` in alphabetical order. The y-axis represents the number of artworks. The figure shows the values of Set A and Set B next to each other. The property pull-down menu (Fig. 1o) shows all available properties for which the objects can be organized, e.g. by dimension height, date, material or depicted subject. The scatterplot presentation (Fig. 1j1) shows comparison of sets with respect to the dual property selection (Fig. 1i) i.e. `material` (y-axis) and `date` (x-axis). This presentation highlights the differences between the two sets with respect to the creation time and what materials they are made of. The table visualization (Fig. 1j2) shows all artworks from Set A. To view all properties from Set B, the user needs to select the tab (Fig. 1m). It is possible to explore the information space by two means: a) alternating between different properties by selecting an item at the property pull down menu (Fig. 1o), or b) visual exploration either by zooming, panning or scrolling. With the different visualizations, the user can flip through different properties to examine multiple collections simultaneously to gather quick insights about vast collections, which is extremely difficult with current tools.

Table 2. Thesauri and collections used in LISA

source (thesaurus coverage)	size	
Collection:		
RKD Archive	82.781	objects
Thesaurus:		
RKD thesaurus (RKD)	11.995	terms
TGN (geographical)	89.000	terms
ULAN (artist)	13.000	people
AAT (art and architecture)	31.000	terms
IconClass (iconographic)	24.331	terms

Implementation

Infrastructure — The LISA application is developed on top of *ClioPatria*, a web application platform for search and annotation across heterogeneous collections. For detailed information on the web server infrastructure and the search strategies across heterogeneous collections, see [14, 24]. Communication between the client and the server is done via requests to the system's HTTP API. Information is sent back from the server in JSON. The implementation of the interface uses (X)HTML, CSS, Javascript and Flash. It is tested on the Firefox 3.0.10 browser. The client side visualization widgets use an extension of the Yahoo User Interface widget (YUI v. 2.7.0) and amChart v. 1.6.5 [7].

Dataset — To enable comparison search with LISA, the server needs to host common thesauri, namely IconClass[8], the Getty Art & Architecture Thesaurus (AAT), the Getty Union List of Artist Names (ULAN) and the Getty Thesaurus of Geographical Names (TGN) [9], as well as collection specific thesauri, such as thesauri from RKD. Table 2 shows the size of collections and thesauri currently used by the application. Collections and thesauri data were converted to an RDF/SKOS representation. To allow information access across collections, specific thesauri are aligned with the common ones. For example, artists' names in the RKD thesauri are linked to artists' names in ULAN. Materials terms in the RKD thesauri are linked with concepts in AAT. Detailed information on the conversion and alignment methods of cultural heritage sources used can be found in [20, 22].

EVALUATION STUDY: THESAURUS-BASED COMPARISON SEARCH INTERFACE EVALUATION

The goal of this study was to evaluate LISA. In particular, we focus on evaluating how well the search, selection and comparison features support experts' comparison search tasks. As a baseline, we use the RKDimages website [2], a popular online cultural heritage archive that contains descriptions, metadata and images of Dutch and Flemish artworks from the 14th-19th century. The RKDimage website contain a comprehensive coverage of different artworks and is widely used as reference. For the purpose of the evaluation, participants can access the same information with LISA as well as with RKDimages website. The research questions for this evaluation are:

---

[6]This is extendable as the current application design takes into account the future addition of more sets, however, since computations are carried out client-side, for more than 1,000 objects the interface becomes slow.

[7]http://www.amChart.com
[8]http://www.iconclass.nl
[9]http://www.getty.edu/research/conducting_research/vocabularies/

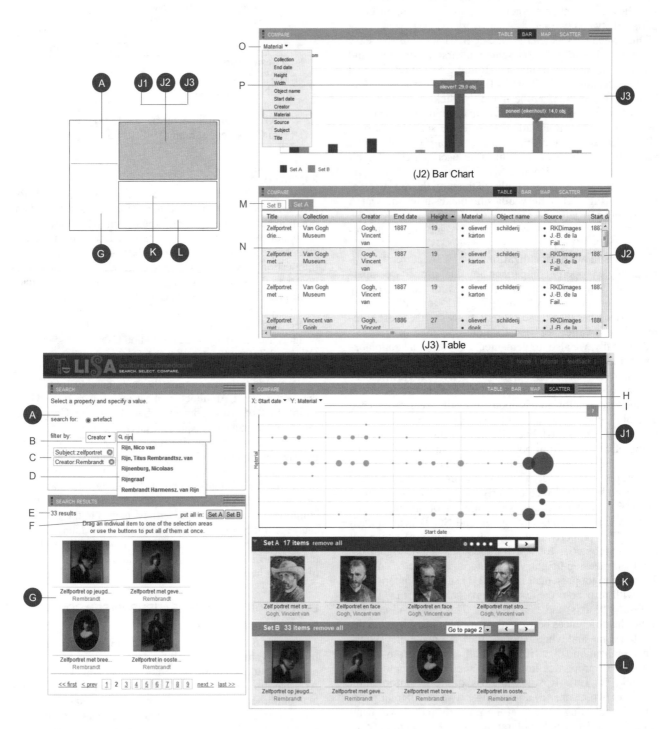

Figure 1. The LISA interface (a) search area, (k) selection area Set A, (l) selection area Set B, (j) comparison area: (j1) Scatterplot (j2) Table (j3) Bar chart
Features: (b) property filter, (c) guided search, (d) autocompletion suggestions, (e) number of search results, (f) selection shortcut, (g) search results, (h) visualization selection options, (i) Scatterplot 2 properties selection,

(j1) The scatterplot shows the distribution of Van Gogh's self portraits and Rembrandt's self portraits with respect to the date and material used. The visualization shows that Rembrandt had consistently painted a small number of self portraits distributed throughout many years using different kinds of materials (e.g. canvas, Oak panel, Mahagony panel). Van Gogh, however, made many self-portraits between 1886 and 1887. In 1887 alone, he made about 11 oilpaint (olieverf) self-portraits.

(j2) The table shows all values of Van Gogh's self-portraits. The smallest height of a van Gogh's self-portrait is 19 cm.

(j3) The bar chart shows the distribution of materials used for Set A and Set B. 29 of Rembrandt's self portraits are made out of oilpaint (olieverf) and 14 are made out of Oak (Paneel Eikenhout).

Table 3. Evaluation Study: Participants demography (total: 12 people)

Age:	21-60 years old (M=39.6, SD=12.1)
Gender:	4 male, 8 female
Affiliation	CH institution(6), museum(2),
	Art historical archive(3), university(1)
Expert role:	researcher(4), curator(2), ICT(2)
	program manager(3), librarian(1)

● Does the LISA tool support searching, selecting and comparing artworks more efficiently than the baseline tool?
● Do users perceive the LISA tool easier to use than the baseline tool?

Setup

The experiments took place at the participant's working place. Each participant was asked to complete comparison search tasks with LISA and RKDimages (within subject design). The experiment had four parts:
● Introduction. Participants were asked demographic questions and for informed consent. Afterwards, they were shown a video demo and were asked to perform trial tasks on the LISA application. As most participants were already regular users of the RKD website, the demo focused on familiarizing the participants with LISA.
● Experiment session. The experiment was divided into two phases. In the first phase, we compared how well the 4 different type of presentations (LISA Table, LISA Bar Chart, LISA Scatterplot, RKDimages) support single property comparison. In the second phase, we compared how well 3 different type of presentations (LISA Table, LISA Scatterplot, RKDimages) support dual property comparison[10]. In total, participants were given 14 comparison tasks (2 tasks per interface). At the completion of each task, participants were ask about how they perceived the ease of use of the interface used. At the end of all tasks, participants gave general impressions about LISA and RKDimages.

User recruitment was based on email invitations and open invitations on a cultural heritage online forum. In total there were 12 cultural heritage experts from seven cultural heritage institutions (see Table 3). Our participants conduct searches within collections frequently for their work (M=4.8, SD= 1.8) [11] and are fairly familiar with the RKDimages website (M=3.8, SD= 2.5) [12]. None of the participants had used the LISA interface prior to this evaluation.

Task

We use two independent variables as dimensions that reflects the complexity of comparison search.
● Number of artworks. We have two conditions: comparing *few* objects (1 artworks per set) and comparing *many* artworks (10-15 artworks per set). We expect that the more artworks there are, the harder it is to perform comparison search.

---

[10]The LISA Bar chart was omitted in the second phase because it is unsuitable for dual property comparison task
[11]Seven point scale, 1: not very often, 7: very often
[12]Seven point scale, 1: very unfamiliar, 7: very familiar

● Number of properties. We have two conditions: *single* property comparison and *dual* property comparison. An example of a comparison search task is as follows:
Use the scatterplot to answer this question: Compare all artworks having the subject depiction "church" from the Stedelijk Museum De Lakenhal with all artworks having the subject depiction "church" from Museum Bredius.
(1) Which artist made the most artworks?
(2) How many of these artworks are paintings and are made after 1612?

Example 1 is a single property comparison task for the property `Artist`. Example 2 is a dual property comparison task for the properties `Object type` and `Date`.

Results

In this section we discuss observations on how well LISA and the RKDimages website support the comparison search tasks conducted by the participants.

Searching and selecting artworks — Prior to the study, we naively assumed that the search, selection and comparison activities are separate and independent. However, during our experiments we observed that the search and selection activities were highly interdependent. Participants conduct a search, make selections and refine the search before being satisfied with the selection result. Only then do participants carry out the more independent comparison activity. This non-linear behavior is also suggested by previous research, such as in [9]. Thus, in our discussions, we describe search and selection activities together and the comparison activity separately.

We analyzed the time performance and the perceived ease of use for searching and selecting artworks. Table 4a. shows the average time it took for participants to complete searching and selecting for (Few and Many) artworks with LISA and RKDimages website. Using the Wilcoxon Sign-rank (WSR) test[13], we found that participants were about two times slower when searching and selecting many artworks using RKDimages (Mdn=2.75 min) than searching and selection few artworks (Mdn=1.12 min) z=-2.04, p<.05, r=-.42. This confirms our expectation that the more artworks there are, the more time it will take to search them using the baseline tool. When participants use LISA for searching and selecting artworks, however, the results were different. We did not find a significant difference when participants were searching and selecting few artworks (Mdn= 1.43 min) compared with many artworks (Mdn=1.15 min). Moreover, when searching and selecting many artworks, RKDimages (Mdn= 2.75 min) is significantly slower than LISA (Mdn= 1.15 min) z=-2.43, p<.05, r=-.49. Thus, we conclude that LISA is more time efficient than RKDimages for searching and selecting many artworks.

Participants also rated the perceived ease of use of LISA and RKDimages for searching and selecting artworks (see Table 4b,c). RKDimages is significantly easier to use when

---

[13] Nonparametric statistics is used throughout the study as not every data meet parametric assumptions.

Table 4. Searching and Selecting artworks with LISA and RKDimages

	LISA	RKDimages
a. Search and select avg. time in min (SD)		
1. FEW	1.38(.41)	1.58(1.19)
2. MANY	1.37(.51)	3.33(1.90)
b. Search - ease of use score (SD)		
1. FEW	5.75(1.22)	5.58(1.38)
2. MANY	6.08(1.08)	4.67(1.78)
c. Select - ease of use score (SD)*		
1. FEW	5.92(1.16)	4.50(1.68)
2. MANY	6.00(0.95)	3.58(1.68)

* 7-Likert point scale, score 1:very difficult, 7:very easy

Few: few objects comparison (1 item/set)

Many: many objects comparison (10-15 items/set)

Table 5. Comparing artworks with LISA and RKDimages

a. Single property comparison avg. time in min. (SD)

	Table	Bar chart	Scatterplot	RKDimages
1. FEW	0.91(.75)	0.94(.34)	1.32(.66)	0.83(0.24)
2. MANY	1.37(.55)	1.19(.36)	1.70(.76)	2.13(1.61)

b. Dual property comparison avg. time in min. (SD)

	Table	Bar chart	Scatterplot	RKDimages
1. FEW	1.14(.71)	-	1.28(.63)	1.06(.40)
2. MANY	2.28(.97)	-	1.39(.65)	2.99(.99)

c. Compare - ease of use score (SD) *

	Table	Bar chart	Scatterplot	RKDimages
1. FEW	4.92(1.68)	5.42(1.08)	4.50(1.78)	2.83(1.47)
2. MANY	5.08(1.38)	4.75(1.54)	4.75(1.76)	2.17(1.47)

* 7-Likert point scale, score 1:very difficult, 7:very easy

searching for few artworks (Mdn=6.0) than when searching for many artworks (Mdn=5.0) z=-2.46, p<.05, r=-.50. When searching with LISA, however, this difference was not significant. Searching for many artworks (Mdn=6.0) is perceived as easy as searching for few artworks (Mdn=6.0). Participants also think that RKDimages (Mdn=5.0) is harder to use than LISA (Mdn=6.0) when they need to search for many artworks z=-2.38, p<.05, r=-.48. Thus, we conclude that LISA is easier to use than RKDimages, especially for searching for many artworks.

We asked the same question for selecting artworks and found congruent results. We found LISA significantly easier to use than RKDimages when selecting few artworks (z=-2.06, p<.05, r=-.42) as well as many artworks (z=-2.69, p<.05, r=-.55). Based on this, we conclude that LISA is easier to use than RKDimages with respect to selecting few as well as many artworks.

For searching and selecting artworks, we found LISA more time efficient and easier to use than RKDimages. We also found that, unlike the time efficiency with the baseline tool, time efficiency with LISA does not suffer much as there are more artworks to search and select. Moreover, overall, participants perceived LISA easier to use than RKDimages for searching and selecting artworks.

Comparing artworks — We use Friedman Analysis of Variance by Ranks (FAVR) to examine if there were any differences in time performance between the different presentations types for single property comparison and dual property comparison tasks (see Table 5).

• Single property comparison search tasks

For single property comparison, we compared participants' time efficiency using four different presentations: LISA-Table, LISA-Bar chart, LISA-Scatterplot and RKDimages. Using the FAVR test, we found no significant difference for the four different presentations. This applies for a single property comparison task for few artworks (χ^2(3)=3.7, p>.05) as well as for many artworks (χ^2(3)=3.0, p>.05) We conclude that all four presentations perform equally with respect to the time spent to conduct single property comparison.

• Dual property comparison search tasks

In dual property comparisons, we found no significant difference between the three presentations for few artworks comparisons (χ^2(2)=2.2, p>.05). However, there is a significant difference between three different presentations (i.e. LISA-Table, LISA-Scatterplot and RKDimages) for many artworks (χ^2(2)=9.5, p<.05). We found significance of time performance between all three presentations. LISA-scatterplot being the fastest (Mdn=1.26 min), followed by LISA-table (Mdn=2.08 min), and RKD images (Mdn=3.02 min) the slowest[14].

We saw clearer trends for the perceived ease of use scores (see Table 5c). We found significant differences for comparison search tasks in few artworks (χ^2(3)=13.07, p<.05) as well as many artworks (χ^2(3)=17.49, p<.05). The WSR post-hoc test confirms that all LISA visualizations are perceived easier to use than RKDimages for comparison.

We conclude that comparing with LISA is more time efficient than with RKDimages mainly for many artworks dual property comparison seach task. However, participants perceive LISA easier to use that RKDimages for few as well as many artworks comparison.

DISCUSSION

The thesaurus-based comparison search tool builds on two important components: the interface and the data. We discuss challenges and improvements with respect to these.

Interface

Searching and selecting artworks — The evaluation study showed that searching and selecting artworks with LISA gives better time performance than with RKDimages. This is mainly because of the ease of use of the thesaurus-based guided search and the selection interface. The thesaurus-based autocompletion enable users to quickly find the correct term to find artworks. This aligns with previous research on the use of thesaurus-based autocompletion for term search [4]. To increase confidence levels when selecting terms from the au-

---

14 WSR post-hoc tests shows LISA Scatterplot - LISA Table (z=-2.12, p<.05, r=-.43), RKDimages - LISA Table (z=-1.96, p<.05, r=-.40), RKDimages - LISA Scatterplot (z=-2.83, p<<.05, r=-.58),

tocompletion suggestions, improvements, such as adding extra information about the terms, e.g. by showing the thesauri hierarchy or descriptions of the terms, could be made [6].

Comparing artworks — We found that, with respect to time spent, LISA shows little improvement on RKDimages for comparison activities. There can be several explanations for this. Our participants are regular RKDimage users, thus they are more experienced in using this application for comparison. Most of them, however, are not used to handling graphs and charts. We observed that participants need to spend time to become familiar with the tool. We acknowledge that we cannot fully eliminate learning effects in a one time evaluation study of a complex tool such as LISA. Many of the participants thought they would be able to handle LISA better once they were accustomed to it. *"I think you have to get used to the system, like to any new system"* [P1], *"This is a new way to present and interact with (museum) collections."* [P14].

Even though LISA did not significantly improve the speed of comparison, participants clearly favor LISA above RKDimages with respect to ease of use. They see the practical benefit of having aggregated results presented automatically rather than computed manually. Before trusting the results, however, they need to understand how the thesaurus-based aggregation works to produce the graphs and charts of the presentations. Participants also appreciated the different presentations as they provide more ways to analyze the same data. *"I think there are different learning and reading styles, so it is useful to have these variations"* [P3].

Additional features — Sometimes experts need to go back and re-examine previous comparison search tasks. Experts may also want to save the visualization results and include them in a report, or may need to inspect the visualization in detail. Our experts listed features such as bookmarking, search history and 'save as' as additional functionalities that LISA should have. Participants also mentioned two important visualization improvements. First, the ability to enlarge the visualization size on demand. This feature is specially useful when dealing with many artworks. Second, more interactivity with the visualization, such as being able to trace back from the visualization to the original artworks.

Data

Based on what we have learned during the LISA implementation and the evaluation study, we identify characteristics of the collection metadata that developers need to be aware of when developing thesaurus-based aggregator services.

Semantic aggregation — Thesaurus-based comparison search should take into account semantic aggregation where narrower/broader relationships exist between terms. For example, to be able to answer the question "How many artworks are paintings?" correctly, the system needs to quantitatively aggregate not only all artworks having `object type:painting`, but also all artworks annotated by the narrower concepts of painting, such as `object type: aquarel`, since Aquarel is a type of a painting.

Inconsistent data — Museum collection metadata may be inconsistent, for example in measurement units. Artwork dimensions, such as height and width, can be specified in different units, e.g. feet, cm or mm. Prior to an aggregation process, metadata needs to be cleaned.

Incomplete metadata — In reality, museum metadata is not always complete. Parts of the collection may have insufficient or missing values. A quantitative aggregation on these data will generate false results. One solution is to check and improve the quality of data automatically as suggested in [23].

Estimated data — In some cases, the metadata contains an estimated value, e.g., the creation date of an artwork is simply unknown. The museum is able to supply only an estimate, e.g. "before AD 400" or "between 600-700". Providing accurate aggregation results based on these estimated data is not possible.

Quality of data alignment — The accuracy of information presented in a thesaurus-based aggregated system also depends on the quality of the data alignment, i.e. linking metadata to terms from individual thesauri and linking terms among different thesauri. Methods for vocabulary alignment are still at a preliminary stage of development, e.g. [21], making it difficult to predict when automatic methods will be of sufficient quality for our experts' needs.

The biggest opportunity for LISA lies in the area of comparison across different collections. At the moment, such tasks are carried out by accessing the different collections individually, and then integrating the data manually. While there is room for improvement by being able to automatically aggregate over multiple collections, the number of errors in the results will also grow when performing computations across collections because of the different schemata and thesauri used to describe the artworks. When dealing with real museum datasets, we believe that the answer needs to come from making the computations more transparent in the interface, allowing the user to examine the data and how the computation is being performed. Thus, if there are errors in the results, the user should be able to trace them, make corrections and even correct the underlying data.

CONCLUSIONS AND FUTURE WORK

We conducted a user-centered design study on a comparison search application for the cultural heritage domain. In a preliminary study, we identified various comparison search use cases, such as learning about collections, planning exhibitions, museometry and qualitative comparison, and identified the challenges users face while performing comparison search, such as searching and selecting terms, and comparisons involving multiple sets and properties. In our evaluation study, we found that our comparison search tool can help users, in particular for efficient searching for terms and selecting artworks. In general, participants perceived the comparison search tool as easier to use than the baseline tool with respect to searching, selecting and comparing artworks. Finally, based on our implementation experience and evaluation study, we identify future improvements to the interface, namely, supporting interactivity visualizations, improving the autocompletion and providing bookmarking and search history functionality. For the data issues, we would be able to extend LISA's functionality to support semantic aggregation. For the other data issues we are dependent on others making the data more reliable. Making the issues more transparent through the LISA interface would be one way of tackling this.

ACKNOWLEDGEMENTS

We thank the cultural heritage experts from Centraal Museum Utrecht, Digital Heritage Netherland (DEN), Efgoed Nederlands, Netherlands Collection Institute (ICN), Publiek Archief Eemland, Netherlands Institute for Art History (RKD), Rijksmuseum Amsterdam, Tropenmuseum, and University of Amsterdam. We thank Hyowon Lee for his feedback during the interface design. This research was supported by the MultimediaN project through the BSIK program of the Dutch Government and by the European Commission contract FP6-027026, KSpace.

REFERENCES

1. http://www.gapminder.org/.

2. http://english.rkd.nl/databases.

3. A. Amin, L. Hardman, J. van Ossenbruggen, and A. van Nispen. Understanding cultural heritage experts' information seeking tasks. In *JCDL'08*, pp 39–47, NY, USA, 2008. ACM.

4. A. Amin, M. Hildebrand, J. van Ossenbruggen, V. Evers, and L. Hardman. Organizing Suggestions In Autocompletion Interfaces. In *ECIR '09*, pp 521–529, 2009.

5. E. Callahan and J. Koenemann. A comparative usability evaluation of user interfaces for online product catalog. In *EC '00*, pp 197–206, NY, USA, 2000. ACM.

6. M. Hildebrand, J. van Ossenbruggen, and L. Hardman. Supporting subject matter annotation using heterogeneous thesauri: A user study in web data reuse. *IJHCS*, 67:887–902, Oct 2009.

7. M. Hildebrand, J. R. van Ossenbruggen, A. K. Amin, L. Aroyo, J. Wielemaker, and L. Hardman. The Design Space Of A Configurable Autocompletion Component. Technical Report INS-E0708, CWI, 2007.

8. E. Hyvonen, et. al. Culturesampo – finnish cultural heritage collections on the semantic web 2.0. In *Proceedings of the 1st International Symposium on Digital humanities for Japanese Arts and Cultures (DH-JAC-2009), Ritsumeikan, Kyoto, Japan*, March 2009.

9. A. Kerne and S. M. Smith. The information discovery framework. In *DIS '04*, pp 357–360, NY, USA, 2004. ACM.

10. A. Kobsa. An empirical comparison of three commercial information visualization systems. In *INFOVIS '01*, pp. 123, Washington, DC, USA, 2001. IEEE Computer Society.

11. J. Lee, H. S. Lee, and P. Wang. An interactive visual interface for online product catalogs. *Electronic Commerce Research*, 4(4):335–358, 2004.

12. S. Perugini, K. McDevitt, R. Richardson, M. A. Pérez-Qui R. Shen, N. Ramakrishnan, C. Williams, and E. A. Fox. Enhancing usability in citidel: multimodal, multilingual, and interactive visualization interfaces. In *JCDL '04*, pp 315–324, NY, USA, 2004. ACM.

13. C. Plaisant, J. Rose, B. Yu, L. Auvil, M. G. Kirschenbaum, M. N. Smith, T. Clement, and G. Lord. Exploring erotics in emily dickinson's correspondence with text mining and visual interfaces. In *JCDL '06*, pp 141–150, NY, USA, 2006. ACM.

14. G. Schreiber, et. al. Semantic annotation and search of cultural-heritage collections: The multimedian e-culture demonstrator. *J. Web Sem.*, 6(4):243–249, 2008.

15. R. Shen, N. S. Vemuri, W. Fan, R. da S. Torres, and E. A. Fox. Exploring digital libraries: integrating browsing, searching, and visualization. In *JCDL '06*, pp 1–10, NY, USA, 2006. ACM.

16. M. Spenke, C. Beilken, and T. Berlage. Focus: the interactive table for product comparison and selection. In *UIST '96*, pp 41–50, NY, USA, 1996. ACM.

17. P. Steiger and M. Stolze. Effective product selection in electronic catalogs. In *CHI '97*, pp. 291–292, NY, USA, 1997. ACM.

18. T. Tenev and R. Rao. Managing multiple focal levels in table lens. In *INFOVIS '97*, pp. 59, Washington, DC, USA, 1997. IEEE Computer Society.

19. M. Theus and S. Urbanek. *Interactive Graphics for Data Analysis*. Computer Science and Data Analysis, 2009.

20. A. Tordai, B. Omelayenko, and G. Schreiber. Semantic excavation of the city of books. In *SAAKM*, 2007.

21. A. Tordai, J. van Ossenbruggen, and G. Schreiber. Combining vocabulary alignment techniques. In *K-CAP '09*, pp 25–32, NY, USA, 2009. ACM.

22. M. van Assem, V. Malaisé, A. Miles, and G. Schreiber. A method to convert thesauri to skos. *The Semantic Web: Research and Applications*, pages 95–109, 2006.

23. A. van den Bosch, M. van Erp, and C. Sporleder. Making a clean sweep of cultural heritage. *IEEE Intelligent Systems*, 24(2):54–63, 2009.

24. J. Wielemaker, M. Hildebrand, J. Ossenbruggen, and G. Schreiber. Thesaurus-based search in large heterogeneous collections. In *ISWC '08*, pp. 695–708, Berlin, Heidelberg, 2008. Springer-Verlag.

25. F. W. Young, P. M. Valero-Mora, and M. Friendly. *Visual Statistics: Seeing Data with Dynamic Interactive Graphics*. Wiley Series, 2006.

Towards Maximizing the Accuracy of Human-Labeled Sensor Data

Stephanie L. Rosenthal
Carnegie Mellon University
Computer Science Department
Pittsburgh PA USA
srosenth@cs.cmu.edu

Anind K. Dey
Carnegie Mellon University
Human-Computer Interaction Institute
Pittsburgh PA USA
anind@cs.cmu.edu

ABSTRACT

We present two studies that evaluate the accuracy of human responses to an intelligent agent's data classification questions. Prior work has shown that agents can elicit accurate human responses, but the applications vary widely in the data features and prediction information they provide to the labelers when asking for help. In an initial analysis of this work, we found the five most popular features, namely uncertainty, amount and level of context, prediction of an answer, and request for user feedback. We propose that there is a set of these data features and prediction information that maximizes the accuracy of labeler responses. In our first study, we compare accuracy of users of an activity recognizer labeling their own data across the dimensions. In the second study, participants were asked to classify a stranger's emails into folders and strangers' work activities by interruptibility. We compared the accuracy of the responses to the users' self-reports across the same five dimensions. We found very similar combinations of information (for users and strangers) that led to very accurate responses as well as more feedback that the agents could use to refine their predictions. We use these results for insight into the information that help labelers the most.

Author Keywords

Labeling Sensor Data, Active Learning

ACM Classification Keywords

H.5.m. Information interfaces and presentation (e.g., HCI): Miscellaneous.

General Terms

Human Factors, Experimentation

INTRODUCTION

When collecting data from users for machine learning-based applications, learning agents must acquire labels to train accurate supervised models. As many labels are hard to sense accurately and implicitly, users themselves often carry the burden of labeling their own data using a diary at the end of the day [5] or with feedback throughout the day [15]. Both of these data collection methods can be prone to

inaccuracies if users forget the context of their activity, do not understand which data the system is requesting a label for, or have limited time to label data.

While active learning provides support for prediction with a limited number of data labels, it still requires that users provide accurate labels and be available when a label is needed [18]. New techniques, like *proactive learning,* take active learning a step further and account for human inaccuracy by creating user models and determining from among a set of users, who to ask based on the need for accuracy [9][6]. Crowd-sourcing the data to websites like Amazon.com's Mechanical Turk or with games like GWAP [30] has also become a popular option for acquiring labels from people other than the actual users or data creators, but can require several people to label the same data in order to ensure accuracy [30][31].

While these techniques address the problem of labeling the data assuming that human inaccuracy is inevitable, we are interested in determining how the learning agent itself can affect the accuracy of the responses it receives. Concretely, the agent can vary the information it provides to labelers about the data as it asks questions, to maximize the accuracy of the labels it collects and the feedback it receives to refine it's predictions. After analyzing previous agents that request classification labels, we focus on a set of information that has been commonly provided to labelers: 1) *varying number of contextual features* of the data point 2) *high/low-level* explanation of those features 3) classification *prediction* 4) *uncertainty* in the prediction and 5) *user feedback* to weigh features used in classification.

In this work, we present a set of studies that explore the impact of agents providing subsets of the above information to labelers with the goal of maximizing the accuracy of the labelers' responses and encouraging feedback that would help a learning agent. We explore and identify the best subset for *people labeling strangers'* email and interruptibility data, in addition to *users labeling their own* physical activity data. Interestingly, these two subsets were nearly identical.

Our contributions are three-fold. First, we contribute a method for determining the combination of information that maximizes the accuracy of human responses by first testing all combinations and then validating the best combination against a combination suggested by experts. Second, we contribute our best combinations for the types of tasks we tested and find that the combinations were nearly identical. Finally, we contribute an understanding of the value of different types of information and reasons for their impact so the information can be used consistently across applications for improving label accuracy.

RELATED WORK

While several different sets of guidelines have been proposed for agents' label-gathering interactions with humans (*e.g.*, [4], [10], [14] [25]), there are seven main types of proposed information: different amounts of context, human-understandable context, uncertainty, predictions, user control and feedback, action disclosure, and social interaction. Our work draws from areas of data collection and corrective feedback in determining which dimensions to focus on and how to implement them. Table 1 outlines these dimensions and previous work that includes different subsets of them. We find that the first five types of information, operationalized and described below, are the most commonly used in current applications. While there is continuing work in understanding socially appropriate times to request labels [15] and in relaying to a user how their action will affect the application [23], we focus on only the most commonly used types of information in this work.

Different Amounts of Context

Many of the guidelines suggest that applications should provide labelers with some *contextual information* about the features of the data to be labeled. However, we found that applications interpret this principle differently. When *BusyBody* asks users to estimate their own interruptibility, it does not explain what it thinks the user is doing [15]. Hoffman *et al.* request help from Wikipedia users to fill in missing summary data as the users are reading an article [13]. When users are asked if the text they are reading in the article *belongs* in the summary, important keywords are not provided in the text. When reading the summary, users *are* provided with excerpts that could be added to make the summary more complete. In studies of interruptibility, it has been shown that people make judgments with relatively small amounts of context (15 seconds) and extra context (30 seconds) does not improve accuracy [12]. We define *sufficient context* such that if fewer features are provided, labeling the data is difficult. *Extra context* includes more features than necessary. In the interruptibility work, 15 seconds of video is sufficient, while 30 seconds is extra.

Levels of Context

Recently, researchers demonstrated that labelers' accuracy can depend on the *level of contextual information* they are provided. When users understand and use their own rules for classification, they are better at making those classifications compared to classifying based on the computers' rules [28][29]. This finding is supported by work in feedback in information retrieval applications [21][22] which mask the *low-level* sensor-level features that computers use and collect (*i.e.,* individual keywords in documents or accelerometer data) and allow users to search for information using *high-level* meaning attributed to the low-level data (*i.e.,* summaries of documents or physical motion inferred from accelerometers). However, because it is often difficult to generate the high-level explanation of context, many applications provide only the low-level raw data, like pictures, to labelers instead of a summary with the assumption that they can find their own meaning [30][31].

Prediction and User Feedback

Other work has focused on making the classification task easier for labelers by providing a classification *prediction*. Here, the user only has to confirm an answer *vs.* generate one, simplifying their work (*e.g.,* [28]). An interface may automatically fill in fields in a form or provide a prediction for which folder to sort a piece of email into (*e.g.,* [8],[11]). Users could also provide *corrective feedback* for incorrect predictions to improve later classification [8]. In the active learning community, Raghavan asked people to label text documents as news articles, sports, etc., and also asked them to pick words (features of the classifier) that should have high weight for each class [20]. Participants knew the article words they were looking for and could identify them easily. The classifier could correctly weight the important features faster than asking for article labels alone, because people had narrowed down the important features. This same method can easily be used for email classification and the other domains. For example, in CueTIP, users see their handwriting and the word prediction and can make corrections [26]. The OOPS toolkit helps users "discover" if the learner's prediction is incorrect and then provides a set of interaction techniques for the user to correct it [16]. Scaffidi allows users to provide feedback by creating rules for the classifier to make better predictions of phone numbers and other personal information [24]. By asking for feedback and providing predictions, an agent can correct errors and use feedback to improve its learning.

Work	Uncertainty	Prediction	Amount of Context	High/Low Context	User Feedback	Action Disclosure	Social Interaction
Horvitz [14]	X	X	X		X		X
Bellotti and Edwards [4]		X	X		X		
Erickson and Kellogg [10]	X		X	X	X	X	
Hoffman et. al [13]	X	X	X	X			
Mankoff et. al [16]		X	X		X		
Cutlotta et. al [8]	X	X		X			

Table 1. Applications provide users with different types of information to help in labeling data. The most popular are Uncertainty, Prediction, Amount and Level of context, and User Feedback.

Uncertainty

Finally, many agents calculate a prediction probability in order to decide whether it should ask for help. Studies of context-aware, expert, and recommender systems all show that providing users with the level of *uncertainty* in a system's predictions improves its overall usability (*e.g.,* [3][17]), even if the learner does not provide the exact uncertainty value [1]. We compare the accuracy of responses from labelers who receive an indication of uncertainty *vs.* those that do not.

While each guideline has been shown to affect usability or accuracy of responses, they are also already commonly calculated in the machine learning process. The learner uses the different weights calculated from *user feedback* on *its contextual features* to make *predictions*, must know *its uncertainty* to determine whether to ask for assistance, and must be able to explain those features to human helpers. Because the learner already calculates these parameters, it should require only minimal additional computation to generate the questions using them compared to high benefit of receiving more accurate responses.

We are interested in determining which *combination* of this popular information maximizes the accuracy of responses to an agent's questions. Additionally, with the recent popularity of crowd-sourcing data labels to people who have not witnessed the generation of the data (*e.g.,* [12], [30], [31], [1]), we are interested in the best way to elicit responses from these strangers as well. Next, we present a set of studies to understand how the content of an agent's questions affect the accuracy of labelers' responses.

STUDY DESIGN

In order to investigate the impact of the varying the content of an agent's questions along the five dimensions presented above, we designed a set of studies that compared the accuracy of labelers' responses based on the information a learning agent provides. To understand information needs for both users labeling their own data and people labeling strangers' data, we developed real tasks for labeler populations – physical activity recognition for users and email sorting and interruptibility estimation for strangers.

Tasks and Materials

Subjects were told that they were testing new technologies that learn by asking questions. They were to complete a primary task, and the application would classify their actions. The application would interrupt their task to ask them for help if it could not confidently label the data itself. They were informed that they could answer the questions if they had time, and that the application would continue to learn whether or not they answered. Participants were told that they would be given a second similar "performance" task that the application could help them complete more quickly if they helped it learn first. They were also reminded that answering was not their primary task and doing so may slow the completion of that task. In this way, we model tradeoffs of time versus improved performance that labelers might consider in real applications.

Figure 1: The agent interrupted a subjects' task to ask which activity there were performing.

User Labels – Physical Activity Coach

The sensors on mobile applications are often hidden and their data is hard to explain, but they capture activities that their users are aware of, such as exercise patterns [7]. In this task, a physical activity coach performs an activity recognition task using sensors from a mobile device to identify exercises the user performs. An application like this one may record users' activities for doctors to analyze physical activity levels, and thus users have an interest in answering its questions to ensure it correctly identifies their activities. We test our physical activity coach's questions to show that users can accurately label their own physical data and can provide feedback to improve its predictions.

Subjects were told they were testing a new physical activity coach on a handheld device that could detect the different activities they performed (Figure 1). The subjects' primary task was to perform each of the 12 physical activities from a list provided (Table 2). Subjects were given all equipment required to complete the activities, including a soccer ball, tennis balls, rackets, step stools, and golf clubs.

They were required to carry a Nokia 770 Internet Tablet that would recognize their activities and beep when it had questions. They were to respond to questions on the tablet using a stylus on a virtual keyboard. We randomly pre-selected 8 out of the 12 activities to ask participants about. Questions were sent from the experimenter's computer, 10-20 seconds after each activity was initiated. Subjects had 12 minutes to complete as many activities as possible, while answering the agent's questions when they had time.

Activity	Description
Walk	Walk around the room once
Soccer	Dribble a soccer ball around the room once
Steps	Step up and down off a stool 10 times
Tennis	Bounce a tennis ball on a racket 10 times
Golf	Putt golf balls on a mini course 5 times
Hula Hoop	Use a hula hoop 10 times
Read	Sit and read 2 pages of a travel book
Toss Ball	Throw a ball in the air 10 times
Bounce Ball	Bounce a ball on the ground 10 times
Jump	Jump up and down 20 times
Jumping Jacks	Do 10 jumping jacks
Push Objects	Push 5 chairs from table to the wall

Table 2. The participants were told that the Physical Activities Coach could detect these tasks.

Strangers' Labels – Email Sorting

While most users do not think of their desktop computers as learning from their actions, word processors learn to spell-check new words and email applications learn which emails are spam and which are not. Because these labels are subjective, the user carries the burden of having to label their own data and may make mistakes. In this task, subjects take notes on a stranger's non-personal emails. The email sorter tries to classify emails in the inbox into a folder. If it is uncertain, it requests help from the subject.

The participants' primary email task is to read provided emails about an upcoming academic conference and consolidate all the changes that need to be made to the conference schedule and website [27]. They were given a spreadsheet with information about conference speakers, sessions, and talks, and asked to make changes to it based on change requests in the email, in 12 minutes. The emails and task were modified from the RADAR dataset [27]. The emails in the data set were labeled with a folder name, which was removed to test the participants. Additionally, we added high-level summaries of the emails and low-level keywords for the agent to use to ask for help.

They were given an email application with the emails and were told that the classifier had sorted most emails into folders based on the type of changes that needed to be made (schedule or website). The email interface was built with Adobe Flex and presented on a 15" Apple MacBook Pro. The participants should try to sort the "Unsorted" emails and answer the questions that popped up automatically when the participant read an email while updating the spreadsheet with the relevant information (primary task).

Stranger's Labels – Interruptibility

With crowd-sourcing technologies widely available today, we conducted an additional task on Amazon.com's Mechanical Turk, an actual system that is often used to pair label requestors with people willing to label data. The labelers on this website have never seen the applications that collect the data; they only fill out forms online for a small fee. These labelers are a perfect example of strangers who are willing to answer short questions like our agents'.

The problem of recognizing when someone is interruptible has been widely studied in the literature (*e.g.*, [12][15]). Specifically it has been shown that strangers are fairly accurate at rating someone else's interruptibility. We recruited subjects from Amazon.com's Mechanical Turk to estimate the interruptibility of office workers from video data previously collected. When the interruptibility video data was collected, office workers made the ratings without specifying who the interrupter was. Our dataset included 586 45-second videos from 5 offices at a university that had been labeled with an interruptibility value from 1 (Highly Interruptible) to 5 (Highly Non-Interruptible) by the five office workers themselves. Twelve videos were selected from the data set and put on the Mechanical Turk website, two randomly chosen from each interruptibility level plus two more from randomly chosen levels. Participants on

Figure 2: The agent asked participants to judge whether people were interruptable in their offices.

Mechanical Turk were asked to rate the person in each of the 12 videos on the same 1-5 scale (Figure 2).

Varying Agent-Provided Information

To understand what information an agent should provide to maximize the accuracy of labelers' responses in each of these tasks, we vary the information the agent provides across the five dimensions presented above, namely providing *uncertainty, different amounts of context, high/low-level context, predictions,* and requesting *user feedback*. We examine all dimensions at once to find dependencies and correlations between them for a 2x3x2x2x2 design. Table 3 describes each dimension, the possible values, and an example on how each was used for each task. Along the dimensions, our content serves as exemplars for the definitions above so our results can be easily generalized to other similar applications and tasks.

Uncertainty

Along this dimension, we varied whether the agent told subjects it was uncertain about which classification to make. Half of the participants were told by the agent that it *"Cannot determine the activity."* while the other half were given no uncertainty information.

Amount of Context

Participants received one of three conditions (split evenly across participants): no context, sufficient context , and extra context. Participants in the sufficient context condition received enough features to identify the label accurately using only that information. On average this was about two pieces of information, and subjects read statements like *"Your feet are leaving the ground."* or *"This email is from X and is about their contact information"*. Participants who received extra context received redundant information and saw statements like *"Your feet are leaving the ground together repeatedly"* or *"This email is from X and about incorrect spelling of their name on the website"*. In the Interruptibility validation, participants were given 15 seconds of video for sufficient context or 30 seconds for extra context; previous work found that people make interruptibility judgments in 15 seconds.

High/Low-Level Context

We also vary the context in terms of the feature level information that is provided. Subjects in the low-level context condition receive information about sensor readings

Dimension	Description	Activity Recognition Example	Email Sorting Example	Interruptibility Estimation Example
Uncertainty	Notify labeler that it is uncertain of the label	"Cannot determine your activity."	"Cannot confidently make a prediction."	"Cannot determine if the person is interruptible."
Amount of Context	Provide varying amounts of contextual information (none, sufficient, extra)	**Sufficient**: "Your feet are leaving the ground." **Extra**: "Your feet are leaving the ground together and repeatedly."	**Sufficient**: "The email has keywords A and B." **Extra**: "The email has keywords A, B, C, and D."	**Sufficient**: (15 seconds of video) **Extra**: (30 seconds of video)
High/Low-Level Context	Give either low (sensor) level context or high (activity) level context	**Low**: "Shaking motion detected." **High**: "Your feet are leaving the ground."	**Low**: "The email has keywords A and B." **High**: "The email is best summarized by F and G."	**Low**: (raw video) **High**: "The door open and two people in the office."
Question	Ask for a label	"What activity are you doing?"	"Where does this email belong?"	"How interruptible is this person?"
Prediction	Share the expected label for the data	"Prediction: Jumping."	Prediction: "Sessions Changes."	"Prediction: 4"
User Feedback	Ask labeler to describe the important features	"How can this action be detected in the future?"	"Why is this folder correct?"	"How did you make that determination?"

Table 3. Scenario Content Dimensions, Description, and Example Sentences for each task

on the activity recognizer, keywords in an email, and raw interruptibility video footage, to help them make their classifications. For instance if someone was jumping, the sensor might read "shaking" - we do not expect users to interpret exact numerical sensor readings or graphs. With high-level context, participants received explanations such as email summaries or body motions like "your feet are leaving the floor" that correspond to sensor readings. Note that if subjects are in the no context condition from the previous dimension, this dimension is not used.

Prediction
Along this dimension, we varied whether users received a prediction from the agent. Half of the users received a correct prediction from the agent (*e.g., "Prediction: Jumping."*) and half did not receive any prediction. Because the agent always gave a correct prediction in our work, we can measure how often a human trusts the agent's prediction but cannot measure the impact of incorrect predictions.

User Feedback
After subjects gave a response to the agent's question, half of them received a follow-up question to describe their actions in the activity or reasons for classifying the email or interruption level so it could be more easily identified in the future: *"How can this activity be detected in the future?"*. We use the quality of this supplemental information as a secondary quantitative measure to compare our conditions when users provide equivalent numbers of correct answers.

Putting it Together
In order to generate questions, we read down this table, top to bottom – provide 1) uncertainty 2) prescribed amount of 3) high/low level context 4) ask question 5) prediction and 6) request for user feedback. For example, when the activity recognizer combines all dimensions above, it might ask a user the following:

Activity Recognizer: "*Cannot determine your activity. Your feet are leaving the ground together repeatedly. What activity are you doing? Prediction: Jumping.*"
Human: *Answers*
Activity Recognizer Follow Up: "*How can this action be detected in the future?*"

Each sentence in this interaction is based on one of the dimensions above. Based on the agent's capability to provide information on the dimensions (*i.e.*, conditions of the study), the corresponding sentence can be removed or changed. For example, if the agent cannot provide high-level information, cannot ask for user feedback and can only provide sufficient context, it might instead ask:

Activity Recognizer: "*Cannot determine your activity. Shaking motion is detected. What activity are you performing? Prediction: Jumping.*"
Human: *Answers, with no follow up*

Each participant experienced one of the 36 possible types of questions from the 2x3x2x2 design space for each task, removing 12 conditions for high/low-level context and the prediction (which is another form of context) when a participant receives the "no context" condition.

METHOD
The study was conducted in phases. For each population (users and strangers), we conducted an *initial* test (activity recognition and email sorting), varying the information that labelers received in all combinations. At the same time, HCI researchers who worked on applications similar to our tasks were brought together to come to a consensus on which information they thought would be best for each of our tasks – which we call the *community advice*. Then, to *validate* our results, a new set of participants completed the same task twice – once with our best combination from the initial test and once with the community advice. We validate against community advice instead of against questions without context for two reasons. We believe, and

will show in our results, that asking for help with no context is confusing and would lead to poor accuracy. Also, it does not reflect what HCI researchers have done in the past when building systems that ask for help. Our community advice reflects a more realistic metric for response accuracy improvement to compare our results against.

After completing this for both users and strangers, we conducted the third interruptibility test to further validate the combination for a larger set of strangers. We chose interruptibility because it is well known in the community and we can draw the following three parallels to the email task. Fogarty *et al.* tested their classifier on strangers, so there was a well-established baseline of accuracy to test against [12]. The raw low-level data (words/video) are human-understandable compared to the accelerometer data in the activity recognition domain. In email, participants could draw context from the emails just as interruptibility participants could use raw video. This is both a feature and a flaw in supplying raw data as there is no context lost in the explanation. Finally, participants in both tasks were tested on their ability to classify against subjective labels. For these reasons, we used the interruptibility task to validate the best combination from the email study.

Procedure
To ensure that all participants in all conditions of all tasks received the same information for the same dimensions, the questions were generated before the study began. We measure the proportion of correct answers labelers provide as well as the quality of their feedback when requested.

Initial Tests
For the *initial* tests, participants were assigned the order of tasks at random, but evenly. Participants were given an explanation of the study and signed a consent form on arrival. Subjects were given 12 minutes to complete their primary task and were told they would receive a "performance" task based on both the completion of the first one and on their responses to the agent.. After completing the task, participants were given a survey about their experiences with the questions. Then, they were given the second primary task with the same instructions and given a second survey. Upon completion, participants were told there was not time to complete the "performance" tasks and were dismissed after being paid $10.

Validation
Before the validation experiments were run, we sought advice from 3 HCI community members who work on projects similar to our email and activity recognition tasks about which information they believe each agent should use when asking for help. The community members understood both the technical data that could be collected from the domains and the usability requirements necessary for effective communication to users. We explained each type of information and how they could be combined together. Each group (email and activity) met separately to discuss the information and then reported their internal consensus about which combination they thought would elicit the most

correct answers. In the end, we had two combinations of information – one for the email sorting task with strangers and one for the activity recognition task with users.

We then analyzed the results from our initial tests to identify our best combinations of the information – one for the email sorting task and one for activity recognition. In both validation tests, participants were randomly but evenly assigned the order they would receive the two types of questions – our best combination *vs.* the community advice. Subjects performed the same procedure as the initial tests, except that they received the same task twice with different combinations of information. When they completed the second survey, they were paid $10 and dismissed.

For reasons given above, we apply the same combinations (ours and community advice) from the email task to the final interruptibility validation. Participants were randomly assigned to receive only one of either our best combination or the community advice and received 12 videos to label. All participants were paid $5 for completing the study.

We validate that our combinations are at least as good as, if not better than, the community advice for each task based on the proportion of correct answers and user opinions.

Participants
Participants, except for the interruptibility task, consisted of 60 Pittsburgh residents ages 18-61 with a variety of occupations including students, bartenders, teachers, and salesmen. 37 subjects completed both initial tests, acting as users in the activity recognition task and as strangers in the email-sorting task. Then, 11 additional subjects completed a validation of the activity recognizer task and 12 more subjects completed the email sorting validation. Only a few participants (15%) had experience with technology that learns, and all spoke fluent English. 180 participants in the Interruptibility task were recruited anonymously on Mechanical Turk, but were only allowed to complete the task once by comparing usernames.

We use this experimental method to find the combination of information that maximizes the accuracy of responses and the amount of feedback from users to label their own data and from others who label strangers' data. We will next describe the measures used to find the best combinations.

Measures
Because a machine-learning agent would benefit more from correct answers rather than incorrect ones, we assessed the user responses primarily based on correctness, but also on the quality of user feedback when available. We also gave subjects surveys about their opinions of the applications, including whether they found them to be annoying.

Users' responses were classified as *correct* answers if their last answer (some users changed their minds) was correct and *incorrect* otherwise. For example, if a subject disagreed with the prediction, but gave an equally correct reference, it was classified as correct. Synonyms were determined to be correct as long as they were not too vague. For example, "putting" was considered synonymous with the activity "golfing", but "swinging arms" was not because it was not an accepted name for the activity (listed on instructions of activities to perform). While we do not expect participants to give exact answers, we also do not expect them to give completely incorrect or opposite values.

If users can provide accurate labels for their data, their ability to give quality, or helpful, *feedback* is of particular interest to possibly speed learning [20]. If users received a request for feedback, their response was coded based on how many features about the data were provided. A value of 0 was given to a response that provided no additional information (*e.g., "I don't know"*). For every piece of valid information, the value increased by 1. For example, "I'm doing jumping jacks if *my arms move up and down* and *my legs go in and out*", would be given a value of 2.

After completing the task, participants were given questionnaires on their *subjective* experiences with each technology. They were asked about whether they thought the application's questions were annoying and whether they found each dimension particularly useful. Responses were coded as either "Yes" or "No". Participants were also asked whether it was easy or hard to answer the questions on a Likert scale from 1 (very easy) to 5 (very hard).

RESULTS
We analyze the results of the activity recognizer initial and validation task to determine a best combination of dimensions for users labeling their own data. Then we analyze the results of the email sorting initial and validation tasks to determine the best combination of dimensions for people labeling strangers' data. We use the results of the interruptibility validation to extend the results beyond a single task and for a broader set of strangers.

Analysis
Initial Test Models - A McNemar test with the Chi-Square statistic was used to analyze the significance of the categorical response (correctness) against the categorical independent variables (our 5 dimensions) for each task. T-tests and ANOVAs were used to analyze the significance of the secondary continuous response (quality of feedback) against the independent variables. Based on the results, we define a combination of information that agents should use to ask questions of labelers to maximize label accuracy.

Validation Models - We conducted a within-subject study to validate that our guidelines result in more correct answers compared to the community input. We used T-tests to analyze the significance of the categorical response (correctness) against the two types of questions (our guidelines and the community advice).

User Labels – Physical Activity Coach
Initial Test Results
We collected 119 responses from participants, including 8 for which participants (6 of them) said they were too busy to respond. When we analyzed the remaining 111 responses

for the effects of the individual dimensions on the proportion of correct labels users provided for their own data, we found that subjects were correct *nearly* 100% of the time and there was *no effect* of any of the dimensions or their combinations. However, we found that when an agent requests user feedback, subjects were able to provide on average of .81 pieces of quality feedback compared to almost 0 pieces without being asked (some subjects provided feedback without prompting). We include user feedback in our best combination, as this is a statistically significant difference (F[6,112] = 8.87, p< 0.001).

We then used the McNemar test on the amount of feedback with all five dimensions as independent variables to analyze the significance. We find that subjects who received sufficient context provide a significantly larger amount of quality feedback (.77 pieces) compared to those provided either no context (.30 pieces) or extra context (.31 pieces) (F[2,2]=5.38, p<.002). Additionally, subjects who received low-level context provided statistically significantly greater amount of feedback (.58 pieces) compared to high-level context (.34 pieces) (F[1,1] = 3.33 p<0.05). There were no significant effects and no combined effects for providing predictions or uncertainty so we use qualitative results to understand the impact of those dimensions.

We find that 25% of subjects who did not receive predictions reported it hard or very hard to answer the questions. Additionally, 0% of subjects with predictions reported the task difficult and 83% thought the questions were useful. There were no effects of uncertainty on the qualitative data so we do not include it in our best combination. Based on these results, we determine that the best combination for a user labeling their own data is the following: ***no uncertainty, do provide sufficient low-level context, predictions, and request user feedback.***

Validation Results
We validate our best combination against the HCI community advice, which varies from our combination in two ways (with differences shown in bold): *do not explain uncertainty, but **provide high-level** and **extra context**, predictions, and request user feedback.*

We collected 113 responses from participants including 11 non-responses. Four participants were too busy to respond at least once. We found that for both conditions, subjects gave correct responses 100% of the time and there were no statistically significant effects on feedback quality, so we use the qualitative results to differentiate the conditions. Subjects found that our dimensions were useful but only 30% realized they were receiving contextual information. Subjects did not prefer either system and could not identify which one learned more, but 70% of participants thought the system using our guidelines was smarter. Users that believe a computer is smarter will respond with more sophistication than to one they think is not as smart [19]. So, we conclude that our combination is at least as good as, if not better than, other combinations of the information.

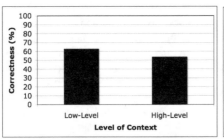 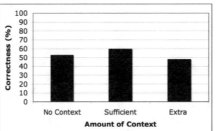 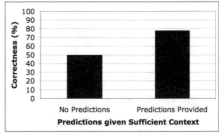

(a) Subjects' Correctness by Level of Context   (b) Subjects' Correctness by Amount of Context   (c) Subjects' Correctness by Prediction

Figure 3: Using results from our study, we developed guidelines along our five dimensions for how an agent should ask questions.

Strangers' Labels – Email Sorting

Initial Results

We collected 153 responses from participants including 13 non-responses. Four participants answered that they were busy at least once. We first analyzed the effects of each individual dimension on the proportion of correct answers. Subjects answered a statistically significant larger proportion of questions correctly when given low-level context (63%) versus high-level context (54%) ($\chi^2[2,2]$ = 10.57, p<.01) (Figure 3a). Subjects had significantly fewer correct answers when they received no context (53%) or extra context (48%) compared to subjects who received sufficient context (60%) and this effect is heightened when combined with the level of context ($\chi^2[4,2]$ = 11.04, p<.01) (Figure 3b). No other single dimension was significant.

To understand how the other three dimensions affected user performance, we analyzed the effects of pairing them with the significant dimension and each other. Subjects provided statistically significantly more correct answers when they received a prediction with sufficient context (78%) compared to when they did not (50%) or when they received other amounts of context (55%) ($\chi^2[2,2]$ = 7.72 p<.01) (Figure 3c). We found that if we provide sufficient context, providing uncertainty increases the proportion of correct answers significantly from 46% to 70% ($\chi^2[4,4]$ = 11.56 p<.01). There is a significant paired effect of prediction with uncertainty ($\chi^2[2,2]$ = 8.70 p<.01). Finally, we found that requesting user feedback resulted in an increase from 30% to 90% in correct answers when paired with uncertainty but a decrease from 87% to 45% when no uncertainty information is provided ($\chi^2[2,2]$ = 12.21 p<.02).

We analyzed the survey responses to understand how useful subjects felt each dimension was. We found that 50% of subjects thought the questions were useful to them during their task while 41% found answering them annoying. A majority of subjects who saw each dimension thought they were useful. 90% of subjects found context useful when they received at least sufficient context, and 100% of subjects who received predictions found them useful. 78% and 71% of subjects who were asked for feedback and who received uncertainty respectively, found it useful. We conclude that the agent should use the following combination when asking strangers questions: *provide uncertainty, sufficient low-level context, predictions, and request user feedback*.

Validation Results

HCI researchers that work in the email domain came to the following consensus on our dimensions (with differences shown in bold): *provide uncertainty, low-level **extra context**, predictions, and **do not request user feedback***.

We collected 301 responses including 4 non-responses. Three participants refused to respond at least once. We found a significant effect of the combination on the proportion of correct responses (t[2,250] = 2.48, p<.01). Subjects who received our combination were 100% correct, while those who received the community advice were 94% correct. A majority (8/11) people preferred the community advice but (7/11) people thought our agent was learning more. When we analyze the dimensions that differed between combinations, more people preferred our context (58% *vs.* 40%) and predictions (63% *vs.* 40%).

Interruptibility Results

Participants in this study were required to answer all 12 questions. Half of our 180 participants estimated the interruptibility for 12 videos with the best combination from the email task and half received the email community's advice. We analyzed the average mean squared error (MSE) of each participant's estimation compared to the true interruptibility across the videos and performed a between-subjects ANOVA analysis to compare the error between the combinations. We removed 16 of the 180 subjects that had MSE results that were more than 3 times the median of the entire data set (average MSE=1.37, outliers > 4.11). Subjects who received our combination had a statistically significant lower average MSE (mean 1.17, std. dev. 0.62) than those who received the community advice (mean 1.42, std. dev. 0.92) (F[1,164] = 6.02, p < 0.01). Subjects who received our combination were correct or off by one level of interruptibility 85% of the time, while subjects that received the community advice were correct 80% of the time. Both of these are better than the previously published interruptibility result, reporting a 65% off-by-one accuracy with only sufficient context.

DISCUSSION

Our results show that we were able to find a combination of information for agents to provide strangers that maximizes labeling accuracy. Additionally, our users were aware of their activity and had no trouble labeling it, so we can find a best combination that maximizes accuracy *and* amount of feedback users give. Next, we discuss differences between users and strangers in each dimension to explain our results.

Benefits of Providing Information to Labelers

We found that each of the five dimensions – amounts of context, level of context, uncertainty, prediction, and requests for user feedback – had a positive effect on the labelers as they were performing their primary task. First, labelers used the context and prediction to match the agent's focus. For example, many labelers used the key words and summaries of the emails when deciding on a label instead of reading the entire email. As a result, the questions did not take as long for labelers to answer compared when they had to pick out the important context themselves. Additionally, labelers checked to confirm their label was consistent with the given context.

Although labelers were frequently interrupted with questions in their 12-minute tasks, they almost always answered when it was prefaced with uncertainty. For example, in the activity recognizer task, one participant who was interrupted only seconds after starting a task said, "It's interrupting me again! Oh, well, I guess it must be hard to distinguish between these [activities]." This shows that users excused the interruption when they felt they could help the agent. However, when we asked participants whether they valued uncertainty, they did not remember if they had received that information and therefore reported it as being not useful. We believe labelers underestimated the usefulness of uncertainty for the usability of the questions.

Finally, when labelers were asked to provide feedback about the label, they sometimes changed their labels to the correct answer when they thought about a reason for the label. While it may be difficult for a system to incorporate such freeform feedback, we find that the agent will benefit from increased response accuracy *just by asking* the question and irrespective of using the response. To make it easier to use such feedback, the agent could ask a multiple-choice question. Overall, we found each piece of information was useful for both user and stranger labelers.

Limitations of These Five Dimensions

While the five dimensions we chose were able to help the labelers focus their answers, they did not provide any new information for users to use in the physical activity task. For example, when users were given context, they already knew what they were doing. As a result, we found that varying the dimensions had little impact on the user's accuracy. We found that users pulled out the tablet and started typing often without even reading the question. We do not, however, believe this is universally true for all user tasks – users may misfile their emails in folders.

Additionally, users had a lot of trouble giving feedback about their physical activities. While they knew that they were golfing and not playing soccer, they were not able to provide much information about what actions constituted the activity like swinging arms or kicking their leg. Often, users thought for a long time about what to write the first time they saw the request for feedback, because they do not usually think about what constitutes a physical activity. Participants had less trouble expressing their feedback in the email and interruptibility tasks, because they had to develop their classification rules while performing the task. While the feedback is useful to a machine learning application, it may be too difficult for labelers to provide if they are not consciously making the classification.

Similar Combinations of Information

We observe that the best combinations for both users and strangers were nearly the same – only differing by uncertainty. We had assumed that because strangers did not know the context the data was drawn from, the agent would need to provide extra context to maximize accuracy compared to users. However, because strangers had some existing domain knowledge about sorting email and determining if someone is interruptible before the study, they did not need as much context to be accurate. We also found that just as users did not require high-level context about their own activities, the strangers did not require high-level context in the email or interruptibility tasks because the raw data (email keywords and video clips) were already human-understandable. This is significant because it reduces computation time for constructing questions, and eliminates the need to translate low-level sensor data into high-level context, allowing more time for processing data.

The only difference between the two combinations is *uncertainty*. Uncertainty offers no help to the labeler but indicates that the classification is hard. Users were aware of the difficulty of activity recognition without the acknowledgement from the system, reporting that they were impressed that a mobile device was able to recognize their activities. Receiving uncertainty did not change the users' opinion and there were no significant changes in accuracy as a result. However, strangers saw human-understandable data and assumed the classification was, in fact, easy. When strangers received uncertainty, we believe they recognized the difficulty of the task and tried harder, resulting in higher accuracy responses. In general, labelers that realize the classification is hard do not require *uncertainty* information.

Accuracy of the Agent

In this work, we wizard-of-oz'd the agents' questions to ensure they were timed correctly and included accurate information. The context that the agents provided *did* accurately represent the data and the high-level context appropriately summarized the sensors. As a result, the labelers could trust and use this data to their advantage when responding. In actual implementations, agents may not always be able to extract this information accurately. It is unclear how labelers would react to incorrect context.

Additionally, the questions were asked in the middle of activities while users were performing them. Because users knew which activity they were currently performing, the agent's information did not affect the user accuracy. If the questions were mistimed or delayed, it is unclear how this would affect the accuracy of users' responses.

While all of the predictions that were provided were the correct, the labelers often did not trust the predictions. This could be because labelers were told the agent asked when it was not confident in its prediction. While the predictions were shown to increase accuracy, we do not believe this is due to their correctness. Rather, they helped labelers narrow down the labels from which they decided on their own.

CONCLUSION

Researchers often instrument an interface or environment with sensors to collect data for learning but it can be difficult to label that data accurately. To automate the process of collecting the most *accurate* labels possible, we use an agent to ask questions. The contribution of this work is three-fold. First, we contribute a two-step method to test combinations of information – an initial step and a validation. While users who label their own data were typically very accurate at labeling their physical activities, we contribute a combination of information that maximizes accuracy *and* the quality of feedback the user provides. Additionally, we found a combination of information that maximizes accuracy of people labeling strangers' data. These more accurate labels and feedback can improve learning. Finally, we observed that the 2 combinations were nearly the same. We believe these validated combinations are applicable far beyond our 3 tasks and could be used today to collect more accurate labels when labelers have domain knowledge about the data they are working with.

This work focuses on a specific set of dimensions for classification problems. Other dimensions may also impact how labelers answer questions and need to be validated using our approach. We would also like to see how well our results apply to other domains and tasks where users and strangers have less domain knowledge about the collected data. Future work is needed to test these questions in long-term data collections and active learning applications and to understand the usability of proactively asking for help.

REFERENCES

1. Amazon.com Mechanical Turk – Artificial, Artificial Intelligence, https://www.mturk.com/mturk/, 2009
2. S. Antifakos, A. Schwaninger, and B. Schiele. Evaluating the Effects of Displaying Uncertainty in Context-aware Applications. *Proc. UbiComp 2004*, 54–69, 2004.
3. S. Banbury, *et al*. Being certain about uncertainty: How the Representation of System Reliability Affects Pilot Decision Making. Proc. *HFES, Aerospace Systems*, 36–39(4), 1998.
4. V. Bellotti and K. Edwards. Intelligibility and accountability: human considerations in context-aware systems. *Human.-Computer Interaction* 16(2), 193-212, 2001.
5. S. Carter, J. Mankoff. When participants do the capturing: the role of media in diary studies. *Proc. CHI 2005*, 899-908, 2005.
6. D. Cohn, L. Atlas and R. Ladner. Improving Generalization with Active Learning. *Machine Learning*. 0885-6125:15(2), 201-221, 1994.
7. S. Consolvo, *et al*. Activity Sensing in the Wild: a Field Trial of Ubifit Garden. *Proc. CHI* 2008, 1797-1806, 2008.
8. A. Culotta, T. Kristjansson, A. McCallum, P. Viola, Corrective Feedback and Persistent Learning for Information Extraction. *Artificial Intelligence*, 170(14-15), 1101-1122, 2006.
9. P. Donmez and J. G. Carbonell. Proactive learning: cost-sensitive active learning with multiple imperfect oracles. *Proc of CIKM '08*, 619-628, 2008.
10. T. Erickson and W. A. Kellogg. Social translucence: an approach to designing systems that support social processes. *ACM ToCHI* 7(1) 59-83, 2001.
11. A. Faulring, *et al*. Successful User Interfaces for RADAR. *CHI 2008 Workshop on Usable Artificial Intelligence*, 2008.
12. J. Fogarty, *et. al*. Predicting human interruptibility with sensors. *ACM ToCHI* 12(1), pp. 119-146, 2005.
13. R. Hoffmann, *et al*. Amplifying community content creation with mixed initiative information extraction. *Proc. CHI '09*, 1849-1858, 2009.
14. E. Horvitz. Principles of mixed-initiative user interfaces. *Proc. of CHI '99*, 159-166, 1999.
15. E. Horvitz, P. Koch, J. Apacible. BusyBody: creating and fielding personalized models of the cost of interruption. *Proc. CSCW 2004*, 507-510, 2004.
16. J. Mankoff, G. Abowd, S.E. Hudson, OOPS: a toolkit supporting mediation techniques for resolving ambiguity in recognition-based interfaces. *Computers & Graphics*, 24(6), 819-834, 2000.
17. S. Mcnee, *et al*. Confidence Displays and Training in Recommender Systems. *Proc. INTERACT*, 176–183, 2003.
18. T. Mitchell. *Machine Learning*. McGraw Hill, 1997.
19. J. Pearson, J., *et. al*. Adaptive language behavior in HCI: how expectations and beliefs about a system affect users' word choice. *Proc. CHI '06*, 1177-1180, 2006.
20. H. Raghavan, O. Madani, R. Jones. Active Learning with Feedback on Features and Instances. Journal of Machine Learning Research 7, 1655-1686, 2006.
21. Y. Rui, *et al*. Relevance Feedback: a Power Tool for Interactive Content-based Image Retrieval. *IEEE Trans. on Circuits/Systems for Video Technology*, 8(5): 644–655, 1998.
22. G. Salton and C. Buckley. Improving Retrieval Performance by Relevance Feedback. *Journal of the American Society for Information Science*, 41(4): 288–297, 1990.
23. T. Salvador and K. Anderson. Practical Considerations of Context for Context Based Systems: An Example from an Ethnographic Case Study of a Man Diagnosed with Early Onset Alzheimer's Disease. *UbiComp 2003*, 243–255, 2003.
24. C. Scaffidi. Topes: Enabling End-User Programmers to Validate and Reformat Data. Technical Report CMU-ISR-09-105, 2009.
25. N. Shadbolt, A. Burton. Knowledge Elicitation. Evaluation of Human Work: Practical Ergonomics Methods, 321-345, 1990.
26. M. Shilman, D. S. Tan, P. Simard, CueTIP: a mixed-initiative interface for correcting handwriting errors. *Proc. UIST '06*. 323-332, 2006.
27. A. Steinfeld, *et al*. The RADAR Test Methodology: Evaluating a Multi-Task Machine Learning System with Humans in the Loop. *Technical Report CMU-CS-06-125*, Carnegie Mellon University, 2006.
28. S. Stumpf, *et al*. Predicting User Tasks: I know What You're Doing. *AAAI 2005 Workshop*, 2005.
29. S. Stumpf, *et al*. Toward Harnessing User Feedback for Machine Learning. *Proc. IUI 2007*, 82 – 91, 2007.
30. L. von Ahn and L. Dabbish. Labeling Images with a Computer Game. ACM Conference on Human Factors in Computing Systems. *Proc. CHI 2004*, 319-326, 2004.
31. L. von Ahn, *et al*. reCAPTCHA: Human-Based Character Recognition via Web Security Measures. *Science*, 1465-1468, 2008.

Mobia Modeler: Easing the Creation Process of Mobile Applications for Non-Technical Users

Florence Balagtas-Fernandez
Media Informatics Group
University of Munich
florence.balagtas@ifi.lmu.de

Max Tafelmayer
Media Informatics Group
University of Munich
max@tafelmayer.de

Heinrich Hussmann
Media Informatics Group
University of Munich
heinrich.hussmann@ifi.lmu.de

ABSTRACT

The development of mobile applications has now extended from mobile network providers into the hands of ordinary people as organizations and companies encourage people to come up with their own software masterpieces by opening up APIs and tools. However, as of the moment, these APIs and tools are only usable by people with programming skills. There is a scarcity of tools that enable users without programming experience to easily build customized mobile applications. We present in this paper a tool and framework that would enable non-technical people to create their own domain-specific mobile applications. The tool features a simple user-interface that features configurable components to easily create mobile applications. As a proof of concept, we focus on the creation of applications in the domain of mobile health monitoring. In the future, we would like to extend our work to cover other domains as well.

Author Keywords

mobile application, modeling tools, domain-specific modeling, user-centered design

ACM Classification Keywords

H.5.2 Information interfaces and presentation: User Interfaces—*Graphical User Interfaces*; D.2.2 Software Engineering: Design Tools and Techniques—*User Interfaces, Evolutionary prototyping*; D.2.6 Programming Environments: Graphical Environments

General Terms

Design, Experimentation, Human Factors

INTRODUCTION

With the mobile phone gaining ground in being the most accessible computing device [5], applications for such devices are no longer limited to be created by mobile phone companies alone, but are now extended to anyone with the right

skills and motivation (e.g. Android platform, iPhone platform). However, like any other programming task, development for mobile devices is a complicated job. Therefore, we proposed [1] to apply the model-driven development approach in creating such applications. In this approach, an application is generated by first creating a model of the application and later on transforming the model to platform-specific code through transformation tools. The main focus of this paper is to discuss the Mobia Modeler which is a tool that enables users without programming experience to easily build mobile applications through modeling. The Mobia Modeler serves as the front end of the Mobia Framework whose two major components are the modeler mentioned, and the Mobia Processor which is responsible for transforming the models into platform specific code. We followed a user-centered iterative design approach in the development of the modeler's user interface. There have been various designs in the past as mentioned in our previous paper [2], which were tested and lead to improvements that were finally applied to the current design. The design of the Mobia Processor and the process that the model goes through in order to generate the final code will also be presented.

RELATED WORK

Various systems allow people with no technical expertise to develop applications. Examples are, ESPranto SDK from Van Herk et al. [10], Vegemite from Lin et al. [7], UI Fin from Puerta et al. [9], and MAKEIT from Holleis et al. [5]. Our work is similar to the researches mentioned in a way that we want to create an environment that would help users with limited technical knowledge, create useful domain specific applications. However, the difference between the Mobia Framework from the mentioned related work is that, the focus is not only on the usability of the modeler for non-programmers, but in the design of the underlying framework as well such that it can be easily extended to support other types of applications for such mobile environments in the future.

MOBIA FRAMEWORK USE-CASE SCENARIO

In order to fully understand how non-technical users can benefit from using a tool like the Mobia Modeler, we present in this section an example scenario in the area of mobile health monitoring.

Increasing Quality of Life with Mobile Health Monitoring

There has been an increased awareness of people with regards to their health. Many technological devices are being created in order to aid people in their goals for better health. Some tools [3] aim to aid people in keeping track of their physical activities and at the same time motivating them through visual and/or audio feedbacks. Others tools [8] help people with existing health problems by monitoring and analyzing physiological signals. However, the problem with these existing applications and tools is that they already contain predefined displays and functionalities. It would be a big help if there was a way to customize these types of applications depending on the type of health related issues that are to be addressed by such applications without the need to do low-level programming. A tool like the Mobia Modeler would be useful in order to achieve this.

Giving the Power to Create: The Target Users

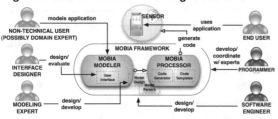

Figure 1. The Mobia Framework and its use cases

As we have mentioned in our conceptual paper [1] about applying domain specific modeling for mobile health monitoring, different types of people can benefit from a tool like the Mobia Modeler. *Domain experts in the field of healthcare* such as doctors, nurses and clinical technicians can create customizable applications for their patients. Other domain experts such as *people in the field of medical research* can also make use of the tool for their own purposes. Other types of users for the Mobia Modeler are *ordinary people* who are just concerned about their own well-being and would like to create their own applications for monitoring their health. For clarification purposes, we want to emphasize that the users we mentioned here are the people who create the application using the Mobia Modeler. They may be the user of the final application (e.g. ordinary people creating applications for themselves), or they may create the application for other users (e.g. healthcare experts creating the application for their patients). Figure 1 shows an overview of the whole Mobia Framework and its use cases.

Health Monitor: A Sample Application

The scenario discussed is adapted from Leijdekkers et al. [6]. A doctor monitors his clinically obese patient by keeping track of his nutrition, physical activities and heart rate. He wants to ensure that his patient is eating the right foods and doing the assigned exercises by getting a daily update on the patient's food intake and physical activities. Since the patient just recently had a heart attack, the doctor wants to ensure that the heart rate does not go over 120 bpm for the next 30 days. In case this happens, the doctor would like to be notified via his pager. He also configures the application

to call an emergency number when the patient's heart rate goes up beyond 150 bpm [6].

THE MOBIA MODELER

The main design idea for the Mobia Modeler is *configuration over combination*. This means that instead of building mobile applications by assembling individual user interface elements on the screen, users can just add components to the model and configure these artifacts based on the application requirements. We call these components *Configurable Components*. The formal definition of configurable components in the context of Mobia is: it is a *logical container for multiple user interface elements that has a clearly defined meaning and acts as a whole, and which functionalities can be modified through simple configuration*. The approach of configurable component-based design has been applied to many areas in software and embedded systems. However, according to Fernando et al. [4], there are still issues that need to be addressed in the design of such systems. The key issues emphasized pertain to the attribute-dependent categorization of components, the development and storage of component configurations, and how to provide guidance to the developer/user to choose the right components [4]. We address the issue of categorization mentioned by Fernando et al. [4] by grouping configurable components in the Mobia Modeler into: Basic, Structure, Sensor and Special (see table in figure 2). The issues of development, storage and developer guidance will be addressed in the next sections.

A Step-by-Step Guide into the Mobia Modeler

The modeler starts with a wizard which helps the user configure the modeler's general user interface and supported functionalities. This is the time where the tool collects domain specific properties (e.g. domain, users) and adapts the tool base on the supplied information. The modeler's interface (figure 3) is composed of three main parts: the Main Area, the Menu Bar and the Side Bar. The *Main Area* is the only view used by the Mobia Modeler for modeling mobile applications. Previous studies [11][2] conducted supports this single view design since it increases the learnability of an application. The *Side Bar* contains elements that represent the different configurable components which are grouped according to the four types mentioned in the previous section, and can be added to the screens in the Main Area. To guide users, not all configurable components are available at a given time. Some are disabled depending on the current state of the model. The sidebar can be adapted indirectly through settings made in the configuration wizard during the creation of a new application. The *Menu Bar* is located at the top of the Mobia Modeler's user interface and contains additional functions. All the menu items shown in figure 3 are already supported in the current version of the Mobia Modeler except for the *Simulation* function. The created model can be saved and loaded either through the server or as a local copy. Components can then be added to the main area depending on the application the user wants to create. Each component can be configured by clicking on the pen symbol (see figure 3) on top of each component. Aside from tool tips, the Mobia Modeler also offers visual hints to the user such as the change in color of a config-

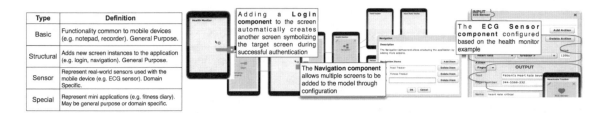

Type	Definition
Basic	Functionality common to mobile devices (e.g. notepad, recorder). General Purpose.
Structural	Adds new screen instances to the application (e.g. login, navigation). General Purpose.
Sensor	Represent real-world sensors used with the mobile device (e.g. ECG sensor). Domain Specific.
Special	Represent mini applications (e.g. fitness diary). May be general purpose or domain specific.

Adding a **Login** component to the screen automatically creates another screen symbolizing the target screen during successful authentication

The **Navigation component** allows multiple screens to be added to the model through configuration

The **ECG Sensor** component configured based on the health monitor example

Figure 2. Examples of Component types

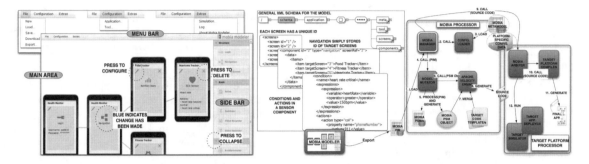

Figure 3. (left) The Mobia Modeler with the Health Monitor sample application model and its (middle) serialized form. (right) The design of the Mobia Processor and the whole code generation process.

urable component if the default values have been changed, or by disabling components in the Side Bar to prevent users from doing invalid moves. Finally, the graphical model can then be serialized into some XML format (see figure 3) that is an important data used for processing the model into code which is the topic of the next section.

From Model to Code: A Look into the Mobia Processor

In our previous paper [1], we have discussed an overview of the initial design of the Mobia Framework including its components. In this section, we will elaborately discuss the Mobia Processor component of the framework and the steps needed to achieve code generation (figure 3).

The process starts when the application model (*Mobia PIM (Platform Independent Model)*) is exported from the Mobia Modeler. The *Mobia Manager* then loads the information from the Mobia PIM into the runtime system of the processor. It then calls the *Configuration Loader* which loads platform specific information (e.g. target platform, code generation templates, *Mobia metamodel*) based on the information specified in the Mobia PIM. The *Mobia metamodel* which is in the form of an XSD file, contains a general description of a model in the Mobia Framework. The Mobia Processor relies on the Mobia metamodel to process the PIM file. For future work, we want to use the Mobia metamodel to easily extend the Mobia Modeler in order to support other domains, or add/modify currently existing components in the modeler's interface. The *Model Mutator* then processes the Mobia PIM and transforms them into *Mobia PSM (Platform Specific Model)*. The difference between Mobia PIM and Mobia PSM is that the Mobia PSM contains additional information that is targeted towards a specific platform. The terminologies PIM and PSM are borrowed from Model-Driven Architecture (http://www.omg.org/mda). The *Model Muta-*

tor then passes the PSM object to the *Apache Velocity Engine* (http://velocity.apache.org/) which merges the information from the PSM and the code templates to generate the final source code. The *Mobia Manager* then calls the *Mobia Arbiter* which is responsible compiling and deploying the final application.

EVALUATION THROUGH QUALITATIVE USER STUDY

A qualitative user study was conducted in order to identify issues that arise from the current design of the Mobia Modeler and find ways to improve it. There were 16 participants in the user study (7 males, 9 females) with the average age of 30. All of the participants have experience in computer usage. 10 of them have no experience in programming, while the other 6 use programming in their respective professions. Although none of the participants have experience in using mobile health monitoring applications, they claim that they understood the concept. In order to *evaluate the different features of the Mobia Modeler*, we observed how the participants interacted with the modeler during the exploration phase and combined it with the participants' answers during the interview (see figure 4). Comparing the views from the two types of participants (programmers and non-programmers or the non-technical people), in terms of understanding the general concepts, usability and design approach of Mobia, it scored higher in the programmers' group as compared to the non-programmers. The variance between the answers of the people in the non-programmers group is also higher which correlates to the different experiences that the participants in this group have.

SUMMARY AND FUTURE WORK

We have presented in this paper the Mobia Modeler which aims to allow non-technical users to create domain-specific mobile applications through modeling methods. We also

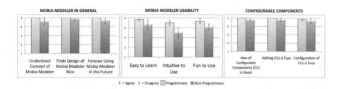

Figure 4. Comparing feedback from non-programmers (non-technical people) and programmers with regards to the Mobia Modeler and its concepts

briefly described the design of the Mobia Processor which works together with the Mobia Modeler in order to generate platform specific code. We combined the use of models and configurable component-based design is our approach. However, our work still has issues which need to be resolved.

- **Provide Richer User Experience and Help.** Users in general are more encouraged to work on a certain task if they see immediate feedback. One thing that is currently missing in the modeler is the simulator that shows the basic functionality of the application being modeled. Another thing that can be added is to provide templates or pre-made models that the user can explore in order to see the capabilities that can be done with the tool. Support for Plug-and-Adapt which automatically adapts the interface based on detected hardware components (similar to [10]) would also ease the initial configuration process.

- **Support for Other Domains and Components.** The underlying Mobia metamodel which is in the form of an XSD file, influences how the Mobia Processor deals with the generated model for code generation. The next plan is to automatically generate and adapt the modeler's interface based on the changes to the metamodel. To further simplify the task, a separate tool may be created such that new domains and its constructs can be added to the modeler without having to manually edit the XSD file.

- **Support for Multiple User Types.** The current target users of the front end (modeler) of the Mobia Framework are novice users. However, as they mature and become semi-skilled users, there should be a way to address their growing needs. More research has to be done in terms of adapting the tool to accommodate this change in expertise.

- **Experience Report.** Getting feedback from the target users/domain experts with regards to the practicality of using the tool for their respective fields is another important thing that needs to be done in the future.

- **Verification and Validation of Generated Artifacts.** Testing and verification of the models generated by the Mobia Modeler and the code generated by the Mobia Processor still needs to be done.

REFERENCES

1. F. Balagtas-Fernandez and H. Hussmann. Applying domain-specific modeling to mobile health monitoring applications. *Information Technology: New Generations, Third International Conference on*, pages 1682–1683, 2009.

2. F. Balagtas-Fernandez and H. Hussmann. Evaluation of user-interfaces for mobile application development environments. In *Human-Computer Interaction. New Trends*, volume 5610/2009, pages 204–213. Springer Berlin/Heidelberg, 2009.

3. F. Buttussi and L. Chittaro. Mopet: A context-aware and user-adaptive wearable system for fitness training. *Artif. Intell. Med.*, 42(2):153–163, 2008.

4. L. F. Friedrich, J. Stankovic, M. Humphrey, M. Marley, and J. Haskins. A survey of configurable, component-based operating systems for embedded applications. *IEEE Micro*, 21(3):54–68, 2001.

5. P. Holleis and A. Schmidt. Makeit: Integrate user interaction times in the design process of mobile applications. In *Pervasive '08: Proceedings of the 6th International Conference on Pervasive Computing*, pages 56–74, Berlin, Heidelberg, 2008. Springer-Verlag.

6. P. Leijdekkers and V. Gay. Personal heart monitoring and rehabilitation system using smart phones. In *ICMB '06: Proceedings of the International Conference on Mobile Business*, page 29, Washington, DC, USA, 2006. IEEE Computer Society.

7. J. Lin, J. Wong, J. Nichols, A. Cypher, and T. A. Lau. End-user programming of mashups with vegemite. In *IUI '09: Proceedings of the 13th international conference on Intelligent user interfaces*, pages 97–106, New York, NY, USA, 2009. ACM.

8. N. Oliver and F. Flores-Mangas. Healthgear: A real-time wearable system for monitoring and analyzing physiological signals. In *BSN '06: Proceedings of the International Workshop on Wearable and Implantable Body Sensor Networks*, pages 61–64, Washington, DC, USA, 2006. IEEE Computer Society.

9. A. Puerta and M. Hu. Ui fin: a process-oriented interface design tool. In *IUI '09: Proceedings of the 13th international conference on Intelligent user interfaces*, pages 345–354, New York, NY, USA, 2009. ACM.

10. R. van Herk, J. Verhaegh, and W. F. Fontijn. Espranto sdk: an adaptive programming environment for tangible applications. In *CHI '09: Proceedings of the 27th international conference on Human factors in computing systems*, pages 849–858, New York, NY, USA, 2009. ACM.

11. M. Q. Wang Baldonado, A. Woodruff, and A. Kuchinsky. Guidelines for using multiple views in information visualization. In *AVI '00: Proceedings of the working conference on Advanced visual interfaces*, pages 110–119, New York, NY, USA, 2000. ACM.

Activity Interface for Physical Activity Motivating Games

Shlomo Berkovsky, Mac Coombe
CSIRO Tasmanian ICT Centre,
Hobart, Australia
firstname.lastname@csiro.au

Richard Helmer
CSIRO Material Science and Engineering
Geelong, Australia
firstname.lastname@csiro.au

ABSTRACT

Contemporary lifestyle is becoming increasingly sedentary with no or little physical activity. We propose a novel design for physical activity motivating games that leverages engagement with games in order to motivate users to perform physical activity as part of traditionally sedentary playing. This paper focuses on the wearable activity interface for physical activity motivating games. We discuss the activity interface design considerations, present physical activity processing details, and analyse some observations of user interaction with the activity interface.

Author Keywords

Serious games, wearable interface, physical activity.

ACM Classification Keywords

H.5.2: User Interfaces, Interaction Styles, I.2.1: Applications and Expert Systems, Games.

General Terms

Design, experimentation, human factors.

INTRODUCTION

According to the World Health Organization, obesity affects over 1.6 billion adults worldwide [5]. One of the reasons for this phenomenon is an increasingly inactive contemporary lifestyle: low amounts of physical activity (sports, exercises) and high amounts of sedentary activity (TV, computer). Since the nature of the sedentary activity is often addictive and self-reinforcing, improving lifestyle by increasing the amount of physical and decreasing the amount of sedentary activity cannot be achieved easily.

Our research of physical activity motivating games presents a novel approach aimed at combating this problem. The activity motivating games leverage engagement of users with games to motivate them to perform physical activity as part of the sedentary playing [1] by adapting the game design such that users gain virtual game related rewards in return for real physical activity they perform. The motivation to perform physical activity is achieved by

modifying the following components of the game and aspects of user interaction with the game:

- *Game motivator*. Users are made aware of the possibility of gaining rewards in return for performing physical activity. Also, the game is modified, such that certain game functionalities are reinforced by the rewards.
- *Activity interface*. Users are provided with an external interface capturing their physical activity. This activity is processed, and converted into virtual game rewards.

These modifications are intended to motivate users as follows. On one hand, the game is modified such that certain features are disabled/diminished. On the other hand, users are made aware of the possibility to perform physical activity and gain game rewards, i.e., enable/reinforce the disabled/diminished features. A composition of these factors combined with existing engagement with the game motivates users to perform physical activity. When performed, the activity is captured by the activity interface and converted into game rewards that enable/reinforce the features. The rewards are visualised by the game interface, such that users remain in control of the amount and timing of the physical activity performed.

We applied the above modifications to a publicly available Neverball game (www.neverball.org). Neverball consists of multiple levels, in which users navigate a ball through a maze-shaped surface and collect coins (see Figure 1) in a limited time. We adapted Neverball by reducing the time allocated to accomplish the levels and motivated users to perform physical activity by offering time based rewards. When the time was perceived to be insufficient, users could pause the game and perform some physical activity. We developed a wearable accelerometer based activity interface, which was configured to recognise jump events, such that for every jump captured, users gained one additional second to accomplish Neverball levels. We conducted an empirical evaluation, which ascertained that activity motivating games can significantly increase the amount of physical activity performed while playing [1].

This paper focuses design and development of the wearable activity interface. The contributions of this paper are three-fold. Firstly, we discuss the design considerations pertaining to the activity interface. Secondly, we present the technical aspects of the conversion of physical activity into game rewards. Thirdly, we present some observations referring to users interaction with the activity interface.

Figure 1. Neverball user interface.

RELATED WORK

Game technologies involving users' physical activity were developed and disseminated in commercial products, like Dance-Dance Revolution developed by Konami, Wii by Nintendo, and PCGamerBike by 3D-Innovations. Dance-Dance Revolution is a dance pad on which users step to control the game. Wii uses an accelerometer-based device, allowing users to control the game by movement. PCGamerBike is a programmable controller using bicycle pedalling motion to control the game. However, these are commercial products providing bodily interfaces to interact with games rather than motivators of physical activity.

The only practical integration of physical activity into computer games was presented by Fujiki *et. al.* [2]. User's physical activity captured by an accelerometer was visualised using a simple race-like game interface. The amount of activity affected the speed of the game character, its standing comparing to others, and the facial expression of the user's avatar. Rather than designing new interfaces and games, physical activity motivating games provide a conceptually new paradigm. If integrated into a variety of existing and future games, it will motivate users to perform physical activity as an integral part of playing [1].

DESIGN AND DEVELOPMENT OF ACTIVITY INTERFACE

There are several factors that need to be considered when designing and developing the wearable activity interface. This section discusses the design considerations and elaborates on the activity processing and conversion details.

Design Considerations

The first consideration refers to the technology used to capture users' physical activity. This can be done using a variety of physical or physiological sensing technologies. For example, consider an accelerometer that measures acceleration, a pedometer that counts steps, or a gyroscope that measures inclination as examples of physical technologies and a heart rate monitor, an ECG reader, or a respiration rate monitor as examples of physiological technologies. To increase accuracy and reliability, activity interfaces can combine several technologies. The selection of the technology determines both the type of activity users perform and location where the activity is measured.

The second consideration refers to the position of the activity interface on the body. In most sensing technologies (mainly physical), the location impacts the accuracy of the

activity data. For example, an accelerometer based activity interfaces should be positioned as close as possible to the user's centre of mass to accurately capture the activity.

The third set of considerations refers to the characteristics of the activity interface, which are as follows:

- *Unobtrusive.* Data transfer from the activity interface to the game should be independent of the user. That is, activity data should not be manually fed in, but rather uploaded automatically upon capture.
- *Wireless.* Users should not be physically connected to the computer on which the game runs, as to not restrict their motion. As such, a wireless transmission of the activity data should be used.
- *Instantaneous.* Activity data should be transferred in real time, i.e., immediately or as soon the connection between the activity interface and the game is established.
- *Compact and wearable.* The activity monitor itself should be compact and lightweight, so as not to interfere with a users' motion. Also, it should be wearable or alternatively attachable to a users' garment.

Activity Monitoring Device

We considered several commercial products when deciding which activity monitors to use. The GT3X developed by Actigraph is an accelerometer based pedometer that requires a cable connection for data upload, thus, restricting users' motion. ForeRunner by Garmin is a wireless exercise monitor that requires users to press a button for data upload, thus, being obtrusive. Pi-Node by Philips is an accurate accelerometer, gyroscope, and magnetometer based motion detector supporting immediate wireless data upload. However, it requires applying complex signal processing techniques and price wise cannot be integrated with physical activity motivating games.

To comply with the design considerations, we use an in-house developed tri-axial accelerometer to capture user's physical activity [3]. The accelerometer is compact (*42x42x10* millimetres) and lightweight (*15* grams). It can be clipped to an elastic band and attached to a user's waist. This way, the activity interface can be easily attached to any garment, does not interfere much with a user's motion, and can be positioned closely to the centre of mass. The three dimensional acceleration signals are wirelessly transmitted *500* times per second using an RF technology to a USB receiver attached to the computer. Figure 2a shows the elastic band, accelerometer, and USB receiver compared to a standard-size magnetic card. Figure 2b shows the activity monitor attached to the user's waist.

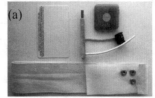

Figure 2. Wearable accelerometer unit used as activity interface: (a) system, (b) on subject.

Physical Activity Data Processing

We process the received acceleration signal to identify users' activity bursts (further referred to as *jumps*). Let us denote by $x(t)$, $y(t)$, and $z(t)$ the three acceleration signals and by X, Y, and Z the respective baseline signals obtained when the accelerometer is still. We approximate the magnitude of the acceleration as follows:

$$AM(t) = [(x(t)-X)^2 + (y(t)-Y)^2 + (z(t)-Z)^2]^{1/2}$$

The acceleration signal can be noisy, as every user's motion is captured. Hence, we use magnitude and time thresholds to identify jumps. If $AM(t)$ exceeds A_{min} for a period of time Δt longer than T_{min}, we identify this as a jump event[1]. The threshold values are calibrated to minimize the number of false positive jumps identified. Figure 3 shows sample acceleration signals captured and respective jump events identified for both low intensity (a) and high intensity (b) activity. The horizontal axis stands for time (in seconds) and vertical for the acceleration.

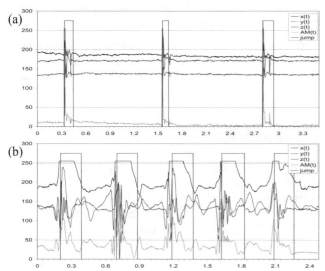

Figure 3. Acceleration processing and jump identification.

Note the differences between low intensity (Figure 3a: *3 jumps in 3.5 seconds*) and high intensity (Figure 3b: *5 jumps in 2.5 seconds*) activities. The high intensity activity signal is considerably noisier and harder to process than the low intensity activity signal. Hence, the values of the A_{min} and T_{min} thresholds need to be calibrated accordingly.

Finally, the identified jumps are converted into virtual rewards in Neverball. We implement a uniform time based reward mechanism, such that for every jump identified by the activity interface, users gain one additional second to accomplish Neverball levels.

USER INTERACTION WITH ACTIVITY INTERFACE

Prior to evaluating the impact of the activity motivating games, we conducted a trial run assessing the accuracy of

---

[1] More accurate signal processing techniques can be applied instead. This one is used as the acceleration approximation.

the activity interface. Two adults and two children were equipped with the activity monitors and requested to jump at various degrees of intensity for the same amount of time. Table 1 presents the number of jumps performed, the number of jumps identified, and the error rate.

	low intensity			high intensity		
	jumps	*counted*	*error*	*jumps*	*counted*	*error*
adults	116	114	1.72%	243	235	3.29%
children	151	148	1.99%	375	362	3.47%

Table 1. Accuracy of activity identification.

As can be seen, activity identification is reasonably accurate both for adults and children at both degrees of intensity. For the low intensity activity, the error rate was less than *2%*. Although the error rate does increase for the high intensity activity, it remains less than *3.5%*. We presume that using state of the art signal processing techniques would further decrease the error rate.

We conducted an experimental evaluation of physical activity motivating games involving *180* users aged *9* to *12* unfamiliar with Neverball. They were divided into two groups: *90* played the normal *sedentary* version of Neverball and *90* played the *active* version of Neverball having the reduced level times. The duration of the playing session in both cases was *20* minutes. Note that the users of both groups used the activity interfaces and were aware of the possibility of gaining one second in return for every jump identified. However, the level times of the *sedentary* users were long enough, such that they had no real motivation to jump.

The results show that activity motivating game increased the amount of activity performed while playing (see Table 2). The *sedentary* group users jumped on average *41.9* times during the playing session, whereas the *active* group users jumped *257.5* times. Similarly, the *sedentary* group users spent on average *95.4%* of time playing and *4.6%* jumping, whereas the *active* group users spent only *76.0%* of time playing and *24.0%* jumping. The differences between the groups were statistically significant.

	sedentary	active
jumps	41.9	257.5
T_{sed}	95.4%	76.0%
T_{act}	4.6%	24.0%

Table 2. Amount of activity performed

In addition to the amount of physical activity performed, it is important to evaluate users' perception of enjoyment of playing the active. No statistically significant difference in the perceived enjoyment of playing (measured on a 6-Likert scale) was observed. Users of the sedentary game reported average enjoyment of *5.52*, whereas users of the active game were very close and reported *5.48*.

The activity interface had a mixed influence on the enjoyment of playing [4]. On one hand, the need to jump interrupted the flow of playing and could have decreased the enjoyment of playing. On the other hand, the activity interface provided users with more control over the game and could have increased the enjoyment. The results might indicate that these factors balanced each other, such that the reported perceived enjoyment did not change considerably.

The post-experiment questionnaire supports this. Users were asked to reflect on the factors that made the playing enjoyable. They were presented with a list of factors and asked to tick those with which they agree. Table 3 shows the number of participants that agreed with two factors of a particular relevance. The first refers to the sedentary playing and the agreement slightly decreases for the *active* group users. The second refers to gaining additional time by jumping and the agreement level increases considerably for the *active* group users. These results indicate that users liked the interaction mode through the activity interface.

I liked to ...	sedentary	active
... control the ball in the maze	65	55
... get more time by jumping	35	60

Table 3. Enjoyment factors.

Another observation refers to the timing of jumping. Figure 4 shows two typical interactions with the activity interface observed for two users playing the same level of Neverball. The horizontal axis stands for the time elapsed from starting the level and vertical for the remaining time. Lines having a negative slope refer to the sedentary playing, whereas lines having a positive slope refer to jumping (the slope depends on the intensity of jumping).

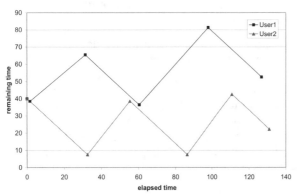

Figure 4. Time-based sedentary/active interaction.

Both users initially had *40* seconds to accomplish the level. The policy of *user1* is referred to as *banking* as the user performs physical activity to gain time in advance of this time being required. We see *user1* jumping after only *1.6* seconds of game play to gain *27* seconds of game time. The second jumping occurs *29.0* seconds later when *user1* still has *36.4* seconds to spare. Then, *user1* gains additional *45* seconds of game playing. Finally, *user1* plays for *28.9* seconds and accomplishes the level at elapsed time of *126.8* seconds still having *52.5* seconds to spare.

The behaviour of *user2* differs considerably as is referred to as an *as needed* policy, since users jump to gain additional time only when the time remaining is low. We see *user2* playing the game for *32.5* seconds until only *7.5* seconds

remain. At this point *user2* jumped to gain additional *31* seconds of game playing before continuing to play with *38.5* seconds to spare. Then, *user2* continued to play until only *7.5* seconds remain before jumping again to gain *35* seconds. Finally, *user2* accomplished the level at elapsed time of *131.1* seconds still having *22.2* seconds to spare.

Comparison between the users shows that *user1* banked the time and jumped even though they had around *40* seconds remaining. Conversely, *user2* exhausted the time and jumped only when *7* seconds remained. Interestingly, the vast majority of users preferred the *as needed* policy and jumped when the remaining time was under *10* seconds.

CONCLUSION AND FUTURE RESEARCH

In this work we present the wearable activity interface for physical activity motivating games. An accelerometer based interface was used to convert the captured user jumps into additional time in Neverball. The evaluation showed that users performed significantly more physical activity and did not report a decrease in the perceived enjoyment of playing the activity motivating version of Neverball.

In the future, we will combine physical and physiological sensing technologies to increase the accuracy of the activity monitor. Also, we will investigate the use of wearable activity interfaces, which will allow users to control the game simultaneously while performing physical activity.

ACKNOWLEDGMENTS

This research is jointly funded by the Australian Government through the Intelligent Island Program and CSIRO. The Intelligent Island Program is administered by the Tasmanian Department of Economic Development, Tourism, and the Arts. We would like to thank Dipak Bhandari and Greg Smith for their help with the development of the activity interface. Special thanks to Robert Kooima and the developers of Neverball.

REFERENCES

1. Berkovsky, S., Freyne, J., Coombe, M., Bhandari, D., Baghaei, N.: Physical Activity Motivating Games: You Can *PLAY, MATE!, Proc. of OZCHI*, Melbourne, 2009.

2. Fujiki, Y., Kazakos, K., Puri, C., Buddharaju, P., Pavlidis, I., Levine, J.: NEAT-o-Games: Blending Physical Activity and Fun in the Daily Routine. *ACM Computers in Entertainment*, vol.6(2), 2008.

3. Helmer, R.J.N., Mestrovic, M.A., Farrow, D., Lucas, S., Spratford, W.: Smart Textiles: Position and Motion Sensing for Sport, Entertainment and Rehabilitation, *Advances in Science and Technology*, vol.60, 2008.

4. Sweetser, P. Wyeth, P.: GameFlow: a Model for Evaluating Player Enjoyment in Games. *ACM Computers in Entertainment*, vol.3(3), 2005.

5. World Health Organization, Obesity and Overweight: Chronic Disease Information Sheet, http://www.who.int/mediacentre/factsheets/fs311/.

Evaluating the Design of Inclusive Interfaces by Simulation

Pradipta Biswas
Computer Laboratory
15 JJ Thomson Avenue
Cambridge CB3 0FD
University of Cambridge, UK
E-mail: pb400@cam.ac.uk

Peter Robinson
Computer Laboratory
15 JJ Thomson Avenue
Cambridge CB3 0FD
University of Cambridge, UK
E-mail: pr10@cam.ac.uk

ABSTRACT

We have developed a simulator to help with the design and evaluation of assistive interfaces. The simulator can predict possible interaction patterns when undertaking a task using a variety of input devices, and estimate the time to complete the task in the presence of different disabilities. In this paper, we have presented a study to evaluate the simulator by considering a representative application being used by able-bodied, visually impaired and mobility impaired people. The simulator predicted task completion times for all three groups with statistically significant accuracy. The simulator also predicted the effects of different interface designs on task completion time accurately.

Categories and Subject Descriptors

D.2.2 [Software Engineering]: Design Tools and Techniques – *user interfaces;* **K.4.2 [Computers and Society]:** Social Issues – *assistive technologies for persons with disabilities*

General Terms

Algorithms, Experimentation, Human Factors, Measurement

Keywords

Human Computer Interaction, Assistive Technology, User Model, Usability Evaluation, Simulator.

1. INTRODUCTION

We have taken a novel approach to designing and evaluating inclusive systems by modelling performance of users with a wide range of abilities. We have developed a simulator that can predict possible interaction patterns when undertaking a task using a variety of input devices, and estimate the time to complete the task in the presence of different disabilities and for different levels of skill [1, 2,

3]. In this paper, we demonstrate its use in evaluating interfaces for an application used by able-bodied, visually impaired and mobility impaired people.

2. THE STUDY

In graphical user interfaces, searching and pointing constitute a significant portion of human computer interaction. Users search for many different artifacts like information in a web page, button with a particular caption in an application, email from a list of mails etc. We can broadly classify searching in two categories.

Text searching includes any search which only involves searching for text and not any other visual artifact. Examples include menu searching, keyword searching in a document, mailbox searching and so on.

Icon Searching includes searching for a visual artifact (such as an icon or a button) along with text search for its caption. The search is mainly guided by the visual artifact and the text is generally used to confirm the target.

We present a study involving an icon searching task. We simulated the task using our simulator and evaluated the predictive power of the model by comparing actual with prediction.

2.1. Experimental design

We conducted trials with two families of icons. The first consisted of geometric shapes with colours spanning a wide range of hues and luminance (Figure 1). The second consisted of images from the system folder in Microsoft Windows to increase the external validity (Figure 2) of the experiment. Each icon bears a caption underneath. The first two letters and length of all the captions were kept same to avoid any pop-out effect of the captions during visual search.

The experiment was a mixed design with two measures and a between-subject factor. The within-subject measures were spacing between icons and font size of captions. We used the following three levels for each measure

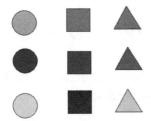

Figure 1. Corpus of Shapes

Figure 2. Corpus of Icons

- Spacing between icons
  - Sparse: 180 pixels horizontally, 230 pixels vertically. This was the maximum separation possible in the screen.
  - Medium: 150 pixels horizontally, 200 pixels vertically.
  - Dense: 120 pixels horizontally, 170 pixels vertically. This was the minimum possible separation without overlapping the icons.
- Font size
  - Small: 10 point.
  - Medium: 14 point as recommended by the RNIB [5].
  - Large: 20 point.

The between-subjects factor is

- Group
  - Able bodied
  - Visually impaired
  - Motor impaired

Each participant undertook 8 trials for each combination of the within-subject measures. The sequence of the trials was randomized using a Latin-square.

2.2. Material
We used a 1280 × 800 LCD colour display driven by a 1.7 GHz Pentium 4 PC running the Microsoft Windows XP operating system. We also used a standard computer Mouse (Microsoft IntelliMouse® Optical Mouse) for clicking on the target.

2.3. Process
The experimental task consisted of shape searching and icon searching tasks. The task was as follows:

1. A particular target (shape or icon with a caption) was shown.

2. A set of 18 candidates for matching was shown.

3. Participants were asked to click on the candidate which was same as the target both in terms of icon and caption.

Each participant did 72 searching and pointing tasks in total. They were trained for the task before start of the actual trial. However one of the participants (P4) retired after undertaking 40 trials.

2.4. Participants
We collected data from 2 able bodied, 2 visually impaired and 3 motor-impaired participants (Table 1). All were expert computer users and used computers more than once a week.

2.5. Simulation
Initially we analyzed the task in light of our cognitive model [1]. Since the users undertook preliminary training, we considered them as expert users. We followed the GOMS analysis technique and identified two sub-tasks

1. Searching for the target.
2. Pointing and clicking on the target.

So the predicted task completion time is obtained by sequentially running the perception model [2] and the motor-behaviour model [3]. The predicted task completion time is the summation of the visual search time (output by the perception model) and the pointing time (output by the motor-behaviour model).

2.6. Results
Figure 3 shows the correlation between actual and predicted task completion times. We also calculated the relative error $\frac{Predicted - Actual}{Actual}$ and show its distribution in Figure 4. The superimposed curve shows a normal distribution with same mean and standard deviation as the relative error.

We found that the correlation is $\rho = 0.7$ ($p < 0.001$) and 56% of the trials have a relative error within ± 40%. The average relative error is + 16% with a standard deviation of 54%. The model did not work for 10% of the trials and the relative error is more than 100% in those cases. For the remaining 90% of the trials the average relative error is + 6% with a standard deviation of 42%.

We also analyzed the effects of font size and icon spacing on the task completion time and investigated whether the prediction reflects these effects as well. So we conducted two 3 × 3 ANOVA (*Spacing × Font × Group*) on the actual and predicted task completion times respectively. We investigated both the within subject effects and results of a multivariate test. In the ANOVAs, we did not consider the trials for which the relative error was more than 100% as the model did not work for those trials. Participant P4 did not also complete the trial, leaving us with 40 rows of data ($N = 40$).

Table 1. List of Participants

	Age	Sex	Impairment
C1	27	M	Able-bodied
C2	30	M	
P1	27	M	Myopia (-4.5 Dioptre)
P2	26	M	Myopia (-5.5 Dioptre)
P3	30	M	Hypokinetic motor impairment resulted from Cerebral Palsy, restricted hand movement, wheelchair user
P4	42	M	Cerebral Palsy, restricted hand movement, also suffering tremor in hand, wheelchair user
P5	45	M	Hyperkinetic motor-impairment resulted from stroke, significant tremor in fingers, wheelchair user

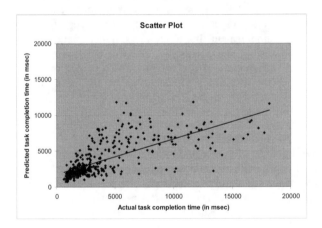

Figure 3. Scatter plot between actual and prediction

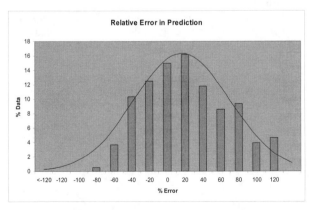

Figure 4. Relative error in prediction

For calculating the within subject effects, the Greenhouse-Geisser correction was used if the Mauchy's test detected violation from sphericity assumption [4] giving fractional values for the degrees of freedom. In this study, the main effect of *Spacing* did not violate sphericity assumption ($W = .854$, $\chi^2 = 5.69$ in actual, $W = .99$, $\chi^2 = 0.374$ in prediction, $p > 0.05$), while the main effect of *Font* ($W = .825$, $\chi^2 = 6.935$ in actual, $W = .836$, $\chi^2 = 6.429$ in prediction, $p < 0.05$) and the interaction effect of *Spacing and Font* ($W = .244$, $\chi^2 = 49.939$ in actual, $W = .539$, $\chi^2 = 21.913$ in prediction, $p < 0.05$) violated sphericity assumption. We have found the following significant effects on both actual and predicted task completion time

- A main effect of *Spacing* ($F_{(2, 74)} = 5.44$, $p < 0.05$) on actual task completion time.
- A main effect of *Spacing* $F_{(2, 74)} = 6.95$, $p < 0.05$) in predicted task completion time.
- An interaction effect of *Spacing and Group* ($F_{(4, 74)} = 3.15$, $p < 0.05$) on actual task completion time.
- An interaction effect of *Spacing and Group* $F_{(4, 74)} = 4.64$, $p < 0.05$) on predicted task completion time.
- An interaction effect of *Font and Group* ($F_{(3.4, 62.97)} = 5.02$, $p < 0.05$) on actual task completion time.
- An interaction effect of *Font and Group* $F_{(3.44, 63.6)} = 3.75$, $p < 0.05$) on predicted task completion time.

The main effect of *Font* and interaction effects between *Font and Group* and *Spacing, Font and Group* do not have significant effects on both actual and predicted task completion times. Figure 5 shows that the effect sizes (η^2) are also fairly similar in the prediction as in the actual. This suggests that the simulator successfully explained the variance in task completion time for different factors. We confirm these effects through a multivariate test (Figure 6), which is not affected by the sphericity assumption. The maximum difference is below 10% in within-subject test and below 20% in multivariate test. As these factors include both interface parameters and physical characteristics of users, we can infer that the simulator has successfully explained the effects of different interface layouts on task completion time for people with visual and motor impairment. Figures 7 and 8 show the effects of font size and spacing for different user groups. In Figures 7 and 8, the points depict the average task completion time and the bars show the standard error at a 95% confidence level. It can be seen from Figures 7 and 8 that the prediction is in line with the actual task completion times for different font sizes and icon spacing.

However the prediction is less accurate in one of the nine conditions - the medium font size and medium spacing for the motor impaired users. We found that, in these cases the model underestimates the task completion times and also fails to capture the variability in task completion times.

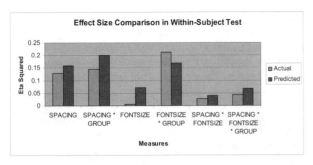

Figure 5. Effect size comparison in ANOVA

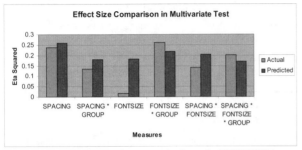

Figure 6. Effect size comparison in MANOVA

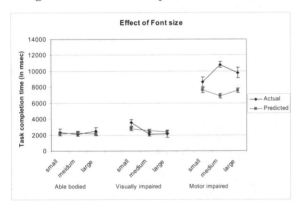

Figure 7. Effect of font size in different user groups

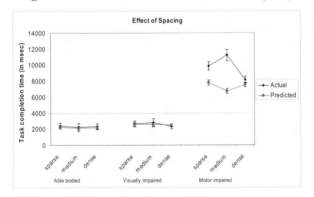

Figure 8. Effect of spacing in different user groups

2.7. Discussion

We have developed a simulator to help with the design and evaluation of assistive interfaces. Choosing a particular interface from a set of alternatives is a significant task for both design and evaluation. In this study, we consid-

ered a representative task and the results showed that the effects of both factors (separation between icons and font size) were the same in the prediction as for actual trials with different user groups. The prediction from the simulator can be reliably used to capture the main effects of different design alternatives for people with a wide range of abilities.

However the model did not work accurately for about 30% of the trials where the relative error is more than 50%. These trials also accounted for an increase in the average relative error from zero to 16%. In particular, the predicted variance in task completion times for motor impaired users was smaller than the actual variance. This can be attributed to many factors; the most important ones are as follows.

- **Effect of usage time - fatigue and learning effects:** The trial continued for about 15 to 20 minutes. A few participants (especially one user in the motor-impaired group) felt fatigue. On the other hand, some users worked more quickly as the trial proceeded. The model did not consider these effects of fatigue and learning. In future we plan to incorporate the usage time into the input parameters of the model.

- **User characteristics**: The variance in the task completion time can be attributed to various factors such as expertise, usage time, type of motor-impairment (hypokinetic vs. hyperkinetic), interest of the participant etc. Currently, the model characterizes the extent of motor-impairment of the user only by measuring the grip strength [3], in future more input parameters may be considered.

3. CONCLUSIONS

We have developed a simulator to help in designing and evaluating inclusive interfaces. We have demonstrated the use of the simulator for a representative task of evaluating an interface layout. The simulator predicted the task completion time with statistically significant accuracy for people with a wide range of abilities.

References

[1] Biswas P. and Robinson P., Automatic Evaluation of Assistive Interfaces, Proceedings of the ACM International Conference on Intelligent User Interfaces (IUI) 2008, pp. 247-256

[2] Biswas P. and Robinson P., Modelling Perception using Image Processing Algorithms, 23rd British Computer Society Conference on Human-Computer Interaction (HCI 09)

[3] Biswas P. and Robinson P., Predicting pointing time from hand strength, In proceedings of Usability and HCI for e-Inclusion, (USAB 2009) LNCS 5889, pp. 428-447

[4] Field A. "Discovering Statistics Using SPSS." SAGE Publications Ltd., 2009.

[5] See it Right, RNIB 2006

Temporal Task Footprinting: Identifying Routine Tasks by Their Temporal Patterns

Oliver Brdiczka
Palo Alto Research Center (PARC)
3333 Coyote Hill Rd, Palo Alto, USA
brdiczka@parc.com

Norman Makoto Su
Department of Informatics
University of California Irvine, USA
normsu@ics.uci.edu

James "Bo" Begole
Palo Alto Research Center (PARC)
3333 Coyote Hill Rd, Palo Alto, USA
begole@parc.com

ABSTRACT

This paper introduces a new representation for describing routine tasks, called *temporal task footprints*. Routines are characterized by their temporal regularity or rhythm. Temporal pattern analysis (T-patterns) can be used to isolate frequent recurrent patterns in routine tasks that appear repeatedly in the same temporal configuration. Using tf-idf statistics, each task can then be defined in terms of its temporal task footprint, a ranked list of temporal patterns along with their typical frequencies. Experimental evaluations using data of 29 days observing and logging 10 subjects showed that temporal task footprints of application windows, email and document usage outperform decision tree and SVMs in recognizing the subjects' tasks.

Categories and Subject Descriptors

H.1.2 User/Machine Systems: Human factors; H.5.2 User Interfaces: Theory and methods

General Terms

Algorithms, Experimentation, Human Factors, Measurement.

Keywords

T-patterns, Temporal patterns, routine task representation, task footprint.

1. INTRODUCTION

Knowledge workers are often involved in multiple tasks that they do on a regular basis and between which they need to switch frequently [9]. As a consequence, task management, maintenance of task context and recovery from interruptions become important problems that a knowledge worker needs to face on a daily basis. User interfaces and systems for managing tasks (e.g., [5]) have been proposed recently to address some of these issues. However, little work has been done on representing the regularity of tasks themselves, i.e. addressing what is commonly designated as "routine" work and its representation as well as automatic recognition.

This paper introduces *temporal task footprints*, a new representation for characterizing routine tasks by incorporating structural time information. A routine task refers to a recurrent activity that is composed of a set of actions to accomplish a job, problem or assignment. Temporal task footprints are not only a good means for recognizing and distinguishing different routine tasks, but can also serve as a *human understandable* representation of tasks for

constructing and sharing workflow knowledge in a company. The temporal task footprints constructed and evaluated in this paper are based on temporal patterns from application and document usage as well as from communication with co-workers.

Routines as a unit of analysis have been examined from an organizational perspective. Feldman and Pentland [6] state the "standard" definition of organizational routines as "repetition, a recognizable pattern of action, multiple participants, and interdependent actions." Routines are repeated over time, seem to be a collection of activities one can categorize, involve multiple people, and are situated in the context created by one's self and other people.

The temporal regularity (its rhythm) of routines, and how awareness of such rhythms can facilitate work has been analyzed in HCI and CSCW research. Begole et al. [1] point out that work patterns differ across time, location, and day of week. By examining past, recurring work rhythms, one can predict future presence based on current events. One can guess, for example, the amount of time needed for a certain individual to prepare and leave for an appointment, prepare for meetings, commute to work, return from lunch and other patterns not captured in an individual's online schedule.

Reddy and Dourish [12] conducted ethnography at a hospital to examine how people use work rhythms to accomplish information seeking. For example, rhythms can provide valuable information between nurses and doctors. The regular rotation of doctors at intervals allows nurses to simply wait, rather than waste resources and time when he or she needs to seek a physician. Finally, specific usage of certain media such as email [3] have been observed to have rhythms (e.g., at the beginning of the day). However, the analyses that have examined the temporal aspects of routines have not addressed *how this temporal information can be used to describe and detect routine tasks*.

Much work has been done in academia concerning automatic task prediction using machine learning methods. The TaskTracer system [5] that has been built within the DARPA CALO project employed task prediction approaches that focus on the selection of different features that are observed and discriminative for each task. After feature selection, tasks are predicted using, for example, a hybrid approach of a naïve Bayesian classifier and support vector machines [14]. Even though recent approaches also focus on the discovery of work procedures or routines [15], the *temporal* information, such as significant duration between task steps that is characteristic for routine tasks, is not considered.

The Microsoft SWISH system [10] constructs a model of a user's tasks based on tf-idf filtered terms in the title of application windows and the windows switching history. A number of clusters of these filtered terms are isolated, corresponding to the user's tasks. This cluster representation is then used for recognition. Again, no duration information between windows is used to characterize a task; windows switching analysis is purely based on building a connected graph from the *sequence* of switches (within a predefined time window T). We believe, however, that duration information is crucial when characterizing routine tasks because these tasks are precisely characterized by their temporal regularity and structure.

This paper intends to build a new task representation that is based on a distribution of temporal patterns characterizing a (routine) task. The employed temporal pattern analysis (T-patterns) is used to isolate frequent recurrent patterns in tasks that appear repeatedly in the same temporal configuration; in other words, the duration between each step remains relatively constant. The tf-idf [13] values of the resulting T-patterns with respect to the routine tasks allows for generating a ranked list of relevant patterns for each task, the temporal task footprint.

The remainder of our paper is structured as follows. First, we briefly introduce the temporal pattern detection (T-pattern analysis) as well as its parameters and outcomes. Based on the detected temporal patterns, the temporal task footprint is defined. Following that, the paper describes the collected data set and the experimental evaluation which has been conducted. A conclusion section sums up this paper.

2. TEMPORAL PATTERN DETECTION

We assume that routine tasks can be characterized by specific recurrent actions that are executed within nearly constant time intervals. In order to detect such patterns, we use a probabilistic temporal pattern detection method, called T-pattern detection [8]. The T-pattern detection algorithm identifies highly significant, hierarchically arranged temporal patterns that are composed of statistically related events that repeatedly appear in the same, relatively invariant, sequence and temporal distance.

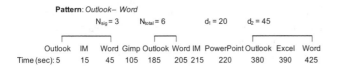

Fig. 1. T-pattern analysis detecting a pattern of the applications Microsoft Word following Microsoft Outlook from 20 to 45 sec.

T-patterns provide significant advantages over traditional sequence analyses by incorporating temporal distance. Indeed, traditional sequential pattern mining techniques [7] or compression-based algorithms (e.g., Lempel-Ziv-Welch) can discover sequential pattern. However, these methods do not take into account the temporal distance among elements of the patterns since the time delays are not modeled. Markov models [11] are not suitable for this problem either, as the first order Markovian assumption does not hold because patterns are constructed as long ($n > 2$) sequences. In addition, Markov model have problems handling patterns that have very long time intervals.

Our implementation of the T-pattern detection algorithm is based on the description by Magnusson [8]. The algorithm identifies a number of T-patterns (N_{sig}) that are significant per task. In addition, the significant minimal and maximal temporal length (d_1 and d_2) for each T-pattern is reported, that is, if A is an earlier component and B is a later component of the same recurring T-pattern, then, after an occurrence of A at t, there is an interval [t + d_1; t + d_2] ($d_2 > d_1 > 0$) that contains at least one occurrence of B. Fig. 1 shows an example

where the use of desktop applications (Outlook, Word, IM, Gimp, etc.) forms the input events. In this example, the T-pattern Outlook-Word is found to have three significant occurrences ($N_{sig} = 3$), marked in the figure with intervals ranging from 20 to 45 seconds. There are additional occurrences of the pattern Outlook-Word (e.g. Outlook at 5 and Word at 205 seconds), but these have not been detected to be significantly recurring. The number of significant occurrences ($N_{sig} = 3$) is a subset of all occurrences ($N_{total} = 6$) of the pattern Outlook-Word.

The T-pattern algorithm can be run on a wide range of time stamped events. In general, these are actions that are executed by a human and reflect his or her behavior in time. In the remainder of this paper, we will focus on PC usage events, i.e. events coming from application windows, window positions, document usage, and email (sender, recipients).

3. TEMPORAL TASK FOOTPRINT

By running the T-pattern analysis on one or several event traces that can be observed when a user works on a routine task, we can extract a number of significant patterns for this task. Table 1 shows a list of such patterns from PC application usage for the task "Expense Reporting." The table reports the pattern, its significance value, number of occurrences (N_{sig}), and minimal as well as maximal intervals (d_1, d_2 in ms).

Pattern	Significance	N_{sig}	d_1	d_2
FIREFOX.EXE – MsgBox – EXCEL.EXE	3.495e-08	3	1985	16812
ACROBAT.EXE – OUTLOOK.EXE – ClipBoardChange	2.666e-07	2	874	3110
OUTLOOK.EXE – ClipBoardChange – WORD.EXE	1.332e-08	4	1709	13858

Table 1. List (excerpt) of significant T-patterns extracted for routine task "Expense Reporting"

The goal of the temporal task footprint is to represent the routine task by incorporating its temporal structure (i.e. its T-patterns) and to make it easily distinguishable from other similar routine tasks.

A basic representation of a routine task could consist of the raw frequencies of occurrence of its significant event patterns. However, this representation has the disadvantage that commonly occurring patterns may unnecessarily make all tasks look similar because their frequencies outweigh those that are characteristic for a particular routine task. To address this problem, we can make use of the term frequency-inverse document frequency measure *tf-idf* [13]. The tf-idf measure is a weight often used in information retrieval and text mining used to evaluate how important a word is to a document in a collection or corpus of documents. The importance increases proportionally to the number of times a word appears in the document but is offset by the frequency of the word in the corpus (e.g., "the" is weighted less than "proposal" in the corpus). In order to adapt tf-idf to our problem, we replace terms by pattern frequencies and document by task frequencies. Thus,

$$tf_{p,T} = \frac{n_{p,T}}{\sum_k n_{k,T}}$$ refers to the normalized occurrence

frequencies of pattern p in task T, while the idf measure for a pattern

p is given by $idf_p = \log \dfrac{|T|}{(|T_p| + 1)}$, where $|T|$ is the total

number of tasks and $|T_p|$ the number of tasks where the pattern p has been observed. The tf-idf measure for a pattern p and task T is defined as: $tfidf_{p,T} = tf_{p,T} * idf_p$. Intuitively, tf-idf scales down commonly occurring patterns and scales up patterns which rarely occur in tasks and therefore are *distinctive* for a task.

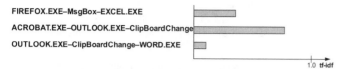

FIREFOX.EXE–MsgBox–EXCEL.EXE

ACROBAT.EXE–OUTLOOK.EXE–ClipBoardChange

OUTLOOK.EXE–ClipBoardChange–WORD.EXE

1.0 tf-idf

Fig. 2. Temporal task footprint for the task "Expense Reporting."

A temporal footprint for a task T is finally defined as a list of temporal patterns p that are weighted by their tf-idf values $tfidf_{p,T}$. Fig. 2 shows an example task footprint for the data from Table 1. Even though the second pattern has the lowest occurrence frequency in the task, it has the highest tf-idf value because it seems to be unique to this task and has not been seen with any other task.

Given a collection of tasks represented by their temporal task footprints, a new candidate task C that has been observed can be recognized/assigned to a task in the collection by evaluating $\arg\max_i [tfidf\_score(C,T_i)]$, where T_i refers to the routine footprints in the collection. The *tfidf_score* is defined by

$$tfidf\_score(C,T_i) = \sum_{p=1}^{N} (tfidf_{p,T_i} \cdot \delta_{p,C}) \text{ where } \quad N$$

refers to the numbers of patterns in the task collection footprint T_i. $\delta_{p,C}$ is 1 if pattern j has been seen in candidate task C and 0 otherwise. The basic idea here is to add up the $tfidf_{p,T_i}$ values only for those patterns p that are shared by T_i and the candidate task C. Finally, the routine task footprint with the highest *tfidf_score* provides the label for the new observed candidate task. In sum, we have adapted tf-idf from measuring the importance of a word in a document, to measuring the importance of a T-pattern (e.g., a temporal pattern of application usage) in a task.

4. EXPERIMENTAL EVALUATION

4.1 Data set

Data was collected in situ by human observation and computer logging of 10 employees working at a research and development company. The human observation allowed us to establish the correct task labels for our time-stamped computer logging data. Table 2 shows the distribution of the informants and their different functions in the company. All but one informant (who was observed for only two whole days due to scheduling constraints) were observed for three whole work days. The observed days were not contiguous; each was separated by a period of one week to one month. The days were selected to contain at least one recurring task. However, the selected recurrent tasks only constituted a small subset of the complete task set that was observed for each user. The remaining tasks could recur during all days of observation (but we did not influence their recurrence in any way). The observer would meet the informant upon their arrival to work and follow the informant as closely as possible until the end of the business day. Using a paper notepad with an electronic LiveScribe pen (www.livescribe.com), the observer would record and label, to the second, user tasks and their start/end times (e.g., 8:15:32am start "Expense Reporting"). A total of 572 different tasks have been observed and labeled, most of which were not been shared across informants. Prior to and during

the observation, logging software was installed on each participant's PC to record application usage.

Accounting Staff	3
IT Staff	2
Library Service Staff	2
Intellectual Property Staff	1
Lab Administration	1
Researcher	1

Table 2. Distribution of informants within the company

The application usage record included: application window, application window position, active document and email sender-recipient. Application window refers to the current application (e.g. EXCEL.EXE) and the current window information (e.g. ConsoleWindow or MessageBox or InternetExplorerPanel1). Note that one normally has several window classes per application; this provides a higher granularity observation of the user's actions. The positions of the application windows (x, y, width, height) were discretized using EM clustering [2]. The cluster numbers of the current application window positions are the input events for the T-pattern analysis. Active document refers to the document that the user is currently working on. Email sender and recipient refer to the event when the user receives, sends or selects an email. Sender and recipient ID of this email are then the input events of the T-pattern analysis.

4.2 Evaluation

The aim of this evaluation was to show that the temporal duration information incorporated in T-patterns and subsequently in temporal task footprints is beneficial for task recognition. Therefore, temporal task footprints have been constructed for the collected data set and compared to the recognition performance of state-of-the-art machine learning algorithms that utilize non-temporal features when recognizing tasks. T-pattern analysis was conducted separately for each task using the data fields of the logging data trace.

We conducted a 3 fold cross-validation, taking one third of a participant's data (= 1 day) for training/constructing the task footprints and two thirds (= 2 days) for testing. In addition to our temporal task footprints, decision trees (J48 [16]) and support vector machines (LibSVM library [4] using radial basis kernel) were employed to learn the task labels from the respective inputs (application window classes, window positions, document usage, email). The obtained classification accuracies are depicted in Table 3. Except for window position patterns, temporal task footprints outperform both decision trees and support vector machines when recognizing the task labels. This is due to the fact that temporal task footprints leverage the temporal information (duration information encoded by the T-patterns) that is not used by J48 and SVMs. This temporal structure information *significantly* improves task recognition except for window positions and sizes. Duration information between different positions and sizes of application windows does not seem to provide much additional information that might improve classification. The best performance for task recognition is obtained when using patterns from document usage. Apparently, sequences of documents and specific durations associated with these are very discriminative between different tasks.

	Temporal Task Footprints	J48	SVM
Application Window Class	51.34%	38.33%	36.93%
Window Positions	26.29%	29.01%	31.44%
Document Usage	63.36%	40.38%	37.38%
Email (sender, recipients)	35.72%	19.21%	24.03%

Table 3. Task recognition accuracies for temporal task footprints, decision trees (J48) and support vector machines (SVM).

The overall low recognition accuracies can be explained by the fact that an ethnographer collected and transcribed the users' tasks in extreme detail. The resulting ground truth therefore contains a large number of task labels and distinguishes tasks at a much lower granularity than most previous work. To illustrate, our data set involved 10 people with 572 different task classes, while TaskTracer [14] used a data set of 8 people with only 107 task classes. Our data set was intended to be very complete and thorough, providing thus some kind of baseline for comparison. We believe that a less fine-grained distinction of tasks (i.e., creating 5-10 routine tasks to be trained and learned per user in a system) will yield better results.

5. CONCLUSION AND FUTURE WORK

This paper introduced a new concept for characterizing routine tasks, called temporal task footprints. Temporal task footprints are based on the assumption that routine tasks are characterized by temporal regularity and repetition of steps that are executed. T-pattern analysis is used to extract these repetitive temporal patterns that are characterized by a relatively constant temporal configuration. The temporal task footprint is further defined by the tf-idf values of the extracted temporal patterns with respect to the corresponding routine tasks. While these footprints can be calculated for a wide variety of tasks and events that are observed, this paper has focused on events from PC usage and routine tasks that haven been executed on PC. Our experimental evaluation involving observation and logging data of 29 days in total from 10 different subjects has shown that temporal task footprints are effective in recognizing routine tasks and outperform standard machine learning methods in this context. This is partly due to the fact that temporal task footprints encode temporal duration information of the observed tasks by incorporating T-patterns. This information is quite discriminative, especially when distinguishing routine tasks that are based on a similar range of events that are observed.

Because temporal task footprints provide a human-readable format for understanding patterns in routine tasks, their utility may go beyond simple task recognition. Temporal task footprints could provide a new way to describe and ultimately share information about routine work. The incorporation of temporal information (T-patterns) in a task representation provides an efficient means to recognize and re-use work routines. Each routine task pattern that is identified may further contain links from its events to related content (e.g., document files or emails). Users can then review their own and their colleagues' patterns, edit and add content (e.g., exchange template files), and execute and re-apply these temporal patterns. In particular, the obtained pattern representations and visualizations can contribute to the re-use of knowledge workflows in a company when training new employees or sharing new work processes with co-workers. By recognizing which routine a user probably engages in, a collection of related patterns can be dynamically recommended. Hence, this pool of temporal task

footprints along with the contained, human-readable, temporal patterns can serve as a data base for defining and sharing workflow information within an organization.

6. REFERENCES

[1] J. B. Begole, J.C. Tang, R. B. Smith, N. Yankelovich. Work rhythms: Analyzing visualizations of awareness histories of distributed groups. In Proc. of CSCW'02, 334–343, 2002.

[2] J. Bilmes, A gentle tutorial of the EM algorithm and its application to parameter estimation for gaussian mixture and hidden Markov models, Technical report TR-97-021, U.C. Berkeley, April 1998.

[3] V. Bellotti, B. Dalal, N. Good, P. Flynn, D. Bobrow, N. Ducheneaut. What a to-do: Studies of task management towards the design of a personal task list manager. In Proc. of CHI'04, 735–742, 2004.

[4] C.C. Chang and C. J. Lin. LIBSVM: a library for support vector machines, 2001. http://www.csie.ntu.edu.tw/~cjlin/libsvm

[5] N. Dragunov, T.G. Dietterich, K. Johnsrude, M. McLaughlin, L. Li, J.L. Herlocker. TaskTracer: a desktop environment to support multi-tasking knowledge workers. In Proc. of IUI '05, 75-82, 2005.

[6] M.S. Feldman, B. T. Pentland. Reconceptualizing organizational routines as a source of flexibility and change. Administrative Science Quarterly 48, 1 (Mar.), 94–118, 2003.

[7] J. Han, H. Cheng, D. Xin, X. Yan. Frequent pattern mining: current status and future directions. In Data Mining and Knowledge Discovery 15:55-86, 2007.

[8] M. S. Magnusson. Discovering hidden time patterns in behavior: T-patterns and their detection. Behavior Research Methods, Instruments, & Computers, 32(1):93–110, 2000.

[9] G. Mark, V.M. Gonzalez, J. Harris. No task left behind?: examining the nature of fragmented work. In Proc. of CHI'05, 321-330, 2005.

[10] N. Oliver, G. Smith, C. Thakkar, A. C. Surendran. SWISH: semantic analysis of window titles and switching history. In Proc. of IUI '06, 194-201, 2006.

[11] L.R. Rabiner. A tutorial on hidden Markov models and selected applications in speech recognition. In Proc. IEEE 2: 257-286, 1989.

[12] M. Reddy, P. Dourish. A finger on the pulse: Temporal rhythms and information seeking in medical work. In Proc. of CSCW'02, 344–353, 2002.

[13] G. Salton, M. McGill (eds). Introduction to Modern Information Retrieval. McGraw-Hill. 1983.

[14] J. Shen, L. Li, T.G. Dietterich, J. L. Herlocker. A hybrid learning system for recognizing user tasks from desk activities and email messages. In Proc. of IUI'06, 86-92, 2006.

[15] J. Shen, E. Fitzhenry, T.G. Dietterich. Discovering frequent work procedures from resource connections. In Proc. of IUI'09, 277-286, 2009.

[16] H. Witten, E. Frank. Data Mining: Practical machine learning tools and techniques, Morgan Kaufmann, San Francisco, 2005. Software available at http://www.cs.waikato.ac.nz/ml/weka/

From Documents to Tasks: Deriving User Tasks from Document Usage Patterns

Oliver Brdiczka

Palo Alto Research Center (PARC)

3333 Coyote Hill Road , Palo Alto, CA, USA

brdiczka@parc.com

ABSTRACT

A typical knowledge worker is involved in multiple tasks and switches frequently between them every work day. These frequent switches become expensive because each task switch requires some recovery time as well as the reconstitution of task context. First task management support systems have been proposed in recent years in order to assist the user during these switches. However, these systems still need a fairly big amount of investment from the user side in order to either learn to use or train such a system. In order to reduce the necessary amount of training, this paper proposes a new approach for automatically estimating a user's tasks from document interactions in an unsupervised manner. While most previous approaches to task detection look at the content of documents or window titles, which might raise confidentiality and privacy issues, our approach only requires document identifiers and the temporal switch history between them as input. Our prototype system monitors a user's desktop activities and logs documents that have focus on the user's desktop by attributing a unique identifier to each of these documents. Retrieved documents are filtered by their dwell times and a document similarity matrix is estimated based on document frequencies and switches. A spectral clustering algorithm then groups documents into tasks using the derived similarity matrix. The described prototype system has been evaluated on user data of 29 days from 10 different subjects in a corporation. Obtained results indicate that the approach is better than previous approaches that use content.

Categories and Subject Descriptors

H.1.2 User/Machine Systems: Human factors; H.5.2 User Interfaces: Theory and methods; I.5 Pattern Recognition: Clustering

General Terms

Algorithms, Experimentation, Measurement.

Keywords

Automatic task identification, document clustering, user task modeling.

1. INTRODUCTION

Work of knowledge workers is characterized by spending short amounts of time in tasks and switching frequently between them [2]. While frequent switches between task contexts lead to long recovery periods and increased stress [5], some dedicated UI and technology

to assist the user in this recovery and switching phases has been proposed in recent years (e.g., [1] or [7]). However, the lack of correctness in the representation of the user's tasks as well as high set-up and maintenance costs in terms of training or learning to use these new systems are still a hurdle for their wide adoption. In this paper, we present a novel approach for constructing a model of a user's tasks without user intervention. The proposed method is based on spectral clustering of document interactions and, in contrast to previous approaches, it does not rely on content of the documents themselves. The correctness of the proposed approach has been evaluated on a large data set of 29 days of desktop work from 10 knowledge workers.

Much research work has focused on automatic task prediction using supervised machine learning. The TaskTracer system [1] which has been built within the DARPA CALO project employed task prediction approaches that focus on the selection of different features that are observed and discriminative for each task. After feature selection, tasks are predicted using a hybrid approach of naïve Bayesian classifier and support vector machines [9]. The used features include windows desktop events, email senders/recipients and window title information. A recent version (TaskTracer2 [10]) includes further features and an improved real-time detection and online learning algorithm. However, these approaches focus on supervised training, i.e. the user needs to invest time to declare his or her current activity during run time and based on given user feedback, a task model and representation is learned and evolved. No a priori model or representation of the user's tasks is acquired from collected observations (without human intervention). An unsupervised approach [8] that uses similar features can detect task switches and is able to identify task boundaries but not the actual tasks themselves.

Rattenbury et al. proposed an automatic task support system, called CAAD [7]. CAAD grouped software artifacts (documents, folders, web pages, people) of a user's interaction contexts into clusters to represent his or her tasks. While CAAD established associations between artifacts and task clusters automatically using an algorithmic approach, it did not focus on the a priori identification of the user's tasks, but rather on the visualization and possible editing of the clusters. Consequently, system evaluations concerned the acceptance of the visualization or approach rather than the accuracy of the task identification.

The Connections system [12] aimed at enhancing search and document retrieval with usage contexts. The idea is to improve content-based search like google desktop by integrating document usage context. Included features are document and file accesses as well as document content. A later system, called Confluence [3], enhances this search by task-based document retrieval. Both systems could show improvements in document search in their evaluations. While these systems do not require any user input concerning his tasks or activities, they do not create a representation of a user's tasks or identify his tasks explicitly.

The Microsoft SWISH system [6] is the most closely related work to ours. SWISH constructs a model of a user's tasks based on tf-idf filtered terms in the title of application windows and windows switching history. A number of clusters of the filtered terms are isolated, corresponding to the user's tasks. Probabilistic Latent Semantic Indexing as well as switching history is used to create a number of clusters corresponding to the user's tasks. While the first SWISH prototype has been evaluated with good results in a lab study, the number of involved users and task was rather small compared to the data set used for evaluation in this paper.

The aim of the approach proposed in this paper is to construct a first representation of the user's tasks based on observed document interactions. The method is completely unsupervised, so no user feedback is necessary. In contrast to previous approaches, the proposed method only leverages document usage information (i.e. switches between documents and document dwell times) and does not intervene with the content of the documents themselves. The extraction and use of content becomes particularly a problem when task representations are shared among co-workers. A user may, for example, not want to share all documents of a task with his subordinates. By using an algorithm that is only based on document identifiers, it is guaranteed that the shared task representation itself will not contain/reveal any sensitive content (e.g., keywords). Links to the actual documents can be included, but will be protected by access right that can be granted or refused. In comparison to most of the previous work, the proposed approach has been applied and evaluated on a big dataset collected from corporate users that were not involved in the research project. The obtained results are promising, outperforming previous content-based approaches.

2. SPECTRAL CLUSTERING OF DOCUMENT INTERACTIONS

The aim of the approach proposed in this paper is to provide a means to discover and re-construct a user's tasks from document interactions *without* using any document content related data. Our prototype system logs document interactions (opening, closing, switching between documents). Similarity scores for documents are further derived based on their co-occurrences. A spectral clustering approach then groups documents into clusters, corresponding to potential user tasks.

2.1 Logging of Document Interactions

Our prototype logs which and when applications get focus on a user's desktop. The path of the document currently displayed in the application window is then extracted. Document information is anonymized by automatically attributing a unique identifier to each extracted document path and only logging this identifier for further analysis. The prototype has been implemented on Windows XP using AutoHotkey (www.autohotkey.com) scripting language. Embedded Visual Basic scripting has been used to query and interact with Microsoft Outlook and Microsoft Office applications. The logging prototype resides in the Windows taskbar and runs in the background on a user's PC. While our prototype is not able to extract document paths from all possible applications, it covers Microsoft Outlook, Microsoft Office applications and Acrobat Reader as well as most utility programs included in Windows XP.

In addition to logging the document identifiers, the prototype also calculates and maintains usage statistics for each document identifier. These include the similarity score to other documents as well as the dwell time for each document. The similarity score is for two documents doc_1 and doc_2 is defined by:

$$sim(doc_1, doc_2) = \frac{\#co-occurences\,of\,doc_1\,and\,doc_2}{\#occurences\,of\,doc_1}$$

A co-occurrence is defined by a direct switch from one document to another on a user's desktop, while an occurrence is defined by a contiguous period of time when one document has focus. The notion dwell time t_{dwell} of a document doc_1 refers to the time a user actively works on a document, i.e.

$$t_{dwell}(doc_1) = t_{focus}(doc_1) - t_{idle}(doc_1),$$

where t_{focus} is the time a document has focus on a user's desktop and t_{idle} is the time no keyboard or mouse events occurred while the document had focus. Similarity score and dwell time are the input for our spectral clustering approach described in the following.

2.2 Spectral Clustering Approach

As soon as enough data is logged, the spectral clustering algorithm is started and run as a background process by the logging prototype that resides in the taskbar. The data processing and spectral clustering algorithm have been implemented in Java using the WEKA machine learning framework [13].

Spectral clustering refers to a class of techniques that rely on the eigenvalues of a similarity matrix to partition points into disjoint clusters, with points in the same cluster that have high similarity and points in different clusters that have low similarity. Spectral clustering has been widely used in machine learning approaches, computer vision and speech processing.

Spectral clustering techniques make use of the spectrum of the similarity matrix of the data to perform dimensionality reduction for clustering in fewer dimensions. We use an implementation of the Shi-Malik algorithm [11] included in the WEKA machine learning framework [13]. Given a set of data points A, the similarity matrix may be defined as a matrix S where S_{ij} represents a measure of the similarity between points in a graph. It partitions data points A into two sets (A_1, A_2) based on the eigenvector v corresponding to the second-smallest eigenvalue of the Laplacian matrix L of S. L is defined by $L = I - D^{-1/2} S D^{-1/2}$ where D is the diagonal matrix $D_{ii} = \sum_j S_{ij}$. Each partitioning step is evaluated by calculating the degree of dissimilarity between the two resulting sets A_1 and A_2, the so called *normalized cut criterion* (*Ncut*). The Ncut criterion computes the weight of the edges connecting the two partitions as a fraction of the total edge connections to all the nodes in the graph. By comparing the Ncut value to a threshold (chosen between 0 and 1), it can be decided whether the current partition should be subdivided and recursively repartition the segmented parts if necessary. The recursive splitting stops as soon as no partition has a Ncut value below the specified threshold. The set of data points A is thus hierarchically subdivided into clusters of points having highest similarity.

Before applying spectral clustering to the document similarity values, we filter the observed documents by their dwell times. The aim is to remove spurious documents that do not belong to any of the user's tasks and therefore the interaction with these documents is limited and of short duration. Only documents with an average dwell time of 25 seconds are considered to be relevant to any of the user's tasks in our approach. The similarity scores of these documents are the input for spectral clustering ($S_{ij}=sim(doc_i,doc_j)$). The threshold for the Ncut criterion has been set to 0.1, admitting only partition splits that cut connections between a rather small fraction of documents. The resulting partitions from the spectral clustering algorithm represent groups of documents with high similarity, i.e. with a high fraction of switches between them. Assuming that the user switches more frequently between documents that relate to a specific user task and less frequently between documents belonging to different user tasks, each of the constructed clusters is considered to correspond to one of the user's tasks.

3. EXPERIMENTAL EVALUATION

In order to evaluate our approach, we adopted a similar evaluation methodology as used in [6]. Data ground truth was obtained by manually labeling user task classes during a large data collection/study involving 10 subjects (cf. section Data Collection). Precision, recall and F-measure have then been estimated for the clusters identified by our method (cf. section Results).

3.1 Data Collection

Data was collected in situ, observing a total of 10 employees working at a research and development company. The subjects were knowledge workers belonging to different departments of the company. The concerned departments included accounting, library service, intellectual property, IT and company administration. None of the subjects was involved in our research project and prototype development. All but one subject (who was observed for only two whole days due to scheduling constraints) were observed for three whole work days. The observed days were not contiguous; each was separated by a period of one week to one month. The days of observation were selected to be ones in which the subject engages in at least one recurring task, such as monthly or weekly status reporting. However, the selected recurrent tasks only constituted a small subset of the complete task set that has been observed for each user. The remaining tasks could also recur during all days of observation (but we did not influence their recurrence in any way). The observer would meet the subject upon their arrival to work and follow the subject as closely as possible until the end of the business day. Using a paper notepad with an electronic LiveScribe pen (www.livescribe.com), the researcher would record and label, to the second, user tasks and their start/end times (e.g., 8:15:32am start "Expense Reporting"). Prior to and during the shadowing, our prototype was installed on each subject's PC to record document usage. User task and document usage data has been anonymized, attributing identifiers to documents and subjects. Our prototype applied the spectral clustering algorithm to the recorded document interactions of each subject, automatically generating document clusters corresponding to the subject's tasks.

3.2 Evaluation and Results

The aim of the evaluation was to assess the quality of the document clusters identified by our clustering method with respect to the actual user tasks (which have been identified and labeled by a human observer as *ground truth*). However, as our method is completely unsupervised, it does not assign any task labels to the identified clusters which subsequently could be used for direct comparison and evaluation with the ground truth. In order to solve this problem, we automatically assign a task label to each cluster by looking at the percentage of documents in the cluster that belong to a specific task label. The task label with the largest percentage of documents in that cluster is assumed to be the task label of the cluster. In order to evaluate the performance, we used the three quantitative measures *precision*, *recall* and *F-measure*. Precision is referring to the fraction of documents in a cluster that belong to the task label of that cluster. Recall designates the fraction of all documents that belong to a task label and appear in the corresponding cluster. The F-measure is the weighted harmonic mean of precision and recall:

$$F-measure = \frac{2*precision*recall}{precision+recall}$$

Higher F-measure generally indicates higher performance of the concerned algorithm.

A high number of different tasks have been observed and labeled for conducting the evaluation. A total number of 572 tasks have been identified by the human observer for the 10 subjects, ranging from 35 (minimum) to 77 (maximum) tasks per subject. Our prototype system identified a total of 219 clusters with a minimum of 9 and a maximum of 52 clusters per subject. Table 1 (last row) indicates the obtained results (precision, recall and F-measure) for the whole data set using the evaluation methodology described earlier in this section. While the obtained overall precision is rather low, our method has a high recall value. The low precision can be explained by the fact that the number of task labels is higher than the number of clusters that have been identified. If there are more task labels than clusters, many documents that belong to tasks that have not been mapped to any cluster add noise to the identified clusters (their task label has never been considered for creating/mapping to a cluster, but they still count as erroneous members of a cluster). However, the clusters that have been identified seem each to have a good correspondence to one particular user task, resulting in a good overall recall value.

	Precision	Recall	F-measure
5 tasks (10 subjects)	0.71	0.77	0.74
All tasks (10 subjects)	0.20	0.76	0.32

Table 1: Average precision, recall and F-measure for the 5 most frequent tasks per subject (50 tasks in total) and all subjects' tasks (572 tasks in total)

The tasks that have been manually identified by an observer were recorded with different levels of granularity, i.e. high-level tasks corresponding to the subject's projects as well as low-level tasks corresponding to basic actions have been recorded. Example tasks that have been labeled are "Proposal for Client X" (high-level) or "Filling out expense web form" (low-level). In order to get to the right granularity of the labeled tasks and to be able to compare with previous approaches, tasks have been ordered according to their total duration, i.e. the accumulative total amount of time the user spent in these tasks. The evaluation of the document clusters identified by our approach has then been conducted on a limited number of these ordered tasks. By limiting the number of tasks that are considered for evaluation, we focus on evaluating higher-level tasks (e.g., projects) in which the subjects spend much of their time. Table 1 (first row) shows the obtained results (precision, recall and F-measure) for the 5 most frequent tasks of each subject. We obtain both good precision and recall for our approach. These results seem to indicate that our approach outperforms previous content-based approaches like SWISH [6] which obtained 0.49 (precision), 0.72

(recall) and 0.58 (F-measure) on a smaller data set of only 4 hours and 5 tasks in total. Thus document switch information and dwell times seem to be sufficient to identify a user's high-level tasks. Figure 1 depicts average precision, recall and F-measure values for an increasing number of user tasks. We see that by including more and more tasks with lower frequencies, the precision gradually drops, while the recall remains quite constant. Our interpretation is that the document clusters identified by our method correspond quite well to specific high-level user tasks. However, as the number of tasks increases and thus their granularity in the data set, not all possible tasks can be isolated by our method. This is also due to the fact that we chose not to force the algorithm to generate a specific number of clusters, but to create the clusters based on the characteristics of logged data.

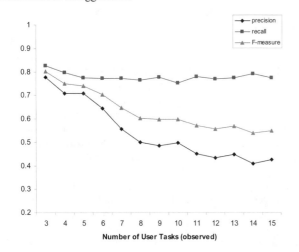

Figure 1: Average precision, recall and F-measure with respect to the number of user tasks

4. CONCLUSION AND FUTURE WORK

This paper introduced a novel approach for automatically constructing a model of a user's tasks based on logged document interactions. In contrast to previous approaches, no content-related data (document text, window titles etc.) is recorded. Identifiers are attributed to logged documents in order to maintain data confidentiality and user privacy. The prototype system and approach has been evaluated on data of 29 work days from 10 subjects. The obtained results show that the proposed approach works well in identifying a smaller set of high-level tasks, while with increasing number of tasks and in particular task granularity, the precision of the isolated clusters gradually decreases. Furthermore, the results seem to indicate that our method outperforms previous content-based approaches like SWISH.

We believe that the proposed approach provides a new efficient means for estimating a first representation of a user's tasks without any need for human intervention or input. Existing task prediction systems like TaskTracer move from tasks to documents/artifacts (top-down) and thus require the user to extensively define and train task labels before use. The proposed move from documents/artifacts to tasks (bottom-up) allows for an easier (semi-) automatic initialization for task prediction. By unobtrusively observing the user for a certain period of time, a first task representation can be constructed without user input. The user may eventually associate labels to the discovered task/document clusters. However, a simple activity/task based organization of work artifacts *without explicit labels and their prediction* has also shown its benefits to users [7]. The user can just choose the pertinent 'task context' (artifact collection) when he or she switches tasks. Each document cluster/task can further be edited by the user and ultimately also be shared among users.

5. REFERENCES

[1]   N. Dragunov, T.G. Dietterich, K. Johnsrude, M. McLaughlin, L. Li, and J.L. Herlocker. TaskTracer: a desktop environment to support multi-tasking knowledge workers. In Proc. of IUI '05, 75-82, 2005.

[2]   V.M. González, G. Mark. Constant, constant, multi-tasking craziness: managing multiple working spheres. In Proc. CHI '04. ACM, New York, NY, 113-120.

[3]   K. Gyllstrom, C. Soules, A. Veitch. Activity put in context: identifying implicit task context within the user's document interaction. In Proc. IIiX'08, 51-56, 2008.

[4]   G. Mark, V.M. Gonzalez, J. Harris. No task left behind?: examining the nature of fragmented work. In Proc. CHI '05. ACM, New York, NY, 321-330.

[5]   G. Mark, D. Gudith, U. Klocke. The cost of interrupted work: more speed and stress. In Proc. CHI '08, 107-110, 2008.

[6]   N. Oliver, G. Smith, C. Thakkar, and A. C. Surendran. SWISH: semantic analysis of window titles and switching history. In Proc. IUI '06, 194-201, 2006.

[7]   T. Rattenbury, J. Canny. CAAD: an automatic task support system. In Proc. CHI'07, 687-696, 2007.

[8]   J. Shen, L. Li, T.G. Dietterich. Real-Time Detection of Task Switches of Desktop Users. In Proc. IJCAI, 2007.

[9]   J. Shen, L. Li, T. G. Dietterich, J. L. Herlocker. A hybrid learning system for recognizing user tasks from desk activities and email messages. In Proc. IUI'06, 86-92, 2006.

[10] J. Shen, J. Irvine, X. Bao, M. Goodman, S. Kolibaba, A. Tran, F. Carl, B. Kirschner, S. Stumpf, T.G. Dietterich. Detecting and correcting user activity switches: algorithms and interfaces. In Proc. IUI'09, 117-126, 2009.

[11] J. Shi, J. Malik. Normalized Cuts and Image Segmentation. IEEE Trans. Pattern Anal. Mach. Intell. 22(8): 888-905, 2000.

[12] C.A. Soules, G. R. Ganger. Connections: using context to enhance file search. SIGOPS Oper. Syst. Rev. 39(5): 119-132, 2005.

[13] H. Witten and E. Frank. Data Mining: Practical machine learning tools and techniques, Morgan Kaufmann, San Francisco, 2005. Software available at http://www.cs.waikato.ac.nz/ml/weka/ (retrieved Sep. 2009)

Towards Intelligent Motion Inferencing in Mathematical Sketching

Salman Cheema
School of EECS
University of Central Florida
salmanc@cs.ucf.edu

Joseph J. LaViola Jr.
School of EECS
University of Central Florida
jjl@cs.ucf.edu

ABSTRACT

We present a new approach for creating dynamic illustrations to assist in the understanding of concepts in physics and mathematics using pen-based interaction. Our approach builds upon mathematical sketching by combining the ability to make associations between handwritten mathematics and free-form drawings with an underlying physics engine. This combination lets users create animations without having to directly specify object behavior with position functions through time, yet still supports writing the mathematics needed to formulate a problem. This functionality significantly expands the capabilities of mathematical sketching to support a wider variety of dynamic illustrations. We describe our approach to creating this mathematical sketching/physics engine fusion and discuss how it provides a foundation for using mathematical sketching in intelligent tutoring systems.

Author Keywords

Pen-based Interfaces, Mathematical Sketching, Sketch Parsing, Sketch Inferencing

ACM Classification Keywords

H.5.2 Information Interfaces and Presentation: User Interfaces—*Interaction styles*; I.2.3 Artificial Intelligence: Deduction and Theorem Proving—*Inference engines*

General Terms

Design, Human Factors

INTRODUCTION

Diagrams are a crucial part of many scientific disciplines. They aid learning by presenting concepts in a visual form [9, 10]. To solve problems, students often sketch a diagram using pencil and paper. The diagram usually includes initial conditions provided in the problem statement. However, such diagrams are static and serve only as a starting point to solving the problem. The answer may be a number or a function that does not necessarily provide much insight

into the underlying concepts. By animating the drawing in a meaningful way, better insight and understanding can be imparted to students. Mathematical sketching is an approach that provides users the ability to animate these diagrams on a pen-based computer by associating them with handwritten mathematics to govern their behavior [5].

Our underlying research goal is to use mathematical sketching as the foundation for intelligent tutoring systems for mathematics and physics. To reach this goal, mathematical sketching needs to evolve to include a firm understanding of the problem, its solution, and a user's input. It can then provide appropriate feedback (using dynamic illustrations) on whether a user's solution is correct or not. In many cases, the information users enter will be insufficient to make a proper animation. Although the current mathematical sketching implementation supports a wide variety of dynamic illustrations [4], it is significantly limited because users must directly specify how objects behave with position and/or rotation functions of time. An inspection of [9, 10] show problems students are asked to solve rarely conform to the dynamic illustration creation scheme provided by mathematical sketching. Thus, mathematical sketching needs to be broadened to include inferencing capabilities to make a proper dynamic illustration, given information that is only indirectly or partially related to providing a behavioral specification for the animation.

In this paper, we present an approach that moves mathematical sketching towards the ability to infer proper dynamic illustrations from incomplete specifications. We combine the ability to make associations between handwritten mathematics and free-form drawings with an underlying physics engine. This combination provides mathematical sketching with more flexibility to support animations without having to directly specify object behavior with position/rotation functions through time, yet still supports writing the mathematics needed to formulate a problem.

RELATED WORK

Systems for recognizing and animating diagrams in terms of basic primitive shapes have been developed by Alvarado [1] and Kara [3]. They allow the representation of a range of problems in specific domains such as mechanical design and vibratory systems by using a simulation backend. However, they are limited in scope because they do not allow the user to write mathematics to govern animation behavior. MathPad^2 [6] sought to overcome these limitations by having users write down the mathematics to govern all aspects of a diagram's animation, but it is also limited in the range of problems that it can represent (e.g. it would be hard to model a collision resolution problem in MathPad[2]). Our approach combines the best elements of [1, 3] with mathematical sketching, providing animations that will work when users provide just the diagram, the diagram with a full mathematical specification, or the diagram with a partial mathematical specification[1].

SYSTEM OVERVIEW

In our system, users can create a dynamic illustration by sketching a diagram and writing down initial conditions and any equations as part of a particular problem. User input takes the form of writing with a stylus on a tablet PC. After drawing the diagram and writing down initial conditions, users can request an analysis of the diagram.

The system attempts to analyze the diagram in terms of its components: convex polygons, circles, springs, and wires. The ink for recognized diagram components is replaced by rectified components. This lets the user know that the system has correctly interpreted the diagram. As the system needs to perform diagram animation with incomplete information, realistic values are assigned to recognized components' attributes based on appearance and position. For example, a shape's default mass is assigned proportional to its enclosed area, in order to provide realistic animated behavior because larger objects are perceived to have more mass.

Users can replace default attributes with proper initial conditions by writing mathematical expressions and making associations with recognized diagram components. To make an association, a lasso gesture is used to select one or more expressions followed by a tap gesture. The user can associate either a constant expression (e.g. $m = 5$) or an equation (e.g. $v(x) = sin(t)$) with any relevant diagram component. The system applies the force of gravity to all components by default. Users may associate any number of constant/variable forces such as push, drag, and reaction forces. Erroneous associations are ignored automatically. For example, it does not make sense to associate velocity equations with wires and springs. Similarly, associating spring constant values with a shape is meaningless. At any time, users can view associations by hovering the stylus over a recognized component.

Allowing users to modify the behavior of the system in this manner has several benefits. First, users can modify default values and behavior as needed for a given problem. Second, users should be able to debug associations and fix errors. Errors can exist in initial conditions, causing incorrect animation that conflicts with the user's intuition. We provide a reset mode that lets users correct and alter existing associations. Finally, our approach allows users to experiment with different initial values and gain better insight into the work-

---

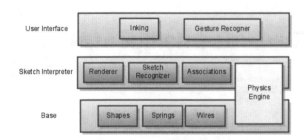

Figure 1. Overview of our system components.

ing of underlying concepts. Consider a projectile problem. It may be instructive to experiment with changing initial velocity or the magnitude of the drag force to see the effects on the range of the projectile.

In keeping with our goal to emulate pencil and paper, existing associations are preserved along different system modes. If users want to alter a part of an expression that is already associated with a diagram component, they do not have to make the association again. We believe that this approach minimizes unnecessary work on the user's part and lets her focus on the problem at hand rather than being encumbered by the user interface.

SYSTEM DESIGN

We use a layered approach for flexibility. A custom 2D rigid body physics engine [7] is used for updating and animating diagram components. See Figure 1 for an overview of the system components.

User Interface

The user interface provides facilities for inking to let the user sketch diagrams and write mathematics in a natural manner. A gesture recognition module recognizes three gestures: lasso, scribble-erase, and tap. The gesture set is limited to provide a simple and accessible user interface. The lasso gesture can be used to select both ink and recognized diagram components. Users can drag and reposition the selection anywhere on the screen. Similarly, the scribble-erase gesture is used to erase ink and diagram components. If users select mathematics and tap a recognized diagram component, an association is made. If no math is selected, the tap gesture will cause a recognized shape to become immobile. We provide options to save/load ink in order to easily recall an old problem for revision or clarification. Instant recognition feedback is provided by means of an online mathematics recognizer [8]. Recognition errors can be fixed by using the scribble erase gesture. The feedback results are also used to make the association which improves performance by not doing unnecessary recognition and minimizes recognition errors by using correctly recognized mathematics.

Sketch Interpreter

The sketch interpreter has components to perform diagram recognition, manage associations, render content, and update the animation. A large part of the physics engine resides

---

[1]A simple example of a partial specification would be writing the appropriate force equations for an object and having the underlying physics engine fill in the details to ensure a plausible animation. The user would not have to write down a numerical routine to solve the differential equation.

in this layer because association information is maintained here. The associations affect initial values and behavior of the physics engine. Therefore the physics engine cannot be decoupled from this layer.

Diagram Recognition

Proper parsing of a diagram is necessary to convert a problem into components that can be animated by the physics engine. From a usability perspective, it is critical that the symbols used to represent diagram components be intuitive and obvious to a physics student. We use circles, convex polygons, springs and wires as basic diagram components. We believe that it is possible to model a wide variety of elementary physics problems using these basic components. This section describes our methodology for recognizing them.

A cusp detector is used to recognize shapes where shapes must be closed strokes. A shape is classified as a polygon if it has more than 2 cusps, otherwise it is classified as a circle. A stroke is a spring if it is not a closed stroke and has three or more self intersections. We employ a line segment intersection test for counting self intersections. Wires are relatively straight lines.

An ink stroke is either a diagram component or part of a mathematical expression. The distinction is important because it is possible to misclassify parts of a mathematical expression as diagram components (e.g. zeros as circles or symbols with self intersections as springs). We use a few simple rules to address these problems. Shapes are separated from mathematics by ensuring that all convex diagram components enclose a minimum area. For springs and wires, at least one end of both must be attached to a shape. Hence recognition proceeds in the following order: shapes, springs, wires, and mathematics.

Associations Management

Associations between mathematics and diagram components are used by the physics engine at runtime to animate a diagram. Associations can include both constant expressions and equations. Constants can modify almost all attributes of a diagram component such as mass, velocity, angular velocity, orientation, position, acceleration, and forces. Constants are applied once, at the start of the animation. It is important to have a mechanism to undo them, because the user can reset the animation and start over with different parameters.

It is possible to write equations for several attributes of diagram components. The physics engine populates the appropriate set of equations with their parameter values at runtime and evaluates them to guide the animation of the diagram. When evaluating equations with errors, any unrecognized parameter is assigned a value of zero. This can yield an incorrect animation but also serves as feedback to the user indicating some error in input is causing abnormal behavior.

Animation of Diagram Components

Diagram components are animated by a custom 2D Rigid Body physics engine [7]. The default animation behavior of all diagram components depends on the standard equations of motion. The engine updates every movable component's position by computing net acceleration and then integrating twice for position. Collision detection and resolution are performed after the update. This step may also involve the computation of rest forces for components that are in resting contact [2]. Lastly, a post processing step is applied that infers unspecified circumstances. Important attributes such as forces and velocity are rendered using arrows. The length of each arrow changes in proportion to the magnitude of the quantity it represents, which lets users observe how important quantities change due to specified initial conditions.

The physics engine has a very open ended design. Much of its behavior can be altered by users. Users may move diagram components by lassoing and dragging. Attributes of diagram components can be altered by associating constants/equations. Users can also specify position or velocity equations as a replacement for standard forces or acceleration equations. In such cases, the system is able to infer what needs to be done to update components' positions. If only velocity is specified, it infers the need to integrate once to update position. If the position equation is specified, it infers that no integration is required. The net force is always computed for display purposes.

Interesting scenarios arise when the default behavior is overridden by user-specified behavior. Consider the following example. Two objects X and Y are part of the diagram. X is moving under standard equations of motion. Y is moving under user-defined equations that specify how its position changes with time. An important question from an animation perspective is what happens if X and Y collide? Clearly the position equations for Y no longer applies. How should the user-defined behavior be changed in order to produce a realistic animation? Our approach is to revert to the standard equations of motion.

Inferencing Unspecified Events

This subsystem is best illustrated by an example. Consider an object attached to some wires. Suppose that the combined tension in all wires is not enough to inhibit motion. How should the system proceed with animation? Clearly the object should move, causing some wires to break. Our approach is to start breaking the wires most opposite to the direction of motion, providing a convincing animation.

Such cases are not specified by users. To incorporate such unseen events into the animation, we have built a simple inferencing system into our physics engine. Inferencing is done after collision resolution. Currently it is limited to detecting if an object is in equilibrium (i.e., will it move?). Such scenarios can occur in a variety of situations involving wires, springs, and inclined plane problems.

EXAMPLE SCENARIO: FREEFALL

Consider a free-fall problem. A student is asked to write down the drag force acting on the body with a coefficient of 0.5 (see Figure 2). The student draws a ball and writes an expression for aerodynamic drag. Upon analysis, the system recognizes and replaces the ball with a circle. The user

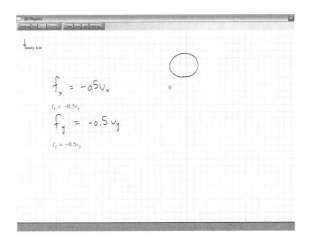

Figure 2. A diagram exploring free fall with aerodynamic drag.

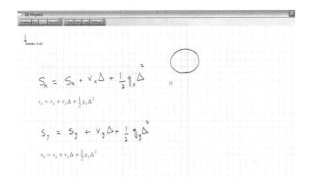

Figure 3. An altered freefall diagram that specifies how the position of the ball changes instead of giving the initial conditions.

associates the drag force with the circle. When run, the animation shows how the velocity and the drag force changes as the ball falls towards the ground. The ball will bounce a few times, losing momentum with each bounce. Eventually it will come to a complete stop on the ground. Note that the student was not asked to find the position equations for the ball, just write an expression for the drag force. In this case, the system infers from the drawing and the mathematics what forces are applied to the ball and that it must fill in the details to ensure a proper animation.

The system also supports the more traditional mathematical sketch creation mechanism. Suppose the student is asked to write down the ball's position equations. In this case, the system detects from the written mathematics that it cannot use the standard equations of motion because position equations have been defined. Instead, it uses the given equations to update the position of the ball. When the ball collides with something while moving, the specified equations become obsolete. The system detects this and the motion of the ball reverts back to the standard equations of motion.

CONCLUSION

We have presented a system that combines mathematical sketching with an underling physics engine to allow cre-

ation of a wider variety of dynamic illustrations to understand physics and mathematics concepts. This fusion provides a mechanism to infer how to make a proper animation given different levels of granularity of user input, from diagram only to complete behavioral specification. Currently our system understands the relationship between acceleration, velocity, and position/orientation. We plan to extend this by building diagrammatic reasoning components into the system. Although we have made strides toward creating a mathematical sketching system suitable for intelligent tutoring, there is still a significant amount of work that needs to be done to make a general solution. Our system needs to develop an understanding of concepts related to the $F = ma$ equation, such as work and kinetic energy, power, momentum, and impulse among others. An evaluation of the performance of system components, such as the shape and gesture recognizers, will help us improve our system. We also plan to get feedback regarding the system's usability and effectiveness by conducting a user study among university physics students.

ACKNOWLEDGEMENTS
This work is supported in part by NSF CAREER Award IIS-0845921.

REFERENCES

1. Alvarado, C.J. *A Natural Sketching Environment: Bringing the Computer into early stages of Mechanical Design* , Master's Thesis, Massachusetts Institute of Technology, 2000

2. Baraff, D., And Witkin, A. *Physically Based Modeling: Principles and Practice* , Siggraph Course Notes, 1997

3. Kara, L.B., Gennari, L., And Stahovich, T.F. *A Sketch-based Tool for Analyzing Vibratory Mechanical Systems* , Journal of Mechanical Design, Volume 130, Issue 10, 2008

4. LaViola, J. Advances in Mathematical Sketching: Moving Toward the Paradigm's Full Potential, *IEEE Computer Graphics and Applications*, 27(1):38-48, January/February 2007.

5. LaViola, J. *Mathematical Sketching: A New Approach to Creating and Exploring Dynamic Illustrations* , PhD Thesis, Brown University, 2005

6. LaViola, J. and R. Zeleznik. MathPad^2: A System for the Creation and Exploration of Mathematical Sketches, *ACM Transactions on Graphics (Proceedings of SIGGRAPH 2004)*, 23(3):432-440, August 2004.

7. Millington, I. *Game Physics Engine Developement* , Morgan Kaufmann, March 2007

8. StarPad. *http://pen.cs.brown.edu/starpad.html*, 2009.

9. Varberg, D. And Purcell, E.J. *Calculus with Analytical Geometry* , Prentice Hall, 1992

10. Young, H.D. *University Physics* , Addison-Wesley Publishing Company, 1992

iSlideshow: a Content-Aware Slideshow System

Jiajian Chen
Georgia Institute of Technology
johnchen@cc.gatech.edu

Jun Xiao, Yuli Gao
HP Labs
{jun.xiao2, yuli.gao}@hp.com

ABSTRACT

We present an intelligent photo slideshow system that automatically analyzes thematic information about the photo collection and utilizes such information to generate compositions and transitions in two modes: story-telling mode and person-highlighting mode. In the story-telling mode the system groups photos by a theme-based clustering algorithm and multiple photos in each theme cluster are seamlessly tiled on a slide. Multiple tiling layouts are generated for each theme cluster and the slideshow is animated by intra-cluster transitions. In the person-highlighting mode, the system first recognizes faces from photos and creates photo clusters for individuals. It then uses face areas as ROI (Regions of Interests) and creates various content-based transitions to highlight individuals in a cluster. With an emphasis on photo content, our system creates slideshows with more fluid, dynamic and meaningful structure compared to existing systems.

Author Keywords

Slideshow, theme clustering, content-based transition, GPU.

ACM Classification Keywords

H.5.1 Information Interfaces and Presentation

General Terms

Algorithms, Design, Human Factors

INTRODUCTION

In this paper, we present iSlideshow, an intelligent photo slideshow system with two photo browsing modes: story-telling and person-highlighting (see Figure 1). In the story-telling mode, we use the theme clustering algorithm to group photos based on time, color and face distance. Then the system generates a sequence of layouts for a theme cluster with increasing number of photos. The photos on a slide are seamlessly tiled on the canvas according to their aspect ratios. We then animate the transition between tile layouts with camera motions.

In the person-highlighting mode we leverage the semantic information of the photos to create interesting and visually appealing transitions. Existing works [2, 5] only apply common camera motion selected from pre-defined templates and do not account for any semantic relationship between photos. Our system uses ROI (e.g., detected face areas) in a photo cluster to create content-based transitions such as water-dropping and spotlighting. The transitions highlight relationship between photos (e.g., the same person) in a cluster of the slideshow.

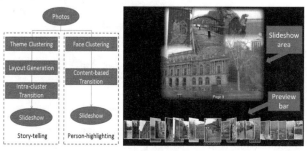

Figure 1. (Left) System Flowchart; (Right) UI Snapshot

THEME CLUSTERING

Time stamp based photo clustering algorithms have been extensively studied in literature [4]. Our algorithm goes beyond that and takes advantage of additional high-level semantic features for better image grouping.

We aim to cluster images into slides by "themes", a concept that is used frequently by graphics designers when they create artifacts from image collections. Theme generally means certain similarities in dimensions such as time, color, people and places. We capture these dimensions using the following functions:

(1) Time distance function $Dt(x,y)$, defined as the absolute difference between the photo-taking time of image x and y.

(2) Color distance function $Dc(x,y)$, defined as the Earth Mover Distance [7] between the color clusters extracted from image x and y.

(3) Face distance function $F(x,y)$, defined as the average distance between faces detected in image x and y.

Due to the variety of similarities one can measure between images, simply computing all metrics on all possible pairs of images in the sequence could lead to a very high computational cost. To reduce the cost, we take advantage of the following locality bias: images that were taken closer in time are more likely to be grouped into a slide than images that were taken further apart in time. This locality property motivates us to restrict the expensive theme-based clustering process within a certain time widow, therefore reducing the computational cost significantly. We describe our theme-based clustering algorithm as the following:

(1) Partition the image sequence into non-overlapping image sub-sequences using a predefined time gap T.

(2) Within each image sub-sequence, a theme graph is constructed by treating all images as nodes, and edges between nodes represent their thematic distance, measured by a linear combination of $Dt(x,y)$, $Dc(x,y)$ and $F(x, y)$.

(3) The graph is then pruned by removing edges whose distances are over a tunable threshold, which is set by the end user to controls the number of output slides.

Finding theme clusters is then cast as finding non-trivial cliques in these theme graphs. Once the theme clusters are found, we simply map each cluster into a single slide.

SEAMLESS TILING

The tiling slideshow [2] places photos with similar topics on a same frame with pre-defined patterns. A drawback of their system is that the aspect ratio of the cells in the pre-defined templates may not comply with the aspect ratio of the photos. Often, images are cropped or transformed. Also, the composed tiling layout includes white space between images that clearly marks the boundaries between cells and are visually disruptive for the coherent scene. We try to improve existing systems with seamless and dynamic tiling.

We use seamless tiling to remove undesired borders between images in the layout. We upscale the photos in each cell in a layout by a small percentage (e.g., 5%) and conduct alpha-blending at the overlapping region of adjacent photos. Before the blending, we also blur the border of each photo using the super-eclipse (round-corner rectangle) to obtain better result in the tiling:

$$\left(\frac{x}{a}\right)^{2/d} + \left(\frac{y}{b}\right)^{2/d} = 1$$

All these operations such as blur and alpha-blending are implemented in GPU. Figure 2 shows an original tiling slide and our seamlessly tiling slide, both with 4 images in the slide.

Figure 2. The original tiling slide (left) and our seamless tiling slide (right), both with 4 photos

DYNAMIC TILING AND INTRA-CLUSTER TRANSITIONS

We use BRIC layout engine to compute the tiling layout [1]. A layout is calculated with constraints of photo aspect ratio, sizes and their relative importance. In addition, BRIC offers stabilized layout and minimize changes of the layout when adding, removing and replacing images. The layout can be recomputed by tuning weighting factors of images and number of images in a cluster. We compute a sequence of layouts for each theme cluster with increasing number of photos, and use intra-cluster transitions to animate these layouts. The procedure is described as the following, assuming a cluster has n images:

(1) Use the first 1, 2, …, or n images from this cluster as input to the layout generator to compute layouts $L1, L2, …, Ln$.

(2) Animate $L1, L2, …, Ln$ in a slideshow with intra-cluster transitions. $L1, L2, …, Ln$ are treated as key frames in the slideshow.

For in-between frames, we compute the position of an image by linearly interpolating its position in two consecutive layouts. The movement and resizing of images in the in-between frames also simulate the camera motion of zooming and panning. Figure 3 illustrates this effect. The system generates 4 layouts for a same theme cluster with 4 images. Each layout is a key frame in the slideshow animation. Images in each layout are seamlessly tiled.

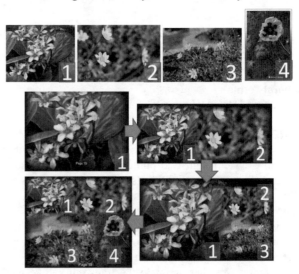

Figure 3. A theme cluster with 4 images (top row) animated by intra-cluster transition that simulates zooming and panning

CONTENT-BASED TRANSITION

Existing systems use motions such as panning and zooming to animate photos, and to transition between consecutive slides. However, for most systems, the animations and transitions are usually selected from a set of predefined effects such as panning, zooming, cross-fade and wipe. The resulting slideshow quickly become repetitive and predictable. In some systems, such as [2], the selection and occurrence of transitions are synchronized with background music, but none of the systems create transitions that dynamically adapt to the content of the photos.

Our approach explores creating content based transitions that can dynamically adapt to the photo content. In the first stage of photo clustering, we detect a list of ROIs or attentive areas, such as faces, and associate them with each photo. To animate two consecutive slides, we use OpenGL to render the photos as textures to screen quads. We created content based transition by manipulating the pixels inside and outside ROIs (Regions of Interest) differently. Specifically, we distort the mapping of pixels between slides, i.e. re-assign texture coordinates of pixels, in the consecutive photos. The normalized texture coordinates of a pixel in a photo are (x,y) in uv texture space, where $0<=x,y<=1$. In the 2D space, the distortion is a 2×1 vector, which is used as a texture coordinate offset for each pixel in the photo. It's defined as follows.

$$\textbf{Distortion}(x, y) = \begin{bmatrix} \Delta_x \\ \Delta_y \end{bmatrix} = \textbf{f}(t, d)$$

Distance d can be computed in many ways such as Euclidean distance or color difference between this pixel and ROI. For example, if the shape of ROI is a circle with center in (x_c, y_c) we choose the following distortion.

$$\textbf{Distortion}(x, y) = \begin{bmatrix} \Delta_x \\ \Delta_y \end{bmatrix} = t\textbf{f}\left(\begin{bmatrix} x-x_c \\ y-y_c \end{bmatrix}\right) = (t|\textbf{f}|)e^{i\theta}$$

The vector $\textbf{f}$ is the distortion speed for that pixel (x,y). We execute the following steps in the GPU shader:

(1) For each pixel in the current photo, use $D(x,y) = t\textbf{f}$ ($t:0\rightarrow1$) to compute the offset vector, then add to its texCoord.

(2) Repeat (1) with reversed time ($t: 1\rightarrow0$) for the next photo.

(3) Blend the two resulting photos based on transition time to achieve the final effect.

The blending function of t specifies the timing of the blending transition for two consecutive frames. We use a linear blending function. Other non-linear blending function such as quadratic functions can also be applied.

We implemented several transitions in the system, including the water-flow, water-dropping, whirlpool-like and spotlighting, as shown in Figure 4.

We choose the following f to obtain the water-dropping effect.

$$|\textbf{f}| = \begin{cases} \sin(k\pi d)\left(\dfrac{d}{r_0}\right)^5 & (if \ d < r_0) \\ \sin(k\pi d) & (otherwise) \end{cases}$$

The direction of f is $(x-x_c, y-y_c)$, d is the Euclidean distance between the pixel and the ROI center. r_0 is the ROI radius. In the water-dropping effect we change only the magnitude of f.

In contrast, we obtain a whirlpool-like effect by changing only its direction (the angle between vector f and the positive x-axis), as shown below.

$$\textbf{Distortion}(x, y) = \left(e^{i\theta t} - 1\right)\begin{bmatrix} x-x_c \\ y-y_c \end{bmatrix}$$

$$\theta = \begin{cases} kd\left(\dfrac{d}{r_0}\right)^5 & (d < r_0) \\ \theta = kd & (otherwise) \end{cases}$$

The water-flow transition is created with a noise map. A noise map is a grey-scale image. We use the grey-scale value of each pixel in the noise map G as the distortion speed when rendering images for in-between frames. We attenuate the distortion by the distance between the pixel and the ROI center, as shown below.

$$|\textbf{f}| = \begin{cases} tG(x,y)\left(\dfrac{d}{r_0}\right)^5 & (d < r_0) \\ tG(x,y) \end{cases}$$

The spotlight transition is created by dimming down the pixels outside of ROI. For this effect, we set D(x,y)=0, but we modify the alpha channel of a pixel based on the distance of the pixel and the ROI center. This effect can be combined with other transitions easily.

The distortion function provides a lot of possibilities to create interesting transitions. Usually changing the magnitude or angle of the distortion vector separately inside and outside ROI creates an illusion that a camera focuses on the ROI and move from frame to frame.

When the normalized ROI in two consecutive photos are not aligned, we can either scale and align ROIs of the two photos (as shown above), or move the ROIs on the photos. The movement of ROI creates an effect that a camera focus is fluidly moving toward the highlighting area from frame to frame in the result video. The moving trajectory could be a curve or line, and the size of the ROI in inter-frame can be decided by a linear interpolation as follows.

ROI of frames between two photos = ROI of the first photo × (1-t) + ROI of the second photo × t. (0<t<1)

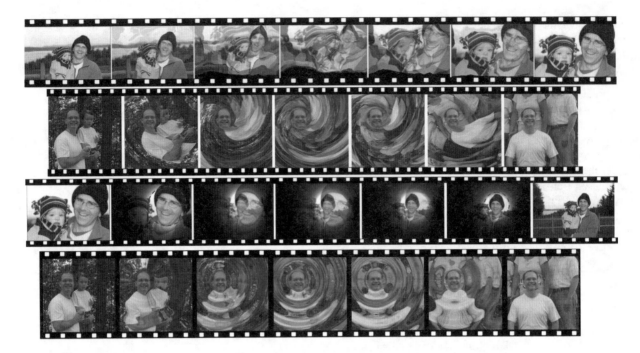

Figure 4. Two photos animated with a waterflow, whirlpool-like, spotlighting and water-dropping effect, from top to bottom. Transitions are generated based on the ROIs, which are detected face areas marked by the red circles.

PILOT USER STUDY

We conducted a comparison pilot study of the iSlideshow system with ACDSee slideshow and the Tiling Slideshow. Fifteen people, who brought their own photos, participated in the study. Each participant was asked to view their photo collections in three slideshow systems. In ACDSee slideshow photos in each cluster are shown one by one. In the tiling slideshow and iSlideshow, multiple photos in each cluster are shown and tiled on a single screen. Participants can view photos in person-highlighting mode in iSlideshow.

The participants then filled out a questionnaire consisting of questions about *Aesthetics, Experience, Atmosphere, Fun and Acceptance* with 1-7 scales. As shown in Figure 5, study participants preferred iSlideshow over other systems, especially in terms of *Aesthetics* and *Fun*. They reported that the dynamic and seamless tiling and various content-based transition effects are fun and fascinating to watch. And they were eager to point out the meaningful connections in and between slides during the interview.

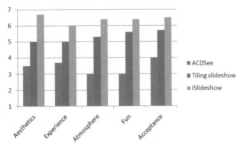

Figure 5. User study results of three systems

CONCLUSION AND FUTURE WORK

We presented a slideshow system that is intelligently aware of image content and relationships between photos. A comparison study of three slideshow systems demonstrated that iSlideshow offers novel and appealing experiences over traditional slideshow applications. We plan to extend content based transitions and ROI framework to use other metadata and incorporate more visual design principles [3, 6] to improve both the layout and the animation of the photo slides.

REFERENCES

1. Atkins, C.B. Blocked recursive image composition. *ACM Multimedia 2008*.

2. Chen, J. C., Chu, W. T., Kuo, J. H., Weng, C. Y. and Wu, J. L. Tiling Slideshow. *ACM Multimedia 2006*.

3. Fogarty, J., Forlizzi, J. and Hudson, S. Aesthetic information collages: generating decorative displays that contain information. *UIST 2001*.

4. Graham, A., Garcia-Molina, H., Paepcke, A., and Winograd, T. Time as essence for photo browsing through personal digital libraries. *JCDL 2002*.

5. Hua, X. S., Lu, L. and Zhang H. J. Photo2Video. *ACM Multimedia 2004*.

6. Lok, S., Feiner, S., and Ngai, G. Evaluation of Visual Balance for Automated Layout. *IUI 2004*.

7. Rubner, Y., Tomasi,C., Guibas, L.J. The Earth Mover's Distance as a Metric for Image Retrieval. *Int. J. Comput. Vision*, Vol. 40, No. 2, 2000, 99-121.

Social Influence of Product Popularity on Consumer Decisions: Usability Study of Flickr Camera Finder

Li Chen
Department of Computer Science
Hong Kong Baptist University, Hong Kong
lichen@comp.hkbu.edu.hk

ABSTRACT

"Product popularity" is in-depth explored in this paper, regarding its practical role within a consumer's decision process. Specifically, the usability evaluation of a novel product finder service (Flickr Camera Finder) shows that users more frequently consulted it, rather than a standard shopping site, to locate popular products. User comments further revealed their credibility concerns and tendency to trust the "popularity" from social resources. Design implications from the experiment are summarized at the end, indicating suggestive directions to integrate social media data to boost current e-commerce decision tools.

Author Keywords

Social influence, product popularity, usability study, Flickr camera finder, consumer decision behavior, e-commerce.

ACM Classification

H5.m. Information interfaces and presentation (e.g., HCI): Miscellaneous.

General Terms

Experimentation, Human Factors, Measurement.

INTRODUCTION

The homepage of an e-commerce website for a specific product category (e.g., digital cameras), covers most of its space to give initial product recommendations, commonly under labels of "most wanted", "popular products", "top ones under $500". These products essentially act as starting points for consumers to get familiar with the product domain, especially when their target is not clear at the start. Indeed, the "product popularity" information has been regarded as one type of important social factors that will impact users' purchase decisions [2]. Sociologists term the effect as "social influence" and point out that it will play a crucial role to assist users in reducing the uncertainty and amount of information that they must process to make a decision [2,5].

However, the question is: do users in reality perceive the popular items credible as displayed in current e-commerce

sites? Given that the credibility is strongly correlated with the user's acceptance intention [4], it is definitely of meaning to explore the issue for the development of convincible social recommendations.

Specifically, in this paper, we study the usability of a novel product finder service, "Flickr Camera Finder", that mainly provides product popularity info based on the analysis of Flickr metadata (i.e., members who have uploaded at least one photo or video with a particular camera over a certain time). By comparing it with standard e-commerce tools, we attempted to answer the following specific concerns: 1) how do users perceive the "popular products" suggested in Flickr Camera Finder, and would it be different from the user perception in a normal e-commerce site? 2) How do popularity-based recommendations practically act within a consumer's whole decision making process? 3) How can user-generated content as from Flickr, be best exploited to generate more effective decision systems to deliver user benefits (such as the improvement on their decision confidence when searching for high-risk products)?

EXPERIMENT METHOD

In order to find answers to above questions, we have performed an empirical study including both of objective user behavior observations and qualitative interviews. The study was launched in July 2009 and 12 participants (3 females) volunteered to join. For each of them, it took around two hours: one hour to test assigned websites and another hour to freely provide any of her/his comments and suggestions. They are mainly Master or PhD students in our department with ages between 20 and 40. All of them have online shopping experiences.

Experimental Procedure

The experiment was designed in a free-choice scenario. That is, two websites were provided as options: Yahoo Shopping (as the representative of standard e-commerce websites, shopping.yahoo.com) and Flickr Camera Finder (www.flickr.com/cameras/). The participant can use either one or both to accomplish the task of "*finding a digital camera you are prepared to buy*". The task was performed after an initial stage of familiarizing themselves with the two websites, so that the choice was completely dependent on their true willingness. Our goal was thus to observe how frequently the subject used Yahoo Shopping (henceforth Yahoo CF) and/or Flickr Camera Finder (henceforth Flickr CF), and what information s/he intentionally relied on to make the choice. It is worth noting that all of our subjects were first-time encounters of the two websites, so their behavior was not biased by any of previous usages.

Each user's interactions with the website(s) including on-screen mouse moves and inputs were all automatically captured by a screen-recorder. After her/his choice was made, a post-study questionnaire was to be filled in, requesting the participant's overall decision confidence and purchase intention, followed by usability assessments of the website(s) s/he just used. A follow-up interview was then conducted and recorded to get her/his verbal comments w.r.t. what s/he liked and disliked most, and what s/he would like to be added or combined for better supports.

Materials

A summary of each website's provided searching facilities and product details was first made in Table 1, from which we can clearly see that Flickr CF mainly supplies popularity-based browsing/sorting, usage trend statistics, and community-shared photos, but lack of feature-based browsing/filtering tools (e.g., by price, megapixels, optical zoom, etc.), product-related recommendations (e.g. "shoppers who viewed this item also viewed ..."), and full product specifications that Yahoo CF gives. One aim of our analysis was then to discover what facilities users consulted at their decision stages. In fact, researchers on consumer behavior indicate that a buyer tends to use two-stage processes to reach her/his decision, where the depth of information processing varies: initial screening of available products to determine which ones are worth considering further; in-depth comparison of selected products before making the purchase decision [3]. It was hence interesting to see whether/how social popularity info practically acted during the processes to help users achieve their final choice.

	Yahoo CF	Flickr CF
Popularity info and browsing/ searching facilities	Most popular products (e.g. "Top Digital Cameras"); Feature-based browsing and filtering facilities (e.g. "Narrow Results"); Searching with keywords ("Shop for"); Product-related recommendations ("Shoppers who viewed this item also viewed")	Most popular and brand popular products (e.g. "Most Popular Cameras in the Flickr Community", "Top 5 xx Cameras in the Community"); Popularity-based sorting (e.g. by "# of items, avg. daily users, activity factor")
Product detail page	Full specifications; Customer rates/reviews; Price comparison	Basic specifications; Usage trend this year; Photos taken with the product

Table 1. Comparison of the two sites' provided facilities and product details (at the time of our experiment).

RESULTS

Flickr CF Usage

To our surprise, all of participants used both websites as a combination to identify their target. 50% of them initially started with Yahoo and the other half began in Flickr CF. Tracing of their actions shows that the general two decision processes [3] (as introduced above) can be further refined into three stages: 1) to screen and select products for in-depth

evaluation; 2) to view the product's details and save it in wish list if near-satisfactory; 3) to compare candidates in the wish list and make the final choice. Accordingly, we measured the frequency of a facility that was used to assist the user in narrowing down to an interested product at the first stage, and the type of product information reviewed respectively at stages two and three.

Credibility of Product Popularity

It first shows that on average 9.67 products were selected to view details, among which 5.42 were first located in Yahoo, and 4.25 were from Flickr CF (*note*: both sites have these products). Figure 1 concretely illustrates where (or through which facility) the product was found (where the percentage was computed as the average application frequency). It can be therefore seen that the standard product searching tool (i.e., feature-based browsing/filtering facility from Yahoo) got highest 39.79% chance enabling the average user to obtain an interested product. The second and third winners come to Flickr CF's popularity-based sorting list (27.51%) and brand popular products (12.18%) respectively.

In comparison, Yahoo's popularity-based recommendations got much less successes (5.28%). Actually, there are only 2 users (out of 12) who consulted the popularity info in Yahoo, versus 9 participants accessing the popularity list in Flickr CF.

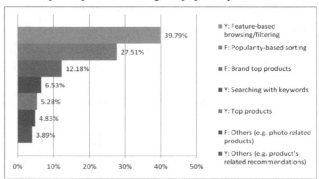

Figure 1. Chance distribution for the location of interested products (*Y* for Yahoo CF, *F* for Flickr CF).

It then came to the question of why people used Flickr CF when the traditional shopping guide was also available, and what their motivations were behind. Post-interviews with all participants disclosed their similar mental activities. That is, their requirements were generally need-based at the start (e.g., looking for a camera that is "*easy to use*", "*easy to carry*", or "*better for photographing night scene*"). They commonly had 2 to 3 preferred brands in mind, besides hard constraints on price range and/or type (e.g., digital SLR). Their goal was hence to find a product best matching to these needs and constraints. For each brand, they first narrowed down to several candidates. At this point, if they had no exact domain knowledge about the brand, they tended to rely on "the most popular ones", since "*popularity is a suitable proxy to measure the product's quality when I am not familiar with a brand or uncertain about what I want*" (as revealed from one user's responses). It was also regarded as "*the best recommendation*" in this condition.

When being asked why they went to Flickr CF to obtain the popularity information, they replied that because it was more credible. They know that Flickr is a social photo-sharing site with millions of active users (e.g., *"I trust the information on the social forum." "I trust Flickr's popularity information because of its large amount of users." "Although this is my first-time using this website, the information sounds credible since it should be based on actual usages."*) They felt that the way of showing popular cameras based on users' uploaded photos is interesting and surprising at the first impression. They were soon used to it to not only look for products for in-depth evaluation, but also employ its usage trend statistics and user-shared photos as important factors to confirm the final choice.

On the contrary, the product popularity on Yahoo Shopping site (e.g., "Top Digital Cameras") was perceived *"less trustworthy"*. As they noted, *"the 'top products' in Yahoo may be only dependent on users' clicks or for companies' promotion purpose." "Flickr is more neutral because it is a consumer-operated website. The information on Yahoo may be not so real since it is more commercial-oriented."* Therefore, it infers that users were inclined to trust the social media site against the standard shopping site, given that the former is seen to be free from commercial interests.

Product Detail Evaluation
As for which product page(s) users went to examine product details, we found 42.86% of products' evaluations were done on Yahoo (of the product's full specifications and customer rates/reviews), 30.44% on Flickr (with usage trend statistics and associated photos), and 26.70% on both product pages. Among all examined products, 45.82% were put into the average user's wish list. The page(s) evaluation respectively contributed 39.09%, 6.25% and 91.67%, to help establish the wish list (the % means the percent of products saved as candidates after the corresponding evaluation, see Figure 2.a). It hence implies that the combination of product details from both Yahoo & Flickr (i.e., the camera's specifications, reviews, plus its usage statistics and images) can mostly likely inspire a serious consideration. The correlation is indeed highly significant ($p < 0.001$) by Pearson coefficients. Another fact is that 91.7% (11 out of 12) users' final choice was from outcomes of such combinative review.

All users further did comparisons among their selected candidates before they made the final choice. In order to understand what features they mainly considered at this last stage, we analyzed pages that were visited near the end. It indicates that 66.7% (8 out of 12) users went to Flickr CF to compare candidates' usage trends or community photos, and 33.3% emphasized product specifications and reviews on Yahoo (see Figure 2.b). Their verbal confirmations additionally verified the factors' dominant effects on their final choice.

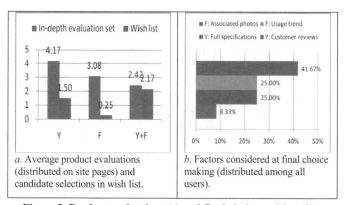

a. Average product evaluations (distributed on site pages) and candidate selections in wish list.

b. Factors considered at final choice making (distributed among all users).

Figure 2. Product evaluations (*a*) and final choice making (*b*).

Usability Scores
Thus, the above results experimentally demonstrate that Flickr CF, as a pure social popularity based product finder, was in fact frequently applied by participants at their different decision stages, in combination with the standard e-store Yahoo CF. Post-measurements of users' decision confidence and purchase intention further shows that 83.3% of them were confident that the product they "purchased" is really the best one and 75% truly intent to purchase it if given the opportunity. It hence reflects a high level of decision quality achieved by our participants after they freely used the two sites.

	Mean (St.d.)		*p* (t-test)
	Yahoo CF	Flickr CF	
"The site is easy to use."	3.75 (0.87)	3.83 (0.72)	0.75
"The site is useful to improve my 'shopping' performance."	3.75 (0.75)	3.75 (0.75)	1
"I would be likely to use it if I had to search for a product in the future."	3.58 (0.67)	3.67 (0.65)	0.81
"I would like to contribute if returning to the site."	3.33 (0.78)	3.75 (0.45)	0.14
Items that users wanted to contribute (the number of users out of all who had overall contribution intention to the site):	PR (3/6); PE (5/6); PP (4/6); RR (2/6);	PR (5/10); PE (3/10); PP (7/10); RR (4/10);	
	PR: product ratings; PE: product reviews; PP: product photos; RR: responses to other reviews		

Table 2. Measurements of users' subjective perceptions (each responded on a 5-point Likert scale from 1 "*strongly disagree*" to "*strongly agree*").

We also measured users' subjective perceptions with the interfaces they just used, including perceived ease of use, perceived usefulness, and return intention and contribution intentions. Since all participants used both sites, a within-subject *t-test* was performed to test the differences if any respecting these criteria. It turns out that Flickr CF obtained similar positive scores to Yahoo CF. Some criteria (such as intention to contribute) were even rated higher although the differences are not significant (see Table 2). As a matter of fact, 10 users explicitly indicated that they would like to contribute content once revisiting Flickr CF, relative to 6 who had such intention to Yahoo. Table 2 lists actual items that they were willing to contribute.

How to convince newcomers to become contributors has always been a challenge to social network sites [1]. The findings from our experiment interestingly suggest that stimulating users to practically experience the benefits of information shared in the social community (e.g., searching for a product based on the info) may likely promote their motivation to contribute (probably driven by the kindness to serve others with similar needs). The reason remains a topic for our future validation and exploration.

Users' Improving Suggestions

We finally collected users' opinions on interface elements and their improving suggestions. Most of them commented that it will be much beneficial to combine both websites into one. That is, Flickr CF can be adopted as a supplementary part to Yahoo (e.g., *"it does not perform like a professional e-commerce site, but the data is useful."*) They suggested that its popularity resources can be embedded into Yahoo to generate "the top products". In addition, the popularity-based sorting tool can be combined with standard feature-based browsing/filtering facilities, to support them when with various preference-certainty levels. Regarding product details, the usage trend statistics and associated photos from Flickr will be valuable references, in addition to static product specifications and customer reviews. Almost all participants were also impressed by the statistical graph that visualizes products' usage trends, perceiving it *"intuitive and easy to understand."*

One user further suggested taking geographical distribution into account, such as separating users in Flickr community by their regions so as to distinguish product differences (*"one camera model was sold in Europe, but probably not in China"*) and cultural impacts (*"people from the same cultural background may have common behavior"*). Another user proposed to add time dimension to compute product popularity, given that old models would be used by more users. He commented that *"popularity should better be compared between products that were released at the same time."*

DESIGN IMPLICATIONS FOR FUTURE WORK

Although more and more attentions have been paid in recent years to developing social recommender systems through utilizing resourceful data from social media sites, most works have focused on objective algorithm accuracy, rather than assessing users' perceptions and true needs of social data in their decision making. As one of beginners, we contributed in this paper to particularly revealing the role of "product popularity" regarding how users perceived and employed it in searching for a high-risk product. The usability study of Flickr CF shows that most users perceived the "product popularity" suggested by it more credible than by a standard e-commerce site, because it is more dependent on a large community's real usages and less of commercial interests. The community information was also found to bring effects at a user's different decision stages. It not only contributed to assisting users in locating interested products, but also actively acted to help them establish wish list and make the

final decision. Moreover, our users, who were all first-time encounters of Flickr CF, expressed positive acceptance scores on it, and more notably higher intention to contribute content to the site against to a normal shopping site.

All in all, according to the experimental results, we believe that the "product popularity" can be well integrated into an adaptive decision support to generate social recommendations, serving users who have unclear objectives at the start. It will induce positive influence on enabling users to be familiar with the product domain and identify candidates among the recommended products, if they trust them. Thus, for the development of a trustworthy social recommender, we suggest including the "product popularity" being originated from social media and connected to consumers' real usages. Furthermore, the popularity can be additionally customized to involve various contextual factors such as contributors' regional properties to dynamically map to the current user's situations. This study also discloses other kinds of product-related social data, like the camera's usage trend statistics and community photos, in guiding users to form a more complete choice confirmation. These data can be hence usefully combined with products' static descriptions to develop more intelligent tradeoff supports [6].

For our future work, we will be engaged in conducting studies to validate the above suggested findings across different product domains and systems. Our ultimate goal is to conclude effective design guidelines to benefit current e-commerce decision tools and recommender interfaces, so that they can optimally improve consumers' subjective perceptions and task performance.

ACKNOWLEDGMENTS

We are grateful to the participants of our user study for their patience and time. We also thank reviewers' comments in improving the quality of the paper.

REFERENCES

1. Burke, M., Marlow, C., and Lento, T. Feed me: motivating newcomer contribution in social network sites. In *Prof. CHI 2009*, ACM Press, 945-954.

2. Cialdini, R. B. and Goldstein, N. J. Social influence: compliance and conformity. *Annual Review of Psychology 55* (2004), 591-621.

3. Haubl, G. and Trifts, V. Consumer decision making in online shopping environments: the effects of interactive decision aids. *Marketing Science 19*, 1 (2000), 4-21.

4. Lazar, J., Meiselwitz, G., and Feng, J. Understanding web credibility: a synthesis of the research literature. *Found. Trends Hum.-Comput. Interact. 1*, 2 (2007), 139-202.

5. Olshavky, R. W. and Granbois, D. H. Consumer decision making: fact or fiction? *Journal of Consumer Research 6* (1979), 93-100.

6. Pu, P. and Chen, L. Integrating tradeoff support in product search tools for e-commerce sites. In *Proc. ACM EC 2006*, ACM Press, 269-278.

Raconteur: From Intent to Stories

Pei-Yu Chi, Henry Lieberman
MIT Media Laboratory
20 Ames St., Cambridge, MA, USA
{peggychi, lieber}@media.mit.edu

ABSTRACT

When editing a story from a large collection of media, such as photos and video clips captured from daily life, it is not always easy to understand how particular scenes fit into the intent for the overall story. Especially for novice editors, there is often a lack of coherent connections between scenes, making it difficult for the viewers to follow the story.

In this paper, we present *Raconteur*, a story editing system that helps users assemble coherent stories from media elements, each annotated with a sentence or two in unrestricted natural language. It uses a Commonsense knowledge base, and the AnalogySpace Commonsense reasoning technique. Raconteur focuses on finding *story analogies* – different elements illustrating the same overall "point", or independent stories exhibiting similar narrative structures.

Author Keywords

Storytelling, media editing, story goal, story analogy, commonsense computing, video, photograph.

ACM Classification Keywords

H5.m. Information interfaces and presentation (e.g., HCI): Miscellaneous.

General Terms

Design, Human Factors

INTRODUCTION

When presenting or editing a large set of material, such as photos and video clips captured from daily life, it is not easy to understand how particular scenes fit into the overall story. Most people therefore choose to present the story by events in chronological order [6], or by location or characters. Although there is software for automating categorization or suggesting keyword tags, it is still challenging to create a coherent higher-level presentation that tells an entertaining story. Novice users often do not pay attention to the "point" being made by showing a given scene, or provide meaningful connections between scenes, making it difficult for the

viewers to follow the story. We believe that an intelligent interface that provides assistance in relating the concrete elements of the scene to the overall story intent, will result in more effective story composition.

We present *Raconteur*, a story editing system that helps users think about material in a story, by showing related scenes or other stories with similar goals. The word "raconteur", by definition, is a person who is skilled in relating stories and anecdotes meaningfully. Similarly, our system tries to understand the narrative goal presented by the user, and find analogous story elements related to the goal.

We aim to create a system that helps a user tell a story by selecting a sequence of media items from a corpus of video, stills, narrations, and other media. We are assuming that each media element is annotated with a sentence or two in unrestricted natural language. The annotation may describe people, events, actions, and intent of the scene. Some annotations may be generated by metadata, transcription of audio, or other means.

A user at first presents a story goal in natural language, for example, "a 4-hour biking challenge on Cape Cod". The objective of the system is to provide a selection of possible matches of the annotated media elements to the story goal, that best help to tell the story. Note that this objective is *not* the same as simple search, keyword matching, subject relevance, or other conventional retrieval problems.

The tools we use for doing this are a large Commonsense knowledge base, Open Mind Common Sense; state-of-the art natural language parsing; and our own unique AnalogySpace inference technique for analogical reasoning. We can only provide a brief description of the knowledge base and inference in this paper; we refer the reader to the references for more detailed explanation of the tools.

For the "biking challenge" example, the system is able to suggest video clips that support relevant themes, such as anticipation and worries, preparation, difficulties, and, finally, the result of success or failure of the trip.

Analogous Story Thinking

We are inspired by how humans understand stories using analogies, which are partial similarities between different situations that support further inferences [4]. Schank proposed the idea of "story skeleton" to explain how we construct and comprehend a story under a certain structure to communicate with each other [11].

For example, a camping, hiking, and biking trip may include challenges (putting a tent up, going through a long and steep path), difficulties or worries (cannot assemble the tent poles, unable to finish the path, get lost on the way, bad weather), and enjoyable experiences (learning the setup, arriving a new place, meeting new friends) of a physical activity with a group of people. Similar points may be presented again and again through the process of developing a story. Superficially different events may illustrate analogous themes, so the ability to make analogies helps tell a story in a coherent way to the audience.

FORMATIVE USER STUDY

Before we present the Raconteur system itself, we describe a formative study to see if users would find presentation of analogous story elements helpful in story construction. In [12], we presented a more extensive user study reporting concrete experience with a previously implemented system for story construction via Commonsense knowledge. The present study is concerned with the value of the new analogical inference. We designed a story-editing interface that shows both the raw set of selected material and the analogous elements we found.

Experimental setup

We asked one participant to collect media (photos or videos) documenting her life experiences for three months. We observed the 30 collected stories, selected and compared similar topics, and specified the key shots in each story.

We summarize three main categories: 1) stories with a clear procedure as a story pattern, e.g. birthday parties that people sing the "Happy Birthday" song, make wishes, cut the cake, etc.; 2) Stories without a clear procedure but with certain expected events; 3) Stories without a clear procedure and expected events, e.g. a camping, hiking, and biking trips that include difficult challenges and new experience of an activity. We chose one story from each of these categories as test cases, including "Hsien's birthday party with a potluck dinner", "Mike's commencement party for his first master's degree", and "A 4-hour biking challenge in Cape Cod". The collector annotated each media element with a sentence or two in English.

5 participants were invited, including 3 males and 2 females, aged between 20-30, experienced with digital media. Participants were asked to edit stories for sharing with their friends. The facilitator first helped them familiarize themselves with the test cases, and then introduced our editing interface and conducted the 3 editing sessions.

Results

We found that when the size of the corpus was large and the story was relatively complex (test case 1&3), presenting the analogous story helped users follow a story pattern better. Especially for test case 3 (a biking trip), participants found the story complex for them to edit, and reported the analogous examples helped them to design the story development. Most participants spent considerable time on

observing the similarity of story content. One participant said, "It was interesting to see how the system presented a new perspective to the story I wanted to tell"; another explained, "The system helped me rethink the similarity and differences between experiences, which I would rarely think to do from just browsing a bunch of files." These findings encouraged us that the analogical reasoning mechanism would prove useful to users in story construction.

DESIGN OF THE RACONTEUR SYSTEM

In this section we present a concrete example of a story of a vacation trip from the collected story base, along with the description of our knowledge representation and inference methods in Raconteur, and the user interface.

Finding Elements Analogous to the Story Goal

A user starts by inputting a story goal, in unrestricted natural language. A simple example is, "*a 4-hour biking challenge on Cape Cod*". First of all, we need to determine the possible patterns to present the goal. Table 1 lists sample narrative goals and media annotations that Raconteur finds for this Cape Cod biking trip example.

Both goal statements and media item annotations are processed using conventional natural language tools such as part of speech tagging. The result is related to knowledge stored in our Open Mind Common Sense knowledge base, and the ConceptNet semantic network [9]. Assertions from that knowledge base relevant to the concept "challenge", after excluding anything that has no connection to "biking" include,

Anticipations and Worries
• "Cape Cod, a peninsula with stunning scenes, is famous for vacation and outdoor activities such as biking." (A1)
• "Before this, I had only experienced long biking trip once. When I promised to take this challenge, I was a little bit nervous and afraid that I couldn't finish the trip." (A2)
Preparation
• "To start a day, we need energy; so first, we went to have a luxurious brunch." (P1)
• "It is important to rent a good bike for the challenge. We came to the rent shop and pick our own bikes." (P1)
• "Then, we biked all the way to the end of the rail trail. This was about six miles, the most difficult part." (P2)
Difficulties
• "It took us a while to find the correct way between the branches. Thanks to the map, or we would get lost." (D1)
• "It was a really long trail… I almost wanted to give up on the half way, especially I had no idea about how long I had biked." (D2)
Results: Successes or Failures
• "As you can see, we were really thrilled when we arrived the beach. Although I already felt one mile was long!" (R1)
• "Surprisingly, it was easier than what I imagined. We were so excited when we arrived the destination." (R2)

Table 1. Multiple story units with similar patterns that Raconteur finds. The number indicates the elements in the same set of patterns.

- Desires (challenge, anticipate something)
- MotivatedByGoal (challenge, test oneself)
- HasProperty (challenge, difficulty)
- Causes (challenge, success)
- Causes (challenge, failure)

One pattern for presenting a challenge involves "*anticipations and worries*", "*preparation*", "*difficulties*" and "*results*" (successes or failures). When Raconteur finds more than one pattern to present the goal, multiple patterns can be considered.

Analogical Inference in Raconteur

Second, Raconteur analyzes the annotation of each media element in natural language, and makes analogical inferences. It uses the AnalogySpace Commonsense reasoning technique [13].

AnalogySpace represents the entire space of OMCS's knowledge through a sparse matrix whose rows are ConceptNet concepts (noun phrases and verb phrases), and whose columns are *features*, one-argument predicates that can be applied to those concepts. A feature generally consists of one of 20 or so two-place relations (kind_of, part_of, etc.) together with another concept. Inference is performed by Principal Component Analysis on this matrix, using the Singular Value Decomposition. This transforms the space by finding those axes that best account for the variation in the matrix. These axes are often semantically meaningful. The reason this is good for computing analogy is that concepts that have similar Commonsense assertions true about them wind up close to each other in the transformed space. Unlike

logical approaches to analogy, it is computationally efficient, and tolerant of vagueness, noise, redundancy, and contradiction.

For example, A1 in Table 1 with descriptions of "*Cape Cod*", "*stunning*", "*famous*", "*vacation*", and "*biking*" infers this piece of material indicates the user's anticipation of the trip; P1 infers the preparation including having brunch, and renting a bike; D1 explains the difficulty of finding the way to avoid getting lost; then R1 shows the excitement of the arrival.

Finally, by finding the elements related to the story goal, we provide different perspectives on telling a story within a set of material. If there is more than one generated pattern that matches the story goal, Raconteur will go through this process to different patterns and present one that contains the most analogous elements in the set.

Raconteur User Interface

The final results of analogous story elements will be shown through the web-based user interface as Figure 1. A user can see the unorganized, sequential material in chronological order as in Figure 1a. The user decides a story goal in English, and then the analogous elements will be shown, as in Figure 1b. The user can drag and drop photos or video clips as desired to create a story.

Discussion

We'd also like to discuss how Raconteur might enable new kinds of storytelling activities. Our model encourages users to think about the story goal instead of directly composing individual elements. To help participants reason how the

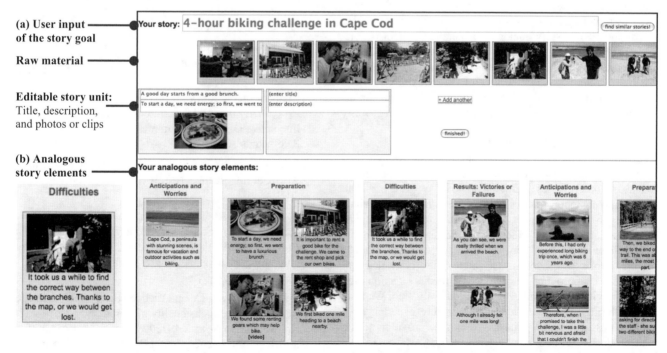

Figure 1. Raconteur interface: (a) the upper part presents the raw material of the unorganized story, and provides the editing interface for users to decide the story goal and the sequence of scenes; (b) the lower part shows the sets of analogous story elements in a pattern that matches the story goal.

pattern and the results were generated, we highlight the keywords that relate to system inferences, allowing users to revise the suggested pattern and explore the space of results. Furthermore, to make the storytelling process closer to the experience of daily conversation, we are also considering integrating our technique in a chat scenario. The storyteller can interact with a partner to talk about the stories, and Raconteur can suggest both story topics and media elements.

RELATED WORK
Cooper et. al. designed a similarity-based analysis to cluster photos by timestamps and content [3]. Joshi and Luo presented a method to infer events and activities from geographical information [5]. However, most of the research work on automatic media organization focuses on analyzing the basic attributes such as time and location; few of them consider the overall story development and story thinking with digital media.

Another emerging research area is to interact with digital media on the level of story composition. ARIA is a software agent that dynamically retrieves related photos based on the content of an email or web page [8]. Barry presented a system that presents contextual information during the process of video capture [1]. The closest system to the present one is Storied Navigation [12], which shares the goal of composing stories from annotated media clips. Our work here differs in the use of the analogy inference technique, and is focused on instantiating narrative goals directly through analogical inference to create better story structures.

We are also aware of several relevant narrative systems such as the storytelling and planning system "Universe," which models the story structure as a set of hierarchical plans and generates plot outlines based on the author's story goal [7]; Riedl and León's story analogous generation system is able to transform existing stories to a novel context [10]; Cheong et. al. presents an authoring interactive narrative framework to help users construct branching story structure [2]. Although rare of these projects incorporate digital media as our goal, they provide insights of story analysis to our work.

CONCLUSION AND FUTURE WORK
We have presented Raconteur, a story editing system that helps users think about material in a story by showing related scenes or other stories with similar goals. We suggest that presenting analogous stories can provide a helpful guideline for users to tell their stories. Our formative user study shows that this kind of analogy finding is particularly helpful in the case where users have large libraries or complex stories. Future work will focus on increasing relevance of suggestions, improving interactivity of media selection and output previews, and conducting detailed evaluation. We also are exploring augmenting the media capture experience as well as post-production editing. We aim for providing a fun and productive environment for storytelling. Maybe it will help your friends become more interested in watching your vacation movies, after all.

REFERENCES
1. Barry, B. and Davenport, G. Documenting Life: Videography and Common Sense. In *Proc. ICME2003*: the 2003 IEEE Intl. Conf. on Multimedia and Expo, IEEE Press (2003), Baltimore, MD, USA.

2. Cheong, Y., Kim, Y. Min, W. and Shim, E. PRISM: A Framework for Authoring Interactive Narratives. In *Proc. ICIDS 2008*: the 1st Joint Intl. Conf. on Interactive Digital Storytelling: Interactive Storytelling, ACM Press (2008), Erfurt, German.

3. Cooper, M., Foote, J., Girgensohn, A., and Wilcox, L. Temporal Event Clustering for Digital Photo Collections. In *Proc. MM'03*: the 11th ACM Intl. Conf. on Multimedia, ACM Press (2003), Berkeley, CA, USA.

4. Gentner, D. Analogy. In *A Companion to Cognitive Science*, Oxford University Press (1998), pp. 107-113.

5. Joshi, D. and Luo, J. Inferring Generic Activities and Events from Image Content and Bags of Geo-tags. In *Proc. CIVR'08*: the 2008 Intl. Conf. on Content-based image and video retrieval, ACM Press (2008), Niagara Falls, Canada.

6. Kirk, D., Sellen, A., Rother, C., and Wood, K. Understanding Photowork. In *Proc. CHI2006*: the 24th Intl. Conf. on Human factors in computing systems, ACM Press (2006), Montréal, Québec, Canada.

7. Lebowitz, M. Story Telling as Planning and Learning. *Poetics 14* (1985), pp. 483-502.

8. Lieberman, H. and Liu, H. Adaptive Linking Between Text and Photos using Common Sense Reasoning. In *Proc. AH2002*: the 2nd Intl. Conf. on Adaptive hypermedia and adaptive web-based systems, ACM Press (2002), London, UK.

9. Liu, H. and Singh, P. ConceptNet: a Practical Commonsense Reasoning Toolkit. In *BT Technology Journal* (2004), 22, 4, 211-226.

10. Riedl, M. and León, C. Generating Story Analogues. In *Proc. AIIDE09*: the 5th Conf. on Artificial Intelligence for Interactive Digital Entertainment, AAAI Press (2009), Palo Alto, CA, USA.

11. Schank, R. Tell Me a Story: A New Look at Real and Artificial Intelligence. Northwestern University Press (1991).

12. Shen, Y.-T., Lieberman, H., and Davenport G. What's Next? Emergent Storytelling from Video Collections. In *Proc. CHI2009*: the 27th Intl. Conf. on Human factors in computing systems, ACM Press (2009), Boston, MA, USA.

13. Speer, R., Havasi, C., and Lieberman, H. AnalogySpace: Reducing the Dimensionality of Common Sense Knowledge. In *Proc. AAAI2008*: the 23rd AAAI Conf. on Artificial intelligence, AAAI Press (2008), Chicago, IL, USA.

Error-Tolerant Version Space Algebra [*]

Eugene R. Creswick
Stottler Henke Associates, Inc.
1107 NE 45th, Suite 310, Seattle, WA, USA
rcreswick@stottlerhenke.com

Aaron M. Novstrup
Stottler Henke Associates, Inc.
1107 NE 45th, Suite 310, Seattle, WA, USA
anovstrup@stottlerhenke.com

ABSTRACT

Application customization has been extensively researched in the field of Programming by Demonstration (PBD), and Version Space Algebra has proven itself to be a viable means of quickly learning precise action sequences from user demonstrations. However, this technique is not capable of handling user error in domains with actions that depend on parameters that accept myriad values. Activities such as image, audio and video editing require user actions that are difficult for users to precisely replicate in different circumstances. Demonstrations that are off by a single pixel or a split-second cause traditional composite Version Spaces to collapse.

We present a method of incorporating error tolerance into Version Space algebra. This approach, termed Error-Tolerant Version Spaces, adapts Version Space Algebra to domains where the tactile capabilities of the user have a much greater chance of prematurely collapsing the hypothesis space that is being learned. The resulting framework is capable of quickly learning in domains where perfectly consistent user input can not be expected. We have successfully applied our technique in the domain of image redaction, allowing our users to quickly specify redactions that can be reliably applied to many images without the entry of explicit parameters.

Author Keywords

Smart Environments, Error Tolerance, Version Spaces, Programming by Demonstration

ACM Classification Keywords

D.2.2 Design Tools and Techniques: User Interfaces; H.1.2 Models and principles: User/Machine Systems

General Terms

Algorithms, Experimentation, Human Factors

---

[*]This work was supported by the Air Force Research Laboratory's Information Directorate (AFRL/RI), Rome, NY, under contract FA8750-09-C-0099.

INTRODUCTION

The field of Programming by Demonstration (PBD) endeavors to enable non-programmers to augment computer interfaces by teaching autonomous agents to perform complex actions that have been demonstrated by users. In its simplest form, programming by demonstration exists in rote recording and playback features in many different environments. Microsoft Office's macro recorder, Emacs macros, and myriad other applications provide recording and playback features that watch a carefully-crafted sequence of user actions and then allow that precise sequence to be repeated at a later time. This approach is definitely of value; however, this form of rote learning does not account for the context of the user actions, nor does it generalize to new circumstances. Therefore, it is possible to do a great deal of damage with recorded macros if they are not created with great care. PBD aims to mitigate this risk by learning "programs" that can run robustly in new execution contexts by generalizing from multiple demonstrations [2, 5].

Many approaches have been proposed for different forms of PBD—we focus on one technique in particular: Version Space Algebra [3].

VERSION SPACE ALGEBRA

Version Space Algebra maintains a set of all possible hypotheses for a given problem domain. These hypotheses are represented in a decomposed form, spread across a hierarchy of version spaces. "Leaf" version spaces are generally trivially simple, consisting of hypotheses about singular values (such as integers, ratios, or strings). These axiomatic version spaces are combined to create more complex composite version spaces by using the following operations:

Union A union of version spaces contains the full set of all valid hypotheses in each of the component version spaces.

Join A join of version spaces contains the cross-product of the valid hypotheses in the component version spaces.

Transform Transforms are used to convert the input and output types of version spaces to match those of other unioned version spaces, or to provide semantics to the tuples that result from a join operation.

The complete description of these operators is out of scope for this paper. Such a description can be found in Tessa Lau's seminal work [3].

Learning is achieved by training the top-level composite version space on a demonstrated (input, output) pair, where the input contains the context of the demonstration, and the output is the desired output state. The top-level version space decomposes the example into sub-input and sub-outputs as necessary, and trains its composite version spaces on the decomposed inputs and outputs. This process continues to the leaves, where the axiomatic version spaces are either narrowed (if the new example is consistent, but different from past examples), collapsed (if the new example is *not* consistent with past examples) or unchanged (if the new example exactly matches past examples). A version space collapse indicates that a hypothesis was discarded and that collapse is propagated up the version space hierarchy, possibly causing other composite version spaces to collapse as well, if they no longer contain valid hypotheses. Lau et. al have shown that this hierarchical structure enables extremely fast learning. In one case, they demonstrated the ability to learn text editing tasks in as little as 1-2 demonstrations [4].

Version Space Algebra has one Achilles' heel that prevents this technique from being applied to many domains: user error during demonstrations can cause version spaces to collapse prematurely. For example, consider the task of drawing rectangles on images of various sizes. This task is particularly important in the area of information redaction. Drawing subsequent rectangles to redact similar content on a series of images at varying resolutions is both time consuming and difficult to do consistently. A user can easily specify the first example by manually dragging a selection tool to specify a rectangular region. The first example will narrow the set of possibilities significantly, but not sufficiently to learn a usable "program" for drawing rectangles. At least one subsequent example must be provided in a different context. In this domain, that means that the user must provide a consistent example on an image of a different size. To do so, the user must draw precisely the same rectangle on a new image. This is extremely difficult to do reliably in all but the simplest cases. Errors of one pixel are sufficient to cause the version space to collapse prematurely, resulting in no benefit at all.

In this paper we present an approach to Version Space Algebra that is tolerant of these types of user error. We start by discussing the limited related work in this area, then we present our initial approach to error tolerant version space algebra, we briefly discuss our specific use cases, and finally we conclude and discuss our goals for subsequent research.

RELATED WORK

User demonstration error can occur in any programming by demonstration domain; however, different approaches are necessary for different domains. Chen and Weld developed CHINLE, a learning system that incorporates techniques for handling errors in demonstrations within widget-based interfaces [1]. CHINLE allows users to detect and fix errors during training by providing the user with a view of the sequence of demonstrations. This view allows the user to retract or correct incorrect demonstrations. This approach works well when the user can readily identify these incorrect demonstrations, but that is not always the case. We are concerned with demonstration errors that are the result of tactile difficulty in precisely specifying an action. In such a situation, it is unlikely that the user will be able to identify an incorrect example from a list of recorded demonstrations.

Numerous PBD techniques have focused on reducing the error of inference engines. Opsis [6] presents users with the choice to create new examples based on old examples, but no generalization is done at all. Rather, "imitation" is used to directly generate programs from user input. Peridot [7, 8] helps users generate interface widgets, including shapes of various sizes and purposes. Peridot uses inferred graphical constraints to allow sloppier user actions, but this is greatly helped because Peridot only needs to deal with the relationships that are typical in user interfaces. In contrast, Error-Tolerant Version Spaces have no such restrictions.

ERROR-TOLERANT VERSION SPACE ALGEBRA

We focus on the domain of image manipulations, and particularly drawing or selecting shapes on an image. This task (shape drawing) arises any time a user needs to specify a selection area, perform a crop, resize, or place an image or other shape within an existing image repeatedly in a predictable way, such as when redacting content. This approach is also applicable to any task where the set of valid user inputs is very high and the parameters to user actions are ordered—such as pixel locations or color selection. In our sample domain the set of inputs is represented by combinations of pixel locations with respect to the loaded image dimensions. Other example use cases include adjusting volume controls, specifying temporal coordinates in video or audio editing, and any application that involves input mechanisms that acquire ordered inputs. The rest of this paper focuses on the task of training an agent to redact rectangular regions of a given input image. To further simplify the text, we only consider selections in one dimension[1].

Error-Tolerant Version Spaces are grounded on the idea that each demonstration is based on a single true hypothesis but the demonstrated values may be perturbed from the true hypothesis by a certain error for the given context of the example. Therefore, error-tolerant version spaces narrow the set of valid hypotheses more conservatively than Lau et. al's Version Spaces [3]. This is accomplished by the addition of two version space functions:

similar $similar(D, H)$ encodes the assumption that for some distance metric d, $d(D, H) < \epsilon$ for any demonstration D, a true hypothesis H, and error tolerance ϵ. If $d < \epsilon$ is true, then $similar(D, H)$ returns true. The purpose of $similar$ is to conservatively narrow the set of valid hypotheses—during training—to the intersection of those hypotheses that are $similar$ to the user's demonstrations.

filter the filter function transforms a set of hypotheses into a (generally smaller, or unit) set of values that represent the most likely valid hypotheses when a version space is

---

[1]Two-dimensional selections are simply a combination of two one-dimensional selections.

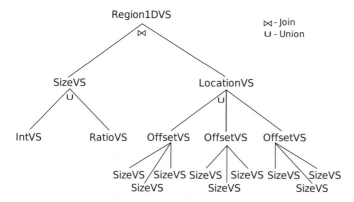

Figure 1. Version Space for one-dimensional regions. IntVS and RatioVS are axiomatic version spaces, the repeated SizeVS instances have been elided for clarity.

evaluated on a real input. We expect that $filter$ will often either be the identity function (in which case no filtering is done) or it will be a strict aggregator (for example, to select the most conservative of, or the average of the incoming hypotheses).

Figure 1 shows a simple version space for learning one-dimensional regions. Regions may have a fixed size or a size relative to the size of the image, and they may be located either a fixed or relative offset from the front (left/top) edge of the image, the back (right/bottom) edge of the image, or the center of the image. The region may be anchored to the location based on the front (left/top) edge, back (right/bottom) edge, or center of the region. This version space is made error tolerant by using a definition of $similar$ to narrow the hypotheses spaces of each of the axiomatic version spaces ($IntVS$ and $RatioVS$). These particular axiomatic version spaces typically only exist in one of three states: (a) Any value, (b) a specific value, or (c) nothing (collapsed). The "Error-Tolerant" versions contain a boundary-set representable region that is determined by intersecting the regions around each example based on the evaluation of $similar$ (and thus on the distance metric d and error tolerance ϵ).

DISCUSSION

Our solution is motivated by a simple model of the errors that users are expected to make, which is based upon our experience implementing and using Error-Tolerant Version Space Algebra for image redaction tasks.

We assume that the size and location of a demonstration are within a fixed, known error bound. Specifically, with an error bound of 2 pixels, we can make some assumptions about the true demonstration that the user meant to provide. For example, if a demonstrated region has a width of 10 pixels, and is centered at 15 pixels from the edge of the image, we can conclude that the true size is no less than 8 and no more than 12. We can also conclude that the left offset of this demonstration was meant to be between 8 and 12 pixels from the left edge of the image, because the demonstration showed a left offset of 10 pixels. We make no assumptions about the distribution of errors. In particular, we do not

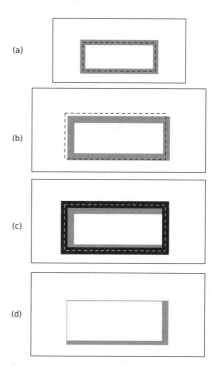

Figure 2. A sequence of demonstrated selections (dashed rectangles), and the valid regions learned from the examples (shaded regions). The outer rectangles represent image borders.

assume that small errors are more likely than large errors, nor do we assume that errors are more likely to be biased in one direction or the other (e.g. making the selection slightly larger than necessary, rather than slightly smaller).

It is important to note that this error model leads to different conclusions than other (also reasonable) models. For example, perhaps users tend to make larger errors with larger images, in which case we would require a relative rather than fixed error tolerance. Alternatively, the error tolerance could apply to the individual end points. In that case, we would assume that the true left endpoint is at least 8 and no more than 12 and the true right endpoint is at least 18 and no more than 22 when the target is the fixed region (10,20) and the error tolerance is 2 units. Note that the region covered by the union of the accepted hypotheses in this second error model is smaller (8 to 22) than the error model we chose to use (8 to 24). This is a point of consideration for certain use cases and demonstrates how the choice of error model can affect the learning properties of the algorithm.

Figure 2 displays a series of two demonstrations on two images of different sizes. In Figure 2 (a), a region is learned around the demonstrated rectangle. In Figure 2 (b), a second demonstration is given; however, because of the changed size, the user is unable to precisely match the same region. Despite the discrepancy, the version space does not collapse. Figure 2 (c) shows that the error tolerant regions around both of the demonstrations do intersect on all sides. Because this intersection is non-empty, the version space still contains hypotheses, which are depicted by the shaded region in Figure 2 (d).

Note that the intersection in Figure 2 (d) is a region, not an individual hypothesis. Instead of collapsing, as a normal version space would, the error-tolerant version space has reduced to a set of tightly clustered hypotheses. A direct comparison between standard and error-tolerant version spaces is impossible, since standard version spaces collapse when given imprecise demonstrations. Nonetheless, it is true that because error-tolerant version spaces do not narrow as quickly, they can require more training examples. The precise number is entirely dependent on the similarity measure used, the error tolerance, and the nature of the examples. In general, however, the maximally acceptable erroneous demonstrations must be observed before the error-tolerant version space achieves perfect learning.

In practice, this has not proven to be a problem, but that may depend greatly on the details of the domain in which this technique is employed. We expect that in the error-tolerant domains where these version spaces are applicable, it may be sufficient to quickly converge to a set of hypotheses clustered around the "true" hypothesis. In preliminary experimental work, we sampled truncated Gaussian models of input region size and user error to generate training/test data. Our results indicate a sizable, but not unreasonable, increase in the number of training examples required to achieve acceptable error as compared to standard version spaces utilizing perfect demonstrations (from an average of two examples with standard version spaces to an average of thirteen with error-tolerant version spaces). These results have been confirmed on a smaller scale by our practical experience with our image redaction tool, where we have found that four or five examples are usually sufficient. We also noted that even with perfect examples, the standard version spaces collapsed prematurely in over 90% of the trials due to rounding errors in the RatioVS.

CONCLUSIONS AND FUTURE WORK

Investigations continue into techniques that will improve upon this research, and we are particularly motivated by the following issues that arose during the development of Error-Tolerant Version Space Algebra:

Redaction error models revealed dependencies When learning conservative redactions on images, we found that the necessary error model revealed dependencies between the component version spaces used to represent redaction size and redaction locations. Because each version space maintained a range of valid hypotheses during most of the learning process, the conservative result (that covered all demonstrations) was not present in the cross-product of the size and location hypotheses, rather the bounds on the location had to be used independently with the largest size possible to ensure complete coverage.

Learning improves with error In fact, learning the correct hypothesis *requires* examples that exhibit the maximum error, as mentioned above. This is undesirable, since it may take significant time for that to happen. However, the degree of error in the generated results is bounded by the error tolerance. Therefore, the executing version spaces always generate results that are within the error tolerance.

Learning does not improve with repeated demonstrations It is reasonable to expect the learning algorithm to converge on the correct hypothesis as evidence accumulates. However, because error-tolerant version spaces only consider whether a hypothesis is *similar* to the user's demonstrations, they gain no information from demonstrations that are *similar* to all of the remaining hypotheses. We envision a probabilistic approach to address this shortcoming. It is also worth noting that when traditional version spaces encounter similar or repeated demonstrations, they either collapse or also learn nothing, respectively.

We have presented an approach to learning with Version Space Algebra when user demonstrations are subject to a form of error that has not previously been addressed. This approach greatly increases the applicability of Version Space Algebra by maintaining version spaces that would have otherwise collapsed prematurely.

REFERENCES

1. J. H. Chen and D. S. Weld. Recovering from errors during programming by demonstration. In *IUI '08: Proceedings of the 13th international conference on Intelligent user interfaces*, pages 159–168, New York, NY, USA, 2008. ACM.

2. A. Cypher, D. C. Halbert, D. Kurlander, H. Lieberman, D. Maulsby, B. A. Myers, and A. Turransky, editors. *Watch what I do: programming by demonstration*. MIT Press, Cambridge, MA, USA, 1993.

3. T. Lau, S. A. Wolfman, P. Domingos, and D. S. Weld. Programming by demonstration using version space algebra. *Machine Learning*, 53(1-2):111–156, 2003.

4. T. A. Lau, P. Domingos, and D. S. Weld. Version space algebra and its application to programming by demonstration. In *ICML '00: Proceedings of the Seventeenth International Conference on Machine Learning*, pages 527–534, San Francisco, CA, USA, 2000. Morgan Kaufmann Publishers Inc.

5. H. Lieberman. *Your Wish is My Command: Programming By Example (Interactive Technologies)*. Morgan Kaufmann, 1st edition, February 2001.

6. A. Michail. Imitation: An alternative to generalization in programming by demonstration systems. Technical report, University of Washington School of Computer Science and Engineering, TR# UW-CSE-98-08-06, 2006.

7. B. A. Myers. *Creating user interfaces by demonstration*. Academic Press Professional, Inc., San Diego, CA, USA, 1988.

8. B. A. Myers. Peridot: creating user interfaces by demonstration. pages 125–153, 1993.

Social Signal Processing: Detecting Small Group Interaction in Leisure Activity

Eyal Dim
The University of Haifa
Mount Carmel, Haifa, 31905, Israel
edim@campus.haifa.ac.il

Tsvi Kuflik
The University of Haifa
Mount Carmel, Haifa, 31905, Israel
tsvikak@mis.haifa.ac.il

ABSTRACT

Social Signal Processing of small groups enables detection of their social context. Monitoring of the social context may be based on position proximity (as a pre-condition for conversation), and on voice communication (an evidence for interaction). Understanding of the social context of a group may allow a system to intervine at the right moment and to suggest relevant services/information. This, in turn, may enhance the group members' experience during leisure activity. This study focuses on assessing the possibility of automatic detection of intra group interaction in a museum environment. It presents analysis and tools that intend to set the foundation for computer aided group iteration during leisure activities.

Author Keywords

Social Signal Processing, Group Modeling, Interrupt Management, Ubiquitous Computing.

ACM Classification Keywords

H.5.3 Group and Organization Interfaces, J.4 Social and Behavioral Sciences.

General Terms

Measurement

INTRODUCTION

Social Signal Processing (SSP) is used to detect human behavior in social context. Studies such as [5] focused mainly on task-oriented groups (e.g. employees in organizations, meetings, shopping, etc.). This study refers to SSP during leisure activities, specifically small groups visiting a museum. The motivation for this work is search for innovative technologies that may enhance museum visitors' experience. Bitgood [1] posits that overwhelming percentage of museum visitors come in groups. He sees the social contact as a very important aspect of informal learning, and sometimes as the most important part of the museum visit experience. Such significant social

opportunities invoke emotions, arousal and pleasure among the museum visitors [2]. Moreover, interaction between visitors is known to deepen the visitors' involvement and increase the intimacy among group members [4]. Therefore if a ubiquitous computing system could identify those groups that are less socially active, and find the right time to suggest social activities, it may have a positive impact on the emotions and feelings experienced by those groups.

Monitoring the group's social behavior may allow determination of its behavioral profile. The history and the current social state of the group may then be used for finding the right time to suggest group activity (e.g. it may be wrong to suggest an activity to a group which is already interacting). Therefore SSP may be used to answer two questions: (1) what is the profile of the group regarding its social interaction, and (2) when is the right time to interrupt the group. SSP measurements for social interactivity may be based on physical proximity as a pre-condition for face-to-face social interaction and on detection of conversation.

Previous studies in cultural heritage focused mainly on exploring the possibility to use novel technologies to support individuals visiting the museum, mainly by improving information delivery. This included adaptation, personalization and various additional aspects such as context-aware support of visitors [7]. Some applications were aimed at using collaborative tools like messaging, voice communication and eavesdropping to enable intra group interaction, as partially surveyed in [3].

The current study is an initial step towards the use of SSP for supporting small, leisure-oriented groups in cultural heritage setting. It focuses on observing small groups of museum visitors and analyzing their behavior in order to suggest ways where technology may be used for reasoning and intervention for enhancing the overall visit experience.

SOCIAL SIGNALS FOR SOCIAL INTERACTION

Setting and Data Collection

58 small groups of visitors, randomly chosen, were observed at the "Yitzhak Livneh-Astonishment" exhibition presented at the Tel-Aviv Museum of Arts. There was no human guidance at the exhibition hall, and the visitors did not use any other guidance device. The data gathered represents obvious group social behaviors. It included: position proximity of group members and duration of voice interaction within 1 minute intervals. Proximity had one of

three states (which was the dominant state during the sampling interval): (i) "Separated" – All group members are separated. (ii) "Joined" – Some group members are together. (iii) "Left" – The group left the exhibition. Voice interaction was recorded within each sampling interval (whether people talked or not). The data was collected for ten minutes for each group (or less if the group left). Four groups that stayed 3 minutes or less at exhibition were omitted from the analysis (resulting in N=54).

Proximity Measurements' Analysis

Position proximity has been analyzed to assess the possibilities for group profiling and interrupt management. Looking at the data, we noticed that there are groups that stay together most of the time, groups that are separated most of the time and groups that occasionally separate. As a first step, we clustered the groups in order to find different group types. We represented the groups using two characteristics: (1) Joined Ratio (JR) defined as percentage of time of being "Joined" out of the total visit time, trying to capture whether group members were in close proximity during the visit (2) Change Ratio (CR): the number of changes from "Joined" to "Separated" and vice versa out of the total visit time, trying to capture if the group has a steady or erratic behavior. We clustered the groups three times, using JR, using CR and using both CR and JR. We used K-mean clustering (trying k=2 through k=6), where k=3 seemed to provide the most intuitive clustering.

Clustering based on JR (Figure 1) shows three distinct behaviors "Joined profile" for groups whose members usually walked in close proximity (■), "Separated profile" for groups that were "Separated" most of the time (•), and "In-between profile" for groups that were sometimes together and sometimes separated (+). The X axis presents the group ID and the Y axis presents the JR. Clustering based on CR (Figure 2) shows other three distinct behaviors: "Steady profile" for groups who usually kept the same proximity – no changes to small changes in proximity, which may be "Joined" or "Separated" (■), "Always changing profile" for groups that were changing their proximity most of the time – erratic groups (•), and "Some changes profile" for groups that head some changes in their proximity status along the visit (+). The X axis presents the group ID and the Y axis presents the CR. Figure 3 presents three profiles resulted from clustering based on combination of CR and JR: the '+' represent the profile of groups that are usually together in close proximity, and their status does not change. The '•' represent the profile of groups that are usually separated and their proximity status has only little changes. The last profile '■' contains the groups that change their proximity very often. The X axis presents the JR and the Y axis presents the CR.

Using Position Proximity for Interrupt Management

The profiles generated by clustering the combined JR and CR representation may be used to decide when to offer group members the opportunity for group activity: (1) the

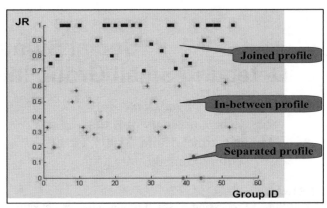
Figure 1. Profiling groups based on Joined Ratio (JR)

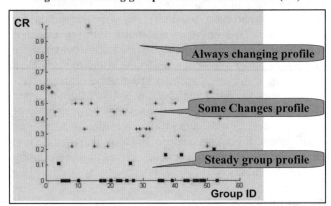
Figure 2. Profiling groups based on Change Ratio (CR)

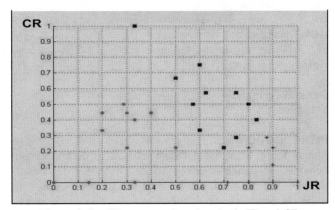
Figure 3. Profiling groups based on both JR and CR

groups that are mostly "Separated", with little changes in their proximity status, may be candidates for group activity suggestions; (2) the groups that change their proximity status erratically may also be candidates for such group activity suggestions; and (3) the groups that are always "Joined" may not require any intervention.

Conversation Duration Measurement and Analysis

Even though it seems that position proximity may help in understanding groups, what if group members in close proximity do not interact at all? This is where voice interaction comes into play. By measuring proximity we may infer interaction while by measuring voice data we can

310

prove interaction. The voice proximity is based on a threshold for cumulative duration of conversation within each predefined time measurement period (a minute in this case). For example, if the threshold is set to 10 seconds, a group having 15 seconds of conversation within a minute, is considered "Joined" (15 > 10 seconds), and a group having 5 seconds of conversation within a minute is considered "Separated" (5 ≤10 seconds). By setting such a Voice Duration Threshold (VDT) we can select our definition for quantified interaction. In addition we replace the position proximity patterns above with *voice proximity* patterns, based on "Joined" / "Separated" states that were defined by the VDT.

As the VDT grows, groups are more "Separated". Analysis of the groups' voice interaction reveals that even a requirement for a VDT of 10 seconds is enough to significantly change the JR of a specific group and transform it from position proximity "Joined" to *voice proximity* "Separated". Table 1 exemplifies this change in behavior. It presents information about 5 groups. Each cell presents the "Joined" or "Separated" state based on proximity to the left of the arrow symbol ("→") and "Joined" or "Separated" state based on VDT of 10 seconds to the right of the arrow symbol. "J" represents a "Joined" state and "S" represents a "Separated" state. Highlighted cells represent minutes where the state changed. If the group left the exhibition the cell is blank. For example the VDT changed the state of group 25 from "Joined" to "Separated" for the total time of presence at the exhibition. Such a change in the determination of "Joined" and "Separated" states could affect the decisions about 'togetherness', if they were based on voice proximity JR criterion rather than on position proximity JR criterion.

Using *Voice Proximity* for Interrupt Management
As shown for group ID 25 in Table 1 above, groups that have been clustered as "Joined" all the time by position proximity (and therefore require no attention, as noted above) may still not interact. In this case, they too may be offered stimuli to increase the opportunity of group activity.

PREDICTION OF BEHAVIORAL PATTERNS
The ability to predict visitors' behavior may allow selection of a course of action regarding encouragement of group activity. We tried two approaches towards such prediction: (1) Using clustering to identify the group's profile and react accordingly; (2) Markov Chain analysis - to assess the status of the next minute, so if it is a "Separated" minute, it is suitable for introduction of group-activity opportunity.

Identifying Group's Profile by K-mean Clustering
Considering the clustering process described earlier, we now have a definition for three distinct group types, represented by three different clusters. Assuming that we have this information, new groups may be assigned to the clusters and inherit the cluster characteristics (e.g. group type). Knowing the group type at early stages of the visit

Group	Minute 1	Minute 2	Minute 3	Minute 4	Minute 5	Minute 6	Minute 7	Minute 8	Minute 9	Minute 10
21	J→J	J→J	J→J	S→S	S→S	J→J	J→J	J→J	J→J	J→J
22	J→J	J→J	J→J	J→J	J→J					
23	S→S	S→S	J→J	S→S	S→S	S→S	J→S	S→S	S→S	S→S
24	J→J	J→S	J→J	J→S	J→J	J→J	J→J			
25	J→S	J→S	J→S	J→S	J→S					

Table 1. The Change from "Joined" to "Separated" States for a VDT of 10 Seconds (J: Joined; S: Separated; →: Proximity status → *Voice Proximity* status changes; based on VDT of 10 seconds per minute.

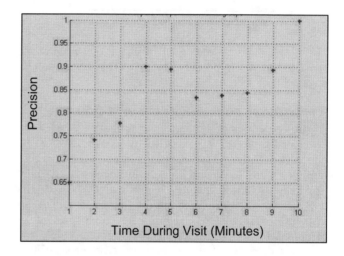

Figure 4. Precision of group profiling - all groups.

may allow us to offer appropriate group services. The question is how fast a system can identify the group's profile, using accumulated data. 10-fold validation was used to assess the precision of the prediction (90% of the data used for training and 10% for testing every time).Figure 4 shows the precision of the prediction (Y axis) as a function of the museum visit duration (X axis). The results show, that from the 4th minute of the visit and on the precision is above 0.8 (in addition, recall is above 0.9 for the groups with low CR, both for "Joined" groups and for "Separated" groups; and as can be expected, the erratic groups are more difficult to predict, and their recall rate exceeds only 0.6 for the worst case minute).

Using Markov Chains for the Next Minute Prediction
Markov Chains analysis is commonly used for prediction based on temporal data [6]. The analysis of the data (using 10-fold validation) focused on finding the optimal number of accumulated data points required for prediction (the K in the analysis). Figure 5 presents the number of errors per prediction (Y axis), based on the size of K (X axis). The solid line with '■' represents a random case, 50% chance of success, compared to the solid line with 'Δ', which shows the improvement gained as a function of the history used.

311

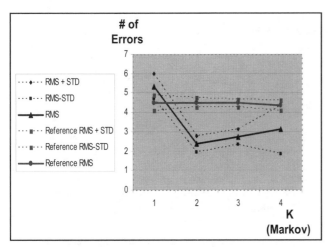

Figure 5. Predicting the next minute.

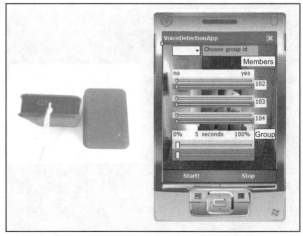

Figure 6. A prototype monitor for group interactive behavior.

The dotted lines at each side of a solid line show the standard deviation of the 10 folds. The best result is received for K=2 (2 minutes history).

A PROTOTYPE FOR GROUP BEHAVIOR MONITOR

A prototype demonstrating such technology has been developed by using data recorded by mobile active RFID tags (developed by 3Tec in Italy, Figure 6 – left). These tags are able to detect the group members' position proximity as well as members' voice activity. The data is analyzed by a group server and transmitted to a PDA for visualization (Figure 6 - right). Each group member is identified by the ID of the mobile tag (e.g. 102), and represented by two bars: the top bar represents position proximity to other group members during the last second, and the bottom one represents if this group member was speaking. The two bars at the bottom part of the screen present the whole group status: the first presents the group's position proximity and the second presents the group's *voice proximity*.

CONCLUSIONS AND FUTURE WORK

This work focused on the possibility to use technology for monitoring and predicting small groups 'togetherness' in a museum environment. This work showed that position proximity and voice proximity patterns can serve as criteria for group profiling. The proximity patterns are group related aspects that may be measured and monitored automatically by currently available technology. These measurements, in turn, may be used to predict the group behavior and trigger the adaptation of a system to better meet the social needs of the small group and its members in leisure activity. In this way it may have a positive impact on the arousal, pleasure and feelings experienced by these groups. Future work will apply the above methodology and tools at the museum.

Acknowledgements. The work was supported by the collaboration project between the Caesarea-Rothschild Institute at the University of Haifa and FBK/irst in Trento and by FIRB project RBIN045PXH.

REFERENCES

1. Bitgood S.: Environmental Psychology in Museums, Zoos, and Other Exhibition Centers. In: R. Bechtel & A. Churchman (eds.), Handbook of Environmental Psychology, John Wiley & Sons, 461-480 (2002).

2. Camarero-Izquierdo C., Garrido-Samaniego M. J., and Silva-García R.: Generating emotions through cultural activities in museums.In Int Rev Public Nonprofit Mark, Springer-Verlag, 6:151-165 (2009).

3. Kuflik T., Stock O., Zancanaro M., Sheidin J., Jbara S., Goren-Bar D., Soffer P.: Supporting Small Groups in the Museum by Context-Aware Communication Services. Proceedings of the 12th International Conference on Intelligent User Interfaces, Honolulu, Hawaii, USA, 305-308 (2007)

4. McManus P.: Towards Understanding the Needs of Museum Visitors. In B. and G.D. Lord (eds.), Manual of Museum Planning (London: HMSO), 35-51 (1991).

5. Olgu´ın Olgu´ın D., Waber B., N., Kim T., Mohan A., Ara K., and Pentland A. (Sandy): Sensible Organizations: Technology and Methodology for Automatically Measuring Organizational Behavior; IEEE Transactions on Systems, Man, and Cybernetics—Part B: Cybernetics, vol. 39. no.1, (2009).

6. Russell S. and Norvig P.: Artificial Intelligence a Modern Approach; 2nd edition, Pearson Education, Inc, New Jersey, USA, (2003).

7. Stock O., Zancanaro M., Busetta P., Callaway C., Kr¨uger A., Kruppa M., Kuflik T., Not E., and Rocchi C.: Adaptive, Intelligent Presentation of Information for the Museum Visitor in PEACH. User Modeling and User-Adapted Interaction, Vol. 18(3), 257–304, (2007).

Toward a Cultural-Sensitive Image Tagging Interface

Wei Dong and Wai-Tat Fu
Applied Cognitive Science Lab
University of Illinois at Urbana-Champaign
405 N. Mathews Avenue, Urbana, IL 61801
wdong@@illinois.edu

ABSTRACT

Do people from different cultures tag digital images differently? The current study examined the relationship between the position and content of tags for digital images created by participants from two cultural groups (European Americans and Chinese). In line with previous findings on cultural differences in attentional patterns, we found cultural differences in the order of the parts of images people chose to tag. European Americans tended to tag main objects first, and tag background objects and overall properties in the images later; in contrast, Chinese tended to tag the overall properties first, and tag the main and background objects later. Based on findings of the current study, we discuss implications on developing a cultural-sensitive algorithm to facilitate the tagging and search process of digital media and data-mining tools to identify user profiles based on their cultural origins.

Author Keywords

Cultural difference, annotation, tagging, image tagging, perception, attention, algorithm

ACM Classification Keywords

H5.m. Information interfaces and presentation (e.g., HCI): Miscellaneous.

General Terms

Human Factors, Experimentation

INTRODUCTION

Innovations in technology have fostered a rapid growth in both personal and public digital media collections, which calls for both better understandings of people's annotating behavior (e.g., adding tags) to digital media and better algorithm implementations to assist indexing and searching of those enormous collections of digital media [7]. Studies have been conducted to better understand *why* and *how* people create tags to digital images [5]. Accordingly, researchers in human-computer interaction have been actively investigating and trying to develop tools [1, 8] to ease the tagging process and provide incentives to motivate people to create tags for digital media [2].

We propose that the contents of tags (*what*) created by users

are also important for three reasons. First, one way to make tagging process easier is to provide algorithms for partially automated tagging, such as suggesting tags that can be added to a piece of digital media [9]. The more the suggestions resemble the actual tags created by human users, the easier can the tagging process be. Second, better search algorithms based on tag contents can provide more visible and direct associations between the effort of creating tags and the benefit of searching from tags, thereby better motivate users to create tags. Third, if patterns can be detected in the content of tags people create, individualized algorithms can be designed to better assist their future tagging and search tasks.

One important aspect is the cultural origin of taggers. Research in perception and cognition suggest that people in different cultures allocate attention differently when viewing images and animations. Westerners tend to focus on main objects and pay less attention to background and contextual information, whereas Easterners have a holistic way of perceiving images, in the sense that they tend to equally spread attention onto every part of an image [6]. For example, it was found that Westerners mention the active focal object more often and describe the inert background objects and overall context less often than Easterners in their first sentences when describing an animation [3]. Westerners are also more likely to detect changes in main objects and less likely to detect contextual changes than Easterners [4].

Based on the assumption that people tend to tag parts of digital images that are more salient and important to them, and weigh these tags as more relevant to the digital media than other ones, the culturally different perceptual patterns may predict different patterns of associations between the sequential position and the content of tags created by people from different cultures. In addition to cultural difference, another reasonable factor that may influence attentional patterns is the kinds of objects depicted in the images, such as animal, humans, or others, as people are naturally inclined to attend to these objects. A study on the effects of culture and object categories on tagging will therefore allow us to tease apart the factors that influence the choice of which parts of the images people prefer to tag.

In this study, we investigated the association between the sequential position and the content of tags created for a same set of digital images by European Americans and Chinese. We also examined the impact of culture and image content on the patterns of those associations. The results will lead to development of algorithms for tools oriented at assisting efficient tagging and searching as well as data mining tools to identify socio-cultural profile of users.

METHOD

A between-subject quasi-experiment design was employed in the current study. Participants were recruited from two cultural groups. All participants were presented the same materials and experienced the same procedure. Participants' responses were compared between the two cultural groups.

Participants

Twenty-one European Americans (9 male, 12 female) and 23 Chinese (8 male, 15 female) were recruited from a university community to participate in the study. All European Americans were born in the United States and English was their first language except for one, who was born in France with French as the first language. None of the European Americans had stayed in an Eastern country for more than 9 months. All Chinese participants had stayed in the US for less than 15 months, with the average time spent in the US being 3.17 months. The two groups were similar in age ($M =$ 21.71 years, $SD = 3.33$ for European Americans, $M = 22.38$ years, $SD = 2.35$ for Chinese), and education level (most had some college education and some had graduated from college). For both cultural groups, participants were very familiar with searching for images on the internet and had some experience in tagging images on websites such as Facebook and Flickr.

Experimental Materials

Sixty digital images were selected from search results using public search engines such as Google. Criteria to select images were 1) photo of real-life objects; 2) there is no language or cultural iconic content in the image; 3) the image contained at least one clear foreground main object and a number of distinguishable background objects; 4) the main object belonged to one of the three categories: human, animal, and still objects; and 5) for a good proportion of the images, there were similarities in either the main objects or the background objects, so that the participants would be invoked to create multiple tags to help distinguish one image from another. There were three groups of digital images, each with 20 images portraying a main object in one of the 3 categories mentioned above.

Procedure

The procedure was the same for all participants, except that the experiment was conducted in English for European Americans and in Chinese for Chinese. We made sure that all participants understood the process of creating tags to images and the purpose of creating the tags. Participants were given the following instructions:

"The purpose to create these tags is to make it easier to search for a particular image in the future. Please imagine that weeks or months later, when you come back to look for a certain image, you can only use tags as your searching cues. The tags you have created should be able to help you find the correct image faster."

Each participant saw one image at a time, at a random order. For each image, participants were asked to create at least one, at most 10 tags to describe the image using a web browser. Participants were also asked to create short, single word tags rather than long ones. European Americans created all tags in English, and Chinese participants created all tags in Chinese.

Coding Procedure

Four steps were taken to code tags into categories. First, three researchers (one from each culture, and one bi-cultural researcher who has spent more than 6 years in each of the two counties) went through all images and agreed on which part is the main object. Second, a coding scheme (Table 1) was developed and the coders were trained. Third, a Chinese coder did the coding for all Chinese tags and 2 European American coders coded the English tags. The bi-cultural researcher coded at least 10% of tags in each language to ensure that all coders have sufficient agreement with the bi-cultural coder. Inter-coder agreements ranged from 81.1% to 87.2%. Lastly, coders discussed the disagreements and reached a consensus on them.

RESULTS

Due to technical difficulties encountered during data collection, data from one Chinese participant was excluded from the analysis. The average number of tags participants created for each image category is in Table 2. On average, European Americans created more tags than Chinese.

The overall percentage of tags coded into each tag category is presented in Table 1. The vast majority of tags (96.2%) created were describing three parts of the images, the main

Tag Category		Coding Criterion	Examples	Percentage
Uncodable		The tag was not a recognizable word or the coder could not associate it to any part of the image		2.3%
Foreground Main Object	Name	The tag described the foreground main objects that were agreed on by the three researchers in the first step of the coding procedure	boy	43.2%
	Property		cute	
	Behavior		running	
Background Object	Name	The tag described any of the objects that were not considered the main object which was decided in the first step of the coding procedure	boats	26.4%
	Property		white	
	Behavior		sailing	
Overall Description		The tag described overall features of the whole image, e.g., place, environment, event, time, emotion conveyed by the image, and photography technical terms	city, sunny, party, morning, joyful, overexposure	26.7%
Relationship		The tag described a relationship between two or more objects in the image	boy-in-park, besides	1.5%

Table 1. Coding scheme for the tags created by participants.

| Culture | Image Category | | | Total |
	Animal	Human	Object	
American	5.27 *(2.54)*	5.42 *(2.44)*	5.34 *(2.44)*	5.35 *(2.46)*
Chinese	3.96 *(1.72)*	4.17 *(1.81)*	4.01 *(1.62)*	4.05 *(1.70)*

Table 2. Average number of tags created for each image category (SDs are provided in parenthesis)

object, the background objects, and overall properties of the image. Thus, only tags from these three categories were included in the analysis reported in the following sections. In addition, given that on average participants only created about 5 tags for each image, the latter tags were so sparse that there was not enough data points to draw powerful conclusions, only the first 5 tag positions (constituting 82.1% of all tags) were included in the following analysis.

Effects of Culture and Tag Position on Tag Category

The percentages of tags in each tag category for each tag position in the two cultures are illustrated in Figure 1. Mixed-design ANOVA with tag position as within-subject variable and culture as between-subject variable revealed interactive effects between culture and tag position for both main object and overall property tag categories (both $F_{4, 132} > 4.56$, $ps < .01$). As we can see from Figure 1(a) and 1(c), European Americans described the main object more often and the overall properties less often in earlier tags than Chinese, whereas the pattern was reversed in latter tags. Only a main effect of tag position ($F_{4, 132} = 19.64$, $p < .001$) emerged in the background object category. Both cultural groups tagged the

background objects to the same extent. The percentages increased to the same extent from earlier tags to latter tags as well. Therefore, culture moderated the effect of tag position on the content of the tags (i.e., which part of image the tags referred to).

Effects of Image Category and Tag Position

We also examined the effect of image category on the sequence of tags because the activeness of the main objects might have an effect on how attention grabbing they were and how early they were tagged. The percentages of tags in each tag category for each tag position in each of the three image categories are illustrated in Figure 2. Repeated measures two-way ANOVA with tag position and image category both as within-subject variables revealed interaction between tag position and image category for all 3 tag categories (all $F_{8, 232} > 3.52$, $ps < .001$), indicating that image category also moderated the effect of tag position on tag contents. Specifically, as we can see in Figure 2, when the main object of the image was active living creatures, participants were more likely to tag the main objects and less likely to tag the overall properties in earlier tags, which could be attributed to the fact that active objects were inherently more likely to grab attention than inert ones.

Predicting Probability of Tag Category from Tag Position, Culture, and Image Category

Three sets of Binary Logistic Regression analyses were conducted using tag position, culture (0 = Chinese, 1 =

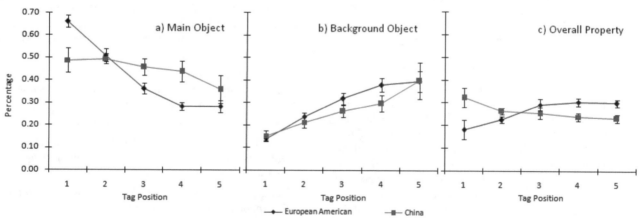

Figure 1. Percentage of tags in each tag category for each tag position in two cultures

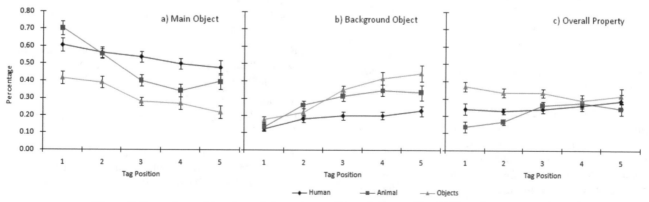

Figure 2. Percentage of tags in each tag category for each tag position in three image categories

European American), image category (represented by two indices: human (1 = human images, 0 = other images) and animal (1 = animal images, 0 = other images), zero on both simply indicated still object category), and their interactions with tag position to predict the logit likelihood of a tag belonging to each of the three tag categories. The regression coefficients are presented in Table 3.

Based on the underlying mechanism of logistic regression, we propose that the logit likelihood of a tag belonging to a particular category can be represented by the following formula, with intercepts in Table 3 representing β_0 and the regression coefficients of each predictor in Table 3 representing the rest of the β's.

Predictive Variables	Outcome Tag Category		
	Main Object	Background Object	Overall Property
Intercept	2.20	-1.99	-3.22
Main Effect			
Culture (C)	-.93	.15	.92
Human (H)	-.60	.20	.79
Animal (A)	-1.07	-.04	1.50
Tag position (T)	-.06	.27	-.23
Interaction Effect			
Culture X Tag position	-.40	.14	.30
Human X Tag position	.12	-.16	.11
Animal X Tag position	-.17	-.05	.31

Table 3. Regression coefficients predicting logit likelihood of tag category

$$\text{logit } (p) = \ln [p / (1-p)]$$

$$= \beta_0 + \beta_C x_C + \beta_H x_H + \beta_A x_A + \beta_T x_T$$

$$+ \beta_{CxT} x_{CxT} + \beta_{HxT} x_{HxT} + \beta_{AxT} x_{AxT}$$

We believe that the logistic equation above will be very useful for improving presentation of results from image search engines. Specifically, given that we know the tag position, the image category (based on some forms of text processing), and the cultural origin of the tagger, one will be able to calculate the probabilities for the tag to fall into each of the three tag categories. The probabilities can then be used to either sort images into categories of outcomes from search engines, or be used as weights to augment the ranking of the degree of match of images to the queries entered by the searcher. Similarly, given that we know the sequential pattern of how a user tag images, we can also implement this algorithm to predict the social-cultural profile of the user to better assist future user-interface interaction. In sum, the current results would be very useful for improving interfaces for categorizing, labeling, and searching of digital images; or in other words, for making interfaces more intelligent.

CONCLUSION AND FUTURE WORK

This study examined the association between the sequential position and the content of tags people created for digital images. Both cultural origins and image categories were found to be moderating this association. The results were convergent with previous findings in cultural difference in

attention and image perception, and provided evidence in support of our hypothesis.

The findings provided implications on cultural specific design of tools that utilize user-generated tags as indices for image searching. Specifically, based on results from our logistic regression analysis, we propose that weightings based on cultural origins and/or image contents could be used in algorithms for search engines to return sets of images better fit the needs of the searcher. Future research is needed to understand whether users from different cultures would also exhibit similar cultural differences in the keywords that they used when they search for images.

We believe that current results will also inform design of data-mining tools to identify different communities of users based on the similar patterns of image tagging behavior. For example, for the same image, users who assign tags in a particular sequence may imply that they are more likely to belong to a particular culture. Of course this will require further research to validate the extent to which this also applies to cultural groups other than European Americans and Chinese.

REFERENCES

1. Girgensohn, A., Adcock, J., Cooper, M., Foote, J. and Wilcox, L. Simplifying the Management of Large Photo Collections. In *Proc. INTERACT 2003*, IOS Press (2003), 196-203.

2. Kustanowitz, J. and Shneiderman, B. Motivating Annotation for Personal Digital Photo Libraries: Lowering Barriers while Raising Incentives. *Tech. Report HCIL-2004-18*, U. Maryland, 2005.

3. Masuda, T. and Nisbett, R. E. Attending Holistically Versus Analytically: Comparing the Context Sensitivity of Japanese and Americans. In *Journal of Personality and Social Psychology, 81*, 5 (2001), 922-934.

4. Masuda, T. and Nisbett, R. E. Culture and Change Blindness. In *Cognitive Science: A Multidisciplinary Journal, 30*, 2 (2006), 381-399.

5. Morgan, A. and Naaman, M. Why We Tag: Motivations for Annotation in Mobile and Online Media. In *Proc. CHI '07*, ACM Press (2007), 971-980.

6. Nisbett, R. E., Peng, K., Choi, I., and Norenzayan, A. Culture and Systems of Thought: Holistic vs. Analytic Cognition. In *Psych. Review, 108* (2001), 291-310.

7. Rodden, K. and Wood, K. How Do People Manage Their Digital Photographs? In *Proc. CHI 2003*, ACM Press (2003), 409-416.

8. Shneiderman, B. and Kang, H. Direct Annotation: A Drag-and-Drop Strategy for Labeling Photos. In *Proc. InfoVis 2000*, IEEE (2000), 88-95.

9. Wenyin,L., Dumais, S., Sun, Y., Zhang, H., Czerwinski, M., and Field, B. Semi-automatic image annotation. In *Proc. INTERACT 2001*, IOS Press (2001), 326-333.

Personalized User Interfaces for Product Configuration

Alexander Felfernig
Graz University of Technology
Applied Software Engineering
Inffeldgasse 16b, A-8010 Graz
alexander.felfernig@ist.tugraz.at

Monika Mandl
Graz University of Technology
Applied Software Engineering
Inffeldgasse 16b, A-8010 Graz
monika.mandl@ist.tugraz.at

Juha Tiihonen
Helsinki University of Technology
Computer Science
and Engineering
02015 TKK, Finland
juha.tiihonen@tkk.fi

Monika Schubert
Graz University of Technology
Applied Software Engineering
Inffeldgasse 16b,
A-8010 Graz
monika.schubert@ist.tugraz.at

Gerhard Leitner
University of Klagenfurt
Interactive Systems
Universitätsstrasse 65-67,
A-9020 Klagenfurt
gerhard.leitner@uni-klu.ac.at

ABSTRACT

Configuration technologies are well established as a foundation of mass customization which is a production paradigm that supports the manufacturing of highly-variant products under pricing conditions similar to mass production. A side-effect of the high diversity of products offered by a configurator is that the complexity of the alternatives may outstrip a user's capability to explore them and make a buying decision. In order to improve the quality of configuration processes, we combine knowledge-based configuration with collaborative and content-based recommendation algorithms. In this paper we present configuration techniques that recommend personalized default values to users. Results of an empirical study show improvements in terms of, for example, user satisfaction or the quality of the configuration process.

Author Keywords

Configuration systems, recommender systems, model-based diagnosis.

ACM Classification Keywords

I.2.5.Expert system tools and techniques.

General Terms

Human Factors, Design, Algorithms

INTRODUCTION

Configuration systems have a long tradition as a successful application area of Artificial Intelligence, see, for example, [1,9,15,18,22]. On an informal level, configuration can be interpreted as a *special case of design activity where the artifact being configured is assembled from instances of a fixed set of well-defined component types which can be*

composed conforming to a set of constraints [18]. Constraints can represent technical restrictions, rules regarding production processes, or restrictions that are related to economic factors. Example domains where product configurators are applied are computers, cars, financial services, railway stations, and complex telecommunication switches.

Although configuration has many advantages such as a significantly lower amount of incorrect quotations and orders, shorter product delivery cycles, and higher productivity of sales representatives [1], customers (users) in many cases have the problem of not understanding the set of offered options in detail and are often overwhelmed by the complexity of those options. The other problem is that users typically do not know exactly which products or components they would like to have. This phenomenon is described by the theory of preference construction [2] which follows from the fact that users do not know their preferences beforehand but rather construct and adapt their preferences within the scope of (in our case) a configuration process. In such a situation it makes sense to support users with recommendations that are, for example, derived from preferences articulated by similar users [23].

In this paper we present functionalities that support personalized configuration of mobile phones and corresponding subscriptions. Our major contribution is the integration of recommendation technologies with knowledge-based configuration (a functionality that is not available in commercial systems).

The remainder of the paper is organized as follows. In the next section we present the recommendation approaches useful for supporting personalized configuration. Thereafter we shortly discuss results of empirical evaluations. Finally, we discuss related work and conclude the paper.

CONFIGURING, RECOMMENDING, ORDERING

In this section we will provide technical details that help to understand how our prototype implementation determines repair alternatives in situations where no solution can be found, how recommendations for features are determined, and how phones are ranked taking into account user preferences.

Supporting configuration tasks. The task of identifying a configuration for a given set of specified customer requirements can be defined as follows:

Definition 1 (configuration task): a configuration task can be defined as a constraint satisfaction problem (V, D, C). $V=\{x_0, x_1, \ldots, x_n\}$ represents a set of finite domain variables and $D=\{dom_0, dom_1, \ldots, dom_n\}$ represents a set of domains dom_i where dom_i is assigned to the variable x_i. Finally, $C = C_{KB} \cup C_R$ where $C_{KB} = \{c_0, c_1, \ldots, c_m\}$ represents a set of domain constraints (the configuration knowledge base) that restrict the possible combinations of values assigned to the variables in V and $C_R = \{r_0, r_1, \ldots, r_q\}$ represents a set of customer requirements.

A simple example for a configuration task is $V=\{styleReq, webUse, GPSReq, pModel, pStyle, pHSDPA, pGPS\}$ where *styleReq* expresses the user's preferred phone style, *webUse* specifies how often the user intends to access internet with the phone, and *GPSReq* specifies whether the user wants to use GPS navigation functionality. Table 1 specifies the existing phone models (*pModel*), their styles a.k.a. form factor (*pStyle*), whether the phone supports fast internet access (*pHSDPA*), and whether the phone supports GPS navigation (*pGPS*). The respective domains are D={{*any, bar, clam*}, {*no, occasional, often*}, {*false, true*}, {*p1, p2, p3*}, {*bar, clam*}, {*true, false*}, {*true, false*}}.

pModel	pStyle	pHSDPA	pGPS
p1	*bar*	*false*	*false*
p2	*clam*	*true*	*true*
p3	*clam*	*true*	*false*

Table 1: Available phone models in working example.

Furthermore, we introduce a set of domain constraints $C_{KB} = \{c_0, c_1, c_2, c_3\}$. Table 1 can be interpreted as a constraint in disjunctive normal form, which yields c_0. The remaining constraints represent the following domain properties:

- c_1: (*webUse = often*) $\rightarrow$ (*pHSDPA=true*) /* *frequent web use requires a fast internet connection* */

- c_2: (*styleReq=any*) OR (*styleReq=pStyle*) /* *the phone should support the user's preferred phone style* */

- c_3: (*GPSReq = true*) $\rightarrow$ (*pGPS = true*) /* *if GPS navigation is required, the phone must support it* */

Finally, an example for customer requirements is $C_R = \{r_0:styleReq=clam, r_1:webUse=often, r_2:GPSReq=false\}$.

On the basis of this definition of a configuration task we can now introduce the definition of a solution for a configuration task (also denoted as *configuration*).

Definition 2 (configuration): a solution (configuration) for a given configuration task (V, D, C) is represented by an instantiation I = $\{x_0 = v_0, x_1 = v_1, \ldots, x_n = v_n\}$, where $v_i \in$ dom_i. A configuration is *consistent* if the assignments in I are consistent with the constraints in C. Furthermore, a configuration is *complete* if all the variables in V have a concrete value. Finally, a configuration is *valid*, if it is both consistent and complete.

An example for a valid configuration is the following: {*styleReq = clam, webUse = often, GPSReq = false, pModel = p3, pStyle=clam, pHDSPA=true, pGPS=false*}.

Diagnosing inconsistent requirements. In situations where no configuration can be found for a given set of requirements, we have to activate a diagnosis functionality [6,7,8,17]. Let us assume the following set of customer requirements $C_R = \{r_1:styleReq = bar, r_2:webUse = often, r_3:GPSReq = true\}$. The setting in C_R does not allow the calculation of a solution; consequently, we have to identify a minimal set of requirements that has to be changed in order to be able to restore consistency. We are interested in minimal changes since we want to keep the original set of requirements the same as much as possible. The calculation of a minimal set of requirements that has to be changed is based on the determination of conflict sets (see the following definition) [11,17].

Definition 3 (conflict set): a conflict set is a set CS $\subseteq C_R$ s.t. $C_{KB} \cup$ CS does not allow the calculation of a solution. Furthermore, CS is said to be minimal if there does not exist a set CS' with CS' $\subset$ CS.

In our working example we can identify the two minimal conflict sets $CS_1=\{r_1, r_2\}$ and $CS_2=\{r_1, r_3\}$. Both are conflict sets since $\{r_1, r_2\} \cup C_{KB}$ as well as $\{r_1, r_3\} \cup C_{KB}$ is inconsistent. Furthermore, both conflict sets are minimal since for both there does not exist a proper subset with the conflict set property (see Definition 3). In order to restore consistency, we have to resolve each of the identified minimal conflict sets. A systematic way to this is to apply the concept of model-based diagnosis [17]. A *customer requirements (CR) diagnosis problem* and a corresponding *CR diagnosis* can be defined as follows.

Definition 4 (CR diagnosis problem and CR diagnosis): a *CR diagnosis problem* is defined as a tuple (C_{KB}, C_R) where C_R is a set of requirements and C_{KB} represents the constraints of the configuration knowledge base. A *diagnosis* for (C_{KB}, C_R) is a set d $\subseteq C_R$, s.t. $C_{KB} \cup (C_R - d)$ is consistent. A diagnosis is *minimal* if there does not exist a diagnosis d'$\subset$ d, s.t. $C_{KB} \cup (C_R - d')$ is consistent.

For determining the complete set of minimal diagnoses we can apply the algorithm proposed by [17]. The core of the concept presented in [17] is the Hitting Set Directed Acyclic Graph (HSDAG) algorithm that is complete in the sense that all the existing diagnoses are found.

Recommending feature values. Beside the calculation of diagnoses in the case that no solution could be found, the recommendation of feature values and the calculation of user-individual rankings for phones are important functionalities. To calculate recommendations for feature values, valid configurations of previous sessions are stored

318

in a database. On the basis of these configurations two basic algorithms are supported in our prototype environment: *nearest neighbors* (see [23]) and *Naïve Bayes voter* [5,23]. The *Naïve Bayes voter* is discussed in detail in [5,23] and is taken into account in this paper. An empirical evaluation of the performance of different feature recommendation algorithms is a goal of future work.

Nearest neighbor based feature value recommendation. The idea of a nearest neighbor algorithm is to determine the neighbor configuration $conf_i$, which is closest to the active user's already specified requirements, and to recommend feature values from this nearest neighbor. The distance between the already specified user requirements and a neighbor configuration $conf_i$ is defined as the sum of individual distances [20] between corresponding feature values, weighted by feature importance weights.

To calculate distances between feature values, *Heterogeneous Value Difference Metric* (*HVDM*) [25] can be applied which help to cope with both symbolic and numeric features. The individual similarity metric to be used for calculating the similarity between two feature values is chosen depending on the basic characteristic of the feature (*less is better*, *more is better*, or *nearer is better* – for details see, for example, [20]). The distance values are normalized to usually be in range 0 to 1. The similarity of symbolic values in a domain is learned automatically [25]. This is done by examining the probability that individual feature values contribute to the classification of the samples - in our case classification of configurations. The higher the probability of a pair of feature values to be present in identically classified configurations, the more similar these feature values are considered [25].

Maintaining the consistency of recommendations. Note that recommendations for feature values must be consistent with the already specified set of customer requirements, i.e., if the user accepts a recommended feature value, this selection should not trigger an inconsistency and the activation of the diagnosis & repair component. In cases where none of the candidate nearest neighbors is able to provide a value that can be recommended, feature recommendation can be omitted.

Similarity-based ranking of phones. For the ranking of phones to be presented to the user we follow a similarity-based approach. We determine the distance of each previous configuration to the user's current configuration, so that phones from nearest configurations are shown first. Phones that are compatible with user requirements are presented to the user.

FIRST EMPIRICAL RESULTS

We have evaluated our prototype configuration environment within the scope of an empirical study with n>500 participants.[1] This study showed significant improvements in terms of qualitative measures such as *trust in a configuration* or the *willingness to buy* [4] as well as in terms of measures such as *prediction quality* of the used similarity measures (precision). In all those dimensions personalized configurator versions outperformed non-personalized versions as they are still in use in commercial environments. One of the major results of this initial study is a clear observation of *decision biases* where selection probabilities significantly changed depending on the configurator version.

RELATED AND FUTURE WORK

Main-stream recommender applications are based on collaborative filtering [13] and content-based filtering [16] approaches. These approaches are predominantly applied to quality and taste products – a very well known example is amazon.com [14]. The application of pure collaborative or content-based recommendation is the exception of the rule – in many cases only hybrid approaches can solve problems such as the ramp-up problem (e.g., for a new user the recommender system does not dispose of rating data which makes the calculation of initial recommendations a challenging task). A discussion of this and further issues regarding the deployment of recommenders can be found in [3].

Configuration systems have a long and successful history in the area of Artificial Intelligence [1,9,15,18,22]. Although these systems support interactive decision processes with the goal to determine configurations that are useful for the customer, the integration of personalization technologies has been ignored with only a few exceptions – see, for example, [5,10]. The goal of the work presented here was to implement and evaluate a system that integrates recommendation technologies that actively support users in a configuration process.

The integration of recommendation technologies with knowledge-based configuration is still in a very early stage. Most of the existing commercial configuration environments are lacking of recommendation functionalities – the study presented in this paper points out potentials for improvements. There exist some contributions that take into account the application of personalization technologies in the configuration context. The authors of [10] introduce an approach to the integration of case-based reasoning methods [12,21] with constraint solving [11] with the goal to adapt nearest neighbors identified for the current problem. There exist a couple of approaches that are similar to [10] – see, for example, [5]. All of those approaches do not provide a clear concept for enabling minimal changes and handling inconsistent feature value recommendations.

---

[1] A detailed discussion of these results has been omitted due to space limitations and will be provided in an extended version of this paper.

CONCLUSIONS

In this paper we provided an overview of basic recommendation techniques that can be used in the context of configuring complex products and services. These techniques show to be useful in terms of improving the user acceptance of the configurator interface.

ACKNOWLEDGEMENTS

The work presented in this paper has been conducted within the research projects WECARE (Austrian Research Promotion Agency) and COSMOS (TEKES Finland).

REFERENCES

1. Barker, V., O'Connor, D., Bachant, J., and Soloway, E. Expert systems for configuration at Digital: XCON and beyond, Communications of the ACM, 32, 3 (1989), 298–318.

2. Bettman, J., Luce, M., and Payne, J. Constructive Consumer Choice Processes, Journal of Consumer Research 25, 3 (1998), 187-217.

3. Burke, R. Hybrid Recommender Systems: Survey and Experiments, Journal of User Modeling and User-Adapted Interaction (UMUAI), 12(4):331□370, 2002.

4. Chen, L., and Pu, P. Trust Building in Recommender Agents, 1st International Workshop on Web Personalization, Recommender Systems and Intelligent User Interfaces (WPRSIUI'05), Reading, UK, 2005, pp. 135-145.

5. Coester, C., Gustavsson, A., Olsson, R., and Rudstroem, A. Enhancing web-based configuration with recommendations and cluster-based help, AH'02 Workshop on Recommendation and Personalized in e-Commerce, 2002, Malaga, Spain.

6. Felfernig, A., Friedrich, G., Jannach, D., and Stumptner, M. Consistency-based diagnosis of configuration knowledge bases, Artificial Intelligence, 2, 152 (2004), 213–234.

7. Felfernig, A., Friedrich, G., Teppan, E., and Isak, K. Intelligent Debugging and Repair of Utility Constraint Sets in Knowledge-based Recommender Applications, 13th ACM International Conference on Intelligent User Interfaces (IUI'08), 2008, Canary Islands, Spain, 218-226.

8. Felfernig, A., Friedrich, G., Schubert, M., Mandl, M., Mairitsch, M., and Teppan, E. Plausible Repairs for Inconsistent Requirements, 21st International Joint Conference on Artificial Intelligence (IJCAI'09), Pasadena, California, USA, 2009, pp. 791-796.

9. Fleischanderl, G., Friedrich, G., Haselboeck, A., Schreiner, H., and Stumptner, M. Configuring Large Systems Using Generative Constraint Satisfaction, IEEE Intelligent Systems, 13, 4 (1998), 59–68.

10. Geneste, L. and Ruet, M. Experience-based Configuration, 17th International Conference on Artificial Intelligence, Workshop on Configuration, Seattle, WA, USA, 2001, pp. 4-10.

11. Junker, U. QuickXPlain: Preferred Explanations and Relaxations for Over-Constrained Problems. 19th National Conference on Artificial Intelligence (AAAI'04), San Jose, AAAI Press, 2004, pp. 167–172.

12. Kolodner, J. Case-based Reasoning, Morgan Kaufmann Publishers, 1993.

13. Konstan, J., Miller, B., Maltz, D., Herlocker, J., Gordon, L. and Riedl, J. GroupLens: applying collaborative filtering to Usenet news Full text. Communications of the ACM, 40,3 (1997),77-87.

14. Linden, G., Smith, B., and York, J. Amazon.com recommendations: Item□to□Item Collaborative Filtering, IEEE Internet Computing, 7(1):76□80, 2003.

15. Mittal, S. and Frayman, F. Towards a Generic Model of Configuration Tasks, 11th International Joint Conference on Artificial Intelligence, Detroit, MI, 1990, pp. 1395–1401.

16. Pazzani, M. A Framework for Collaborative, Content-Based and Demographic Filtering. Artificial Intelligence Review, 1999, 13(5-6):393–408.

17. Reiter, R. A theory of diagnosis from first principles. AI Journal, 23(1):57–95, 1987.

18. Sabin, D. and Weigel, R. Product Configuration Frameworks – A Survey, IEEE Intelligent Systems, 13, 4 (1998), pp. 42–49.

19. Samuelson, W. and Zeckhauser, R. Status quo bias in decision making, Journal of Risk and Uncertainty 108, 2 (1988), 370–392.

20. McSherry, D. Similarity and Compromise. Intl. Conference on Case-based Reasoning (ICCBR'03), pages 291-305, 2003, Trondheim, Norway.

21. Smyth, B., and Keane, M. Using Adaptation Knowledge to Retrieve and Adapt Design Cases, Journal of Knowledge-based Systems, 9, 2 (1996), 127-135.

22. Stumptner, M. An overview of knowledge-based configuration, AI Communications (AICOM), 10, 2 (1997), 111–126.

23. Tiihonen, J. and Felfernig, A. Towards Recommending Configurable Offerings, International Journal of Mass Customization, to appear, 2009.

24. Tversky, A. and Kahneman, D. Choices, values, and frames, American Psychologist 39 (1984), 341–350.

25. Wilson, D. and Martinez, T. Improved Heterogenous Distance Functions, Journal of Artificial Intelligence Research, 6 (1997), 1-34.

Intelligent Food Planning: Personalized Recipe Recommendation

Jill Freyne and Shlomo Berkovsky
CSIRO Tasmanian ICT Centre
Hobart, Australia
firstname.lastname@csiro.au

ABSTRACT

As the obesity epidemic takes hold, many medical professionals are referring users to online systems aimed at educating and persuading users to alter their lifestyle. The challenge for many of these systems is to increase initial adoption and sustain participation for sufficient time to have real impact on the life of their users. In this work we present some preliminary investigation into the design of a recipe recommender, aimed at educating and sustaining user participation, which makes tailored recommendations of healthy recipes. We concentrate on the two initial dimensions of food recommendations: data capture and food-recipe relationships and present a study into the suitability of varying recommender algorithms for the recommendation of recipes.

Author Keywords

Recommender systems, personalization, food, recipe, collaborative filtering

ACM Classification Keywords

H.5.m Information Interfaces and Presentation: Miscellaneous

General Terms

Algorithms, Performance

INTRODUCTION

With over 1.6 billion adults worldwide classified as obese [8], health care professionals are investigating the use of online systems to influence the general public to change their attitude and behaviour toward a healthy lifestyle. Weight loss systems have progressed from paper recording of diet and exercise to online systems, in which informative content and intelligent services are used to persuade users to alter their behaviour. In these systems users often provide explicit reporting on diet and exercise and browse health related content such as recipes, exercise plans and others. Thus, there is a huge scope for rich user modelling and personalized content delivery services to both sustain user participation with the system and influence their behaviour.

When adopting a healthy lifestyle, many users lack the skills and knowledge required to affect change. With the aid of personalized recommendations we aim to equip users with relevant information to adopt and sustain a healthier lifestyle. One such personalized service, ideally suited to informing diet and lifestyle, is a personalized meal planner. This planner could exploit explicit food preferences, food diary entries, and user browsing behaviour, as well as various other sources, to inform its recipe recommendations.

The domain of food is varied and complex and presents a large challenge to recommendations. To start with, thousands of food items exist, with almost 1000 different vegetables alone. Secondly, food items are rarely eaten in isolation, with a more common consumption tending to be in the combination of dishes. Given the number of food items in existence, the number of possible combinations is exponentially large. Finally, and more complexly, user's opinion on food items can vary quite significantly based on several factors including whether a food item is cooked or raw, if cooked how it is cooked, what quantity of it is included in a recipe and many others. For example, a person may like smoked salmon, but not grilled salmon or may like salmon for dinner, but not for breakfast.

Several recipe recommender systems have been developed in the past. For example, Sobecki et al [9] presented a hybrid recommender using fuzzy reasoning to recommend recipes, Lawrence et al [5] generated recommendations for new food products that might be appealing to supermarket customers, and Svensson et al [10] provided recipe based grocery shopping recommendations. Unlike our work, the above treated the recipe/product as core items and did not break them down into individual food components.

The area of case-based reasoning has seen numerous works in the area of recipe construction from individual ingredients. The Chef [2] and Julia [4] systems both require extensive domain knowledge to create recipes from core ingredients, while the work by Zhang et al [11] exploits existing techniques (e.g., active learning) and knowledge sources (e.g., WordNet) to construct recipes.

The challenges for recipe recommendations are three fold. Firstly, given the number of *recipes* and *foods items*, what

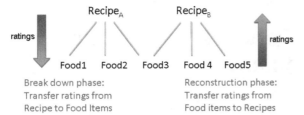

Break down phase:
Transfer ratings from
Recipe to Food Items

Reconstruction phase:
Transfer ratings from
Food items to Recipes

Figure 1. Menu food relationships

practical solution exists for gathering sufficient user modelling information on which to base recommendations? In this work we look at ratings on recipes and food items. Secondly, what are the relationships between a recipe and its component foods? If a system is aware of a recipe rating, what assumptions can be made about its ingredients or vice versa. Finally, can preferences on combinations and cooking methods be worked into a recipe recommender?

In this work we concentrate on the first two challenges: data capture and food-recipe relationships. We present a preliminary study into the suitability of varying recommender algorithms for the recommendation of recipes. The study is based on 8701 preferences and ratings provided by 183 users on recipes and food items. We examine the accuracy of content based and collaborative filtering algorithms and compare them with hybrid recommender strategies, which dismantle recipes into their components in order to make accurate recommendations. We show that solicitation of recipe ratings, which are transferred to food ratings through a food's inclusion in recipe, is an accurate and effective method of capturing food preferences.

RECOMMENDER STRATEGIES

The aim of this work is to uncover which recommender algorithms are suitable for personalized recipe recommendations. We focus on two data gathering strategies: the first is a fine grained food item strategy that gathers explicit ratings on individual food items, the second is a higher level strategy that gathers ratings on recipes. Regardless of whether ratings are gathered on food items or recipes, the output of the recommender algorithms is a *recipe recommendation*.

Before delving into the details of the individual strategies, we explain how we relate foods to recipes and vice versa. In this work, we adopted a simple recipe to food item relationship strategy shown in Figure 1. We ignore all weights, cooking processes and combination effects and consider all food items to be equally weighted within a recipe. Accordingly, we transfer ratings gathered on food items equally to recipes containing these foods and vice versa from recipe ratings to associated foods.

In order to compare our recommender strategies, we implement a baseline algorithm *random* which assigns a randomly generated prediction score to a recipe. The following strategies generate personalized predictions and encompass a pure content based algorithm, a collaborative filtering algorithm and three hybrid algorithms which consist of both content based and collaborative strategies. The strategies are named according to the item types on which their input is based

and on the recommender strategies they use. The two strategies which are applied to ratings gathered on *food items* are the $food_{cb}$ and $food_h$ strategy. The $food_{cb}$ strategy assigns scores for a target recipe r_t for a user u_a based on the average of all the ratings provided by u_a on food items $food_1, ..., food_j$ of r_t.

$$pred(u_a, r_t) = \frac{\sum_{j \epsilon r_t} rat(u_a, food_j)}{j} \qquad (1)$$

The $food_{cb}$ strategy can only make predictions for recipes on which it has information pertaining to the included food items. As mentioned, a huge number of food items exist and gathering a reasonable portion of explicit user preferences on individual food items is unrealistic from a user effort perspective. In order to increase the amount of knowledge held by the system on food items, i.e., reduce the data sparsity, our food hybrid strategy, $food_h$, exploits collaborative filtering to make predictions for unrated food items before carrying out the content matching step. Briefly, a set of N similar users, *neighbours*, is identified using Pearson's correlation algorithm shown in Equation 2 and predictions for food items not rated by u_a are generated using Equation 3.

$$sim(u_a, u_b) = \frac{\sum_{i=1}^{k}(u_{a_i} - \overline{u_a})(u_{b_i} - \overline{u_b})}{\sqrt{\sum_{i=1}^{k}(u_{a_i} - \overline{u_a})^2 \sum_{i=1}^{k}(u_{b_i} - \overline{u_b})^2}} \qquad (2)$$

$$rat(u_a, food_i) = \frac{\sum_{n \epsilon N} sim(u_a, u_n) rat(u_n, food_i)}{\sum_{n \epsilon N} sim(u_a, u_n)} \qquad (3)$$

With this more densely populated food ratings the content-based prediction step from Equation 1 is used to generate a prediction for r_t.

In contrast, we also investigate the use of strategies which are applicable to situations were ratings are requested on *recipes* rather than on food items. We implemented four recipe based strategies. The first one, $recipe_{cf}$, is a standard collaborative filtering algorithm assigning predictions to recipes based on the weighted ratings of a set of k neighbours as seen in Equations 2 and 3, where the items in question are recipes rather than food items.

The second, a content based strategy $recipe_{cb}$, breaks down each recipe r_i rated by u_a into food items $food_1, ..., food_x$ (see Figure 1) and assigns the ratings provided by u_a to each food item according to Equation 4.

$$rat(u_a, food_i) = \frac{\sum_{l \; s.t. \; food_i \epsilon r_l} rat(u_a, r_l)}{l} \qquad (4)$$

The strategy then applies the same content based algorithm from Equation 1 to construct a score for the target recipe r_t.

We also implemented two recipe hybrid strategies. The first one, $recipe_{hr}$, identifies a set of N neighbours based on *ratings* provided on recipes. Then, it uses Equation 4 to break down each recipes rated by u_a into foods, Equation 3 to predict as many food ratings as possible, and Equation 1 to generate a score for r_t. The seconds one, $recipe_{hf}$, differs only from $recipe_{hr}$ in its neighbour selection step. Here user similarity is computed based on overlapping items in the food

Table 1. Rating spread

hate	dislike	neutral	like	love
1935	2300	2145	1037	384

matrix established after the recipe break down step rather than on the recipe ratings as in $recipe_{hr}$.

EVALUATION

In order to test the above recommendation strategies, we gathered user preferences from a set of users, who were taking part in a study on healthy living social technologies [1].

Set-up

The corpus of recipes used was sourced from the CSIRO Total Wellbeing Diet Book [7]. We extracted 136 recipes which were categorised into *breakfast & lunch*, *soups & salads*, *seafood*, *chicken & pork*, *beef & veal*, *lamb*, and *vegetables*. This set corresponded to 337 food items which were in turn classified into *breads & cereals*, *dairy*, *vegetables*, *general grocery*, and *meat & fish*. On average, each recipe was made up of 9.98 food items and the average number of recipes that each food item was found in was 4.12.

We gathered opinions of 183 users regarding the available recipes and foods over a period of 3 weeks. Users were asked to provide initial preferences on either 20 recipes or 30 foods with the type requested determined randomly. All ratings were captured on a 5-Likert scale, spanning from "Hate" to "Love". In order to obtain a broad spread of items for each user, preferences were requested from randomly selected items in each of the above mentioned recipe or food item categories. Once an initial preference set was gathered, users were asked to periodically provide ratings on additional 20 recipes or 30 foods, depending on their seed set type. In total 8701 preferences were gathered with an average of 47.54 per user. Table 1 shows the spread of ratings over the dataset.

Methodology

We conducted a traditional leave one out off-line analysis, which took each rating of a $\{user_i, r_t, rating\}$ tuple from a user profile and used a set of recommender algorithms to generate predictions. For users who provided ratings on food items, the appropriate strategies were $food_{cb}$, $food_h$ and $random$. For users who provided ratings on recipes, the $recipe_{cb}$, $recipe_{cf}$, $recipe_{hr}$, $recipe_{hf}$ and $random$ strategies were used. The accuracy of the recommendations has been evaluated using the MAE measure[1] [3].

Results

Figure 2 shows the normalized MAE for each strategy. As expected, the $random$ algorithm performed worst with an MAE of 3.88. The poorest performer of the personalized strategies was the collaborative filtering algorithm $recipe_{cf}$.

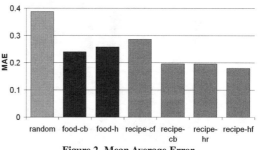

Figure 2. Mean Average Error

This is not surprising given that collaborative filtering algorithms suffer from the cold start problem and the recipe matrix was only 17% populated. The strategies whose input ratings were food based, $food_{cb}$ and $food_h$, fare similarly with an MAE of 0.24 and 0.26, respectively. We note here that the $food_h$ strategy introduced a level of noise to the food rating matrix resulting in a slightly (but significantly) higher MAE than the pure content based strategy $food_{cb}$. This finding is in line with that of Melville et al, who also used content boosted collaborative filtering [6].

The three hybrid recipe based strategies return the lowest MAE of below 0.2 with the $recipe_{hf}$ strategy the most accurate. We do not see an equivalent decrease in accuracy when we compare the $recipe_{cb}$ and $recipe_{hr}$ strategies as we see with the analogous food based strategies $food_{cb}$ and $food_h$. We do however see a difference in accuracy between the two hybrid strategies, $recipe_{hr}$ and $recipe_{hf}$, which differ in the neighbour determination timing. It seems that more accurate neighbour determination and food prediction occurs when neighbours are based on *implied* user ratings on foods rather than on recipes. The differences in MAE are significant at $p < 0.05$ across all pairings except the $recipe_{cb}$ and $recipe_{hr}$ pairs.

The closeness the recipe strategies $recipe_{cb}$, $recipe_{hr}$ and $recipe_{hf}$ is in part due to the coverage of foods in the food matrix. In 7% of simulations the food matrix contained ratings for all the foods in target recipe, such that all three strategies returned the same prediction. Similarly, in 50% of simulations the collaborative filtering was unable to make predictions on any additional food items in the target recipe, again returning the same prediction in all three strategies.

Comparing strategies varying only on the ratings matrix used shows that recommendations made on transferred food ratings outperformed the actual food rating algorithms across the board. The $recipe_{cb}$ strategy has a relative 25% improvement in accuracy over the $food_{cb}$ strategy and similarly the $recipe_{hr}$ and $recipe_{hf}$ strategies have a 25-28% improvement over the $food_h$ strategy. This shows that the decomposition of recipes into food items is beneficial for the purposes of recommendation generation even with a naive break down and reconstruction applied. Also, this shows that ratings on individual food items are not necessarily required for recipe recommendations even if the reasoning occurs on them.

The second aspect pertaining to the practicality of data gathering for food recommendations is algorithm coverage [3].

---

[1]The aim of the live-user trial was not to judge the accuracy of the recommendations, but to gather preferences to run off-line analysis and bootstrap future studies.

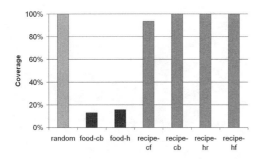

Figure 3. Coverage

We wish to find an algorithm which has reasonable accuracy and coverage across all users even for low number of ratings. Figure 3 shows the percentage of simulations where each algorithm was able to generate a prediction. The notable outliers are $food_{cb}$ and $food_h$ algorithms, which have very low coverage of 13% and 16%, respectively. Apart from the $recipe_{cf}$ algorithm, which has a 96% coverage, all other algorithms can generate predictions for all user item pairs.

CONCLUSIONS AND FUTURE WORK

As with all recommender technologies, a balance needs to be struck between accuracy, coverage and the workload of the users in providing information. This work presented an initial analysis as to the practicality of gathering food preferences and making recipe recommendations. We found that high coverage and reasonable accuracy can be achieved through content based strategies with a simple break down and construction used to relate recipes and food items. We found only marginal improvement in accuracy when collaborative filtering is employed to boost the rating matrix density. In conclusion, we have shown that even a naive recipe break down into food items with reasoning on the latter provides more accurate recommendations than a collaborative filtering algorithm using a sparse matrix.

Our future work includes an investigation into more intelligent means of reasoning on food ratings when recipe ratings are known, and vice versa, on recipe ratings when food ratings are known. Our first consideration concerns the impact of mixed ratings on recipes. For example, when breaking down recipes, a food item may receive a positive rating in one recipe and a negative in another, which are currently just averaged. However, more appropriate combinations would consider whether an ingredient in a positively and a negatively recipe should maintain only the positive rating, as it is unlikely to be the cause of the dislike in the negatively rated recipe. Furthermore, here we operate a simplistic idea of what a recipe recommender needs to do. We are, however, aware that making recipe recommendations is a far more complicated task in reality and we aim to investigate group recommendations, sequential recommendations, and diversification of recommendations.

ACKNOWLEDGMENTS

This research is jointly funded by the Australian Government through the Intelligent Island Program and CSIRO. The Intelligent Island Program is administered by the Tasmanian Department of Economic Development, Tourism and the Arts. The authors thank Nilufar Baghaei, Stephen Kimani, Dipak Bhandari and Greg Smith for their help with the development of the experimental eHealth family portal.

REFERENCES

1. N. Baghaei, J. Freyne, S. Kimani, G. Smith, S. Berkovsky, D. Bhandari, N. Colineau, and C. Paris. SOFA: An Online Social Network for Engaging and Motivating Families to Adopt a Healthy Lifestyle. In *Proceedings of 21st Annual OzChi Conference*, pages 269–272, 2009.

2. K. Hammond. CHEF: A Model of Case-Based Planning. In *Proceedings of the Fifth National Conference on Artificial Intelligence*, volume 1, 1986.

3. J. L. Herlocker, J. A. Konstan, L. G. Terveen, and J. T. Riedl. Evaluating collaborative filtering recommender systems. *ACM Trans. Inf. Syst.*, 22(1):5–53, 2004.

4. T. Hinrichs. Strategies for adaptation and recovery in a design problem solver. In *Proceedings Second Workshop on case-based reasoning, Pensacola Beach, Florida, Morgan-Kauffman*, 1989.

5. R. D. Lawrence, G. S. Almasi, V. Kotlyar, M. S. Viveros, and S. S. Duri. Personalization of supermarket product recommendations. *Data Min. Knowl. Discov.*, 5(1-2):11–32, 2001.

6. P. Melville, R. Mooney, and R. Nagarajan. Content-boosted collaborative filtering for improved recommendations. In *Proceedings of the National Conference on Artificial Intelligence*, pages 187–192. Menlo Park, CA.

7. M. Noakes and P. Clifton. The CSIRO Total Wellbeing Diet Book 2, 2006.

8. W. H. Organization. Chronic disease information sheet. http://www.who.int/mediacentre/factsheets/fs311/en/index.html accessed Sept 2009.

9. J. Sobecki, E. Babiak, and M. Slanina. Application of hybrid recommendation in web-based cooking assistant. In *Proceedings of the Tenth Conference on Knowledge-Based Intelligent Information and Engineering Systems*, pages 797–804, 2006.

10. M. Svensson, J. Laaksolahti, K. Höök, and A. Waern. A recipe based on-line food store. In *IUI '00: Proceedings of the 5th international conference on Intelligent user interfaces*, pages 260–263, 2000.

11. Q. Zhang, R. Hu, B. Namee, and S. Delany. Back to the future: Knowledge light case base cookery. Technical report, Technical report, Dublin Institute of Technology, 2008.

A Natural Language Interface of Thorough Coverage by Concordance with Knowledge Bases

Yong-Jin Han   Tae-Gil Noh   Seong-Bae Park   Se Young Park   Sang-Jo Lee
Kyungpook National University
Daegu 702-701, Korea
{yjhan,tgnoh,sbpark,sypark,sjlee}@sejong.knu.ac.kr

ABSTRACT

One of the critical problems in natural language interfaces is the discordance between the expressions covered by the interface and those by the knowledge base. In the graph-based knowledge base such as an ontology, all possible queries can be prepared in advance. As a solution of the discordance problem in natural language interfaces, this paper proposes a method that translates a natural language query into a formal language query such as SPARQL. In this paper, a user query is translated into a formal language by choosing the most appropriate query from the prepared queries. The experimental results show a high accuracy and coverage for the given knowledge base.

Author Keywords

natural language interface, knowledge base, ontology, knowledge concordance

ACM Classification Keywords

H.5.2 Information Interfaces and Presentation: User Interfaces—*Natural Language*

General Terms

Algorithms, Experimentation

INTRODUCTION

Various types of query interfaces have been proposed to improve the accessibility of knowledge bases. Each type has its own method to allow the users to easily write formal queries. Such methods include menu-driven interfaces, graphical query composers, and natural language interfaces [1]. Among them, the natural language query interface allows more precise query expressions. This is because the users are more familiar with word-based query interfaces than other graphical- or menu-driven interfaces. As a result, there have been many previous works on natural language interface (NLI) which translates natural language queries into formal language queries [5].

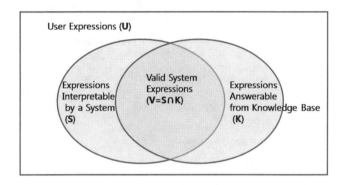

Figure 1. Mismatch between expressions which are interpretable by a NLI system and those answerable by a knowledge base.

Most NLIs are based on syntactic parsing and semantic analysis in direction from natural language to formal language [2, 3, 6, 4]. Their main problem is that the current natural language understanding methods are not sufficient to process various natural language expressions. Even the state-of-the-art parsers produce many parsing errors, and these errors are then propagated to the semantic analysis and query understanding.

The problem of the legacy NLI systems can be explained by Figure 1. S is a set of expressions that are interpretable by a NLI system, and K is a set of expressions that are answerable by a knowledge base. The capability of an interface is defined as an intersection, V, between S and K. There is a critical area ($K - S$) which the system fails in, but is indeed answerable by a knowledge base. In the previous interfaces, this area corresponds to the expressions which are failed syntactically or semantically in their analysis. One way to reduce $K - S$ is to expand S. However, this requires highly accurate natural language processing techniques, which is in general impractical.

In order to solve this problem, this paper proposes a novel method for NLI. The main idea of the method is to generate S from K, instead of expanding S to cover as much K as possible. Even if a user query can be accurately analyzed, it can not be answered by the knowledge base when it falls out of K. Therefore, what is important is to focus on the user queries which can be answered by the knowledge base.

The benefits of the proposed method are two-fold. First, it can answer nearly all queries obtainable from a knowledge

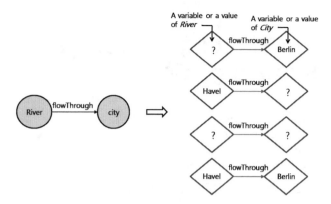

Figure 2. Generating formal queries from ontology schema.

base, since the queries are systemically generated from the schema of the knowledge base. Second, unexpected complex queries can be processed by combining the prepared simple queries.

QUERIES FROM AN ONTOLOGY
Schema-Level Query Group

This paper focuses on ontologies as knowledge bases, since ontologies are widely used and easily applicable to various applications. An ontology is represented as a directed graph. Entities of an ontology are nodes of the graph, and the relationships among entities are edges. In the ontology, the nodes represent *concepts*, *instances*, *data types*, or *data values*, while the edges represent *predicates*. Thus, each edge has a subject and an object node. All facts described in an ontology are expressed as graphs.

Valid queries for the ontology are also expressed as graphs in the same way as the facts are described if they can be answered by the ontology. All valid queries can be regarded as subgraphs of the ontology and they can be automatically generated from the ontology. Even if it is possible to directly generate all subgraphs in the instance level, the number of subgraphs in the instance level would be extremely large. Therefore, it is better to generate the queries for the ontology in the schema level rather than in the instance level.

Actual formal queries can be made by replacing the concept of a relation with a variable or a value. Figure 2 shows how actual queries are generated from the ontology schema. This figure depicts that there could be four actual queries when two concepts *River* and *City* are connected by a predicate *flowThrough*. The left hand side of this figure is a subgraph of an ontology. It describes that a *River* flows through a *City*. However, it is transformed into a query by replacing any concept with an instance or a variable. For instance, when *River* becomes a variable and *City* is replaced by an instance "Berlin" of *City*, it becomes a query of "What river flows through Berlin?"

As shown in Figure 2, many actual formal queries could be generated from a relation or relations within the ontology. Therefore, each meaningful subgraph can be regarded as a

set of actual queries, and it is called as 'schema-level query group' in this paper. The basic assumption of this paper is that if a natural language query by users is answerable by an ontology, there is at least one schema-level query group which is equivalent to the user query. Since schema-level query groups are known, the queries for the ontology can be all generated before the users' query time. If a NLI handles all the schema-level query groups, then it can answer all user queries for the ontology and is the specialized NLI for the ontology.

For an ontology with a moderate size, it is impractical to generate directly all kinds of schema-level query groups with multiple relations even if the number is finite. However, a complex query is explained as a combination of simple queries. Since it is tractable to prepare all possible simple queries, all valid queries for the ontology can be generated in advance at least using the simple queries.

Natural Language Queries from Schema-Level Query Group

Since a natural language query is a sentence which consists of words, it can not be matched directly with any schema-level query group which is a graph. In order to make it possible, natural language queries for each schema-level query group should be prepared in advance.

Natural language expressions for a predicate are various while concepts or instances have a strict form. For instance, Figure 2 expresses only the queries of which verb is 'flow', since it is based on the predicate 'flowThrough'. Thus, one possible query from this schema-level query group is "What river flows through Berlin?" However, a user can ask "What river passes by Berlin?" which is semantically same. This query can not be correctly analyzed only with the schema-level query groups, since the predicate 'pass' is not found in the ontology. One way to cope with this problem is to prepare in advance the natural language queries for each schema-level query group as various as possible. Then, the user query can be compared with these natural language queries from schema-level query groups.

For the easy matching between user queries and prepared natural language queries, the prepared queries are normalized, and then the normalized forms are archived. Let us consider the following example query.

> What river flows through Berlin? $\Rightarrow$
> <what><C:River><flow><through><I:City>

The normalized query is a sequence of tokens. The token can be a lexical string or a semantic code. The lexical string of a word is the base form of the word which can be obtained by a lexical analyzer. In the example above, <what>, <flow>, and <through> are lexical strings. A semantic code is a token which expresses the type of ontology entities. The type is one of concept (C), instance (I), or data type (D)[1]. The semantic code <C: River> implies the word 'river' corresponds to a concept River, and <I:City> means

---

[1]Since data values are not available in the schema level, only data types are considered for a semantic code.

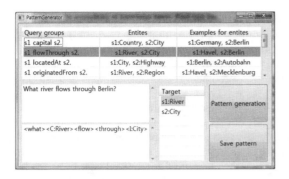

Figure 3. A screen-shot of *PatternGenerator*, a program to generate normalized queries from a schema-level query group.

that 'Berlin' is an instance of a concept `City`. A dictionary is needed to transform a word like 'river' or 'Berlin' into a semantic code such as `<C: River>` or `<I:City>`. This dictionary can be built automatically from the ontology.

To prepare normalized queries, the method needs to collect some number of natural language queries for each schema level query group. Thus, we developed *PatternGenerator*, a program that enables human experts to input equivalent sentences for each schema-level query group. Figure 3 shows a screen-shot of *PatternGenerator*. It lists all schema-level query groups. When the user provides a natural language query for a schema-level query group, *PatternGenerator* generates its normalized queries. If multiple normalized queries are made due to the ambiguity of natural language, it allows the user to choose the correct one from the normalized queries. The chosen normalized query is then saved in the archive of normalized queries.

TRANSLATION OF USER QUERY INTO FORMAL QUERY

A natural language query from a user is translated into a formal query by finding the schema-level query group which matches best with the user query. This is done actually by comparing the user query with the normalized forms of schema-level query groups. A user query should be also normalized to be compared with the prepared normalized queries. The normalizing process of a user query is equal to that explained in the previous section.

Due to the ambiguity of natural language, a user query can be understood in various ways. That is, a user query is analyzed into a set of normalized forms, Q. When P is a set of all possible normalized queries, a pair of the correct meaning of the user query, q^*, and its corresponding normalized query, p^*, is determined by

$$(q^*, p^*) = \underset{(q,p) \in Q \times P}{\arg \max} \, Sim(q, p), \qquad (1)$$

where $Sim(q, p)$ is the similarity between $p \in P$ and $q \in Q$. $Sim(q, p)$ is a normalized alignment similarity between q and p. That is,

$$Sim(q, p) = \frac{AlignScore(q, p)}{||p||}. \qquad (2)$$

In this paper, a standard alignment method [7] is used for

$AlignScore(q, p)$. When two normalized queries p_1 and p_2 have the same alignment similarity with a given user query q, that is, $AlignScore\,(q, p_1) = AlignScore(q, p_2)$, the function Sim prefers the shorter normalized query to the longer one as $AlignScore\,(q, p)$ is divided by the length of p, $||p||$. This is because the shorter one has less irrelevant tokens than the longer one.

When a user query is a sentence that contains two or more predicates, it has to be matched with two or more normalized queries. When a user query Q consists of n predicates, that is, $Q = Q_1 Q_2 \ldots Q_n$, all Q_i's should be matched at the same time with one of the schema-level query groups within P. Note that each Q_i can be analyzed into a number of normalized forms. If Q_i is analyzed into m normalized forms on average, Q has m^n members. Thus, Equation (1) has to investigate $m^n \cdot |P|$ candidates while just $m \cdot |P|$ candidates are considered for a user query with a single predicate. This can be computationally intractable. One solution to this problem is to assume that each Q_i is independent one another. Then, the best pair of (q_i^*, p_i^*) for each Q_i can be obtained by Equation (1). Therefore, the best normalized form for a complex Q is just $q_1^* q_2^* \ldots q_n^*$. This considers only $n \cdot m \cdot |P|$ candidates.

The fact that the most similar normalized query is found implies that the best schema-level query group for the user query is chosen. Then, a formal query equivalent to the user query can be also generated automatically and easily from the chosen schema-level query group.

EXPERIMENTS

For the experiments, an ontology about books [8] is used as the target knowledge base. The ontology is designed to express various knowledge about books with 11 predicates. Thus, the proposed method has 11 schema-level query groups. The performance of the proposed method is measured by the accuracy which is defined by

$$Acc = \frac{\text{No. of queries which produces a correct answer}}{\text{No. of all queries}}.$$

In order to see how many normalized queries for each schema-level query group are actually needed, 531 natural language queries are constructed by four graduate students from the ontology. Among them, 223 queries have just one predicate and 146 queries have two predicates. The remaining 162 queries have three predicates.

Figure 4 shows how accuracy changes according to the number of normalized queries for each schema-level query group. The curve labeled as 'single' in this figure is the accuracy for the queries with one predicate. Those labeled as 'dual' and 'triple' are the accuracies for two and three predicates respectively. The accuracy of 'single' is far higher than those of 'dual' and 'triple'. This coincides with our intuition. When the proposed method is treated as a classification problem, the problem is regarded as finding the most suitable query group for the given query. The search space for 'single' is smaller than 'dual' or 'triple'. This figure shows that all accuracies increase monotonically as the number of normal-

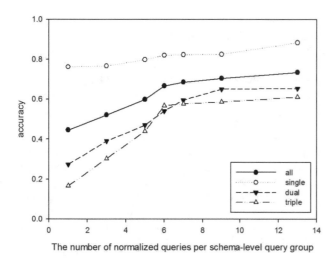

Figure 4. Accuracy change according to the number of normalized queries per schema-level query group.

ized queries increases. Note that they are saturated when the numbers of normalized queries are larger than 10. That is, the number of normalized queries for each schema-level is bounded and the human labor for producing them is also bounded. It is a reasonable level of work for human experts to write 10 natural queries for each schema-level query group.

To evaluate the performance of the proposed method in the real world, additional 102 queries are prepared by another four graduate students who are different from those in the first experiments. They prepared the queries without prior knowledge about the ontology. The large portion of queries, a half of the 102 queries, is out of the scope of the ontology. For instance, they asked about yearly earning of a publisher or an original work of a certain movie, but the ontology has no such information.

The proposed method correctly answered 44 queries. It achieves 43.1 % of accuracy. The accuracy seems somewhat low, but is actually high, since the half of the queries is not answerable from the ontology by any other method. When considering only 51 queries answerable by the ontology, the accuracy goes up to 86.2 %. This result says that the proposed method thoroughly covers the scope of the ontology and reasonably meets users' needs.

In addition, the accuracy in this experiment is far higher than that in the first experiment shown in Figure 4. This is because most of the casual users ask factoid questions that usually have just a single predicate. In our experiment, only 10% of the queries have three predicates. The accuracy is impressive when it is compared with previous systems like ORAKEL [3]. They report the accuracy of around 70% in a similar scenario. Since answerable queries are systemically prepared in advance before query time, the accuracy of the proposed method is higher than that of legacy NLIs.

CONCLUSION

One major problem of natural language interfaces is the discordance between queries covered by the interfaces and those covered by the knowledge base. This paper proposed a novel method to overcome this problem. We prepared all possible queries for the knowledge base and a set of corresponding normalized queries for the problem. The proposed method thoroughly covers possible questions for the knowledge base. The effectiveness of the proposed method is shown by evaluating it with a real world knowledge base. The experiments show the number of normalized queries by the human pattern builder is bounded and high accuracy of 86.2% is achieved. As for future works, we aim at testing the method on various ontologies, and also at developing interactive methods that can guide users to the types of queries which can be answered by the system and the knowledge base.

Acknowledgement

This work was supported in part by KEIT through IT Leading R&D Support Project.

REFERENCES

1. L. Androutsopoulos. Natural language interfaces to databases - an introduction. *Journal of Natural Language Engineering*, 1:29–81, 1995.

2. L. T. C. Thompson, R. Mooney. Learning to parse natural language database queries into logical form. In *Proceedings of the 13th National Conference on Artificial Intelligence*, pages 1050–1055, 1996.

3. P. Cimiano, P. Haase, and J. Heizmann. Porting natural language interfaces between domains: An experimental user study with the ORAKEL system. In *Proceedings of the 12th International Conference on Intelligent User Interfaces*, pages 180–189, 2007.

4. A. Frank, H. Krieger, F. Xu, H. Uszkoreit, B. Crysmann, B. Jörg, and U. Schafer. Question answering from structured knowledge sources. *Journal of Appied Logic*, 5(1):20–48, 2007.

5. E. Kaufmann and A. Bernstein. How useful are natural language interface to the semantic web for casual end-users? In *Proceedings of the 6th International Semantic Web Conference*, pages 281–294, 2007.

6. V. Lopez, M. Pasin, and E. Motta. Aqualog: an ontology-portable question answering system for the semantic web. In *Proceedings of the European Semantic Web Conference*, pages 546–562, 2007.

7. A. Moustafa. *JAligner: Open source Java implementation of Smith-Waterman*, 2009 (accessed July 23, 2009).

8. T. Noh, Y. Han, J. Son, H. Song, H. Yoon, J. Lee, S. Lee, K. Kim, Y. Lee, S. Park, S. Park, and S. Lee. Experience search: Accessing the emergent knowledge from annotated blog postings. In *Proceedings of the 2009 IEEE International Conference on Social Computing*, pages 639–644, 2009.

Exploratory Information Search by Domain Experts and Novices

Ruogu Kang and *Wai-Tat Fu*
Applied Cognitive Science Lab
Human Factors Division and Beckman Institute
University of Illinois at Urbana-Champaign
{kang57, wfu}@illinois.edu

ABSTRACT

The arising popularity of social tagging system has the potential to transform traditional web search into a new era of social search. Based on the finding that domain expertise could influence search behavior in traditional search engines, we hypothesized and tested the idea that domain expertise would have similar influence on search behavior in a social tagging system. We conducted an experiment comparing search behavior of experts and novices when they searched using a tradition search engine and a social tagging system. Results from our experiment showed that experts relied more on their own domain knowledge to generate search queries, while novices were influenced more by social cues in the social tagging system. Experts were also found to conform to each other more than novices in their choice of bookmarks and tags. Implications on the design of future social information systems are discussed.

Author Keywords

Social search, exploratory search, domain expertise.

ACM Classification Keywords

H.3.3 Information Search and Retrieval: Search Process. H5.4. Information interfaces and presentation (e.g., HCI): User Issues.

General Terms

Experimentation, Human Factors, Performance

INTRODUCTION

As information search is becoming one of the most prominent activities for Web users, Web search has evolved into a social activity that involve exploring, learning, and sharing of information [9] in addition to simple query-based fact retrieval. Though search engines are good for direct fact retrievals, exploratory search often involves an iterative process of exploration and goal refinement as knowledge is incrementally acquired during the process [3, 7]. Previous

research suggested that social search environment could facilitate users' information search by providing information cues (e.g., social tags) from others that direct users to the right information (e.g., [4, 7]). It is therefore reasonable to assume that for exploratory search, social information systems such as delicious (www.delicious.com) may be more desirable than traditional search engines such as Google (www.google.com).

Results from prior research have already shown that domain expertise would influence users' search behavior, reflected on their search queries and success rate. White et al. [10] found that domain experts generated longer queries and used more domain specific vocabularies. They also suggested that domain experts are more successful in their search than novices. Duggan and Payne [2] suggested that greater knowledge could increase the ability of users to select more related information. Similarly, Hsieh-Yee [6] found that subject knowledge would play an important role affecting experienced searchers' reliance on their own language, indicating that when users were searching in their domain, they used more of their own terms. However, none of these results shows how experts and novices search differently in a social context. Some researchers [8] proposed that social search systems can potentially improve learning compared with the keyword-based search engines, but there is still a lack of understanding on how domain expertise of users may affect their exploratory search behavior in a social search environment.

As social tagging systems allow users to see other users' interpretation of the same information contents, we hypothesize that domain expertise will impact not only what information they select from the Web, but also influence how they interpret contents tagged by others, and how they assign tags to the information contents. In other words, domain expertise may play a pivotal role in influencing the *sharing and understanding* of information in the iterative exploratory searching cycles as users are interacting with a social tagging system.

METHOD

We used a 2 × 2 between-subject design to investigate users' search behavior when users with different levels of domain expertise searched in different search environments. While Google provides a traditional search environment for keyword-based queries, delicious provides a social search environment with tagged bookmarks saved by other users, which allow users to conduct either tag-based or keyword-based queries. Under the assumption that domain expertise might influence users' exploratory search process, we expected that experts and novices could have different search performance when they performed exploratory search using the two interfaces.

Participants

48 participants were recruited for the study (22 female, 26 male, M = 24.4 years). All participants were skilled computer users with more than 10 years of computer usage experience. All participants reported Google as their most familiar search engine and that they performed Internet searches with an average frequency of 3.95 on a 5-point scale (interpreted as "use search engine several times a day"). 24 of the participants claimed to have expert knowledge in finance or related area (such as holding an advanced degree or have employment experiences in the finance industry). The other 24 did not have any professional knowledge in finance or related fields. Expert and novice participants were randomly assigned to one of the two interfaces. Each condition has 12 subjects.

We designed a short survey with 5 questions to test their knowledge of finance and economics as well as their familiarity of the current financial crisis on a 5-point scale. A sample question is: "I know the causes and backgrounds of the current financial crisis". We found a high reliability for the self-report questions (Cronbach's alpha = 0.921). A knowledge test was then used to test participants' domain knowledge about the financial crisis. Questions in the knowledge test were generated from online quizzes and textbooks on financial crisis. The test was reviewed by two graduate students major in finance and one professional who had been working in a financial holding company for more than 15 years.

The Exploratory Search Tasks

We used "financial crisis" as the topic for our exploratory search task. Participants were asked to imagine that they were to collect information from the Web to give a talk on the topic of financial crisis. They were encouraged to explore information using their assigned search tools (Google or delicious) to enrich their knowledge. During the search process they were asked to *save and tag* useful websites as bookmarks as much as they needed. In delicious, they could save websites as bookmarks in their assigned web account; in Google, they could save bookmarks into a given folder and create tags for each saved bookmark. They were instructed to search, read, and select information, but not to spend too much time on each page to keep a good balance between exploration and understanding a specific document.

Procedure

Upon their arrival at the facility, participants were first debriefed about the task and the goal of the research. They were then asked to read and sign the consent form for participating in the experiment. Participants then filled out a general survey about experience in computer, demographics and the short survey on their background knowledge. Each participant was randomly assigned to the Google or delicious condition. Participants performed the exploratory search task individually and were given a maximum of 1.5 hours for their task. Camtasia recorder was used to record all on-screen actions of the participants. After finishing the search task, they completed the knowledge questionnaire. The knowledge questionnaire was given after the search task to avoid potential priming effect on their search performance by the knowledge questions. The whole experiment took about 2 hours.

RESULTS

Domain Experts vs. Novices

From the self-reported domain knowledge, we found significant difference between experts and novices (M = 3.8 and 2.87 on a 5-point scale, p<0.001). Consistent with the self-reported ratings, we also found a significant difference on the knowledge test score between experts and novices (p<0.05).

Search Strategy

In order to see how domain knowledge influenced their search performance in the social environment, we first looked at the search strategies of the experts and novices in the social condition. Participants could use tag-based queries (selecting tags from the popular tags list or from other users' tags attached to each website title) or keyword-based queries (entering keywords in keyword search box) in delicious; but they could only use keyword-based queries in Google. ANOVA results showed that the interaction effect of expertise × search strategy was significant (F (1,38) = 5.349, p < 0.05). As shown in Figure 1, experts used more keyword-based search, while novices used more tag-based search. This result is consistent with results from previous research [6] that experts were more likely to come up with their own keyword-based queries to search, but novices relied more on using other users' tags to search.

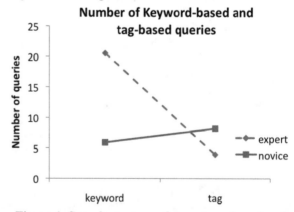

Figure 1. Search strategy of experts and novices in delicious

In other words, experts tended to rely more on knowledge in their heads and novices tended to rely more on knowledge in the environment when they performed the information search.

Consensus on Tag Choice

As the result above indicated, domain knowledge influenced how user searched for information. We analyzed their tags in order to find out whether domain knowledge would influence their interpretation of information. Among the 48 participants, 3 participants have invalid tags (e.g., "bookmark 1"). The other 45 participants created 3046 tags in total. On average, every participant created 2.73 tags on each bookmark (SD = 1.76). After getting rid of stop words and invalid tags, the number of distinctive tags is 1384. As the number of distinctive tags was much fewer than the total number of tags, we speculated that the higher proportion of shared tags could be caused by: (1) social effect on tag choices in delicious, and/or (2) participants with similar knowledge background might have similar interpretation to information about one topic. In order to investigate which factor drove tag sharing, we performed a 2 (interface) × 2 (expertise) ANOVA using the number of users sharing each tag as dependent variable.

Results showed that the main effect of interface and expertise were significant (F (1,5528) = 54.75, p < 0.001; F(1,5528) = 7.65, p < 0.05). The interaction effect of interface × expertise was also significant (F (1, 5528) = 45.75, p < 0.001). As shown in Figure 2, the interaction effect illustrated that experts using delicious shared more tags than novices (F (1, 2764) = 70.30, p<0.001), but we could not find any difference between experts and novices when they were using Google (F (1,2764) = 0.35, p = 0.55).

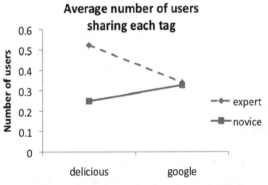

Figure 2. Sharing of tags in Google and delicious

This result indicated that experts were more likely to agree with each other than novices in tag choices. Although it might seem surprising that experts had higher level of agreement on their tag choices even though they tended to search using their own queries, the result could be explained by their specific knowledge structures that influenced them to assign the same tags to the Web documents. Indeed, experts in the same domain were likely to share more common semantic representations of the same topic [4, 5]. Therefore when experts were in a social environment, they tended to use similar tags as other experts. In contrast, novices tended to have more diverse interpretation to a topic, and might be more likely to use different tags to describe the bookmarks. In Google, experts and novices did not have this difference,

possibly because of the mediation of the query suggestions provided by Google. Given that we did not collect data on query suggestions in this experiment, their effect could not be assessed; but their effects will be studied in our future study.

Consensus on Bookmark Selection

To further explore whether or not the social search environment could benefit users, we examined the bookmarks saved by participants. 48 participants selected 1170 bookmarks in total (M = 24.9 bookmarks/participant, SD = 13.4). Among those 1170 bookmarks, 363 bookmarks were saved by more than 2 participants. The most popular bookmark was saved by 11 users (the wikipedia page on subprime mortgage crisis).

We divided all bookmarks into two groups: we called those bookmarks shared by more than two people *popular* bookmarks and the rest of them *unique* bookmarks. We were interested in finding out whether participants with different level of domain expertise and the use of different interfaces might differ in their sharing of popular or unique bookmarks. To this end, we performed a 2 (popular/unique) × 2 (interface) × 2 (expertise) ANOVA using the number of participants sharing each bookmark as dependent variables. Results from the ANOVA showed that the main effects of shared frequency and interface were significant (F (1, 484) = 43.63, p < 0.001 and F (1, 484) = 21.11, p < 0.001), but the main effect of expertise was not significant. The interaction of shared frequency × interface and expertise × interface were both significant (F (1, 484)=11.74, p < 0.001; F (1,484)=7.14, p<0.05). The three-way interaction of shared frequency × interface × expertise was not significant.

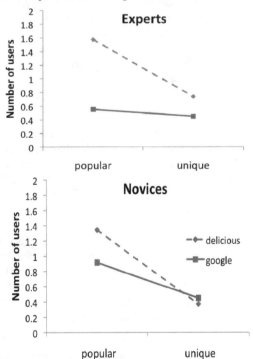

Figure 3. Bookmark sharing of experts and novices

Since the main effect of expertise did not reach significance, we carried out separate ANOVAs on each of the two expertise groups. The interaction effect of shared frequency × interface was significant in both experts and novices ($p < 0.05$). As shown in Figure 3, both experts and novices shared more general bookmarks when using delicious than when they were using Google ($p<0.001$ and $p<0.05$). For unique bookmarks, experts shared more in delicious compared to Google, though the difference was only marginally significant ($p = 0.14$). Novices did not show this difference in sharing unique information ($p = 0.42$). We also examined the contents of these bookmarks. We found that most of the unique bookmarks were either specific web sites describing a particular event, or professional websites developed for finance professionals. Therefore, the unique bookmarks were closer to experts' knowledge, which facilitated experts' bookmark selection but impeded novices' bookmark selection as novices might not have the background knowledge to judge whether or not they were relevant information [10].

In summary, delicious was able to support both experts and novices in finding general information in a particular topic domain, even though novices did not share more tags. In other words, novices in a social tagging system were still able to find information they needed, but could not interpret the information correctly, as reflected by their more diversified tag choices. Traditional search engine could help novices' information search by providing query suggestions, but could not assist experts' search.

CONCLUSION AND DISCUSSION
Based on the empirical data from a laboratory experiment, we found preliminary evidence supporting that domain expertise can facilitate exploratory information search in social tagging systems for both *sharing* and *understanding*. Specifically, we found that experts shared more bookmarks and tags related to the assigned topic in delicious compared to Google. Experts also shared more tags than novices when they were both searching in delicious.

As experts used more keyword-based queries than novices in delicious and novices used more tag-based queries, we believe that experts were more likely to utilize knowledge in their head to search for information, and novices relied more on information in the environment. The results provided further support that social information websites can facilitate sharing of useful information among novice users, and they do seem to have potential to augment the exploratory search of information, especially for users who have little knowledge on the topic. Although Google provides automated query suggestions that might be similar to social cues, how experts and novices utilize the recommended queries still needs investigation.

Our results also provided some implication to the design of future social information systems. Most current tagging systems recommended tags only based on the use frequency, which may lead to the "vocabulary problems" that make finding the right information difficult. Incorporating quality

of tags as part of the algorithm that determines which tag should be presented would definitely benefit information seekers to use high-quality tags as navigational cues to find more related information. Since domain experts have professional knowledge in their domain, it is reasonable to consider that tags created by domain experts would have higher quality. Also, tags created by experts might have greater potential to facilitate other's searching than "good tags" generated by computer algorithms, because expert-created tags can support the exchange of users' understanding to the information. As we found experts shared more information in delicious, it is possible to identify experts in a social tagging system by certain data mining techniques that match the tagging and searching behavioral patterns of users. By putting more weight into the tags created by experts, one could reduce the potential drawbacks caused by the "vocabulary problem" and increase the effectiveness of information sharing in social tagging systems.

REFERENCES
1. Cattuto, C., Loreto. V., and Pietronero. L. (2007). Semiotic Dynamics and Collaborative Tagging. *Proc. National Academy of Sciences,* 104(5), 1461-1464.

2. Duggan, G.B. and S.J. Payne. (2008). Knowledge in the Head and on the Web: Using Topic Expertise to Aid Search. *Proc. CHI 2008*, ACM, 39-48.

3. Fu, W.-T. (2008). The Microstructures of Social Tagging: a Rational Model. *Proc. CSCW 2008*, ACM, 229-238.

4. Fu, W.-T., Kannampallil, T. G., Kang, R. (2010). Facilitating Exploratory Search by Model-Based Navigational Cues, *Proc. IUI 2010*. ACM, in press.

5. Fu, W.-T., Kannampallil, T. G., Kang, R. (2009). A Semantic Imitation Model of Social Tag Choices. *Proc. 2009 IEEE SocialCom,* in press.

6. Hsieh-Yee, I. (1993). Effects of Search Experience and Subject Knowledge on the Search Tactics of Novice and Experienced Searchers. *Journal of the American Society for Information Science,* 44(3), 161-174.

7. Kang, R., Kannampallil, T. G., He, J., Fu, W.-T. (2009). Conformity out of Diversity: Dynamics of Information Needs and Social Influence of Tags in Exploratory Information Search. *Proc. HCII 2009*, 155-164.

8. Kammerer, Y., Nairn, R., Pirolli, P. L., Chi, E. H. (2009). Signpost from the Masses: Learning Effects in an Exploratory Social Tag Search Browser. *Proc. CHI 2009*, ACM, 625-634.

9. Marchionini, G. (2006). Exploratory Search: from Finding to Understanding. *Commun. ACM 49*, 4, 41-46.

10. White, R.W., S.T. Dumais, and J. Teevan. (2009). Characterizing the Influence of Domain Expertise on Web Search Behavior. *Proc. WSDM 2009,* ACM, 132-141.

Using Language Complexity to Measure Cognitive Load for Adaptive Interaction Design

M. Asif Khawaja
NICTA/CSE UNSW
Sydney, Australia
asif.khawaja@nicta.com.au

Fang Chen
NICTA/CSE, EET UNSW
Sydney, Australia
fang.chen@nicta.com.au

Nadine Marcus
CSE UNSW
Sydney, Australia
nadinem@cse.unsw.edu.au

ABSTRACT

An adaptive interaction system, which is aware of the users' current cognitive load, can change its response, presentation and interaction flow to improve users' experience and their task performance. In this paper, we propose a novel speech content analysis approach for measuring users' cognitive load, based on their language and dialogue complexity. We have analysed the transcribed speech of operators working in computerized incident control rooms and involved in highly complex bushfire management tasks in Australia. The resulting patterns of language complexity show significant differences between the speech from cognitively low load and high load tasks. We also discuss the value of using this approach of cognitive load measurement for user interface evaluation and interaction design improvement.

Author Keywords

Cognitive Load, Measurement, Language Complexity Measures, Interaction design.

ACM Classification Keywords

H.5.2 User Interfaces: Evaluation methodology, Natural language, theory and methods.

General Terms

Human Factors, Measurement, Performance

INTRODUCTION

When a person performs a particular problem-solving task, it imposes a mental load on the person's working memory, known as Cognitive Load [1]. It is caused by the limited capacity of the person's working memory and his/her ability to process new information [2]. Users of an interaction system can experience high cognitive demands, especially in data-intense and time-critical situations. These demands may be attributable to either the complexity of the task being carried out or by the complex interaction design of the system, as in multimodal or multimedia interfaces,

which may contain large amounts of information presented at once [3]. For example, high intensity control room situations such as air traffic control rooms, require operators to manage a number of such interfaces, switching from one application interface to another, often over multiple screens and in time-critical scenarios. Operators will frequently use radios or mobile phones, make and answer calls, and speak to their co-located colleagues while completing their tasks. This can result in very high cognitive load and hinder the users' ability to perform the task to the best of their ability.

An understanding of the users' cognitive load will enable us to alleviate these problems by implementing strategies to adjust the interaction system's response, presentation, and flow of interaction material as per their cognitive load, thus helping them complete tasks more effectively. But, measuring a user's cognitive load perfectly and in real time is not a trivial task. Many studies have attempted to measure cognitive load using several methods including physiological, performance, and self-reporting subjective measures [1,4-7]. However, such measures can be physically or psychologically intrusive, can sometimes only be measured post hoc and may disrupt the normal flow of the interaction. Though they may be useful approaches in research situations but are often unsuitable for deployment in real-life applications.

Some behavioral measures of load, for example speech features, like pitch, prosody, pauses, and disfluencies have also been found to vary under high levels of cognitive load [8-10]. These measures allow non-intrusive analysis as they are based on speech data generated by users while they complete the task. Linguistic and grammatical features may also be extracted from spoken or written input and are highly unobtrusive. The content of the language or the manner in which it is delivered can both be analyzed for patterns [11], which may be indicative of high load situations. Such features have been used before for purposes other than cognitive load measurement [12-14].

Speech pauses including both silent as well as filled pauses have also been studied as a potential measure of cognitive load [9,15]. In psychology, the pauses during natural speech have been linked to a person's cognitive and thinking processes, i.e. if producing a response requires a particular amount of cognitive energy, then the more time it takes to produce the response, the more cognitive energy is required to do so [16]. The studies showed that the number and the time duration of pauses is directly proportional to the users' experienced level of cognitive load. Our previous work evaluated the use of some linguistic features for measuring cognitive load, including negative emotions, perceptive and cognitive phrases, feelings etc. showing significant differences between low and high cognitive load tasks [17].

In this paper, we present a novel speech content analysis approach for measuring users' cognitive load, based on their language complexity. We analysed the speech contents of members of bushfire management teams working in computerized incident control rooms and involved in several convoluted bushfire management simulation tasks around Australia. The objective was to analyse how their use of language and its complexity varies for tasks of different difficulty levels. We converted their speech conversations into text transcriptions and analysed them for language complexity. The complexity of a written or spoken text or transcript can be measured by two major factors: *semantic difficulty* and *syntactic complexity* [18]. Semantic difficulty observes the use of words, their frequencies, and their lengths (both in syllables as well as alphabets/characters). Syntactic complexity observes primarily the sentence length, which is considered as the best indicator of text or language complexity [18]. Long sentences have more chances to contain more clauses, and therefore communicate more information and varying ideas; hence the longer the sentences, the more complex the language and more difficult to comprehend it. Together, both these factors contribute to the complexity of a text or transcript.

We analyse some complexity measures and present results showing significant differences in the language complexity between the speech from cognitively low load and high load tasks. The selection of these measures was motivated by the fact that there is large amount of speech data available in fields such as bushfire management. Spoken communication is an integral part of this activity and is always available for analysis. Additionally, use of linguistic features can supplement other signal based speech features and/or methods to measure cognitive load non-intrusively. We also contend that the value of language complexity features as a proxy to cognitive load is very high, specifically for user interface evaluation and interaction design improvement.

STUDY AND METHOD
We used the same data set as collected in our study from previous work (for specific details of the study and its design, the participants, data collection, coding and cleaning methods refer to [17]). In brief, the study involved several training bushfire management tasks carried out by bushfire incident management teams. Each team was involved in tasks of different difficulty levels and comprised of three team members, an incident controller (IC), planner, and operation officer, all operating collaboratively from a computerized incident control room. During the tasks, their speech was recorded, and later transcribed, cleaned, and coded by bushfire management experts for two task difficulty/ load levels:

- 'low load': routine tasks, no time pressure;
- 'high load': challenging tasks, time constraints, and a lot of unexpected events and breakdowns happening.

Complexity Measures
For our current analysis, we used six language complexity measures including Lexical Density, Complex Word Ratio, Gunning Fog Index, Flesch-Kincaid Grade, SMOG Grade, and Lexile Level. These are also known as readability measures [19] and have been used by many studies [18-21] for purposes other than cognitive load measurement. Though mostly used with written texts such as articles, essays etc., these measures may also be applied to transcripts of spoken texts. While written texts involve a considerable amount of editing, spoken texts are the result of more spontaneous speech where there is no opportunity to edit in the same way. Hence these measures may actually show more drastic language complexity differences for spoken texts than written texts.

Lexical Density is the estimated measure of content per functional and lexical units or lexemes in total text [22]. In simple words, it is a measure of the ratio of unique words to the total number of words.

Complex words are the words with three or more syllables. A word can be divided into syllables and each syllable is a sound that can be said without interruption and is usually a vowel which can have consonants before and/or after it [23]; for example, the word 'density' has three syllables. Complex Word Ratio is the measure of the ratio of complex words to the total number of words.

Gunning Fog Index calculates the syntactic complexity of language using sentence lengths and complex words and implies that short and simple sentences in plain English achieve a better score (lower value) than long sentences in complicated language [19,23-24]. Flesch-Kincaid Grade calculates the language difficulty using average sentence lengths and average syllables per word [25]. It estimates the number of years of education required to understand the written or transcribed text. The SMOG Grade [26] also estimates the number of education years needed to fully comprehend the text. It uses sentences and complex words to calculate it. The emphasis on full comprehension distinguishes this measurement from other complexity measures. Lexile Level also measures the comprehension complexity of any written or spoken text [18]. A Lexile measure is the numeric representation of a text's difficulty ranging from 200L for easy to above 1700L for complicated texts. It uses mean sentence lengths and mean log word frequency to calculate it. Note that all six measures involve both basic language complexity factors: semantic difficulty and syntactic complexity as discussed earlier.

We processed the bushfire transcription data using an advanced text analyzer software tool [23]. The tool automatically calculated a value for each of the above six language complexity measures from each bushfire management operator's speech for their cognitively low load and high load tasks separately.

HYPOTHESES

We expected that as the task difficulty (and so the cognitive load) increases, both the lexical density or the vocabulary richness and the use of complex words (words with three or more syllables) decrease. This is because we expect people to use a variety of different words when working in an easy task situation because they have the cognitive resources available to search and select from a richer pool of words. When dealing with high load situations, their vocabulary richness and the use of complex words would decrease.

We also expected that for Gunning Fog, Flesch-Kincaid, SMOG Grade, and Lexile measures, their measurement values would increase with the task difficulty. Our intuition was that when dealing with easy tasks, people use short, and complete sentences. For more difficult tasks, they will have to focus more attention on the task itself than speaking, resulting in long, complicated, and often incomplete sentences containing several clauses and ideas.

RESULTS AND DISCUSSION

We analyzed the complexity measures for the significant differences between low load and high load tasks, using dependent means t-Test with alpha = 0.05. Results showed that as expected, the bushfire management operators' lexical density decreased significantly from low cognitive tasks to high cognitive tasks (decreased by 4.8%, p < 0.04). Unexpectedly, the complex word ratio showed a significant positive correlation with cognitive load or task difficulty (increased by 17%, p < 0.0001).

For Gunning Fog Index, the mean score for low load tasks was 5.78 compared to 7.08 for high load tasks, a significant increase by 22.5% (p < 0.0001). Flesch-Kincaid Grade showed a significant increase of 42% from a mean value of 2.79 under low load tasks to 3.96 under high load (p < 0.0004). Similarly, SMOG Grade also showed an increase from mean value of 6.76 to 7.51 between low and high load tasks, a significant increase by 11% (p < 0.0003). Finally, for the Lexile Level, the mean score for low load tasks was 712L compared to 905L for high load tasks, again a significant increase by 27% (p < 0.0004). All results, with exception to the complex word ratio, are found to be in line with our hypotheses and are summarized in Table 1.

These results suggest that while communicating and interacting via speech, users' language and its complexity aspects show different patterns under different cognitive load situations and that the complexity measures presented, along with other potential features proposed in other studies, can be successfully implemented in a cognitive load measurement system.

Measure	Low Load	High Load	Difference	p-value
Lexical Density	67.3	64.2	−4.8%	0.04
Complex Word Ratio	0.052	0.061	+17%	0.0001
Gunning Fog Index	5.78	7.08	+22.5%	0.0001
Flesch-Kincaid Grade	2.79	3.96	+42%	0.0004
SMOG Grade	6.76	7.51	+11%	0.0003
Lexile Level	712	905	+27%	0.0004

Table 1. Summary of Complexity Measures under Low vs. High Cognitive Load Tasks; Differences significant for p<0.05.

It was interesting to find out that in contrast to our hypothesis about the complex word ratio, there was an increasing trend. This could be due to the complex and critical nature of the bushfire management task with operators using more complex words. We assume the same feature behavior in similar task situations but this trend may not persist with less critical task situations. Also though the results apply across a variety of people and roles, these are specific for this combination of tasks, in a bushfire management scenario. These results may vary for other types of application scenarios, e.g. in road or air traffic management, though it is expected to have some common trends across these application areas.

This knowledge about users' experienced cognitive load using the proposed complexity measures and other linguistic and grammatical parameters explored earlier, may enable us to use this approach to measuring cognitive load as a post-hoc analysis methodology for user interface evaluation and systems' interaction design improvement. For example, we could use two different speech-supported interaction systems used by the same user for the same task and then see which one causes higher cognitive load. The results may enable us to improve the interaction design for the interface or system that is causing higher cognitive load.

When appropriate technology for automatic speech recognition is available, we may be able to analyze the proposed features in real-time, enabling the interaction systems to achieve the adaptive response to users' cognitive load. For example in case of bushfire management control room situation, based on the operator's measured cognitive load, the interaction system could be able to adapt any number of aspects of the task, from fairly simple changes such as highlighting critical screens, and showing controlled reminders, to more complex or subtle changes such as sorting and prioritizing task checklists, or filtering email messages, and redirecting phone calls to less cognitively loaded operators and so on.

CONCLUSION AND FUTURE WORK

This study has provided encouraging evidence for the use of language complexity measures as indicators of increased cognitive load. They offer a promising contribution to the set of potential implicit interactive features specifically in the domain of bushfire management. Though not trivial, identification of such features could help develop intelligent interaction systems that adapt to difficulties experienced by the user in real-time to ensure optimal user performance and experience. However, these features require cross-application validation and verification before they are tested in other contexts.

For future work, we intend to investigate more grammatical and language parameters including parts of speech and their varying structure and relationship under varying cognitive load situations. We also intend to validate all the potential language and grammatical features of cognitive load and develop a potential feature set common to different application areas enabling us to develop an application-adaptive cognitive load measurement system.

ACKNOWLEDGMENTS

We thank Christine Owen and Gregory Hickey from University of Tasmania and the Bushfire CRC, for helping us in the collection and coding of the bushfire speech data.

REFERENCES

1. Chandler, P. and Sweller, J., Cognitive load theory and the format of instruction. *Cognition and Instruction 8*,4 (1991), 293-332.
2. Paas, F., Tuovinen, J. E., et al. Cognitive load measurement as a means to advance cognitive load theory. *Educational Psychologist 38*, 1 (2003), 63-71.
3. Mayer, R. E., *Multimedia learning*. Cambridge, UK: Cambridge University Press, 2001.
4. Kramer, A. F., Physiological metrics of mental workload: a review of recent progress. *Multiple task performance*, Damos, D. L., Ed., (1991), 279-328.
5. Ark, W., et al.; The Emotion Mouse. *HCI: Ergonomics and User Interfaces 1*; Eds. Bullinger and Ziegler. London, Lawrence Erlbaum Assoc., 1 (1999), 818-823.
6. Windell, D. and Wiebe, N.; A comparison of two mental workload instruments in multimedia instruction. In *Proc. HFES 2006*, Human Factors and Ergonomics Society Press, Santa Monica, CA, USA, 2006.
7. Novak, D., et al. Using psychophysiological measurements in physically demanding virtual environments. *Proc. Interact 2009*; Eds T. Gross et al., Part I, LNCS 5726, pp. 490-493, 2009.
8. Yin, B., et al. Speech-based cognitive load monitoring system, *Proc. ICASSP'08*, IEEE Press, 2041-2044, 2008
9. Berthold, A. and Jameson, A., Interpreting Symptoms of Cognitive Load in Speech Input. In *User Modeling 99*, Springer Wien New York, 1999.
10. Muller, C., et al., Recognizing time pressure and cognitive load on the basis of speech: An experimental study, in *Proc. 8th International Conference on User Modeling*, 2001, pp. 24-33.
11. Kettebekov, S. Exploiting prosodic structuring of coverbal gesticulation, *Proc. ICMI2004*, ACM Press, pp. 105-112, 2004.
12. Sexton J. and Helmreich, R., *Analyzing Cockpit Communication: The links between language, performance, error, and workload*. University of Texas Team Research Project, Austin, USA, 2000.
13. Stirman, S. W., and Pennebaker J. W.; Word use in the poetry of suicidal and nonsuicidal poets. *Psychosomatic Medicine 63*, Amer. psychosomatic society press, 2001.
14. Kramer, A. et al. Using Linguistic Features to Measure Presence in Computer-Mediated Communication, *Proc. CHI2006*, ACM Press, (2006).
15. Khawaja, M. A., Ruiz, N., Chen, F. Potential Speech Features for Cognitive Load Measurement. *Proc. OzCHI 2007*, ACM Press, 2007.
16. Schilperoord, J. On the cognitive status of pauses in discourse production, T. Olive and C. M. Levy Eds., *Contemporary tools and techniques for studying writing 10*, pp. 61-88, 2001, London: Kluwer Academic Publishers, 2001.
17. Khawaja, M. A., Chen, F., and et al. Cognitive Load Measurement from User's Linguistic Speech Features for Adaptive Interaction Design. In *Proc. Interact 2009*; Eds T. Gross et al., Part I, LNCS 5726, pp. 485-489, 2009.
18. Lennon C. and Burdick H., The Lexile Framework as an approach for reading measurement and success; April 2004, http://www.lexile.com; Last accessed: July 2008.
19. Reck, P. and et el., Generating and rendering readability scores for Project Gutenberg texts, In *Proc. Corpus Linguistics Conference*, Birmingham, UK, 2007, Article #120.
20. Sokolova, M. and et el., Comparative analysis of text data in successful face-to-face and electronic negotiations, *Group Decision and Negotiation 15*, pp. 127-140, Springer 2006.
21. Kun-Moo Rhee and Eunil Kim, A Statistical Analysis of Text for Inferring Authenticity, *Proc. 53rd Session of International Statistical Institute*, Seoul, 2001. http://isi.cbs.nl/iamamember/index.htm
22. Ure, J. Lexical density and register differentiation. *Applications of Linguistics*, Perren and Trim (Eds), London: Cambridge University Press. 1971, pp. 443-452
23. Advanced Text Analyser, *UsingEnglish*, http://www.usingenglish.com; Last accessed: Sept. 2009
24. Gunning, R. *The Technique of Clear Writing*. McGraw-Hill, 1952.
25. Flesch, R. F., A New Readability Yardstick, *Journal of Applied Psychology, 32*, 1948, pp. 221-233.
26. McLaughlin, G. H., SMOG Grading - A new readability formula, *Journal of Reading*, May 1969, pp. 639-646.

Activity Awareness in Family-Based Healthy Living Online Social Networks

Stephen Kimani, Shlomo Berkovsky, Greg Smith, Jill Freyne, Nilufar Baghaei, Dipak Bhandari
CSIRO Tasmanian ICT Center
GPO Box 1538, Hobart, 7001, Australia
firstname.lastname@csiro.au

ABSTRACT

Social relationships and family involvement play an important role in health management. Activity awareness is useful in decision-making and stimulating motivation and action. In this paper, we propose a novel user interface that provides activity awareness in the context of a family-oriented healthy living social network. It is intended to increase family members' interaction with healthy living social networks. The interface has elements through which family members can record, track, and view healthy living activities in the real world and on the online social network. A user study showed that the activity awareness interface increased interaction with healthy living content underpinning the social network, led to higher levels of learning in relation to healthy living, and impacted on specific healthy living activities. There was also considerable appreciation of and interaction with the activity awareness user interface elements.

Author Keywords

Activity awareness, user interface, user interaction, online social networks, families, healthy living, evaluation.

ACM Classification Keywords

H.5.2 User Interfaces: Graphical user interfaces (GUI), Evaluation/methodology.

General Terms

Design, Experimentation, Human Factors

INTRODUCTION

The World Health Organization predicts that by 2030, three-quarters of all deaths in the world will be due to chronic non-communicable diseases [10]. The lifestyle which people adopt has a bearing on their health and wellbeing. There is thus the need and opportunity for IT solutions that support people to manage their lifestyles. Prior research indicates that there is a positive correlation between social relationships and health, and that family involvement is important in health management [1].

Awareness has been defined as "*an understanding of the activities of others, which provides a context for your own activity*" [2]. It is useful in decision-making [3] and can enable people to make sense of activity of others and tailor their own activity accordingly [2]. Prior research in activity awareness has mainly focused on the context of work and office environments [4]. There are some activity awareness efforts that have involved the family context [7,8]. These efforts, however, focus on strengthening the links between family members by supporting communication and connectedness.

In our research, we focus on ways to increase family members' interaction with healthy living online social networks and as a means of encouraging them to adopt a healthy lifestyle. We propose a novel activity awareness user interface integrated with a family-oriented healthy living social application supporting families to adopt a healthy lifestyle. The healthy living social application [5] consists of two main components: content component and social component. The content component provides access to health-related resources drawn primarily from the CSIRO Total Wellbeing Diet book [6]. The social component provides social support features, such as blogs through which users can publish messages visible to the community, forums for online discussions, activity feeds with updates on the features/pages users are using, visiting or viewing, and others.

To develop the activity awareness interface, we have adopted a design process that involves HCI experts, domain experts (health and nutrition specialists), and potential users. The interface comprises visual elements, through which family members can record and track their healthy living activities. It also comprises elements, through which family members can view their own performance of healthy living activities in the real world and on the online social network and compare it with the performance of other users. A user study involving 92 families showed that the activity awareness interface increased user interaction with the health-related content and led to higher level of learning about healthy living and impact on specific healthy living activities. There was also considerable appreciation of and interaction with the activity awareness user interface elements.

ACTIVITY AWARENESS USER INTERFACE

The users of the family-oriented healthy living online social network application are families. We consider the set of all these users as the community. We represent the community by $C=\{F_1, F_2, ..., F_n\}$, where F_i denotes family i and n is the number of families in the community. A family F_i is represented by $F_i=\{fm_{i1}, fm_{i2}, ..., fm_{ik}\}$, where fm_{ij} is member j of family F_i and k is the number of family members in F_i.

The activity awareness user interface includes elements for supporting two categories of healthy living activities: online social activities using the system, and healthy living activities in the real world.

Online social activities using the system

While interacting with the social network, users can perform various activities (see a partial list in Table 1). We have assigned a weight w_l to each activity l. The weights reflect the importance of activities to the sustainability of the social network and efforts involved in performing them, and are in line with the weighting schema proposed in [9].

Social activity identifier	Social activity	w_l
22	View forum post	1
1	Update activity diary	3
40	Write blog entry	2

Table 1. Sample social activities and their weights.

An individual user performance of social activities, s_{ij}, of user fm_{ij} is computed by

$$s_{ij} = \sum_{l=1}^{n_l} w_l * f_{ij,l} \quad (1);$$

where $f_{ij,l}$ is the frequency (number of times performed) of social activity l weighted w_l. and n_l is the number of social activities supported by the social network. A family performance s_i of social activities is computed by

$$s_i = \sum_{m=1}^{k_i} s_{im} \quad (2);$$

where k_i is the number of family members in F_i. The community performance S is computed by

$$S = \sum_{f=1}^{n} s_i \quad (3);$$

where n is the number of families in the community. We use $max(s_{ij})$ and $av(s_{ij})$ to represent the top and average individual user performances in the community. Similarly, we compute performances related to a specific social activity l. These will be denoted by $s_{ij,l}$, $s_{i,l}$, and S_l.

In order to support online social activities, the activity awareness user interface comprises a *scorecard* (Figure 1-right) and *performance graph* (Figure 2-right) of social activities. The scorecard helps users track their performance in interacting with the social network, and compare their performance with the top and average performance in the

community. The performance graph shows the distribution of social activities across the entire community.

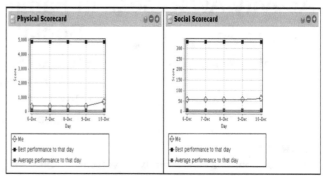

Figure 1: Scorecards.

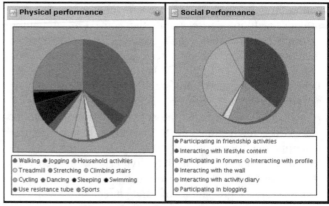

Figure 2: Performance graphs.

Healthy living activities in the real world

In order to support healthy living activities in the real world, the activity awareness user interface comprises an *activity diary*, and a scorecard (Figure 1-left) and performance graph (Figure 2-left) of physical activities. The activity diary enables users to record their healthy living activities in the real world. Each entry in the diary is self-reported by the user and can have one of the following four intensity levels and corresponding weights: mild (1), moderate (2), moderate plus (3), hard (4).

An individual user performance of physical activities, p_{ij}, of user fm_{ij} is computed by

$$p_{ij} = \sum_{e=1}^{n_e} i_{ij,e} * d_{ij,e} \quad (4);$$

where n_e is the number of entries in the user's activity diary, $i_{ij,e}$ is the intensity and $d_{ij,e}$ is the duration of the activity.

Similarly to the online social activities, the following performances of physical activities can be computed: family performance p_i, community performance P, top and average performance $max(p_{ij})$ and $av(p_{ij})$, and individual, family and community performance of a specific physical activity m, respectively, $p_{ij,m}$, $p_{i,m}$, and P_m.

USER STUDY

We conducted a user study to evaluate the contribution of the activity awareness user interface in increasing user interaction with the healthy living social network. We were targeting families of 4 individuals (2 parents and 2 children) familiar with online social networks. We recruited 368 participants from 92 families. Participants were partitioned into two groups: group A - without activity awareness interface (177 users) and group B - with activity awareness interface (191 users). The study had 3 main stages. In the *pre-interaction stage* all the participants filled out a demographics questionnaire. In the *interaction stage* participants were asked to interact regularly with the social network over a period of 3 weeks (July-August 2009). The system logged data about users' interaction with the social network during this period. In the *post-interaction stage* participants filled out a user experience questionnaire. At this stage we got responses from 239 users (110 in group A, 129 in group B).

Experimental results

In this subsection, we present the results of the study.

1. Interaction stage results

Interaction: Users in the group B exhibited a higher interaction with the system (M=46.35[1]) than in group A (M=43.60). It is worth noting that on the whole the interaction levels of parents and children were comparable, with an average interaction of 46.7 for parents, and of 45.1 for children.

Usage of features: Activity diary was among the most used features (see *Diary save* and *Diary add* in Figure 3). Users in group B had a significantly higher interaction with content (M=10.17), than in group A (M=6.8); t(366)=2.336, p=0.02[2].

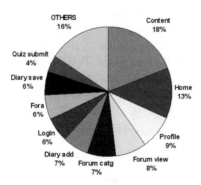

Figure 3: Usage of system features.

Direct navigation to content: Users in group B exhibited a significantly higher number of clicks on activity feeds on the social network homepage taking users directly to the

---

[1] We use M to represent the mean

[2] We use the notation to represent our independent-samples two-tailed t-tests

content (M=0.42), than participants in group A (M=0.22); t(366)=2.385, p=0.018.

Interaction with specific types of content: Group B exhibited higher interaction with all content types than group A (Figure 4). The difference was statistically significant for recipes (t(366)=2.386, p=0.018), and shopping lists (t(366)=2.607, p=0.010).

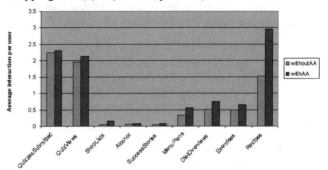

Figure 4: Interaction with specific content types.

2. Post-interaction stage results

Ease of access to health resources: Users in group B reported a significantly higher ease of access to health resources (M=2.23), than in group A (M=2.01); t(237)=2.290, p=0.023.

Learning about healthy living: A significantly higher number of users in group B reported that using the system enabled them to learn about healthy living (M=1.9), than in group A (M=1.69); t(237)=2.023, p=0.044.

Impact on healthy living activities: A significantly higher number of users in group B reported that using the system had an impact on alcohol and smoking management in their families (M=0.29), than in group A (M=0.14); t(237)=2.976, p=0.003. A higher number was also observed impact on physical activities (M=0.46 vs. M=0.34). Although in the latter difference was not significant, it was very close; t(237)=1.908, p=0.058.

Most liked social features: The graphs of physical activities were among the most liked social features. Other social features that were liked include: forums and updating profiles.

DISCUSSION

Inclusion of the activity awareness interface increased interaction of users with the social network. Our research suggests that activity awareness is relevant to the following aspects of interaction:

Influence on users' access to content:
- Direct navigation to content from the homepage: showing the most frequently visited content in the activity feed inspired users to visit the content.
- Interaction with the healthy living content: showing scorecards and performance graphs motivated users to view the content.

To support this, group B reported a significantly higher measure of ease of access to resources than group A.

Learning about healthy living: The performance graphs and scorecards motivated learning. Users in group B reported that activity awareness interface enabled them to get feedback on their progress, set goals, compare with others, and discover new activities. As a result, users became more aware of themselves and others and could learn from this what to do to improve their health and lifestyle.

Impact on specific healthy living activities: Users in group B reported high measures of impact on smoking/alcohol management and exercise. Users indicated that the activity awareness interface helped them to identify areas they needed to improve and to see that other people were making progress.

Feature usage and appreciation: As was observed in the previous section, there was high utility of the activity awareness interface. The graphs of physical activities were among the most liked social network features.

CONCLUSIONS AND FUTURE WORK

This paper has described an activity awareness user interface in family-based healthy living social networks. The interface added value to user interaction with family-based healthy living social network, increased interaction with content, and led to higher levels of learning about healthy living and greater impact on lifestyle activities. There was also significant appreciation and utility of the activity awareness interface elements.

In the future we will develop and incorporate interaction mechanisms for implicitly capturing real-world user activities. This will involve the use of devices with activity monitors in order to automatically sense and capture user's physical activities. We will also conduct further analysis of the data to establish whether there were gender differences

ACKNOWLEDGMENTS

This research is jointly funded by the Australian Government through the Intelligent Island Program and CSIRO. The Intelligent Island Program is administered by the Tasmanian Department of Economic Development, Tourism, and the Arts. The authors wish to thank Nathalie Colineau and Cécile Paris for their thoughts and comments regarding this research work.

REFERENCES

1. MacLean, S.L., Guzzetta, C.E., White, C., Fontaine, D., Eichorn, D.J. and Meyers, T.A. Family presence during cardiopulmonary resuscitation and invasive procedures: Practices of critical care and emergency nurses. American Journal of Critical Care 12 (2003), 246-257.

2. Dourish, P., Bellotti, V. Awareness and coordination in shared workspaces. Proc. CSCW'99, ACM Press (1992).

3. Cannon-Bowers, J.A., Salas, E. and Converse, S.A. Shared mental models in expert decision-making teams. In: Castellan, N.J., Jr. (ed.) Current issues in individual and group decision making, Erlbaum (1993), 221-246.

4. Elliot, K. and Carpendale, S. Awareness and Coordination: A Calendar for Families. Technical Report 2005-791-22, Department of Computer Science, University of Calgary, Calgary, Alberta, Canada (2005).

5. Baghaei, N., Freyne, J., Kimani, S., Smith, G., Berkovsky, S., Bhandari, D., Colineau, N. and Paris, C.. SOFA: An Online Social Network for Engaging and Motivating Families to Adopt a Healthy Lifestyle. Australian conference on Computer-Human Interaction (OZCHI'09), (2009).

6. Noakes, M., Clifton, P.: The CSIRO Total Wellbeing Diet. Penguin, Australia. (2005).

7. Mynatt, E., Rowan, J., Jacobs, A. and Craighill, S. Digital Family Portraits: Supporting Peace of Mind for Extended Family Members. Proc. CHI'01, ACM Press (2001).

8. Khan, V. and Markopoulos, P. Busy families' awareness needs. IJHS 67, 2 (2009), 139-153.

9. Vassileva J. Adaptive Incentive Mechanism for Sustainable Online Community. Proc. of Workshop Sustaining Community at GROUP'05, (2005).

10. World Health Organization, Factsheet 311, http://www.who.int/mediacentre/factsheets/fs3

A $3 Gesture Recognizer – Simple Gesture Recognition for Devices Equipped with 3D Acceleration Sensors

Sven Kratz
Deutsche Telekom Laboratories
TU Berlin
Ernst-Reuter-Platz 7
10587 Berlin, Germany
sven.kratz@telekom.de

Michael Rohs
Deutsche Telekom Laboratories
TU Berlin
Ernst-Reuter-Platz 7
10587 Berlin, Germany
michael.rohs@telekom.de

ABSTRACT

We present the $3 Gesture Recognizer, a simple but robust gesture recognition system for input devices featuring 3D acceleration sensors. The algorithm is designed to be implemented quickly in prototyping environments, is intended to be device-independent and does not require any special toolkits or frameworks. It relies solely on simple trigonometric and geometric calculations. A user evaluation of our system resulted in a correct gesture recognition rate of 80%, when using a set of 10 unique gestures for classification. Our method requires significantly less training data than other gesture recognizers and is thus suited to be deployed and to deliver results rapidly.

Author Keywords

Gesture recognition, recognition rates, classifier, user interfaces, rapid prototyping, 3D gestures

ACM Classification Keywords

H5.2 [Information interfaces and presentation]: User interfaces – *Input devices and strategies*. I5.2. [Pattern Recognition]: Design methodology – *Classifier design and evaluation*. I5.5 [Pattern Recognition]: Implementation – Interactive Systems.

General Terms

Algorithms, Measurement, Performance, Experimentation

INTRODUCTION AND RELATED WORK

An increasing number of mobile devices are equipped with 3D accelerometers, which calls for suitable methods for 3D gesture recognition on these platforms. Gesture input for mobile devices can be a way to overcome the limitations of miniature input facilities and small displays, since the range of movement is not restricted by the size of the device. An example would be to perform gestures on a keypad-locked mobile phone to immediately start intended applications.

The Nintendo Wii [2] controller is a prominent and commercially successful example for a new generation of game consoles that use acceleration sensors for input to allow for more natural interaction.

Our work is based on previous work by Wobbrock et al. [8], who developed a simple "$1 Recognizer" using basic geometry and trigonometry. The "$1 Recognizer" is targeted at user interface prototyping for 2D touch-screen-based gesture recognition and therefore focuses on ease of implementation on novel hardware platforms. (The authors provide a pseudocode implementation of the complete recognizer in the paper.) We extend and modify Wobbrock et al.'s algorithm to work with 3D acceleration data. Instead of capturing exact pixel positions on a touch screen, acceleration data is of much lower quality because it is prone to noise, and additionally, drift error accumulates as the path of a gesture entry is integrated. We extend Wobbrock's original algorithm with a scoring heuristic to lower the rate of false positives. Using actual user input, we present an evaluation of the performance of Wobbrock's modified algorithm, and show that this method is well suited to implement 3D gesture recognition in rapid prototyping environments.

Past contributions [5, 7] in the area adopt established, but highly complex techniques (Hidden Markov Models, Neural Networks) for gesture recognition. Rabiner [6] is the standard introduction to implementing HMM-based classifiers. The gesture recognizers of Schlömer et al. [5] and Kratz et al. [7] feature good recognition rates, but only use a small gesture vocabulary. Moreover, these recognizers require relatively large gesture training sets. Producing repetitive movements can be a nuisance for the user. In contrast, our approach produces good results with about five training examples per gesture. Other past contributions focus on finding appropriate gestures for certain application domains (e.g., VCR control) [4] and mostly use "flat" 2D gestures.

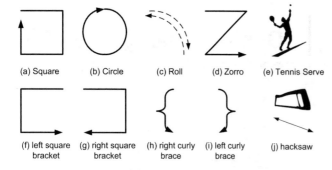

(a) Square   (b) Circle   (c) Roll   (d) Zorro   (e) Tennis Serve

(f) left square bracket   (g) right square bracket   (h) right curly brace   (i) left curly brace   (j) hacksaw

Figure 1. The reference gesture vocabulary containing the gesture classes used for the preliminary evaluation. (b) describes a clockwise circular motion, (c) a wrist rolling motion (e) stands for a gesture resembling the serve of a tennis player and (j) represents a repeated rapid forward-backwards motion.

The major contribution of this work is the creation a simple gesture recognizer that is designed to recognize "true" 3D Gestures, i.e. gestures which are not limited to shapes that can be drawn in a 2D plane. The advantage of true 3D gesture recognition is that more natural movements, such a tennis serve or boxing punches can be input by the user.

Like the "$1 Recognizer," our approach is quick and cheap to implement, does not require library support, needs only minimal parameter adjustment and minimal training, and provides a good recognition rate. It is therefore very valuable for user interface prototyping and rapid application development. It can also easily be integrated into mobile interfaces that take advantage of other modalities, like speech, or touch-based interaction with RFID/NFC.

THE $3 GESTURE RECOGNIZER

Extending Wobbrock's [8] work, we present a gesture recognizer that can recognize gestures from 3D acceleration data as input. To test our algorithm we used acceleration samples obtained from a Nintendo Wii Controller (WiiMote). The WiiMote features an ADXL 330 Accelerometer [1] and the acceleration data can be sent, as in our case, via a Bluetooth connection to a PC. Our algorithm is by no means limited to the WiiMote. It can be used in any acceleration-enabled device, for instance modern smart-phones.

Gesture Trace

In contrast to [7], we do not modify or pre-process the raw acceleration data in any way (filtering, smoothing, etc.). To determine the current change in acceleration, we subtract the current acceleration value reported by the WiiMote from the previous one. We thus obtain an *acceleration delta*. By summation of the acceleration deltas, we obtain a *gesture trace T* which can be plotted in 3D space (Figure 1 gestures (e),(j)), or projected into a 2D plane (gestures (a)-(d), (f)-(i)) to obtain a graphical representation of the gesture [3].

Gesture Class Library

The *gesture class library L* contains a predefined number of gesture traces for each *gesture class G*. We also refer to these traces as *training gestures*.

Gesture Recognition Problem

The basic task of our algorithm is to find the best matching gesture class G from the gesture class library L, for a given input gesture I. (Example representatives of gesture classes is given in Figure 1.) To find a matching gesture class, we compare the trace t_i of I to the traces of all training gestures $t_{G_k} \in L$ and generate a score table that lists the comparison score of t_i and each t_{G_k}. A heuristic then is applied to the score table to determine if a gesture has been recognized.

Resampling

For optimal classification, the original gesture trace T needs to be resampled to have a number N of points equal to that of the template gestures. This is because the gesture input duration and movement speeds can vary between users, even for the same intended gesture. Resampling ensures that the points are re-distributed to be at equal distances from each other.

In our case $N = 150$, which is slightly above the average amount of acceleration deltas received while users enter a gesture with the WiiMote. Setting N to a lower value decreases the gesture recognition precision, while choosing a higher N just increases the computation time for gesture recognition, without a significant gain in accuracy.

Resampling is performed using piecewise linear interpolation, in which a resampled gesture trace T_N consisting of N equidistant points t_N is created. The locations of the T_N are built up by successive addition of the points t_k of the original gesture trace T to generate N equidistant segments connecting the new points t_N of T_N.

Rotation to "Indicative Angle" and Rescaling

To correct for rotational errors during gesture entry, the resampled gesture trace T_N is rotated once along the gesture's *indicative angle*. Like Wobbrock, we define the indicative angle as the angle between the gesture's first point p_0 and its centroid $c = (\bar{x}, \bar{y}, \bar{z})$. The angle is determined by taking the arcus cosine of the normalized scalar product of p_0 and c:

$$\theta = acos(\frac{p_0 \bullet c}{\|p_0\| \|c\|})$$

The rotation along the indicative angle is then performed using the unit vector of the vector orthogonal to p_0 and c. The orthogonal vector is obtained using the cross product of P_0 and c:

$$v_{axis} = \frac{p_0 \times c}{\|p_0 \times c\|}$$

The trace T_N is the rotated using v_{axis} and ϑ to obtain the rotated trace T_{N_ϑ}.

After rotation, T_{N_θ} is scaled to fit in a normalized cube of 100^3 units, to compensate for scaling differences between gestures. The algorithm has now finished preprocessing the original user input and has obtained a gesture T_M, which is ready for matching with candidate gestures from the gesture class library.

Search for Minimum Distance at Best Angle

Like Wobbrock, we use the average MSE (Mean Square Error) to calculate the path distance d between T_M and candidate gesture from the gesture class library. We convert the path distance to a $[0, 1]$ scale using a version of Wobbrock's scoring equation adapted to three dimensions, where d signifies the path distance and l the side length of the cube that T_M was scaled to in the rescaling step.

$$Score = 1 - \frac{d}{0.5\sqrt{3l^2}}$$

Following Wobbrock's discussion of rotation invariance of path distances, we have adapted a Golden Section Search (GSS) using the Golden Ratio $\varphi = 0.5(-1+\sqrt{5})$ to approximate the local minimum path distance within an angular range of $[-180° \ldots 180°]$, for rotation around the three axis of the coordinate system, signified by the angles α, β and γ. We define a minimum cutoff angle for GSS of $2°$, in order to guarantee that the approximate minimum is found after exactly 11 iterations of GSS. We compared this approach to a brute-force implementation of the angle search and found that the result of GSS lies within $5°$ of the optimal rotation angle in the majority of cases.

The GSS-based minimum distance approximation is repeated for each trace of every gesture class in the library. The result is a table sorted by matching scores with the corresponding gesture class ID.

Scoring Heuristic

Wobbrock's original algorithm did not feature a heuristic to reduce the occurance of false positives, which is a common problem for simple gesture recognition algorithms operating on large gesture vocabularies [8]. The matches obtained from gestures entered as 3D acceleration data are not as precise as strokes entered on a touch screen. To compensate for the weaker matches, we have developed our own scoring heuristic, which processes the score table described in the previous section. Using this heuristic, we achieved a considerable reduction of false recognitions compared to Wobbrock's original strategy of selecting the gesture candidate with the highest matching score to determine the recognized gesture.

After sorting the score table by maximum score, our heuristic determines the recognized gesture with the following rules:

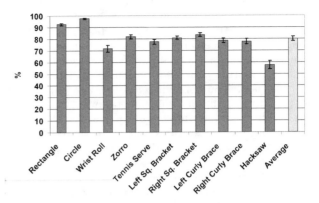

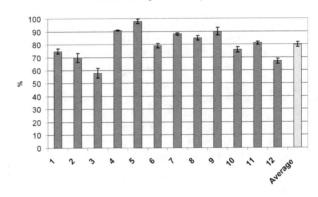

Figure 2. Average correct recognition rates with standard error, sorted by gesture class (top) and by user (bottom).

- ε is defined as the threshold score.

- Iff the highest-scoring candidate in the score table has a score $> 1.1\varepsilon$, return this candidate's gesture ID.

- Iff, within the top three candidates in the score table, two candidates exist of the same gesture class and have a score $> 0.95\varepsilon$, respectively, return the gesture ID of these two candidates.

- Else, return "Gesture not recognized!".

EVALUATION OF THE $3 GESTURE RECOGNIZER

To get an initial estimate of the gesture recognition performance of our method, we evaluated the 3$ gesture recognition algorithm with twelve participants, who were compensated for their effort.

Our reference gesture vocabulary contained all of the gestures utilized by [7] as well as a subset of Wobbrock's unistroke gestures [8], as displayed in Figure 1, totaling 10 unique gesture classes. We chose this particular set of gestures to make our study comparable to the previous work. Each user was asked to enter each gesture class in the reference set 15 times using a WiiMote. The gesture data was recorded and stored on a PC.

The actual gesture recognition was performed offline using the stored gestures entered by the users. From each gesture class, the first five entered gestures of a particular gesture class were chosen as the training set for that class. The remaining gestures were input into our gesture recognition algorithm. Knowing the gesture class of the tested gesture beforehand, we recorded the number of times the gestures were correctly recognized, incorrectly recognized or not recognized at all.

Our evaluation resulted in average (correct) recognition rate of 80%. Between test subjects, the recognition rate varied between 58% and 98%, with a standard deviation of 11.4. As can be seen in Figure 2, the recognition rate was fairly constant across all users and gestures, with gesture class (b) having the highest average recognition rate and gesture class (j) being the most error-prone gesture. We speculate that the low recognition rate of gesture class (j) is due to the ambiguity of that gesture, as users varied the "sawing motion", which they were expected to perform, considerably. Notably, users commented that gesture classes (h) and (i) were the most uncomfortable gestures to perform. Furthermore, our results indicate that our scoring heuristic functioned acceptably, as only about 8% of all detected gestures were false positives.

Our gesture recognition algorithm yielded a lower correct recognition rate than those obtained with the system featured in [7]. In spite of this, we deem our correct recognition rate to be fully acceptable given that we used substantially simpler methods, and, which is more important, twice as many gesture classes with a significantly smaller gesture training set per class to achieve this recognition rate.

It is likely that the nearly 20% lower recognition rate of our method compared to [8] is influenced by the following factors. Gestures in 3D space are more difficult for a human to re-produce perfectly than in 2D, even for simple 2D shapes. More important, the equipment which we used to capture the gesture information was far from perfect, and may have contributed to the reduced recognition rate.

Limits of the $3 Gesture Recognizer

As it is a simple algorithm, the $3 Gesture Recognizer has several limitations. For one, in contrast to more refined methods such as those based on HMMs, it cannot be used to detect gestures in a continuous motion stream. Only gestures which are explicitly started and stopped by the user can be recognized. A further limitation is the size of the gesture vocabulary. Not only does the number of false positive recognitions rise together with the size of the gesture vocabulary, but also the computational overhead ($O(N \cdot M)$), where N is the amount of motion samples, and M is the number of

training gestures in the gesture class library). This is due to the intensive use of trigonometric functions, increases as well, which limits the maximum practicable size of the gesture vocabulary to about 10-15 gestures. These limitations, however do not represent an impediment for the use of our recognizer in its target domain — rapid prototyping of gesture-based interfaces.

DISCUSSION AND FUTURE WORK

We presented a simple, easy-to-implement gesture recognizer for input devices equipped with 3D acceleration sensors. The idea behind our gesture recognition algorithm is to provide a quick and cheap way to implement gesture recognition for true 3D gestures (such as the reference gesture (e)). Our method does not require any advanced software frameworks or toolkits. The gesture set is not fixed but can be specified by as needed, even at runtime. An example application area for our gesture recognizer is user interface prototyping.

In an initial evaluation of our algorithm, we obtained gesture recognition rates which are comparable to those of more advanced approaches. The advantage of our system is that it is specifically targeted for use in prototype environments, in which gesture-based interfaces (or multimodal interfaces using gestures as one of multiple components), are needed that provide quick results with little coding and minimal training data.

REFERENCES

1. Analog Devices ADXL330, http://tr.im/GTHc.

2. Nintendo inc. http://wii.nintendo.com.

3. S. Kallio, J. Kela, J. Mäntyjärvi, and J. Plomp. Visualization of hand gestures for pervasive computing environments. In *Proc. AVI '06*, pages 480–483, New York, NY, USA, 2006. ACM.

4. J. Kela, P. Korpipää, J. Mäntyjärvi, S. Kallio, G. Savino, L. Jozzo, and S.D. Marca. Accelerometer-based gesture control for a design environment. *Personal Ubiquitous Computing*, 10(5):285–299, 2006.

5. L. Kratz, M. Smith, and F.J. Lee. Wiizards: 3d gesture recognition for game play input. In *Proc. Future Play '07*, pages 209–212, New York, NY, USA, 2007. ACM.

6. LR Rabiner. A tutorial on hidden Markov models and selected applications inspeech recognition. *Proceedings of the IEEE*, 77(2):257–286, 1989.

7. T. Schlömer, B. Poppinga, N. Henze, and S. Boll. Gesture recognition with a wii controller. In *Proc. TEI '08*, pages 11–14, New York, NY, USA, 2008. ACM.

8. J.O. Wobbrock, A.D. Wilson, and Y. Li. Gestures without libraries, toolkits or training: a $1 recognizer for user interface prototypes. In *Proc. UIST '07*, pages 159–168, New York, NY, USA, 2007. ACM.

A Multimodal Labeling Interface for Wearable Computing

Shanqing Li and Yunde Jia
Beijing Laboratory of Intelligent Information Technology,
School of Computer Science, Beijing Institute of Technology, Beijing, P.R.China
{shanqingli, jiayunde}@bit.edu.cn

ABSTRACT

Under wearable environments, it is not convenient to label an object with portable keyboards and mice. This paper presents a multimodal labeling interface to solve this problem with natural and efficient operations. Visual and audio modalities cooperate with each other: an object is encircled by visual tracking of a pointing gesture, and meanwhile its name is obtained by speech recognition. In this paper, we propose a concept of virtual touchpad based on stereo vision techniques. With the touchpad, the object encircling task is achieved by drawing a closed curve on a transparent blackboard. The touch events and movements of a pointing gesture are robustly detected for natural gesture interactions. The experimental results demonstrate the efficiency and usability of our multimodal interface.

Author Keywords

Multimodal labeling, virtual touchpad, wearable computing.

ACM Classification Keywords

H.5.2. Information interfaces and presentation: User Interfaces –User-centered design.

General Terms

Design, Human Factors

INTRODUCTION

Wearable computing has been one of the important research topics in human computer interaction. To be adaptive to new environments and meet user-specific demands, the ability of learning new concepts and categories is very essential for wearable computers. Therefore, new training samples are necessary to update classification models. However, it is not convenient to label an object under wearable environments with portable keyboards and mice. The multimodal provides a most promising way of labeling an object naturally and efficiently: encircling its silhouette by the movements of a pointing gesture, and meanwhile denoting its name from the wearer's voice.

Multimodal interactions have attracted much attention in recent years for wearable/mobile computing [1-6]. Yang et

al. [1] presented a tourist assistant system which integrates speech and gestures to interpret intentions and provides assistance for a tourist. Keaton et al. [2] reported a wearable system called SNAP&TELL to recognize objects including outdoor landmarks by combining real-time gesture tracking and audio-based control commands. Kolsch et al. [3] described an augmented reality interface with the HandVu wearable system, providing efficient access to information encountered in urban environments. Heidemann et al. [4] proposed a multimodal interaction approach for augmented reality scenarios. Either pointing gesture or speech can be used to select objects and manipulate menus. An object is selected by pointing gesture, and its label has still to be typed by a keyboard. Based on this work [4], Bekel et al. [5] further introduced a self-organizing map and MPEG-7 features to achieve pre-categorizations for interactive labeling. In those systems, visual and audio modalities are both used for manipulation commands performing in a sequential order. The complementary characteristics of two modalities are not used completely. Harada [6] presented a VoiceLabel system for collecting ground truth data for building activity inference models on mobile devices. The segmentation of recorded data and recognition of spoken labels have to be performed offline.

In this paper, visual and audio modalities cooperate with each other in a most complementary manner to achieve efficient object labeling tasks. When an object is encircled by a user's pointing gesture, its name can be obtained by speech recognition at the same time. Visual tracking of pointing gesture and speech recognition are performed in real-time for object labeling. To track the pointing gesture robustly under wearable environments, the local binary pattern (LBP) features and depth maps are used to indicate visual cues of the pointing gesture. And furthermore, we propose a concept of virtual touchpad to perform object encircling in a more intuitive approach. The depth maps play an important role in our work: (1) to generate proposal distributions as heuristic information for importance sampling which makes particle filter tracking more robust, (2) to calculate 3D positions of the index fingertip. Voice commands are recognized by a HMM-based method. The experimental results demonstrate that the proposed interface works robustly and efficiently in wearable environments.

SYSTEM CONFIGURATION

The multimodal labeling interface is shown in Figure 1. The hardware is composed of four parts: stereo machine, head-mounted display (HMD), wearable computer and Bluetooth microphone. The stereo machine developed in our lab [7] obtains gray images and depth maps at video rate. The cameras use wide-angle CMOS lenses (about 80°) to capture a wide range of scene and recover dense depth maps within a close distance. A Motorola H680 Bluetooth microphone provides a wireless connection to the wearable computer. The computing results are displayed on the HMD.

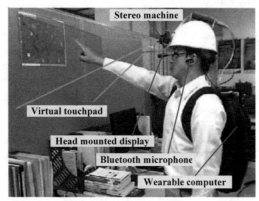

Figure 1. Multimodal labeling system setup.

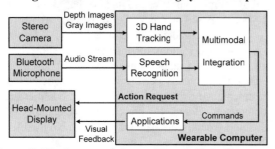

Figure 2. Block map of the multimodal labeling system.

The system architecture is shown in Figure 2. The pointing gesture is tracked by combining the depth maps and LBP features under the particle filter framework. The recovered 3D position of index fingertip is used to determine whether the index fingertip touches the virtual touchpad or not. The audio processor performs HMM-based speech recognition algorithms to obtain object names from audio streams in a natural way. The multimodal integration module analyzes the results of the two input modalities and verifies whether a complete task is formed correctly. If all parameters are available, an executable command is immediately sent to applications. If not, an action request for parameters is sent to the wearer through the HMD.

VISION INTERFACE

Pointing Gesture Tracking

Particle filters offer a probabilistic framework for dynamic state estimation. The tracking framework uses the process density $p(s_t \mid s_{t-1})$ and the observation density $p(z_t \mid s_t)$ to compute the posterior state-density $p(s_t \mid z_t)$ at time t. The shape model for pointing gesture is described as a cardboard model, and the state vector is defined as

$$\bar{s} = [P_x, P_y, \alpha_x \cos\theta - 1, \alpha_y \cos\theta - 1, -\alpha_y \sin\theta, \alpha_x \sin\theta]^T \quad (1)$$

where P_x and P_y are the translation parameters, α_x and α_y are the scaling parameters, θ is the rotation angle. The gesture is divided into several patches and the local binary pattern features are extracted to describe the gesture appearance.

Besides factored sampling based on the spatial-temporal consistence, importance sampling uses knowledge from current t time to generate samples in a heuristic way. In this paper, two sampling strategies are simultaneously employed for better tracking performance. That is, some samples are generated by factored sampling with spatial-temporal consistence, and the others by importance sampling according to the depth maps. We assume that the wearer's hand is the closest object to the head-mounted cameras. The centroid $p = (x, y)$ of segmented hand region is used to generate the importance function

$$g(p) = N(p, \sigma) \quad (2)$$

where $N(\cdot)$ represents the normal distribution, and σ is the covariance which can be set manually.

To measure and weight all newly generated samples, we use support vector machine (SVM) to train a classifier with manually labeled samples. With the SVM classifier, the distance d from the separating hyperplane is used to calculate sample weights by the sigmoidal function

$$\pi_t = \frac{1}{1 + \exp(-d)} , \quad \text{with } d = W\phi(x) + b \quad (3)$$

where W and b are the SVM model parameters. To achieve rotation and scale invariance, we first transform the sample to a unified scale space, then calculate the rotation-invariant LBP features following the approach by Ojala et al. [8].

Virtual Touchpad

During encircling an object with a pointing gesture, it is very important to indicate the start and end states. A simple way is to use several gestures for different states, as described in an early version of our system [9], but the wearer has to memorize and transform predefined hand gestures correctly. A more natural method is to simulate the operations of drawing closed curves on a blackboard for object encircling. Hereby, we define a virtual touchpad which is a plane in front of a head-mounted stereo camera and paralleling to the image plane, similar to a transparent blackboard. With the touchpad, the object encircling is naturally performed as follows: (1) put the pointing gesture on the board, (2) move the pointing gesture to encircle an object quickly, (3) detach the pointing gesture from the board when an encircling process ends.

With hand tracking results and depth maps, we can directly calculate the 3D positions of the index fingertip. Under wearable environments, depth maps of a pointing gesture commonly lose partial data, which potentially lead to wrong results. To solve this problem, we calculate the hand plane in 3D space with point mass in segmented hand regions and the method of least squares

$$H: a_1x + b_1y + c_1z + d_1 = 0 \qquad (4)$$

The imaging model of a camera, indicating a line passing the index fingertip, camera lens and its imaging point, is given by

$$L: A[R,t](x,y,z,1)^T = \lambda(u,v,1)^T \qquad (5)$$

where A is the camera intrinsic matrix, R is the rotation matrix, t is the translation matrix, λ is a constant variant, $(x,y,z,1)$ and $(u,v,1)$ are positions of index fingertip in 3D space and image space, respectively. Therefore, the 3D position of an index fingertip is defined as the intersect point of the hand plane H and the line L.

Assume that D indicates the distance between the virtual touchpad and the camera lens, and d represents the depth value of an index fingertip. As shown in Figure 3(a), a touching event of the pointing gesture can be converted to checking whether the condition $d \geq D$ is satisfied. To indicate that the index fingertip "touches" the surface, a green cross will be rendered on the fingertip as feedbacks.

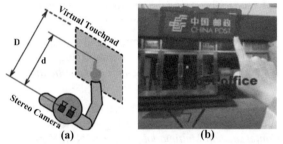

Figure 3. Sketch maps for (a) virtual touchpad, and (b) multimodal labeling.

AUDIO INTERFACE

Speech input is very efficient for wearable computing devices. We developed a speech recognition system based on the HTK open resource library of Cambridge University. The toolkit is based on hidden Markov models, where each monophone is represented as a five-state HMM. When speech utterances are sent to the recognition engine, acoustic analysis is performed to extract the MFCC (Mel Frequency Cepstral Coefficient) vectors. Next, the system performs recognition algorithms to produce an n-best list of textual transcripts constrained by a predefined grammar. Finally, the transcripts are parsed into an n-best list of alternative interpretations ranked by their associated recognition probabilities. The interpretation with the highest probability is chosen as the final result. For about 100 isolated words, the recognition rate is up to 98%.

MULTIMODAL LABELING

In our system, the visual and audio modalities work in a coordinated manner for efficient interactions. The visual modality tracks the pointing gesture and encircles an object of interest, and meanwhile its name is determined by speech recognition. The labeling approach is shown in Figure 3(b). When a modality is activated, the other modality is checked

for available parameters. For example, when a voice command is identified, the multimodal labeling module tries to find the object region encircled by the wearer. If the region exists, a new sample is labeled successfully; otherwise, an action request to encircle an object is sent to the wearer by the HMD.

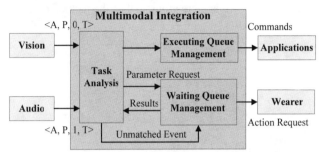

Figure 4. Block maps for multimodal integration.

We present a time-stamped task-oriented integration scheme for a solution of multimodal integration of two heterogeneous modalities, as shown in Figure 4. The input parameters are described as $< A,P,M,T >$, where A denotes the action name, P the parameters for interactions, M the used modality, and T the time when the interaction occurs. The task analysis module checks and integrates the input parameters from two modalities. An executable command is generated if all parameters are correctly assigned. Otherwise, a parameter request is sent to the waiting queue management module. The management module returns the matched parameters, or otherwise sends an action request to the wearer by the HMD.

EVALUATION

In our experiments, the CPU frequency is 2.0 GHz and the stereo machine can capture 320×240 gray images and recover depth maps at video rate (30fps). A 240-frame sequence of about 8 seconds is collected to evaluate the tracking performance of the proposed algorithm. The comparison results between the tracked fingertips and the ground truth data are shown in Figure 5, in which 120 frames are chosen with an equal interval sampling strategy. The ground truth values are manually labeled 3D positions of the index fingertip. The mean error and standard error of distances are 0.046m and 0.043m, respectively.

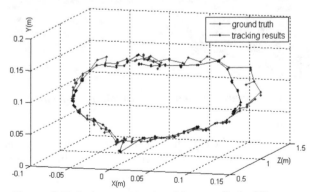

Figure 5. Pointing gesture tracking results in 3D space.

To evaluate the efficiency of the multimodal labeling system, we encircle several circle regions with different radius and give the name "circle". Object encircling and naming are performed with different modalities. Visual and audio modalities cooperate with each other at the same time in our system. The comparison results in Figure 6 show that the proposed approach is more efficient than the method of using keyboards and mice.

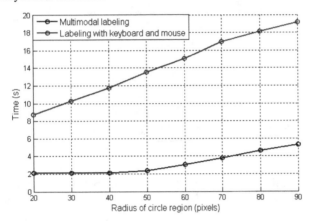

Figure 6. Efficiency comparison results for two methods.

APPLICATION

The multimodal labeling interface can be widely used in many applications, especially for online learning under wearable computing environments. With the labeled samples yielded by our labeling interface, object classifiers can be directly trained for online interactions. We use the SURF (features) [10] to detect and describe local invariant features of common objects in our campus. The descriptors are invariant to scale and rotation transformations, and can also handle the part-occlusion problems. The object models are composed of several images with significantly different viewpoints which are efficiently selected by our multimodal labeling interface. Some snapshots of object recognition under different conditions are shown in Figure 7.

Figure 7. Snapshots of object recognition applications.

CONCLUSIONS

A multimodal labeling interface is proposed for wearable computing in this paper. An efficient object labeling mode is provided by cooperating visual and audio modalities in a complementary manner. We also proposed a concept of virtual touchpad for natural object encircling. Visual tracking of a pointing gesture and speech recognition are performed in real-time and integrated by a time-stamped task-oriented fusion scheme. The experimental results and applications demonstrate the robustness and usability of our multimodal labeling interface under wearable environments.

ACKNOWLEDGMENTS

This work was partially supported by the Natural Science Foundation of China (90920009, 60905006), and the Chinese High-Tech Program (2009AA01Z323).

REFERENCES

1. Yang, J., Yang, W., Denecke, M. and Waibel, A. 1999. Smart Sight: a tourist assistant system, *International Symposium on Wearable Computers*, 73-78.

2. Keaton, T., Dominguez, S.M., and Sayed, A.H. 2002. SNAP&TELL: A multi-modal wearable computer interface for browsing the environment, *International Symposium on Wearable Computers*, 75-82.

3. Kolsch, M., Bane, R., Hollerer, T., and Turk, M. 2006. Multimodal interaction with a wearable augmented reality system, *IEEE Computer Graphics and Applications*, 62-71.

4. Heidemann, G., Bax, I., and Bekel, H. 2004. Multimodal interaction in an augmented reality scenario. *International Conference on Multimodal interfaces*, New York, 53-60.

5. Bekel, H., Heidemann, G., and Ritter, H. 2005. Interactive image data labeling using self-organizing maps in an augmented reality scenario. *Neural Netw.* 18(5-6), 566-574.

6. Harada, S., Lester, J., Patel, K., Saponas, T. S., Fogarty, J., Landay, J. A., and Wobbrock, J. O. 2008. VoiceLabel: using speech to label mobile sensor data. *International Conference on Multimodal Interfaces*. New York, 69-76.

7. Jia, Y., Zhang, X., Li, M., and An L. 2004. A Miniature Stereo Vision Machine (MVSM-III) for Dense Disparity Mapping, *International Conference on Pattern Recognition*, Cambridge, 728-731.

8. Ojala, T., Pietikainen, M., and Maenpaa, T. 2002. Multiresolution gray-scale and rotation invariant texture classification with local binary patterns, *Pattern Analysis and Machine Intelligence*, 24(7), 971-987.

9. Liu, Y., Liu, X., and Jia, Y. 2006. Hand-Gesture Based Text Input for Wearable Computers. *International Conference on Computer Vision Systems*, Washington, 8.

10. Bay, H., Tuytelaars, T., Gool, L.V. 2006. SURF: Speeded up robust features, *European Conference on Computer Vision* (1), 404-417.

Avara: A System to Improve User Experience in Web and Virtual World

Jalal Mahmud
IBM Almaden Research
Center
San Jose, CA 95120
jumahmud@us.ibm.com

Yun-Wu Huang
IBM T.J. Watson Research
Center
Hawthorne, NY 10532
ywh@us.ibm.com

John Ponzo
IBM T.J. Watson Research
Center
Hawthorne, NY 10532
jponzo@us.ibm.com

Roger Pollak
IBM T.J. Watson Research
Center
Hawthorne, NY 10532
pollak@us.ibm.com

ABSTRACT

3D virtual world software is becoming a popular medium for entertainment, social interaction and commerce. To the best of our knowledge, there is no system available to facilitate the bridging between Web applications and virtual world systems in the form of information sharing, data collection and control propagation. As a result, user experience in a Web interface is not sensitive to state changes of virtual world avatars or objects. Similarly, a virtual world environment does not provide Web context-rich user experience. We address this issue and propose a bridging and context sharing architecture between the Web and virtual world applications such that Web applications can control, monitor and collect information from artifacts in the virtual worlds, and vice versa. We also implemented this architecture using existing Web and virtual world technologies. Based on this implementation, we illustrate some novel applications and present a user study to illustrate the value of the system.

ACM Classification Keywords

H.5.2 Information Interfaces and Presentation: User Interfaces

General Terms

Algorithms, Design, Human Factors, Experimentation

Author Keywords

3D Web, Virtual World, Second Life, Bridging

INTRODUCTION

Recent years have seen a trend for increasing popularity of 3D virtual world software such as Second Life [10]. Al-

though virtual world software is mostly used for entertainment and social interaction, some of them have seen emerging presence of 3D stores (e.g., [10], [1]) offering virtual shopping experiences.

Most current e-commerce systems rely on Web interface to display content and interact with the users. 3D virtual world systems also have user interfaces. But the presentation of their user interfaces is generally too complex to be modeled by typical Web pages. Virtual world interfaces therefore are based on different technologies and their creation requires different skills than typical Web interfaces. As a result, even a company may have an e-commerce system that has both the Web interface and virtual world interface, these two interfaces are not tightly coupled and offer different user experiences and serve different functions. Moreover, context of a Web user (e.g., users preferences for a particular item), who also has a virtual world avatar is not propagated to the virtual world environment. For example, users preferences and browsing history in Web pages are not used to present the virtual world store items to them. Similarly, current Web-based applications do not leverage the contextual information from virtual world (e.g., users virtual world preferences) to enhance Web users experience. Thus, there is a gap between users experience in Web and virtual world interfaces. To our knowledge, there is no such system available to bridge this gap and improve user experience.

In this paper, we propose a bridging system so that a Web application can tightly couple with a virtual world application and one can retrieve information and receive events from the other. We call this system *Avara* (*Avara* stands for Across virtual and real applications). Avara allows contextual information to be collected and propagated from both the interfaces. Using such information, both Web and virtual world environment can be adaptive to the changes in one another. We also present a preliminary user study based on the implementation of the system. Our study illustrates that sharing and propagating contexual information from Web to virtual world and vice versa by Avara system can improve user experience in both applications.

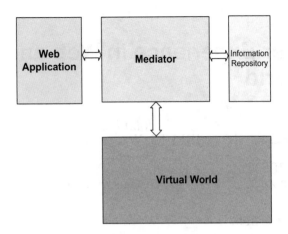

Figure 1. High Level System Architecture

The Web application may make requests to retrieve the properties and meta-information of 3D presentation of its objects in the virtual world, or send information to the virtual world. The Web application may use this 3D information to enrich user experience or enhance knowledge about its displayed objects.

Virtual World Interface is a 3D virtual world client application. For example, in Second Life, the world and the marketplace are virtual world Interfaces. Virtual world objects state and contextual data are periodically sent to the mediator from the virtual world interface.

Mediator communicates with Web applications and virtual world Interfaces. Mediator receives request to propagate and receive contextual data from both Web and virtual world interface. Mediator can access information repository for quick storage and retrieval of the meta data.

RELATED WORK

There are prior research to bridge real world applications/objects and virtual world. For example, [4] illustrates an approach to connect physical objects with virtual representations or computational function, via various types of tags, e.g., RFID tags. Recently, [6] develops a concept of service between services in virtual worlds (VW) and services in the real world (RW). In [6], authors show through examples how messaging, web publishing, and real time multimedia services in a virtual world can be bridged with corresponding services in Real world. Mirco et al. describe an approach to bridge the divide between real world and virtual world by mapping real world activities (e.g., sitting, walking, running) in the virtual world [7]. Using this approach, it is possible to automatically translate users current actions and movements in real life to the virtual life of their avatars. GVU research project's [3] client software bridges locations in physical space with corresponding places in virtual space.

The fundamental difference between our research and all of these approaches is that our work presents a tight coupling between Web applications (e.g., an e-commerce application) and 3D virtual world such that contextual information and meta data can be collected and propagated from both the interfaces. Using such information, both Web and virtual world environment can be adaptive to the changes in one another. None of the above mentioned research focuses on improving user experience in Web and virtual world by context sharing and propagating. Our research illustrates that both Web applications and virtual world applications can be context sensitive and adaptive to improve user experience.

THE AVARA ARCHITECTURE

The system architecture, depicted in Figure 1, is based on the mediator pattern in which a Web application and a virtual world system communicate through the Mediator which knows how to interface with the Web Application and the virtual world systems.

Web applications are the most common front-end process of today's enterprise computing. An object presented in Web application may have a 3D presentation in a virtual world.

THE AVARA BRIDGING FRAMEWORK

The bridging framework of *Avara* is based on an object mapping model and a communication model that enable the sharing of information across the Web and the virtual worlds.

The Avara Object Mapping Model

Object mapping defines the relation between Web objects and virtual world objects. The relation can be one-to-one, one-to-many or many-to-one. Each Web object is associated with Web data that is stored in Information Repository. Similarly, each virtual world object is associated with meta-data stored in Information Repository. The stored data is retrievable by the URL of its associated object. The stored data may include information that captures the state of the object it models, hence is dynamic in nature as it can change frequently. For example, the stored data of a Web object may include a textual discription, an image and a hyperlink, whereas that of a virtual world object may include the size, color and spatial location of this virtual world object. Currently, the mapping rules have to be manually inserted into the information repository. These rules are static in nature, meaning that once the relations are stored in Information Repository, they do not change until the objects they model are removed or their relations are changed. In future, we will explore better approaches to derive mapping rules, e.g., detection of similar objects and insert mapping rules into the information repository automatically.

The Avara Communication Model

We use message passing to propagate information from Web and virtual world and vice versa. Currently we do not support time-critical data propagation. Instead, our system relies on message passing based on the *store-and-forward* pattern adopted by the Mediator. Request messages (e.g., request to retrieve a users virtual world preference information) are constructed by both Web applications and virtual world interfaces and are sent to the mediator. Information repository can be accessed to serve those requests. Mediator processes the requests and sends response message back to the requesting application.

Figure 2. A Virtual World Store of *Avara*

THE AVARA IMPLEMENTATION

We implemented a prototype system based on the *Avara* bridging architecture. We built an example e-commerce application which has both a Web interface and a virtual world interface. This section describes the implementation details of this system.

We implemented Mediator as a server-side Web application deployed in a remote Web server based on Apache Tomcat [2]. The various components in Mediator are implemented using PHP [9]. Information Repository is implemented using MySQL [8] database to store mapping relations and cached Web data and virtual world meta-data in relational tables. The Web interface is implemented using HTML, XML and JavaScript. Our virtual world interface is implemented in Second Life [10], a very popular virtual world system. All virtual world components are implemented using the Second Life scripting language called the Linden Scripting Language [5].

AVARA APPLICATIONS

Virtual-Context Aware Web Interface

Consider a user "James" who has registered his Second life Avatar "Mahmud Vella" to the Web interface of a virtual store. He takes his avatar to the virtual store. The store has few sensor objects placed at each counter, and each of them senses whether any avatar speaks about a 3D object, or touches or even moves closer to the object. In such cases, sensor object makes a PreferenceUpdate request with appropriate parameters. The parameters of this request are as follows:

AvatarName: Name of the Avatar
ObjectName: Name of the 3D Object
Location: Location Vector
EventName: Name of the Preference Event (e.g. Touch, Speak, Move Close).

The preference update request is then sent to the Mediator. Each preference event is associated with a weight which we have set apriori and stored in the database. Mediator retreives the weight of the preference event from the database and makes a RepositoryUpdate request to update the rating for the relation: (AvatarName, ObjectName) by the weight value for the event. Continuing with our example, the avatar "Mahmud Vella" touches the virtual object "SLObject_1". Therefore the rating value of the relation ("Mahmud Vella", "SLObject_1") is increased by the weight of the event "Touch". Then the avatar speaks about the object "SLObject_2" and the rating of the relation ("Mahmud Vella", "SLObject_2") is increased by the weight of the event "Speak". Now the user opens the Web page for this store. The user signs in and finds that the item "Object_2" is recommended to him. In this example, weight of the event "Speak" is higher than the event "Touch", therefore the rating of the relation ("Mahmud Vella", "SLObject_2") is higher than that of the other relation. As the user "James" signs in, the system retrieves the avatar name for this user and gets the most preferable virtual world object by comparing all the rating values for this avatar. Then it takes the best one, gets the Web page product name for that 3D virtual world object, and recommends that product to the user.

The simple scenario described above illustrates how our system can exploit virtual world context to make intelligent context-aware Web interface.

Web-Context Aware Virtual Interface

Consider the user "James" who has registered to our hypothetical store "Web-VStore". Each time the user clicks an item, searches an item or adds the item to the shopping cart, the rating of the corresponding relation is increased. Let us assume that, the user accessed the item "Object_1" the highest number of times in a given period. Therefore, the rating of the relation ("James","Object_1") becomes higher than the rating of any other relation of the form ("James", X), for all Object X in the store.

Next, the user opens the virtual world "Second Life" and his avatar "Mahmud Vella" visits the virtual world store "Web-VStore". The store has few 3D sensor objects placed at each counter, and each of them senses the presence of any avatar. As one of the sensor detects the avatars presence, it makes a request to get the preference for the user of that avatar, and sends that request to the mediator which then accesses the information repository to get the mapping of the user for that avatar and the rating of each relations of the form (UserName, ObjectName). For this example, mediator finds that the rating of the relation ("James", "Object_1") is the highest. It then uses the mapping of Web object and 3D artifacts, and returns the relation ("Mahmud Vella", "SLObject_1") to the controller of the object "SLObject_1". The controller recommends that object to the avatar by changing the visual property (e.g. display text).

USER STUDY

We did a user study of our system. The goal of this study was to justify whether context sharing and propagation by

Avara can improve user experience. We used 3 participants in our study. They were familiar with Web browsing. They also used some Virtual Worlds, e.g., Second Life previously. We introduced them with Avara, its Web and Virtual World interface, before the start of the study. We asked them to do the following tasks:

- Task 1: Select an item from the Avara Web interface and add that item to the shopping cart. Then, visit the Avara Virtual World interface (i.e. Second Life store of Avara), and find that item.

- Task 2: Visit the virtual world store of Avara, select an item, add that item to the virtual world shopping cart. Then, find the same item from Web interface of Avara.

- Task 3: Click/Search an item from the Avara Web interface, and then, visit the Avara Virtual World interface (i.e. Second Life store of Avara), and find that item.

- Task 4: Visit the virtual world store of Avara, speak about an item. Then, find the same item from Web interface of Avara.

Each of the task was done in the following ways:

- - without using the context sharing service of Avara, i.e. contextual information was not propagated from Web to virtual world and vice versa.

- - using context sharing service of Avara, i.e. contextual information was propagated between Web and virtual worlds.

Our participants mentioned that they could find the item more easily when they used Avara's context sharing feature. This is because an item added to the shopping cart by the user in Avara's Web interface was recommended to the corresponding Avatar in Virtual World interface, and vice versa. They also mentioned that a context preserving and sharing system could help improving their experience in both Web and 3D virtual world by recommending the relevant tasks. They also suggested to use context sharing service for bridging real time communications (e.g., chat service) in both Web and virtual world. We also measured the service latency of Avara system in each of the cases. This service latency is the sum of the following:

- - Web access delay to make a HTTP request to server. This is not different from the delay of a typical client Web page sending a HTTP request to the Web server

- - Computation delay at Avara Server. This is the delay for database lookups.

- - Virtual World delay caused by virtual world sensors, and objects.

On average, our participants observed approximately 5-10 seconds service latency when they used Avara's context sharing and propagating service. They mentioned that Avara would be more useful to them if the delay could be reduced. We also seperately measured each component of the delay, and found that virtual world delay was the most contributing

factor to service latency. In future, we will focus on how to reduce this delay. One possibility is to minimize the number of sensors in virtual world.

CONCLUSION AND FUTURE WORK

In this paper, we present the *Avara* architecture that bridges the Web and virtual world applications such that Web applications can control, monitor and collect information from artifacts in the virtual worlds, and vice versa. Leveraging this architecture, an e-commerce application can achieve a wider reach of customers while providing them with rich shopping experience. Furthermore, an *Avara*-based system can gather both virtual world customer knowledge information and virtual world contextual and state information.

There are possible avenues of future research. Our architecture supports asynchronous message passing between Web applications and 3D virtual world clients to propagate state and meta data. However, there are cases when states and meta data have to be propagated synchronously (e.g., connecting a 3D world chat instance to a real world chat program). Towards that, We will extend the architecture with a Web Feed [11] to support synchronous communication. We would also like to address challanges in virtual world constraints including scalability, network latency and programmability.

REFERENCES

1. www.activeworlds.com/.

2. www.apache.org.

3. http://arsecondlife.gvu.gatech.edu/.

4. B. L. Harrison, K. P. Fishkin, A. Gujar, D. Portnov, and R. Want. Bridging physical and virtual worlds with tagged documents, objects and locations. In *CHI '99: CHI '99 extended abstracts on Human factors in computing systems*, pages 29–30. ACM, 1999.

5. J. Heaton. *Introduction to Linden Scripting Language for Second Life*. Heaton Research, Inc., 2007.

6. R. Jana, A. Basso, Y.-F. Chen, G. D. Fabbrizio, D. Gibbon, B. Renger, and B. Wei. Bridging communication services connecting virtual worlds to real world: a service providers perspective. In *MobEA 2008, in conjunction with WWW 2008*, 2008.

7. M. Musolesi, E. Miluzzo, N. D. Lane, S. B. Eisenman, T. Choudhury, and A. T. Campbell. Integrating sensor presence into virtual worlds using mobile phones. In *SenSys '08: Proceedings of the 6th ACM conference on Embedded network sensor systems*, pages 383–384, New York, NY, USA, 2008. ACM.

8. www.mysql.com.

9. www.php.net.

10. http://secondlife.com.

11. http://en.wikipedia.org/wiki/Web_feed.

Supporting Exploratory Information Seeking by Epistemology-based Social Search

Yuqing Mao
School of Computer Engineering
Nanyang Technological University,
Singapore
maoy0002@ntu.edu.sg

Haifeng Shen
School of Computer Science,
Engineering and Mathematics
Flinders University, Adelaide, Australia
hfshen@csem.flinders.edu.au

Chengzheng Sun
School of Computer Engineering
Nanyang Technological
University, Singapore
czsun@ntu.edu.sg

ABSTRACT

Formulating proper keywords and evaluating search results are common difficulties in exploratory information seeking. Reusing and refining others' successful searches are pragmatic directions to tackle these difficulties. In this paper, we present a novel epistemology-based social search solution, where search epistemologies are effectively shared, reused, and refined by others with the same or similar search interests through novel user interfaces. We have developed a prototype system *Baijia* and experimental results show that an epistemology-based social search system outperforms a conventional search engine in supporting exploratory information seeking.

Author Keywords World Wide Web, exploratory information seeking, epistemology-based social search.

ACM Classification Keywords
H5.3. Information interfaces and presentation (e.g., HCI): Group and Organization Interfaces.

General Terms Design, Human Factors

INTRODUCTION

The WWW has a higher degree of freedom than conventional media because it is possible for anyone to publish any information at any time from any place. Furthermore, search engines such as Google and Yahoo make it easy for people to seek information on the WWW. However, conventional search engines are facing difficulties such as formulating proper keywords and evaluating search results in supporting exploratory information seeking (EIS).

On the one hand, the relevance of the information to be returned by a search engine relies on the accuracy of the keywords to describe a search goal. In EIS, formulating proper keywords out of a vague search goal is not easy. On the other hand, the ranking of the result pages based on the PageRank or HITS algorithm may not well reflect the quality precedence in EIS.

Social search has been increasingly adopted to address these difficulties in recent years by utilizing the wisdom of crowds: as many people search for the same or similar in-formation, reusing others' successful searches is a pragmatic solution. Previous work [3] has suggested that social search could be immensely valuable for an EIS process which combines foraging and sensemaking [10]. Since it is generally difficult and time-consuming to start an EIS process from the scratch, it would be more efficient and fruitful to simply take advantage of others' successful searches for the same or similar goal.

Existing work in this direction mainly revolves around mining relationships between queries and result pages or sharing tags on commonly interested search results. On the one hand, they emphasize on reusing others' searches but do not provide mechanisms to refine them. On the other hand, different work addresses the reusing of a different isolated aspect of others' searches, such as keywords, results, or certain type of meta-information about results. Our solution focuses on not only reusing but also refining others' contributions, and provides a novel platform and interfaces for people to share their intimate knowledge and Web search experiences (not just search results).

In this paper, we present a novel epistemology-based social search solution to EIS, where search epistemologies – aggregated and well-structured information packages derived from successful search processes, such as queries, results, rankings, annotations, comments, and evaluations, contributed by a mass of searchers – are effectively shared, reused, and refined by others with the same or similar search interests. We have developed a prototype system *Baijia* and conducted a set of experiments based on automatically generated epistemologies to validate the solution. The results show that an epistemology-based social search system outperforms a conventional search engine in sup-porting EIS.

The remainder of this paper is organized as follows. First, we review the related work on social search. Next, we de-scribe our epistemology-based social search solution. After that, we present the experiments with the prototype system and discuss the results. Finally, we conclude the paper with a summary of major contributions and future work.

RELATED WORK

The idea of reusing others' successful searches has emerged with the rise of search engines. For example, users will see the keyword suggestions from a search engine (e.g., Google) when they type incomplete keywords in the search box. Query expansion and query substitution are often used to provide query suggestions by enhancing and modifying queries in search logs [7].

Considering explicit feedback would interrupt users' natural searching behaviors, most research work is based on mining implicit feedback from users, e.g., the collaborative filtering technique used in recommender systems [5] and the community search assistant [4], where a group of users search collaboratively by using query recommendation based on a query graph. Although research in these directions does reuse others' searches, it is not regarded as genuine social search because users are not explicitly engaged in reusing processes [1]. These research areas mainly study reusing optimal queries by analyzing query logs and search results from search engines.

Social networks and social media Web sites like blogs and collaborative tagging systems have been increasingly popular, where sharing is regarded as the "heart and soul", e.g., sharing bookmarks by Delicious[1], photos by Flickr[2], and videos by Youtube[3]. However, tags are generally different from keywords submitted to a search engine, and extra efforts are needed to facilitate search of tags [6]. MrTaggy [2] is such a social search system recommending others' tags.

Social-ranking-based search engines exemplified by Scour[4], allow users to manually re-rank search results through voting and editing and to share their re-rankings with others. Q&A systems like Yahoo! Answers allows a user to seek help from others regarding a specific question. Some research work does not focus on reusing others' contributions but on collaboratively performing a common Web search task by a group of invited users. For example, SearchTogether [8] allows groups of people to communicate and share search results in real time.

Our epistemology-based social search solution supports not only reusing but also more importantly refining others' contributions by means of well-structured epistemologies that are far more comprehensive than isolated queries, results, tags, or rankings.

AN EPISTEMOLOGY-BASED SOCIAL SEARCH SYSTEM
In the following sections, we will elaborate the epistemology-based social search solution by referring to the *Baijia* prototype system.

Epistemology Generation and Refinement
In an EIS process, the user usually needs to formulate a set of queries eis = {$q_1, q_2... q_n$}, and the epistemology of this search *Epi(eis)* is defined as:

---

[1] http://www. delicious.com

[2] http://www. flickr.com

[3] http://www. youtube.com

[4] http://www.scour.com

$$Epi(eis) = Epi(q_1)\cdots \oplus Epi(q_i)\cdots \oplus Epi(q_n) \oplus Epi(extra),$$

where $Epi(q_i)$ is the epistemology for q_i ($1\leq i \leq n$), *Epi(extra)* is the epistemology for information that is not acquired through these queries, e.g., from authoritative websites, and '$\oplus$' is the operator to construct the epistemology for an EIS process out of those for constituent queries. Each $Epi(q_i)$ is based on the user's interaction with the system, such as pages selected by the user and the user's ranking and comments on the pages.

Figure 1 shows an epistemology window in *Baijia*. When the user submits a query to the system, the entry for the query will be added automatically to the epistemology, and the user can add selected pages for this entry by dragging them to the epistemology. Selected pages in an epistemology will be ranked and commented by other users, and therefore the system will re-rank the pages in each epistemology dynamically. While most previous work focused on providing more relevant pages for a specific query, *Baijia* can discover related queries in the epistemology repository. As such, our solution can better support EIS because users can get the required information quickly and easily even if they start with not-so-relevant queries.

Furthermore, the system supports refinement of epistemologies and notification of updates of interested epistemologies. One can create an initial epistemology entry in the repository and then subscribe to it by clicking the "subscribe it!" button. The system will send a notification to the user when the epistemology is refined by others. One can subscribe (with proper authentication and authorization) to any epistemology no matter who has actually created it.

Epistemology Search and Reuse
Search results come from our epistemology repository and the result pages returned by a search engine (currently

Figure 1. A window of epistemology generation and refinement

Google through its API). The epistemology search engine adjusts the weights between the epistemologies and the results from the search engine according to the level of agreement between the queries and each epistemology. The agreement is defined based on the summation of queries match of all epistemic concepts, each of which is contributed by user i, and the match is based on the similarity between all elements of the concept and the queries:

$$Agree(Epi, queries) = \sum_i \sum_k (w_1 \times sim(q, q_k) +$$
$$w_2 \times sim(tags, q_k) + w_3 \times sim(comments, q_k) +$$
$$w_4 \times \sum_j sim(p_j, q_k) + \cdots) , q_k \in queries, p_j \in pages,$$

where w_i is the weight assigned to an element of the epistemology according to its importance, e.g., an element such as a comment or a page with a higher user ranking will be assigned a heavier weight.

The similarity between two elements can be measured by various methods. In *Baijia*, it is measured with the Kullback-Liebler divergence (KL-divergence) between two language models. We also adopted Jelinek-Mercer (JM) as a smoothing technique to address the data sparseness problem in language models.

These measurements are applied to the sorting of related epistemologies. If no matches of epistemologies are found, results from the search engine are given a higher priority, and the most relevant epistemologies are listed for reference. Furthermore, as the computation is based on the queue of queries, the epistemologies are re-ranked dynamically while the user continuously submits queries. Figure 2 shows a window of related epistemologies in *Baijia*.

Baijia also supports real-time sharing of search epistemologies: users can perform collaborative work on selected epistemologies with friends in real time through the instant messenger built in the system.

EXPERIMENTS

The main purpose of setting up experiments is to validate how much an epistemology-based social search system can

Figure 2. Epistemology search and reuse

outperform a conventional search engine in supporting EIS. The studies of human factors in epistemology-based social search and usability of the system (including user evaluation) are currently ongoing.

Procedure

We selected the AOL query logs [9] as the base of our experiments. As the URL clicking can be regarded as the positive feedback, it is possible to reproduce users' search processes out of the query logs. As such, we have simulated users' interactions with epistemologies and search results (based on user ID).

First, to simulate the contribution from users, we extracted every user's exploratory searches from one's contextually related queries. Then, to simulate the sharing of epistemologies, we retrieved the epistemology repository for relevant search epistemologies. An epistemology is relevant to an exploratory search if its queries are similar to the search queries, and the selected pages of the epistemology completely/partially match the clicked URLs of the search. Finally, to simulate the refinement of epistemologies, a score is assigned to every clicked URL to represent the evaluation from the current user. URLs that are repeatedly clicked are given higher scores and the selected URLs of every epistemology are re-ranked according to the scores.

Metrics

We adopt existing metrics of Mean Average Precision (MAP) and Normalized Discounted Cumulative Gain (NDCG) to evaluate the performance of search engines, and introduce new metrics of Epistemology Acquisition Rate (EAR) and Interactive Search Entropy (ISE) to compare the performance of our epistemology-based social search system *Baijia* with that of the AOL search engine. With these metrics, we are able to test the conjecture that the system can provide higher precision, shorter search time, and better quality of search results.

EAR is the ratio of users' searches that can successfully retrieve relevant epistemologies. This metric is introduced to measure how many searches can benefit from the epistemologies in the repository. ISE is to measure the performance of a search system in supporting EIS in terms of the total number of queries issued in an exploratory search process. It represents the interaction times between users and the system.

Results

The EAR value of *Baijia* is shown in Table 1, which increases as more exploratory searches are imported. Thus it can be seen that *Baijia* is self-reinforcing because the more searchers contribute to the epistemology repository, the more likely new searchers will reuse previous epistemologies.

In Table 2, we illustrate the average ISE for both *Baijia* and AOL. As about 26.3% of all exploratory searches were unsuccessful in the dataset (without clicking any URLs), and about 25.9% of all successful searches are one-step searches (such a search task requires no exploration at all), they should

Number of exploratory searches imported	Epistemology repository size	EAR
20,000	7,612	18.35%
200,000	74,634	29.67%
400,000	151,392	34.20%
800,000	311,167	39.93%
1,201,497	480,254	42.52%

Table 1. Epistemology repository size and EAR at different stages

ISE	*Baijia*	AOL
Overall	1.5563	2.3734
Exclusive of unsuccessful searches	2.1924	3.7080
Exclusive of unsuccessful and one-step searches	3.0331	5.2076

Table 2. ISE of *Baijia* and AOL

be excluded for the comparison study. After excluding unsuccessful searches and one-step searches, we can see a noticeable improvement of average ISE.

Figure 3 shows the MAP scores of *Baijia* as compared to those of AOL (the original data). The results show that increase of the number of exploratory searches imported leads to improvement of MAP scores in *Baijia* while the MAP scores of AOL are steady.

Figure 4 shows NDCG@10 of *Baijia* and AOL. It can be seen that *Baijia* has obviously achieved a better ranking performance than that of AOL. This is because *Baijia* re-ranks the search results according to users' judgments, and the re-ranked results are more approximate to those of the perfect algorithm (ranking based on part of users' evaluation).

CONCLUSIONS AND FUTURE WORK

Conventional search engines are incompetent in the situations where users have difficulties in formulating proper keywords and must struggle to evaluate search results. In this paper, we present a novel epistemology-based social search

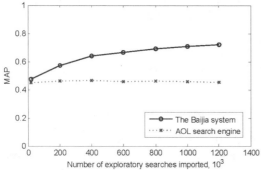

Figure 3. MAP scores of *Baijia* and AOL

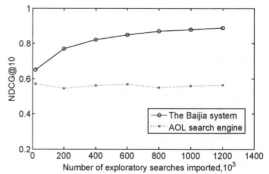

Figure 4. NDCG@10 of *Baijia* and AOL

approach to supporting EIS. With the *Baijia* prototype system we have designed and implemented, we show how an epistemology can be generated from a search process, and how it can be effectively shared, reused, and refined by others. Through the experimental evaluation, we show that an epistemology-based social search system outperforms a conventional search engine in supporting EIS.

Currently, we are conducting user studies to validate the proposed approach, including user interface evaluation and usability study.

REFERENCES

1. Agichtein, E., Brill, E., Dumais, S. Improving web search ranking by incorporating user behavior information. In *Proc. SIGIR'06*, ACM Press (2006), 19–26.

2. Chi, Ed H. Information Seeking Can Be Social. *Computer*, 42, 3(2009), 42-46, 2009.

3. Evans, B. M., Chi, E. H. Towards a model of understanding social search. In *Proc. CSCW'08*, ACM Press (2008), 485-494.

4. Glance, N. S. Community search assistant. In *Proc. IUI'01*, ACM Press (2001), 91-96.

5. Herlocker, J., Konstan, J., and Riedl, J. Explaining Collaborative Filtering Recommendations. In *Proc. CSCW'00*, ACM Press (2000), 241-250.

6. Heymann, P., Koutrika, G. and Garcia-Molina, H. Can social bookmarking improve web search? In *Proc. WSDM'08*, ACM Press (2008), 195-205.

7. Jones, R., Rey, B., Madani, O. and Greiner, W. Generating query substitutions. In *Proc. WWW'06*, ACM Press (2006), 387-396.

8. Morris, M. R. and Horvitz, E. SearchTogether: an interface for collaborative web search. In *Proc. UIST'07*, ACM Press (2007), 3-12.

9. Pass, G., Chowdhury, A. and Torgeson, C. A Picture of Search. In *Proc. of the 1st International Conference on Scalable Information Systems*. Infoscale 2006.

10. Russell, D. M., Stefik, M. J., Card, S. K., The cost structure of sensemaking. In *Proc. CHI'93*, ACM Press (1993), 269-276.

Ocean of Information: Fusing Aggregate & Individual Dynamics for Metropolitan Analysis

Mauro Martino, Francesco Calabrese, Giusy Di Lorenzo, Clio Andris, Liang Liu, Carlo Ratti
Senseable City Laboratory, Massachusetts Institute of Technology
E-mail: {mmartino,fcalabre,giusy,clio,liuliang,ratti}@mit.edu

ABSTRACT

In this paper, we propose a tool to explore human movement dynamics in a Metropolitan Area. By analyzing a mass of individual cell phone traces, we build a Human-City Interaction System for understanding urban mobility patterns at different user-controlled temporal and geographic scales. We solve the problems that are found in available tools for spatio-temporal analysis, by allowing seamless manipulability and introducing a simultaneous\multi-scale visualization of individual and aggregate flows. Our tool is built to support the exploration and discovery of urban mobility patterns and the daily interactions of millions of people. Moreover, we implement an intelligent algorithm to evaluate the level of mobility homophily of people moving from place to place.

Author Keywords

Graph visualization, exploratory spatial data analysis, visual analysis, intelligent human information interaction, cellphone data analysis.

ACM Classification Keywords

H.3.1 [Content Analysis and Indexing]: Abstracting methods; H5.m. Information interfaces and presentation (e.g., HCI): Miscellaneous.

General Terms

Design, Human Factors, Algorithms

INTRODUCTION

Collecting and analyzing massive amount of human mobility data has revealed interesting patterns in human dynamics [1], urban planning [10], and the spreading of viruses [11]. However, the tools needed to easily select and visualize massive mobility datasets and perform simple queries and selections to allow explanatory spatio-temporal data analysis are still lacking. The following tools and visualizations excel at displaying specific dimensions of the problem of spatio-temporal visual data analysis through using cell phone data.

Tools reference

MobiVis [5] (Figure 1.c) , MobileMiner [6] (Figure 1.d) and GeoTime [7] (Figure 1.e) are 3 tools that use data mining techniques for the analysis of mobile communication data. Developing tools from scratch with the required flexibility is difficult, time-consuming and requires skills not possessed by

many engaged in geovisualization [8]. For this reason, tools have been developed that allow different interactive visualizations. MobiVis is a visual analytics system designed for exploring and discovering mobile data. The principal quality of this tool is to visualize complex social-spatial-temporal data and to filter the data with ontology graphs and interactive timecharts. MobiVis is suitable for both the expert and new user but is not compatible with other programs.

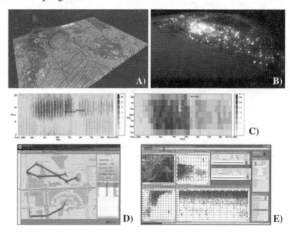

Figure 1. Examples of visualizations of urban dynamics and visual analysis tools for exploring and understanding social-spatial-temporal mobile data.

MobileMiner is a tool to show a working data mining system on real mobile communication data. It is a good reference for understanding how to customize these types of programs for specific functions. In this case, data mining techniques are integrated into a mobile communication business solution. GeoTime is a tool for displaying and working with data over both space and time within a single, highly interactive 3D view. More importantly it operates with GIS and offers automated geo and temporal navigation. The principal concept is that individual frames of movement are translated into a continuous spatiotemporal representation.

Visualization references

Real Time Rome [3] (Figure 1.a) and UrbanMobs [4] (Figure1.b) introduce a 3D perspective view and provide a sense of the collective emotions of a city. Aggregated data from cell phones is mapped onto the geography of the city during two special events over the summer of 2006: the World Cup finals match between Italy and France, and a Madonna concert. The visualizations show peaks in the volume of calls during stirring moments (such as Italy scoring a goal during the World Cup match) in a sense revealing the emotional signature of the city as well as where people are congregating. Similarly, Orange Labs and Faber Novel developed

UrbanMobs as a tool to showcase popular emotion cartography through the analysis and visualization of citywide cellular network traffic activity. Both examples signal a shift in both the aesthetic qualities of visualizing dynamic urban data and in the methodology of positioning cell phones within urban space according to the location of cell phone towers that service those calls. This methodology may lose the detail of GPS data but in tapping into the network infrastructure of cell phones, it can harness vast amounts of data representing large swaths of the city, thus increasing the scale of representation.

In this paper, we propose the tool *Ocean of Information,* to explore the interactions between human and the city in a Metropolitan Area. By analyzing a mass of individual cell phone traces, we propose to build a Human-City Interaction system for understanding urban mobility patterns at both the individual and aggregate level, and furthermore, to work towards understanding large-scale dynamic human mobility patterns. Our most prominent innovations include:

• *combining aggregated mobility patterns and individual traces in real time;*

• *building interactive tools for discovering patterns in large scale mobility data sets;*

• *visualizing massive dynamic datasets in both spatial and temporal scale.*

• *automatic detection of homophily between mobility patterns of people's traces.*

Ocean of Information introduces improvements compared with similar tools, including temporal window-linked timelines and map manipulations. The sequential presentation of data, the 3D point of view and the ability to represent small multiple designs [9] increase the capacity of our tool to compare data and detect patterns in relation to the other reviewed tools.

3 DATASET

The dataset used in this project consists of cellular phone location data anonymously collected by AirSage1 for close to one million cellphone users of one telecom operator in eastern Massachusetts, USA. This aggregated information is used to model, evaluate and analyze the location, movement and flow of people in the city. To guarantee anonymity, each user is identified with an encrypted unique identification number (ID). Moreover, the ID is reset every day in order to avoid the possibility of tracking people over a long period of time. The database for each user contains a measure of their geographic location in latitude/longitude, for each time they connect to the cell network.

Since, the location measurements collected for every user are often noisy and inconsistently sampled, we processed the raw data to extract a set of meaningful places and trips between those places. We define a *trajectory* as a sequence of chronological location points for each user. A sub-trajectory is obtained by segmenting the trajectory with a spatial threshold ΔS, thus

$$Traj_i = \{p_1 \to p_2 \to \dots \to p_n\}$$
where $p_i \in P, t_{i+1} > t_i$
and $distance(p_i, p_{i+1}) < \Delta S, \quad \forall i = 1, \dots n$.

The segmentation aims at removing spatial gaps between two recorded points (p_i, p_{i+1}) of more than ΔS into a time interval ΔT. If a gap is found, p_i becomes the end point of the last sub-trajectory, and

p_{i+1} becomes the starting point of the new sub-trajectory. Once sub-trajectories are detected, we first resample with a constant sampling time Tc and then apply to them a low pass filter in order to eliminate some measurement noise contained in the data. For each sub-trajectory we determine the time at which the user stops traveling, and call the location stop S. St is a geographic region where the user stayed over a certain time interval. A stop can occur when the user remains in a certain geospatial region for a period. The extraction of a stop depends on two parameters: time distance threshold (Tth) and a spatial distance threshold (Sth). Therefore, a single stop s can be regarded as a virtual location characterized by a group of consecutive location points

$$P = \{p_s \to p_{s+1} \to \dots \to p_n\}$$
where:
$$\max(distance(p_i, p_j)) < S_{th} \dots \forall s \leq i, j \leq n$$
$$t_n - t_s > T_{th}$$

Once the stops have been detected, we want to identify the user's landmarks, and travel path throughout the day. To detect these landmarks, we group nearby stops and create a grid of 200 by 200 meter cells. The pixel size can be manipulated to best reflect the scope of activity in the area.

4 TOOL DESIGN

In light of the above discussion, we identified the following specific design requirements to guide the design and implementation of this tool. The visualizations should be interactive but simple, allowing the user to explore the evolution of the event in space and time. Same maps are not meant to be visual analytics tools, so they should not provide quantitative details on the data, but other maps provide quantitative details. Inspired by Norman's work [2], we use color, saturation, and luminosity to improve the aesthetic and emotional impact of the project.

*Digital Skin*a

The patch graph movement represents the aggregate data; the color of the patches changes in relation to the number of people in each area (projected as a patch onto the floor).

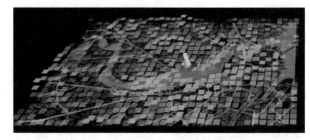

Figure 2. 3d control view; visualization of cell mobile activity in Boston in the July, 4, 2009; color represents cell mobile activity density, height represents current number of calls, and the 3 boxes represent the position of 3 different users (height and color of bars are selected to increase the distinguishability).

The patch graph movement represents the aggregate data; the color of the patches changes in relation to the number of people in each area (projected as a patch onto the floor). The data are displayed dynamically over time and in geographic space in order to represent flows of activity (i.e. pedestrians and cars). The visualizations attempt to represent activity in almost real-time with a 5 minute delay. The patches should create a *"digital skin"* of urban spaces, with a simple and clear visual language system. They should convey the social dynamics of a crowd, which are real phenomena, using informational data. The user should perceive the former, not the latter. They should establish a strong relationship between the crowd and the urban landscape. For this reason, we considered the spatial representation of the information as a given, reflecting the geographic nature of the data.

Multiview and Interactive Areas

Figure 3. Multi view. A) In the left a top view where the color lines represent the trajectory in the space of the users that are in selected area. B) In the center there are the interactive visualization of density of people (is possible change the percentage and select the absolute or relative value, the yellow dots represent the region area where it has the minimum value of the selected percentage. C) In the right the interactive area (You can select one or more areas of space and view (in the view at the top and in the view below left) the people at that point in time are present in the square.

Multiview is the basis for explanatory data visualization and analysis, since it helps the user search, locate and find new information with no prior knowledge. We selected multiviews to help make sense of the large volume of data.

Each view is linked to the others using the CMV (coordinate multiview view) technique and changed automatically while interacting and querying the data. Moreover, we added an interactive area to query information about different locations in the city at the same time.

5 INTELLIGENT INTERACTION

As described above, the tool allows visualizing the massive amount of information contained in the close to 1 million traces, by combining aggregate behaviors and individual traces. However, to allow easily detecting similar mobility patterns in the data, we further introduce intelligent components to measure how much users move similarly in the environment. This measure is then associated to a particular place and time interval, and allows for creating maps that illustrate at a give time which areas of the city are aggregating more similar people.

5.1 MOBILITY HOMOPHILY

Given an area C, and a time interval T, let us consider all traces that cross this area in the time interval T. For each of those traces, we can determine the location and time of the stop preceding time T, and the location and time of the stop following that. If we group together those locations and times for all traces, we can derive the following sets:

$$before(C,T) = \left\{ (B_1, Tb_1, nb_1), \ldots, (B_n, Tb_n, nb_n) \right\}$$

$$after(C,T) = \left\{ (A_1, Ta_1, na_1), \ldots, (A_m, Ta_m, na_m) \right\}$$

where the tripe (B_1, Tb_1, nb_1) represents nb_1 traces who have passed through location B_1 at time Tb_1. For every trace t will then exist two indexes i and j so that

$$t \in (B_i, Tb_i, nb_i) \text{ and } t \in (A_j, Ta_j, na_j).$$

We can then define the following mobility homophily index as follows

$$h(C,T) = \frac{1}{n\,m} \sum_i \sum_j \frac{\#\text{traces in } (B_i, Tb_i, nb_i) \text{ and } (A_j, Ta_j, na_j)}{\min\{nb_i, na_j\}}$$

The index ranges from 0 to 1 and represents how much a given area, at a given time, brings together people that behave similarly from a mobility point of view. Repeating this computation for every area in the city, and consecutive time intervals, we can create a map showing at a give time which areas are aggregating more similar people.

5.2 PANELS

The tool is designed to help answer questions regarding human movement dynamics in the city. To do this, we characterize each trace with succinct variables: distance, duration, speed, tortousity. The following view is of downtown Boston. Aggregate-data interaction allows for the selection and visualization of grouped individual traces for a population density distribution over space and time. The density of users in an area is evaluated by summing the number of users that fall into the area at a given time. Individual-data interaction deals with the selection and visualization of individual traces based on geographic location and time.

The following panels illustrate different scenes of the visualization.

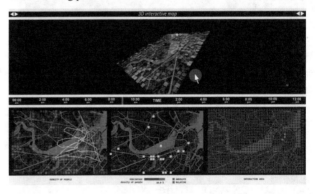

Panel 1: 3D visualization of density distribution of people over time. The user is able to adjust the viewpoint of the 3D scene. Changing the viewpoint permits the user to view and zoom around the scene. For example, the user could view an alignment of two different lines, or two objects of the same shading overlapping from a particular view.

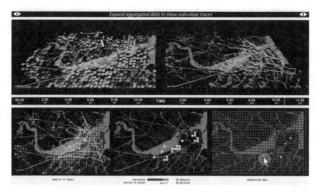

Panel 2: A large scale rendering of downtown traces. This image allows the user to examine tortousity and envision activity space by the spread of each individual trace. The user manipulates the view by interactively selecting specific areas (wherein all the traces that pass through that geographic area are highlighted). The user can also interactively select individual traces with traditional union and intersection functions. The temporal frame in use adds an extra element, as when the trajectories are selected at time t, they will remain in place at time t+x for a smooth comparative analysis.

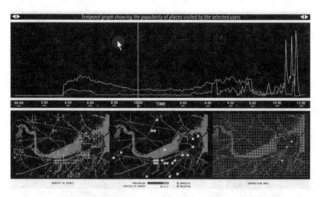

Panel 3: The places where Mobility Homophily is high are shown on the map (bottom center), together with a temporal graph showing the popularity of places visited by the users passing the selected areas (top); each line in the top graph denotes the Mobility Homophily for each user (the color are the same at the color the vi use to connoted the user in the other visualization).

6 CONCLUSION AND FUTURE WORK

In this paper, we have proposed a tool to explore human movement dynamics in a Metropolitan Area. By analyzing a mass of individual cell phone traces, we have built a Human-City Interaction System for understanding urban mobility patterns at malleable temporal and geographic scales. The tool enables the incorporation of different advanced data analysis methods, and provides a unified interface for performing sophisticated analytic tasks. To test the potential

of the tool associated to the used dataset, we have implemented an intelligent algorithm to evaluate the level of mobility homophily of people moving from places to places.

ACKNOWLEDGEMENTS

The work described in this paper has been supported by AirSage.

REFERENCES

1. González, M. C., Hidalgo, C. A., and Barabási, A. L. (2008). Understanding individual human mobility patterns. *Nature* 453, pp. 779-782.

2. D.Norman. Emotional Design: Why we love (or hate) everyday things. Basic Books, 2004

3. J. Reades, F. Calabrese, A. Sevtsuk, and C. Ratti. Cellular census: Explorations in urban data collection. *IEEE Pervasive Computing Magazine*, 6(3):30–38, 2007.Hancock, J. T., Toma, C., and Ellison, N. (2007). The truth about lying in online dating profiles. *CHI 2007*. ACM, New York, NY.

4. Orange Labs and Faber Nove. UrbanMobs, http://www.fabernovel.com, Revised in 30 August 2009.

5. Z. Shen, K. Ma. MobiVis - A Visualization System for Exploring Mobile Data. *Visualization & Interface Design Innovation* (VIDi), 2007.

6. T. Wang, B. Yang, J. Gao. MobileMiner: A Real World Case Study of Data Mining in Mobile Communication. *SIGMOD 2009*.

7. T. Kapler and W. Wright. GeoTime Information Visualization. *InfoVis 2004*.

8. J.A. Dykes, "Exploring spatial data representation with dynamic graphics", *Computers and Geosciences 23 (*4), pp. 345-370, 1997.

9. Tufte, E., Envisioning Information, Graphics Press, Cheshire, CT, 1990.

10. Reades J, Calabrese F, Ratti C, 2009, "Eigenplaces: analysing cities using the space – time structure of the mobile phone network" *Environment and Planning B: Planning and Design 36*(5) 824 – 836

11. P. Wang, M.C. González, C.A. Hidalgo and A.-L.Barabási Understanding the spreading patterns of mobile phones viruses, Science 324, 1071-1076 (2009).

Vocabulary Navigation Made Easier

Sonya Nikolova[1], Xiaojuan Ma[1], Marilyn Tremaine[2] and Perry Cook[1]

[1]Princeton University
Princeton, NJ 08540 U.S.A.
{nikolova,xm,prc}@cs.princeton.edu

[2]Rutgers University
Piscataway, NJ 08854 U.S.A.
tremaine@caip.rutgers.edu

ABSTRACT

It is challenging to search a dictionary consisting of thousands of entries in order to select appropriate words for building written communication. This is true both for people trying to communicate in a foreign language who have not developed a full vocabulary, for school children learning to write, for authors who wish to be more precise and expressive, and especially for people with lexical access disorders. We make vocabulary navigation and word finding easier by augmenting a basic vocabulary with links between words based on human judgments of semantic similarity. In this paper, we report the results from a user study evaluating how our system named ViVA performs compared to a widely used assistive vocabulary in which words are organized hierarchically into common categories.

Author Keywords

Visual vocabularies, assistive communication, semantic networks, adaptive user interfaces.

ACM Classification Keywords

H5.2. Information interfaces and presentation (e.g., HCI): User Interfaces. Evaluation/methodology

General Terms

Design, Experimentation, Human Factors

INTRODUCTION

Searching for words in electronic dictionaries occurs in a variety of contexts. Examples include searching for words to communicate in a foreign language, using a thesaurus to get ideas for better word choices when writing, searching for words as part of a game, e.g., crossword puzzles, and searching for words in assistive vocabularies that help people with language impairments to communicate. Navigating a vocabulary consisting of thousands of entries is particularly challenging for individuals with lexical access disorders like those caused by aphasia, a cognitive disorder. Many existing assistive communication vocabularies have a lexical

organization scheme based on a simple list of words. Some word collections are organized in hierarchies which often leads to deep and confusing searches; others are simply a list of arbitrary categories which causes excessive scrolling and a sense of disorganization. Static vocabulary organizations hurt the usability and adoption of assistive communication tools and ultimately fail to help users engage in practical communication. Our research goal is to develop techniques for vocabulary organization that enable effective word finding tailored to meet individual user needs.

We have designed a visual vocabulary for people with aphasia which enables efficient word finding by modeling a speaker's "mental lexicon", where words are stored and organized in ways that allow efficient access and retrieval. Due to damaged semantic links in their mental lexicon, people with aphasia have persistent difficulties accessing and retrieving words that express intended concepts. The Visual Vocabulary for Aphasia (ViVA) attempts to compensate for some of these impaired links by organizing words in a dynamic semantic network where connections between words reflect semantic association measures, human judgments of semantic similarity, and past vocabulary usage.

Previously, we showed with a simulation that a simple prediction algorithm can shorten browsing distances between words needed to form a sentence by incorporating prior word usage statistics [8]. In this paper, we present results from a study investigating how evocation, a semantic association measure, guides users in finding words in ViVA. To demonstrate ViVA's potential, we compare searching for words in ViVA to searching for words in Lingraphica [6], a commonly used assistive vocabulary.

BACKGROUND

Existing assistive vocabularies consist of thousands of words which a user browses in searching for individual concepts which once found are assembled linearly into a phrase. There have been efforts to improve on the traditional linear syntax and word finding by providing phrase starters and semantic rather than syntactic schemas (e.g. [1, 6, 9]). Despite this assistance, the user still has to search through the vocabulary to find most of the concepts she wishes to express. The words in such vocabularies are mostly organized in hierarchies of categories of common words such as *food*, *leisure* and *clothes*. While hierarchies provide consistent structure, they can be challenging to navigate because the user often has to traverse multiple categories at different levels of the hierarchy to create a simple phrase. This process can take considerable time and effort, and users can easily get lost or distracted [2, 3]. Personalizing the vocabulary by creating user-specific categories and shortcuts addresses some of these issues, but it also introduces an additional burden for the user.

To make word finding more efficient, we propose an organization based on theories that explain how the human mind organizes words. People with lexical access disorders can be thought of as experiencing severe case of the tip-of-the-tongue (TOT) phenomenon. While for most people TOT results in short-term inability to retrieve words due to temporarily impaired semantic connections, this problem is persistent for people with aphasia. Experimental evidence — including evidence from TOT states induced in the laboratory — suggests that words are organized in a speaker's mental lexicon by various similarity relations, in particular phonological and semantic similarity. For example, subjects in word association experiments overwhelmingly respond with *husband* to the stimulus *wife* [7]. Semantic priming [10], a robust and powerful tool for the experimental investigation of cognitive processes, relies on the semantic relatedness of the prime and an experimental target: responses to the target are faster when it is related to the prime as in the classic case *doctor-nurse*. Spreading network activation models [4] assume that presenting a prime stimulus word activates the corresponding representation in lexical memory and that this activation spreads to other related nodes, thus facilitating the processing of related target words.

We apply these theories to building semantic networks which overlay a basic hierarchical vocabulary. The semantic links between words reflect associations based on the measure of evocation, i.e. how much one word brings to mind another word. Evocation is particularly valuable, because it encodes cross-part-of-speech connections such as the intuitive association among *traffic*, *congested*, and *stop*. The evocation data incorporated in our vocabulary was collected through an online experiment described in [8].

THE VISUAL VOCABULARY FOR APHASIA

The visual vocabulary for aphasia (ViVA) attempts to improve word finding by building semantic networks which incorporate word association measures drawn from WordNet [5], a large-scale lexical database, human judgments of evocation, and vocabulary usage statistics. Thus, ViVA compensates for impaired semantic connections, guides a user's search for words, and adapts over time to better suit users' past actions and future needs.

As its core vocabulary, ViVA uses the vocabulary hierarchy of Lingraphica [6], a successful commercial assistive communication tool for people with aphasia. Lingraphica's vocabulary organization attempts to mimic real-life situations by grouping words according to shared contexts (which provides some semantic associations). If you need to find *milk*, for example, you find the *kitchen* category, then *fridge*, then *dairy*, and then finally, *milk*. We chose Lingraphica's

vocabulary as our basic organization, because it is a well-structured vocabulary of commonly used words which has evolved over time incorporating feedback from aphasic users and experts such as speech-language pathologists.

Theoretical evaluation of ViVA, which simulated vocabulary usage and sentence construction, showed that ViVA improves on average 52% of the paths between needed words by making them shorter [8]. While these results are encouraging, presenting a changing set of related words to an actual user while she navigates the vocabulary and takes decisions about what to click on next may be overwhelming. To investigate this issue, we conducted a preliminary experiment evaluating ViVA with able users. We present the results from a study examining whether and how users take advantage of the provided word associations and whether they help them find words faster as well as improve their experience with navigating the vocabulary. If users spend less time and perform fewer clicks to find words, we expect that search path efficiency will lead to less cognitive load and more effective word search.

EXPERIMENT METHODOLOGY

Task and Participants

We recruited sixteen people (seven female) from the Princeton University campus. Participants were asked to find a total of 164 missing words in 78 phrases using the two vocabularies described next. They were given a tutorial on how to navigate the first vocabulary (order was counterbalanced) and asked to complete the first five phrases as practice. Participants were allowed to skip words and phrases, and were asked to work as quickly as possible. After completing the first set of 39 phrases, participants were presented with the second vocabulary, the differences between the two conditions were highlighted, and they were asked to complete another practice set before proceeding to complete the remaining phrases. At the end of the study the investigator asked background questions and inquired about participants' impressions of the two vocabularies. The study took approximately 60 minutes and participants were compensated $10.

LG Vocabulary Condition

The first vocabulary which we call LG is a subset of Lingraphica's hierarchy. It consists of 270 words chosen such that it is possible to navigate to all missing words. Figure 1 illustrates the LG vocabulary interface. The user browses the vocabulary hierarchy by clicking on the arrow-down button associated with the different categories. Once the user has found the icon for a missing word, she can click on the plus button associated with it and the choice is reflected in the lower portion of the screen where the phrase and the missing words, indicated by a question mark icon, are displayed (see Figure 1).

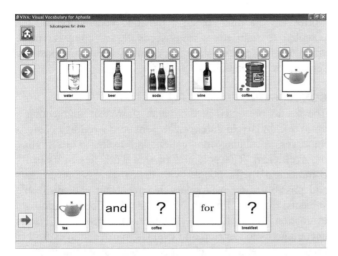

Figure 1: Subcategories for *drinks* in the LG vocabulary. *Tea* has already been found and added to the phrase.

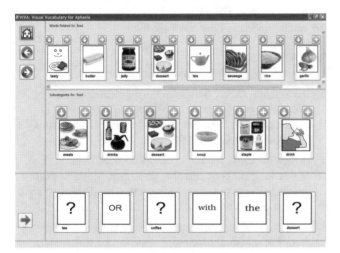

Figure 2: Related words in ViVA are displayed above the basic hierarchy, e.g. *tea* and *dessert* are associated with *food*.

ViVA Vocabulary Condition

The second vocabulary, ViVA, inherits the LG hierarchy of 270 words but also provides associations between words based on the evocation data collected by [8]. The ViVA user interface is similar to the LG interface. The difference is that words related to the concept the user has clicked on are displayed in a related-words panel (see Figure 2).

In the ViVA condition, 50% of the missing words in all phrases were directly associated or in other words, the second word in a pair of consecutive words in a phrase was displayed in the first word's related-words panel; 36% of the words were strongly associated or there was a path between them through a common related word; 14% of the words were moderately associated or there was a path between them through two levels of common related words. This setup allowed us to study people's satisfaction of having the word that they are looking for appear immediately as well as observe whether they utilize the alternatives paths available through the related-words panel.

Quantitative and Qualitative Measures

The phrases were constructed so that the optimal paths between missing words and the number of missing words per phrase were consistent across conditions. We automatically logged all clicks users performed in order to keep track of the paths that participants took to find each missing word. We also recorded how long it took participants to complete each phrase and which words were skipped. At the end of the experiment, participants were asked to fill out a questionnaire collecting their demographic information, language background, and comments on their experience with the two vocabularies.

RESULTS

Within-subjects analysis of variance (ANOVA) showed that it took significantly less time to complete all phrases using ViVA compared to using LG ($F(1, 31) = 35.46$, $p < .01$). For both conditions, it took significantly longer if being tested first indicating an order effect ($F(1, 31) = 33.70$, $p < .01$). This was anticipated because both vocabularies rely on the same hierarchy. Once participants became familiar with the vocabulary structure and locations of common categories (e.g. food), finding words became faster.

LG benefited significantly more from the order effect ($F(1,15) = 8.58$, $p < .05$); less words were skipped when it was tested second (down to a mean of 2.63 skipped words from a mean of 6.38). With LG, participants could find a word only by traversing the hierarchy. This was challenging for words located in uncommon categories, e.g. *sleep* is under *dictionary* → *actions* → *daily routines* → *inhale* → *sleep*. ViVA provided alternative paths to words and people did not have to know the exact category. For example, many people did not know *milk* was under *house* → *kitchen* → *refrigerator* → *diary*, but could still find it through related words such as *coffee* and *tea*. As a result, less words were skipped with ViVA ($F(1,31) = 15.70$, $p < .01$).

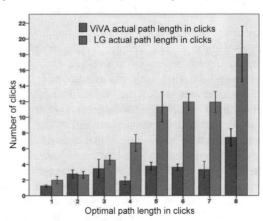

Figure 3: Fewer clicks were required to find the missing words when using ViVA.

ANOVA results also showed that significantly fewer clicks were required to find a word in ViVA than in LG (Figure 3: $F(1, 83) = 33.70$, $p < .01$). In LG, the actual number of clicks used in the study increased consistently as the optimal path length (shortest path in the hierarchy) increased (F(1, 83) = 10.82, p < .05). The actual path length in ViVA was not affected by the hierarchy's optimal path length in the same way, indicating that people took shorter paths enabled by the provided related words.

All participants agreed that having related words helped them find words faster and most thought that finding words in ViVA was less confusing than searching in LG. With ViVA people tended to search for words via related words instead of trying to locate what category the word should belong to. Five people commented that they did that without analyzing the associations and merely utilized what was given. For example, two participants always got to *food* by finding it in the related words for *eat* instead of going to *dictionary*, *things* and then *food*.

DISCUSSION AND FUTURE WORK

Augmenting a basic vocabulary hierarchy with word association data helped users find words more efficiently. Even though the number of missing words and the optimal path to find them was consistent across conditions, it was unreasonable to do a pairwise comparison of the average time participants took to complete each phrase. This is explained by the fundamental challenge present in organizing words in categories. While the user can find *eggs* and *cigarette* in the same number of clicks, *eggs* is easier to reach via the optimal path *things* → *house* → *kitchen* → *refrigerator* → *eggs*. The word *cigarette*, on the other hand, can only be reached along the less intuitive path *things* → *house* → *living room* → *ashtray* → *cigarette*. Different users expect to find things in different contexts depending on individual idiosyncrasies in word knowledge. Thus, it is important to provide a vocabulary structure which reflects user preferences and vocabulary usage in addition to general word associations which can still serve as a framework to a dynamic semantic network. Improving and evaluating ViVA within this framework is part of our future work.

The experiment we described serves as a stepping stone to further evaluation with people with lexical access impairments. It was necessary to evaluate our vocabulary navigation approach, first, with able users in order to test our research assumptions about the value of related words abstracting from the challenges inherent to working with people who experience communication difficulties. Showing significant difference in user performance and satisfaction with fluent English speakers who have intact mental lexicons suggests aphasic people can benefit even more from a tool that aims to compensate for impaired semantic connections. There are a number of interesting issues to consider in evaluating ViVA further. It is unclear how much cognitive load an adaptive vocabulary structure would add to the interaction. On one hand, stability of the user interface is important for people who are already overwhelmed due to age-related difficulties of using technology (people with aphasia tend to be older) and the inability to find or associate words. On the other hand, a dynamic vocabulary has the potential to help users find words faster, compose more complex phrases, explore the vocabulary better, and possibly serve for rehabilitation.

CONCLUSION

The results presented in this paper show that augmenting a basic vocabulary hierarchy with semantic word associations improves vocabulary navigation and makes word finding more efficient. The potential of this work lies in assisting communication for people with lexical access impairments and possibly foreign language learners. Our choice of able subjects, fluent in English, makes the described preliminary evaluation inconclusive. However, the positive results encourage us to develop and evaluate our techniques further involving target users such as people who have aphasia.

ACKNOWLEDGMENTS

We would like to thank our participants, Vyenna Song, Microsoft Research, the Kimberley and Frank H. Moss '71 Research Fund, and Lingraphicare Inc.

REFERENCES

1. AssistiveWare. http://www.assistiveware.com/.

2. Beukelman, D.R & Mirenda, P. Augmentative and alternative communication: Management of severe communication disorders in children and adults. Brooks Publishing Company, 1998.

3. Boyd-Graber, J., Nikolova, S., Moffatt, K., Kin, K., Lee, J., Mackey, L., Tremaine, M., & Klawe, M. Participatory design with proxies: developing a desktop-PDA system to support people with aphasia. Proc. CHI '06, 151–160.

4. Collins, A. M. & Loftus, E. F. A spreading-activation theory of semantic processing. Psychological Review, 82(6):407–428, November 1975.

5. Fellbaum, C. A Semantic Network of English Verbs. In WordNet: An Electronic Lexical Database. MIT Press, Cambridge, MA, 1998.

6. Lingraphicare Inc. http://www.aphasia.com/.

7. Moss, H. & Older, L. Birkbeck Word Association Norms. Psychology Press, 1996.

8. Nikolova, S., Boyd-Graber, J. Fellbaum, C. & Cook, P. Better Vocabularies for Assistive Communication Aids: Connecting Terms using Semantic Networks and Untrained Annotators. In Proc. ASSETS'09, 171–178.

9. Patel, R., Pilato, S. & Roy, D. Beyond linear syntax: An image-orientation communication aid. Assistive Technology Outcomes and Benefits, 1(1):57–67, 2004.

10. Swinney, D. Lexical access during sentence comprehension: (Re)consideration of context effects. Journal of Verbal Learning and Verbal Behavior, (18):645–659, 1979.

An Intuitive Texture Picker

Wai-Man Pang
Spatial Media Group, Computer Arts Lab.,
University of Aizu, Japan
wmpang@u-aizu.ac.jp

ABSTRACT

Color and texture are basic elements in digital graphics. Selection of color with a picker is convenient in many of the image editing softwares. However, more organized and intelligent GUI for texture pattern selection is still missing. In this paper, we attempt to fill this gap with the introduction of several robust techniques in building an intuitive texture picking GUI. By arranging patterns according to their visual similarities, texture picker with plane and circular layout are presented. Additional functionality include content-based texture searching which can quickly find similar patterns of given sample. Preliminary response to the proposed interface is positive in general, while further improvements are required, for example, on building a hierarchy to facilitate high to low level selection for huge amount of texture patterns.

Author Keywords

Texture Pattern Picker, Texture Selection GUI, Texture Similarity, Multidimensional Scaling

ACM Classification Keywords

H.5.2 Information Interfaces and Presentation: Graphical user interfaces (GUI)

General Terms

Design, Algorithms, Human Factors

INTRODUCTION

Selection of colors from color panels or pickers exists in various painting or image editing tools. Some of them look like Figure 1. The design of color panels is largely according to the science of color and color models which have been extensively studied in the last decades [2, 7, 5]. Recently, more advanced methods are proposed to help artist in choosing color combinations with harmonic consideration [3, 8].

However, textures or screens, which are used as frequent as colors in some artistic tools, are not accompanied with similarly convenient graphical user interface for selection. Many

of the existing texture selection panels in image editing softwares present all available textures in thumbnails plainly, for example in GIMP, we can refer to Figure 2. More advanced ones may provide a directory like structure to categorize textures manually. An advantage of this is that it may allow a text search on texture. However, we should agree that its usability is limited and may not fulfill the needs of artists or normal users to improve productivities. We can imagine how annoying for a user to choose a single texture among hundreds of different texture patterns.

Therefore, in this paper, we propose an intuitive user interface for selection of texture patterns, which we refer it as a *texture picker*. We make use of texture analysis metrics and dimensionality reduction technique to efficiently present textures in an organized manner. Also, content-based search of texture becomes possible. Some of the critical features of our proposed user interface are listed below :

- Organizing textures automatically : texture database can be expanded without manual categorization

- Intuitive texture picker : showing similar patterns in neighbor to ease selection

- Content-based texture searching : seek similar texture with extracted or drawn texture sample

To the best of our knowledge, this research is the first work in revolutionizing the texture picking interface and functionalities. We apply our technique mainly on the use of manga production, in which lots of screens (texture patterns) are used in preparing black and white manga drawings, though

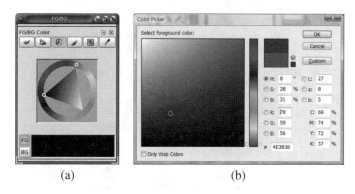

(a)   (b)

Figure 1. Color pickers (a) from open source image editor "GIMP", (b) from PhotoShop®.

the technique itself is general enough to be applicable to all kinds of textures.

TEXTURE PICKER INTERFACE DESIGN

Our interface design references the traditional color pickers. Figure 3 shows screenshots of our GUI. Figure 3 (a) is a circular arrangement of texture, which resembles the Hue channel of color. Same as color, it represents a smooth change among texture patterns. Figure 3 (b) shows another layout which flattens all the textures in a 2D region. Again, textures are placed according to their visual similarities. A slider bar on the right is responsible for adjusting the intensity (tone) of the selected pattern. We can find the final appearance of the chosen texture in Figure 5.

The content-based search window is shown in Figure 6. We can search a texture by drawing a sample (pencil icon button) or by extracting a sample from an existing image (dropper icon button). With a given sample pattern, a list of visually similar candidates will be displayed at the bottom in descending order. We can do an opposite to seek textures with greatest dissimilarity or contrast.

PROPOSED METHOD

In Figure 4, we illustrate the major procedures in our proposed method. They are texture feature computation, dimensionality reduction, layout arrangement and visualization. In the following of this section, we will introduce the technical details of these procedures.

Texture Organization with Similarity Metrics

The proposed texture picker relies on a proper texture similarity metric that is visually consistent to our perception. Currently, we are employing Gabor wavelets [6] to quantify the texture characteristics. As it is effective in texture identification for normal textures or manga screens from our previous experiences [10].

Consider a texture $I(x, y)$, we can obtain its Gabor wavelet

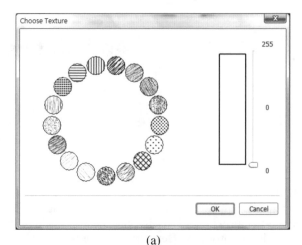

(a)

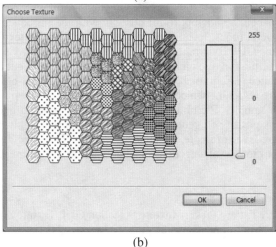

(b)

Figure 3. Our proposed pickers. (a) Circular layout, (b) plane layout.

feature $[\mu_{m,n}, \sigma_{m,n}]_{m=1,\cdots,4,n=1,\cdots,4}$ in a per-pixel manner,

$$
\mu_{m,n} = \int \int |W_{m,n}(x,y)|\, dxdy,
$$

$$
\sigma_{m,n} = \sqrt{\int \int (|W_{m,n}(x,y)| - \mu_{m,n})^2\, dxdy}. \quad (1)
$$

where $W_{m,n}$ is the Gabor wavelets on multiple scales and orientations. By averaging Gabor wavelet feature of all pixels or a number of sample pixels, we obtain the 32D representative feature vector of the texture, with 16 mean values (μ) and 16 standard deviation values (σ).

The similarity of textures is, therefore, obtained by measuring the norm-2 distance of the representative texture feature vectors between a pair of textures. The smaller the value, the more similar the texture pair is. Therefore, our system requires no manual operations in organizing the textures, and they can be categorized and displayed according to the texture visual appearance.

Layout Algorithm of Texture Picker

As shown in Figure 3, our texture picker is layouted in a 2D plane or a circular manner. However, we have to note that

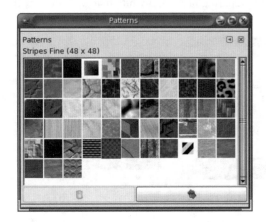

Figure 2. Texture pattern pickers from "GIMP".

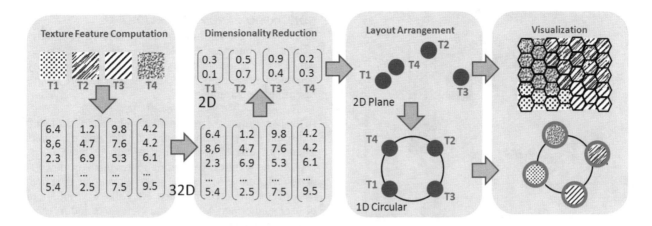

Figure 4. Procedures of texture picker formation.

our texture feature is in a high-dimensional space, which is 32D instead of 2D or 1D circular. In order to arrange them in a 2D or circular layout, we must rely on a dimensionality reduction scheme. Remind that our texture picker intends to manage similar patterns in neighbor, while dissimilar patterns farther away from each other. With this requirement, we employ classical multi-dimensional scaling (MDS) [4] to achieve such a distance relationship between patterns. It is efficient in reducing the dimensionality of the data while maintaining the relative distance among data in their original space. Another advantage of classical MDS is its linear nature, so we can obtain a fast and yet satisfactory solution.

To solve the problem, MDS tries to formulate the relations of a high dimensional vector p with a lower dimensional vector q. Suppose there are n different patterns in the database. We can have p_i as a m-dimensional feature vector, in our case m is 32, of the i-th pattern and d_{ij} is the distance between screens p_i and p_j. Here the distance is measured with Euclidean distance. Let the point q_i in 2D space be associated with the pattern p_i. We further assume that the centroid of all data points lies at the origin, i.e. $\sum_i^n p_i = \mathbf{0}$. Here is the formulation of MDS that relates the projected coordinate q_i and d_{ij} in a matrix form,

$$QQ^T = -\frac{1}{2}[I - \frac{1}{n}[\mathbf{1}]]D^2[I - \frac{1}{n}[\mathbf{1}]] \qquad (2)$$

Here, Q is a $m \times n$ matrix with projected coordinate vectors as columns, D is the dissimilarity matrix which stores the feature distances between all pairs of textures d_{ij} and $[\mathbf{1}]$ is a matrix with all elements being 1. Since D is symmetric, so as the right hand side of Equation 2. Then, by performing singular value decomposition (SVD), we have the following equation,

$$QQ^T = V\Lambda V^T$$
$$Q = V\Lambda^{1/2} \qquad (3)$$

Here Λ is diagonal matrix with all the eigenvalues. Then, we extract the major components by truncating Q into $\hat{Q}$ with dimension $2 \times n$, by keeping the first two rows. Then, the columns of $\hat{Q}$ form all q_i, which are the projected coordinates of the i-th texture in the 2D space. Usually, as there

is no specific meaning in scale of distance between all q_i, we usually normalized it within $([0, 1] \times [0, 1])$.

Result from MDS can be directly used for the 2D plane layout by resampling with a hexagonal grid structure. Each grid is assigned to the nearest texture pattern. However, to map the result further to a circular layout as in Figure 3, it needs further processing to order the 2D projected coordinates into 1D circular. The requirements to this ordering is to include every pattern exactly once and to put similar patterns together, substantially different patterns further away. As similarities can now be represented by distance between two different patterns, our problem now is similar to the famous "Traveling Salesman Problem" (TSP) in combinatorial optimization [1].

We can treat each pattern as a node with position as its 2D projected coordinate. Then, our objective is to find a tour connecting all the nodes exactly once from the complete graph. One difference on our objective to TSP is that we are not required to finish the tour with the shortest overall path, but we want to keep the short edges in the complete graph as much as possible.

We are, therefore, defining our objective function to give better advantage to edge which is shorter than the mean edge distance m :

$$h(\xi) = \sum_{\varepsilon \in \xi} e^{\frac{l_\varepsilon - m}{m}} \qquad (4)$$

here ξ is the set of all edges included in the tour, l_ε is the length of a particular edge ε. By employing simulated annealing optimization algorithm proposed in solving TSP [9], we can obtain an optimized result iteratively. In each iteration, the selection of edges in edge set ξ is constrained, so that the edges form a tour (i.e. the last node will connects back to first node and each node is included only once). The optimization stops after the objective value is lower than a threshold or a number of iterations is completed.

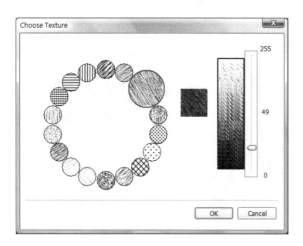

Figure 5. Interface selected with proper texture pattern and intensity.

Texture Searching

Searching of similar and dissimilar texture patterns can be easily achieved, as each texture is now quantified by a texture feature vector. We first compute the texture feature of the search target pattern. Then, by computing the norm-2 distance with each texture pattern feature in the database, we will know the similarity of the target pattern to each of them. We can even order their similarity based on the distance value. In the search result panel, candidate textures are presented from best match to the poorest, like as shown at bottom of Figure 6.

IMPLEMENTATION AND PRELIMINARY RESULTS

Our current implementation is done with wxWidgets, an open source GUI SDK, and running on a PC with Windows Vista. It is a part in a self-developed image editing tool specific for manga production from real photographs. Preliminary user responses are satisfactory. In general, they think that the system is convenient for them to select proper textures more quickly. However, some users report that using the texture picker is still time consuming for them to locate a texture when there is a large number of textures. While the searching function helps them a lot in reducing the amount of candidate required to screen out.

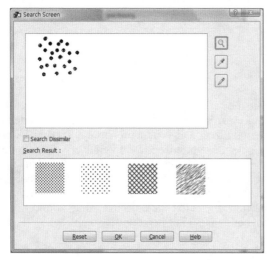

Figure 6. Texture searching window.

CONCLUSION AND FUTURE WORK

In current stage, we limit the use of screens or texture patterns to be bitonal (i.e. black and white). However, the whole idea can be simply extended to color textures by appending 2 more components in the texture feature vector representing the chrominance.

In the near future, we prepare to introduce a hierarchy of textures and group textures based on their visual similarities. Therefore, when the number of textures is huge, users can explore the textures from group representatives down to individual textures. Moreover, to further validate the effectiveness of the proposed interface, we will carry out a number of user studies and collect more comments and information from users who tried our proposed texture picker.

REFERENCES

1. D. L. Applegate, R. E. Bixby, V. Chvatal, and W. J. Cook. *The Traveling Salesman Problem: A Computational Study (Princeton Series in Applied Mathematics)*. Princeton University Press, January 2007.

2. B. Berlin and P. Kay. *Basic Color Terms: Their Universality and Evolution*. Center for the Study of Language and Inf, March 1999.

3. D. Cohen-Or, O. Sorkine, R. Gal, T. Leyvand, and Y.-Q. Xu. Color harmonization. *ACM Transactions on Graphics (Proceedings of ACM SIGGRAPH)*, 25(3):624–630, 2006.

4. T. F. Cox and M. A. A. Cox. *Multidimensional Scaling*. Chapman & Hall, 1994.

5. J. Krause. *Color Index: Over 1,000 Color Combinations, CMYK and RGB Formulas, for Print and Web Media*. F & W Publications, Incorporated, 2002.

6. B. S. Manjunath and W. Y. Ma. Texture features for browsing and retrieval of image data. *IEEE Transactions on Pattern Analysis and Machine Intelligence*, 18(8):837–842, 1996.

7. Y. Matsuda. *Color design*. Asakura Shoten. (in Japanese)., 1995.

8. F. Nack, A. Manniesing, and L. Hardman. Colour picking: the pecking prder of form and function. In *MULTIMEDIA '03: Proceedings of the eleventh ACM international conference on Multimedia*, pages 279–282, New York, NY, USA, 2003. ACM.

9. W. Press, S. Teukolsky, W. Vetterling, and B. Flannery. *Numerical Recipes in C*. Cambridge University Press, Cambridge, UK, 2nd edition, 1992.

10. Y. Qu, W.-M. Pang, T.-T. Wong, and P.-A. Heng. Richness-preserving manga screening. *ACM Transactions on Graphics (SIGGRAPH Asia 2008 issue)*, 27, 2008. 155:1-155:8.

Automatic Generation of Research Trails in Web History

Elin Rønby Pedersen
Google, Inc.
Mountain View, CA 94035
USA
elinp@google.com

Karl Gyllstrom
Dept. of Computer Science,
University of N. Carolina,
Chapel Hill, NC 27599, USA
karl@cs.unc.edu

Shengyin Gu
Dept. of Computer Science,
University of California,
Davis, CA 95616, USA
gus@cs.ucdavis.edu

Peter Jin Hong
Google, Inc.
Mountain View, CA 94045
USA
peterjinhong@google.com

ABSTRACT

We propose the concept of research trails to help web users create and reestablish context across fragmented research processes without requiring them to explicitly structure and organize the material. A research trail is an ordered sequence of web pages that were accessed as part of a larger investigation; they are automatically constructed by filtering and organizing users' activity history, using a combination of semantic and activity based criteria for grouping similar visited web pages. The design was informed by an ethnographic study of ordinary people doing research on the web, emphasizing a need to support research processes that are fragmented and where the research question is still in formation. This paper motivates and describes our algorithms for generating research trails.

Research trails can be applied in several situations: as the underlying mechanism for a research task browser, or as feed to an ambient display of history information while searching. A prototype was built to assess the utility of the first option, a research trail browser.

Author Keywords

Web history, automatic clustering, semantic clustering, activity based computing, task browser, ethnography.

ACM Classification Keywords

H.3.3. Information Search and Retrieval, clustering

General Terms

Algorithms, Design, Experimentation, Human Factors.

INTRODUCTION

We recently conducted an ethnographic study, which indicated that ordinary people are engaged in extensive research and investigations on the web, but conduct this activity in ways that are distinct from traditional models of scholarly and investigative research [12]. Thus, the study confirmed findings widely reported in other studies of information work such as the importance of context in the user experience and the difficulty establishing and maintaining it: people typically ask, "Where is all the stuff I just worked on?" or "Where was I?" [7]. But the study also highlighted important differences in both goals and quality criteria from traditional scholarly and investigative research leading to the concept of *early research* as an important but underserved area. According to the study, early research is characterized by the following four properties.

For personal consumption: It is done for own consumption, done to get an answer or understand an issue, and finished as soon as the answer is found or the researcher abandons the task for more important or more enjoyable pursuits. Material is collected but is minimally processed or organized.

Fragmented process: Substantial work effort may go into a task but it is done in small installments, possibly spread over long time with many other activities interspersed. This leads to some time wasted in finding where to pick up from the previous round.

Topic sliding: Substantial user effort is invested in a single thematic exploration, though the theme may change slightly during the research process as the researcher learns more about the domain. It is often difficult to determine a specific task for a given user activity, even when we were able to ask the user right there in the moment.

Premature structure: Early researchers are typically working with vague or very open questions, and they only gradually build sufficient understanding of the domain; while they might be tempted to apply their normal organizing techniques (putting into folder, devising labeling schemes, etc.) they quickly realize their effort is wasted and sometimes even counter-productive as their organizational scheme may reflect an outdated understanding.

Based on these findings, we suggest that people would greatly benefit from tools that would allow them to browse through previous research sessions to effectively and efficiently provide a context for their work and enabling them to easily pick up where they last left off. Research trails are one such tool; they group together events that the user perceive as belonging to the same research task and represent them as temporally ordered lists of segments.

RELATED WORK

Revisitation of previously viewed web page is common, with one study reporting that it accounts for 81% [3] of web visits. Unfortunately, support for re-finding web pages is poor. Bookmarks are simple tools for keeping references to pages, but require that users immediately recognize the value of a page, and are rarely used [3]. Most web browsers retain the users' browsing history, and in addition to client-based history tools the user can also use server-based tools (like Google Web History). These enable users to search for entries in their web history using text queries, akin to web searches. Though useful, existing browsing history tools are limited by their simplicity: with no intuitive abstractions built upon them, managing them is cumbersome, and finding information within them grows more difficult with size. Users often elect to re-find information by issuing new web queries rather than search their history [7].

There have been attempts to improve the usefulness of web history through better visualization. This often takes the form of page thumbnails displayed with some meaningful structure, including path-based [6], hub-and-spoke [4], and 3D [15]. LeeTiernan et al. showed clustering of pages by URL similarity and temporal proximity to be effective visualization tools [9]. Won et al. studied users' problems with using web history as a tool to re-find pages, and used the findings to inform the design of a contextual history search tool [14]. This tool provides more flexibility with filtering by date ranges, and gives contextual cues such as thumbnails. Eyebrowse records and displays users' web page visits, computes aggregated statistics and visualizes the information for users [11]. Ideally we should look for a combination of making the history easily browsable and also reducing the amounts of data by filtering only stuff that the users have invested some minimal amount of effort in.

Personalized and task-based search have been applied with some success. Umea [8] and TaskTracer [5] improve the process of keeping files organized according to task, but require users to predefine tasks, which is not easy or obvious in early-stage research. Some personalized search assists users in re-finding previously viewed information, first by building semantic profiles from terms appearing in pages from their web history or PC, then applying these profiles to add or rank results (e.g., [2, 10, 13]). Research trails are similar to personalized search in that we use data from users' web history to help re-find information, although our focus is separating history according to users' tasks, as a usable abstraction. This can also be used to re-establish working contexts, rather than simply find single web pages.

DESIGN OF RESEARCH TRAILS
We propose the concept of research trails to help the web researchers create and reestablish context across fragmented work processes without requiring them to explicitly structure and organize the material.

Supporting context: The researcher is helped by showing where he or she is in the ongoing activity. While it might seem obvious to think of overview techniques, like bird's eye view, this may be of limited practical value due to sheer complexity. Looking at the user data, we can isolate two situations where contextual assistance would be desired: "what did I leave unfinished?" and "where did I leave off last time I worked on this?" So we choose to anchor the representation in the "now", showing the researcher how he

or she got there. Consequently, the research trails are one-dimensional strings of visited pages, starting from the most recent and going back in time.

Combining semantic and activity based signals: We extract both activity-based and semantic information from available sources of user activity, each type of information potentially being noisy and error-prone, for instance, using semantic analysis to determine similarity between visited pages (limited to those that lend themselves to semantic analysis). Careful combination of the two approaches allows us to mitigate flaws, e.g., using timely proximity (segment membership) to compensate for lack of semantic specificity of pages: they are tentatively assumed to be related to all topics in the same segment.

Designing with room for ambiguity: The ability to handle ambiguity – though an essential aspect of human capability – often gets left out when computing tools are designed. Research trails accommodate ambiguity in at least two areas. First, while each research trail is about strongly related work, we allow topic sliding since we only require local relatedness; thus, the first and the last segment of the trail can potentially be quite different, reflecting the development of insight the researcher went through. Second, relatedness is perceived at many different levels, and not only the theme or topic of the work can be important but also the timely proximity of events, e.g. a researcher would talk about "the work I was doing when I got the email from my sister about sitting in the Paris café"). While our semantic algorithms would allow us to split timely clustered page visits that cover different tasks or themes, we chose to support a so-called "virtual split" (explained later) thereby providing some level of contextual richness by timely affinity.

ALGORITHMS FOR TRAIL CONSTRUCTION
We apply two different perspectives on a user's web history. An *activity-based* perspective focuses on how a user interacts with data, e.g., how long a page is viewed; and a *semantic* perspective focuses on the material the user worked on, e.g., how data are related to each other by text contents. We also define three main entities: *event*, *segment* and *topic*. An event is a page visit from a user's activity history. A segment is a temporal clustering of events. A topic is a semantic descriptor obtained from a suitable statistical/linguistic technique.

Activity Analysis of Events
Events are temporally clustered into distinct periods of activity, denoted as segments. When more than M (e.g., $M=5$) minutes transpire between two consecutive events, a segment boundary is produced. Each segment includes the events within its two boundaries. Besides providing a first rough segmentation of work periods, the activity-based segmentation is also used to cluster events with little text content such as events dominated by images. These events are often related to their temporal neighbors and may "borrow" trail membership from them.

Semantic Analysis of Events

Semantic analysis of events provides each event with *topic vector*, which is a list of its coverage of an automatically determined set of topics. Some events have substantial contents that can be subject to semantic analysis for detection of relationship between events. Exceptions are pages with a lot of visuals and very little textual material to feed to the analysis, and pages that cannot be retrieved for analysis. We use the value *unknown* as algorithmically different from a zero value, and try to engage secondary methods for determining topical relations.

We generate a *segment topic vector* simply by averaging the topic vectors of each event in the segment.

Coherence within Segments

We are interested in segment coherence, i.e., the extent to which events within a segment have topical similarity. Topical similarity between two events is computed as the cosine similarity between their topic vectors. As we know that many segments reflect multi-tasking, we are interested in also capturing bi-focal work. Thus, we calculate *segment coherence* by combining two qualities called *average coherence* (*AC*) and *maximum coherence* (*MC*). Average coherence is calculated by averaging the similarity for all pairs of events within a segment. To compute maximum coherence we determine the maximum similarity that each event e in segment S shares with any other event in S, and computing the average of each of these maximums. High AC and MC indicate a mono-focal segment; high MC but low AC suggest multi-focal segment; while low AC and MC indicate a diffuse segment.

Virtual Segment Split

A multi-focal segment can be potentially split into *virtual sub-segments* to achieve better coherence within virtual sub-segments. However, we do not physically split the segments, we merely identify the sub-segments, assign topic vectors for them, and compute similarities using sub-segments when building trails.

We use a brute-force algorithm for virtual splitting, beginning by randomly divide the segment into two equal sized sub-segments. For each event in the segment, we attempt to move it over to the other sub-segment. The attempt is successful, if after the operation, it improves the average coherence for both sub-segments. The algorithm terminates when all events in the segment are processed. The process can be iterated.

Provisions to Handle Topical Slide

We tailored the trail creation method to allow for topic sliding, requiring only strong local semantic similarity among consecutive segments. This would allow a research trail to have little or no semantic similarity between the first and the last segment, provided similarity remains strong within subsequences of the trail.

More specifically, trails are created in the following way. Each segment S, which is not already in a previous trail, can start a trail. We add S to its trail. Then for all segments after S up to a time limit, we check if the next segment N should become part of the trail. N will be added to the trail, if N is not previously consumed and is similar to any of the last W segments in the trail, subject to a similarity threshold.

In the case of virtual split of multi-focal segments, we compute similarity against each sub-segment. If one of these similarities is above a certain threshold, the entire segment will be included in the trail, but only the sub-segment will be considered in the subsequent trail building. In this way, a multi-focal segment can belong to several trails. This leads to an operational definition of research:

- Research happens when we have trails of at least length L (e.g., $L=3$) with an overall net duration of at least T (e.g., $T=60$ min); net duration is the sum of segment durations.

- Research with significant topical sliding is characterized as *early research*. And conversely, *mature research* is research with little topical sliding

IMPLEMENTATION OF A RESEARCH TRAIL BROWSER

We have implemented and done preliminary evaluation of a research trail browser that the users can invoke from the new tab page. The implementation consists of two modules: an initialization module that builds the semantic model based on the user's Google web history and a trail browser module, consisting of a *user interface*, and a *model server* that handles the background processing for the user interface.

Initialization Module

The initialization module captures users' activity history, detects linguistic topics, and translates temporal segmentation and topic clusters into research trails. We used Google history data in this prototyping effort providing event types like query, query-click, and page visit, and derived user activity data from time stamps attached to them. History data is used to recreate the corresponding web content (caveat: pages might have changed since they were originally visited), and essential content is extracted for subsequent processing by a topic detection algorithm.

We apply the Latent Dirichlet Allocation [1] topic-detecting algorithm to the extracted web page content. This produces a list of *μ-topics* (a μ-topic is a list of prominent words ordered according to their importance to the topic), and for each page, a vector of real values between zero and one, reflecting the relative strength of semantic relationship between the page and the μ-topics.

Trail Browser Module

User Interface: The interface is fitted to the New Tab page that exists in many browsers; in addition to the usual services, such as most recently visited or most visited pages, the user sees a list of the most recent research trails; other research trails can be shown as well on request. The user can view the trails, their segments, as well as all the events (visited paged).

Model Server: When a user makes a request to see the trails, the server gets the request and queries the database. To be efficient, the trails are computed only once and stored in the server side database. The server sends the trails in XML format for the user interface module to process and display.

Preliminary Assessment

During the development of the prototype, the algorithms were continually assessed and checked towards web histories, which had been volunteered by colleagues. We conducted a preliminary assessment of the research trail method in an end-to-end experiment involving on three users. In this experiment, we presented the segments and the research trails. For segments, we also attached associated attributes such as its time stamps, duration, topic summary, coherence values, etc. Users could explore trails and segments, and inspect the corresponding web pages.

We found that the segment definition naturally captures the concept of a work session, as perceived by the user. Majority of the segments reflected a single task session, where both average coherence and maximum coherence were high. In cases of multi-tasking, we observed that maximum coherence was high and average coherence was low which matched our expectation. This version of experiment did not include the virtual segment split.

We also found that segments in trails are mostly related and coherent locally, that is, within the "trail windows". Topic sliding was observed in some cases and seems well supported. Sometimes we observed unrelated segments in trails (false positive), and some related segments were not included (false negative). The latter would sometimes be grouped with another trail of very similar research tasks. One direction of improvement is to merge similar trails and adjust similarity threshold in the trail construction algorithm so we get fewer trails but they would map better to users' perceived research tasks.

SUMMARY AND FUTURE WORK

Our ethnographic study described *early research* as a common activity that is not well supported by current tools. The study informed our design of *research trailing*, a method that automatically filters and reorganizes users' activity history (browsing as well as general interaction history) into trails of related work. The trailing method is robust against gradual shifts in research direction.

An extensive evaluation of the prototype and the algorithms is in progress, and the results will guide further design. Ideally the research trails would be visualized with screen snapshots to facilitate fast browsing. Manipulation of trails by criteria, including time, duration, recency etc., is also desirable. While such features are essential to a fulfilling user experience, they are not crucial for demonstrating the research trail concept.

Other potential future designs include: graceful degradation when less user activity detail is captured; capturing richer activity data, e.g., user activity on visited page, by moving the trail building from server to client; "mixed initiative" approaches that would let user further process the research trails, clean them up, name them and categorize them; and finally, implementation of incremental update of the topic model.

REFERENCES

1. Blei, D. M., Ng, A. Y., and Jordan, M. I. Latent Dirichlet allocation. In Journal of Machine Learning Research 3, 2003

2. Chirita, P., Firan, C., and Nejdl, W. Personalized query expansion for the web. In Proc. SIGIR '07, ACM, 2007.

3. Cockburn, A., and Mckenzie, B. What do web users do? An empirical analysis of web use. In International Journal of Human-Computer Studies, 54, 2000.

4. Cockburn, A., Greenberg, S., Mckenzie, B., Jasonsmith, M., and Kaasten, S. Webview: A graphical aid for revisiting web pages. In Proc. OZCHI '99, 1999.

5. Dragunov, A.N., Dietterich, T.G., Johnsrude, K., McLaughlin, M., Li, L., and Herlocker, J. TaskTracer: A Desktop Environment to Support Multi-tasking Knowledge Workers. In Proc. IUI'05. ACM 2005

6. Hightower, R. et al. Graphical Multiscale Web Histories: A Study of PadPrints, Proc. Hypertext, 1998.

7. Jones, W., Dumais, S., and Bruce, H. Once found, what then? A study of "keeping" behaviors in the personal use of web information. In ASIST, 39(1), 2002.

8. Kaptelinin, V. UMEA: translating interaction histories into project contexts. In Proc. CHI '03. ACM, 2003.

9. LeeTiernan, S., Farnham, S., and Cheng, L. Two methods for auto-organizing personal web history. In Proc. CHI '03, 2003. ACM.

10. Luxenburger, J., Elbassuoni, S., and Weikum, G. Matching task profiles and user needs in personalized web search. In Proc. CIKM 2008, ACM, 2008.

11. Moore, B., Van Kleek, M., and Karger, D. Eyebrowse. http://eyebrowse.csail.mit.edu/

12. Pedersen, E.R. Habits of Ordinary Web Researchers. Under review (expected 2010).

13. Qiu, F. and Cho, J. Automatic identification of user interest for personalized search. In Proc. WWW '06, ACM, 2006.

14. Won, S.S., Jin, J., and Hong, J.J. Contextual web history: using visual and contextual cues to improve web browser history. In Proc. CHI '09. ACM, 2009

15. Yamaguchi, T., Hattori, H., Ito, T, and Shintani, T. On a web browsing support system with 3d visualization. In Proc. WWW Alt. '04, ACM, 2004

Balancing Error and Supervision Effort in Interactive-Predictive Handwriting Recognition*

Nicolás Serrano, Albert Sanchis, and Alfons Juan
DSIC/ITI, Universitat Politècnica de València
Camí de Vera, s/n, 46022 València, Spain
{nserrano, asanchis, ajuan}@iti.upv.es

ABSTRACT

An effective approach to transcribe handwritten text documents is to follow an interactive-predictive paradigm in which both, the system is guided by the user, and the user is assisted by the system to complete the transcription task as efficiently as possible. This approach has been recently implemented in a system prototype called GIDOC, in which standard speech technology is adapted to handwritten text (line) images: HMM-based text image modeling, n-gram language modeling, and also confidence measures on recognized words. Confidence measures are used to assist the user in locating possible transcription errors, and thus validate system output after only supervising those (few) words for which the system is not highly confident. However, a certain degree of supervision is required for proper model adaptation from partially supervised transcriptions. Here, we propose a simple yet effective method to find an optimal balance between recognition error and supervision effort.

Author Keywords

Computer-assisted text transcription, confidence measures, document analysis, handwriting recognition.

ACM Classification Keywords

H.5.m Information Interfaces and Presentation: Miscellaneous—*Interactive-predictive systems*; I.5.5 Pattern Recognition: Implementation—*Interactive systems*; I.7.5 Document and Text Processing: Document Capture—*OCR; Document analysis.*

General Terms

Algorithms, Experimentation, Human Factors

*Work supported by the EC (FEDER/FSE) and the Spanish Government under the MIPRCV "Consolider Ingenio 2010" program (CSD2007-00018), the iTransDoc (TIN2006-15694-CO2-01), iTrans2 (TIN2009-14511) and MITTRAL (TIN2009-14633-C03-01) projects, and the FPU scholarship AP2007-02867. Also supported by the Generalitat Valenciana under grant Prometeo/2009/014, and the UPV under grant 20080033.

INTRODUCTION

Transcription of handwritten text in (old) documents is an important, time-consuming task for digital libraries. It might be carried out by first processing all document images off-line, and then manually supervising system transcriptions to edit incorrect parts. However, state-of-the-art technologies for automatic page layout analysis, text line detection and handwritten text recognition are still far from perfect [8, 2, 1], and thus post-editing automatically generated output is not clearly better than simply ignoring it.

A more effective approach to transcribe old text documents is to follow an interactive-predictive paradigm in which both, the system is guided by the user, and the user is assisted by the system to complete the transcription task as efficiently as possible. Following this approach, a system prototype called GIDOC (Gimp-based Interactive transcription of old text DOCuments) is being developed to provide user-friendly, integrated support for interactive-predictive page layout analysis, text line detection and handwriting transcription [4, 6].

GIDOC is designed to work with (large) collections of homogeneous documents, that is, of similar structure and writing styles. They are annotated sequentially, by (partially) supervising hypotheses drawn from statistical models that are constantly updated with an increasing number of available annotated documents. And this is done at different annotation levels. For instance, at the level of page layout analysis, GIDOC uses a novel text block detection method in which conventional, memoryless techniques are improved with a "history" model of text block positions [4]. Similarly, at the level of text line image transcription, GIDOC includes a handwriting recognizer which is steadily improved with a growing number of supervised transcriptions [6].

Here we will focus on the handwriting recognition part of GIDOC. As in the most advanced handwriting recognizers today, it is based on standard speech technology adapted to handwritten text images; that is, HMM-based text image modeling and n-gram language modeling. Each text line image is processed in turn, by first predicting its most likely transcription, and then locating and editing system errors. In order to reduce the effort in locating these errors, GIDOC again resorts to standard speech technology and, in particular, to confidence measures (at word level), which are calculated as posterior word probabilities estimated from word graphs [7]. Recognized words for which the system is not confident enough are marked as possible errors and the user is asked to only supervise and correct, if needed, each of them. Clearly, this partial supervision approach does not guarantee perfect transcriptions though, if (hopefully minor) recognition errors can be tolerated in non-supervised parts, it might result in considerable supervision effort reduction.

In this paper, we study how to automatically balance recognition error and supervision effort. Our starting point is [6], where we have recently compared several model adaptation techniques from partially supervised transcriptions. It has been shown that it is better not to adapt models from all data, but only from high-confidence parts, or just simply from supervised parts. More importantly, it has been shown that a certain degree of supervision is required for model adaptation though, it remains unclear how to adjust it properly. In this work, we propose a simple yet effective method to find an optimal balance between recognition error and supervision effort. The user decides on a maximum tolerance threshold for the recognition error (in non-supervised parts), and the system adjusts the required supervision effort on the basis of an estimate for this error. In what follows, we first briefly describe GIDOC. Then, the proposed balancing method is presented and tested on a real transcription task.

GIDOC OVERVIEW

GIDOC is a first attempt to provide user-friendly, integrated support for interactive-predictive page layout analysis, text line detection and handwritten text transcription [4, 6]. It is built as a set of plug-ins for the well-known GNU Image Manipulation Program (GIMP), which has many image processing features already incorporated and, what is more important, a high-end user interface for image manipulation. To run GIDOC, we must first run GIMP and open a document image. GIMP will come up with its high-end user interface, which is often configured to only show the main toolbox (with docked dialogs) and an image window. GIDOC can be accessed from the menubar (see Fig. 1).

As shown in Fig. 1, the GIDOC menu includes six entries, though here only the last one, *Transcription,* is briefly described (see [4, 6] for more detailed descriptions). The *Transcription* entry opens an interactive transcription dialog (also shown in Fig. 1), which consists of two main sections: the image section, in the middle part, and the transcription section, in the bottom part. A number of text line images are displayed in the image section together with their transcriptions, if available, in separate editable text boxes within the transcription section. The *current* line to be transcribed is selected by placing the edit cursor in the appropriate editable box. Its corresponding baseline is emphasized (in blue color) and, whenever possible, GIDOC shifts line images and their transcriptions so as to display the current line in the central part of both the image and transcription sections. It is assumed that The user transcribes or supervises text lines, from top to bottom, by entering text and moving the edit cursor.

Note that each editable text box has a button attached to its left, which is labeled with its corresponding line number. By clicking on it, its associated line image is extracted, preprocessed, transformed into a sequence of feature vectors, and

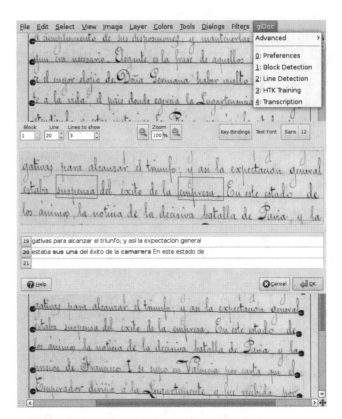

Figure 1. Interactive Transcription dialog over an image window.

Viterbi-decoded using HMMs and a language model previous trained. As shown in Fig. 1, words in the current line for which the system is not highly confident are emphasized (in red) in both the image and transcription sections. It is then up to the user to supervise emphasized words.

BALANCING ERROR AND SUPERVISION EFFORT

As said in the introduction, in this paper we propose a simple yet effective method to find an optimal balance between recognition error and supervision effort. As usual, recognition error is measured in terms of Word Error Rate (WER); that is, as the average number of elementary editing operations needed to produce a reference (correctly transcribed) word from recognized words. This is done by computing a minimum edit (Levenshtein) distance path between the reference and recognized transcriptions of each text line image. For instance, consider the example shown in Fig. 2. Four elementary editing operations are required to transform the recognized transcription into its reference: substitution of "sus" for "suspensa", deletion of "una", substitution of "camarera" for "empresa", and insertion of ".". As there are 12 reference words in this simple example, the resulting WER is $\frac{1}{3}$; i.e. one editing operation every three reference words.

Given a collection of reference-recognized transcription pairs, its WER may be simply expressed as:

$$WER = \frac{E}{N}$$

where E is the total number of editing operations required to transform recognized transcriptions into their corresponding

374

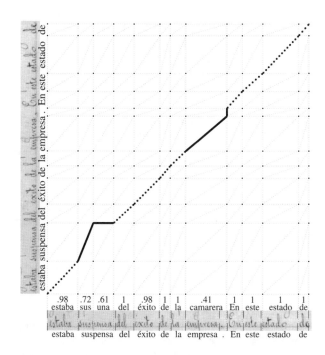

Figure 2. Example of minimum edit distance path between the recognized and true transcriptions of a text line image.

references, and N is the total number of reference words. In this work, however, we need to decompose these three variables additively, as

$$WER = WER^+ + WER^-$$
$$E = E^+ + E^- \quad \text{and} \quad N = N^+ + N^-$$

where the superscripts $^+$ and $^-$ denote supervised and unsupervised parts, respectively, and thus

$$WER^+ = \frac{E^+}{N} \quad \text{and} \quad WER^- = \frac{E^-}{N}$$

In order to balance error and supervision effort, we propose the system to ask for supervision effort only when WER^- becomes greater than a given, maximum tolerance threshold, say WER^*. However, as we do not know the values of E^- and N^-, they have to be estimated from available data. A reasonable estimate for N^- is simply

$$\hat{N}^- = \frac{N^+}{R^+} R^-$$

where R^+ and R^- denote the number of recognized words in the supervised and unsupervised parts, respectively. Similarly, a reasonable estimate for E^- is

$$\hat{E}^- = \frac{E^+}{R^+} R^-$$

and thus the desired estimate for WER^- is

$$\widehat{WER}^- = \frac{\frac{E^+}{R^+} R^-}{N^+ + \frac{N^+}{R^+} R^-}$$

Each recognized word will be accepted without supervision if it does not lead to a WER^- estimate greater that WER^*.

Note that the above estimate for WER^- is pessimistic, since it assumes that, on average, correction of unsupervised parts requires similar editing effort to that required for supervised parts. However, the user is asked to supervise recognized words in increasing order of confidence, and hence unsupervised parts should require less correction effort. In order to better estimate WER^-, we may group recognized words by their level of confidence c, from 1 to a certain maximum level C, and compute a c-dependent estimate for E as above,

$$\hat{E}_c^- = \frac{E_c^+}{R_c^+} R_c^-$$

where E_c^+, R_c^+ and R_c^- are c-dependent versions of E^+, R^+ and R^-, respectively. The global estimate for E is obtained by simply summing these c-dependent estimates,

$$\hat{E}^- = \sum_{c=1}^{C} \hat{E}_c^-$$

and, therefore, the estimate for WER^- becomes

$$\widehat{WER}^- = \frac{\sum_{c=1}^{C} \frac{E_c^+}{R_c^+} R_c^-}{N^+ + \frac{N^+}{R^+} R^-}$$

which reduces to the previous, pessimistic estimate when only a single confidence level is considered ($C = 1$).

EXPERIMENTS

During its development, GIDOC has been used by a paleography expert to annotate blocks, text lines and transcriptions on a new dataset called GERMANA [3]. GERMANA is the result of digitizing and annotating a 764-page Spanish manuscript from 1891, in which most pages only contain nearly calligraphed text written on ruled sheets of well-separated lines. The example shown in Fig. 1 corresponds to the page 144. GERMANA is solely written in Spanish up to page 180; then, the manuscript includes many parts that are written in languages different from Spanish.

Due to its sequential book structure, the very basic task on GERMANA is to transcribe it from the beginning to the end, though here we only consider its transcription up to line 3700 (page 177). For this part, we consider its transcription under four tolerance thresholds on the recognition error (in unsupervised parts): 0% (fully supervised), 9% (one recognition error per line, on average), 18%, and 27%.

We divided GERMANA into consecutive blocks of 100 lines each (37 blocks). The first two blocks were used to train initial image and language models from fully supervised transcriptions. Then, from block 3 to 37, each new block was recognized, partially supervised as discussed in the preceding section for $C = 4$ confidence levels, and added to the previous training set. The first three confidence levels correspond, respectively, to the first three words in each line that were recognized with smaller confidence; the remaining recognized words were all grouped into the fourth level. Re-training of image and language models was carried out from only high confidence parts [6]. On the other hand, simulation of user supervision actions on each recognized word was done in accordance with the user interaction model described in [6]. The results are shown in Fig. 3 (left) in terms of WER on transcribed lines (excluding the first 200).

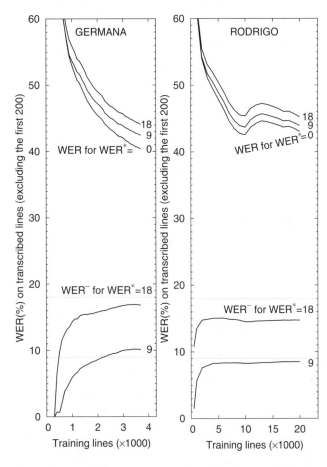

Figure 3. Word Error Rate (WER) on transcribed lines (excluding the first 200), as a function of the (number of) training lines, for varying tolerance thresholds on the recognition error (in unsupervised parts). Left: GERMANA dataset. Right: RODRIGO dataset.

From the results in Fig. 3 (left), it becomes clear that the proposed balancing method takes full advantage of the allowed tolerance to reduce supervision effort. Moreover, the total WER of the system trained with partial transcriptions does not deviate significantly from that of the fully supervised system. The average user effort reduction ranges from 29% (for $WER^* = 9\%$) to 49% (for $WER^* = 18\%$). That is, if one recognition error per line is allowed on average ($WER^* = 9\%$), then the user will save a 29% of the supervision actions that are required in the case of a fully supervised system. Here, supervision actions refers to elementary editing operations, and also to check that a correctly recognized word is certainly correct.

In order to better assess the proposed method, a larger experiment was also conducted on another handwritten text database, RODRIGO, which is comparable in size to GERMANA, but it is completely written in Spanish and comes from a much older manuscript, from 1545 [5]. RODRIGO comprises about 20K lines that were divided into blocks of 1000 lines each, except for the first 1000 lines, which were

divided into the line blocks 1-100, 101-200, 201-500 and 501-1000. The experiment and results, shown in Fig. 3 (right), are analogous to those described above for GERMANA.

Although the results presented in Fig. 3 are quite satisfactory, we have observed that the proposed balancing method does not clearly favor supervision of low confidence words over those recognized with high confidence. We think that this is mainly due to the fact that it works on a word-by-word basis and, in order to decide whether are given word has to be supervised or not, its contribution to the current estimate of WER^- is not as important as the closeness of this estimate to WER^*. We think that this behavior can be alleviated by using more confidence levels or, more directly, by working on a line-by-line basis. That is, by first assuming that all recognized words in a line are not supervised, and then supervising words in increasing order of confidence while the current estimate of WER^- is above WER^*.

CONCLUDING REMARKS

A simple yet effective method has been proposed to find an optimal balance between recognition error and supervision effort in interactive-predictive handwriting recognition. The user decides on a maximum tolerance threshold for the recognition error (after supervision), and the system adjusts the required supervision effort on the basis of an estimate for this error. Empirical results have been reported showing the effectiveness of the proposed method. Current work is underway to develop improved variants of this method. In particular, it would be interesting to allow the user to adjust the maximum tolerance threshold dynamically, perhaps with system assistance.

REFERENCES

1. R. Bertolami and H. Bunke. Hidden Markov model-based ensemble methods for offline handwritten text line recognition. *Patt. Rec.*, 41:3452–3460, 2008.

2. L. Likforman-Sulem, A. Zahour, and B. Taconet. Text line segmentation of historical documents: a survey. *IJDAR*, 9:123–138, 2007.

3. D. Pérez et al. The GERMANA database. In *ICDAR*, pages 301–305, Barcelona (Spain), 2009.

4. O. Ramos, N. Serrano, and A. Juan. Interactive-predictive detection of handwritten text blocks. In *DRR XVII*, San Jose (USA), 2010.

5. N. Serrano, F. Castro, and A. Juan. The RODRIGO database. In *LREC*, 2010. (submitted).

6. N. Serrano, D. Pérez, A. Sanchis, and A. Juan. Adaptation from partially supervised handwritten text transcriptions. In *ICMI-MLMI*, Cambridge (USA), 2009.

7. L. Tarazón et al. Confidence Measures for Error Correction in Interactive Transcription of Handwritten Text. In *ICIAP*, Vietri sul Mare (Italy), 2009.

8. A. H. Toselli et al. Integrated handwriting recognition and interpretation using finite-state models. *IJPRAI*, 18(4):519–539, 2004.

The Why UI: Using Goal Networks to Improve User Interfaces

Dustin A. Smith
MIT Media Lab
20 Ames St; Cambridge, MA 02139
dustin@media.mit.edu

Henry Lieberman
MIT Media Lab
20 Ames St; Cambridge, MA 02139
lieber@media.mit.edu

ABSTRACT

People interact with interfaces to accomplish goals, and knowledge about human goals can be useful for building intelligent user interfaces. We suggest that modeling high, *human-level* goals like "repair my credit score", is especially useful for coordinating workflows between interfaces, automated planning, and building introspective applications.

We analyzed data from 43Things.com, a website where users share and discuss goals and plans in natural language, and constructed a goal network that relates *what* goals people have with *how* people solve them. We then label goals with specific details, such as *where* the goal typically is met and *how long* it takes to achieve, facilitating plan and goal recognition. Lastly, we demonstrate a simple application of goal networks, deploying it in a mobile, location-aware to-do list application, ToDoGo, which uses goal networks to help users plan where and when to accomplish their desired goals.

Author Keywords

Learning Goal Networks, Plan Recognition, To-Do Lists

ACM Classification Keywords

H.5.2 Information Interfaces and Presentation: User Interfaces—*Natural Language*; H.4.1 Information Systems Applications: Office Automation—*Workflow Management*

General Terms

Design, Human Factors, Theory

INTRODUCTION

People interact with interfaces to solve problems to accomplish goals, and knowledge about human goals can be useful for building intelligent user interfaces. In previous work, goal knowledge has used in recommendation systems, for disambiguating natural language queries in search engines [8] and in the more general problem of building **plan recognition** systems, which try to infer the user's goals from an incomplete and mixed sequence of observed behaviors.

Goals are desired world states and people can describe them in natural language: "[I want to] click the 'okay' button", "start the movie", and "entertain my date". As you can see, goals can span different temporal granularities and their English descriptions can abstract away many important details: of those three descriptions, each contained roughly the same number of words. A goal library is required to map between the *interface-level* goals, about clicking buttons and performing actions in the interface, to the *human-level* goals, the kind that people regularly communicate with each other.

To date, work on modeling user goals has either involved costly knowledge engineering efforts to manually encode the plan knowledge, or automated efforts which learn single plans at a time from user behaviors. Here, we investigate a third option: processing a natural language plan corpus, constructed by a community of people. This approach has the potential of acquiring broad coverage of "human level" goals automatically, through the automated construction of a machine interpretable goal network. In this paper, we explain our approach for deriving a goal network from text and present an example application that uses this goal knowledge. In addition to kind of applications where this goal knowledge is immediately useful, our method of recognizing English description of sub-goals can be used to attach goal networks to descriptions of interface level goals.

GOALS IN USER INTERFACES

There are many uses of goal knowledge in user interfaces. When the application is aware of the user's goal, knowledge about the relationships between goals is useful for automated planning, to coordinate workflows that span multiple interfaces and to build introspective applications.

Automated Planning

Goals can either be inferred by the system (plan recognition), or communicated explicitly by the user. Plan recognition systems attempt to infer the user's active goals and plans based on some partial observation of his or her actions. If the system infers correctly, it tries to help the user by automating the task when it can. See [1] for a review of plan recognition in IUIs. An example of explicit communication through natural language is Roadie [7], a consumer electronics interface where users speak their intentions, such as "I want to watch the news", and the system attempts to understand the goal in order to create and execute a plan.

Modeling tasks between interfaces or within interfaces

Imagine pursuing the goal of "buying a home": In between searching for the perfect house, you may spend time calling realtors, repairing your credit score, applying for mortgages, etc. Each of these tasks involves a variety of subtasks, different tools and interfaces (web browsers, cell phones, financial software, etc), which are all oblivious to your larger workflow. Similarly, when a single application can do many different tasks, like a smart phone or a word processing program, it can be useful to predict which feature subset the user is interested in, depending on his or her goals. A broad library relating human goals to interface actions will be essential for this kind of interface behavior.

Introspective applications

When people make their goals explicit and detailed, it facilitates accomplishing them; however, paradoxically people commonly fail to formulate explicit goals for the domains they most value and formulate more specific goals for the domains they value less [10]. One could imagine a "self-reflective" interface that helps the user to self-regulate (verifying that one's behavior aligns with one's goals), or allows them to reflect upon a longitudinal perspective of how their goals change over time. Again, to achieve this, it will be important to know relations between goals and actions.

ACQUIRING AND USING PLAN LIBRARIES

All plan recognition systems require a hypothesis space, a library of plans; and, designing and acquiring a plan library is an arduous task. Generally, plans are handcrafted by knowledge engineers or learned by observing the user's behavior. TaskTracer [9] for example, monitors a user's interactions with Microsoft WinXP and Office, asks the user to label a few tasks and then uses these labels to classify the user's later actions. *End-user programming* is when the system learns a specific plan from the user's explicit behavior, with the goal of automatically executing that plan in the future. Typically, such plan libraries are small and confined to the tasks the user has taught the system. An interesting exception is the CoScripter learning by example project, where users can explore and exchange web scripts in an online script repository [2]. Such script repositories still require annotating scripts with the goals it helps to accomplish.

Learning plans from a natural language corpus

Our goal is to create a plan library that covers the breadth of everyday human goals and actions. Fortunately, in recent years several websites have appeared which focus on codifying (in English) and exchanging descriptions of procedural problem-solving knowledge: 43things.com, eHow.com, wikiHow.com, hassleme.co.uk; and more targeted knowledge acquisition efforts like OMICS [6]. The knowledge in these resources is encoded in natural languages and requires challenging transformations before they can be used in interface applications. We focused on the knowledge from 43Things.com, a free online community of users who list, compare and discuss each other's goals, with the objective of improving time management and problem solving skills.

It may seem at first that the high-level or frivolous goals mentioned in 43Things might have little to do with the concrete details of a user interface. That might indeed be the case for some entries; but, there are many applications where users indeed record life goals, such as calendars, to-do lists, and project management software, even if the software has no operations for directly achieving those goals. Second, a large goal like "buy a house" might have subgoals like "find a real estate agent" that are directly satisfiable by software operations. Third, we might imagine creating corpora that are more focused on lower level goals, such as "get bibliography into IUI format", which might also encounter the same problems of incompletely described or missing steps, etc. The same sort of analysis techniques presented here will prove relevant.

MINING A GOAL NETWORK FROM TEXT

We downloaded the 43things.com corpus, which contains data about a wide range of *goal statements* including "buy a house" and "travel to Hong Kong". Some statements have "how I did it" stories by people who have achieved the goal and describe how they did, how long it took, and the way achieving the goal made him or her feel. We called these stories *plan statements*. At the time of acquiring a snapshot of the database (Fall 2008) it contained over 2.5 million goal statement entries and $22,528$ plan statements about $9,304$ distinct goals.

The 43Things corpus does not contain explicit relations between goal statements, so the global graph structure must be inferred. Our approach was to look within the text of each plan statement to detect other goal statements. Consider this plan statement by someone who accomplished the goal "eat better":

> i hate eating healthy! i do, i do. i plan to **lose 50 pounds** though, and that is the inspiration you need. everyone needs something to look forward to...

Here, the goal to ''lose 50 pounds" matched another goal in the database. Our procedure looks at the text and recognizes these embedded goals. We looked for a list of subgoals available from 43thing goal statements as well as a filtered list of public todo-lists from Tadalist.com. Because the statements were contributed by thousands of different authors, our mining approach must handle noisy text. Our approach[1] is:

Preprocessing the English Plans First, we corrected misspellings, stripped non-words, segmented phrases and sentences using the Punkt tokenizer, labeled each token with its part of speech and stemmed word root.

Building a directed weighted goal graph For each plan statement, each step of $p \in P_i$ for goal statement i is compared with each stemmed goal statement j to see if the tokens are a *longest common subsequence*[2] If the goal occurs as a subsequence, a directed edge (i, j) is added to the goal

---

[1]Code available from http://web.media.mit.edu/~dustin/goals

[2]A **subsequence** is like a **substring** that permits gaps in between the successive elements (comparing only tokens, not POS tags).

graph, given a *support* weight equal to the ratio of plans that goal occurred in $w(i,j) = \frac{\sum_{p \in P_i} hasSeq(p,j)}{|P_i|}$.

Divisive graph clustering The last step produced a large directed weighted graph with 3335 nodes and 6406 edges and 69 components. We consolidated some of the nodes and removed some of the outliers. Graph clustering looks at the relational structure (between goals), while regular object clustering looks at internal features describing the goals (*e.g.*, the overlapping words between two plans, the duration of the goals, etc). We clustered this large data set using a stochastic flow clustering algorithm [4].

Extracting verb-phrases and locations with rules We filtered the tagged plan descriptions with hand-authored Regular Expression Chunking rules to extract verb phrases and prepositional phrases that were indicative of a location. The rules matched syntactic tags with particular tokens, but yielded many false positives due to the problems of the tagger.

ANALYZING A CORPUS OF HUMAN GOALS

The GOALS themselves contain meta-data specifying the number of users pursuing the goal and the number of people who voted on the goal as 'worth doing' or 'not worth doing'. We analyzed this and our learned graph structure to answer some questions:

Which goals are most popular?

The number of people who have picked a particular goal follows a power-law distribution with its characteristic thick tail: of the $2,524,563$ unique goal strings, 88.8% of them are listed by 1 or no people, yet each goal is pursued by 2.6 people on average. The top goals: *lose weight* $(32,504)$; *stop procrastinating* $(24,100)$; *write a book* $(22,342)$; *fall in love* $(22,091)$; and *be happy* $(19,498)$.

Which goals are most controversial?

Users of 43Things.com also have the option to vote on each other's goals, indicating whether they view the goal as "Worth it" or "Not worth it". We used this voting data to try and capture the notion of goals that were the most polarizing. We approximated this using **entropy**, which measures uncertainty—in our case, measuring the community's uncertainty about whether or not a goal is "worth it". Here are some controversial goals:

GOAL	WORTH IT	NOT WORTH IT
don't shave for a few days	149	55
try soy milk or rice milk	122	45
gamble in Vegas	38	14
lose the game	239	89
be a better girlfriend	30	11
own a house	248	12

Table 1. Listed are the top five most controversial goals (highest entropy of worth it ratings). "own a house" was added for an ongoing comparison.

Which goals in the goal network are most central?

After clustering the goals into a goal network, we looked for nodes that had an important role in the structure of the graph. One metric is the **closeness centrality**, measuring the mean shortest path of one node (goal) to all other nodes, which generalizes easily to weighted graphs. The most central goals in our inferred goal network are: *beat depression* (0.212), *be more confident* (0.200), *be happy with myself* (0.196), *have better sex* (0.182), and *find my soulmate* (0.17931). These goals are at the center of influence of the network, and–assuming goals lead to each other–should have the most significance in "opening the most doors" to other goals in the graph.

EXAMPLE INTERFACE

We put the goal knowledge to work in a mobile, location-aware to-do list application, ToDoGo.

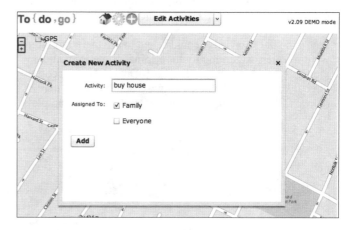

Figure 2. The user describes their goal, "buy house" to the to-do list program (side-stepping the problem of plan recognition).

Figure 3. Using the background goal knowledge, the system infers plausible sub-goals for the goal "buy house", including "see relator" and "apply for mortgage". The user selects the appropriate tasks.

To-do lists make plan recognition trivial because the user is already explicitly declaring his or her goal. Several recent projects have worked to automate to-do lists [3]. They

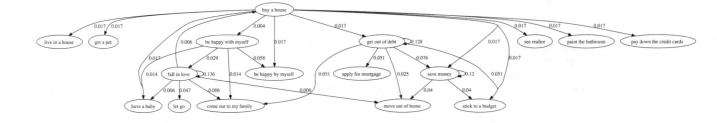

Figure 1. This subgraph shows nodes related to the goal *buy a house*. The weight in the directed arrow indicates the ratio of the parent goal's plan statement the embedded goal appeared.

work by mapping the parsed to-do list entry into actions that can be solved by an automated agent. This is challenging because many to-do list entires are abbreviated and not all entries are tasks that can be automated [5].

Plan and goal knowledge could be put to use in a straightforward manner: Returning to our original scenario, you communicate your goal "buy house" to ToDoGo . Using a corpus of goal knowledge, ToDoGo suggests sub-goals that may be relevant , looks up surrounding points of interests and plots them on a local map.

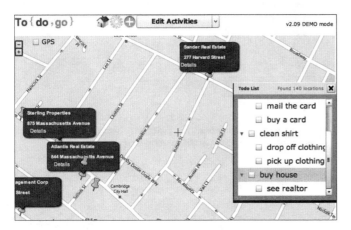

Figure 4. ToDoGo uses default knowledge about events, knowing that "see relator" takes place at real estate office, it queries local points of interests by category and presents them on a map

CONCLUSION

This paper argues for building programs that are sensitive to a user's goals. We first analyzed a corpus of plans and goals. Then we showed how we used natural language processing techniques to transform collaboratively collected semi-structured text into a goal graph to be used for plan recognition. Finally we showed how these could be useful in a mobile to-do list application.

ACKNOWLEDGEMENTS

We thank the anonymous reviewers for their helpful comments and suggestions on the first draft, and Josh Petersen from 43things.com.

REFERENCES

1. M. G. Armentano and A. Amandi. Plan recognition for interface agents. *Artificial Intelligence Review*, 28(2):131–162, Aug 2007.

2. C. Bogart, M. Burnett, A. Cypher, and C. Scaffidi. End-user programming in the wild: A field study of coscripter scripts. *IEEE Symposium on Visual Languages and Human-Centric Computing, 2008. VL/HCC 2008*, pages 39–46, 2008.

3. K. Conley and J. Carpenter. Towel: Towards an intelligent to-do list. In *Proceedings of the AAAI Spring Symposium on Interaction Challenges for Artificial Assistants*, 2007.

4. S. Dongen. Graph clustering by flow simulation. *Ph.D. Thesis*, Jan 2000.

5. Y. Gil and V. Ratnakar. Automating to-do lists for users: Interpretation of to-dos for selecting and tasking agents. *Proceedings of the Twenty-Third AAAI Conference on Artificial Intelligence*, page 7, Apr 2008.

6. R. Gupta and K. Hennacy. Commonsense reasoning about task instructions. *AAAI-05 Workshop on modular construction of human-like intelligence. Pittsburgh, PA, July*, 10:05–08, 2005.

7. H. Lieberman and J. Espinosa. A goal-oriented interface to consumer electronics using planning and commonsense reasoning. *Knowledge-Based Systems*, 20(6):592–606, 2007.

8. M. Strohmaier, M. Kröll, and C. Körner. Intentional query suggestion: making user goals more explicit during search. *Proceedings of the 2009 workshop on Web Search Click Data*, pages 68–74, 2009.

9. S. Stumpf, X. Bao, A. Dragunov, T. Dietterich, J. Herlocker, K. Johnsrude, L. Li, and J. Shen. Predicting user tasks: I know what you're doing. In *20th National Conference on Artificial Intelligence (AAAI-05), Workshop on Human Comprehensible Machine Learning*, 2005.

10. P. Whitmore. *The Maieutics of Goal Articulation: Motivating the choices of the highest import*. PhD thesis, Stanford University, March 2000.

A Multimodal Dialogue Mashup for Medical Image Semantics

Daniel Sonntag
German Research Center for AI
Saarbrücken, Germany
daniel.sonntag@dfki.de

Manuel Möller
German Research Center for AI
Kaiserslautern, Germany
manuel.moeller@dfki.de

ABSTRACT

This paper presents a multimodal dialogue mashup where different users are involved in the use of different user interfaces for the annotation and retrieval of medical images. Our solution is a mashup that integrates a multimodal interface for speech-based annotation of medical images and dialogue-based image retrieval with a semantic image annotation tool for manual annotations on a desktop computer. A remote RDF repository connects the annotation and querying task into a common framework and serves as the semantic backend system for the advanced multimodal dialogue a radiologist can use.

Author Keywords

Design, Touchscreen Interface, Collaborative Environments

ACM Classification Keywords

H.5.2 User Interfaces: Input Devices and Strategies, Natural Language, Graphical HCIs, Prototyping

General Terms

Design, Theory

INTRODUCTION

In contemporary, daily hospital work, clinicians can only manually search for "similar" images using outdated desktop search applications. After considering the relevant categories of similarity, they subsequently apply one filter after the other. For instance, a clinician first sets a filter for the imaging modality (e.g., CT angiography), the second filter for the procedure (e.g., coronary angiography), and so on. In addition to the fact that this approach is quite time-consuming, it is neither possible to formulate complex and semantically integrated search queries in a convenient way, nor can a radiologist easily annotate images with anatomy or disease information. Hence, the need exists for a seamless integration of medical images and different user applications by direct access to image semantics. Semantic image re-

trieval using formal ontologies can provide the basis for the help in decision support and computer-aided diagnosis.

Adequate (multimodal) user interfaces play a significant role in achieving this goal. Automatic detection of image semantics seems to be feasible, but is too error-prone (at least on the desired annotation level where multiple layers of tissue have to be annotated at different image resolutions). Accordingly, our major challenge is the so-called knowledge acquisition bottleneck. We cannot easily acquire the necessary medical knowledge about the image contents.

In this contribution, we define a *mashup* as a Web application that combines data and functionality from two or more sources into a single integrated application. We focus on the HCI aspect of the integrated application when addressing advanced dialogical interaction with semantic (medical) image repositories. In particular, we address the knowledge acquisition bottleneck problem by concerning ourselves with the question how to mash-up

- a multimodal interface for speech-based annotations (manual and semi-automatic annotation),
- a semantic image annotation tool RadSem for manual annotations on a desktop computer typically performed by medical students,
- statistical image region annotation (automatic annotation),

into a common framework that benefits from manual, semi-automatic, and automatic image annotations. A remote RDF repository which stores the semantic image information and connects the annotation and querying task into a common framework makes the mashup unique. The system supports the full range of multimodal interaction patterns, such as deictic or cross-modal references in the context of the annotation. We will also demonstrate the image retrieval (querying) functionality of the multimodal dialogue interface.

INTERACTION DESIGN AND PRINCIPLES

Experience shows that decisions made in the early phases of the development of a multimodal system prevail throughout the life-cycle of the project. We learned some lessons which we use as guidelines in the development of our mashup system. Some partners in the project contributed their experience from earlier projects [8, 5] where different sub-components were integrated to multimodal interaction systems. We also learned some lessons which we use as guidelines in the development of our *semantic* mashup [4, 7].

Multimodality: More modalities allow for more natural communication, which normally employs multiple channels of expression. It is also the case that more modalities constrain the interpretation and, hence, enhance robustness. For the medical image annotation step, predefined speech recognition grammars work quite well. In addition, the touchscreen display allows for new information presentation and aggregation concepts.

Representation and Standards: In a complex interaction system, a common ground of terms and structures is absolutely necessary. A shared representation and a common knowledge base ease the dataflow within the system and avoid costly and error-prone transformation processes. The ontology-based representation combines formal dialogue and image semantics grammars with a RDF repository[1] using the SPARQL query standard.

Interface: Semantic representations and standards facilitate the design of interface structures. The desktop and touchscreen interface both communicate with the RDF repository while using the same SPARQL interface.

Encapsulation: Encapsulate the multimodal dialogue interface proper from the application backend as far as possible. This is the most important part. Multiple user interfaces (cf. next two subsections) can be connected to the dialogue system. The system also acts as middleware between the multimodal interface and the RDF repository.

Desktop Annotation and Example: For the semantic annotation on a regular desktop workstation we developed a new medical semantic annotation and retrieval tool RadSem [3]. It consists of a component that implements a method to annotate images and upload/maintain a remote RDF repository of the images and image semantics. For annotations, we reuse existing reference ontologies and terminologies. For anatomical annotations, we use the Foundational Model of Anatomy (FMA) ontology [6]. To express features of the visual manifestation of a particular anatomical entity or disease of the current image, we use fragments of RadLex [2]. Diseases are formalized using the International Classification of Diseases (ICD-10)[2]. Figure 1 shows the graphical user interface of the annotation tool. Images can be segmented into *regions of interest* (ROI). Each of these regions can be annotated independently with anatomical concepts (e.g., "lymph node"), with information about the visual manifestation of the anatomical concept (e.g., "enlarged"), and with a disease category using ICD-10 classes (e.g., "Nodular lymphoma" or "Lymphoblastic"). However, any combination of anatomical, visual, and disease annotations is allowed and multiple annotations of the same region are possible. In order to ease the task of finding appropriate annotations, we use *auto-completing* combo-boxes. While typing in a search term, concept names with matching prefixes are shown in a drop down box and can be selected. An diagram of the human body shows the current body region to simplify navigation in the data set.

---

[1]We use Sesame, see http://www.openrdf.org.

[2]http://www.who.int/classifications/apps/icd/icd10online

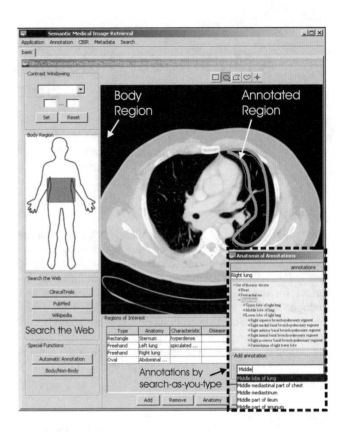

Figure 1. Desktop Interface of the Annotation Tool

Touchscreen Annotation and Retrieval: In this scenario, the user (radiologist) stands in front of the touchscreen installation. The interactive system is based on a generic framework for implementing multimodal dialogue systems (ODP platform, available at http://www.semvox.de). Technically, the generic framework follows a programming model which eases the interface to external third-party components (e.g., the automatic speech recognizer (ASR), natural language understanding (NLU), or synthesis component (TTS)) while using ontology concepts in a model-based design. We implemented several interfaces for the multimodal framework: the multimodal touchscreen interface, the event bus, the speech dialogue system, and the application backend as remote RDF repository (see figure 2). The *multimodal touchscreen interface* is implemented as a native application using a special window manager for pointing gestures on a touchscreen display. The client provides means to connect to the dialogue system via the *event bus*, to notify it of occurred events, to record and playback audio streams, and to render the received display data obtained from the *dialogue system*. The dialogue system contains an ontology-based rule engine for processing dialogue grammars and an external service connector to third-party components.

COMBINED SCENARIO

Consider a radiologist at his daily work. The diagnostic analysis of medical images typically concentrates around three questions: i) what is the anatomy? ii) what is the name of the body part? iii) is the statement normal or abnormal? To satisfy the radiologist's information need, he can formulate

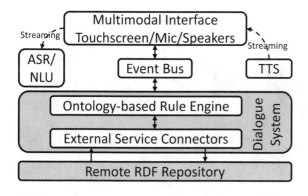

Figure 2. Multimodal Dialogue Architecture

the questions in natural speech when a respective image annotation exists, or, most importantly, we help him annotate the respective images and image regions during the patient finding process. Thereby, we give an account of the research questions (a) what kind of information is relevant for his daily tasks (a combination of annotation and retrieval) and (b) at what stage of the workflow should selected information items be offered and aggregated/annotated (in the finding process while using a touchscreen speech interface).

The mashup allows us to annotate medical images with ontology-based medical concepts (RadLex); these are directly transferred to a remote RDF Repository (Sesame). At this point, the radiologist can (1) access the images and image (region) annotations (a summary can also be synthesized), (2) complete them, and (3) refine existing annotations while using a multimodal dialogue shell. Finally, the RDF repository is updated again. See figure 3.

Multimodal Example Dialogue
1. **U:** "Show me the CTs, last examination, patient XY." (retrieval stage)
2. **S:** Shows corresponding patient CT study picture series.
3. **U:** "Show me the internal organs: lungs, liver, then spleen."
4. **S:** Shows patient images according to referral record.
5. **U:** "Annotate with lymph node enhancement (+ pointing gesture on region)"; so *lymphoblastic* (expert finding)."
6. **S:** "Region has been annotated."
7. **S:** "And replace the characteristic of the other by RadLex: shrunken."
8. **S:** "Region characteristic has been updated."
   → The radiologist switches to another patient with a broken finger and asks for a summary (retrieval stage).
9. **S:** "This is a summary of the fracture: ... "
10. **S:** "Five corresponding CTs will be displayed."
   → The radiologist switches to the differential diagnosis of the suspicious case (first patient), before the next organ (liver) is examined and the image annotations can be completed.

A variety of multimodal interaction patterns are implemented in this dialogue, e.g., the resolution of multimodal references. In (5), a deictic reference is resolved, whereby in (7) an exophoric reference is given by "the other". The command "annotate with" is an implicit reference in the context of the CT image in the current focus. Last but not least, the system builds an own anaphoric reference "corresponding" in (10). Interestingly, "five" is the result of a retrieval function that condenses the results to a single value, i.e., the amount of all results. Chai et al. [1] describe a probabilistic

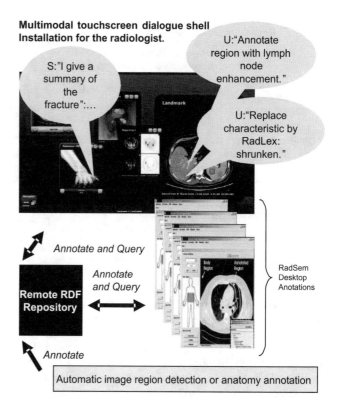

Figure 3. Combined Medical Scenario

approach to reference resolution where the referring expression is given by a user in speech inputs. We use a production rule system which decreases the relevance of specific referents in the course of the dialogue. In all these references, the ontological context plays the major role for ambiguity resolution (e.g., "the other" can only refer to a single second region annotation in the same image). Hence, the semantic knowledge acquisition process is not only necessary in order to capture the relevant image semantics, but also to allow the radiologist to engage in a natural speech dialogue.

KNOWLEDGE ACQUISITION PROCESS
Our knowledge acquisition process for annotating images is incremental. We will first describe the common ontologies used as representation basis, before explaining the function of the remote RDF repository as an incremental semantic knowledge base.

Common Ontologies: Figure 4 gives an overview of the general structure of our medical ontology hierarchy. It consists of several components each modeling different aspects of the domain of our use case. It is structured across four different layers, based on the assumption that those elements at higher levels are more stable, shared among more people, and thus change less often than those at lower levels. Wherever applicable, we reused background knowledge from existing ontologies. Our ontology hierarchy starts with the *Representational Ontologies*. They define the vocabulary with which the other ontologies are represented. The *Upper Ontology* describes very general concepts which are the same across all domains. The *Information Element Ontol-*

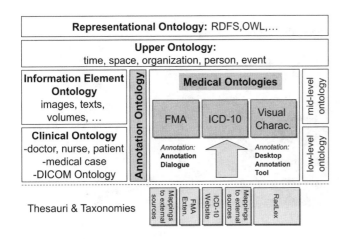

Figure 4. Medical Ontology Hierarchy

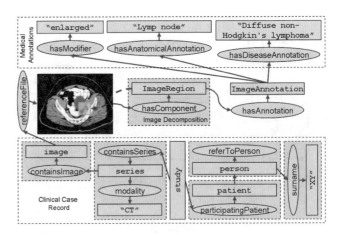

Figure 5. Result Example Graph

ogy represents the information elements that we want to annotate. These can be images, 3D image volumes, time series data and regions/segments of these. We use the *Clinical Ontologies* to specify roles and domain specific abstract data aggregations (like Electronic Health Records) from clinical practice. For example, the concepts nurse, doctor, patient, and medical case belong to these ontologies. For the *Medical Ontologies*, a separation into mid- and low-level ontologies is not so clear since they usually cover a broad spectrum of concepts ranging from very abstract ones like "heart" (which are not very likely to change) to macromolecules (which are updated and added frequently). In any case, the dialogue system maps the ASR output to one ontology instance (similar to [3]).

Remote RDF Repository: The semantic image repository, a triple store setup at the remote RDF repository site, is based on two VMWare instances which differentiate between development and production environment. (Both systems use the open source triple store Sesame.) A direct access to the RDF statements is possible while using the query language SPARQL. This allows us to specify queries of almost arbitrary complexity. They can span from patient metadata to image annotations to medical domain knowledge and are used to translate the dialogue questions.

Representation of Queries: The query example is an indirect translation of the clinician's dialogue question, "Show me the CTs, last examination, patient XY."

```
SELECT ?person ?patient ?imageURL
WHERE {
  ?person mao:surname ?var0 .
  FILTER (regex(?var0, "XY", "i")) .
  ?patient mdo:referToPerson ?person.
[...]
  ?series mdo:modality "CT".
  ?series mdo:containsImage ?image.
  ?image mdo:referenceFile ?imageURL.
[...]
}
```

Representation of Answers: Figure 5 shows a graphical representation of the graph that is retrieved when using the query.

CONCLUSIONS

We presented a dialogue mashup that integrates a multimodal interface for speech-based annotations of medical images and dialogue-based image retrieval with a semantic image annotation tool for manual annotations on a desktop computer. Incremental and dialogue-based image annotation can save large amounts of expert user time compared to outdated single-stage desktop-based approaches, as individual expert user tests show. We combined natural language processing and interface technology with ontology-based media annotations and ontology-based query interfaces. The common annotation and dialogue querying framework will now be tested in the University Hospital in Erlangen, where several medical students and radiologists will conduct usability studies with us.

Acknowledgements: This research has been supported by the research program THESEUS in the MEDICO project, which is funded by the German Federal Ministry of Economics and Technology under the grant number 01MQ07016. The responsibility for this publication lies with the authors.

REFERENCES

1. J. Y. Chai, P. Hong, and M. X. Zhou. A probabilistic approach to reference resolution in multimodal user interfaces. In J. Vanderdonckt, N. J. Nunes, and C. Rich, editors, *IUI*, pages 70–77. ACM, 2004.

2. C. P. Langlotz. Radlex: A new method for indexing online educational materials. *RadioGraphics*, 26:1595–1597, 2006.

3. M. Möller, S. Regel, and M. Sintek. Radsem: Semantic annotation and retrieval for medical images. In *Proc. of ESWC2009*, June 2009.

4. S. Oviatt. Ten myths of multimodal interaction. *Communications of the ACM*, 42(11):74–81, 1999.

5. N. Reithinger, D. Fedeler, A. Kumar, C. Lauer, E. Pecourt, and L. Romary. MIAMM - A Multimodal Dialogue System Using Haptics. In *Advances in Natural Multimodal Dialogue Systems*. Springer, 2005.

6. C. Rosse and J. L. V. Mejino. *Anatomy Ontologies for Bioinformatics: Principles and Practice*, volume 6, chapter The Foundational Model of Anatomy Ontology, pages 59–117. Springer, December 2007.

7. D. Sonntag, R. Engel, G. Herzog, A. Pfalzgraf, N. Pfleger, M. Romanelli, and N. Reithinger. *SmartWeb Handheld—Multimodal Interaction with Ontological Knowledge Bases and Semantic Web Services*, LNCS volume 4451, pages 272–295. Springer, 2007.

8. W. Wahlster. SmartKom: Symmetric Multimodality in an Adaptive and Reusable Dialogue Shell, *Proc. of the Human Computer Interaction Status Conference*, pages 47–62, Berlin, Germany, 2003. DLR.

Finding Your Way in a Multi-dimensional Semantic Space with Luminoso

Robert Speer
MIT Media Lab
Cambridge, MA, USA
rspeer@mit.edu

Catherine Havasi
MIT Media Lab
Cambridge, MA, USA
havasi@mit.edu

Nichole Treadway
MIT EECS
Cambridge, MA, USA
knt@mit.edu

Henry Lieberman
MIT Media Lab
Cambridge, MA, USA
lieber@media.mit.edu

ABSTRACT

We present Luminoso, a tool that helps researchers to visualize and understand a dimensionality-reduced semantic space by exploring it interactively. It also streamlines the process of creating such a space, by inputting text documents and optionally including common-sense background information. This interface is based on the fundamental operation of "grabbing" a point, which simultaneously allows a user to rotate their view using that data point, view associated text and statistics, and compare it to other data points. This also highlights the point's neighborhood of semantically-associated points, providing clues for reasons as to why the points were classified along the dimensions they were. We show how this interface can be used to discover trends in a text corpus, such as free-text responses to a survey.

Author Keywords

n-dimensional visualization, common sense, svd, natural language processing

ACM Classification Keywords

I.6.9 Simulation, Modeling, and Visualization: Visualization

General Terms

Design, Experimentation

INTRODUCTION

Language and language understanding plays a large role in the world of human-computer interaction. Users express their opinions en masse on surveys, in forums, and in dialogue systems, creating a need for systems which can help others visualize and understand the meaning of large collections of such data. When working with the semantics of natural language data, we often need to make sense of data that can be measured in many different dimensions – thousands of dimensions or more. This leaves two related problems: how to express the data in such a way that a computer can make sense of it, and how to further generalize the data so that a human can understand and work with it.

A straightforward computational way to model word co-occurrence among a corpus of documents, for example, is the "bag of words" model, where each document is described with the number of times each word occurs in it. This can easily create a feature space of tens of thousands of features, one for each word that appears in the corpus. In our work, we tend to use not just a bag of words for our semantic models; we also include background common sense knowledge from ConceptNet to provide the models with more "intuition" [7]. This, of course, makes the size of the feature space even larger. A common next step is to use dimensionality reduction to reduce the size of the feature space. Using an algorithm such as truncated SVD reduces the high-dimensional data to a vector space with many fewer dimensions, so that perhaps only 20 or 50 dimensions are necessary to represent the structure of the data.

These vectors, with 20 dimensions or so, are much easier to work with and compare to each other, and they make generalizations that give them more representational power than the original vector space. This is the core idea behind latent semantic analysis (LSA). When a semantic network of background common-sense knowledge is added in, it is also the idea behind AnalogySpace [8], a representation discussed further in the referenced paper.

Luminoso is an interactive application that aids a researcher in exploring these semantic spaces in a way that is intuitive for discovering semantic patterns from the dimensionality-reduced data. It enables them to create a vector space from a folder of input documents, using either an AnalogySpace-based model or a plain bag-of-words model, and then to explore that space interactively on a two-dimensional computer screen. The goal is to help the researcher understand their data by exploring this space, using an intuitive mouse operation we refer to as *grabbing*, which simultaneously lets them visualize the semantic neighborhood of the grabbed data point and use that point to N-dimensionally rotate their viewpoint. Other features of the interface help the user understand the space better, such as by using vectors with known semantics as "signposts".

Using Luminoso is a form of data mining that focuses on interactive exploration of the data. The importance of user participation in data mining has been observed by others [2], because an unsupervised algorithm to detect correlations in data will tend to find correlations that are spurious and irrelevant. An involved user, however, can guide this process

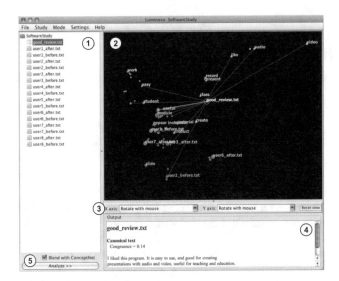

Figure 1. The overall interface to Luminoso, with labeled parts: (1) The document pane, allowing documents to be selected and new documents to be added to the study. (2) The viewer pane, providing a two-dimensional view into the SVD space. (3) The axis controls, with which the user can fix one or both of the axes to represent particular directions in the space. (4) The output pane, showing information about the selected point. (5) The "Analyze" button, which runs the SVD and updates the view. The "Blend with ConceptNet" option may be replaced with an interface for blending with any external data set in a future version.

toward relevant results by using their intuitive sense of what is interesting.

A use case for Luminoso that we focus on is to understand large quantities of people's suggestions and feedback at once. Survey forms frequently contain free-response spaces where people can write a paragraph to explain their views, but after a large enough number of people reply to such a survey, the free-response feedback tends to be ignored. Nobody has the time to read it all. By loading that data into Luminoso, however, one can visualize the major clusters of responses, view representative responses from each cluster, and even include known data about emotion or affect as signposts to understand the tone of the data.

CREATING THE SPACE

In order to display a representative space with Luminoso, we must first analyze the textual input used to create the space. We do this using a series of techniques designed to find patterns in natural language data – including patterns that appear within the input data, that come from a corpus of background knowledge, and that become apparent in the conjunction of both. We can use these techniques to draw general conclusions about the meaning of the data, cluster information in a variety of semantically informed ways, and make inferences across different types of information.

Natural language is a mode of input that can be handled particularly well by our techniques of common sense reasoning. We amplify the power of LSA, which is based only on the co-occurrence of words among the input documents, by including additional information about the se-

mantic connections between words from ConceptNet. The additional knowledge this provides can help to better organize the words and phrases that appear in the input documents into a semantic space. It can recognize when two different words are semantically close to each other, such as "audio" and "video", even when this is not apparent from the distribution of word occurrences in the documents. It can also distinguish words that appear in different topic areas that exist independently of the input data, such as "action verbs", "household items", "computer terminology", and "things people don't want". This kind of information gives the vector space more power to represent the rough meaning of a document.

Applying common sense

ConceptNet [6] is a semantic network created using the information collected by the collaborative Open Mind Common Sense project. Using a representation that expresses knowledge as relations between words and short phrases, it describes the meanings of the words people use in terms of other words. The information contained in ConceptNet includes relations between everyday objects ("Books are used for reading."), information on people's priorities and goals ("People want to be respected."), and affectual information ("Arguments make people angry.").

AnalogySpace [8] refers to the technique of reasoning over such a semantic network by representing it as a matrix and performing singular value decomposition on it. Information in ConceptNet can easily be transformed into a matrix representation that relates its nodes (concepts such as "dog" or "taking pictures") to their neighboring edges (features such as "...has four legs" and "...is used for enjoyment"). Singular value decomposition expresses these concepts and features in terms of a core set of *axes*, or principal components, that are selected by the algorithm to represent the most variance in the data. The effect is to summarize the provided common-sense knowledge in terms of its large-scale patterns, using moderate-sized vectors (typically 50 to 100 dimensions) to represent each concept and each feature.

INTERACTING WITH LUMINOSO

The first step in interacting with Luminoso is to load the input documents. The container that holds documents and their analysis is called a *study*. The user can use the document tree to add documents to analyze (or they can use their operating system to drop documents into the folder representing the study). One or more of these documents can be marked as "canonical", with effects that will be described later.

The user can choose whether to blend the data with ConceptNet in order to provide background information about semantics. Once the input is set up, the "Analyze" button creates the blend (if necessary), performs the SVD, and displays the results in the viewer window.

The "grabbing" operation

Many of the ways that a user interacts with the Luminoso visualization is centered around an operation we call "grab-

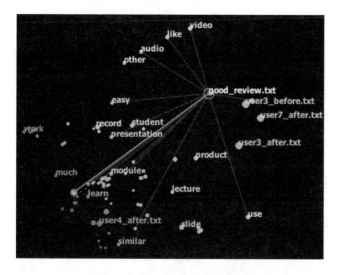

Figure 2. The selected point is a canonical document representing the expected content of a good review. The gray line connecting the point to the origin is always shown, as a reference for comparing with other points.

bing". This operation combines the action of selecting or focusing on a point with the ability to use that point to shift one's perspective in the N-dimensional space. The key idea is that a point you grab is a point you want to understand more about. Thus, not only does "grabbing" a point make information specific to that point visible in the interface, it also lets you find a projection of the data in which you can see the point and its related data better, following the visualization principle of focus-plus-context.

Grabbing a concept and dragging it uses that concept's position to change the projection of the data. It also displays information about the point being grabbed, such as the document's text if it represents a document, and blue lines representing the other terms and documents that the selected point is connected to.

While the point is being held, Luminoso changes the colors of all points to show their amount of correlation with the grabbed point. The colors represent the range of cosine similarity, from -1.0 to 1.0, on a "heat" scale: the most related points glow white or yellow, while unrelated points are a more neutral orange, and diametrically opposed points appear in dark red, as shown in Figure 2.

One way to benefit from this kind of interaction is to add documents with known semantic values into the space. These documents, known as canonical documents, can act as "signposts" when exploring the space. In the interface, a gray axis connects the canonical document point to the origin, informing you that a particular direction corresponds to a particular meaning, no matter what projection you are looking at at the time. When working with a data set of software reviews, for example, a useful canonical document to create is one you construct to represent an idealized good review. Having such a document with a known semantic value, other documents can then be compared to it – either by their

location, using the similarity color scale, or by actually locking the X or Y axis of the view on a canonical document.

Congruence

A common use for a canonical document is to test whether the input documents generally "agree" with it semantically. As a way of assisting experimentation, the interface presents a statistic called *congruence* in the info pane when a canonical document point is grabbed. Congruence measures how much that canonical document aligns with the other documents in the study, which can also be seen as describing whether that document is typical or atypical among the input data. This value can be compared between different runs of Luminoso or between different canonical documents.

The congruence of a document is calculated by comparing the distribution of cosine similarities between that document and all others, with the distribution of cosine similarities between all pairs of documents. The congruence is expressed as a Z-value (the difference in means over the standard error), so that it is scale-free.

GRAPHICALLY REPRESENTING N-DIMENSIONAL DATA

After using SVD to describe the data according to its principal components, one is left with vectors with a moderate number of dimensions. At this point, it is Luminoso's job to present this data understandably on a two-dimensional computer screen, so that the researcher can explore the resulting space, see whether it captures the patterns in the input data that it was intended to capture, and discover new patterns along the way.

The data can be represented as a sort of N-dimensional scatter plot. Each word, phrase, common-sense feature, or document in the input corresponds to a point in this space, which will use Luminoso to explore.

At any given time, Luminoso will project all the points in the N-dimensional space onto a two-dimensional plane, which the user can see a part of in a window on their computer screen. The user can change their viewport into this plane much like they would change their viewport in another 2-D interface such as Google Maps: the user can pan by dragging the right mouse button, or zoom using the mouse wheel or a laptop's equivalent "scrolling" gesture.

We represent each point as a small circle, at the appropriate location in the 2-D projection. The size of each circle increases with the number of times the item appears in the input, in order to draw attention to more significant inputs. Every point has a text label, describing a concept, a common-sense feature, or the name of a document, but not all of these labels can be displayed at once – the result would be incomprehensible clutter as many thousands of labels competed for screen space. Instead, only a subset of the labels are shown, determined interactively using the mouse pointer. The labels are chosen so as to set a maximum on the density of labels per unit of screen space. Additional points in a "full" area of the screen go unlabeled. The maximum density of labels decreases with the square of the distance from the mouse pointer. The effect is that, if the user wants to see the label of a point that is currently unlabeled, they can do so by moving the mouse closer to it.

Pressing the left mouse button will select the nearest point and "grab" it, which makes a number of useful things happen, one of which is that the user can use the grabbed point as a handle with which they can transform their view of the N-dimensional space. When the user grabs and drags a point, the view transforms (by stretching and rotating) in such a way that the point's projection onto the screen follows the mouse pointer, while the origin stays in the same place. The following section describes how this occurs.

Transforming the view

When using Luminoso, it is important to be able to fluidly change the projection of the points onto the screen, in order to see the structure of the data in many dimensions. Frequently, the user is looking for something specific – she wants to place a particular point in a particular location on the screen, and then examine where other points fall around it. For this reason, we allow the user to determine the projection by grabbing points and putting them in particular places on the screen.

The current projection can be described by two vectors in N-dimensional space: a vector $\mathbf{x}$ that represents the current X-axis, and a vector $\mathbf{y}$ that represents the current Y-axis. We add or subtract a small multiple of the grabbed point's vector from the X and Y vectors, which has the effect of stretching and rotating the space until the point is in the desired place. We also include an option to gradually re-orthogonalize the vectors over time, making these transformations into true rotations that preserve distances and angles.

Related work

Duffin and Barrett [4] describe an interface for rotating a projection, which differs from ours in that the user rotates the space by clicking and dragging a representation of an axis, instead of by clicking and dragging points in the space.

Buja et al. [1] describe the theory of projecting N-dimensional data onto a 2-dimensional view. This paper is largely concerned with creating "tours" of the space, or animations that trace a path between all possible projections of the N axes, but also mentions the ability to rotate particular axes using the "spider" interface.

Buja et al.'s paper provides a survey of existing software for multi-dimensional visualizations, such as GGobi [3], which performs singular value decomposition and allows visualizing the space using 2-D tours and spiders.

APPLICATIONS

Increasingly, the commercial world has become interested in computational linguistics as a way to solve the problem of understanding customer feedback. Focus groups, consumer surveys, and other opportunities to communicate with customers often involve understanding their spoken or written text and "reading between the lines" to understand the patterns. Thus blending common sense with customer-

generated free text can often yield insights that normal statistics miss.

The OMCS project worked with a large software company to analyze the data from their user tests [5]. In addition to rating various aspects of the software on a scale from 1 to 7, the users provided short-answer responses to various questions about their perception of the software. This free text data was considerably more expressive and informative than the numeric ratings, but the data was difficult to analyze automatically by computer. Blending with ConceptNet and exploring the results using Luminoso helped to draw general conclusions from the sparse data contained in the free text.

Luminoso can also be used to help users create and develop specialized semantic networks, such as biological or medical information resources, by providing a visualizer which shows the layout, focus, and coverage of the developing resource. As a semantic network gets larger, a multidimensional projection such as that provided by Luminoso becomes a crucial part of visualizing the data.

REFERENCES

1. A. Buja, D. Cook, D. Asimov, and C. Hurley. Computational methods for high-dimensional rotations in data visualization. In C. R. Rao, editor, *Handbook of statistics: Data mining and data visualization*, pages 391 – 415. Lavoisier, April 2005.

2. A. Ceglar, J. F. Roddick, and P. Calder. Guiding knowledge discovery through interactive data mining. pages 45–87, 2003.

3. D. Cook and D. F. Swayne. *Interactive and Dynamic Graphics for Data Analysis: With R and GGobi*. Springer, December 2007.

4. K. L. Duffin and W. A. Barrett. Spiders: A new user interface for rotation and visualization of n-dimensional point sets. In *In Proceedings of the Conference on Visualization (Los Alamitos*, pages 205–211. IEEE Computer Society Press, 1994.

5. C. Havasi. *Discovering Semantic Relations Using Singular Value Decomposition Based Techniques*. PhD thesis, Brandeis University, June 2009.

6. C. Havasi, R. Speer, and J. Alonso. ConceptNet 3: a flexible, multilingual semantic network for common sense knowledge. In *Recent Advances in Natural Language Processing*, Borovets, Bulgaria, September 2007.

7. C. Havasi, R. Speer, J. Pustejovsky, and H. Lieberman. Digital intuition: Applying common sense using dimensionality reduction. *IEEE Intelligent Systems*, July 2009.

8. R. Speer, C. Havasi, and H. Lieberman. AnalogySpace: Reducing the dimensionality of common sense knowledge. *Proceedings of AAAI 2008*, October 2008.

A Multi Faceted Recommendation Approach for Explorative Video Retrieval Tasks

David Vallet, Martin Halvey, David Hannah and Joemon M. Jose

Department of Computing Science
University of Glasgow
{dvallet, halvey, davidh, jj}@dcs.gla.ac.uk

ABSTRACT

In this paper we examine the use of multi faceted recommendations to aid users while carrying out exploratory video retrieval tasks. These recommendations are integrated into ViGOR (Video Grouping, Organisation and Retrieval), a system which employs grouping techniques to facilitate video retrieval tasks. Two types of recommendations based on past usage history are utilised, the first attempts to couple the multi-faceted nature of explorative video retrieval tasks with the current user interests in order to provide global recommendations, while the second exploits the organisational features of ViGOR in order to provide recommendations based on a specific aspect of the user's task.

Author Keywords: Video, collaborative, recommendation, exploratory, search.

ACM Classification Keywords: H.5.1 Multimedia Information Systems, H.5.3 Group and Organization Interfaces

General Terms: Design, Experimentation, Human Factors

INTRODUCTION

Current state of the art systems that are used to organise and retrieve video are insufficient for dealing with the vast and swiftly growing volumes of video that are currently being created. Specifically, there is a growing need to create tools and techniques to aid users in the difficult task of searching for video; this is particularly true online with the increasing growth of web-based video storage and search systems. Current video retrieval systems rely on textual descriptions or methods that use low-level descriptors to find relevant videos. Neither of these methods has proved to be sufficient to overcome the difficulties associated with video search. The difference between the low-level data representation of videos and the high level concepts that people associate with video, commonly known as the semantic gap, provides difficulties for using these low-level features. We propose that many of the problems associated with searching large collections of video can be eased through the use of recommendation techniques. Recommendation techniques offer a solution that allows systems to circumnavigate the problems associated with the semantic gap [3] and the unreliability of textual descriptions.

To that end, we have extended our existing recommendation techniques that exploit both the implicit and explicit actions involved in previous user searches [3]. This extension in itself is an innovation as it allows us to provide recommendations that support complex and explorative search tasks. However, the main goal of this work is to assist users in completing their difficult search tasks, by creating a predictive model that exploits both the implicit and explicit actions involved in previous user searches to provide multi-faceted recommendations. To achieve this we provide recommendations to users using two novel techniques: 1) a global recommendation that relates to the overall goal of the search task that they are carrying out and 2) a local recommendation that relates to the particular aspect of a search task that users are exploring at that time. We believe that our approach of modelling multiple aspects of user needs via implicit user interactions can result in improved user performance in terms of task completion and reduce the user effort involved in finding relevant videos.

SYSTEM DESCRIPTION

Figure 1 shows the ViGOR interface, ViGOR comprises of a search panel (A), results display area (B), workspace (C) and playback panel (D). The users enter a text based query in the search panel to begin their search. The result panel is where users can view the search results (b). Additional information about each video shot can be easily retrieved. Placing the mouse cursor over a video keyframe for longer than 3 seconds will result in any text associated with that video being displayed to the user (we will hence forth refer to this action as tooltip) (f). Users can play, pause, stop and navigate through the video as they can on a normal media player. Like the MediaGLOW [1] and EGO [4] systems, the most important element of ViGOR is the provision of a workspace (C). In MediaGLOW and EGO the workspace is only used to cluster images, however as has been discussed previously [2] the difficulties relating to video and image search are somewhat different and the approach of using groups in a workspace is an extremely useful solution for video search. Groups can be created by clicking on the create group button. Users must then select a textual label for the group. Drag-and-drop techniques allow the user to drag videos into a group or reposition the group in the workspace. Any video can belong to multiple groups simultaneously. The workspace is designed as a potentially ever expanding space to accommodate a large number of groups. Each group can also be used as a starting point for further search queries. Users can select particular videos and can choose to view an expansion of the group that contains similar videos based on a number of different features (d). As the ViGOR system uses the YouTube API as a backend, the features available to expand the group are mainly standard YouTube features. The interface offers three expansion options (e): 1) related videos; 2) videos from the same user 3) and text expansion, which is the result of a new search using text extracted from the selected videos.

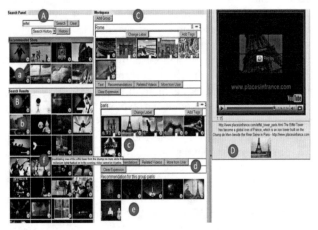

Figure 1. Interface of the video retrieval system

Extending ViGOR with recommendations

Some of the interface components of ViGOR allow users of the system to provide explicit and implicit feedback, which is then used to provide recommendations to future users. Explicit feedback is given by users adding a video to a group (c). Implicit feedback is given by users playing a video (D), highlighting a video using the tooltip (f) or submitting a search query (A). In this extended interface, users also have two options to receive recommendations. The users are presented with global recommendations of video shots that might match their search criteria based on their interactions (a). Users may also retrieve localised recommended videos via an extra expansion option available in the group (d, e). These recommendations are localised to each group and are based on the interactions of previous users with videos that the current user has selected.

A MULTI-FACETED RECOMMENDATION APPROACH

The goal of our recommendation approach is twofold: 1) to exploit the organisational functionalities provided by ViGOR as a new source of implicit and explicit information; and 2) to take into consideration the ambiguous and multi-faceted nature of explorative video tasks. We follow a graph-based approach for the representation of past user interactions, based on previous work [3]. In this approach, a user session s is represented as a set of queries Q_s, which were input by the user, the set of multimedia documents D_s the user accessed during the session, and a set of groups or aspects G_s the user created during the search session.

Queries, documents and groups are the nodes $N_s = Q_s \cup D_s \cup G_s$ of our graph representation $G_s = (N_s, W_s)$. The arcs of this graph representation, W_s, are of the form (n_i, n_j, u, w_s) and indicate that at least one action led the user u from the node n_i to n_j. Note that the only action that can lead to a group node $g \in G_s$ is the action of assigning a document node to the group. The weight value w_s represents the probability that node n_j was relevant to the user for the given session. This value is either given explicitly by the user, or estimated by means of the implicit evidence obtained from the interactions of the user with that node, following a previously developed implicit model [3].

Finally, all the session graphs are aggregated into a single graph $G = (N, W)$, where $N = \bigcup_s N_s$ and $W = \bigcup_s W_s$, which constitutes a global pool of usage information that collects all the implicit and explicit relevance evidence of users from past sessions. The nodes of the implicit pool are all the nodes involved in any past interaction $N = \bigcup_s N_s$, whereas the weighted links W are of the form (n_i, n_j, w), where $n_i, n_j \in N$ and w combines the probabilities of all the session-based values. As weight values are considered probabilities of relevance of the node n_j to the user, we opt for a simple aggregation of these probabilities, this is $w = \frac{\sum_s w_s}{|w_s|}$. Each link will thus represent the overall implicit (or explicit, if available) relevance that all users whom actions or soft links led from node n_i to n_j, gave to node n_j.

Global Recommendation

The global recommendation approach is based on the status of the current user session. As the user interacts with the system, a session graph $G_s = (N_s, W_s)$ is constructed, where in this case s is the current user's ongoing session. This graph is the input for the global recommendation algorithm presented next. This recommendation approach has the main goal of exploiting the implicit pool in order to retrieve similar nodes that were somewhat relevant to other users and. We define the global recommendation as:

$$gr(n, N_s) = \sum_{\substack{n_i \in N_s \\ p = n_i \leadsto n_j \to n \\ length(p) < D_{MAX}}} lr'(n_i) \cdot \xi^{length(p)-1} \cdot w(n_j, n)$$

Where $n_i \leadsto n_j$ denotes the existence of a path from n_i to n_j in the graph, taking link directionality into consideration. $n_j \to n$ means that n is adjacent to n_j. $w(n_j, n)$ is the probability weight, given by the implicit pool. $lr'(n_i) \in [0,1]$ is a weighing function that follows our previous implicit model [3] based on the relevance of this node to the outgoing user's session, obtained from the user's implicit and explicit feedback. $Length(p)$ is counted as the number of links in path p, which must be less than a maximum length D_{MAX}, set to 5 in for our evaluation. Finally, ξ is a length reduction factor, set to 0.8, which allows us to give more importance to those documents that directly follow the interaction sequence.

Local Group Recommendation

The local group recommendation focuses on a single group, and tries to recommend more documents that could aid the user in expanding the aspect of the task represented by this group. This recommendation approach exploits the representation in the implicit pool of the different aspects created by previous users. In this case, the local group recommendation tries to find similar aspects that previous users could have created and then rank their related documents. The input of the local group recommendation is the set of documents D_g that the current user has selected within an aspect group $g \in G$. On the first step of this approach, related aspect groups from the implicit pool are searched for, this is achieved by ranking the related groups panels $n_g \in G$ with the global recommendation approach, using the set of selected documents as input, and ranking only group nodes. Thus, the related groups can be ranked as $gr(n_g, D_g)$, were the local relevance of the selected documents is set to 1, i.e. $lr'(d_g) = 1, d_g \in D_g$. We limited the expansion distance D_{MAX} to 3, in order to constraint the search to more related groups.

On the second step of this approach, the implicit pool is exploited in order to rank the top nodes related to the set of ranked group nodes n_g. The ranking approach in this second step is to rank higher those documents that belong to more related aspects created by previous users. This ranking can be also implemented by tuning the global recommendation approach in the following way. The input of the ranking approach will be the ranked set of related groups, $n_g \in G$. The local relevance of the input is the ranking given by the previous step: $lr'(n_g) = gr(n_g, D_g)$. Thus, the final ranking is obtained from $gr(n, n_g)$.

EXPERIMENTAL METHODOLOGY

In order to evaluate our multi-faceted approach for video recommendation a user evaluation was conducted, the goal of which was to answer a number of research questions.

R1 Does the user performance improve or diminish with ViGOR that provides recommendations in comparison with the same system without recommendations? Are these recommendation approaches effective enough?

R2 Does the provision of recommendations impact on the effort involved for users in searching and exploring a video collection?

R3 Do the users use different types of recommendations, i.e. global recommendations vs. local recommendations, at different stages of their task or is the use of these tools independent of the stage of the task?

Experimental Design

For the purposes of this evaluation, the YouTube API was used to provide access to YouTube's video collection. Four simulated work task situations were created in order to provide broad, ambiguous, open ended tasks for the users. The system provides recommendations based on logs from a previous evaluation of ViGOR that also used YouTube [2] and four simulated tasks. The tasks defined in this evaluation had some similarities. However, the new tasks for this evaluation are broader than the tasks for the previous evaluation and might contain only some aspects related to the tasks from the previous evaluation. The four evaluated tasks are:

Task 1 Politics: A task of finding videos containing leading world figures.

Task 2 Travel: A task of finding video clips about locations in Europe that you would like to visit.

Task 3 Culture: A task of finding videos that illustrate Scottish culture.

Task 4 News: A task of finding videos illustrating news stories from 2008.

A between subjects design was adopted for this evaluation. Two systems were evaluated; ViGOR with and without recommendations. Tasks and interfaces were assigned using a Latin square design. The participants were given ten minutes training on their search system carrying out training tasks. Users had a maximum of 20 minutes to complete each task. For each participant their interaction with the system was logged and the videos they marked as relevant were stored. 24 participants took part in our evaluation. The participants consisted of 18 males and 6 females with an average age of 28.78 years (median: 28) and an advanced proficiency with English. The participants indicated that they regularly interacted with and searched for multimedia. They were paid a sum of £12 for their participation, which took approximately 2 hours.

RESULTS

Task Performance

A direct comparison between the two interfaces found that on average users of the recommendation system marked 27.15 videos as being relevant (i.e. add them to groups) in comparison with 19.6 videos for users of the system without recommendations. This is an increase of 38.47% in the number of retrieved relevant videos. In addition to this, users of the recommendation system created more groups or aspects of the task on average, 5.4, as opposed to 4.67 for the system without recommendations, this is an increase of 15.63%. It was found that system was a significant variable for the number of videos retrieved (2 way ANOVA, $F=6.94$, $p=0.01$). Overall, these results show that users are retrieving more videos and examining more aspects of their task using ViGOR with recommendations.

A further analysis was performed on the interaction logs. Users of ViGOR with recommendations have more user interactions with the system overall in comparison with users of the ViGOR baseline system. However, much of this difference is due to the increased use of the tooltip functionality of the recommendation system; this is a lightweight functionality which is of low cost for the user to carry out. In terms of more heavyweight user actions such as querying the system or viewing a video, there are small differences between the two systems, with no statistically significant differences. One major noticeable difference in the user interactions is the way that the users use the expansion functionalities. In the recommendation system the three YouTube related expansions are used less frequently than in the baseline ViGOR system. This is to be expected as this system offers one more expansion option. However, the new recommendation expansion is used almost as frequently as the YouTube related expansion. Users appear to find the recommendations useful and exploit this resource. A more direct comparison of the recommendation techniques shows that the global recommendation techniques are selected as relevant more often than the local recommendations.

Thus far we have seen that the user performance improves with the use of the recommendations, this addresses the first of our research questions, as we were able to exploit past noisy implicit information to benefit the users in their explorative and multi-faceted tasks. It has also been shown that the user interactions increase while using the recommendation system, however most of this increase is due to an increase in the use of the lightweight tooltip function, this may just be as a result of the extra results and options that are presented to the users of the recommendation system. This addresses our second research question pertaining to user effort.

User Interactions

In an attempt to gain a further insight into the differences between the user interactions with the two types of recommendation approaches, we plotted a cumulative distribution for selecting each type of recommendation against time (see Figure 2). We do not show any of the other three expansions actions in this figure, as they follow a similar distribution to the local recommendation. A pair wise t-test revealed that the differences between the recommendation distributions were statistically significant. Users select examples from the global recommendations early in the task, it is not until later in the task that the users appear to select examples from the local expansions and add them to groups. This illustrates a difference in user behaviour, it appears that at the beginning users are more interested in

the overall global task, but as the task progresses users become more interested in the details of each aspect, thus providing an answer for our third research question.

DISCUSSION AND CONCLUSIONS

In this paper we have presented our approach for providing multi faceted recommendations by extending our implicit feedback recommendation approach [3]. In order to evaluate this approach for providing recommendations and indeed the concept of multi-faceted recommendations for videos search, the recommendation algorithms were integrated into our ViGOR system. The unique organisational features available in ViGOR allow richer and multi-faceted recommendations.

The results of our evaluation have highlighted the promise of multi-faceted recommendations for video search tasks. Our recommendation approach based on implicit feedback coupled with an innovative video search interface has improved user performance and highlighted the promise of multi-faceted recommendations based on collaborative implicit feedback for alleviating many problems associated with online video search, and indeed could be applied to numerous other video search paradigms.

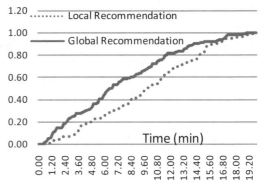

Figure 2. Cumulative distribution of selection of recommendations over time

Acknowledgements. This research was supported by the European Commission under contract FP6-027122-SALERO and by the Spanish Ministry of Science and Education (TIN2008-06566-C04-02).

REFERENCES

1. Girgensohn, A., Shipman, F., Wilcox, L., Turner, T., and Cooper, M. MediaGLOW: organizing photos in a graph-based workspace. In *Proc.* IUI 2009, 419 - 424.

2. Halvey, M., Vallet, D., Hannah, D., and Jose, J. M. ViGOR: a grouping oriented interface for search and retrieval in video libraries. In *Proc. JCDL 2009*, 87-96.

3. Hopfgartner, F., Vallet, D., Halvey, M., and Jose, J. Search trails using user feedback to improve video search. In *Proc. ACM MM 2008*, 339-348.

4. Urban, J. and Jose, J.M. A Personalised Multimedia Management and Retrieval Tool. In the International Journal of Intelligent Systems, 21(7), 725-745, 2006.

Evaluating Automatic Warning Cues for Visual Search in Vascular Images

Boris W. van Schooten
Faculty of EEMCS
University of Twente
schooten@ewi.utwente.nl

Betsy M.A.G. van Dijk
Faculty of EEMCS
University of Twente
bvdijk@ewi.utwente.nl

Anton Nijholt
Faculty of EEMCS
University of Twente
anijholt@ewi.utwente.nl

Johan H.C. Reiber
Leiden University
Medical Center
j.h.c.reiber@lumc.nl

ABSTRACT

Visual search is a task that is performed in various application areas. Search can be aided by an automatic warning system, which highlights the sections that may contain targets and require the user's attention. The effect of imperfect automatic warnings on overall performance ultimately depends on the interplay between the user and the automatic warning system. While various user studies exist, the different studies differ in several experimental variables including the nature of the visualisation itself. Studies in the medical area remain relatively rare, even though there is a growing interest in medical screening systems. We describe an experiment where users had to perform a visual search on a vascular structure, traversing a particular vessel linearly in search of possible errors made in an automatic segmentation. We find that only the case in which the warning system generates only false positives improves user time and error performance. We discuss this finding in relation to the findings of other studies.

Author Keywords

visual search, automatic warning system, magnetic resonance angiography, image segmentation

ACM Classification Keywords

H.5.2 Information Interfaces and Presentation: User Interfaces—*Graphical user interfaces (GUI)*

General Terms

Human Factors, Performance, Reliability

INTRODUCTION

Visual search tasks are performed in various areas: finding weapons in x-rayed baggage [4], targets from a moving vehicle [14] or on aerial photographs [10, 11], cancer areas in mammograms [5, 9], polyps in colonoscopy [6], or low-credibility areas in automatic medical image segmentations [8, 7]. In many cases, automatic warning systems have been devised that highlight potential targets. Such systems are

imperfect: failure may be either a false positive (false alarm) or false negative (a missed item). A detection system may be tuned to produce either more false positives or false negatives. Some medical systems can be tuned to produce near zero false positives or negatives [6, 9]. Especially the absence of false negatives is often seen as a prerequisite for their medical applicability.

However, the presence of failures (especially false alarms) in alarm systems (for both visual search tasks and other tasks) are known to cause problems for users, such as over- or under-reliance. While various studies have been made, experimental variables vary widely among different application areas: the presence or absence of a moving scene or navigation, the prevalence of false positives or negatives, whether the search is self-terminating or not (that is, whether the search ends when the target is found), task difficulty (examined in [10]), target rarity [4], the level of information about the system given to the users, and of course the task itself, which varies widely in nature. While some of these variables have been examined, most have not, and we can expect different applications to have quite different outcomes. These are too many variables to examine all at once, and the research coverage remains as yet spotty. Examining different application areas is still a very meaningful exercise.

We examine a new application involving vascular image analysis, more specifically, 3D magnetic resonance angiography (MRA) segmentation, as performed routinely by radiologists. Vascular segmentation involves determining the thickness of the inside of the vessel (the lumen), which enables analysis of possible pathological narrowings or widenings. While a vessel is tortuous, it can basically be navigated linearly (from one end to the other), as can for example the colon in colonoscopy. So, the task can be characterised as relatively easy, non-self-terminating, involving simple navigation, with users given information about presence of false positives or negatives. We examine in particular the effect of the presence of false positives versus false negatives.

RELATED WORK

Studies of generic self-terminating target finding tasks with target highlighting found that imperfect highlighting often increased rather than decreased overall user response time, due to suboptimal increase in response time for the cases where the wrong target was highlighted [3, 12]. For some non-self-terminating tasks, users were also found to spend more time double-checking the data in case of false positives, resulting in increased overall response times in the presence of warnings [1]. Overall, user performance is suboptimal, even when users have a good estimate of the system's reliability [2, 11].

Wickens et al. [13] found that distinction of visual elements by highlighting helps focussed attention (attention to one target) but hinders integrative attention (where all targets need to be interpreted in an integrated way). Another detrimental effect is called *attention tunneling*, which means the highlights distract the user from seeing other elements in the scene. Yeh et al. [14] found that, even if highlighting of one target served to predict with 100% accuracy a target in the vicinity rather than the highlighted target itself, performance worsened.

Studies on the reliance (or trust) of users on (visual and non-visual) automatic warnings as related to the failure rate of the warning system has been studied fairly extensively. One common finding is that false positives are more damaging to trust and hence performance than false negatives [10]. Maltz et al. [10] also finds that target cueing works best if the targets are otherwise very difficult to detect.

None of these studies were conducted in the medical domain. One of the rare medical studies in this area, done by Freer et al. [5], seems to contradict some of these findings. It indicates a positive effect on clinical outcome in a mammogram-reading study with as much as 97.4% false positives. Freer et al. use a double-reading scheme, taken from medical practice, but used by none of the other studies: each mammogram is first examined as a plain image, before the warning highlights are shown, reducing any possible effect of attention tunneling. Additionally Freer et al.'s task is difficult (experts miss 50% or more of targets), unlike most of the other experiments. This shows that studies in the medical domain may have different outcomes due to differences in experimental variables, which are implicitly assumed in the other domains. This makes it worthwhile to study other medical tasks more closely.

EXPERIMENTAL DESIGN

Our task consists of checking the correctness of automatic segmentations of vessels in MRA scans. A typical segmentation algorithm determines a vessel's location by drawing a line through the (density) center of the vessel, called the centerline. Then, it determines the thickness of the inside of the vessel (the lumen) based on the centerline.

We used a software phantom approach. The MRA data is artificially generated, along with segmentations with artificially generated segmentation errors. This way it is easy to generate dozens of cases with a clear distinction between correct and erroneous, an unambiguous ground truth, and similar difficulty levels. A vessel is constructed using a sum of sine waves. Three distractors vessels were added in each phantom. Thickness of the vessel was varied in a stylized manner with thinner and thicker areas. When looking at a cross-section, density in the center of the vessel was highest, gradually lowering towards the boundaries of the vessel, and

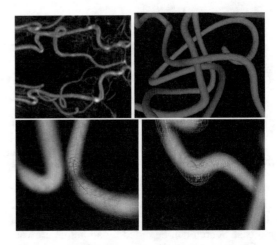

Figure 1. Illustration of the visual stimuli used. Top left: real-life data. Top right: typical software phantom as used in our experiment. Bottom: stimuli as presented to the users. Bottom left: with thickness error in the center and marked as potential error. Bottom right: with veering error in the center but not marked.

zero outside of the vessel. No noise or other distractors were added, neither were bifurcations present. See figure 1.

Errors are simply defined as a deviation between the segmentation and the densest parts of the volume. Only three error types exist: a veering away of the centerline and segmentation from the vessel, the segmentation being thinner than the vessel, and the segmentation being thicker.

We use direct volume rendering (DVR) to visualise the volume data, with a yellow line indicating the centerline, and a brown mesh indicating the segmentation. The warning system highlights parts of the centerline and mesh in red to indicate possible errors.

We chose controls to be as simple as possible without sacrificing user control. Control is with the mouse only. One major choice we made is to base navigation on the centerline. The camera is always centered around a point on the centerline, and rotates so that the vessel is viewed from the side. The centerline is navigated by rolling the mouse wheel, or by clicking on a centerline point with the middle mouse button (MMB). The user can specify relative rotation using a two-axis valuator scheme controlled with the right mouse button (RMB). The camera is zoomed in close to the vessel so details can be seen clearly. The user can simply click on a section of the vessel with the left mouse button (LMB) to indicate a segmentation error. The appropriate section is highlighted in green.

We compare user performance (time taken and error rate) for the following four conditions:

1. NONE - no suspicious areas (baseline)

2. PAR (paranoid suspicious areas) yields only false positives - the user only has to search within the suspicious areas

3. CON (conservative suspicious areas) yields only false

negatives - the user can simply click the suspicious areas but has to search the rest for missed errors

4. PER (perfect detection) - while not realistic, this indicates an upper limit to performance of suspicious areas. It is basically an interaction task rather than an interpretation task.

Note that it is not easy to compare a false positives condition with a false negatives one in absolute terms, because the situation is asymmetric. What we can do is compare if either are faster than NONE. We chose conditions to have 6-8 errors with 1-2 false positives or negatives.

We used a within-subjects design. All users received the same set of software phantoms in the same order, but with different, randomly ordered and counterbalanced, conditions. The users had to complete 6 trials per condition, totaling 24 trials. Total duration of the main experiment was 10-20 minutes. A short subjective survey was conducted at the end. The survey questions we asked are the following:

usedsuspar (did you use the paranoid-mode suspicious areas to find errors?) {4:All the time, 3:some of the time, 2:learned to ignore them during the session, 1:ignored them}
usedsuscon (did you use the conservative-mode suspicious areas to find errors?) {4:All the time, 3:some of the time, 2:learned to ignore them during the session, 1:ignored them}
suspar (5-point scale, from strongly prefer PAR (5) to strongly prefer NONE (1))
suscon (5-point scale, from strongly prefer CON (5) to strongly prefer NONE (1))
susparcon (5-point scale, from strongly prefer PAR (5) to strongly prefer CON (1))

Because we used somewhat stylised models, medical laypersons could easily do the task. Since our research concerns usability involving novel interaction techniques, we asked experts on user interfaces rather than medical experts to perform our experiment. We recruited 8 unpaid subjects from the Human Media Interaction department of our CS faculty. Age ranged between 25 and 51; 7 were male and 1 female. They had already done a similar experiment several days earlier, involving DVR visualisation, with and without suspicious area highlighting, along with two other visualisations. This meant they already had experience with the visualisation and controls. Training for this experiment consisted of a 4-minute interactive tutorial, explaining the differences between the four conditions. Users were told whether to expect false positives or negatives, but not how many of these they could expect. The sessions were conducted in a quiet room, with the users seated at a distance of about 70 cm from the 24" display. An experimenter was seated behind them.

RESULTS

We shall begin with time performance. We expect time performance effects to be multiplicative rather than additive, so we transformed the data using the log transform. We used a second transformation to increase statistical sensitivity. It is based on the fact that the sequence of software phantoms used for the trials was the same for all users. We divided the time for each trial by the overall average of that trial over all users (note that all conditions occurred equally often for each trial in the sequence). This has the effect of normalising for variations in trial difficulty.

Though PER is meant as a baseline condition, we first used repeated-measures ANOVA with Sidak posthoc analysis over all conditions including PER. The ANOVA yields $F(3, 21) = 214.052, p < 0.0005$. PER is, as we might expect, very significantly different from the others: $p < 0.0005$. It is almost twice as fast as the NONE condition, which shows that there may be quite a lot to gain from suspicious areas. We disregard it from here on.

We performed a second repeated-measures ANOVA on the remaining three conditions, which yields $F(2, 14) = 5.172, p = 0.021$. A Sidak post-hoc analysis reveals that PAR is significantly faster than NONE ($p = 0.038$). The other comparisons (NONE-CON, CON-PAR) are not significant ($p >= 0.391$). This shows that PAR does provide benefit. Mean performance over all users is given below.

condition:	NONE	CON	PAR	PER
mean trial time (sec):	36.8	35.0	34.0	19.7

We analysed error rate by means of a χ^2 table, assuming that trials are independent events. User errors (mistakes) were very rare events, with a total of 17 mistakes, which makes them difficult to analyse. We found that three mistakes resulted from a cognitive slip, as admitted by the user in question, resulting in 2 false positives and 1 false negative in a particular short section of vessel under the PAR condition. These were the only false positives in the dataset.

We classify trials into two classes: trials with one or more mistakes and trials without mistakes. See the table below.

cond.	total trials	total segm. errors	total nr. mistakes	total nr. trials w/ mistakes
none	48	336	6	6
con	48	336	7	5
par	48	336	1 (+3)	1 (+1)

It appears that the PAR condition might result in fewer mistakes, but the values are a bit low for a χ^2 analysis. If we include the cognitive slip, a chi-square analysis on trials with mistakes v trials without mistakes results in $\chi^2(2, N = 144) = 2.198, p = 0.333$. If we consider deletion of the cognitive slip valid, the same analysis results in $\chi^2(2, N = 144) = 3.818, p = 0.148$, and one on total number of user mistakes v total number of correctly selected segmentation errors yields $\chi^2(2, N = 1008) = 4.491, p = 0.106$. While we cannot say that PAR produces significantly less mistakes than the other conditions, it appears at least that CON and PAR do not seem to result in *more* mistakes than NONE.

For a summary of the subjective survey results, see table 1. The sample is a bit small for serious statistical analysis, but it is clear that all users used the suspicious areas, and mostly

variable	nr. users:	1	2	3	4	5	average
usedsuspar		-	-	3	5		3.62
usedsuscon		-	-	1	7		3.88
suspar		-	-	-	4	4	4.50
suscon		-	-	2	1	5	4.38
susparcon		-	2	-	3	3	3.88

Table 1. Subjective variable statistics. Number of users who selected each item on each survey scale, and the average value.

preferred them. We can at least conclude that users did not find the suspicious area marking annoying. There was little difference in preference between PAR and CON, although PAR was preferred more often than CON, and most users would prefer it over CON as well. However, a larger sample would be required to test if there is a significant difference here.

CONCLUSIONS

We conducted an experiment involving the manual verification of automatic segmentations of MRA images, with help of an imperfect automatic warning system that highlights possible errors in the segmentation. We compared user time and error performance as well as subjective preference for the following conditions: no warning highlights, only false positives (paranoid), only false negatives (conservative), and perfect highlighting. We found that users perform significantly faster with paranoid highlighting than with no highlighting, and they make insignificantly less errors. There were no other significant differences. Users also prefer suspicious areas over no suspicious areas, and appear to prefer paranoid over conservative highlighting.

This contradicts most previous findings, which generally indicate that especially paranoid highlighting is often detrimental for both speed and error rate. While false positive rate was fairly low (about 20%), other experiments demonstrated a detrimental effect for similar rates [1, 14]. Somehow, it appears our results more closely follow a rationally based cognitive model: for the false positives case users will have to search only the marked areas, and hence, search space is much reduced, in contrast to the false negatives case, where it is less reduced. Our contradictory result cannot be explained by high difficulty or low target prevalence (the task was easy, as is illustrated by the low error rate). A possible explanation is the system reliability information given to the users. However, previous studies also showed a detrimental effect under similar reliability levels, when the users did have an accurate estimate of system reliability [2, 11]. The difference in outcome may alternatively be explained by a difference in task domain or visual stimuli. We argue that further experiments will be necessary to more thoroughly cover this research area.

ACKNOWLEDGEMENTS

This work was carried out under the NWO (Netherlands Organization for Scientific research) Multivis project (N 643.100.602), which is part of the NWO VIEW program.

REFERENCES

1. S. R. Dixon, C. D. Wickens, and J. S. McCarley. On the independence of compliance and reliance: are automation false alarms worse than misses? *Human factors*, 49(4):564–72, 2007.

2. N. Ezer, A. D. Fisk, and W. A. Rogers. Age-related differences in reliance behavior attributable to costs within a human-decision aid system export. *Human Factors*, 50(6):853–863, 2008.

3. D. L. Fisher and K. C. Tan. Visual displays: The highlighting paradox. *Human Factors*, 31(1):17–30, 1989.

4. M. S. Fleck and S. R. Mitroff. Rare targets are rarely missed in correctable search. *Psychological Science*, 18(11):943–947, 2007.

5. T. W. Freer and J. M. Ulissey. Screening mammography with computer-aided detection: prospective study of 12,860 patients in a community breast center. *Radiology*, 220:781–786, 2001.

6. W. Hong, F. Qiu, and A. Kaufman. A pipeline for computer aided polyp detection. *IEEE Transactions on Visualization and Computer Graphics*, 12(5):861–868, 2006.

7. K. Levinski, A. Sourin, and V. Zagorodnov. 3D visualization and segmentation of brain MRI data. In *GRAPP 2009*, pages 111–118, 2009.

8. J. H. Levy, R. R. Broadhurst, S. Ray, E. L. Chaney, and S. M. Pizer. Signaling local non-credibility in an automatic segmentation pipeline. In *Proceedings of the International Society for Optical Engineering meetings on Medical Imaging, Volume 6512*, 2007.

9. F. J. López-Aligué, I. Acevedo-Sotoca, A. García-Manso, C. J. García-Orellana, and R. Gallardo-Caballero. Microcalcifications detection in digital mammograms. In *EMBC 2004, vol.3*, 2004.

10. M. Maltz and D. Shinar. New alternative methods of analyzing human behavior in cued target acquisition. *Human Factors*, 45(2):281–295, 2003.

11. S. Rice. Examining single and multiple-process theories of trust in automation. *Journal of General Psychology*, 136(3):303–319, 2009.

12. F. P. Tamborello and M. D. Byrne. Adaptive but non-optimal visual search behavior with highlighted displays. *Cognitive Systems Research*, 8(3):182–191, 2007. Cognitive Modeling.

13. C. D. Wickens and A. D. Andre. Proximity compatibility and information display: Effects of color, space, and objectness on information integration. *Human Factors*, 32(1):61–77, 1990.

14. M. Yeh and C. D. Wickens. Display signaling in augmented reality: Effects of cue reliability and image realism on attention allocation and trust calibration. *Human Factors*, 43(3):355–365, 2001.

Automatic Configuration of Spatially Consistent Mouse Pointer Navigation in Multi-Display Environments

Manuela Waldner, Christian Pirchheim, Ernst Kruijff, Dieter Schmalstieg
Institute for Computer Graphics and Vision, Graz University of Technology, Austria
{waldner | pirchheim | kruijff | schmalstieg}@icg.tugraz.at

ABSTRACT

Multi-display environments combine displays of various form factors into a common interaction space. Cross-display navigation techniques have to provide transitions to move the mouse pointer across display boundaries to reach distant display locations. A spatially consistent description of display relationships thereby supports fluid cross-display navigation. In this paper, we present two spatially consistent navigation techniques for seamless cross-display navigation in multi-user multi-display environments. These navigation techniques are automatically configured from a spatial model of the environment, which is generated in a camera-assisted calibration step. We describe the implementation in a distributed system and present results of a comparative experiment.

Author Keywords

multi-display environment, cross-display mouse navigation.

ACM Classification Keywords

H.5.2 Information Interfaces and Presentation: User Interfaces—*Input devices and strategies (e.g., mouse, touchscreen)*

General Terms

Design, Experimentation, Human Factors

INTRODUCTION

Inexpensive large-format displays, such as large monitors and projectors, make it attractive to combine personal workspaces into an interactive teamspace operated by multiple collaborators. Such a multi-display environment (MDE) can be composed of displays of various form factors arranged arbitrarily in the environment.

To allow all users to operate all display spaces in the environment, cross-display navigation techniques to redirect user input to distant displays are required. Previous work has shown that cross-display mouse pointer navigation perfor-

mance is affected by discontinuities in the spatial display arrangement [10, 7] and the user's location within the environment [6, 8]. *Spatially consistent* mouse pointer navigation techniques aim to accommodate for these discontinuities by creating cross-display *transitions* taking the spatial display arrangement into account. However, cross-display navigation solutions so far have either been restricted to a fixed environment with manual configuration of transitions [6] or by tracking the location of the user in a known display environment [8]. Ad-hoc usage of MDEs requires that users do not need to configure the navigation space manually while still having the flexibility to re-assemble the MDE according to their preferences. It also requires that users are not enforced to apply expensive and obtrusive head-worn tracking systems.

In this paper, we present methods for automatic generation of spatially consistent mouse pointer navigation frames and cross-display transitions for multi-user MDEs. To obtain the navigation frames, we rely on a three-dimensional model of the display environment, obtained in an automatic display registration process, and a user location estimation which does not require the user to wear head tracking devices. We implemented and evaluated two spatially consistent mouse pointer navigation techniques: *free navigation*, which creates 2D navigation frames from the estimated user locations and *path navigation*, which creates point-to-point mappings between virtually connected edge regions.

RELATED WORK

A popular approach to achieve seamless cross-display navigation is to virtually connect ("stitch") adjacent display edges, such as in MightyMouse [4], PointRight [6], Desktop Rover[1], and Synergy[2]. They all require the user to specify edge connections offline manually. In contrast to stitching, MouseEther [1] aims to minimize the visual discontinuity in motor space introduced by monitor bezels and display size-resolution mismatches on multi-monitor setups. Perspective Cursor [8] extends this approach to heterogeneous multi-display environments. As their display setup is non-planar, they require a 3D model of the environment and employ 3 DOF head-tracking to retrieve the user's position in the environment. Instead of implicitly triggering a transition by crossing connected display edges, pointer warping techniques (*e.g.* [2]) and interactive miniature views (*e.g.* [4, 3]) allow the user to redirect input explicitly to a target display.

---

[1] http://www.neslosoftware.com/desktopRover.html
[2] http://synergy2.sourceforge.net/

SPATIAL DISPLAY MODEL

To generate mouse pointer navigation frames automatically, the system needs to know the spatial display topology, as well as the user locations towards the displays for location-aware navigation control. Creating 3D models of display surfaces is a common technique for smart projector systems (*c.f.*, [5]) which usually employ the geometric information solely for compensation of projected imagery. However, this information has also high value for interaction techniques in MDEs – in particular for mouse pointer navigation. Our camera-assisted calibration step registers multiple projected displays, as well as monitors, to a common metric coordinate system and approximates display geometries by a polygonal model. If display arrangements change, as devices are added or removed, users can request a partial re-calibration. A full calibration step typically takes less than a minute.

Since we are interested in computer operation using conventional mouse and keyboard, it is reasonable to assume that users are seated at a known desk with a private "home" display. This assumption works well for conference rooms and open-plan offices. By default, monitors with connected mouse pointers are treated as private displays, accessible only for the host mouse pointer. Projected displays are public. We estimate user head locations to be at a certain distance from their home display's center with a viewing direction perpendicular to the display surface. As each user is uniquely associated with a personal mouse, our system is provided with a simple but sufficient identity management.

CROSS-DISPLAY NAVIGATION TECHNIQUES

Conventional stitching of desktops uses a very simple model of the display space. Displays are assumed to lie in one plane, with no gaps and no rotation between displays, as well as uniform resolution. Since this is clearly not adequate to represent more complex MDEs, Perspective Cursor [8] attempts to replace stitching with mouse navigation that operates in a perspectively correct space around the user. It builds on the idea of a mouse *ether* [1] accounting for the movement in the space between displays. This results in a perceived continuous movement in the real world, and was found to improve performance and pointing accuracy.

However, switching from a stitched planar to perspective navigation also incurs a number of problems: Due to perspective foreshortening, the mouse cursor will be subject to nonlinear control/display gain, in particular for displays viewed at a strongly oblique angle. In addition, if the user has to turn head and body to operate a (horizontal) display, this results in a dynamic change of the perspective navigation map or a non-intuitive mouse movement direction when using a static map. Occluded display regions and displays facing away from the user are inaccessible due to the perspective representation. Finally, perspective cursor control requires the user to navigate display-less space blindly. However, recent research [7] has shown that warping the mouse pointer across large gaps between displays is superior to a mouse ether approach. This finding is particularly important for multi-user setups, which often employ spatially separated displays (*e.g.*, a conference table in the center and surrounding wall displays). These considerations motivated us to investigate alternatives for navigation in complex MDE layouts, which combine the use of three-dimensional structure with the efficiency of warping.

Free Navigation

In a nutshell, *free navigation* works similar to perspective cursor navigation, but warps the mouse cursor across display-less space. First, a perspective map of all displays is computed from the estimated user location. The map is set up in such a way that navigation on the home display is not altered by this procedure. However, navigation in all other displays is subject to perspective effects. At runtime, each incoming mouse motion event is evaluated relative to this perspective mapping and converted to the target display's native pixel coordinates using per-display homographies. Unlike perspective cursor navigation, the user cannot navigate in display-less space. Instead, when leaving the display, the last motion on the source display is extrapolated to a ray. If this ray intersects other displays' edges, the intersection point closest to the current position is converted to the target display's device coordinates and input redirection is triggered (Figure 1).

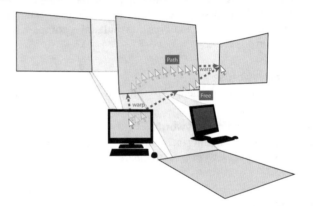

Figure 1. Exemplary mouse pointer paths for free navigation and path navigation. The areas connecting adjacent displays represent edge connections for path navigation

Path Navigation

Path navigation combines aspects of stitching and free navigation. Like stitching, navigation within a display operates in the normal 2D space of the display without any perspective effect. Like free navigation, it uses the spatial display model as reference frame to compute the mouse pointer paths. However, it does not incorporate the user perspective but rather creates a common navigation frame valid for all user locations. Warping across display boundaries is based on a set of edges connecting displays pair-wise in 3D (Figure 1). The connection algorithm starts by considering all possible display pairs and their closest edges. For each candidate pair, connecting edge intervals are computed from normal projections of the closest edges' corner points on the adjacent edge and vice versa. If the resulting interval is empty or smaller than a given threshold on both edges, the candidate is discarded. Otherwise, the normal distance of the edges at the midpoint of the intersection interval is used as a proximity measure. Spatial properties of adjacent displays, such as connection of non-opposite edges or normal vectors facing away from each other, lead to penalties of the proximity score. Overlapping edge intervals are prioritized according to their proximity scores, so intervals with lower scores are trimmed or removed. Connected edge intervals between neighboring displays are visualized by pair-wise color-coded lines along the connected edge intervals.

The main advantage of path navigation is that it works equally well from any location within the environment and thereby creates a consistent navigation space for multiple users. Table 1 shows a continuum of cross-display navigation techniques from conventional stitching to Perspective Cursor [8].

Navigation technique	movement across displays	reference frame	movement in display
Perspective cursor	continuous	spatial	perspective
Free navigation	warping	spatial	perspective
Path navigation	warping	spatial	standard
Stitching	warping	device	standard

Table 1. Comparison of cross-display navigation techniques.

Implementation

Our mouse pointer navigation framework is implemented in the distributed MDE framework *Deskotheque* [9]. Input redirection is based on an extended version of the open-source mouse pointer sharing tool *Synergy*. In its original implementation, Synergy enables a single mouse and keyboard pair to be shared across multiple machines based on a client-server framework architecture. We added two major extensions to Synergy. As first extension, we implemented a navigation framework on top of the Synergy server which maintains the spatial descriptions of display relationships. As each mouse device is controlled by its own server process, the spatial descriptions of display relationships can be issued separately for each mouse pointer and user, respectively. This assures that each user is provided the appropriate 2D map for free navigation and that multiple users can employ different navigation modes simultaneously. As second extension, we added a coordination of multiple Synergy client instances on public host machines for the X Windows implementation. Multiple pointers on a single machine are coordinated by a "floor control", sequentially assigning the exclusively available core pointer functionality to the present pointers. Multiple pointers are rendered by a plug-in for the *Compiz*[3] window manager.

EXPERIMENT

We compared the implemented navigation techniques in a single-user experiment on a representative multi-user MDE. Twenty users (11 male, 9 female, aged 23 to 48) participated in the experiment. No participant was familiar with the system or the employed display setup. The setup consisted of four XGA projections and two single-monitor workstations of 24" with 1920x1200 pixels as shown in Figure 2. Displays were driven by commodity desktop computers connected via gigabit ethernet. The users were seated in front of the left workstation monitor, with mouse and keyboard

---

[3]http://www.compiz.org/

placed in front of the monitor. The right monitor was private and therefore not accessible. There were no occlusions of displays from the user's point of view.

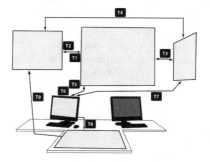

Figure 2. Experimental setup with transitions T1-T9.

We compared the following navigation techniques: free navigation (*free*), path navigation (*path*), a world-in-miniature control (*WIM*) to select the target display in the 3D model of the environment (similar to ARIS [3]), and a pointer warping technique (*warp*) redirecting the mouse pointer to a target display by pressing a keyboard shortcut. For *path*, navigation cues for the connected edge intervals were displayed. For each technique, users were asked to accomplish a target selection task starting from the home display. Targets appeared sequentially at different display locations, resulting in nine different transitions (*T1-T9*), illustrated in Figure 2. Each block was preceded by a short training phase. The order of navigation techniques and target appearances was balanced. Overall, the study lasted approximately one hour for each participant.

For task completion time, we measured the time between two target selections. Additionally, we collected subjective ratings of each technique on a seven-point Likert scale in a post-experiment questionnaire. Main effect and interaction analysis were performed at $\alpha = .05$ and Bonferroni adjustments were applied for post-hoc comparisons. One user test was declared as outlier and not included in the results.

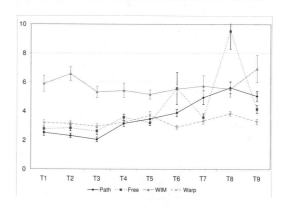

Figure 3. Task completion times (s) of all navigation techniques (average and standard error) for transitions T1 to T9.

A 4(navigation technique) x 9(transition) repeated measures ANOVA on target selection times showed main effects for navigation technique ($F_{3,54} = 33.801, p < .001$) and transition ($F_{8,114} = 18.439, p < .001$). There is also an interaction between navigation technique and transition ($F_{24,432} = 8.099, p < .001$). Overall, path was significantly faster than free. Warp was also faster than free, while WIM was the slowest technique overall. On average, path was faster than free for transitions between wall displays (T1-T4), which is significant for T2. It was also faster for accessing the tabletop display (T8). In contrast, free was faster than path for navigation *from* the tabletop display to the left projection wall (T9) and for navigation between monitor and the right projection wall (T7). Both, warp and WIM had almost uniform completion times across all transitions. Results are shown in Figure 3.

From the post-experiment questionnaire, we found no significant differences across preference scores ($F_{3,54} = 3.241, p = .461$). In an interview at the end of the experiment three users reported they preferred path navigation due to the given structure implied by the constraint, visualized paths, while three other users assessed path navigation as "exhausting" caused by the restrictive paths. Feedback for free navigation was similarly diverse: seven users rated free navigation as very intuitive while two users stated they did not understand the concept of free navigation at all. The main point of criticism was the mouse mapping on the table, leading to targeting difficulties on the tabletop display.

Path navigation seems to be more suitable for simple navigation tasks, such as between adjacent displays. In contrast, free navigation was superior for long and complex paths (T7 and T9) but had lower performance than path navigation overall. This contradicts findings by Nacenta *et al.* [8], who showed that perspective-based navigation is generally faster than stitching. Similar to our experiment, this difference was more distinct for complex navigation tasks. However, as Perspective Cursor was evaluated on a typical single-user workspace, there are two major differences in the experimental setup potentially leading to the divergent overall result: First, in their setup all displays were directly facing the user and, second, physical gaps between adjacent displays were comparably small. In our experiment, navigation to targets on the tabletop display (T8), which was partially located outside the user's field of view, caused serious problems for some of the participants. Many users mentioned a non-intuitive mapping of pointer movement on the table. This mapping is caused by the static perspective map, where the representation of the tabletop display is skewed and rotated relative to the actual device space (Figure 1). Navigation from the center wall to the monitor (T6) caused similar difficulties, as users sometimes involuntarily navigated to the tabletop display. It is probably sufficient to let users access displays located outside their immediate workspace exclusively by explicit pointer warping, which was the fastest technique in our experiment to access the tabletop display.

CONCLUSION

Deriving 2D mouse pointer navigation frames and transitions automatically from a 3D description of display spaces allows us to quickly build MDEs for collaborative workspaces tailored to the group size, architectural constraints, and the task to be accomplished by the team. Each team member is provided his or her own mouse and keyboard pair and can choose the preferred cross-display navigation technique, which is configured per mouse pointer. Our experiment has shown that estimating user positions and viewing directions from the 3D model is sufficient, as long as the displays are placed in front of the user. The results furthermore indicate that the "optimal" cross-display navigation technique depends on the user preference, which is strongly diverse, as well as the complexity of the display setup and the required mouse pointer travels. In the future we aim to extend our MDE to support more sophisticated tasks, like relocating content, in combination with the presented navigation techniques.

ACKNOWLEDGEMENTS
This work was funded by the Austrian Science Fund FWF (Y193 and W1209-N15) and FFG BRIDGE 822716.

REFERENCES

1. P. Baudisch, E. Cutrell, K. Hinckley, and R. Gruen. Mouse ether: accelerating the acquisition of targets across multi-monitor displays. In *Ext. Abstracts CHI 2004*, pages 1379–1382. ACM, 2004.

2. H. Benko and S. Feiner. Pointer warping in heterogeneous multi-monitor environments. In *Proc. GI 2007*, pages 111–117. ACM, 2007.

3. J. T. Biehl and B. P. Bailey. ARIS: An Interface for Application Relocation in an Interactive Space. In *Proc. GI 2004*, pages 107–116, 2004.

4. K. S. Booth, B. D. Fisher, C. J. R. Lin, and R. Argue. The "mighty mouse" multi-screen collaboration tool. In *Proc. UIST 2002*, pages 209–212. ACM, 2002.

5. M. Brown, A. Majumder, and R. Yang. Camera-Based Calibration Techniques for Seamless Multiprojector Displays. *IEEE Transactions on Visualization and Computer Graphics*, 11(2):193–206, 2005.

6. B. Johanson, G. Hutchins, T. Winograd, and M. Stone. PointRight: Experience with Flexible Input Redirection in Interactive Workspaces. In *Proc. UIST 2002*, pages 227–234, 2002.

7. M. A. Nacenta, R. L. Mandryk, and C. Gutwin. Targeting across displayless space. In *Proc. CHI 2008*, pages 777–786. ACM, 2008.

8. M. A. Nacenta, S. Sallam, B. Champoux, S. Subramanian, and C. Gutwin. Perspective Cursor: Perspective-Based Interaction for Multi-Display Environments. In *Proc. CHI 2006*, pages 289–298, 2006.

9. C. Pirchheim, M. Waldner, and D. Schmalstieg. Improving spatial awareness in multi-display environments. In *Proc. VR 2009*, pages 123–126, 2009.

10. R. Su and B. P. Bailey. Put them where? towards guidelines for positioning large displays in interactive workspaces. In *Proc. GI 2005*, pages 337–349, 2005.

User Interface for Filtering Videos Interconnecting High Level and Intellectual Metadata

Arne Berger

University of Technology Chemnitz, Strasse der Nationen 62, Chemnitz, Germany
firstname.secondname@informatik.tu-chemnitz.de

ABSTRACT

We present a user interface that combines the requirements needed for information search in a professional environment with the possibilities for multimedial queries based on automatically generated fuzzy high level metadata.

Author Keywords

user interface, filtering, interactive information retrieval

ACM Classification Keywords

H5.2. Information interfaces and presentation

General Terms

Design, Experimentation, Human Factors

TECHNICAL INTRODUCTION

The core of our projects efforts is a retrieval engine (6.) that incorporates fuzzy high level metadata from our attempts to solve the recognition of persons and objects in video broadcasts via facial and voice recognition as well as OCR in the lower third of the screen. Those automatically generated high-level metadata are added to a intellectually annotated database to improve the retrieval outcome.

TEXT BASED VS. GRAPHICALLY RICH QUERIES

In typical local TV stations in Germany, archivists, editors and cutters access their video repositories through text based search interfaces. These frontends help the users to retrieve videos, based on specific intellectually annotated metadata. Those interfaces are poorly customizable and lack adaptability for heterogenous user groups. On the other hand, algorithms that automatically generate high level metadata and novel retrieval engines based on those, are developed to facilitate better search results in insufficiently annotated multimedial data. Sketch based image search engines, engines that focus on drilldowns in content clusters or tools that search based on the color distribution of the images show todays possibilities but are not advanced enough to solve everyday retrieval tasks. (9, 10, 11, 12.) Known-item queries can still be better solved via text-only searches. Still, most queries are so vague, that users need to reformulate their queries substantially (2).

Users begin their search for an item with a small query and reformulate it step by step after inspecting the results to find matching results for the image in mind.

During this process, users form a mental string of reformulation. This string gets obscured by repetitive editing, hence previous versions of the text based query get lost. Furthermore a modal gap occurs, as users repeatetly need to switch between query editing and result browsing. Our search interface tries to bridge this gap via the implementation of filtering. It also incorporates a vivid way to visualize the users string of query reformulation.

RELATED WORK

Shneiderman et. al. proposed filtering as a visual representation of query formulation (5.). Cutrell et. al. among others successfully evaluated the usability of those systems for constantly growing multimedial repositories (3.). Hearst et. al. published and evaluated ways of drilling down search results with the help of faceted metadata (4.) in a step by step manner, while visualizing the reformulation process.

COMBINED INTERFACE

As previous work has shown (1.) users from local TV stations are interested in using customizable retrieval interfaces for their retrieval tasks in the stations broadcasting archive. As there are 70 possible intellectually annotated metadata fields for the videos (8.) evaluation showed, that users want to search only in customized subsets, according to their needs. Therefore our interface allows users to group metadata fields into distinct search widgets. Each widget is suitable for one distinct query.

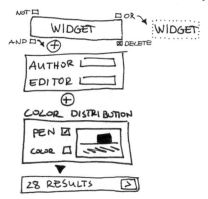

Figure 1. Exemplary Widgets + Combination

This idea may be expanded to multimedial query formulation based on fuzzy high level metadata. User interviews revealed that users are in despair for having better search results, because intellectual annotated metadata are not sufficient. Users are also looking for less restricted ways to formulate queries in their daily work. They are aware of the chances and drawbacks of automatically annotated metadata and are willing to sacrifice their current fixed retrieval systems for a more open way to formulate queries.

For the purpose of evaluating the interface, the following basic set of widgets have been included in the interface:

Text based Widgets (corresponding metadata fields): Title (Title, Serial Title), Production (Production Number, Date OR Period of Recording, Place of Recording, …), Broadcast (Station, Date & Time of Broadcast, Period of Broadcast, Duration of Broadcast, Rerun, …), Persons (Author, Editor, Actor, …)

Graphical Widgets based on High Level Metadata: OCR in the lower third of the screen, Distinction if there is a Person Visible, Color Distribution.

The widgets for text based search are only examples. Based on the users profession or their personal work style, the respective widgets and their corresponding metadata fields may vary widely. The amount of available widgets for multimedial queries will grow according to the advancement of our research. At a later stage of our project face, speaker and resulting person recognition will be included in the retrieval system. User interviews indicate, that users find it plausible to use new developed widgets in the same way as the current ones for query reformulation. Furthermore they are eager to use them as well as they are constantly reporting suggestions. Most of these widgets, taken for themself would not automatically justify a stand alone application. Formulated in widgets and combined in one query formulation and reformulation flow, they are much more of a help. Developers may create or customize widgets according to emerging user needs or technical possibilities. Dependent on previously used widgets, the system may suggest widgets for the next reformulation step.

To visually formulate a multi term query, the widgets may be ordered next to each other. Our proposal lets users position widgets vertically below each other, to combine query terms for reformulation. Our findings show that when users drill down results by adding a widget in order to add another query term for reformulation, they expect widgets to be AND-ed when connected vertically, as single queries from within a widget are also AND-ed, as users expected. Accordingly, for OR as well as NOT, separate options are included in each widget to act accordingly. Removing a search widget eliminates this query term. For a single term known item search users may just use one widget.

EVALUATION
We evaluated our interface against a classic expert search were all available metadata fields have been present with 30 users (7.). Participants liked our approach more, learned and explored its advantages fast and retrieved better results.

Figure 2. Interface

ACKNOWLEDGEMENT
This work was accomplished in conjunction with the project sachsMedia, which is funded by the Entrepreneurial Regions program of the German Federal Ministry of Education and Research.

REFERENCES
1. Berger, A., Kürsten, J., Eibl, M.: „Visual String of Reformulation". Proceedings of HCI International 2009, LNCS Springer Heidelberg. 2009

2. Bates, M.J.: „The Design of Browsing and Berrypicking Techniques for the online search interface." University of California Los Angeles, 1989

3. Cutrell E., Robbins D.: „Fast, flexible filtering with phlat" Proceedings of the SIGCHI conference, 2006

4. Yee, K-P., Swearingen, K., Li, K., Hearst, M., „Faceted Metadata for Image Search and Browsing", Proceedings of the SIGCHI conference 2003

5. Shneiderman, B., Young, D.: „A Graphical Filter/Flow Representation of Boolean Queries", American Society for Information Science. Vol. 44. pp. 327-339, 1993

6. Wilhelm, T., Kürsten, J., Eibl, M.: „The Xtrieval Framework at CLEF 2008: ImageCLEF photographic retrieval task", CLEF 2008 Workshop, 2008.

7. Wittig, A.,: „Implementation und Evaluation einer GUI für Multimedia-Archive", TU Chemnitz, 2008

8. Regelwerk Mediendokumentation, http://rmd.dra.de

9. http://labs.systemone.at/retrievr

10. http://xcavator.net

11. http://www.cuil.com

12. http://www.quintura.com

Isn't it Great? You Can *PLAY, MATE!*

Shlomo Berkovsky, Mac Coombe, Jill Freyne, and Dipak Bhandari
CSIRO Tasmanian ICT Center
GPO Box 1538, Hobart, 7001, Australia
firstname.lastname@csiro.au

ABSTRACT

The addictive nature of game playing contributes to an increasingly sedentary lifestyle. In this demonstration we showcase *PLAY, MATE!*, a novel mixed reality game design that motivates players to perform physical activity as part of playing. According to the *PLAY, MATE!* design, players gain virtual game rewards in return for the real physical activity they perform. We demonstrate the application of the *PLAY, MATE!* design to an open source game and allow participants to experience physical activity motivating games in person.

Author Keywords

Game interaction, activity motivation, bodily interface.

ACM Classification Keywords

H.5.2: User Interfaces, Interaction Styles, I.2.1: Applications and Expert Systems, Games.

General Terms

Human factors.

INTRODUCTION

Contemporary lifestyle is becoming increasingly sedentary with little physical (sports, exercises) and much sedentary (TV, computers) activity. We present a novel approach aimed at combating this problem in the context of computer games. Rather than changing the amount of physical and sedentary activity a person sets out to perform, we propose *PLAY, MATE!*, a novel design of mixed reality games that leverages the engagement of players with games in order to motivate them to perform physical activity while playing [1]. According to the *PLAY, MATE!* design, at any point in time players can perform some physical activity, which will instantaneously reinforce the game features. Empirical evaluation showed that *PLAY, MATE!* motivates players to perform physical activity, decreases sedentary playing time, and does not affect the perceived enjoyment of playing [1]. In this demonstration we showcase the application of *PLAY, MATE!* to the Neverball game and let the participants to experience physical activity motivating games.

DESIGN AND APPLICATION OF *PLAY, MATE!*

The goal of the *PLAY, MATE!* design is to change the sedentary nature of game playing to include certain aspects of physical activity. The physical activity is introduced as an integral part of playing, such that the existing engagement of players with the game is leveraged to motivate them to perform physical activity. The motivation is achieved by modifying the following game components and aspects of interaction with the game:

- *Game motivator.* Players are made aware of the possibility of gaining virtual game related rewards in return for performing real physical activity. The game is modified in order to motivate players to perform physical activity, such that certain game features can be enabled or reinforced by the rewards.
- *Activity interface.* Players are provided with an external interface capturing the physical activity performed and converting it into virtual game rewards.
- *Game control.* Since performing physical activity and controlling the game simultaneously could be too complicated, players are given supplementary control over the flow of the game.

Using these modifications, *PLAY, MATE!* motivates players to perform physical activity as follows. On one hand, the game is modified such that certain features are disabled or diminished. On the other hand, players are made aware of the fact that performing physical activity will gain them game rewards, i.e., enable or reinforce these features. These two factors, combined with the existing engagement with the game and enjoyment of playing, motivate players to perform physical activity. When performed, the physical activity is captured by the activity interface, processed, and converted into game rewards, which instantaneously enable or reinforce the game features.

We applied the *PLAY, MATE!* design to an open source game Neverball (www.neverball.org). In Neverball, players are required to navigate a ball to a target point through an obstacle course and collect the required number of coins, in a limited time (Figure 1-left). Control over the ball is achieved by inclining the obstacle course, which causes the ball to roll. We applied a time based physical activity motivator. The initial time allocated to accomplish Neverball levels was reduced and players were made aware of the possibility of gaining extra time in return for performing physical activity.

Figure 1. Accelerometer (left) and Neverball interface (right).

We used a compact (*42x42x10* mm) and lightweight (*15* g) tri-axial accelerometer as the interface to capture the player's physical activity [2]. The accelerometer was attached to the player's waist, so as not to interfere with the player's normal motion, using an elastic band (see Figure 1-right) and wirelessly transmitted the measured acceleration signal to a receiver attached to the computer running Neverball. We filtered out noise and abnormal activity spikes, performed time based normalization, and discretised the acceleration signal into activity bursts. For every burst captured players gained one extra second to accomplish Neverball levels. The remaining time was instantaneously visualised, such that players were in control of the amount of physical activity they performed.

In summary, players interacted with the activity motivating version of Neverball in the following way. Players were motivated by the reduced time motivator and the awareness of the possibility of gaining extra time in return for performing physical activity. When the remaining time was perceived to be insufficient, players could pause the game and perform some physical activity. The physical activity was instantaneously captured by the accelerometer, transmitted to Neverball, and visualised. When the remaining time was perceived to be sufficient, players could resume sedentary playing.

We conducted an empirical evaluation aimed at assessing the acceptance of *PLAY, MATE!*. The main indicators of acceptance were the amount of physical activity performed while playing and the perceived enjoyment of playing [3]. The evaluation involved 180 young players aged 9 to 12 and 104 adults. The results demonstrated a good acceptance of the activity motivating games. In particular, the evaluation showed that (1) players were successfully motivated to perform more physical activity, (2) players decreased their sedentary playing time and increased their active time, (3) although realistically perceiving the performed physical activity, players did not report a decrease in the enjoyment of playing (4) less skilled players performed more physical activity than more skilled players, and (5) adults preferred the activity motivating games over the sedentary games.

These results demonstrate the potential of physical activity motivating games and call for future research on player-tailored application of *PLAY, MATE!* to various types of games and for a longitudinal study assessing the attitudinal and behavioural change introduced by physical activity motivating games.

SUMMARY

We presented the *PLAY, MATE!* design for physical activity motivating computer games. The main idea underpinning the design is that the players' engagement with games can be leveraged in order to motivate them to perform physical activity as part of playing. According to the design, physical activity is introduced as part of sedentary playing, such that performing real physical activity enables the players to gain virtual game rewards. Experimental evaluation involving real players showed that physical activity motivating games can indeed motivate players to perform physical activity, whereas they do not decrease the perceived enjoyment of playing.

This demonstration will let the participants to experience the attractiveness of physical activity motivating games in person. They will be equipped with the accelerometer, informed about the activity motivating version of Neverball and their ability to gain extra time in return for performing physical activity, and will be offered the opportunity of a short playing session. While playing, the participants will not be directed regarding when and how much physical activity they should perform. Hence, the choice between sedentary and active playing will be left at their own discretion. In a sense, it will be a live demonstration of the persuasive power of the activity motivating games.

ACKNOWLEDGMENTS

This research is jointly funded by the Australian Government through the Intelligent Island Program and CSIRO. The Intelligent Island Program is administered by the Tasmanian Department of Economic Development, Tourism, and the Arts. We would like to thank Robert Kooima and the developers of Neverball.

REFERENCES

1. Berkovsky, S., Freyne, J., Coombe, M., Bhandari, D., Baghaei, N.: Physical Activity Motivating Games: You Can *PLAY, MATE!*, *Proc. of OZCHI*, Melbourne, 2009.

2. Helmer, R.J.N., Mestrovic, M.A., Farrow, D., Lucas, S., Spratford, W.: Smart Textiles: Position and Motion Sensing for Sport, Entertainment and Rehabilitation, *Advances in Science and Technology*, vol.60, 2008.

3. Sweetser, P. Wyeth, P.: GameFlow: a Model for Evaluating Player Enjoyment in Games. *ACM Computers in Entertainment*, vol.3(3), 2005.

Understanding Web Documents Using Semantic Overlays

Grégoire Burel
Department of Computer Sciences
University of Sheffield, Sheffield, UK
G.Burel@dcs.shef.ac.uk

Amparo E. Cano
Department of Computer Sciences
University of Sheffield, Sheffield, UK
A.Cano@dcs.shef.ac.uk

ABSTRACT

The Ozone Browser is a platform independent tool that enables users to visually augment the knowledge presented in a web document in an unobtrusive way. This tool supports the user comprehension of Web documents through the use of Semantic Overlays. This tool uses linked data and lightweight semantics for getting relevant information within a document. The current implementation uses a JavaScript bookmarklet.

Author Keywords

Web Augmentation, Semantic Web, Semantic Overlays.

ACM Classification Keywords

H.5.4 Hypertext/Hypermedia: User issues; Navigation.

General Terms

Design, Human Factors

INTRODUCTION

Web documents enable the storage of information (text and media) in a syntactic fashion with hyperlinks providing the formal structure necessary for connecting them together. Because Web documents use hyperlinks for referring to different types of related information, a Web document cannot be seen as a self-contained information. As a consequence, when reading a Web document, a user must use hyperlinked information coupled with their own background knowledge in order to understand a particular document. Although, all this information helps the comprehension of a reader by enhancing their background knowledge, the activities of collecting this information is time consuming and inefficient. Since the information is purely syntactic, a document may contain information and hyperlinks irrelevant for the comprehension task. In this case, the user must filter relevant from irrelevant information as the available links are explored. Moreover, each linked document presents additional links to be followed leading to information overload.

This paper introduces Ozone Browser[1] (OB), a platform independent tool that enables users to visually augment the knowledge presented in a web document in an unobtrusive way[2]. This process of *Web Augmentation* provides contextual information that helps the user to understand a specific document without requiring them to search manually for contextual information. This approach uses semantic information to provide an accurate and meaningful knowledge augmentation to the user. In order to improve the user experience, the proposed system satisfies the following requirements: Platform independence, Document independence, In-situ Augmentation, Unobtrusive Augmentation, Contextual Augmentation, Good Precision and Recall, Usability (user friendly information visualisation). The following section introduces the concept of *Web Augmentation* and how it can be used for assisting the user in comprehending Web documents. It also describes the different existing approaches. The second section introduces the conceptual model used in OB for performing Web Augmentation and describes OB, our Web Augmentation system.

WEB AUGMENTATION

A comprehension task can be supported by adding and displaying relevant external knowledge on the top of an existing web document. This information can be displayed using an overlay that adds information layered above existing information. Bouvin[1] defines this approach with the term *Web Augmentation*. *Web Augmentation* is a hypermedia augmentation tool that adds information to an existing Web document directly or indirectly with the purpose of helping the user to associate, organise or structure information found on the web. Although Bouvin describes different types of augmentation, the concept introduced by Bouvin matches the requirements of an application supporting users comprehension of Web Documents.

LINKED-DATA WEB AUGMENTATION

Different strategies have been pursued for performing Web Augmentation. The different approaches can be divided in three categories: 1) *Syntactic Augmentation:* The methods based on this idea uses the information pointed by the hyperlinks available within a document for augmenting a document[5] . These approaches generally ignore the users browsing context or try to extracts the meaning of the web document as they are accessed thus generating a Web Augmenta-

---

[1]Sparks Ozone Browser, http://oak.dcs.shef.ac.uk/sparks/.

tion with a low accuracy; 2) *Annotation Augmentation:* The use of collaborative annotation for providing the augmentation generates a better accuracy compared to the previous purely syntactic method since it relies on users to manually augment web document[3]. Unfortunately, this method generates a very low recall and it requires manually annotated document in order to work properly; 3)*Ontological Web Augmentation:*Semantics web technologies have been recently used for augmenting web documents[3][4] . In this paper we present a new approach to *Web Augmentation*. This approach relies on the concept of Semantic Overlays (SO). The presented technique uses linked data and efficient visualization strategies to present relevant information to the user.

SEMANTIC OVERLAYS

A Semantic Overlay (SO) can be defined as a visual, contextual and interactive knowledge augmentation layer. This layer augments a web document by adding contextual knowledge to it and presenting it to the user in an unobtrusive and human friendly manner. This approach encompasses the two main requirements of an accurate Web Augmentation: 1) *Accurate and contextual knowledge retrieval*; 2) *User friendly unobtrusive presentation.*

Contextual Knowledge Gathering

In order to provide an accurate Web Augmentation, a semantic overlay uses Semantic Web ontologies as its knowledge representation model since ontologies represent information which allows a precise augmentation. In order to provide in place and accurate augmentation, the current SO implementation relies on RDFa[2]. By following a Semantic Web approach to the problem of Web Augmentation, SO uses linked-data[3] for retrieving contextual knowledge related to a particular piece of information. This approach provides accurate information compared to the syntactic approaches.

Unobtrusive Knowledge Visualization

SO does not replace or change the content of an underlining document. A SO is a contextual layer that appears not only on top of the document but also above the information of the document that requires augmentation. This strategy enables a more contextual augmentation. In order to generate a meaningful representation, the current SO implementation relies on the automatic selection of a visualization given the data to be represented. The method use visualization plugins that specifies the handled information.

OZONE BROWSER

Ozone Browser (OB) is implemented as JavaScript bookmarklet (a bookmarklet is a small JavaScript application embedded in in a URI). In order to perform the augmentation of a Web document, OB performs four different tasks: 1) The Browser's bookmarklet is applied on an HTML+RDFa document; 2) OB extracts the local context through the extraction of the embedded semantics contained in the document;

[2]RDFa, http://www.w3.org/TR/xhtml-rdfa-primer/.

[3]Linked Data, http://linkeddata.org.

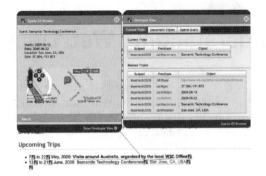

Figure 1. Ozone Browser in Action: a) the summary of an event; b) the related developers view

3) External knowledge bases are accessed and the SO is generated; 4) The SO is applied on top of the document. The current implementation has two experimental views. The first one display the information from a Twitter[4] account (recent tweets). The second one displays specific information about events (a summary with a map) found in a page (Figure 1.a). A developer view is also implemented (Figure 1.b) for displaying the semantic information presented in the page and querying them[2].

CONCLUSION

OB returns accurate informations in a user friendly way. It is expected to release a public platform for enabling users to create their own visualisation and to personalise the overlay according to the user interests.

ACKNOWLEDGEMENTS

The research leading to these results has received funding from the EU project WeKnowIt[5] (ICT-215453).

REFERENCES

1. N. Bouvin. Unifying strategies for Web augmentation. In *The Tenth ACM Conference on Hypertext and hypermedia*, pages 91–100. ACM, 1999.

2. G. Burel, A. Cano, and V. Lanfranchi. Ozone browser: Augmenting the web with semantic overlays. In *5th Workshop on Scripting and Development for the Semantic Web*, 2009.

3. F. Ciravegna, A. Dingli, and D. Petrelli. Melita: Active document enrichment using adaptive information extraction from text. In *First International Semantic Web Conference Posters*, 2002.

4. J. Domingue, M. Dzbor, and E. Motta. Collaborative semantic web browsing with magpie. In *The 1st European Semantic Web Symposium*, 2004.

5. L. Holmquist. Focus+ context visualization with flip zooming and the zoom browser. In *CHI'97 extended abstracts on Human factors in computing systems: looking to the future*, page 264. ACM, 1997.

[4]Twitter, http://twitter.com.

[5]WeKnowIt, http://www.weknowit.eu/.

Context-aware Intelligent Recommender System

Mehdi Elahi
Stockholm University
melahi@kth.se

ABSTRACT

This demo paper presents a context-aware recommendation system. The system mines data from user's web searches and other sources to improve the presentation of content on visited web pages. While user is browsing the internet, a memory resident agent records and analyzes the content of the webpages that were either searched for or visited in order to identify topic preferences. Then, based on such information, the content of requested web page is ranked and classified with different styles. The demo shows how a music weblog can be modified automatically based on user's affinities.

Author Keywords

Recommendation systems, recommenders, context-aware, fuzzy logic, classification, active learning

ACM Classification Keywords

I.2.7 [Natural Language Processing]: Text analysis.

General Terms

Algorithms, Human Factors, Languages, Performance

INTRODUCTION

Internet is a huge network of about 1 trillion (as in 1,000,000,000,000) unique URLs on the web at the moment [1]. Daily needs and necessities require us to go through many websites such as news agencies or online shops taking a long time to read and find the appropriate information. The system addressed in this demo shall be an approach to solve the problem of irrelevant, redundant, unsolicited and low-value information [2]. The demo learns the affinities in music, fashion, sports and other fields of interest when surfing online. The intelligence behind classifies the content into favored and unfavored blocks. Finally, the appearance of the page is revised highlighting favorite parts [2].

INTELLIGENT CORE

Monitoring, analyzing and categorizing someone's taste is not an easy task. As a result, the system should be sufficiently quick and active performing fundamental functionalities such as learning, classifying and re-presenting.

The intelligent core understands and records the client activities to predict the preferences. The classification algorithm, later on, separates the textual content to desired and undesired and, at the end, the text is regenerated accordingly.

Learning Method

The learning method consists of analyses of activities such as searching or reading online and, then, logging and updating these information. The mined data is saved in a secure database on the local computer in the form of extracted keywords. These keywords will be the comparison factors for further classification process.

Fuzzy System

Fuzzy Logic is a reasoning approach logically constructed by decision making with imprecise probabilistic information. Assuming that we have a number of learning sets (inputs), the fuzzy logic decides the most appropriate direction to find the relevant results (outputs) [4]. Figure 1 shows how the fuzzy system can separate the input text blocks by increasing, decreasing or keeping the ranking list, provided that the input to be found favorite or unfavorite.

Artificial Neuron

Different techniques are available to be employed for implementation of the idea. However, the simpler the technique utilized, the faster the result achieved.

One of the basic and effective classifiers is an artificial neuron with a step function so-called "Perceptron". In this method, the input variables are weighted by a single layer of neurons and the output values are calculated by a step function.

IMPLEMENTATION

Demo was implemented in Java. The input data is taken off the webpage requested by the user and, then, the font size and the color are changed based on the ranking.

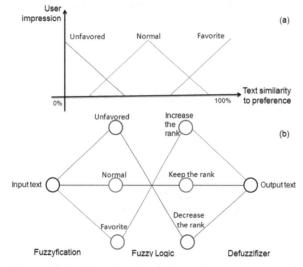

Figure 1. (a) Categories of input text, (b) Fuzzy system [4]

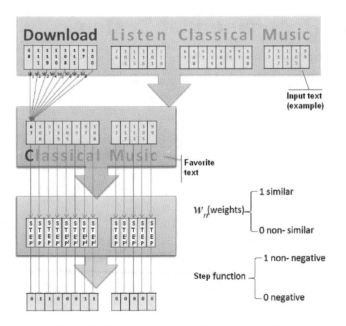

Figure 2. Example of textual data analyses [5]

Keywords Extraction

Textual data are collection of sentences representing particular information. Although each individual word in a sentence holds a meaningful concept, some of these words (keywords) play significant roles compared to others. Therefore every topic can be expressed in summary by their corresponding keywords [5].

Data mining

When extraction step is finished, the keywords are compared and weighted all together based on their similarities. Figure 2 illustrates how the process is performed for an example of two phrases. It is assumed that the user is interested in "classical music" and a new phrase "download and listen to classical music" is compared to determine whether it is a kind of favorite topic or not. A layer of Perceptrons is used to rank the letters and final decision is made, afterward.

DEMO OVERVIEW

Figure 3 is a screenshot of the demo applied for a music weblog [6]. The content of the page has a number of text blocks each of which introducing a free music database. Suppose that the demo is running on the computer of a user interested in "classical music" and uninterested in "metal music". As soon as entering the weblog, the recommender application imports the text data and finds the most similar blocks to "classical music" and highlights the message. On the other hand, the most unfavored part being "metal music concert" is understated by re-coloring the font. This modification of style will simplify and improve the quality of finding the relevant online information.

Figure 3. Demonstration of context-aware recommender

CONCLUSION

This demo paper presents the high possible potentials of the context-aware recommender systems saving the time and increasing the efficiency of reading. It also hints future applications such as intelligent web browsers with novel ideas behind.

ACKNOWLEDGMENTS

I would like to thank Magnus Jändel (FOI) supervising my thesis work. Also a big thanks goes to thesis examiner Annika Waern (Stockholm University) providing a pleasant working atmosphere and stimulating discussions.

REFERENCES

1. Official Google Blog: we knew the web was big…, access date:2009/11/20, http://googleblog.blogspot.com/2008/07/we-knew-web-was-big.html.

2. Orman, L., (1984). Fighting Information Pollution with Decision Support Systems. *Journal of Management Information Systems*, 1(2), pp. 64-71

3. Jändel, M. and Elahi, M. (2009). "Tribal Taste: Mobile Multiagent Recommender System", To Appear in the Proceedings of the *International Conference on Intelligent User Interfaces* 8-11 Feb., Sanibel Island, Florida, USA.

4. Cornelius, P.(2007), "Neural Networks", Based on original lecture notes by Nedelko Grbic, 1999, Department of Signal Processing, Blekinge institute of Technology, Sweden

5. Elahi, M. (2009). "A Mobile Peer-to-Peer Recommender System", Master thesis work at Department of Computer and Systems Sciences, Stockholm University, Sweden

Mobile Mentor: Weight Management Platform

Jill Freyne, Dipak Bhandari, Shlomo Berkovsky and Lyle Borlase
CSIRO Tasmanian ICT Center
GPO Box 1538
Hobart, 7001, Australia
firstname.lastname@csiro.au

Chris Campbell and Steve Chau
Verdant Health
2/149A Macquarie Street
Hobart, 7000, Australia
firstname@verdant.com.au

ABSTRACT

In recent years health care professionals have been investigating the use of ICT technologies in order to influence the general public to change their attitude and behaviour toward a healthier lifestyle. We present Mobile Mentor, a platform aimed at supporting individuals on goal driven programs through personalized mobile technology. This demonstration focuses on a weight loss prototype, Weight Management Mentor, which supports self regulation through the collection of real time diet and exercise data, self reflection and awareness through its graphical feedback mechanisms, and interaction with a health practitioner or advisor through a central server.

Author Keywords

Mobile interaction, personalized diet, tailoring

ACM Classification Keywords

H5.m. Information interfaces and presentation (e.g., HCI): Miscellaneous.

General Terms

Design

INTRODUCTION

With over 1.6 billion adults worldwide classified as obese or overweight [2], a huge drive is ongoing into the development of effective weight loss programs and tools. A wide range of programs exist which vary in the level of professional and social support provided to participants. Many weight loss programs require users to record their dietary intake and many have progressed from pen and paper recording to digital systems, where informative content and additional services and features can be used to persuade users to alter their behaviour [1]. Here we present a tool, Weight Management Mentor (WMM), designed to maximise the support offered to users through mobile technology. WMM is a convenient and easy to use tool which allows users to record their progress and receive real time feedback. It also prompts and encourages users when they appear to be struggling with their diet.

WEIGHT MANAGEMENT MENTOR

WMM is a mobile support tool for individuals engaged in a weight loss program. In addition to allowing users to simply and conveniently track their weight, food intake and exercise through a mobile device, WMM prompts users to reflect on various aspects of their lives which may be impacting on their diet and their compliance to the weight loss program through questions posed on the mobile device. These wellbeing indicators include fitness, motivation, stress levels, fatigue, sleep patterns, and other parameters.

WMM can act as an intermediary between a dieter and their professional support team. All of the information provided to WMM by participants is uploaded to a central server such that the support team can easily access a user's account and monitor their progress before (or instead of) a scheduled meeting. WMM provides the facility for shorter meetings as progress can be judged in advance or, on programs where no regular meetings occur, discussions can happen virtually with both parties informed of progress.

WMM acts as a reminder and encourager to participants on a diet. As WMM is a data gathering tool, users are expected to interact with it several times a day. If a participant fails to enter data when WMM expects it to, the system will alert the user and prompt for data entry. In this way users, who have strayed from a diet, will be reminded of their diet commitment and encouraged to comply in future.

In a typical usage scenario of WMM, users interact with the tool three times a day: morning, afternoon and evening. However, these interactions can be customized to suit user preferences. Each interaction can contain information from WMM, questions which require responses, and feedback based on these responses. The information presented and questions posed depend on multiple factors including the time of day, previous information provided, and stage in the diet program. The questions are informed by the amount of time a user is likely to have to interact with WMM and their applicability to the time of day. For example, a typical daily interaction of a user in the early stages of a weight loss program with WMM would be as follows:

Morning interaction

Good morning <name>. Welcome to day 2 of your weight loss plan, its early days but you are doing great!

You may have experienced interrupted sleep last night, this is normal when you start to diet. If you'd like more information on sleep and diet click <URL>.

Q1. How well did you sleep last night? (see Fig. 1-left)
Q2. How many hours sleep did you get?
Q3. What is your weight today?
Q4. Have you planned your meals today?
Q5. Have you planned your exercise?

Today's featured article relates to <URL>. If you have a few moments consider reading this helpful information.

Figure 1. WMM Information Gathering

Afternoon interaction
Q6. What have you eaten so far today?
- Breakfast (see Fig. 1-center)
- Snack
- Lunch
- Confectionary, sodas

Evening Interaction
Q7. What have you eaten since this afternoon?
- Dinner
- Snack
- Alcohol (type, serve, amount)
- Confectionary, sodas
Q8: Did you do any exercise today? (see Fig. 1-right)
- Type, duration, intensity
Q9. How stressful was your day?
Q10. What were the key sources of stress?
Q11. How do you think you did today?

<name> you've done well today. You've completed the required amount of exercise and stuck with your diet.

WMM creates graphs in real time based on the data received in order to allow users and their professional support to view progress on several dimensions including weight loss (Fig. 2-left), dietary intake, exercise, program

compliance (Fig. 2-centre), engagement with WMM and a summary of their daily input (Fig. 2-right)

The concept demonstrator for WMM was developed as an iPhone application. WMM system backend comprises of an IIS 6.0 server and an SQL Server 2005 database. WMM user responses are communicated to the WMM server via a web service over a 3G mobile network upon submission. User data is processed on the server side and the application fetches the feedback information via a .NET web service.

Figure 2. WMM Feedback and Summary

FUTURE WORK
While WMM is adaptive to the responses of users there is much scope to increase its intelligence through learning and personalization, primarily in information delivery, prompting and feedback delivery features. Immediate plans include a live user analysis of the interface, interaction modalities and effectiveness of WMM to assist users in complying with a diet program.

ACKNOWLEDGMENTS
This research is funded by the Australian Government through the Tasmanian Research Partnership Program, the Intelligent Island Program and CSIRO. The Intelligent Island Program is administered by the Tasmanian Department of Economic Development, Tourism, and the Arts. The authors thank Manny Noakes, Gilly Hendrie, and Emily Brindal for their help with the development of the platform and WMM prototype.

REFERENCES
1. Lee, G., Tsai, C., Griswold W.G., Raab, F., Patrick, K.: PmEB: a Mobile Phone Application for Monitoring Caloric Balance, *CHI Extended Abstracts*, 2006.

2. World Health Organization. Obesity and Overweight Information Sheet, www.who.int/factsheets/fs311

Relevant TV Program Retrieval using Broadcast Summaries

Jun Goto[1]   Hideki Sumiyoshi[1]   Masaru Miyazaki[1]   Hideki Tanaka[1]

Masahiro Shibata[1]   Akiko Aizawa[2]

[1]NHK Science and Technology Research Labolatories   [2]National Institute of Informatics

ABSTRACT

On-demand services for TV program, which provide users with past programs on demand, are becoming popular. It is therefore necessary to find a means of efficiently searching for programs that users want to view, from huge program archives. This paper proposes an automatic method of retrieving programs related to the one being viewed by the user. To that end, we compute similarity between program summaries and closed captions obtained from broadcasting by weighting significant words such as compound words and named entities. Additionally our method provides inter-program relationship labels to indicate why the results of relevant programs were chosen. The results of an evaluation showed that the method recommended relevant programs with higher accuracy than baseline methods and indicated appropriate relationship labels for related programs.

ACM Classification Keywords

H3.3. Information Search and Retrieval: Search process.

General Terms

Languages, Algorithms

INTRODUCTION

On-demand services for TV program, which provide users with past programs over the Internet, are becoming popular [1]. It is therefore necessary to find a means of efficiently searching for programs that users want to view from huge program archives.

In related studies of TV program retrieval, there are metadata-based methods using keywords annotated by broadcasting station such as performer name and genre [2], and rating-based methods using evaluation and selection given by customers, such as movie ratings [3]. The metadata-based method is useful for making rough classifications; it is not, however, enough to retrieve programs which have relevant content because of a lack of kind and resolution of the metadata. The rating-based methods are effective for recommendation; it is, however, generally difficult to obtain such rich rating data of users.

In this paper, we propose a summary-based method to automatically retrieve programs related to a query program that the user selected by considering compound words and named entities in summaries as a part of Electronic Program Guide (EPG) and in closed captions.

TV PROGRAM RETRIEVAL BASED ON SUMMARIES

In program retrieval using broadcast summaries, the similarities using only word statistics such as tf-idf based cosine or Okapi BM25 are not very effective because broadcast summaries are too short to obtain reliable statistics. Therefore, we add weights to semantically significant words, such as named entities (NEs) and compound words. These words are important to give relevant programs higher rankings. We propose to use the similarity between a query program Q and a relevant program D given by (1).

$$S(D,Q) = \sum_n \sum_{t^{(n)} \in Q} w_{ne}(t^{(n)}) \times w_{ng}(n) \times S_{BM}(t^{(n)}, D) \quad (1)$$

The similarity is based on n-gram adding the weights w_{ng} for compound words and w_{ne} for NEs. The term $t^{(n)}$ is an n-gram included in Q, and n is the number of word chains in the n-gram (n=1-3). The score S_{BM} stands for the score based on Okapi BM25.

Scoring based on Okapi BM25

Our method uses the score based on Okapi BM25 [4], given by (2) because it can modify parameters such as the weights of word frequencies in the query program Q and the database DB and the weights of normalized items based on the length of summaries.

$$S_{BM}(t^{(n)}, D) = \frac{(k_1+1)tf_d}{k_1((1-b)+b \cdot dl/dl_{av})+tf_d} \frac{(k_3+1)tf_q}{k_3+tf_q} \log\left(\frac{M-m+0.5}{m+0.5}\right) \quad (2)$$

M: # in DB, m: # of including $t^{(n)}$, tf_d and tf_q: frequency of $t^{(n)}$ in D and Q, dl: length of D, dl_{av}: average length of programs in DB, $k1, k3$ and b: constant parameters.

Extension to n-gram

We extend word to n-gram in BM25 and sum all of the n-gram scores to weight compound words. For example, if *graduate school* occurs in two summaries, the total score of *graduate school* is calculated by summing up 1-gram scores of *graduate* and of *school*, and the 2-gram score of *graduate school*. Thus the score of *graduate school* will get a higher score than one in which the words *graduate* and *school* appear separately. Note that if n is large, the scores will rise too high, so we use a damping weight $w_{ng}=1/n$.

Weighting by Extended Named Entity

Common nouns and proper names might have similar scores in BM25 if words have the same frequencies. For that reason, we apply weightings w_{ne} that utilize NEs. Many studies have only used person name, organization and location as NEs. However these general NEs are not enough to grasp the content. Therefore, we use extended named entities (ENEs) [5] for weighting.

In a preliminary experiment, we chose five types of ENE tags: person name (PN), job title (JT), organization (ORG), living things such as animal or plant (LT), and location (GPE). Based on the results of experiment, the w_{ne} of PN was set to 1.0; JT 1.2, LT 1.3, ORG 1.1 and GPE 1.1. ENEs are shown as italics in the following EPG example.

> The world's fastest *monkey* is in *Cameroon* in *Central Africa*. Long-legged and exceptionally stylish, it's the *Patas monkey*. It runs at 50 kph over the savanna. ....We look at the secrets of the performance of these *top athletes* and their unique child-raising habits.

Relationship Label

Relationship labels (R-labels) indicates the relationship between the query and retrieved programs. This enables the user to know why each program was recommended. The R-Label $L(D,Q)$ given by (3) takes advantage of the S_{BM} and w_{ne} calculated in the retrieval steps for each n-gram.

$$L(D,Q) = \arg\max_{t^{(n)}} (S_{BM}(t^{(n)}, D) \times w_{ne}(t^{(n)})) \quad (3)$$

The n-gram $t^{(n)}$ with the greatest S_{BM} weighted by w_{ne} is selected as the R-label. Since different n-grams appear depending on the query program, the retrieval results might have different R-labels even for the same program.

EXPERIMENTS

Implementation of Experimental System

We prototyped a TV program retrieval system based on the proposed method and applied it to 2218 program summaries from NHK On-Demand [1] as program database.

The ENE recognizer was created by using our in-house ENE corpus as training data and Conditional Random Fields as the machine learning method. The features of learning included the letters of morpheme, reading, part of speech, and ID in a concept dictionary. The accuracy when applied to the summaries for dramas and movies was an F-measure of 0.91.

To present the retrieved results, we developed an interface that gathers relevant programs with the same R-labels into one category (see Figure 1). In this example, science programs and variety shows related to one topic of news show "*Action of anti-pollen in house*" appear as results with R-labels such as *hay fever*, *specialist*, and *infectious disease*.

Evaluation

We performed an experiment evaluating the accuracy of the retrieval result and quality of R-labels. The accuracy was whether the user felt that the retrieved programs were related to the query program. The quality of R-labels was whether the label was appropriate for the relationship between the query program and retrieved programs.

Ten test subjects evaluated the top 20 programs in the retrieval results. We set the correct data the programs which more than five subjects judged as relevant. The query programs were 13 programs in different genres and five news topics. Note that five news topics used their closed captions as summaries instead of the summaries.

Figure 1: Example retrieval result

Table1: Evaluation of retrieval results

	P@3	P@5	P@10	P@20
tf-idf	0.722	0.656	0.544	0.461
BM25	0.741	0.689	0.589	0.478
Proposed	0.796	0.700	0.606	0.514

Table 2: Evaluation of relationship labels

Relevant	Almost relevant	Not relevant
0.558	0.404	0.038

Accuracy of retrieval was evaluated with precision at rank (P@rank). We compared proposed method with the tf-idf based cosine similarity and pure Okapi BM25. The proposed method was evaluated more highly than the baseline methods (see Table 1). The weighting of ENEs and compound words based on n-gram boosted the ordering of programs containing those representations.

To evaluate the quality of R-Label, we performed a subjective evaluation (relevant; almost relevant; not relevant) for relevant programs. The results revealed that 96.2% of the R-labels were judged to be relevant or almost relevant (See Table 2). This is thought to be because our method could choose R-Labels that have semantic meanings, such as compound words and ENEs.

CONCLUSION

We proposed a summary-based method to retrieve relevant TV programs with relationship labels. Evaluations showed that our method retrieved relevant programs with higher accuracy than baseline methods and indicated appropriate relationship labels for related programs.

REFERENCES

1. https://www.nhk-ondemand.jp/

2. Y. Mizoguchi, T. Nakamoto, K. Asakawa, S. Nagano, M. Inaba and T. Kawamura: TV Navigation Agent for Measuring Semantic Similarity between Programs, Proceedings of AWESOME'07, pp75-84 (2007).

3. T. Raiko, A. Ilin and J. Karhunen: Principal Component Analysis for Large Scale Problems with Lots of Missing Values, Proceedings of ECML2007, pp 691-698 (2007).

4. S. Robertson and S. Walker: Okapi/ Keenbow at TREC-8, Proceedings of TREC-8, pp151-162 (1999).

5. S. Sekine : Extended Named Entity Ontology with Attribute Information, Proceeding of LREC2008 (2008).

MagiTact: Interaction with Mobile Devices Based on Compass (Magnetic) Sensor

Hamed Ketabdar
Quality and Usability Lab,
Deutsche Telekom Laboratories,
TU Berlin
Ernst-Reuter-Platz 7
10587 Berlin, Germany
hamed.ketabdar@telekom.de

Kamer Ali Yüksel
Technical University of Berlin
Ernst-Reuter-Platz 7
10587, Berlin, Germany
kamer.yuksel@telekom.de

Mehran Roshandel
Deutsche Telekom
Laboratories,
Ernst-Reuter-Platz 7
10587 Berlin, Germany
mehran.roshandel@telekom.de

ABSTRACT

In this work, we present a new technique for efficient use of 3D space around a mobile device for interaction with the device. Around Device Interaction (ADI) enables extending interaction space of small mobile and tangible devices beyond their physical boundary. Our proposed method is based on using compass (magnetic field) sensor integrated in mobile devices (e.g. iPhone 3GS, G1 Android). In this method, a properly shaped permanent magnet (e.g. in the shape of a rod, pen or a ring) is used for interaction. The user makes coarse gestures in the 3D space around the device using the magnet. Movement of the magnet affects the magnetic field sensed by the compass sensor integrated in the device. The temporal pattern of the gesture is then used as a basis for sending different interaction commands to the mobile device. Zooming, turning pages, accepting/rejecting calls, clicking items, controlling a music player, and game interaction are some example use cases. The proposed method does not impose changes in hardware specifications of the mobile device, and unlike optical methods is not limited by occlusion problems.

Author Keywords

Around Device Interaction, Mobile Devices, Compass (Magnetic) Sensor, Magnet, Movement-Based Gestures.

ACM Classification Keywords

I.5.4 [Computing Methodologies]: Pattern Recognition, Applications – *Signal processing.*

General Terms

Algorithms

INTRODUCTION: AROUND DEVICE INTERACTION

Around Device Interaction (ADI) is being increasingly investigated as an efficient interaction technique for mobile and tangible devices. ADI provides possibility of extending interaction space of small mobile devices beyond their physical boundary allowing effective use of 3D space around the device for interaction. This can be especially useful for small tangible/wearable mobile or controller

devices such cell phones, wrist watches, headsets, etc. In these devices, it is extremely difficult to operate small buttons and touch screens. However, the space beyond the device can be easily used, no matter how small the device is. ADI can be also very useful for interaction when the device screen is not in the line of user's sight.

ADI concept can allow coarse movement-based gestures made in the 3D space around the device to be used for sending different interaction commands such as turning pages (in an e-book or calendar), changing sound volume, zooming, rotation, etc. ADI techniques are based on using different sensory inputs such as camera [1], infrared distance sensors [2], touch screen at the back of device [3], electric field sensing [4], etc.

In this work, we propose ADI based on interaction with compass (magnetic) sensor integrated in some mobile devices, using a properly shaped magnetic material. The user takes the magnet which can be in shape of a rod, pen or ring in hand, and draws coarse gestures in 3D space around the device (Fig. 1). These gestures can be interpreted as different interaction commands by the device. In the next section, we describe our approach in more detail.

OUR APPROACH: INTERACTION BASED ON MAGNETIC FIELD SENSOR

In this work, we demonstrate our initial investigations towards using compass (magnetic field) sensor integrated in mobile devices (e.g. iPhone 3GS, G1 Android) for ADI. In our method, we use a regular magnetic material in a proper shape to be taken in hand (e.g. rod shaped, pen, ring), to influence compass (magnetic) sensor by different movement-based gestures, and hence interact with the device. We demonstrate the use of this interaction in different applications such as turning pages, zooming, reacting to a call alert, and music playback.

In the Introduction, we mentioned to a few methods for ADI. Getting useful information from magnetic sensor is algorithmically much simpler than implementing computer vision techniques. Our simple yet effective approach also does not suffer from illumination variation and occlusion problems. Our technique does not impose changes or adding huge number of extra sensors to mobile devices. For mobile devices such as iPhone and G1 Android, it is only necessary to have a properly shaped magnet as an extra accessory. In addition, considering the fact that the back of mobile device is usually covered by hand, optical ADI techniques (e.g. camera and infra-red based) can face difficulties for using the space at the back of device. However, since the interaction in our method is based on magnetic field (which can pass through hand), the space at the back of device can be efficiently used for interaction.

GESTURE RECOGNITION BASED ON MAGNETIC FIELD

The gestures are created based on moving the magnet (a rod or ring) by hand in the space around the device along different 3D trajectories. The gestures studied in this work are mainly based on movement of magnet in front or at the back of device in different directions with different periodicities.

The compass (magnetic) sensors provides a measure of magnetic field strength along x, y, and z directions. The values change over a range of -128 to 128. The compass sensor can be affected by the magnetic fields around the device, most importantly the earth's magnetic field. In order to decrease the influence of these factors in gesture recognition, we calculate derivative of the signals over time. This is achieved by subtracting two consecutive values, and acts as a high pass filter which allows only evidences related to gestures appear at the output. The gestures are generated by rather fast movement of magnet (resulting in fast changes in magnetic field), therefore their evidence can be passed through a high pass filter.

The next processing step is feature extraction. The features we have used are mainly based on average strength of magnetic field in different directions, average piecewise correlation between field strength in different directions, and zero crossing rate (for different directions). All the features are extracted from high pass filtered signals. The beginning and end of each gesture is identified based on change of magnitude signal over a threshold. The mentioned features are extracted over a window marked by the beginning and end of gesture.

Final classification of gestures is done based on extracted features using a heuristically designed binary decision tree. The decision tree algorithm can run faster on the mobile device as compared to some statistical machine learning algorithms. Correlation between different directions, magnitude in different directions and zero crossing rate are used as basis for decision making and classification.

Initial evaluation of the algorithm has shown convincing gesture recognition results for 6 gestures and 5 users,

reaching an accuracy over 90%. This is still initial results and at the demo level. Although actual interaction with our demo seems quite satisfactory, our ongoing studies show potential for obtaining even better classification results.

IMPLEMENTATION

We have implemented a demo application based on the presented method for iPhone 3GS. The interaction is used to turn pages left-right or up-down in a photo view and document view application, as well as zooming a map in and out. Zooming functionality can be also achieved using space at the back of device, so that the screen doe not get occluded. The application can also demonstrate rejecting/accepting a call using our interaction method. This functionality can be achieved even when the phone is in a bag or pocket, and facilitates dealing with unexpected calls in an improper situation (e.g. office, meeting). In addition, the application demonstrates interacting with a music player for changing sound volume or music track.

REFERENCES

[1] Starner, T. and Auxier, J. and Ashbrook, D. and Gandy, M, The gesture pendant: A self-illuminating, wearable, infrared computer vision system for home automation control and medical monitoring, International Symposium on Wearable Computing, 2000, pp. 87-94.

[2] Hinckley, K., Pierce, J., Sinclair, M., and Horvitz, E. 2000. Sensing techniques for mobile interaction. In Proc. of

UIST '00. ACM, pp. 91-100.

[3] Baudisch, P. and Chu, G. Back-of-device interaction allows creating very small touch devices. In Proc. of CHI '09.

[4] Theremin, L.S. The Design of a Musical Instrument Based on Cathode Relays. Reprinted in Leonardo Music J., No. 6, 1996, 49-50.

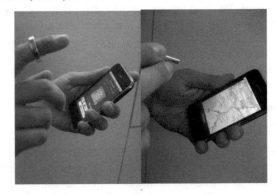

Figure 1

Smart Ring: Controlling Call Alert Functionality Based on Audio and Movement Analysis

Hamed Ketabdar
Quality and Usability Lab, Deutsche Telekom
Laboratories, TU Berlin
Ernst-Reuter-Platz 7, 10587, Berlin, Germany
hamed.ketabdar@telekom.de

Kamer Ali Yüksel
Technical University of Berlin
Ernst-Reuter-Platz 7, 10587, Berlin, Germany
kamer-ali.yuksel@telekom.de

ABSTRACT

In this work, we present a method for controlling call alert functionality in mobile phones. It has happened for almost everybody experiencing a situation that call alert functionality is not proper for actual ambient context, leading to missing a phone call or disturbing others by a loud ring. In this work, we use audio and physical movement analysis to distinguish between different situations in which a mobile phone may ring, and adjust the call alert functionality accordingly. Considering the fact that mobile phones are usually carried in a pocket or bag, capturing ambient audio is not usually practically perfect. The novelty in our work is using information about physical movements of user of mobile device in addition to analysis of ambient audio. Analysis of user movements is based on information captured by acceleration sensors integrated in mobile phone. The call alert functionality is then adjusted based on a combination of ambient audio level and physical activities of user.

Author Keywords

Call Alert Functionality, Ambient Audio, Physical Movements, Acceleration Sensors, Ambient Context

ACM Classification Keywords

I.5.4 [Computing Methodologies]: Pattern Recognition, Applications – Signal processing.

General Terms

Algorithms

INTRODUCTION

Mobile phones have become an essential in our lives. They are used frequently in many situations and places ranging from home, work, outdoor, partying, restaurants, etc. Besides such a widespread use of mobile phones, some unpleasant experiences are also associated with them. Almost everybody has experienced missing some important calls, or disturbing others by a very loud phone ring in an improper situation [1]. These unpleasant cases are usually due to the fact that the call alert functionality is not proper

for the actual situation of mobile phone's user. If the call alert is in "vibration" mode, or too low volume ring, the user may not realize the call alert if he is in a noisy place such as a restaurant or party, or just walking in a crowded street. The user may decide then to increase the ring volume, however this does not solve the problem. Soon when he is back at work or a quiet place, the loud ring starts disturbing his colleagues! A potential solution for this problem would be adjusting call alert functionality based on the actual situation of user and ambient context.

There has been research on context aware mobile devices which can adapt to actual context [2, 3]. Controlling call alert functionality can be a case of such adaption/adjustment. Contextual data is these approaches are usually collected using several external sensors (e.g. microphone for ambient noise, acceleration sensors for movements). However, using internally integrated sensory inputs (such as embedded microphone) can be challenging, and on the other hand more practical as it does not impose wearing extra sensory units. For instance in [4] ambient noise level is measured using embedded microphone in mobile device, and loudness of the noise is then estimated. The call alert functionality is then adjusted based on a reverse relation with loudness of ambient noise. However, the main practical drawback in such an approach (using embedded microphone) is capturing ambient audio. As the phone is usually carried in a pocket or bag, audio information captured by the mobile phone's microphone is not always a proper representative of the ambient audio. According to our experiments, a majority of captured audio content is components caused by friction between the phone and materials inside a pocket or bag. These components can practically hide ambient audio information. This issue can become more problematic especially when the user is engaged in physical activities such as walking. Additionally, physical activity itself may also affect user perception of call alerts.

Considering above argument, in this work we propose a method for adjusting call alert functionality (using embedded sensors in a mobile phone) which takes into account physical activities of user, in addition to ambient audio analysis. Information about physical activities of user is captured using acceleration sensor integrated in mobile

415

phone. The alert is adjusted based on a weighted combination of activity level of user (movement level of mobile device) and ambient audio captured by embedded microphone. Ambient audio gains a higher share when mobile device movements are insignificant, and hence the captured audio content is more reliable.

ADJUSTING CALL ALERTS

As already mentioned, we use a combination of audio data captured by microphone, and movement related data captured by accelerometers integrated in mobile phone. Accelerometer sensor which is integrated in many new mobile devices (e.g. iPhone, G1 Android, etc.) captures acceleration of device along the three axis. It is traditionally used for rotating screen when the phone is rotated. Acceleration data can also deliver some information about movements of the device, and user movements assuming that the device is carried by the user. Activity level of user can affect his perception of call alerts, as being engaged in high physical activities such as running or walking can increase the chance of missing calls.

Combination of audio and movement related data provides a score which is used for call alert adjustment. Call alert strength has a reverse relation with this score. In combination of audio and movement data for call alert adjustment, the basic idea is to weight ambient audio data based on its reliability. As a mobile phone is usually carried in a pocket or bag, audio data during carriage can be heavily biased by the components caused by rubbing against materials inside the pocket or bag. In contrast, ambient audio can be captured in a more reliable when the phone is outside e.g. on a table.

The reliability is determined based on movement level of device, i.e. activity level of its user assuming that the phone is carried by the user. If movement of the device is not significant, we assume that audio data is reliable as a measure of ambient noise. On the other hand, if movement of device is significant, the weight of ambient audio data is reduced in the adjustment process, and movement level of device (user) is used as main factor for adjusting call alerts. For instance, a long continues walk of user can indicate being outdoor, therefore need for stronger call alert. If the user is running, call alert should be even stronger! Estimating movement level of device, and ambient audio level are described in the next sections.

ESTIMATING MOVEMENT LEVEL OF MOBILE DEVICE

In order to estimate movement level of mobile device, low pass components of the acceleration signals which are mainly due to gravity force are removed (high pass filter). The magnitude of acceleration is then calculated using 3 axis acceleration components. The magnitude acceleration is then processed over a window of 10 seconds, and some features mainly based on average magnitude and average rate of change is calculated. A weighted sum of these features is used as basis for estimating movement level of device.

AMBIENT AUDIO ESTIMATION

Audio samples are obtained from microphone integrated in the device. We use root-mean-square (RMS) of the audio signal over a window of 10 seconds as a measure of loudness.

IMPLEMENTATION

We have implemented the presented method on iPhone 3G mobile device. Audio is captured at 8KHz, and acceleration data is captured at 50Hz rate. The strength of call alert for actual situation is obtained in reverse relation with the score estimated from ambient audio and device movement. In this relation, there is also a tuning factor which can be adjusted to enhance the relation. If the call alert strength is below a threshold, the alert functionality is switched to vibration mode, otherwise the strength of call alert is mapped to level of ring volume. The demo application automatically simulates call alert situations every 20 seconds, and the call alert functionality is adjusted accordingly. The demo application has been tested in different indoor and outdoor situations providing higher satisfaction with call alert functionality.

ACKNOWLEDGMENTS

We would like to thank Tim Polzehl, Mehran Roshandel and Matti Lyra for helpful discussions.

REFERENCES

[1] Monk, A., Carroll, J., Parker, S., Blythe, M., Why are mobile phones annoying? Behaviour & Information Technology, Vol. 23, no. 1, pp. 33-41. Jan.-Feb. 2004

[2] Daniel Siewiorek, Asim Smailagic, Junichi Furukawa, Neema Moraveji, Kathryn Reiger, and Jeremy Shaffer, SenSay: A Context-Aware Mobile Phone, Proceedings of the 7th IEEE International Symposium on Wearable Computers, 2003.

[3] A Khalil, K Connelly, Context-aware Configuration: A study on improving cell phone awareness, Lecture Notes in Computer Science, 2005, Springer.

[4] Chris Mitchell, Adjust Your Ring Volume For Ambient Noise, MSDN Magazine, October 2007.

ActivityMonitor: Assisted Life Using Mobile Phones

Hamed Ketabdar
Quality and Usability Lab, Deutsche Telekom
Laboratories, TU Berlin
Ernst-Reuter-Platz 7, 10587, Berlin, Germany
hamed.ketabdar@telekom.de

Matti Lyra
School of Informatics, University of Sussex
104 Ditchling Rise, BN1 4QR Brighton
East Sussex, England
matti.lyra@gmail.com

ABSTRACT

In this work, we present a system and methodology for using mobile phones for monitoring physical activities of a user, and its applications in assisting elderly and people with need for special care and monitoring. The method is based on processing acceleration data provided by accelerometers integrated in mobile phones. This information is sent to a monitoring server, analyzed and presented as different health related factors for assistance, monitoring and healthcare purposes. A monitoring agent can use a desktop application to observe pattern of physical activities of several users in a live manner, and receive warnings in case of unexpected physical conditions. The data can be also stored offline for longer term analysis of physical behaviour and health. The desktop application also provides different options for managing, browsing, and searching activity related data.

Author Keywords

Assisted Life, Live Activity Monitoring, Mobile Phones, Acceleration Sensor, Health Related Factors, Desktop Application

ACM Classification Keywords

I.5.4 [Computing Methodologies]: Pattern Recognition, Applications – Signal processing.

General Terms

Algorithms

INTRODUCTION

Mobile phone are wide spread devices in our daily life. Almost everybody has a mobile phone and carries this device regularly during a major part of his daily life. Considering such a popularity and user friendliness of mobile phones, we present a demo application which can turn mobile phones to devices for constantly monitoring physical activities of a user. Such an application can send information related to physical activity pattern of user and related health factors to a server for monitoring purposes. On the server side, a monitoring agent can use a desktop application to visualize and analyse the data sent to the

server in live or offline manner. This can be especially useful for people who are in constant need for assistance and monitoring, such as elderly or people with movement or psychological disorders. In addition to this group of users, healthy people can also benefit form such an application by constantly receiving reports on details of their activity level and energy consumption.

Regarding the issue of heath care and activity analysis, there are a few commercial applications especially for iPhone platform [1,2]. These applications use data provided by GPS to analyse amount of activity during sports. However, they are dependent on availability of GPS signal for activity level estimation. In many indoor places, GPS signal is not available. In addition, user position information is not strongly correlated with amount or pattern of user activity. In contrast, acceleration information can be strongly correlated with amount and pattern of force exerted by user, and thus more directly related to amount and pattern of user activity. There has been research on using acceleration sensors for human activity analysis [3, 4, 5], however these systems impose wearing extra sensory, analysis, and communication units. The user should also be usually within a limited range of communication devices. Considering the fact that a mobile phone is usually equipped with all these sensory and communication facilities, and more importantly carried comfortably and regularly by users during their daily life, we propose to use mobile phones for remote activity monitoring and assistance purposes. The remote monitoring can be performed everywhere data access services are available.

ACCELERATION DATA AND ACTIVITY ANALYSIS

Acceleration sensor which is integrated in mobile devices such as iPhone 3G and G1 Android provides acceleration data along the 3 axis. As the device is carried by the user, the acceleration data can deliver information about activity pattern of user. In this work, we assume that the mobile phone is carried in pant pocket.

The acceleration pattern sensed by the mobile device can be due to multiple sources such as physical activity pattern of user, movement of a vehicle, and gravity force. The components caused by physical activities of user are usually higher frequency components, while the rest contribute as low frequency components. Therefore, the first step is preprocessing acceleration signals using a high pass filter. This removes components caused by gravity force and movements of a vehicle.

The next step in activity level estimation and classification is feature extraction. For activity level estimation, the magnitude of acceleration is calculated using 3 axis acceleration components. The magnitude acceleration is then processed over a window of 10 seconds, and some features mainly based on average magnitude value and average rate of change is calculated. A weighted sum of these features is used as basis for estimating activity level of user. For activity classification, a similar feature extraction process is performed over sliding windows of 10 seconds with 30% overlap. Features which are used for activity classification are based on magnitude, and rate of change of acceleration along different axis, as well as piecewise correlation between acceleration values along different axis. A simple Multi-Layer Perceptron (MLP) classifier is then used for training and classification. We have 5 main classes of "mobile phone not carried by user", "no activity", "resting", "walking", and "high activity". We have also used a simple heuristically designed binary decision tree for the classification leading to comparable results.

IMPLEMENTATION OF THE SYSTEM

We have used an iPhone 3G as mobile device. Linear acceleration data is provided along x, y, and z axis at 50Hz sampling rate. The acceleration data is sent to a server using available connection (e.g. Wi-Fi, GPRS, etc.). We have developed a desktop application which analyzes this data and presents it as different activity and health related factors to an agent (Figure 1). The analysis mainly includes estimation of general activity level, and classification of activities into certain categories. The desktop application allows observing activity pattern, activity level, activity category, energy consumption estimates, periodicity and several other statistics in real time. It also provides the possibility to store this data, browse it over time, or search it for a certain activity category in a custom time span. In addition, it provides the possibility to check for certain irregularities such as long periods of very low or very high activity, and issue warnings for the monitoring agent. This feature makes the monitoring process semi or full automatic, and allows the agent to monitor several users simultaneously.

ACKNOWLEDGMENTS

We would like to thank Michael Rohs, Shiva Sundaram, and Christine Kühnel for helpful discussions.

REFERENCES

[1] http://www.runkeeper.com

[2] http://www.mapmyride.com

[3] Song, K., Wang, Y., Remote activity monitoring of the elderly using a two-axis accelerometer, CACS Automatic Control Conference, Taiwan, Nov. 2005.

[4] Wang, S., Yang, J., Chen, X., Human activity recognition with user-free accelerometers in the sensor networks, Neural Networks and Brain, Vol. 2, pp. 1212-1217, 2005.

[5] http://www.minisun.com/

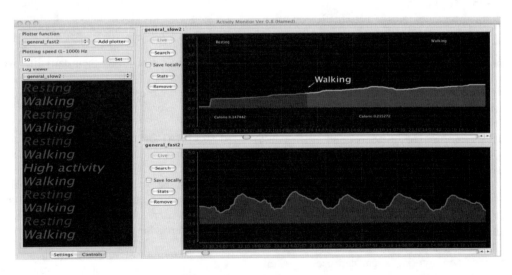

Figure 1. ActivityMonitor Desktop

The $3 Recognizer: Simple 3D Gesture Recognition on Mobile Devices

Sven Kratz
Deutsche Telekom Laboratories, TU Berlin
Ernst-Reuter-Platz 7
10587 Berlin, Germany
sven.kratz@telekom.de

Michael Rohs
Deutsche Telekom Laboratories, TU Berlin
Ernst-Reuter-Platz 7
10587 Berlin, Germany
michael.rohs@telekom.de

ABSTRACT

We present the $3 Gesture Recognizer, a simple but robust gesture recognition system for input devices featuring 3D acceleration sensors. The algorithm is designed to be implemented quickly in prototyping environments, is intended to be device-independent and does not require any special toolkits or frameworks, but relies solely on simple trigonometric and geometric calculations. Our method requires significantly less training data than other gesture recognizers and is thus suited to be deployed and to deliver results rapidly.

Author Keywords

Gesture recognition, recognition rates, classifier, user interfaces, rapid prototyping, 3D gestures

ACM Classification Keywords

H5.2 [Information interfaces and presentation]: User interfaces – *Input devices and strategies*. I5.2. [Pattern Recognition]: Design methodology – *Classifier design and evaluation*. I5.5 [Pattern Recognition]: Implementation – Interactive Systems

General Terms

Algorithms, Performance

INTRODUCTION AND RELATED WORK

An increasing number of mobile devices are equipped with 3D accelerometers, which calls for suitable methods for 3D gesture recognition on these platforms. Gesture input for mobile devices can be a way to overcome the limitations of miniature input facilities and small displays, since the range of movement is not restricted by the size of the device. Our work is based on previous work by Wobbrock et al. [4], who developed a simple "$1 Recognizer" using basic geometry and trigonometry. The "$1 Recognizer" is targeted at user interface

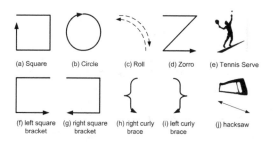

Figure 1. The reference gesture vocabulary containing the gesture classes used for the preliminary evaluation. (b) describes a clockwise circular motion, (c) a wrist rolling motion, (e) a gesture resembling a tennis serve and (j) a rapid forward-backwards motion.

prototyping for 2D touch-screen-based gesture recognition and therefore focuses on ease of implementation on novel hardware platforms. Our contribution is in extending and modifying Wobbrock et al.'s algorithm to work with 3D acceleration data. Instead of capturing exact pixel positions on a touch screen, acceleration data is of much lower quality because it is prone to noise, and additionally, drift error accumulates as the path of a gesture entry is integrated. We extend Wobbrock's original algorithm with a scoring heuristic to lower the rate of false positives. The major contribution of this work is the creation a simple gesture recognizer that is designed to recognize "true" 3D Gestures, i.e. gestures which are not limited to shapes that can be drawn in a 2D plane. The advantage of true 3D gesture recognition is that more natural movements, such a tennis serve or boxing punches can be input by the user. Like the "$1 Recognizer," our approach is quick and cheap to implement, does not require library support, needs only minimal parameter adjustment and minimal training, about 5 samples per gesture provide good recognition results. It is therefore very valuable for user interface prototyping and rapid application development. It can also easily be integrated into mobile interfaces that take advantage of other modalities, like speech, or touch-based interaction with RFID/NFC.

THE $3 GESTURE RECOGNIZER

Extending Wobbrock's [4] work, we present a gesture recognizer that can recognize gestures from 3D acceleration data as input. A detailed description of the algorithm we developed can be found in [2]. Our demo is implemented in Objective-C as an iPhone 3GS application, and in Java running on the Android platform, but the method is by no means limited to these devices.

Gesture Trace and Gesture Class Library

In contrast to [3], modification or pre-processing of the raw acceleration data in any way (filtering, smoothing, etc.) is not required by our method. To determine the current change in acceleration, we subtract the current acceleration value reported by the device's acceleration sensor from the previous one. We thus obtain an *acceleration delta*. By summation of the acceleration deltas, we obtain a *gesture trace T* (which can be plotted in a 3D space (Figure 1 (e),(j)) or projected into a 2D plane (gestures (a)-(d), (f)-(i)) to obtain a graphical representation of the gesture [1]. The *gesture class library L* contains a predefined number of *training gesture* traces for each *gesture class G*.

Gesture Recognition Problem

The basic task of our algorithm is to find the best matching gesture class from the gesture class library. To find a matching gesture class, we compare the gesture trace entered by the user to all known gesture traces stored the gesture class library and thus generate a score table that lists the comparison score of the entered gesture with the known gestures. A heuristic is then applied to the score table to determine if a gesture has been correctly recognized.

Resampling

For optimal classification, the gesture trace needs to be resampled to have a number of points equal to the template gestures. Furthermore, our resampling method ensures that the points are re-distributed to be at equal distances from each other.

Rotation to "Indicative Angle" and Rescaling

To correct for rotational errors during gesture entry, the resampled gesture trace is rotated once along the gesture's *indicative angle*. Like Wobbrock, we define the indicative angle as the angle between the gesture's first point p_0 and its centroid $c = (\bar{x}, \bar{y}, \bar{z})$. After rotation, the gesture trace is scaled to fit into a normalize cube, to compensate for scaling differences between gestures. After these pre-processing steps, we have converted the original user input to a gesture that is ready for matching with candidates from the gesture class library.

Search for Minimum Distance at Best Angle

We use the average MSE (Mean Square Error) as distance measure between the gesture entered by the user and candidate gestures in the gesture class library. To compensate for rotational differences, we adapted a Golden Section Search (GSS). This type of search uses the Golden Ratio ($\varphi = 0.5(-1 + \sqrt{5})$) to iteratively estimate the optimal rotation around three axis of the coordinate system. The end result of GSS is a table

sorted by matching scores with the corresponding gesture class ID.

Scoring Heuristic

Wobbrock's original algorithm did not feature a heuristic to reduce the occurance of false positives, which is a common problem for simple gesture recognition algorithms operating on large gesture vocabularies [4]. The matches obtained from gestures entered as 3D acceleration data are not as precise as strokes entered on a touch screen. To compensate for the weaker matches, we have developed our own scoring heuristic, which processes the score table described in the previous section. After sorting the score table by maximum score, our heuristic determines the recognized gesture with the following rules:

- ε is defined as the threshold score.
- Iff the highest-scoring candidate in the score table has a score $> 1.1\varepsilon$, return this candidate's gesture ID.
- Iff, within the top three candidates in the score table, two candidates exist of the same gesture class and have a score $> 0.95\varepsilon$, respectively, return the gesture ID of these two candidates.
- Else, return "Gesture not recognized!".

Using this heuristic, we achieved a considerable reduction of false recognitions compared to Wobbrock's original strategy of selecting the gesture candidate with the highest matching score to determine the recognized gesture.

SUMMARY

We present a simple, easy-to-implement gesture recognizer for input devices equipped with 3D acceleration sensors. The idea behind our gesture recognition algorithm is to provide a quick and cheap way to implement gesture recognition for true 3D gestures (such as the reference gesture (e)), for devices equipped with 3D acceleration sensors. Our method does not require any advanced software frameworks or toolkits. An example application area for our gesture recognizer is user interface prototyping.

REFERENCES

1. Sanna Kallio, Juha Kela, Jani Mäntyjärvi, and Johan Plomp. Visualization of hand gestures for pervasive computing environments. In *Proc. AVI '06*, pages 480–483. ACM, 2006.

2. Sven Kratz and Michael Rohs. A $3 gesture recognizer – simple gesture recognition for devices equipped with 3d acceleration sensors. In *Proc. IUI'10*, 2010.

3. Thomas Schloemer, Benjamin Poppinga, Niels Henze, and Susanne Boll. Gesture recognition with a wii controller. In *Proc. TEI '08*, pages 11–14. ACM, 2008.

4. Jacob O. Wobbrock, Andrew D. Wilson, and Yang Li. Gestures without libraries, toolkits or training: a $1 recognizer for user interface prototypes. In *Proc. UIST '07*, pages 159–168, New York, NY, USA, 2007. ACM.

The RelFinder User Interface: Interactive Exploration of Relationships between Objects of Interest

Steffen Lohmann
Carlos III University
of Madrid
Leganés, Spain
slohmann@inf.uc3m.es

Philipp Heim
University of Stuttgart
Stuttgart, Germany
philipp.heim@vis.uni-
stuttgart.de

Timo Stegemann
University of
Duisburg-Essen
Duisburg, Germany
timo.stegemann@uni-due.de

Jürgen Ziegler
University of
Duisburg-Essen
Duisburg, Germany
juergen.ziegler@uni-due.de

ABSTRACT

Being aware of the relationships that exist between objects of interest is crucial in many situations. The RelFinder user interface helps to get an overview: Even large amounts of relationships can be visualized, filtered, and analyzed by the user. Common concepts of knowledge representation are exploited in order to support interactive exploration both on the level of global filters and single relationships. The RelFinder is easy-to-use and works on every RDF know-ledge base that provides standardized SPARQL access.

ACM Classification Keywords

H.5.2 User Interfaces: Graphical user interfaces (GUI)

General Terms

Human Factors, Management, Design

INTRODUCTION

Today's world is complex, and so are the relationships within most knowledge domains. Especially non-obvious relationships can easily be overlooked and therefore not considered in decision making or similar processes. This might result in wrong decisions and unwanted conse-quences. Algorithms that detect and extract relationships between objects of interest help to reduce this risk [1]. However, such algorithms only provide benefit when combined with sophisticated user interfaces that assist in the analysis and exploration of the found relationships. We developed the RelFinder user interface in order to cope with these challenges. In the following, we describe how it supports the interactive exploration of even large amounts of relationships.

THE RELFINDER USER INTERFACE

The Adobe Flex based user interface of the RelFinder offers an interactive visualization of relationships between given objects of interest. The relationships are found by an algorithm consisting of several SPARQL queries that can be applied to arbitrary RDF knowledge bases [2]. The labels of the objects are entered in input boxes in the upper part of the sidebar (see Fig. 1). They are then mapped to unique objects of the knowledge base by executing an

automatic (if possible) or manual (if not) disambiguation. These user-given objects serve as starting nodes in a graph that is drawn in the presentation area of the user interface. The starting nodes (indicated by a stronger border) are elliptically arranged in the graph visualization and are either directly connected with each other or indirectly via further objects that were found in between by the algorithm. The links between the objects are visualized as labeled and directed edges in accordance with their representation in the knowledge base[1]. Thus, relationships in the graph visualization follow the well-known subject-predicate-object schema making them easy to read.

The graph visualization and the sidebar offer sophisticated functionality for the interactive exploration of the found relationships. Whereas graph interaction takes place mainly on the level of single objects and relationships, the sidebar also supports the exploration on a more global level, as described in the following.

Filtering Relationships on Four Dimensions

The sidebar offers four types of filters that facilitate the exploration of the graph visualization by highlighting or removing certain elements. The first two filters are based on type information derived from the knowledge base:

- **Class Filter**: Objects in knowledge bases are typically assigned to certain classes (e.g., in RDF via `rdf:type`). These classes can be helpful in filtering objects that are not of interest. In Fig. 1, for instance, all objects belonging to the class `GrandPrixDrivers` of the YAGO ontology[2] have been removed from the graph.

- **Link Filter**: Links between objects are usually of a certain type that can also be used for filtering. In Fig. 1, five links of type `companyType` have been removed from the graph as they were not of interest to the user.

The two remaining filters use properties that characterize the topology of relationships:

- **Length Filter**: Relationships found by the algorithm are typically of different lengths, i.e., the number of objects the relationships consist of varies. This value is used by

---

[1] Actually, edge labels are also handled as nodes in the graph layout for readability reasons.
[2] http://www.mpi-inf.mpg.de/yago-naga/yago/

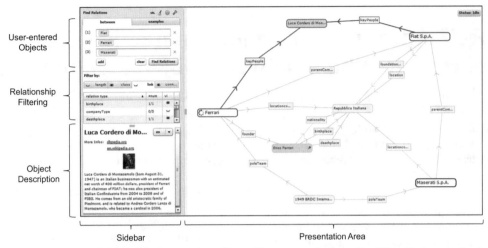

User-entered Objects

Relationship Filtering

Object Description

Sidebar

Presentation Area

Figure 1. Screenshot of the RelFinder user interface with an example from the DBpedia knowledge base.

the length filter. In Fig. 1, direct relationships (i.e., those without any objects) were removed from the visualization since the user was only interested in indirect ones.

- **Connectivity Filter**: The found relationships can also be classified according to the number of user-given objects (i.e., starting nodes in the graph) they connect. In Fig. 1, only relationships that contain the object ("Repubblica Italiana") connect all three user-given objects. The connectivity filter usually gains in importance when the number of user-given objects increases. This filter can then be used, for instance, to remove less connected relationships or to highlight those relationships that connect all user-given objects.

Direct Exploration of the Relationship Graph

Besides the filtering features offered in the sidebar, the graph visualization can also be directly explored on the level of single objects and relationships. On this level, the RelFinder provides the following interaction support:

- **Red Thread**: If an object node is selected, a "red thread" through the graph is drawn highlighting all relationships that contain this object (Fig. 1). That helps the user to visually track relationships within the graph.

- **Pick & Pin**: Single object nodes can be picked and repositioned, making it possible to decouple relationships from the automatic layout and analyze them separately (repositioned nodes are indicated by a needle symbol).

- **Infobox**: Additional information about the selected object (such as an image and a short description) is shown in the lower part of the sidebar. This information is gathered from the knowledge base by searching for well-known descriptors (e.g., `foaf:Image` or `rdfs:comment`).

In general, all visible objects that belong to the same class as the selected one are highlighted in the graph (by using the above-mentioned class filter). This helps to create some awareness of further objects that might be of interest to the user. In Fig. 1, for instance, another object ("Enzo Ferrari")

is highlighted that also belongs to the class `Person` of the DBpedia ontology[3].

DISCUSSION

The described features of the RelFinder assist users in exploring relationships between given objects of interest. The RelFinder therefore fills the gap between algorithms that find relationships within knowledge bases and their efficient usage in the context of real-world scenarios. In particular, it aims to facilitate the separation of relevant relationships from irrelevant ones and the discovery on non-obvious relationships by offering innovative visual features.

We tested the RelFinder against several RDF knowledge bases (e.g., DBpedia, LOD[4], LinkedMDB[5]) and evaluated it in a small user study. In sum, it shows that the interface is easy-to-use even for non-experts and very suitable to get a quick overview on relationships between objects of interest. Drawbacks are long response times in some cases or many irrelevant relationships in others. However, these are rather issues of the accessed knowledge bases than the RelFinder.

The RelFinder implements several further features that cannot be detailed here, such as an automatic initial filtering of relationships or a correction of false disambiguations. The accessed knowledge bases can easily be configured and new ones can be added via a settings menu or an XML-file. The current version of the RelFinder is accessible at [3].

REFERENCES

1. Sheth, A.P., Ramakrishnan, C. Relationship Web: Blazing Semantic Trails between Web Resources. *IEEE Internet Computing 11*, 4 (2007), 77-81.

2. Heim, P., Hellmann, S., Lehmann, J., Lohmann, S., Stegemann, T. RelFinder – Revealing Relationships in RDF Knowledge Bases. *Proc. SAMT* (2009), 182-187.

3. RelFinder: http://relfinder.semanticweb.org

---

[3] http://wiki.dbpedia.org/Ontology/

[4] http://linkeddata.org/

[5] http://linkedmdb.org/

Interactive Machine Translation using a Web-based Architecture *

Daniel Ortiz-Martínez   Luis A. Leiva   Vicent Alabau   Francisco Casacuberta

ITI - Instituto Tecnológico de Informática
Universidad Politécnica de Valencia
Camino de Vera s/n, 46022 - Valencia, Spain
{dortiz,luileito,valabau,fcn}@iti.upv.es

ABSTRACT

In this paper we present a new way of translating documents by using a Web-based system. An interactive approach is proposed as an alternative to post-editing the output of a machine translation system. In this approach, the user's feedback is used to validate or to correct parts of the system output that allow the generation of improved versions of the rest of the output.

Author Keywords

Computer Assisted Translation, Interactive Machine Translation, Statistical Machine Translation

ACM Classification Keywords

H.5.3 Group and Organization Interfaces: Web-based interaction; I.2.7 Natural Language Processing: Machine translation

General Terms

Design, Algorithms, Experimentation

INTRODUCTION

Computer-Assisted Translation (CAT) is an alternative approach to Machine Translation, integrating human expertise into the automatic translation process. Interactive Machine Translation (IMT) [1] can be considered as a special type of the CAT paradigm. In this framework, a human interacts with a system until the output desired by the human is completely generated. In this way of working the system provides an initial translation of a given source sentence on screen. Then the user validates a prefix of such system translation, introducing the next character(s) of the desired translation to correct some of the errors produced by the system; whereupon the system provides a suffix that best completes the prefix validated by the user. This process is repeated

*This work has been supported by the Spanish research programme Consolider Ingenio 2010: MIPRCV (CSD2007-00018), the Regional research programme PROMETEO/2009/014, the EC (FEDER) and the Spanish MEC grant TIN2006-15694-CO2-01.

until the desired translation has been completely generated. The IMT framework was later extended in [5], in which the possibility of *rejecting* a given suffix was introduced.

The WWW with its universal access to information and instant communication between users has created a physical and geographical freedom for translators that was inconceivable in the past [2]. The above mentioned interactive framework for CAT is shown to work quite well by a Web-based architecture. In similar web-based natural language processing systems [4], the user's feedback has shown to improve system accuracy, and increase both system ergonomics and user's acceptability.

Predictive interaction is approached in such a way that both the main and the feedback data streams help each-other to optimize overall performance and usability. Since the users operate within a Web browser, the system also provides cross-platform compatibility and requires neither computational power nor disk space on the client's machine.

DEMO DESCRIPTION

The proposed system coordinates client-side scripting with server-side technologies. At first, the Web interface loads an index of all available corpora. Each corpus consists of a Web document that is parsed from an automatically generated Translation Memory eXchange (TMX) file[1]. The user then navigates to a page and begins to translate the document by text segments. She can make corrections with the keyboard and also accomplish some mouse operations. User's feedback is then processed by the Interactive CAT engine.

Figure 1. Interactive CAT system architecture.

Figure 1 shows a diagram of the IMT system architecture. More interaction modes are being currently researched.

[1]TMX is an open XML standard for the exchange of translation documents.

source	Para ver la lista de recursos:
interaction-0	To view the resources list:
interaction-1	To view |a list of resources
interaction-2	To view a list i ng resources:
interaction-3	To view a listing o f resources:
acceptance	To view a listing of resources:

(a) User Interactions

(b) Demo Interface

Figure 2. 2(a) IMT session to translate a Spanish sentence into English and 2(b) implemented interface for the demo system. On interaction-0, the system suggests a translation. On interaction-1, the user moves the mouse to validate (VP) the first eight characters "To view" and rejects (R) the next word; then the system suggests completing the sentence with "a list of resources". On interaction-2 the user moves again the mouse to accept the next six characters and presses the key *i* (KS). interaction-3 is similar to interaction-2. Finally, the user completely accepts (A) the present suggestion.

User Interaction Protocol

The protocol that rules the interaction process has the following steps:

1. The system proposes a full translation of the selected text segment.

2. The user validates the longest prefix of the translation which is error-free and/or corrects the first error in the suffix. Corrections are entered by amendment keystrokes or mouse-clicks operations.

3. In this way, a new extended consolidated prefix is produced based on the previous validated prefix and the interaction amendments. Using this new prefix, the system suggests a suitable continuation of it.

4. Steps 2 and 3 are iterated until the user-desired translation is produced.

System Interaction Modes

Our proposed system works both at full-word and character level, that is, the user can introduce modifications to the system by interacting with minimum and atomic text parts, respectively. The types of operations that can be carried out are grouped in 4 categories:

Validate prefix (VP) The text at the left of the mouse pointer is validated

Key stroke (KS) The next character of the desired translation is inserted

Reject (R) The received suffix is wrong.

Accept (A) The text is finally correct.

Figure 2(a) shows an example of a typical IMT session involving the 4 interaction modes that have been described above (key stroke operations are represented with framed boxes and reject operations are represented with vertical bars).

TECHNOLOGY

In this section we describe the technology used to implement the IMT server and the Web interface needed to communicate both client and server sides.

Interactive CAT Server

The IMT server is based on the phrase-based statistical machine translation (SMT) approach [3] to generate the suffixes completing the consolidated prefixes given by the user.

State-of-the-art SMT systems use a log-linear combination of features to generate their translations. Among the features typically used in this log-linear combination, the most important of them are the statistical language model and the statistical translation model. Fully automatic SMT systems require certain modifications for its use in the IMT framework [1].

Web Interface

Client-Server communication is made asynchronously via Ajax, providing thus a richer interactive experience, and Server-Engine communication is made through binary sockets. All corrections are stored in plain text logs on the server, so the user can retake them in any moment, also allowing other users to help to translate the full document(s).

EVALUATION RESULTS

Experimental results were carried out on two different tasks: the Xerox and the European Union corpora [1]. The results suggest that the proposed techniques can reduce the typing effort needed to produce a high-quality translation of a given source text by as much as 80% with respect to the effort needed to simply type the whole translation.

REFERENCES

1. S. Barrachina, O. Bender, F. Casacuberta, J. Civera, E. Cubel, S. Khadivi, A. L. Lagarda, H. Ney, J. Tomás, E. Vidal, and J. M. Vilar. Statistical approaches to computer-assisted translation. *Computational Linguistics*, 35(1):3–28, 2009.

2. O. Craciunescu, C. Gerding-Salas, and S. Stringer-O'Keeffe. Machine translation and computer-assisted translation: a new way of translating? *Translation Journal*, 8(3), 2004.

3. P. Koehn, F. J. Och, and D. Marcu. Statistical phrase-based translation. In *Proc. of the HLT/NAACL*, pages 48–54, Edmonton, Canada, May 2003.

4. V. Romero, L. A. Leiva, A. H. Toselli, and E. Vidal. Interactive multimodal transcription of text images using a web-based demo system. In *Proceedings of IUI*, 2009.

5. G. Sanchis-Trilles, D. Ortiz-Martínez, J. Civera, F. Casacuberta, E. Vidal, and H. Hoang. Improving interactive machine translation via mouse actions. In *EMNLP 2008: conference on Empirical Methods in Natural Language Processing*, 2008.

Haptic Augmented Reality Dental Trainer with Automatic Performance Assessment

Phattanapon Rhienmora[*], Kugamoorthy Gajananan[*], Peter Haddawy[*],
Siriwan Suebnukarn[**], Matthew N. Dailey[*], Ekarin Supataratarn[*], Poonam Shrestha[*]
[*]School of Engineering and Technology, Asian Institute of Technology
phattanapon.rhienmora@ait.asia
[**]Faculty of Dentistry, Thammasat University
ssiriwan@tu.ac.th

ABSTRACT

We developed an augmented reality (AR) dental training simulator utilizing a haptic (force feedback) device. A number of dental procedures such as crown preparation and opening access to the pulp can be simulated with various shapes of dental drill. The system allows students to practise surgery in the correct postures as in the actual environment by combining 3D tooth and tool models upon the real-world view and displaying the result through a video see-through head mounted display (HMD). The system monitors the important features such as applied forces and tool movement that characterize the quality of the procedure. Automatic performance assessment is achieved by comparing outcome and process features of a student with the best matching expert. Moreover, we incorporated kinematic feedback and hand guidance by haptic device. The result from an initial evaluation shows that the simulator is promising for supplemental training.

Author Keywords

Dental surgical training, augmented reality, haptic device, automatic performance assessment.

ACM Classification Keywords

H.5.1 Multimedia Information Systems: Artificial, augmented, and virtual realities. H.5.2 User Interfaces: Haptic I/O. H.5.2 User Interfaces: Training, help, and documentation.

General Terms

Algorithms, Design, Experimentation, Human Factors

INTRODUCTION AND BACKGROUND

Traditional methods for dental surgical training rely on practicing procedural skills on plastic teeth or live patients under the supervision of dental experts. The limitations of this approach include a lack of real-world challenging cases, unavailability of expert supervision, and the subjective manner of surgical skills assessment based on the number of errors and task completion time. Recently, haptic VR simulators for dental surgery have been introduced

[1,3]. The advantages of these simulators are that the students are able to practice procedures as many times as they want at no incremental cost and that the training can take place anywhere.

However, some important functionalities are still missing in current VR dental simulators. Firstly, the realism of graphics and haptic display is limited. Some simulators use surface based tooth model, ignoring the internal structure of the real tooth. Many others provide only a spherical shaped tool for simplicity of collision detection and haptic rendering. Secondly, most of them are not co-located; users have to look at the monitor instead of their operating hands which results in an unrealistic simulation and makes hand-eye coordination difficult. Thus, skills accquired from this kind of simulator might not transfer well to the operating room. Thirdly, current simulators do not provide automatic assessment functionality which prevents students from tracking their own progress and the simulator itself from being an effective self-training tool. Finally, many beneficial features available only in simulation have not yet exploited, for example, kinematic feedback and hand guidance. We describe our solutions for these problems in the following sections.

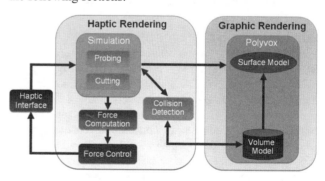

Figure 1. Overall system architecture.

VOLUMETRIC-BASED DENTAL SIMULATOR

Figure 1 shows the overall architecture of the simulator. We generate volumetric tooth model from a patient's CT scan and preserve volume density that represent tooth internal structure in an occupancy grid data structure. For different shapes of virtual dental tool, equally sampled volumetric points are utilized. The collision detection between sample points on the tool and the tooth occupany grid is fast enough to maintain the system stability. Once a collision is detected, we compute force feedback based on the number of immersed sample points and the tooth density at the colliding region. This technique allows an operator to feel different hardness of tooth anatomy with various shapes of dental drill such as sphere, cone, flat end cylinder, and round end cylinder. If the cutting is detected, the tooth's volume is modified according to the drill's shape

AUGMENTED REALITY DISPLAY

To improve the realism of the simulator, we changed our previous VR dental simulator [2] to an AR environemnt by using a video see-through head-mounted display (HMD) with a camera attached at the front (see Figure 2) and the ARToolKit library. Within the AR environment, the haptic device is co-located with the 3D graphics, giving the operator a more realistic and natural way to practise dental surgery where hand-eye coordination is crucial. Real-time head tracking is made possible by continuously grabing camera images, detecing AR markers, and 3D object registration with help from ARToolKit. Other commercially available co-located displays rely on a CRT monitors and a translucent mirror; they are relatively large for mobility and require additional hardware for head tracking.

Figure 2. Our AR approach for co-located display.

AUTOMATIC PERFORMANCE ASSESSMENT

Previously [2] we demonstrated the ability of hidden Markov models (HMM) to distinguish between novice and expert performance in the virtual tooth preparation but the number of trial data (ten) was relatively small. Recently we conducted another experiment and collected a total of 384 trial data from 32 dentists with different levels of expertise who performed virtual opening access operation. Each trial was given a subjective score based on common criterias from two experts. For each score group, we built and trained models with the same process features as in the previous work [2]. However, beside process data, the volumetric outcome of the tooth is now considered as another criterion for automatic assessment by finding the best matching outcome whose score is already known. With these methods, the system can automatically assign performance score for a new trial with a high accuracy.

KINEMATIC FEEDBACKS AND HAND GUIDANCE

During simulation, the system can displays kinematic feedback such as force utilization in three axes of each procedure stage, and tool/mirror movement patterns (see Figure 3). By dividing students into groups that obtained different kinematic feedback during training session, we found that students who received kinematic feedbacks performed more effectively than those who did not receive them on the retention test session.

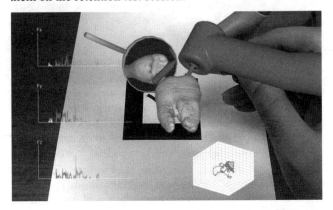

Figure 3. AR environment with kinematic feedback.

Lastly, the system allows students to practice a procedure by holding the haptic device that automatically moves along an expert's path. We found that this hand-over-hand technique is simple yet powerful in a virtual dental training.

CONCLUSION AND FUTURE WORK

In summary, we demonstrate an intelligent dental training simulator that introduces new functionalities and addresses limitations of current research and commercially available dental simulators. We plan to combine the current setup with a usual physical mouth or phantom head for better realism. Moreover, additional training strategies will be explored in the near future.

ACKNOWLEDGMENTS

This research was supported by the National Electronics and Computer Technology Center (NT-B-22-MS-14-50-04) and Office of the Higher Education Commission, Thailand.

REFERENCES

1. Kim, L., Hwang, Y., Park, S. H. and Ha, S. Dental training system using multi-modal interface. *Computer-Aided Design & Applications*, vol. 2, no. 5, pp. 591–598, 2005.

2. Rhienmora, P., Haddawy, P., Suebnukarn, S. and Dailey, M.N. Providing Objective Feedback on Skill Assessment in a Dental Surgical Training Simulator. *Proc. AIME 2009*, pp. 305-314, 2009.

3. Yau, H. T., Tsou, L. S. and Tsai, M. J. Octree-based virtual dental training system with a haptic device. *Computer-Aided Design & Applications*, vol. 3, pp. 415–424, 2006.

QuickWoZ: A Multi-purpose Wizard-of-Oz Framework for Experiments with Embodied Conversational Agents

Jan Smeddinck, Kamila Wajda, Adeel Naveed, Leen Touma, Yuting Chen, Muhammad Abu Hasan,
Muhammad Waqas Latif, Robert Porzel
Digital Media, FB 3, University of Bremen
confetti | porzel@informatik.uni-bremen.de

ABSTRACT

Herein we describe the QuickWoZ system, a Wizard-of-Oz (WoZ) tool that allows for the remote control of the behavior of animated characters in a 3D environment. The complete scene, character, behaviors and sounds can be defined in simple XML documents, which are parsed at runtime, so that setting up an experiment can be done without programming expertise. Quick selection lists and buttons enable the *wizard* to easily control the agents' behavior and allow for fast reactions to the subjects' input. The system is tailored for experiments with embodied conversational agents (ECAs) featuring multimodal interaction and was designed as a rapid prototyping system for evaluating the impact of an agent's behavior on the user.

Author Keywords

HCI, embodiment, conversational agents, evaluation

ACM Classification Keywords

H5.2. Information interfaces and presentation: Graphical user interfaces (GUI)

General Terms

Experimentation, Measurement

INTRODUCTION

ECAs featuring natural language and other natural modalities processing capabilities promise interactional benefits as an HCI metaphor, but their development as a suitable intelligent user interface remains a challenging enterprise. In order to explore various aspects and implications of HCI systems – without the need to develop the system first – WoZ experiments have been employed as a suitable tool for testing and evaluating the interaction with the system [5]. Such experiments, therefore, allow the compilation of user requirements concerning ECAs [4]. Typical WoZ-tools are often difficult to use and designed for a single purpose. Additionally, we noted a complete lack of systems offering means to include natural 3D motion and animation of the character. This motivated the

creation of this a more generally applicable system – based on popular formats and open definition files – that enables the designer to record and import libraries of movements, which can be combined with each other and more modalities such as text-to-speech audio. In the following we describe the architecture of the QuickWoZ system and discuss some of the implications concerning future improvements that are motivated by its experimental employment for testing the impact of agent character traits and gestural behavior on user expectations of ECA systems.

RELATED WORK

As noted above a whole range of tools for controlling 2D virtual characters and voice-based systems exists [4], but none that allow for integrating fully embodied 3D animation of ECAs. Additionally, a host of studies exist that examine the potential effects of an agent's design and personality on the interaction [3,6]. The work presented herein can be thought of as an enabling tool to further this type of study by the creation of a more generally usable WoZ system that allows the wizard to control 3D embodied agents within their environments.

FRAMEWORK AND PIPELINE

The framework and pipeline were designed for specific types of experimental settings, where the goal is to test not only the effects of the verbal but also the non-verbal behavior of an agent. Given its particular construction, however, the system can also be employed for different purposes as it is intuitively adaptable. For this reason, QuickWOZ can be seen as a multi-purpose experimental framework that could be swiftly applied (without programming) to a large number of possible experiments.

QuickWoZ is programmed in C# and uses Ogre3D with the C# wrapper library MOGRE for .NET integration as the visual engine, supporting both DirectX and OpenGL rendering [7]. The sound streaming is managed with the BASS.NET library [1]. With these basic technologies QuickWoZ supports the creation of scenes, characters and animations with all industry standard 3D modeling and animation tools and the most common sound file formats.

Funded by the DFG within the SFB 637.

An arbitrary amount of QuickWoZ instances can be synchronized through a relay-server. All engine-controlling functions that are influencing a given scene are then automatically synchronized, while user interface actions run in a different thread and are not synchronized. This allows for one client to be put into full-screen mode, while the instance on the wizard's computer runs the engine in window mode. The experiment operators can thereby easily observe the exact behavior of the agent as it is presented to experiment participants.

In order to obtain natural human-like animations in comparably short time we decided to capture animations with a motion capture suit. Inverse-kinematics, physically, or behaviorally driven animations can be used alternatively. These animations were mapped to a biped skeleton in a 3D character animation software and skinned with a simple humanoid body. Ogre exporter tools exist for all common 3D-modeling and -animation suites and can be used to generate the necessary meshes and skeleton binaries. The animations in the skeleton file can be linked to the according sound files via XML documents. Next to such a library of movements and gestures, natural language responses of the agent can be prerecorded and distorted with audio filters to mimic the sound of a computer-synthesized voice or spoken directly by the wizard using online distortion filters.

As other WoZ tools, the QuickWoZ system will typically be running on two or more computers in different rooms. The connection can be set up in the 'Options' panel of the menu bar. To be able to control the prerecorded libraries, the operator first has to start Ogre and synch the two machines using the accordant 'Synch'-button. In the 'File' panel, the wizard can load an XML expression file whose content appears as alphabetically sorted list on the right side of the window. In order to play an animation the wizard can double-click an expression from the list after running Ogre. To find an expression from the list in short time, the operator can also use the search bar on the right top of the application. As depicted in Figure 1, individual buttons are offered for the most frequently used animations which are automatically generated from the expression list. In case the user asks a question which was not prerecorded, the wizard can use the 'push to talk' button which activates a prerecorded animation and the answering is done live by a speaker using sound distortion filters.

The QuickWoZ system has been employed in an experiment testing the impact of the character traits and gestures of an agent on user-expectations and trust. In this case, two wizards controlled the agent together: One selected the behaviors as replies to user requests and the other one acted as a "live speaker", when no prepared answer was available as a matching response to user requests. For this test, live speech was achieved using an external sound-distortion tool. For the next version of the QuickWoZ system we plan to integrate this functionality

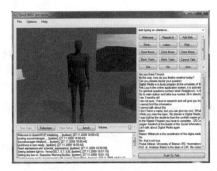

Figure 1. Screenshot of a QuickWoZ sample scene with quick-play buttons on the top right.

into the core system. The deployment of the system delivered valuable feedback both in terms of the experimental design as well as for the architecture of the system. The tool ran stable and allowed for variable length synchronized sessions. The illusion of the ECA was such that none of the participants noticed that they were interacting with a wizard-system and not a real one.

CONCLUSION AND FUTURE WORK

The outcome of the deployment showed that the QuickWoZ system provided an appropriate illusion of a real naturally behaving artificial intelligent. Participants described the system as an engaging interaction experience. The next version of QuickWoZ will include real-time filters for microphone sound-distortion so that the number of tools required by a wizard drops to one and future experiments can be handled by a single wizard in a more convenient manner. Also, we will add speech synthesis technology to enable faster extensions with more expressive capabilities for different characters.

REFERENCES

1. BASS audio library (http://www.un4seen.com/).

2. Cassell, J. and Ryokai, K. 2001. Making Space for Voice: Technologies to Support Children's Fantasy and Storytelling. *Personal Ubiquitous Comput.* 5, 3 2001.

3. Cassell, J. and T. Bickmore. External Manifestations of Trustworthiness in the Interface. Communications of the ACM, 43(12):50-56, 2000.

4. Dahlback, N., Jonsson, A., Ahrenberg, L. Wizard of OZ studies-Why and How, In Readings in intelligent user interfaces (1993), 610-619.

5. Francony, J.-M., E. Kuijpers, and Y. Polity. Towards a methodology for Wizard of Oz experiments. In 3rd Conference on Applied NLP, 1992.

6. Kraemer, N., N. Simons, and S. Kopp. The effects of an embodied conversational agent's nonverbal behavior on user's evaluation and behavioral mimicry. In Proc. Of 7th IVA, LNAI 4722, Springer-Verlag, 2007.

7. MOGRE .NET wrapper for Ogre3D. http://www.ogre3d.org/wiki/index.php/MOGRE

Agents as Intelligent User Interfaces for the Net Generation

Han Yu, Yundong Cai, Zhiqi Shen, Xuehong Tao, Chunyan Miao
Nanyang Technological University, Singapore
{yuha0008, ydcai, zqshen}@ntu.edu.sg, xuehongtao@gmail.com, ascymiao@ntu.edu.sg

ABSTRACT

Riding on the back of the rapid expansion of the Internet, online virtual worlds which combine the prowess of interactive digital media and social networks have attained a high level of acceptance among the Net Generation users. This development prompted researchers to look into the potential of embedding learning contents into virtual worlds to create virtual learning environments (VLEs) that suit the need of the Net Generation learners. However, the special characteristics of virtual worlds that make them popular also pose great challenges to educators who wish to leverage their power. These challenges call for more sophisticated human computer interaction (HCI) mechanisms to assist learners to navigate the intriguing landscape of VLEs. In this paper, we demonstrate a teachable remembrance agent which acts as an intelligent user interface to provide innovative ways for students to interact with VLEs.

Author Keywords

Teachable Agent, Remembrance Agent, Interface Agent, Virtual Learning Environment, Virtual World.

ACM Classification Keywords

H5.m. Information interfaces and presentation (e.g., HCI): Miscellaneous.

General Terms

Human Factors.

INTRODUCTION

Since leading researchers identified the important applications of virtual worlds in e-learning [1], VLE research has been gaining momentum. Learning in such environments typically involves letting students explore in an open and immersive manner. In a VLE, students engage in avatar based interactions (ABIs) with the environment just like in online virtual worlds. Over the years, many new HCI mechanisms have emerged to enhance the students' sense of immersion in VLEs [2]. However, the mainstream ABIs in the existing virtual worlds still focus on helping users navigate the virtual environments in a more life-like manner. They are essentially surrogates of the traditional menu based user interfaces. In our view, HCI mechanisms should not be constrained to enhancing the effectiveness of

interaction between the users and the system but should also play a part in helping the users achieve their desired objectives in the target system. Combined with intelligent agent technologies, ABI has the potential to provide deeper levels of interaction between the users and the VLE.

In order to promote active user involvement in VLEs, we propose an amazing agent as an intelligent user interface (AIUI) demonstration. A teachable remembrance agent would accompany each student during their exploration process in a VLE. This agent is designed to take on the roles of both an interface agent and a learning companion. It rewards the student with the sense of achievement gained from teaching a virtual character to become more knowledgeable in the subject of learning and help the student to repeat and reflect upon what he/she has learnt in the VLE to help them build up the learning scaffold on their own. Through the novel HCI mechanisms with the proposed agent, we aim to enhance the student's learning experience in VLEs.

In the subsequent sections, we further illustrate the design of the interactions between the student and the proposed agent and highlight our plans for future development.

STUDENT AGENT INTERACTION DESIGN

The proposed agent is placed into a VLE which allows students to learn high school level science concepts. Its interaction mechanisms with the student are designed based on the learning by teaching others theory [3] and the principle of associative recall in remembrance agents [4]. Initially proposed to assist information retrieval applications, a remembrance simulates human associative memory which we find helpful in VLEs. According to the Assimilation Theory, learning depends on what a student already knows. Therefore, we incorporate interaction mechanisms that enable the proposed agent to stimulate the student's memory at the appropriate time during the process of learning.

In order to remind the students of what they have learnt, the proposed agent must record the situation under which certain knowledge is acquired by a student. This process consists of two parts: 1) autonomous recording by the agent; 2) manual input by the student. The interface between the student and the remembrance component of the agent is in the form of a science diary in which the student can write down notes and take pictures to practice recording scientific observations. In the background, the agent records the situational information related to the learning activity (e.g. time, location, other participants etc.) into a persistent store. At the same time, the agent monitors the student's progress in accomplishing the learning task. If it senses the student is being stuck at certain point, it will start to progressively offer hints to help the student build up the connection between the current problem and the previous knowledge. In this way, the avatar provides predictive aiding to the students not only to help them navigate the system but also complete learning tasks.

The hints offered are in the form of generated speech with subtitles and they are progressively more explicit. The use of multiple resources (i.e. visual and audio) helps attract the attention from the student. For example, at first, the hint given could be associated with the time and location in the VLE where the student first acquired the knowledge related to the current problem; if the student still failed to recall after a predefined duration, more information related to the situation under which the learning occurred is offered (e.g. any other friends who were with the student at that time etc.); if the student still failed to recall, the required knowledge would be included in the hint explicitly. A student progress monitor module is built into the agent to enable it to come up with a prediction about whether the student needs assistance according the time the student spent on any particular learning task without successfully completing it. This way, the agent stores knowledge which should be held in the student's short term memory and reinforces it at the appropriate time to help the student internalize the knowledge into his/her long term memory.

Learning by teaching others is a well known educational theory. Studies in peer-assisted tutoring [5], computerized learning companions [6] and classroom teaching [7] have all supported the effectiveness of learning by teaching. When in a position to prepare to instruct others instead of just learning for one's own knowledge gain, the students often take on a higher sense of responsibility. The proposed agent incorporates the learning by teaching process into the learning tasks to interactively reinforce the knowledge just acquired by the student.

The proposed agent monitors the student's progress during a learning task. Once it is completed, the agent would compose an open-ended question based on the observed result for the student. The interface then allows the student to teach the agent through two mechanisms: 1) by directly manipulating a cognitive map which illustrates the causal relations among the concepts; and 2) by specifying fuzzy rules which define quantitative relations among the concepts. Once the fuzzy rules are entered by the students, the agent checks for conflicting rules and raise them to the student for further modifications. With the concept cognitive map and fuzzy rule set being expanded as more learning activities are carried out, the agent will occasionally pose questions to the student during subsequent learning tasks that are related to known concepts. When generating these questions, an error bias is introduced to cause the agent to randomly make conceptual mistakes which require the student to identify and correct. By allowing the student to visually manipulate the knowledge taught to the agent, this ABI mechanism replaces memory with visual information. This ABI mechanism not only enables the student to reflect deeply on the concept learnt but also to derive satisfaction from having an impact on another autonomous entity (i.e. the agent).

CONCLUSIONS AND FUTUREWORK

By incorporating specially designed HCI mechanisms, we enable interface agents in VLEs to have the ability to embed advanced learning theories into their interactions with the students. In this way, the students are not only able to get directions on how to use the functionalities of a VLE, but are also able to enjoy an enhanced learning experience by following the interactions initiated by the proposed agent. In future development, we will consider more sophisticated user models which could facilitate the addition of complex agent affect modeling. Through this development, the agent would be able to estimate the student's emotional state more accurately and choose an appropriate emotional response to elicit an optimal emotional state in the student to carry on the learning task.

REFERENCES

1. Bainbridge, W. S. (2007). The Scientific Research Potential of Virtual Worlds. *Science, 317*, 472 - 476.
2. Dede, C. (2009). Immersive Interfaces for Engagement and Learning. *Science, 323*(5910), 66-69.
3. Sinclair, G., & Beverley, H. (1989). *Peer Tutoring - A Guide to Learning by Teaching*: Nichols Publishing.
4. Rhodes, B. J., & Starner, T. (1996). *Remembrance Agent - A continuously running automated information retrieval system*. The First International Conference on the Practical Application of Intelligent Agents and Multi Agent Technology (PAAM).
5. Cohen, P. A., Kulik, J. A., & Kulik, C.-L. C. (1982). Educational Outcomes of Peer Tutoring: A Meta-analysis of Findings. *American Educational Research Journal, 19*, 237-248.
6. Chan, T.-W., & Chou, C.-Y. (1997). Exploring the Design of Computer Supports for Reciprocal Tutoring. *International Journal of Artificial Intelligence in Education, 8*, 1-29.
7. Sherin, M. (2002). When Teaching Becomes Learning. *Cognition & Instruction, 20*, 119-150.

Workshop: Eye Gaze in Intelligent Human Machine Interaction

Elisabeth André

Institute for Informatics,
Augsburg University
Universitätsser. 6a
86159 Augsburg, Germany
andre@informatik.uni-augsburg.de

Joyce Y. Chai

Department of Computer Science and Engineering
Michigan State University
3115 Engineering Building
East Lansing, MI 48824
jchai@cse.msu.edu

ABSTRACT

This workshop brought researchers from academia and industry together to share recent advances and discuss research directions and opportunities for next generation of intelligent human machine interaction that incorporate eye gaze.

Author Keywords

Eye Gaze, Intelligent Human Machine Interaction

ACM Classification Keywords

H.5.m. Information interfaces and presentation (e.g., HCI): Miscellaneous.

General Terms

Algorithms, Design, Experimentation, Human Factors, Languages, Measurement, Theory

INTRODUCTION

Eye gaze serves multiple functions in human-human communication. The speaker may use gaze to reference an object in the environment, or to indicate attention to the listener, and or to manage who has the floor, among other functions.

Researchers have long been interested in the role of eye gaze in human machine interaction. It has been used as a pointing mechanism in direct manipulation interfaces, for example, to assist users with "locked-in syndrome". It has also been used to reflect information needs in web search and tailor information presentation. Based on joint attention indicated by eye gaze, it has been used as a facilitator in computer supported human-human communication. In conversational interfaces, eye gaze has been used to improve language understanding and intention recognition. It has also been incorporated in multimodal behavior of embodied conversational agents. Recent work on human robot interaction has further explored eye gaze in incremental language processing, visual scene processing, and conversation engagement and grounding. Given the recent advances in eye tracking technology and the availability of non-intrusive and high performance eye tracking devices, there has never been a better time to explore new opportunities to incorporate eye gaze in intelligent and natural human machine communication.

Topics

This workshop brought researchers from academia and industry together to share recent advances and discuss research directions and opportunities for next generation of human machine interaction that incorporate eye gaze. The workshop addresses the following areas:

- Empirical studies of eye gaze in human-human communication which have implications in human machine communication. Examples include new empirical findings of eye gaze in human language processing, in human vision processing, and in conversation management.
- Algorithms and systems that incorporate eye gaze for human computer interaction and human robot interaction. Examples include gaze-based feedback to information systems, gaze-based attention modeling, incorporating gaze for automated language processing, controlling gaze behavior for embodied conversation agents or robots to enable grounding, turn-taking, and engagement.
- Applications that demonstrate the value of incorporating eye gaze in practical systems to enable intelligent human machine communication.

Workshop on Social Recommender Systems

Ido Guy
IBM Haifa Research Lab
Mt. Carmel, Haifa
31905, Israel

ido@il.ibm.com

Li Chen
Department of Computer Science
Hong Kong Baptist University
224 Waterloo Road,
Kowloon Tong, Hong Kong
lichen@comp.hkbu.edu.hk

Michelle X. Zhou
IBM China Research Lab
Bld 19, Shangdi Zhong Guan Cun
Software Park, Beijing, China

mxzhou@cn.ibm.com

ABSTRACT

This workshop brought researchers from academia and industry together to share recent advances and discuss research directions for recommender systems in social media and Web 2.0. With social media sites becoming ubiquitous, the challenges and opportunities for recommendation technologies become greater, setting the grounds for new research and innovation.

Author Keywords

Recommender Systems, Social Media, Social Web, Web 2.0

ACM Classification Keywords

H.5.3 Information Interfaces and Presentation: Group and Organization Interfaces – Collaborative computing; H.3.3 Information Search and Retrieval – Information filtering.

General Terms

Algorithms, Design, Experimentation, Human Factors, Measurement, Theory

INTRODUCTION

Social media sites have become tremendously popular in recent years. These sites include photo and video sharing sites such as Flickr and YouTube, blog and wiki systems such as Blogger and Wikipedia, social tagging sites such as Delicious, social network sites (SNSs), such as MySpace and Facebook, and micro-blogging sites such as Twitter.. Millions of users are active daily in these sites, creating rich information online that has not been available before. Yet, the abundance and popularity of social media sites floods users with huge volumes of information and hence poses a great challenge in terms of information overload. In addition, most of user-generated contents are unstructured (e.g., blogs and wikis). It hence raises open questions of how such information can be exploited for personalization.

Social Recommender Systems (SRSs) aim to alleviate information overload over social media users by presenting the most attractive and relevant content, often using personalization techniques adapted for the specific user. SRSs also aim at increasing adoption, engagement, and

participation of new and existing users of social media sites. Traditional techniques, such as content-based methods and collaborative filtering are being used separately and jointly to support effective recommendations. Yet, the social media platform allows incorporating new techniques that take advantage of the new information becoming publicly available in social media sites, such as the explicit connections between individuals in SNSs, the tags people are using to classify items, and the content they create. In addition to recommending content to consume, new types of recommendations emerge within social media, such as of people and communities to connect to, to follow, or to join.

The fact that much of the information within social media sites – tags, comments, ratings, connections, content, and sometimes even message correspondence – is public, enabling more transparency in social recommender systems. New techniques for explanations that try to reason a recommendation provided to a user are being exploited, aiming at increasing users' trust in the system and stimulating more active participation. On the other hand, incorporating user feedback – both explicit and implicit – to improve recommendations and keep them attractive over time is another important challenge for SRSs.

Indeed, explaining the rationale behind recommendations as well as presenting recommendation results is an important aspect of social recommender systems. Because of the diverse information used in making recommendation (e.g., social network as well as content relevance), effective mechanisms must be in place to explain the recommendation rationale and results to users. Not only will such an explanation help instill users' trust in recommended items, but it also provides an opportunity for users to provide feedback for adaptive recommendations (e.g., deleting unwanted information sources to be used for making recommendations). In addition to providing recommendations to individuals, social recommender systems are also often targeted for communities. Community recommendations need to take into account the entire set of community members, the aggregation of their diverse needs for constructing community preference models, the analysis of their collective behavior, and the different content already consumed by the community.

Another main challenge in the area of Recommender Systems is the evaluation of provided recommendations. Social media presents opportunities for new evaluation techniques, for example by leveraging tags as interest indicators of specific topics or specific items, or by harnessing the crowds that are actively participating in the sites. Developing new evaluation techniques and applying them on social recommender systems are essential to compare different recommendation methods and reach more effective systems.

OBJECTIVES AND TOPICS

This workshop brought together researchers and practitioners around the emerging topic of recommender systems within social media in order to: (1) share research and techniques used to develop effective social media recommenders, from algorithms, through user interfaces, to evaluation (2) identify next key challenges in the area, and (3) identify new cross-topic collaboration opportunities.

The workshop addressed the following areas:

Social recommender technologies and applications

- Model of recommendation context (e.g., types of information needed) for social recommender systems

- New algorithms suitable for social recommender systems
- New recommender applications for social media sites, e.g., people and community recommenders
- Recommendations for individuals and communities
- Social recommender systems in the enterprise
- Diversity and novelty in social recommender systems
- Recommendations for diverse user groups (e.g., new users of social media sites versus frequent users)

User interfaces in social recommender systems (SRS)

- Transparency and explanations in SRS
- Adaption and personalization for SRS
- User feedback in SRS
- Trust and reputation in SRS
- Social awareness and visualization

Evaluation

- Evaluation methods and evaluations of SRS
- User studies
.

Visual Interfaces to the Social and Semantic Web (VISSW 2010)

Siegfried Handschuh
Digital Enterprise Research
Institute
National University of
Ireland, Galway
IDA Business Park
Galway, Ireland
siegfried.handschuh@deri.org

Tom Heath
Talis Information Ltd
Knights Court, Solihull
Parkway,
Birmingham Business Park
B37 7YB, United Kingdom
tom.heath@talis.com

VinhTuan Thai
Digital Enterprise Research
Institute
National University of
Ireland, Galway
IDA Business Park
Galway, Ireland
vinhtuan.thai@deri.org

Ian Dickinson
Epimorphics Ltd
United Kingdom
i.j.dickinson@gmail.com

Lora Aroyo
VU Amsterdam
The Netherlands
l.m.aroyo@cs.vu.nl

Valentina Presutti
Semantic Technology
Laboratory (STLab)
National Research Council
(CNR), Italy
valentina.presutti@istc.cnr.it

ABSTRACT

Recent innovations in the Social and Semantic Web fields have resulted in large amounts of data created, published and consumed by users of the Web. This vast amount of data exists in a variety of formats, from the traditional ones such as text, image, video to the more recent additions such as streams of status information from Twitter and Facebook. The ability to easily integrate such vast amounts of data raises significant and exciting research challenges, not least of which how to provide effective access to and navigation across heterogeneous data sources on different platforms (e.g. computers, mobile devices, set-top boxes). Building on the success of the VISSW2009 workshop, the IUI2010 workshop on Visual Interfaces to the Social and Semantic Web aims to bring together researchers and practitioners from different fields to discuss the latest research results and challenges in designing, implementing, and evaluating intelligent interfaces supporting access, navigation and publishing of different types of contents on the Social and Semantic Web. This paper outlines the context of the workshop and provides an overview of the research to be presented at the event.

Author Keywords

Visual interfaces, Social and Semantic Web

ACM Classification Keywords

H.5.2 Information Interfaces and Presentation: User Interfaces—*Graphical user interfaces (GUI)*

General Terms

Design, Human Factors, Documentation

INTRODUCTION

The continued growth and importance of the Social Web has resulted in ever increasing volumes of data created, published and consumed by users. This vast amount of data takes many forms, including text, images, video and more recently streams of status information from applications such as Twitter and Facebook. Not only is this data accessible through more traditional means, such as desktop and laptop computers, but also via diverse platforms such as mobile phones and set-top boxes that bring unique constraints in terms of computing resources and user interfaces. Through the increasing availability of Web APIs, data that has traditionally been coupled with a specific application may now be exposed through novel interfaces developed by third parties, providing functionality not previously anticipated by the data owner.

In tandem with the growth of the Social Web, the Web at large has experienced a significant evolution into a Web not just of linked documents, but also of Linked Data. This development, which exploits the Semantic Web technology stack, allows relationships to be expressed between items in distributed data sets, paving the way for integration of raw data from multiple, heterogeneous sources. Coupled with the increasing availability of APIs that expose structured (if not linked) data from the Social Web, application developers have a wealth of data available to them upon which they can build compelling visual interfaces.

The ability to easily integrate vast amounts of data from across the Social and Semantic Web raises significant and exciting research challenges, not least of which how to provide effective access to and navigation across vast, heterogeneous and interconnected data sources. However, the need for intelligent and visual human interfaces to this evolving Web is not limited simply to the modalities of searching and browsing, important as these are. As the Web becomes increasingly populated with data, continues to evolve from a read-mainly to a read-write medium, and the level of social interaction supported on the Web increases, there is also a pressing need to support end-users who engage in a wide range of online tasks, such as publishing and sharing their own data on the Web.

OBJECTIVES

Building on the success of the VISSW2009 workshop[1] at IUI2009 [1], we anticipate the VISSW 2010 workshop[2] to be of interest to researchers and practitioners in the following areas:

- Human-Computer Interaction

- Intelligent User Interfaces

- Personal Information Management

- Information Visualization

- Social, Mobile and Ubiquitous Computing

- Linked Data and Semantic Web

The workshop is a forum to discuss the latest research results and challenges in designing, implementing, and evaluating intelligent interfaces in the context of the Social and Semantic Web. The workshop will serve as an opportunity for researchers to gain feedback on their work, and to identify potential collaborations with their peers. We believe that the potential for fostering links between a variety of facets of the IUI community will help to ensure an exciting workshop program.

TOPICS

Topics of interest for workshop discussion include:

- Interfaces

  - Novel visualisation of structured, linked and aggregated data, originating from multiple sources.

  - Novel interfaces for high-volume transient data, e.g. feeds, streams and sensors.

  - 'Living' interfaces to constantly evolving data, vocabularies, and emerging links between them.

  - Task-centric interfaces for structured and/or Linked Data.

  - Interface components for displaying/interacting with aggregated, heterogeneous Linked Data, e.g. components for displaying provenance information.

  - Lightweight components and processes for casual users to publish/share their own content on the Web.

  - Ontology-based visualization of collections of data.

- Interaction Paradigms

  - Novel interaction paradigms for textual, photos, music, videos, etc. on alternative platforms (e.g. mobile devices, set-top boxes, shared/public displays).

  - Novel interaction paradigms with structured, linked and aggregated data.

  - Investigation of task-centric interaction paradigms beyond search and browse.

  - Ontology-based interaction with collections of data.

  - Semantic models for interaction and their reuse on the web

- Empirical Studies and Evaluation

  - Empirical studies that can guide the development of interfaces for Linked Data.

  - Use cases which present novel visualization requirements and expose interesting interaction challenges on the Social and Semantic Web.

  - Lessons learned from user-studies, pilot systems and live deployments in the Social and Semantic Web.

SUBMISSIONS

It is our belief that this workshop has the potential for fostering links between diverse but highly related facets of the IUI community.

In fact, the workshop has attracted submissions on a variety of topics, such as:

- Ontology Based Queries Investigating a Natural Language Interface

- How Last.fm Illustrates the Musical World: User Behavior and Relevant User-Generated Content

- Gaining Musical Insights: Visualizing Multiple Listening Histories

- Cross-media Retrieval System based on Association among Heterogeneous Media

Further details about accepted papers can be found on the workshop webpage.

REFERENCES

1. S. Handschuh, T. Heath, and V. Thai . *Visual interfaces to the social and the semantic web (VISSW 2009)*. In Proceedings of the 13th International Conference on Intelligent User Interfaces (Sanibel Island, Florida, USA, February 08 - 11, 2009). IUI '09. ACM, New York, NY, 499-500.

---

[1]http://www.smart-ui.org/events/vissw2009/
[2]http://www.smart-ui.org/events/vissw2010/

1st International Workshop on Semantic Models for Adaptive Interactive Systems (SEMAIS 2010)

Tim Hussein
University of Duisburg-Essen
tim.hussein@uni-due.de

Stephan Lukosch
Delft University of Technology
s.g.lukosch@tudelft.nl

Juergen Ziegler
University of Duisburg-Essen
juergen.ziegler@uni-due.de

Alan Dix
Lancaster University
alan@hcibook.com

ABSTRACT

The International Workshop on Semantic Models for Adaptive Interactive Systems (SEMAIS 2010) aims to identify emerging trends in interactive system design using semantic models.

Author Keywords

Semantic Models, Interface Design, Model-driven User Interfaces, Usability, Adaptive Interactive Systems.

ACM Classification Keywords

H.5.2. [Information Interfaces and Presentation]: User Interfaces – Graphical User Interfaces, User-centered Design.

General Terms

Design, Human Factors

INTRODUCTION

Semantic technologies and, in particular, ontologies as formal, shareable representations of a domain of interest play an increasingly important role also for the design and development of user interfaces and more generally interactive systems. Semantic models can serve a number of different purposes in this context. They can be used as application or interface models *in model-driven desi*gn and generation of user interfaces [1,3,5,9]. Ontologies can also be applied for representing the various kinds of context information for context-aware and adaptive systems [2,10]. In particular, they have promise to provide a technique for representing external physical context factors such as location, time or technical parameters and 'internal' context such as user interest profiles or interaction context in a consistent, generalized manner [4,6-8]. Owing to these properties, semantic models can also contribute to bridging gaps, e.g., between user models, context-aware interfaces and model-driven UI generation.

There is, therefore, a considerable potential for using semantic models as a basis for adaptive interactive systems. The range of potential adaptations is wide comprising, for example, context- and user-dependent recommendations, interactive assistance when performing application-specific tasks, adaptation of the application functionality, or adaptive retrieval support. Furthermore, a variety of reasoning and machine learning techniques exist, that can be employed to achieve adaptive system behavior.

The workshop will address, among others, the following research issues:

- Representing user models, domain knowledge and interaction context by means of semantic models
- Cognitively or neurally founded reasoning techniques such as activation spreading for semantic user models
- Context-aware interaction based on semantic models
- Adaptation strategies and techniques based on semantic models for e.g. recommender systems, adaptive retrieval, collaboration support systems and others
- Generating explanations or visualizations to increase user confidence and support traceability
- Scalability of semantic model-based interactive systems.
- Semantic model-driven UI development
- Generation and evolution of semantic models for interactive systems

Evaluation approaches for adaptive interaction

Objectives of the Workshop

The workshop generally aims at sharing experiences and identifying a set of shared research issues that need to be addressed in future research. Specifically, we intend to

- Bring together researchers within the IUI, HCI and Semantic Web communities to initiate future collaboration
- Identify and structure approaches and techniques for semantic model-based interaction and adaptation with the aim of developing a conceptual framework
- Identify the potential for building and sharing sharing ontologies or semantic model-based components for adaptive UIs and, possibly, to start an initiative for developing them
- Identify evaluation methods and criteria for semantic model-based interactive systems

Participants and Workshop Attraction

The target audience for this workshop will be researchers from the HCI and AI communities and the intersecting area of intelligent user interfaces which is the focus of the conference. We also intend to attract persons from the Semantic Web community with an interest in user interface issues such as the SWUI group. We also expect the workshop to be of interest for researchers in the area of ubiquitous and context-aware systems.

We will solicit contributions using all usual channels incl. announcements in mailing lists, conferences and personal contacts. The targeted size of the workshop will be a maximum of 15 participants to enable a sufficiently broad but also focussed discussion.

ORGANIZERS

Alan Dix is professor of computing at Lancaster University. He has worked in diverse aspects of HCI, from physical and affective aspects of interaction to formal modeling and interface architecture, and he is author of one of the principal textbooks in the area. His interest in intelligent interaction has included a dot.com spin-out, as well as more academic research, focused most recently on data-detectors to mine semantics and spreading activation to model context..

Tim Hussein is a research assistant and PhD student at the University of Duisburg-Essen. His main research interests include context-aware interaction and recommendation techniques based on ontologies. In two funded research projects, WISE and CONTici, he was responsible for context-adaptive human-computer interaction based on ontologies.

Stephan Lukosch is assistant professor at the Delft University of Technology. His current research interests include intelligent collaboration support, collaborative storytelling as well as design patterns and approaches for computer-mediated interaction. His articles appeared in various journals including IJHCS, J.UCS and IJCIS. He was program chair of CRIWG'05, served on various program committees and recently organized a minitrack context-adaptive collaboration at HICSS.

Jürgen Ziegler is professor for interactive systems and interaction design at the University of Duisburg-Essen. His main areas of research are context-adaptive interaction, information visualization and user interfaces for semantic data. Recent work in the CONTici project addresses ontology-based context models for adaptive cooperation support. He has served in many functions for leading HCI conferences and has also been a workshops chair for CHI twice.

REFERENCES

1. Bauer, M. and Baldes, S. An Ontology-based Interface for Machine Learning. In *Proc. IUI* 2005. ACM Press (2005), 314-316.

2. Chen, H., Finin, T., and Joshi, A. An Ontology for Context-aware Pervasive Computing Environments. *The Knowledge Engineering Review, 18,3* (2003), 197–207.

3. Crampes, M. and Ranwez, S. Ontology-supported and Ontology-driven Conceptual Navigation on the World Wide Web. In *Proc. Hypertext 2000,* ACM Press (2000), 191–199.

4. Dix, A., Catarci, T., Habegger, B., Ioannidis, Y., Kamaruddin, A., Katifori, A., Lepouras, G., Poggi, A., and Ramduny-Ellis, D. Intelligent Context-sensitive Interactions on Desktop and the Web. Proceedings of Context in Advanced Interfaces. In *AVI 2006 Workshop*, ACM Press (2006), 23-27.

5. Gurevych, I., Merten, S., and Porzel, R. Automatic Creation of Interface Specifications from Ontologies. In *SEALTS 2003*, Association for Computational Linguistics (2003), 59-66.

6. Hussein, T. and Ziegler, J. Adapting Web Sites by Spreading Activation in Ontologies. In *Proc. ReColl 2008.*

7. Katifori, A., Vassilakis, C., and Dix, A. Ontologies and the Brain: Using Spreading Activation through Ontologies to Support Personal Interaction. *Cognitive Systems Research* (in press).

8. Lukosch, S., Veiel, D., and Haake, J.M. Enabling Context-adaptive Collaboration for Knowledge-intense Processes. In *Proc. ICEIS 2009*, Springer (2009), 34-41

9. Paraiso, E. C. Ontology-based Utterance Interpretation for Intelligent Conversational Interfaces. In *SAC 2008*, ACM Press (2008), 1578–1582.

10. Strang, T. and Linnhoff-Popien, C. A Context Modeling Survey. In *Proc. Workshop on Advanced Context Modelling, Reasoning and Management 2004.*

Workshop on Intelligent Visual Interfaces for Text Analysis

Shixia Liu
IBM Research China
liusx@cn.ibm.com

Michelle X. Zhou
IBM Research China
mxzhou@cn.ibm.com

Giuseppe Carenini
University of British
Columbia
carenini@cs.ubc.ca

Huamin Qu
Hong Kong University of
Science and Technology
huamin@cse.ust.hk

ABSTRACT

This workshop brought together researchers and practitioners from both text analytics and interactive visualization communities to explore, define, and develop intelligent visual interfaces that help enhance the consumption and quality of complex text analysis results. Using this workshop as a starting point, we aim to foster closer, interdisciplinary relationships among researchers from text analytics and interactive visualization communities, so they can combine their expertise together to better tackle the difficult problems that face the text analytics community today.

Author Keywords

Text Analytics, Interactive Visualization, Visual Analytics.

ACM Classification Keywords

H.5.2 [User Interfaces]: Graphical user interfaces (GUI), Interaction styles;

General Terms

Algorithms, Design, Experimentation, Human Factors

INTRODUCTION

Most of the world's information is contained in the form of text documents. To help people cope with the ever increasing amounts of text information, researchers have developed a wide array of text analysis technologies [1]. However, consuming the complex analysis results of these technologies may be non-trivial, especially for average users who are not computer experts, let alone text analytics experts. Furthermore, such results may be inaccurate or contain ambiguous or even misleading information. To help users better interpret text analysis results and discover opportunities to improve the results, researchers have been integrating text analytics technologies with interactive visualization technologies [2].

Such efforts roughly fall into two categories. On the one hand, researchers from the text analytics community use basic visualizations (e.g., bar chart, pie chart) to display their final analysis results. On the other hand, researchers from the information visualization community focus on illustrating simple analysis results (e.g., tf–idf measure of keywords). There are a few efforts that tightly integrate state-of-the-art text analytics with interactive visualization to maximize the value of both.

With the current far-from-perfect text analysis technologies, we believe that it is critical to create a "smart" interactive environment where human analysts and computers can work collaboratively. On the one hand, computers interpret/track the human analysis process as a context to better understand the needs of analysts or average users and assist them in their information consuming tasks (e.g., finding a particular piece of text information for decision making). On the other hand, human analysts or average users could use computer-presented information as a context to better articulate their needs (e.g., issuing follow-up data inquiries) and help human analysts or average users actively involve in the text process and provide their feedback (e.g., interactively merging topics in an LDA-based analysis).

OBJECTIVES AND TOPICS

This workshop aims to achieve to main objectives: 1) Identify key research issues and challenges in designing and developing intelligent visual interface for text analysis; and 2) Establish and grow a community that consists of researchers and practitioners from multiple disciplines (e.g., text analytics and visualization) to tackle the difficult problems of text analytics and initiate proper collaboration among different teams.

This workshop addressed the following research areas:

- Novel, intelligent interfaces for text analytics
- Visual and interactive text analytics
- Collaborative visual text analytics
- Scalable visual text analytics
- Visual representations and interaction techniques to allow users to see, explore, and understand large amounts of textual information
- Techniques to support production, presentation, and dissemination of text analysis results to a variety of audiences
- Data representations and transformations that convert conflicting and dynamic textual data in ways that support visualization and analysis
- User studies concerning intelligent interfaces for text analysis
- Evaluation methods for text analysis techniques and systems

REFERENCES

1. http://en.wikipedia.org/wiki/Text_mining
2. http://en.wikipedia.org/wiki/Interactive_visualization

2nd Multimodal Interfaces for Automotive Applications (MIAA 2010)

Michael Feld, Christian Müller
German Research Center for Artificial Intelligence
Stuhlsatzenhausweg 3
66123 Saarbrücken, Germany
{michael.feld, christian.mueller}@dfki.de

Tim Schwartz
Cluster of Excellence, Multimodal
Computing and Interaction
University of the Saarland
Germany
schwarz@cs.uni-sb.de

ABSTRACT
This paper summarizes the main objectives of the 2nd IUI workshop on multimodal interfaces for automotive applications (MIAA 2010).

Keywords: multimodal interfaces, human-machine-interaction, automotive applications

ACM Classification: H.5.1 Multimedia Information Systems. – Evaluation – Methodology; H.5.2 [Information interfaces and presentation]: User Interfaces. - Graphical user interfaces, Natural Language, User-centered design, Voice I/O, Interaction styles, Haptic I/O, Ergononmics; J7 [Computers in other systems]: Command and Control, Consumer Products

General terms: Design, Reliability, Experimentation, Human Factors

INTRODUCTION
The technology we interact with is no longer static, but will react completely different depending on who is using it. Personal computers and mobile devices have already been affected by this development in recent years. As vehicles are accumulating more advanced technological components, it is clear that they are heading in the same direction. But not only because a certain degree of customizability is expected today: As cars host such a large range of accessories and devices on little space, a seamless interaction between user and system entails an enormous benefit with respect to usability.

The basis for a modern human-machine interaction concept is a user-centric design that focuses on the needs of the target users. An advanced user-adaptive system however goes further: There it is not sufficient to develop the interface on the drawing board with a specific target group in mind and then implement a set of fixed interactions for that group, but to also incorporate the actual state of the user and its interrelations with the context in the dialog system. This can be done for example by adjusting system output to the cognitive load of the user or enable different input methods depending on what interactions related to other tasks such as driving or communicating with passengers are being performed in parallel.

MAIN OBJECTIVES OF THE WORKSHOP
One research aspect of such user-adaptive systems is the acquisition of knowledge. Different functions will be able to provide different degrees of service and personalization depending on what is known about the subject. The highest level of service can be accomplished when we know exactly whom we are dealing with, i.e. if the user identifies himself by some credentials, voice identification or an ID token. There are several examples where such tokens are incorporated into car keys, ID cards or other common accessories. In that case, we can look up basic information in a local database. With more vehicles being equipped with Internet access, such information can also be looked up on web services, enabling an easier sharing of preferences when multiple cars are used. The greater challenge however is the situation when the user does not identify himself, either because he is in a hurry, because he is not a regular driver of the car (imagine a car rental service) or because he is simply joining in some other car and not driving at all. Explicit information input – while generally less desirable because of the overall discomfort generated by entering it – is not a realistic option for the driver. In this case, we can still fuel our systems with knowledge from probabilistic models, typically based on sensor information. The same applies to most of the rapidly changing aspects of user state. Such non-intrusive information acquisition methods have a strong potential for in-car applications. While many other scenarios suffer the problem of difficult instrumentation, in the automotive field, we are dealing with a rather small and well-defined interaction space (i.e. a single seat), where it is easier to place cameras and other sensors. In addition, there are already many existing sensors available to be exploited, for instance weight and temperature sensors. Also, while the speech of a user is typically used only as a primary input to control a system, there is much more information we can obtain about the speaker from his voice, like age, gender, emotion, cognitive load and even the level of alcohol in his blood.

The collection of data from external sources is not the only aspect related to user knowledge acquisition. When we have many pieces of information from many different sources, an intelligent fusion mechanism needs to be designed that also takes into account context parameters. This is of particular importance whenever uncertainty is involved. When we consider for example the attention state of driver, we may have some the visuals of the person's eyes as one cue, while other cues are derived from reaction times and driving style. Then again, the time of day and duration of driving play a role as context parameters. In the end, we need to come up with a single value – preferably annotated by a meaningful confidence value – that an application or driving assistance function can make use of to adapt itself to this circumstance. There are many different ways of how such fusion of information can be done. One option is logical inference systems, which work quite well for fact knowledge. Rule engines may be another choice, and they are preferred in cases where complex inferences based on expert knowledge is needed, or when are they serve to model rules set by laws, a case that is omnipresent in automotive system design.

A different area of research addresses the question of how user knowledge is represented. In order to provide an accessible platform for other services, a certain degree of content is needed with respect to how the data is retrieved and possibly updated. Semantic knowledge representation in the form of ontologies is certainly a state-of-the-art solution here, yet there are few examples of public ontologies that focus on the driver and passengers as a special case of a user and that also take incorporate context aspects like car features and the current driving situation. The fact that information sharing between cars like with the car2x paradigm is becoming increasingly important for new safety and convenience features too requires us to think about the privacy aspects of data sharing too. Essentially there need to be methods to ensure that no sensitive data leaves the car or is "desensitized" on its way out. Further, in car systems we have the contrast of lengthy driving on the one hand and highly fluctuating information on the other, which makes the dimension of time another essential issue for knowledge representation. Services have to know the validity period of a datum, and may need to access data from already passed points in time.

The final objective in the design process of personalized in-car systems is the realization of the actual adaptation concepts. Eventually every aspect of multimodal input and output is adaptable: The way gestures are recognized, the type of output produced, the speed of voice output, the temperature settings and window operation mode, and the elements presented on the screen. The motivation behind it may vary between settings. It can serve to ensure an intuitive usage by making a system react like the user expects it to. It can also be used to customize functions to the user's preferences. Adaptation may be employed to compensate a physical or mental handicap of the user, or simply to reduce his cognitive load while driving. Identifying places where adaptation can be useful is the first step, followed by the identification of

those characteristics in the user model that it should be based on. Then an adaptation strategy has to be chosen, which will determine the result visible to the user. Strategies can range from very function-specific effects, like the choice of roads in a navigation component, to generic ones, such as the increasing of font size for people with a bad visual acuity. Generic adaptation components are a further pertinent topic for further research. The selection of strategies typically comes along with a conflict resolution mechanism in case multiple strategies are in conflict or compete for a single output modality. This can avoid for instance that a user is presented with a long sequence of spoken output while the screen remains unused. How far an adaptation can go largely depends on the confidence in the underlying information.

The car HMI is subject to much stricter rules and undergoes a more rigorous testing than interfaces in other areas. Therefore, a formal specification of the HMI on multiple layers of abstraction is necessary in the design phase. However, current methods often do not include adaptivity as part of such a specification, hence new procedures have to be developed and existing ones need to be extended to incorporate these aspects. In a similar manner, current industry standard evaluation methods may also need to be updated.

Adaptation does not end when the user is confronted with a personalized output. Most of the time, uncertainty is involved to some extent in the process, hence the result may not always be appropriate, or it may be difficult to understand – up to the case where the user mistakes adaptive behavior for a system malfunction. The user's reaction to this at least partially autonomous decision of the system to adapt the way it did may provide important cues as to whether the intended goal was reached. Moreover, it can shed some light on the user's model of the system and his learning process. Trying to find out about the user's view of an adaptive system and using this information to improve the learning and make the behavior more transparent is subject to ongoing research. Future systems are expected to be much more user-friendly when they approach adaptivity with this meta-level aspect in mind.

REFERENCES

[1] Brandherm, B. und Jameson, A. (2004). An Extension of the Differential Approach for Bayesian Network Inference to Dynamic Bayesian Networks. International Journal of Intelligent Systems, 19(8), 727–748.

[2] Heckmann, D. (2005). Ubiquitous User Modeling. Department of Computer Science, Saarland University.

[3] Müller, C. (2005). Zweistufige kontextsensitive Sprecherklassifikation am Beispiel von Alter und Geschlecht [Two-layered Context-Sensitive Speaker Classification on the Example of Age and Gender]. Ph.D. thesis, Computer Science Institute, Saarland University

Author Index

NOTES

NOTES

NOTES

NOTES